AN INDEX
TO BOOK REVIEWS
IN THE HUMANITIES

VOLUME 13

1972

PHILLIP THOMSON

WILLIAMSTON, MICHIGAN

STANDARD BOOK NUMBER: 0-911504-13-3

INTERNATIONAL STANDARD SERIAL NUMBER:
     US ISSN 0073-5892

LIBRARY OF CONGRESS CATALOG CARD NUMBER:
     62-21757

PRINTED IN THE U.S.A.

THIS VOLUME OF THE INDEX CONTAINS DATA COLLECTED UP TO 31 DECEMBER 1972.

THIS IS AN INDEX TO BOOK REVIEWS IN HUMANITIES PERIODICALS. WITH THE LAST VOLUME OF THIS INDEX (VOLUME 12, DATED 1971) THE FORMER POLICY OF SELECTIVELY INDEXING REVIEWS OF BOOKS IN CERTAIN SUBJECT CATEGORIES ONLY WAS DROPPED IN FAVOR OF A POLICY OF INDEXING ALL REVIEWS IN THE PERIODICALS INDEXED, WITH THE ONE EXCEPTION OF CHILDREN'S BOOKS--THE REVIEWS OF WHICH WILL NOT BE INDEXED. EVERY PERIODICAL INDEXED DATED AFTER 1 JANUARY 1971 HAS HAD ALL REVIEWS INDEXED. MANY OF THE PERIODICALS INDEXED IN THIS VOLUME WITH EARLIER DATES HAVE ALSO HAD ALL REVIEWS INDEXED, BUT IN THIS VOLUME WE HAVE MADE NO ATTEMPT TO IDENTIFY THESE ISSUES IN THE LIST OF PERIODICALS INDEXED BEGINNING ON PAGE III. IT SHOULD THEREFORE BE ASSUMED THAT ALL PERIODICALS SHOWN IN THAT LIST WITH DATES EARLIER THAN 1971 WERE INDEXED UNDER THE OLD RULES OF INCLUSION. THOSE RULES CAN BE FOUND ON THIS PAGE IN ANY VOLUME OF THIS INDEX SPINE-DATED 1970 OR EARLIER.

THE FORM OF THE ENTRIES USED IS AS FOLLOWS:

    AUTHOR. TITLE.
        REVIEWER. IDENTIFYING LEGEND.

THE AUTHOR'S NAME USED IS THE NAME THAT APPEARS ON THE TITLE-PAGE OF THE BOOK BEING REVIEWED, AS WELL AS WE ARE ABLE TO DETERMINE, EVEN THOUGH THIS NAME IS KNOWN TO BE A PSEUDONYM. THE TITLE ONLY IS SHOWN; SUBTITLES ARE INCLUDED ONLY WHERE THEY ARE NECESSARY TO IDENTIFY A BOOK IN A SERIES. THE IDENTIFYING LEGEND CONSISTS OF THE PERIODICAL, EACH OF WHICH HAS A CODE NUMBER, AND THE DATE AND PAGE NUMBER OF THE PERIODICAL WHERE THE REVIEW IS TO BE FOUND. PMLA ABBREVIATIONS ARE ALSO SHOWN (WHEN A PERIODICAL HAS SUCH AN ABBREVIATION, BUT SUCH ABBREVIATIONS ARE LIMITED TO FOUR LETTERS) IMMEDIATELY FOLLOWING THE CODE NUMBER OF THE PERIODICAL. TO LEARN THE NAME OF THE PERIODICAL IN WHICH THE REVIEW APPEARS, IT IS NECESSARY TO REFER THE CODE NUMBER TO THE NUMERICALLY-ARRANGED LIST OF PERIODICALS BEGINNING ON PAGE III. THIS LIST ALSO SHOWS THE VOLUME AND NUMBER OF THE PERIODICALS INDEXED.

REVIEWS ARE INDEXED AS THEY APPEAR AND NO ATTEMPT IS MADE TO HOLD THE TITLE UNTIL ALL THE REVIEWS ARE PUBLISHED. FOR THIS REASON IT IS NECESSARY TO REFER TO PREVIOUS AND SUBSEQUENT VOLUMES OF THIS INDEX TO BE SURE THAT THE COMPLETE ROSTER OF REVIEWS OF ANY TITLE IS SEEN. AS AN AID TO THE USER, AN ASTERISK (*) HAS BEEN ADDED IMMEDIATELY FOLLOWING ANY TITLE THAT WAS ALSO INDEXED IN VOLUME 12 (1971) OF THIS INDEX.

AUTHORS WITH HYPHENATED SURNAMES ARE INDEXED UNDER THE NAME BEFORE THE HYPHEN, AND THE NAME FOLLOWING THE HYPHEN IS NOT CROSS-INDEXED. AUTHORS WITH MORE THAN ONE SURNAME, BUT WHERE THE NAMES ARE NOT HYPHENATED, ARE INDEXED UNDER THE FIRST OF THE NAMES AND THE LAST NAME IS CROSS-INDEXED. WHEN ALPHABETIZING SURNAMES CONTAINING UMLAUTS, THE UMLAUTS ARE IGNORED. EDITORS ARE ALWAYS SHOWN IN THE AUTHOR-TITLE ENTRY, AND THEY ARE CROSS-INDEXED (EXCEPT WHERE THE EDITOR'S SURNAME IS THE SAME AS THAT OF THE AUTHOR). TRANSLATORS ARE SHOWN ONLY WHEN THEY ARE NECESSARY TO IDENTIFY THE BOOK BEING REVIEWED (AS IN THE CLASSICS), AND THEY ARE NOT CROSS-INDEXED UNLESS THE BOOK BEING REVIEWED HAS NO AUTHOR OR EDITOR. CERTAIN REFERENCE WORKS AND ANONYMOUS WORKS THAT ARE KNOWN PRIMARILY BY THEIR TITLE ARE INDEXED UNDER THAT TITLE AND THEIR EDITORS ARE CROSS-INDEXED.

A LIST OF ABBREVIATIONS USED IS SHOWN ON PAGE II.

ABBREVIATIONS

```
ANON ..............ANONYMOUS
APR ...............APRIL
AUG ...............AUGUST
BK ................BOOK
COMP(S) ...........COMPILER(S)
CONT. .............CONTINUED
DEC ...............DECEMBER
ED(S) .............EDITOR(S) [OR]
                      EDITION(S)
FASC ..............FASCICULE
FEB ...............FEBRUARY
JAN ...............JANUARY
JUL ...............JULY
JUN ...............JUNE
MAR ...............MARCH
NO. (OR #) ........NUMBER
NOV ...............NOVEMBER
OCT ...............OCTOBER
PREV ..............PREVIOUS VOLUME OF
                      THIS INDEX
PT ................PART
REV ...............REVISED
SEP ...............SEPTEMBER
SER ...............SERIES
SUPP ..............SUPPLEMENT
TRANS .............TRANSLATOR(S)
VOL ...............VOLUME
* (ASTERISK) ......THIS TITLE WAS ALSO
                      SHOWN IN THE VOLUME
                      OF THIS INDEX IM-
                      MEDIATELY PRECEDING
                      THIS ONE
```

THE PERIODICALS IN WHICH THE REVIEWS
APPEAR ARE IDENTIFIED IN THIS INDEX BY A
NUMBER. TO SUPPLEMENT THIS NUMBER, AND
TO PROMOTE READY IDENTIFICATION, PMLA
ABBREVIATIONS ARE ALSO GIVEN FOLLOWING
THIS NUMBER. EVERY ATTEMPT WILL BE MADE
TO INDEX THOSE ISSUES SHOWN HERE AS
"MISSING" IN A LATER VOLUME OF THIS
INDEX. EVERY PERIODICAL INDEXED IN THIS
VOLUME WITH A COVER DATE AFTER 1 JANUARY
1971 HAS HAD ALL REVIEWS APPEARING THERE-
IN INDEXED; MANY OF THE PERIODICALS
INDEXED WITH EARLIER COVER DATES HAVE
ALSO HAD ALL REVIEWS INDEXED, BUT THESE
ARE NOT INDICATED BELOW. IT SHOULD
THEREFORE BE ASSUMED THAT ALL PERIODICALS
SHOWN BELOW WITH COVER DATES EARLIER
THAN 1971 WERE INDEXED UNDER THE OLD
RULES OF INCLUSION.
  THE FOLLOWING IS A LISTING OF THE
PERIODICALS INDEXED IN VOLUME 13:

  5 - ARION. AUSTIN, TEXAS. QUARTERLY.
        SPRING69 THRU WINTER69 (VOL
        8 COMPLETE)
  9(ALAR) - ALABAMA REVIEW. UNIVERSITY,
        ALABAMA. QUARTERLY.
        JAN69 THRU OCT69 (VOL 22
        COMPLETE)
 14 - AMERICAN ARCHIVIST. LAWRENCE,
        KANSAS. QUARTERLY.
        JAN69 THRU OCT69 (VOL 32
        COMPLETE)
 19(AGR) - AMERICAN-GERMAN REVIEW.
        PHILADELPHIA. BI-MONTHLY.
        VOL35#1 THRU VOL 36#6 (BOTH
        VOLS COMPLETE)
 24 - AMERICAN JOURNAL OF PHILOLOGY.
        BALTIMORE. QUARTERLY.
        JAN71 THRU OCT71 (VOL 92
        COMPLETE)
 27(AL) - AMERICAN LITERATURE. DURHAM,
        NORTH CAROLINA. QUARTERLY.
        MAR71 THRU JAN72 (VOL 43
        COMPLETE)
 31(ASCH) - AMERICAN SCHOLAR. WASHING-
        TON, D.C. QUARTERLY.
        WINTER71/72 THRU AUTUMN72
        (VOL 41 COMPLETE)
 32 - SLAVIC REVIEW. SEATTLE, WASH.
        QUARTERLY.
        MAR71 THRU DEC71 (VOL 30
        COMPLETE)
 35(AS) - AMERICAN SPEECH. NEW YORK.
        QUARTERLY.
        MAY68 & OCT 68 (VOL 43 #2&3)
 37 - THE AMERICAS. WASHINGTON, D.C.
        MONTHLY.
        JAN69 THRU NOV-DEC69 (VOL 21
        COMPLETE)
 38 - ANGLIA. TÜBINGEN, GERMANY. QUAR-
        TERLY.
        BAND 87 COMPLETE
 39 - APOLLO. LONDON. MONTHLY.
        JAN69 THRU DEC69 (VOLS 89 &
        90 COMPLETE)
 42(AR) - ANTIOCH REVIEW. YELLOW SPRINGS,
        OHIO. QUARTERLY.
        SPRING69 THRU WINTER69/70
        (VOL 29 COMPLETE)
 44 - ARCHITECTURAL FORUM. NEW YORK.
        MONTHLY.
        JAN-FEB69 THRU DEC69 (VOLS
        130 & 131 COMPLETE)

 45 - ARCHITECTURAL RECORD. NEW YORK.
        MONTHLY.
        JAN69 THRU DEC69 (VOLS 145 &
        146 COMPLETE)
 46 - ARCHITECTURAL REVIEW. LONDON.
        MONTHLY.
        JAN69 THRU DEC69 (VOLS 145 &
        146 COMPLETE)
 50(ARQ) - ARIZONA QUARTERLY. TUCSON.
        SPRING69 THRU WINTER69 (VOL
        25 COMPLETE)
 52 - ARCADIA. BERLIN. THREE YEARLY.
        BAND 4 COMPLETE
 54 - ART BULLETIN. NEW YORK. QUARTERLY.
        MAR69 THRU DEC69 (VOL 51
        COMPLETE)
 55 - ART NEWS. NEW YORK. MONTHLY.
        JAN69 THRU FEB70 (VOL 67
        #9&10, VOL 68 COMPLETE) [VOL
        68 BEGINS WITH MAR69 ISSUE]
 56 - ART QUARTERLY. DETROIT.
        SPRING69 THRU WINTER69 (VOL
        32 COMPLETE)
 57 - ARTIBUS ASIAE. ASCONA, SWITZER-
        LAND. QUARTERLY.
        VOL 31 COMPLETE
 58 - ARTS MAGAZINE. NEW YORK. MONTHLY.
        SEP/OCT69 THRU SUMMER70 (VOL
        44 COMPLETE)
 61 - ATLANTIC MONTHLY. BOSTON.
        JAN72 THRU DEC72 (VOLS 229 &
        230 COMPLETE)
 63 - AUSTRALASIAN JOURNAL OF PHILOSOPHY.
        SYDNEY. THREE YEARLY.
        MAY71 THRU DEC71 (VOL 49
        COMPLETE)
 67 - AUMLA [JOURNAL OF THE AUSTRALASIAN
        UNIVERSITIES LANGUAGE AND LIT-
        ERATURE ASSN.] CHRISTCHURCH,
        N.Z. TWICE YEARLY.
        MAY71 & NOV71 (#35 & 36)
 69 - AFRICA. LONDON. QUARTERLY.
        JAN69 THRU OCT69 (VOL 39
        COMPLETE)
 70(ANQ) - AMERICAN NOTES & QUERIES.
        NEW HAVEN, CONN. MONTHLY.
        SEP71 THRU JUN72 (VOL 10
        COMPLETE)
 71(ALS) - AUSTRALIAN LITERARY STUDIES.
        HOBART, TASMANIA. TWICE
        YEARLY.
        MAY72 & OCT72 (VOL 5 #3&4)
 72 - ARCHIV FÜR DAS STUDIUM DER NEUEREN
        SPRACHEN UND LITERATUREN.
        BRAUNSCHWEIG, GERMANY. SIX
        YEARLY.
        BAND 208 COMPLETE
 75 - BABEL. GERLINGEN, GERMANY. QUAR-
        TERLY.
        1/1969 THRU 4/1969 (VOL 15
        COMPLETE)
 78(BC) - BOOK COLLECTOR. LONDON.
        QUARTERLY.
        SPRING70 THRU WINTER70 (VOL
        19 COMPLETE)
 86(BHS) - BULLETIN OF HISPANIC STUDIES.
        LIVERPOOL. QUARTERLY.
        JAN71 THRU OCT71 (VOL 48
        COMPLETE)
 89(BJA) - THE BRITISH JOURNAL OF AES-
        THETICS. LONDON. QUARTERLY.
        WINTER71 THRU AUTUMN71 (VOL
        11 COMPLETE)
 90 - BURLINGTON MAGAZINE. LONDON.
        MONTHLY.
        JAN69 THRU DEC70 (VOLS 111 &
        112 COMPLETE)

208(FS) - FRENCH STUDIES. OXFORD, ENG-
 LAND. QUARTERLY.
  JAN71 THRU OCT71 (VOL 25
  COMPLETE)
219(GAR) - GEORGIA REVIEW. ATHENS, GA.
 QUARTERLY.
  SPRING69 THRU WINTER69 (VOL
  23 COMPLETE)
220(GL&L) - GERMAN LIFE AND LETTERS.
 OXFORD, ENGLAND. QUARTERLY.
  OCT70 THRU JUL71 (VOL 24
  COMPLETE)
221(GQ) - GERMAN QUARTERLY.
  JAN70 THRU NOV70 (VOL 43
  COMPLETE)
222(GR) - GERMANIC REVIEW. NEW YORK.
 QUARTERLY.
  JAN70 THRU NOV70 (VOL 45
  COMPLETE)
231 - HARPER'S MAGAZINE. NEW YORK.
 MONTHLY.
  JAN72 THRU DEC72 (VOLS 244
  & 245 COMPLETE)
238 - HISPANIA. QUARTERLY.
  MAR70 THRU DEC70 (VOL 53
  COMPLETE)
240(HR) - HISPANIC REVIEW. PHILADELPHIA.
 QUARTERLY.
  JAN70 THRU OCT70 (VOL 38
  COMPLETE)
241 - HISPANÓFILA. CHAPEL HILL, N.C.
 THREE YEARLY.
  JAN71 THRU SEP71 (#41-43)
244(HJAS) - HARVARD JOURNAL OF ASIATIC
 STUDIES. CAMBRIDGE, MASS.
 ANNUAL.
  VOL 29 COMPLETE
249(HUDR) - HUDSON REVIEW. NEW YORK.
 QUARTERLY.
  SPRING71 THRU WINTER71/72
  (VOL 24 COMPLETE)
255(HAB) - HUMANITIES ASSOCIATION BULLE-
 TIN. FREDERICTON, N.B.,
 CANADA. TWICE YEARLY.
  WINTER69 & SPRING69 (VOL 20
  #1&2)
258 - INTERNATIONAL PHILOSOPHICAL QUAR-
 TERLY. NEW YORK.
  MAR69 THRU DEC69 (VOL 9
  COMPLETE)
263 - INTER-AMERICAN REVIEW OF BIBLIO-
 GRAPHY. WASHINGTON, D.C.
 QUARTERLY.
  JAN-MAR71 THRU OCT-DEC71
  (VOL 21 COMPLETE)
269(IJAL) - INTERNATIONAL JOURNAL OF
 AMERICAN LINGUISTICS. BALTI-
 MORE. QUARTERLY.
  JAN69 THRU OCT69 (VOL 35
  COMPLETE)
270 - INTERNATIONAL P.E.N. LONDON.
 QUARTERLY.
  VOL 20 COMPLETE
273(IC) - ISLAMIC CULTURE. NARAYANGUDA,
 HYDERABAD-DECCAN, INDIA.
 QUARTERLY.
  JAN69 THRU OCT69 (VOL 43
  COMPLETE)
275(IQ) - ITALIAN QUARTERLY. RIVERSIDE,
 CALIFORNIA.
  SUMMER69 THRU WINTER70 (VOL
  13 #49-51)
276 - ITALICA. NEW YORK. QUARTERLY.
  SPRING70 THRU WINTER70 (VOL
  47 COMPLETE)
285(JAPQ) - JAPAN QUARTERLY. TOKYO.
  JAN-MAR70 THRU OCT-DEC70
  (VOL 17 COMPLETE)

287 - JEWISH FRONTIER. NEW YORK. MONTHLY.
  JAN69 THRU DEC69 (VOL 36
  COMPLETE)
290(JAAC) - JOURNAL OF AESTHETICS AND ART
 CRITICISM. BALTIMORE. QUAR-
 TERLY.
  FALL69 THRU SUMMER70 (VOL
  28 COMPLETE)
292(JAF) - JOURNAL OF AMERICAN FOLKLORE.
 QUARTERLY.
  JAN-MAR70 THRU OCT-DEC70
  (VOL 83 COMPLETE)
293(JAST) - JOURNAL OF ASIAN STUDIES.
 ANN ARBOR, MICH. QUARTERLY.
  NOV69 THRU AUG70 (VOL 29
  COMPLETE)
295 - JOURNAL OF MODERN LITERATURE.
 PHILADELPHIA. FIVE YEARLY.
  VOL 2 #1 THRU VOL 2 #3
296 - JOURNAL OF CANADIAN FICTION. FRED-
 ERICTON, N.B., CANADA. QUAR-
 TERLY.
  WINTER72 THRU FALL72 (VOL 1
  COMPLETE)
297(JL) - JOURNAL OF LINGUISTICS. READ-
 ING, ENGLAND. TWICE YEARLY.
  APR69 & OCT69 (VOL 5 COM-
  PLETE)
301(JEGP) - JOURNAL OF ENGLISH AND GER-
 MANIC PHILOLOGY. URBANA, ILL.
 QUARTERLY.
  JAN71 THRU OCT71 (VOL 70
  COMPLETE)
302 - JOURNAL OF ORIENTAL STUDIES. HONG
 KONG. TWICE YEARLY.
  JAN69 THRU JUL70 (VOLS 7 &
  8 COMPLETE)
303 - JOURNAL OF HELLENIC STUDIES.
 LONDON. ANNUAL.
  VOL 90 COMPLETE
308 - JOURNAL OF MUSIC THEORY. NEW
 HAVEN, CONN. TWICE YEARLY.
  SPRING67 THRU WINTER70 (VOLS
  11 THRU 14 COMPLETE)
311(JP) - JOURNAL OF PHILOSOPHY. NEW
 YORK. BI-WEEKLY.
  13JAN72 THRU 21DEC72 (VOL
  69 COMPLETE)
313 - JOURNAL OF ROMAN STUDIES. LONDON.
 ANNUAL.
  VOL 60 COMPLETE
315(JAL) - JOURNAL OF AFRICAN LANGUAGES.
 LONDON. THREE YEARLY.
  VOL 7 PT 3 & VOL 8 COMPLETE
317 - JOURNAL OF THE AMERICAN MUSICOLOGI-
 CAL SOCIETY. RICHMOND, VA.
 THREE YEARLY.
  SPRING71 THRU FALL71 (VOL
  24 COMPLETE)
318(JAOS) - JOURNAL OF THE AMERICAN
 ORIENTAL SOCIETY. BALTIMORE.
 QUARTERLY.
  JAN-MAR70 THRU OCT-DEC70
  (VOL 90 COMPLETE)
319 - JOURNAL OF THE HISTORY OF PHILOSO-
 PHY. BERKELEY, CALIF. QUAR-
 TERLY.
  JAN72 THRU OCT72 (VOL 10
  COMPLETE)
320(CJL) - CANADIAN JOURNAL OF LINGUIS-
 TICS. TORONTO. TWICE YEARLY.
  FALL69 & SPRING70 (VOL 15
  COMPLETE)
322(JHI) - JOURNAL OF THE HISTORY OF
 IDEAS. NEW YORK. QUARTERLY.
  JAN-MAR69 THRU OCT-DEC69
  (VOL 30 COMPLETE)

325 - JOURNAL OF THE SOCIETY OF ARCHIV-
ISTS. LONDON. TWICE YEARLY.
APR69 THRU OCT70 (VOL 3
#9&10, VOL 4 #1&2)

328 - JUDAISM. NEW YORK. QUARTERLY.
WINTER69 THRU FALL69 (VOL
18 COMPLETE)

329(JJQ) - JAMES JOYCE QUARTERLY. TULSA,
OKLAHOMA.
FALL71 THRU SUMMER72 (VOL
9 COMPLETE)

330(MASJ) - MIDCONTINENT AMERICAN STUDIES
JOURNAL. LAWRENCE, KANSAS.
TWICE YEARLY.
SPRING69 & FALL69 (VOL 10
COMPLETE [ISSUE DATED FALL68
MISSING]

331 - JOURNAL OF CANADIAN STUDIES/REVUE
D'ÉTUDES CANADIENNES. PETER-
BOROUGH, ONT., CANADA. QUAR-
TERLY.
FEB69 THRU NOV69 (VOL 4
COMPLETE)

340(KR) - KENYON REVIEW. GAMBIER, OHIO.
FIVE YEARLY.
1969/1 THRU 1970/1 (VOL 31
COMPLETE & VOL 32 #1) [CEASED
PUBLICATION WITH ISSUE DATED
1970/1]

350 - LANGUAGE. BALTIMORE. QUARTERLY.
MAR71 THRU DEC71 (VOL 47
COMPLETE)

351(LL) - LANGUAGE LEARNING. ANN ARBOR,
MICH. TWICE YEARLY.
JUN70 & DEC70 (VOL 20 COM-
PLETE)

353 - LINGUISTICS. THE HAGUE. MONTHLY.
APR69 THRU DEC69 (#47-55)

354 - THE LIBRARY. LONDON. QUARTERLY.
MAR69 THRU DEC69 (VOL 24
COMPLETE)

355 - LIBRARY ASSOCIATION RECORD. LON-
DON. MONTHLY.
JAN69 THRU DEC69 (VOL 71
COMPLETE)

356 - LIBRARY QUARTERLY. CHICAGO.
JAN71 THRU OCT71 (VOL 41
COMPLETE)

361 - LINGUA. AMSTERDAM. QUARTERLY.
VOL 23 #1 THRU VOL 24 #4

362 - THE LISTENER. LONDON. WEEKLY.
6JAN72 THRU 28DEC72 (VOLS
87 & 88 COMPLETE)

363 - LITURGICAL ARTS. NEW YORK. QUAR-
TERLY.
NOV69 THRU AUG70 (VOL 38
COMPLETE)

364 - LONDON MAGAZINE. LONDON. BI-
MONTHLY.
APR/MAY71 THRU FEB/MAR72
(VOL 11 COMPLETE)

368 - LANDFALL. CHRISTCHURCH, N.Z.
QUARTERLY.
MAR69 THRU DEC69 (VOL 23
COMPLETE)

377 - MANUSCRIPTA. ST. LOUIS, MO. THREE
YEARLY.
MAR71 THRU NOV71 (VOL 15
COMPLETE)

381 - MEANJIN. PARKVILLE, VICTORIA,
AUSTRALIA. QUARTERLY.
VOL 29 COMPLETE

382(MAE) - MEDIUM AEVUM. OXFORD, ENGLAND.
THREE YEARLY.
1971/1 THRU 1971/3 (VOL 40
COMPLETE)

385(MQR) - MICHIGAN QUARTERLY REVIEW.
ANN ARBOR.
WINTER72 THRU FALL72 (VOL 11
COMPLETE)

390 - MIDSTREAM. NEW YORK. MONTHLY.
JAN69 THRU DEC69 (VOL 15
COMPLETE)

393(MIND) - MIND. LONDON. QUARTERLY.
JAN70 THRU OCT70 (VOL 79
COMPLETE)

396(MODA) - MODERN AGE. CHICAGO. QUAR-
TERLY.
WINTER71 THRU FALL71 (VOL
15 COMPLETE)

397(MD) - MODERN DRAMA. LAWRENCE, KANSAS.
QUARTERLY.
SEP67 THRU FEB70 (VOL 10
#2-4, VOLS 11 & 12 COMPLETE)

398 - MODERN POETRY STUDIES. BUFFALO,
N.Y. SIX YEARLY.
VOL 3 #1-3

399(MLJ) - MODERN LANGUAGE JOURNAL. MIL-
WAUKEE, WISC. MONTHLY.
JAN70 THRU DEC70 (VOL 54
COMPLETE)

400(MLN) - MODERN LANGUAGE NOTES. BALTI-
MORE. SIX YEARLY.
JAN70 THRU DEC70 (VOL 85
COMPLETE)

401(MLQ) - MODERN LANGUAGE QUARTERLY.
SEATTLE, WASH.
MAR70 THRU DEC70 (VOL 31
COMPLETE)

402(MLR) - MODERN LANGUAGE REVIEW. LON-
DON. QUARTERLY.
JAN71 THRU OCT71 (VOL 66
COMPLETE)

405(MP) - MODERN PHILOLOGY. CHICAGO.
QUARTERLY.
AUG69 THRU MAY70 (VOL 67
COMPLETE)

406 - MONATSHEFTE. MADISON, WISC. QUAR-
TERLY.
SPRING71 THRU WINTER71 (VOL
63 COMPLETE)

410(M&L) - MUSIC & LETTERS. LONDON.
QUARTERLY.
JAN71 THRU OCT71 (VOL 52
COMPLETE)

412 - MUSIC REVIEW. CAMBRIDGE, ENGLAND.
QUARTERLY.
FEB71 THRU NOV71 (VOL 32
COMPLETE)

414(MQ) - MUSICAL QUARTERLY. NEW YORK.
JAN68 THRU OCT69 (VOLS 54
& 55 COMPLETE)

415 - MUSICAL TIMES. LONDON. MONTHLY.
JAN70 THRU DEC71 (VOLS 111
& 112 COMPLETE)

418(MR) - THE MASSACHUSETTS REVIEW.
AMHERST, MASS. QUARTERLY.
WINTER71 THRU AUTUMN71 (VOL
12 COMPLETE)

424 - NAMES. POTSDAM, N.Y. QUARTERLY.
MAR68 THRU DEC69 (VOLS 16 &
17 COMPLETE)

432(NEQ) - NEW ENGLAND QUARTERLY. BRUNS-
WICK, MAINE.
MAR70 THRU DEC70 (VOL 43
COMPLETE)

440 - BOOK WORLD. CHICAGO & WASHINGTON.
WEEKLY.
2JAN72 THRU 28MAY72 (VOL 6
#1-22) [CEASED PUBLICATION
WITH 28MAY72 ISSUE]

441 - THE NEW YORK TIMES. DAILY.
1JAN72 THRU 31DEC72

442(NY) - THE NEW YORKER. WEEKLY.
1JAN72 THRU 30DEC72 (VOL 47
#46-53, VOL 48 #1-45) [VOL
48 BEGINS WITH ISSUE DATED
26FEB72]
445(NCF) - NINETEENTH-CENTURY FICTION.
BERKELEY, CALIF. QUARTERLY.
JUN68 THRU MAR70 (VOLS 23 &
24 COMPLETE)
447(N&Q) - NOTES & QUERIES. LONDON.
MONTHLY.
JAN70 THRU DEC70 (VOL 17
COMPLETE)
448 - NORTHWEST REVIEW. EUGENE, OREGON.
THREE YEARLY.
SUMMER68 THRU SUMMER70 (VOL
10 COMPLETE)
453 - THE NEW YORK REVIEW OF BOOKS.
BI-WEEKLY.
27JAN72 THRU 14DEC72 (VOL
17 #12/VOL 18#1 THRU VOL 19
#10) [VOL 19 BEGINS WITH
ISSUE DATED 20JUL72]
461 - ORBIS. PHILADELPHIA. QUARTERLY.
SPRING68 THRU WINTER70
(VOLS 12 & 13 COMPLETE)
462(OL) - ORBIS LITTERARUM. COPENHAGEN.
QUARTERLY.
VOL 23 #2 THRU VOL 25 #4
468 - PAKISTAN HORIZON. KARACHI. QUAR-
TERLY.
VOL 21 #1&2
470 - PAN PIPES. DES MOINES, IOWA.
QUARTERLY.
NOV68 THRU JAN70 (VOL 61
COMPLETE, VOL 62 #1&2)
473(PR) - PARTISAN REVIEW. NEW YORK.
QUARTERLY.
1/1971 THRU WINTER71/72
(VOL 38 COMPLETE)
477 - PERSONALIST. LOS ANGELES. QUAR-
TERLY.
WINTER69 THRU AUTUMN69 (VOL
50 COMPLETE)
479(PHQ) - PHILOSOPHICAL QUARTERLY. ST.
ANDREWS, SCOTLAND.
JAN70 THRU OCT70 (VOL 20
COMPLETE)
481(PQ) - PHILOLOGICAL QUARTERLY. IOWA
CITY, IOWA.
JAN70 THRU OCT70 (VOL 49
COMPLETE)
482(PHR) - PHILOSOPHICAL REVIEW. ITHACA,
N.Y. QUARTERLY.
JAN70 THRU OCT70 (VOL 79
COMPLETE)
483 - PHILOSOPHY. LONDON. QUARTERLY.
JAN70 THRU OCT70 (VOL 45
COMPLETE)
484(PPR) - PHILOSOPHY & PHENOMENOLOGICAL
RESEARCH. BUFFALO, N.Y.
QUARTERLY.
SEP69 THRU JUN70 (VOL 30
COMPLETE)
485(PE&W) - PHILOSOPHY EAST AND WEST.
HONOLULU. QUARTERLY.
JAN-APR68 THRU OCT69 (VOLS
18 & 19 COMPLETE)
486 - PHILOSOPHY OF SCIENCE. EAST LAN-
SING, MICH. QUARTERLY.
APR65 & JUL-OCT65, MAR68
THRU DEC69 (VOL 32 #2&3/4,
VOLS 35 & 36 COMPLETE)
487 - PHOENIX. TORONTO. QUARTERLY.
SPRING70 THRU WINTER70
(VOL 24 COMPLETE)

490 - POETICA. MÜNCHEN. QUARTERLY.
JAN68 THRU OCT68 (VOL 2
COMPLETE)
491 - POETRY. CHICAGO. MONTHLY.
OCT71 THRU SEP72 (VOLS 119
& 120 COMPLETE) [VOL 120 BE-
GINS WITH ISSUE DATED APR72]
493 - POETRY REVIEW. LONDON. QUARTERLY.
SPRING70 THRU WINTER70/71
(VOL 61 COMPLETE)
497(POLR) - POLISH REVIEW. NEW YORK.
QUARTERLY.
WINTER68 THRU AUTUMN69
(VOLS 13 & 14 COMPLETE)
502(PRS) - PRAIRIE SCHOONER. LINCOLN,
NEBRASKA. QUARTERLY.
SPRING68 THRU WINTER69/70
(VOLS 42 & 43 COMPLETE)
503 - THE PRIVATE LIBRARY. PINNER, MID-
DLESEX, ENGLAND. QUARTERLY.
SPRING68 & WINTER68 THRU
AUTUMN69 (NEW SER VOL 1 #1,
VOL 1 #4, VOL 2 #1-3)
[ISSUES DATED SUMMER68 &
AUTUMN68 MISSING]
505 - PROGRESSIVE ARCHITECTURE. NEW YORK.
MONTHLY.
JAN68 THRU DEC69 (VOLS 49 &
50 COMPLETE)
513 - PERSPECTIVES OF NEW MUSIC. PRINCE-
TON, N.J. TWICE YEARLY.
FALL-WINTER68 & SPRING-SUMMER
69 (VOL 7 COMPLETE)
517(PBSA) - PAPERS OF THE BIBLIOGRAPHICAL
SOCIETY OF AMERICA. NEW
HAVEN, CONN. QUARTERLY.
JAN-MAR71 THRU OCT-DEC71
(VOL 65 COMPLETE)
518 - PHILOSOPHICAL BOOKS. LEICESTER,
ENGLAND. THREE YEARLY.
JAN70 THRU OCT71 (VOLS 11 &
12 COMPLETE)
529(QQ) - QUEEN'S QUARTERLY. KINGSTON,
ONT., CANADA.
SPRING70 THRU WINTER70 (VOL
77 COMPLETE)
536 - RATIO. OXFORD, ENGLAND. TWICE
YEARLY.
JUN70 & DEC70 (VOL 12 COM-
PLETE)
541(RES) - REVIEW OF ENGLISH STUDIES.
LONDON. QUARTERLY.
FEB70 THRU NOV70 (VOL 21
COMPLETE)
542 - REVUE PHILOSOPHIQUE DE LA FRANCE
ET DE L'ÉTRANGER. PARIS.
QUARTERLY.
JAN-MAR68 THRU JUL-DEC69
(VOLS 158 & 159 COMPLETE)
543 - REVIEW OF METAPHYSICS. NEW HAVEN,
CONN. QUARTERLY.
SEP69 THRU JUN70 (VOL 23
COMPLETE)
545(RPH) - ROMANCE PHILOLOGY. BERKELEY,
CALIF. QUARTERLY.
AUG69 THRU MAY71 (VOLS 23 &
24 COMPLETE)
546(RR) - ROMANIC REVIEW. NEW YORK.
QUARTERLY.
FEB70 THRU DEC70 (VOL 61
COMPLETE)
548(RCSF) - RIVISTA CRITICA DI STORIA
DELLA FILOSOFIA. FIRENZE,
ITALY. QUARTERLY.
JAN-MAR68 THRU OCT-DEC69
(VOLS 23 & 24 COMPLETE)

550(RUSR) - RUSSIAN REVIEW. HANOVER, N.H. QUARTERLY.
JAN70 THRU OCT70 (VOL 29 COMPLETE)

551(RENQ) - RENAISSANCE QUARTERLY. NEW YORK.
SPRING70 THRU WINTER70 (VOL 23 COMPLETE)

555 - REVUE DE PHILOLOGIE. PARIS. TWICE YEARLY.
VOL 44 COMPLETE

561(SATR) - SATURDAY REVIEW. NEW YORK. WEEKLY.
1JAN72 THRU 23 DEC72 (VOL 55 COMPLETE)

563(SS) - SCANDINAVIAN STUDIES. QUARTERLY.
WINTER71 THRU AUTUMN71 (VOL 43 COMPLETE)

564 - SEMINAR. TORONTO. TWICE YEARLY.
SPRING68 THRU FALL69 (VOLS 4 & 5 COMPLETE)

566 - THE SCRIBLERIAN. PHILADELPHIA. TWICE YEARLY.
AUTUMN70 & SPRING71 (VOL 3 COMPLETE)

568(SCN) - SEVENTEENTH-CENTURY NEWS. NEW YORK. QUARTERLY.
SPRING71 THRU WINTER71 (VOL 29 COMPLETE)

569(SR) - SEWANEE REVIEW. SEWANEE, TENN. QUARTERLY.
WINTER71 THRU AUTUMN71 (VOL 79 COMPLETE)

570(SQ) - SHAKESPEARE QUARTERLY. NEW YORK.
WINTER68 THRU AUTUMN69 (VOLS 19 & 20 COMPLETE)

571 - THE SHAVIAN. LONDON. THREE YEARLY.
SPRING-SUMMER68 THRU WINTER 69/70 (VOL 3 #9&10, VOL 4 #1&2)

572 - SHAW REVIEW. UNIVERSITY PARK, PA. THREE YEARLY.
JAN68 THRU SEP69 (VOLS 11 & 12 COMPLETE)

574(SEEJ) - SLAVIC AND EAST EUROPEAN JOURNAL. MADISON, WISC. QUARTERLY.
SPRING71 THRU WINTER71 (VOL 15 COMPLETE)

575(SEER) - SLAVONIC AND EAST EUROPEAN REVIEW. LONDON. QUARTERLY.
JAN71 THRU OCT71 (VOL 49 COMPLETE)

576 - JOURNAL OF THE SOCIETY OF ARCHITECTURAL HISTORIANS. PHILADELPHIA. QUARTERLY.
MAR68 THRU DEC69 (VOLS 27 & 28 COMPLETE)

577(SHR) - SOUTHERN HUMANITIES REVIEW. AUBURN, ALA. QUARTERLY.
WINTER70 THRU FALL70 (VOL 4 COMPLETE)

578 - SOUTHERN LITERARY JOURNAL. CHAPEL HILL, N.C. TWICE YEARLY.
SPRING72 & FALL72 (VOL 4 #2, VOL 5 #1)

579(SAQ) - SOUTH ATLANTIC QUARTERLY. DURHAM, N.C.
WINTER71 THRU AUTUMN71 (VOL 70 COMPLETE)

581 - SOUTHERLY. SYDNEY, AUSTRALIA. QUARTERLY.
1971/1, 1971/2 & 1971/4 (VOL 31 #1, 2 & 4) [ISSUE DATED 1971/3 MISSING]

582(SFQ) - SOUTHERN FOLKLORE QUARTERLY. GAINESVILLE, FLA.
MAR68 THRU DEC69 (VOLS 32 & 33 COMPLETE)

583 - SOUTHERN SPEECH JOURNAL. WINSTON-SALEM, N.C. QUARTERLY.
WINTER67 THRU SUMMER70 (VOL 33 #2-4, VOLS 34 & 35 COMPLETE)

584(SWR) - SOUTHWEST REVIEW. DALLAS, TEXAS. QUARTERLY.
WINTER71 THRU AUTUMN 71 (VOL 56 COMPLETE)

587 - SOVIET STUDIES. GLASGOW. QUARTERLY.
JAN68 THRU APR70 (VOL 19 #3&4, VOLS 20 & 21 COMPLETE)

589 - SPECULUM. CAMBRIDGE, MASS. QUARTERLY.
JAN71 THRU OCT71 (VOL 46 COMPLETE)

590 - SPIRIT. SOUTH ORANGE, N.J. QUARTERLY.
SPRING70 THRU WINTER71 (VOL 37 COMPLETE)

592 - STUDIO INTERNATIONAL. LIVERPOOL. MONTHLY.
JAN68 THRU NOV69 (VOLS 175-177 COMPLETE, VOL 178 #913-916)

593 - SYMPOSIUM. SYRACUSE, N.Y. QUARTERLY.
SPRING71 THRU WINTER71 (VOL 25 COMPLETE)

595(SCS) - SCOTTISH STUDIES. EDINBURGH. TWICE YEARLY.
VOL 15 COMPLETE

596(SL) - STUDIA LINGUISTICA. LUND, SWEDEN. TWICE YEARLY.
VOLS 22 & 23 COMPLETE

597(SN) - STUDIA NEOPHILOLOGICA. UPPSALA, SWEDEN. TWICE YEARLY.
VOLS 40 & 41 COMPLETE

598(SOR) - THE SOUTHERN REVIEW. BATON ROUGE, LA. QUARTERLY.
WINTER72 THRU AUTUMN72 (VOL 8 COMPLETE)

606(TAMR) - TAMARACK REVIEW. TORONTO. QUARTERLY.
#54 THRU #57

607 - TEMPO. LONDON. QUARTERLY.
WINTER67/68 THRU AUTUMN70 (#83-94)

613 - THOUGHT. BRONX, N.Y. QUARTERLY.
SPRING68 THRU WINTER69 (VOLS 43 & 44 COMPLETE)

617(TLS) - TIMES LITERARY SUPPLEMENT. LONDON. WEEKLY.
7JAN72 THRU 29DEC72 (#3645-3695)

619(TC) - TWENTIETH CENTURY. LONDON. QUARTERLY.
1968/2 THRU VOL 177 #1042 (VOL 176 #1037-1040, VOL 177 #1041 & 1042)

627(UTQ) - UNIVERSITY OF TORONTO QUARTERLY.
JAN69 THRU JUL70 (VOL 38 #2-4, VOL 39 COMPLETE)

637(VS) - VICTORIAN STUDIES. BLOOMINGTON, IND. QUARTERLY.
SEP69 THRU JUN70 (VOL 13 COMPLETE)

639(VQR) - VIRGINIA QUARTERLY REVIEW. CHARLOTTESVILLE, VA.
WINTER70 THRU AUTUMN70 (VOL 46 COMPLETE)

646(WWR) - WALT WHITMAN REVIEW. DETROIT.
           QUARTERLY.
                MAR68 THRU DEC69 (VOLS 14 &
                15 COMPLETE)
650(WF) - WESTERN FOLKLORE. BERKELEY,
           CALIF. QUARTERLY.
                JAN68 THRU OCT69   (VOLS 27
                & 28 COMPLETE)
651(WHR) - WESTERN HUMANITIES REVIEW.
           SALT LAKE CITY. QUARTERLY.
                WINTER71 THRU AUTUMN71 (VOL
                25 COMPLETE)
656(WMQ) - WILLIAM & MARY QUARTERLY.
           WILLIAMSBURG, VA.
                JAN70 THRU OCT70 (VOL 27
                COMPLETE)
659 - CONTEMPORARY LITERATURE. MADISON,
           WISC. QUARTERLY.
                WINTER72 THRU AUTUMN72 (VOL
                13 COMPLETE)
661 - WORKS. NEW YORK.
                SPRING69 THRU SUMMER70 (VOL
                2 #1-3)
676(YR) - YALE REVIEW. NEW HAVEN, CONN.
           QUARTERLY.
                AUTUMN70 THRU SUMMER71 (VOL
                60 COMPLETE)
677 - THE YEARBOOK OF ENGLISH STUDIES.
           LONDON. ANNUAL.
                VOL 2 COMPLETE

AARNES, S.A. "AESTHETISK LUTHERANER" OG
ANDRE STUDIER I NORSK SENROMANTIKK.
H.S. NAESS, 563(SS):SPRING71-199
AARNES, S.A., ED. NORSK LITTERATUR-
KRITIKK FRA TULLIN TIL A.H. WINSNES.
L. ASKELAND, 563(SS):SUMMER71-300
AARON, W. STRAIGHT.
A. STORR, 440:21MAY72-3
441:30JUL72-21
AARSLEFF, H. THE STUDY OF LANGUAGE IN
ENGLAND, 1780-1860.*
K. TOGEBY, 545(RPH):FEB70-362
A. WARD, 541(RES):MAY70-250
AARTS, F.G.A.M., ED. THE PATER NOSTER
OF RICHARD ERMYTE.*
A.I. DOYLE, 179(ES):JUN70-249
T.P. DUNNING, 597(SN):VOL41#2-465
ABBAGNANO, N. CRITICAL EXISTENTIALISM.
(N. LANGIULLI, ED & TRANS)
J. ASHMORE, 484(PPR):MAR70-468
W.A.J., 543:JUN70-737
A. MANSER, 479(PHQ):JUL70-279
G.J. STACK, 319:JUL72-376
ABBAS, I. - SEE AŞ-ŞAFADĪ, Ḥ.A.
VAN ABBÉ, D. GOETHE.
617(TLS):20OCT72-1262
ABBEY, E. SUNSET CANYON.
V. CUNNINGHAM, 362:24AUG72-248
ABBOTT, G.F. MACEDONIAN FOLKLORE.
R. PIONTKOVSKY, 104:SPRING71-128
ABBOTT, K. WHERE THE SUN BEGAN.
L. CLARK, 493:WINTER70/71-370
ABDO, D.A. ON STRESS AND ARABIC PHONOL-
OGY.
F.S. ANSHEN, 350:DEC71-955
ABDULLA, J.J. & E.N. MC CARUS. KURDISH
BASIC COURSE, DIALECT OF SULAIMANIA,
IRAQ.
E.R. ONEY, 318(JAOS):APR-JUN70-295
ABDULLA, J.J. & E.N. MC CARUS, EDS. KUR-
DISH READERS.
E.R. ONEY, 318(JAOS):APR-JUN70-295
ABÉ, K. THE RUINED MAP.
J. HUNTER, 362:9MAR72-317
617(TLS):17MAR72-295
ABEL-STRUTH, S. MUSIKPÄDAGOGIK. (VOL 1)
412:FEB71-76
ABELARD, P. PETRUS ABAELARDUS, "DIALEC-
TICA." (2ND ED) (L.M. DE RIJK, ED)
O. BIRD, 589:JUL71-510
ABELLIO, R. MA DERNIÈRE MÉMOIRE.
617(TLS):14JUL72-792
ABELS, J. MAN ON FIRE.
J.S. LONG, 584(SWR):SUMMER71-290
ABENDROTH, W. A SHORT HISTORY OF THE
EUROPEAN WORKING CLASS.
617(TLS):2JUN72-636
ABERCROMBIE, D. ELEMENTS OF GENERAL
PHONETICS.*
K. HADDING-KOCH, 361:VOL23#1-87
T.F. MITCHELL, 297(JL):APR69-153
J. POSTHUMUS, 179(ES):JUN70-275
ABERCROMBIE, P.B. THE BROU-HA-HA.
J. HUNTER, 362:9MAR72-317
617(TLS):17MAR72-295
ABERNETHY, F.E. J. FRANK DOBIE.
D.W. HATLEY, 582(SFQ):SEP68-268
ABRAHAM À SANCTA CLARA. WUNDERLICHER
TRAUM VON EINEM GROSSEN NARRENNEST.
(A. HAAS, ED)
W.F. SCHERER, 406:FALL71-294
ABRAHAM, G., ED. THE NEW OXFORD HISTORY
OF MUSIC.* (VOL 4: THE AGE OF HUMAN-
ISM, 1540-1630.)
M. PETERSON, 470:NOV68-65
ABRAHAM, G. SLAVONIC AND ROMANTIC MUSIC.
B. KRADER, 414(MQ):OCT69-573

ABRAHAM, P. & OTHERS. ROMAIN ROLLAND.
W.T. STARR, 207(FR):DEC69-337
ABRAHAM, S. & F. KIEFER. A THEORY OF
STRUCTURAL SEMANTICS.
Y. BAR-HILLEL, 361:VOL23#4-397
ABRAHAMOWICZ, Z. KATALOG DOKUMENTÓW
TURECKICH.
A.L. HORNIKER, 318(JAOS):OCT-DEC70-
568
ABRAHAMS, P. WILD CONQUEST.
J. CAREW, 441:2APR72-7
ABRAHAMS, R.D. & G. FOSS. ANGLO-AMERICAN
FOLKSONG STYLE.
M. PETERSON, 470:JAN70-45
ABRAHAMSEN, D. OUR VIOLENT SOCIETY.
H.D. GRAHAM, 639(VQR):SUMMER70-509
ABRAMS, C. THE LANGUAGE OF CITIES.*
D. MACDONALD, 442(NY):6MAY72-129
ABRAMS, M.H. NATURAL SUPERNATURALISM.
R.M. ADAMS, 249(HUDR):WINTER71/72-687
ABRAMS, P. THE ORIGINS OF BRITISH SOCI-
OLOGY 1834-1914.
G. HAWTHORN, 637(VS):DEC69-233
ABRAMSON, D.E. NEGRO PLAYWRIGHTS IN THE
AMERICAN THEATRE, 1925-1959.*
S. REDDING, 27(AL):JAN72-678
ABSALOM, R.N.L. PASSAGES FOR TRANSLA-
TION FROM ITALIAN.
M. BORELLI, 399(MLJ):MAY70-363
ABSE, D. SELECTED POEMS.*
E. NELSON, 590:WINTER71-41
ABSE, D. A SMALL DESPERATION.
R. MATHIAS, 448:SUMMER70-135
ABU HAKIMA, A.M. HISTORY OF EASTERN
ARABIA, 1750-1800.
R.G. LANDEN, 318(JAOS):APR-JUN70-272
ABŪ MA'SHAR. ALBUMASARIS, "DE REVOLU-
TIONIBUS NATIVITATUM."* (D. PINGREE,
ED) [SHOWN IN PREV UNDER ED]
J.G. GRIFFITHS, 123:DEC70-402
C. MUGLER, 555:VOL44FASC2-333
ABUN-NASR, J.M. A HISTORY OF THE MAGH-
RIB.
617(TLS):29SEP72-1172
ABZUG, B. BELLA!
S. HARRINGTON, 441:2JUL72-5
G. VIDAL, 453:10AUG72-8
ACE, G. THE BETTER OF GOODMAN ACE.
441:6FEB72-40
ACEVES, P. & M. EINARSSON-MULLARKY,
COMPS. FOLKLORE ARCHIVES OF THE WORLD.
R.L. WELSCH, 292(JAF):JUL-SEP70-369
ACHEBE, C. GIRLS AT WAR AND OTHER STOR-
IES.
D.A.N. JONES, 362:30MAR72-426
617(TLS):3MAR72-247
ACHEBE, C. & OTHERS. THE INSIDER.
617(TLS):3MAR72-247
ACHESON, D. GRAPES FROM THORNS.
A. KAZIN, 441:28MAY72-2
ACHESON, D. PRESENT AT THE CREATION.*
R.A. ESTHUS, 377:JUL71-117
ACHINSTEIN, P. LAW AND EXPLANATION.
617(TLS):11FEB72-160
ACKERLEY, J.R. MY FATHER AND MYSELF.
42(AR):SPRING69-112
ACKERMAN, J.S. PALLADIO.
P.G. HAMBERG, 290(JAAC):FALL69-101
J.F. O'GORMAN, 576:MAR68-80
ACKERMAN, J.S. PALLADIO'S VILLAS.
J.F. O'GORMAN, 576:MAR68-80
W. SMITH, 56:AUTUMN69-317
39:JUL69-83
ACKERMANN, I. VERGEBUNG UND GNADE IM
KLASSISCHEN DEUTSCHEN DRAMA.
W. EMMERICH, 222(GR):NOV70-307
F.M. FOWLER, 220(GL&L):OCT70-107
ACKRILL, J.L. - SEE ARISTOTLE

ACORN, M. I'VE TASTED MY BLOOD.*
    M. HORNYANSKY, 627(UTQ):JUL70-335
ACOSTA, O. & R. SOSA. ANTOLOGÍA DEL
    CUENTO HONDUREÑO.
    S. MENTON, 238:MAR70-160
ACOSTA, O.Z. THE AUTOBIOGRAPHY OF A
    BROWN BUFFALO.
    J. KANON, 561(SATR):11NOV72-67
"ACTA GERMANICA." (VOL 1)
    F. WIEDEN, 564:SPRING68-69
ACTON, H. MEMOIRS OF AN AESTHETE 1939-
    1969.* (BRITISH TITLE: MORE MEMOIRS
    OF AN AESTHETE.)
    G. STEINER, 442(NY):1JAN72-63
ACTON, H.B. KANT'S MORAL PHILOSOPHY.
    C.L. TEN, 63:MAY71-114
    K. WARD, 518:JAN71-1
ACTON, H.B., ED. THE PHILOSOPHY OF
    PUNISHMENT.
    R.S. DOWNIE, 483:OCT70-341
ADAM, A. GRANDEUR AND ILLUSION.
    617(TLS):14APR72-406
ADAM, C. BIBLIOGRAFÍA Y DOCUMENTOS DE
    EZEQUIEL MARTÍNEZ ESTRADA.
    S.R. WILSON, 240(HR):OCT70-446
ADAM, R. WHAT SHAW REALLY SAID.
    F.P.W. MC DOWELL, 397(MD):DEC68-341
ADAM, T. CLEMENTIA PRINCIPIS.
    F. LASSERRE, 182:VOL23#10-556
ADAMS, A.B. GERONIMO.
    441:6FEB72-40
ADAMS, B.B. - SEE BALE, J.
ADAMS, H.M. CATALOGUE OF BOOKS PRINTED
    ON THE CONTINENT OF EUROPE, 1501-1600
    IN CAMBRIDGE LIBRARIES.
    J.W. JOLLIFFE, 354:MAR69-63
ADAMS, I. & OTHERS. THE REAL POVERTY
    REPORT.
    P. GRADY, 99:MAY72-12
ADAMS, J.D. THE "POPULUS" OF AUGUSTINE
    AND JEROME.
    617(TLS):17NOV72-1405
ADAMS, M.M. & N. KRETZMANN - SEE OCKHAM,
    WILLIAM OF
ADAMS, R.M. STENDHAL.
    M. LEBOWITZ, 340(KR):1969/3-389
ADAMS, R.N. CRUCIFIXION BY POWER.*
    617(TLS):4AUG72-915
ADAMS, R.P. FAULKNER.*
    M. MILLGATE, 405(MP):FEB70-299
    O.W. VICKERY, 191(ELN):SEP70-69
ADAMS, T.W. AKEL.
    617(TLS):7JAN72-4
ADAMSON, D. - SEE SENCOURT, R.
ADAMSON, J. PIPPA'S CHALLENGE.
    J.E. BRODY, 441:14AUG72-29
    441:6AUG72-20
ADAMSON, R. CANTICLES ON THE SKIN.
    J. TULIP, 581:1971/1-72
ADBURGHAM, A. WOMEN IN PRINT.
    617(TLS):2JUN72-628
ADCOCK, F. HIGH TIDE IN THE GARDEN.*
    I. WEDDE, 364:DEC71/JAN72-118
ADDINGTON, A.C. THE ROYAL HOUSE OF
    STUART.
    617(TLS):15SEP72-1053
ADELMAN, B. DOWN HOME.
    S. SCHWARTZ, 441:3DEC72-16
ADELMAN, C. GENERATIONS.
    N. SCHREIBER, 561(SATR):2SEP72-58
ADELMANN, F.J. FROM DIALOGUE TO EPI-
    LOGUE.
    W.A.J., 543:MAR70-552
ADELSON, A. SDS.
    M. BREASTED, 561(SATR):12FEB72-75
ADELSTEIN, M.E. FANNY BURNEY.
    C. DE ST. VICTOR, 481(PQ):JUL70-332

ADEN, J.M. SOMETHING LIKE HORACE.*
    M.J. MC GANN, 123:DEC71-456
    H.D. WEINBROT, 481(PQ):JUL70-367
ADERETH, M. COMMITMENT IN MODERN FRENCH
    LITERATURE.
    P.A. FORTIER, 207(FR):FEB70-509
ADKINS, A.W.H. FROM THE MANY TO THE
    ONE.*
    L. PEARSON, 124:APR71-277
ADLER, A. RÜCKZUG IN EPISCHER PARADE.
    J. HORRENT, 545(RPH):FEB71-554
ADLER, G.M. LAND PLANNING BY ADMINIS-
    TRATIVE REGULATION.
    W.R.B. HILL, 99:MAY72-64
ADLER, H.G. PANORAMA. EREIGNISSE.
    G. FISCHER, 270:VOL20#2-38
ADLER, K. PHONETICS AND DICTION IN SING-
    ING.
    A. BLYTH, 415:FEB70-164
ADLER, M.J. & C. VAN DOREN. HOW TO READ
    A BOOK. (REV)
    C. LEHMANN-HAUPT, 441:25DEC72-15
ADLER, P. A HOUSE IS NOT A HOME.
    A. WHITMAN, 231:MAY72-102
ADLER, R. TOWARD A RADICAL MIDDLE.
    N. MILLS, 651(WHR):WINTER71-86
ADOLFSSON, H. - SEE GUY DE BAZOCHES
ADOLPH, R. THE RISE OF MODERN PROSE
    STYLE.*
    J.I. COPE, 401(MLQ):MAR70-92
    O.F. SIGWORTH, 50(ARQ):WINTER69-362
ADORNO, T.W. ALBAN BERG.
    T. SOUSTER, 607:SPRING69-65
ADORNO, T.W. & OTHERS. ÜBER WALTER BEN-
    JAMIN.
    J. GUILLONNEAU, 98:AUG-SEP69-675
    S. ROSENFELD, 221(GQ):MAR70-293
ADRADOS, F.R - SEE UNDER RODRÍGUEZ
    ADRADOS, F.
ADY, E. POEMS OF ENDRE ADY. (A.N. NYER-
    GES, TRANS; J.M. ÉRTAVY-BARÁTH, ED)
    E.E. GEORGE, 32:JUN71-448
AELFRIC. HOMILIES OF AELFRIC.* (VOLS
    1&2) (J.C. POPE, ED)
    A. CAMPBELL, 541(RES):FEB70-68
    C. CLARK, 179(ES):DEC70-545
    E.G. STANLEY, 447(N&Q):JUL70-262
AEPLY, J. UNE FILLE À MARIER.
    D. TAILLEUX, 207(FR):APR70-863
AESCHYLUS. ÉSQUILO: "AS SUPLICANTES."
    (A.P.Q.F. SOTTOMAYOR, ED & TRANS)
    A.F. GARVIE, 487:AUTUMN70-276
AFFRON, C. PATTERNS OF FAILURE IN "LA
    COMÉDIE HUMAINE."
    617(TLS):18AUG72-973
"AFRICA 1971."
    617(TLS):31MAR72-378
"AFRICA SOUTH OF THE SAHARA." (2ND ED)
    617(TLS):10MAR72-268
AGAR, H. BRITAIN ALONE.
    617(TLS):29DEC72-1571
AGEE, J. THE COLLECTED POEMS OF JAMES
    AGEE.
    617(TLS):9JUN72-659
AGEE, J. THE COLLECTED SHORT PROSE OF
    JAMES AGEE.* (R. FITZGERALD, ED)
    617(TLS):9JUN72-659
AGEL, J., ED. THE RADICAL THERAPIST.
    E. WILLIS, 453:31AUG72-7
AGRICOLA, E. SYNTAKTISCHE MEHRDEUTIGKEIT
    (POLYSYNTAKTIZITÄT) BEI DER ANALYSE DES
    DEUTSCHEN UND DES ENGLISCHEN.
    J.C. MC KAY, 350:MAR71-219
AGUILAR PIÑAL, F. IMPRESOS CASTELLANOS
    DEL SIGLO XVI EN EL BRITISH MUSEUM.
    K. WHINNOM, 86(BHS):JUL71-270

AGUILERA, R. INTENCIÓN Y SILENCIO EN EL
QUIJOTE.
617(TLS):1DEC72-1445
AGUS, I.A. THE HEROIC AGE OF FRANCO-
GERMAN JEWRY.
R. CHAZAN, 589:JAN71-120
AGWANI, M.S. COMMUNISM IN THE ARAB
EAST.*
W. LAQUEUR, 32:SEP71-673
AHERN, J.F. POLICE IN TROUBLE.
P. ADAMS, 61:JUL72-96
J. HOLT, 561(SATR):5AUG72-51
453:6APR72-34
AHLSTROM, S.E. A RELIGIOUS HISTORY OF
THE AMERICAN PEOPLE.
M.E. MARTY, 441:29OCT72-40
617(TLS):22DEC72-1545
AHMAD, Q-U-D. THE WAHABI MOVEMENT IN
INDIA.*
H. MALIK, 293(JAST):MAY70-717
AIDOO, A.A. NO SWEETNESS HERE.*
J. CAREW, 441:2APR72-7
AIKEN, A. COURAGE PAST.
617(TLS):7APR72-402
AIKEN, C. USHANT.*
M. SCHORER, 61:FEB72-98
AIKEN, H.D. & OTHERS. THE UNIVERSITY AND
THE NEW INTELLECTUAL ENVIRONMENT.
B. TROTTER, 529(QQ):SPRING70-134
AIKEN, J. A CLUSTER OF SEPARATE SPARKS.
N. CALLENDAR, 441:9APR72-41
AIKEN, J. DIED ON A RAINY SUNDAY.
617(TLS):10NOV72-1375
AINSLIE, T. CANADA PRESERVED. (S.S.
COHEN, ED)
E.P. HAMILTON, 432(NEQ):MAR70-166
G.F.G. STANLEY, 656(WMQ):JAN70-180
AIRD, A. THE AUTOMOTIVE NIGHTMARE.
E. ROTHSCHILD, 362:29JUN72-871
617(TLS):18AUG72-963
AITCHISON, J. SOUNDS BEFORE SLEEP.
J. FULLER, 362:24FEB72-251
617(TLS):28JAN72-94
AITKEN, A.J., A. MC INTOSH & H. PÁLSSON,
EDS. EDINBURGH STUDIES IN ENGLISH AND
SCOTS.
M.H. SHORT, 677:VOL2-228
AITKEN, E. - SEE TOLSTOJ, L.
AITKEN, W.R. A HISTORY OF THE PUBLIC
LIBRARY MOVEMENT IN SCOTLAND TO 1955.
R.E. HELD, 356:OCT71-343
AITMATOV, C. POVESTI GOR I STEPEI.
617(TLS):7APR72-384
AITMATOV, C. THE WHITE STEAMSHIP.
617(TLS):18AUG72-961
AKENSON, D.H. & L.F. STEVENS. THE CHANG-
ING USES OF THE LIBERAL ARTS COLLEGE.
G.L. PLAYE, 356:JAN71-64
AKERMAN, R. THE TRUTH ABOUT FORT FUS-
SOCKS.
617(TLS):27OCT72-1274
AKHMANOVA, O.S. - SEE SMIRNITSKY, A.L.
AKIMOV, V. VLADIMIR AKIMOV ON THE DIL-
EMMAS OF RUSSIAN MARXISM, 1895-1903.*
(J. FRANKEL, ED)
I. GETZLER, 32:MAR71-145
A. WILDMAN, 550(RUSR):APR70-215
AKINJOGBIN, I.A. DAHOMEY AND ITS NEIGH-
BOURS 1708-1818.
W.J. ARGYLE, 69:APR69-202
AKITA, G. FOUNDATIONS OF CONSTITUTIONAL
GOVERNMENT IN MODERN JAPAN, 1868-1900.*
N.R. BENNETT, 302:JUL69-277
AKPAN, N.U. THE STRUGGLE FOR SECESSION,
1966-1970.
617(TLS):25AUG72-981

AKRIGG, G.P.V. SHAKESPEARE AND THE EARL
OF SOUTHAMPTON.
T.P. LOGAN, 399(MLJ):MAR70-211
M. MACLURE, 627(UTQ):JUL70-365
S. SCHOENBAUM, 401(MLQ):MAR70-115
P.L. STEWART, 219(GAR):SPRING69-112
"AKTEN ZUR DEUTSCHEN AUSWÄRTIGEN POLI-
TIK." (SER B, VOL 4, PT 1)
F.L. CARSTEN, 575(SEER):OCT71-625
AKULA, K. TOMORROW IS YESTERDAY.*
G. ROPER, 627(UTQ):JUL69-360
AKURGAL, E. THE BIRTH OF GREEK ART.
J. BOARDMAN, 123:DEC70-379
AL-AZM, S.J. THE ORIGINS OF KANT'S
ARGUMENTS IN THE ANTINOMIES.
617(TLS):19MAY72-569
ALADÁR, T. FÉNYBEN ÉS SÖTÉTBEN.
I. REJTŐ, 270:VOL20#1-19
ALAIN-FOURNIER. LE GRAND MEAULNES.*
(R. GIBSON, ED)
A.M. BEICHMAN, 399(MLJ):FEB70-137
ALAZRAKI, J. LA PROSA NARRATIVA DE JORGE
LUIS BORGES.*
F. DAUSTER, 240(HR):JUL70-345
R. LIMA, 238:MAR70-157
ALBERT, W. THE TURNPIKE ROAD SYSTEM IN
ENGLAND 1663-1840.
617(TLS):14JUL72-822
ALBERTI, R. YEAR OF PICASSO.
D.L. SHIREY, 441:10DEC72-47
ALBERTS, R.C. THE GOLDEN VOYAGE.*
F.S. ALLIS, JR., 432(NEQ):MAR70-163
A.L. JENSEN, 656(WMQ):OCT70-677
ALBERTS, W.J., ED. DE STADSREKENINGEN
VAN ARNHEM. (VOL 1)
D.W. JELLEMA, 589:OCT71-721
ALBERTSEN, E. RATIO UND "MYSTIK" IM WERK
ROBERT MUSILS.
W. HOFFMEISTER, 221(GQ):NOV70-796
ALBERTSEN, L.L. DAS LEHRGEDICHT.
H.J. SCHUELER, 222(GR):MAR70-152
ALBERTSON, C. ANGLO-SAXON SAINTS AND
HEROES.
E.V. STACKPOOLE, 613:AUTUMN68-470
ALBERTSON, P. & M. BARNETT, EDS. MANAG-
ING THE PLANET.
S.B. SHEPARD, 441:19NOV72-52
ALBIACH, A.M. - SEE UNDER MARTÍNEZ ALBI-
ACH, A.
ALBINI, J.L. THE AMERICAN MAFIA.
W. SHEED, 453:20JUL72-23
ALBINI, U., ED. PERI POLITEIAS.
S. USHER, 303:VOL90-220
ALBORG, J.L. HISTORIA DE LA LITERATURA
ESPAÑOLA.* (VOL 1) (2ND ED)
M.C. PEÑUELAS, 241:SEP71-78
DE ALBORNOZ, A. LA PRESENCIA DE MIGUEL
DE UNAMUNO EN ANTONIO MACHADO.
R. GULLÓN, 546(RR):APR70-160
ALBOUY, P. LA CRÉATION MYTHOLOGIQUE CHEZ
HUGO.
J-P. RICHARD, 98:MAY69-387
ALBOUY, P. MYTHES ET MYTHOLOGIES DANS
LA LITTÉRATURE FRANÇAISE.
G. MEAD, 207(FR):FEB70-506
J. SEZNEC, 208(FS):APR71-243
ALBRECHT, G. & OTHERS. LEXIKON DEUTSCH-
SPRACHIGER SCHRIFTSTELLER VON DEN
ANFÄNGEN BIS ZUR GEGENWART. (6TH ED)
G.K. FRIESEN, 400(MLN):APR70-394
G. HAY, 462(OL):VOL25#4-361
ALBRECHT, M.V. & E. ZINN, EDS. OVID.
S. VIARRE, 555:VOL44FASC1-150
ALBRIGHT, J. WHAT MAKES SPIRO RUN?
W. JACOBSON, 440:14MAY72-1

3

ALBRIGHT, W.F. & T.O. LAMBDIN. THE CAM-
BRIDGE ANCIENT HISTORY. (REV) (VOL 1,
CHAPTER 4)
  A. SALONEN, 318(JAOS):OCT-DEC70-525
ALCALÁ GALIANO, A. LITERATURA ESPAÑOLA
SIGLO XIX. (V. LLORENS, ED & TRANS)
  191(ELN):SEP70(SUPP)-153
ALCINA FRANCH, J. POESÍA AMERICANA PRE-
COLOMBINA.
  R. LESLIE, 86(BHS):OCT71-364
ALCOTT, A.B. THE LETTERS OF A. BRONSON
ALCOTT.* (R.L. HERRNSTADT, ED)
  C.H. FOSTER, 432(NEQ):DEC70-680
ALDCROFT, D.H., ED. THE DEVELOPMENT OF
BRITISH INDUSTRY AND FOREIGN COMPETI-
TION, 1875-1914.
  B. SUPPLE, 637(VS):DEC69-221
ALDCROFT, D.H. & P. FEARON, EDS. BRITISH
ECONOMIC FLUCTUATIONS 1790-1939.
  617(TLS):4AUG72-920
ALDERSON, F. BICYCLING.
  617(TLS):13OCT72-1237
ALDERSON, W.L. & A.C. HENDERSON. CHAUCER
AND AUGUSTAN SCHOLARSHIP.
  H.N. DAVIES, 677:VOL2-245
ALDING, P. DESPITE THE EVIDENCE.*
  N. CALLENDAR, 441:2APR72-22
ALDISS, B.W. THE MOMENT OF ECLIPSE.
THE SOLDIER ERECT.*
  M. FELD, 364:JUN/JUL71-156
ALDOUS, T. BATTLE FOR THE ENVIRONMENT.
  617(TLS):23JUN72-727
ALDRED, C. JEWELS OF THE PHARAOHS.
  617(TLS):21JAN72-72
ALDRICH, P. RHYTHM IN SEVENTEENTH-
CENTURY ITALIAN MONODY.
  L. GUSHEE, 308:SPRING67-117
ALDRIDGE, A.O., ED. COMPARATIVE LITERA-
TURE.*
  C.S. BROWN, 131(CL):SUMMER71-265
  J. FUEGI, 399(MLJ):NOV70-536
ALDRIDGE, A.O., ED. THE IBERO-AMERICAN
ENLIGHTENMENT.
  617(TLS):8DEC72-1503
ALDRIDGE, J.W. THE DEVIL IN THE FIRE.
  A. BROYARD, 441:20JAN72-45
  G. DAVENPORT, 441:16JAN72-6
  G.A. PANICHAS, 385(MQR):FALL72-292
  B. WEBER, 561(SATR):11MAR72-71
  453:27JAN72-38
ALDRIDGE, J.W. IN THE COUNTRY OF THE
YOUNG.*
  G.A. PANICHAS, 396(MODA):FALL71-416
  639(VQR):SUMMER70-CXII
ALDRITT, K. THE MAKING OF GEORGE ORWELL.
  D. LIVINGSTONE, 150(DR):AUTUMN70-405
  F. ODLE, 619(TC):1969/2-49
ALDRITT, K. THE VISUAL IMAGINATION OF
D.H. LAWRENCE.
  M. ALLOTT, 677:VOL2-327
ALEKSEEV, M.P. STIXOTVORENIE PUŠKINA
"JA PAMJATNIK SEBE VOZDVIG..."
  J.P. PAULS, 574(SEEJ):SPRING71-68
ALEXANDER, A. GIOVANNI VERGA.
  617(TLS):14JUL72-794
ALEXANDER, D.B. & T. WEBB. TEXAS HOMES
OF THE NINETEENTH CENTURY.*
  J.W. RUDD, 576:MAY68-155
ALEXANDER, H.E. MONEY IN POLITICS.
  W.V. SHANNON, 441:15OCT72-38
  442(NY):15APR72-147
ALEXANDER, J.J.G. NORMAN ILLUMINATION AT
MONT ST MICHEL, 966-1100.
  R. BRANNER, 589:APR71-360
ALEXANDER, J.J.G. & A.C. DE LA MARE. THE
ITALIAN MANUSCRIPTS IN THE LIBRARY OF
MAJOR J.R. ABBEY.
  I. TOESCA, 39:NOV69-450

ALEXANDER, J.T. AUTOCRATIC POLITICS IN
A NATIONAL CRISIS.*
  P. AVRICH, 550(RUSR):JUL70-337
  P. DUKES, 575(SEER):OCT71-619
ALEXANDER, N. POISON, PLAY AND DUEL.
  617(TLS):30JUN72-739
ALEXANDER, P.J., ED. THE ORACLE OF
BAALBEK.
  H.W. PARKE, 303:VOL90-221
ALEXANDER, W.M. JOHANN GEORG HAMANN.
  M.J.V., 543:SEP69-123
ALEXANDERSON, B. TEXTKRITISCHER KOMMEN-
TAR ZUM HIPPOKRATISCHEN PROGNOSTIKON
UND BEMERKUNGEN ZU GALENS PROGNOSTIKON-
KOMMENTAR.
  L.R. LIND, 121(CJ):FEB-MAR71-264
ALEXANDERSON, B. TEXTUAL REMARKS ON
PTOLEMY'S "HARMONICA" AND PORPHYRY'S
COMMENTARY.
  E.K. BORTHWICK, 123:DEC71-367
ALEXANDRE, P. THE DUEL.
  J. ARDAGH, 440:1MAY72-10
  J. LACOUTURE, 441:14MAY72-31
  T. LASK, 441:15APR72-33
  442(NY):22JUL72-79
ALEXANDRIAN, S. ANDRÉ BRETON PAR LUI
MEME.
  617(TLS):21APR72-442
ALEXANDRIAN, S. SURREALIST ART.
  R. SHATTUCK, 453:1JUN72-23
ALEXANDROVA, V. LITERATURA I ZHINZ'.
  P. ROSSBACHER, 550(RUSR):APR70-230
ALEXIOU, S., N. PLATON & H. GUANELLA.
ANCIENT CRETE.*
  D.K. HAWORTH, 127:FALL70-114
  D. STRONG, 39:SEP69-269
  R.F. WILLETTS, 303:VOL90-246
ALEXIS, P. "NATURALISME PAS MORT."
(B.H. BAKKER, ED)
  617(TLS):20OCT72-1262
AL-FĀRĀBĪ. KITĀB AL-ALFĀZ AL-MUSTA'MALAH
FĪ AL-MANTIQ. (M. MAHDI, ED)
  M.E. MARMURA, 318(JAOS):OCT-DEC70-554
ALFIERI, V.E. FILOSOFIA E FILOLOGIA.
  P. DI VONA, 548(RCSF):JAN/MAR69-118
ALFÖLDI, A. THE CONVERSION OF CONSTAN-
TINE AND PAGAN ROME.
  W.H.C. FREND, 123:JUN71-300
ALFÖLDY, G. FASTI HISPANIENSES.
  J. GAGÉ, 182:VOL23#1/2-46
ALFÖLDY, G. DIE PERSONENNAMEN IN DER
RÖMISCHEN PROVINZ DALMATIA.
  J.J. WILKES, 313:VOL60-247
ALFONSI, P. & P. PESNOT. SATAN'S NEEDLE.
  A. GOTTLIEB, 441:21MAY72-36
ALFONSO EL SABIO. GENERAL ESTORIA. (2ND
PT, VOL 2) (A.G. SOLALINDE, L.A. KASTEN
& V.R.B. OELSCHLÄGER, EDS)
  F. RICO, 545(RPH):AUG70-216
ALFONSO EL SABIO. LAPIDARIO. (M. BREY
MARIÑO, ED)
  A.R. CLEMENTE, 400(MLN):MAR70-287
ALFONSO, P. THE SCHOLAR'S GUIDE. (J.R.
JONES & J.E. KELLER, EDS & TRANS)
  A.I. BAGBY, JR., 589:JUL71-521
ALI, S.A. - SEE AMEER ALI, S.
ALI, T. THE COMING BRITISH REVOLUTION.
  R. WOLLHEIM, 362:27JAN72-119
  617(TLS):18FEB72-172
ALIGHIERI, D. - SEE UNDER DANTE ALIGHIERI
ALINEI, M.L. SPOGLI ELETTRONICI DELL'-
ITALIANO DELLE ORIGINI E DEL DUECENTO.
(VOL 2)
  G.E. SANSONE, 276:WINTER70-441
ALINSKY, S.D. REVEILLE FOR RADICALS.*
  N. MILLS, 651(WHR):WINTER71-86

4

ALKEMA, C.J. ALKEMA'S COMPLETE GUIDE TO
CREATIVE ART FOR YOUNG PEOPLE.
617(TLS):14JUL72-821
ALKER, H. BLOCKFLÖTEN BIBLIOGRAPHIE 2.
N. O'LOUGHLIN, 415:MAR70-283
ALKON, P.K. SAMUEL JOHNSON AND MORAL
DISCIPLINE.
J. GAGEN, 405(MP):AUG69-94
502(PRS):FALL68-280
ALLAN, D.J. THE PHILOSOPHY OF ARIS-
TOTLE.
H.D. RANKIN, 63:AUG71-225
ALLAN, M. PALGRAVE OF ARABIA.
617(TLS):21APR72-455
ALLCHIN, B. & R. THE BIRTH OF INDIAN
CIVILIZATION.*
J.W. SPELLMAN, 293(JAST):NOV69-179
ALLDAY, E. STEFAN ZWEIG.
617(TLS):28APR72-468
ALLEMANN, B. GOTTFRIED BENN.
J. BOUVERESSE, 98:AUG-SEP69-713
ALLEN, C. & R.W. JOHNSON, EDS. AFRICAN
PERSPECTIVES.
617(TLS):10MAR72-268
ALLEN, D. - SEE CREELEY, R.
ALLEN, D.C. THE HARMONIOUS VISION.
(ENLARGED ED)
J.R. MC ADAMS, 568(SCN):WINTER71-61
ALLEN, D.G.C. WILLIAM SHIPLEY.*
R. EDWARDS, 39:MAY69-404
ALLEN, G.W. WILLIAM JAMES.
A.J. RECK, 483:JAN70-80
ALLEN, G.W. MELVILLE AND HIS WORLD.
617(TLS):21JAN72-53
ALLEN, J.J. DON QUIXOTE: HERO OR FOOL?*
F.G. SALINERO, 238:MAY70-335
ALLEN, M. POE AND THE BRITISH MAGAZINE
TRADITION.*
J. RAEBURN, 385(MQR):SUMMER72-222
ALLEN, R. VALHALLA AT THE OK.
S. MARTINEAU, 99:JUL-AUG72-44
ALLEN, R.E. PLATO'S "EUTHYPHRO" AND THE
EARLIER THEORY OF FORMS.*
G. ANAGNOSTOPOULOS, 319:JUL72-354
A.J. BOYLE, 63:DEC71-331
D.E. HAHM, 124:APR71-268
ALLEN, R.H. AN ANNOTATED ARTHUR SCHNITZ-
LER BIBLIOGRAPHY.
C. HILL, 397(MD):DEC67-322
ALLEN, R.L. THE VERB SYSTEM OF PRESENT-
DAY AMERICAN ENGLISH.*
D.L.F. NILSEN, 353:JUL69-112
ALLEN, R.V., ED. YEARBOOK ON INTERNA-
TIONAL COMMUNIST AFFAIRS: 1968.*
H. HANAK, 575(SEER):APR71-323
J.S. RESHETAR, JR., 550(RUSR):APR70-
239
ALLEN, V.L. THE SOCIOLOGY OF INDUSTRIAL
RELATIONS.
617(TLS):14JAN72-47
ALLEN, W. TRANSLATING FOR KING JAMES.
J.H. HARWELL, 569(SR):SPRING71-285
ALLEN, W. THE URGENT WEST.*
R. BERMAN, 340(KR):1969/3-378
R. LEHAN, 445(NCF):JUN69-123
ALLEN, W.S. VOX GRAECA.*
D.M. JONES, 123:JUN71-295
ALLENTUCK, M., ED. THE ACHIEVEMENT OF
ISAAC BASHEVIS SINGER.*
M. FRIEDBERG, 32:MAR71-220
ALLERDYCE, G., ED. THE PLACE OF FASCISM
IN EUROPEAN HISTORY.
G. BARRACLOUGH, 453:19OCT72-37
ALLEY, R. PICASSO: THE THREE DANCERS.
B.M.B. PETRIE, 90:MAR69-161
ALLEY, R.S. SO HELP ME GOD.
M.E. MARTY, 441:6AUG72-7

ALLILUYEVA, S. ONLY ONE YEAR.* (RUSSIAN
TITLE: TOL'KO ODIN GOD.)
A. TOLSTOY, 550(RUSR):JAN70-87
B.D. WOLFE, 550(RUSR):JAN70-88
ALLISON, A.F., COMP. THOMAS DEKKER C.
1572-1632.
617(TLS):17NOV72-1404
ALLISON, G.H. EASY THAI.
T.W. GETHING, 399(MLJ):OCT70-463
ALLISON, G.T. ESSENCE OF DECISION.
R. STEEL, 453:19OCT72-43
ALLISON, H.E. LESSING AND THE ENLIGHT-
ENMENT.*
K.S. GUTHKE, 564:FALL68-171
M.J.V., 543:SEP69-123
ALLOTT, M. - SEE KEATS, J.
ALLOWAY, L. THE VENICE BIENNALE 1895-
1968.
C.R. BRIGHTON, 89(BJA):WINTER71-105
J. RUSSELL, 592:JUL/AUG69-46
ALLSOP, K. IN THE COUNTRY.
617(TLS):29DEC72-1586
"ALMANACH BIBLIOTEKI NARODOWEJ."
D. WELSH, 104:SPRING71-125
DE ALMEIDA, M.A. MEMÓRIAS DE UM SARGENTO
DE MILÍCAS. (D. DAMASCENO, ED)
191(ELN):SEP69(SUPP)-135
ALMERICH. LA FAZIENDA DE ULTRA MAR. (M.
LAZAR, ED)
A. VARVARO, 545(RPH):NOV69-239
ALONGE, R. IL TEATRO DEI ROZZI DI SIENA.
L.G. CLUBB, 131(CL):WINTER71-55
ALONSO, A. DE LA PRONUNCIACIÓN MEDIEVAL
A LA MODERNA EN ESPAÑOL. (VOL 2)
H.T. STURCKEN, 238:DEC70-1019
ALPERS, K. BERICHT ÜBER STAND UND
METHODE DER AUSGABE DES ETYMOLOGICUM
GENUINUM (MIT EINER AUSGABE DES BUCH-
STABEN L).
N.G. WILSON, 123:DEC71-453
ALPERS, P.J. THE POETRY OF "THE FAERIE
QUEENE."
G.K. HUNTER, 148:SPRING70-91
ALSDORF, L. DIE ĀRYĀ-STROPHEN DES PALI-
KANONS METRISCH HERGESTELLT UND TEXT-
GESCHICHTLICH UNTERSUCHT.
L.A. SCHWARZSCHILD, 318(JAOS):OCT-
DEC70-586
ALSTON, P.L. EDUCATION AND THE STATE IN
TSARIST RUSSIA.*
W.K. MEDLIN, 550(RUSR):JUL70-340
ALTABÉ, D.F. TEMAS Y DIÁLOGOS.
V. BURBRIDGE, 238:DEC70-1029
ALTER, P. DIE IRISCHE NATIONALBEWEGUNG.
617(TLS):3MAR72-242
ALTER, R. FIELDING AND THE NATURE OF
THE NOVEL.*
M.C. BATTESTIN, 219(GAR):SPRING69-100
A. SHERBO, 173(ECS):SUMMER70-560
P. STEVICK, 141:WINTER70-76
C. TRACY, 529(QQ):SPRING70-140
ALTHUSSER, L. FOR MARX.
N. LOBKOWICZ, 32:JUN71-423
ALTICK, R.D. & J.F. LOUCKS 2D. BROWN-
ING'S ROMAN MURDER STORY.*
P. HONAN, 405(MP):NOV69-207
J.F. HULCOOP, 402(MLR):JAN71-180
ALTMAN, D. HOMOSEXUAL.
J. JOHNSTON, 441:20FEB72-5
ALTMANN, A., ED. MOSES MENDELSSOHNS
FRÜHSCHRIFTEN ZUR METAPHYSIK.
G. DARMS, 182:VOL23#9-454
W.H. WERKMEISTER, 319:JUL72-363
ALTON, W.G. WOODEN TOYS THAT YOU CAN
MAKE.
617(TLS):4AUG72-926

AMORT, C. & I.M. JEDLICKA. THE CANARIS
 FILE.
  R.F. STAAR, 32:DEC71-894
AMORY, M. BIOGRAPHY OF LORD DUNSANY.
  S. HEANEY, 362:28SEP72-408
  617(TLS):9JUN72-647
AMPE, A., ED. DEN TEMPEL ONSER SIELEN.
  E. COLLEDGE, 402(MLR):JAN71-233
AMPHILOCHIUS. AMPHILOCHII ICONIENSIS
 "IAMBI AD SELEUCUM."* (E. OBERG, ED)
  R. BROWNING, 123:MAR71-137
AN SU-GIL. PUKKANDO.
  270:VOL20#4-100
ANANIA, M. THE COLOR OF DUST.
  J. ATLAS, 491:OCT71-45
ANATOLI, A. - SEE UNDER KUZNETSOV, A.
ANCESCHI, L. LE ISTITUZIONI DELLA
 POESIA.*
  S. FEDERICI, 484(PPR):DEC69-312
ANDERSCH, A. EFRAIM: EIN ROMAN.
  C. BURGAUNER, 220(GL&L):JAN71-210
ANDERSCH, A. EFRAIM'S BOOK.
  D.J. GORDON, 676(YR):SPRING71-428
  J. HUNTER, 362:10FEB72-188
  617(TLS):10MAR72-265
ANDERSEN, D. & H. SMITH. A CRITICAL
 PALI DICTIONARY. (VOL 2, FASC 5)
  L.A. SCHWARZSCHILD, 318(JAOS):APR-JUN
  70-408
ANDERSEN, H.C. DAGBØGER 1825-1875. (VOL
 1 ED BY H.V. LAURIDSEN; VOL 5 ED BY T.
 GAD & K. WEBER)
  617(TLS):4FEB72-120
ANDERSEN, H.C. A VISIT TO PORTUGAL,
 1866. (G. THORNTON, ED & TRANS)
  617(TLS):15SEP72-1062
ANDERSEN, T. - SEE MALEVICH, K.S.
ANDERSEN, W. CÉZANNE'S PORTRAIT DRAW-
 INGS.
  617(TLS):14APR72-414
ANDERSON, B.R.O. JAVA IN A TIME OF
 REVOLUTION.
  617(TLS):11AUG72-941
ANDERSON, C.R. MELVILLE IN THE SOUTH
 SEAS.
  J.G. RIEWALD, 179(ES):DEC70-571
ANDERSON, D.M. - SEE CRESCI, G.F.
ANDERSON, F. & K.M. SANDERSON, EDS. MARK
 TWAIN: THE CRITICAL HERITAGE.
  617(TLS):10MAR72-280
ANDERSON, G.H., ED. CHRIST AND CRISIS
 IN SOUTHEAST ASIA.
  C.W. KEGLEY, 293(JAST):FEB70-488
ANDERSON, G.H., ED. STUDIES IN PHILIP-
 PINE CHURCH HISTORY.
  D.V. HART, 293(JAST):AUG70-994
ANDERSON, J. DEATH & FRIENDS.*
  W. DICKEY, 249(HUDR):SPRING71-159
  G.H. HARTMAN, 441:30JUL72-4
ANDERSON, J. MISSION TO THE EAST COAST
 OF SUMATRA IN 1823. ACHEEN AND THE
 PORTS ON THE NORTH AND EAST COASTS OF
 SUMATRA.
  617(TLS):22DEC72-1565
ANDERSON, J.A. & F.J. GROTEN, JR. LATIN.
  M.F. MC NAMARA, 124:DEC70-134
ANDERSON, J.K. MILITARY THEORY AND PRAC-
 TICE IN THE AGE OF XENOPHON.
  C.W.J. ELIOT, 124:DEC70-124
  C.G. STARR, 122:JAN71-74
ANDERSON, J.M. THE REALM OF ART.
  A. SHIELDS, 290(JAAC):SPRING70-398
  H.R. WACKRILL, 39:MAR69-246
ANDERSON, J.N.D. MORALITY, LAW AND
 GRACE.
  617(TLS):24MAR72-342
ANDERSON, J.Q. THE LIBERATING GODS.
  V.C. HOPKINS, 27(AL):NOV71-449

ANDERSON, J.Q., ED. WITH THE BARK ON.
  D.J. MC MILLAN, 650(WF):JAN69-56
ANDERSON, J.R.L. RECKONING IN ICE.
  617(TLS):7JAN72-17
ANDERSON, M. FAMILY STRUCTURE IN NINE-
 TEENTH CENTURY LANCASHIRE.
  617(TLS):28JUL72-894
ANDERSON, M.D. GREY SISTERS.
  617(TLS):21APR72-438
ANDERSON, M.D. HISTORY AND IMAGERY IN
 BRITISH CHURCHES.
  617(TLS):28JAN72-102
ANDERSON, M.M. THE FESTIVALS OF NEPAL.
  617(TLS):1SEP72-1034
ANDERSON, O. A LIBERAL STATE AT WAR.
  V. CROMWELL, 325:OCT69-590
ANDERSON, P. UN-MAN AND OTHER NOVELLAS.
  617(TLS):13OCT72-1235
ANDERSON, R.R. SPANISH AMERICAN MODERN-
 ISM.
  D.L. SHAW, 402(MLR):OCT71-912
ANDERSON, S. SHERWOOD ANDERSON'S MEM-
 OIRS.* (R.L. WHITE, ED)
  42(AR):FALL69-447
ANDERSON, S. A STORY TELLER'S STORY.
 (R.L. WHITE, ED)
  W.B. RIDEOUT, 191(ELN):SEP69-70
ANDERSON, V. THE LAST OF THE ECCENTRICS.
  617(TLS):14JUL72-792
ANDERSON, W. CASTLES OF EUROPE.*
  90:NOV70-774
ANDERSON, W.C. THE HEADSTRONG HOUSEBOAT.
  441:30APR72-28
ANDERSON, W.C. HURRICANE HUNTERS.
  M. LEVIN, 441:26NOV72-39
ANDERSON, W.D. & T.D. CLARESON, EDS.
 VICTORIAN ESSAYS.
  M.S., 155:SEP69-190
ANDERSON, W.J.V. & D. CROSS. STEAM IN
 SCOTLAND. (VOL 2) (B. STEPHENSON, ED)
  617(TLS):22DEC72-1566
ANDERSON, W.L. EDWIN ARLINGTON ROBINSON.
  D.T. CORKER, 677:VOL2-324
  P.R. YANNELLA, 399(MLJ):APR70-293
ANDERSON, W.S. THE ART OF THE "AENEID."
  M.P. CUNNINGHAM, 122:JUL71-215
  G.E. DUCKWORTH, 24:APR71-343
  R.A. HORNSBY, 124:SEP70-26
ANDERSSON, T. FOREIGN LANGUAGES IN THE
 ELEMENTARY SCHOOL.
  S.I. ARELLANO, 238:MAY70-350
  E.H. RATTE, 207(FR):APR70-854
  L.V. SIMPSON, 399(MLJ):APR70-282
ANDERSSON-SCHMITT, M. MANUSCRIPTA
 MEDIAEVLIA UPSALIENSIS.
  L.S. THOMPSON, 563(SS):AUTUMN71-439
ANDIC, F., S. ANDIC & D. DOSSER. A THE-
 ORY OF ECONOMIC INTEGRATION FOR DEVEL-
 OPING COUNTRIES.
  617(TLS):15SEP72-1066
ANDICS, H. RULE OF TERROR.
  R.H. MC NEAL, 550(RUSR):JUL70-352
ANDO, T. BUNRAKU THE PUPPET THEATER.
  M. PRESS, 285(JAPQ):OCT-DEC70-479
ANDRADE, J.M.P. - SEE UNDER PITA ANDRADE,
 J.M.
ANDRAE, F., ED. VOLKSBÜCHEREI UND
 NATIONALSOZIALISMUS.
  E. DEJUNG, 182:VOL23#19/20-833
ANDRÉ, J. - SEE OVID
ANDRÉ, J. - SEE PLINY
ANDREACH, R.J. THE SLAIN AND RESURRECTED
 GOD.
  J. FEASTER, 295:VOL2#3-417
ANDREEV, J.A. REVOLJUCIJA I LITERATURA.
  L.A. FOSTER, 574(SEEJ):SUMMER71-224
ANDRES, S. DIE VERSUCHUNG DES SYNESIOS.
  617(TLS):25FEB72-208

ANDRÉSEN, B.S. PRE-GLOTTALIZATION IN
ENGLISH STANDARD PRONUNCIATION.
A.W. JONES, 597(SN):VOL41#1-225
M. SCHUBIGER, 179(ES):JUN69-317
ANDRESKI, S. SOCIAL SCIENCES AS SORCERY.
617(TLS):13OCT72-1220
ANDREWES, A. THE GREEKS.*
R.J. HOPPER, 123:JUN71-244
ANDREWES, L. SERMONS. (G.M. STORY, ED)
M. MAC LURE, 627(UTQ):JUL69-368
ANDREWS, E.D. & F. VISIONS OF THE HEAV-
ENLY SPHERE.
P. LITTLEFIELD, 432(NEQ):JUN70-315
ANDREWS, J.C. THE SOUTH REPORTS THE
CIVIL WAR.
639(VQR):AUTUMN70-CXLVIII
ANDREWS, K. NATIONAL GALLERY OF SCOT-
LAND: CATALOGUE OF ITALIAN DRAWINGS.*
A. NEUMEYER, 290(JAAC):SUMMER70-560
W. VITZTHUM, 90:NOV69-691
ANDREWS, K.R., ED. THE LAST VOYAGE OF
DRAKE AND HAWKINS.
617(TLS):12MAY72-536
ANDREWS, M. THE BLACK PALACE.
M. LEVIN, 441:7MAY72-32
ANDREWS, M. CARACOL REEF.
617(TLS):7JUL72-783
ANDREWS, W. ARCHITECTURE IN MICHIGAN.*
K. MARZOLF, 576:DEC69-301
ANDRIETTE, E.A. DEVON AND EXETER IN THE
CIVIL WAR.
617(TLS):28JAN72-109
ANDRIEUX, M. DAILY LIFE IN VENICE AT THE
TIME OF CASANOVA.
617(TLS):24NOV72-1436
ANDRO, P., A. DAUVERGNE & L.M. LAGOUTTE.
LE MAI DE LA RÉVOLUTION.
C.W. COLMAN, 399(MLJ):OCT70-468
ANDRONIKOS, M. TOTENKULT.*
P. CHANTRAINE, 555:VOL44FASC1-121
ANDRZEJEWSKI, J. THE APPEAL.*
I. WEDDE, 364:OCT/NOV71-149
ANFUSO, N. & A. GIANUARIO. CLAUDIO MON-
TEVERDI.
J.A.W., 410(M&L):APR71-200
ANGELELLI, I. - SEE FREGE, G.
ANGELL, A. POLITICS AND THE LABOUR
MOVEMENT IN CHILE.
617(TLS):3NOV72-1347
ANGELL, R. THE SUMMER GAME.
C. LEHMANN-HAUPT, 441:6JUN72-43
R. ROBINSON, 440:14MAY72-4
T. SOLOTAROFF, 441:11JUN72-1
453:18MAY72-37
ANGELOV, D. BOGOMILSTVOTO V B"LGARIJA.
E. NIEDERHAUSER, 104:FALL71-440
ANGLO, S. MACHIAVELLI.
L. PERTILE, 402(MLR):JUL71-696
ANGLO, S. SPECTACLE, PAGEANTRY, AND
EARLY TUDOR POLICY.
M. LEVINE, 551(RENQ):WINTER70-470
ANGLO, S. - SEE "THE GREAT TOURNAMENT
ROLL OF WESTMINSTER"
ANGOFF, C. MEMORANDA FOR TOMORROW.
G. DAVIDSON, 502(PRS):WINTER69/70-417
ANGOFF, C. MEMORY OF AUTUMN.*
H.U. RIBALOW, 287:JAN69-27
ANIKST, A. TEATR EPOKHI SHEKSPIRA.
A. GLASSE, 570(SQ):WINTER68-97
ANIKST, A. TEORIA DRAMY OD ARISTOTELA
DO LESSINGA.
M. RIESER, 290(JAAC):WINTER69-253
ANING, B.A. AN ANNOTATED BIBLIOGRAPHY OF
MUSIC AND DANCE IN ENGLISH-SPEAKING
AFRICA.
A.P. MERRIAM, 187:SEP72-544

ANKUM, J.A., R. FEENSTRA & W.F. LEEMANS,
EDS. SYMBOLAE IURIDICAE ET HISTORICAE
MARTINO DAVID DEDICATAE. (VOL 2)
J.J. FINKELSTEIN, 318(JAOS):APR-JUN
70-243
ANNENKOV, P.V. THE EXTRAORDINARY
DECADE.* (A.P. MENDEL, ED)
H.W. DEWEY, 385(MQR):WINTER72-61
ANNIS, V.L. THE ARCHITECTURE OF ANTIGUA
GUATEMALA 1543-1773.
F.L. PHELPS, 37:AUG69-37
"THE ANNUAL OF THE BRITISH SCHOOL AT
ATHENS." (NO. 66, 1971)
617(TLS):11AUG72-952
ANOBILE, R.J., ED. WHY A DUCK?
617(TLS):7JUL72-770
ANSART, P. SAINT-SIMON.
G.M. BRAVO, 548(RCSF):JUL/SEP69-345
ANSCOMBE, G.E.M. & G.H. VON WRIGHT - SEE
WITTGENSTEIN, L.
ANSEL, W. HITLER AND THE MIDDLE SEA.
617(TLS):3NOV72-1308
ANSERMET, E. ECRITS SUR LA MUSIQUE.
(J-C. PIGUET, ED)
617(TLS):27OCT72-1280
ANSHEN, R.N. - SEE TEILHARD DE CHARDIN,
P.
ANSON, P., ED. CANADA FIRST.
F. SUTHERLAND, 102(CANL):WINTER71-98
ANSON, R.S. MC GOVERN.
L.W. KOENIG, 561(SATR):3JUN72-62
R.R. LINGEMAN, 441:4JUN72-1
617(TLS):30JUN72-736
ANSTETT, J-J. - SEE SCHLEGEL, F.
ANTAL, E. DIE FUNKTIONEN DER WERBUNG IM
SYSTEM DER ZENTRALEN WIRTSCHAFTSLEN-
KUNG.
A. BRZESKI, 32:SEP71-694
ANTAL, E. & J. HARTHAN - SEE KLINGENDER,
F.
ANTHONY, D. BLOOD ON A HARVEST MOON.
N. CALLENDAR, 441:20FEB72-27
H. FRANKEL, 561(SATR):25MAR72-104
ANTHONY, E. THE POELLENBERG INHERITANCE.
N. CALLENDAR, 441:7MAY72-34
ANTHONY, E.M., J.T. GANDOUR, JR. & U.
WAROTAMASIKKHADIT. FOUNDATIONS OF
THAI. (BK 2, PTS 1&2)
T.W. GETHING, 293(JAST):NOV69-205
ANTHONY, P. VAR THE STICK.
617(TLS):11FEB72-145
ANTHONY, S. THE DISCOVERY OF DEATH IN
CHILDHOOD AND AFTER.
617(TLS):14JUL72-826
ANTIN, P. RECUEIL SUR SAINT JÉRÔME.
W.H.C. FREND, 123:MAR71-135
ANTISERI, D. DAL NEOPOSITIVISMO ALLA
FILOSOFIA ANALITICA.
A. PASQUINELLI, 548(RCSF):JUL-SEP68-
364
ANTON, H. MYTHOLOGISCHE EROTIK IN
KELLERS SIEBEN LEGENDEN UND IM SINNGE-
DICHT.
J.M. LINDSAY, 67:NOV71-255
ANTON, J.P., ED. NATURALISM AND HISTORI-
CAL UNDERSTANDING.
L. ARMOUR & J.R. HORNE, 486:MAR68-73
ANTON, J.P. - SEE PAPANOUTSOS, E.
BROTHER ANTONINUS. THE ROSE OF SOLI-
TUDE.*
S. MC PHERSON, 448:SUMMER68-104
ANTONOVYCH-RUDNYCKA, M., ED. AN ANTHOL-
OGY OF RUSSIAN POETRY.
C.H. ANDRUSYSHEN, 627(UTQ):JUL69-495
P.A. KERSTEN, 574(SEEJ):WINTER71-516

ANZAI HITOSHI, SHIRAISHI KAZUKO & TANI-
KAWA SHUNTARO. THREE CONTEMPORARY
JAPANESE POETS.
    617(TLS):4AUG72-910
APEL, W. HARVARD DICTIONARY OF MUSIC.
(2ND ED)
    B.H. HAGGIN, 249(HUDR):AUTUMN71-495
    A.H. KING, 415:DEC70-1221
APFEL, E. ANLAGE UND STRUKTURE DER
MOTETTEN IM CODEX MONTPELLIER.
    G.A.A., 410(M&L):APR71-195
APOLLINAIRE, G. APOLLINAIRE ON ART.
(L.C. BREUNIG, ED)
    R. DOWNES, 441:31DEC72-6
    617(TLS):27OCT72-1277
APOLLINAIRE, G. CALLIGRAMMES. [CONCOR-
DANCE]
    G. REES, 208(FS):OCT71-483
APOLLINAIRE, G. OEUVRES COMPLÈTES. (A.
BALLAND & J. LECAT, EDS)
    P. VIALLANEIX, 98:JAN69-41
APOLLONIUS. APOLLONIO RODIO, "LE ARGO-
NAUTICHE." (BKS 1&2) (G. POMPELLA,
ED & TRANS)
    G. GIANGRANDE, 123:DEC70-399
APPEL, A., JR. - SEE NABOKOV, V.
APPELHANS, P. UNTERSUCHUNGEN ZUR SPÄT-
MITTELALTERLICHEN MARIENDICHTUNG.
    O. SAYCE, 402(MLR):OCT71-934
APPERSON, G.L. ENGLISH PROVERBS AND
PROVERBIAL PHRASES.
    E.G. STANLEY, 447(N&Q):MAY70-187
APPLEBY, J. SKATE.
    S. BLACKBURN, 440:30JAN72-12
    V. CUNNINGHAM, 362:27APR72-564
    J.D. HOUSTON, 441:20FEB72-29
    T. LASK, 441:29JAN72-27
    617(TLS):19MAY72-565
APPLEBY, J.T. THE TROUBLED REIGN OF
KING STEPHEN.
    M. ALTSCHUL, 589:OCT71-723
APPLEMAN, P. IN THE TWELFTH YEAR OF THE
WAR.
    M. MUDRICK, 249(HUDR):SPRING71-185
APPLEMAN, P. SUMMER LOVE AND SURF.
    N. JACOBS, 447(N&Q):DEC70-476
    B.D.S., 502(PRS):FALL69-326
APPLETON, W.W. - SEE CIBBER, C.
APPLEYARD, J.A. COLERIDGE'S PHILOSOPHY
OF LITERATURE.
    N. BROOKE, 447(N&Q):MAY70-193
APTEKAR, J. ICONS OF JUSTICE.
    R.O. IREDALE, 541(RES):NOV70-488
    J. MAZZARO, 141:SPRING70-155
    P. THOMSON, 402(MLR):JAN71-177
    K. WILLIAMS, 301(JEGP):JUL71-536
APTER, D.E. SOME CONCEPTUAL APPROACHES
TO THE STUDY OF MODERNIZATION.
    A. WEINGROD, 293(JAST):MAY70-681
AQUIN, H. POINT DE FUITE.
    617(TLS):19MAY72-583
AQUIN, H. PROCHAIN EPISODE.
    J.R. SORFLEET, 296:SPRING72-92
AQUIN, R. MYSTICISM IN GABRIELA MISTRAL.
    H. CASTILLO, 238:DEC70-1024
IBN 'ARABĪ - SEE FILED UNDER IBN
ARAGON. HENRI MATISSE.
    J. BERGER, 441:3DEC72-2
ARAGON, L. HISTORY OF THE U.S.S.R. FROM
LENIN TO KHRUSHCHEV.
    W.V. WALLACE, 587:OCT68-270
ARAKIN, V.D. MAL'GAŠSKIJ JAZYK.
    J. KNAPPERT, 353:SEP69-109
ARAPOFF, N. WRITING THROUGH UNDERSTAND-
ING.
    H.D. BROWN, 351(LL):DEC70-273
ARBASINO, A. LA BELLA DI LODI.
    617(TLS):4AUG72-909

ARBASINO, A. SESSANTA POSIZIONI.
    617(TLS):3NOV72-1344
ARBASINO, A. I TURCHI.
    617(TLS):18AUG72-976
ARBAUGH, G.E. & G.B. KIERKEGAARD'S
AUTHORSHIP.
    M.H., 477:SUMMER69-412
ARBERRY, A.J. ASPECTS OF ISLAMIC CIVILI-
ZATION.
    A.A.A. FYZEE, 273(IC):OCT69-306
ARBERRY, A.J. - SEE AL-MUTANABBĪ,
A.T.A.H.
"DIANE ARBUS."
    S. SCHWARTZ, 441:3DEC72-5
    442(NY):23DEC72-80
ARCANGELI, G. LE POESIE.
    617(TLS):11FEB72-146
ARCARI, P.M. IDEE E SENTIMENTI POLITICI
DELL'ALTO MEDIOEVO.
    J.D. ADAMS, 589:JAN71-122
ARCHER, F. A LAD OF EVESHAM VALE.
    617(TLS):29DEC72-1591
ARCHER, F. THE SECRETS OF BREDON HILL.
    617(TLS):14JAN72-49
ARCHER, M. COMPANY DRAWINGS IN THE INDIA
OFFICE LIBRARY.
    617(TLS):8DEC72-1508
ARCHER, M.S., ED. STUDENTS, UNIVERSITY
AND SOCIETY.
    617(TLS):3NOV72-1309
ARCHILOCHUS. ARCHILOCO. (G. TARDITI,
ED & TRANS)
    C. MEILLIER, 555:VOL44FASC2-305
"ARCHIVES DES LETTRES CANADIENNES."
(VOL 4)
    J-L. MAJOR, 627(UTQ):JUL70-425
"THE ARCHIVES OF THE ROYAL INSTITUTION OF
GREAT BRITAIN." (VOLS 1&2)
    617(TLS):18FEB72-198
ARCINIEGAS, G. LATINOAMÉRICA. (C.D.
MC VICKER & O.N. SOTO, EDS) TEMAS DE
ARCINIEGAS. (O.N. SOTO & C.D. MC VICK-
ER, EDS)
    L.F. LYDAY, 399(MLJ):JAN70-56
ARDEN, L. THE TWILIGHT'S LAST GLEAMING.
    M. LEVIN, 441:14MAY72-37
ARDEN, W. DIE TO A DISTANT DRUM.
    N. CALLENDAR, 441:7MAY72-34
ARDIES, T. THIS SUITCASE IS GOING TO
EXPLODE.
    N. CALLENDAR, 441:23JUL72-22
    617(TLS):13OCT72-1235
ARDLEY, G. BERKELEY'S RENOVATION OF
PHILOSOPHY.
    D.M. ARMSTRONG, 479(PHQ):APR70-181
    I. TIPTON, 393(MIND):JUL70-474
ARENDT, H. CRISES OF THE REPUBLIC.
    P. GREEN, 441:7MAY72-27
    442(NY):10JUN72-132
ARENDT, H. ON VIOLENCE.*
    H.D. GRAHAM, 639(VQR):SUMMER70-509
ARENDT, H. - SEE BENJAMIN, W.
ARENSKIJ, K., ED. PIS'MA V XOLLIVUD.
    S.P. HILL, 574(SEEJ):WINTER71-512
ARETHAS. ARETHAE "SCRIPTA MINORA."
(VOL 1) (L.G. WESTERINK, ED)
    R. BROWNING, 123:DEC70-331
"ARETINO'S DIALOGUES." (R. ROSENTHAL,
TRANS)
    A. MORAVIA, 441:30APR72-27
AREY, J.A. THE SKY PIRATES.
    F.J. COOK, 561(SATR):11MAR72-68
ARGENIO, R. - SEE ENNIUS
ARGENTI, P.P. THE RELIGIOUS MINORITIES
OF CHIOS.*
    J. RICHARD, 182:VOL23#19/20-882

ARGOV, D. MODERATES AND EXTREMISTS IN
THE INDIAN NATIONALIST MOVEMENT, 1883-
1920.
H.F. OWEN, 293(JAST):FEB70-478
ARGYRIS, C. THE APPLICABILITY OF ORGANI-
ZATIONAL SOCIOLOGY.
617(TLS):1DEC72-1456
ARIAN, E. BACH, BEETHOVEN AND BUREAU-
CRACY.
T. LASK, 441:14APR72-40
ARIAS-LARRETA, A. LITERATURAS ABORÍGENES
DE AMÉRICA. (9TH ED)
D. GIFFORD, 86(BHS):APR71-177
ARIOSTO, L. ORLANDO FURIOSO. (J. HAR-
INGTON, TRANS; R. MC NULTY, ED)
617(TLS):60CT72-1195
ARISTOPHANES. ARISTOPHANIS, "ACHARNEN-
SES, AVES, ECCLESIAZUSAE, EQUITES,
LYSISTRATA, NUBES, PAX, PLUTUS, RANAE
THESMOPHORIAZUSAE, VESPAE." (J. VAN
LEEUWEN, ED)
P. CHANTRAINE, 555:VOL44FASC1-128
ARISTOPHANES. CLOUDS.* (K.J. DOVER, ED)
C. SEGAL, 24:JAN71-100
ARISTOPHANES. THE LYSISTRATA OF ARIS-
TOPHANES. (S. SMITH, TRANS; ILLUS-
TRATED BY A. BEARDSLEY)
617(TLS):14JAN72-25
ARISTOTLE. ARISTOTE, "ÉCONOMIQUE."*
(B-A. VAN GRONINGEN & A. WARTELLE, EDS
& TRANS)
M-I. FINLEY, 123:DEC70-315
P. LOUIS, 555:VOL44FASC1-129
ARISTOTLE. ARISTOTE, "HISTOIRE DES ANI-
MAUX." (VOL 3, BKS 8-10) (P. LOUIS,
ED & TRANS)
C. MUGLER, 555:VOL44FASC2-323
J. STANNARD, 124:SEP70-22
ARISTOTLE. ARISTOTELE, "GLI ANALITICI
PRIMI." (M. MIGNUCCI, ED & TRANS)
P-M. HUBY, 123:MAR71-33
P. LOUIS, 555:VOL44FASC2-327
ARISTOTLE. ARISTOTLE ON THE ART OF FIC-
TION. (L.J. POTTS, ED & TRANS)
R.A. SWANSON, 399(MLJ):APR70-289
ARISTOTLE. ARISTOTLE'S "POETICS."* (L.
GOLDEN, TRANS; O.B. HARDISON, JR., ED)
E.H. DUNCAN, 290(JAAC):SPRING70-402
R.A. SWANSON, 399(MLJ):APR70-289
ARISTOTLE. "CATEGORIES" AND "DE INTERPRE-
TATIONE." (J.L. ACKRILL, ED & TRANS)
J. BRUNSCHWIG, 542:APR-JUN69-268
ARISTOTLE. MAQĀLA TASHTAMIL 'ALĀ FUSŪL
MIN KITĀB AL-ḤAYAWĀN LI-ARISṬŪ/TRACT
COMPRISING EXCERPTS FROM ARISTOTLE'S
BOOK OF ANIMALS. (J.N. MATTOCK, ED &
TRANS)
F.E. PETERS, 124:OCT70-58
ARISTOTLE. DE PARTIBUS ANIMALUM I [AND]
DE GENERATIONE ANIMALUM I. (D.M.
BALME, ED & TRANS)
617(TLS):22SEP72-1124
ARISTOTLE. "POÉTICA" DE ARISTÓTELES
TRADUCIDA DE LATIN. (J.P.M. RIZO,
TRANS; M. NEWELS, ED)
L.J. FRIEDMAN, 545(RPH):NOV70-372
ARIZA, A.K. & I.F. - SEE OLMO, L.
ARKOUN, M. - SEE MISKAWAYH
ARMACOST, M.H. THE POLITICS OF WEAPONS
INNOVATION.
E. HONEGGER, 182:VOL23#13/14-682
ARMAH, A.K. WHY ARE WE SO BLEST?
J. CAREW, 441:2APR72-7
A. HISLOP, 440:2APR72-8
C.R. LARSON, 561(SATR):18MAR72-73

ARMATO, R.P. & J.M. SPALEK, EDS. MEDI-
EVAL EPIC TO THE "EPIC THEATER" OF
BRECHT.
E. SPEIDEL, 447(N&Q):JUN70-238
W.B. WARDE, JR., 577(SHR):SPRING70-
193
ARMBRISTER, T. A MATTER OF ACCOUNTABIL-
ITY.*
J.E. DORNAN, JR., 396(MODA):SPRING71-
197
ARMENGOL, P.O. - SEE UNDER ORTIZ ARMEN-
GOL, P.
ARMENS, S. ARCHETYPES OF THE FAMILY IN
LITERATURE.
A.C. KIRSCH, 570(SQ):AUTUMN68-398
ARMOUR, L. THE CONCEPT OF TRUTH.
R.A. STANWAY, 150(DR):SPRING70-127
ARMSTRONG, A.H., ED. THE CAMBRIDGE HIS-
TORY OF LATER GREEK AND EARLY MEDIEVAL
PHILOSOPHY.*
C. MC GRATH, 613:WINTER68-630
R.T. WALLIS, 123:JUN71-233
ARMSTRONG, B.G. CALVINISM AND THE
AMYRAUT HERESY.
W.F. CHURCH, 551(RENQ):AUTUMN70-294
A.J. KRAILSHEIMER, 208(FS):OCT71-452
W.J. ONG, 377:JUL71-104
ARMSTRONG, D.M. A MATERIALIST THEORY OF
THE MIND.
T. NAGEL, 482(PHR):JUL70-394
ARMSTRONG, E. RONSARD AND THE AGE OF
GOLD.*
V.E. GRAHAM, 627(UTQ):JUL69-379
M.A. SCREECH, 447(N&Q):JAN70-39
I. SILVER, 546(RR):FEB70-54
ARMSTRONG, H.F. PEACE AND COUNTERPEACE.*
617(TLS):29DEC72-1571
ARMSTRONG, I., ED. THE MAJOR VICTORIAN
POETS: RECONSIDERATIONS.*
R.L. BRETT, 541(RES):NOV70-515
R. LANGBAUM, 184(EIC):OCT70-451
W.D. SHAW, 637(VS):JUN70-458
ARMSTRONG, I., ED. VICTORIAN SCRUTINIES.
617(TLS):22SEP72-1106
ARMSTRONG, J. THE PARADISE MYTH.
D.C. ALLEN, 551(RENQ):SPRING70-93
J.B. BEER, 541(RES):NOV70-524
G.R. HIBBARD, 447(N&Q):NOV70-430
ARMSTRONG, J.B. FACTORY UNDER THE ELMS.
676(YR):AUTUMN70-XXVIII
ARMSTRONG, V.I., COMP. I HAVE SPOKEN.*
617(TLS):21JUL72-829
ARNDT, N. DIE SHITOMIRER ARNDTS.
W. KIRCHNER, 32:SEP71-671
ARNDT, W. - SEE PUSHKIN, A.S.
ARNGART, O., ED. THE MIDDLE ENGLISH
"GENESIS AND EXODUS."*
G. BAUER, 72:BAND208HEFT2-139
A. RYNELL, 179(ES):FEB70-52
ARNHEIM, M.T.W. THE SENATORIAL ARISTO-
CRACY IN THE LATER ROMAN EMPIRE.
617(TLS):23JUN72-720
ARNHEIM, R. TOWARDS A PSYCHOLOGY OF ART.
ART AND VISUAL PERCEPTION.
H.R. WACKRILL, 39:MAR69-246
ARNHEIM, R. VISUAL THINKING.
H. OSBORNE, 89(BJA):SUMMER71-305
W.S. RUSK, 127:SPRING71-326
VON ARNIM, A. ERZÄHLUNGEN. (K.
KRATZSCH, ED)
I.C., 191(ELN):SEP70(SUPP)-97
VON ARNIM, L.A. DAS LOCH ODER DAS WIED-
ERGEFUNDENE PARADIES. [TOGETHER WITH]
VON EICHENDORFF, J. DAS INCOGNITO ODER
DIE MEHREREN KÖNIGE ODER ALT UND NEU.
(G. KLUGE, ED)
I.C., 191(ELN):SEP70(SUPP)-93

ARNOLD, A. PROSA DES EXPRESSIONISMUS.
617(TLS):22SEP72-1109
ARNOLD, A.J. PAUL VALÉRY AND HIS CRIT-
ICS.
A.G. ENGSTROM, 517(PBSA):OCT-DEC71-
425
ARNOLD, B. A CONCISE HISTORY OF IRISH
ART.
D. FITZ-GERALD, 39:MAY69-406
A. NEUMEYER, 290(JAAC):SPRING70-393
ARNOLD, D. & N. FORTUNE, EDS. THE
BEETHOVEN COMPANION.*
J.V.C., 410(M&L):JUL71-319
S. SADIE, 415:JUN71-554
ARNOLD, D. & N. FORTUNE, EDS. THE
MONTEVERDI COMPANION.*
M. PETERSON, 470:NOV68-65
ARNOLD, E. FORESTS OF THE NIGHT.*
S. BLACKBURN, 440:2JAN72-2
ARNOLD, H.L., ED. LITERATURBETRIEB IN
DEUTSCHLAND.
617(TLS):7APR72-399
ARNOLD, H.L. & F.J. GORTZ - SEE GRASS, G.
ARNOLD, J. PATTERNS OF FASHION. (2ND
ED)
617(TLS):8DEC72-1513
ARNOLD, M. MATTHEW ARNOLD'S ESSAYS IN
CRITICISM.* (1ST SER) (T.M. HOCTOR,
ED)
P. VEYRIRAS, 677:VOL2-318
ARNOLD, M. ESSAYS RELIGIOUS AND MIXED.
(R.H. SUPER, ED)
617(TLS):25AUG72-988
ARNOLD, O. GHOST GOLD.
W. GARD, 584(SWR):SPRING71-199
ARNOLD, P., D. STEINHILBER & H. KUTHMANN.
CATALOGUE OF GERMAN COINS SINCE 1800.
617(TLS):1DEC72-1469
ARNOLD, R. & K. HANSEN. PHONETIK DER
ENGLISCHEN SPRACHE.
G. SCHERER, 38:BAND87HEFT3/4-423
ARNOTT, P.D. THE ROMANS AND THEIR WORLD.
J.H. REID, 124:APR71-276
ARNTZEN, H. DIE ERNSTE KOMÖDIE.
C.P. MAGILL, 220(GL&L):OCT70-109
ARON, R. MARXISM AND THE EXISTENTIAL-
ISTS.
R.J.B., 543:SEP69-124
ARONSON, E. THE SOCIAL ANIMAL.
561(SATR):28OCT72-83
ARONSON, J. THE PRESS AND THE COLD WAR.*
P.S. GILLETTE, 32:DEC71-892
ARONSON, T. THE COBURGS OF BELGIUM.
R.D., 619(TC):1968/4&1969/1-95
ARONSON, T. QUEEN VICTORIA AND THE BONA-
PARTES.
442(NY):24JUN72-95
617(TLS):7JUL72-785
ARORA, S.K. & H.D. LASSWELL. POLITICAL
COMMUNICATION.
D.J. ELKINS, 293(JAST):NOV69-180
ARP, J. ARP ON ARP. (M. JEAN, ED)
R. SHATTUCK, 453:18MAY72-24
ARPS, L.W. & E.E. KINGERY. HIGH COUNTRY
NAMES.
R.A. MOHL, 424:MAR68-52
ARRABAL, F. THÉÂTRE IV.
F. TONELLI, 207(FR):MAR70-726
ARRIVÉ, M. - SEE JARRY, A.
ARROM, J.J. HISPANOAMÉRICA.
E.M. ALDRICH, JR., 238:MAR70-172
"ARROW-ODD: A MEDIEVAL NOVEL." (P. ED-
WARDS & H. PÁLSSON, TRANS)
G.S. LANE, 563(SS):WINTER71-89
P. SCHACH, 301(JEGP):OCT71-707
ARROWSMITH, P., ED. TO ASIA IN PEACE.
617(TLS):31MAR72-351

"ART TREASURES IN FRANCE."
R.E. SPEAR, 207(FR):MAR70-725
S. SPECTOR, 58:MAY70-14
"ART TREASURES IN ITALY."
S. SPECTOR, 58:MAY70-14
"ART TREASURES IN SPAIN."
J.F. MOFFITT, 127:SUMMER71-428
S. SPECTOR, 58:MAY70-14
"ART TREASURES OF MEDIEVAL FINLAND."
J. BECKWITH, 39:SEP69-267
ARTAUD, A. COLLECTED WORKS. (VOL 3)
617(TLS):10MAR72-285
ARTHOS, J. MILTON AND THE ITALIAN CITIES.
J.M. STEADMAN, 275(IQ):SUMMER69-92
ARTHOS, J. SHAKESPEARE: THE EARLY
WRITINGS.
617(TLS):28JUL72-867
ARTHUR, E. & D. WITNEY. THE BARN.
H. KRAMER, 441:3DEC72-34
442(NY):16DEC72-152
ARTHUR, N. AUXILIARY VERBS IN MYANG OF
NORTHERN THAILAND.
J.A. MATISOFF, 293(JAST):FEB70-492
ARTOLA GALLEGO, M. LA ESPAÑA DE FERNANDO
VII.
191(ELN):SEP70(SUPP)-149
ARTOLA GALLEGO, M. - SEE FERNÁNDEZ DE
CÓRDOVA, F.
ARVEILLER, R. ETUDE SUR LE PARLER DE
MONACO.
P. DEGUISE, 207(FR):DEC69-366
ARVON, H. GEORGES LUKÁCS, OU LE FRONT
POPULAIRE EN LITTÉRATURE.
Z. TAR, 32:JUN71-426
"AS I CROSSED A BRIDGE OF DREAMS."* (I.
MORRIS, TRANS)
617(TLS):5MAY72-524
ASCLEPIUS OF TRALLES. COMMENTARY TO
NICOMACHUS' INTRODUCTION TO ARITHMETIC.
(L. TARÁN, ED)
C. MUGLER, 555:VOL44FASC2-332
ASCOLI, G.I. SCRITTI SULLA QUESTIONE
DELLA LINGUA. (G. GRASSI, ED)
M.S. BRESLIN, 545(RPH):NOV69-251
ASH, C.V. & E.S. ROHMER. MASTER OF
VILLAINY.
D.J. ENRIGHT, 362:21DEC72-867
ASHBEE, C.R. FRANK LLOYD WRIGHT: THE
EARLY WORK.
W.R. HASBROUCK, 44:JUN69-84
ASHBERY, J. THE DOUBLE DREAM OF SPRING.*
F. MORAMARCO, 651(WHR):WINTER71-96
639(VQR):AUTUMN70-CXXXII
ASHBERY, J. THREE POEMS.
P. DALE, 561(SATR):8JUL72-57
R. HOWARD, 491:AUG72-296
P. ZWEIG, 441:9APR72-4
ASHBY, E. & M. ANDERSON. THE RISE OF
THE STUDENT ESTATE IN BRITAIN.*
676(YR):SPRING71-XIV
ASHDOWN, C. THE ADVENTURES OF ROMNEY
PRINGLE.
N. CALLENDAR, 441:10DEC72-56
ASHE, G. & OTHERS. THE QUEST FOR AMERI-
CA.
617(TLS):21JAN72-77
ASHER, R. RICHARD ASHER TALKING SENSE.
(F.A. JONES, ED)
617(TLS):3NOV72-1349
ASHLEY, M. CHARLES II.*
617(TLS):7JAN72-10
ASHMEAD, A.H. & K.M. PHILLIPS, JR. COR-
PUS VASORUM ANTIQUORUM. (FASC 1)
617(TLS):11FEB72-165
ASHMOLE, E. THE INSTITUTION, LAWS AND
CEREMONIES OF THE MOST NOBLE ORDER OF
THE GARTER.
617(TLS):18FEB72-190

ASHTON, D. RICHARD LINDNER.
  S. FRANK, 58:SUMMER70-14
ASHTON, D. NEW YORK.
  C.W. CASEWIT, 440:30APR72-15
ASHTON, D. - SEE PICASSO, P.
ASHTON, T.L. BYRON'S HEBREW MELODIES.
  617(TLS):19MAY72-573
ASHTON-WARNER, S. SPEARPOINT.
  B. DE MOTT, 561(SATR):16SEP72-97
  P. MARIN, 441:24SEP72-59
ASHTON-WARNER, S. THREE.
  P. CRUTTWELL, 249(HUDR):SPRING71-177
ASIMOV, I. ASIMOV'S BIOGRAPHICAL ENCY-
  CLOPEDIA OF SCIENCE AND TECHNOLOGY.
  E. EDELSON, 440:30APR72-11
ASIMOV, I. THE GODS THEMSELVES.
  617(TLS):13OCT72-1235
DE ASÍS FERNÁNDEZ, F. A PRINCIPIO DE
  CUENTAS.
  R. SQUIRRU, 37:JUL69-40
ASLANAPA, O. TURKISH ART AND ARCHITEC-
  TURE.
  617(TLS):10MAR72-279
ASLIN, E. THE AESTHETIC MOVEMENT.
  P. GAY, 31(ASCH):AUTUMN72-660
ASPENSTRÖM, W. SKÅL.
  L. SJÖBERG, 563(SS):SUMMER71-304
ASPILLERA, P.S. BASIC TAGALOG FOR FOR-
  EIGNERS AND NON-TAGALOGS.
  A.M. STEVENS, 293(JAST):FEB70-499
ASPINALL, A. - SEE GEORGE III
ASPINALL, A. - SEE GEORGE IV
ASPLAND, C.W. A SYNTACTICAL STUDY OF
  EPIC FORMULAS AND FORMULAIC EXPRESSIONS
  CONTAINING THE -ANT FORMS IN TWELFTH
  CENTURY FRENCH VERSE.
  P. NYKROG, 589:OCT71-724
  P. RICKARD, 382(MAE):1971/2-190
  D.J.A. ROSS, 402(MLR):OCT71-891
ASPLER, T. THE STREETS OF ASKELON.
  617(TLS):7JUL72-783
ASPREA, L. IL PREVITOCCIOLO.
  617(TLS):4FEB72-120
ASQUITH, C. DIARIES, 1915-18.
  C.E. BARON, 97(CQ):SUMMER68-274
ASTALDI, M-L. MANZONI.
  617(TLS):4FEB72-134
ASTROM, P., COMP. WHO'S WHO IN CYPRIOTE
  ARCHAEOLOGY.
  617(TLS):31MAR72-370
ASTUDILLO Y A., R. LAS ELEGÍAS DE LA
  CARNE.
  R. SQUIRRU, 37:JUL69-40
ASTURIAS, M.A. THE BEJEWELED BOY.*
  P. ADAMS, 61:JAN72-96
  J. YGLESIAS, 61:AUG72-83
ASTURIAS, M.A. STRONG WIND.
  H.L. JOHNSON, 238:MAR70-162
ASTUTO, P.L. EUGENIO ESPEJO (1747-1795),
  REFORMADOR ECUATORIANO DE LA ILUSTRA-
  CIÓN.
  H. MONCAYO, 263:OCT-DEC71-459
"ATHENIAN." INSIDE THE COLONELS' GREECE.
  617(TLS):7APR72-395
ATKINS, J.W.H. ENGLISH LITERARY CRITI-
  CISM: THE RENASCENCE.
  W.A. SESSIONS, 399(MLJ):JAN70-49
ATKINSON, A.B. UNEQUAL SHARES.
  W.G. RUNCIMAN, 362:14DEC72-835
ATKINSON, B. BROADWAY.*
  J.T. NARDIN, 27(AL):NOV71-497
ATKINSON, B. THIS BRIGHT LAND.
  J.K. TERRES, 441:9APR72-23
ATKINSON, B. - SEE O'CASEY, S.
ATKINSON, H. THE RECKONING.
  N. CALLENDAR, 441:9JUL72-30
ATTAL, J-P. L'IMAGE MÉTAPHYSIQUE.
  A. MARISSEL, 207(FR):APR70-848

ATTERBURY, P., ED. NICHOLSON'S GUIDES
  TO THE WATERWAYS. (VOL 1)
  617(TLS):7APR72-402
"ATTI DEL PRIMO SIMPOSIO INTERNAZIONALE
  DI PROTOSTORIA ITALIANA."*
  R.M. OGILVIE, 123:DEC71-459
"ATTICA."
  B. NELSON, 441:17DEC72-1
ATWOOD, E.B. THE REGIONAL VOCABULARY OF
  TEXAS.
  E. KOLB, 179(ES):AUG70-376
ATWOOD, M. THE ANIMALS IN THAT COUNTRY.*
  H. MAC CALLUM, 627(UTQ):JUL69-343
ATWOOD, M. THE EDIBLE WOMAN.*
  G. JONAS, 606(TAMR):#54-75
  G. ROPER, 627(UTQ):JUL70-341
ATWOOD, M. THE JOURNALS OF SUSANNA
  MOODIE.
  M. DOYLE, 491:MAR72-356
  A.W. PURDY, 102(CANL):WINTER71-80
ATWOOD, M. POWER POLITICS.
  D. ALLEN, 491:JUL72-235
  M. DOYLE, 491:MAR72-356
ATWOOD, M. PROCEDURES FOR UNDERGROUND.
  D. BARBOUR, 150(DR):AUTUMN70-433
  P. STEVENS, 102(CANL):AUTUMN71-91
ATWOOD, M. SURFACING.
  P. MORLEY, 296:FALL72-99
ATWOOD, M. - SEE TRAILL, W.
AUB, M. LAS BUENAS INTENCIONES. LA
  CALLE DE VALVERDE. JUSEP TORRES CAM-
  PALANS. VIDA Y OBRA DE LUIS ALVAREZ
  PETREÑA.
  617(TLS):4FEB72-117
AUBIN, P. LE PROBLÈME DE LA "CONVERSION."
  J. TROUILLARD, 542:APR-JUN69-281
AUBINEAU, M. - SEE GRÉGOIRE DE NYSSE
AUBREY, J. AUBREY ON EDUCATION. (J.E.
  STEPHENS, ED)
  H. TREVOR-ROPER, 362:23MAR72-380
AUBRY, C. THE MAGIC FIDDLER AND OTHER
  LEGENDS OF FRENCH CANADA.
  A. EMERY, 627(UTQ):JUL69-408
AUCHINCLOSS, L., ED. FABLES OF WIT AND
  ELEGANCE.
  T. LASK, 441:25SEP72-39
AUCHINCLOSS, L. I COME AS A THIEF.
  T.R. EDWARDS, 453:5OCT72-21
  G. HICKS, 441:3SEP72-6
  J. KANON, 561(SATR):26AUG72-60
  T. LASK, 441:25SEP72-39
  E. WEEKS, 61:SEP72-107
  442(NY):26AUG72-78
AUCHINCLOSS, L. EDITH WHARTON.*
  617(TLS):5MAY72-509
AUCHINCLOSS, L. A WORLD OF PROFIT.
  42(AR):SUMMER69-261
AUDEMARS, P. STOLEN LIKE MAGIC AWAY.
  617(TLS):4FEB72-135
AUDEN, W.H. A CERTAIN WORLD.*
  M.K. SPEARS, 676(YR):AUTUMN70-90
AUDEN, W.H. CITY WITHOUT WALLS.*
  G.S. FRASER, 473(PR):WINTER71/72-469
  R. HOWARD, 491:OCT71-34
  M.K. SPEARS, 676(YR):AUTUMN70-90
AUDEN, W.H. COLLECTED LONGER POEMS.*
  H. SERGEANT, 175:SPRING69-33
  M.K. SPEARS, 676(YR):AUTUMN70-90
AUDEN, W.H. EPISTLE TO A GODSON.
  C. BEDIENT, 441:24SEP72-4
  A. BROYARD, 441:29SEP72-45
  F. KERMODE, 362:26OCT72-551
AUDEN, W.H. SECONDARY WORLDS.
  M.I., 619(TC):1968/4&1969/1-91
  H. SERGEANT, 175:SUMMER69-71
  M.K. SPEARS, 676(YR):AUTUMN70-90
AUDET, N. LA TÊTE BARBARE.
  J-L. MAJOR, 627(UTQ):JUL69-484

12

AUDRIC, J. ANGKOR AND THE KHMER EMPIRE.
617(TLS):21APR72-436
AUERBACH, E. GESAMMELTE AUFSÄTZE ZUR
ROMANISCHEN PHILOLOGIE.
A.G. REICHENBERGER, 546(RR):APR70-161
AUERBACH, E. & C.K. ADAMS. PAINTINGS AND
SCULPTURE AT HATFIELD HOUSE.
617(TLS):14JAN72-42
AUGUET, R. CRUELTY AND CIVILIZATION.
617(TLS):22DEC72-1564
SAINT AUGUSTINE. KING ALFRED'S VERSION
OF ST. AUGUSTINE'S "SOLILOQUIES."*
(T.A. CARNICELLI, ED)
J.J. CAMPBELL, 301(JEGP):JUL71-526
A. HUDSON, 541(RES):NOV70-474
E.G. STANLEY, 447(N&Q):MAR70-109
SAINT AUGUSTINE. THE CITY OF GOD AGAINST
THE PAGANS. (VOL 3, BKS 8-11) (D.S.
WIESEN, TRANS)
J. ANDRÉ, 555:VOL44FASC2-354
SAINT AUGUSTINE. CITY OF GOD AGAINST THE
PAGANS. (VOL 7, BKS 21-22) (W.M.
GREEN, TRANS)
617(TLS):19MAY72-584
SAINT AUGUSTINE. CONCERNING THE CITY OF
GOD AGAINST THE PAGANS. (D. KNOWLES,
ED)
617(TLS):18AUG72-974
SAINT AUGUSTINE. LA LUMIÈRE INTÉRIEURE.
(J-C. FRAISSE, ED & TRANS)
A. FOREST, 542:APR-JUN69-283
AUJAC, G. STRABON ET LA SCIENCE DE SON
TEMPS.
D.R. DICKS, 123:DEC70-328
AUJAC, G. & F. LASSERRE - SEE STRABO
AULT, W.O. OPEN-FIELD FARMING IN MEDIE-
VAL ENGLAND.
617(TLS):15SEP72-1071
AUNG, M.H. - SEE UNDER HTIN AUNG, M.
AURELIAN OF RÉOMÉ. THE DISCIPLINE OF
MUSIC (MUSICA DISCIPLINA).* (J. PONTE,
TRANS)
A. CLARKSON, 308:WINTER68-281
AURENHAMMER, H. MARTINO ALTOMONTE.
N. LYNTON, 90:FEB69-97
AURENHAMMER, H. LEXIKON DER CHRISTLICHEN
IKONOGRAPHIE. (PT 6)
P.P. FEHL, 290(JAAC):FALL69-100
AUSTIN, A. THE PRESIDENT'S WAR.*
D.I. DAVIDSON, 61:FEB72-96
AUSTIN, C. - SEE EURIPIDES
AUSTIN, C. - SEE MENANDER
AUSTIN, D. MALTA AND THE END OF THE
EMPIRE.
617(TLS):14JAN72-49
AUSTIN, N. THE GREEK HISTORIANS.
H.D. WESTLAKE, 123:JUN71-297
AUSTIN, P.B. ON BEING SWEDISH.*
R.C. ELLSWORTH, 529(QQ):WINTER70-657
AUSTIN, W.W. MUSIC IN THE TWENTIETH
CENTURY.
R. SWIFT, 308:SPRING67-165
AUSUBEL, N., ED. A TREASURY OF JEWISH
FOLKLORE.
617(TLS):19MAY72-584
AUTY, P. TITO.*
F.W.D. DEAKIN, 575(SEER):OCT71-626
AUTY, R., J.L.I. FENNELL & J.S.G. SIM-
MONS, EDS. OXFORD SLAVONIC PAPERS.*
(NEW SER, VOL 1)
W.B. EDGERTON, 550(RUSR):JAN70-110
AUTY, R., J.L.I. FENNELL & J.S.G. SIM-
MONS, EDS. OXFORD SLAVONIC PAPERS.
(NEW SER, VOL 2)
L.R. LEWITTER, 402(MLR):JAN71-238

AUTY, R., J.L.I. FENNELL & J.S.G. SIM-
MONS, EDS. OXFORD SLAVONIC PAPERS.
(NEW SER, VOL 3)
D.S., 410(M&L):JUL71-317
AUTY, R. & A.E. PENNINGTON - SEE UNBE-
GAUN, B.O.
AVALLE-ARCE, J.B. - SEE DE CERVANTES
SAAVEDRA, M.
AVASTHI, A., ED. MUNICIPAL ADMINISTRA-
TION IN INDIA.
617(TLS):1SEP72-1033
AVASTHY, R.S. THE MUGHAL EMPEROR HUM-
AYUN.
S.A. AKBAR, 273(IC):JAN69-71
LADY AVEBURY - SEE CASSON, H. & J. GREN-
FELL
AVERY, G.C. INQUIRY AND TESTAMENT.*
O.F. BEST, 221(GQ):JAN70-119
AVI-YONAH, M. THE HOLY LAND.
617(TLS):29DEC72-1574
AVINERI, S. THE SOCIAL AND POLITICAL
THOUGHT OF KARL MARX.
P.P. RESTUCCIA, 484(PPR):JUN70-627
B.B. SELIGMAN, 390:JAN69-74
W.A. SUCHTING, 63:DEC71-338
AVIS, W.S. & OTHERS, EDS. DICTIONARY OF
CANADIAN ENGLISH: THE SENIOR DICTION-
ARY.*
P.W. ROGERS, 529(QQ):SPRING70-111
AVIS, W.S. & OTHERS, EDS. A DICTIONARY
OF CANADIANISMS ON HISTORICAL PRINCI-
PLES.*
P.W. ROGERS, 529(QQ):SPRING70-111
617(TLS):13OCT72-1209
AVNERI, Z., ED. GERMANIA JUDAICA. (VOL
2)
D. DEMANDT, 182:VOL23#19/20-884
AVNI, A.A. THE BIBLE AND ROMANTICISM.
F.P. BOWMAN, 208(FS):OCT71-471
J.S.P., 191(ELN):SEP70(SUPP)-52
AVRAM, H.D. & OTHERS. CONVERSION OF
RETROSPECTIVE CATALOG RECORDS TO MACH-
INE-READABLE FORM.
C.A. SHEPHERD, 356:JAN71-66
AVRICH, P. KRONSTADT 1921.*
A. ASCHER, 550(RUSR):OCT70-465
E. MAWDSLEY, 575(SEER):JAN71-161
R.G. SUNY, 32:MAR71-150
639(VQR):SUMMER70-CX
AVRICH, P. THE RUSSIAN ANARCHISTS.
J.A. NEWTH, 587:OCT68-260
AVRICH, P. - SEE KROPOTKIN, P.
AWOONOR, K. THIS EARTH, MY BROTHER...*
J. CAREW, 441:2APR72-7
617(TLS):24MAR72-325
AXELOS, K. HÉRACLITE ET LA PHILOSOPHIE.
G.B. KERFERD, 123:JUN71-289
AXTELL, J.L. - SEE LOCKE, J.
"AYE D'AVIGNON." (S.J. BORG, ED)
R. TAYLOR, 399(MLJ):MAY70-381
AYER, A.J. METAPHYSICS AND COMMON SENSE.
R. BAMBROUGH, 111:30JAN70-92
A.R. WHITE, 518:MAY70-1
AYER, A.J. THE ORIGINS OF PRAGMATISM.
D. GREENLEE, 322(JHI):OCT-DEC69-603
J.W. ROTH, 319:JUL72-375
R.J. ROTH, 258:JUN69-297
H.S. THAYER, 479(PHQ):JAN70-80
AYER, A.J. PROBABILITY AND EVIDENCE.
L. KOLAKOWSKI, 362:7SEP72-310
617(TLS):31MAR72-359
AYER, A.J. BERTRAND RUSSELL.
L. KOLAKOWSKI, 362:7SEP72-310
J. RACHELS, 441:22OCT72-6
617(TLS):14JUL72-795

BAHLKE, G.W. THE LATER AUDEN.*
  G.L. BRUNS, 590:WINTER71-37
  E. MENDELSON, 677:VOL2-337
BAHLMAN, D.W.R. - SEE HAMILTON, E.W.
BAILBÉ, J. AGRIPPA D'AUBIGNÉ, POÈTE DES
  "TRAGIQUES."*
  F. GRAY, 207(FR):MAR70-698
BAILBÉ, J.M. LE ROMAN ET LA MUSIQUE EN
  FRANCE SOUS LA MONARCHIE DE JUILLET.
  R. CHAMBERS, 67:MAY71-132
BAILEY, B.L. JAMAICAN CREOLE SYNTAX.*
  F. ANSHEN, 35(AS):OCT68-233
BAILEY, D. MY BARENESS IS NOT JUST MY
  BODY.
  R.G. ADAMS, 198:SPRING72-111
BAILEY, D.R.S. - SEE UNDER SHACKLETON
  BAILEY, D.R.
BAILEY, D.W. BRITISH MILITARY LONGARMS,
  1715-1815.
  617(TLS):25AUG72-1005
BAILEY, F.L., WITH H. ARONSON. THE
  DEFENCE NEVER RESTS.*
  P. WALL, 441:23JAN72-4
  617(TLS):11AUG72-954
BAILEY, H.W., ED. SAKA DOCUMENTS.
  (PORTFOLIOS 1-4)
  M.J. DRESDEN, 318(JAOS):APR-JUN70-360
BAILEY, J. THE WIRE CLASSROOM.
  V. CUNNINGHAM, 362:14SEP72-344
  617(TLS):1DEC72-1467
BAILEY, J.H. THE ICARUS COMPLEX.
  M. LEVIN, 441:12NOV72-67
BAILEY, J.O. THE POETRY OF THOMAS
  HARDY.*
  D. KRAMER, 579(SAQ):SUMMER71-421
  H. OREL, 301(JEGP):JAN71-177
BAILEY, P. TALKING TO MYSELF.
  441:16APR72-20
BAILEY, P. TRESPASSES.*
  F.P.W. MC DOWELL, 659:SUMMER72-361
BAILEY, R.W. & D.M. BURTON. ENGLISH
  STYLISTICS.
  S.R. LEVIN, 399(MLJ):JAN70-41
  S. ULLMANN, 545(RPH):MAY71-639
BAILLIE, I.F. & S.J. SHEEHY, EDS. IRISH
  AGRICULTURE IN A CHANGING WORLD.
  617(TLS):25FEB72-229
BAILY, F. JOURNAL OF A TOUR IN UNSETTLED
  PARTS OF NORTH AMERICA IN 1796 AND
  1797. (J.D.L. HOLMES, ED)
  J.L. WRIGHT, JR., 656(WMQ):JUL70-500
BAINBRIDGE, B. HARRIET SAID...
  V. CUNNINGHAM, 362:12OCT72-482
  617(TLS):6OCT72-1184
BAINE, R.M. DANIEL DEFOE AND THE SUPER-
  NATURAL.
  M.E. NOVAK, 541(RES):MAY70-215
  J.J. RICHETTI, 301(JEGP):APR71-318
  A. SHERBO, 173(ECS):SUMMER70-560
BAINTON, R.H. ERASMUS OF CHRISTENDOM.*
  A.W. GODFREY, 363:NOV69-29
BAIRD, J. THE DOME AND THE ROCK.
  R. BUTTEL, 295:VOL2#3-431
  H.H. WAGGONER, 405(MP):MAY70-392
BAIRD, T. PEOPLE WHO PULL YOU DOWN.
  639(VQR):SUMMER70-LXXXIX
BAJEC, A. & OTHERS, EDS. SLOVAR SLOVEN-
  SKEGA KNJIŽNEGA JEZIKA. (PT 1)
  R.G.A. DE BRAY, 575(SEER):APR71-282
BAJPAI, S.C. THE NORTHERN FRONTIER OF
  INDIA.
  617(TLS):10NOV72-1377
BAKELANTS, L. LA VIE ET LES OEUVRES DE
  GISLAIN BULTEEL D'YPRES, 1555-1611.
  (G. CAMBIER, ED)
  E.J. KENNEY, 123:DEC70-408

BAKER, A.R.H., ED. PROGRESS IN HISTORI-
  CAL GEOGRAPHY.
  617(TLS):28JUL72-875
BAKER, H. THE RACE OF TIME.
  A.A., 477:SUMMER69-421
BAKER, H.D.R. A CHINESE LINEAGE VILLAGE.
  K.H-K. CHANG, 318(JAOS):OCT-DEC70-621
  N. DIAMOND, 293(JAST):NOV69-147
BAKER, I. GRAVE DOUBT.
  N. CALLENDAR, 441:31DEC72-18
BAKER, I. - SEE UNDER LM
BAKER, J.T. THOMAS MERTON, SOCIAL
  CRITIC.
  J.E. JENSEN, 70(ANQ):MAR72-109
BAKER, L. BRAHMIN IN REVOLT.
  442(NY):4MAR72-115
BAKER, N. GOVERNMENT AND CONTRACTORS.
  617(TLS):21APR72-451
BAKER, R. POOR RUSSELL'S ALMANAC.
  G. MARX, 441:30JAN72-2
BAKER, R. THE TERROR OF TOBERMORY.
  617(TLS):17MAR72-317
BAKER, R.J.S. ADMINISTRATIVE THEORY AND
  PUBLIC ADMINISTRATION.
  617(TLS):2JUN72-638
BAKER, T. MEDIEVAL LONDON.*
  M. WEINBAUM, 589:APR71-362
BAKER, W. JACQUES PRÉVERT.
  A.H. GREET, 399(MLJ):APR70-283
BAKER, W.E. SYNTAX IN ENGLISH POETRY,
  1870-1930.
  J.R. BENNETT, 141:FALL69-384
BAKEWELL, K.G.B. A MANUAL OF CATALOGUING
  PRACTICE.
  617(TLS):21APR72-456
BAKEWELL, P.J. SILVER MINING AND SOCIETY
  IN COLONIAL MEXICO, ZACATECAS 1546-
  1700.
  617(TLS):7JUL72-782
BAKHTIN, M. RABELAIS AND HIS WORLD.
  E.K. BEAUJOUR, 207(FR):OCT69-190
  T.M.G., 543:JUN70-737
BAKKER, B.H. - SEE ALEXIS, P.
BAKKER, D.M. SAMENTREKKING IN NEDER-
  LANDSE SYNTACTISCHE GROEPEN.
  M.C. VAN DEN TOORN, 361:VOL23#2-199
BAKOŠ, M. & OTHERS, EDS. CHESHKO-RUSSKIE
  I SLOVATSKO-RUSSKIE LITERATURNYE OT-
  NOSHENIIA (KONETS XVIII-NACHALO XX V.).
  J.V. HANEY, 32:JUN71-446
AL-BAKRI, A.'U. THE GEOGRAPHY OF AL-
  ANDALUS AND EUROPE. (A.R.A. AL-HAJJI,
  ED)
  M.A.M. KHAN, 273(IC):OCT69-308
BAKUNIN, M. MICHEL BAKOUNINE ET SES
  RELATIONS AVEC SERGEJ NEČAEV 1870-1872.
  (A. LEHNING, ED)
  617(TLS):4FEB72-119
BAKUNIN, M. BAKUNIN ON ANARCHY. (S.
  DOLGOFF, ED)
  E. CAPOUYA, 561(SATR):4MAR72-88
BAL, W. INTRODUCTION AUX ÉTUDES DE LIN-
  GUISTIQUE ROMANE.
  F.P. MARTÍ, 596(SL):VOL22#1-64
BAL, W. - SEE PIGAFETTA, F. & D. LOPEZ
BALAKIAN, A. ANDRÉ BRETON.*
  D. SCHIER, 109:FALL/WINTER71/72-133
  R. SHATTUCK, 453:1JUN72-19
  617(TLS):21APR72-442
BALAKIAN, A. THE SYMBOLIST MOVEMENT.*
  E. KERN, 131(CL):SPRING71-180
BALANDIER, G. DAILY LIFE IN THE KINGDOM
  OF THE KONGO FROM THE 16TH TO THE 18TH
  CENTURY. (FRENCH TITLE: LA VIE QUOTID-
  IENNE AU ROYAUME DE KONGO DU XVIE AU
  XVIIIE SIÈCLE.)
  J. VANSINA, 69:JAN69-62

15

BALANDIER, G. SENS ET PUISSANCE.
617(TLS):7JAN72-7
BALASSA, B. & OTHERS. THE STRUCTURE OF
PROTECTION IN DEVELOPING COUNTRIES.
617(TLS):15SEP72-1066
BALASUBRAHMANYAM, S.R. EARLY CHOLA
TEMPLES.
617(TLS):12MAY72-552
BALAWYDER, A. CANADIAN SOVIET RELATIONS
BETWEEN THE WORLD WARS.
J.L. GRANATSTEIN, 99:SEP72-16
BALD, R.C. JOHN DONNE.* (W. MILGATE,
ED)
W. BENNETT, 493:AUTUMN70-258
E. LE COMTE, 301(JEGP):JAN71-154
F. MANLEY, 579(SAQ):SUMMER71-416
617(TLS):29DEC72-1581
BALDICK, R. DINNER AT MAGNY'S.*
R. FREEDMAN, 440:20FEB72-7
BALDUINO, A. LETTERATURA ROMANTICA DAL
PRATI AL CARDUCCI.
W.T.S., 191(ELN):SEP69(SUPP)-119
BALDUINO, A. - SEE FOSCOLO, U.
BALDWIN, J. NO NAME IN THE STREET.
D. CAUTE, 362:18MAY72-659
B. DE MOTT, 561(SATR):27MAY72-63
M. KEMPTON, 453:29JUN72-3
M. WATKINS, 441:28MAY72-17
E. WEEKS, 61:JUN72-108
617(TLS):28APR72-469
BALDWIN, J. ONE DAY, WHEN I WAS LOST.
617(TLS):17NOV72-1390
BALDWIN, J.W. MASTERS, PRINCES, AND
MERCHANTS.
J.A. BRUNDAGE, 589:OCT71-726
BALDWIN, M. THE CELLAR.
V. CUNNINGHAM, 362:6APR72-458
617(TLS):19MAY72-565
BALDWIN, M.W. ALEXANDER III AND THE
TWELFTH CENTURY.*
J.A. WAHL, 377:MAR71-38
BALDWIN, R.E. ECONOMIC DEVELOPMENT AND
EXPORT GROWTH.
D. WALKER, 69:JAN69-89
BALDWIN, T.W. ON THE COMPOSITIONAL GEN-
ETICS OF THE COMEDY OF ERRORS.
J.P. REDDINGTON, 570(SQ):WINTER68-88
BALE, J. JOHN BALE'S "KING JOHAN."
((B.B. ADAMS, ED)
G.R. PROUDFOOT, 541(RES):NOV70-484
BALESTRINI, N. VOGLIAMO TUTTO.
617(TLS):29SEP72-1139
BALFOUR, C. INDUSTRIAL RELATIONS IN THE
COMMON MARKET.
617(TLS):3NOV72-1347
BALFOUR, J. THE TINY TOTS.
617(TLS):3MAR72-239
BALINKY, A. MARX'S ECONOMICS.
D.F. GORDON, 32:SEP71-692
BALINT, M. & J. DUPONT - SEE FERENCZI, S.
BALL, A. YESTERDAY IN BATH.
617(TLS):7JUL72-785
BALL, J. THE FIRST TEAM.
M. LEVIN, 441:20FEB72-26
617(TLS):26MAY72-612
BALL, J. FIVE PIECES OF JADE.
N. CALLENDAR, 441:12MAR72-40
617(TLS):13OCT72-1235
BALL, N. SPARROWS. WATER-PIPES & MOON-
LIGHT.
D. BARBOUR, 150(DR):SPRING70-112
BALL, P.M. THE CENTRAL SELF.
L. LERNER, 184(EIC):JAN70-89
"BALLAD OF THE HIDDEN DRAGON." (M.
DOLEŽELOVÁ-VELINGEROVÁ & J.I. CRUMP,
TRANS)
617(TLS):23JUN72-730
BALLAIRA, G. - SEE TIBERIUS

BALLANCHE, P.S. LA VISION D'HÉBAL.
(A-J-L. BUSST, ED)
B. JUDEN, 208(FS):JUL71-341
BALLAND, A. & J. LECAT - SEE APOLLINAIRE,
G.
BALLARD, E.G. SOCRATIC IGNORANCE.
M-A. VINCENT-VIGUIER, 542:APR-JUN68-
294
BALLARD, J.G. LOVE AND NAPALM.
P. THEROUX, 441:29OCT72-56
BALLOU, E.B. THE BUILDING OF THE HOUSE.*
639(VQR):SUMMER70-CXVI
BALME, D.M. - SEE ARISTOTLE
BALOG, P. THE COINAGE OF THE MAMŪLK
SULTANS OF EGYPT AND SYRIA.
A.L. UDOVITCH, 318(JAOS):APR-JUN70-
288
BALOTĂ, N. URMUZ.
V. NEMOIANU, 574(SEEJ):FALL71-398
BALSAMO, L. LA STAMPA IN SARDEGNA NEI
SECOLI XV E XVI.
D.E. RHODES, 354:JUN69-167
BALSDON, J.P.V.D. LIFE AND LEISURE IN
ANCIENT ROME.*
B. BALDWIN, 487:AUTUMN70-280
M.L. CLARKE, 313:VOL60-219
J.H. D'ARMS, 24:OCT71-715
P.G. WALSH, 123:JUN71-265
639(VQR):SPRING70-LXXV
BALSEIRO, J.A. THE AMERICAS LOOK AT
EACH OTHER.*
A.O. ALDRIDGE, 141:SUMMER70-254
H.E. LEWALD, 149:SEP71-273
BALSEIRO, J.A. SEIS ESTUDIOS SOBRE RUBÉN
DARIO.*
C.D. WATLAND, 546(RR):FEB70-71
BALTAZAR, E.R. GOD WITHIN PROCESS.
R. LAUDER, 142:FALL71-487
BALTRUSAITIS, J. LA QUÊTE D'ISIS.
G. LASCAULT, 98:JAN69-54
BALTZELL, W.J. - SEE MAC DOWELL, E.
BALYUZI, H.M. 'ABDU'L-BAHÁ.
617(TLS):7APR72-397
DE BALZAC, H. CORRESPONDANCE.* (VOL 5)
(R. PIERROT, ED)
A-R. PUGH, 402(MLR):JAN71-188
DE BALZAC, H. LE PÈRE GORIOT.* (P.W.
LOCK, ED)
C.C., 191(ELN):SEP69(SUPP)-57
C.F. COATES, 399(MLJ):JAN70-46
BAMBARA, T.C. GORILLA, MY LOVE.
A. BROYARD, 441:11OCT72-41
C-D.B. BRYAN, 441:15OCT72-31
561(SATR):18NOV72-97
BAMBROUGH, R., ED. PLATO, POPPER AND
POLITICS.*
I.M. CROMBIE, 447(N&Q):JUL70-279
BAMBROUGH, R. REASON, TRUTH AND GOD.
A-R.C. DUNCAN, 529(QQ):AUTUMN70-468
A.C. EWING, 393(MIND):JAN70-154
R. HEPBURN, 479(PHQ):JUL70-313
D.Z. PHILLIPS, 518:JAN70-1
BAMM, P. ALEXANDER THE GREAT.
R.M. ERRINGTON, 303:VOL90-249
E-A. FREDRICKSMEYER, 124:DEC70-130
BANASEVIĆ, N., ED. PROCEEDINGS OF THE
FIFTH CONGRESS OF THE INTERNATIONAL
COMPARATIVE LITERATURE ASSOCIATION:
BELGRADE, 1967.
A.O.A., 149:MAR71-108
BANCES CANDAMO, F. THEATRO DE LOS THEAT-
ROS DE LOS PASADOS Y PRESENTES SIGLOS.
(D.W. MOIR, ED)
617(TLS):4AUG72-914
BANCQUART, M-C. ANATOLE FRANCE POLÉ-
MISTE.
D. BRESKY, 131(CL):SUMMER71-273

16

BANCQUART, M-C. - SEE BOUILHET, L. & L.
COLET
BANCZEROWSKI, J. KONSONANTENALTERNATION
IM OSTLAPPISCHEN UNTER DEM ASPEKT DER
VERSTÄRKUNG-LENIERUNG.
  K. BERGSLAND, 350:DEC71-954
BANDERA GÓMEZ, C. EL "POEMA DE MÍO CID."
  T. MONTGOMERY, 545(RPH):AUG70-213
  J. SZERTICS, 238:MAY70-334
BANDI, H-G. & OTHERS. THE ART OF THE
STONE AGE.
  617(TLS):26MAY72-599
BANDINELLI, R.B. - SEE UNDER BIANCHI
BANDINELLI, R.
BANERJI, J.M. HISTORY OF FIRUZ SHAH
TUGHLUQ.
  H.K. SHERWANI, 273(IC):JUL69-240
BANERJI, S.C. KĀLIDĀSA-KOŚA.
  L. ROCHER, 318(JAOS):APR-JUN70-410
BANERJI, S.C., ED. SADUKTI-KARNĀMRTA OF
ŚRĪDHARADĀSA.
  L. STERNBACH, 318(JAOS):APR-JUN70-352
"ANTONIO BANFI E IL PENSIERO CONTEMPOR-
ANEO."
  P. PICCONE, 484(PPR):MAR70-473
BANHAM, R. THE ARCHITECTURE OF THE WELL-
TEMPERED ENVIRONMENT.*
  H. WRIGHT, 44:NOV69-63
BANHAM, R. LOS ANGELES.*
  F. CARNEY, 453:1JUN72-26
BANKS, L.R. THE BACKWARD SHADOW.
  F.P.W. MC DOWELL, 659:SUMMER72-361
BANKS, R. WAITING TO FREEZE.
  J. TIPTON, 661:SUMMER70-120
BANKS, R., W. MATTHEWS & N. SMITH. 15
POEMS.
  W. WITHERUP, 502(PRS):WINTER69/70-422
BANNER, J.M., JR. TO THE HARTFORD CON-
VENTION.
  D.A. BERNSTEIN, 432(NEQ):DEC70-661
  S.G. KURTZ, 656(WMQ):JUL70-479
  639(VQR):AUTUMN70-CXLVII
BANNERMAN, D.A. & W.M. HANDBOOK OF THE
BIRDS OF CYPRUS AND MIGRANTS OF THE
MIDDLE EAST.
  617(TLS):9JUN72-667
BANNISTER, R. RAY STANNARD BAKER.
  F.D. MITCHELL, 330(MASJ):SPRING69-88
BANTA, M., WITH R. GOTTESMAN & D.J. NORD-
LOH - SEE HOWELLS, W.D.
BANTOCK, G.H. T.S. ELIOT AND EDUCATION.*
  R.C. STEPHENS, 677:VOL2-334
BANTOCK, M. GRANVILLE BANTOCK.
  617(TLS):21JUL72-840
BANTON, M. RACIAL MINORITIES.
  617(TLS):17NOV72-1400
BANULS, A. HEINRICH MANN.
  B-A. SØRENSEN, 462(OL):VOL24#4-305
  U. WEISSTEIN, 400(MLN):OCT70-759
BAPTISTA GUMUCIO, M. NARRADORES BOLIVI-
ANOS.
  A. GUZMÁN, 263:APR-JUN71-214
BAR-ZOHAR, M. SPIES IN THE PROMISED
LAND.
  617(TLS):13OCT72-1222
BARAKA, I.A. [L. JONES], ED. AFRICAN
CONGRESS.
  M. KILSON, 441:12MAR72-27
BARALT, R.M. OBRAS LITERARIAS. (G.
DÍAZ-PLAJA, ED)
  191(ELN):SEP69(SUPP)-148
BARANY, G. STEPHEN SZÉCHENYI AND THE
AWAKENING OF HUNGARIAN NATIONALISM,
1791-1841.
  P. BODY, 497(POLR):AUTUMN69-115
  P. HANÁK, 32:SEP71-683
BARASH, A. PICTURES FROM A BREWERY.
  617(TLS):14JUL72-793

BARAZ, M. L'ÊTRE ET LA CONNAISSANCE
SELON MONTAIGNE.
  I.D. MC FARLANE, 208(FS):JUL71-325
BARBA, P.A. - SEE UNDER TREHER, C.M.
BARBEAU, A.T. THE INTELLECTUAL DESIGN
OF JOHN DRYDEN'S HEROIC PLAYS.
  E. ROTHSTEIN, 301(JEGP):JAN71-157
BARBER, J.D. THE PRESIDENTIAL CHARACTER.
  B. MAZLISH, 441:8OCT72-30
  B. MOYERS, 561(SATR):5AUG72-49
BARBER, R. THE KNIGHT AND CHIVALRY.*
  W.R. THOMSON, 651(WHR):AUTUMN71-363
BARBERI, F. IL FRONTESPIZIO NEL LIBRO
ITALIANO DEL QUATTROCENTO E DEL CIN-
QUECENTO.
  N. BARKER, 78(BC):WINTER70-540
BARBÉRIS, P. BALZAC ET LE MAL DU SIÈCLE.
  617(TLS):18AUG72-973
BARBI, M. & V. PERNICONE - SEE DANTE
ALIGHIERI
BARBIER, C.P. - SEE MALLARMÉ, S.
BARBIERI, F. CORPUS PALLADIANUM. (VOL
2: THE BASILICA.)
  617(TLS):29DEC72-1577
BARBOUR, I. ISSUES IN SCIENCE AND RELI-
GION.
  S.A.S., 543:DEC69-341
BARBOUR, P.L., ED. THE JAMESTOWN VOYAGES
UNDER THE FIRST CHARTER, 1606-1609.
  K.R. ANDREWS, 551(RENQ):WINTER70-464
  R.R. BEEMAN, 656(WMQ):JAN70-165
BARBOUR, P.L. POCAHONTAS AND HER WORLD.
  639(VQR):AUTUMN70-CXLVI
BARBU, Z. SOCIETY, CULTURE AND PERSONAL-
ITY.
  617(TLS):21APR72-445
BARBUDO, A.S. - SEE UNDER SÁNCHEZ BAR-
BUDO, A.
DE LA BARCA, P.C. - SEE UNDER CALDERÓN DE
LA BARCA, P.
BARCATA, L. CHINA IN THE THROES OF THE
CULTURAL REVOLUTION.
  P.K.T. SIH, 396(MODA):WINTER71-103
BARCIA, J.R. & M.A. ZEITLIN - SEE UNDER
RUBIA BARCIA, J. & M.A. ZEITLIN
BARDENS, D. THE LADYKILLER.
  617(TLS):17NOV72-1402
BARDON, H. - SEE CATULLUS
BARFIELD, L. NORTHERN ITALY BEFORE ROME.
  617(TLS):6OCT72-1189
BARFIELD, O. WHAT COLERIDGE THOUGHT.
  617(TLS):11AUG72-943
BARFORD, P. MAHLER SYMPHONIES AND
SONGS.*
  E. SAMS, 415:MAR71-245
BARILLI, R. POETICA E RETORICA.*
  617(TLS):18AUG72-967
BARK, J. & D. PFORTE, EDS. DIE DEUTSCH-
SPRACHIGE ANTHOLOGIE. (VOL 2)
  S. MEWS, 301(JEGP):JAN71-130
BARKER, C.M. HEALING IN DEPTH. (H.I.
BACH, ED)
  617(TLS):26MAY72-613
BARKER, E.S. WESTERN LIFE AND ADVEN-
TURES, 1889 TO 1970.
  W. GARD, 584(SWR):AUTUMN71-VI
BARKER, G. AT THURGARTON CHURCH.
  T. BLACKBURN, 493:SUMMER70-171
BARKER, G. POEMS OF PLACES AND PEOPLE.*
  N. RENNIE, 364:AUG/SEP71-120
BARKER, J.W. MANUEL II PALAEOLOGUS
(1391-1425).*
  D.M. NICOL, 303:VOL90-270
BARKER, M.A. & OTHERS. A COURSE IN URDU,
YBTYDAI WRDU.
  V. MILTNER, 353:SEP69-89

17

BARKER, N. STANLEY MORISON.
    R. STONE, 362:17AUG72-214
    617(TLS):1SEP72-1023
BARKER, N., ED. TO GEOFFREY KEYNES.
    617(TLS):21JUL72-852
BARKER, N. - SEE MORISON, S.
BARKER, P., ED. ONE FOR SORROW, TWO FOR
  JOY.
    617(TLS):8DEC72-1506
BARKER, R., ED. STUDIES IN OPPOSITION.
    617(TLS):28JAN72-84
BARKER, W. N.S. KHRUSHCHEV.
    M. MC CAULEY, 575(SEER):JAN71-168
BARKIN, K.D. THE CONTROVERSY OVER GERMAN
  INDUSTRIALIZATION.
    H.M. ADAMS, 396(MODA):WINTER71-108
BARLACH, E. DIE BRIEFE. (VOL 1) (F.
  DROSS, ED)
    A. WERNER, 19(AGR):VOL35#3-27
BARLEY, M.W. THE HOUSE AND THE HOME.
    J. STAFFORD, 440:12MAR72-13
BARLOW, F. EDWARD THE CONFESSOR.
    617(TLS):20OCT72-1255
BARMASH, I. NET NET.
    M. LEVIN, 441:16APR72-30
BARNABY, F. MAN AND THE ATOM.
    617(TLS):26MAY72-613
BARNARD, C.N. HEART ATTACK.
    441:30APR72-28
    617(TLS):4AUG72-922
BARNARD, D.S., JR. - SEE GOODMAN, N.
BARNARD, E., ED. EDWIN ARLINGTON ROBIN-
  SON.
    J.T. FLANAGAN, 579(SAQ):WINTER71-129
BARNARD, F.M. - SEE VON HERDER, J.G.
BARNARD, G.C. SAMUEL BECKETT.
    R. PEARCE, 295:VOL2#3-442
BARNARD, H.C. EDUCATION AND THE FRENCH
  REVOLUTION.
    D. BRADSHAW, 208(FS):APR71-246
BARNAVE, J. POWER, PROPERTY AND HISTORY.
  (E. CHILL, ED & TRANS)
    C.B.A. BEHRENS, 453:27JAN72-29
BARNDS, W.J. INDIA, PAKISTAN AND THE
  GREAT POWERS.
    617(TLS):30JUN72-736
BARNES, H.G. GOETHE'S "DIE WAHLVERWANDT-
  SCHAFTEN."
    K.A. DICKSON, 564:SPRING69-67
    K. HARRIS, 221(GQ):NOV70-793
    F. RADANDT, 405(MP):AUG69-72
BARNES, J. HENRY KINGSLEY AND COLONIAL
  FICTION.
    L. KRAMER, 71(ALS):OCT72-433
BARNES, J. THE ONTOLOGICAL ARGUMENT.
    617(TLS):13OCT72-1234
BARNES, J., ED. THE WRITER IN AUSTRALIA.*
    M. WILDING, 402(MLR):JUL71-678
BARNES, M. & J. BERKE. MARY BARNES.*
    J. KOVEL, 441:2JUL72-13
    C. LEHMANN-HAUPT, 441:3APR72-39
BARNES, P. PAWNS.
    R. SHERRILL, 440:9JAN72-10
    441:9JAN72-28
    442(NY):29JAN72-95
BARNES, T.D. TERTULLIAN.
    617(TLS):14APR72-422
BARNES, W. A BIBLIOGRAPHY OF ELIZABETH
  BARRETT BROWNING.
    J. CARTER, 78(BC):SPRING70-101
BARNET, R.J. ROOTS OF WAR.
    H.S. COMMAGER, 453:5OCT72-7
    T. LASK, 441:9JUN72-38
    W.O. PFAFF, 440:28MAY72-5
    R. STEEL, 441:11JUN72-3
    E.B. TOMPKINS, 561(SATR):20MAY72-68

BARNETT, C. THE COLLAPSE OF BRITISH
  POWER.
    617(TLS):14JUL72-789
BARNETT, D. THE PERFORMANCE OF MUSIC.
    617(TLS):28JUL72-893
BARNETT, D.A., ED. CHINESE COMMUNIST
  POLITICS IN ACTION.
    J.D. OLANDER, 293(JAST):FEB70-436
BARNETT, G.L., ED. EIGHTEENTH-CENTURY
  BRITISH NOVELISTS ON THE NOVEL.
    A. SHERBO, 173(ECS):SUMMER70-560
BARNHART, C.L., ED. THE AMERICAN COLLEGE
  DICTIONARY. THE WORLD BOOK DICTIONARY.
    617(TLS):13OCT72-1209
BARNOUW, E. A TOWER IN BABEL.* THE
  GOLDEN WEB.* THE IMAGE EMPIRE.* [ALSO
  SHOWN IN PREV UNDER THE SERIES TITLE:
  A HISTORY OF BROADCASTING IN THE UNITED
  STATES.]
    L. ROSS, 453:9MAR72-25
BARNSLEY, J.H. THE SOCIAL REALITY OF
  ETHICS.
    617(TLS):29SEP72-1147
BARNSTONE, W. - SEE MAO TSE-TUNG
BARO, G. CLAES OLDENBURG: DRAWINGS AND
  PRINTS.
    E. KOKKIMEN, 58:NOV69-12
BAROIN, J., ED. SIMON DE POUILLE.*
    D.J.A. ROSS, 402(MLR):JAN71-182
BARON, H. FROM PETRARCH TO LEONARDO
  BRUNI.*
    A. BULLOCK, 551(RENQ):SPRING70-48
BARON, S. THE DESERT LOCUST.
    617(TLS):18AUG72-975
BARON, S.H., ED & TRANS. THE TRAVELS OF
  OLEARIUS IN SEVENTEENTH-CENTURY RUSSIA.
    B. UROFF, 574(SEEJ):SUMMER71-255
BARONE, M., G. UJIFUSA & D. MATTHEWS.
  THE ALMANAC OF AMERICAN POLITICS.
    E. DREW, 441:4JUN72-3
    617(TLS):29SEP72-1176
BARR, M-M.H., WITH F.A. SPEAR. QUARANTE
  ANNÉES D'ÉTUDES VOLTAIRIENNES.
    A.R. DESAUTELS, 207(FR):FEB70-507
I BARRAQUER, A.V. - SEE UNDER VIDAL I
  BARRAQUER, A.
BARRATT, J. & M. LOUW, EDS. INTERNATION-
  AL ASPECTS OF OVERPOPULATION.
    617(TLS):18AUG72-978
BARRAULT, J-L. SOUVENIRS POUR DEMAIN.
  MISE EN SCÈNE DE PHÈDRE.
    617(TLS):16JUN72-685
BARRELL, J. THE IDEA OF LANDSCAPE AND
  THE SENSE OF PLACE 1730-1840.
    617(TLS):9JUN72-654
BARRÈRE, D.B. THE KUMUHONUA LEGENDS.
    K. LUOMALA, 292(JAF):OCT-DEC70-471
BARRETT, C. - SEE WITTGENSTEIN, L.
BARRETT, F.A. & A.L. THORPE. DERBY
  PORCELAIN 1750-1848.
    617(TLS):3MAR72-240
BARRETT, S. PRIVATE VIEW.
    617(TLS):3NOV72-1305
BARRETT, W. TIME OF NEED.
    A. BROYARD, 441:27SEP72-49
BARRETT, W.E. THE SHAPE OF ILLUSION.
    F. SWEENEY, 441:24SEP72-56
BARRETT, W.H. TALES FROM THE FENS. MORE
  TALES FROM THE FENS.
    E.W. BAUGHMAN, 650(WF):OCT68-280
BARRETTE, P. - SEE "ROBERT DE BLOIS'S
  'FLORIS ET LYRIOPÉ'"
BARRETTE, P. & T. BRAUN. SECOND FRENCH.
    J. HELLERMANN, 207(FR):FEB70-543
BARRETTE, P. & M. FOL. UN CERTAIN STYLE
  OU UN STYLE CERTAIN?
    W. STAAKS, 207(FR):FEB70-543

BARROLL, J.L., ED. SHAKESPEARE STUDIES.
(VOL 1)
R.A. FOAKES, 570(SQ):WINTER68-87
BARROLL, J.L., ED. SHAKESPEARE STUDIES.
(VOL 2)
H.W. DONNER, 597(SN):VOL40#1-247
G.A. SMITH, 570(SQ):SPRING69-237
BARROLL, J.L., ED. SHAKESPEARE STUDIES.
(VOL 3)
T.P. LOGAN, 399(MLJ):MAR70-211
BARROS, J. THE LEAGUE OF NATIONS AND THE
GREAT POWERS: THE GREEK-BULGARIAN INCI-
DENT, 1925.
L.A.D. DELLIN, 32:DEC71-923
BARROW, J. SKETCHES OF THE ROYAL SOCIETY
AND ROYAL SOCIETY CLUB.
617(TLS):18FEB72-198
BARRUTIA, R. LINGUISTIC THEORY OF LAN-
GUAGE LEARNING AS RELATED TO MACHINE
TEACHING.
C.N. STAUBACH, 399(MLJ):DEC70-617
BARSTOW, S. WATCHERS ON THE SHORE.
502(PRS):WINTER68/69-367
BART, B.F. FLAUBERT.
M. SACHS, 593:FALL71-306
BARTER, A.R. LEARNING LANGUAGES.*
D.H. KELLY, 124:MAY71-312
BARTH, J. CHIMERA.
P. ADAMS, 61:OCT72-135
C. LEHMANN-HAUPT, 441:20SEP72-49
L. MICHAELS, 441:24SEP72-35
M. WOOD, 453:19OCT72-33
442(NY):30SEP72-125
BARTH, J. GILES GOAT-BOY.
J.L. MC DONALD, 145(CRIT):VOL13#3-5
BARTH, J. LOST IN THE FUNHOUSE.*
L.T. LEMON, 502(PRS):SUMMER69-231
BARTH, J.R. COLERIDGE AND CHRISTIAN
DOCTRINE.*
J. COLMER, 677:VOL2-296
R. EBERWEIN, 141:SPRING70-160
BARTHELME, D. CITY LIFE.*
639(VQR):AUTUMN70-CXXIX
BARTHELME, D. SADNESS.
A. BROYARD, 441:27OCT72-43
C.T. SAMUELS, 441:5NOV72-27
J. SEELYE, 561(SATR):25NOV72-66
R. TODD, 61:DEC72-126
M. WOOD, 453:14DEC72-12
BARTHELME, D. UNSPEAKABLE PRACTICES,
UNNATURAL ACTS.*
I. SADOFF, 448:SUMMER70-141
BARTHES, R. CRITICAL ESSAYS.
R. LOCKE, 441:30JUN72-36
E.W. SAID, 441:30JUL72-5
BARTHES, R. MYTHOLOGIES. (A. LAVERS, ED
& TRANS)
P.N. FURBANK, 362:24AUG72-246
R. LOCKE, 441:30JUN72-36
E.W. SAID, 441:30JUL72-5
442(NY):9SEP72-128
453:18MAY72-37
617(TLS):24MAR72-330
BARTHES, R. S/Z.
J. CULLER, 402(MLR):JAN71-191
N. SILVERSTEIN, 295:VOL2#1-154
BARTHES, R. SADE FOURIER LOYOLA.
617(TLS):24MAR72-330
BARTHOLOMEW, J.C. & OTHERS - SEE "THE
TIMES CONCISE ATLAS OF THE WORLD"
BARTLETT, V. CENTRAL ITALY.
617(TLS):24MAR72-339
BARTLETT, W.H. BARTLETT'S CANADA. (TEXT
BY J. TYRWHITT)
T. EMERY, 627(UTQ):JUL70-384

BARTÓK, B. BÉLA BARTÓK: LETTERS.* (J.
DEMÉNY, ED)
A. CROSS, 415:DEC71-1173
W. SARGEANT, 442(NY):20MAY72-124
BARTÓK, B. RUMANIAN FOLK MUSIC.* (B.
SUCHOFF, ED)
P.H.L., 414(MQ):OCT68-542
B. SAROSI, 607:SPRING68-31
BARTOLOZZI, B. NEW SOUNDS FOR WOODWIND.
A. HACKER, 607:WINTER67/68-29
BARTON, J., COMP. THE HOLLOW CROWN.
617(TLS):7JAN72-21
BARTON, J. - SEE SHAKESPEARE, W.
BARTON, S. MONUMENTAL FOLLIES.
617(TLS):15SEP72-1071
BARTONĚK, A., ED. STUDIA MYCENAEA.*
P. CHANTRAINE, 555:VOL44FASC1-120
BARTOSZEWSKI, W. & Z. LEWIN, EDS. RIGHT-
EOUS AMONG NATIONS.
W. KOREY, 32:MAR71-181
BARTZ, P.M. SOUTH KOREA.
617(TLS):10NOV72-1377
BARZINI, L. FROM CAESAR TO THE MAFIA.*
M. PEI, 396(MODA):FALL71-438
BARZUN, J. BERLIOZ AND THE ROMANTIC CEN-
TURY. (3RD ED)
N. SUCKLING, 208(FS):APR71-219
BASDEKIS, D. UNAMUNO AND SPANISH LITERA-
TURE.
P.G. EARLE, 546(RR):OCT70-233
"BASIC CARPENTRY ILLUSTRATED."
B. GLADSTONE, 441:3DEC72-99
BASKIN, L. FIGURES OF DEAD MEN.
M.S. YOUNG, 39:APR69-330
BASKIN, W. DICTIONARY OF SATANISM.
617(TLS):19MAY72-585
BASS, A. THE ARAPAHO WAY.
G.S. NICKERSON, 650(WF):JAN68-66
BASS, G.F. & OTHERS. CAPE GELIDONYA: A
BRONZE AGE SHIPWRECK.*
R.R. STIEGLITZ, 318(JAOS):OCT-DEC70-
541
BASSAN, F. POLITIQUE ET HAUTE SOCIÉTÉ À
L'ÉPOQUE ROMANTIQUE.
191(ELN):SEP70(SUPP)-52
BASSANI, G. BEHIND THE DOOR.
P. SOURIAN, 441:1OCT72-7
442(NY):7OCT72-157
BASSANI, G. L'ODORE DEL FIENO.
617(TLS):21JUL72-835
BASSO, A., ED. LA MUSICA. (PT 2)
J.A.W., 410(M&L):JUL71-326
BASTIN, M.L. TSHIBINDA ILUNGA.
J. VANSINA, 69:JAN69-99
BASTLUND, K. JOSÉ LUIS SERT.
S. VON MOOS, 44:JAN-FEB69-83
P. ZUCKER, 505:FEB68-186
BATAILLE, G. MY MOTHER.
J. HUNTER, 362:13APR72-493
617(TLS):21APR72-439
BATAILLE, G. OEUVRES COMPLÈTES. (VOLS
1-4)
617(TLS):3MAR72-233
BATAILLE, M. LE CHAT SAUVAGE.
617(TLS):7JAN72-17
BATAILLE, M. CITY OF FOOLS.*
J.T. BURNS, 505:NOV68-160
BATCHELOR, J. EXISTENCE AND IMAGINATION.
L. LE SAGE, 397(MD):FEB69-450
BATCHELOR, R.E. UNAMUNO NOVELIST.
617(TLS):29SEP72-1167
BATE, W.J. THE BURDEN OF THE PAST AND
THE ENGLISH POET.*
B. BOYCE, 191(ELN):MAR71-242
617(TLS):15SEP72-1049
BATE, W.J. COLERIDGE.
W.J.B. OWEN, 541(RES):AUG70-370
BATE, W.J. - SEE JOHNSON, S.

19

BATE, W.J. & A.B. STRAUSS - SEE JOHNSON,
S.
BATEMAN, R. THEMATIC STAMP COLLECTING.
617(TLS):5MAY72-529
BATES, D. A GUST OF PLUMES.
617(TLS):11FEB72-153
BATES, H.E. THE BLOSSOMING WORLD.*
442(NY):8JAN72-86
BATES, H.E. THE SONG OF THE WREN.
617(TLS):21JUL72-835
BATES, H.E. THE WORLD IN RIPENESS.
617(TLS):13OCT72-1214
BATES, R. CHANGES.
H. MAC CALLUM, 627(UTQ):JUL69-345
BATES, R. NORTHROP FRYE.
P.C. NOEL-BENTLEY, 296:SUMMER72-78
BATESON, F.W. ESSAYS IN CRITICAL DIS-
SENT.
J. CAREY, 362:1JUN72-725
617(TLS):4FEB72-123
BATESON, F.W. THE SCHOLAR-CRITIC.
J. CAREY, 362:1JUN72-725
617(TLS):9JUN72-654
BATESON, G. STEPS TO AN ECOLOGY OF MIND.
D.W. HARDING, 453:19OCT72-29
BATHO, G.R., ED. A CALENDAR OF THE
SHREWSBURY AND TALBOT PAPERS. (VOL 2)
617(TLS):21JUL72-853
BATLLORI, M. & V.M. ARBELOA - SEE VIDAL I
BARRAQUER, A.
BATTAGLIA, S. L'IDEOLOGIA LETTERARIA DI
GIACOMO LEOPARDI.
W.T.S., 191(ELN):SEP70(SUPP)-135
BATTCOCK, G., ED. MINIMAL ART.
W. TUCKER, 592:JUL/AUG69-51
BATTENHOUSE, R.W. SHAKESPEAREAN TRAG-
EDY.*
L.F. DEAN, 131(CL):FALL71-375
R.M. FRYE, 191(ELN):JUN71-319
K. MUIR, 402(MLR):APR71-388
BATTERSBY, M. THE DECORATIVE THIRTIES.
617(TLS):30JUN72-740
BATTERSBY, M. THE WORLD OF ART NOUVEAU.
B. HILLIER, 592:MAR69-152
BATTESTIN, M.C. - SEE FIELDING, H.
BATTISCOMBE, G. QUEEN ALEXANDRA.
639(VQR):SPRING70-LXVII
BATTISTI, E. CIMABUE.
J. GARDNER, 90:JAN70-52
BATTS, M. HANDBUCH DER DEUTSCHEN LIT-
ERATURGESCHICHTE.* (VOL 2)
D.H. GREEN, 402(MLR):APR71-439
BATTS, M.S. & M.G. STANKIEWICZ, EDS.
ESSAYS ON GERMAN LITERATURE IN HONOUR
OF G. JOYCE HALLAMORE.*
H. WETZEL, 627(UTQ):JUL69-388
IBN BAṬṬŪṬA. THE TRAVELS OF IBN BATTUTA,
A.D. 1325-1354. (VOL 3) (H.A.R. GIBB,
ED & TRANS)
617(TLS):21APR72-455
BAUDELAIRE, C. OEUVRES COMPLÈTES.*
(M.A. RUFF, ED)
C. ROSENBERG, 50(ARQ):AUTUMN69-282
BAUDELAIRE, C. PETITS POÈMES EN PROSE.
(M. ZIMMERMAN, ED) PETITS POÈMES EN
PROSE.* (R. KOPP, ED)
J.S. PATTY, 207(FR):DEC69-346
BAUDISCH, G. DAS PATRIARCHALE DORF IM
ERZÄHLWERK VON JANKO M. VESELINOVIĆ.
M. COOTE, 574(SEEJ):FALL71-394
BAUDOUIN DE COURTENAY. A BAUDOUIN DE
COURTENAY ANTHOLOGY. (E. STANKIEWICZ,
ED & TRANS)
617(TLS):13OCT72-1230
BAUDOUIN, L., ED. LA RECHERCHE AU
CANADA FRANÇAIS.
D.M. HAYNE, 208(FS):JUL71-359

BAUDRILLARD, J. LE SYSTÈME DES OBJETS.
J.V. ALTER, 149:MAR71-105
BAUER, C. PANORAMA DE LA FRANCE MODERNE.
E.C. KNOX, 399(MLJ):JAN70-61
BAUER, G. ZUR POETIK DES DIALOGS.*
B. PIKE, 301(JEGP):JAN71-128
BAUER, G. & S., EDS. GOTTHOLD EPHRAIM
LESSING.
R.K. ANGRESS, 221(GQ):NOV70-783
BAUER, G.H. SARTRE AND THE ARTIST.*
W. ALBERT, 207(FR):APR70-838
E. KERN, 401(MLQ):JUN70-263
I. KOBERNICK, 290(JAAC):SUMMER70-558
BAUER, K. DER SECHSTE SINN.
G. FISCHER, 270:VOL20#3-64
BAUER, P.T. DISSENT ON DEVELOPMENT.
617(TLS):7JUL72-772
BAUER, W. THE PRICE OF MORNING.*
H. MAC CALLUM, 627(UTQ):JUL69-350
BAUFLE, J-M. & J-P. VARIN. PHOTOGRAPHING
WILDLIFE.
617(TLS):13OCT72-1237
BAUGHAN, P.E. THE CHESTER AND HOLYHEAD
RAILWAY. (VOL 1)
617(TLS):22DEC72-1566
BAUGHMAN, E.W. TYPE AND MOTIF-INDEX OF
THE FOLK-TALES OF ENGLAND AND NORTH
AMERICA.
J. VAN HAVER, 179(ES):FEB69-121
BAUM, G. MAN BECOMING.
R. LAUDER, 142:FALL71-487
BAUM, R. RECHERCHES SUR LES OEUVRES
ATTRIBUÉES À MARIE DE FRANCE.
F. LYONS, 208(FS):JUL71-315
BAUMANN, G. ARTHUR SCHNITZLER.
I. SEIDLER, 133:1969/3-354
BAUMANN, W. THE ROSE IN THE STEEL DUST.*
W.M. CHACE, 598(SOR):WINTER72-225
BAUMGART, W., ED. VON BREST-LITOVSK ZUR
DEUTSCHEN NOVEMBER-REVOLUTION.
617(TLS):19MAY72-581
BAUMGÄRTEL, E. DIE ALMANACHE, KALENDER
UND TASCHENBÜCHER (1750-1860) DER
LANDESBIBLIOTHEK COBURG.
N.H. SMITH, 182:VOL23#1/2-1
BÄUML, F.H., ED. KUDRUN.
P. SALMON, 402(MLR):JUL71-700
BAUSINGER, H. FORMEN DER "VOLKSPOESIE."*
D.J. WARD, 221(GQ):NOV70-806
BAUSINGER, H. & W. BRÜCKNER, EDS. KON-
TINUITÄT?
W. VEIT, 67:NOV71-257
BAUTIER, R-H. THE ECONOMIC DEVELOPMENT
OF MEDIEVAL EUROPE.
617(TLS):11FEB72-165
BAUTIER, R-H. & G. LABORY - SEE DE
FLEURY, A.
BAWCUTT, P.J. - SEE DOUGLAS, G.
BAWDEN, C.R. THE MODERN HISTORY OF
MONGOLIA.*
G.M. FRITERS, 293(JAST):MAY70-712
BAWDEN, N. ANNA APPARENT.
D.A.N. JONES, 362:28SEP72-418
M. LEVIN, 441:15OCT72-43
617(TLS):6OCT72-1185
BAWDEN, N. THE BIRDS ON THE TREES.*
F.P.W. MC DOWELL, 659:SUMMER72-361
BAWDEN, N. DEVIL BY THE SEA.
617(TLS):6OCT72-1185
BAXANDALL, L. MARXISM AND AESTHETICS.
D.L. GELPI, 613(WINTER69-611
R.G. GOLDY, 290(JAAC):FALL69-109
BAXT, G. THE AFFAIR AT ROYALTIES.
N. CALLENDAR, 441:18JUN72-31
BAXT, G. BURNING SAPPHO.
617(TLS):29SEP72-1174
BAXTER, C. THE JANA SANGH.
B.D. GRAHAM, 293(JAST):AUG70-967

BAXTER, J.K. THE LION SKIN.
  A. RODDICK, 368:MAR69-84
BAXTER, W.H., JR. BASIC STUDIES IN
MUSIC.
  C. WHITTENBERG, 308:WINTER68-300
BAYER, E. & OTHERS. SAECULUM WELTGE-
SCHICHTE. (VOLS 1&2)
  J. KELLENS, 182:VOL23#6-314
BAYER, H. VISUAL COMMUNICATION, ARCHI-
TECTURE, PAINTING.
  R. BOYD, 44:MAR69-76
BAYERDÖRFER, H-P. POETIK ALS SPRACH-
THEORETISCHES PROBLEM.
  G. WIENOLD, 490:JUL68-426
BAYERSCHMIDT, C.F. SIGRID UNDSET.
  S. ARESTAD, 563(SS):SPRING71-206
  R.D. SPECTOR, 222(GR):NOV70-315
BAYET, J. CROYANCES ET RITES DANS LA
ROME ANTIQUE.
  617(TLS):11FEB72-158
BAYET, J. HISTOIRE POLITIQUE ET PSYCHO-
LOGIQUE DE LA RELIGION ROMAINE. (2ND
ED)
  A. ERNOUT, 555:VOL44FASC2-364
BAYLEN, J.O. & A. CONWAY - SEE REID, D.A.
BAYLEY, D.H. THE POLICE AND POLITICAL
DEVELOPMENT IN INDIA.
  R.N. BLUE, 293(JAST):AUG70-966
BAYLEY, P. EDMUND SPENSER.
  617(TLS):12MAY72-541
BAYNES, J. THE HISTORY OF THE CAMERON-
IANS. (VOL 4)
  617(TLS):4FEB72-132
BAYNES, J.C.M. THE SOLDIER IN MODERN
SOCIETY.
  617(TLS):23JUN72-703
BAYNHAM, H. FROM THE LOWER DECK.
  639(VQR):AUTUMN70-CL
BAYONAS, A.C. THE IDEA OF LEGISLATION IN
THE EARLIER PLATONIC DIALOGUES.
  P. SOMVILLE, 542:APR-JUN68-287
BAZANOV, V.G., ED. YESENIN I RUSSKAYA
POEZIYA.
  G. MC VAY, 575(SEER):JAN71-145
BAZANT, J. ALIENATION OF CHURCH WEALTH
IN MEXICO. (M.P. COSTELOE, ED & TRANS)
  617(TLS):8DEC72-1503
BAZELL, C.E. & OTHERS, EDS. IN MEMORY
OF J.R. FIRTH.*
  E.C. GARCÍA, 545(RPH):MAY71-612
  G. NICKEL, 72:BAND208HEFT3-203
BAZIN, A. WHAT IS CINEMA? (VOL 2) (H.
GRAY, ED & TRANS)
  L. BRAUDY, 441:13FEB72-27
BAZIN, G. THE BAROQUE.
  J. AGNEW, 39:JUN69-482
BAZIN, G. THE HISTORY OF WORLD SCULP-
TURE.*
  90:JUN70-424
BAZIN, H. CRI DE LA CHOUETTE.
  617(TLS):24NOV72-1415
BAZIN, H. JOUR [SUIVI DE] LA POURSUITE
D'IRIS.
  617(TLS):11FEB72-146
BAZIN, H. TRISTAN. (FRENCH TITLE: LES
BIENHEUREUX DE LA DÉSOLATION.)
  V. CUNNINGHAM, 362:27APR72-564
  617(TLS):2JUN72-623
DE BAZOCHES, G. - SEE UNDER GUY DE
BAZOCHES
BAZYLOW, L. HISTORIA ROSJI.
  L.R. LEWITTER, 575(SEER):JUL71-482
  W. SUKIENNICKI, 550(RUSR):OCT70-477
BAZYLOW, L. POLITYKA WEWNĘTRZNA CARATU
I RUCHY SPOŁECZNE W ROSJI NA POCZĄTKU
XX WIEKU.
  M.K. DZIEWANOWSKI, 32:MAR71-144

BEACH, E.L. DUST ON THE SEA.
  M. LEVIN, 441:22OCT72-46
BEACH, J.D. INTRODUCTION TO LOGIC.
  J. CAULFIELD, 363:AUG70-132
BEAL, J.R. MARSHALL IN CHINA.
  H.M. ADAMS, 396(MODA):SPRING71-204
BEAN, G.E. AEGEAN TURKEY.*
  H. PLOMMER, 576:MAR68-77
BEAN, G.E. TURKEY BEYOND THE MEANDER.
  617(TLS):24MAR72-339
BEAN, L.H. HOW TO PREDICT THE 1972
ELECTION.
  441:24SEP72-52
BEARD, J. AMERICAN COOKERY.
  N. HAZELTON, 441:3DEC72-96
BEARD, J.F. - SEE COOPER, J.F.
BEARDMORE, G. & J. - SEE "ARNOLD BENNETT
IN LOVE"
BEARDSLEY, A. THE LETTERS OF AUBREY
BEARDSLEY.* (H. MAAS, J.L. DUNCAN &
W.G. GOOD, EDS)
  617(TLS):14JAN72-25
BEARDSLEY, M.C. THE POSSIBILITY OF
CRITICISM.
  P. JONES, 89(BJA):SPRING71-197
  J. REICHERT, 385(MQR):SPRING72-141
BEARDSLEY, M.C. & H.M. SCHUELLER, EDS.
AESTHETIC INQUIRY.
  H.R. WACKRILL, 39:MAR69-246
BEARDSMORE, R.D. MORAL REASONING.
  R.F.D., 543:MAR70-552
  P. PALMER, 479(PHQ):JUL70-306
  E. TELFER, 518:JAN70-3
BEARE, G. THE BEE STING DEAL.
  N. CALLENDAR, 441:27AUG72-14
  442(NY):14OCT72-184
BEARE, G. CHAIN OF INFAMY.
  617(TLS):29DEC72-1588
BEATON, C. THE HAPPY YEARS.
  E.S. TURNER, 362:1JUN72-727
  617(TLS):26MAY72-594
BEATTY, C. GATE OF DREAMS.
  617(TLS):16JUN72-690
BEATTY, R.C. WILLIAM BYRD OF WESTOVER.
  G. CORE, 578:SPRING72-117
BEAU, M. LA COLLECTION DES DESSINS
D'HUBERT ROBERT AU MUSÉE DE VALENCE.
  P. CONISBEE, 90:SEP70-632
BEAUJOUR, E.K. THE INVISIBLE LAND.
  R. SHELDON, 32:DEC71-911
  617(TLS):24MAR72-341
BEAUJOUR, M. LE JEU DE RABELAIS.
  D. STONE, JR., 207(FR):DEC69-356
BEAULIEU, M. JE TOURNE EN ROND MAIS
C'EST AUTOUR DE TOI.
  R. ROBIDOUX, 627(UTQ):JUL70-435
DE BEAUMARCHAIS, P.A.C. BEAUMARCHAIS,
CORRESPONDENCE. (VOL 1) (B.N. MORTON,
ED)
  E.J. ARNOULD, 208(FS):JAN71-92
  E. STURM, 207(FR):APR70-841
  D. WALKER, 67:MAY71-130
DE BEAUMARCHAIS, P.A.C. BEAUMARCHAIS,
CORRESPONDENCE. (VOL 2) (B.N. MORTON,
ED)
  E.J. ARNOULD, 208(FS):JAN71-92
  D. WALKER, 67:MAY71-130
DE BEAUMARCHAIS, P.A.C. LE MARIAGE DE
FIGARO. (J.R. RATERMANIS, ED)
  E.J. ARNOULD, 208(FS):OCT71-466
  R. NIKLAUS, 546(RR):APR70-146
BEAUREGARD, L. TOPONYMIE DE LA RÉGION
MÉTROPOLITAINE DE MONTRÉAL.
  S.A. STOUDEMIRE, 424:SEP69-238
BEAURLINE, L.A. - SEE SUCKLING, J.
BEAURLINE, L.A. & F. BOWERS - SEE DRY-
DEN, J.

DE BEAUVOIR, S. THE COMING OF AGE.
  A. BROYARD, 441:22MAY72-37
  R. COLES, 442(NY):19AUG72-68
  E. HARDWICK, 441:14MAY72-1
  E. JANEWAY, 61:JUN72-94
  V.S. PRITCHETT, 453:20JUL72-3
DE BEAUVOIR, S. OLD AGE.
  P. BEER, 362:16MAR72-345
  617(TLS):7APR72-388
DE BEAUVOIR, S. TOUT COMPTE FAIT.
  617(TLS):10NOV72-1359
DE BEAUVOIR, S. LA VIEILLESSE.
  T.H. ADAMOWSKI, 150(DR):AUTUMN70-394
BEAZLEY, E. THE COUNTRYSIDE ON VIEW.
  617(TLS):14JAN72-49
BEAZLEY, E. & L. BRETT. NORTH WALES.
  617(TLS):3NOV72-1349
BEAZLEY, J.D. PARALIPOMENA. (2ND ED)
  617(TLS):3NOV72-1349
BEBBINGTON, G. LONDON STREET NAMES.
  617(TLS):8DEC72-1513
BEBEY, F. AGATHA MOUDIO'S SON.
  617(TLS):3MAR72-248
BEC, P., ED & TRANS. NOUVELLE ANTHOLOGIE
  DE LA LYRIQUE OCCITANE DU MOYEN ÂGE.
  A. ALSDORF-BOLLÉE, 72:BAND208HEFT2-
  147
BECATTI, G. THE ART OF ANCIENT GREECE
  AND ROME FROM THE RISE OF GREECE TO THE
  FALL OF ROME.*
  G.M.A. HANFMANN, 54:DEC69-392
  D. STRONG, 39:APR69-322
BECCARI, A. MAESTRO ANTONIO DA FERRARA
  (ANTONIO BECCARI), "RIME." (L. BEL-
  LUCCI, ED)
  N. ILIESCU, 589:OCT71-721
BECCARIA, G.L. SPAGNOLO E SPAGNOLI IN
  ITALIA.
  T.M. ROSSI, 545(RPH):AUG70-181
BECH, G. DAS GERMANISCHE REDUPLIZIERTE
  PRÄTERITUM.
  A.L. LLOYD, 350:SEP71-711
BECK, A. - SEE HÖLDERLIN, F.
BECK, L.W. EARLY GERMAN PHILOSOPHY.*
  R.J.B., 543:JUN70-738
BECK, R.A. & OTHERS. PLAY PRODUCTION IN
  THE HIGH SCHOOL.
  B.L. LUSTY, 583:SPRING70-280
BECK, R.N. PERSPECTIVES IN PHILOSOPHY.
  (2ND ED)
  M.B.M., 543:JUN70-738
BECK, S. SIMCA'S CUISINE.
  N. HAZELTON, 441:3DEC72-96
BECK, W. JOYCE'S "DUBLINERS."
  639(VQR):SUMMER70-XCVIII
DE BECK-AGULAR, V.D. & H. KURZ - SEE
  BONET, J.
BECKER, G.J. - SEE DE GONCOURT, E.
BECKER, J. SCHNEE.
  617(TLS):7JAN72-6
BECKER, T. GOVERNMENT ANARCHY AND THE
  POGONOGO ALTERNATIVE.
  G. COWAN, 441:20AUG72-2
BECKERMAN, W., ED. THE LABOUR GOVERN-
  MENT'S ECONOMIC RECORD, 1964-1970.
  P. TOWNSEND, 362:27APR72-558
  617(TLS):6OCT72-1191
BECKETT, R.B. - SEE CONSTABLE, J.
BECKETT, S. THE LOST ONES.
  J. HUNTER, 362:29JUN72-874
  J. MC ELROY, 441:29OCT72-4
  C. RICKS, 453:14DEC72-42
  617(TLS):11AUG72-935
BECKETT, S. MORE PRICKS THAN KICKS.
  C. RICKS, 453:14DEC72-42
BECKETT, S. WATT.
  L. JANVIER, 98:APR69-312

BECKFORD, W. VATHEK. (R. LONSDALE, ED)
  P. FAULKNER, 677:VOL2-292
BECKHAM, B. RUNNER MACK.
  M. WATKINS, 441:17SEP72-3
BECKMANN, G.M. & O. GENJI. THE JAPANESE
  COMMUNIST PARTY 1922-1945.*
  F. NODA, 293(JAST):FEB70-446
BECKMANN, H. THORNTON WILDER.
  K. TETZELI VON ROSADOR, 72:BAND208
  HEFT1-49
BÉDARD, R-J. L'AFFAIRE DU LABRADOR.
  J-C. BONENFANT, 627(UTQ):JUL69-456
"BEDE'S ECCLESIASTICAL HISTORY OF THE
  ENGLISH PEOPLE." (B. COLGRAVE & R.A.B.
  MYNORS, EDS)
  P.H. BLAIR, 382(MAE):1971/1-58
  P. MEYVAERT, 589:JAN71-135
LORD BEDFORD, WITH G. MIKES. HOW TO RUN
  A STATELY HOME.
  617(TLS):14JAN72-49
BEDINI, S.A. THE LIFE OF BENJAMIN BAN-
  NEKER.
  B. QUARLES, 561(SATR):4MAR72-76
  A. WHITMAN, 441:27FEB72-36
  E.M. YODER, JR., 440:13FEB72-13
  453:9MAR72-34
BEECHING, J., H. GUEST & M. MEAD. PEN-
  GUIN MODERN POETS 16.
  C. KIZER, 491:FEB72-291
  P. LESTER, 493:AUTUMN70-250
VAN BEEK, M. AN ENQUIRY INTO PURITAN
  VOCABULARY.
  A. HUME, 541(RES):AUG70-356
BEER, A. - SEE ROHR, H.
DE BEER, G. HANNIBAL.*
  A.E. ASTIN, 313:VOL60-208
  H.H. SCULLARD, 123:JUN71-299
  639(VQR):SUMMER70-CIV
BEER, G. MEREDITH.
  A. WRIGHT, 677:VOL2-317
DE BEER, G. JEAN-JACQUES ROUSSEAU AND
  HIS WORLD.
  617(TLS):10NOV72-1367
DE BEER, G. & A-M. ROUSSEAU, EDS. VOL-
  TAIRE'S BRITISH VISITORS.
  G. MAY, 546(RR):FEB70-61
BEER, J. BLAKE'S HUMANISM.
  D.V.E., 191(ELN):SEP69(SUPP)-19
  D. HIRST, 402(MLR):JAN71-179
  C. TAYLOR, 141:WINTER69-100
BEER, J. BLAKE'S VISIONARY UNIVERSE.
  M. BOTTRALL, 148:AUTUMN70-286
  D. DOUGLAS, 67:NOV71-238
  D. HIRST, 677:VOL2-294
BEER, P. THE ESTUARY.*
  I. WEDDE, 364:FEB/MAR72-148
  617(TLS):14JAN72-32
BEER, P. AN INTRODUCTION TO THE META-
  PHYSICAL POETS.
  617(TLS):20OCT72-1243
BEERBOHM, M. THE BODLEY HEAD MAX BEER-
  BOHM. (D. CECIL, ED)
  J.D. HAINSWORTH, 67:MAY71-112
BEERBOHM, M. A PEEP INTO THE PAST. (R.
  HART-DAVIS, ED)
  442(NY):4NOV72-196
  617(TLS):15SEP72-1043
BEESTON, A.F.L. WRITTEN ARABIC.*
  T. DRURY, 399(MLJ):APR70-292
BEET, E.A. MATHEMATICAL ASTRONOMY FOR
  AMATEURS.
  617(TLS):31MAR72-378
VAN BEETHOVEN, L. LUDWIG VAN BEETHOVENS
  KONVERSATIONSHEFTE. (VOL 5) (K-H.
  KÖHLER & G. HERRE, WITH P. PÖTSCHNER,
  EDS)
  A. TYSON, 415:AUG70-804

"LUDWIG VAN BEETHOVEN: AUTOGRAPH MISCEL-
LANY FROM CIRCA 1786 TO 1799."* (J.
KERMAN, ED)
   J.A.W., 410(M&L):APR71-194
BEGIASHVILI, A.F. SOVREMENNAYA ANGLII-
SKAYA LINGVISTICHESKAYA FILOSOFIYA.
   T. O'HAGAN, 587:JUL68-139
BÉGUIN, A. & Y. BONNEFOY, EDS. LA QUÊTE
DU GRAAL.
   T. TODOROV, 98:MAR69-195
BÉHAR, H. ETUDE SUR LA THÉÂTRE DADA ET
SURRÉALISTE.
   H.S. GERSHMAN, 397(MD):FEB69-449
BEHLER, E. & R. STRUC - SEE SCHLEGEL, F.
BEHLMER, R. - SEE SELZNICK, D.O.
BEHN, H. - SEE GIDDINGS, R.W.
BEHR, C.A. AELIUS ARISTIDES AND THE
SACRED TALES.
   I. AVOTINS, 24:APR71-347
BEHRE, F. STUDIES IN AGATHA CHRISTIE'S
WRITINGS.
   H. KOZIOL, 72:BAND208HEFT4/6-424
   B.M.H. STRANG, 597(SN):VOL41#1-232
   A. ZETTERSTEN, 596(SL):VOL22#2-132
BEHRMAN, J.R. SUPPLY RESPONSE IN UNDER-
DEVELOPED AGRICULTURE.
   E. VAN ROY, 293(JAST):FEB70-496
BEHRMAN, S.N. DUVEEN.
   T. LASK, 441:8SEP72-36
   617(TLS):13OCT72-1218
BEHRMAN, S.N. PEOPLE IN A DIARY.
   H. CLURMAN, 441:25JUN72-7
   E. FREMONT-SMITH, 561(SATR):22JUL72-
52
   T. LASK, 441:23JUN72-39
BEHRMAN, S.N. TRIBULATIONS AND LAUGHTER.
   617(TLS):1SEP72-1017
BEICHMAN, A. NINE LIES ABOUT AMERICA.
   B. DE MOTT, 441:8OCT72-33
   C. LEHMANN-HAUPT, 441:29MAY72-15
   A. RYAN, 362:16NOV72-681
   617(TLS):3NOV72-1307
BEIER, U. CONTEMPORARY ART IN AFRICA.*
   G.I. JONES, 69:APR69-191
BEIKIRCHER, H. KOMMENTAR ZUR VI. SATIRE
DES A. PERSIUS FLACCUS.
   C. DESSEN, 24:OCT71-759
   E.J. KENNEY, 123:DEC70-410
BEISNER, R.L. THE ANTI-IMPERIALISTS,
1898-1900.
   A. RAPPAPORT, 340(KR):1969/2-277
BEISSEL, H. FACE IN THE DARK.
   F. COGSWELL, 102(CANL):AUTUMN71-96
"BEITRÄGE ZUR SPRACHWISSENSCHAFT, VOLKS-
KUNDE UND LITERATURFORSCHUNG, WOLFGANG
STEINITZ ZUM 60. GEBURTSTAG AM 28.
FEBRUAR 1965 DARGEBRACHT."
   V. RŪĶE-DRAVIŅA, 353:APR69-101
BEKKER, H. THE NIBELUNGENLIED.
   H. WEDDIGE, 72:BAND208HEFT4/6-374
BEKKERS, J.A.F. - SEE MORRIS, J.
BEKU BONG. KIN NICHI-SEI DEN.
   H.C. KIM, 293(JAST):MAY70-710
BELAVAL, Y., ED & TRANS. CONFESSIO
PHILOSOPHI.
   L. PRENANT, 542:JUL-SEP68-397
BELBEN, R. BOGIES.
   V. CUNNINGHAM, 362:24AUG72-248
BELENITSKY, A. CENTRAL ASIA.
   P.O. HARPER, 57:VOL31#4-326
BELIAVSKAYA, I.A. BOURGEOIS REFORMISM
IN THE U.S.A. (1900-1914).
   N.N. BOLKHOVITINOV, 432(NEQ):MAR70-
143
BELL, A. DANCING THE GAY LIB BLUES.
   J. JOHNSTON, 441:20FEB72-5

BELL, A.C. CHRONOLOGICAL CATALOGUE OF
HANDEL'S WORKS.
   A. HICKS, 415:JAN70-48
   412:FEB71-84
BELL, C. THE CONVENTIONS OF CRISIS.
   617(TLS):14JAN72-49
BELL, C. & H. NEWBY. COMMUNITY STUDIES.
   617(TLS):22SEP72-1124
BELL, C.G. THE HALF GODS.
   R.M. BAINE, 219(GAR):SUMMER69-252
BELL, D.R. BERTRAND RUSSELL.
   617(TLS):21APR72-457
BELL, G. VILLAINS GALORE.
   617(TLS):14APR72-427
BELL, G. & A. KOECHLIN. GEORGE BELL/AL-
PHONS KOECHLIN; BRIEFWECHSEL 1933-54.
(A. LINDT, ED)
   F.F. BRUCE, 182:VOL23#23/24-975
BELL, J., ED. RHYMES OF NORTHERN BARDS.
   617(TLS):18FEB72-194
BELL, J.B. THE MYTH OF THE GUERRILLA.*
   442(NY):8JAN72-86
BELL, J.B. THE SECRET ARMY.*
   J.W. BOYLE, 99:APR72-48
BELL, M. THE ESCAPE INTO YOU.
   R. HOWARD, 491:AUG72-296
   V. YOUNG, 249(HUDR):WINTER71/72-671
BELL, M. A PROBABLE VOLUME OF DREAMS.*
   R. HOWARD, 340(KR):1970/1-130
   A. OSTRIKER, 473(PR):1971/2-218
   S. TUDOR, 590:FALL70-36
   639(VQR):SPRING70-XLVI
BELL, M.D. HAWTHORNE AND THE HISTORICAL
ROMANCE OF NEW ENGLAND.
   J.H. MC ELROY, 27(AL):JAN72-658
BELL, Q. BLOOMSBURY.*
   R. MORPHET, 592:JUL/AUG68-49
BELL, Q. VICTORIAN ARTISTS.*
   K. ROBERTS, 90:OCT70-704
BELL, Q. VIRGINIA WOOLF. (VOL 1)
   N. ANNAN, 362:15JUN72-794
   617(TLS):30JUN72-735
BELL, Q. VIRGINIA WOOLF. (VOL 2)
   N. ANNAN, 362:26OCT72-543
   617(TLS):27OCT72-1278
BELL, Q. VIRGINIA WOOLF. (VOLS 1&2
BOUND IN ONE VOL)
   B. DE MOTT, 561(SATR):9DEC72-67
   C. LEHMANN-HAUPT, 441:7DEC72-71
   M. ROSENTHAL, 441:5NOV72-1
BELL, S.H. THE THEATRE IN ULSTER.
   617(TLS):7JUL72-770
BELLEN, H. STUDIEN ZUR SKLAVENFLUCHT IM
RÖMISCHEN KAISERREICH.
   F. LASSERRE, 182:VOL23#21/22-944
BELLER, M. PHILEMON UND BAUCIS IN DER
EUROPÄISCHEN LITERATUR.*
   K. STACKMANN, 52:BAND4HEFT1-93
BELLEZZA, D. INVETTIVE E LICENZE.
   617(TLS):11FEB72-146
BELLI, A. ANCIENT GREEK MYTHS AND MODERN
DRAMA.*
   R. COHN, 397(MD):DEC69-319
BELLINATI, C. & S. BETTINI. L'EPISTOL-
ARIO MINIATO DI GIOVANNI DA GAIBANA.
   C. NORDENFALK, 90:JUN70-403
BELLOC, H. BELLOC: A BIOGRAPHICAL AN-
THOLOGY.* (H. VAN THAL & J.S. NICKER-
SON, EDS)
   R. ROBINSON, 67:MAY71-113
BELLORI, G.P. THE LIVES OF ANNIBALE AND
AGOSTINO CARRACCI.
   K. GARLICK, 39:JUL69-84
BELLOW, A. THE ILLUSTRATED HISTORY OF
THE GUITAR.
   T.F. HECK, 317:SUMMER71-310

BELLOW, S. MR. SAMMLER'S PLANET.*
S. SANDERS, 111:29MAY70-199
42(AR):WINTER69/70-587
639(VQR):SPRING70-XL
BELLOW, S. MOSBY'S MEMOIRS AND OTHER
STORIES.*
R. LACY, 448:SUMMER70-139
S. PINSKER, 328:SUMMER69-377
BELLUCCI, L. - SEE BECCARI, A.
BELOFF, M. IMPERIAL SUNSET. (VOL 1)
J.L. GODFREY, 639(VQR):SUMMER70-499
BELYJ, A. VOSPOMINANIJA O A.A. BLOKE.
V. TERRAS, 574(SEEJ):SPRING71-123
BELZ, C. THE STORY OF ROCK.*
R.S. DENISOFF, 292(JAF):OCT-DEC70-478
M. HARRISON, 415:JAN71-36
42(AR):WINTER69/70-590
639(VQR):SUMMER70-CXV
BEN-GURION, D. ISRAEL.*
617(TLS):29DEC72-1574
BEN-ISRAEL, H. ENGLISH HISTORIANS ON THE
FRENCH REVOLUTION.
D.V.E., 191(ELN):SEP69(SUPP)-6
BENAMOU, M. & E. IONESCO. MISE EN TRAIN.
R. BOSWELL, 399(MLJ):MAR70-216
BENAY, J.G. & R. KUHN, EDS. PANORAMA DU
THÉÂTRE NOUVEAU.* (VOLS 1&2)
J. DECOCK, 207(FR):FEB70-547
BENAY, J.G. & R. KUHN, EDS. PANORAMA
DU THÉÂTRE NOUVEAU.* (VOLS 3&4)
J. DECOCK, 207(FR):FEB70-547
J. DECOCK, 399(MLJ):JAN70-52
BENCHLEY, N. THE HUNTER'S MOON.
M. LEVIN, 441:22OCT72-46
BENDER, B.W. SPOKEN MARSHALLESE.
J.L. FISCHER, 350:SEP71-734
BENDER, E.J. BIBLIOGRAPHIE: CHARLES
NODIER.
A.G.E., 191(ELN):SEP70(SUPP)-79
C. KING, 78(BC):WINTER70-535
BENDER, K-H. KÖNIG UND VASALL.
W.M. HACKETT, 545(RPH):AUG70-228
J. SCHULZE, 490:APR68-275
BENDER, R.M. & C.L. SQUIER, EDS. THE
SONNET.
J.W. BENNETT, 570(SQ):SPRING68-177
BÉNÉ, C. ÉRASME ET SAINT AUGUSTIN.
A. HYMA, 551(RENQ):SPRING70-57
E-W. KOHLS, 182:VOL23#7-321
BENEDETTI, J. GILLES DE RAIS.
617(TLS):4FEB72-122
BENEDIKT, M. MOLE NOTES.
V. YOUNG, 249(HUDR):WINTER71/72-669
BENEDIKT, M. SKY.*
L.L. MARTZ, 676(YR):SPRING71-403
F. MORAMARCO, 651(WHR):SUMMER71-282
J. VERNON, 651(WHR):SPRING71-193
BENEDIKZ, P.M. DURHAM TOPOGRAPHICAL
PRINTS UP TO 1800.
P.C.G. ISAAC, 354:DEC69-356
BENESCH, O. COLLECTED WRITINGS. (VOL 2)
(E. BENESCH, ED)
617(TLS):3MAR72-240
BENESCH, O. COLLECTED WRITINGS. (VOL 3)
(E. BENESCH, ED)
617(TLS):27OCT72-1277
BENESCH, O. GERMAN PAINTING FROM DÜRER
TO HOLBEIN.*
M. LEVEY, 90:MAR70-179
BENÉT, M.K. SECRETARY.
617(TLS):6OCT72-1202
BÉNÉZÉ, G. GÉNÉREUX ALAIN.
M. BARTHÉLEMY-MADAULE, 542:OCT-DEC68-
494
BENGIS, I. COMBAT IN THE EROGENOUS ZONE.
L.C. POGREBIN, 441:12NOV72-46
G. STUTTAFORD, 561(SATR):23DEC72-60
M. WATKINS, 441:29NOV72-47

BENGTSON, H. GRUNDRISS DER RÖMISCHEN
GESCHICHTE, MIT QUELLENKUNDE.* (VOL 1)
J-C. DUMONT, 555:VOL44FASC1-164
BENGTSON, H. INTRODUCTION TO ANCIENT
HISTORY.
E.N. BORZA, 124:FEB71-200
BENGTSON, H. & OTHERS. THE GREEKS AND
THE PERSIANS.
N.G.L. HAMMOND, 123:DEC70-368
BENGTSSON, A. ADVENTURE PLAYGROUNDS.
617(TLS):1SEP72-1034
BÉNICHOU, P. NERVAL ET LA CHANSON FOLK-
LORIQUE.*
A. FAIRLIE, 208(FS):OCT71-475
BÉNICHOU, P. ROMANCERO JUDEO-ESPAÑOL DE
MARRUECOS.
I.J. LÉVY, 238:MAR70-146
C. SMITH, 402(MLR):JAN71-203
BENÍTEZ CLAROS, R., ED. VERDORES DEL
PARNASO.
A. NOUGUÉ, 182:VOL23#4-165
K. WHINNOM, 86(BHS):APR71-164
BENJAMIN, W. ANGELUS NOVUS. URSPRUNG
DES DEUTSCHEN TRAUERSPIELS.
S. WEBER, 98:AUG-SEP69-699
BENJAMIN, W. ILLUMINATIONS.* (H. ARENDT,
ED)
M. JAY, 390:FEB69-68
BENJAMIN, W. ILLUMINATIONS. ESSAIS SUR
BERTOLD BRECHT.
P. MISSAC, 98:AUG-SEP69-681
BENN, G. GOTTFRIED BENN: SELECTED
POEMS. (F.W. WODTKE, ED)
R. GRIMM, 406:WINTER71-395
BENN, G. GESAMMELTE WERKE. (D. WELLERS-
HOFF, ED) UN POÈTE ET LE MONDE.
J. BOUVERESSE, 98:AUG-SEP69-713
"GOTTFRIED BENN." (E. LOHNER, ED)
J-C. BRUCE, 406:SUMMER71-166
R-E. LORBE, 301(JEGP):APR71-340
BENNETT, A. THE LOOT OF THE CITIES.
N. CALLENDAR, 441:10DEC72-56
BENNETT, A.M.H. - SEE BROWN, J.A.C.
"ARNOLD BENNETT IN LOVE." (G. & J.
BEARDMORE, EDS)
M. DRABBLE, 362:21DEC72-868
BENNETT, B.V. PIANO CLASSES FOR EVERY-
ONE.
F. DAWES, 415:JUL70-714
BENNETT, D.N. PARENTS SHOULD BE HEARD.
617(TLS):17MAR72-317
BENNETT, E.M. RECOGNITION OF RUSSIA.
R.P. BROWDER, 32:JUN71-400
E.B. TOMPKINS, 550(RUSR):OCT70-467
BENNETT, G. NELSON THE COMMANDER.
T. LASK, 441:17NOV72-47
E. WEEKS, 61:NOV72-126
617(TLS):12MAY72-536
BENNETT, H. NO MORE PUBLIC SCHOOL.
441:16APR72-22
BENNETT, H.S. ENGLISH BOOKS AND READERS,
1475 TO 1557. (2ND ED)
P.K.J. WRIGHT, 355:JUL69-224
BENNETT, H.S. ENGLISH BOOKS AND READERS,
1603 TO 1640.*
L.A. BEAURLINE, 301(JEGP):APR71-286
A. BRAUER, 182:VOL23#13/14-641
H. FLETCHER, 356:JAN71-63
K. KOLLER, 568(SCN):WINTER71-70
P. MORGAN, 402(MLR):OCT71-862
78(BC):WINTER70-442
BENNETT, J.A.W. CHAUCER'S "BOOK OF
FAME."*
S-W. HOLTON, 597(SN):VOL41#1-176
J.M. NEWTON, 97(CQ):SUMMER69-300

BENNETT, J.A.W. & G.V. SMITHERS, WITH N.
DAVIS, EDS. EARLY MIDDLE ENGLISH
VERSE AND PROSE.
G. BAUER, 38:BAND87HEFT1-86
BENNETT, J.C. & OTHERS. STORM OVER
ETHICS.
R.J. TAPIA, 613:AUTUMN68-460
BENNETT, J.W. "MEASURE FOR MEASURE" AS
ROYAL ENTERTAINMENT.*
A.A., 477:SUMMER69-417
M. SRIGLEY, 597(SN):VOL40#1-243
BENNETT, W.A. ASPECTS OF LANGUAGE AND
LANGUAGE TEACHING.
B. EBLING, 207(FR):MAR70-704
BENOIT. CHRONIQUE DES DUCS DE NORMANDIE.
(VOL 3) (C. FAHLIN, ED)
F. KOENIG, 545(RPH):FEB70-366
BENOIT, F. LE SYMBOLISME DANS LES
SANCTUAIRES DE LA GAULE.
C.B. PASCAL, 124:JAN71-171
BENOT, Y. DIDEROT.
617(TLS):22SEP72-1118
BENSON, F.R. WRITERS IN ARMS.
D.E.S. MAXWELL, 402(MLR):JAN71-174
BENSON, M. AT THE STILL POINT.*
F. MC GUINNESS, 364:AUG/SEP71-143
BENSON, R.L. THE BISHOP-ELECT.*
R.E. SULLIVAN, 377:MAR71-36
BENTHALL, J. SCIENCE AND TECHNOLOGY IN
ART TODAY.
561(SATR):23DEC72-68
BENTHAM, J. THE CORRESPONDENCE OF JEREMY
BENTHAM. (VOLS 1&2) (T.L.S. SPRIGGE,
ED)
K.T.A., 191(ELN):SEP69(SUPP)-13
BENTLEY, E. BERNARD SHAW.
W. TYDEMAN, 148:SPRING70-92
BENTLEY, E. THE THEATRE OF COMMITMENT.
R. COHN, 397(MD):SEP68-214
571:WINTER68/69-34
BENTLEY, E., ED. THE THEORY OF THE
MODERN STAGE.
T.F. MARSHALL, 149:JUN71-190
BENTLEY, E., ED. THIRTY YEARS OF
TREASON.*
J. DUNN, 362:27APR72-553
617(TLS):2JUN72-625
BENTLEY, G.E. THE SEVENTEENTH CENTURY
STAGE.
W. ANGUS, 529(QQ):SPRING70-133
BENTLEY, G.E., JR., ED. BLAKE RECORDS.
J.B. BEER, 402(MLR):OCT71-872
BENTLEY, N. THE VICTORIAN SCENE.
A.B., 155:MAY69-120
K. ROBERTS, 90:OCT70-704
"NICOLAS BENTLEY'S TALES FROM SHAKE-
SPEARE."
617(TLS):18AUG72-977
BENTON, K. SPY IN CHANCERY.
617(TLS):29SEP72-1174
BENTON, R., ED. DIRECTORY OF MUSIC
RESEARCH LIBRARIES. (PT 2)
J.A.W., 410(M&L):JUL71-316
BENTON, W.A. WHIG-LOYALISM.
R. KETCHAM, 432(NEQ):JUN70-320
L.F.S. UPTON, 656(WMQ):JAN70-161
BENVENISTE, É. LE VOCABULAIRE DES INSTI-
TUTIONS INDO-EUROPÉENNES.
W. DRESSLER, 350:MAR71-209
A. ERNOUT, 555:VOL44FASC2-278
BENWARD, B. SIGHTSINGING COMPLETE.
P. HARDER, 308:SPRING67-164
BENWARD, B. TEACHER'S DICTATION MANUAL
IN EAR TRAINING.
P. HARDER, 308:SPRING67-160
BENZI, M. LES DERNIERS ADORATEURS DU
PEYOTL.
617(TLS):22SEP72-1094

BEONIO-BROCCHIERI FUMAGALLI, M.T. THE
LOGIC OF ABELARD.
O. BIRD, 589:JUL71-510
BÉRANGER, J. LES HOMMES DE LETTRES ET
LA POLITIQUE EN ANGLETERRE DE LA RÉVO-
LUTION DE 1688 À LA MORT DE GEORGE IER.
C. WINTON, 301(JEGP):JUL71-557
BERAZALUCE, A.M. - SEE TEIJEIRO, A.
BERBEROVA, N. THE ITALICS ARE MINE.*
T. PACHMUSS, 574(SEEJ):SPRING71-80
G. STRUVE, 550(RUSR):JAN70-92
BERCKMAN, E. THE FOURTH MAN ON THE ROPE.
N. CALLENDAR, 441:30APR72-36
617(TLS):28APR72-500
BERESFORD, A. FOOTSTEPS ON SNOW.
617(TLS):13OCT72-1217
BERESFORD, M. NEW TOWNS OF THE MIDDLE
AGES.*
W. CREESE, 576:MAR69-75
BERETTA, G. CONTRIBUTO ALL'OPERA NOVEL-
LISTICA DI GIOVANNI SERCAMBI CON IL
TESTO DI 14 NOVELLE INEDITE.
F.B. AGENO, 545(RPH):MAY70-605
BERG, A. ALBAN BERG: LETTERS TO HIS
WIFE.* (B. GRUN, ED & TRANS)
M-C., 410(M&L):JUL71-306
M. CARNER, 415:MAY71-442
C. ROSEN, 441:2JAN72-3
BERG, K. STUDIES IN TUSCAN TWELFTH-CEN-
TURY ILLUMINATION.*
C. NORDENFALK, 90:JUN70-401
BERG, L. LOOK AT KIDS.
617(TLS):22SEP72-1124
BERG, L. & L. FACE TO FACE.
617(TLS):5MAY72-524
BERG, S. & R. MEZEY, EDS. NAKED POETRY.*
J.C. DE VANY, 590:SPRING70-41
BERGAMINI, D. JAPAN'S IMPERIAL CON-
SPIRACY.*
N. BLIVEN, 442(NY):25MAR72-128
BERGAMINI, J. THE TRAGIC DYNASTY.*
E.C. THADEN, 550(RUSR):JUL70-352
BERGER, B. & H. RUPP - SEE KOSCH, W.
BERGER, J. ART AND REVOLUTION.
A. FALCONER, 592:JUL/AUG69-44
A. LEONG, 574(SEEJ):SUMMER71-253
BERGER, J. G.
L. BRAUDY, 441:10SEP72-5
P.N. FURBANK, 362:8JUN72-767
R. JELLINEK, 441:29SEP72-43
K. MILLER, 453:30NOV72-40
617(TLS):9JUN72-645
BERGER, J. THE LOOK OF THINGS.
A. FORGE, 362:3FEB72-161
BERGER, J. THE MOMENT OF CUBISM AND
OTHER ESSAYS.
M. SHEPHERD, 619(TC):1969/2-55
BERGER, J. SELECTED ESSAYS AND ARTICLES.
(N. STANGOS, ED)
617(TLS):9JUN72-645
BERGER, K. ODILON REDON.*
R. PICKVANCE, 90:SEP69-570
BERGER, P.L. A RUMOR OF ANGELS.
S.O.H., 543:DEC69-341
BERGÈRE, M-C. LA BOURGEOISIE CHINOISE ET
LA RÉVOLUTION DE 1911.
T-L. KENNEDY, 293(JAST):FEB70-431
BERGES, R. THE BACKGROUNDS AND TRADI-
TIONS OF OPERA. (2ND ED)
J.A.W., 410(M&L):JUL71-330
BERGH, B., ED. DEN HELIGA BIRGITTAS
REVELACIONES BOK VII.
M-J. RONDEAU, 555:VOL44FASC1-175
BERGHAHN, V.R. DER TIRPITZ-PLAN.
617(TLS):9JUN72-664
BERGIN, T.G., ED. FROM TIME TO ETERNITY.
J.C. MATHEWS, 546(RR):FEB70-43

BERGMAN, G. KORTFATTAD SVENSK SPRÅKHIS-
TORIA.
    B. HELLSTRÖM, 270:VOL20#1-24
BERGONZI, B. T.S. ELIOT.
    617(TLS):1DEC72-1454
BERGONZI, B. ANTHONY POWELL.
    617(TLS):30JUN72-757
BERGSTEN, B. - SEE NIVER, K.R.
BERGSTEN, G. THOMAS MANN'S "DOCTOR
FAUSTUS."*
    H.A. BASILIUS, 290(JAAC):WINTER69-257
    K.W. JONAS, 399(MLJ):APR70-298
BERGSTEN, G. & S., EDS. LYRIK I TID OCH
OTID.
    W.A. BERENDSOHN, 182:VOL23#17/18-804
BERGSVEINSSON, S. ISLÄNDISCH-DEUTSCHES
WÖRTERBUCH.
    H. BENEDIKTSSON, 353:SEP69-83
BERKELEY, E. & D.S. DR. ALEXANDER GARDEN
OF CHARLES TOWN.*
    G.F. FRICK, 656(WMQ):JUL70-493
BERKELEY, G. ANTOLOGIA DEGLI SCRITTI
FILOSOFICI. (T.E. JESSOP, ED)
    E. RONCHETTI, 548(RCSF):JAN/MAR69-113
BERKELEY, H. CROSSING THE FLOOR.
    617(TLS):14APR72-413
BERKELEY, J. LULWORTH AND THE WELDS.
    617(TLS):10MAR72-285
BERKMAN, T. TO SEIZE THE PASSING DREAM.
    M. LEVIN, 441:19MAR72-40
    R. LYNN, 561(SATR):15JUL72-52
BERKOVITS, I. ILLUMINATED MANUSCRIPTS IN
HUNGARY: XI-XVI CENTURIES. (REV BY A.
WEST)
    H.R. ARCHER, 32:JUN71-460
BERLE, A.A. POWER.
    D. GERMINO, 639(VQR):WINTER70-160
BERLEANT, A. THE AESTHETIC FIELD.
    C. LYAS, 89(BJA):SUMMER71-289
BERLIN, I. FATHERS AND CHILDREN.
    617(TLS):22DEC72-1553
BERLIN, I. FOUR ESSAYS ON LIBERTY.*
    639(VQR):AUTUMN70-CLII
BERLIN, S. PRIDE OF THE PEACOCK.
    617(TLS):21JUL72-836
BERLIOZ, H. THE MEMOIRS OF HECTOR BER-
LIOZ.* (D. CAIRNS, ED & TRANS)
    639(VQR):SUMMER70-CIV
BERLIOZ, H. LES SOIRÉES DE L'ORCHESTRE.
LES GROTESQUES DE LA MUSIQUE. A TRAV-
ERS CHANTS. (ALL ED BY L. GUICHARD)
    617(TLS):18FEB72-169
BERLIOZ, H. TRAITÉ D'INSTRUMENTATION ET
D'ORCHESTRATION. VOYAGE MUSICAL EN
ALLEMAGNE ET EN ITALIE. LES SOIRÉES
DE L'ORCHESTRE. LES GROTESQUES DE LA
MUSIQUE. A TRAVERS CHANTS. MÉMOIRES.
LES MUSICIENS ET LA MUSIQUE.
    617(TLS):18FEB72-169
BERMAN, H. & M. ZLOTOVER. ZLOTOVER
STORY.
    N. BENTWICH, 287:MAR69-25
BERMAN, M. THE POLITICS OF AUTHENTI-
CITY.*
    P. BROOKS, 441:10SEP72-36
    617(TLS):21JAN72-66
BERMANT, C. THE COUSINHOOD.
    442(NY):24JUN72-94
    617(TLS):17MAR72-308
BERMANT, C. ROSES ARE BLOOMING IN PIC-
ARDY.
    J. HUNTER, 362:9MAR72-317
    617(TLS):31MAR72-352
BERMEJO MARCOS, M. DON JUAN VALERA,
CRÍTICO LITERARIO.
    C.C. DE COSTER, 240(HR):OCT70-437

BERNAC, P. THE INTERPRETATION OF FRENCH
SONG.*
    R. CRICHTON, 415:JUN70-608
BERNAD, M.A. HISTORY AGAINST THE LAND-
SCAPE.
    C.O. HOUSTON, 293(JAST):FEB70-507
BERNAL, I., R. PINA-CHAN & F. CAMARA-
BARBACHANO. 3,000 YEARS OF ART AND
LIFE IN MEXICO.
    J.B. LYNCH, 127:SUMMER71-426
BERNAL, J.D. THE EXTENSION OF MAN.
    617(TLS):7APR72-400
BERNANOS, G. COMBAT POUR LA LIBERTÉ.
(J. MURRAY, ED)
    617(TLS):18FEB72-177
BERNANOS, G. JOURNAL D'UN CURÉ DE CAM-
PAGNE. (E.M. O'SHARKEY, ED)
    E. BEAUMONT, 208(FS):JUL71-354
BERNARD DE VENTADOUR. CHANSONS D'AMOUR.
(M. LAZAR, ED & TRANS)
    G. MERMIER, 207(FR):OCT69-195
BERNARD OF CLAIRVAUX. BERNARDO DI CHI-
ARAVALLE: GRAZIA E LIBERO ARBITRIO.
BERNARDO DI CHIARAVALLE: LE LETTERE
CONTRO PIETRO ABELARDO. (A. BABOLIN,
ED OF BOTH)
    D. LUSCOMBE, 382(MAE):1971/1-66
BERNARD, G. LE SECRÉTARIAT D'ÉTAT ET LE
CONSEIL ESPAGNOL DES INDES (1700-1808).
    617(TLS):29SEP72-1171
BERNARD, J-P. LES ROUGES.
    B.J. YOUNG, 99:JUN72-33
BERNARD, R. ILLEGAL ENTRY.
    N. CALLENDAR, 441:13FEB72-34
BERNARDO, G.A., COMP. BIBLIOGRAPHY OF
PHILIPPINE BIBLIOGRAPHIES, 1953-1961.
(N.P. VERZOSA, ED)
    J.K. MUSGRAVE, 293(JAST):MAY70-741
BERNARI, C. UN FORO NEL PARABREZZA.
    617(TLS):4FEB72-135
BERNATH, M., H. JABLONOWSKI & W. PHILIPP
- SEE "FORSCHUNGEN ZUR OSTEUROPÄISCHEN
GESCHICHTE" (VOL 15)
BERND, C.A. - SEE STORM, T. & P. HEYSE
BERNDTSON, A. ART, EXPRESSION AND
BEAUTY.
    E.H. DUNCAN, 290(JAAC):SUMMER70-557
    D.B. KUSPIT, 484(PPR):DEC69-304
BERNE, E. WHAT DO YOU SAY AFTER YOU SAY
HELLO?
    A. BROYARD, 441:17JUL72-31
    J.S. GORDON, 441:10CT72-44
BERNHARD, T. DER ITALIENER. MIDLAND IN
STILFS. GEHEN.
    617(TLS):29SEP72-1139
BERNSTEIN, B. CLASS, CODES AND CONTROL.
(VOL 1)
    M. DOUGLAS, 362:9MAR72-312
BERNSTEIN, B. THE STICKS.
    J. KANON, 561(SATR):2SEP72-50
"EDUARD BERNSTEINS BRIEFWECHSEL MIT
FRIEDRICH ENGELS."* (H. HIRSCH, ED)
    A. LASSERRE, 182:VOL23#15/16-727
BERNSTEIN, K. THE SENATOR'S RANSOM.
    N. CALLENDAR, 441:23JAN72-26
BERNSTEIN, M.H. - SEE CHAPMAN, J.J.
BERNT, G. DAS LATEINISCHE EPIGRAMM
IM ÜBERGANG VON DER SPÄTANTIKE ZUM
FRÜHEN MITTELALTER.
    P.G. WALSH, 123:DEC70-402
BÉROUL. THE ROMANCE OF TRISTRAN.* (VOL
2) (A. EWERT, ED)
    E.M. KENNEDY, 382(MAE):1971/3-280
    T.B.W. REID, 208(FS):JAN71-53
BERQUE, J. EGYPT.
    617(TLS):270CT72-1272
BERRIGAN, D. AMERICA IS HARD TO FIND.
    H. MITGANG, 441:70CT72-35

BERRIGAN, D. THE TRIAL OF THE CATONS-
VILLE NINE.
639(VQR):AUTUMN70-CLII
BERRIGAN, D., WITH L. LOCKWOOD. ABSURD
CONVICTIONS, MODEST HOPES.
H. MITGANG, 441:7OCT72-35
BERRIGAN, T. IN THE EARLY MORNING RAIN.*
D. LEHMAN, 491:JAN72-224
F. MORAMARCO, 651(WHR):SUMMER71-280
BERRIO, A.G. - SEE UNDER GARCÍA BERRIO,
A.
BERRY, F. THE SHAKESPEARE INSET.
F.D. HOENIGER, 570(SQ):AUTUMN68-396
BERRY, J. SOCIAL WORK WITH CHILDREN.
617(TLS):13OCT72-1237
BERRY, R. THE ART OF JOHN WEBSTER.
617(TLS):29SEP72-1162
BERRY, W. FARMING.
W. DICKEY, 249(HUDR):SPRING71-159
W.H. PRITCHARD, 491:DEC71-159
BERRY, W. OPENINGS.
R. MORAN, 598(SOR):WINTER72-243
G. OWEN, 577(SHR):SPRING70-186
BERRY, W. & E. CHUDACOFF. EIGHTEENTH-
CENTURY IMITATIVE COUNTERPOINT.
T. CLIFTON, 308:SPRING70-133
BERRYMAN, J. BERRYMAN'S SONNETS.*
H. SERGEANT, 175:SPRING69-33
BERRYMAN, J. DELUSIONS, ETC.
A. ALVAREZ, 441:25JUN72-1
J. BAYLEY, 362:28DEC72-901
P. DALE, 561(SATR):8JUL72-57
BERRYMAN, J. THE DREAM SONGS.*
L.P. VONALT, 569(SR):SUMMER71-464
639(VQR):SPRING70-XLIV
BERRYMAN, J. HIS TOY, HIS DREAM, HIS
REST.*
J. MC MICHAEL, 598(SOR):WINTER72-213
J. MAZZARO, 340(KR):1969/2-259
W.P. TURNER, 619(TC):1969/2-45
BERRYMAN, J. LOVE AND FAME.*
G. BURNS, 584(SWR):SPRING71-207
G.S. FRASER, 473(PR):WINTER71/72-469
C. JAMES, 362:20JAN72-87
F. MORAMARCO, 651(WHR):SUMMER71-283
BERSANI, J. & OTHERS. LA LITTÉRATURE
EN FRANCE DEPUIS 1945.
W.G. MOORE, 402(MLR):OCT71-907
BERSON, L.E. THE NEGROES AND THE JEWS.*
M. KEMPTON, 453:29JUN72-3
VON BERTALANFFY, L. GENERAL SYSTEM
THEORY.
617(TLS):17MAR72-299
BERTALOT, E.U. ANDRÉ GIDE ET L'ATTENTE
DE DIEU.
R. GOLDTHORPE, 402(MLR):OCT71-902
M. LINDSAY, 399(MLJ):MAR70-197
BERTEAUT, S. PIAF.
R.R. LINGEMAN, 441:28JUL72-31
R. SEAVER, 561(SATR):12AUG72-52
J. STAFFORD, 453:10AUG72-22
A. WHITMAN, 441:6AUG72-4
442(NY):8JUL72-76
BERTELLI, S. GIANNONIANA.
P. ZAMBELLI, 548(RCSF):OCT-DEC69-469
BERTHOFF, A.E. THE RESOLVED SOUL.*
M. SHAPIRO, 301(JEGP):OCT71-665
BERTHOFF, R. AN UNSETTLED PEOPLE.*
676(YR):SUMMER71-XXII
BERTHOFF, W. THE FERMENT OF REALISM.
R. NARVESON, 502(PRS):SPRING69-135
BERTHOFF, W. FICTIONS AND EVENTS.*
L. GRAVER, 561(SATR):8JAN72-36
W.H. PRITCHARD, 249(HUDR):WINTER
71/72-709
BERTI, E. IL "DE RE PUBLICA" DI CICERONE
E IL PENSIERO POLITICO CLASSICO.
A. GRILLI, 548(RCSF):APR-JUN68-227

BERTI, E. LA FILOSOFIA DEL PRIMO ARIS-
TOTELE.
J. BRUNSCHWIG, 542:APR-JUN68-284
BERTI, L. MASACCIO.
M. DAVIES, 90:APR69-227
DE BERTIER DE SAUVIGNY, G. METTERNICH ET
LA FRANCE APRÈS LE CONGRÈS DE VIENNE.
(VOL 3)
617(TLS):4AUG72-912
BERTINI, F. - SEE PLAUTUS
BERTOCCI, P.A. THE PERSON GOD IS.*
J. HOWIE, 518:OCT71-1
BERTON, P. THE IMPOSSIBLE RAILWAY.
M. RICHLER, 441:12NOV72-48
BERTON, P. THE LAST SPIKE.
P. GEORGE, 99:JAN-FEB72-71
BERTON, P. THE NATIONAL DREAM.
P.B. WAITE, 150(DR):WINTER70/71-563
102(CANL):WINTER71-106
BERTRAM, P. SHAKESPEARE AND "THE TWO
NOBLE KINSMEN."
C. HOY, 405(MP):AUG69-83
BERTRAND, M. L'OEUVRE DE JEAN PRÉVOST.
P. BRODIN, 546(RR):OCT70-235
BERTUCCIOLI, G. LA LETTERATURA CINESE.
(NEW ED)
E. CARBONARO, 302:JAN70-252
BESER, S. LEOPOLDO ALAS, CRÍTICO LITER-
ARIO.*
J. DOWLING, 238:MAR70-149
R. GUTIÉRREZ GIRARDOT, 72:BAND208
HEFT3-238
BESHIR, M.O. THE SOUTHERN SUDAN.
J. BUXTON, 69:JUL69-308
BESSELL, R. INTERVIEWING AND COUNSEL-
LING.
617(TLS):7APR72-400
BESSER, G.R. BALZAC'S CONCEPT OF GENIUS.
D. ADAMSON, 208(FS):JUL71-342
P. CITRON, 546(RR):DEC70-309
BESSET, M. NEW FRENCH ARCHITECTURE.*
G.E. KIDDER SMITH, 576:MAY69-150
BESSET, M. WHO WAS LE CORBUSIER?
C. NIVOLA, 44:DEC69-60
BESSETTE, G. UNE LITTÉRATURE EN ÉBUL-
LITION.
J-C. BONENFANT, 627(UTQ):JUL69-459
BESSINGER, J.B., JR., ED. A CONCORDANCE
TO "BEOWULF."*
W.F. BOLTON, 541(RES):MAY70-189
A. CAMPBELL, 447(N&Q):MAR70-116
G. GRABAND, 72:BAND208HEFT2-123
BESSINGER, J.B. JR. & S.J. KAHRL, EDS.
ESSENTIAL ARTICLES FOR THE STUDY OF
OLD ENGLISH POETRY.*
H. GNEUSS, 72:BAND208HEFT3-214
J. TORRINGA, 179(ES):DEC69-603
BEST, A.M. - SEE CHAPPUYS, C.
BEST, G. MID-VICTORIAN BRITAIN, 1851-
1875.*
441:16APR72-22
BEST, G. - SEE CHURCH, R.W.
BEST, R.I. & M.A. O'BRIEN, EDS. THE BOOK
OF LEINSTER, FORMERLY LEBAR NA NÚACHON-
GBÁLA. (VOL 5)
R.T. MEYER, 589:OCT71-727
BEST, T.W. THE HUMANIST ULRICH VON HUT-
TEN.*
R.S. SYLVESTER, 551(RENQ):WINTER70-
455
"BEST POEMS OF 1966." [BORESTONE MOUN-
TAIN POETRY AWARDS XIX]
N. JACOBS, 447(N&Q):FEB70-71
"BEST POEMS OF 1967." [BORESTONE
MOUNTAIN POETRY AWARDS XX]
N. JACOBS, 447(N&Q):DEC70-476

"BEST POEMS OF 1968." [BORESTONE
MOUNTAIN POETRY AWARDS XXI]
N. JACOBS, 447(N&Q):DEC70-476
BESTERMAN, T., ED. STUDIES ON VOLTAIRE
AND THE EIGHTEENTH CENTURY. (VOL 67)
J.H. BRUMFITT, 208(FS):OCT71-461
BESTERMAN, T., ED. STUDIES ON VOLTAIRE
AND THE EIGHTEENTH CENTURY. (VOL 68)
D. WILLIAMS, 208(FS):OCT71-462
BESTERMAN, T., ED. STUDIES ON VOLTAIRE
AND THE EIGHTEENTH CENTURY. (VOLS 84 &
86)
617(TLS):30JUN72-751
BESTERMAN, T., ED. STUDIES ON VOLTAIRE
AND THE EIGHTEENTH CENTURY. (VOLS 87-
90)
617(TLS):22SEP72-1118
BESTERMAN, T. - SEE DE VOLTAIRE, F.M.A.
BÉTEILLE, A. CASTES.
R.W. NICHOLAS, 293(JAST):AUG70-950
BETHELL, L. THE ABOLITION OF THE
BRAZILIAN SLAVE TRADE.
D. CARNEIRO, 263:JAN-MAR71-67
BETHELL, N. GOMUŁKA.
E. MICKIEWICZ, 32:MAR71-182
BETHELL, N. THE WAR HITLER WON.
617(TLS):8DEC72-1478
BETHGE, E. - SEE BONHOEFFER, D.
BETJEMAN, J. LONDON'S HISTORIC RAILWAY
STATIONS.
G. ANNAN, 362:6JUL72-22
617(TLS):15SEP72-1050
BETJEMAN, J. A PICTORIAL HISTORY OF ENG-
LISH ARCHITECTURE.
442(NY):9DEC72-178
617(TLS):15SEP72-1050
BETJEMAN, J., ED. POCKET GUIDE TO ENG-
LISH PARISH CHURCHES.
J. KILLICK, 46:JAN69-71
BETJEMAN, J. & J.S. GRAY. VICTORIAN AND
EDWARDIAN BRIGHTON FROM OLD PHOTO-
GRAPHS.
617(TLS):23JUN72-730
BETJEMAN, J. & D. VAISEY. VICTORIAN AND
EDWARDIAN OXFORD FROM OLD PHOTOGRAPHS.
G. ANNAN, 362:6JAN72-24
617(TLS):14JAN72-43
BETTERTON, T. - SEE UNDER GILDON, C.
BETTS, D. THE RIVER TO PICKLE BEACH.
J. YARDLEY, 441:21MAY72-12
BETTS, R.R. ESSAYS IN CZECH HISTORY.*
H. KAMINSKY, 32:MAR71-172
BEUGNOT, B. JEAN-LOUIS GUEZ DE BALZAC.
J. BRODY, 546(RR):FEB70-59
BEUMANN, H. & OTHERS, EDS. KAROLUS MAG-
NUS ET LEO PAPA.
L. FALKENSTEIN, 182:VOL23#3-105
BEURDELEY, C. & M. GIUSEPPE CASTIGLIONE.
J. CANADAY, 441:3DEC72-90
BEVAN, E.D. A CONCORDANCE TO THE PLAYS
AND PREFACES OF BERNARD SHAW.
617(TLS):2JUN72-633
BEVERIDGE, H. - SEE JAHĀNGĪR
BEVINGTON, D. TUDOR DRAMA AND POLITICS.*
J. VAN DORSTEN, 541(RES):AUG70-344
N. RABKIN, 301(JEGP):JAN71-149
BEVINGTON, D.M., ED. TWENTIETH-CENTURY
INTERPRETATIONS OF "HAMLET."
A.L. FRENCH, 184(EIC):JAN70-98
J.O. WOOD, 570(SQ):SPRING69-236
BEWICK, T. BEWICK TO DOVASTON. (G.
WILLIAMS, ED)
P.C.G. ISAAC, 354:JUN69-171
BEWLEY, M. MASKS AND MIRRORS.
M. LEBOWITZ, 598(SOR):SUMMER72-696
BEYER, C-J. - SEE MONTESQUIEU
BEYER, O. - SEE MENDELSOHN, E.

BEYLEN, R. THE WAY TO THE SUN.
M. LEVIN, 441:16JAN72-43
DE BEZE, C. 1688 REVOLUTION IN SIAM.
(E.W. HUTCHINSON, TRANS)
D.K. WYATT, 293(JAST):FEB70-494
BHAERMAN, S. & J. DENKER. NO PARTICULAR
PLACE TO GO.
E.Z. FRIEDENBERG, 453:4MAY72-21
T. LASK, 441:7APR72-36
J. PATENAUDE, 561(SATR):29APR72-53
"THE BHAGAVAD GĪTĀ." (E. DEUTSCH, ED &
TRANS)
R. ROCHER, 293(JAST):NOV69-183
"THE BHAGAVAD GITA." (A. STANFORD,
TRANS)
J.L. HALIO, 598(SOR):SPRING72-453
BHAGWATI, J.N. & P. DESAI. INDIA.
617(TLS):15SEP72-1066
BHARGAVA, D. JAINA ETHICS.
P.S. JAINI, 293(JAST):FEB70-503
D.W. MITCHELL, 485(PE&W):OCT69-467
BHARIER, J. ECONOMIC DEVELOPMENT IN IRAN
1900-1970.
617(TLS):11FEB72-164
BHATIA, J. THE LATCHKEY KID.
A. MONTAGNES, 99:JAN-FEB72-75
BHATTACHARYA, H.S. REALS IN THE JAINA
METAPHYSICS.
A. BHARATI, 318(JAOS):APR-JUN70-349
BHUTTO, Z.A. THE MYTH OF INDEPENDENCE.
W. WILCOX, 293(JAST):AUG70-977
BIAŁOSTOCKI, J. STIL UND IKONOGRAPHIE.
J. MONTAGU, 54:JUN69-197
BIANCHI, E.C. THE RELIGIOUS EXPERIENCE
OF REVOLUTIONARIES.
W. DAVISON, 441:5NOV72-20
BIANCHI, L. CARISSIMI, STRADELLA, SCAR-
LATTI E L'ORATORIO MUSICALE.
G. ROSE, 377:FALL71-485
BIANCHI, U., ED. STUDI DI STORIA RE-
LIGIOSA DELLA TARDA ANTICHITĀ.
C.B. PASCAL, 122:APR71-141
BIANCHI BANDINELLI, R. ROME.*
617(TLS):24MAR72-338
BIANCO, L. ORIGINS OF THE CHINESE REVO-
LUTION, 1915-1949.*
R. STEEL, 440:9APR72-1
617(TLS):6OCT72-1187
BIASIN, G-P. THE SMILE OF THE GODS.*
T.G. BERGIN, 401(MLQ):SEP70-392
D. HEINEY, 131(CL):FALL71-366
G. RIMANELLI, 275(IQ):FALL69-73
F. ROSENGARTEN, 276:AUTUMN70-319
BIBAUW, J., ED. HOMMAGES A MARCEL
RENARD.
A. ERNOUT, 555:VOL44FASC1-142
BIBBY, C. SCIENTIST EXTRAORDINARY.
617(TLS):3NOV72-1301
BIBBY, G. LOOKING FOR DILMUN.*
W.S. RUSK, 127:SPRING71-326
676(YR):AUTUMN70-XXX
PRINCESSE BIBESCO. ECHANGES AVEC PAUL
CLAUDEL.
617(TLS):17MAR72-300
"BIBLIA PAUPERUM." (E. SOLTÉSZ, ED)
J. BECKWITH, 39:SEP69-267
A. HEIMANN, 90:FEB69-94
"BIBLIOGRAPHIE ANNUELLE DE L'HISTOIRE DE
FRANCE DU CINQUIÈME SIÈCLE À 1945."
(1968)
N. HAMPSON, 208(FS):OCT71-496
"BIBLIOTHECA BARBADIENSIS."
R. CAVE, 78(BC):WINTER70-531
BICKERMAN, E.J. CHRONOLOGY OF THE
ANCIENT WORLD.*
S-I. OOST, 122:APR71-143
BIDA, C. & V. RICH. LESYA UKRAINKA.
C.H. ANDRUSYSHEN, 627(UTQ):JUL69-490

BIDAULT, G. RESISTANCE.
A. DE RIENCOURT, 461:SUMMER68-611
BIDDIS, M. - SEE DE GOBINEAU, J.A.
BIDWELL, C.E. OUTLINE OF CZECH MORPHOL-
OGY.
Z.P. MEYERSTEIN, 574(SEEJ):WINTER71-
524
BIDWELL, C.E. OUTLINE OF SLOVENIAN MOR-
PHOLOGY.
G.M. ERAMIAN, 104:SUMMER71-251
K.E. NAYLOR, 574(SEEJ):SPRING71-102
BIDWELL, C.E. OUTLINE OF UKRAINIAN MOR-
PHOLOGY. OUTLINE OF BIELORUSSIAN MOR-
PHOLOGY.*
H. ANDERSEN, 361:VOL24#4-404
BIDWELL, C.E. THE SLAVIC LANGUAGES.
(2ND ED) A MORPHO-SYNTACTIC CHARACT-
ERIZATION OF THE MODERN SLAVIC LAN-
GUAGES. OUTLINE OF BIELORUSSIAN MOR-
PHOLOGY. (REV)
G.M. ERAMIAN, 104:SUMMER71-251
BIDWELL, C.E. THE STRUCTURE OF RUSSIAN
IN OUTLINE.
P. REIAL, 104:FALL71-420
C.E. TOWNSEND, 574(SEEJ):SPRING71-96
BIEBUYCK, D. & K.C. MATEENE, EDS & TRANS.
THE MWINDO EPIC FROM THE BANYANGA
(CONGO REPUBLIC).
G. CALAME-GRIAULE, 315(JAL):VOL8PT2-
126
VON BIEDERMANN, F., ED. GOETHES GE-
SPRÄCHE. (VOLS 1&2) (REV BY W. HERWIG)
N.H. SMITH, 182:VOL23#19/20-860
BIELATOWICZ, J. LITERATURA NA EMIGRACJI.
J.R. KRZYŻANOWSKI, 574(SEEJ):WINTER
71-513
BIELEFELD, E. ARCHAEOLOGIA HOMERICA.
(VOL C)
P. CHANTRAINE, 555:VOL44FASC2-301
BIELEFELD, E. SCHMUCK.
F.M. COMBELLACK, 122:JAN71-44
BIELER, M. DER PASSAGIER.
617(TLS):2JUN72-623
BIEN, P. KAZANTZAKIS AND THE LINGUISTIC
REVOLUTION IN GREEK LITERATURE.
617(TLS):10NOV72-1362
BIENEK, H. THE CELL.
L.J. DAVIS, 441:19NOV72-59
BIERLAIRE, F. LA FAMILIA D'ÉRASME.
R.C. PETRY, 551(RENQ):SUMMER70-168
BIGGS-DAVISON, J. AFRICA - HOPE DEFER-
RED.
617(TLS):19MAY72-564
BIGONGIARI, P. ANTIMATERIA.
617(TLS):29SEP72-1166
BIGONGIARI, P. POESIA FRANCESE DEL NOVE-
CENTO.
J-M. GARDAIR, 98:APR69-304
BIGSBY, C.W.E. CONFRONTATION AND COMMIT-
MENT.
R. HOGAN, 397(MD):SEP69-217
BILENCHI, R. IL BOTTONE DI STALINGRADO.
617(TLS):17NOV72-1387
BILENCHI, R. IL CONSERVATORIO DI SANTA
TERESA. RACCONTI. RÉCITS.
J-M. GARDAIR, 98:OCT69-888
BILIK, J.H. LEARNING TO HEAR.
P. HARDER, 308:SPRING67-160
BILLIAS, G.A., ED. GEORGE WASHINGTON'S
OPPONENTS.
B. KNOLLENBERG, 656(WMQ):APR70-320
BILLINGS, H., ED. EDWARD DAHLBERG.*
J. HARRIS, 328:SUMMER69-374
BILLINGTON, J.H. THE ICON AND THE AXE.*
T. RIHA, 587:APR68-581

BILLY, A. UN SINGULIER BÉNÉDICTIN
L'ABBÉ PRÉVOST - AUTEUR DE "MANON LES-
CAUT."
R.F. O'REILLY, 207(FR):MAR70-696
BINDER, F.M. THE COLOR PROBLEM IN EARLY
AMERICA AS VIEWED BY JOHN ADAMS, JEF-
FERSON, AND JACKSON.
G.W. MULLIN, 656(WMQ):JAN70-167
R.M. SPECTOR, 432(NEQ):MAR70-168
BING, R. 5,000 NIGHTS AT THE OPERA.
D. HENAHAN, 441:22OCT72-1
I. KOLODIN, 561(SATR):4NOV72-80
T. LASK, 441:3NOV72-39
617(TLS):27OCT72-1283
BING, S. ARTISTIC AMERICA, TIFFANY
GLASS, AND ART NOUVEAU.
639(VQR):AUTUMN70-CLIV
BINGHAM, C. CORONET AMONG THE GRASS.
M. LEVIN, 441:23JUL72-21
617(TLS):21APR72-450
BINGHAM, C. JAMES V.
617(TLS):4FEB72-137
BINGHAM, M. SHERIDAN.
T. LASK, 441:29DEC72-22
617(TLS):5MAY72-520
BINGHAM, S. THE WAY IT IS NOW.
P. ADAMS, 61:MAR72-108
J. HENDIN, 441:2APR72-6
BINNEY, J. THE LEGACY OF GUILT.
J. THOMSON, 368:JUN69-194
BIRCH, A.H. REPRESENTATION.
617(TLS):11FEB72-151
BIRD, H. WAR FOR THE WEST 1790-1813.*
617(TLS):21JUL72-829
BIRD, W.R. ANGEL COVE.
E. ZIMMER, 296:SUMMER72-85
BIRDSALL, V.O. WILD CIVILITY.
A. BARTON, 677:VOL2-271
BIRDWELL, R. MOUNT HOREB.
M. LEVIN, 441:9JUL72-28
BIRDWHISTELL, R.L. KINESICS AND CONTEXT.
617(TLS):11FEB72-149
BIRENBAUM, W.M. SOMETHING FOR EVERYBODY
IS NOT ENOUGH.
R. GROSS, 440:26MAR72-10
N. POSTMAN, 441:5MAR72-4
BIRKE, J. - SEE GOTTSCHED, J.C.
BIRKENMAYER, S.S. NIKOLAJ NEKRASOV.*
J.A. POSIN, 550(RUSR):JAN70-108
BIRKMAIER, E.M., ED. THE BRITANNICA
REVIEW OF FOREIGN LANGUAGE EDUCATION.
(VOL 1)
J.G. MIRSKY, 238:DEC70-1027
J.A. RALLO, 276:AUTUMN70-326
BIRKNER, H-J. SCHLEIERMACHERS CHRIST-
LICHE SITTENLEHRE IM ZUSAMMENHANG
SEINES PHILOSOPHISCH-THEOLOGISCHEN SYS-
TEMS.
M.J.V., 543:SEP69-124
BIRKS, T. BUILDING THE NEW UNIVERSITIES.
617(TLS):14APR72-415
BIRLEY, A. SEPTIMIUS SEVERUS.*
R. PAYNE, 561(SATR):18MAR72-76
BIRMINGHAM, S. THE LATE JOHN MARQUAND.
J.W. ALDRIDGE, 561(SATR):17JUN72-63
E. WEEKS, 61:JUL72-94
441:20AUG72-20
BIRNBAUM, H. & J. PUHVEL, EDS. ANCIENT
INDO-EUROPEAN DIALECTS.*
J. GONDA, 353:JUL69-95
BIRNBAUM, N. TOWARD A CRITICAL SOCIOL-
OGY.
T. BOTTOMORE, 453:6APR72-31
617(TLS):11FEB72-149
BIRNEY, E. RAG AND BONE SHOP.*
F. COGSWELL, 102(CANL):SUMMER71-96

BIRREN, F., ED. A GRAMMAR OF COLOR. THE
COLOR PRIMER.
P. SLOANE, 58:FEB70-14
BIRREN, F. PRINCIPLES OF COLOR.
P. SLOANE, 58:FEB70-14
BIRSTEIN, A. SUMMER SITUATIONS.
S. BEAUMAN, 441:5MAR72-7
A. BROYARD, 441:28FEB72-33
A.Z. SILVER, 561(SATR):4MAR72-86
BISCO, R.L., ED. DATA BASES, COMPUTERS,
AND THE SOCIAL SCIENCES.
C.A. SHEPHERD, 356:JAN71-71
BISHOP, E. THE COMPLETE POEMS OF ELIZA-
BETH BISHOP.*
T. HARRISON, 364:APR/MAY71-163
BISHOP, I. "PEARL" IN ITS SETTING.*
C.R. BLYTH, 589:JAN71-126
BISHOP, J.L., ED. STUDIES OF GOVERNMEN-
TAL INSTITUTIONS IN CHINESE HISTORY.
D.W. MITCHELL, 485(PE&W):JAN69-90
BISHOP, T.A.M. ENGLISH CAROLINE MINUS-
CULE.
617(TLS):7JAN72-20
BISSETT, B. DRIFTING INTO WAR.
R. GIBBS, 198:SUMMER72-129
BISSETT, B. LEBANON VOICES.
D. BARBOUR, 150(DR):SPRING70-112
BISSETT, B. NOBODY OWNS TH EARTH.
F. DAVEY, 99:JUL-AUG72-44
BISSETT, B. OF TH LAND DIVINE SERVICE.*
D. BARBOUR, 150(DR):SPRING70-112
H. MAC CALLUM, 627(UTQ):JUL69-352
BITTER, W., ED. EVOLUTION.
V. RÜFNER, 182:VOL23#10-518
BITTMAN, L. THE DECEPTION GAME.
441:10DEC72-48
BITZER, H. GOETHE ÜBER DEN DILETTANTIS-
MUS.
E. BAHR, 406:SUMMER71-180
BIVAR, A.D.H. CATALOGUE OF THE WESTERN
ASIATIC SEALS IN THE BRITISH MUSEUM.
(VOL 2)
B. BUCHANAN, 318(JAOS):OCT-DEC70-546
BLACK, C. DEATH'S HEAD.
N. CALLENDAR, 441:10SEP72-40
617(TLS):21JUL72-851
BLACK, E.R. ALTERNATIVE IN SOUTHEAST
ASIA.
W.C. JOHNSTONE, 639(VQR):SPRING70-352
MARUYAMA SHIZUO, 285(JAPQ):APR-JUN70-
215
F.N. TRAGER, 293(JAST):AUG70-983
BLACK, J.R. YOUNG JAPAN.
293(JAST):MAY70-745
BLACK, K. RICHES AND FAME AND THE
PLEASURE OF SENSE.*
M. LEVIN, 441:2JAN72-16
BLACK, L. RANSOM FOR A NUDE.
O.L. BAILEY, 561(SATR):25NOV72-70
N. CALLENDAR, 441:24SEP72-41
BLACK, M. THE LABYRINTH OF LANGUAGE.*
C.E. CATON, 479(PHQ):APR70-186
BLACK, M. MARGINS OF PRECISION.
R. KIRK, 518:OCT71-3
BLACK, P. THE BIGGEST ASPIDISTRA IN THE
WORLD.
F. DILLON, 362:2NOV72-608
617(TLS):17NOV72-1397
BLACK, P. THE MIRROR IN THE CORNER.
J. CRAWLEY, 362:16MAR72-347
617(TLS):2JUN72-628
BLACK, R.D.C. & R. KONEKAMP - SEE JEVONS,
W.S.
"THE BLACK TITAN."
H.W. CRUSE & C. GIPSON, 453:30NOV72-
22
BLACKBURN, H. WOMEN'S SUFFRAGE.
617(TLS):18FEB72-180

BLACKBURN, J. FOR FEAR OF LITTLE MEN.
617(TLS):14APR72-427
BLACKBURN, R., ED. IDEOLOGY IN SOCIAL
SCIENCE.
617(TLS):3NOV72-1309
BLACKBURN, T. THE FOURTH MAN.*
I. WEDDE, 364:DEC71/JAN72-118
BLACKLEY, F.D. & G. HERMANSEN, EDS. THE
HOUSEHOLD BOOK OF QUEEN ISABELLA OF
ENGLAND.
617(TLS):4AUG72-926
BLACKMORE, H.L. HUNTING WEAPONS.
617(TLS):25AUG72-1005
BLACKSTOCK, C. THE JUNGLE.
M. LEVIN, 441:16JAN72-43
BLACKSTOCK, P.W. THE SECRET ROAD TO
WORLD WAR II.
N. GRANT, 550(RUSR):JAN70-96
BLACKWELL, W.L. THE INDUSTRIALIZATION OF
RUSSIA.
J.P. MC KAY, 32:SEP71-667
BLADES, J. PERCUSSION INSTRUMENTS AND
THEIR HISTORY.*
G. OLDHAM, 415:SEP71-857
J.A.W., 410(M&L):JUL71-325
BLAINEY, A. THE FARTHING POET.*
K. TILLOTSON, 155:JAN69-42
BLAIR, J.M. ECONOMIC CONCENTRATION.
S.P. LEE & P. PASSELL, 441:10SEP72-31
BLAIR, K.H. A REVIEW OF SOVIET LITERA-
TURE.
R.R. MILNER-GULLAND, 587:JUL69-115
BLAIR, W. - SEE TWAIN, M.
BLAIS, M-C. THE MANUSCRIPTS OF PAULINE
ARCHANGE.
H. MC PHERSON, 606(TAMR):#57-84
BLAKE, N.F. - SEE "THE HISTORY OF REYNARD
THE FOX"
BLAKE, N.M. NOVELISTS' AMERICA.
F. MORAMARCO, 330(MASJ):FALL69-83
BLAKE, R. MADE IN HEAVEN.
M. LEVIN, 441:21MAY72-31
BLAKE, R.L.V.F. - SEE UNDER FFRENCH
BLAKE, R.L.V.
BLAKE, V.B. & R. GREENHILL. RURAL ON-
TARIO.
P. RUSSELL, 96:FEB70-60
BLAKE, W. THE BOOK OF THEL. (N. BOGEN,
ED)
617(TLS):29SEP72-1145
BLAKE, W. EUROPE. [A FACSIMILE]
R.N. ESSICK, 340(KR):1970/1-190
BLAKE, W. EUROPE, A PROPHECY. SONGS OF
INNOCENCE AND OF EXPERIENCE. (BOTH ED
BY G. KEYNES)
G.E. BENTLEY, JR., 627(UTQ):APR70-274
BLAKE, W. THE GATES OF PARADISE.* THE
LETTERS OF WILLIAM BLAKE. (BOTH ED BY
G. KEYNES)
G.E. BENTLEY, JR., 627(UTQ):APR70-274
D.V.E., 191(ELN):SEP69(SUPP)-23
BLAKE, W. ILLUSTRATIONS TO THE "DIVINE
COMEDY" OF DANTE.
M. BUTLIN, 90:SEP69-570
G. GRIGSON, 39:OCT69-352
BLAKE, W. THERE IS NO NATURAL RELIGION.
617(TLS):28APR72-470
"THE BLAKE COLLECTION OF MRS. LANDON K.
THORNE."
617(TLS):28APR72-470
BLAKEMORE, H. & C.T. SMITH, EDS. LATIN
AMERICA.
617(TLS):9JUN72-656
BLAKISTON, G. LORD WILLIAM RUSSELL AND
HIS WIFE 1815-1846.
C. SYKES, 362:23MAR72-385
617(TLS):17MAR72-300

BLAMIRES, D.   DAVID JONES.*
    N. BALAKIAN, 441:17SEP72-30
BLAMIRES, H.   WORD UNHEARD.*
    G. SMITH, 27(AL):MAY71-300
    B.C. SOUTHAM, 184(EIC):JAN70-104
BLANCH, J.M.L. - SEE UNDER LOPE BLANCH,
    J.M.
BLANCH, R.J., ED.   STYLE AND SYMBOLISM
    IN "PIERS PLOWMAN."*
    R.J. PEARCY, 577(SHR):FALL70-380
    B.C. RAW, 447(N&Q):SEP70-357
BLANCQUART, M-C. - SEE VALLÈS, J.
BLAND, D., ED.   GESTA GRAYORUM.
    E. JONES, 447(N&Q):JUN70-236
BLANKENSHIP, W.D.   THE HELIX FILE.
    N. CALLENDAR, 441:13AUG72-20
BLASER, W.   MIES VAN DER ROHE.
    617(TLS):24NOV72-1414
BLASS, B.A., D.D. JOHNSON & W.W. GAGE.
    A PROVISIONAL SURVEY OF MATERIALS FOR
    THE STUDY OF NEGLECTED LANGUAGES.
    V.E. HANZELI, 399(MLJ):DEC70-615
    M.D. MC KEE, 315(JAL):VOL8PT1-60
BLATT, F., ED.   NOVUM GLOSSARIUM MEDIAE
    LATINITATIS.
    J.W. FUCHS, 361:VOL23#2-205
BLATT, T.B.   THE PLAYS OF JOHN BALE.*
    J. VAN DORSTEN, 541(RES):AUG70-344
"BLÄTTER FÜR DIE KUNST, 1892-1919."
    W.H. PERL, 221(GQ):MAY70-521
BLAXLAND, G.   THE BUFFS.
    617(TLS):28JUL72-900
BLAZEK, D.   ALL GODS MUST LEARN TO KILL.
    J. HOPPER, 661:SPRING69-97
BLAZICEK, O.J.   BAROQUE ART IN BOHEMIA.
    K. GARLICK, 39:JUN69-487
BLAZQUEZ, J.M.   TARTESSOS Y LOS ORIGINES
    DE LA COLONIZACION FENICIA EN OCCI-
    DENTE.
    E.C. KINGSBURY, 318(JAOS):OCT-DEC70-
    542
BLEECK, O.   THE PROCANE CHRONICLE.
    N. CALLENDAR, 441:30JAN72-24
BLEGEN, T.C.   THE KENSINGTON RUNIC STONE.
    H.A. ROE, 589:JAN71-126
BLEIKER, J.   ZUR MORPHOLOGIE UND SPRACH-
    GEOGRAPHIE DER VERBEN "HABEN, SEIN,
    TUN" IM SCHWEIZERDEUTSCHEN.
    R.E. KELLER, 402(MLR):APR71-425
    W.G. MOULTON, 301(JEGP):APR71-368
    W.G. MOULTON, 350:DEC71-938
    M. SZADROWSKY, 182:VOL23#8-410
BLEILER, E.H. - SEE "'CARMEN' BY GEORGES
    BIZET"
BLESSING, R.A.   WALLACE STEVENS' WHOLE
    HARMONIUM.
    R. BUTTEL, 295:VOL2#3-431
    P.L. MARIANI, 418(MR):WINTER71-162
    D.E. STANFORD, 27(AL):MAY71-301
LADY BLESSINGTON.   LADY BLESSINGTON'S
    "CONVERSATIONS OF LORD BYRON."   (E.J.
    LOVELL, JR., ED)
    D.V.E., 191(ELN):SEP70(SUPP)-28
    W.P. ELLEDGE, 191(ELN):DEC69-148
    J.J. MC GANN, 405(MP):NOV69-203
BLICQ, A.   THE RISE AND FALL OF MARRIED
    CHARLIE.
    P. GROSSKURTH, 102(CANL):SPRING71-83
BLISH, J.   AND ALL THE STARS A STAGE.
    R. BRYDEN, 362:30NOV72-760
BLISH, J.   THE DAY AFTER JUDGEMENT.
    E. MORGAN, 362:20APR72-524
    617(TLS):23JUN72-705
BLISH, J., ED.   NEBULA AWARD STORIES 5.
    617(TLS):12MAY72-537
BLISHEN, B.R. & OTHERS, EDS.   CANADIAN
    SOCIETY.
    F.J.K. GRIEZIC, 529(QQ):WINTER70-654

BLISHEN, E.   A CACKHANDED WAR.
    617(TLS):25AUG72-987
BLISS, A.   AS I REMEMBER.*
    R. ANDERSON, 415:AUG70-803
    A. PAYNE, 607:SUMMER70-35
BLISS, A.J., ED.   SIR ORFEO.   (2ND ED)
    H. WEINSTOCK, 597(SN):VOL41#1-211
BLISS, I.S.   EDWARD YOUNG.
    H. PETTIT, 566:SPRING71-73
BLIT, L.   THE ORIGINS OF POLISH SOCIAL-
    ISM.
    617(TLS):25FEB72-210
BLIVEN, B., JR.   UNDER THE GUNS.
    P. ADAMS, 61:AUG72-92
    T. LASK, 441:5AUG72-23
    441:17SEP72-44
    442(NY):26AUG72-79
"BERNARD BLOCH ON JAPANESE."   (R.A.
    MILLER, ED)
    J.J. CHEW, JR., 350:DEC71-965
    E-D. COOK, 320(CJL):SPRING70-154
BLOCH, E.   MAN ON HIS OWN.*
    J.M. CAMERON, 453:29JUN72-31
BLOCH, E.   ON KARL MARX.
    J.M. CAMERON, 453:29JUN72-31
BLOCH, E.M.   GEORGE CALEB BINGHAM.
    G. HOOD, 56:SUMMER69-197
BLOCH, R.   THE ANCIENT CIVILIZATION OF
    THE ETRUSCANS.
    R.R. HOLLOWAY, 124:APR71-274
BLOCH, R.   NIGHT WORLD.
    O.L. BAILEY, 561(SATR):26AUG72-62
    N. CALLENDAR, 441:6AUG72-24
BLOCK, H.   HERBLOCK'S STATE OF THE UNION.
    P. ADAMS, 61:OCT72-135
    W.V. SHANNON, 441:29OCT72-44
BLOCK, L.   RONALD RABBIT IS A DIRTY OLD
    MAN.
    M. LEVIN, 441:16JAN72-43
BLODGETT, H.W. & S. BRADLEY - SEE WHIT-
    MAN, W.
BLOK, A.   SELECTED POEMS.   (A. PYMAN, ED)
    617(TLS):2JUN72-641
BLOK, A.   SELECTED POEMS OF ALEKSANDR
    BLOK.*   (J.B. WOODWARD, ED)
    R. KEMBALL, 550(RUSR):APR70-239
BLOK, A.   THE TWELVE AND OTHER POEMS.*
    J. ATLAS, 491:OCT71-45
    J. BERNARDIN, 493:AUTUMN70-254
    C. COLLINS, 32:JUN71-440
BLOK, A. & A. BELYJ.   PEREPISKA.*
    V. TERRAS, 574(SEEJ):SPRING71-123
BLOKHINTSEV, D.   THE PHILOSOPHY OF QUAN-
    TUM MECHANICS.
    H.P.K., 543:MAR70-553
BLOM, E.   EVERYMAN'S DICTIONARY OF
    MUSIC.   (5TH ED REV BY J. WESTRUP)
    617(TLS):3NOV72-1349
BLOM-COOPER, L. & G. DREWRY.   FINAL
    APPEAL.
    617(TLS):20OCT72-1250
BLOMQVIST, J.   GREEK PARTICLES IN HELLEN-
    ISTIC PROSE.*
    F.W. HOUSEHOLDER, 121(CJ):FEB-MAR71-
    263
    É. DES PLACES, 555:VOL44FASC2-322
    S. USHER, 123:DEC70-403
BLOMSTEDT, Y.   K.J. STÅHLBERT - VALTIO-
    MIESELÄMÄKERTA.
    M. RINTALA, 32:MAR71-194
BLONDEL, J-F.   ENTENTE CORDIALE.
    617(TLS):21JAN72-71
BLONDEL, M. & L. LABERTHONNIÈRE.   COR-
    RESPONDANCE PHILOSOPHIQUE.
    L. JERPHAGNON, 542:OCT-DEC68-491
BLONDELL, J.   CENTER DOOR FANCY.
    M. LEVIN, 441:22OCT72-46

BLOODWORTH, D. ANY NUMBER CAN PLAY.
A. BROYARD, 441:22DEC72-28
617(TLS):10NOV72-1375
BLOOM, A. GOD AND MAN.
617(TLS):28JAN72-107
BLOOM, A. - SEE KOJÈVE, A.
BLOOM, A. - SEE PLATO
BLOOM, E.A. & L.D. JOSEPH ADDISON'S
SOCIABLE ANIMAL.
617(TLS):14APR72-412
BLOOM, H. BLAKE'S APOCALYPSE.
E.J. ROSE, 651(WHR):AUTUMN71-362
BLOOM, H. YEATS.*
J.L. ALLEN, JR., 295:VOL2#1-148
K. CONNELLY, 676(YR):SPRING71-394
A. GROSSMAN, 639(VQR):SUMMER70-520
W.H. PRITCHARD, 473(PR):1971/1-107
H. VENDLER, 301(JEGP):OCT71-691
BLOOM, M.T. ROGUES TO RICHES.
441:20FEB72-24
BLOOMFIELD, L. A LEONARD BLOOMFIELD
ANTHOLOGY. (C.F. HOCKETT, ED)
H. HOIJER, 350:DEC71-911
617(TLS):10MAR72-261
BLOOMFIELD, M.W. ESSAYS AND EXPLORA-
TIONS.
P.W. ROGERS, 529(QQ):WINTER70-644
BLOOMFIELD, R. THE SUFFOLK POET, SELEC-
TIONS FROM THE CORRESPONDENCE OF.
(W.H. HART, ED)
J. COTTON, 503:AUTUMN69-128
BLOT, J. LA JEUNE GÉANTE.
J. NANTET, 98:APR69-383
BLOTNER, J., COMP. WILLIAM FAULKNER'S
LIBRARY.
J.G. RIEWALD, 179(ES):DEC69-622
BLOUNT, T. CHARLES DICKENS: THE EARLY
NOVELS.
S. MARCUS, 155:MAY69-126
BLUESTONE, M. & N. RABKIN, EDS. SHAKE-
SPEARE'S CONTEMPORARIES. (2ND ED)
T.P. LOGAN, 399(MLJ):OCT70-454
BLÜHER, K.A. SENECA IN SPANIEN.*
H. ETTINGHAUSEN, 86(BHS):JAN71-66
BLUM, H. DIE ANTIKE MNEMOTECHNIK.
D. NEWTON-DE MOLINA, 184(EIC):JUL70-
353
BLUM, R. BIBLIOGRAPHIA.
F.J. WITTY, 356:JAN71-74
BLUM, R. OLD GLORY AND THE REAL-TIME
FREAKS.
W. SCHOTT, 441:23APR72-4
BLUM, W. CURIOSI UND REGENDARII.
W. LIEBESCHUETZ, 313:VOL60-229
BLUME, F. CLASSIC AND ROMANTIC MUSIC.
617(TLS):15DEC72-1538
BLUME, O. MÖGLICHKEITEN UND GRENZEN DER
ALTENHILFE.
U. LEHR, 182:VOL23#21/22-928
BLÜMEL, C. GREEK SCULPTORS AT WORK.
(REV TRANS)
J. BOARDMAN, 90:APR70-247
R.M. COOK, 123:DEC71-464
BLUMENBERG, W. KARL MARX.
617(TLS):19MAY72-578
BLUMENSON, M. THE PATTON PAPERS: 1885-
1940.
J. BUNTING 3D, 61:APR72-107
G.A. CRAIG, 441:9APR72-2
C. LEHMANN-HAUPT, 441:20MAR72-39
S.L.A. MARSHALL, 440:26MAR72-4
L. MORTON, 561(SATR):19FEB72-65
BLUMENTHAL, A.L. LANGUAGE AND PSYCHOL-
OGY.
E.A. ESPER, 350:DEC71-979
BLUMENTHAL, H. FRANCE AND THE UNITED
STATES.
639(VQR):AUTUMN70-CLI

BLUNT, A. THE PAINTINGS OF NICOLAS
POUSSIN.
E. WATERHOUSE, 90:APR69-224
BLUNT, A. PICASSO'S GUERNICA.
B. PETRIE, 90:SEP69-571
639(VQR):WINTER70-XXVI
BLUNT, A. NICOLAS POUSSIN.
J.M. BROWN, 290(JAAC):FALL69-99
H. DANIEL, 592:MAR69-150
E. WATERHOUSE, 90:APR69-224
BLUNT, A. SICILIAN BAROQUE.
H. HONOUR, 46:NOV69-404
D. MACK SMITH, 90:SEP69-569
J. WILTON-ELY, 39:JUL69-80
592:NOV68-231
BLUNT, W. THE DREAM KING.
G. ABRAHAM, 415:FEB71-141
BLY, R., ED. FORTY POEMS TOUCHING ON
RECENT AMERICAN HISTORY.
H. TAYLOR, 651(WHR):AUTUMN71-371
BLY, R. THE LIGHT AROUND THE BODY.*
H. ZINNES, 502(PRS):SUMMER68-176
BLY, R. - SEE NERUDA, P. & C. VALLEJO
BLYTH, A. COLIN DAVIS.
617(TLS):8DEC72-1513
BLYTH, H. CARO.
617(TLS):6OCT72-1205
BO, D. - SEE PERSIUS
BOARDMAN, J. ARCHAIC GREEK GEMS.*
R. HIGGINS, 39:MAY69-405
J.J. POLLITT, 124:SEP70-24
BOARDMAN, J. ENGRAVED GEMS.*
J.J. POLLITT, 124:SEP70-24
BOASE, A.M., ED. THE POETRY OF FRANCE.*
(VOL 4)
J.A. DUNCAN, 402(MLR):JAN71-194
BOASE, T.S.R. ST. FRANCIS OF ASSISI.
E.A. LEBANO, 399(MLJ):MAR70-217
BOATRIGHT, M.C. & W.A. OWENS. TALES FROM
THE DERRICK FLOOR.
W. GARD, 584(SWR):WINTER71-91
BOATWRIGHT, H. - SEE IVES, C.
BOATWRIGHT, J. - SEE CARTER, T.H.
BOBROWSKI, J. & H. BIENEK. SELECTED
POEMS.*
J. SYMONS, 364:FEB/MAR72-160
BOCCACCIO, G. IL CORBACCIO. (T. NUR-
MELA, ED)
A. SCAGLIONE, 545(RPH):NOV70-369
BOCCACCIO, G. THE DECAMERON. (G.H.
MC WILLIAM, TRANS)
617(TLS):17NOV72-1405
BOCHEŃSKI, J.M. & T.J. BLAKELEY, EDS.
BIBLIOGRAPHIE DER SOWJETISCHEN PHILOSO-
PHIE. (FASC 4-7)
G. MASTROIANNI, 548(RCSF):APR/JUN69-
234
BODARD, L. GREEN HELL.* (BRITISH TITLE:
MASSACRE ON THE AMAZON.)
P. ADAMS, 61:FEB72-110
S. KLAIDMAN, 440:23JAN72-10
R. LYNN, 441:12MAR72-34
B.J. MEGGERS, 561(SATR):19FEB72-70
G. PHELPS, 362:13APR72-492
453:27JAN72-38
BODARD, L. LES PLAISIRS DE L'HEXAGONE.
617(TLS):21APR72-447
BODDE, D. CHINA'S FIRST UNIFIER. (2ND
ED)
C-Y. CHENG, 485(PE&W):JUL68-220
BODE, C. MENCKEN.
639(VQR):WINTER70-XIX
BODE, C. - SEE THOREAU, H.D.
BODEA, C. THE ROMANIANS' STRUGGLE FOR
UNIFICATION, 1834-1849.
V.F. BROWN, 32:JUN71-418

BODEN, M.A. PURPOSIVE EXPLANATION IN
PSYCHOLOGY.
617(TLS):29DEC72-1579
BODINI, V. SEGNI E SIMBOLI NELLA "VIDA
ES SUEÑO."
W.M. WHITBY, 240(HR):OCT70-430
BØDKER, L. INTERNATIONAL DICTIONARY OF
REGIONAL EUROPEAN ETHNOLOGY AND FOLK-
LORE. (VOL 2)
R.M. DORSON, 650(WF):JUL68-218
BOEHM, R. - SEE HUSSERL, E.
BOEHRINGER, R. DER GENIUS DES ABEND-
LANDES.
F.G. CRONHEIM, 402(MLR):JUL71-713
BOELEN, B.J. EXISTENTIAL THINKING.
B. MURCHLAND, 484(PPR):JUN70-624
BOER, C. - SEE "THE HOMERIC HYMNS"
BOERNER, P. TAGEBUCH.
H.T. BETTERIDGE, 402(MLR):JUL71-708
W. EMMERICH, 406:SUMMER71-170
BOESCHENSTEIN, H. GERMAN LITERATURE OF
THE NINETEENTH CENTURY.*
L. JENNINGS, 406:WINTER71-407
BOESCHENSTEIN, H. GOTTFRIED KELLER.
S. POWELL, 402(MLR):JUL71-710
C. STEINER, 406:SPRING71-84
BOESIGER, W. LE CORBUSIER.
617(TLS):24NOV72-1414
BOESIGER, W. & H. GIRSBERGER. LE COR-
BUSIER, 1910-1965.*
P.H. MITARACHI, 505:APR68-226
BOETHIUS, A.M.S. [BOEZIO, S.] DE CONSOL-
ATIONE PHILOSOPHIE. (S. SIERRA, ED)
G. LARAS, 548(RCSF):JUL-SEP68-359
BOGAERT, R. BANQUES ET BANQUIERS DANS
LES CITÉS GRECQUES.*
R.J. HOPPER, 123:DEC71-422
S.C. HUMPHREYS, 303:VOL90-252
BOGAN, L. THE BLUE ESTUARIES.
W. HEYEN, 502(PRS):FALL69-323
BOGARD, T. CONTOUR IN TIME.
C. LEHMANN-HAUPT, 441:26OCT72-45
J.C. OATES, 441:29OCT72-5
BOGART, L. SILENT POLITICS.
441:19MAR72-16
BOGDAN, M. & OTHERS, EDS. DICTIONAR
ENGLEZ-ROMÂN.
P.V. VEHVILAINEN, 104:SUMMER71-271
BOGEN, J. WITTGENSTEIN'S PHILOSOPHY OF
LANGUAGE.
617(TLS):29SEP72-1153
BOGEN, N. - SEE BLAKE, W.
BOGER, L.A. THE DICTIONARY OF WORLD
POTTERY AND PORCELAIN.
617(TLS):14APR72-429
BOGGS, J.S. THE NATIONAL GALLERY OF
CANADA.
617(TLS):14JAN72-42
BOGOJAVLENSKY, M. REFLECTIONS ON NIKOLAI
GOGOL.
Y. LOURIA, 104:SUMMER71-264
BOHLÄNDER, C. & K.H. HOLLER. RECLAMS
JAZZFÜHRER.
R.T.B., 410(M&L):OCT71-428
BOHM, P. & A.V. KNEESE, EDS. THE ECONOM-
ICS OF ENVIRONMENT.
617(TLS):24MAR72-327
BÖHMER, M. UNTERSUCHUNGEN ZUR MITTEL-
HOCHDEUTSCHEN KREUZZUGSLYRIK.*
D.H. GREEN, 402(MLR):JAN71-210
BOHNE, F. - SEE BUSCH, W.
BOILEAU-DESPRÉAUX, N. OEUVRES. (VOLS
1&2) (J. VERCRUYSSE & S. MENANT, EDS)
H.T. BARNWELL, 208(FS):JUL71-333
DE BOILEU, L. RECOLLECTIONS OF LABRADOR
LIFE. (T.F. BREDIN, ED)
102(CANL):SPRING71-120

BOIME, A. THE ACADEMY AND FRENCH PAINT-
ING IN THE NINETEENTH CENTURY.*
P. GAY, 31(ASCH):AUTUMN72-660
BOLD, A. THE STATE OF THE NATION.
C. KIZER, 491:FEB72-291
BOLES, J.B. THE GREAT REVIVAL, 1787-
1805.
N.H. SONNE, 441:6AUG72-6
BOLIN, L. SPAIN: THE VITAL YEARS.
J.F. THORNING, 613:SPRING69-150
BOLINGER, D. ASPECTS OF LANGUAGE.*
R. POSNER, 545(RPH):NOV70-329
R.H. ROBINS, 361:VOL24#4-392
BÖLL, H. AUFSÄTZE, KRITIKEN, REDEN.
P. PROCHNIK, 220(GL&L):APR71-290
BOLLA, K., E. PÁLL & F. PAPP. KURS
SOVREMENNOGO RUSSKOGO JAZYKA. (F.
PAPP, ED)
C.V. CHVANY, 574(SEEJ):FALL71-358
BOLLACHER, M. DER JUNGE GOETHE UND
SPINOZA.
H.B. NISBET, 402(MLR):OCT71-943
BOLLACK, J. EMPÉDOCLE.
S. KOFMAN, 98:JUN69-525
BOLTÉ, M. & M. EASTMAN. HAUNTED NEW
ENGLAND.
H. FRANKEL, 561(SATR):25MAR72-104
BOLTON, I. THE WHIRLIGIG OF TIME.*
G. WEALES, 249(HUDR):WINTER71/72-716
BOLTON, W.F., ED. THE ENGLISH LANGUAGE.*
(VOL 1)
V.E. HANZELI, 399(MLJ):OCT70-458
BOLTON, W.F. A HISTORY OF ANGLO-LATIN
LITERATURE, 597-1066.* (VOL 1)
J. ANDRÉ, 555:VOL44FASC1-174
J.E. CROSS, 597(SN):VOL41#2-447
F.L. UTLEY, 545(RPH):NOV70-343
BOLTON, W.F. A SHORT HISTORY OF LITERARY
ENGLISH.
G. BAUER, 38:BAND87HEFT3/4-418
BOLTON, W.F. & D. CRYSTAL, EDS. THE
ENGLISH LANGUAGE. (VOL 2)
V.E. HANZELI, 399(MLJ):OCT70-458
V. SALMON, 677:VOL2-229
V.J. SCATTERGOOD, 447(N&Q):APR70-146
BOMBACI, A. THE KUFIC INSCRIPTION IN
PERSIAN VERSES IN THE COURT OF THE
ROYAL PALACE OF MAS'ŪD III AT GHAZNI.
L. GOLOMBEK, 318(JAOS):APR-JUN70-290
BOMBACI, A. - SEE FUZŪLĪ
BOMBELLES, J.T. ECONOMIC DEVELOPMENT OF
COMMUNIST YUGOSLAVIA, 1947-1964.
S. LAMED, 104:SPRING71-110
P.F. SUGAR, 575(SEER):APR71-313
BÖMER, F. P. OVIDIUS NASO, "METAMOR-
PHOSEN:" BUCH I-III - KOMMENTAR.
M.P. CUNNINGHAM, 124:DEC70-131
BONARD, O. LA PEINTURE DANS LA CRÉATION
BALZACIENNE.
H.J. HUNT, 208(FS):APR71-216
B. VANNIER, 400(MLN):MAY70-615
BONARJEE, N.B. UNDER TWO MASTERS.
N. MAXWELL, 453:23MAR72-8
BONAVIA-HUNT, N.A. HORACE THE MINSTREL.
R. ANDERSON, 415:MAR70-282
M. PLATNAUER, 123:DEC70-401
BONAVIRI, G. LA DIVINA FORESTA.
G. CARSANIGA, 270:VOL20#2-41
BOND, B. THE VICTORIAN ARMY AND THE
STAFF COLLEGE 1854-1914.
617(TLS):27OCT72-1294
BOND, D.F., COMP. A REFERENCE GUIDE TO
ENGLISH STUDIES. (2ND ED)
H.C. WOODBRIDGE, 517(PBSA):JUL-SEP71-
319
BOND, M.F. GUIDE TO THE RECORDS OF PAR-
LIAMENT.
617(TLS):7JAN72-10

BOND, R.P. THE TATLER.
617(TLS):9JUN72-654
BOND, W.H., ED. EIGHTEENTH-CENTURY
STUDIES IN HONOR OF DONALD F. HYDE.
L. HARTLEY, 517(PBSA):APR-JUN71-192
BOND, W.H. - SEE JACKSON, W.A.
BONEBAKKER, S.A. SOME EARLY DEFINITIONS
OF THE TAWRIYA AND ṢAFADĪ'S "FAḌḌ AL-
XITĀM'AN AT-TAWRIYA WA-'L-ISTIXDĀM."
J.A. BELLAMY, 318(JAOS):APR-JUN70-299
BONET, E. & OTHERS. BULLS AND BULL-
FIGHTING.
617(TLS):4AUG72-926
BONET, J. TAMBIÉN EN PALMA CRECEN LOS
NIÑOS. (V.D. DE BECK-AGULAR & H.
KURZ, EDS)
E.J. NEUGAARD, 399(MLJ):JAN70-56
BONG, B. - SEE UNDER BEKU BONG
BONGARD, W. ART AND COMMERCE.
R. KUDIELKA, 592:MAR68-160
BONHAM-CARTER, V. - SEE LAWSON, G.
BONHOEFFER, D. CHRIST THE CENTER.
R.G.K., 543:DEC69-342
BONHOEFFER, D. LETTERS AND PAPERS FROM
PRISON. (E. BETHGE, ED)
617(TLS):28JAN72-103
BONNARD, G.A. - SEE GIBBON, E.
BONNEFOY, Y. L'ARRIÈRE-PAYS.
617(TLS):21JUL72-839
BONNELL, P. & F. SEDWICK. CONVERSATION
IN GERMAN.
R.C. CLARK, 221(GQ):MAR70-307
"BONNER GELEHRTE."
G. NEUMANN, 72:BAND208HEFT3-196
BONNET, H. - SEE SAND, G.
BONNET, M. - SEE COMTE DE LAUTRÉAMONT
BONNEVILLE, H. LE POÈTE SÉVILLAN JUAN DE
SALINAS (1562?-1643).
R.O. JONES, 86(BHS):APR71-162
E.L. RIVERS, 400(MLN):MAR70-291
BONNEY, R. KEDAH 1771-1821.
617(TLS):22DEC72-1565
DE BONO, E. LATERAL THINKING.
E. EDELSON, 440:9APR72-6
BONTEMPO, J.D. - SEE UNDER DOMINGOS BON-
TEMPO, J.
VAN DEN BOOGAARD, N.H.J., ED. RONDEAUX
ET REFRAINS DU XIIE SIÈCLE AU DÉBUT DU
XIVE.
J. FOX, 382(MAE):1971/2-199
N. WILKINS, 208(FS):OCT71-442
"THE BOOK OF COUNSEL." (M.S. EDMONSON,
TRANS)
W.S. MERWIN, 453:20APR72-16
"A BOOK OF MASQUES: IN HONOR OF ALLARDYCE
NICOLL."* (T.J.B. SPENCER & S.M.
WELLS, EDS)
R.W. DENT, 570(SQ):AUTUMN68-403
"BOOK-AUCTION RECORDS." (VOL 68, 1970/
71) (G.R. DORMAN, COMP)
617(TLS):25AUG72-1004
BOON, L.P. CHAPEL ROAD.
617(TLS):11AUG72-935
DE BOOR, H., H. MOSER & C. WINKLER, EDS.
SIEBS, DEUTSCHE AUSSPRACHE. (19TH ED)
B.J. KOEKKOEK, 399(MLJ):NOV70-524
BOORMAN, H.L., ED. BIOGRAPHICAL DICTION-
ARY OF REPUBLICAN CHINA. (VOLS 3&4)
M. BERNAL, 453:23MAR72-31
617(TLS):28JAN72-90
BOORMAN, H.L., WITH R. HOWARD, EDS. BIO-
GRAPHICAL DICTIONARY OF REPUBLICAN
CHINA.* (VOLS 1&2)
M. BERNAL, 453:23MAR72-31
BOORMAN, S. JOHN TORONTO.
R.S. HARRIS, 627(UTQ):JUL70-401

BOORMAN, S.A. THE PROTRACTED GAME.
M. LINDSAY, 293(JAST):AUG70-926
639(VQR):SPRING70-LXXVI
BOOTH, A.D., ED. MACHINE TRANSLATION.
L.J. COHEN, 479(PHQ):APR70-187
BOOTH, E. & W. WINTER. BETWEEN ACTOR AND
CRITIC. (D.J. WATERMEIER, ED)
C.D. PEAVY, 27(AL):JAN72-660
BOOTH, M.R., ED. ENGLISH PLAYS OF THE
NINETEENTH CENTURY.* (VOLS 1&2)
R. DAVIES, 627(UTQ):JUL70-368
G. ROWELL, 541(RES):NOV70-531
BOOTH, S. THE BOOK CALLED HOLINSHED'S
"CHRONICLES."*
W.G. ZEEVELD, 551(RENQ):SPRING70-86
BOOTH, S. AN ESSAY ON SHAKESPEARE'S
SONNETS.
M. CHARNEY, 301(JEGP):APR71-296
D.J. PALMER, 148:WINTER70-383
C. SCHAAR, 551(RENQ):SUMMER70-198
BOOTH, W. - SEE CRANE, R.S.
BOOTON, K. QUITE BY ACCIDENT.
N. CALLENDAR, 441:1OCT72-43
BOPP, L. PSYCHOLOGIE DES FLEURS DU MAL.
(VOL 4)
G.D. SAUNDERS, 402(MLR):APR71-412
BORCHARDT, R. DER LEIDENSCHAFTLICHE
GÄRTNER.
E.A. WIRTZ, 220(GL&L):OCT70-105
BORCHERT, W. THE MAN OUTSIDE.
J.M. MORSE, 249(HUDR):AUTUMN71-540
BORD, J. & C. MYSTERIOUS BRITAIN.
617(TLS):8DEC72-1483
BORDAZ, J. TOOLS OF THE OLD AND NEW
STONE AGE.
617(TLS):31MAR72-371
BOREA, E. DOMENICHINO.
C. WHITFIELD, 90:MAY70-319
BOREL, J. SÉRAPHITA ET LE MYSTICISME
BALZACIEN. MÉDECINE ET PSYCHIATRIE
BALZACIENNES.
617(TLS):18AUG72-973
BOREL, J-P. INTRODUCCIÓN A ORTEGA Y GAS-
SET.
D. BASDEKIS, 238:SEP70-575
E. SARMIENTO, 86(BHS):OCT71-356
BOREN, H.C. THE GRACCHI.*
D. EARL, 313:VOL60-209
W.O. MOELLER, 121(CJ):DEC70-JAN71-173
BORG, S.J. - SEE "AYE D'AVIGNON"
BORGES, J.L. THE ALEPH AND OTHER STOR-
IES.* (N.T. DI GIOVANNI, WITH J.L.
BORGES, EDS & TRANS)
M. MUDRICK, 249(HUDR):SPRING71-185
BORGES, J.L. BORGES: SUS MEJORES PÁGIN-
AS. (M. ENGUÍDANOS, ED)
D.T. JAÉN, 238:DEC70-1031
BORGES, J.L. DR. BRODIE'S REPORT.
F. ALEGRÍA, 561(SATR):26FEB72-59
A. BROYARD, 441:4JAN72-35
E.R. MONEGAL, 441:7MAY72-4
E. WEEKS, 61:FEB72-107
M. WOOD, 453:1JUN72-32
J. YGLESIAS, 61:AUG72-83
BORGES, J.L. A PERSONAL ANTHOLOGY. (A.
KERRIGAN, ED)
D. HOLBROOK, 619(TC):1968/2-55
BORGES, J.L. SELECTED POEMS 1923-1967.
(N.T. DI GIOVANNI, ED)
P. ADAMS, 61:MAR72-110
F. ALEGRÍA, 561(SATR):26FEB72-59
E.R. MONEGAL, 441:7MAY72-4
M. WOOD, 453:1JUN72-32
BORGES, J.L. A UNIVERSAL HISTORY OF
INFAMY.
P. ADAMS, 61:DEC72-144

BORGES, J.L., WITH M. GUERRERO. THE
BOOK OF IMAGINARY BEINGS.* (N.T. DI
GIOVANNI, ED & TRANS)
639(VQR):SPRING70-LXX
BORI, I. & E. KÖRNER. KASSÁK IRODALMA
ÉS FESTÉSZETE.
G. RÓNAY, 270:VOL20#3-68
BORLAND, H. SWEDISH FOR STUDENTS.
A.L. RICE, 563(SS):SPRING71-193
VON BORMANN, A. NATURA LOQUITUR.
E. STOPP, 402(MLR):JAN71-222
BORNÄS, G., ED. TROIS CONTES FRANÇAIS DU
XIIIE SIÈCLE TIRÉS DU RECUEIL DES VIES
DES PÈRES.
F. LECOY, 597(SN):VOL41#2-413
BORNE, A. LE FACTEUR CHEVAL.
D. GROJNOWSKI, 98:DEC69-1111
BORNECQUE, J-H. VERLAINE PAR LUI-MÊME.
G. ZAYED, 207(FR):DEC69-342
BORNEMAN, E. SEX IM VOLKSMUND.
617(TLS):11FEB72-160
BORNITZ, H-F. HERODOT-STUDIEN.*
H.R. IMMERWAHR, 303:VOL90-207
BORNMANN, F. - SEE CALLIMACHUS
BORODINA, M.A. PROBLEMY LINGVISTIČESKOJ
GEOGRAFII.
P.F. DEMBOWSKI, 545(RPH):AUG69-97
BOROS, F. MAGYAR-CSEHSZLOVÁK KAPCSOLA-
TOK 1918-1921-BEN.
M.D. FENYO, 32:DEC71-924
BORST, C.V., ED. THE MIND/BRAIN IDENTITY
THEORY.
E. HINDESS, 518:MAY71-1
BORY, J-L. LA RÉVOLUTION DE JUILLET.
617(TLS):29SEP72-1149
BORZA, E.N. TRAVEL AND COMMUNICATIONS IN
CLASSICAL TIMES.
C.D. HAMILTON, 122:OCT71-263
BÖSCHENSTEIN, B. STUDIEN ZUR DICHTUNG
DES ABSOLUTEN.
J.L. SAMMONS, 221(GQ):MAR70-244
BOSCHINI, M. LA CARTA DEL NAVEGAR PITOR-
ESCO.
F.H., 90:APR69-231
A.S. HARRIS, 56:SPRING69-93
BOSE, A., ED. CALCUTTA ESSAYS ON SHAKE-
SPEARE.
R.H. WEST, 570(SQ):AUTUMN68-400
BOSE, B., ED. AN ANTHOLOGY OF BENGALI
WRITING.
617(TLS):8DEC72-1513
BOSE, D. THE PROBLEMS OF INDIAN SOCIETY.
F.L. NITZBERG, 293(JAST):MAY70-722
BOSE, T.C. AMERICAN SOVIET RELATIONS
1921-1933.
G. STERN, 587:OCT69-253
BOŠKOVIĆ-STULLI, M. NARODNA PREDAJA O
VLADAREVOJ TAJNI.*
P. ARANT, 292(JAF):JAN-MAR70-89
BOSKOVITS, M. TUSCAN PAINTINGS OF THE
EARLY RENAISSANCE.
592:JUL/AUG69-54
BOŠNJAK, M. SLAVENSKA INKUNABULISTIKA.
J.S.G. SIMMONS, 78(BC):AUTUMN70-394
BOSQUET, A. CONVERSATIONS WITH DALÍ.
J.K. HOBHOUSE, 58:MAR70-14
BOSQUET, A. NOTES POUR UN AMOUR.
617(TLS):21APR72-441
BOSTON, R. BRITISH CHARTISTS IN AMERICA
1839-1900.
617(TLS):22SEP72-1096
BOSWELL, J. THE CORRESPONDENCE AND OTHER
PAPERS OF JAMES BOSWELL RELATING TO THE
MAKING OF THE "LIFE OF JOHNSON."* (M.
WAINGROW, ED)
481(PQ):JUL70-331

BOTKINE, V. LETTRES SUR L'ESPAGNE. (A.
ZVIGUILSKY, ED & TRANS)
J. WEINER, 238:SEP70-580
BOTSFORD, K. DOMINGUÍN.
L. COLLINS, 441:10SEP72-44
BÖTTCHER, I. - SEE HARSDÖRFER, G.P.
BÖTTCHER, K., ED. ROMANTIK.
J.D. ZIPES, 222(GR):JAN70-75
BÖTTCHER, K. & R. SAMARIN, EDS. INTER-
NATIONALE BIBLIOGRAPHIE ZUR GESCHICHTE
DER DEUTSCHEN LITERATUR VON DEN AN-
FÄNGEN BIS ZUR GEGENWART.
K.L. BERGHAHN, 406:SUMMER71-157
BOTTIGHEIMER, K.S. ENGLISH MONEY AND
IRISH LAND.
617(TLS):10MAR72-266
BOTTINEAU, Y. NOTRE-DAME DE PARIS AND
THE SAINTE CHAPELLE.
J. BECKWITH, 39:SEP69-267
BOUBAT, E. WOMAN.
617(TLS):19MAY72-585
BOUCHARD, I. L'EXPÉRIENCE APOSTOLIQUE DE
PAUL CLAUDEL D'APRÈS SA CORRESPONDANCE.
J-C. BONENFANT, 627(UTQ):JUL70-413
BOUCHER, P. CHARLES COCHON DE LAPPARENT.
H. MITCHELL, 182:VOL23#21/22-950
DU BOUCHET, A. QUI N'EST PAS TOURNÉ VERS
NOUS.
617(TLS):21JUL72-839
BOUDREAULT, M. RYTHME ET MÉLODIE DE LA
PHRASE PARLÉE EN FRANCE ET AU QUÉBEC.
P. WRENN, 627(UTQ):JUL69-385
BOUGHNER, D.C. THE DEVIL'S DISCIPLE.*
W.A. ARMSTRONG, 551(RENQ):AUTUMN70-
333
K.J. ATCHITY, 276:SUMMER70-216
M. VALENCY, 546(RR):FEB70-56
BOUGLÉ, C. ESSAYS ON THE CASTE SYSTEM.
617(TLS):22SEP72-1119
BOUILHET, L. & L. COLET. LETTRES DE
LOUIS BOUILHET À LOUISE COLET. (M-C.
BANCQUART, ED)
P. DEGUISE, 207(FR):DEC69-344
BOULANGER, D. LA BARQUE AMIRALE.
617(TLS):21JUL72-851
BOULBY, M. HERMANN HESSE.*
G.W. FIELD, 564:SPRING69-65
BOULEZ, P. BOULEZ ON MUSIC TODAY.*
J. HARVEY, 415:JUN71-557
O.W. HENRY, 187:MAY72-286
C. ROSEN, 453:10FEB72-31
BOULGER, J.D., ED. TWENTIETH CENTURY
INTERPRETATIONS OF "THE RIME OF THE
ANCIENT MARINER."
D.V.E., 191(ELN):SEP70(SUPP)-31
BOULLE, P. EARS OF THE JUNGLE. (FRENCH
TITLE: LES OREILLES DE JUNGLE.)
A. BROYARD, 441:30NOV72-45
M. LEVIN, 441:24DEC72-14
617(TLS):2JUN72-623
BOULLÉE, E.L. ARCHITECTURE; ESSAI SUR
L'ART.
P. GUERRE, 98:NOV69-978
BOULOISEAU, M. LA RÉPUBLIQUE JACOBINE.
617(TLS):22SEP72-1113
BOULTON, J.T., ED. JOHNSON: THE CRITICAL
HERITAGE.
617(TLS):20OCT72-1241
BOULTON, J.T. - SEE BURKE, E.
BOULTON, J.T. - SEE LAWRENCE, D.H.
BOULTON, L. THE MUSIC HUNTER.
M. PETERSON, 470:MAY69-32
BOULTON, W.B. THE AMUSEMENTS OF OLD
LONDON.
617(TLS):18FEB72-199
BOUMA, J.A. - SEE PAULINUS
BOUQUET, M. SOUTH EASTERN SAIL.
617(TLS):1SEP72-1033

BOURAOUI, H.A. TREMBLÉ.
L. WELCH, 150(DR):AUTUMN70-416
BOURCIEZ, E. & J. PHONÉTIQUE FRANÇAISE.
R.W. NEWMAN, 207(FR):APR70-857
BOURDEAUX, M. PATRIARCH AND PROPHETS.
B.R. BOCIURKIW, 32:MAR71-164
BOURDEAUX, M. RELIGIOUS FERMENT IN
RUSSIA.
M. KLIMENKO, 32:JUN71-403
BOURDON, D. CHRISTO.
A. BROYARD, 441:6APR72-45
BOURGEOIS, B. L'IDÉALISME DE FICHTE.
A. MEDINA, 484(PPR):SEP69-153
DU BOURGUET, P. EARLY CHRISTIAN ART.
J. CANADAY, 441:3DEC72-90
BOURGUINA, A.M. RUSSIAN SOCIAL DEMO-
CRACY: THE MENSHEVIK MOVEMENT.*
J. BARBER, 575(SEER):APR71-320
R.C. ELWOOD, 550(RUSR):APR70-230
BOURGY, V. LE BOUFFON SUR LA SCÈNE
ANGLAISE AU XVIe SIÈCLE (C. 1495-
1594).*
J.A.B. SOMERSET, 402(MLR):OCT71-854
BOURLAND, G.W. REFUGEES FROM NOWHERE.
J. HOPPER, 661:SPRING69-105
BOURMOV, A. OEUVRES CHOISIES. (VOL 1)
G. SOTIROFF, 104:SUMMER71-291
BOURNE, K. & D.C. WATT, EDS. STUDIES IN
INTERNATIONAL HISTORY.
V. CROMWELL, 325:APR69-507
BOUTON, C. - SEE FLAUBERT, G.
BOUTON, J. BALL FOUR.*
T.R. EDWARDS, 473(PR):1971/3-330
BOVILL, E.W. THE NIGER EXPLORED.
K. FOLAYAN, 69:JUL69-314
BOWDEN, R.H. POEMS FROM ITALY.
J. SMITH, 493:WINTER70/71-363
BOWEN, C.D. FAMILY PORTRAIT.
639(VQR):AUTUMN70-CXLII
BOWEN, D. THE IDEA OF THE VICTORIAN
CHURCH.
P. GROSSKURTH, 627(UTQ):APR69-310
BOWEN, E.G. BRITAIN AND THE WESTERN SEA-
WAYS.
617(TLS):29SEP72-1168
BOWEN, J. A HISTORY OF WESTERN EDUCA-
TION. (VOL 1)
617(TLS):9JUN72-657
BOWEN, J.D., ED. INTERMEDIATE READINGS
IN TAGALOG.
H. MC KAUGHAN, 399(MLJ):MAR70-205
BOWEN, J.D. - SEE DECANEY, F.R.
BOWERING, G. THE GANGS OF KOSMOS.
D. BARBOUR, 150(DR):SPRING70-112
A. SHUCARD, 102(CANL):SPRING71-80
BOWERING, G. GEORGE, VANCOUVER.
D. FETHERLING, 606(TAMR):#57-80
BOWERING, G. AL PURDY.
D. BARBOUR, 99:MAY72-68
BOWERING, G., ED. THE STORY SO FAR.*
J.G. MOSS, 296:WINTER72-79
BOWERING, G. TOUCH.
J.L. NUGENT, 198:WINTER72-109
BOWERING, P. ALDOUS HUXLEY.*
S. DICK, 529(QQ):AUTUMN70-456
J. GINDIN, 191(ELN):DEC69-155
BOWERS, F. SCRIABIN.
G.A., 410(M&L):JUL71-311
P. BANHAM, 651(WHR):SUMMER71-277
BOWERS, F., ED. STUDIES IN BIBLIOGRAPHY.
(VOL 21)
R. DONALDSON, 354:JUN69-156
BOWERS, F., ED. STUDIES IN BIBLIOGRAPHY.
(VOL 25)
617(TLS):2JUN72-640
BOWERS, F. - SEE CRANE, S.

BOWERSOCK, G.W. GREEK SOPHISTS IN THE
ROMAN EMPIRE.*
T.R.S. BROUGHTON, 487:WINTER70-359
A.F. NORMAN, 122:APR71-124
R.A. PACK, 24:APR71-337
BOWES, P. CONSCIOUSNESS AND FREEDOM.
E. DEUTSCH, 311(JP):20APR72-224
BOWETT, D.W. THE SEARCH FOR PEACE.
617(TLS):14APR72-424
BOWIE, T. - SEE WARNER, L.
BOWLES, C. A VIEW FROM NEW DELHI.
N.D. PALMER, 293(JAST):FEB70-477
BOWLES, P. THE THICKET OF SPRING.
V. THOMSON, 453:18MAY72-35
BOWLES, P. WITHOUT STOPPING.
A. BROYARD, 441:21MAR72-43
A. PRYCE-JONES, 440:26MAR72-12
C.T. SAMUELS, 441:9APR72-32
V. THOMSON, 453:18MAY72-35
442(NY):25MAR72-131
617(TLS):13OCT72-1227
BOWLES, P. - SEE MRABET, M.
BOWLEY, A.H. A MEMOIR OF PROFESSOR SIR
ARTHUR BOWLEY (1869-1957) AND HIS
FAMILY.
617(TLS):19MAY72-584
BOWMAN, F.P. - SEE CONSTANT, A-L.
BOWMAN, F.P. - SEE LÉVI, E.
BOWNESS, A. CONTEMPORARY BRITISH PAINT-
ING.
W.C. LIPKE, 54:DEC69-402
BOWNESS, A. MODERN EUROPEAN ART.
617(TLS):15SEP72-1044
BOWNESS, A. - SEE "ALAN DAVIE"
BOWRA, C.M. HOMER.
617(TLS):23JUN72-720
BOWYER, C. THE FLYING ELEPHANTS.
617(TLS):1DEC72-1469
BOXER, A. NO ADDRESS.
R.G. ADAMS, 198:SUMMER72-122
BOXER, C.R. THE PORTUGUESE SEABORNE
EMPIRE, 1415-1825.*
639(VQR):SUMMER70-CVI
BOXILL, R. SHAW AND THE DOCTORS.*
D.R. BECKER, 572:MAY69-82
BOYANCÉ, P. - SEE EPICURUS
BOYCE, D.G. ENGLISHMEN AND IRISH TROUB-
LES.
617(TLS):29SEP72-1148
BOYD, A. HOLY WAR IN BELFAST.
O.D. EDWARDS, 441:9APR72-7
BOYD, A. THE RISE OF THE IRISH TRADE
UNIONS 1729-1970.
617(TLS):14APR72-416
BOYD, A.F. ASPECTS OF THE RUSSIAN NOVEL.
617(TLS):16JUN72-680
BOYD, J.D. THE FUNCTION OF MIMESIS AND
ITS DECLINE.*
S.L. BARTKY, 290(JAAC):FALL69-109
R. BOYLE, 613:SUMMER69-295
G.S. ROUSSEAU, 481(PQ):JAN70-134
BOYD, J.P. - SEE JEFFERSON, T.
BOYER, F. LE MONDE DES ARTS EN ITALIE
ET LA FRANCE DE LA RÉVOLUTION ET DE
L'EMPIRE.*
J. SEZNEC, 208(FS):APR71-210
BOYERS, R. & R. ORRILL, EDS. LAING AND
ANTI-PSYCHIATRY.
617(TLS):3NOV72-1303
BOYLE, A. ONLY THE WIND WILL LISTEN.
H. GREENE, 362:2NOV72-565
617(TLS):17NOV72-1397
BOYLE, H.J. THE GREAT CANADIAN NOVEL.
M. LEVIN, 441:26NOV72-38
BOYLE, J.A., ED. THE CAMBRIDGE HISTORY
OF IRAN.* (VOL 5)
K.A. LUTHER, 318(JAOS):OCT-DEC70-572

BOYLE, K. TESTAMENT FOR MY STUDENTS.
E. NELSON, 590:FALL70-42
M.L. ROSENTHAL, 491:NOV71-99
BOYNTON, L. THE ELIZABETHAN MILITIA,
1558-1683.
H.J. WEBB, 551(RENQ):SUMMER70-196
BOZZO, C.D. CORPUS DELLA SCULTURA ALTO-
MEDIEVALE IV LA DIOCESE DI GENOVA.
T.S.R. BOASE, 90:JAN69-37
BRAATEN, C.E. - SEE TILLICH, P.
BRABHAM, J., WITH E. HAYWARD. WHEN THE
FLAG DROPS.
J. DURSO, 441:3DEC72-40
BRACHER, K.D. THE GERMAN DICTATORSHIP.*
G. BARRACLOUGH, 453:19OCT72-37
K. GLASER, 396(MODA):SUMMER71-331
BRACKEN, H.M. THE EARLY RECEPTION OF
BERKELEY'S IMMATERIALISM 1710-1733.
E. RONCHETTI, 548(RCSF):APR-JUN68-246
BRADBROOK, M.C. LITERATURE IN ACTION.
J.G. MOSS, 296:FALL72-90
617(TLS):29DEC72-1578
BRADBROOK, M.C. SHAKESPEARE'S PRIMITIVE
ART.
L.F. BALL, 570(SQ):AUTUMN69-479
BRADBROOK, M.C. THE TRAGIC PAGEANT OF
"TIMON OF ATHENS."
L.F. BALL, 570(SQ):AUTUMN69-478
BRADBURY, F. HISTORY OF OLD SHEFFIELD
PLATE AND OF THE ANTIQUE SILVER AND
WHITE OR BRITANNIA METAL TRADE.
C. OMAN, 39:JUN69-487
BRADBURY, M. THE SOCIAL CONTEXT OF
MODERN ENGLISH LITERATURE.*
G. GERSH, 99:SEP72-33
BRADBURY, M. & OTHERS, EDS. THE PENGUIN
COMPANION TO AMERICAN LITERATURE.
N. BALAKIAN, 441:28JAN72-42
R. PLANT, 441:5NOV72-31
BRADBURY, M. & D. PALMER, EDS. METAPHYS-
ICAL POETRY.
E. MINER, 568(SCN):SPRING71-13
BRADDY, H. HAMLET'S WOUNDED NAME.
A.L. HASTINGS, 570(SQ):SPRING68-186
BRADDY, H. MEXICO AND THE OLD SOUTHWEST.
J.T. BRATCHER, 584(SWR):SUMMER71-298
BRADFORD, E. CLEOPATRA.
617(TLS):14JAN72-49
BRADING, D.A. MINERS AND MERCHANTS IN
BOURBON MEXICO 1763-1810.
617(TLS):7JUL72-782
BRADLEY, H. AND MISS CARTER WORE PINK.
617(TLS):28JAN72-89
BRADLEY, J.F.N. CZECHOSLOVAKIA.
617(TLS):14JAN72-41
BRADSHAW, G. SOUFFLÉS QUICHES MOUSSES &
THE RANDOM EGG.
N. MAGID, 440:13FEB72-5
BRADSHAW, K. & D. PRING. PARLIAMENT AND
CONGRESS.
617(TLS):7APR72-392
BRADSTREET, A. POEMS OF ANNE BRADSTREET.
(R. HUTCHINSON, ED)
W.J. SCHEICK, 165:FALL72-204
BRADY, J. L'OEUVRE DE EMILE ZOLA, ROMAN
SUR LES ARTS.
R.T. DENOMMÉ, 207(FR):DEC69-339
BRAEM, H.M. EUGENE O'NEILL. EDWARD
ALBEE.
K. TETZELI VON ROSADOR, 72:BAND208
HEFT1-49
BRAET, H. L'ACCUEIL FAIT AU SYMBOLISME
EN BELGIQUE, 1885-1900.*
J. MATTHEWS, 546(RR):OCT70-230
BRAGG, M. JOSH LAWTON.
J.G. FARRELL, 362:13JUL72-57
617(TLS):14JUL72-793

BRAGG, M. A PLACE IN ENGLAND.* THE
NERVE.*
F.P.W. MC DOWELL, 659:SUMMER72-361
BRAGG, M. WITHOUT A CITY WALL.
K.J. ATCHITY, 340(KR):1969/5-675
BRAHMS, J. FOLK SONGS FOR WOMEN'S
VOICES. (V. GOTWALS & P. KEPPLER, EDS)
412:NOV71-364
BRAILSFORD, D. SPORT AND SOCIETY: ELIZA-
BETH TO ANNE.
N. FARMER, JR., 551(RENQ):WINTER70-
461
BRAIMAH, J.A. & J.R. GOODY. SALAGA.
R.G. THOMAS, 69:OCT69-425
BRAIN, R. BANGWA KINSHIP AND MARRIAGE.
617(TLS):28JUL72-874
BRAIN, R. & A. POLLOCK. BANGWA FUNERARY
SCULPTURE.
E.H. GOMBRICH, 453:4MAY72-35
BRAINE, J. THE QUEEN OF A DISTANT COUN-
TRY.
D.A.N. JONES, 362:26OCT72-557
617(TLS):27OCT72-1273
BRAINE, J. THE VIEW FROM TOWER HILL.*
(BRITISH TITLE: STAY WITH ME TILL
MORNING.)
F.P.W. MC DOWELL, 659:SUMMER72-361
BRAITHWAITE, D. FAIRGROUND ARCHITECTURE.
W. KIDNEY, 505:SEP68-184
BRAITHWAITE, E. MASKS.
E.J., 619(TC):1968/3-53
BRAITHWAITE, E.R. RELUCTANT NEIGHBORS.
O. COOMBS, 441:17SEP72-4
617(TLS):13OCT72-1220
BRÄKER, U. THE LIFE STORY AND REAL
ADVENTURES OF THE POOR MAN OF TOGGEN-
BURG.
E. MASON, 402(MLR):OCT71-945
BRAMELD, T. JAPAN.
G.W. HEWES, 293(JAST):FEB70-451
BRAMSTED, E.K. GERMANY.
617(TLS):15SEP72-1055
BRANCH, E.M. - SEE TWAIN, M.
BRANCO, T.M.S.D. - SEE UNDER SCHEDEL DE
CASTELLO BRANCO, T.M.
BRAND, S. - SEE "THE LAST WHOLE EARTH
CATALOG"
BRANDABUR, E. A SCRUPULOUS MEANNESS.
M. SHECHNER, 329(JJQ):WINTER71-280
BRANDEL, M. THE MAN WHO LIKED WOMEN.
M. LEVIN, 441:5NOV72-40
442(NY):11NOV72-190
VON BRANDENSTEIN, C.G. NARRATIVES FROM
THE NORTH WEST OF WESTERN AUSTRALIA IN
THE NGARLUMA AND JINDJIPARNDI LAN-
GUAGES.
A. CAPELL, 67:MAY71-140
BRANDES, D. DIE TSCHECHEN UNTER DEUT-
SCHEM PROTEKTORAT. (VOL 1)
H. HANAK, 575(SEER):JAN71-163
S.Z. PECH, 32:MAR71-175
BRANDIS, T. MITTELHOCHDEUTSCHE, MITTEL-
NIEDERDEUTSCHE UND MITTELNIEDERLÄND-
ISCHE MINNEREDEN.*
C.F. BAYERSCHMIDT, 222(GR):JAN70-63
H. BUSSMANN, 182:VOL23#17/18-788
O. SAYCE, 402(MLR):APR71-437
BRANDON, J.R., ED. ON THRONES OF GOLD.
639(VQR):AUTUMN70-CLVI
BRANDON, J.R. THEATRE IN SOUTHEAST ASIA.
MAUNG HTIN AUNG, 397(MD):FEB68-438
BRANDON, O. THE PASTOR AND HIS MINISTRY.
617(TLS):31MAR72-378
BRANDT, E., ED. ANTIKE GEMMEN IN DEUT-
SCHEN SAMMLUNGEN.* (VOL 1, PT 1)
J. BOARDMAN, 303:VOL90-264

37

BRANDT, T.O. DIE VIELDEUTIGKEIT BERTOLT
BRECHTS.*
  G.E. BAHR, 221(GQ):MAR70-294
BRANDT, W. DIE ERZÄHLKONZEPTION HEIN-
RICHS VON VELDEKE IN DER "ENEIDE."
  D.H. GREEN, 402(MLR):OCT71-926
BRANFMAN, F., COMP. VOICES FROM THE
PLAIN OF JARS.
  N. CHOMSKY, 561(SATR):2SEP72-49
  G. EMERSON, 453:10AUG72-19
BRANIGAN, K. THE FOUNDATIONS OF PALATIAL
CRETE.
  J.W. GRAHAM, 124:DEC70-125
  C. RENFREW, 123:DEC71-434
BRANNEN, N.S. SŌKA GAKKAI.
  J-K-C. OH, 293(JAST):FEB70-451
BRANNER, R., ED. CHARTRES CATHEDRAL.
  J. HARVEY, 90:AUG70-548
BRANSON, D. JOHN FIELD AND CHOPIN.
  W. SARGEANT, 442(NY):20MAY72-127
  617(TLS):26MAY72-611
BRANT, I. IMPEACHMENT.
  H. MITGANG, 561(SATR):13MAY72-83
  E.M. YODER, JR., 440:7MAY72-1
BRANT, S. DAS NARRENSCHIFF. (2ND ED)
(M. LEMMER, ED)
  E.H. ZEYDEL, 221(GQ):JAN70-115
BRASCH, H. BEWAHRTE HEIMAT. (G.P. LAND-
MANN, ED)
  F.G. CRONHEIM, 402(MLR):JUL71-713
BRASHER, T.L. WHITMAN AS EDITOR OF THE
BROOKLYN "DAILY EAGLE."*
  C. GOHDES, 579(SAQ):SUMMER71-433
BRASSAÏ. PICASSO AND COMPANY.*
  D. HALL, 39:MAY69-404
BRATCHER, J.T. & L.H. KENDALL, JR. A
SUPPRESSED CRITIQUE OF WISE'S SWINBURNE
TRANSACTIONS.
  617(TLS):10MAR72-284
BRATHWAITE, E. THE DEVELOPMENT OF CREOLE
SOCIETY IN JAMAICA 1770-1820.
  617(TLS):30JUN72-745
BRATHWAITE, E. ISLANDS.*
  D. GRANT, 148:SUMMER70-186
  639(VQR):SPRING70-LII
BRATHWAITE, E. MASKS.
  D. GRANT, 148:SUMMER70-186
  H. SERGEANT, 175:SPRING69-33
BRATHWAITE, E. RIGHTS OF PASSAGE.*
  D. GRANT, 148:SUMMER70-186
BRATUS, B.V. THE FORMATION AND EXPRES-
SIVE USE OF DIMINUTIVES.*
  O. FRINK, 574(SEEJ):SUMMER71-236
BRAUCHER, B. PROMISES TO KEEP.
  J. DURSO, 441:3DEC72-44
BRAUDEL, F. CIVILISATION MATÉRIELLE ET
CAPITALISME. (VOL 1)
  C.J. BEYER, 207(FR):DEC69-373
BRAUDEL, F. THE MEDITERRANEAN. (VOL 1)
  J.H. PLUMB, 441:31DEC72-8
BRAUDY, L. NARRATIVE FORM IN HISTORY
AND FICTION.
  M.C. BATTESTIN, 401(MLQ):DEC70-508
  J.A. DUSSINGER, 301(JEGP):OCT71-676
  S. GUBAR, 191(ELN):JUN71-331
  676(YR):WINTER71-XVIII
BRAUDY, L. JEAN RENOIR.
  A. SARRIS, 441:3SEP72-18
BRAUER, G.C., JR. JUDAEA WEEPING.
  H.R. MOEHRING, 124:JAN71-172
BRAUER, J.C., ED. THE IMPACT OF THE
CHURCH UPON ITS CULTURE.
  G.M., 477:SUMMER69-429
BRAUER, J.C. - SEE TILLICH, P.
BRAUKÄMPER, U. DER EINFLUSS DES ISLAM
AUF DIE GESCHICHTE UND KULTURENTWICK-
LUNG ADAMAUAS.
  P. KRÜGER, 182:VOL23#4-181

BRAULT, G.J. EARLY BLAZON.
  617(TLS):18AUG72-966
BRAULT, J. MÉMOIRE.
  J-L. MAJOR, 627(UTQ):JUL69-478
BRAULT, J. & B. LACROIX - SEE GARNEAU,
H.S-D.
BRAUN, E. - SEE MEYERHOLD, V.E.
BRAUN, H. AN INTRODUCTION TO ENGLISH
MEDIEVAL ARCHITECTURE.
  J. BECKWITH, 39:SEP69-267
  S. BLUTMAN, 505:APR69-186
BRAUN, K. & P. IDEN, EDS. NEUES
DEUTSCHES THEATER.
  617(TLS):26MAY72-611
BRAUN, L. DIE CANTICA DES PLAUTUS.
  F. LASSERRE, 182:VOL23#6-295
BRAUN, R.J. TEACHERS AND POWER.
  M.D. FANTINI, 441:28MAY72-3
  J. HERNDON, 561(SATR):29JUL72-64
BRAUNECK, M., ED. DAS DEUTSCHE DRAMA VOM
EXPRESSIONISMUS BIS ZUR GEGENWART.
  V. SANDER, 406:FALL71-300
BRAUNECK, M., ED. SPIELTEXTE DER WANDER-
BÜHNE. (VOLS 1&3)
  E.A. METZGER, 301(JEGP):JUL71-496
BRAUTIGAN, R. THE ABORTION.*
  W.H. PRITCHARD, 249(HUDR):SUMMER71-
  360
BRAUTIGAN, R. IN WATERMELON SUGAR.
A CONFEDERATE GENERAL FROM BIG SUR.*
  M. FELD, 364:AUG/SEP71-150
BRAUTIGAN, R. REVENGE OF THE LAWN.*
  J.G. FARRELL, 362:13JUL72-57
  J. HENDIN, 441:16JAN72-7
BRAUTIGAN, R. ROMMEL DRIVES ON DEEP
INTO EGYPT.*
  639(VQR):AUTUMN70-CXXXIV
BRAUTIGAN, R. TROUT FISHING IN AMERICA.
  M. FELD, 364:AUG/SEP71-150
  K. SEIB, 145(CRIT):VOL13#2-63
BRAVO, F. THE OPERA MEDICINALIA.
  L.S. THOMPSON, 263:APR-JUN71-222
BRAVO VILLASANTE, C. UNA VIDA ROMÁNTICA -
LA AVELLANEDA.
  191(ELN):SEP70(SUPP)-153
BRAY, C. SHADOW OF A RUNNING MAN.
  J. HUNTER, 362:21DEC72-869
BRAYBROOKE, D. THREE TESTS FOR DEMOCRA-
CY.
  T.E. FLANAGAN, 150(DR):SPRING70-143
BRAZEAU, J.R. AN OUTLINE OF CONTEMPORARY
FRENCH CANADIAN LITERATURE.
  A. SIROIS, 296:SPRING72-77
BREATHNACH, B. FOLK MUSIC AND DANCES OF
IRELAND.
  617(TLS):17MAR72-309
BRECHER, E.M. & OTHERS. LICIT AND ILLI-
CIT DRUGS.
  561(SATR):25NOV72-72
BRECHER, J. STRIKE!
  S.P. LEE & P. PASSELL, 441:20AUG72-4
  R.R. LINGEMAN, 441:23AUG72-43
BRECHER, M. THE FOREIGN POLICY SYSTEM
OF ISRAEL.
  617(TLS):1SEP72-1028
BRECHER, M. INDIA AND WORLD POLITICS.*
  A. STEIN, 293(JAST):NOV69-181
BRÉCHON, R. LE SURRÉALISME.
  617(TLS):21APR72-442
BRECHT, B. ÜBER REALISMUS. (W. HECHT,
ED)
  617(TLS):29SEP72-1169
BRECKENRIDGE, J.D. LIKENESS.
  G.M.A. HANFMANN, 124:NOV70-89
  127:SUMMER71-424
BREDIN, T.F. - SEE DE BOILEU, L.

BREDIUS, A. REMBRANDT: THE COMPLETE
EDITION OF THE PAINTINGS.* (3RD ED
REV BY H. GERSON)
A. DORN, 58:DEC69/JAN70-16
G. MARTIN, 39:SEP69-266
A. WERNER, 340(KR):1970/1-121
C. WHITFIELD, 592:JUL/AUG69-50
BRÉE, G. CAMUS AND SARTRE.
A. MEMMI, 441:13AUG72-6
442(NY):30SEP72-127
BRÉE, G. MARCEL PROUST AND DELIVERANCE
FROM TIME. (2ND ED)
L.B. PRICE, 207(FR):MAR70-686
C. SAVAGE, 219(GAR):WINTER69-553
BRÉE, G. THE WORLD OF MARCEL PROUST.
M.J. FRIEDMAN, 593:SPRING71-87
BRÉE, G. & P. SOLOMON, EDS. CHOIX
D'ESSAIS DU VINGTIÈME SIÈCLE.
J. CRUICKSHANK, 208(FS):APR71-242
BREEDEN, E.M. CALL BACK THE LOVELY
APRIL.
617(TLS):9JUN72-667
BREGLIA, L. ROMAN IMPERIAL COINS.*
M.H. CRAWFORD, 313:VOL60-265
R.J. ROWLAND, JR., 121(CJ):OCT-NOV70-
90
BRÉHIER, E. THE NINETEENTH CENTURY.
M.B.M., 543:SEP69-124
BREIN, F. - SEE JÜTHNER, J.
BREKLE, H.E. & L. LIPKA, EDS. WORTBIL-
DUNG, SYNTAX UND MORPHOLOGIE.
R.W. ZANDVOORT, 179(ES):FEB70-77
BRELICH, A. PAIDES E PARTHENOI. (VOL 1)
J. FONTENROSE, 124:JAN71-165
BREMER, J.M. HAMARTIA.
L. GOLDEN, 122:APR71-125
G.M. KIRKWOOD, 24:OCT71-711
D. DE MONTMOLLIN, 487:AUTUMN70-277
BRENCHLEY, D.R. & C. SHRIMPTON, COMPS.
TRAVEL IN THE TURNPIKE AGE.
W.B. STEPHENS, 325:APR70-83
BREND, R.M. A TAGMEMIC ANALYSIS OF
MEXICAN SPANISH CLAUSES.*
W.H. HAVERKATE, 361:VOL24#1-75
BRENNAN, B.P. WILLIAM JAMES.*
D.C. MATHUR, 484(PPR):SEP69-143
BRENNAN, M.M., ED & TRANS. BABIO: A
TWELFTH CENTURY PROFANE COMEDY.*
M.P. CUNNINGHAM, 399(MLJ):JAN70-47
C. WITKE, 545(RPH):FEB70-351
BRENNER, A. THE WIND THAT SWEPT MEXICO.
617(TLS):21JAN72-62
BRENNER, H. DIE KUNSTPOLITIK DES NATION-
ALSOZIALISMUS. AKTIONEN, BEKENNTNISSE,
PERSPEKTIVEN. ZUR TRADITION DER SOZ-
IALISTISCHEN LITERATUR IN DEUTSCHLAND.
L. RICHARD, 98:AUG-SEP69-749
BRENNER, H. - SEE LACIS, A.
BRENTANO, C. BRIEFE AN EMILIE LINDER,
MIT ZWEI BRIEFEN AN APOLLONIA DIEPEN-
BROCK UND MARIANNE VON WILLEMER. (W.
FRÜHWALD, ED)
E. STOPP, 402(MLR):APR71-461
BRERETON, G. PRINCIPLES OF TRAGEDY.
H.T. BARNWELL, 208(FS):JUL71-361
N. DENNY, 541(RES):AUG70-379
S.G. PUTT, 175:AUTUMN69-107
D.D. RAPHAEL, 447(N&Q):APR70-157
BRERO, C. & R. GANDOLFO - SEE PACOTTO, G.
BRESKY, D. THE ART OF ANATOLE FRANCE.
J.A. WALKER, 627(UTQ):JUL70-351
BRESLIN, J.E. WILLIAM CARLOS WILLIAMS.*
W. SUTTON, 27(AL):NOV71-472
BRESSY, N. SAUVAGINE.
A. BROYARD, 441:18APR72-49
M. LEVIN, 441:21MAY72-31
BRETNOR, R. DECISIVE WARFARE.
R.J. LENG, 385(MQR):WINTER72-64

BRETON, A. & P. SOUPAULT. LES CHAMPS
MAGNÉTIQUES. (NEW ED)
617(TLS):21APR72-442
BRETÓN DE LOS HERREROS, M. OBRA DISPER-
SA. (VOL 1) (J.M. DÍEZ TABOADA & J.M.
ROZAS, EDS)
191(ELN):SEP69(SUPP)-150
BRETT. FOR THE WEST COAST.
R. GIBBS, 198:SUMMER72-129
BRETT, C.E.B., COMP. HISTORIC BUILDINGS,
GROUPS OF BUILDINGS, AREAS OF ARCHI-
TECTURAL IMPORTANCE IN THE GLENS OF
ANTRIM.
617(TLS):15SEP72-1050
BRETT, G. KINETIC ART.
C. BARRETT, 592:JUL/AUG68-57
BRETT-EVANS, D., ED. MAKERS OF THE
TWENTIETH CENTURY.
H. RIDLEY, 220(GL&L):APR71-289
BREUNIG, L.C. GUILLAUME APOLLINAIRE.
S. BATES, 399(MLJ):NOV70-543
BREUNIG, L.C. - SEE APOLLINAIRE, G.
BREUNINGER, M. FUNKTION UND WERTUNG DES
ROMANS IM FRÜHVIKTORIANISCHEN ROMAN.
K. TETZELI VON ROSADOR, 72:BAND208
HEFT4/6-396
BREWER, J.T. & W.W. MOELLEKEN. DEUTSCHE
PERSPEKTIVEN.
K. KEETON, 399(MLJ):JAN70-33
BREWSTER, D. THE HEART'S GROWN BRUTAL.
V. CUNNINGHAM, 362:12OCT72-482
G. DAVIS, 441:17SEP72-48
617(TLS):6OCT72-1185
BREWSTER, E. PASSAGE OF SUMMER.*
T. MARSHALL, 529(QQ):SUMMER70-294
BREWSTER, E. SUNRISE NORTH.
B. BARTLETT, 198:FALL72-118
BREY MARIÑO, M. - SEE ALFONSO EL SABIO
BRÉZILLON, M. DICTIONNAIRE DE LA PRÉ-
HISTOIRE.
P. AUBERY, 207(FR):APR70-853
BRIAN, D. MURDERERS AND OTHER FRIENDLY
PEOPLE.
J.D. O'HARA, 440:30JAN72-13
BRICE, G. DESCRIPTION DE LA VILLE DE
PARIS ET DE TOUT CE QU'ELLE CONTIENT DE
PLUS REMARQUABLE. (P. CODET, ED)
617(TLS):25AUG72-989
BRICHANT, C., ED. FRENCH FOR THE HUM-
ANITIES.
R.E. LEAKE, JR., 399(MLJ):OCT70-457
BRICHANT, C.D. CHARLES DE GAULLE.
R. MERKER, 207(FR):DEC69-372
BRICKNER, R.P. BRINGING DOWN THE HOUSE.
E. BAKER, 441:30JAN72-6
T. LASK, 441:4FEB72-33
BRIDBURY, A.R. HISTORIANS AND THE OPEN
SOCIETY.
617(TLS):24NOV72-1437
BRIDENBAUGH, C. & R. NO PEACE BEYOND THE
LINE.
C. MAC INNES, 441:21MAY72-6
617(TLS):29DEC72-1584
BRIDGELAND, M. PIONEER WORK WITH MAL-
ADJUSTED CHILDREN.
617(TLS):7JAN72-9
BRIDGES-ADAMS, W. A BRIDGES-ADAMS LETTER
BOOK. (R. SPEAIGHT, ED)
617(TLS):6OCT72-1205
BRIDGMAN, R. GERTRUDE STEIN IN PIECES.*
M.J. HOFFMAN, 27(AL):NOV71-467
BRIDGWATER, P. NIETZSCHE IN ANGLOSAXONY.
617(TLS):24NOV72-1432
BRIDSON, D.G. THE FILIBUSTER.
617(TLS):15DEC72-1535

BRIEGER, P., M. MEISS & C.S. SINGLETON.
ILLUMINATED MANUSCRIPTS OF "THE
DIVINE COMEDY."
L.E. BOYLE, 363:MAY70-108
BRIEGLEB, K. - SEE HEINE, H.
BRIET, S. MADAME RIMBAUD.
S.I. LOCKERBIE, 208(FS):JUL71-344
BRIGANTI, G. GASPAR VAN WITTEL, E L'ORI-
GINE DELLA VEDUTA SETTECENTESCA.
W. BARCHAM, 54:JUN69-189
BRIGG, E. STAND UP AND FIGHT.
617(TLS):25AUG72-987
BRIGGS, A. 1851.
617(TLS):14JUL72-826
BRIGGS, P. 200,000,000 YEARS BENEATH THE
SEA.
441:6FEB72-40
BRIGGS, P. WILL CALIFORNIA FALL INTO THE
SEA?
561(SATR):28OCT72-83
BRIGGS, S. & A., EDS. CAP AND BELL.
Q. BELL, 362:23NOV72-714
BRIGHAM, B. HEAVED FROM THE EARTH.
D. ALLEN, 491:JUL72-235
F. MORAMARCO, 651(WHR):SUMMER71-279
BRIGHT, W., ED. SOCIOLINGUISTICS.
A.D. SHVEITSER, 269(IJAL):JUL69-278
BRIGHT, W., ED. STUDIES IN CALIFORNIAN
LINGUISTICS.
K.V. TEETER, 361:VOL24#4-407
BRIGHTFIELD, M.F. VICTORIAN ENGLAND IN
ITS NOVELS (1840-1870).
R.A. COLBY, 445(NCF):DEC69-356
K. GRAHAM, 541(RES):NOV70-530
BRIGNANO, R.C. RICHARD WRIGHT.*
J.R. BRYER, 27(AL):JAN72-672
L.J. BUDD, 579(SAQ):WINTER71-131
BRILLAT-SAVARIN, J.A. THE PHYSIOLOGY OF
TASTE.* (M.F.K. FISHER, ED & TRANS)
R.S. PIRIE & R. SENNETT, 441:6FEB72-
27
442(NY):22JAN72-100
BRILLIANT, R. THE ARCH OF SEPTIMIUS
SEVERUS IN THE ROMAN FORUM.
A.G. MC KAY, 124:JAN71-170
BRINDLE, R.S. - SEE UNDER SMITH BRINDLE,
R.
BRINDLEY, J.F. FRENCH FIGHTERS OF WORLD
WAR TWO. (VOL 1)
617(TLS):11FEB72-165
617(TLS):28JUL72-900
BRINGMANN, K. UNTERSUCHUNGEN ZUM SPÄTEN
CICERO.
F. LASSERRE, 182:VOL23#19/20-873
BRINKERHOFF, D.M. A COLLECTION OF
SCULPTURE IN CLASSICAL AND EARLY
CHRISTIAN ANTIOCH.
J.A. GAERTNER, 124:APR71-273
BRINKLEY, G.A. THE VOLUNTEER ARMY AND
ALLIED INTERVENTION IN SOUTH RUSSIA,
1917-1921.
R.S. FELDMAN, 587:OCT68-265
BRINKMANN, R. ARNOLD SCHÖNBERG: DIE
KLAVIERSTUCKE OP. II.
R.T.B., 410(M&L):APR71-206
BRINKMANN, R.D. KEINER WEISS MEHR.
T. WEYR, 19(AGR):VOL35#4-31
BRINNIN, J.M. SKIN DIVING IN THE VIRGINS
AND OTHER POEMS.*
R.B. SHAW, 491:MAR72-342
BRINNIN, J.M. THE SWAY OF THE GRAND
SALOON.*
E.S. TURNER, 362:13JUL72-56
A. WAUGH, 441:9JAN72-30
617(TLS):4AUG72-920
BRINNIN, J.M. - SEE STEIN, G.
BRINNIN, J.M. & B. READ, EDS. THE
MODERN POETS.
J. ATLAS, 491:DEC71-169

BRINSMEAD, E. THE HISTORY OF THE PIANO-
FORTE.
R. ANDERSON, 415:AUG70-808
BRION-GUERRY, L. L'ANNÉE 1913.
617(TLS):19MAY72-568
BRISSENDEN, R.F., ED. STUDIES IN THE
EIGHTEENTH CENTURY.
D.I.B. SMITH, 627(UTQ):JAN70-188
BRISSMAN, B. SWING LOW.
M. LEVIN, 441:10SEP72-40
BRISTER, C. THIS IS MY KINGDOM.
617(TLS):6OCT72-1193
BRISTOL, R.P. SUPPLEMENT TO CHARLES
EVANS' AMERICAN BIBLIOGRAPHY.
E. WOLF 2D, 517(PBSA):APR-JUN71-186
"BRITAIN 1972."
617(TLS):31MAR72-378
BRITTAIN, F. IT'S A DON'S LIFE.
617(TLS):18AUG72-962
BRITTEN, B. & I. HOLST - SEE PURCELL, H.
BRITTON, K. PHILOSOPHY AND THE MEANING
OF LIFE.*
L. HOLBOROW, 393(MIND):OCT70-634
BROAD, R. & R.J. JARRETT. COMMUNITY
EUROPE TODAY.
617(TLS):28JUL72-861
BROADHEAD, H.D. TRAGICA.*
H. LLOYD-JONES, 123:DEC70-304
D. YOUNG, 487:WINTER70-356
BROADIE, F. AN APPROACH TO DESCARTES'S
"MEDITATIONS."
T. KEEFE, 518:JAN71-6
H.W. SCHNEIDER, 319:APR72-223
BROCH, H. BERGROMAN. (F. KRESS & H.A.
MAIER, EDS)
617(TLS):25FEB72-226
"HERMANN BROCH - DANIEL BRODY: BRIEF-
WECHSEL 1930-1951." (B. HACK & M.
KLEISS, EDS)
617(TLS):25FEB72-226
BROCHIER, J-J. - SEE NIZAN, P.
BROCK, P. PACIFISM IN EUROPE TO 1914.
617(TLS):24NOV72-1413
BROCK, P. RADICAL PACIFISTS IN ANTE-
BELLUM AMERICA.
42(AR):SUMMER69-266
BROCKETT, O.G. HISTORY OF THE THEATRE.
A.C. HARRISON, 583:WINTER69-183
"BROCKHAUS ENZYKLOPÄDIE." (VOL 8)
K.E.H. LIEDTKE, 399(MLJ):OCT70-454
BROCKLEHURST, B. RESPONSE TO MUSIC.*
B. RAINBOW, 415:MAY71-447
BRODER, D.S. THE PARTY'S OVER.
E. DREW, 441:4JUN72-3
T. LEWIS, 440:12MAR72-12
BRODEUR, P. DOWNSTREAM.
A. BROYARD, 441:23MAR72-45
R.E. LYNCH, 561(SATR):1APR72-76
S.K. OBERBECK, 440:23APR72-11
BRODIN, D. MARCEL AYMÉ.
S.M. BELL, 208(FS):OCT71-489
BRODIN, G. TERMINI DIMOSTRATIVI TOSCANI.
M. SANDMANN, 72:BAND208HEFT3-229
BRODIN, P. ECRIVAINS AMÉRICAINS D'AU-
JOURD'HUI DES ANNÉES 60.
B.L. KNAPP, 207(FR):DEC69-359
BRODINE, V. & M. SELDEN, EDS. OPEN
SECRET.
R.J. BARNET, 453:16NOV72-14
J. CHACE, 441:10DEC72-2
BRODSKY, I. OSTANOVKA V PUSTYNE.
C. BROWN, 32:SEP71-708
BRODY, E. MUSIC IN OPERA.
L. SALTER, 415:JUN71-554
BRØGGER, A.W. & H. SHETELIG. THE VIKING
SHIPS. (NEW ED)
617(TLS):19MAY72-584

BROICH, U. STUDIEN ZUM KOMISCHEN EPOS.
  H-J. ZIMMERMANN, 72:BAND208HEFT4/6-
  383
BROIDO, E. MEMOIRS OF A REVOLUTIONARY.*
  (V. BROIDO, ED & TRANS)
  I. GETZLER, 587:OCT68-260
BROMBERT, V. STENDHAL.*
  M. LEBOWITZ, 340(KR):1969/3-389
  K.G. MC WATTERS, 546(RR):FEB70-64
  G. MAY, 401(MLQ):MAR70-125
  J.S.P., 191(ELN):SEP70(SUPP)-83
  F.W. SAUNDERS, 208(FS):APR71-215
  P. ZUCKERMAN, 400(MLN):MAY70-618
BROME, V. FRANK HARRIS.
  E. FORD, 571:WINTER69/70-69
BROMMER, F. DIE METOPEN DES PARTHENON.
  E.B. HARRISON, 124:OCT70-60
BROMSEN, M.A., ED. JOSÉ TORIBIO MEDINA,
  HUMANISTA DE AMÉRICA.
  E. DE GANDÍA, 263:OCT-DEC71-452
BRONFENBRENNER, U., WITH J.C. CONDRY,
  JR., EDS. TWO WORLDS OF CHILDHOOD.*
  639(VQR):AUTUMN70-CLVI
BRONGER, D. DER KAMPF UM DIE SOWJETISCHE
  AGRARPOLITIK, 1925-1929.
  O.A. NARKIEWICZ, 587:JAN69-398
BRONK, W. THE EMPTY HANDS.*
  J. HOPPER, 661:SUMMER70-123
BRONK, W. THAT TANTALUS.
  S.F. MORSE, 385(MQR):FALL72-297
BRONOWSKI, J. WILLIAM BLAKE AND THE AGE
  OF REVOLUTION.
  617(TLS):28APR72-470
BRONSON, B.H. THE BALLAD AS SONG.*
  639(VQR):AUTUMN70-CXXXVI
BRONSON, B.H. FACETS OF THE ENLIGHTEN-
  MENT.
  E.A. BLOOM, 402(MLR):APR71-395
  R. LONSDALE, 541(RES):AUG70-365
  R.G. SAISSELIN, 290(JAAC):SUMMER70-
  560
  D.I.B. SMITH, 627(UTQ):JAN70-188
BROOK, D. FLIGHT FROM THE OBJECT.
  C.R. BRIGHTON, 89(BJA):WINTER71-105
BROOK, G.L. THE LANGUAGE OF DICKENS.*
  N. PAGE, 155:SEP70-250
BROOK-SHEPHERD, G. THE LAST HABSBURG.
  H. LEDERER, 19(AGR):VOL36#2-27
BROOKE, C. MEDIEVAL CHURCH AND SOCIETY.
  617(TLS):25FEB72-214
BROOKE, C. THE STRUCTURE OF MEDIEVAL
  SOCIETY.
  617(TLS):11FEB72-165
BROOKE, D. THE LOVE LIFE OF A CHELTEN-
  HAM LADY.*
  442(NY):22JAN72-100
BROOKE, I. MEDIEVAL THEATRE COSTUME.
  J. BECKWITH, 39:SEP69-267
BROOKE, J. KING GEORGE III.
  J. CANNON, 362:9NOV72-642
  J.H. PLUMB, 453:14DEC72-44
  617(TLS):60CT72-1199
BROOKE, J. & M. SORENSEN - SEE GLAD-
  STONE, W.E.
BROOKE, N. SHAKESPEARE'S EARLY TRAGE-
  DIES.
  W.C. FERGUSON, 529(QQ):SPRING70-131
  E.A.J. HONIGMANN, 447(N&Q):APR70-148
  A.P. RIEMER, 67:MAY71-86
BROOKE, R.B., ED & TRANS. SCRIPTA
  LEONIS, RUFINI ET ANGELI SOCIORUM S.
  FRANCISCI.*
  E. COLLEDGE, 382(MAE):1971/1-62
BROOKE, S. QUEEN OF THE HEAD HUNTERS.
  A. BROYARD, 441:14APR72-41
  L.E. SISSMAN, 442(NY):3JUN72-108
BROOKE, Z.N., WITH A. MOREY & C.N.L.
  BROOKE - SEE FOLIOT, G.

BROOKE-ROSE, C. A ZBC OF EZRA POUND.
  D. DONOGHUE, 362:23NOV72-718
  617(TLS):2JUN72-624
BROOKHOUSE, C., ED. "SIR AMADACE" AND
  "THE AVOWING OF ARTHUR."*
  A.J. BLISS, 597(SN):VOL41#2-471
BROOKNER, A. GREUZE.
  J. CANADAY, 441:3DEC72-90
  617(TLS):13OCT72-1218
BROOKS, C. A SHAPING JOY.*
  G. CORE, 578:FALL72-177
  T. LASK, 441:19APR72-49
  E.W. SAID, 441:10DEC72-4
  L.P. SIMPSON, 598(SOR):SUMMER72-XI
BROOKS, G. THE WORLD OF GWENDOLYN
  BROOKS.
  A. GAYLE, JR., 441:2JAN72-4
BROOKS, M.Z. NASAL VOWELS IN CONTEMPOR-
  ARY STANDARD POLISH.
  D. FIALOVÁ, 575(SEER):APR71-284
  W. JASSEM, 361:VOL24#4-401
BROOKS, P. THE HOUSE OF LIFE.
  J. HAY, 440:26MAR72-6
  J. JOHNSON, 441:30APR72-30
  D. MC CORD, 561(SATR):25MAR72-108
  E. WEEKS, 61:APR72-124
BROOKS, P. THE NOVEL OF WORLDLINESS.
  V. MYLNE, 208(FS):OCT71-464
  P. STEWART, 207(FR):MAR70-690
  W. WRAGE, 399(MLJ):MAR70-210
BROOKS, P.C. RESEARCH IN ARCHIVES.
  M.L. RADOFF, 14:OCT69-383
BROOKS, V.W. & L. MUMFORD. THE VAN WYCK
  BROOKS-LEWIS MUMFORD LETTERS. (R.E.
  SPILLER, ED)
  639(VQR):AUTUMN70-CXL
BROPHY, B. IN TRANSIT.*
  F.P.W. MC DOWELL, 659:SUMMER72-361
BROSE, O.J. FREDERICK DENISON MAURICE.
  441:5MAR72-10
  617(TLS):23JUN72-717
BROTHERS, J. & S. HATCH. RESIDENCE AND
  STUDENT LIFE.
  617(TLS):7JUL72-768
BROTHERSTON, G. MANUEL MACHADO.*
  M.H. GUERRA, 399(MLJ):FEB70-128
BROTHWELL, D. & P. FOOD IN ANTIQUITY.
  D.E. EICHHOLZ, 123:MAR71-111
  J. PERCIVAL, 313:VOL60-236
BROUDY, H.S. THE REAL WORLD OF THE
  PUBLIC SCHOOLS.
  442(NY):7OCT72-160
BROUWERS, J. DE TOTELTUIN.
  A. DIXOH, 270:VOL20#3-67
BROWDER, C. ANDRÉ BRETON, ARBITER OF
  SURREALISM.
  E. DEBERDT-MALAQUAIS, 546(RR):FEB70-
  73
BROWER, B. THE LATE GREAT CREATURE.
  P. ADAMS, 61:MAR72-108
  A. HISLOP, 440:12MAR72-5
  C. LEHMANN-HAUPT, 441:10MAR72-39
  J. SEELYE, 441:12MAR72-4
  P. WOOD, 561(SATR):22APR72-86
  442(NY):1APR72-106
BROWER, R.A. HERO AND SAINT.
  F. KERMODE, 441:10DEC72-35
  L.C. KNIGHTS, 453:5OCT72-3
  617(TLS):7APR72-390
BROWER, R.A. & W.H. BOND - SEE HOMER
BROWER, R.H. & E. MINER. FUJIWARA
  TEIKA'S SUPERIOR POEMS OF OUR TIME.
  E.A. CRANSTON, 318(JAOS):APR-JUN70-
  377
BROWN, C. COME SOFTLY TO MY WAKE.
  617(TLS):7JAN72-6

41

BROWN, C. THE LIFE & LOVES OF MR. JIVE-
ASS NIGGER.*
42(AR):WINTER69/70-588
BROWN, C.C. - SEE "SĚJARAH MĚLAYU OR
MALAY ANNALS"
BROWN, C.H. WILLIAM CULLEN BRYANT.
441:13FEB72-16
442(NY):29JAN72-95
BROWN, D. AMERICAN COOKING: THE NORTH-
WEST.
N. MAGID, 440:20FEB72-6
BROWN, D. BURY MY HEART AT WOUNDED
KNEE.*
W. ALLEN, 362:6JAN72-23
617(TLS):21JUL72-829
BROWN, D. OVERLAND TO INDIA.
C.W. CASEWIT, 440:30APR72-4
BROWN, D.G. ACTION.
A.C. DANTO, 482(PHR):OCT70-582
D.S. SHWAYDER, 479(PHQ):JUL70-288
L.M.G. SMITH, 627(UTQ):JUL69-418
P.F. STRAWSON, 393(MIND):JUL70-441
BROWN, E. THE CANDLE OF THE WICKED.
N. CALLENDAR, 441:6AUG72-24
BROWN, F.M. & B. HEINEMAN. JAMAICA AND
ITS BUTTERFLIES.
617(TLS):18AUG72-975
BROWN, G. & W. JASSEY. INTRODUCCIÓN AL
ENSAYO HISPANOAMERICANO.
M.S. STABB, 238:MAR70-173
BROWN, G.H. & H. KEITH. NEW ZEALAND
PAINTING.
90:SEP70-652
BROWN, G.M. GREENVOE.
J. HUNTER, 362:1JUN72-736
M. LEVIN, 441:17SEP72-42
BROWN, G.M. POEMS NEW AND SELECTED.
I. WEDDE, 364:DEC71/JAN72-118
BROWN, H. PROSE STYLES.
R. POSNER, 545(RPH):AUG69-118
BROWN, I. A CHARM OF NAMES.
617(TLS):29SEP72-1164
BROWN, I.D. & M. DOLLEY. COIN HOARDS OF
GREAT BRITAIN AND IRELAND.
617(TLS):10NOV72-1377
BROWN, J. THE CHANCER.
617(TLS):7JUL72-783
BROWN, J. FORGETTING.
D. BARBOUR, 150(DR):SPRING70-112
BROWN, J. TOWARD A CHEMISTRY OF REEL
PEOPLE.
F. DAVEY, 99:JUL-AUG72-45
BROWN, J. & D. PHILLIPS, EDS. WEST COAST
SEEN.*
M. ATWOOD, 102(CANL):WINTER71-75
D. BARBOUR, 150(DR):SPRING70-112
BROWN, J.A.C. PEARS MEDICAL ENCYCLO-
PEDIA. (REV BY A.M.H. BENNETT)
617(TLS):7JAN72-22
BROWN, J.M. THE ORDEAL OF A PLAYWRIGHT.*
(N. COUSINS, ED)
T.F. MARSHALL, 27(AL):NOV71-471
BROWN, J.P. THE LEBANON AND PHOENICIA.
(VOL 1)
S.I. OOST, 122:APR71-133
BROWN, J.R. MODERN BRITISH DRAMATISTS.
R. GASKELL, 397(MD):MAY69-101
502(PRS):WINTER68/69-366
BROWN, J.R. SHAKESPEARE'S PLAYS IN PER-
FORMANCE.
M. ROSENBERG, 570(SQ):SPRING69-235
BROWN, J.R. THEATRE LANGUAGE.
617(TLS):29DEC72-1569
BROWN, J.R. & B. HARRIS, EDS. STRATFORD-
UPON-AVON STUDIES. (VOL 8: LATER
SHAKESPEARE.)
S. SCHOENBAUM, 570(SQ):SPRING69-233

BROWN, J.R. & B. HARRIS, EDS. STRATFORD-
UPON-AVON STUDIES. (VOL 9: ELIZABETHAN
THEATRE.)
M.O. HINMAN, 570(SQ):AUTUMN68-399
BROWN, J.R. & B. HARRIS, EDS. STRATFORD-
UPON-AVON STUDIES.* (VOL 10: AMERICAN
THEATRE.)
M. HARTMAN, 397(MD):FEB69-455
BROWN, J.W. THE RISE OF BIBLICAL CRITI-
CISM IN AMERICA, 1800-1870.
C.A. HOLBROOK, 432(NEQ):MAR70-172
BROWN, L. TELEVISION.*
L. ROSS, 453:9MAR72-25
BROWN, L.R. WORLD WITHOUT BORDERS.
442(NY):18NOV72-247
561(SATR):23DEC72-68
BROWN, M. THE POLITICS OF IRISH LITERA-
TURE.
617(TLS):7JUL72-764
BROWN, M.H., ED. PAPERS OF THE YUGOSLAV-
AMERICAN SEMINAR ON MUSIC.
D.S., 410(M&L):APR71-203
BROWN, M.J.E. SCHUBERT SYMPHONIES.
R. ANDERSON, 415:NOV70-1111
412:MAY71-182
BROWN, O. EXHIBITION.*
L. WADDINGTON, 592:MAR68-164
BROWN, P. AUGUSTINE OF HIPPO.*
M.T. CLARK, 258:MAR69-148
G.M., 477:SUMMER69-398
R.J. O'CONNELL, 613:SUMMER68-308
BROWN, P. RELIGION AND SOCIETY IN THE
AGE OF SAINT AUGUSTINE.
617(TLS):26MAY72-608
BROWN, P.L. ASTRONOMY IN COLOUR.
617(TLS):7JUL72-785
BROWN, P.L. WHAT STAR IS THAT?
617(TLS):25FEB72-229
BROWN, R. SOME DEATHS IN THE DELTA.
R.B. SHAW, 491:MAR72-342
BROWN, R. & C.D. ROLLINS, EDS. CONTEM-
PORARY PHILOSOPHY IN AUSTRALIA.
A.G.N. FLEW, 63:MAY71-97
A.R. WHITE, 479(PHQ):JUL70-280
BROWN, R.A. THE NORMANS AND THE NORMAN
CONQUEST.*
676(YR):SPRING71-XXII
BROWN, R.E. CARL BECKER ON HISTORY AND
THE AMERICAN REVOLUTION.
G.A. RAWLYK, 529(QQ):WINTER70-643
BROWN, R.E. HANS HENNY JAHNNS "FLUSS
OHNE UFER."
T.P. FREEMAN, 222(GR):MAR70-139
A. HUYSSEN, 406:SPRING71-87
BROWN, R.M. THE ECUMENICAL REVOLUTION.
G.M., 477:SUMMER69-415
BROWN, S.C. DO RELIGIOUS CLAIMS MAKE
SENSE?
J. HICK, 518:MAY70-3
T. MAUTNER, 63:AUG71-231
R.C. WALLACE, 479(PHQ):OCT70-412
BROWN, S.H. LING.
V.G. VARTAN, 441:10SEP72-3
BROWN, S.L. SURNAMES ARE THE FOSSILS OF
SPEECH.
O. WHITTAKER, 424:JUN68-185
BROWN, T.A. THE AESTHETICS OF ROBERT
SCHUMANN.*
J. RETI-FORBES, 219(GAR):SUMMER69-263
BROWN, T.H. FRENCH.
B. EBLING, 207(FR):OCT69-147
BROWN, W. THE GOOD AMERICANS.
W.A. BENTON, 656(WMQ):JUL70-499
BROWN, W.R. IMAGEMAKER.
W. BLAIR, 27(AL):NOV71-470
BROWN, W.S. THE AMPHIBIOUS CAMPAIGN FOR
WEST FLORIDA AND LOUISIANA, 1814-1815.
C.B. BROOKS, 656(WMQ):JAN70-157

BROWNE, E.M. THE MAKING OF T.S. ELIOT'S
PLAYS.*
C.H. SMITH, 191(ELN):DEC70-148
639(VQR):WINTER70-XVIII
BROWNE, G.A. 11 HARROWHOUSE.
N. CALLENDAR, 441:9APR72-38
L.J. DAVIS, 440:30APR72-10
BROWNE, M.D. THE WIFE OF WINTER.
P. PETTINGELL, 491:JAN72-234
BROWNE, R. ATHMANI.
M. LEVIN, 441:8OCT72-42
BROWNE, R.B. & OTHERS, EDS. FRONTIERS
OF AMERICAN CULTURE.
H.T. MESEROLE, 27(AL):NOV71-493
M.E. RUCKER, 50(ARQ):SPRING69-93
BROWNE, R.B. & D. PIZER, EDS. THEMES
AND DIRECTIONS IN AMERICAN LITERATURE.
A.C. KERN, 651(WHR):WINTER71-91
BROWNE, T. THOMAS BROWNE, "RELIGIO
MEDICI."
P.G. STANWOOD, 568(SCN):SUMMER/AUTUMN
71-49
BROWNE, T. SIR THOMAS BROWNE: SELECTED
WRITINGS. (G. KEYNES, ED)
T. HERRING, 67:MAY71-121
BROWNING, D. EL SALVADOR.
617(TLS):21JAN72-62
BROWNING, E. I CAN'T SEE WHAT YOU'RE
SAYING.
617(TLS):8DEC72-1484
BROWNING, E.B. DIARY BY E.B.B. (P. KEL-
LEY & R. HUDSON, EDS)
M.G. WIEBE, 529(QQ):WINTER70-649
BROWNING, R. THE COMPLETE WORKS OF
ROBERT BROWNING. (VOL 1) (R.A. KING,
JR. & OTHERS, EDS)
T.J. COLLINS, 637(VS):JUN70-441
M. HANCHER, 677:VOL2-312
BROWNING, R. MEDIEVAL AND MODERN GREEK.
D.Q. ADAMS, 350:DEC71-943
G.M. MESSING, 589:JAN71-129
BROWNING, R. POETICAL WORKS 1833-1864.*
(I. JACK, ED)
P. HONAN, 402(MLR):JUL71-676
BROWNING, R. & E.B. BARRETT. THE LETTERS
OF ROBERT BROWNING AND ELIZABETH BAR-
RETT BARRETT, 1845-1846.* (E. KINTNER,
ED)
W.D. SHAW, 627(UTQ):APR70-289
639(VQR):SPRING70-LXVI
BROWNING, R.M. UMGANG MIT GEDICHTEN.
K.H. VAN D'ELDEN, 399(MLJ):MAR70-202
BROWNJOHN, A. SAND GRAINS ON A TRAY.*
J. SMITH, 493:SPRING70-89
BROWNJOHN, A. WARRIOR'S CAREER.
617(TLS):15DEC72-1524
BROWNLOW, K. THE PARADE'S GONE BY.
R. GIROUX, 200:MAR69-174
BROWNRIGG, R. WHO'S WHO IN THE NEW TES-
TAMENT.*
617(TLS):25FEB72-225
BROWNSTEIN, M. BRAIN STORMS.
V. YOUNG, 249(HUDR):WINTER71/72-669
BROWNSTEIN, M. HIGHWAY TO THE SKY.
J. ATLAS, 491:OCT71-45
BROWNSTONE, C. ASSOCIATED PRESS COOK-
BOOK.
N. HAZELTON, 441:3DEC72-96
BRÚ, H. THE OLD MAN AND HIS SONS.
E. SCHÜRER, 563(SS):AUTUMN71-446
BRUCCOLI, M. & J. BRYER - SEE FITZGERALD,
F.S.
BRUCCOLI, M.J., ED. ERNEST HEMINGWAY,
CUB REPORTER.
639(VQR):AUTUMN70-CXXXVII
BRUCCOLI, M.J. - SEE CHARVAT, W.
BRUCCOLI, M.J., WITH J.M. ATKINSON - SEE
FITZGERALD, F.S. & H. OBER

BRUCE, C. THE NEWS AND THE SOUTHAMS.
W.H. KESTERTON, 627(UTQ):JUL69-399
BRUCE, G. THE COLLECTED POEMS OF GEORGE
BRUCE.
H. CARRUTH, 249(HUDR):SUMMER71-335
BRUCE, G., ED. SHORT STORIES OF THE
FIRST WORLD WAR.
G. EWART, 364:FEB/MAR72-180
BRUCE, G. THE WARSAW UPRISING.
617(TLS):15SEP72-1061
BRÜHL, C. STUDIEN ZU DEN LANGOBARDISCHEN
KÖNIGSURKUNDEN.
I. MÜLLER, 182:VOL23#9-504
BRUMBAUGH, R.S. THE PHILOSOPHERS OF
GREECE.
J.S. MORRISON, 123:JUN71-222
BRUMBERG, A., ED. IN QUEST OF JUSTICE.
B.R. BOCIURKIW, 550(RUSR):JUL70-328
S.F. COHEN, 441:23JUL72-6
L. LIPSON, 32:DEC71-897
L.M. TIKOS, 418(MR):SPRING71-349
BRUMBY, C. THE ART OF PROLONGING THE
MUSICAL TONE.
I. KEMP, 607:AUTUMN69-41
BRUMFITT, J.H. - SEE DE VOLTAIRE, F.M.A.
BRUNDAGE, J.A. MEDIEVAL CANON LAW AND
THE CRUSADER.
J.W. BALDWIN, 589:JAN71-131
BRUNEAU, C. L'EPOQUE RÉALISTE. (PT 2)
(M. PIRON, ED)
617(TLS):24NOV72-1430
BRUNER, J.S. THE RELEVANCE OF EDUCATION.
(A. GIL, ED)
617(TLS):22SEP72-1091
BRUNÉS, T. THE SECRETS OF ANCIENT
GEOMETRY - AND ITS USE.
617(TLS):4FEB72-133
BRUNET, J. ALBERT LABERGE, SA VIE ET
SON OEUVRE.
J-C. BONENFANT, 627(UTQ):JUL70-409
BRUNET, M. LES CANADIENS APRÈS LA CON-
QUÊTE, 1759-1775.
J-C. BONENFANT, 627(UTQ):JUL70-403
BRUNET, M. QUÉBEC/CANADA ANGLAIS.
J-C. BONENFANT, 627(UTQ):JUL69-462
BRUNIUS, N., G.O. ERIKSSON & R. REMBE.
SWEDISH THEATRE.
B. STEENE, 397(MD):MAY69-109
BRUNNER, F. & OTHERS. VOM WESEN DER
SPRACHE.
M. SANDMANN, 545(RPH):NOV70-361
BRUNNER, K. ALTENGLISCHE GRAMMATIK.
(3RD ED)
G.H.V. BUNT, 179(ES):DEC70-546
BRUNOT, F. LA DOCTRINE DE MALHERBE
D'APRÈS SON COMMENTAIRE SUR DESPORTES.
J.D. BIARD, 208(FS):OCT71-453
BRUNVAND, J.H. THE STUDY OF AMERICAN
FOLKLORE.*
A.L. CAMPA, 582(SFQ):MAR69-55
BRUST, A. DRAMEN. (H. DENKLER, ED)
617(TLS):7JUL72-784
BRUSTEIN, R. REVOLUTION AS THEATRE.*
G.A. PANICHAS, 396(MODA):FALL71-416
BRUSTEIN, R. THE THEATRE OF REVOLT.
G.W. BRANDT, 402(MLR):OCT71-888
BRUTUS. CONFESSIONS OF A STOCKBROKER.
G. WHEELER, 440:2APR72-7
BRUYERE, T.B. & S.J. ROBIE. FOR GOURMETS
WITH ULCERS.
N. MAGID, 440:13FEB72-5
BRUZZI, A. LA FORMAZIONE DELLE "MAXIMES"
DI LA ROCHEFOUCAULD ATTRAVERSO LE ED-
IZIONI ORIGINALI.
E.D. JAMES, 208(FS):JAN71-77
BRY, A., ED. INSIDE PSYCHOTHERAPY.
W. SCHOTT, 561(SATR):19AUG72-61
441:9JAN72-28

BRYAN, C.D.B. THE GREAT DETHRIFFE.
   D.J. GORDON, 676(YR):SPRING71-428
   617(TLS):29DEC72-1573
BRYANT, A. THE GREAT DUKE, OR THE INVIN-
CIBLE GENERAL.*
   D.C. ACHESON, 441:10DEC72-54
   T. LASK, 441:17NOV72-47
BRYANT, D. ELLA PRICE'S JOURNAL.
   M. LEVIN, 441:24DEC72-14
   G. STUTTAFORD, 561(SATR):28OCT72-83
BRYANT, G. HEALEY WILLAN CATALOGUE.
   J. BECKWITH, 99:DEC72-32
BRYANT, J.H. THE OPEN DECISION.*
   M. BEEBE, 27(AL):NOV71-488
   J.L. BROWN, 659:SUMMER72-395
   R.A. CHRISTMAS, 651(WHR):SUMMER71-276
   G. CUOMO, 418(MR):AUTUMN71-837
BRYDEN, J.R. & D.G. HUGHES, COMPS. AN
INDEX OF GREGORIAN CHANT.*
   I.D. BENT, 415:OCT70-1002
BRYER, J.R. THE CRITICAL REPUTATION OF
F. SCOTT FITZGERALD.
   W.G. FRENCH, 330(MASJ):SPRING69-90
BRYER, J.R., ED. FIFTEEN MODERN AMERICAN
AUTHORS.*
   J. KUEHL, 399(MLJ):APR70-303
BRYER, V., COMP. PROFESSOR PERCIVAL
ROBSON KIRBY M.A., D. LITT., F.R.C.M.
   A.P. MERRIAM, 187:SEP72-544
BRYLOWSKI, W. FAULKNER'S OLYMPIAN
LAUGH.*
   J.L. ROBERTS, 502(PRS):WINTER68/69-
   359
BRYSON, N. THE SWIMMER AND OTHER POEMS.
   G. CAVALIERO, 111:30JAN70-93
BRYUSOV, V.Y. RASSKAZY I POVESTI. MOY
PUSHKIN.
   G. DONCHIN, 575(SEER):OCT71-618
BRZEZINSKI, Z. BETWEEN TWO AGES.*
   J. GILBERT, 473(PR):1971/1-112
   H.L. ROBERTS, 676(YR):WINTER71-287
BRZEZINSKI, Z. THE FRAGILE BLOSSOM.
   R. HALLORAN, 561(SATR):5FEB72-67
   H.S. STOKES, 441:9APR72-6
BUCCELLATI, G. THE AMORITES OF THE UR
III PERIOD.
   W.L. MORAN, 318(JAOS):OCT-DEC70-529
BUCCI, M. MIRÓ.
   617(TLS):7JAN72-18
BUCHAN, A. THE RIGHT TO WORK.
   617(TLS):3MAR72-258
BUCHAN, D. THE BALLAD AND THE FOLK.
   617(TLS):27OCT72-1292
BUCHANAN, C. MAIDEN.
   J. CATINELLA, 561(SATR):27MAY72-68
   J.R. FRAKES, 440:9JAN72-2
   A. GOTTLIEB, 441:9JAN72-6
   R.R. LINGEMAN, 441:26JAN72-39
BUCHANAN, G. MINUTE-BOOK OF A CITY.
   617(TLS):29SEP72-1146
BUCHANAN, J.D. THE PROFESSIONAL.
   N. CALLENDAR, 441:15OCT72-42
   617(TLS):26MAY72-612
BUCHANAN, J.M. & N.E. DEVLETOGLOU. ACA-
DEMIA IN ANARCHY.
   C.P. IVES, 396(MODA):WINTER71-96
BUCHANAN, M. GREENSHARDS.
   J. HUNTER, 362:13APR72-493
   617(TLS):12MAY72-537
BUCHDAHL, G. METAPHYSICS AND THE PHIL-
OSOPHY OF SCIENCE.
   R.G. SWINBURNE, 518:OCT70-1
BUCHER, F. THE PAMPLONA BIBLES.*
   D. MINER, 70(ANQ):SEP71-12
BUCHER, L.M., WITH M. RASCOVICH. BUCHER:
MY STORY.
   J.E. DORNAN, JR., 396(MODA):SPRING71-
   197

BÜCHNER, G. DANTONS TOD. (R.C. COWEN,
ED)
   R.P. ROSENBERG, 221(GQ):NOV70-812
BÜCHNER, G. SÄMTLICHE WERKE UND BRIEFE.
(VOL 2) (W.R. LEHMANN, ED)
   617(TLS):21JAN72-60
BUCHNER, H. & O. PÖGGELER - SEE HEGEL,
G.W.F.
BUCK, A. DIE HUMANISTISCHE TRADITION IN
DER ROMANIA.
   R. HESS, 72:BAND208HEFT4/6-446
   V.A. TUMINS, 551(RENQ):SPRING70-82
BÜCKING, J. KULTUR UND GESELLSCHAFT IN
TIROL UM 1600.
   T.A. BRADY, JR., 182:VOL23#3-109
BUCKINGHAM, W.J., ED. EMILY DICKINSON:
AN ANNOTATED BIBLIOGRAPHY.*
   F.L. MOREY, 517(PBSA):OCT-DEC71-421
BUCKLE, H.T. ON SCOTLAND AND THE SCOTCH
INTELLECT. (H.J. HANHAM, ED)
   617(TLS):18FEB72-175
BUCKLE, R. NIJINSKY.
   A. CROCE, 441:8OCT72-27
   D. HARRIS, 561(SATR):7OCT72-95
   617(TLS):14JAN72-35
BUCKLE, R. NIJINSKY ON STAGE.
   617(TLS):14JAN72-35
BUCKLER, E. OX BELLS AND FIREFLIES.*
   G. ROPER, 627(UTQ):JUL69-355
BUCKLEY, V. POETRY AND THE SACRED.
   J.S., 619(TC):1968/4&1969/1-91
BUCKLEY, W.F., JR., ED. DID YOU EVER SEE
A DREAM WALKING?
   H. GOW, 396(MODA):SUMMER71-319
BUCKLEY, W.F., JR. INVEIGHING WE WILL
GO.
   J.P. ROCHE, 441:8OCT72-40
BUCKMASTER, H. THE WALKING TRIP.
   N. CALLENDAR, 441:12MAR72-40
   617(TLS):29SEP72-1174
BUCYK, J., WITH R. CONWAY. HOCKEY IN MY
BLOOD.
   J. DURSO, 441:3DEC72-40
BUDD, L.J. ROBERT HERRICK.
   B. NEVIUS, 27(AL):JAN72-666
BUDGEN, F. JAMES JOYCE AND THE MAKING OF
"ULYSSES."
   617(TLS):12MAY72-541
BUDICK, S. DRYDEN AND THE ABYSS OF
LIGHT.*
   V.M. HAMM, 301(JEGP):OCT71-670
   W. MYERS, 402(MLR):OCT71-866
BUDYONNY, S. THE PATH OF VALOUR.
   617(TLS):24NOV72-1441
BUEB, B. NIETZSCHES KRITIK DER PRAK-
TISCHEN VERNUNFT.
   D. HOWARD, 182:VOL23#19/20-837
BUECHNER, F. THE ENTRANCE TO PORLOCK.*
   639(VQR):SPRING70-XLI
BUECHNER, F. LION COUNTRY.*
   W.H. PRITCHARD, 249(HUDR):SUMMER71-
   361
BUECHNER, F. OPEN HEART.
   R. BRYDEN, 362:30NOV72-760
   T.R. EDWARDS, 453:20JUL72-20
   C. LEHMANN-HAUPT, 441:19MAY72-37
   G. MALKO, 561(SATR):29JUL72-64
   C. OZICK, 441:11JUN72-4
   P. THEROUX, 440:28MAY72-4
   442(NY):22JUL72-78
   617(TLS):29DEC72-1588
BUEHNE, S.Z., J.L. HODGE & L.B. PINTO,
EDS. HELEN ADOLF FESTSCHRIFT.
   H.B. WILLSON, 221(GQ):MAR70-249
BUELL, F. THESEUS AND OTHER POEMS.
   R. LATTIMORE, 249(HUDR):AUTUMN71-503

BUELL, J. THE SHREWSDALE EXIT.
  O.L. BAILEY, 561(SATR):28OCT72-89
  N. CALLENDAR, 441:1OCT72-43
BUELOW, G.J. THOROUGH-BASS ACCOMPANIMENT
  ACCORDING TO JOHANN DAVID HEINICHEN.*
  A. COHEN, 308:WINTER67-281
BUFFIÈRE, F., ED & TRANS. ANTHOLOGIE
  GRECQUE. (PT 1, VOL 12)
  J.W. SHUMAKER, 124:JAN71-160
BUFFINGTON, R. THE EQUILIBRIST.*
  C. BUSH, 447(N&Q):FEB70-72
BUFORD, T.O., ED. TOWARD A PHILOSOPHY
  OF EDUCATION.
  S.O.H., 543:DEC69-367
BUGAENKO, P.A. A.V. LUNACHARSKII I LIT-
  ERATURNOE DVIZHENIE 20-KH GODOV.
  S. FITZPATRICK, 587:APR69-527
BUGLER, J. POLLUTING BRITAIN.
  617(TLS):23JUN72-727
BUHNE, R. JEREMIAS GOTTHELF UND DAS
  PROBLEM DER ARMUT.*
  H. BOESCHENSTEIN, 221(GQ):MAR70-287
VAN BUITENEN, J.A.B. - SEE RĀMĀNUJA
BUITENHUIS, P. THE GRASPING IMAGINA-
  TION.*
  B.A. RICHARDS, 677:VOL2-321
  K.B. VAID, 27(AL):NOV71-461
BUKHARIN, N. IMPERIALISM AND WORLD
  ECONOMY.
  617(TLS):16JUN72-683
BUKHARIN, N.I. PUT' K SOTSIALIZMU V
  ROSSII. (S. HEITMAN, ED)
  D. MULHOLLAND, 32:MAR71-147
BUKOWSKA-GROSSE, E. & E. KOSCHMIEDER,
  EDS. POLNISCHE VOLKSMÄRCHEN.
  A. DE VINCENZ, 72:BAND208HEFT4/6-478
BUKOWSKI, C. AT TERROR STREET AND AGONY
  WAY.
  R. BROTHERSON, 661:FALL/WINTER69-105
  A. OSTRIKER, 473(PR):1971/2-218
BUKOWSKI, C. ERECTIONS, EJACULATIONS,
  EXHIBITIONS AND GENERAL TALES OF ORDI-
  NARY MADNESS.
  T.R. EDWARDS, 453:5OCT72-21
BULATOVIC, M. THE WAR WAS BETTER.
  J. HITREC, 441:16JUL72-34
  V.D. MIHAILOVICH, 561(SATR):13MAY72-
  84
BULGAKOV, M. BELAJA GVARDIJA.
  J.P. MANSON, 574(SEEJ):FALL71-373
BULGAKOV, M. BLACK SNOW. (M. GLENNY,
  TRANS) THE HEART OF A DOG. (M.
  GLENNY, TRANS) HEART OF A DOG. (M.
  GINSBURG, TRANS)
  Z. YURIEFF, 574(SEEJ):SPRING71-73
BULGAKOV, M. DIABOLIAD AND OTHER STOR-
  IES. (E. & C.R. PROFFER, EDS)
  P. ADAMS, 61:MAY72-113
  M. BERMAN, 441:23JUL72-7
  E. LEVIN, 561(SATR):29APR72-59
  617(TLS):1SEP72-1013
BULGAKOV, M. THE EARLY PLAYS OF MIKHAIL
  BULGAKOV. (E. PROFFER, ED)
  P. ADAMS, 61:MAY72-113
  M. BERMAN, 441:23JUL72-7
  E. LEVIN, 561(SATR):29APR72-59
BULGAKOV, M. FLIGHT.
  H. OULANOFF, 574(SEEJ):SPRING71-114
BULGAKOV, M. THE WHITE GUARD.*
  K. FITZLYON, 364:APR/MAY71-168
  H. MUCHNIC, 453:23MAR72-37
BULGAKOV, V.F. THE LAST YEAR OF LEO
  TOLSTOY.*
  K. FITZLYON, 364:DEC71/JAN72-139
BULL, F. SAINT DAVID'S DAY.
  617(TLS):4AUG72-910

BULL, G., WITH P. HOBDAY & J. HAMWAY.
  INDUSTRIAL RELATIONS.
  617(TLS):15SEP72-1051
"BULLETIN DE L'INSTITUT D'ARCHÉOLOGIE."
  (VOL 30)
  G. SOTIROFF, 104:SUMMER71-289
BULLITT, O.H. - SEE ROOSEVELT, F.D. &
  W.C. BULLITT
BULLOCK, H.A. A HISTORY OF NEGRO EDUCA-
  TION IN THE SOUTH FROM 1619 TO THE
  PRESENT.
  C.A. HANGARTNER, 377:JUL71-114
BULLOCK, J. THEM AND US.
  617(TLS):28APR72-501
BULLOCK, M. GREEN BEGINNING BLACK END-
  ING.
  A. MONTAGNES, 99:JAN-FEB72-75
BULLOUGH, G., ED. NARRATIVE AND DRAMATIC
  SOURCES OF SHAKESPEARE.* (VOLS 4&5)
  N. BROOKE, 179(ES):DEC70-553
BULLOUGH, G. SHAKESPEARE THE ELIZABETH-
  AN.
  L.F. BALL, 570(SQ):AUTUMN69-478
BULWER-LYTTON, E. ENGLAND AND THE ENG-
  LISH. (S. MEACHAM, ED)
  617(TLS):18FEB72-175
BUM-SUCK, C. - SEE UNDER CHA BUM-SUCK
BUMKE, J. DIE WOLFRAM VON ESCHENBACH-
  FORSCHUNG SEIT 1945.
  S.M. JOHNSON, 301(JEGP):OCT71-709
BUMSTEAD, J.M. HENRY ALLINE 1784-1784.
  617(TLS):12MAY72-536
BUNGE, M., ED. QUANTUM THEORY AND REAL-
  ITY.
  J. BUB, 486:DEC68-425
  A. FINE, 482(PHR):APR70-295
BUNGERT, H. FORMEN DER EINSAMKEIT IM
  ZEITGENÖSSISCHEN AMERIKANISCHEN ROMAN.
  H. FRIEDL, 72:BAND208HEFT4/6-420
BUNJES, R. THE PRAETORIUS ORGAN.
  P. WILLIAMS, 415:JUL70-713
BUNKER, B. PORTRAIT OF SHEFFIELD.
  617(TLS):17NOV72-1405
BUNNIK, R. PRIESTS FOR TOMORROW.
  J.M. PETULLA, 142:WINTER71-121
BUNTING, B. HOUSES OF BOSTON'S BACK
  BAY.*
  S.M. SHERMAN, 576:MAY69-145
BUNTING, B. TAOS ADOBES.
  G. KUBLER, 576:MAY68-151
BUNTING, B. - SEE FORD, F.M.
BUNTING, J. THE LIONHEADS.
  P. ADAMS, 61:MAY72-112
  T. LASK, 441:6MAY72-37
  M. LEVIN, 441:16APR72-30
  M. RUSS, 561(SATR):29APR72-76
BUNTING, W.H. PORTRAIT OF A PORT.
  T. SEVERIN, 440:30JAN72-7
BUNYAN, J. THE HOLY WAR MADE BY SHADDAI
  UPON DIABOLUS FOR THE REGAINING OF THE
  METROPOLIS OF THE WORLD, OR THE LOSING
  AND TAKING AGAIN OF THE TOWN OF MAN-
  SOUL. (J.F. FORREST, ED)
  J.J. MC MANMON, 405(MP):AUG69-90
BUNYAN, J. THE ORIGIN OF FORCED LABOR IN
  THE SOVIET STATE 1917-1921.
  J. KEEP, 575(SEER):APR71-309
  S. SWIANIEWICZ, 587:APR69-551
BURCHARD, R.C. JOHN UPDIKE.
  N.Y. YATES, 27(AL):NOV71-484
BURCHELL, S.C. UPSTART EMPIRE.
  617(TLS):14JAN72-43
BURCHFIELD, R.W. - SEE "A SUPPLEMENT TO
  THE OXFORD ENGLISH DICTIONARY"
BURCKHARDT, C.J. RICHELIEU AND HIS AGE.*
  (VOLS 1-3) (VOL 1 ABRIDGED BY E. & W.
  MUIR)
  442(NY):9SEP72-125

BURCKHARDT, C.J. - SEE VON HOFMANNSTHAL,
H. & C.J. BURCKHARDT
BURCKHARDT, C.J. & M. RYCHNER. BRIEFE
1926-1965.
F.G. CRONHEIM, 402(MLR):JUL71-715
BURCKHARDT, J. BRIEFE. (VOL 7)
V-L. TAPIÉ, 182:VOL23#1/2-51
BURCKHARDT, S. SHAKESPEAREAN MEANINGS.
T.P. LOGAN, 399(MLJ):MAR70-211
BURD, V.A. - SEE RUSKIN, J.
BURFORD, A. CRAFTSMEN IN GREEK AND
ROMAN SOCIETY.
617(TLS):11AUG72-952
BURFORD, A. THE GREEK TEMPLE BUILDERS AT
EPIDAUROS.
A.T. HODGE, 124:SEP70-24
A.T. HODGE, 487:WINTER70-365
H. PLOMMER, 123:JUN71-269
BURG, D. & A. BOYARS - SEE DANIEL, Y.
BURG, D. & G. FEIFER. SOLZHENITSYN.
617(TLS):10NOV72-1369
BÜRGEL, J.C. AVERROES, "CONTRA GALENUM."
S. HAMARNEH, 318(JAOS):APR-JUN70-406
BURGER, H. - SEE WEISE, C.
BURGER, H.O. RENAISSANCE HUMANISMUS
REFORMATION.
T.W. BEST, 221(GQ):NOV70-785
D. BLAMIRES, 402(MLR):OCT71-935
BURGER, I.B. CREATIVE PLAY ACTING. (2ND
ED)
J.H. DAVIS, 397(MD):DEC67-321
BURGESS, A. MF.*
M. FELD, 364:DEC71/JAN72-162
F.P-W. MC DOWELL, 659:SUMMER72-361
W.H. PRITCHARD, 249(HUDR):SUMMER71-
366
BURGESS, A. THE NOVEL NOW. (REV)
617(TLS):21APR72-439
BURGESS, A. ONE HAND CLAPPING.
P. ADAMS, 61:MAR72-108
R.P. BRICKNER, 441:12MAR72-4
A. FOOTE, 440:5MAR72-7
H.T. MOORE, 561(SATR):12FEB72-73
442(NY):18MAR72-154
BURGESS, A. SHAKESPEARE.
G. NEVIN, 493:WINTER70/71-372
C.T. PROUTY, 676(YR):SPRING71-456
BURGESS, A. URGENT COPY.
571:SUMMER69-35
BURGESS, A. - SEE ROSTAND, E.
BURGESS, A. & F. HASKELL. THE AGE OF THE
GRAND TOUR.
M. LEVEY, 592:MAR68-155
BURGESS, G.S. CONTRIBUTION À L'ÉTUDE DU
VOCABULAIRE PRÉ-COURTOIS.
G.J. BRAULT, 589:APR71-362
P. MENARD, 382(MAE):1971/3-275
S. ULLMANN, 402(MLR):OCT71-892
BÜRGIN, H. & H-O. MAYER. THOMAS MANN.*
I.B. JONAS, 399(MLJ):OCT70-466
BURIAN, J. THE SCENOGRAPHY OF JOSEF
SVOBODA.
617(TLS):14JAN72-35
BÜRKE, B., ED. DAS NEUNTE BUCH (THETA)
DES LATEINISCHEN GROSSEN METAPHYSIK-
KOMMENTARS VON AVERROES.
J. JOLIVET, 182:VOL23#5-196
F.E. PETERS, 124:DEC70-135
BURKE, E. THE CORRESPONDENCE OF EDMUND
BURKE. (VOL 8) (P.J. MARSHALL & J.A.
WOODS, EDS)
J.T. BOULTON, 447(N&Q):MAR70-107
BURKE, E. A PHILOSOPHICAL ENQUIRY INTO
THE ORIGIN OF OUR IDEAS OF THE SUBLIME
AND BEAUTIFUL. (J.T. BOULTON, ED)
E.H. DUNCAN, 290(JAAC):FALL69-113

BURKE, J.L. LAY DOWN MY SWORD AND
SHIELD.
M. LEVIN, 441:16JAN72-43
BURKE, K. THE COMPLETE WHITE OXEN.*
H.N. SCHNEIDAU, 340(KR):1969/3-406
BURKE, P. CULTURE AND SOCIETY IN RENAIS-
SANCE ITALY 1420-1540.
617(TLS):11AUG72-948
BURKHARD, A. GRILLPARZER IM AUSLAND.
H. ADOLF, 149:SEP71-279
C. HAMMER, JR., 399(MLJ):OCT70-453
W.E. YATES, 402(MLR):JAN71-225
BURKHEAD, J. & J. MINER. PUBLIC EXPENDI-
TURE.
617(TLS):3MAR72-250
BURKLE, H.R. THE NON-EXISTENCE OF GOD.
W.A.J., 543:MAR70-553
BURLAND, B. THE SAILOR AND THE FOX.
M. LEVIN, 441:31DEC72-18
BURLAND, C.A. THE GODS OF MEXICO.
M.S. YOUNG, 39:APR69-330
BURLAND, C.A. SECRETS OF THE OCCULT.
617(TLS):24NOV72-1441
BURLEY, R. & F.C. CARRUTHERS. EDWARD
ELGAR.
617(TLS):18AUG72-964
BURLIN, R.B. THE OLD ENGLISH ADVENT.*
T.P. DUNNING, 597(SN):VOL41#2-452
R.T.P. FARRELL, 541(RES):FEB70-66
R. WOOLF, 382(MAE):1971/1-60
BURMEISTER, J. RUNNING SCARED.
617(TLS):10NOV72-1375
BURMEISTER, K.H. ACHILLES PIRMIN GASSER
(1505-77). (VOLS 1&2)
J-J. DAETWYLER, 182:VOL23#19/20-835
BURN, A.R. THE ROMANS IN BRITAIN. (2ND
ED)
P. SALWAY, 123:DEC70-412
BURN, A.R. THE WARRING STATES OF
GREECE.*
J.K. DAVIES, 123:DEC70-404
"THE FRANK P. & HARRIET C. BURNAP COL-
LECTION OF ENGLISH POTTERY."
G. WILLS, 39:FEB69-159
BURNELL, G. THE GOLDEN THREAD OF REAL-
ITY.
M.H., 477:SUMMER69-408
BURNET, M. DOMINANT MAMMAL.
617(TLS):7APR72-400
BURNETT, A.P. CATASTROPHE SURVIVED.
617(TLS):31MAR72-374
BURNEY, C. MUSIC, MEN AND MANNERS IN
FRANCE AND ITALY, 1770.* (H.E. POOLE,
ED)
S. SADIE, 415:JUN70-606
BURNEY, C. & D.M. LANG. THE PEOPLE OF
THE HILLS.
617(TLS):18FEB72-182
BURNEY, F. THE JOURNALS AND LETTERS OF
FANNY BURNEY (MADAME D'ARBLAY). (J.
HEMLOW, C.D. CECIL & A. DOUGLAS, EDS)
P. BEER, 362:22JUN72-839
617(TLS):15DEC72-1531
BURNHAM, J. BEYOND MODERN SCULPTURE.
J. BENTHALL, 592:MAR69-148
BURNIAUX, C. L'AMOUR DE VIVRE.
J-L. DUMONT, 207(FR):FEB70-532
BURNLEY, J., ED. PENGUIN MODERN STORIES
10.
V. CUNNINGHAM, 362:2MAR72-283
BURNS, A., ED. TO DEPRAVE AND CORRUPT.
617(TLS):22SEP72-1083
BURNS, A. DREAMERIKA!
617(TLS):5MAY72-526
BURNS, E.B. A HISTORY OF BRAZIL.
D. CARNEIRO, 263:OCT-DEC71-461
BURNS, E.L.M. GENERAL MUD.
102(CANL):AUTUMN71-102

46

BURNS, J.M. ROOSEVELT: THE SOLDIER OF
FREEDOM, 1940-45.*
R. POLENBERG, 639(VQR):AUTUMN70-663
BURNS, J.M. UNCOMMON SENSE.
E. DREW, 441:4JUN72-3
M.R. KONVITZ, 561(SATR):12FEB72-70
R.J. WALTON, 440:16JAN72-3
BURNS, P.L. - SEE WILKINSON, R.J.
BURNS, R. THE POEMS AND SONGS OF ROBERT
BURNS. (J. KINSLEY, ED)
D.V.E., 191(ELN):SEP69(SUPP)-27
BURNS, R.I. THE CRUSADER KINGDOM OF
VALENCIA.*
J.F. POWERS, 613:AUTUMN68-477
BURNS, R.M., ED. ONE COUNTRY OR TWO.
S. LANGDON, 99:OCT/NOV72-84
BURNSHAW, S. IN THE TERRIFIED RADIANCE.
J. DICKEY, 441:24SEP72-4
BURNSHAW, S. THE SEAMLESS WEB.*
L. FEDER, 385(MQR):SPRING72-138
J.H. HAGSTRUM, 149:SEP71-271
D.C. MUECKE, 67:MAY71-116
W.S. RUSK, 127:SPRING71-326
H. VENDLER, 418(MR):AUTUMN71-834
BURR, S.E., JR. NAPOLEON'S DOSSIER ON
AARON BURR.
R. SVENNINGSEN, 14:JUL69-275
BURROUGHS, E.R. THE MOON MAID.
V. CUNNINGHAM, 362:14SEP72-344
BURROUGHS, W.S. THE WILD BOYS.*
J. HUNTER, 362:1JUN72-736
617(TLS):2JUN72-622
BURROW, J.A., ED. GEOFFREY CHAUCER.
H. BOYD, 180(ESA):SEP70-415
S.S. HUSSEY, 447(N&Q):JUN70-227
BURROW, J.A. - SEE "SIR GAWAIN AND THE
GREEN KNIGHT"
BURROWS, D., WITH R. GOTTESMAN & D.J.
NORDLOH - SEE HOWELLS, W.D.
BURROWS, J.F. JANE AUSTEN'S "EMMA."
F. MC COMBIE, 447(N&Q):MAY70-200
W.D. SCHAEFER, 445(NCF):SEP69-248
BURROWS, R. THE NATURALIST IN DEVON AND
CORNWALL.
617(TLS):17MAR72-317
BURRUS, E.J. LA OBRA CARTOGRÁFICA DE LA
PROVINCIA MEXICANA DE LA COMPAÑÍA DE
JESÚS (1567-1967).
A.P. NASATIR, 377:JUL71-106
BURRUS, E.J. - SEE LINCK, W.
BURRUS, E.J. & G.P. HAMMOND, EDS. HOMEN-
AJE A DON JOSÉ MARÍA DE LA PEÑA Y
CÁMARA.
C.L. RILEY, 377:MAR71-47
BURSCHELL, F. SCHILLER.
H. MEYER, 222(GR):MAR70-153
BURSILL-HALL, G.L. SPECULATIVE GRAMMARS
OF THE MIDDLE AGES.
617(TLS):29SEP72-1164
BURSILL-HALL, G.L. - SEE THOMAS OF ERFURT
BURSSENS, A. PROBLEMEN IN INVENTARISA-
TIE VAN DE VERBALE STRUKTUREN IN HET
DHO ALUR (NOORDOOST-KONGO).
A.N. TUCKER, 315(JAL):VOL8PT2-125
BURSTON, W.H. - SEE "JAMES MILL ON EDU-
CATION"
BURTON, E. THE EARLY VICTORIANS AT HOME,
1837-1861.
617(TLS):21JUL72-841
BURTON, H.M. DICKENS AND HIS WORKS.
D. BROWN, 155:MAY69-125
BURTON, M., ED. ENCYCLOPAEDIA OF ANIMALS
IN COLOUR.
617(TLS):10NOV72-1376
BURTON, S.H. THE WEST COUNTRY.
617(TLS):22SEP72-1124

BURTON-BROWN, T. THIRD MILLENNIUM DIF-
FUSION.
617(TLS):22DEC72-1564
BURTT, E.A. IN SEARCH OF PHILOSOPHIC
UNDERSTANDING.
M. LEBOWITZ, 340(KR):SEP66-553
BURWICK, F. - SEE DE QUINCEY, T.
BURY, A. MAURICE-QUENTIN DE LA TOUR.
617(TLS):15DEC72-1520
BUSCH, F. ERZÄHLER-, FIGUREN- UND LESER-
PERSPEKTIVE IN HENRY JAMES' ROMAN "THE
AMBASSADORS."
H. FRIEDL, 72:BAND208HEFT4/6-411
BUSCH, M. & G. EDEL, EDS. ERZIEHUNG ZUR
FREIHEIT DURCH FREIHEITSENTZUG.
W. KURTH, 182:VOL23#13/14-657
BUSCH, W. SÄMTLICHE BRIEFE. (F. BOHNE,
ED)
K. WEIMAR, 182:VOL23#5-230
BUSH, D. MATTHEW ARNOLD.
617(TLS):21JAN72-59
BUSH, D. ENGLISH LITERATURE IN THE
EARLIER SEVENTEENTH CENTURY 1600-1660.
(2ND ED)
T.A. BIRRELL, 179(ES):AUG70-359
BUSH, D. PAGAN MYTH AND CHRISTIAN TRA-
DITION IN ENGLISH POETRY.
R.G. LUNT, 541(RES):FEB70-65
BUSH, D., J.E. SHAW & A.B. GIAMATTI. A
VARIORUM COMMENTARY ON THE POEMS OF
JOHN MILTON.* (VOL 1) [SHOWN IN PREV
UNDER MILTON, J.]
J.M.P., 568(SCN):SPRING71-1
J.T. SHAWCROSS, 568(SCN):SPRING71-1
R. VOITLE, 579(SAQ):SUMMER71-422
BUSH, J.W. VENETIA REDEEMED.
R.J. MARAS, 613:SUMMER69-318
BUSH, M.H. REVOLUTIONARY ENIGMA.
D.R. GERLACH, 656(WMQ):OCT70-672
BUSH, S. THE CHINESE LITERATI ON PAINT-
ING.
617(TLS):7JUL72-761
BUSH, V. PIECES OF THE ACTION.
617(TLS):10MAR72-264
BUSHBY, J. GUNNER'S MOON.
617(TLS):29SEP72-1176
BUSHRUI, S.B., ED. SUNSHINE AND THE
MOON'S DELIGHT.
617(TLS):9JUN72-662
BUSIGNANI, A. POLLOCK.
617(TLS):7JAN72-18
BUSSABARGER, R.F., B.D. ROBINS & A. TAU.
THE EVERYDAY ART OF INDIA.
W.G. ARCHER, 592:NOV69-190
BUSSE, H. CHALIF UND GROSSKÖNIG.
J. VAN ESS, 182:VOL23#8-436
BUSSMANN, H. - SEE EILHART VON OBERG
BUSST, A-J-L. - SEE BALLANCHE, P.S.
BUSTARD, R. AUSTRALIAN LIZARDS.
617(TLS):30JUN72-754
BUSZA, A. CONRAD'S POLISH LITERARY BACK-
GROUND.*
J.R. KRZYZANOWSKI, 627(UTQ):JUL69-386
BUTCHER, F. MANY LIVES, ONE LOVE.
441:24SEP72-52
BUTCHER, H.J. & D.E. LOMAX, EDS. READ-
INGS IN HUMAN INTELLIGENCE.
617(TLS):15SEP72-1063
BUTCHVAROV, P. THE CONCEPT OF KNOWLEDGE.
K. LEHRER, 311(JP):1JUN72-312
BUTKUS, D., WITH R.W. BILLINGS. STOP-
ACTION.
J. DURSO, 441:3DEC72-44
LORD BUTLER. THE ART OF THE POSSIBLE.*
P. JOHNSON, 441:19NOV72-2
BUTLER, B. THE DISCOVERY OF AMERICA.
J. HOPPER, 661:SPRING69-109

47

BUTLER, C. THE PRINCIPLES OF MUSIK IN
SINGING AND SETTING.
I. SPINK, 415:MAR71-241
J.A.W., 410(M&L):APR71-207
BUTLER, E. MASON-MAC.
617(TLS):13OCT72-1228
BUTLER, J. THE GARBAGEMAN.
G. WOODCOCK, 296:FALL72-94
BUTLER, M. MARIA EDGEWORTH.
617(TLS):22SEP72-1112
BUTLER, P. - SEE RACINE, J.
BUTLER, S. CHARACTERS.* (C.W. DAVES,
ED)
J.H.P. PAFFORD, 402(MLR):APR71-394
BUTLER, S. ERNEST PONTIFEX, OR THE WAY
OF ALL FLESH. (D.F. HOWARD, ED)
J. REES, 402(MLR):OCT71-882
BUTLER, S. HUDIBRAS. (J. WILDERS, ED)
H. CASTROP, 38:BAND87HEFT2-267
R. QUINTANA, 405(MP):AUG69-88
BUTLER, W. THE BONE HOUSE.
J.G. FARRELL, 362:13JUL72-57
BUTLIN, M., ED. THE BLAKE-VARLEY SKETCH-
BOOK OF 1819 IN THE COLLECTION OF
M.D.E. CLAYTON-STAMM.
D.V.E., 191(ELN):SEP70(SUPP)-21
G. KEYNES, 111:25OCT69-24
BUTLIN, M. WATERCOLOURS FROM THE TURNER
BEQUEST: 1819-1945.
E. JOLL, 39:DEC69-546
BUTOR, M. ESSAIS SUR LES ESSAIS.
R.D. COTTRELL, 399(MLJ):APR70-304
BUTOR, M. INVENTORY.* (R. HOWARD, ED)
J. BEHAR, 340(KR):1969/3-400
BUTOR, M. PORTRAIT DE L'ARTISTE EN JEUNE
SINGE.
G. LASCAULT, 98:JAN69-54
BÜTOW, H. ALLE TRÄUME DIESER WELT.
P. LAYTON, 270:VOL20#1-17
BUTT, J. POPE, DICKENS AND OTHERS.*
M.S., 155:SEP69-180
BUTT, J. & K. TILLOTSON. DICKENS AT
WORK.
K.J. FIELDING, 155:JAN69-49
BUTTERFIELD, R.W. THE BROKEN ARC.*
A. GALPIN, 659:WINTER72-106
BUTTERWORTH, B., COMP. THE GROWTH OF
INDUSTRIAL ART.
H. KRAMER, 441:3DEC72-34
BUTTERWORTH, E.A.S. THE TREE AT THE
NAVEL OF THE EARTH.
617(TLS):3MAR72-255
BUTTERWORTH, M. THE BLACK LOOK.
N. CALLENDAR, 441:25JUN72-30
BUTTINGER, J. VIETNAM: A DRAGON EMBAT-
TLED.*
F.J. CORLEY, 613:AUTUMN69-478
BUTTITTA, I. LA PAGLIA BRUCIATA.
G. CARSANIGA, 270:VOL20#1-21
BÜTTNER, L. BÜCHNERS BILD VOM MENSCHEN.*
R.F. GREEN, 182:VOL23#1/2-26
BUTWELL, R. SOUTHEAST ASIA, TODAY AND
TOMORROW. (2ND ED)
W. LEVI, 293(JAST):AUG70-982
BUXÓ, J.P. UNGARETTI, TRADUCTOR DE GÓN-
GORA.*
A. ILLIANO, 131(CL):SUMMER71-269
BUXTON, E. PROMISE THEM ANYTHING.
R. LASSON, 441:22OCT72-44
BUXTON, J. BYRON AND SHELLEY.
E.E.B., 191(ELN):SEP69(SUPP)-27
BUYSSENS, E. LES DEUX ASPECTIFS DE LA
CONJUGAISON ANGLAISE AU XXe SIÈCLE.
R.A.W. BLADON, 179(ES):OCT70-470
BUYSSENS, E. LINGUISTIQUE HISTORIQUE.*
K.E. ZIMMER, 545(RPH):FEB70-342

BUZZATI, D. UN CASO CLINICO. (P.R.
RAFFAELE & M. GAMBONE, EDS)
L.M. FERRARI, 399(MLJ):MAR70-208
R. STURM, 276:AUTUMN70-333
BUZZATI, D. LE NOTTI DIFFICILI.
617(TLS):2JUN72-623
BUZZATI, D. POEMA A FUMETTI.
F.J. FATA, 275(IQ):WINTER70-71
"BYELARUSKAYA SAVIETSKAYA ENTSYKLAPEDYA."
(VOLS 1-4)
617(TLS):30JUN72-743
BYGRAVE, M. & OTHERS, EDS. TIME OUT'S
BOOK OF LONDON.
617(TLS):30JUN72-752
BYKOV, V. THE ORDEAL.
E. MORGAN, 362:23MAR72-393
617(TLS):14APR72-427
BYRD, C.K. BOOKS IN SINGAPORE.
J.M. ECHOLS, 356:APR71-183
BYRNES, R.F. POBEDONOSTSEV.*
N.D. ROODKOWSKY, 613:AUTUMN69-474
BYROM, M. PUNCH AND JUDY.
617(TLS):23JUN72-730
"BYZANTINOBULGARIA." (VOL 2)
G. SOTIROFF, 104:SUMMER71-290

CABALLERO, R.F. - SEE UNDER FLORES CABAL-
LERO, R.
CABALLERO CALDERÓN, E. CAÍN.
E. ECHEVARRÍA, 263:JAN-MAR71-72
L.F. LYDAY, 263:JUL-SEP71-340
CABANIS, J. CHARLES X.
617(TLS):29SEP72-1149
CABANNE, P. DIALOGUES WITH MARCEL
DUCHAMP.*
R. SHATTUCK, 453:1JUN72-22
CABLE, J. GUNBOAT DIPLOMACY.
617(TLS):21JAN72-71
CABLE, M. THE AVENUE OF PRESIDENTS.
639(VQR):SPRING70-LXXIV
CABRERA INFANTE, G. THREE TRAPPED TIG-
ERS.*
J. UPDIKE, 442(NY):29JAN72-91
J. YGLESIAS, 61:AUG72-84
CABRERA INFANTE, G. TRES TRISTES TIGRES.
A. ADELL, 270:VOL20#3-62
CADEL, G. NOIRS ET BLANCS.
S.O. MEZU, 207(FR):DEC69-370
CADELL, E. HOME FOR THE WEDDING.
M. LEVIN, 441:16JAN72-43
CADOGAN, A. THE DIARIES OF SIR ALEXANDER
CADOGAN 1938-1945.* (D. DILKS, ED)
M. GILBERT, 441:16APR72-12
M. PANTER-DOWNES, 442(NY):28OCT72-148
E.M. YODER, JR., 440:19MAR72-8
CADOT, M. LA RUSSIE DANS LA VIE INTEL-
LECTUELLE FRANÇAISE 1839-1856.
E.K. BEAUJOUR, 207(FR):FEB70-535
CAESAR. 55 AND 54 B.C. - CAESAR'S EXPE-
DITIONS TO BRITAIN. (D.A.S. JOHN, ED)
M.F. MC NAMARA, 124:OCT70-63
CAFLISCH, L. LA PROTECTION DES SOCIÉTÉS
COMMERCIALES ET DES INTÉRÊTS INDIRECTS
EN DROIT INTERNATIONAL PUBLIC.
H.J. HAHN, 182:VOL23#19/20-843
CAGE, J. NOTATIONS.
V.M. AMES, 290(JAAC):SUMMER70-559
C. CARDEW, 592:JUL/AUG69-42
T. SOUSTER, 607:SUMMER69-34
CAGE, J. SILENCE.* A YEAR FROM MONDAY.*
B. DENNIS, 607:WINTER68/69-37
"CAHIERS ANDRÉ GIDE 3: LE CENTENAIRE."
617(TLS):15SEP72-1045

CAHN, E.B. ADRIAN DE VRIES UND SEINE
KIRCHLICHEN BRONZEKUNSTWERKE IN SCHAUM-
BURG.
C. AVERY, 90:JAN69-39
CAHN, S.M. FATE, LOGIC, AND TIME.
R. MC INERNY, 613:AUTUMN68-467
CAIDIN, M. DESTINATION MARS.
T. STURGEON, 441:3SEP72-20
CAIDIN, M. MARYJANE TONIGHT AT ANGELS
TWELVE.
N. CALLENDAR, 441:1OCT72-43
CAILLOIS, R. LES JEUX ET LES HOMMES.
J. EHRMANN, 98:JUL69-579
CAINAS PONZOA, A. DESNUDEZ.
M.A. CASARTELLI, 263:JUL-SEP71-341
CAIRNS, D. - SEE BERLIOZ, H.
CAIZZI, F.D. - SEE UNDER DECLEVA CAIZZI,
F.
CALAHANE, V.H., ED. THE IMPERIAL COLLEC-
TION OF AUDUBON ANIMALS.
W. BLUNT, 90:JUN69-398
CALARCO, N.J. TRAGIC BEING.*
W. ANGUS, 529(QQ):SPRING70-133
T. ROGERS, 175:AUTUMN69-110
C.H. SMITH, 397(MD):DEC69-324
DE CALATCHI, R. ORIENTAL CARPETS.
M.H. BEATTIE, 39:FEB69-161
M.H. BEATTIE, 39:MAR69-245
CALBOLI, G. CORNIFICIANA 2.
A. MICHEL, 555:VOL44FASC1-147
CALDER, N. THE RESTLESS EARTH.
P. ADAMS, 61:AUG72-92
CALDER, N. TECHNOPOLIS.
J. WREN-LEWIS, 619(TC):VOL177#1042-53
CALDER-MARSHALL, A. LEWD, BLASPHEMOUS
AND OBSCENE.
617(TLS):3NOV72-1346
CALDERÓN, E.C. - SEE UNDER CABALLERO CAL-
DERÓN, E.
CALDERÓN, E.C. - SEE UNDER CORREA CALDER-
ÓN, E.
CALDERÓN DE LA BARCA, P. A CRITICAL EDI-
TION OF CALDERÓN'S "LOS CABELLOS DE
ABSALÓN."* (H.F. GIACOMAN, ED)
V.R. CRAIG, 238:SEP70-571
CALDERÓN DE LA BARCA, P. LA HIJA DEL
AIRE. (G. EDWARDS, ED)
617(TLS):4AUG72-914
CALDERWOOD, J.L. & H.R. TOLIVER. FORMS
OF POETRY.
A. RODWAY, 447(N&Q):JUL70-269
CALDWELL, H. MACHADO DE ASSIS.*
M.I. ABREU, 593:WINTER71-408
CALDWELL, O.J. A SECRET WAR.
M. COPELAND, 561(SATR):20MAY72-67
CALDWELL, T. CAPTAINS AND THE KINGS.
M. LEVIN, 441:14MAY72-36
CALERO, R.C. - SEE UNDER CARBALLO CALERO,
R.
CALHOUN, J.C. THE PAPERS OF JOHN C. CAL-
HOUN. (VOL 5) (W.E. HEMPHILL, ED)
617(TLS):28APR72-498
CALIC, E., ED. SECRET CONVERSATIONS WITH
HITLER.
G. BARRACLOUGH, 453:2NOV72-32
CALIN, W. THE EPIC QUEST.*
P. JONIN, 545(RPH):NOV69-236
CALISHER, H. HERSELF. STANDARD DREAM-
ING.
W. ABRAHAMS, 561(SATR):14OCT72-75
R. KIELY, 441:1OCT72-3
C. LEHMANN-HAUPT, 441:9NOV72-49
E. WEEKS, 61:OCT72-132
CALISHER, H. THE NEW YORKERS.
N.L. MAGID, 340(KR):1969/5-714
C. OZICK, 390:NOV69-77
"CALL THEM CANADIANS."
A. EMERY, 627(UTQ):JUL69-408

CALLADO, A. DON JUAN'S BAR.
M. LEVIN, 441:9APR72-42
CALLAHAN, J.F. AUGUSTINE AND THE GREEK
PHILOSOPHERS.
A.H. ARMSTRONG, 313:VOL60-230
CALLAHAN, N. CARL SANDBURG.*
J.T. FLANAGAN, 27(AL):MAR71-142
CALLAHAN, N. GEORGE WASHINGTON, SOLDIER
AND MAN.
441:10DEC72-48
LADY CALLCOTT. LITTLE ARTHUR'S HISTORY
OF ENGLAND.
617(TLS):7JAN72-10
CALLEBAT, L. SERMO COTIDIANUS DANS LES
MÉTAMORPHOSES D'APULÉE.
C.C. SCHLAM, 124:NOV70-93
CALLEY, W.L., WITH J. SACK. BODY COUNT.
617(TLS):10MAR72-264
CALLIMACHUS. CALLIMACHI "HYMNUS IN
DIANAM." (F. BORNMANN, ED)
G. GIANGRANDE, 123:DEC71-354
A.H. GRIFFITHS, 303:VOL90-214
CALLOT, É. CIVILISATION ET CIVILISA-
TIONS.
C. SCHUWER, 542:JAN-MAR69-115
CALLOW, P. BARE WIRES.
617(TLS):4AUG72-910
CALLOW, P. FLESH OF MORNING.*
F. MC GUINESS, 364:JUN/JUL71-148
CALLOW, P. YOURS.
J.G. FARRELL, 362:7SEP72-312
617(TLS):15SEP72-1042
CALTHROP, K. READING TOGETHER.
617(TLS):4FEB72-137
CALVETTI, C.G. SPINOZA, I PRESUPPOSTI
TEORETICI DELL'IRENISMO ETICO.
P. DI VONA, 548(RCSF):JUL/SEP69-340
CALVIN, A.D., ED. PROGRAMMED INSTRUC-
TION.
A.S. CARTON, 399(MLJ):MAY70-375
CALVIN, H. TAKE TWO POPES.
617(TLS):25AUG72-1005
CALVOCORESSI, P. & G. WINT. TOTAL WAR.
D. SCHOENBRUN, 441:17DEC72-4
617(TLS):14JUL72-789
CAMBIER, G. - SEE BAKELANTS, L.
CAMBON, G. DANTE'S CRAFT.*
D.J.B. ROBEY, 402(MLR):JAN71-200
CAMBON, G. GIUSEPPE UNGARETTI.
C.W. MACLEOD, 447(N&Q):FEB70-74
L. REBAY, 276:SPRING70-103
"CAMBRIDGE LATIN COURSE UNIT 2."
617(TLS):25FEB72-229
"CAMBRIDGE LATIN COURSE UNIT 3."
617(TLS):11AUG72-954
CAMDEN, W. THE HISTORY OF THE MOST RE-
NOWNED AND VICTORIOUS PRINCESS ELIZA-
BETH (LATE QUEEN OF ENGLAND). (W.T.
MAC CAFFREY, ED)
617(TLS):18FEB72-175
CAMERON, A. AGATHIAS.
W.E. KAEGI, JR., 124:JAN71-161
CAMERON, A. CLAUDIAN.
639(VQR):AUTUMN70-CXL
CAMERON, A. THE IDENTITY OF OEDIPUS THE
KING.*
M.J. O'BRIEN, 24:APR71-370
R.P. WINNINGTON-INGRAM, 303:VOL90-204
CAMERON, A., R. FRANK & J. LEYERLE, EDS.
COMPUTERS AND OLD ENGLISH CONCORDANCES.
617(TLS):4FEB72-136
CAMERON, A.S. CHINESE PAINTING TECH-
NIQUES.
P. HARDIE, 39:APR69-327
CAMERON, G. ROSE.
617(TLS):23JUN72-704

CAMERON, I. THE IMPOSSIBLE DREAM.
441:20FEB72-24
617(TLS):7JUL72-782
CAMERON, I. THE MOUNTAINS AT THE BOTTOM
OF THE WORLD.
M. LEVIN, 441:5NOV72-41
CAMERON, K. - SEE DE RIVAUDEAU, A.
CAMERON, K.N., ED. SHELLEY AND HIS
CIRCLE, 1773-1822.* (VOLS 3&4)
P.H. BUTTER, 402(MLR):OCT71-876
J. CLUBBE, 579(SAQ):WINTER71-122
R.H. FOGLE, 639(VQR):SUMMER70-525
CAMERON, R. AUSTRALIA.*
617(TLS):16JUN72-690
CAMERON, W.J., ED. POEMS ON AFFAIRS OF
STATE. (VOL 5)
617(TLS):4AUG72-910
CAMI. LES EXPLOITS GALANTS DU BARON DE
CRAC.
617(TLS):29SEP72-1161
CAMP, J. PORTRAIT OF BUCKINGHAMSHIRE.
617(TLS):27OCT72-1296
CAMP, J., X.J. KENNEDY & K. WALDROP, EDS.
PEGASUS DESCENDING.*
G. SOULE, 109:SPRING/SUMMER72-149
617(TLS):7APR72-392
CAMPANA, D. ORPHIC SONGS.
J.A. MOLINARO, 276:SPRING70-100
CAMPANELLA, T. APOLOGIA DI GALILEO. (L.
FIRPO, ED)
M. DEL PRA, 548(RCSF):JAN/MAR69-109
CAMPANELLA, T. METAFISICA. (G. DI
NAPOLI, ED)
G. ERNST, 548(RCSF):APR/JUN69-214
CAMPBELL, A. & I. DAWSON, EDS. THE
LIBRARY TECHNICIAN AT WORK.
R.C. ELLSWORTH, 356:APR71-191
CAMPBELL, B. & J. FERGUSON-LEES. A
FIELD GUIDE TO BIRD'S NESTS.
617(TLS):15DEC72-1541
CAMPBELL, C. TOWARD A SOCIOLOGY OF
IRRELIGION.
617(TLS):28APR72-471
CAMPBELL, D.A. THE DRESS OF THE ROYAL
ARTILLERY. (C.W. IKIN, ED)
617(TLS):4FEB72-137
CAMPBELL, H.D. & C.E. BAUER. PROGRAMMED
FRENCH READERS. (BKS 1&2)
W.R. JONES, 207(FR):OCT69-146
CAMPBELL, J. MYTHS TO LIVE BY.
E. WILSON, JR., 561(SATR):24JUN72-68
442(NY):3JUN72-111
CAMPBELL, J.L. - SEE MAC CORMICK, D.
CAMPBELL, K. BODY AND MIND.
K. WARD, 518:OCT71-5
CAMPBELL, K. THUNDER ON SUNDAY.
N. CALLENDAR, 441:12NOV72-67
617(TLS):7JUL72-783
CAMPBELL, N., COMP. TENNYSON IN LINCOLN.
(VOL 1)
617(TLS):26MAY72-606
CAMPBELL, O.J., WITH E.G. QUINN, EDS.
A SHAKESPEARE ENCYCLOPAEDIA.
D. MEHL, 38:BAND87HEFT3/4-457
CAMPBELL, P. FAT TUESDAY TAILS.
V. CUNNINGHAM, 362:9NOV72-643
617(TLS):24NOV72-1441
CAMPBELL, R. - SEE OSWALD, R.G.
CAMPBELL, R.N. NOUN SUBSTITUTES IN MOD-
ERN THAI.
T.W. GETHING, 293(JAST):MAY70-732
CAMPBELL, T.D. ADAM SMITH'S SCIENCE OF
MORALS.*
J.R. LINDGREN, 319:OCT72-481
CAMPION, R. THE INVISIBLE WORM.
441:1OCT72-38

CAMPION, T. THE WORKS OF THOMAS CAM-
PION.* (W.R. DAVIS, ED)
D.C.B., 412:MAY71-191
I. SPINK, 415:MAY70-508
DEL CAMPO, X. NARRATIVA JOVEN DE MÉXICO.
R.M. REEVE, 238:MAY70-346
DE CAMPOS, D.R. - SEE UNDER REDIG DE
CAMPOS, D.
CAMPOS, J. TEATRO Y SOCIEDAD EN ESPAÑA
(1780-1820).
191(ELN):SEP70(SUPP)-150
CAMPS, W.A. AN INTRODUCTION TO VIRGIL'S
"AENEID."*
R.G. AUSTIN, 313:VOL60-261
M.L. CLARKE, 123:MAR71-47
G.E. DUCKWORTH, 24:JAN71-124
M.C.J. PUTNAM, 121(CJ):FEB-MAR71-278
CAMUS, A. A HAPPY DEATH.* (FRENCH
TITLE: LA MORT HEUREUSE.)
A. BROYARD, 441:13JUN72-45
E. CAPOUYA, 561(SATR):15APR72-63
J.D. O'HARA, 440:14MAY72-4
P. SOURIAN, 441:11JUN72-4
J. UPDIKE, 442(NY):21OCT72-157
J. WEIGHTMAN, 453:15JUN72-6
CANADAY, J. CULTURE GULCH.
M. LAVANOUX, 363:NOV69-28
CANCIK, H. UNTERSUCHUNGEN ZU SENECAS.
E. WITZENRATH, 490:JUL68-421
CANDAMO, F.B. - SEE UNDER BANCES CANDAMO,
F.
CANETTI, E. MACHT UND ÜBERLEBEN. DIE
GESPALTENE ZUKUNFT.
617(TLS):22DEC72-1560
CANFIELD, C. UP AND DOWN AND AROUND.*
617(TLS):21JUL72-852
CANFORA, F. SIMMACO E AMBROGIO, O DI UN'
ANTICA CONTROVERSIA SULLA TOLLERANZA E
SULL' INTOLLERANZA.
S.I. OOST, 122:OCT71-293
CANFORA, L. PER LA CRONOLOGIA DI DEMOS-
TENE.
D.M. MACDOWELL, 123:DEC70-321
CANGIOTTI, G. PÍO BAROJA, "OSSERVATORE"
DEL COSTUME ITALIANO.
C.A. LONGHURST, 86(BHS):JAN71-80
CANNEY, M.A. AN ENCYCLOPAEDIA OF RELI-
GIONS.
J.J. FARBER, 124:APR71-273
CANNING, J., ED. 100 GREAT MODERN LIVES.
617(TLS):22SEP72-1124
CANNING, V. FIRECREST.
N. CALLENDAR, 441:14MAY72-35
617(TLS):4FEB72-135
CANNING, V. THE RAINBIRD PATTERN.
617(TLS):8DEC72-1507
CANNING, V. THE RUNAWAYS.
M. LEVIN, 441:13FEB72-32
CANNON, G. - SEE JONES, W.
CANNON, J. THE FOX-NORTH COALITION.
G. NIEDHART, 182:VOL23#15/16-755
CANNON, L. THE MC CLOSKEY CHALLENGE.
G. WILLS, 440:5MAR72-4
CANO, J.L. LA POESÍA DE LA GENERACIÓN
DEL 27.
H.F. GRANT, 86(BHS):JAN71-83
CANTOR, N.E., ED. PERSPECTIVES ON THE
EUROPEAN PAST.
617(TLS):24NOV72-1437
CANTORE, E. ATOMIC ORDER.
R.H.K., 543:JUN70-739
CANTWELL, R. THE HIDDEN NORTHWEST.
441:8OCT72-38
CAPEL, V. THE MUSIC LOVER'S ALL-IN-ONE
GRAMOPHONE BOOK.
M. GOFF, 415:JUL70-714

CAPEL MARGARITO, M. LA CAROLINA CAPITAL
DE LAS NUEVAS POBLACIONES.
J. NADAL, 86(BHS):JUL71-276
CAPLAN, H. OF ELOQUENCE. (A. KING & H.
NORTH, EDS)
G.M.A. GRUBE, 124:MAY71-313
617(TLS):21JUL72-849
"CAPOLAVORI NELLA RACCOLTA DELLE STAMPE
DELLA PINACOTECA NAZIONALE DI BOLOGNA."*
(VOL 1)
K. ANDREWS, 90:MAY69-309
CAPONE, G. DRAMMI PER VOCI.
M. FRATTI, 397(MD):MAY69-104
CAPORALE, R. & A. GRUMELLI, EDS. THE
CULTURE OF UNBELIEF.
617(TLS):7APR72-397
CAPOVILLA, G. CALLIMACO.*
R. RIEKS, 182:VOL23#8-422
CAPP, B.S. THE FIFTH MONARCHY MEN.
617(TLS):18AUG72-969
CAPRIOLI, S. INDAGINI SUL BOLOGNINI.
D.E. QUELLER, 589:JAN71-133
DE CARAMAN-CHIMAY, T. VIOLETS FOR THE
EMPEROR.
617(TLS):10NOV72-1377
CARASSUS, E. - SEE VALLÈS, J.
CARBALLIDO, E. THE NORTHER.
J. RUTHERFORD, 86(BHS):APR71-181
CARBALLO CALERO, R. HISTORIA DA LITERA-
TURA GALEGA CONTEMPORÁNEA. (VOL 1)
191(ELN):SEP69(SUPP)-140
CARBONELL, R. EL HOMBRE SOBRE EL
ARMARIO Y OTROS CUENTOS. (L.C. DE
MORELOS & A. LAFORA, EDS)
S.J. WILLIAMS, JR., 399(MLJ):JAN70-52
CÁRDENAS, D.N. EL ESPAÑOL DE JALISCO.
J.R. CRADDOCK, 240(HR):OCT70-422
CARDEW, C., ED. SCRATCH MUSIC.
617(TLS):27OCT72-1280
CARDEW, M. PIONEER POTTERY.
S. PETERSON, 139:SEP/OCT69-8
CARDINAL, H. THE UNJUST SOCIETY.
N. SHIPLEY, 529(QQ):SUMMER70-292
CARDINAL, R. & R.S. SHORT. SURREALISM.
R. SHATTUCK, 453:1JUN72-22
CARDUNER, J. LA CRÉATION ROMANESQUE
CHEZ MALRAUX.
J.V. ALTER, 207(FR):DEC69-328
J. DALE, 208(FS):JUL71-355
R.D. RECK, 399(MLJ):NOV70-547
CARDUS, N. FULL SCORE.
R. ANDERSON, 415:MAR71-245
J.A.W., 410(M&L):JAN71-88
CARDWELL, D.S.L. FROM WATT TO CLAUSIUS.
617(TLS):4FEB72-133
CARDWELL, M. - SEE DICKENS, C.
CARE, N.S. & R.H. GRIMM, EDS. PERCEPTION
AND PERSONAL IDENTITY.
R.H. KANE, 484(PPR):JUN70-624
M.B.M., 543:JUN70-754
CARELESS, J.M.S., ED. COLONISTS AND
CANADIENS 1760-1867.
P. OLIVER, 99:JAN-FEB72-73
CARELL, P. SCORCHED EARTH.
R.L. GARTHOFF, 32:SEP71-669
CARENS, J.F. - SEE GOGARTY, O.S.
CAREY, G. A FARAWAY TIME AND PLACE.
J.B. BOLES, 70(ANQ):APR72-124
CAREY, J., ED. ANDREW MARVELL.*
S. GILL, 447(N&Q):JUL70-272
CAREY, J. & A. FOWLER - SEE MILTON, J.
CAREY, R. THE MEMOIRS OF ROBERT CAREY.
(F.H. MARES, ED)
617(TLS):1DEC72-1452
CARGO, R.T., ED. BAUDELAIRE CRITICISM
1950-1967.*
F.E. HYSLOP, JR., 207(FR):OCT69-180
R.B. WEBER, 577(SHR):SUMMER70-283

CARIDI, R.J. THE KOREAN WAR AND AMERICAN
POLITICS.
R.Y. KOEN, 293(JAST):AUG70-946
CARLÉ, M.D. DEL CONCEJO MEDIEVAL CASTEL-
LANO-LEONÉS.
R.I. BURNS, 589:JAN71-134
CARLETON, W.G. TECHNOLOGY AND HUMANISM.
D.H. STEWART, 651(WHR):SPRING71-184
CARLISLE, C.J. SHAKESPEARE FROM THE
GREENROOM.*
A. FREEMAN, 551(RENQ):WINTER70-485
CARLISLE, H. VOYAGE TO THE FIRST OF
DECEMBER.
C. LEHMANN-HAUPT, 441:2FEB72-41
M. LEVIN, 441:23JAN72-36
P. THEROUX, 440:23JAN72-2
A. WHITMAN, 561(SATR):12FEB72-74
442(NY):19FEB72-115
CARLISLE, O., ED. POETS ON STREET COR-
NERS.*
R. KEMBALL, 550(RUSR):JAN70-103
CARLO, A.M. - SEE MILLARES CARLO, A.
CARLS, C.D. ERNST BARLACH.
A. WERNER, 58:DEC69/JAN70-12
CARLSON, E.W., ED. THE RECOGNITION OF
EDGAR ALLAN POE.
R. LEHAN, 445(NCF):JUN68-117
CARLSON, L.H. - SEE GREENWOOD, J. & H.
BARROW
CARLSSON, L. LE DEGRÉ DE COHÉSION DES
GROUPES SUBST. + DE + SUBST. EN FRAN-
ÇAIS CONTEMPORAINE ÉTUDIÉ D'APRÈS LA
PLACE ACCORDÉE À L'ADJECTIF ÉPITHÈTE.
S. ANDERSSON, 596(SL):VOL22#1-66
CARLTON, C. A DESCRIPTIVE SYNTAX OF THE
OLD ENGLISH CHARTERS.
R.B. MITCHELL, 382(MAE):1971/2-181
CARLTON, R.G. - SEE OKINSHEVICH, L.
CARLUT, C. LA CORRESPONDANCE DE FLAU-
BERT.
B.F. BART, 399(MLJ):JAN70-48
C.A. BURNS, 208(FS):APR71-223
CARLUT, C. & W. MEIDEN. FRENCH FOR ORAL
AND WRITTEN REVIEW.
M. WALTER, 399(MLJ):DEC70-616
CARLYLE, T. THE LETTERS OF THOMAS CAR-
LYLE TO HIS BROTHER ALEXANDER, WITH
RELATED FAMILY LETTERS.* (E.W. MARRS,
JR., ED)
D.V.E., 191(ELN):SEP70(SUPP)-30
G.B. TENNYSON, 637(VS):MAR70-366
R. TRICKETT, 447(N&Q):MAY70-195
CARLYLE, T. & J.W. THE COLLECTED LETTERS
OF THOMAS AND JANE WELSH CARLYLE.*
(VOLS 1-4) (C.R. SANDERS, ED)
F.W. HILLES, 676(YR):SUMMER71-569
"'CARMEN' BY GEORGES BIZET." (E.H.
BLEILER, TRANS)
W. DEAN, 415:MAR71-246
J.W.K., 410(M&L):APR71-181
CARMICHAEL, H. THE QUIET WOMAN.
N. CALLENDAR, 441:10SEP72-40
DEL CARMIN, P.E.D. - SEE UNDER EULOGIO DE
LA VIRGEN DEL CARMIN, P.
CARMONA, A. DUES CATALUNYES.
191(ELN):SEP70(SUPP)-150
DE CARMOY, G. THE FOREIGN POLICIES OF
FRANCE 1944-1968.
B.H. SMITH, 396(MODA):SUMMER71-325
CARNAP, R. THE LOGICAL STRUCTURE OF THE
WORLD & PSEUDO-PROBLEMS IN PHILOSOPHY.
B.C. VAN FRAASSEN, 486:SEP68-298
CARNAP, R. & R.C. JEFFREY, EDS. STUDIES
IN LOGIC AND PROBABILITY. (VOL 1)
617(TLS):17MAR72-303
CARNICELLI, T.A. - SEE SAINT AUGUSTINE

CARNICER, R. ENTRE LA CIENCIA Y LA
MAGIA MARIANO CUBÍ.
G.J.G. CHEYNE, 86(BHS):APR71-169
CARNOCHAN, W.B. LEMUEL GULLIVER'S MIRROR
FOR MAN.*
P. HARTH, 401(MLQ):MAR70-118
C.J. RAWSON, 541(RES):MAY70-217
"CAROLINGIAN CHRONICLES." (B.W. SCHOLZ,
WITH B. ROGERS, TRANS)
O. MURRAY, 382(MAE):1971/3-314
CARPENTER, C.A. BERNARD SHAW AND THE ART
OF DESTROYING IDEALS.*
A.P. BARR, 141:WINTER70-82
C.A. BERST, 401(MLQ):MAR70-128
L. CROMPTON, 502(PRS):WINTER69/70-414
L. CROMPTON, 572:SEP69-130
R. ROBERTSON, 529(QQ):WINTER70-652
T. ROGERS, 175:AUTUMN69-110
CARPENTER, D. GETTING OFF.*
J.M. MORSE, 249(HUDR):AUTUMN71-535
CARPENTER, E. CANTUAR.
617(TLS):28JAN72-106
CARPENTER, N.C. JOHN SKELTON.
W.N. KING, 219(GAR):WINTER69-547
CARPENTIER, A. WAR OF TIME.*
F. DONAHUE, 584(SWR):WINTER71-99
CARPENTIER, C. FLIGHT ONE.
M. LEVIN, 441:12NOV72-67
CARPENTIER, H. & J. BROF, EDS. DOORS
AND MIRRORS.
A. BROYARD, 441:27JUL72-33
DA CARPI, U. THESAURO DE SCRITTORI,
1535.
D. CHAMBERS, 503:AUTUMN69-130
CARPOZI, G., JR. ORDEAL BY TRIAL.
441:30APR72-28
CARR, E.H. THE OCTOBER REVOLUTION.*
R.V. DANIELS, 550(RUSR):JUL70-339
CARR, J.D. THE HUNGRY GOBLIN.
O.L. BAILEY, 561(SATR):26AUG72-62
N. CALLENDAR, 441:16JUL72-32
CARR, J.L. THE HARPOLE REPORT.
617(TLS):16JUN72-677
CARR, L. A CATALOGUE OF THE VANDER POEL
DICKENS COLLECTION AT THE UNIVERSITY
OF TEXAS. (2ND ED)
T.D. SMITH, 155:SEP70-251
CARR, R. SPAIN 1808-1939.
J. BÉCARUD, 98:JUN69-551 [AND CONT IN]
98:JUL69-657
CARRÀ, M., WITH P. WALDBERG & E. RATHKE.
METAPHYSICAL ART.
617(TLS):1DEC72-1448
CARRARA, G.M.A. OPERE SCELTE. (G. GIR-
ALDI, ED)
H.H. DAVIS, 551(RENQ):AUTUMN70-303
CARRASCO URGOITI, M.S. EL PROBLEMA
MORISCO EN ARAGÓN AL COMIENZO DEL REIN-
ADO DE FELIPE II (ESTUDIO Y APÉNDICES
DOCUMENTALES).
J. CASEY, 86(BHS):APR71-161
CARRASQUER, F. "IMÁN" Y LA NOVELA HIS-
TÓRICA DE RAMÓN J. SENDER.
C.L. KING, 238:MAR70-151
LE CARRÉ, J. THE NAIVE AND SENTIMENTAL
LOVER.*
A. COOPER, 561(SATR):8JAN72-34
D. JOHNSON, 440:9JAN72-4
C. LEHMANN-HAUPT, 441:5JAN72-39
F.P.W. MC DOWELL, 659:SUMMER72-361
E. WEEKS, 61:FEB72-107
G. WOLFF, 441:9JAN72-7
CARRICK, A.V. A HISTORY OF AMERICAN
SILHOUETTES.
M.S. YOUNG, 39:APR69-328
CARRIER, R. IL EST PAR LÀ, LE SOLEIL.
R. SUTHERLAND, 102(CANL):AUTUMN71-87

CARRIER, R. LA GUERRE, YES SIR!*
D. BAILEY, 606(TAMR):#55-88
CARRIKER, R.C. FORT SUPPLY, INDIAN TER-
RITORY.
W. GARD, 584(SWR):SPRING71-199
CARRINGTON, D. GRANITE ISLAND.
617(TLS):5MAY72-512
CARROL, P. - SEE DAHLBERG, E.
CARROLL, D.B. HENRI MERCIER AND THE
AMERICAN CIVIL WAR.
617(TLS):22SEP72-1114
CARROLL, J., ED. THE EGO AND HIS OWN.*
J. DUNN, 362:10FEB72-186
CARROLL, J., ED. SAMUEL RICHARDSON: A
COLLECTION OF CRITICAL ESSAYS.
J. STEDMOND, 627(UTQ):JUL70-369
A. WRIGHT, 677:VOL2-281
CARROLL, J. - SEE STIRNER, M.
CARROLL, L. ALICE IN WONDERLAND. (D.J.
GRAY, ED)
J. GARDNER, 441:30JAN72-3
CARROLL, L. THROUGH THE LOOKING GLASS
AND WHAT ALICE FOUND THERE.
617(TLS):15DEC72-1525
CARROLL, P. ODES.*
P. COOPER, 340(KR):1970/1-143
639(VQR):SPRING70-L
CARROLL, P., ED. THE YOUNG AMERICAN
POETS.*
J.C. DE VANY, 590:SPRING70-41
CARROLL, P.N. PURITANISM AND THE WIL-
DERNESS.
D.D. HALL, 432(NEQ):MAR70-156
K.J. HANSEN, 529(QQ):SPRING70-141
N. PETTIT, 656(WMQ):JUL70-481
639(VQR):WINTER70-XXIII
CARRUBBA, R.W. THE EPODES OF HORACE.
T.A. SUITS, 124:NOV70-91
CARRUTH, H. FOR YOU.*
W. DICKEY, 249(HUDR):SPRING71-159
CARSON, E. THE ANCIENT AND RIGHTFUL
CUSTOMS.
617(TLS):16JUN72-692
CARSON, G. MEN, BEASTS AND GODS.
M. BATES & R. WYKES, 441:12NOV72-54
CARSTEN, F.L. REVOLUTION IN CENTRAL
EUROPE, 1918-1919.
617(TLS):21APR72-444
CARTER, A. THE INFERNAL DESIRE MACHINES
OF DOCTOR HOFFMAN.
V. CUNNINGHAM, 362:25MAY72-693
617(TLS):2JUN72-622
CARTER, A.E. VERLAINE.
A.F.B. CLARK, 627(UTQ):JUL70-352
CARTER, B.G. HISTORIA DE LA LITERATURA
HISPANOAMERICANA A TRAVÉS DE SUS
REVISTAS.
J.S. BRUSHWOOD, 240(HR):OCT70-445
CARTER, C. THE BLIZZARD OF '91.
617(TLS):21JAN72-78
CARTER, C.H. THE WESTERN EUROPEAN POW-
ERS, 1500-1700.*
D.P. JORDAN, 356:OCT71-351
CARTER, D.T. SCOTTSBORO.
J.P. DIGGINS, 340(KR):1969/3-427
W.B. GATEWOOD, JR., 219(GAR):FALL69-
408
W.M. TUTTLE, JR., 330(MASJ):FALL69-81
CARTER, H. THE STUDY OF URBAN GEOGRAPHY.
617(TLS):28JUL72-875
CARTER, H. THE TOMB OF TUTANKHAMEN.
P. ADAMS, 61:OCT72-135
CARTER, H.H., ED. THE PORTUGUESE BOOK
OF JOSEPH OF ARIMATHEA.*
V.M. LAGORIO, 377:MAR71-39
K.S. ROBERTS, 240(HR):APR70-238

CARTER, J. ABC FOR BOOK COLLECTORS.
(REV)
617(TLS):18AUG72-976
CARTER, J. - SEE HOUSMAN, A.E.
CARTER, J.M. THE BATTLE OF ACTIUM.
W.O. MOELLER, 124:JAN71-168
CARTER, L. TOLKIEN.
P.J. CALLAHAN, 502(PRS):FALL69-316
CARTER, S. 3D. BLAZE OF GLORY.
441:9JAN72-28
CARTER, T.H. ESSAYS AND REVIEWS. (J.
BOATWRIGHT, ED)
G. CORE, 219(GAR):WINTER69-544
CARTEY, W. WHISPERS FROM A CONTINENT.*
C.M. BROWN, 340(KR):1969/3-395
CARTIER-BRESSON, H. THE FACE OF ASIA.
S. SCHWARTZ, 441:3DEC72-20
CARTIER-BRESSON, H. MAN AND MACHINE.
617(TLS):14APR72-429
CARTON, A.S. THE "METHOD OF INFERENCE"
IN FOREIGN LANGUAGE STUDY.
T. MUELLER, 399(MLJ):MAY70-378
CARTON, F. - SEE COTTIGNIES, F.
CARTWRIGHT, F.F., WITH M.D. BIDDISS.
DISEASE AND HISTORY.
617(TLS):4AUG72-922
CARTWRIGHT, M.T. DIDEROT CRITIQUE D'ART
ET LE PROBLÈME DE L'EXPRESSION.*
M. HOBSON, 402(MLR):JAN71-186
CARVALHO, J.D. - SEE UNDER DE SOUSA CAR-
VALHO, J.
DE CARVALHO-NETO, P. HISTORIA DEL FOLK-
LORE IBEROAMERICANO.
E. GARRIDO DE BOGGS, 263:APR-JUN71-
203
CARY, L. & R. MAPES. THE SOCIOLOGY OF
PLANNING.
617(TLS):11FEB72-166
"THE MARY FLAGLER CARY MUSIC COLLECTION."
J.A.W., 410(M&L):OCT71-443
CARY, O. NIHON TO NO TAIWA.
T. KANO, 293(JAST):FEB70-450
CASADO NIETO, M. LA TURBIA CORRIENTE.
R.L. SHEEHAN, 238:MAY70-341
CASALS, P. JOYS AND SORROWS.
R. ANDERSON, 415:JAN71-34
CASANOVA, A. VATICAN II ET L'EVOLUTION
DE L'EGLISE.
H. PEYRE, 207(FR):MAR70-721
CASANOVA, G. HISTORY OF MY LIFE.* (VOLS
1-12) (W.R. TRASK, TRANS)
617(TLS):1SEP72-1009
CASEY, K., ED. WINTER'S TALES FROM IRE-
LAND 2.
617(TLS):29DEC72-1573
CASEY, M. OBSCENITIES.
D. HOFFMAN, 441:14MAY72-2
N. ROSTEN, 561(SATR):12AUG72-58
CASEY, R.G. AUSTRALIAN FOREIGN MINISTER.
(T.B. MILLAR, ED)
617(TLS):2JUN72-617
CASINI, P. L'UNIVERSO-MACCHINA.
G. GORI, 548(RCSF):JUL/SEP69-332
CASKEL, W. & G. STRENZIOK. ĞAMHARAT AN-
NASAB. (VOLS 1&2)
S.D. GOITEIN, 318(JAOS):OCT-DEC70-548
CASO GONZÁLEZ, J., ED. LA VIDA DE LAZAR-
ILLO DE TORMES, Y DE SUS FORTUNAS Y
ADVERSIDADES.
F. RICO, 240(HR):OCT70-405
CASOTTI, M.W. IL VIGNOLA.
T.K. KITAO, 54:DEC69-400
CASSEDY, J.H. DEMOGRAPHY IN EARLY AMERI-
CA.
J. MODELL, 656(WMQ):OCT70-682
B.E. STEINER, 432(NEQ):SEP70-482
639(VQR):SUMMER70-CVIII

CASSELL, R.A., ED. FORD MADOX FORD:
MODERN JUDGEMENTS.
617(TLS):15DEC72-1525
CASSERLEY, H.C. FAMOUS RAILWAY PHOTOGRA-
PHERS: H.C. CASSERLEY.
617(TLS):29SEP72-1176
CASSERLEY, H.C. RAILWAYS SINCE 1939.
617(TLS):21APR72-458
CASSIDY, F.G. DANE COUNTY PLACE-NAMES.
E.C. EHRENSPERGER, 424:SEP69-239
CASSIDY, F.G. JAMAICA TALK.
617(TLS):30JUN72-745
CASSIDY, F.G. & R.B. LE PAGE, EDS. A
DICTIONARY OF JAMAICAN ENGLISH.*
617(TLS):13OCT72-1209
CASSILL, R.V. LA VIE PASSIONNÉE OF
RODNEY BUCKTHORNE.
R. LACY, 448:SUMMER70-122
CASSINELLI, C.W. & R.B. EKVALL. A TIBET-
AN PRINCIPALITY.
P. CARRASCO, 293(JAST):FEB70-457
CASSIRER, E. FILOSOFIA DELLE FORME SIM-
BOLICHE. (VOL 3)
E. BECCHI, 548(RCSF):OCT-DEC68-473
CASSON, H. & J. GRENFELL. NANNY SAYS.
(LADY AVEBURY, ED)
617(TLS):1DEC72-1469
CASSON, J. LEWIS AND SYBIL.
617(TLS):8DEC72-1482
CASTANEDA, C. JOURNEY TO IXTLAN.
R. JELLINEK, 441:14OCT72-35
J. KANON, 561(SATR):11NOV72-67
P. RIESMAN, 441:22OCT72-7
CASTANEDA, C. A SEPARATE REALITY.*
P. RIESMAN, 441:22OCT72-7
CASTANEDA, C. THE TEACHINGS OF DON
JUAN.*
D. PRINGLE, 96:DEC69-48
P. RIESMAN, 441:22OCT72-7
CASTANIEN, D.G. EL INCA GARCILASO DE LA
VEGA.
A. SOONS, 238:MAR70-161
CASTEDO, L. A HISTORY OF LATIN AMERICAN
ART AND ARCHITECTURE.
J. BARNITZ, 58:FEB70-14
A•W. GODFREY, 363:AUG70-133
J.B. LYNCH, 127:SUMMER71-426
G. PONTIERO, 86(BHS):APR71-176
CASTELLET, J.M. & J. MOLAS. OCHO SIGLOS
DE POESIA CATALANA.
A. TERRY, 86(BHS):JUL71-282
CASTELLI, E., ED. IL MITO DELLA PENA.
G.M., 477:SUMMER69-401
M.M. MILBURN, 319:OCT72-502
CASTELLI, E. SIMBOLI E IMMAGINI.
G.M., 477:SUMMER69-407
CASTELLO, J.A. REALIDADE E ILUSÃO EM
MACHADO DE ASSIS.
H. CALDWELL, 263:OCT-DEC71-464
CASTELOT, A. NAPOLEON.*
G.M. FRASER, 440:5MAR72-1
J.H. PLUMB, 441:12MAR72-2
CASTIGLIONE, B. THE BOOK OF THE COUR-
TIER. (G. BULL, TRANS)
O. RAGUSA, 399(MLJ):APR70-283
CASTILE, R. THE WAY OF TEA.
617(TLS):22DEC72-1561
CASTILLO, H., ED. ESTUDIOS CRITICOS
SOBRE EL MODERNISMO.*
R. ESQUENAZI-MAYO, 238:MAR70-154
E-F. LONNE, 263:OCT-DEC71-437
CASTILLO, O.R. LET'S GO!*
G. DAVENPORT, 249(HUDR):WINTER71/72-
696
CASTILLO-PUCHE, J.L. HEMINGWAY, ENTRE
LA VIDA Y LA MUERTE.
E. RUIZ-FORNELLS, 238:MAR70-153

CASTLE, C., ED. NOËL.
    617(TLS):8DEC72-1482
CASTORINA, E. LA POESIA D'ORAZIO.*
    A. MICHEL, 555:VOL44FASC1-149
CASTRITIUS, H. STUDIEN ZU MAXIMINUS
DAIA.
    T.D. BARNES, 123:DEC71-461
    A.R. BIRLEY, 313:VOL60-215
    S.I. OOST, 122:OCT71-290
CASTRO, A. EL PENSAMIENTO DE CERVANTES.
    617(TLS):1DEC72-1445
CASTRO, A. THE SPANIARDS.
    617(TLS):25FEB72-214
CATALÁN, D. SIETE SIGLOS DE ROMANCERO
(HISTORIA Y POESÍA).
    C. SMITH, 86(BHS):JUL71-261
CATALANO, P. LINEE DEL SISTEMA SOVRAN-
NAZIONALE ROMANO, UNIVERTÀ DI TORINO,
MEMORIE DELL'ISTITUTO GIURIDICO. (PT
1)
    A. HUS, 555:VOL44FASC1-172
"CATALOG OF THE ARABIC COLLECTION."
[HOOVER INSTITUTION]
    S.R. BRUNSWICK, 356:APR71-181
"CATALOGO DELLE EDIZIONI DI TESTI CLAS-
SICI ESISTENTI NELLE BIBLIOTECHE DEGLI
ISTITUTI STRANIERI DI ROMA."
    123:DEC70-414
"CATALOGS OF THE TURKISH AND PERSIAN COL-
LECTIONS." [HOOVER INSTITUTION]
    S.R. BRUNSWICK, 356:APR71-181
"CATALOGUE OF BOOKS PRINTED IN THE XVTH
CENTURY NOW IN THE BRITISH MUSEUM."
(PT 10)
    617(TLS):24MAR72-344
"CATALOGUE OF MANUSCRIPTS ACQUIRED SINCE
1925." (VOL 3) [NATIONAL LIBRARY OF
SCOTLAND]
    K.J. FIELDING, 637(VS):MAR70-362
    S. NOWELL-SMITH, 354:SEP69-267
CATE, C. ANTOINE DE SAINT-EXUPÉRY.*
    P. DICKINSON, 364:JUN/JUL71-151
ST. CATERINA DA SIENA. IL DIALOGO DELLA
DIVINA PROVVIDENZA [OVVERO] LIBRO DELLA
DIVINA DOTTRINA. (G. CAVALLINI, ED)
    A. BIZZICCARI, 276:SUMMER70-202
CATFORD, J.C. A LINGUISTIC THEORY OF
TRANSLATION.
    C. GOOD, 353:OCT69-118
CATHER, W. THE KINGDOM OF ART. (B.
SLOTE, ED)
    M.R. BENNETT, 502(PRS):SUMMER68-178
CATHER, W. THE WORLD AND THE PARISH.*
(W.M. CURTIN, ED)
    T. MARTIN, 27(AL):NOV71-465
    G. WEALES, 598(SOR):SUMMER72-681
CATLIN, G. FOR GOD'S SAKE GO.
    617(TLS):2JUN72-619
CATLING, P.S. THE SURROGATE.
    617(TLS):19MAY72-565
CATTAFI, B. L'ARIA SECCA DEL FUOCO.
    617(TLS):21JUL72-839
CATTANEO, M.A. LIBERTÀ E VIRTÚ NEL PEN-
SIERO DI ROBESPIERRE.
    A. NEGRI, 548(RCSF):JAN/MAR69-98
CATTAUI, G. CLAUDEL: LE CYCLE DES COÛ-
FONTAINE ET LE MYSTÈRE D'ISRAËL.*
    L. BOLLE, 98:MAR69-287
    W.H. MATHESON, 207(FR):OCT69-172
CATTEL, N.R. THE DESIGN OF ENGLISH.
    G. NICKEL, 72:BAND208HEFT3-211
CATTON, B. WAITING FOR THE MORNING
TRAIN.
    P. ADAMS, 61:DEC72-144
    W. SCHOTT, 441:10DEC72-52
CATUDAL, H.M., JR. STEINSTÜCKEN.
    N. ASCHERSON, 453:20APR72-26

CATULLUS. CATULLI CARMINA. (H. BARDON,
ED & TRANS)
    M.L. DANIELS, 124:JAN71-165
CATULLUS. THE COMPLETE POEMS FOR AMERI-
CAN READERS. (R. MYERS & R.J. ORMSBY,
TRANS)
    D.P. HARMON, 124:FEB71-203
CATULLUS. THE POEMS OF CATULLUS.* (J.
MICHIE, TRANS)
    M.L. CLARKE, 123:JUN71-290
"CATULLUS."* (C. & L. ZUKOFSKY, TRANS)
    B. RAFFEL, 5:AUTUMN69-435
CATULLUS & HORACE. ROMAN LYRIC POETRY:
CATULLUS AND HORACE. (A.G. MC KAY &
D.M. SHEPHERD, EDS)
    W.S. ANDERSON, 124:NOV70-90
    T.P. WISEMAN, 313:VOL60-267
CAUDILL, H.M. MY LAND IS DYING.*
    R. CASSIDY, 561(SATR):1JAN72-30
    F. GRAHAM, JR., 441:7MAY72-8
    C. TOMKINS, 442(NY):10JUN72-125
CAUDWELL, C. ROMANCE AND REALISM. (S.
HYNES, ED)
    R. FULLER, 362:6JAN72-21
    617(TLS):28APR72-470
CAUDWELL, C. STUDIES AND FURTHER STUDIES
IN A DYING CULTURE.
    R. FULLER, 362:6JAN72-21
CAUSLEY, C. FIGURE OF EIGHT.
    J. HEADLAM, 493:SPRING70-91
CAUTE, D. THE OCCUPATION.*
    M. FELD, 364:DEC71/JAN72-162
CAVAFY, C.P. PASSIONS AND ANCIENT DAYS.*
    R. LATTIMORE, 249(HUDR):AUTUMN71-508
    S. SPENDER, 453:15JUN72-12
CAVALLINI, G. - SEE ST. CATERINA DA SIENA
CAVALLO, A.S. TAPESTRIES OF EUROPE AND
OF COLONIAL PERU IN THE MUSEUM OF FINE
ARTS, BOSTON.
    D. KING, 39:DEC69-539
CAVAÑA, A.M. - SEE UNDER MORETO Y CAVAÑA,
A.
CAVE, R. THE PRIVATE PRESS.
    617(TLS):16JUN72-696
CAVE, R., D. CHAMBERS & P. HOY, EDS.
PRIVATE PRESS BOOKS 1967.
    S. CARTER, 354:SEP69-269
CAVE, T.C. DEVOTIONAL POETRY IN FRANCE,
C. 1570-1613.*
    C.E. RATHÉ, 399(MLJ):FEB70-126
    J. ZELDIN, 551(RENQ):AUTUMN70-300
CAVELL, S. MUST WE MEAN WHAT WE SAY?
    42(AR):FALL69-446
CAVIGELLI, P. DIE GERMANISIERUNG VON
BONADUZ IN GESCHICHTLICHER UND SPRACH-
LICHER SCHAU.*
    R.E. KELLER, 402(MLR):APR71-426
    W.G. MOULTON, 301(JEGP):APR71-368
    W.G. MOULTON, 350:DEC71-938
CAVINA, A.O. CARLO SARACENI.
    B. NICOLSON, 90:MAY70-312
CAVITCH, D. D.H. LAWRENCE AND THE NEW
WORLD.*
    M. BELL, 191(ELN):MAR71-237
    W. WATSON, 584(SWR):WINTER71-106
    P.L. WILEY, 659:SPRING72-249
    G.J. ZYTARUK, 141:FALL70-365
CAWLEY, A.C., ED. CHAUCER'S MIND AND
ART.*
    M.W. BLOOMFIELD, 676(YR):SPRING71-438
    R.T. DAVIES, 447(N&Q):FEB70-65
CAWS, M.A. ANDRÉ BRETON.
    R. SHATTUCK, 453:1JUN72-23
CAWS, M.A. THE POETRY OF DADA AND SUR-
REALISM.
    P. BROOME, 67:NOV71-249
    S. LAWALL, 418(MR):SPRING71-354
    R. SHATTUCK, 453:1JUN72-23

CAWS, P. THE PHILOSOPHY OF SCIENCE.
T. MISCHEL, 486:SEP69-322
CAZDEN, R.E. GERMAN EXILE LITERATURE IN
AMERICA 1933-1950.
C.E. LLOYD, 517(PBSA):JUL-SEP71-325
F. REICHMANN, 356:JAN71-69
L.S. THOMPSON, 263:APR-JUN71-206
CAZENAVE, M. LE PHILTRE ET L'AMOUR.
F. LYONS, 208(FS):JUL71-315
CAZENEUVE, J. LUCIEN LÉVY-BRUHL.
617(TLS):22SEP72-1094
CECCHETTI, G. IL VERGA MAGGIORE.
G. CAMBON, 276:AUTUMN70-317
CECCHIN, S.A. PATRIOS POLITEIA.
S.I. OOST, 122:OCT71-289
CECIL, D. VISIONARY AND DREAMER.*
D.V.E., 191(ELN):SEP70(SUPP)-11
L. HERRMANN, 90:NOV70-765
L. STEVENSON, 639(VQR):SPRING70-359
CECIL, D. - SEE BEERBOHM, M.
CECIL, R. THE MYTH OF THE MASTER RACE.
D. SCHOENBAUM, 441:29OCT72-55
617(TLS):17NOV72-1400
CELA, C.J. AL SERVICIO DE ALGO.
J. ALBERICH, 86(BHS):APR71-174
CELA, C.J. DICCIONARIO SECRETO. (VOL 2)
617(TLS):11FEB72-160
CELA, C.J. VÍSPERAS, FESTIVIDAD Y OCTAVA
DE SAN CAMILO DEL AÑO 1936 EN MADRID.
A. ADELL, 270:VOL20#1-23
CELAN, P. NINETEEN POEMS BY PAUL CELAN.
(M. HAMBURGER, TRANS)
617(TLS):21APR72-441
CELAN, P. SELECTED POEMS. (M. HAMBURGER
& C. MIDDLETON, TRANS)
617(TLS):8DEC72-1509
CELAN, P. SPEECH-GRILLE AND SELECTED
POEMS.* (J. NEUGROSCHEL, TRANS)
G. DAVENPORT, 249(HUDR):WINTER71/72-
700
CELANT, G. ARTE POVERA.
J. MOFFITT, 127:FALL70-124
CELATI, G. COMICHE.
617(TLS):25AUG72-1005
CELAYA, G. EXPLORACIÓN DE LA POESÍA.
617(TLS):14APR72-419
CÉLINE, L-F. CASTLE TO CASTLE.
N. DENNIS, 453:10FEB72-3
B. WRIGHT, 619(TC):1969/2-47
CÉLINE, L-F. GUIGNOL'S BAND.
N. DENNIS, 453:10FEB72-3
CÉLINE, L-F. NORTH.
A. BROYARD, 441:12JAN72-45
N. DENNIS, 453:10FEB72-3
R. SEAVER, 561(SATR):5FEB72-57
P. WEST, 440:30JAN72-3
442(NY):4MAR72-114
617(TLS):1SEP72-1017
CELLINI, B. - SEE SHAKESPEARE, W.
CENDRARS, B. PLANUS. (N. ROOTES, ED &
TRANS)
617(TLS):14APR72-408
CENTLIVRE, S. A BOLD STROKE FOR A WIFE.
(T. STATHAS, ED)
A. SHERBO, 402(MLR):OCT71-867
CERNUDA, L. PERFIL DEL AIRE. (D. HAR-
RIS, ED)
617(TLS):7JUL72-769
CERONE, P. EL MELOPEO TRACTADO DE
MUSICA THEORICA Y PRATICA.
R. STEVENSON, 317:FALL71-477
DE CERVANTES SAAVEDRA, M. EXEMPLARY
STORIES. (C.A. JONES, TRANS) EL IN-
GENIOSO HIDALGO DON QUIJOTE DE LA
MANCHA.
617(TLS):1DEC72-1445

DE CERVANTES SAAVEDRA, M. LA GALATEA.
(B. CINTI, ED)
M. HERNÁNDEZ ESTEBAN, 202(FMOD):
NOV69-102
DE CERVANTES SAAVEDRA, M. OCHO ENTRE-
MESES. (J.B. AVALLE-ARCE, ED)
E. COUGHLIN, 238:DEC70-1030
DE CERVANTES SAAVEDRA, M. LOS TRABAJOS
DE PERSILES Y SIGISMUNDA. (J.B.
AVALLE-ARCE, ED)
J. LOWE, 86(BHS):JAN71-67
ČERVENKA, Z. THE NIGERIAN WAR, 1967-
1970.
617(TLS):25AUG72-981
CERVERA VERA, L. EL CONJUNTO PALACIAL
DELA VILLA DE LERMA.
E. ROSENTHAL, 576:DEC69-305
CERVI, M. THE HOLLOW LEGIONS.
617(TLS):25AUG72-991
CÉSAIRE, A. CADASTRE.
C. FRANÇOIS, 207(FR):APR70-864
CHA BUM-SUCK. PROXY.
O HWA-SOP, 270:VOL20#4-103
CHAADAEV, P.Y. THE MAJOR WORKS OF PETER
CHAADAEV.* (R.T. MC NALLY, ED & TRANS)
M. RAEFF, 104:SPRING71-129
CHAADAEV, P.Y. PHILOSOPHICAL LETTERS &
APOLOGY OF A MADMAN. (M-B. ZELDIN,
TRANS)
M. RAEFF, 104:SPRING71-129
J.L. WIECZYNSKI, 32:SEP71-664
639(VQR):SUMMER70-CXVI
CHADWICK, H. EARLY CHRISTIAN THOUGHT AND
THE CLASSICAL TRADITION.*
P. LANGLOIS, 555:VOL44FASC1-154
CHADWICK, M.H. THE HEROIC AGE.
W.M.A. GRIMALDI, 613:AUTUMN69-473
CHADWICK, N.K. & V. ZHIRMUNSKY. ORAL
EPICS OF CENTRAL ASIA.*
J.A. NEWTH, 587:JUL69-116
D. SINOR, 293(JAST):NOV69-176
CHAFE, W.L. MEANING AND THE STRUCTURE OF
LANGUAGE.*
D. IANNUCCI, 651(WHR):SUMMER71-272
CHAIKIN, J. THE PRESENCE OF THE ACTOR.
R. GILMAN, 441:6AUG72-5
CHAILLEY, J. EXPLIQUER L'HARMONIE.
N. CAZDEN, 308:SPRING68-119
CHAILLEY, J. THE MAGIC FLUTE, MASONIC
OPERA.* (H. WEINSTOCK, TRANS)
617(TLS):12MAY72-542
CHAKRAVARTI, N.R. THE INDIAN MINORITY
IN BURMA.
617(TLS):15DEC72-1526
CHAKRAVARTI, P.C. THE EVOLUTION OF
INDIA'S NORTHERN BORDERS.
617(TLS):10NOV72-1377
CHAKRAVORTY, J. THE IDEA OF REVENGE IN
SHAKESPEARE, WITH SPECIAL REFERENCE TO
"HAMLET."
P.N. SIEGEL, 402(MLR):JAN71-178
CHALIAPIN, F.I. CHALIAPIN: AN AUTOBIOG-
RAPHY AS TOLD TO MAXIM GORKY. (N.
FROUD & J. HANLEY, EDS & TRANS)
M.L. HOOVER, 32:MAR71-211
CHALKER, J. THE ENGLISH GEORGIC.*
M. REIK, 566:AUTUMN70-32
A.J. SAMBROOK, 301(JEGP):JAN71-161
CHALLINOR, J. THE HISTORY OF BRITISH
GEOLOGY.
617(TLS):7JAN72-21
CHALLINOR, R. THE LANCASHIRE AND CHE-
SHIRE MINERS.
617(TLS):1DEC72-1469
CHALLINOR, R. & B. RIPLEY. THE MINERS'
ASSOCIATION.
W.H. MAEHL, JR., 637(VS):JUN70-450

CHALMERS, G. AN APOLOGY FOR THE BELIEV-
ERS IN THE SHAKESPEARE-PAPERS. A SUP-
PLEMENTAL APOLOGY.
617(TLS):18FEB72-178
CHAMBERLIN, E.R. LIFE IN WARTIME BRIT-
AIN.
617(TLS):24NOV72-1441
CHAMBERS, D., ED. PRIVATE PRESS BOOKS
1970.
617(TLS):16JUN72-696
CHAMBERS, R. GÉRARD DE NERVAL ET LA
POÉTIQUE DU VOYAGE.*
M. MAURIN, 207(FR):MAR70-687
CHAMBERS, R.W. & M. DAUNT, EDS. A BOOK
OF LONDON ENGLISH 1384-1425.
N. DAVIS, 382(MAE):1971/1-75
CHAMBERS, W.W. & J.R. WILKIE. A SHORT
HISTORY OF THE GERMAN LANGUAGE.
J.T. WATERMAN, 406:FALL71-287
"CHAMBERS TWENTIETH CENTURY DICTIONARY."
(REV) (A.M. MACDONALD, ED)
617(TLS):7JUL72-785
617(TLS):13OCT72-1209
CHAMFORT, S.R.N. MAXIMES ET PENSÉES,
CARACTÈRES ET ANECDOTES. (J. DAGEN,
ED)
N. SUCKLING, 208(FS):OCT71-468
CHAMIER, G. A SOUTH-SEA SIREN. (J.
STEVENS, ED)
K.L. GOODWIN, 67:MAY71-122
CHAMOUX, F. GREEK ART.
R. HIGGINS, 39:FEB69-160
CHAMPAGNE, A. LES LA VÉRENDRYE ET LE
POSTE DE L'OUEST.
W.J. ECCLES, 656(WMQ):JAN70-170
CHAMPIGNY, R. POUR UNE ESTHÉTIQUE DE
L'ESSAI.*
L. WELCH, 290(JAAC):FALL69-102
CHAMPION, L.S. THE EVOLUTION OF SHAKE-
SPEARE'S COMEDY.
T. HAWKES, 676(YR):AUTUMN70-130
CHAN, H-L. THE HISTORIOGRAPHY OF THE
CHIN DYNASTY.
C. HANA, 182:VOL23#23/24-1000
CHAN, W-T. AN OUTLINE AND AN ANNOTATED
BIBLIOGRAPHY OF CHINESE PHILOSOPHY.
293(JAST):MAY70-744
CHAN, W-T. & OTHERS. THE GREAT ASIAN
RELIGIONS.
L. ROTHENHEBER, 318(JAOS):OCT-DEC70-
603
"CHAN-KUO TS'E." (J.I. CRUMP, JR.,
TRANS)
639(VQR):AUTUMN70-CLVI
CHANCELLOR, C. - SEE THOMPSON, H.Y.
CHAND, T. MATERIAL AND IDEOLOGICAL FAC-
TORS IN INDIAN HISTORY.
H.A.A., 273(IC):OCT69-305
CHANDLER, A. A DREAM OF ORDER.*
S.M. SMITH, 677:VOL2-305
CHANDLER, A.D., JR. & S.E. AMBROSE - SEE
EISENHOWER, D.D.
CHANDLER, G. VICTORIAN AND EDWARDIAN
LIVERPOOL AND THE NORTH WEST FROM OLD
PHOTOGRAPHS.
617(TLS):1SEP72-1033
CHANDLER, R. THE MIDNIGHT RAYMOND
CHANDLER.
L.E. SISSMAN, 442(NY):11MAR72-123
CHANDOS, J., ED. IN GOD'S NAME.
617(TLS):28JAN72-101
CHANDRA, G.S.S. APRIL IN NANJANGUD.
N. RENNIE, 364:AUG/SEP71-120
CHANEY, D. PROCESSES OF MASS COMMUNICA-
TION.
617(TLS):4AUG72-911

CHANEY, W.A. THE CULT OF KINGSHIP IN
ANGLO-SAXON ENGLAND.*
F. BARLOW, 382(MAE):1971/2-179
CHANG, H. THE ETYMOLOGIES OF 3000 CHIN-
ESE CHARACTERS IN COMMON USAGE.
WANG FANG-YU & H.C. FENN, 293(JAST):
AUG70-911
CHANG, J.K. INDUSTRIAL DEVELOPMENT IN
PRE-COMMUNIST CHINA.*
R. MYERS, 293(JAST):AUG70-897
CHANG, K-C. FENGPITOU, TAPENKENG, AND
THE PREHISTORY OF TAIWAN.
W.G. SOLHEIM 2D, 293(JAST):FEB70-422
CHANNON, H. CHIPS. (R.R. JAMES, ED)
571:WINTER68/69-37
"LA CHANSON DE ROLAND." (G. MOIGNET,
TRANS)
G.S. BURGESS, 402(MLR):JUL71-685
J. FAIGAN, 67:MAY71-127
CHANTOUX, A., A. GONTIER & A. PROST.
GRAMMAIRE GOURMANTCHÉ.
G. MANESSY, 315(JAL):VOL8PT2-120
CHANTRAINE, H. FREIGELASSENE UND SKLAVEN
IM DIENST DER RÖMISCHEN KAISER.
A.E. GORDON, 124:NOV70-95
CHANTRAINE, P. DICTIONNAIRE ÉTYMOLOGIQUE
DE LA LANGUE GRECQUE.* (VOLS 1&2)
G.M. MESSING, 122:JUL71-194
CHAO, Y.R. LANGUAGE AND SYMBOLIC SYS-
TEMS.*
C-Y. CHENG, 485(PE&W):OCT69-455
J. FOUGHT, 399(MLJ):APR70-301
R. POSNER, 545(RPH):NOV70-329
J. VACHEK, 361:VOL23#2-194
CHAPIN, H. TO THE END OF WEST.
D. ALLEN, 491:JUL72-236
CHAPIN, W. WASTED.
G. DAVIS, 441:21MAY72-40
CHAPLIN, S. THE SMELL OF SUNDAY DINNER.
617(TLS):28JAN72-109
CHAPMAN, A., ED. STEAL AWAY.
E. & N. FONER, 453:20APR72-39
CHAPMAN, G. THE DREYFUS TRIALS.
617(TLS):25AUG72-991
CHAPMAN, G. THE PLAYS OF GEORGE CHAPMAN:
THE COMEDIES. (A. HOLADAY, ED)
G.W. WILLIAMS, 579(SAQ):WINTER71-119
CHAPMAN, G.W., ED. ESSAYS ON SHAKE-
SPEARE.
R. KIMBROUGH, 570(SQ):WINTER68-91
CHAPMAN, H.W. CAROLINE MATILDA.*
C. HIBBERT, 440:2APR72-3
CHAPMAN, J.J. THE COLLECTED WORKS OF
JOHN JAY CHAPMAN. (M.H. BERNSTEIN, ED)
R.B. HOVEY, 399(MLJ):OCT70-451
CHAPMAN, R. THE VICTORIAN DEBATE.
P. COLLINS, 155:MAY69-119
CHAPPELL, W. A SHORT HISTORY OF THE
PRINTED WORD.
617(TLS):18AUG72-976
CHAPPELOW, A. SHAW - "THE CHUCKER-OUT."
L. CLARK, 619(TC):VOL177#1042-55
T.F. EVANS, 571:WINTER69/70-66
E. REUBEN, 637(VS):JUN70-437
R. ROBERTSON, 529(QQ):WINTER70-652
S. WEINTRAUB, 441:24SEP72-44
CHAPPLE, J.A.V. & A. POLLARD - SEE GAS-
KELL, E.C.S.
CHAPPUYS, C. CLAUDE CHAPPUYS: POÉSIES
INTIMES. (A.M. BEST, ED)
V.E. GRAHAM, 546(RR):FEB70-51
CHAPUT-ROLLAND, S. REGARDS 1968.
J-C. BONENFANT, 627(UTQ):JUL70-415
CHAPUT-ROLLAND, S. THE SECOND CONQUEST.
A.N. RASPA, 150(DR):WINTER70/71-553
CHAR, R. LE NU PERDU.
617(TLS):28JAN72-94

CHAR, R. & C. FELD. PICASSO; HIS RECENT
DRAWINGS, 1966-1968.
B. PETRIE, 90:NOV70-766
CHARBONNEAUX, J., R. MARTIN & F. VILLARD.
ARCHAIC GREEK ART 620-480 B.C.*
617(TLS):31MAR72-370
DE CHARDIN, P.T. - SEE UNDER TEILHARD DE
CHARDIN, P.
CHAREST, G.J. FOREIGN LANGUAGE TEACH-
ING.
E.D. ALLEN, 399(MLJ):MAY70-363
CHARLES, A.M. - SEE KNEVET, R.
CHARLES, G. THE DESTINY WALTZ.*
F.P.W. MC DOWELL, 659:SUMMER72-361
442(NY):16SEP72-125
CHARLES-PICARD, G. L'ARCHÉOLOGIE, DÉCOU-
VERTE DES CIVILISATIONS DISPARUES.
P. AUBERY, 207(FR):APR70-853
CHARLESTON, R.J. MEISSEN AND OTHER
EUROPEAN PORCELAIN [BOUND TOGETHER
WITH] AYERS, J. ORIENTAL PORCELAIN.
617(TLS):3NOV72-1311
CHARLESTON, R.J., ED. WORLD CERAMICS.
G. WILLS, 39:AUG69-162
CHARLESWORTH, J.H., ED. JOHN AND QUMRAN.
617(TLS):1SEP72-1034
CHARLESWORTH, M.J. PHILOSOPHY OF
RELIGION: THE HISTORIC APPROACHES.
617(TLS):3MAR72-255
CHARLOT, J., ED. LES FRANÇAIS ET DE
GAULLE.
617(TLS):29SEP72-1134
CHARLTON, D.G., ED. FRANCE.
617(TLS):14JUL72-825
CHARLTON, W. AESTHETICS.
S.E. MARSHALL, 518:MAY71-3
S.R. SUTHERLAND, 89(BJA):SUMMER71-288
CHARNEY, M. - SEE SHAKESPEARE, W.
CHARPENTRAT, P. L'ART BAROQUE.
M. SANDOZ, 56:SPRING69-104
CHARPENTRAT, P. LIVING ARCHITECTURE:
BAROQUE.*
J. WASSERMAN, 576:MAR69-73
CHARRIÈRE, H. PAPILLON.
N.C. MILLS, 676(YR):SPRING71-440
CHARTERIS, L. THE SAINT AND THE PEOPLE
IMPORTERS.
N. CALLENDAR, 441:2APR72-22
CHARTERS, M. VICTOR VICTIM.
L. WOODS, 606(TAMR):#56-85
CHARTERS, S. THE BLUESMEN.
J. GREENWAY, 650(WF):JAN69-68
CHARVAT, W. THE PROFESSION OF AUTHOR-
SHIP IN AMERICA, 1800-1870.* (M.J.
BRUCCOLI, ED)
E. CURRENT-GARCIA, 577(SHR):SUMMER70-
287
R. LEHAN, 445(NCF):JUN69-123
S. NOWELL-SMITH, 354:DEC69-354
CHARYN, J. AMERICAN SCRAPBOOK.
L. HABER, 390:OCT69-78
CHARYN, J. EISENHOWER, MY EISENHOWER.*
W.H. PRITCHARD, 249(HUDR):SUMMER71-
357
DE CHASCA, E. EL ARTE JUGLARESCO EN EL
"CANTAR DE MÍO CID."*
T. MONTGOMERY, 545(RPH):AUG70-213
CHASE, A. ARBOL DEL TIEMPO.
G. CARVAJAL, 37:MAY69-43
CHASE, A. THE BIOLOGICAL IMPERATIVES.
R. BAZELL, 453:2NOV72-38
CHASE, G. CONTEMPORARY ART IN LATIN
AMERICA.
C.I. CALKIN, 263:APR-JUN71-205
CHASINS, A. MUSIC AT THE CROSSROADS.
T. LASK, 441:14APR72-40

CHASSÉ, C. THE NABIS AND THEIR PERIOD.
J. HOUSE, 90:OCT70-711
S. WHITFIELD, 592:JUL/AUG69-44
CHASSERIAU, T. ILLUSTRATIONS FOR OTHELLO.
S. SPECTOR, 58:APR70-14
CHASTEL, A. THE MYTH OF THE RENAISSANCE,
1420-1520.
639(VQR):WINTER70-XXV
CHATAGNIER, L.J. & H.R. IMAGES DE LA
FRANCE CONTEMPORAINE.
J. DECOCK, 207(FR):MAR70-712
DE CHATEAUBRIAND, F-R. CHATEAUBRIAND'S
TRAVELS IN AMERICA. (R. SWITZER,
TRANS)
C-S. BOSTELMANN, 656(WMQ):JUL70-504
DE CHATEAUBRIAND, F-R. VIE DE RANCÉ.
(M-F. GUYARD, ED)
D.G. CHARLTON, 208(FS):APR71-213
DE CHATEAUBRIAND, F-R. VOYAGE EN ITALIE.
(J-M. GAUTIER, ED)
M. GUTWIRTH, 207(FR):FEB70-521
R. SWITZER, 399(MLJ):MAR70-206
CHATELET, F. PLATON.
J. BRUNSCHWIG, 542:APR-JUN68-283
CHATHAM, J.R. & E. RUIZ-FORNELLS. DIS-
SERTATIONS IN HISPANIC LANGUAGES AND
LITERATURES.
F.P. HEBBLETHWAITE, 263:JAN-MAR71-64
L.S. THOMPSON, 517(PBSA):APR-JUN71-
197
CHATMAN, S. THE LATER STYLE OF HENRY
JAMES.
617(TLS):18AUG72-957
CHATMAN, S. & S.R. LEVIN, EDS. ESSAYS ON
THE LANGUAGE OF LITERATURE.
K.D. UITTI, 545(RPH):NOV69-214
CHATTERJEE, B., ED. ESSAYS ON SHAKE-
SPEARE.
B.A.W. JACKSON, 570(SQ):WINTER68-92
CHATTERJEE, B. JOHN KEATS.
617(TLS):30JUN72-741
CHATTERJI, B.R. INDIAN CULTURAL INFLU-
ENCE IN CAMBODIA. (2ND ED)
K. BHATTACHARYA, 57:VOL31#2/3-224
CHATTERJI, P.C. FUNDAMENTAL QUESTIONS
IN AESTHETICS.
R. SAW, 89(BJA):WINTER71-96
CHATTERJI, S.K. THE ORIGIN AND DEVELOP-
MENT OF THE BENGALI LANGUAGE.
L.A. HERCUS, 67:NOV71-276
CHATZIOIANNOU, K.P. TA EN DIASPORA.
D.M. NICOL, 123:DEC71-459
CHAUCER, G. CHAUCER: GENERAL PROLOGUE,
"THE CANTERBURY TALES." (P. HODGSON,
ED)
R.T. DAVIES, 447(N&Q):FEB70-65
CHAUCER, G. TROILUS AND CRISEYDE. (N.
COGHILL, TRANS) A CHOICE OF CHAUCER'S
VERSE. (N. COGHILL, ED)
617(TLS):10NOV72-1364
CHAUCHARD, P. LA MORALE DU CERVEAU.
C. PRÉVOST, 542:JAN-MAR69-117
CHAUDHURI, H. THE PHILOSOPHY OF INTEG-
RALISM. (2ND ED)
N.L. CHOBOT, 485(PE&W):OCT68-337
CHAUDHURI, M.A. THE CIVIL SERVICE IN
PAKISTAN.
W. WILCOX, 293(JAST):AUG70-979
CHAUDHURI, M.A. GOVERNMENT AND POLITICS
IN PAKISTAN.
B. SINGH, 293(JAST):FEB70-505
CHAUDHURI, N.C. THE INTELLECTUAL IN
INDIA.
M.L. CORMACK, 293(JAST):FEB70-463
CHAUDHURI, P., ED. ASPECTS OF INDIAN
ECONOMIC DEVELOPMENT.
617(TLS):15SEP72-1066

DE CHAULIAC, G. - SEE UNDER GUY DE
CHAULIAC
CHAURAND, J. HISTOIRE DE LA LANGUE FRAN-
ÇAISE.
S. ULLMANN, 208(FS):OCT71-504
CHAUSSERIE-LAPRÉE, J-P. L'EXPRESSION
NARRATIVE CHEZ LES HISTORIENS LATINS.
A. ERNOUT, 555:VOL44FASC2-340
M. HAMMOND, 24:OCT71-733
A.M. WARD, 124:JAN71-167
CHAYANAM, D. THAI KAP SONGKHRAM LOK
KHRANG THI SONG.
E.T. FLOOD, 293(JAST):AUG70-988
"CHECKLIST OF BRITISH PARLIAMENTARY PAP-
ERS IN THE IRISH UNIVERSITY PRESS 1000-
VOLUME SERIES 1801-1899."
617(TLS):25AUG72-1006
CHEDID, A. L'AUTRE.
S. MAX, 207(FR):MAR70-727
CHEETHAM, J. SOCIAL WORK WITH IMMI-
GRANTS.
617(TLS):15DEC72-1526
CHEETHAM, J.H. & J. PIPER. WILTSHIRE.
G. GRIGSON, 46:MAR69-228
CHEETHAM, N. A HISTORY OF MEXICO.
617(TLS):21JAN72-62
CHEEVER, J. BULLET PARK.
G. GREENE, 340(KR):1969/4-564
CHEFFINS, R.I. THE CONSTITUTIONAL PRO-
CESS IN CANADA.
J.A. CORRY, 529(QQ):SUMMER70-279
CHEJNE, A.G. THE ARABIC LANGUAGE.
F.J. ZIADEH, 399(MLJ):MAY70-361
CHEKHOV, A. THE ISLAND. (L. & M. TER-
PAK, TRANS)
T.G. WINNER, 32:MAR71-205
CHEKHOV, A.P. THREE STORIES. (L.S.K.
LE FLEMING, ED)
J.L. CONRAD, 574(SEEJ):SUMMER71-233
CHEN, K.C. VIETNAM AND CHINA 1938-1954.
J. YIN, 293(JAST):AUG70-925
639(VQR):SUMMER70-CXIV
CHEN, L-C. & H.D. LASSWELL. FORMOSA,
CHINA AND THE UNITED NATIONS.
L-S. TAO, 293(JAST):MAY70-695
CHEN, N-R. & W. GALENSON. THE CHINESE
ECONOMY UNDER COMMUNISM.*
R.M. FIELD, 293(JAST):AUG70-933
CHENERY, H.B., WITH OTHERS, EDS. STUDIES
IN DEVELOPMENT PLANNING.
617(TLS):15SEP72-1066
CHENEY, C.R. & M.G. - SEE POPE INNOCENT
III
CHENG, C-Y. THE MACHINE-BUILDING INDUS-
TRY IN COMMUNIST CHINA.
617(TLS):10NOV72-1361
CHÊNG TÊ-K'UN. ARCHAEOLOGY IN SARAWAK.
W.G. SOLHEIM 2D, 293(JAST):MAY70-738
CHERNAIK, W.L. THE POETRY OF LIMITATION.
H. KELLIHER, 541(RES):MAY70-208
H.H.R. LOVE, 67:NOV71-234
A. LOW, 568(SCN):SPRING71-10
CHESLER, P. WOMEN AND MADNESS.
S.R. MADDI, 561(SATR):23DEC72-61
A. RICH, 441:31DEC72-1
CHESNEAUX, J. THE POLITICAL AND SOCIAL
IDEAS OF JULES VERNE.
617(TLS):17NOV72-1391
CHESNEY, K. THE ANTI-SOCIETY.*
676(YR):SPRING71-XXVII
CHESNEY, K. THE VICTORIAN UNDERWORLD.
A.B., 155:SEP70-244
CHESSER, E. STRANGE LOVES.* (BRITISH
TITLE: THE HUMAN ASPECTS OF SEXUAL
DEVIATION.)
D. GREENBURG, 441:16JAN72-27

CHESTERTON, G.K. SELECTED STORIES. (K.
AMIS, ED)
D.A.N. JONES, 362:26OCT72-557
617(TLS):15DEC72-1525
CHETHAM, C.S. & OTHERS. MODERN PAINTING,
DRAWING AND SCULPTURE COLLECTED BY
LOUISE AND JOSEPH PULITZER, JR. (VOL
3)
617(TLS):1SEP72-1033
CHETWODE, P. KULU.
617(TLS):1SEP72-1034
CHEVALIER, D. KLEE.
617(TLS):28JUL72-888
CHEVALIER, J-C. HISTOIRE DE LA SYNTAXE.*
A. LORIAN, 545(RPH):MAY70-581
CHEVALIER, M. LOS TEMAS ARIOSTESCOS EN
EL ROMANCERO Y LA POESÍA ESPAÑOLA DEL
SIGLO DE ORO.
M.S. GILDERMAN, 238:MAR70-148
C. SMITH, 86(BHS):JUL71-270
CHEVALIER, M. & R. DOISNEAU. MY PARIS.
561(SATR):7OCT72-77
CHEVALLEY-SABATIER, L. GUSTAVE FLAUBERT
ET SA NIÈCE CAROLINE.
617(TLS):2JUN72-627
CHEVALLIER, R. DICTIONNAIRE DE LA LIT-
TÉRATURE LATINE.
J. ANDRÉ, 555:VOL44FASC2-370
CHEVIGNY, B.G., ED. TWENTIETH-CENTURY
INTERPRETATIONS OF "ENDGAME."
S. STERNLICHT, 149:SEP71-278
CHEVIGNY, P. COPS AND REBELS.
D. BURNHAM, 441:16JUL72-6
CHEVREUL, M.E. THE PRINCIPLES OF HAR-
MONY AND CONTRAST OF COLORS AND THEIR
APPLICATIONS TO THE ARTS.
K. CROWN, 54:DEC69-408
CHI PING-FENG. CH'ING-MO KO-MING YU
CHUN-HSIEN TI LUN-CHENG.
F.F. WONG, 293(JAST):FEB70-428
CHIA-CHIEN, W. - SEE UNDER WANG CHIA-
CHIEN
CHIAPUSSO, J. BACH'S WORLD.*
S. DAW, 415:JUN70-606
CHIARINI, M. CLAUDE LORRAIN; SELECTED
DRAWINGS.
G. MARTIN, 39:DEC69-540
CHIARO DAVANZATI. RIME. (A. MENICHETTI,
ED)
F.B. AGENO, 545(RPH):AUG69-127
CHIAROMONTE, N. THE PARADOX OF HISTORY.*
E. THOMAS, 364:JUN/JUL71-158
CHIBNALL, M. - SEE ORDERIC VITALIS
CHICHESTER, F. THE ROMANTIC CHALLENGE.*
T. SEVERIN, 440:2APR72-4
CHIH, T. - SEE UNDER TS'AO CHIH
CHILCOTT, T. A PUBLISHER AND HIS CIRCLE.
617(TLS):27OCT72-1270
CHILD, H. - SEE JOHNSTON, E.
CHILDERHOUSE, J.R. WINTER RACEHORSE.
G. ROPER, 627(UTQ):JUL69-360
CHILDRESS, A., ED. BLACK SCENES.
G. WEALES, 441:11JUN72-8
CHILDRESS, J.F. CIVIL DISOBEDIENCE AND
POLITICAL OBLIGATION.
617(TLS):19MAY72-580
CHILDS, D. GERMANY SINCE 1918.*
G. BARRACLOUGH, 453:2NOV72-32
CHILDS, J.R. FOREIGN SERVICE FAREWELL.
639(VQR):WINTER70-XX
CHILL, E. - SEE BARNAVE, J.
CHIN, R. & S. AI-LI. PSYCHOLOGICAL RE-
SEARCH IN COMMUNIST CHINA.
G. RAZRAN, 293(JAST):AUG70-928
"CHINA!"
S.R. SCHRAM, 441:7MAY72-2
CHING, F. - SEE DURDIN, T., J. RESTON &
S. TOPPING

CHIPP, H.B., ED. THEORIES OF MODERN
ART.
B. GOLDMAN, 290(JAAC):FALL69-111
CHIRASSI, I. ELEMENTI DI CULTURE PRE-
CEREALI NEI MITI E RITI GRECI.
P.N. LOCKHART, 124:OCT70-60
DE CHIRICO, G. THE MEMOIRS OF GIORGIO DE
CHIRICO.*
G. EWART, 364:DEC71/JAN72-146
617(TLS):21APR72-442
CHISHOLM, A.R. A STUDY OF CHRISTOPHER
BRENNAN'S "THE FOREST OF NIGHT."*
G.A. WILKES, 581:1971/2-155
CHITTY, E.N. & A.B. - SEE GREEN, E.
CHITWOOD, O.P. RICHARD HENRY LEE,
STATESMAN OF THE REVOLUTION.
E.G. EVANS, 656(WMQ):JAN70-172
CHLOROS, A.G. YUGOSLAV CIVIL LAW.
W.J. WAGNER, 32:DEC71-921
CHMIELEWSKI, E. THE POLISH QUESTION IN
THE RUSSIAN STATE DUMA.
R.F. LESLIE, 575(SEER):OCT71-621
CHOI IN-HUN. KWANGJANG.
270:VOL20#4-96
CHOKSEY, R.D. MOUNTSTUART ELPHINSTONE:
THE INDIAN YEARS 1796-1827.
617(TLS):21JUL72-853
CHOMSKY, C. THE ACQUISITION OF SYNTAX
IN CHILDREN FROM 5 TO 10.
E.V. CLARK, 350:SEP71-742
CHOMSKY, N. ASPECTS OF THE THEORY OF
SYNTAX.*
G. NICKEL, 72:BAND208HEFT3-206
F.C.C. PENG, 353:JUN69-91
CHOMSKY, N. CARTESIAN LINGUISTICS.*
H.E. BREKLE, 353:JUN69-74
V. SALMON, 297(JL):APR69-165
K.D. UITTI, 545(RPH):AUG69-75
CHOMSKY, N. LANGUAGE AND MIND.
R.J.B., 543:DEC69-342
CHOMSKY, N. PROBLEMS OF KNOWLEDGE AND
FREEDOM.*
G. STEINER, 441:9JAN72-23
617(TLS):31MAR72-359
CHOMSKY, N. STUDIES ON SEMANTICS IN
GENERATIVE GRAMMAR.
617(TLS):7JUL72-773
CHOMSKY, N. TOPICS IN THE THEORY OF
GENERATIVE GRAMMAR.
I. BELLERT, 353:OCT69-107
CHONG-JU, S. - SEE UNDER SUH CHONG-JU
CHOPIN, K. THE COMPLETE WORKS OF KATE
CHOPIN.* (P. SEYERSTED, ED)
G. ARMS, 27(AL):MAR71-136
CHOPRA, B.R. KINGDOM OF THE PUNJAB
(1839-45).
B.G. GOKHALE, 318(JAOS):OCT-DEC70-602
CHOPRA, S. UN MEDIATION IN KASHMIR.
617(TLS):22SEP72-1124
CHORON, J. SUICIDE.
P. ADAMS, 61:APR72-129
W.H. GASS, 453:18MAY72-3
I. HOWE, 231:JUN72-102
CHOW TSE-TUNG, ED. WEN-LIN.
R. BARICOVICH, 485(PE&W):JAN69-84
CHRÉTIEN DE TROYES. DER PERCEVALROMAN
("LI CONTES DEL GRAAL"). (3RD ED) (A.
HILKA, ED; REV BY G. ROHLFS)
P. MÉNARD, 545(RPH):AUG69-137
CHRÉTIEN DE TROYES. YVAIN OU LE CHEV-
ALIER AU LION. (J. NELSON, ED)
W.F. KLEIN, 399(MLJ):FEB70-137
CHRIST, J. STAAT UND STAATSRAISON BEI
FRIEDRICH NAUMANN.
G. STRAUSS, 182:VOL23#9-507
CHRIST, K. ANTIKE NUMISMATIK, EINFÜHRUNG
UND BIBLIOGRAPHIE.
M.H. CRAWFORD, 313:VOL60-265

CHRIST, W. & OTHERS. MATERIALS AND
STRUCTURE OF MUSIC.
P. NELSON, 308:WINTER68-289
CHRISTENSEN, D., WITH H-J. JORDAN - SEE
"KATALOG DER TONBANDAUFNAHMEN M 1 -
M 2000 DER MUSIKETHNOLOGISCHEN ABTEIL-
UNG, MUSEUM FÜR VÖLKERKUNDE BERLIN"
CHRISTENSEN, D.E., ED. HEGEL AND THE
PHILOSOPHY OF RELIGION.
L.D. EASTON, 319:OCT72-483
CHRISTENSEN, E.M. EN FORTOLKNING AF
"HØJT FRA TRAEETS GRØNNE TOP."*
P.M. MITCHELL, 462(OL):VOL25#4-362
CHRISTENSON, C.V. KINSEY.*
P.A. ROBINSON, 61:MAY72-99
CHRISTENSON, R.M. & OTHERS. IDEOLOGIES
AND MODERN POLITICS.
617(TLS):5MAY72-507
CHRISTESEN, C.B., ED. ON NATIVE GROUNDS.*
T. STURM, 368:JUN69-179
CHRISTIAN, C.W. & G.R. WITTIG, EDS. RADI-
CAL THEOLOGY: PHASE TWO.
G.M., 477:SUMMER69-409
CHRISTIAN, R., ED. THE NATURE-LOVER'S
COMPANION.
617(TLS):17MAR72-317
CHRISTIAN, R. OLD ENGLISH CUSTOMS.
617(TLS):15DEC72-1541
CHRISTIAN, R.F. TOLSTOY: A CRITICAL
INTRODUCTION.*
S. MC LAUGHLIN, 574(SEEJ):SPRING71-69
R.E. MATLAW, 550(RUSR):OCT70-472
T. REDPATH, 402(MLR):APR71-478
CHRISTIAN, W.A. OPPOSITIONS OF RELIGIOUS
DOCTRINES.
617(TLS):19MAY72-585
CHRISTIANSEN, P.G. THE USE OF IMAGES BY
CLAUDIUS CLAUDIANUS.
F. LASSERRE, 182:VOL23#6-297
CHRISTIE, A. ELEPHANTS CAN REMEMBER.
N. CALLENDAR, 441:26NOV72-36
617(TLS):1DEC72-1467
CHRISTIE, A. NEMESIS.*
N. CALLENDAR, 441:13FEB72-34
CHRISTIE, J.D. - SEE KNIGHT, W.F.J.
CHRISTOFF, P.K. THE THIRD HEART.
M. RAEFF, 32:JUN71-393
CHROMATIUS. CHROMACE D'AQUILÉE, "SER-
MONS." (VOL 1) (J. LEMARIÉ & H. TAR-
DIF, EDS)
W.H.C. FREND, 123:DEC71-454
"THE CHRONICLE OF FU CHIEN." (M.C.
ROGERS, ED & TRANS)
J-S. TAO, 293(JAST):FEB70-426
CHRYSOSTOM, J. JEAN CHRYSOSTOME, "LET-
TRES À OLYMPIAS." (A-M. MALINGREY,
ED & TRANS)
É. DES PLACES, 555:VOL44FASC2-332
CHU, D. & E. SKINNER. A GLORIOUS AGE IN
AFRICA.
N. WEYL, 396(MODA):SPRING71-217
CHUBATYI, M. [N. CHUBATY] ISTORIIA
KHRYSTYIANSTVA NA RUSY-UKRAÏNI. (VOL
1)
O.P. BACKUS 3D & H.A. STAMMLER, 32:
JUN71-361
CHUGHTAI, M.A.R. THE HOUSE OF TAIMUR.
617(TLS):21JAN72-77
CHUKOVSKAYA, L. GOING UNDER.
J. HUNTER, 362:27JUL72-118
617(TLS):11AUG72-935
CHULL, P. - SEE UNDER PAIK CHULL
"CHUNG-KUO TA-LU FO-CHIAO TZU-LIAO HUI-
PIEN."
D.C. YU, 293(JAST):FEB70-439
CHURCH, G. & C.D. CARNES. THE PIT.
A. BROYARD, 441:28NOV72-47

CHURCH, R.W. THE OXFORD MOVEMENT. (G. BEST, ED)
617(TLS):18FEB72-175
CHURCHILL, W.S. YOUNG WINSTON'S WARS. (F. WOODS, ED)
617(TLS):15SEP72-1065
CHUTE, B.J. THE STORY OF A SMALL LIFE.
M. LEVIN, 441:20FEB72-26
CIANCI, G. LA SCUOLA DI CAMBRIDGE.
H. BREDIN, 89(BJA):WINTER71-99
CIBBER, C. AN APOLOGY FOR THE LIFE OF COLLEY CIBBER. (B.R.S. FONE, ED)
E.L. AVERY, 405(MP):NOV69-194
CIBBER, C. THE CARELESS HUSBAND. (W.W. APPLETON, ED)
C.M. TAYLOR, 50(ARQ):SPRING69-80
CICERO. CICÉRON, "DISCOURS." (VOL 16, PT 1) (P. GRIMAL, ED & TRANS)
R.G.M. NISBET, 123:MAR71-61
CICERO. M. TULLI CICERONIS "PRO C. RABIRIO POSTUMO ORATIO." (I.C. GIAR-DINA, ED)
R.G.M. NISBET, 123:MAR71-133
CICERO. M. TULLI CICERONIS "PRO L. MURENA ORATIO." (C. MACDONALD, ED)
R.G. SCHETTLER, 124:DEC70-130
CICERO. M. TULLI CICERONIS PRO P. QUINCTIO ORATIO. (T.E. KINSEY, ED)
617(TLS):14APR72-422
CICERO. THE NATURE OF THE GODS. (H.C.P. MC GREGOR, TRANS)
617(TLS):18AUG72-977
CICERO. ON MORAL OBLIGATION.* (J. HIG-GINBOTHAM, ED & TRANS)
J.P.V.D. BALSDON, 5:AUTUMN69-446
CICERO. ON OLD AGE; ON FRIENDSHIP.* (H.G. EDINGER, ED & TRANS)
J.M. SNYDER, 121(CJ):OCT-NOV70-89
CICERO. ORATIONES IN CATILINAM. (A. HAURY, ED)
H. OPPERMANN, 182:VOL23#10-559
CICERO. THIRTY-FIVE LETTERS OF CICERO. (D. STOCKTON, ED)
P.R. POUNCEY, 124:FEB71-203
CIENCIAŁA, A.M. POLAND AND THE WESTERN POWERS, 1938-1939.*
R. DĘBICKI, 497(POLR):SPRING69-109
ČINNOV, I. METAFORY.
V. TERRAS, 574(SEEJ):SPRING71-81
ČINNOV, I. PARTITURA.
V. TERRAS, 574(SEEJ):WINTER71-511
CINTI, B. - SEE DE CERVANTES SAAVEDRA, M.
CIOBANU, F. & F. HASAN. FORMAREA CUVIN-TELOR ÎN LIMBA ROMÂNĂ. (VOL 1)
K. KAZAZIS, 104:WINTER71-560
CIONE, E. FEDE E RAGIONE NELLA STORIA.
E. NAMER, 542:JUL-DEC69-493
CIORAN, E.M. THE TEMPTATION TO EXIST.*
L.B. CEBIK, 219(GAR):FALL69-400
CIORANESCU, A. BIBLIOGRAPHIE DE LA LITTÉRATURE FRANÇAISE DU DIX-HUITIÈME SIÈCLE.
F. NIES, 72:BAND208HEFT3-235
E. ZIMMERMANN, 182:VOL23#7-324
ČIRKOV, N.M. O STILE DOSTOEVSKOGO. O STILE DOSTOEVSKOGO: PROBLEMATIKA, IDEI, OBRAZY.
J. GLAD, 574(SEEJ):FALL71-376
CISNEROS, A. THE SPIDER HANGS TOO FAR FROM THE GROUND.*
G. BROTHERSTON, 86(BHS):OCT71-367
"THE CITIZEN KANE BOOK" - SEE UNDER KAEL, P.
"CIVILIZATION AND SCIENCE, IN CONFLICT OR COLLABORATION?"
617(TLS):23JUN72-702

CIXOUS, H. L'EXIL DE JAMES JOYCE OU L'ART DU REMPLACEMENT.
L. FINAS, 98:NOV69-992
CIXOUS, H. NEUTRE.
617(TLS):2JUN72-623
CLAERBAUT, D. BLACK JARGON IN WHITE AMERICA.
M.K. SPEARS, 453:16NOV72-32
CLAGETT, M. - SEE ORESME, N.
CLAIBORNE, C. THE NEW YORK TIMES INTER-NATIONAL COOK BOOK.
N. MAGID, 440:20FEB72-6
CLAIBORNE, C. & V. LEE. THE CHINESE COOKBOOK.
N. HAZELTON, 441:3DEC72-96
CLAIR, C. - SEE NICHOLS, J.
CLAIR, P. & F. GIRBAL - SEE DE CORDEMOY, G.
CLAIRMONT, C. THE JOURNALS OF CLAIRE CLAIRMONT, 1814-1827.* (M.K. STOCKING, WITH D.M. STOCKING, EDS)
E.E.B., 191(ELN):SEP69(SUPP)-30
CLAPHAM, J. ANTONÍN DVOŘÁK.*
K.M. KOMMA, 182:VOL23#17/18-806
CLAPHAM, J. SMETANA.
617(TLS):25AUG72-1003
CLAPHAM, S. PRIMULAS.
617(TLS):11FEB72-165
CLARAC, P. L'AGE CLASSIQUE II 1660-1680.
R. SWITZER, 399(MLJ):APR70-280
CLARE, P. THE STRUGGLE FOR THE GREAT BARRIER REEF.
S. MANTELL, 231:JUL72-94
617(TLS):14JAN72-45
CLARFIELD, G.H. TIMOTHY PICKERING AND AMERICAN DIPLOMACY, 1795-1800.
J.G. CLIFFORD, 432(NEQ):JUN70-323
R. ERNST, 656(WMQ):JAN70-174
CLARÍN. DOÑA INÉS. (L. LIVINGSTONE, ED)
C.W. BUTLER, 238:MAR70-176
"CLARION."
T. STURGEON, 441:5MAR72-36
CLARK, A.M. SIR WALTER SCOTT: THE FORMA-TIVE YEARS.
K.C., 191(ELN):SEP70(SUPP)-41
CLARK, C., ED. THE PETERBOROUGH CHRON-ICLE, 1070-1154. (2ND ED)
N.E. ELIASON, 402(MLR):OCT71-848
R.M. WILSON, 382(MAE):1971/2-185
CLARK, C. RIVER OF DISSOLUTION.
J. SANKEY, 619(TC):1969/2-44
CLARK, C. & S. RUSH. HOW TO GET ALONG WITH BLACK PEOPLE.
441:9JAN72-28
CLARK, E. BALDUR'S GATE.
P. CRUTTWELL, 249(HUDR):SPRING71-177
P.E. GRAY, 676(YR):AUTUMN70-101
W. SULLIVAN, 569(SR):AUTUMN71-634
639(VQR):AUTUMN70-CXXVIII
CLARK, E.E. INDIAN LEGENDS FROM THE NORTHERN ROCKIES.
G.S. NICKERSON, 650(WF):JAN68-66
CLARK, G. MAY YOUR FIRST LOVE BE YOUR LAST.
J.M. ROBSON, 627(UTQ):JUL70-384
CLARK, G.H., ED. SELECTIONS FROM HELLEN-ISTIC PHILOSOPHY.
J-P. DUMONT, 542:APR-JUN69-274
CLARK, H. THE ETHICAL MYSTICISM OF ALBERT SCHWEITZER.
W.A.J., 543:SEP69-125
CLARK, J.P. THE EXAMPLE OF SHAKESPEARE.
617(TLS):7JAN72-16

CLARK, J.R. FORM AND FRENZY IN SWIFT'S
  "TALE OF A TUB."*
    E. KREUTZER, 72:BAND208HEFT4/6-387
    M.K. STARKMAN, 566:AUTUMN70-21
    P. THORPE, 141:FALL70-361
CLARK, J.W. EARLY ENGLISH. (2ND ED)
    J. VACHEK, 353:JUL69-105
CLARK, K. THE DRAWINGS OF LEONARDO DA
  VINCI IN THE COLLECTION OF HER MAJESTY
  THE QUEEN AT WINDSOR CASTLE. (2ND ED,
  REV WITH THE ASSISTANCE OF C. PED-
  RETTI)
    C. GOULD, 39:OCT69-351
CLARK, K. A FAILURE OF NERVE.
    K.W. FORSTER, 551(RENQ):AUTUMN70-287
CLARK, L. SARK DISCOVERED. (REV)
    617(TLS):19MAY72-585
CLARK, L. ALFRED WILLIAMS.
    H. MAXWELL, 619(TC):1969/2-50
CLARK, P. & P. SLACK, EDS. CRISIS AND
  ORDER IN ENGLISH TOWNS 1500-1700.
    J.P. COOPER, 362:17AUG72-215
    617(TLS):23JUN72-706
CLARK, R.W. THE HUXLEYS.*
    D.H. ERICKSEN, 50(ARQ):SPRING69-88
CLARK, T. AIR.
    D. LEHMAN, 491:JAN72-224
CLARK, T. & R. PADGETT. BUN.
    J. HOPPER, 661:SPRING69-107
CLARK, T.W., ED. THE NOVEL IN INDIA.
    I.J. CATANACH, 67:NOV71-243
CLARK, W.B., ED. NAVAL DOCUMENTS OF THE
  AMERICAN REVOLUTION. (VOL 3)
    A.M. PATTERSON, 14:OCT69-387
CLARK, W.B., ED. NAVAL DOCUMENTS OF THE
  AMERICAN REVOLUTION. (VOL 4)
    S.G. MORSE, 432(NEQ):DEC70-657
CLARKE, A. THE ECHO AT COOLE.
    H. SERGEANT, 175:SPRING69-33
CLARKE, A. THE END OF A SHADOW.
    617(TLS):7APR72-384
CLARKE, A. THE MEETING POINT.
    A. HISLOP, 440:21MAY72-5
    M. LEVIN, 441:9APR72-42
    442(NY):22APR72-142
CLARKE, A. TIRESIAS.
    617(TLS):1DEC72-1459
CLARKE, A. WHEN HE WAS FREE AND YOUNG
  AND HE USED TO WEAR SILKS.
    A. BOXILL, 198:FALL72-117
CLARKE, A.C. THE WIND FROM THE SUN.
    617(TLS):13OCT72-1235
CLARKE, C. RIVER OF DISSOLUTION.*
    M. ALLOTT, 677:VOL2-327
    K. MC LEOD, 541(RES):NOV70-521
    A. RUDRUM, 529(QQ):AUTUMN70-454
CLARKE, D.C. ALLEGORY, DECALOGUE, AND
  DEADLY SINS IN "LA CELESTINA."
    J. BURKE, 238:MAR70-146
CLARKE, D.H. EAST COAST PASSAGE.
    617(TLS):7APR72-402
CLARKE, J. THE LIFE AND TIMES OF GEORGE
  III.
    617(TLS):6OCT72-1199
CLARKE, J.H., ED. MALCOLM X.
    H.A. LARRABEE, 432(NEQ):DEC70-638
    639(VQR):SPRING70-LXX
CLARKE, M.W. CHIEF BOWLES AND THE TEXAS
  CHEROKEES.
    W. GARD, 584(SWR):AUTUMN71-VI
CLARKE, N. BLUFF YOUR WAY IN WINE.
    C. DRIVER, 362:7DEC72-801
CLARKE, S. & A.H. - SEE SÁNCHEZ FERLOSIO,
  R.
CLARKSON, A. HUNGER TRACE.
    G. WOODCOCK, 102(CANL):WINTER71-88
CLARKSON, A. A LOVER MORE CONDOLING.
    G. ROPER, 627(UTQ):JUL69-359

CLARKSON, E. HALIC.
    639(VQR):AUTUMN70-CLVI
CLARKSON, L.A. THE PRE-INDUSTRIAL ECON-
  OMY IN ENGLAND 1500-1750.
    617(TLS):24MAR72-321
CLAROS, R.B. - SEE UNDER BENÍTEZ CLAROS,
  R.
CLAUDEL, P. & A. MEYER. CLAUDEL ET L'AM-
  ÉRIQUE, II. (E. ROBERTO, ED)
    R.J. NELSON, 207(FR):FEB70-513
CLAUDIAN. DE RAPTU PROSERPINAE.* (J.B.
  HALL, ED)
    O.A.W. DILKE, 487:WINTER70-368
    H.L. LEVY, 24:APR71-381
    H.L. LEVY, 124:SEP70-27
CLAUS, H. NATUURGETROUWER.
    270:VOL20#3-66
CLAVEL, M. LE TIERS DES ÉTOILES.
    617(TLS):22DEC72-1549
CLAVELIN, M. LA PHILOSOPHIE NATURELLE DE
  GALILÉE.
    A. PACCHI, 548(RCSF):OCT-DEC69-462
CLAVELL, J.C. - SEE UNDER COSTA CLAVELL,
  J.
CLAVIR, J. & J. SPITZER, EDS. THE CON-
  SPIRACY TRIAL.
    617(TLS):18FEB72-186
CLAYPOOLE, H.G.C. INTRODUCTION TO
  COARSE FISHING.
    617(TLS):13OCT72-1236
CLAYTON, J.J. SAUL BELLOW.
    A.D. HOOK, 447(N&Q):MAR70-117
CLAYTON, M. THE COLLECTOR'S DICTIONARY
  OF THE SILVER AND GOLD OF GREAT BRITAIN
  AND NORTH AMERICA.
    617(TLS):11FEB72-150
CLAYTON, S. SABBATICAL.
    E. MORGAN, 362:20APR72-524
    617(TLS):28APR72-500
CLAYTON, T. - SEE SUCKLING, J.
CLEAGE, A.B., JR. BLACK CHRISTIAN
  NATIONALISM.
    A. LAHR, 561(SATR):8APR72-61
CLEAGE, A.B., JR. THE BLACK MESSIAH.
    J. MC DONNELL, 142:FALL71-469
CLEARY, J. THE NINTH MARQUESS.
    M. LEVIN, 441:14MAY72-37
CLEAVER, E. SOUL ON ICE.
    H.A. LARRABEE, 432(NEQ):DEC70-638
CLEEVE, B. THE TRIUMPH OF O'ROURKE.
    M. LEVIN, 441:12MAR72-41
CLEGG, A.B., ED. THE CHANGING PRIMARY
  SCHOOL.
    617(TLS):10MAR72-285
CLEGG, H.A. THE SYSTEM OF INDUSTRIAL
  RELATIONS IN GREAT BRITAIN.
    617(TLS):1SEP72-1034
CLEGG, J. DICTIONARY OF SOCIAL SERVICES.
    617(TLS):2JUN72-641
CLEMEN, W. A COMMENTARY ON SHAKESPEARE'S
  "RICHARD III."
    M. MINCOFF, 179(ES):AUG70-355
CLEMEN, W. SHAKESPEARE'S DRAMATIC ART.
    617(TLS):5MAY72-517
CLEMENS, D.S. YALTA.*
    F.C. POGUE, 32:SEP71-669
CLEMENS, W.H. CHAUCER'S EARLY POETRY.
    H. BOYD, 180(ESA):SEP70-415
CLÉMENT, F. & P. LAROUSSE. DICTIONNAIRE
  DES OPÉRAS. (REV BY A. POUGIN)
    S. SADIE, 415:FEB70-164
CLEMENTS, A.L. THE MYSTICAL POETRY OF
  THOMAS TRAHERNE.*
    R.L. COLIE, 301(JEGP):JUL71-546
    B. DRAKE, 401(MLQ):DEC70-492
    C.M. SICHERMAN, 551(RENQ):WINTER70-
    491

61

CLEMENTS, R.J. - SEE DONADONI, E.
CLEMO, J. THE ECHOING TIP.
617(TLS):7JAN72-6
CLEMOES, P. RHYTHM AND COSMIC ORDER IN
OLD ENGLISH CHRISTIAN LITERATURE.
T.A. SHIPPEY, 677:VOL2-231
CLEMOES, P. & K. HUGHES, EDS. ENGLAND
BEFORE THE CONQUEST.
617(TLS):3MAR72-243
CLENDENNING, J. - SEE ROYCE, J.
CLEVELAND, J. THE POEMS OF JOHN CLEVE-
LAND. (B. MORRIS & E. WITHINGTON, EDS)
A.M. CHARLES, 405(MP):FEB70-288
S. SHRAPNEL, 97(CQ):SUMMER68-281
CLEVERDON, D. THE GROWTH OF "MILK WOOD."
H. SERGEANT, 175:AUTUMN69-111
CLIFFORD, D. & T. JOHN CROME.*
F.W. HAWCROFT, 90:DEC69-765
CLIFFORD, F. A WILD JUSTICE.
M. LEVIN, 441:9JUL72-28
442(NY):12AUG72-77
617(TLS):26MAY72-612
CLIFFORD, J.L., ED. MAN VERSUS SOCIETY
IN EIGHTEENTH-CENTURY BRITAIN.
K.T.A., 191(ELN):SEP69(SUPP)-12
E.A. BLOOM, 402(MLR):JUL71-666
H. ERSKINE-HILL, 447(N&Q):MAR70-103
CLIFFORD, M. WASHINGTON COOKBOOK.
N. HAZELTON, 441:3DEC72-96
CLIFTON, L. GOOD NEWS ABOUT EARTH.
N. ROSTEN, 561:12AUG72-58
CLIFTON-TAYLOR, A. THE PATTERN OF ENG-
LISH BUILDING. (REV)
617(TLS):5MAY72-508
CLINE, C.L. - SEE MEREDITH, G.
CLINTON-BADDELEY, V.C. TO STUDY A LONG
SILENCE.
617(TLS):28APR72-500
CLIVE, G. THE BROKEN ICON.
617(TLS):8DEC72-1509
CLIVE, J. & T. PINNEY - SEE MACAULAY,
T.B.
CLOETE, S. A VICTORIAN SON.
E.S. TURNER, 362:3FEB72-154
617(TLS):28JAN72-89
"THE CLOISTERS APOCALYPSE."
617(TLS):28JAN72-108
CLOSS, A., ED. TWENTIETH-CENTURY GERMAN
LITERATURE.*
J.C. HAMMER, 221(GQ):JAN70-102
E. STOPP, 402(MLR):APR71-473
CLOSS, A. & W.T. PUGH, EDS. THE HARRAP
ANTHOLOGY OF GERMAN POETRY. (2ND ED)
J.C. HAMMER, 221(GQ):NOV70-792
CLOUGH, S.B. & S. SALADINO. A HISTORY
OF MODERN ITALY.
S. HUGHES, 613:AUTUMN69-477
CLOYD, E.L. JAMES BURNETT, LORD MONBOD-
DO.
H. TREVOR-ROPER, 362:28SEP72-407
CLUBB, L.G. ITALIAN PLAYS (1500-1700)
IN THE FOLGER LIBRARY.
B. MITCHELL, 276:WINTER70-435
A. SCAGLIONE, 545(RPH):FEB71-561
CLUBB, O.E. CHINA AND RUSSIA.*
J. ISRAEL, 440:16JAN72-7
CLUBBE, J. VICTORIAN FORERUNNER.
M.S., 155:JAN70-59
P. TURNER, 541(RES):MAY70-249
CLUNE, H.W. THE ROCHESTER I KNOW.
441:31DEC72-19
CLURMAN, H. ON DIRECTING.
A. SZOGYI, 441:19NOV72-28
COATE, H.H.J. & L. OATES. A GRAMMAR OF
NGARINJIN.
C. YALLOP, 67:MAY71-139

COATES, A. CHINA, INDIA, AND THE RUINS
OF WASHINGTON.
P. ADAMS, 61:JUN72-112
COATES, A. RIZAL.
J.N. SCHUMACHER, 293(JAST):NOV69-208
COATES, K. & T. TOPHAM. THE NEW UNION-
ISM.
617(TLS):1DEC72-1464
COATES, P. GEORGE ROBEY.
617(TLS):25FEB72-229
COBB, C.W. FEDERICO GARCIA LORCA.
M.G. CHRISTOPHERSEN, 577(SHR):WINTER
70-96
COBB, R. REACTIONS TO THE FRENCH REVO-
LUTION.
P.N. FURBANK, 362:10AUG72-182
617(TLS):16JUN72-679
COCHISE, N. & A.K. GRIFFITH. THE FIRST
HUNDRED YEARS OF NIÑO COCHISE.*
617(TLS):21JUL72-829
COCHRAN, T.C. BUSINESS IN AMERICAN LIFE.
441:6AUG72-20
COCHRANE, A.L. EFFECTIVENESS AND
EFFICIENCY.
617(TLS):21APR72-458
COCKBURN, C. BESTSELLER.
M. DRABBLE, 362:29JUN72-872
617(TLS):14JUL72-796
COCKBURN, H. MEMORIALS OF HIS TIME.
617(TLS):18FEB72-181
COCKBURN, J.S. & T.F.T. BAKER, EDS. THE
VICTORIA HISTORY OF THE COUNTIES OF
ENGLAND: A HISTORY OF THE COUNTY OF
MIDDLESEX. (VOL 4)
617(TLS):7APR72-391
COCKBURN, R.H. THE NOVELS OF HUGH
MAC LENNAN.
D. BARBOUR, 102(CANL):SUMMER71-75
COCKCROFT, J.D. INTELLECTUAL PRECURSORS
OF THE MEXICAN REVOLUTION, 1900-1913.
P. KELSO, 50(ARQ):WINTER69-360
COCKE, R. PIER FRANCESCO MOLA.
617(TLS):5MAY72-508
COCKSHUT, A.O.J. THE ACHIEVEMENT OF WAL-
TER SCOTT.
K.C., 191(ELN):SEP70(SUPP)-41
COCKX-INDESTEGE, E. & G. GLORIEUX. BEL-
GICA TYPOGRAPHICA 1541-1600. (VOL 1)
J.W. JOLLIFFE, 354:SEP69-263
CODET, P. - SEE BRICE, G.
CODY, J. AFTER GREAT PAIN.*
617(TLS):2JUN72-624
CODY, R. THE LANDSCAPE OF THE MIND.
J. REES, 447(N&Q):APR70-153
J. ROBERTSON, 541(RES):NOV70-490
L.G. SALINGAR, 551(RENQ):AUTUMN70-327
639(VQR):SPRING70-LX
COE, R.N. - SEE STENDHAL
COE, T. DON'T LIE TO ME.
N. CALLENDAR, 441:3SEP72-22
COFFEY, T.M. IMPERIAL TRAGEDY.*
R.A. MILLER, 676(YR):SUMMER71-576
COFFIN, A.B. ROBINSON JEFFERS.*
F.I. CARPENTER, 27(AL):NOV71-477
COFFIN, T.P. & H. COHEN, EDS. FOLKLORE
IN AMERICA.*
C.P. AUSER, 650(WP):JAN69-53
COGER, L.I. & M.R. WHITE. READERS
THEATRE HANDBOOK.
B. WHITAKER, 583:SPRING69-238
COGGAN, D. WORD AND WORLD.
617(TLS):28APR72-501
COGHILL, N. CHAUCER'S IDEA OF WHAT IS
NOBLE.
617(TLS):10NOV72-1364
COGHILL, N. SHAKESPEARE'S PROFESSIONAL
SKILLS.
A. GÉRARD, 179(ES):JUN70-251

COGHILL, N. - SEE CHAUCER, G.
COGNY, P. MAUPASSANT.
  D. FREIMANIS, 207(FR):DEC69-338
COGSWELL, F. THE CHAINS OF LILLIPUT.
  W. PROUTY, 198:SUMMER72-116
COGSWELL, F. IMMORTAL PLOWMAN.
  M. DOYLE, 491:MAR72-356
COGSWELL, F., ED & TRANS. ONE HUNDRED
  POEMS OF MODERN QUEBEC.
  P. STRATFORD, 102(CANL):SUMMER71-88
COGSWELL, F. STAR-PEOPLE.
  H. MAC CALLUM, 627(UTQ):JUL69-351
COHEN, C. CIVIL DISOBEDIENCE.*
  H.A. BEDAU, 311(JP):6APR72-179
COHEN, D. & H. ZAFRANI. GRAMMAIRE DE
  L'HÉBREU VIVANT.
  P.O. SAMUELSDORFF, 361:VOL24#3-307
COHEN, H. A BUNDLE OF TIME.*
  R.J. DRAKEFORD, 571:SUMMER69-28
COHEN, L. SELECTED POEMS 1956-68.
  H. MAC CALLUM, 627(UTQ):JUL69-340
COHEN, L.J. THE IMPLICATIONS OF INDUC-
  TION.*
  R. ACKERMANN, 311(JP):24FEB72-103
  H.E. KYBURG, JR., 311(JP):24FEB72-106
  R.G. SWINBURNE, 518:JAN71-4
COHEN, M. JOHNNY CRACKLE SINGS.
  S. ATHERTON, 296:WINTER72-87
  D. BARBOUR, 99:JAN-FEB72-80
COHEN, M. KORSONILOFF.
  G. ROPER, 627(UTQ):JUL70-340
COHEN, M., ED. 101 PLUS 5 FOLK SONGS FOR
  CAMP.
  B.G. LUMPKIN, 650(WF):JAN68-59
COHEN, M., ED. TO HELL WITH SKIING!
  J. GREENWAY, 650(WF):JAN69-68
COHEN, R. GIRAUDOUX.*
  J.D. ERICKSON, 397(MD):FEB70-436
  A.G. RAYMOND, 207(FR):DEC69-335
COHEN, R. THE UNFOLDING OF "THE SEAS-
  ONS."
  C.J. RAWSON, 677:VOL2-283
  566:AUTUMN70-30
COHEN, R.S. & M.W. WARTOFSKY, EDS. BOS-
  TON STUDIES IN THE PHILOSOPHY OF SCI-
  ENCE. (VOL 5)
  R.H.K., 543:JUN70-751
COHEN, S. FOLK DEVILS AND MORAL PANICS.
  617(TLS):8DEC72-1506
COHEN, S. & L. TAYLOR. PSYCHOLOGICAL
  SURVIVAL.
  617(TLS):24NOV72-1416
COHEN, S.J. - SEE "DORIS HUMPHREY"
COHEN, S.S. - SEE AINSLIE, T.
COHEN, W.I. AMERICA'S RESPONSE TO CHINA.
  R. STEEL, 440:9APR72-1
COHN, H. THE TRIAL AND DEATH OF JESUS.*
  617(TLS):14JUL72-823
COHN, H.J., ED. GOVERNMENT IN REFORMA-
  TION EUROPE, 1520-1560.
  617(TLS):10MAR72-285
COHN, M. - SEE "HANNAH SENESH: HER LIFE
  AND DIARY"
COHN, R. EDWARD ALBEE.
  A.P. HINCHLIFFE, 148:SPRING70-95
COHN, R., ED. CASEBOOK ON "WAITING FOR
  GODOT."
  J. FLETCHER, 397(MD):MAY69-99
COHN, S.H. ECONOMIC DEVELOPMENT IN THE
  SOVIET UNION.
  M. BORNSTEIN, 32:DEC71-900
DE COINCI, G. - SEE UNDER GAUTIER DE
  COINCI
COINDREAU, M.E. THE TIME OF WILLIAM
  FAULKNER.* (G.M. REEVES, ED & TRANS)
  J. EARLY, 584(SWR):SUMMER71-293
  W.L. MINER, 27(AL):NOV71-478

COKE, V.D. THE PAINTER AND THE PHOTO-
  GRAPH FROM DELACROIX TO WARHOL.
  P. GAY, 31(ASCH):AUTUMN72-660
COLBY, A.M. THE PORTRAIT IN TWELFTH-
  CENTURY FRENCH LITERATURE.
  C. MÉLA, 545(RPH):FEB71-529
COLBY, V. & R.A. THE EQUIVOCAL VIRTUE.
  K.J. FIELDING, 637(VS):MAR70-362
COLDSTREAM, J.N. GREEK GEOMETRIC POT-
  TERY.*
  R. HIGGINS, 39:NOV69-450
  E. VERMEULE, 121(CJ):OCT-NOV70-83
COLE, B. THE VISITORS.
  R. DURGNAT, 493:WINTER70/71-366
COLE, M. & S. BLACK. CHECKING IT OUT.
  441:9APR72-34
COLE, T. DEMOCRITUS AND THE SOURCES OF
  GREEK ANTHROPOLOGY.*
  D. FURLEY, 303:VOL90-239
COLE, W. THE FORM OF MUSIC.
  J. HORTON, 415:FEB70-163
COLE, W. KYOTO IN THE MOMOYAMA PERIOD.
  R. KOSTKA, 576:MAR69-75
COLEMAN, A., ED. CINCO MAESTROS.
  E. ECHEVARRÍA, 238:MAR70-175
COLEMAN, A. OTHER VOICES.
  J. DÍAZ, 241:JAN71-77
  D.R. HARRIS, 86(BHS):JAN71-87
COLEMAN, A.R. VICTORIAN LADY ON THE
  TEXAS FRONTIER.* (C.R. KING, ED)
  W. GARD, 584(SWR):SPRING71-199
COLEMAN, E.S., ED. STIMMEN AUS DEM
  STUNDENGLAS.
  I.L. CARLSON, 221(GQ):MAY70-530
COLEMAN, T. GOING TO AMERICA.
  P. ADAMS, 61:JUN72-113
  C. SIMMONS, 441:2AUG72-37
COLEMAN, T. PASSAGE TO AMERICA.
  R. MITCHISON, 362:22JUN72-838
  617(TLS):22SEP72-1096
COLEMAN, V. LIGHT VERSE.
  P.M. BATES, 96:APR70-64
COLEMAN, V. PARKING LOTS.
  R. GIBBS, 198:SUMMER72-129
COLERIDGE, A. CHIPPENDALE FURNITURE.*
  C. MUSGRAVE, 90:JUL70-472
COLERIDGE, S.T. COLERIDGE'S VERSE: A
  SELECTION. (W. EMPSON & D. PIRIE, EDS)
  617(TLS):15DEC72-1524
COLERIDGE, S.T. COLLECTED LETTERS OF
  SAMUEL TAYLOR COLERIDGE. (VOLS 5&6)
  (E.L. GRIGGS, ED)
  D. DONOGHUE, 362:30MAR72-427
  617(TLS):31MAR72-354
COLERIDGE, S.T. THE COLLECTED WORKS OF
  SAMUEL TAYLOR COLERIDGE: THE FRIEND.*
  (B.E. ROOKE, ED)
  I.H.C., 191(ELN):SEP70(SUPP)-33
  639(VQR):WINTER70-XVIII
COLERIDGE, S.T. THE COLLECTED WORKS OF
  SAMUEL TAYLOR COLERIDGE: THE WATCHMAN.*
  (L. PATTON, ED)
  639(VQR):SUMMER70-XCVI
COLES, R. FAREWELL TO THE SOUTH.
  J. YARDLEY, 441:6AUG72-3
  442(NY):2SEP72-71
  561(SATR):21OCT72-80
COLES, R. MIGRANTS, SHARECROPPERS,
  MOUNTAINEERS. THE SOUTH GOES NORTH.
  H.M. CAUDILL, 453:9MAR72-21
  C. LEHMANN-HAUPT, 441:18FEB72-37
  M. PIERCY, 441:13FEB72-1
  H.L. VAN BRUNT, 561(SATR):8APR72-69
COLES, W.A. - SEE VAN BRUNT, H.
COLETTE. JOURNEY FOR MYSELF.*
  N. HALE, 441:1OCT72-6
  442(NY):28OCT72-160

63

COLETTE. LA NAISSANCE DU JOUR. (C.
PICHOIS, ED)
   H. GODIN, 208(FS):APR71-236
COLETTE. THE OTHER WOMAN.*
   N. HALE, 441:10CT72-6
   N. RYAN, 561(SATR):1APR72-74
COLETTE. PLACES.*
   N. HALE, 441:10CT72-6
COLGRAVE, B., ED & TRANS. THE EARLIEST
LIFE OF GREGORY THE GREAT, BY AN ANONY-
MOUS MONK OF WHITBY.*
   D.F. HEIMANN, 121(CJ):OCT-NOV70-78
COLGRAVE, B.' & R.A.B. MYNORS - SEE
"BEDE'S ECCLESIASTICAL HISTORY OF THE
ENGLISH PEOPLE"
COLIE, R.L. "MY ECCHOING SONG."
   R.J. BAUER, 568(SCN):SUMMER/AUTUMN71-
   43
   P. LEGOUIS, 191(ELN):MAR71-225
   M. SHAPIRO, 301(JEGP):OCT71-665
COLLANTES, J. LA ESTRUCTURA DE LA
IGLESIA.
   G. MAY, 182:VOL23#1/2-9
COLLARD, A. NUEVA POESÍA.
   E.J. GATES, 546(RR):APR70-137
   E.L. RIVERS, 400(MLN):MAR70-296
   E.A. WILSON, 240(HR):APR70-227
COLLARD, E. NINETEENTH CENTURY POTTERY
AND PORCELAIN IN CANADA.*
   G.W., 39:MAY69-405
COLLART, J. - SEE PLAUTUS
"COLLECT BRITISH STAMPS." (NEW ED)
   617(TLS):25AUG72-1006
"THE JOHN COLLIER READER."
   T. LASK, 441:25NOV72-33
COLLINGWOOD, P. THE TECHNIQUES OF RUG
WEAVING.
   L. BLUMENAU, 139:JUL/AUG69-6
COLLINGWOOD, R.G. THE ARCHAEOLOGY OF
ROMAN BRITAIN. (REV BY I. RICHMOND)
   G. WEBSTER, 313:VOL60-245
COLLINGWOOD, R.G. FAITH AND REASON.
(L. RUBINOFF, ED)
   R.E. ROBLIN, 484(PPR):JUN70-628
   D.V. WADE, 627(UTQ):JUL69-427
COLLINS, D.A. THOMAS CORNEILLE.
   J.M. CABAUD, 546(RR):APR70-134
   Q.M. HOPE, 399(MLJ):NOV70-534
COLLINS, F., JR. THE PRODUCTION OF MEDI-
EVAL CHURCH MUSIC-DRAMA.
   617(TLS):28JUL72-884
COLLINS, G.R. & C.C. CAMILLO SITTE AND
THE BIRTH OF MODERN CITY PLANNING.
   C. TUNNARD, 576:MAR68-87
COLLINS, H.F. LE CHARMANT PAYS DE
FRANCE.
   R-M. DAELE-GUINAN, 207(FR):MAR70-715
COLLINS, J. THE EMERGENCE OF THE PHIL-
OSOPHY OF RELIGION.
   J.J. SIKORA, 613:SPRING68-149
   G.C. STEAD, 479(PHQ):APR70-188
COLLINS, L. & D. LAPIERRE. O JERUSALEM!
   M.M. BERNET, 561(SATR):10JUN72-60
   T. LASK, 441:13MAY72-33
   D. SCHOENBRUN, 441:14MAY72-7
   E. WEEKS, 61:JUL72-93
   442(NY):24JUN72-94
   617(TLS):13OCT72-1222
COLLINS, M. SHADOW OF A TIGER.
   N. CALLENDAR, 441:80CT72-46
COLLINS, P. - SEE DICKENS, C.
COLLINS, R.O. KING LEOPOLD, ENGLAND AND
THE UPPER NILE.
   N-R. BENNETT, 637(VS):DEC69-223
COLLINSON, F. THE TRADITIONAL AND
NATIONAL MUSIC OF SCOTLAND.
   M.W. CLARKE, 650(WF):JAN69-60

COLLIOT, R. ADENET LE ROI, "BERTE AUS
GRANS PIÉS."
   J. GILDEA, 589:JAN71-137
   W. ROTHWELL, 182:VOL23#6-271
COLLIS, L. A PRIVATE VIEW OF STANLEY
SPENCER.
   T. DRIBERG, 362:23MAR72-389
   617(TLS):24MAR72-328
COLLUTHUS. COLLUTO, "IL RATTO DI
ELENA."* (E. LIVREA, ED & TRANS)
   F.M. COMBELLACK, 122:JAN71-48
COLOMBO, J.R. THE GREAT SAN FRANCISCO
EARTHQUAKE AND FIRE.
   J.R. SORFLEET, 198:SPRING72-116
COLOMBO, J.R. NEO POEMS.*
   J. CHRISTY, 102(CANL):AUTUMN71-84
   M. DOYLE, 491:MAR72-356
   150(DR):AUTUMN70-431
COLOMBO, U. ALESSANDRO MANZONI. (PT 1)
   W.T.S., 191(ELN):SEP69(SUPP)-125
COLQUHOUN, P. A TREATISE ON THE POLICE
OF THE METROPOLIS. A TREATISE ON THE
COMMERCE AND POLICE OF THE RIVER
THAMES.
   617(TLS):18FEB72-191
COLTER, C. THE RIVERS OF EROS.
   J. CATINELLA, 561(SATR):27MAY72-68
   G. DAVIS, 441:17SEP72-48
   M. WATKINS, 441:14JUL72-32
COLUMELLA. COLUMELLE, "DE L'AGRICUL-
TURE."* (BK 10) (E. DE SAINT-DENIS,
ED & TRANS)
   F.R.D. GOODYEAR, 123:MAR71-59
COLUMELLA. L. IVNI MODERATI COLVMELLAE,
"RES RUSTICA." (FASC 3&8) (S. HEDBERG,
ED)
   J. ANDRÉ, 555:VOL44FASC2-346
COLVILLE, J.R. MAN OF VALOUR.
   J. GRIGG, 362:13JAN72-58
   617(TLS):14JAN72-29
COLVIN, C. - SEE EDGEWORTH, M.
COLVIN, H.M., ED. BUILDING ACCOUNTS OF
KING HENRY III.
   617(TLS):11FEB72-165
COMAN, D.R. THE ENDLESS ADVENTURE.
   441:31DEC72-19
COMAY, J. WHO'S WHO IN THE OLD TESTA-
MENT.*
   617(TLS):25FEB72-225
COMBE, T.G.S. & P. RICKARD, EDS. THE
FRENCH LANGUAGE.
   G. PRICE, 208(FS):JAN71-119
COMBELLACK, F.M. - SEE QUINTUS OF SMYRNA
COMBÈS, M. LE CONCEPT DE CONCEPT FORMEL.
   P.F. STRAWSON, 393(MIND):APR70-311
COMBS, J.A. THE JAY TREATY.
   A.H. BOWMAN, 656(WMQ):OCT70-678
   A. NORMAN, 432(NEQ):SEP70-513
COMBS, J.H. FOLK-SONGS OF THE SOUTHERN
UNITED STATES.
   P.H. KENNEDY, 582(SFQ):DEC69-370
COMELIAU, C. CONDITIONS DE LA PLANIFICA-
TION DU DÉVELOPPEMENT.
   T. PANG, 182:VOL23#10-537
COMENIUS, J.A. ORBIS PICTUS.
   P.E.D., 503:WINTER68-185
COMERCHERO, V. NATHANAEL WEST.*
   B. LEE, 447(N&Q):FEB70-79
COMETTI, E. - SEE DAL VERME, F.
COMMELIN, I. BEGIN ENDE VOORTGANGH.
   617(TLS):14JAN72-37
COMIRE, A., ED. SOMETHING ABOUT THE
AUTHOR. (VOL 1)
   J.M. SHAW, 70(ANQ):FEB72-92
COMMONER, B. THE CLOSING CIRCLE.*
   J. CAREY, 362:3FEB72-154
   617(TLS):24MAR72-327

"COMMUNICATIONS 10." (1967)
    E.C. KNOX, 207(FR):MAR70-719
COMNENA, A. THE "ALEXIAD" OF ANNA COM-
NENA. (E.R.A. SEWTER, TRANS)
    J.E. SEAVER, 124:SEP70-28
"THE COMPACT EDITION OF THE OXFORD ENG-
LISH DICTIONARY."*
    617(TLS):13OCT72-1209
"THE COMPLETE SUNDAY LECTIONARY AND MASS
BOOK."
    617(TLS):14APR72-426
"THE COMPLETE WORK OF RAPHAEL."
    A. WERNER, 58:APR70-10
COMPTON, P. CARDIGAN OF BALACLAVA.
    617(TLS):27OCT72-1294
COMPTON-BURNETT, I. THE LAST AND THE
FIRST.*
    G. WEALES, 249(HUDR):WINTER71/72-716
CONACHER, D.J. EURIPIDEAN DRAMA.*
    H.C. BALDRY, 123:DEC71-345
CONACHER, J.B. THE ABERDEEN COALITION,
1852-1855.
    V. CROMWELL, 325:APR70-79
    N. GASH, 637(VS):JUN70-439
CONANT, J.B. MY SEVERAL LIVES.
    H.W. DODDS, 639(VQR):AUTUMN70-670
CONARROE, J. WILLIAM CARLOS WILLIAMS'
"PATERSON."*
    W. SUTTON, 27(AL):NOV71-472
"THE CONCERNED PHOTOGRAPHER 2."
    S. SCHWARTZ, 441:3DEC72-20
CONCHE, M. MONTAIGNE OU LA CONSCIENCE
HEUREUSE. (NEW ED)
    R. GRACE, 399(MLJ):JAN70-54
DE CONCHES, G. - SEE UNDER GUILLAUME DE
CONCHES
CONDER, J.J. A FORMULA OF HIS OWN.*
    H.P. VINCENT, 432(NEQ):DEC70-669
    639(VQR):AUTUMN70-CXXXVII
CONDON, R. ARIGATO.
    R. BRYDEN, 362:30NOV72-760
    N. CALLENDAR, 441:29OCT72-59
    442(NY):21OCT72-167
    617(TLS):8DEC72-1477
CONDON, R. THE VERTICAL SMILE.*
    617(TLS):28APR72-500
CONE, E.T. MUSICAL FORM AND MUSICAL
PERFORMANCE.
    M. PETERSON, 470:MAY69-32
CONE, J.H. A BLACK THEOLOGY OF LIBERA-
TION.
    J. MC DONNELL, 142:FALL71-469
CONFINO, M. L'ASSOLEMENT TRIENNAL EN
RUSSIE AUX XVIIIE-XIXE SIÈCLES.
    M. MC CAULEY, 575(SEER):JUL71-474
CONFINO, M. SYSTÈMES AGRAIRES ET PROGRÈS
AGRICOLE.
    F-X. COQUIN, 32:DEC71-880
CONGAR, Y.M-J. A HISTORY OF THEOLOGY.
    W.A.J., 543:SEP69-125
CONGDON, K. THE CHRISTMAS TREE.
    J. HOPPER, 661:SPRING69-109
CONGDON, K., ED. MAGAZINE.
    J. HOPPER, 661:SPRING69-109
CONGREVE, W. THE COMPLETE PLAYS OF
WILLIAM CONGREVE. (H. DAVIS, ED)
    U. BROICH, 38:BAND87HEFT1-95
    G. SORELIUS, 597(SN):VOL40#1-249
CONGREVE, W. LOVE FOR LOVE. (M.M. KEL-
SALL, ED)
    P. ROBERTS, 447(N&Q):JUN70-237
CONLON, K. MY FATHER'S HOUSE.
    617(TLS):30JUN72-737
CONLON, P.M. PRÉLUDE AU SIÈCLE DES
LUMIÈRES EN FRANCE.
    A. MARTIN, 67:MAY71-128
CONN, S. STOATS IN THE SUNLIGHT.
    E.J., 619(TC):1968/3-53

CONNELL, E.S., JR. THE DIARY OF A RAP-
IST.
    J. BOATWRIGHT, 340(KR):SEP66-563
CONNELL-SMITH, G. & H.A. LLOYD. THE
RELEVANCE OF HISTORY.
    617(TLS):24NOV72-1437
CONNERS, B.F. DON'T EMBARRASS THE BUREAU.
    N. CALLENDAR, 441:18JUN72-32
CONNOLLY, E. LEOPOLDO PANERO.
    G. CONNELL, 86(BHS):APR71-173
CONNOLLY, R., ED. THE BEATLES YEARS.
    617(TLS):14JUL72-826
CONNOR, S.V. & O.B. FAULK. NORTH AMERICA
DIVIDED.
    441:6FEB72-40
CONNOR, T. IN THE HAPPY VALLEY.*
    C. MOLESWORTH, 491:MAY72-107
    I. WEDDE, 364:DEC71/JAN72-118
CONNOR, W.R. THE NEW POLITICIANS OF
FIFTH-CENTURY ATHENS.
    617(TLS):31MAR72-376
CONNOR, W.R. THEOPOMPUS AND FIFTH-
CENTURY ATHENS.*
    F-M. WASSERMANN, 121(CJ):OCT-NOV70-76
CONNORS, D.F. THOMAS MORTON.
    D.B. SHEA, JR., 656(WMQ):JUL70-486
CONOLLY, V. BEYOND THE URALS.
    P-G. FRANCK, 293(JAST):FEB70-456
CONOMIS, N.C. - SEE LYCURGUS
CONOVER, D. ONE MAN'S ISLAND.
    617(TLS):16JUN72-697
CONQUEST, R., ED. AGRICULTURAL WORKERS
IN THE U.S.S.R.
    A.E. ADAMS, 550(RUSR):JAN70-108
CONQUEST, R. THE GREAT TERROR.
    G.H. BOLSOVER, 575(SEER):APR71-315
    A. NOVE, 587:APR69-536
CONQUEST, R., ED. RELIGION IN THE
U.S.S.R.
    M. KLIMENKO, 32:JUN71-403
CONQUEST, R. - SEE YAKIR, P.
CONRAD, J. JOSEPH CONRAD'S LETTERS TO
R.B. CUNNINGHAME GRAHAM. (C.T. WATTS,
ED)
    E.A. BOJARSKI, 149:SEP71-275
    H.J. LASKOWSKY, 136:WINTER69/70-125
    E.W. SAID, 637(VS):JUN70-429
    639(VQR):WINTER70-XXI
CONRAD, J. TYPHOON. (U. MURSIA, ED)
    S. HANNESTAD, 136:FALL69-125
CONROY, M.C. IMAGERY IN THE SERMONS OF
MAXIMUS, BISHOP OF TURIN.
    H. SAVON, 555:VOL44FASC1-162
CONROY, P. THE WATER IS WIDE.
    A. BROYARD, 441:13JUL72-37
    J. HASKINS, 441:24SEP72-10
CONSTABLE, J. JOHN CONSTABLE'S CORRES-
PONDENCE.* (VOL 6) (R.B. BECKETT, ED)
    K. GARLICK, 90:SEP70-635
CONSTABLE, T.J. HIDDEN HEROES.
    617(TLS):28JUL72-900
CONSTANT, A-L. ELIPHAS LEVI VISIONNAIRE
ROMANTIQUE. (F.P. BOWMAN, ED)
    J.S.P., 191(ELN):SEP70(SUPP)-66
CONSTANT, B. (PAR LUI-MÊME).
    P. DE MAN, 98:JUL69-608
CONSTANTINE, A., JR. KNOW YOUR WOODS.
    B. GLADSTONE, 441:3DEC72-99
CONSTANTINESCU, M. ÉTUDES D'HISTOIRE
TRANSYLVAINE.
    J.C. CAMPBELL, 104:WINTER71-578
CONSTANTINESCU, M. & OTHERS. ÉTUDES
D'HISTOIRE CONTEMPORAINE DE LA ROU-
MANIE.
    J.C. CAMPBELL, 104:WINTER71-578

CONSTANTINESCU, M. & V. LIVEANU. SUR
QUELQUES PROBLÈMES D'HISTOIRE. PROB-
LEMS OF HISTORY AND SOCIAL THEORY.
  J.C. CAMPBELL, 104:WINTER71-578
"CONTEMPORARY AMERICAN PAINTING AND
SCULPTURE."
  M.S. YOUNG, 39:APR69-329
"CONTES ET NOUVELLES D'AUJOURD'HUI."
  A. SZOGYI, 207(FR):MAR70-716
CONTI, P.G. L'AUTORE INTENZIONALE.
  W.T.S., 191(ELN):SEP69(SUPP)-123
"CONTRIBUTI DELL'ISTITUTO DI FILOLOGIA
MODERNA." (SER FRANCESE, VOL 5)
  G. HAINSWORTH, 208(FS):JUL71-368
"CONTRIBUTIONS TO ANTHROPOLOGY: LINGUIS-
TICS I (ALGONQUIAN)."
  W. COWAN, 269(IJAL):JUL69-270
CONWAY, D. MAGIC.
  617(TLS):12MAY72-557
CONZE, E. BUDDHIST THOUGHT IN INDIA.
  P.J.H., 543:JUN70-739
CONZE, E. THIRTY YEARS OF BUDDHIST
STUDIES.*
  P.J.H., 543:DEC69-343
COOK, A. ENACTMENT.
  M. AUGEN, 385(MQR):SUMMER72-224
COOK, A.S., COMP. A CONCORDANCE TO
"BEOWULF."
  A. CAMPBELL, 447(N&Q):MAR70-116
COOK, D. ALBERT'S MEMORIAL.
  E. MORGAN, 362:27JAN72-120
  617(TLS):28JAN72-85
COOK, L. A FEELING OF DISQUIET.
  J. HUNTER, 362:1JUN72-736
COOK, R., ED. FRENCH CANADIAN NATIONAL-
ISM.
  G.F.G. STANLEY, 529(QQ):AUTUMN70-440
COOK, R. THE MAPLE LEAF FOR EVER.
  102(CANL):AUTUMN71-102
COOK, R. JONATHAN SWIFT AS A TORY PAM-
PHLETEER.
  J.J. STATHIS, 219(GAR):SPRING69-110
COOK, R. & K. SOUTHERN GREECE.*
  L.H. JEFFERY, 447(N&Q):JUL70-268
COOK, R.A. FLINT FROM THE FIRE.
  J.E. TALMADGE, 219(GAR):SUMMER69-266
COOK, S. & G. LEAN. THE LITTLE BLACK AND
WHITE BOOK.
  617(TLS):24MAR72-334
COOKE, A.M. A HISTORY OF THE ROYAL
COLLEGE OF PHYSICIANS OF LONDON. (VOL
3)
  617(TLS):16JUN72-694
COOKE, D. - SEE RÉTI, R.
COOKE, J.E., ED. ALEXANDER HAMILTON.
  J.F. COSTANZO, 613:SUMMER68-310
COOKE, J.R. PRONOMINAL REFERENCE IN
THAI, BURMESE, AND VIETNAMESE.*
  F.K. LEHMAN, 293(JAST):MAY70-733
COOKE, K. A.C. BRADLEY AND HIS INFLUENCE
IN TWENTIETH-CENTURY SHAKESPEARE CRITI-
CISM.
  617(TLS):13OCT72-1216
COOKE, M.G. THE BLIND MAN TRACES THE
CIRCLE.
  E.E.B., 191(ELN):SEP70(SUPP)-26
COOKES, A. THE SOUTHAMPTON POLICE FORCE
1836-1856.
  617(TLS):18AUG72-977
COOKRIDGE, E.H. GEHLEN.
  N. ASCHERSON, 453:1JUN72-3
  R.G. DEINDORFER, 561(SATR):24JUN72-61
  C. FELIX, 441:16APR72-3
  617(TLS):14JAN72-30
COOKRIDGE, E.H. SPY TRADE.
  441:8OCT72-38
COOKSON, T., ED. SHAW.
  617(TLS):25AUG72-988

COOLIDGE, C. SPACE.
  D. LEHMAN, 491:JAN72-224
COOLIDGE, O. GEORGE BERNARD SHAW.
  M.B. WEINTRAUB, 572:JAN69-39
COOMBES, D. STATE ENTERPRISE.
  617(TLS):2JUN72-637
COOMBS, H. & P. - SEE SKINNER, J.
COON, C.S. THE HUNTING PEOPLES.*
  617(TLS):22SEP72-1094
COONEY, T. HOMAGE TO ANAIS.
  F.A. RANA, 296:FALL72-97
COONS, W.R. ATTICA DIARY.
  442(NY):26AUG72-79
COOPER, B. SEX WITHOUT TEARS.
  T. STURGEON, 441:17SEP72-41
COOPER, C. CONRAD AND THE HUMAN DILEMMA.
  J. FEASTER, 295:VOL2#3-417
COOPER, D. THE DEATH OF THE FAMILY.*
  H. LOMAS, 364:AUG/SEP71-136
COOPER, D. PICASSO: THEATRE.
  G. BARO, 592:NOV68-228
  B. PETRIE, 90:SEP69-571
COOPER, D.M., COMP. SEVEN RUSSIAN PLAY-
LETS.
  W. JASZCZUN, 574(SEEJ):SPRING71-129
COOPER, G.L. 3D. ZUR SYNTAKTISCHEN
THEORIE UND TEXTKRITIK DER ATTISCHEN
AUTOREN.
  F. LASSERRE, 182:VOL23#21/22-945
COOPER, J.E.S. - SEE SHANSKII, N.M.
COOPER, J.F. THE LETTERS AND JOURNALS OF
JAMES FENIMORE COOPER.* (VOLS 5&6)
(J.F. BEARD, ED)
  O. ØVERLAND, 179(ES):JUN69-312
  J.H. PICKERING, 445(NCF):DEC68-351
COOPER, J.I. MONTREAL.
  G. TULCHINSKY, 529(QQ):SUMMER70-293
COOPER, M. BEETHOVEN: THE LAST DECADE,
1817-1827.*
  B.H. HAGGIN, 249(HUDR):SUMMER71-317
  J. KERMAN, 415:APR70-391
  639(VQR):SUMMER70-CI
COOPER, M. THE CAMERON STORY.
  J. HUNTER, 362:27JUL72-118
COOPER, M., ED. THE CONCISE ENCYCLOPEDIA
OF MUSIC AND MUSICIANS. (2ND ED)
  617(TLS):3MAR72-253
COOPER, P. THE AUTOBIOGRAPHICAL MYTH OF
ROBERT LOWELL.*
  T. PARKINSON, 27(AL):NOV71-482
COOPER, P. IN DEEP.
  502(PRS):WINTER68/69-367
COOPER, R.G. ENGLISH SLIPWARE DISHES
1650-1850.*
  G. WILLS, 39:FEB69-159
COOPER, S.M., JR. THE SONNETS OF ASTRO-
PHEL AND STELLA.
  W. MAYNARD, 541(RES):MAY70-195
  J. REES, 402(MLR):OCT71-857
COOPER, W. BROTHERS.
  P. THEROUX, 440:23APR72-8
COOPER, W. HAIR.
  P. ADAMS, 61:JAN72-96
COOPERMAN, S. CAPPELBAUM'S DANCE.*
  F. COGSWELL, 102(CANL):AUTUMN71-96
  D. FETHERLING, 606(TAMR):#57-80
COOPERMAN, S. THE DAY OF THE PARROT AND
OTHER POEMS.*
  C. ALEXANDER, 502(PRS):FALL69-320
COOPERMAN, S. THE OWL BEHIND THE DOOR.*
  H. MAC CALLUM, 627(UTQ):JUL69-352
COOPERMAN, S. WORLD WAR I AND THE AMERI-
CAN NOVEL.*
  L. GILHOOLEY, 613:AUTUMN68-441
COOPERSMITH, S., ED. FRONTIERS OF
PSYCHOLOGICAL RESEARCH.
  S.A.S., 543:DEC69-364
COOPLAND, G.W. - SEE DE MÉZIÈRES, P.

COOTE, J. A PICTURE HISTORY OF THE
OLYMPICS.
  B. GLANVILLE, 441:20AUG72-19
COOVER, R. PRICKSONGS AND DESCANTS.*
  639(VQR):SPRING70-XL
COPE, J. THE STUDENT OF ZEND.
  617(TLS):1SEP72-1013
COPE, T. IZIBONGO - ZULU PRAISE POEMS.
  D.P. KUNENE, 315(JAL):VOL8PT1-50
COPEAU, J. & R. MARTIN DU GARD. CORRES-
PONDANCE. (C. SICARD, ED)
  617(TLS):1SEP72-1017
COPI, I.M. THE THEORY OF LOGICAL TYPES.
  617(TLS):30JUN72-757
COPLAND, A. THE NEW MUSIC 1900/1960.
  (2ND ED)
  M. PETERSON, 470:JAN69-31
  S. WALSH, 607:SPRING69-63
COPLESTON, F.C. A HISTORY OF MEDIEVAL
PHILOSOPHY.
  617(TLS):24NOV72-1439
COPLEY, F.O. LATIN LITERATURE FROM THE
BEGINNINGS TO THE CLOSE OF THE SECOND
CENTURY A.D.*
  J.E.A. CRAKE, 487:WINTER70-366
  J.J. SAVAGE, 24:JUL71-479
  F.A. SULLIVAN, 122:OCT71-276
COPPEL, A. THE LANDLOCKED MAN.
  M. LEVIN, 441:9APR72-42
  442(NY):7OCT72-159
COPPER, B. A SONG FOR EVERY SEASON.
  617(TLS):28JAN72-109
COPPLESTONE, T. MODERN ART MOVEMENTS.
  D. IRWIN, 39:SEP69-271
COQUERY-VIDROVITCH, C., ED. BRAZZA ET
LA PRISE DE POSSESSION DU CONGO.
  P. SALMON, 182:VOL23#13/14-686
CORBEIL, J-C. LES STRUCTURES SYNTAXIQUES
DU FRANÇAIS MODERNE.
  N.C.W. SPENCE, 208(FS):OCT71-502
  K. TOGEBY, 545(RPH):FEB71-546
CORBETT, J.A., ED. PRAEPOSITINI CRE-
MONENSIS TRACTATUS DE OFFICIIS.
  F. BROOMFIELD, 382(MAE):1971/3-314
  M.E. JEGEN, 377:JUL71-103
CORBETT, P.B. PETRONIUS.
  J.P. SULLIVAN, 124:DEC70-133
CORBIN, H. CREATIVE IMAGINATION IN THE
ṢŪFISM OF IBN 'ARABĪ.
  N. HEER, 589:OCT71-730
CORBIN, H. EN ISLAM IRANIEN. (VOLS 1&2)
  617(TLS):8DEC72-1508
CORBOZ, A. INVENTION DE CAROUGE.
  P. CHARPENTRAT, 98:MAY69-431
DE CORDEMOY, G. OEUVRES PHILOSOPHIQUES.
  (P. CLAIR & F. GIRBAL, EDS)
  G. GORI, 548(RCSF):OCT-DEC69-466
CORDER, J.W., ED. SHAKESPEARE 1964.
  B.A.W. JACKSON, 570(SQ):WINTER68-92
CORDERO, F. OPUS. L'EPISTOLA AI ROMANI.
  617(TLS):9JUN72-650
CORDEY, P. & J-L. SEYLAZ, EDS. BENJAMIN
CONSTANT.
  B.C. FINK, 207(FR):FEB70-519
  M. HOBSON, 208(FS):JAN71-96
DE CÓRDOBA, S. GARCILASO A LO DIVINO.
  (G.R. GALE, ED)
  617(TLS):22SEP72-1111
DE CÓRDOVA, F.F. - SEE UNDER FERNÁNDEZ
DE CÓRDOVA, F.
CORE, G., ED. SOUTHERN FICTION TODAY.*
  639(VQR):WINTER70-XV
CORE, G. - SEE STEWART, R.
CORE, G. - SEE SULLIVAN, W., C.H. HOLMAN
& L.D. RUBIN, JR.

CORIPPUS. FLAVII CRESCONII CORIPPI
"JOHANNIDOS" LIBRI VIII. (J. DIGGLE &
F.R.D. GOODYEAR, EDS)
  G.W. SHEA, 24:JUL71-502
  R.A. TUCKER, 124:DEC70-134
CORLEY, E. ACAPULCO GOLD.
  M. LEVIN, 441:24DEC72-14
CORLEY, E. FAREWELL, MY SLIGHTLY TAR-
NISHED HERO.
  M. LEVIN, 441:2JAN72-16
CORMAN, C. - SEE PONGE, F.
CORMIER, L. THE SILENT COWBOYS OF THE
EAST.
  M. DOYLE, 491:MAR72-356
CORNELISEN, A. VENDETTA OF SILENCE.*
  W. GUZZARDI, JR., 561(SATR):29JAN72-
68
  617(TLS):14APR72-409
CORNELL, L.L. KIPLING IN INDIA.
  W.D. SCHAEFER, 445(NCF):SEP68-251
CORNER, B.C. & C. BOOTH, EDS. CHAIN OF
FRIENDSHIP.
  617(TLS):22SEP72-1096
CORNET, J. ART OF AFRICA.*
  617(TLS):31MAR72-368
CORNFORTH, M. THE OPEN PHILOSOPHY AND
THE OPEN SOCIETY.
  Z.A. JORDAN, 483:JAN70-78
CORNISH, J. SHERBOURNE STREET.*
  G. ROPER, 627(UTQ):JUL69-362
CORNISH, J. A WORLD TURNED TURTLE.
  G. ROPER, 627(UTQ):JUL70-343
  G. WOODCOCK, 102(CANL):WINTER71-88
"THE CORNISH ORDINALIA." (M. HARRIS,
TRANS)
  N. DENNY, 382(MAE):1971/3-305
  R.G. THOMAS, 402(MLR):APR71-383
CORNMAN, J.W. MATERIALISM AND SENSA-
TIONS.
  617(TLS):7JUL72-779
CORNMAN, J.W. & K. LEHRER. PHILOSOPHICAL
PROBLEMS AND ARGUMENTS.
  J. PERRY, 482(PHR):OCT70-578
CORNYN, W.S. & D.H. ROOP. BEGINNING
BURMESE.
  R.B. JONES, 399(MLJ):MAR70-209
  J. OKELL, 318(JAOS):APR-JUN70-399
CORONEL, M.D. STORIES AND LEGENDS FROM
FILIPINO FOLKLORE.
  M. HAGLER, 292(JAF):OCT-DEC70-482
  D.V. HART, 293(JAST):FEB70-507
CORREA, G. REALIDAD, FICCIÓN Y SÍMBOLO
EN LAS NOVELAS DE PÉREZ GALDÓS.*
  V.A. CHAMBERLIN, 238:MAR70-149
  G. GILLESPIE, 240(HR):APR70-234
CORREA CALDERÓN, E. - SEE GRACIÁN, B.
CORRIGAN, B., ED. ITALIAN POETS AND
ENGLISH CRITICS, 1755-1859.
  G. CAMBON, 191(ELN):DEC69-146
  K. KROEBER, 275(IQ):SUMMER69-91
CORRINGTON, J.W. THE LONESOME TRAVELER.
  J.P. DEGNAN, 340(KR):1969/2-272
CORSTIUS, H.B. EXERCISES IN COMPUTA-
TIONAL LINGUISTICS.
  J.E. GRIMES, 350:DEC71-975
CORSTIUS, J.B. INTRODUCTION TO THE COM-
PARATIVE STUDY OF LITERATURE.
  S.L. FLAXMAN, 131(CL):SPRING71-174
CORSTIUS, J.C.B. HET POËTISCH PROGRAMMA
VAN TACHTIG.
  C.O. JELLEMA, 52:BAND4HEFT2-215
CORTAZAR, E.R., ED. SELECCIONES FOLKLÓR-
ICAS CODEX.
  M.S. EDMONSON, 650(WF):OCT68-279
CORTÁZAR, J. PAMEOS Y MEOPAS.
  617(TLS):16JUN72-678

CORTÁZAR, J. 62: A MODEL KIT.
   L. BERSANI, 441:26NOV72-7
   A. BROYARD, 441:24NOV72-39
CORTLAND, P. THE SENTIMENTAL ADVENTURE.
   M. SACHS, 546(RR):FEB70-67
CORWIN, A.F. SPAIN AND THE ABOLITION OF
   SLAVERY IN CUBA, 1817-1886.
   J.B. WARREN, 37:JUN69-40
CORY, D. EVEN IF YOU RUN.
   A. BROYARD, 441:12MAY72-43
   N. CALLENDAR, 441:25JUN72-30
CORY, D. TAKE MY DRUM TO ENGLAND.
   617(TLS):7JAN72-17
COSGRAVE, P. THE PUBLIC POETRY OF ROBERT
   LOWELL.*
   D. KALSTONE, 441:17SEP72-47
COSIN, J. JOHN COSIN: A COLLECTION OF
   PRIVATE DEVOTIONS.* (P.G. STANWOOD,
   WITH D. O'CONNOR, EDS)
   R. DANIELLS, 102(CANL):WINTER71-99
   M. FIXLER, 405(MP):NOV69-185
COSMAN, M.P. THE EDUCATION OF THE HERO
   IN ARTHURIAN ROMANCE.*
   S. EISNER, 50(ARQ):AUTUMN69-283
DA COSTA, F. THE ANTIQUITY OF THE ART OF
   PAINTING.* (G. KUBLER, ED)
   J.D. HOAG, 551(RENQ):SUMMER70-176
COSTA CLAVELL, J. ROSALÍA DE CASTRO.
   191(ELN):SEP70(SUPP)-154
COSTA DU RELS, A. LA LAGUNA H.3.
   E. ECHEVARRÍA, 238:MAY70-345
COSTELLO, D.F. THE DESERT WORLD.
   442(NY):9SEP72-126
COSTELOE, M.P. CHURCH WEALTH IN MEXICO.
   L.N. MC ALISTER, 377:MAR71-44
COSTELOE, M.P. - SEE BAZANT, J.
COSTER, C.H. LATE ROMAN STUDIES.
   F.M. CLOVER, 122:OCT71-279
COSTISELLA, J. L'ESPRIT RÉVOLUTIONNAIRE
   DANS LA LITTÉRATURE CANADIENNE-FRAN-
   ÇAISE.
   J-C. BONENFANT, 627(UTQ):JUL69-458
COTELO, R. NARRADORES URUGUAYOS.
   G. FIGUEIRA, 263:JUL-SEP71-344
COTRONEO, G. JEAN BODIN TEORICO DELLA
   STORIA.
   F.P. DE MICHELIS, 548(RCSF):JAN/MAR
      69-108
COTTIGNIES, F. CHANSONS ET PASQUILLES.
   (F. CARTON, ED)
   F. DELOFFRE, 545(RPH):NOV70-366
COTTIN, M. - SEE GAUTIER, T.
COTTINO-JONES, M. AN ANATOMY OF BOCCAC-
   CIO'S STYLE.
   T.M. GREENE, 276:SPRING70-95
COTTLE, B. THE PENGUIN DICTIONARY OF
   SURNAMES.
   H. CARLSON, 424:SEP68-303
COTTRELL, J. & F. CASHIN. RICHARD BUR-
   TON.
   D. GODDARD, 441:10SEP72-42
   617(TLS):2JUN72-635
COTTRELL, R.D. BRANTÔME.
   S.L. ENGLAND, 402(MLR):JUL71-687
COUCH, J.P. GEORGE ELIOT IN FRANCE.*
   M. SACHS, 207(FR):APR70-839
   W.D. SCHAEFER, 445(NCF):MAR69-490
COULET, H. LE ROMAN JUSQU'À LA RÉVOLU-
   TION. (VOL 1)
   L.K. LUXEMBOURG, 207(FR):DEC69-363
COULSON, J. - SEE OSTLER, G.
COULSON, J. & OTHERS -- SEE "OXFORD
   ILLUSTRATED DICTIONARY"
COUPER, J. STANISLAS LÉPINE, SA VIE,
   SON OEUVRE.
   J. HOUSE, 90:SEP70-635

COUPERIN, F. L'ART DE TOUCHER LE CLAVE-
   CIN.
   J.A.W., 410(M&L):JUL71-333
COUPLAND, R. THE INDIAN PROBLEM: 1833-
   1935.
   B. SINGH, 293(JAST):NOV69-182
COURCELLE, P. LATE LATIN WRITERS AND
   THEIR GREEK SOURCES.
   R. BROWNING, 123:DEC71-411
   S.E. SMETHURST, 529(QQ):AUTUMN70-457
COURLANDER, H. NEGRO FOLK MUSIC USA.
   M. HARRISON, 415:JAN71-36
DE COURSAC, P.G. - SEE UNDER GIRAULT DE
   COURSAC, P.
COURT, D. & A. JACKSON, EDS. PAEDIATRICS
   IN THE SEVENTIES.
   617(TLS):28JUL72-879
DE COURTENAY, B. - SEE UNDER BAUDOUIN DE
   COURTENAY
COURTNEY, W.F. THE READER'S ADVISER.
   (VOL 1) (11TH ED)
   C-A. TOASE, 355:JUL69-225
COUSINS, F.W. THE SOLAR SYSTEM.
   617(TLS):25AUG72-1006
COUSINS, N. - SEE BROWN, J.M.
COUSINS, P.M. JOEL CHANDLER HARRIS.*
   S.B. BROOKES, 191(ELN):DEC69-153
COUSTEAU, J-Y. & P. DIOLE. DIVING FOR
   SUNKEN TREASURE.
   617(TLS):3MAR72-241
COUSTILLAS, P., ED. COLLECTED ARTICLES
   ON GEORGE GISSING.
   W.D. SCHAEFER, 445(NCF):SEP69-250
COUSTILLAS, P. GEORGE GISSING AT ALDER-
   LEY EDGE.
   P.J. KEATING, 637(VS):JUN70-393
COUSTILLAS, P. GISSING'S WRITINGS ON
   DICKENS.
   P.J. KEATING, 637(VS):JUN70-393
   M-S., 155:SEP70-253
COUSTILLAS, P. - SEE GISSING, G.
COUTINHO, A. AN INTRODUCTION TO LITERA-
   TURE IN BRAZIL.*
   O.T. MYERS, 399(MLJ):NOV70-538
COUTINHO, A. A TRADIÇÃO AFORTUNADA (O
   ESPÍRITO DE NACIONALIDADE NA CRÍTICA
   BRASILEIRA).
   F. ELLISON, 238:MAR70-158
   191(ELN):SEP69(SUPP)-131
COUTTS-SMITH, K. DADA.
   R. SHATTUCK, 453:1JUN72-23
COUTTS-SMITH, K. THE DREAM OF ICARUS.
   L.A. BURMAN, 89(BJA):SPRING71-208
COUTURIER, M. RECHERCHES SUR LES STRUC-
   TURES SOCIALES DE CHÂTEAUDUN, 1525-
   1789.
   617(TLS):3MAR72-243
COVA, P.V. LA CRITICA LETTERARIA DI
   PLINIO IL GIOVANE.*
   A. HUS, 555:VOL44FASC1-153
COVERT, P. CAGES.
   442(NY):1JAN72-64
COWAN, A. HERE BE DRAGONS.
   617(TLS):9JUN72-649
COWAN, H.K.J. GRAMMAR OF THE SENTANI
   LANGUAGE.*
   A-R. PENCE, 350:SEP71-736
COWAN, I.B., ED. THE ENIGMA OF MARY
   STUART.*
   G.M. FRASER, 440:12MAR72-7
COWAN, J.C. D.H. LAWRENCE'S AMERICAN
   JOURNEY.*
   P.L. WILEY, 659:SPRING72-249
COWAN, J.L. PLEASURE AND PAIN.
   E.J.C., 543:SEP69-126
COWAN, J.L., ED. STUDIES IN THOUGHT AND
   LANGUAGE.
   N.J. BLOCK, 311(JP):3AUG72-427

COWAN, L. THE SOUTHERN CRITICS.
L.P. SIMPSON, 598(SOR):SUMMER72-XI
COWAN, M.H., ED. A COLLECTION OF CRITI-
CAL ESSAYS ON "THE SOUND AND THE FURY."
D. HOLBROOK, 619(TC):1968/2-56
COWDREY, H.E.J. THE CLUNIACS AND THE
GREGORIAN REFORM.*
G. CONSTABLE, 589:APR71-364
COWEN, I. JEWS IN REMOTE CORNERS OF THE
WORLD.
441:13FEB72-16
COWEN, J. - SEE MALORY, T.
COWEN, R.C. HANDBUCH DER DEUTSCHEN LIT-
ERATURGESCHICHTE: BIBLIOGRAPHIEN.
(VOL 9)
M.B. BENN, 402(MLR):OCT71-951
COWEN, R.C. - SEE BÜCHNER, G.
COWIE, P. SEVENTY YEARS OF CINEMA.
B. BERGSTEN, 200:AUG-SEP69-429
COWLES, V. THE RUSSIAN DAGGER.
B.F. OPPEL, 32:SEP71-663
COWLEY, F. A CRITIQUE OF BRITISH EMPIRI-
CISM.*
F.A. OLAFSON, 482(PHR):JUL70-429
COWLEY, J. OF MEN AND ANGELS.
M. LEVIN, 441:24DEC72-14
COWLEY, M. A MANY-WINDOWED HOUSE. (H.D.
PIPER, ED)
J. LYDENBERG, 27(AL):JAN72-673
COWLEY, M. THINK BACK ON US...
M.M., 502(PRS):SUMMER69-235
COWPER, R. KULDESAK.
617(TLS):23JUN72-705
COX, H. THE FEAST OF FOOLS.
G. LECKIE, 639(VQR):SPRING70-365
COX, J.S. & G - SEE UNDER STEVENS COX,
J. & G.
COX, R.G., ED. THOMAS HARDY: THE CRITI-
CAL HERITAGE.
L. STEVENSON, 676(YR):AUTUMN70-126
COXE, G.H. WOMAN WITH A GUN.
N. CALLENDAR, 441:5MAR72-34
COZZENS, J.G. MORNING, NOON AND NIGHT.
P.H. POROSKY, 448:SUMMER70-142
CRABB, R. EMPIRE ON THE PLATTE.
N. YOST, 502(PRS):SPRING68-80
CRABBE, G. GEORGE CRABBE: TALES 1812,
AND OTHER SELECTED POEMS. (H. MILLS,
ED)
J. WILTSHIRE, 97(CQ):SPRING68-185
CRABBE, J. HI-FI IN THE HOME.
P.J.P., 412:MAY71-189
CRABTREE, C. INDUSTRIAL RELATIONS ACT.
617(TLS):28JAN72-88
CRAFT, R. STRAVINSKY.
A. BROYARD, 441:15JUN72-43
S. KARLINSKY, 441:2JUL72-1
H. KELLER, 362:26OCT72-547
617(TLS):22DEC72-1557
CRAGG, G.R., ED. THE CAMBRIDGE PLATON-
ISTS.*
J.W. YOLTON, 393(MIND):APR70-304
639(VQR):WINTER70-XXVIII
CRAGG, K. THE EVENT OF THE QUR'ĀN.
617(TLS):26MAY72-608
CRAHAY, R. LA RELIGION DES GRECS.
A.W.H. ADKINS, 123:JUN71-238
CRAIG, B. SEPTEMBER CAN BE DANGEROUS IN
EDINBURGH.
N. CALLENDAR, 441:6FEB72-38
CRAIG, B.M., ED. "LA CREACION," "LA
TRANSGRESSION" AND "L'EXPULSION" OF THE
"MISTERE DU VIEL TESTAMENT."
A. FOULET, 545(RPH):FEB71-558
CRAIG, C. CHRISTOPH MARTIN WIELAND AS
THE ORIGINATOR OF THE MODERN TRAVESTY
IN GERMAN LITERATURE.
A.R. SCHMITT, 301(JEGP):OCT71-724

CRAIG, D. DOUBLE TAKE.
N. CALLENDAR, 441:2JUL72-15
617(TLS):28APR72-500
CRAIG, D. - SEE DICKENS, C.
CRAIG, E. P.S. YOUR NOT LISTENING.
J. HERNDON, 441:19NOV72-42
C. LEHMANN-HAUPT, 441:1DEC72-41
561(SATR):9DEC72-80
CRAIG, G.Y. - SEE SCHAFER, W.
CRAIG, J. IF YOU WANT TO SEE YOUR WIFE
AGAIN...
N. CALLENDAR, 441:23JAN72-26
H. FRANKEL, 561(SATR):29JAN72-73
CRAIG, J. THE PRO.
G. ROPER, 627(UTQ):JUL69-360
CRAIGIE, W.A. & A.J. AITKEN, EDS. A DIC-
TIONARY OF THE OLDER SCOTTISH TONGUE.
(A-N)
617(TLS):13OCT72-1209
CRAIGIE, W.A. & J.R. HULBERT, EDS. A
DICTIONARY OF AMERICAN ENGLISH ON HIS-
TORICAL PRINCIPLES.
617(TLS):13OCT72-1209
CRAIK, W.A. THE BRONTË NOVELS.
T.C. MOSER, 191(ELN):SEP69-63
CRAMER, C.H. AMERICAN ENTERPRISE.
561(SATR):16DEC72-68
CRAMPA, J. LABRAUNDA.* (VOL 3, PT 1:
THE GREEK INSCRIPTIONS, PT 1)
D.M. LEWIS, 123:MAR71-118
CRANDALL, C., ED. SWETNAM THE WOMAN-
HATER.
A. LOW, 568(SCN):WINTER71-74
CRANE, I. THE THINK TRAP.
D.A.N. JONES, 362:16MAR72-348
CRANE, R.S. THE IDEA OF THE HUMANITIES.
(W. BOOTH, ED)
L.T. LEMON, 502(PRS):SUMMER68-175
H. TROWBRIDGE, 173(ECS):SPRING70-398
CRANE, S. THE COMPLETE NOVELS OF STEPHEN
CRANE. (T.A. GULLASON, ED)
E. SOLOMON, 445(NCF):SEP68-245
CRANE, S. THE NOTEBOOK OF STEPHEN
CRANE. (D.J. & E.B. GREINER, EDS)
639(VQR):WINTER70-XV
CRANE, S. THE POEMS OF STEPHEN CRANE.
(J. KATZ, ED)
O. FRYCKSTEDT, 597(SN):VOL40#1-255
CRANE, S. SULLIVAN COUNTY TALES AND
SKETCHES. (R.W. STALLMAN, ED)
B.D.S., 502(PRS):SPRING69-140
CRANE, S. THE WORKS OF STEPHEN CRANE.*
(VOLS 1&7) (F. BOWERS, ED)
J. MAYHALL, 453:10AUG72-28
639(VQR):WINTER70-IX
CRANE, S. THE WORKS OF STEPHEN CRANE.
(VOLS 4&9) (F. BOWERS, ED)
J. MAYHALL, 453:10AUG72-28
CRANE, S. THE WORKS OF STEPHEN CRANE.*
(VOLS 5&6) (F. BOWERS, ED)
W.B. DILLINGHAM, 27(AL):NOV71-462
J. MAYHALL, 453:10AUG72-28
A. TURNER, 579(SAQ):AUTUMN71-607
CRANE, T.F. ITALIAN POPULAR TALES.
W.H. JANSEN, 582(SFQ):DEC69-367
C. SPERONI, 275(IQ):FALL69-79
CRANMER, P. THE TECHNIQUE OF ACCOMPANI-
MENT.
G. MOORE, 415:JUL70-709
CRANSTON, E. - SEE "THE IZUMI SHIKIBU
DIARY"
CRAPANZANO, V. THE FIFTH WORLD OF
FORSTER BENNETT.
P. ADAMS, 61:JUL72-96
W. BRANDON, 561(SATR):1JUL72-50
T. LASK, 441:20MAY72-35
442(NY):10JUN72-131
453:15JUN72-35

CRAPULLI, G. & E.G. BOSCHERINI. RICERCHE
LESSICALI SU OPERE DI DESCARTES E SPIN-
OZA.
S. DECLOUX, 182:VOL23#23/24-967
CRASHAW, R. THE COMPLETE POETRY OF
RICHARD CRASHAW. (G.W. WILLIAMS, ED)
G.W. HUOTT, 568(SCN):SUMMER/AUTUMN71-
40
CRASTER, E. THE HISTORY OF ALL SOULS
COLLEGE LIBRARY. (E.F. JACOB, ED)
617(TLS):21JAN72-76
CRAVEN, A.B. VICTORIAN AND EDWARDIAN
YORKSHIRE FROM OLD PHOTOGRAPHS.
G. ANNAN, 362:6JAN72-24
617(TLS):14JAN72-43
CRAWFORD, J.P.W. SPANISH DRAMA BEFORE
LOPE DE VEGA. (REV)
D.R. LARSON, 545(RPH):FEB70-359
CRAWFORD, M. & K. ARMSTRONG. THE FEN-
IANS.
102(CANL):WINTER71-107
CRAWFORD, M.H. ROMAN REPUBLICAN COIN
HOARDS.
H.C. BOREN, 487:WINTER70-357
C.D. HAMILTON, 122:APR71-141
H.B. MATTINGLY, 313:VOL60-231
CRAWFORD, R.A. ANDREW LAW, AMERICAN
PSALMODIST.*
M. PETERSON, 470:JAN69-31
CRAWFORD, S.G. LOG OF THE S.S. THE MRS.
UNGUENTINE.*
A. BROYARD, 441:12DEC72-49
D.K. MANO, 441:27AUG72-2
CRAWFORD, T. LOST NEIGHBOURHOOD.
M. DOYLE, 491:MAR72-356
CRAWFURD, J. A DESCRIPTIVE DICTIONARY OF
THE INDIAN ISLANDS AND ADJACENT COUN-
TRIES.
617(TLS):22DEC72-1565
CRAWLEY, T.E. THE STRUCTURE OF "LEAVES
OF GRASS."
H.W. BLODGETT, 27(AL):NOV71-454
CRAWLEY, W. IS IT GENUINE?
617(TLS):7JAN72-8
CREASEY, J. A SPLINTER OF GLASS.
N. CALLENDAR, 441:23JUL72-22
CREED, R.P., ED. OLD ENGLISH POETRY.*
B. MITCHELL, 541(RES):MAY70-185
R.E. PALMER, JR., 141:FALL69-393
CREEDY, J., ED. THE SOCIAL CONTEXT OF
ART.
A. HANNAY, 89(BJA):SUMMER71-296
CREELEY, R. PIECES.*
J. MAZZARO, 340(KR):1970/1-163
R. MORAN, 598(SOR):WINTER72-243
CREELEY, R. A QUICK GRAPH. (D. ALLEN,
ED)
M.L. ROSENTHAL, 491:NOV71-99
CREELEY, R. ST. MARTINS.*
V. YOUNG, 249(HUDR):WINTER71/72-669
CREELEY, R. WORDS.
R.H. BAYES, 448:SUMMER68-123
CREIGHTON, D. CANADA'S FIRST CENTURY,
1867-1967.*
G.F.G. STANLEY, 529(QQ):AUTUMN70-440
P.B. WAITE, 150(DR):SUMMER70-279
CREMER, F.W. DIE CHALDÄISCHEN ORAKEL
UND JAMBLICH DE MYSTERIIS.
L.H. FELDMAN, 124:NOV70-89
J.G. GRIFFITHS, 123:MAR71-39
CRESCI, G.F. ESSEMPLARE DI PIN SORTI
LETTERE, 1578. (A.S. OSLEY, ED)
D. CHAMBERS, 503:AUTUMN69-130
CRESCI, G.F. A RENAISSANCE ALPHABET.
(D.M. ANDERSON, ED)
617(TLS):14JAN72-48

CRESPELLE, J-P. LES MAÎTRES DE LA BELLE
EPOQUE.
H. DE LEY, JR., 207(FR):OCT69-159
CRESSEY, D.R. CRIMINAL ORGANIZATION.
617(TLS):31MAR72-357
CRESSWELL, M.J. & G.E. HUGHES. AN INTRO-
DUCTION TO MODAL LOGIC.
R.H.K., 543:JUN70-739
CRESTI, C. LE CORBUSIER.
617(TLS):7JAN72-18
CRESWELL, J. BRITISH ADMIRALS OF THE
EIGHTEENTH CENTURY.
617(TLS):3NOV72-1308
CREWDSON, H.A.F. THE WORSHIPFUL COMPANY
OF MUSICIANS. (2ND ED)
F. HOWES, 415:DEC71-1175
CREWS, H. CAR.
C. LEHMANN-HAUPT, 441:2MAR72-41
J. YARDLEY, 441:27FEB72-5
442(NY):1APR72-104
CREWS, H. KARATE IS A THING OF THE
SPIRIT.*
V. CUNNINGHAM, 362:3FEB72-156
617(TLS):25FEB72-209
CRICHTON, M. THE TERMINAL MAN.
A. COOPER, 561(SATR):6MAY72-89
T.R. EDWARDS, 453:20JUL72-20
C. LEHMANN-HAUPT, 441:9MAY72-43
T. STURGEON, 441:30APR72-32
E. WEEKS, 61:MAY72-108
442(NY):13MAY72-145
617(TLS):1DEC72-1467
CRICHTON, R. THE CAMERONS.
C. LEHMANN-HAUPT, 441:3NOV72-41
W. SCHOTT, 441:19NOV72-4
P. THEROUX, 561(SATR):4NOV72-74
442(NY):11NOV72-189
CRICHTON SMITH, I. FROM BOURGEOIS LAND.
W.H. PRITCHARD, 491:DEC71-159
J. SMITH, 493:SPRING70-89
CRICHTON SMITH, I. HAMLET IN AUTUMN.
617(TLS):20OCT72-1249
CRICHTON SMITH, I. LOVE POEMS & ELEGIES.
617(TLS):29SEP72-1146
CRICK, B. POLITICAL THEORY AND PRACTICE.
R. CROSSMAN, 362:7DEC72-800
617(TLS):8DEC72-1476
CRIPPA, R. STUDI SULLA COSCIENZA ETICA
E RELIGIOSA DEL SEICENTO.
P. DI VONA, 548(RCSF):JAN-MAR68-108
CRIQUI, F. MOTS ET CONCEPTS.
A. TUKEY, 207(FR):DEC69-366
CRISAFULLI, A.S., ED. LINGUISTICS AND
LITERARY STUDIES IN HONOR OF HELMUT A.
HATZFELD.
E. GIANTURCO, 131(CL):WINTER71-60
CRITCHLEY, T.A. & P.D. JAMES. THE MAUL
AND THE PEAR TREE.
617(TLS):7JAN72-5
CROCE, A. THE FRED ASTAIRE & GINGER
ROGERS BOOK.
J. KANON, 561(SATR):16DEC72-58
D. MC DONAGH, 441:17DEC72-2
CROCKER, L.G., ED. THE AGE OF ENLIGHT-
ENMENT.
D.G., 173(ECS):SPRING70-422
CROCKER, L.G. DIDEROT.
G. SOLINAS, 548(RCSF):JAN/MAR69-93
CROCKER, L.G. JEAN-JACQUES ROUSSEAU.*
(VOL 1)
A.J. KNODEL, 173(ECS):SUMMER70-567
CROCKER, L.G. ROUSSEAU'S "SOCIAL CON-
TRACT."
J.S. SPINK, 208(FS):OCT71-465
P.M. SPURLIN, 401(MLQ):SEP70-385
CROCKER, R. A HISTORY OF MUSICAL STYLE.
J. PRUETT, 308:SPRING67-144

CROCKER, W.R. AUSTRALIAN AMBASSADOR.
617(TLS):7APR72-395
CROFT-MURRAY, E. DECORATIVE PAINTING IN
ENGLAND 1537-1837. (VOL 2)
617(TLS):21APR72-443
CROLL, M.W. "ATTIC" AND BAROQUE PROSE
STYLE. (J.M. PATRICK & R.O. EVANS,
WITH J.M. WALLACE, EDS)
A.H. LANNER, 568(SCN):SPRING71-8
CROLL, M.W. STYLE, RHETORIC, AND RHY-
THM.* (J.M. PATRICK & OTHERS, EDS)
J.R. BENNETT, 179(ES):DEC70-573
CROMPTON, L. SHAW THE DRAMATIST.*
A.P. BARR, 141:WINTER70-82
R.H. CHAPMAN, 191(ELN):MAR70-233
F.P.W. MC DOWELL, 572:SEP69-122
617(TLS):4AUG72-917
CRONE, G.R. THE DISCOVERY OF THE EAST.
617(TLS):25FEB72-214
CRONIN, S. THE MC GARRITY PAPERS.
617(TLS):10NOV72-1355
CRONIN, V. NAPOLEON BONAPARTE.*
G.M. FRASER, 440:5MAR72-1
J.H. PLUMB, 441:12MAR72-2
CRONJE, S. THE WORLD AND NIGERIA.
F. WYNDHAM, 362:23NOV72-716
CRONNE, H.A. THE REIGN OF STEPHEN 1135-
54.
C.R. YOUNG, 589:OCT71-732
CRONNE, H.A. & R.H.C. DAVIS, EDS. REGES-
TA REGUM ANGLO-NORMANNORUM 1066-1154.
(VOL 3)
C.A.F. MEEKINGS, 325:APR69-498
CRONT, G. INSTITUȚII MEDIEVALE ROMÂN-
EȘTI.*
K. HITCHINS, 575(SEER):JUL71-470
CROOK, J.M. THE BRITISH MUSEUM.
617(TLS):14APR72-415
CROOK, J.M. THE GREEK REVIVAL.
617(TLS):15DEC72-1520
CROOK, J.M. VICTORIAN ARCHITECTURE.
617(TLS):18FEB72-196
CROPSEY, J. - SEE HOBBES, T.
CROS, E. PROTÉE ET LE GUEUX.
F. SCHALK, 72:BAND208HEFT1-76
R.W. TRUMAN, 402(MLR):APR71-418
CROSBY, D.H. - SEE VON KLEIST, H.
CROSBY, J.O. EN TORNO A LA POESÍA DE
QUEVEDO.
E.S. MORBY, 240(HR):JAN70-95
H. SIEBER, 400(MLN):MAR70-305
CROSBY, J.O. - SEE DE QUEVEDO, F.
CROSBY, S.M. THE APOSTLE BAS-RELIEF AT
SAINT-DENIS.
617(TLS):28JUL72-888
CROSS, A. THE THEBAN MYSTERIES.*
617(TLS):28APR72-500
CROSS, J.E. AELFRIC AND THE MEDIAEVAL
HOMILIARY.
C. CLARK, 179(ES):JUN70-247
CROSS, K.G.W. & R.T. DUNLOP. A BIBLIO-
GRAPHY OF YEATS CRITICISM 1887-1965.
617(TLS):17MAR72-311
CROSS, R.K. FLAUBERT AND JOYCE.
441:30JAN72-33
CROSSMAN, C.L. THE CHINA TRADE.
T. LASK, 441:2DEC72-37
CROSSMAN, R. INSIDE VIEW.
D. OWEN, 362:4MAY72-593
617(TLS):19MAY72-572
CROSSMAN, R. THE STRUCTURE OF MIND.
J. HARRISON, 393(MIND):JUL70-469
CROUCH, B., ED. OVERCOMING LEARNING
DIFFICULTIES.
617(TLS):5MAY72-529
CROUCH, M. THE NESBIT TRADITION.
617(TLS):8DEC72-1488

CROUZET, F., ED. CAPITAL FORMATION IN
THE INDUSTRIAL REVOLUTION.
617(TLS):29DEC72-1576
CROW, C.M. PAUL VALÉRY.
617(TLS):29SEP72-1143
CROW, D., ED. AFVS OF WORLD WAR ONE.
BRITISH AFVS 1919-40.* BRITISH AND
COMMONWEALTH AFVS 1940-46.
617(TLS):4FEB72-113
CROW, D. BRITISH AND COMMONWEALTH AR-
MOURED FORMATIONS (1919-46).
617(TLS):21JUL72-853
CROW, D. THE VICTORIAN WOMAN.*
442(NY):22APR72-143
CROW, J.A. GREECE.
F.M. COMBELLACK, 124:NOV70-89
CROWDER, M. WEST AFRICA UNDER COLONIAL
RULE.
H. DESCHAMPS, 69:JAN69-81
CROWE, B. CONCISE DICTIONARY OF SOVIET
TERMINOLOGY, INSTITUTIONS AND ABBREVI-
ATIONS.
M. BENSON, 574(SEEJ):SPRING71-96
D.B. CROCKETT, 32:MAR71-223
CROWE, C. THE TWICE-BORN.
M. LEVIN, 441:10CT72-42
CROWE, J. ANOTHER WAY TO DIE.
N. CALLENDAR, 441:18JUN72-32
CROWE, J. A TOUCH OF DARKNESS.
N. CALLENDAR, 441:290CT72-59
CROWELL, N.B. THE CONVEX GLASS.*
P. HONAN, 405(MP):NOV69-207
P.F. MATTHEISEN, 637(VS):SEP69-108
CROWLEY, D.J. I COULD TALK OLD-STORY
GOOD.
S.W. MINTZ, 650(WF):OCT68-285
CROWLEY, F.K. FORREST 1847-1918. (VOL 1)
617(TLS):2JUN72-617
CROWLEY, J.D. - SEE DEFOE, D.
CROWTHER, P.A., COMP. A BIBLIOGRAPHY OF
WORKS IN ENGLISH ON EARLY RUSSIAN
HISTORY TO 1800.
R. HELLIE, 32:JUN71-454
CROZIER, A. THE NOVELS OF HARRIET BEECH-
ER STOWE.*
E.B. KIRKHAM, 432(NEQ):JUN70-333
CROZIER, B., ED. ANNUAL OF POWER AND
CONFLICT 1971.
617(TLS):1SEP72-1029
CROZIER, B. FRANCO.*
J.F. THORNING, 613:SPRING69-151
CROZIER, R.C., ED. CHINA'S CULTURAL
LEGACY AND COMMUNISM.
S.C. CHU, 293(JAST):AUG70-927
CRUICKSHANK, J., ED. FRENCH LITERATURE
AND ITS BACKGROUND.* (VOLS 1-6)
H-J. NEUSCHÄFER, 72:BAND208HEFT4/6-
442
CRUICKSHANK, J., ED. FRENCH LITERATURE
AND ITS BACKGROUND. (VOL 4)
J.S.P., 191(ELN):SEP70(SUPP)-53
CRUM, M., ED. FIRST-LINE INDEX OF ENG-
LISH POETRY 1500-1800 IN MANUSCRIPTS
OF THE BODLEIAN LIBRARY OXFORD.
J. KINSLEY, 354:SEP69-262
C.A. ZIMANSKY, 481(PQ):JUL70-290
CRUM, M. - SEE KING, H.
CRUMMEY, R.O. THE OLD BELIEVERS AND THE
WORLD OF ANTICHRIST.
S. BLANC, 575(SEER):JAN71-149
M. RAEFF, 104:FALL71-433
S-A. ZENKOVSKY, 32:JUN71-390
639(VQR):SUMMER70-CXI
CRUMP, G.M., ED. POEMS ON AFFAIRS OF
STATE. (VOL 4)
P.K. ELKIN, 67:MAY71-97
CRUMP, J.I., JR. - SEE "CHAN-KUO TS'E"

DE LA CRUZ, S.J.I. - SEE UNDER INÉS DE LA
CRUZ, S.J.

CRVENKOVSKI, D. & V. GRUIK. MAL MAKEDON-
SKO-ANGLISKI REČNIK/A LITTLE MACEDON-
IAN-ENGLISH DICTIONARY.
K.E. NAYLOR, 574(SEEJ):SPRING71-104

CRYSTAL, D. LINGUISTICS.
617(TLS):4FEB72-136

CRYSTAL, D. & D. DAVY. INVESTIGATING
ENGLISH STYLE.
W.O. HENDRICKS, 350:DEC71-990

CSAPODI, C. & K. CSAPODI-GÁRDONYI, EDS.
BIBLIOTHECA CORVINIANA.
T.R. MARK, 32:MAR71-182

CSATKAI, A. OLD TRADE-SIGNS IN HUNGARY.
617(TLS):28JUL72-900

CUADRA, P.A. POESÍA ESCOGIDA.
H. PEÑA, 263:APR-JUN71-193

CUDWORTH, C. HANDEL.
617(TLS):7APR72-402

"CUESTIONARIO PROVISIONAL PARA EL ESTUDIO
COORDINADO DE LA NORMA LINGÜÍSTICA
CULTA DE LAS PRINCIPALES CIUDADES DE
IBEROAMÉRICA Y DE LA PENÍNSULA IBÉRICA.
(VOL 1)
P. BOYD-BOWMAN, 238:MAR70-153

CUGUSI, P. <C. SALLUSTI CRISPI> EPIS-
TULAE AD CAESAREM.
R.E.A. PALMER, 24:APR71-339

CULL, D. CANCER RISING.
M. DOYLE, 491:MAR72-356

CULLEN, L.M. AN ECONOMIC HISTORY OF
IRELAND SINCE 1600.
617(TLS):16JUN72-692

CULLEN, P. SPENSER, MARVELL, AND RENAIS-
SANCE PASTORAL.*
R.L. COLIE, 301(JEGP):JUL71-538

CULLMANN, O. VORTRÄGE UND AUFSATZE
1925-62. (K. FRÖHLICH, ED)
D.H. WALLACE, 182:VOL23#7-335

CULVER, D.C. BIBLIOGRAPHY OF CRIME AND
CRIMINAL JUSTICE 1927-1931. BIBLIOGRA-
PHY OF CRIME AND CRIMINAL JUSTICE 1932-
1937.
617(TLS):18FEB72-191

CUMING, G.J. & D. BAKER, EDS. POPULAR
BELIEF AND PRACTICE.
617(TLS):24MAR72-342

CUMMING, C.E. STUDIES IN EDUCATIONAL
COSTS.
617(TLS):25FEB72-229

CUMMING, J. A CONTRIBUTION TOWARDS A
BIBLIOGRAPHY DEALING WITH CRIME AND
COGNATE SUBJECTS.
617(TLS):18FEB72-191

CUMMING, W.P., R.A. SKELTON & D.B. QUINN.
THE DISCOVERY OF NORTH AMERICA.*
L.B. WRIGHT, 441:16JUL72-23

CUMMINGS, E.E. SELECTED LETTERS OF E.E.
CUMMINGS. (F.W. DUPEE & G. STADE,
EDS)
E. NELSON, 590:SPRING70-42
617(TLS):17NOV72-1403

CUNLIFFE, B.W., ED. RICHBOROUGH: FIFTH
REPORT OF THE EXCAVATIONS OF THE ROMAN
FORT AT RICHBOROUGH, KENT.
G.C. BOON, 313:VOL60-247

CUNNINGHAM, I.C. - SEE HERODAS

CUNNINGHAM, J.V. COLLECTED POEMS AND
EPIGRAMS.*
V. YOUNG, 249(HUDR):WINTER71/72-681

CUNNINGHAM, J.V., ED. THE PROBLEM OF
STYLE.
P.F. DEMBOWSKI, 545(RPH):AUG69-134

CUNNINGTON, P. & C. LUCAS. COSTUME FOR
BIRTHS, MARRIAGES AND DEATHS.
617(TLS):15SEP72-1043

CUNQUEIRO, Á. UN HOMBRE QUE SE PARECÍA
A ORESTES.
J.W. KRONIK, 238:MAR70-152

CUOMO, G. AMONG THIEVES.
L.D. CLARK, 50(ARQ):SUMMER69-170

CURLE, A. MYSTICS AND MILITANTS.
617(TLS):25AUG72-1000

CURLEY, E.M. SPINOZA'S METAPHYSICS.
G.H.R. PARKINSON, 483:OCT70-342
P. SELIGMAN, 319:JAN72-91

CURRAN, C.P. JAMES JOYCE REMEMBERED.*
A. MAC GILLIVRAY, 613:AUTUMN69-471
P. RECONDO, 202(FMOD):NOV69-104
T. ROGERS, 175:SUMMER69-73

CURRAN, S. SHELLEY'S "CENCI."
D.H. REIMAN, 301(JEGP):OCT71-682
676(YR):SUMMER71-XXIV

CURRENT, W. & V. SCULLY. PUEBLO ARCHI-
TECTURE OF THE SOUTHWEST.
W. GARD, 584(SWR):SUMMER71-V

CURREY, R.N. - SEE PHIPSON, T.

CURRY, R., ED. RADICALISM, RACISM, AND
PARTY REALIGNMENT.
639(VQR):SUMMER70-CX

CURRY-LINDAHL, K. LET THEM LIVE.
S.B. SHEPARD, 441:19NOV72-52

CURTAYNE, A. FRANCIS LEDWIDGE.
S. HEANEY, 362:28SEP72-408

CURTIN, J. MYTHS AND FOLK-LORE OF IRE-
LAND.
T.B. UNTHANK, 582(SFQ):MAR69-61

CURTIN, P.D. THE ATLANTIC SLAVE TRADE.
C.R. BOXER, 656(WMQ):APR70-317
P.E.H. HAIR, 86(BHS):JAN71-94

CURTIN, W.M. - SEE CATHER, W.

CURTIS, A. SWEELINCK'S KEYBOARD MUSIC.*
P.H.L., 414(MQ):JUL69-418

CURTIS, E.S. PORTRAITS FROM NORTH AMERI-
CAN INDIAN LIFE.
P. ADAMS, 61:NOV72-130

CURTIS, J.R. WORDSWORTH'S EXPERIMENTS
WITH TRADITION.
617(TLS):6OCT72-1186

CURTIS, M., WITH B. GILBERT. KEEP OFF
MY TURF.
J. DURSO, 441:3DEC72-44

CURTIS, R.A., ED. THE GENIUS OF WILLIAM
HOGARTH.
617(TLS):9JUN72-667

CURTIS, R.L. TRISTAN STUDIES.
F. LYONS, 208(FS):JUL71-315

CURTISS, T.Q. VON STROHEIM.*
G. MILLAR, 362:1JUN72-726

CURTISS, U. LETTER OF INTENT.*
617(TLS):7JUL72-783

CUTHBERTSON, T. ANYBODY'S BIKE BOOK.
BIKE TRIPPING.
H.C. GARDNER, 441:4JUN72-8

CUTILEIRO, J. A PORTUGUESE RURAL SOCI-
ETY.
617(TLS):19MAY72-580

CUTRIGHT, P.R. LEWIS AND CLARK.
H.L. CARTER, 656(WMQ):APR70-333

CUTT, J. TAXATION AND ECONOMIC DEVELOP-
MENT IN INDIA.
J. HURD 2D, 293(JAST):MAY70-727

CUTT, T. - SEE PETRONIUS

CUTT, T. - SEE PLAUTUS

CUTTLER, C.D. NORTHERN PAINTING.*
D.L. EHRESMANN, 127:FALL70-116

CUTTS, J.P. THE SHATTERED GLASS.
A.E. CRAVEN, 50(ARQ):AUTUMN69-285
W.F. MC NEIR, 149:JUN71-168

CVETAEVA, M. PROZA. STIXOTVORENIJA.
J.P. MANSON, 574(SEEJ):FALL71-373

CVETKO, D., ED. INTERNATIONAL MUSICOL-
OGICAL SOCIETY: REPORT OF THE TENTH
CONGRESS, LJUBLJANA, 1967.
   M.T., 410(M&L):JAN71-73
CVETKOVA, B. PAMETNA BITKA NA NARODITE.
   E. NIEDERHAUSER, 104:FALL71-441
CYNK, J.B. HISTORY OF THE POLISH AIR
FORCE.
   617(TLS):4AUG72-926
CZACHOWSKA, J. & I. MACIEJEWSKA, EDS.
LEOPOLD STAFF, W KRĘGU LITERACKICH
PRZYJAŹNI.
   J.T. BAER, 497(POLR):SUMMER68-80
CZERWINSKI, E. & J. PIEKALKIEWICZ, EDS.
THE SOVIET INVASION OF CZECHOSLOVAKIA.
   N. ASCHERSON, 453:10AUG72-16
CZIGÁNY, M. HUNGARIAN LITERATURE IN
ENGLISH TRANSLATION PUBLISHED IN GREAT
BRITAIN 1830-1968.
   D.M. JONES, 575(SEER):APR71-290

VAN DAALEN, D.H. THE REAL RESURRECTION.
   617(TLS):17NOV72-1399
DABNEY, V. VIRGINIA.
   C. PHILLIPS, 441:27FEB72-40
D'ABRERA, B. BUTTERFLIES OF THE AUSTRAL-
IAN REGION.
   617(TLS):18AUG72-975
DADIÉ, B.B. CLIMBIÉ.
   617(TLS):3MAR72-248
DAGEN, J. - SEE CHAMFORT, S.R.N.
DAGHLIAN, P.B., ED. ESSAYS IN EIGH-
TEENTH-CENTURY BIOGRAPHY.*
   C.J. RAWSON, 447(N&Q):MAR70-104
DAHL, L. LINGUISTIC FEATURES OF THE
STREAM-OF-CONSCIOUSNESS TECHNIQUES OF
JAMES JOYCE, VIRGINIA WOOLF AND EUGENE
O'NEILL.
   W. FÜGER, 72:BAND72HEFT4/6-414
   M.H. SHORT, 677:VOL2-333
DAHL, R. SELECTED STORIES OF ROALD
DAHL.*
   J.P. DEGNAN, 340(KR):1969/2-272
DAHLBERG, E. BECAUSE I WAS FLESH. THE
EDWARD DAHLBERG READER. (P. CARROL,
ED) EPITAPHS OF OUR TIMES.
   J. HARRIS, 328:SUMMER69-374
DAHLBERG, E. THE CONFESSIONS OF EDWARD
DAHLBERG.*
   G. BURNS, 584(SWR):SUMMER71-295
DAHLHAUS, C., ED. DAS DRAMA RICHARD
WAGNERS ALS MUSIKALISCHES KUNSTWERK.
   R.H., 410(M&L):OCT71-428
DAHLHAUS, C. SCHÖNBERG, VARIATIONEN FÜR
ORCHESTER.
   W.M. STROH, 513:FALL-WINTER68-145
DAHLHAUS, C. RICHARD WAGNERS MUSIKDRAM-
EN.
   617(TLS):21JUL72-840
DAHLHEIM, W. STRUKTUR UND ENTWICKLUNG
DES RÖMISCHEN VÖLKERRECHTS IM 3. UND 2.
JAHRHUNDERT V. CHR.
   J.A.O. LARSEN, 313:VOL60-218
   E.T. SALMON, 124:SEP70-27
   R. VILLERS, 555:VOL44FASC1-170
DAHLIE, H. BRIAN MOORE.*
   D. CAMERON, 529(QQ):SUMMER70-282
DAICHES, D. ROBERT BURNS AND HIS WORLD.
   442(NY):22JAN72-100
DAICHES, D. MORE LITERARY ESSAYS.
   P. ROBERTS, 541(RES):AUG70-386
DAICHES, D., ED. THE PENGUIN COMPANION
TO ENGLISH LITERATURE. (BRITISH TITLE:
THE PENGUIN COMPANION TO LITERATURE:
BRITAIN AND THE COMMONWEALTH.)
   N. BALAKIAN, 441:28JAN72-42   [CONT]

[CONTINUING]
   R. PLANT, 441:5NOV72-31
   617(TLS):7JUL72-780
DAICHES, D. TWO WORLDS. A THIRD WORLD.
   617(TLS):28JAN72-89
DAICHES, D. & A. THORLBY, EDS. LITERA-
TURE AND WESTERN CIVILIZATION. (VOL 1)
   617(TLS):28JUL72-895
"THE DAILY POCKET LECTIONARY AND MASS
BOOK."
   617(TLS):14APR72-426
DAIN, A. - SEE TACITUS, A.
DAIN, F.R. EDUCATION IN THE WILDERNESS.
   Q.M. WILSON, 377:MAR71-52
DAIN, P. THE NEW YORK PUBLIC LIBRARY.
   H. LEHMANN-HAUPT, 441:26NOV72-48
DAINTREY, A. FRAGONARD'S "LE BILLET
DOUX."
   D. SUTTON, 39:JUN69-414
DAITZ, S.G. THE JERUSALEM PALIMPSEST OF
EURIPIDES.
   J. PERADOTTO, 124:DEC70-123
   N.G. WILSON, 123:DEC71-349
DAIX, P. & G. BOUDAILLE. PICASSO: THE
BLUE AND ROSE PERIODS.
   J. LOPEZ-REY, 39:MAR69-244
DAKERS, L. CHURCH MUSIC AT THE CROSS-
ROADS.*
   B. RAINBOW, 415:AUG70-805
DAKIN, D. THE UNIFICATION OF GREECE
1770-1923.
   617(TLS):13OCT72-1232
DAKIN, D.M. A SHERLOCK HOLMES COMMEN-
TARY.
   617(TLS):7APR72-391
DAL, E., ED. DANISH BALLADS AND FOLK
SONGS.*
   D.W. PATTERSON, 582(SFQ):MAR68-70
D'ALBERTI, S. PIRANDELLO ROMANZIERE.
   R. DOMBROSKI, 405(MP):FEB70-295
   A. VICARI, 276:SPRING70-97
DALE, A.M. COLLECTED PAPERS.
   D.A. CAMPBELL, 487:AUTUMN70-281
   T. COLE, 24:OCT71-718
   D.A. KIDD, 67:MAY71-67
   H. LLOYD-JONES, 123:DEC71-407
DALE, C. A DARK CORNER.*
   J.W. HUGHES, 561(SATR):22APR72-87
   442(NY):25MAR72-131
DALE, D.C. THE UNITED NATIONS LIBRARY.
   P. KRUSE, 356:APR71-180
DALE, J.B. & M.L. COURS PRÉPARATOIRE DE
FRANÇAIS, DEUXIÈME CYCLE.
   E. POPPER, 207(FR):DEC69-376
DALE, K. BRAHMS.*
   J. WARRACK, 415:JUL71-670
DALE, P. MORTAL FIRE.*
   J. SMITH, 493:WINTER70/71-363
D'ALESSANDRO, V. "FIDELITAS NORMANNOR-
UM."
   D.J.A. MATTHEW, 589:JAN71-139
D'ALESSIO, R.H. - SEE UNDER HENZO D'ALES-
SIO, R.
"SALVATORE DALI: CARMEN."
   ATIRNOMIS, 58:NOV69-10
DALLAS, I. THE BOOK OF STRANGERS.
   617(TLS):1DEC72-1467
DALLAS, R. SHADOW SHOW.
   J.E.P. THOMSON, 368:JUN69-184
DALLA VALLE, D. DE THÉOPHILE A MOLIÈRE.
   G. HAINSWORTH, 208(FS):APR71-195
DALLIN, A. & G.W. BRESLAUER. POLITICAL
TERROR IN COMMUNIST SYSTEMS.
   B. HARASYMIW, 104:WINTER71-585
D'ALMEIDA, M. & G. LACLÉ. KÉTÉYOULI,
L'ÉTUDIANT NOIR.
   S.O. MEZU, 207(FR):DEC69-370

73

DALRYMPLE, J. PINAFORE FARM COOKBOOK.
N. MAGID, 440:20FEB72-8
DALTON, D. JANIS.
P. MARIN, 441:20FEB72-4
N. SCHREIBER, 440:27FEB72-11
453:27JAN72-38
DALTON, D., ED. ROLLING STONES.
617(TLS):15SEP72-1071
DALTON, O.M. THE TREASURE OF THE OXUS
WITH OTHER EXAMPLES OF EARLY ORIENTAL
METAL-WORK. (3RD ED)
E.M. YAMAUCHI, 318(JAOS):APR-JUN70-
340
DAL VERME, F. SEEING AMERICA AND ITS
GREAT MEN. (E. COMETTI, ED & TRANS)
J.W. MANIGAULTE, 656(WMQ):JAN70-179
DALZIEL, M. - SEE LENNOX, C.
DAMASCENO, D. - SEE DE ALMEIDA, M.A.
DAMERAU, N. POLNISCHE GRAMMATIK.
R.A. ROTHSTEIN, 497(POLR):AUTUMN69-
106
DAMIANI, B.M. - SEE DELICADO, F.
DAMÍANOV, S. FRANTSIÍA I B"LGARSKATA
NATSIONALNA REVOLÍUTSIÍA.
K. HITCHINS, 104:SUMMER71-293
DAMMANN, R. DER MUSIKBEGRIFF IM DEUT-
SCHEN BAROCK.
P.H.L., 414(MQ):APR69-246
DAMODARAN, K. INDIAN THOUGHT.
S.K. SAKSENA, 485(PE&W):JAN-APR68-110
DAMON, P., ED. LITERARY CRITICISM AND
HISTORICAL UNDERSTANDING.
H.W. DONNER, 597(SN):VOL41#1-207
A. RODWAY, 447(N&Q):JUL70-269
DANA, D. - SEE MISTRAL, G.
DANBY, M. A SINGLE GIRL.
J. HUNTER, 362:21SEP72-376
DANCE, F.E.X., ED. HUMAN COMMUNICATION
THEORY.
R.H.K., 543:MAR70-572
DANCE, S. THE WORLD OF DUKE ELLINGTON.
617(TLS):21JAN72-65
D'ANCONA, P.D. & E. AESCHLIMANN. THE
ART OF ILLUMINATION.
J.J.G. ALEXANDER, 90:APR70-247
M.M. SHEEHAN, 363:FEB70-74
DAND, C.H. THE MIGHTY AFFAIR.
617(TLS):3MAR72-242
DANEK, W. MATEJKO I KRASZEWSKI - DWIE
KONCEPCJE DZIEJÓW POLSKI.
D. WELSH, 104:SPRING71-128
DANEMAN, M. A CHANCE TO SIT DOWN.*
E. FEINSTEIN, 364:FEB/MAR72-177
M. LEVIN, 441:11JUN72-34
DANEU, A. L'ARTE TRAPANESE DEL CORALLO.
R. WILDHABER, 182:VOL23#21/22-937
D'ANGELO, E. THE PROBLEM OF FREEDOM AND
DETERMINISM.
R.H.K., 543:MAR70-554
DANGERFIELD, G. VICTORIA'S HEIR.
617(TLS):21JUL72-841
DANIEL, G.B., JR., ED. RENAISSANCE AND
OTHER STUDIES IN HONOR OF WILLIAM LEON
WILEY.
L.J. FRIEDMAN, 545(RPH):NOV69-256
I.D. MC FARLANE, 208(FS):JUL71-317
J.E. WHITE, JR., 207(FR):DEC69-358
W.V. WORTLEY, 546(RR):APR70-130
DANIEL, M.L. JOÃO GUIMARÃES ROSA.
G.M. MOSER, 238:MAR70-158
DANIEL, N. ISLAM, EUROPE AND EMPIRE.
H.A.B. RIVLIN, 318(JAOS):APR-JUN70-
304
DANIEL, S. & P. MC GUIRE, EDS. THE
PAINT HOUSE.
617(TLS):24NOV72-1416

DANIEL, Y. PRISON POEMS. (D. BURG &
A. BOYARS, EDS)
S. HOOD, 362:24FEB72-248
I. WEDDE, 364:FEB/MAR72-148
DANIELLS, R. ALEXANDER MACKENZIE AND THE
NORTHWEST.
R. HAIG-BROWN, 102(CANL):SPRING71-87
DANIÉLOU, A. NORTHERN INDIAN MUSIC.
N. SORRELL, 293(JAST):FEB70-486
DANIELS, J. KUWAIT JOURNEY.
617(TLS):28JAN72-109
DANIELS, J. THE RANDOLPHS OF VIRGINIA.
N. BURT, 441:12NOV72-4
DANIELS, K., COMP. ÜBER DIE SPRACHE.
E. WILHELM, 462(OL):VOL23#3-250
DANIELS, M.F., COMP. WYNDHAM LEWIS.
617(TLS):15DEC72-1535
DANIELS, R.V. RED OCTOBER.
I. GETZLER, 587:OCT69-255
DANIELS, S. HOW 2 GERBILS 20 GOLDFISH
200 GAMES 2,000 BOOKS AND I TAUGHT THEM
HOW TO READ.
N. HENTOFF, 442(NY):5FEB72-101
DANIELSSON, B. JOHN HART'S WORKS ON
ENGLISH ORTHOGRAPHY AND PRONUNCIATION
(1551, 1569, 1570).* (PT 2)
A.A. PRINS, 179(ES):DEC69-609
DANISCHEWSKY, M. OUT OF MY MIND.
617(TLS):22DEC72-1554
"TREVOR DANNATT: BUILDINGS AND INTERÍORS,
1951-72."
617(TLS):24NOV72-1441
DANNENFELDT, K.H. LEONHARD RAUWOLF.
T. HERNDON, 551(RENQ):AUTUMN70-307
DANSEREAU, P., ED. CHALLENGE FOR SUR-
VIVAL.
R.O. EARL, 529(QQ):AUTUMN70-458
DANTE ALIGHIERI. DANTE: THE SELECTED
WORKS. (P. MILANO, ED)
617(TLS):14APR72-429
DANTE ALIGHIERI. THE DIVINE COMEDY.
(G.L. BICKERSTETH, TRANS)
N.J. PERELLA, 545(RPH):NOV70-368
DANTE ALIGHIERI. THE PARADISO.* (J.
CIARDI, TRANS) THE DIVINE COMEDY:
INFERNO.* (C.S. SINGLETON, TRANS)
T.G. BERGIN, 676(YR):SUMMER71-614
DANTE ALIGHIERI. RIME DELLA MATURITÀ E
DELL'ESILIO. (M. BARBI & V. PERNICONE,
EDS)
K. FOSTER, 400(MLN):JAN70-92
"DANTE ALIGHIERI: ESTUDIOS REUNIDOS EN
CONMEMORACION DEL VII CENTENARIO DE
SU NACIMIENTO (1265-1965)."
R. BRÄNDLI, 545(RPH):NOV69-258
"DANTE STUDIES." (VOLS 84-86) (A.L.
PELLEGRINI, ED)
M. SHAPIRO, 545(RPH):FEB71-536
DANTISCO, L.G. - SEE UNDER GRACIÁN DAN-
TISCO, L.
DANTO, A.C. ANALYTICAL PHILOSOPHY OF
HISTORY.
G. MATTHEWS, 393(MIND):JAN70-153
A.E. MUSGRAVE, 483:APR70-163
DANTON, J.P. BETWEEN M.L.S. AND PH.D.
F. WEZEMAN, 356:JUL71-263
DANZIG, A. & P. SCHWED, EDS. THE FIRE-
SIDE BOOK OF TENNIS.
F. TUPPER, 441:22OCT72-26
DARBELNET, J. PENSÉE ET STRUCTURE.
G.B. DANIEL, 399(MLJ):OCT70-443
W. STAAKS, 207(FR):DEC69-384
D'ARCH SMITH, T. LOVE IN EARNEST.*
L. ORMOND, 677:VOL2-319
DARIS, S., ED. PAPIRI MILANESI (P. MED.)
I.N. 1-12. (2ND ED)
A. BLANCHARD, 555:VOL44FASC1-132

DARLING, A. LOLA MONTEZ.
442(NY):12AUG72-78
DARLINGTON, C.D. THE EVOLUTION OF MAN
AND SOCIETY.*
N. WEYL, 396(MODA):SUMMER71-315
D'ARMS, J.H. ROMANS ON THE BAY OF
NAPLES.
639(VQR):AUTUMN70-CLV
DARTT, R.L., COMP. G.A. HENTY.
617(TLS):12MAY72-556
DARWIN, E. THE ESSENTIAL WRITINGS OF
ERASMUS DARWIN. (D. KING-HELE, ED)
D.V.E., 191(ELN):SEP70(SUPP)-35
DARYUSH, E. VERSES: SEVENTH BOOK. SEL-
ECTED POEMS.
617(TLS):21APR72-441
DAS, D. THE VANISHING MAHARAJAS.
617(TLS):27OCT72-1297
DAS GUPTA, A. MALABAR IN ASIAN TRADE,
1740-1800.
W.E. CHEONG, 302:JAN69-113
DAS GUPTA, J.B. JAMMU AND KASHMIR.
R.S. WHEELER, 293(JAST):AUG70-975
DASHTI, A. IN SEARCH OF OMAR KHAYYÁM.
617(TLS):14JAN72-46
DA SILVA, A. THE ART OF CHINESE LAND-
SCAPE PAINTING IN THE CAVES OF TUN-
HUANG.
E.J. LAING, 56:SUMMER69-201
DASSONVILLE, M. RONSARD.* (VOL 1)
L.W. JOHNSON, 551(RENQ):SUMMER70-186
DASSONVILLE, M. RONSARD.* (VOL 2)
K.M. HALL, 402(MLR):OCT71-895
DATOR, J.A. SŌKA GAKKAI.
J.K-C. OH, 293(JAST):FEB70-451
DATTA, V.N. AMRITSAR.
B.N. RAMUSACK, 293(JAST):MAY70-728
DAUBE, D. ROMAN LAW: LINGUISTIC, SOCIAL,
AND PHILOSOPHICAL ASPECTS.*
G. CRIFÒ, 313:VOL60-194
J. CROOK, 123:DEC70-361
DAUBENY, P. MY WORLD OF THEATRE.*
J. ELSOM, 364:AUG/SEP71-158
D'AUBIGNÉ, A. LES TRAGIQUES. (I.D.
MC FARLANE, ED)
K.M. HALL, 208(FS):APR71-193
IBN DAUD, A. THE BOOK OF TRADITION
(SEFER HA-QABBALAH).
M.I., 619(TC):1968/4&1969/1-96
DAUGERT, S.M. - SEE SHARMA, I.C.
DAULTE, F. FRENCH WATERCOLOURS OF THE
19TH CENTURY.
K.R., 90:JUN70-423
DAUNICHT, R. LESSING IM GESPRÄCH.
J.A. KRUSE, 182:VOL23#17/18-795
DAUNICHT, R. - SEE LENZ, J.M.R.
DAUSTER, F.N. HISTORIA DEL TEATRO HIS-
PANOAMERICANO: SIGLOS XIX Y XX.
R.M. REEVE, 238:MAR70-155
D'AUVERGNE, M. - SEE UNDER MARTIAL
D'AUVERGNE
DAVANZATI, C. - SEE UNDER CHIARO DAVAN-
ZATI
D'AVANZO, M.L. KEATS'S METAPHORS FOR THE
POETIC IMAGINATION.
I.H.C., 191(ELN):SEP70(SUPP)-37
DAVENANT, W. THE SHORTER POEMS AND
SONGS FROM THE PLAYS AND MASQUES.
(A.M. GIBBS, ED)
617(TLS):17NOV72-1398
DAVENPORT, F.G., JR. THE MYTH OF SOUTH-
ERN HISTORY.*
L.P. SIMPSON, 27(AL):NOV71-490
DAVES, C.W. - SEE BUTLER, S.
DAVEY, F. EARLE BIRNEY.
D. BARBOUR, 99:MAY72-68
P.C. NOEL-BENTLEY, 296:SPRING72-84

DAVID, C., W. WITTKOWSKI & L. RYAN.
KLEIST UND FRANKREICH. (W. MÜLLER-
SEIDEL, ED)
W. HOFFMEISTER, 406:FALL71-279
W.H. MC CLAIN, 301(JEGP):JUL71-509
DAVID, J. & H. HARRINGTON, EDS. GROWING
UP AFRICAN.
441:12MAR72-39
DAVID, L. TED KENNEDY.
C. KILPATRICK, 561(SATR):13MAY72-79
R.R. LINGEMAN, 441:4JUN72-1
DAVID, M. LETTERATURA E PSICANALISI.
G-P. BIASIN, 400(MLN):JAN70-100
DAVID, P., ED & TRANS. CHINESE CONNOIS-
SEURSHIP.
617(TLS):7JUL72-761
DAVIDS, R.C. HOW TO TALK TO BIRDS AND
OTHER UNCOMMON WAYS OF ENJOYING NATURE
THE YEAR ROUND.
441:8OCT72-38
A.C. AMES, 440:28MAY72-11
DAVIDSON, B. AFRICA IN HISTORY. THE
LOST CITIES OF AFRICA.
N. WEYL, 396(MODA):SPRING71-217
DAVIDSON, B. IN THE EYE OF THE STORM.
617(TLS):1DEC72-1451
DAVIDSON, B. INDICT AND CONVICT.
617(TLS):26MAY72-613
DAVIDSON, C. BIRACIAL POLITICS.
C.V. WOODWARD, 453:14DEC72-37
DAVIDSON, C. WHAT BLACK POLITICIANS ARE
SAYING.
N.I. HUGGINS, 441:12NOV72-42
DAVIDSON, I. BRITAIN AND THE MAKING OF
EUROPE.
617(TLS):28JUL72-861
"ALAN DAVIE." (A. BOWNESS, ED)
R. HUGHES, 592:MAR68-165
DAVIE, D. COLLECTED POEMS 1950-1970.
617(TLS):22DEC72-1548
DAVIE, G.E. - SEE RITCHIE, A.D.
DAVIE, M. IN THE FUTURE NOW.
617(TLS):1SEP72-1012
DAVIES, D.I. & K. HERMAN, EDS. SOCIAL
SPACE.
B.N. AGGER, 99:JUL-AUG72-38
DAVIES, E. THOUGHTS ON SOME QUESTIONS
RELATING TO WOMEN, 1860-1908.
617(TLS):18FEB72-180
DAVIES, G. & M.F. KEELER, EDS. BIBLIO-
GRAPHY OF BRITISH HISTORY (STUART
PERIOD, 1603-1714). (2ND ED)
617(TLS):3MAR72-257
DAVIES, G.A. A POET AT COURT.
617(TLS):7JUL72-784
DAVIES, H. BODY CHARGE.
D-A.N. JONES, 362:6JUL72-22
617(TLS):4AUG72-909
DAVIES, H. THE GLORY GAME.
D. BLANCHFLOWER, 362:23NOV72-724
DAVIES, H. THE RISE AND FALL OF JAKE
SULLIVAN.
F.P.W. MC DOWELL, 659:SUMMER72-361
DAVIES, J.D. BEGINNING NOW.
617(TLS):14APR72-426
DAVIES, J.P., JR. DRAGON BY THE TAIL.
J. GITTINGS, 453:16NOV72-7
J.C. THOMSON, JR., 441:29OCT72-3
442(NY):23SEP72-131
DAVIES, L. CÉSAR FRANCK AND HIS CIRCLE.
W. DEAN, 415:NOV70-1109
DAVIES, L. PATHS TO MODERN MUSIC.*
P. EVANS, 415:SEP71-861
W. SARGEANT, 442(NY):1JAN72-59
DAVIES, L. RAVEL ORCHESTRAL MUSIC.
A.E.F. DICKINSON, 607:SUMMER70-37
G.W. HOPKINS, 415:SEP70-896

DAVIES, L.P. GIVE ME BACK MYSELF.
N. CALLENDAR, 441:23JAN72-28
DAVIES, M. ROGIER VAN DER WEYDEN.
J. CANADAY, 441:3DEC72-90
DAVIES, M.R. & V.A. LEWIS. MODELS OF
POLITICAL SYSTEMS.
617(TLS):17MAR72-312
DAVIES, N. WHITE EAGLE, RED STAR.
441:8OCT72-38
617(TLS):1SEP72-1021
DAVIES, P.W., COMP. A HISTORY OF NATION-
AL WOMAN'S RIGHTS MOVEMENT FOR TWENTY
YEARS.
617(TLS):18FEB72-180
DAVIES, R. FIFTH BUSINESS.*
K. DOBBS, 606(TAMR):#57-76
W.F. HALL, 102(CANL):SUMMER71-80
G. ROPER, 296:WINTER72-33
DAVIES, R. STEPHEN LEACOCK.
D. BARBOUR, 102(CANL):SUMMER71-75
DAVIES, R. THE MANTICORE.
W. KENNEDY, 441:19NOV72-4
C. LEHMANN-HAUPT, 441:15NOV72-49
442(NY):9DEC72-176
DAVIES, R. A VOICE FROM THE ATTIC.
J.R. SORFLEET, 296:SPRING72-92
DAVIES, R. - SEE LEACOCK, S.
DAVIES, W. HEALTH OR HEALTH SERVICE?
617(TLS):31MAR72-378
DAVIES, W. DYLAN THOMAS.
617(TLS):15SEP72-1048
DAVIES, W. - SEE THOMAS, D.
DAVIN, D. BRIDES OF PRICE.
D.A.N. JONES, 362:28SEP72-418
617(TLS):15SEP72-1041
DAVIS, A., COMP. LOMA 1970.
617(TLS):14JUL72-821
DAVIS, A. PACKAGE AND PRINT.
C. BANKS, 592:SEP68-119
G.W., 503:SPRING68-41
DAVIS, A.K., JR. MATTHEW ARNOLD'S LET-
TERS.
S.M.B. COULLING, 637(VS):SEP69-100
DAVIS, A.Y. & OTHERS. IF THEY COME IN
THE MORNING.*
441:12MAR72-38
DAVIS, C. THE PRODUCER.
D. ADLER, 441:5MAR72-4
A. BROYARD, 441:7FEB72-33
DAVIS, C.C. THAT AMBITIOUS MR. LEGARÉ.
R.D. JACOBS, 578:SPRING72-122
DAVIS, D., C. WILMER & R. WELLS. SHADE
MARINERS. (G. SPIRO, ED)
G. CAVALIERO, 111:30JAN70-93
DAVIS, D.C. ENGLISH BOTTLES AND DECAN-
TERS 1650-1900.
617(TLS):21APR72-457
DAVIS, D.S. SHOCK WAVE.
O.L. BAILEY, 561(SATR):9SEP72-75
N. CALLENDAR, 441:30JUL72-22
T. LASK, 441:22JUL72-25
DAVIS, E. VISION FUGITIVE.
H. LOMAS, 364:DEC71/JAN72-168
J. SCHWARTZ, 590:SUMMER70-42
DAVIS, G. BANDAGING BREAD.
L.L. MARTZ, 676(YR):SPRING71-403
DAVIS, G. COMING HOME.
P. RAND, 441:9JAN72-7
DAVIS, G. TOUCHING.*
W.H. PRITCHARD, 249(HUDR):SUMMER71-
355
DAVIS, G.N. GERMAN THOUGHT AND CULTURE
IN ENGLAND 1700-1770.
I.M. KIMBER, 402(MLR):OCT71-939
481(PQ):JUL70-394
DAVIS, H. JONATHAN SWIFT.
P. DANCHIN, 179(ES):JUN70-261
DAVIS, H. - SEE CONGREVE, W.

DAVIS, H.B. NATIONALISM AND SOCIALISM.*
Z.A.B. ZEMAN, 587:JUL69-113
DAVIS, H.H. THE DARK WAY TO THE PLAZA.
502(PRS):WINTER68/69-365
DAVIS, J. THE PAPERS OF JEFFERSON DAVIS.
(VOL 1) (H.M. MONROE, JR. & J.T.
MC INTOSH, EDS)
441:19MAR72-16
DAVIS, J.A. BEEVER & COMPANY.
639(VQR):WINTER70-XXVIII
DAVIS, J.G. OPERATION RHINO.
617(TLS):9JUN72-667
DAVIS, J.W., D.J. HOCHNEY & W.K. WILSON,
EDS. PHILOSOPHICAL LOGIC.
R.H.K., 543:JUN70-754
DAVIS, K.S. FDR.
J.D. BARBER, 441:31DEC72-3
C. LEHMANN-HAUPT, 441:21DEC72-33
DAVIS, L.J. COWBOYS DON'T CRY.*
K.J. ATCHITY, 340(KR):1969/5-675
DAVIS, L.J. A MEANINGFUL LIFE.*
E. MORGAN, 362:18MAY72-660
617(TLS):21JUL72-851
DAVIS, M. THREE MINUTES TO MIDNIGHT.
N. CALLENDAR, 441:6FEB72-38
H. FRANKEL, 561(SATR):29JAN72-73
DAVIS, M.S. WHO DEFENDS ROME?
441:23JUL72-16
DAVIS, N., ED. NON-CYCLE PLAYS AND FRAG-
MENTS.
D. BEVINGTON, 589:OCT71-733
G. WICKHAM, 677:VOL2-235
DAVIS, N. - SEE "SIR GAWAIN AND THE GREEN
KNIGHT"
DAVIS, O. THE STEPS OF THE SUN.
M. LEVIN, 441:30JAN72-26
DAVIS, R.M., ED. THE NOVEL.
J.H. SIMS, 577(SHR):FALL70-373
DAVIS, S. THE DECIPHERMENT OF THE
MINOAN LINEAR A AND PICTOGRAPHIC
SCRIPTS.*
O. MASSON, 555:VOL44FASC2-297
DAVIS, W., ED. PICK OF PUNCH.
Q. BELL, 362:23NOV72-714
617(TLS):20OCT72-1264
DAVIS, W.R. IDEA AND ACT IN ELIZABETHAN
FICTION.
R.P. ASHLEY, 191(ELN):DEC70-141
G.R. HIBBARD, 551(RENQ):AUTUMN70-318
M. LAWLIS, 301(JEGP):APR71-288
DAVIS, W.R. - SEE CAMPION, T.
DAVISON, D. W.H. AUDEN.
E. MENDELSON, 677:VOL2-337
DAVISON, J.A. FROM ARCHILOCHUS TO PIN-
DAR.
N.V. DUNBAR, 123:DEC70-291
D.E. GERBER, 121(CJ):DEC70-JAN71-178
DAVISON, P., ED. SONGS OF THE BRITISH
MUSIC HALL.
617(TLS):9JUN72-667
DAVISON, W. HALFPENNY CHAPBOOKS.
617(TLS):17MAR72-302
DAWE, L.B. CHRIST CHURCH, LANCASTER
COUNTY, VIRGINIA, 1732, AND THE LIFE
AROUND IT.
639(VQR):AUTUMN70-CLV
DAWES, F. DEBUSSY PIANO MUSIC.
G.W. HOPKINS, 607(WINTER69/70-41
E. LOCKSPEISER, 415:MAY70-507
412:NOV71-362
DAWIDOWICZ, L.S., ED. THE GOLDEN TRADI-
TION.*
E. MENDELSOHN, 497(POLR):WINTER69-72
DAWSON, C. THE DIVIDING OF CHRISTENDOM.
THE GODS OF REVOLUTION.
617(TLS):28JUL72-881

DAWSON, C. HIS FINE WIT.
  M. COOKE, 676(YR):WINTER71-294
  L. MADDEN, 637(VS):JUN70-435
  S.M. SMITH, 677:VOL2-298
DAWSON, C. THOMAS LOVE PEACOCK.
  L. MADDEN, 637(VS):JUN70-435
DAWSON, C.M. & T. COLE, EDS. STUDIES IN
  LATIN POETRY.
  G.P. GOOLD, 487:WINTER70-367
  L.I. LINDO, 122:APR71-127
  K. QUINN, 67:MAY71-73
  G.B. TOWNEND, 123:JUN71-216
DAWSON, G.E. & L. KENNEDY-SKIPTON. ELIZ-
  ABETHAN HANDWRITING 1500-1650.*
  M. CRUM, 354:SEP69-265
  R.A. FOAKES, 570(SQ):SPRING68-184
  P.E. JONES, 325:APR69-508
DAWSON, R. IMPERIAL CHINA.
  617(TLS):8DEC72-1508
DAWSON, W.S. DRAMA AND THE DRAMATIC.
  S. WELLS, 402(MLR):OCT71-845
DAY, B. PILGRIMS OF PEACE.
  H. MAC CALLUM, 627(UTQ):JUL69-353
DAY, C. THE DUTCH IN JAVA.
  W.F. VELLA, 293(JAST):FEB70-489
DAY, D. & M. LOWRY - SEE LOWRY, M.
DAY, M. FORTY ACRES.
  J. WOMACK, JR., 453:31AUG72-12
DAY, P.D. EASTERN CHRISTIAN LITURGIES.
  617(TLS):12MAY72-557
DAY, R.A. TOLD IN LETTERS.
  D.G. SPENCER, 613:SUMMER68-302
DAY LEWIS, C. THE WHISPERING ROOTS AND
  OTHER POEMS.*
  T. BLACKBURN, 493:SUMMER70-171
  R.B. SHAW, 491:MAR72-342
DEACON, R. A HISTORY OF THE RUSSIAN
  SECRET SERVICE.
  617(TLS):28JUL72-866
DEAKIN, M. THE CHILDREN ON THE HILL.
  L. HUDSON, 362:25MAY72-690
  617(TLS):9JUN72-657
DEAL, B.H. SUMMER GAMES.
  M. LEVIN, 441:13FEB72-32
"DEALING WITH DRUG ABUSE."
  J.M. MARKHAM, 441:21MAY72-33
  617(TLS):15DEC72-1527
DE AMICIS, E. AMORE E GINNASTICA.
  617(TLS):5MAY72-509
DEAN, V.M. NEW PATTERNS OF DEMOCRACY IN
  INDIA.
  D.B. ROSENTHAL, 293(JAST):FEB70-504
DEAN, W. HANDEL AND THE OPERA SERIA.*
  A. HICKS, 415:JAN71-31
  J.A.W., 410(M&L):JAN71-85
  412:MAY71-183
DEAN, W. THE INDUSTRIALIZATION OF SÃO
  PAULO, 1880-1945.
  D. CARNEIRO, 263:JAN-MAR71-68
DEAN, W.G., ED. ECONOMIC ATLAS OF ON-
  TARIO.
  G. CURNOE, 96:DEC70/JAN71-64
  A. ROTSTEIN, 96:DEC70/JAN71-64
DEARDEN, J.S. & K.G. THORNE. RUSKIN &
  CONISTON.
  617(TLS):17MAR72-317
DEARNLEY, C. ENGLISH CHURCH MUSIC 1650-
  1750.*
  P.J.D., 410(M&L):JAN71-78
  N. FORTUNE, 415:DEC70-1223
DEARNLEY, M. THE POETRY OF CHRISTOPHER
  SMART.
  A. TIBBLE, 175:SUMMER69-69
DEBENEDETTI, G. IL ROMANZO DEL NOVE-
  CENTO.
  617(TLS):12MAY72-554

DEBICKI, A.P. ESTUDIOS SOBRE POESÍA
  ESPAÑOLA CONTEMPORÁNEA.
  M. JATO MACÍAS, 238:SEP70-576
DEBORIN, G. SECRETS OF THE SECOND WORLD
  WAR.
  617(TLS):2JUN72-618
DEBRAY, R. THE CHILEAN REVOLUTION.*
  (BRITISH TITLE: CONVERSATIONS WITH
  ALLENDE.)
  D. KURZMAN, 561(SATR):22JAN72-61
  D. SEERS, 441:20FEB72-6
DEBRECZENY, P. & J. ZELDIN, EDS & TRANS.
  LITERATURE AND NATIONAL IDENTITY.
  A. LEVIN, 32:SEP71-702
  N. MORAVCEVICH, 574(SEEJ):FALL71-380
DE BRUYNE, E. THE ESTHETICS OF THE MID-
  DLE AGES.
  G.W. OLSEN, 613:WINTER69-610
DEBUSSY, C. MONSIEUR CROCHE ET AUTRES
  ÉCRITS.* (F. LESURE, ED)
  G.W. HOPKINS, 415:OCT71-965
  R.H.M., 410(M&L):OCT71-426
DECANEY, F.R. TECHNIQUES AND PROCEDURES
  IN SECOND LANGUAGE TEACHING. (J.D.
  BOWEN, ED)
  E.D. ALLEN, 399(MLJ):APR70-281
DÉCAUX, E. PETITE GRAMMAIRE POLONAISE.*
  C.A. WERTZ, 104:WINTER71-569
DECK, J. ONE MORNING FOR PLEASURE.
  J.G., 502(PRS):SUMMER69-233
DECK, J. RANCHO PARADISE.
  E. HOAGLAND, 441:17SEP72-36
  R.R. LINGEMAN, 441:28AUG72-27
DECK, J.N. NATURE, CONTEMPLATION AND THE
  ONE.*
  A.C. LLOYD, 482(PHR):JAN70-145
DECKERS, M-C. LE VOCABULAIRE DE TEILHARD
  DE CHARDIN.
  H. GODIN, 208(FS):APR71-241
DECLEVA CAIZZI, F., ED. ANTISTHENIS
  FRAGMENTA.
  R. LAURENTI, 548(RCSF):JAN-MAR68-103
DE CONDE, A. HALF BITTER, HALF SWEET.
  J. MANGIONE, 441:6FEB72-41
DECTER, M. THE NEW CHASTITY AND OTHER
  ARGUMENTS AGAINST WOMEN'S LIBERATION.
  C. LEHMANN-HAUPT, 441:26SEP72-49
  A. RICH, 453:30NOV72-34
  G. STADE, 441:15OCT72-5
  L. WOLFE, 561(SATR):21OCT72-72
  442(NY):7OCT72-159
DEDERING, S. - SEE AŞ-ŞAFADĪ, H.A.
DEDIJER, V. THE BATTLE STALIN LOST.*
  P.N. HEHN, 32:DEC71-920
DEDIO, A. DAS DRAMATISCHE WERK VON LADY
  GREGORY.*
  K. SPINNER, 179(ES):OCT70-464
DEDRICK, D.E. - SEE MORETO Y CAVAÑA, A.
DEELMAN, C. THE GREAT SHAKESPEARE
  JUBILEE.
  L. FOX, 570(SQ):WINTER68-99
DEETERS, W. QUELLEN ZUR HOF- UND FAMIL-
  IENFORSCHUNG IM NIEDERSÄCHSISCHEN
  STAATSARCHIV IN STADE.
  C.A.F. MEEKINGS, 325:APR69-506
DE FALCO, J. THE HERO IN HEMINGWAY'S
  SHORT STORIES.
  H. STRAUMANN, 179(ES):APR69-221
DE FALCO, V. & M. KRAUSE - SEE HYPSICLES
DEFOE, D. THE FORTUNES AND MISFORTUNES
  OF THE FAMOUS MOLL FLANDERS. (G.A.
  STARR, ED)
  617(TLS):11FEB72-148
DEFOE, D. A JOURNAL OF THE PLAGUE YEAR.
  (L. LANDA, ED)
  O.M. BRACK, JR., 481(PQ):JUL70-337
  R.J. MERRETT, 677:VOL2-276

DEFOE, D. THE LIFE, ADVENTURES, AND
PYRACIES, OF THE FAMOUS CAPTAIN SIN-
GLETON ETC. (S.K. KUMAR, ED)
   R.J. MERRETT, 677:VOL2-276
   J.H. SIMS, 568(SCN):WINTER71-79
DEFOE, D. ROBINSON CRUSOE. (J.D. CROW-
LEY, ED)
   617(TLS):7JUL72-764
DEFRÉMERY, C., B.R. SANGUINETTI & V.
MONTEIL - SEE IBN KHALDUN
DE FUSCO, R. IL CODICE DELL' ARCHITET-
TURA ANTOLOGIA DI TRATTATISTI.
   S. LANG, 46:MAR69-226
DEGENHARDT, I. STUDIEN ZUM WANDEL DES
ECKHARTSBILDES.
   M.J.V., 543:SEP69-127
DE GEORGE, R.T., ED. ETHICS AND SOCIETY.
   G.J. WARNOCK, 479(PHQ):JUL70-304
DE GEORGE, R.T. THE NEW MARXISM.*
   H.B., 543:SEP69-128
   E. KAMENKA, 550(RUSR):JAN70-97
DE GEORGE, R.T. SOVIET ETHICS AND MORAL-
ITY.*
   A. VUCINICH, 550(RUSR):JUL70-342
DEGÉRANDO, J-M. THE OBSERVATION OF SAV-
AGE PEOPLES.
   S. MORAVIA, 548(RCSF):OCT-DEC69-472
DEIGHTON, L. BOMBER.*
   P. CRUTTWELL, 249(HUDR):SPRING71-177
DEIGHTON, L. CLOSE-UP.
   J. HUNTER, 362:29JUN72-874
   M. LEVIN, 441:25JUN72-28
   442(NY):24JUN72-94
   617(TLS):16JUN72-677
DEIGHTON, L. DECLARATIONS OF WAR.*
   G. EWART, 364:FEB/MAR72-180
DEISS, J.J. THE ROMAN YEARS OF MARGARET
FULLER.*
   639(VQR):SUMMER70-CV
DE JONGH, B. THE COMPANION GUIDE TO
SOUTHERN GREECE.
   617(TLS):24MAR72-339
DEKMEJIAN, R.H. EGYPT UNDER NASIR.
   M. COPELAND, 441:21MAY72-2
DELACROIX, E. EUGÈNE DELACROIX: SELECTED
LETTERS 1813-1863.* (J. STEWART, ED &
TRANS)
   A. WERNER, 31(ASCH):WINTER71/72-158
DELAISSÉ, L.M.J. A CENTURY OF DUTCH
MANUSCRIPT ILLUMINATION.*
   K.G. BOON, 90:JUN69-389
DELAMARRE, M.J-B. LE BERGER DANS LA
FRANCE DES VILLAGES.
   P. VOSSELER, 182:VOL23#13/14-697
DELANY, P. BRITISH AUTOBIOGRAPHY IN THE
SEVENTEENTH CENTURY.
   D. DOUGLAS, 541(RES):AUG70-384
   S. GOLDING, 301(JEGP):JUL71-555
   R.E. KELLEY, 481(PQ):JUL70-311
   D. NOVARR, 191(ELN):JUN71-321
DELATTRE, R.A. BEAUTY AND SENSIBILITY IN
THE THOUGHT OF JONATHAN EDWARDS.
   J.W. DIXON, JR., 290(JAAC):SUMMER70-
   546
   W.A.J., 543:DEC69-343
   A.A. MAURER, 479(PHQ):OCT70-399
DE LAURA, D.J. HEBREW AND HELLENE IN
VICTORIAN ENGLAND.*
   H. EBEL, 637(VS):JUN70-415
   W. ROBBINS, 191(ELN):DEC70-143
DELAVENAY, E. D.H. LAWRENCE. (VOL 1)
   P. DELANY, 441:10DEC72-4
   R. LOCKE, 441:2OCT72-39
   617(TLS):16JUN72-680
DELBAERE-GARANT, J. HENRY JAMES.
   L. EDEL, 27(AL):JAN72-662
DELBO, C. NONE OF US WILL RETURN.
   S.K.J., 502(PRS):WINTER68/69-364

DELDERFIELD, R.F. GOD IS AN ENGLISHMAN.*
   P. CRUTTWELL, 249(HUDR):SPRING71-177
DELDERFIELD, R.F. TO SERVE THEM ALL MY
DAYS.
   M. LEVIN, 441:8OCT72-42
   442(NY):4NOV72-195
DELEBECQUE, E. - SEE XENOPHON
DELEKAT, L. KATOCHE, HIERODOULIE UND
ADOPTIONSFREILASSUNG.
   J. OATES, 318(JAOS):APR-JUN70-319
DELEUZE, G. NIETZSCHE ET LA PHILOSOPHIE.
   J. GRANIER, 542:JAN-MAR69-91
VAN DELFT, L. LA BRUYÈRE MORALISTE.
   617(TLS):4FEB72-134
DE LIBERO, L. DI BRACE IN BRACE.
   617(TLS):29SEP72-1166
DELIBES, M. PARÁBOLA DEL NÁUFRAGO.
   J.W. DÍAZ, 238:DEC70-1024
DELIBES, M. SMOKE OF THE GROUND.
   M. LEVIN, 441:20AUG72-24
DELICADO, F. LA LOZANA ANDALUZA. (B.M.
DAMIANI, ED)
   P.N. DUNN, 86(BHS):APR71-158
DELIEB, E. THE GREAT SILVER MANUFACTORY.
   617(TLS):21JAN72-77
DE LILLO, D. END ZONE.
   T.R. EDWARDS, 441:9APR72-1
   C. LEHMANN-HAUPT, 441:22MAR72-49
   S.K. OBERBECK, 440:16APR72-11
   R. SALE, 453:29JUN72-28
   442(NY):6MAY72-145
DE LEVITA, D. THE CONCEPT OF IDENTITY.
   S.A.S., 543:DEC69-343
DELLA CORTE, F. CATONE CENSORE. (2ND
ED)
   H.H. SCULLARD, 123:JUN71-300
DELLEPIANE, A.B. PRESENCIA DE AMÉRICA
EN LA OBRA DE TIRSO DE MOLINA.
   R.W. TYLER, 238:DEC70-1021
DELLEPIANE, A.B. ERNESTO SÁBATO, EL
HOMBRE Y SU OBRA.
   S. LIPP, 238:MAR70-156
DELMAN, D. SUDDEN DEATH.
   N. CALLENDAR, 441:19NOV72-61
DELMAN, D. A WEEK TO KILL.
   N. CALLENDAR, 441:30JUL72-22
DEL MAR, N. RICHARD STRAUSS.* (VOL 2)
   J. TAVENER, 607:AUTUMN69-45
DELMER, S. THE COUNTERFEIT SPY.
   H.H. RANSOM, 561(SATR):26FEB72-74
DE LOACH, A., ED. THE EAST SIDE SCENE.
   K. CONGDON, 37:AUG69-40
DELOFFRE, F. LA NOUVELLE EN FRANCE À
L'ÂGE CLASSIQUE.
   B. MORRISSETTE, 546(RR):APR70-135
DELOFFRE, F. - SEE DE MARIVAUX, P.C.D.
DELOFFRE, F. & M. GILOT - SEE DE MARI-
VAUX, P.C.D.
DELORIA, V., JR. CUSTER DIED FOR YOUR
SINS.*
   617(TLS):21JUL72-829
DELSTON, E. OF LOVE REMEMBERED.
   M. LEVIN, 441:16JAN72-43
DELUMEAU, J. LA CIVILISATION DE LA
RENAISSANCE.
   D. REUILLARD, 98:AUG-SEP69-835
DE LUNA, B.N. JONSON'S ROMISH PLOT.*
   A. LEGGATT, 627(UTQ):APR70-287
   N. PLATZ, 38:BAND87HEFT2-259
DELVING, M. A SHADOW OF HIMSELF.
   N. CALLENDAR, 441:12MAR72-40
   617(TLS):7JUL72-783
DEMARAY, J.G. MILTON AND THE MASQUE
TRADITION.
   G. BULLOUGH, 175:SPRING69-28
   I. DONALDSON, 541(RES):MAY70-248
   L. NATHANSON, 405(MP):FEB70-285

DEMARIA, F. PAMPA ROJA.
C.A. SALATINO, 37:MAY69-40
"THE DEMAUNDES JOYOUS." (J. WARDROPER, ED)
617(TLS):10MAR72-284
DEMBO, L.S., ED. NABOKOV.
H. FINK, 104:SPRING71-85
DEMBOWSKI, P.F., ED. AMI ET AMILE.
P.R. GRILLO, 207(FR):MAR70-700
DEMÉNY, J. - SEE BARTÓK, B.
DEMETRIO, F. SYMBOLS IN COMPARATIVE
RELIGION AND THE GEORGICS.
E. DE SAINT-DENIS, 555:VOL44FASC2-338
DEMETRIO Y RADAZA, F. THE VILLAGE, EARLY
CAGAYAN DE ORO IN LEGEND AND HISTORY.
TOWARDS A SURVEY OF PHILIPPINE FOLKLORE
AND MYTHOLOGY.
D.V. HART, 293(JAST):AUG70-994
DEMETRIO, J.K. GREEK SCHOLARSHIP IN
SPAIN AND LATIN AMERICA.
F. MÁRQUEZ-VILLANUEVA, 545(RPH):
AUG69-140
DEMETZ, P., T. GREENE & L. NELSON, JR.,
EDS. THE DISCIPLINES OF CRITICISM.
R.A. SAYCE, 184(EIC):JAN70-81
DEMETZ, P. & W.T.H. JACKSON, EDS. AN
ANTHOLOGY OF GERMAN LITERATURE 800-
1750.
E.S. DICK, 399(MLJ):OCT70-462
DE MILLE, A. LIZZIE BORDEN.
M.G. SWIFT, 151:JAN69-70
DEMING, R.H., ED. JAMES JOYCE: THE
CRITICAL HERITAGE.*
E.W. MELLOWN, 579(SAQ):WINTER71-126
DEMKO, G.J. THE RUSSIAN COLONIZATION OF
KAZAKHSTAN, 1896-1916.
F-X. COQUIN, 32:JUN71-430
DEMORIZI, E.R. - SEE UNDER RODRÍGUEZ
DEMORIZI, E.
DEMOS, J. A LITTLE COMMONWEALTH.
B.E. STEINER, 432(NEQ):SEP70-482
J.J. WATERS, 656(WMQ):OCT70-657
DEMOS, J., ED. REMARKABLE PROVIDENCES,
1600-1760.
T. LASK, 441:26MAY72-35
DE MOTT, B. SUPERGROW.* SURVIVING THE
70'S.*
J.P. DEGNAN, 249(HUDR):AUTUMN71-541
DENAT, A. VU DES ANTIPODES, SYNTHÈSES
CRITIQUES.
G. TREMBLEY, 207(FR):MAR70-680
DEN BOER, J. LEARNING THE WAY.
H. CARLILE, 448:SUMMER70-124
DEN BOER, J. TRYING TO COME APART.
H. TAYLOR, 651(WHR):AUTUMN71-370
A. WILLIAMSON, 491:FEB72-296
DENDLE, B.J. THE SPANISH NOVEL OF RELIG-
IOUS THESIS, 1876-1936.
J. DEVLIN, 238:MAY70-336
DENEAUVE, J. LAMPES DE CARTHAGE.
A.R. NEUMANN, 182:VOL23#6-291
DENHAM, H.M. THE IONIAN ISLANDS TO
RHODES.
617(TLS):25AUG72-993
DENKLER, H. DRAMA DES EXPRESSIONISMUS.*
E.M. CHICK, 222(GR):MAR70-141
DENKLER, H., ED. EINAKTER UND KLEINE
DRAMEN DES EXPRESSIONISMUS.
R.K., 221(GQ):JAN70-145
DENKLER, H. - SEE BRUST, A.
DENNETT, D.C. CONTENT AND CONSCIOUS-
NESS.*
N.J.H. DENT, 479(PHQ):OCT70-403
R.H-K., 543:JUN70-740
T. NAGEL, 311(JP):20APR72-220
J.J.C. SMART, 393(MIND):OCT70-616

DENNIS, B. EXPERIMENTAL MUSIC IN
SCHOOLS.
G. WINTERS, 607:SPRING70-43
DENNIS, N. AN ESSAY ON MALTA.
617(TLS):30JUN72-752
DENNIS, N. EXOTICS.
R. DURGNAT, 493:WINTER70/71-366
DENNIS, P. DECISION BY DEFAULT.
617(TLS):14JUL72-789
DENNIS, P. 3 D.
P. SHOWERS, 441:10DEC72-30
DENOMMÉ, R.T. NINETEENTH-CENTURY FRENCH
ROMANTIC POETS.
C.C., 191(ELN):SEP70(SUPP)-54
P. DEGUISE, 207(FR):MAR70-688
DENT, A. DONKEY.
617(TLS):18AUG72-975
DENT, A., ED. WORLD OF SHAKESPEARE: ANI-
MALS AND MONSTERS.
617(TLS):28JUL72-900
DENT, P. PROXIMA CENTAURI.
617(TLS):13OCT72-1217
D'ENTRÈVES, A.P. - SEE PASSERIN D'EN-
TRÈVES, A.
DENY, J. & OTHERS, EDS. PHILOLOGIAE
TURCICAE FUNDAMENTA. (VOLS 1&2)
G. LAZARD, 182:VOL23#11/12-607
DE PATER, W.A. LES "TOPIQUES" D'ARISTOTE
ET LA DIALECTIQUE PLATONICIENNE.
M.I. PARENTE, 548(RCSF):APR-JUN68-243
DE PORTE, A.W. DE GAULLE'S FOREIGN
POLICY, 1944-1946.
G.W. BAER, 461:FALL68-909
DE QUINCEY, T. SELECTED ESSAYS ON RHET-
ORIC. (F. BURWICK, ED)
G. PHIFER, 583:WINTER68-162
DERCSÉNYI, D. HISTORICAL MONUMENTS IN
HUNGARY.
H.R. ARCHER, 32:JUN71-460
DERECSKEY, S. THE HUNGARIAN COOKBOOK.
N. HAZELTON, 441:3DEC72-96
DE RIENZO, G. FOGAZZARO E L'ESPERIENZA
DELLA REALTÀ.
R.A. HALL, JR., 276:SUMMER70-218
DE RIJK, L.M. LOGICA MODERNORUM.
N. KRETZMANN, 482(PHR):APR70-262
DE RIJK, L.M. - SEE ABELARD, P.
DESAI, P.B. SIZE AND SEX COMPOSITION OF
POPULATION IN INDIA: 1901-1961.
G.B. SIMMONS, 293(JAST):AUG70-963
DESBOROUGH, V.R.D. THE GREEK DARK AGES.
617(TLS):22SEP72-1110
DESCARTES, R. PHILOSOPHICAL LETTERS.
(A. KENNY, ED & TRANS)
T. KEEFE, 518:JAN71-15
DESCHAMPS, N. - SEE HÉMON, L.
DESCHOUX, M. PHILOSOPHIE DU SAVOIR
SCIENTIFIQUE.
A. MERCIER, 182:VOL23#4-129
DESCOTES, M. RACINE.
C. FRANÇOIS, 207(FR):FEB70-524
R.C. KNIGHT, 208(FS):JUL71-334
DESCOTES, M.E. LA LÉGENDE DE NAPOLÉON
ET LES ÉCRIVAINS FRANÇAIS DU XIXE
SIÈCLE.
J-L. CORNUZ, 207(FR):FEB70-520
DES GAGNIERS, J. L'ILE-AUX-COUDRES.
J-C. BONENFANT, 627(UTQ):JUL70-415
DESGRAVES, L. & OTHERS, EDS. RÉPERTOIRE
BIBLIOGRAPHIQUE DES LIVRES IMPRIMÉS EN
FRANCE AU XVIE SIÈCLE. (BKS 1-3)
E. ZIMMERMANN, 182:VOL23#7-327
DE SHIELDS, J.T. TALL MEN WITH LONG
RIFLES.
W. GARD, 584(SWR):AUTUMN71-VI

DÉSILETS, A. HECTOR-LOUIS LANGEVIN, UN
PÈRE DE LA CONFÉDÉRATION CANADIENNE
(1826-1906).
J-C. BONENFANT, 627(UTQ):JUL70-404
DESMOND, A. SCHUMANN SONGS.
617(TLS):21JUL72-853
DESMONDE, K. DOLLS AND DOLLS HOUSES.
617(TLS):21APR72-457
DESSAIN, C.S. - SEE NEWMAN, J.H.
DESSEN, C.S. IUNCTURA CALLIDUS ACRI.*
J.C. BRAMBLE, 123:MAR71-46
DESSOIR, M. AESTHETICS AND THEORY OF
ART.
E. SCHAPER, 89(BJA):SUMMER71-311
DETIENNE, M. LES MAÎTRES DE LA VÉRITÉ
DANS LA GRÈCE ARCHAÏQUE.
A.W.H. ADKINS, 123:JUN71-220
DETTWEILER, F., H. KÖLLNER & P.A. RIEDL,
EDS. STUDIEN ZUR BUCHMALEREI UND
GOLDSCHMIEDEKUNST DES MITTELALTERS.
C.M. KAUFFMANN, 90:FEB69-94
DEUEL, L. FLIGHTS INTO YESTERDAY.*
B.L. TRELL, 124:MAR71-243
DE DEUGD, C. HET METAFYSISCH GRONDPAT-
ROON VAN HET ROMANTISCHE LITERAIRE
DENKEN.
P. HADERMANN, 52:BAND4HEFT2-210
DE DEUGD, C. THE SIGNIFICANCE OF SPIN-
OZA'S FIRST KIND OF KNOWLEDGE.
P. DI VONA, 548(RCSF):OCT-DEC68-461
DEUTSCH, A. - SEE "THE BHAGAVAD GÎTÂ"
DEUTSCH, H.C. THE CONSPIRACY AGAINST
HITLER IN THE TWILIGHT WAR.
W.J. MILLER, 377:MAR71-48
DEUTSCHER, I. MARXISM IN OUR TIME. (T.
DEUTSCHER, ED)
617(TLS):16JUN72-676
DEUTSCHER, I. RUSSIA, CHINA AND THE
WEST.
M. MC CAULEY, 575(SEER):APR71-317
639(VQR):AUTUMN70-CLI
DEUTSCHMAN, P. THE ADIPOSE COMPLEX.
M. LEVIN, 441:12NOV72-67
VON DEUTZ, R. - SEE UNDER RUPERT VON
DEUTZ
DEVASTHALI, G.V. - SEE VARADARĀJA
DEVEREUX, E.J. A CHECKLIST OF ENGLISH
TRANSLATIONS OF ERASMUS TO 1700.
D. CRANE, 447(N&Q):JUN70-228
DEVI, R. DANCE DIALECTS OF INDIA.
617(TLS):16JUN72-697
DEVINE, D. DEAD TROUBLE.*
N. CALLENDAR, 441:6FEB72-38
DEVINE, D. THREE GREEN BOTTLES.
O.L. BAILEY, 561(SATR):25NOV72-70
N. CALLENDAR, 441:29OCT72-59
617(TLS):14APR72-427
DE VRIES, P. INTO YOUR TENT I'LL CREEP.*
D.A.N. JONES, 362:10AUG72-184
P. WOOD, 561(SATR):8JAN72-35
617(TLS):28JUL72-864
DE VRIES, P. WITHOUT A STITCH IN TIME.
R.R. LINGEMAN, 441:23NOV72-33
P. SHOWERS, 441:24DEC72-3
DE VRIES, W. & V.L. TARRANCE. THE
TICKET-SPLITTER.
E. DREW, 441:4JUN72-3
DEWDNEY, J.C. TURKEY.
617(TLS):21APR72-455
DEWEY, J. THE EARLY WORKS, 1893-1894.
(VOL 4)
H.W. SCHNEIDER, 319:OCT72-485
DE WOLFE, I., ED. CIVILIA - THE END OF
SUB URBAN MAN.
617(TLS):18FEB72-196

DEYERMOND, A.D. EPIC POETRY AND THE
CLERGY.
C. BANDERA, 593:FALL71-309
G.B. GYBBON-MONYPENNY, 86(BHS):JAN71-
60
D.G. PATTISON, 382(MAE):1971/1-68
K.R. SCHOLBERG, 238:DEC70-1019
DEYERMOND, A.D. THE MIDDLE AGES.
617(TLS):14APR72-419
DEZETTEL, L.M. MASONS AND BUILDERS LIB-
RARY. (VOL 1)
B. GLADSTONE, 441:3DEC72-99
DHARAMPAL. INDIAN SCIENCE AND TECHNOLOGY
IN THE EIGHTEENTH CENTURY.
617(TLS):21JAN72-78
DIAKIN, V.S. RUSSKAIA BURZHUAZIIA I
TSARIZM V GODY PERVOI MIROVOI VOINY
(1914-1917).
M.F. HAMM, 32:JUN71-397
DIAMOND, A.S. PRIMITIVE LAW PAST AND
PRESENT.
617(TLS):23JUN72-715
DIAMOND, N. K'UN SHEN.
M.L. COHEN, 293(JAST):MAY70-696
DIAMOND, R.E. OLD ENGLISH.
M. RIGBY, 402(MLR):JUL71-654
DIAS, P.V. VIELFALT DER KIRCHE IN DER
VIELFALT DER JÜNGER, ZEUGEN UND
DIENER.
F.F. BRUCE, 182:VOL23#6-261
DÍAZ, J.I. - SEE UNDER IGLESIAS DÍAZ, J.
DÍAZ-PLAJA, G. - SEE BARALT, R.M.
DÍAZ SÁNCHEZ, R. CUMBOTO.
H.L. JOHNSON, 238:MAY70-348
639(VQR):SPRING70-XLIV
DÍAZ VALCÁRCEL, E. FIGURACIONES EN EL
MES DE MARZO.
617(TLS):22SEP72-1122
DIBBEN, A.A. COVENTRY CITY CHARTERS.
S. BOND, 325:OCT70-152
DIBELIUS, U. MODERNE MUSIK 1945-1965.
W.M. STROH, 513:FALL-WINTER68-146
DI BIASE, C. AUTOBIOGRAFISMO E ARTE IN
NICCOLÒ TOMMASEO. IL DIZIONARIO DEI
SINONIMI DI NICCOLÒ TOMMASEO.
W.T.S., 191(ELN):SEP69(SUPP)-129
DI BONA, J.E. CHANGE AND CONFLICT IN THE
INDIAN UNIVERSITY.
S. MATHAI, 293(JAST):AUG70-969
DI CESARE, M.A. VIDA'S "CHRISTIAD" AND
VERGILIAN EPIC.
P. PASCAL, 545(RPH):FEB70-355
DICKENS, C. THE BEDSIDE DICKENS. (J.W.
GARROD, COMP)
J.G., 155:JAN70-61
DICKENS, C. BOOTS AT THE HOLLY-TREE INN
AND OTHER STORIES. COMPLETE PLAYS AND
SELECTED POEMS.
A.B., 155:SEP70-244
DICKENS, C. A CHRISTMAS CAROL.
617(TLS):15DEC72-1525
DICKENS, C. A CHRISTMAS CAROL. (P. COL-
LINS, ED)
617(TLS):3MAR72-256
DICKENS, C. CHARLES DICKENS' UNCOLLECTED
WRITINGS FROM HOUSEHOLD WORDS 1850-
1859. (H. STONE, ED)
K.J. FIELDING, 637(VS):DEC69-216
J. HAGAN, 445(NCF):DEC69-361
DICKENS, C. HARD TIMES. (D. CRAIG, ED)
K.J. FIELDING, 155:SEP69-189
DICKENS, C. THE LETTERS OF CHARLES
DICKENS. (VOL 2) (M. HOUSE & G.
STOREY, EDS)
I. JACK, 111:30JAN70-96
M.S., 155:SEP70-242
639(VQR):SPRING70-LXVII

DICKENS, C. MARTIN CHUZZLEWIT. (P.N. FURBANK, ED)
  A. EASSON, 155:JAN69-51
DICKENS, C. THE MYSTERY OF EDWIN DROOD. (M. CARDWELL, ED) THE POSTHUMOUS PAPERS OF THE PICKWICK CLUB. (R.L. PATTEN, ED) THE OLD CURIOSITY SHOP. (A. EASSON, ED) AMERICAN NOTES FOR GENERAL CIRCULATION. (J.S. WHITLEY & A. GOLDMAN, EDS)
  617(TLS):11AUG72-946
DICKENS, C. OLIVER TWIST.* (K. TILLOTSON, ED)
  F. BOWERS, 445(NCF):SEP68-226
DICKENS, C. & W.M. THACKERAY. THE LOVING BALLAD OF LORD BATEMAN.
  M.S., 155:JAN70-60
DICKEY, J. DELIVERANCE.*
  M. CAVELL, 473(PR):1971/1-117
  W. EYSTER, 569(SR):SUMMER71-469
  P.E. GRAY, 676(YR):AUTUMN70-101
  639(VQR):SUMMER70-LXXXVIII
DICKEY, J. THE EYE-BEATERS, BLOOD, VICTORY, MADNESS, BUCKHEAD AND MERCY.*
  G.S. FRASER, 473(PR):WINTER71/72-469
  T. LUCAS, 590:FALL70-39
DICKEY, J. SORTIES.*
  W. HEYEN, 561(SATR):11MAR72-70
  D. KALSTONE, 441:23JAN72-6
DICKEY, J. SPINNING THE CRYSTAL BALL.
  G. CORE, 219(GAR):SUMMER70-250
DICKEY, R.P. RUNNING LUCKY.*
  F. MORAMARCO, 651(WHR):WINTER71-99
DICKEY, W. MORE UNDER SATURN.
  V. YOUNG, 249(HUDR):WINTER71/72-672
DICKINSON, E. THE COMPLETE POEMS OF EMILY DICKINSON. (T.H. JOHNSON, ED)
  E.L. JONES, 67:MAY71-110
DICKINSON, G.S. A HANDBOOK OF STYLE IN MUSIC.
  E. SAMS, 415:AUG70-807
  412:FEB71-74
DICKINSON, H. MYTH ON THE MODERN STAGE.*
  R. COHN, 397(MD):DEC69-319
DICKINSON, H.T. BOLINGBROKE.*
  D. RUBINI, 566:SPRING71-65
DICKINSON, P. THE LIZARD IN THE CUP.
  S. BLACKBURN, 440:14MAY72-13
  A. BROYARD, 441:31MAR72-27
  N. CALLENDAR, 441:14MAY72-35
  617(TLS):14APR72-427
DICKINSON, P. MORE THAN TIME.*
  L. CLARK, 493:WINTER70/71-370
DICKINSON, R.D.N. THE CHRISTIAN COLLEGE IN DEVELOPING INDIA.
  617(TLS):7APR72-402
DICKINSON, S., ED. MOTHER'S HELP.
  617(TLS):21JUL72-853
DICKS, D.R. EARLY GREEK ASTRONOMY TO ARISTOTLE.
  P.A. MAC KAY, 124:JAN71-164
  J.S. MORRISON, 123:JUN71-224
DICKSON, H.E. "GENTLEMEN, MORE DOLCE PLEASE!"
  V. FORD, 432(NEQ):JUN70-309
DICKSON, L. H.G. WELLS.*
  S. DICK, 529(QQ):AUTUMN70-456
  M.W. STEINBERG, 627(UTQ):JUL70-349
DICKSON, P. THE GREAT AMERICAN ICE CREAM BOOK.
  N. HAZELTON, 441:3DEC72-96
  R. LASSON, 441:15OCT72-6
  C. LEHMANN-HAUPT, 441:19DEC72-45
DICKSON, P. THINK TANKS.*
  L. IAQUINTA, 561(SATR):18MAR72-82
DICKSTEIN, M. KEATS AND HIS POETRY.*
  617(TLS):22SEP72-1106

"DICTIONNAIRE ABRÉGÉ DU SURRÉALISME."
  R.S. SHORT, 208(FS):JUL71-353
DIDEROT, D. DENIS DIDEROT: SUR L'ART ET LES ARTISTES. (J. SEZNEC, ED)
  J.R. LOY, 546(RR):FEB70-63
DIDEROT, D. DIDEROT'S LETTERS TO SOPHIE VOLLAND. (P. FRANCE, TRANS)
  617(TLS):1DEC72-1469
DIDEROT, D. SALONS.* (VOL 4) (J. SEZNEC, ED)
  A. BROOKNER, 90:JUN69-397
  H. DIECKMANN, 54:SEP69-307
DIEHL, G. VAN DONGEN.
  592:JUL/AUG69-54
DIEHL, S. ZAUBEREI UND SATIRE IM FRÜHWERK NESTROYS.
  J.D. BARLOW, 406:SPRING71-88
DIEKSTRA, F.N.M., ED. A DIALOGUE BETWEEN REASON AND ADVERSITY.
  A.J. BLISS, 597(SN):VOL41#2-466
  C. SISAM, 541(RES):MAY70-190
DIENST, R-G. RICHARD LINDNER.*
  S. FRANK, 58:SUMMER70-14
DIÉNY, J-P. AUX ORIGINES DE LA POÉSIE CLASSIQUE EN CHINE.
  J.D. FRODSHAM, 293(JAST):AUG70-913
DIETRICH, N. & B. THOMAS. HOWARD.
  A.E. HOTCHNER, 561(SATR):1APR72-65
  J. SEELYE, 441:25JUN72-2
  G. VIDAL, 453:20APR72-11
DIETRICH, W.D. DIE STÄDTE DER ENGLISCHEN KANALKÜSTE.
  M. BLACKSELL, 182:VOL23#21/22-959
DIETSCHY, M. LE CAS ANDRÉ SUARÈS.*
  S.D. BRAUN, 207(FR):OCT69-176
DIETZ, K. DIE REZEPTION DES VORKONSONANTISCHEN "L" IN ROMANISCHEN LEHNWÖRTERN DES MITTELENGLISCHEN UND SEINE REFLEXE IM NEUENGLISCHEN STANDARD.*
  H. WEINSTOCK, 597(SN):VOL41#2-460
DIEZ DE MEDINA, F. MATEO MONTEMAYOR.
  G. FRANCOVICH, 263:APR-JUN71-216
DIEZ DE MEDINA, F. OLLANTA, EL JEFE KOLLA.
  E. GUILLERMO, 263:OCT-DEC71-466
DÍEZ TABOADA, J.M. & J.M. ROZAS - SEE BRETÓN DE LOS HERREROS, M.
DIGBY, G.W., WITH W. HEFFORD. THE DEVONSHIRE HUNTING TAPESTRIES.
  617(TLS):14JUL72-821
DIGBY, K. LOOSE FANTASIES. (V. GABRIELI, ED)
  M. CRUM, 541(RES):AUG70-383
DIGGINS, J.P. MUSSOLINI AND FASCISM.
  A. WHITMAN, 231:APR72-102
  442(NY):1APR72-106
DIGGLE, J. - SEE EURIPIDES
DIGGLE, J. & F.R.D. GOODYEAR - SEE CORIPPUS
DIHM, J. KOŚCIUSZKO NIEZNANY.
  G.J. LERSKI, 32:SEP71-680
DIJKSTRA, B. THE HIEROGLYPHICS OF A NEW SPEECH.*
  C. BENSON, 27(AL):MAY71-302
  639(VQR):AUTUMN70-CXXXIV
DIK, S.C. COORDINATION.
  P.H. MATTHEWS, 361:VOL23#4-349
DIKE, D.A. & D.H. ZUCKER - SEE SCHWARTZ, D.
DILKS, D. - SEE CADOGAN, A.
DILLARD, J.L. BLACK ENGLISH.
  P. ADAMS, 61:SEP72-110
  T.C. BAMBARA, 441:3SEP72-3
  C. LEHMANN-HAUPT, 441:29AUG72-35
  M.K. SPEARS, 453:16NOV72-32
DILLARD, R.H.W. NEWS OF THE NILE.*
  H. TAYLOR, 651(WHR):AUTUMN71-369

DILLENBERGER, J. SECULAR ART WITH SACRED
THEMES.
B. BETTINSON, 363:AUG70-137
DILLIGAN, R.J. & T.K. BENDER, COMPS. A
CONCORDANCE TO THE ENGLISH POETRY OF
GERARD MANLEY HOPKINS.
R. DEROLEZ, 179(ES):OCT70-476
DILLON, J. THE ADVERTISING MAN.
C. LEHMANN-HAUPT, 441:15SEP72-37
M. LEVIN, 441:10SEP72-40
DILTHEY, W. IL SECOLO XVIII E IL MONDO
STORICO.
R. PARENTI, 548(RCSF):JAN-MAR68-109
DIMOCK, E.C., JR. THE PLACE OF THE
HIDDEN MOON.
T.J. HOPKINS, 318(JAOS):APR-JUN70-351
DI NAPOLI, G. - SEE CAMPANELLA, T.
DINGLE, H. SCIENCE AT THE CROSSROADS.
G. STADLEN, 362:28SEP72-411
DINNEEN, F.P. AN INTRODUCTION TO GENERAL
LINGUISTICS.*
J. KRÁMSKÝ, 353:OCT69-100
DIOGENES LAËRTIUS. LIVES OF THE PHILOSO-
PHERS. (A.R. CAPONIGRI, TRANS)
H.S. LONG, 124:NOV70-87
DION, R. LES ANTHROPOPHAGES DE L'"ODYS-
SÉE."
F.M. COMBELLACK, 122:JAN71-47
DIONISOTTI, C. GEOGRAFIA E STORIA DELLA
LETTERATURA ITALIANA.
C. FAHY, 402(MLR):JUL71-693
DIONISOTTI, C. GLI UMANISTI E IL VOLGARE
FRA QUATTRO E CINQUECENTO.
A. SCAGLIONE, 545(RPH):AUG69-120
DIÓSZEGI, V., ED. POPULAR BELIEFS AND
FOLKLORE TRADITION IN SIBERIA.
W. EBERHARD, 292(JAF):JAN-MAR70-82
DIÓSZEGI, V. TRACING SHAMANS IN SIBERIA.
S.P. DUNN, 550(RUSR):JUL70-353
A. FARKAS, 32:JUN71-380
DI PALMA, R. THE GALLERY GOERS.
J. NAIDEN, 491:MAY72-115
"DIRECTORY OF SELECTED SCIENTIFIC INSTI-
TUTIONS IN MAINLAND CHINA."
617(TLS):4FEB72-133
DIRLMEIER, F. ZUR CHRONOLOGIE DER
GROSSEN ETHIK DES ARISTOTELES.
H.S. LONG, 124:FEB71-199
DISBROW, D.W. SCHOOLS FOR AN URBAN
SOCIETY.
Q.M. WILSON, 377:MAR71-52
DISNEY, D.M. THE DAY MISS BESSIE LEWIS
DISAPPEARED.
N. CALLENDAR, 441:13AUG72-20
DI STEFANO, G. SINCRONIA E DIACRONIA
NEL ROMANZERO.
C. SMITH, 86(BHS):APR71-154
DISTLER, P.F. LATIN IV.
M. FINNEGAN, 121(CJ):DEC70-JAN71-177
DITTMANN, L. STIL, SYMBOL, STRUKTUR.
A. WERNER, 56:SPRING69-101
"DIVERSITY AMONG LIVING THINGS."
617(TLS):30JUN72-754
DIVINE, R.A., ED. THE CUBAN MISSILE CRI-
SIS.
R. STEEL, 453:19OCT72-43
DIX, C.M. ANTHONY BURGESS.
617(TLS):3MAR72-252
"DIX-HUITIÈME SIÈCLE." (NO. 1, 1969)
M.H. WADDICOR, 208(FS):OCT71-456
DIXON, N. GEORGIAN PISTOLS.
617(TLS):25AUG72-1005
DIXON, P. RHETORIC.
617(TLS):21JUL72-849

DIXON, P. THE WORLD OF POPE'S SATIRES.
T.R. EDWARDS, 141:FALL69-383
R. PARKIN, 173(ECS):SPRING70-419
C.J. RAWSON, 447(N&Q):OCT70-399
R. TRICKETT, 541(RES):MAY70-221
DIXON, R.M.W. WHAT IS LANGUAGE?
G. NICKEL, 72:BAND208HEFT3-201
DIXON, R.M.W. & J. GODRICH. RECORDING
THE BLUES.
W.R. FERRIS, JR., 187:JAN72-132
M. HARRISON, 415:SEP70-898
DIXON, V. - SEE LOPE DE VEGA
DJILAS, M. LAND WITHOUT JUSTICE.
N. ASCHERSON, 453:30NOV72-15
DJILAS, M. THE STONE AND THE VIOLETS.
N. ASCHERSON, 453:30NOV72-15
M. LEVIN, 441:16JUL72-30
E. WASIOLEK, 561(SATR):25MAR72-100
442(NY):25MAR72-131
DMITRIEV, S.S., ED. GRANOVSKII, TIMOFEI
NIKOLAEVICH.
R. WORTMAN, 32:JUN71-389
DMYTRYSHYN, B., ED. IMPERIAL RUSSIA.*
L. KOCHAN, 587:APR69-564
DOBBS, B. DRURY LANE.
617(TLS):18AUG72-978
DOBBS, K. READING THE TIME.
J.M. ROBSON, 627(UTQ):JUL69-425
DOBRÉE, B. RUDYARD KIPLING.*
W.D. SCHAEFER, 445(NCF):SEP68-251
DOBSON, E.J. ENGLISH PRONUNCIATION 1500-
1700. (2ND ED)
H. KOZIOL, 179(ES):OCT70-492
A. RYNELL, 597(SN):VOL41#2-476
E.G. STANLEY, 447(N&Q):JAN70-38
DOBSON, W.A.C.H. THE LANGUAGE OF THE
BOOK OF SONGS.
A. LONSDALE, 447(N&Q):JUL70-276
DOBYNS, S. CONCURRING BEASTS.
R.D. SPECTOR, 561(SATR):11MAR72-80
DOCKSTADER, F.J. SOUTH AMERICAN INDIAN
ART.
M.S. YOUNG, 39:APR69-331
DOCTOROW, E.L. THE BOOK OF DANIEL.*
D.A.N. JONES, 362:17FEB72-221
617(TLS):18FEB72-173
"DOCUMENTS OF MOSCOW 1966 ALL-UNION CON-
FERENCE OF EVANGELICAL CHRISTIAN-BAP-
TISTS."
M. KLIMENKO, 32:JUN71-403
DODD, A.H. LIFE IN WALES.
617(TLS):30JUN72-757
DODD, C.H. POLITICAL DEVELOPMENT.
617(TLS):9JUN72-666
DODD, W. THE BEAUTIES OF SHAKESPEAR.
617(TLS):18FEB72-178
DODDS, E.R. PAGAN AND CHRISTIAN IN AN
AGE OF ANXIETY.
P. LANGLOIS, 555:VOL44FASC1-156
DODGE, B. - SEE "THE FIHRIST OF AL-NADÎM"
DODGE, E.S. BEYOND THE CAPES.*
617(TLS):4FEB72-132
DODGSON, J.M. THE PLACE NAMES OF CHE-
SHIRE. (PT 4)
617(TLS):30JUN72-752
DODSON, C.J., E. PRICE & I.T. WILLIAMS.
TOWARDS BILINGUALISM.
G.R. TUCKER, 399(MLJ):NOV70-544
DOE, B. SOUTHERN ARABIA.
617(TLS):5MAY72-523
DOERFLINGER, F. SLOW BOAT THROUGH
PENNINE WATERS.
617(TLS):7APR72-402
VAN DOESBURG, T. PRINCIPLES OF NEO-
PLASTIC ART.
S. ABERCROMBIE, 505:OCT69-218

DŌGEN. DOGEN'S SHOBOGENZO ZUIMONKI.
(R. MASUNAGA, TRANS)
617(TLS):24MAR72-342
DOHERTY, F.M. BYRON.
D.V.E., 191(ELN):SEP70(SUPP)-27
DOHRMAN, R. THE LAST OF THE MAIDENS.
639(VQR):WINTER70-VIII
"DOKUMENTY SOVETSKO-ITAL'IANSKOI KONFER-
ENTSII ISTORIKOV, 8-10 APRELIA 1968
GODA."
A. GERSCHENKRON, 32:DEC71-853
DOLEZALEK, G. DAS IMBREVIATURBUCH DES
ERZBISCHÖFLICHEN GERICHTSNOTARS HUBAL-
DUS AUS PISA, MAI BIS AUGUST 1230.
D.E. QUELLER, 589:JAN71-141
DOLEŽEL, L. & R.W. BAILEY, EDS. STATIS-
TICS AND STYLE.*
D.R. TALLENTIRE, 402(MLR):JAN71-164
DOLEŽEL, L., P. SGALL & J. VACHEK, EDS.
PRAGUE STUDIES IN MATHEMATICAL LINGUIS-
TICS. (VOL 2)
F. SALTER, 104:SUMMER71-266
DOLEŽELOVÁ-VELINGEROVÁ, M. & J.I. CRUMP -
SEE "BALLAD OF THE HIDDEN DRAGON"
DÖLGER, F. & J. KARAYANNOPULOS. BYZAN-
TINISCHE URKUNDENLEHRE.* (PT 1)
N. OIKONOMIDES, 303:VOL90-265
DOLGOFF, S. - SEE BAKUNIN, M.
DOLTO, F. LE CAS DOMINIQUE.
617(TLS):4FEB72-122
DOMHOFF, G.W. FAT CATS AND DEMOCRATS.
W.V. SHANNON, 441:15OCT72-38
G. VIDAL, 453:10AUG72-8
DOMIN, H. WOZU LYRIK HEUTE?
L. BULLOCK, 270:VOL20#1-16
DOMINGOS BONTEMPO, J. SINFONIA NO. 1/
OPUS 11. (F. DE SOUSA, ED)
R. STEVENSON, 414(MQ):JAN68-111
DOMÍNGUEZ ORTIZ, A. THE GOLDEN AGE OF
SPAIN 1516-1659.
617(TLS):3MAR72-243
DOMINIC, R.B. THERE IS NO JUSTICE.
N. CALLENDAR, 441:2JAN72-16
DOMMANGET, M. AUGUSTE BLANQUI.*
H. MESMER, 182:VOL23#4-183
DOMMEN, A.J. CONFLICT IN LAOS.
617(TLS):11FEB72-143
DONADONI, E. A HISTORY OF ITALIAN LIT-
ERATURE. (R.J. CLEMENTS, ED)
R. ANDREWS, 402(MLR):OCT71-909
DONAHUE, J.W., JR. DRAMATIC CHARACTER IN
THE ENGLISH ROMANTIC AGE.
N. BERLIN, 418(MR):SPRING71-343
DONALD, D. CHARLES SUMNER AND THE RIGHTS
OF MAN.*
676(YR):SUMMER71-XVIII
DONALDSON, E.T. SPEAKING OF CHAUCER.
M.W. BLOOMFIELD, 676(YR):SPRING71-438
D.S. BREWER, 677:VOL2-241
DONALDSON, I. THE WORLD UPSIDE-DOWN.*
C.T. PROBYN, 566:AUTUMN70-31
DONALDSON-EVANS, L.K. POÉSIE ET MÉDITA-
TION CHEZ JEAN DE LA CEPPÈDE.
C.E. HOLMES, 551(RENQ):WINTER70-445
DONAT, J., ED. WORLD ARCHITECTURE 4.
N. MILLER, 505:AUG68-156
DONCEEL, J. - SEE MARÉCHAL, J.
DONIACH, N.S., ED. THE OXFORD ENGLISH-
ARABIC DICTIONARY OF CURRENT USAGE.
617(TLS):13OCT72-1231
DONINGTON, R. THE INSTRUMENTS OF MUSIC.
(3RD ED)
412:MAY71-184
DONINI, G. LA POSIZIONE DI TUCIDIDE
VERSO IL GOVERNO DEI CINQUEMILA.
H.D. WESTLAKE, 123:JUN71-183

DONNE, J. IGNATIUS HIS CONCLAVE.* (T.S.
HEALY, ED)
W. VON KOPPENFELS, 72:BAND208HEFT3-
215
617(TLS):29DEC72-1581
DONNE, J. THE SATIRES, EPIGRAMS AND
VERSE LETTERS OF JOHN DONNE.* (W.
MILGATE, ED)
617(TLS):29DEC72-1581
DONNELLY, A.S. THE RUSSIAN CONQUEST OF
BASHKIRIA 1552-1740.
M.L. ENTNER, 293(JAST):NOV69-177
DONNELLY, M.C. THE NEW ENGLAND MEETING
HOUSES OF THE SEVENTEENTH CENTURY.
E.P. DEAN, 432(NEQ):MAR70-158
DONNELLY, P.J. BLANC DE CHINE.
G. REITLINGER, 90:JAN70-54
DONNITHORNE, A. CHINA'S ECONOMIC SYSTEM.
C. RISKIN, 293(JAST):NOV69-148
DONNO, E.S., ED. ELIZABETHAN MINOR
EPICS.
W. BLISSETT, 179(ES):1969SUPP-XCVI
DONNO, E.S. - SEE MARVELL, A.
DONOGHUE, D. THE DIVINE UNIVERSE.*
R. GROGAN, 184(EIC):JUL70-344
J.S., 619(TC):1968/3-54
H. SERGEANT, 175:SUMMER69-71
DONOGHUE, D. JONATHAN SWIFT.*
P. CRUTTWELL, 184(EIC):OCT70-479
C.J. HORNE, 67:MAY71-103
C.J. RAWSON, 541(RES):NOV70-504
D.T. TORCHIANA, 481(PQ):JUL70-383
DONOGHUE, D. YEATS.
617(TLS):17MAR72-311
DONOGHUE, M.R. FOREIGN LANGUAGES AND THE
ELEMENTARY SCHOOL CHILD.
G.C. LIPTON, 207(FR):FEB70-539
DONOSO, R. FRANCISCO A. ENCINA, SIMULA-
DOR.
C.H. GARDINER, 263:JUL-SEP71-333
DONOVAN, J. THE BUSINESSMAN'S INTERNA-
TIONAL TRAVEL GUIDE.
C.W. CASEWIT, 440:30APR72-4
DONOVAN, M.J. THE BRETON LAY.*
G.C. BRITTON, 447(N&Q):AUG70-317
W.H.W. FIELD, 401(MLQ):SEP70-372
DÖNT, E. PLATONS SPÄTPHILOSOPHIE UND DIE
AKADEMIE.
H.S. LONG, 123:JAN71-159
DONZÉ, R. LA GRAMMAIRE GÉNÉRALE ET
RAISONNÉE DE PORT-ROYAL.
K.D. UITTI, 545(RPH):AUG69-75
DOOLITTLE, J. ALFRED DE VIGNY.
L.M. PORTER, 546(RR):APR70-151
DÖPP, S. VIRGILISCHER EINFLUSS IM WERK
OVIDS.
O.C. PHILLIPS, JR., 122:JAN71-72
DOR, M. DIE WEISSE STADT.
T. WEYR, 19(AGR):VOL36#1-31
DORÉ, G. THE RARE AND EXTRAORDINARY
HISTORY OF HOLY RUSSIA.
617(TLS):17NOV72-1405
DORÉ, G. & B. JERROLD. LONDON.
617(TLS):28JAN72-86
DOREY, T.A., ED. ERASMUS.
H.C. SCHNUR, 124:APR71-278
DOREY, T.A., ED. TACITUS.
B. WALKER, 313:VOL60-258
DORFLES, G. L'ESTETICA DEL MITO DA
VICO A WITTGENSTEIN.
R.W. KRETSCH, 290(JAAC):FALL69-105
DORFMAN, D. BLAKE IN THE NINETEENTH
CENTURY.*
D.V.E., 191(ELN):SEP70(SUPP)-22
J.E. GRANT, 481(PQ):JUL70-328
W.H. STEVENSON, 184(EIC):APR70-251

DORFMAN, E. THE NARREME IN THE MEDIEVAL
    ROMANCE EPIC.*
    M. CHAPLIN, 86(BHS):JAN71-58
    J.H. MARTIN, 131(CL):FALL71-362
    R. SCHOLES, 481(PQ):JAN70-137
    F.L. UTLEY, 350:MAR71-247
DORMAN, C.C. CARLISLE (CITADEL) RAILWAY
    SCENE.
    617(TLS):24NOV72-1441
DORMAN, G.R. - SEE "BOOK-AUCTION RECORDS"
D'ORMESSON, J. LA GLOIRE DE L'EMPIRE.
    617(TLS):7APR72-384
DORN, E. GUNSLINGER. (BK 1)
    R. DURGNAT, 493:SUMMER70-162
    N. MARTIEN, 473(PR):1971/1-122
DORN, E. GUNSLINGER. (BK 2)
    R. DURGNAT, 493:SUMMER70-162
    N. MARTIEN, 473(PR):1971/1-122
    639(VQR):AUTUMN70-CXXXII
DORN, J.H. WASHINGTON GLADDEN.
    R.W. RESH, 330(MASJ):SPRING69-89
DORNBERG, J. THE NEW TSARS.
    B.M. COHEN, 561(SATR):3JUN72-60
DÖRRIE, H. DIE SCHÖNE GALATEA.
    J.E. NYENHUIS, 124:SEP70-22
DORRIS, G.E. PAOLO ROLLI AND THE ITALIAN
    CIRCLE IN LONDON, 1715-1744.
    G. COSTA, 131(CL):WINTER71-92
    H.S. NOCE, 405(MP):AUG69-92
DORSON, R.M. THE BRITISH FOLKLORISTS.*
    J. KISSANE, 637(VS):DEC69-237
DORSON, R.M., ED. PEASANT CUSTOMS AND
    SAVAGE MYTHS.
    J. KISSANE, 637(VS):DEC69-237
DORWART, R.A. THE PRUSSIAN WELFARE
    STATE BEFORE 1740.
    617(TLS):15SEP72-1055
DOS PASSOS, J. ONE MAN'S INITIATION:
    1917.
    S.H. FRANK, 577(SHR):WINTER70-93
DOSTOEVSKY, F.M. THE NOTEBOOKS FOR "THE
    IDIOT." (E. WASIOLEK, ED)
    R.A. PEACE, 447(N&Q):OCT70-397
DOSTOEVSKY, F.M. THE NOTEBOOKS FOR "THE
    POSSESSED." (E. WASIOLEK, ED)
    T. PACHMUSS, 550(RUSR):JAN70-109
DOUBROVSKY, S. LA DISPERSION.
    J.V. ALTER, 207(FR):MAR70-728
DOUCETTE, L.E. EMERY BIGOT.*
    568(SCN):WINTER71-76
DOUCHIN, J-L. LE SENTIMENT DE L'ABSURDE
    CHEZ GUSTAVE FLAUBERT.
    A. FAIRLIE, 208(FS):JUL71-343
DOUGHTY, O. & R. WAHL - SEE ROSSETTI,
    D.G.
DOUGLAS, G. THE SHORTER POEMS OF GAVIN
    DOUGLAS. (P.J. BAWCUTT, ED)
    P.J. FRANKIS, 541(RES):FEB70-75
    K. WITTIG, 38:BAND87HEFT3/4-454
DOUGLAS, J. MANDALAS.
    D. FETHERLING, 606(TAMR):#57-80
DOUGLAS, M. DEALING.*
    W.H. PRITCHARD, 249(HUDR):SUMMER71-
    355
DOUGLAS, P.H. IN THE FULLNESS OF TIME.
    A.J. MIKVA, 441:16JUL72-26
DOUGLAS, R. WORKING WITH R.V.W.
    617(TLS):29SEP72-1163
DOUGLAS, W.O. HOLOCAUST OR HEMISPHERIC
    CO-OP.*
    D. KURZMAN, 561(SATR):22JAN72-61
DOUGLAS, W.O. INTERNATIONAL DISSENT.*
    M. ZUCKERT, 109:FALL/WINTER71/72-142
DOUGLAS, W.W. WORDSWORTH.
    K.K., 191(ELN):SEP69(SUPP)-47
    L. WALDOFF, 301(JEGP):JAN71-163
DOUGLASS, D. PIT LIFE IN CO. DURHAM.
    617(TLS):7APR72-401

DOUGLASS, F. THE LANGUAGE OF THE CLASSI-
    CAL FRENCH ORGAN.*
    P. WILLIAMS, 415:JAN70-47
DOUGLASS, W.A. DEATH IN MURÉLAGA.
    617(TLS):19MAY72-580
DOULIS, T. THE QUARRIES OF SICILY.*
    639(VQR):WINTER70-IX
DOVER, K.J. ARISTOPHANIC COMEDY.
    E. SEGAL, 441:15OCT72-36
DOVER, K.J. LYSIAS AND THE CORPUS LYSIA-
    CUM.*
    W.G. ARNOTT, 123:DEC71-359
    J.J. SHERIDAN, 487:AUTUMN70-263
    R. WEIL, 555:VOL44FASC2-319
DOVER, K.J. - SEE ARISTOPHANES
DOW, F.D.M. A STUDY OF CHIANG-SU AND
    CHE-CHIANG GAZETTEERS OF THE MING
    DYNASTY.
    L.C. GOODRICH, 293(JAST):AUG70-918
    A.Y.C. LUI, 302:JUL70-408
DOW, H. FRANK DALBY DAVISON.
    L. KRAMER, 71(ALS):OCT72-433
DOW, S. CONVENTIONS IN EDITING.*
    D.M. LEWIS, 123:JUN71-309
DOWDEN, W.S. JOSEPH CONRAD.
    J. FEASTER, 295:VOL2#3-417
DOWDEY, C. ROBERT E. LEE.
    A. CONWAY, 67:NOV71-275
DOWDEY, C. THE VIRGINIA DYNASTIES.
    639(VQR):WINTER70-XXI
DOWLING, B. HATHERLEY.
    A. RODDICK, 368:MAR69-84
DOWNES, K. ENGLISH BAROQUE ARCHITECTURE.
    D. STILLMAN, 576:MAR68-75
DOWNES, K. CHRISTOPHER WREN.
    617(TLS):28JAN72-98
DOWNEY, S.B. THE EXCAVATIONS AT DURA-
    EUROPOS, FINAL REPORT III.* (PT 1,
    FASC 1: THE HERACLES SCULPTURE.)
    M.A.R. COLLEDGE, 123:DEC71-462
DOWNIE, R.S. & E. TELFER. RESPECT FOR
    PERSONS.*
    B. MAYO, 518:MAY70-4
DOWNING, A.F., E. MAC DOUGALL & E. PEAR-
    SON. SURVEY OF ARCHITECTURAL HISTORY
    IN CAMBRIDGE.* (REPORT 2)
    F. KOEPER, 576:DEC68-305
DOWNING, A.J. COTTAGE RESIDENCES, RURAL
    ARCHITECTURE, AND LANDSCAPE GARDENING.
    S. BLUTMAN, 576:DEC68-307
DOWNS, R.B. & F.B. JENKINS, EDS. BIBLI-
    OGRAPHY.*
    G. BARBER, 447(N&Q):JUL70-273
DOXAT, J. DRINKS AND DRINKING.
    617(TLS):21JAN72-77
DOXIADIS, C.A. EKISTICS.
    S. ABERCROMBIE, 505:MAR69-170
DOYLE, C. EARTH MEDITATIONS: 2.
    A. RODDICK, 368:MAR69-84
DOYLE, C. EARTH MEDITATIONS: ONE TO
    FIVE.
    C. MOLESWORTH, 491:MAY72-107
DOZOIS, G., ED. A DAY IN THE LIFE.
    T. STURGEON, 441:14MAY72-34
DRABBLE, M. THE NEEDLE'S EYE.
    M. ELLMANN, 362:30MAR72-428
    K. FRASER, 442(NY):16DEC72-146
    T. LASK, 441:10JUN72-33
    J.C. OATES, 441:11JUN72-23
    R. SALE, 453:5OCT72-34
    617(TLS):31MAR72-353
DRABBLE, M. WORDSWORTH.
    J. COLMER, 402(MLR):APR71-399
    K.K., 191(ELN):SEP70(SUPP)-47
DRABBLE, M. & B.S. JOHNSON, EDS. LONDON
    CONSEQUENCES.
    J. HUNTER, 362:4MAY72-596

DRAGE, C.L. & W.N. VICKERY, EDS. AN
EIGHTEENTH-CENTURY RUSSIAN READER.
  M. BERMAN, 574(SEEJ):SUMMER71-218
  I.P. FOOTE, 402(MLR):JAN71-239
  G.S. SMITH, 575(SEER):OCT71-613
DRAHT, V.H. TYPISCH DEUTSCH? (2ND ED)
  K.W. MOERSCHNER, 221(GQ):MAR70-311
DRAKE, D.B. CERVANTES: A CRITICAL BIBLI-
OGRAPHY. (VOL 1)
  J.B. AVALLE-ARCE, 400(MLN):MAR70-303
DRAKE, M. POPULATION AND SOCIETY IN
NORWAY 1735-1865.
  S. GROENNINGS, 563(SS):SPRING71-189
DRAKE, R. FLANNERY O'CONNOR.
  E. KRICKEL, 219(GAR):SUMMER69-246
DRANGE, T. TYPE CROSSINGS.*
  R.H.K., 543:MAR70-554
DRANSFIELD, M. STREETS OF THE LONG
VOYAGE.
  J. TULIP, 581:1971/1-72
DRAPER, A. THE DEATH PENALTY.
  617(TLS):28APR72-500
DRAPER, E. BIRTH CONTROL IN THE MODERN
WORLD.
  617(TLS):20OCT72-1264
DRAPER, R.P., ED. D.H. LAWRENCE: THE
CRITICAL HERITAGE.*
  M. ALLOTT, 677:VOL2-327
DREES, L. OLYMPIA.*
  T.W. JACOBSEN, 121(CJ):DEC70-JAN71-
174
DREITZEL, H. PROTESTANTISCHER ARISTO-
TELISMUS UND ABSOLUTER STAAT.
  G. STRAUSS, 182:VOL23#8-442
DRERUP, H. GRIECHISCHE BAUKUNST IN
GEOMETRISCHER ZEIT.
  J. BOARDMAN, 123:MAR71-143
DRESCHER, H.W. - SEE MACKENZIE, H.
DRESDEN, S. UMANESIMO E RINASCIMENTO.
  R. PARENTI, 548(RCSF):JUL-SEP68-360
"DRESS REGULATIONS FOR THE ARMY 1900."
  617(TLS):2JUN72-641
DRESSLER, W. STUDIEN ZUR VERBALEN
PLURALITÄT.
  F. BADER, 555:VOL44FASC2-292
  J. GONDA, 361:VOL24#2-194
  A. MORPURGO-DAVIES, 123:MAR71-91
DRETSKE, F.I. SEEING AND KNOWING.*
  J.J.E., 543:MAR70-555
  G.J. WARNOCK, 393(MIND):APR70-281
DREW, J.H. KENILWORTH.
  617(TLS):1SEP72-1033
DREW, P. THE POETRY OF ROBERT BROWNING.*
  M.G. WIEBE, 529(QQ):WINTER70-649
DREXLER, R. ONE OR ANOTHER.
  M. MUDRICK, 249(HUDR):SPRING71-185
DREXLER, R. TO SMITHEREENS.
  S. BLACKBURN, 440:19MAR72-5
  A. BROYARD, 441:21FEB72-25
  S. KEMPTON, 441:27FEB72-5
  M. WOOD, 453:10AUG72-14
DREYFUS, H.L. WHAT COMPUTERS CAN'T DO.
  M. GARDNER, 440:23JAN72-12
DREYFUS, J., GENERAL ED. TYPE SPECIMEN
FACSIMILES II.
  617(TLS):25AUG72-1004
DRIEBERG, T. INDIRA GANDHI.
  617(TLS):1SEP72-1029
DRIMMER, M., ED. BLACK HISTORY.
  N. WEYL, 396(MODA):SPRING71-217
DRISCOLL, P. THE WILBY CONSPIRACY.
  O.L. BAILEY, 561(SATR):30SEP72-80
  N. CALLENDAR, 441:12NOV72-66
  C. LEHMANN-HAUPT, 441:24OCT72-45
  442(NY):14OCT72-184
DRIVER, C.J. DEATH OF FATHERS.
  D.A.N. JONES, 362:16MAR72-348
  617(TLS):10MAR72-265

DRÖGEMÜLLER, H-P. SYRAKUS.*
  H.D. WESTLAKE, 123:MAR71-97
DRONKE, P. THE MEDIEVAL LYRIC.
  T.R.H., 131(CL):WINTER71-67
DRONKE, P. POETIC INDIVIDUALITY IN THE
MIDDLE AGES.*
  R.M. WILSON, 402(MLR):APR71-380
DRONKE, U. - SEE "THE POETIC EDDA"
DROSS, F. - SEE BARLACH, E.
VON DROSTE-HÜLSHOFF, A. GEDICHTE. (C.
REINIG, ED)
  T.T. KARST, 221(GQ):NOV70-828
VON DROSTE-HÜLSHOFF, A. DIE JUDENBUCHE.
(H. RÖLLEKE, ED)
  J.M. MC GLATHERY, 301(JEGP):OCT71-731
DROWER, E.S., ED & TRANS. A PAIR OF
NAṢORAEAN COMMENTARIES.
  J.C. GREENFIELD, 318(JAOS):APR-JUN70-
339
DROZ, E. CHEMINS DE L'HÉRÉSIE.
  T. KLEIN, 182:VOL23#6-308
DRUMMOND, C. A DEATH AT THE BAR.
  617(TLS):13OCT72-1235
DRUMOND, C. CONTRIBUIÇÃO DO BORORO A
TOPONÍMIA BRASÍLICA.
  J.A. DABBS, 424:MAR68-57
DRUMMOND, J. FAREWELL PARTY.
  617(TLS):7JAN72-17
DRURY, A. & F. MAROON. COURAGE AND HESI-
TATION.
  E. DREW, 441:9JAN72-3
DRUTMAN, I. - SEE FLANNER, J.
DRYDEN, E.A. MELVILLE'S THEMATICS OF
FORM.
  W. GLICK, 141:WINTER70-79
  R. LEHAN, 445(NCF):DEC69-372
DRYDEN, J. AURENG-ZEBE. (F.M. LINK, ED)
  617(TLS):26MAY72-613
DRYDEN, J. FOUR TRAGEDIES.* FOUR COME-
DIES.* (L.A. BEAURLINE & F. BOWERS,
EDS OF BOTH)
  P.K. ELKIN, 67:NOV71-210
  P. HARTH, 405(MP):MAY70-379
DRYDEN, J. THE WORKS OF JOHN DRYDEN:
PROSE 1668-1691. (S.H. MONK, WITH
A.E.W. MAURER, EDS)
  617(TLS):16JUN72-678
DRYDEN, J. THE WORKS OF JOHN DRYDEN.*
(VOL 3: POEMS 1685-1692.) (E. MINER &
OTHERS, EDS)
  G. MC FADDEN, 481(PQ):JUL70-340
DRYDEN, J. THE WORKS OF JOHN DRYDEN.*
(VOL 10) (M.E. NOVAK & G.R. GUFFEY,
EDS)
  J.R. CLARK, 568(SCN):WINTER71-74
DUANE, A. BLOOD MOTHER.
  M. LEVIN, 441:26NOV72-38
DUBASHINSKIJ, I.A. VILJAM SHEKSPIR.
  A. GLASSE, 570(SQ):WINTER68-97
DUBÉ, J-C. CLAUDE-THOMAS DUPUY, INTEN-
DANT DE LA NOUVELLE-FRANCE, 1678-1738.
  J-C. BONENFANT, 627(UTQ):JUL70-402
DUBE, W-D. THE EXPRESSIONISTS.
  617(TLS):22DEC72-1550
DUBERMAN, M. BLACK MOUNTAIN.
  E.Z. FRIEDENBERG, 453:16NOV72-35
  J. JEROME, 561(SATR):21OCT72-70
  C. LEHMANN-HAUPT, 441:7NOV72-37
  H. LEIBOWITZ, 441:29OCT72-37
DUBERMAN, M. THE UNCOMPLETED PAST.
  42(AR):WINTER69/70-589
DUBLER, A-M. DIE KLOSTERHERRSCHAFT HER-
METSCHWIL VON DEN ANFÄNGEN BIS 1798.
  G. ZIMMERMANN, 182:VOL23#8-446
DUBOIS, J. GRAMMAIRE STRUCTURALE DU
FRANÇAIS: NOM ET PRONOM.* GRAMMAIRE
STRUCTURALE DU FRANÇAIS: LE VERBE.
  R.W. NEWMAN, 207(FR):FEB70-545

DUBOIS, M.M. LA LITTÉRATURE ANGLAISE DU
MOYEN AGE, 500-1500.
D.S. BREWER, 179(ES):FEB70-59
DU BOIS, S.G. HIS DAY IS MARCHING ON.
H.W. CRUSE & C. GIPSON, 453:30NOV72-
22
DU BOIS, W.E.B. THE SEVENTH SON. (J.
LESTER, ED)
H.W. CRUSE & C. GIPSON, 453:30NOV72-
22
DUBOS, R. A GOD WITHIN.
W. ARNOLD, 441:24DEC72-10
442(NY):23SEP72-132
DU BOULAY, F.R.H. & C.M. BARRON, EDS.
THE REIGN OF RICHARD II.
617(TLS):7JUL72-778
DUBY, G. L'EUROPE DES CATHÉDRALES,
1140-1280.
P. GUERRE, 98:MAR69-265
DUCASSE, C.J. TRUTH, KNOWLEDGE AND CAUS-
ATION.
P.H. HARE, 484(PPR):JUN70-619
DUCASSE, I. - SEE UNDER COMTE DE LAUTRÉA-
MONT
DUCHAC, R. LA JEUNESSE DE TOKYO.
R.J. SMITH, 293(JAST):FEB70-446
"RAYMOND DUCHAMP-VILLON."
A. ELSEN, 90:AUG69-523
DUCHÊNE, F. THE CASE OF THE HELMETED
AIRMAN.
617(TLS):15SEP72-1048
DUCHÊNE, R. MME. DE SÉVIGNÉ.
A. LEVI, 208(FS):JAN71-76
DUCHROW, U. CHRISTENHEIT UND WELTVERANT-
WORTUNG.
F.F. BRUCE, 182:VOL23#9-465
DUCKETT, E. MEDIEVAL PORTRAITS FROM EAST
AND WEST.
V. CRONIN, 440:16APR72-6
DUCKWORTH, A.M. THE IMPROVEMENT OF THE
ESTATE.
617(TLS):14APR72-412
DUCKWORTH, G.E. VERGIL AND CLASSICAL
HEXAMETER POETRY.
G.P. GOOLD, 124:SEP70-26
E.J. KENNEY, 123:JUN71-200
W.C. SCOTT, 122:OCT71-271
DUCLOS, J. ANARCHISTES D'HIER ET D'AU-
JOURD'HUI.
J.A. GREEN, 207(FR):MAR70-719
DUCREY, P. LE TRAITEMENT DES PRISONNIERS
DE GUERRE DANS LA GRÈCE ANTIQUE DES
ORIGINES À LA CONQUÊTE ROMAINE.*
P. GAUTHIER, 555:VOL44FASC1-116
M. OSTWALD, 24:JUL71-484
DUCROT, N. - SEE "ANDRÉ KERTÉSZ"
DUDEK, L. COLLECTED POETRY.
M. DAGG, 198:SUMMER72-111
F.W. WATT, 99:JAN-FEB72-82
DUDLEY, D.R., ED & TRANS. URBS ROMA.*
D.E. STRONG, 90:JAN69-37
DUDLEY, D.R., ED. VIRGIL.*
M.L. CLARKE, 123:DEC70-335
DUDLEY, D.R. THE WORLD OF TACITUS.*
B. BALDWIN, 121(CJ):OCT-NOV70-87
D. HENRY, 122:APR71-118
DUDLEY, D.R. & D.M. LANG, EDS. THE
PENGUIN COMPANION TO LITERATURE: CLAS-
SICAL AND BYZANTINE AND ORIENTAL AND
AFRICAN.
R. PLANT, 441:5NOV72-31
617(TLS):7JUL72-780
DUERDEN, D. & C. PIETERSE, EDS. AFRICAN
WRITERS TALKING.
617(TLS):29DEC72-1573
DUFF, D. VICTORIA AND ALBERT.
P. QUENNELL, 441:26NOV72-5

DUFFY, J. A HISTORY OF PUBLIC HEALTH IN
NEW YORK CITY, 1625-1866.
J.H. CASSEDY, 656(WMQ):JUL70-505
DUFFY, M. THE EROTIC WORLD OF FAERY.
617(TLS):10NOV72-1370
DUFOUR, P. PICASSO, 1950-1968.
639(VQR):WINTER70-XXV
DUFOURNET, J. LA DESTRUCTION DES MYTHES
DANS LES MÉMOIRES DE PH. DE COMMYNES.
H.F. WILLIAMS, 593:FALL71-304
DUFRENNE, M. ESTHÉTIQUE ET PHILOSOPHIE.
G. GILLAN, 484(PPR):SEP69-154
DUFRENNE, M. POUR L'HOMME.
C.A. KELBLEY, 258:SEP69-460
DUGAN, A. COLLECTED POEMS.*
T. HARRISON, 364:APR/MAY71-163
B. QUINN, 491:FEB72-301
DUGGAN, A. KNIGHT WITH ARMOUR. THE
LADY FOR RANSOM.
617(TLS):31MAR72-352
DUGGAN, M.A., E.F. MC CARTAN & M.R.
IRWIN, EDS. THE COMPUTER UTILITY.
A. BOOKSTEIN, 356:JUL71-258
DUGMORE, R. PUTTENHAM UNDER THE HOG'S
BACK.
617(TLS):24NOV72-1441
DUHAMEL, R. LE ROMAN DES BONAPARTE.
J-C. BONENFANT, 627(UTQ):JUL70-408
DUHEM, P. TO SAVE THE PHENOMENA.
R. NIALL & D. MARTIN, 483:OCT70-344
DUHNKE, H. DIE KPD VON 1933 BIS 1945.
617(TLS):2JUN72-636
DUKE, M.H. FREUD.
617(TLS):21APR72-457
DUKES, P. THE EMERGENCE OF THE SUPER-
POWERS.
J.M. KITCH, 575(SEER):JAN71-158
DUKORE, B.F. - SEE SHAW, G.B.
DULANEY, P.S. THE ARCHITECTURE OF HIS-
TORIC RICHMOND.
J. MAASS, 576:OCT69-231
DULLES, A., ED. GREAT SPY STORIES FROM
FICTION.
J. WALT, 136:SPRING70-144
DULLES, F.R. AMERICAN POLICY TOWARD
COMMUNIST CHINA.
R. STEEL, 440:9APR72-1
DULONG, M. - SEE "THE TRINITY COLLEGE
APOCALYPSE"
DUMAS, A. DIETRICH BONHOEFFER.
W. KOCH, 182:VOL23#11/12-592
DUMAS, A. LES TROIS MOUSQUETAIRES. LE
COMTE DE MONTE CRISTO. (R.D. DE SALES,
ED OF BOTH)
L.D. NEWMAN, 207(FR):DEC69-378
"DUMBARTON OAKS PAPERS, NO. 25."
617(TLS):15SEP72-1071
DUMÉRY, H. FAITH AND REFLECTION.* (L.
DUPRÉ, ED)
142:FALL71-490
DUMÉZIL, G. HEUR ET MALHEUR DU GUER-
RIER.
A. ERNOUT, 555:VOL44FASC2-363
F. VIAN, 555:VOL44FASC2-295
DUMÉZIL, G. IDÉES ROMAINES.
A. ERNOUT, 555:VOL44FASC2-362
DUMONT, L. RELIGION, POLITICS AND
HISTORY IN INDIA.
617(TLS):22SEP72-1119
DUMONT, R. STEFAN ZWEIG ET LA FRANCE.
K-A. HORST, 52:BAND4HEFT2-212
DUMUR, G., ED. HISTOIRE DES SPECTACLES.
R. COHN, 397(MD):SEP67-217
DUNBAR, J. J.M. BARRIE.*
B. BENSTOCK, 659:WINTER72-116
DUNBAR, W.F. THE MICHIGAN RECORD IN
HIGHER EDUCATION.
Q.M. WILSON, 377:MAR71-52

DUNCAN, H.D. CULTURE AND DEMOCRACY.
D. DE NEVI, 186(ETC.):MAR69-86
DUNCAN, J.S. NOT A ONE-WAY STREET.
D. MYERS, 99:JUN72-36
DUNCAN, N.W. 79TH ARMOURED DIVISION.
617(TLS):25AUG72-1006
DUNCAN, R. BENDING THE BOW.*
H. ZINNES, 502(PRS):FALL69-317
DUNCAN, R. DERIVATIONS.
T. BLACKBURN, 493:SPRING70-85
DUNCAN, R. TRIBUNALS.
H. CARRUTH, 249(HUDR):SUMMER71-332
DUNCAN, R. - SEE GANDHI, M.
VAN DEN DUNGEN, P.H.M. THE PUNJAB TRA-
DITION.
617(TLS):3NOV72-1349
DUNLAP, W. HISTORY OF THE RISE AND PRO-
GRESS OF THE ARTS OF DESIGN IN THE
UNITED STATES.
G.A. PERRET, 58:APR70-14
DUNLOP, D.M. ARAB CIVILIZATION TO A.D.
1500.
617(TLS):4FEB72-130
DUNLOP, J.E., ED. LATIN PASTORALS.
H.G. EDINGER, 124:DEC70-132
DUNN, C.M. - SEE RAMUS, P.
DUNN, D. THE HAPPIER LIFE.
617(TLS):9JUN72-651
DUNN, D. THE MAKING OF NO, NO, NANETTE.
441:21MAY72-29
DUNN, J. MODERN REVOLUTIONS.
A. RYAN, 362:16MAR72-346
617(TLS):28APR72-464
DUNN, J. THE POLITICAL THOUGHT OF JOHN
LOCKE.
N.S. FIERING, 656(WMQ):APR70-312
P.M.S. HACKER, 393(MIND):JAN70-150
J.J. JENKINS, 483:JUL70-244
D.O. THOMAS, 518:JAN70-30
639(VQR):WINTER70-XXIV
DUNNETT, A.M., ED. ALISTAIR MACLEAN IN-
TRODUCES SCOTLAND.
561(SATR):70CT72-103
DUNNING, J.H. & E.V. MORGAN, EDS. AN
ECONOMIC STUDY OF THE CITY OF LONDON.
617(TLS):20OCT72-1264
DUNNING, T.P. & A.J. BLISS - SEE "THE
WANDERER"
LORD DUNSANY. THE CURSE OF THE WISE
WOMAN. MY TALKS WITH DEAN SPANLEY.
S. HEANEY, 362:28SEP72-408
617(TLS):9JUN72-647
DUNSEATH, T.K. SPENSER'S ALLEGORY OF
JUSTICE IN BOOK FIVE OF "THE FAERIE
QUEENE."*
A.C. HAMILTON, 149:JUN71-163
W.J.B. OWEN, 551(RENQ):AUTUMN70-323
DUPEE, F.W. & G. STADE - SEE CUMMINGS,
E.E.
DUPEYRON-MARCHESSOU, H. WILLIAM CARLOS
WILLIAMS ET LE RENOUVEAU DU LYRISME.
C. BENSON, 27(AL):MAY71-302
DUPIN, J. L'EMBRASURE.
617(TLS):11FEB72-146
DUPRÉ, C. THE CHILD OF JULIAN FLYNN.
D.A.N. JONES, 362:8JUN72-768
DUPRÉ, L. - SEE DUMÉRY, H.
DUPRIEZ, B. L'ÉTUDE DES STYLES.
M. DAVIES, 402(MLR):JUL71-652
DUQUESNE, J. A CHURCH WITHOUT PRIESTS?
E.A.R., 543:SEP69-128
DURÁN, M. GENIO Y FIGURA DE AMADO NERVO.
J. GOETZINGER, 238:MAR70-161
DURÁN, M. PROGRAMMED SPANISH DICTIONARY.
L.A. SHARPE, 399(MLJ):JAN70-63
DURANT, G.M. BRITAIN, ROME'S MOST
NORTHERLY PROVINCE.
P. SALWAY, 123:DEC70-377

DURANT, W. & A. ROUSSEAU AND REVOLUTION.
J.F. COSTANZO, 613:SPRING69-145
MADAME DE DURAS. OLIVIER, OU LE SECRET.
(D. VIRIEUX, ED)
617(TLS):7JUL72-784
DURAS, M. DESTROY...
I. WEDDE, 364:OCT/NOV71-149
DURAS, M. L'AMOUR.
617(TLS):14APR72-409
DURBIN, P.R. LOGIC AND SCIENTIFIC IN-
QUIRY.
T.D.Z., 543:DEC69-344
VON DÜRCKHEIM, K. THE WAY OF TRANSFOR-
MATION.
617(TLS):17MAR72-317
DURDIN, T., J. RESTON & S. TOPPING. THE
NEW YORK TIMES REPORT FROM RED CHINA.
(F. CHING, ED)
J.K. FAIRBANK, 453:24FEB72-3
S.R. SCHRAM, 441:7MAY72-2
DÜRER, A. THE LITTLE PASSION.
617(TLS):4FEB72-124
DURHAM, M. THE MAN WHO LOVED CAT DANC-
ING.
C. LEHMANN-HAUPT, 441:15AUG72-37
M. LEVIN, 441:30JUL72-23
617(TLS):10NOV72-1375
DÜRING, I., ED. NATURPHILOSOPHIE BEI
ARISTOTELES UND THEOPHRAST.
P.M. HUBY, 123:JUN71-229
DURKHEIM, E. EMILE DURKHEIM: SELECTED
WRITINGS. (A. GIDDENS, ED & TRANS)
617(TLS):28JUL72-876
DURLING, R.J. A CATALOGUE OF SIXTEENTH
CENTURY PRINTED BOOKS IN THE NATIONAL
LIBRARY OF MEDICINE.
F.N.L. POYNTER, 354:JUN69-168
DUROCHE, L.L. ASPECTS OF CRITICISM.*
H. KNUST, 149:MAR71-94
DURR, R.A. POETIC VISION AND THE PSYCHE-
DELIC EXPERIENCE.*
A.L. CLEMENTS, 301(JEGP):JUL71-564
D. HUBBLE, 402(MLR):JUL71-651
E. KRIEGER, 400(MLN):DEC70-939
676(YR):AUTUMN70-VI
DURRANT, G. WILLIAM WORDSWORTH.*
B.D. CHEADLE, 180(ESA):MAR71-129
R.E.C. HOUGHTON, 541(RES):AUG70-368
K.K., 191(ELN):SEP70(SUPP)-48
L.J. SWINGLE, 102(CANL):AUTUMN71-90
DURRANT, G. WORDSWORTH AND THE GREAT
SYSTEM.*
A.J. HARTLEY, 150(DR):WINTER70/71-565
J. STILLINGER, 301(JEGP):JAN71-166
G. WOODCOCK, 102(CANL):SUMMER71-67
DURRELL, G. BIRDS, BEASTS, AND RELA-
TIVES.
639(VQR):WINTER70-XX
DURRELL, G. CATCH ME A COLOBUS.
441:10CT72-38
561(SATR):70CT72-103
617(TLS):1DEC72-1466
DURRELL, L. NUMQUAM.*
F.P.W. MC DOWELL, 659:SUMMER72-361
DÜRRENMATT, F. KOMÖDIEN III. PORTRÄT
EINES PLANETEN. DER STURZ. PLAY
STRINDBERG.
617(TLS):27OCT72-1285
DURRY, M., ED. LUCAIN.
O.C. PHILLIPS, JR., 124:MAR71-240
DURSO, J. YANKEE STADIUM.
R. KAHN, 441:3DEC72-44
DURZAK, M. HERMANN BROCH.*
J. MC CORMICK, 221(GQ):MAR70-296
DURZAK, M. DER DEUTSCHE ROMAN DER GEGEN-
WART.
617(TLS):24MAR72-341

DURZAK, M. DER JUNGE STEFAN GEORGE.*
A. CLOSS, 402(MLR):JAN71-230
DUSSART-DEBÈFVE, S. DIE SPRACHE DER
PREDIGTEN JOHANNES TAULERS NACH DER
WIENER HANDSCHRIFT NR. 2744.
C.E. REED, 350:SEP71-714
DUSSEL, E. LES ÉVÊQUES HISPANO-AMÉRI-
CAINS, DÉFENSEURS ET ÉVANGÉLISATEURS
DE L'INDIEN, 1504 À 1620.
J. SPECKER, 182:VOL23#4-140
DUTT, N.K. ORIGIN AND GROWTH OF CASTE
IN INDIA.
O.M. LYNCH, 293(JAST):FEB70-503
DUTTON, B. LA "VIDA DE SAN MILLÁN DE LA
COGOLLA" DE GONZALO DE BERCEO.
O.T. MYERS, 240(HR):APR70-211
DUTTON, B., L.P. HARVEY & R.M. WALKER,
COMPS. CASSELL'S NEW COMPACT SPANISH-
ENGLISH, ENGLISH-SPANISH DICTIONARY.
H.H. CARTER, 238:SEP70-590
DUTTON, T.E. SALMON AND SEA TROUT FISH-
ING.
617(TLS):1SEP72-1034
DUTU, A. COORDINATE ALE CULTURII
ROMÂNEŞTI ÎN SECOLUL XVIII (1700-1821).
K. HITCHINS, 32:JUN71-417
V. NEMOIANU, 104:SUMMER71-292
DUTU, A. EXPLORARI IN ISTORIA LITERA-
TURII ROMANE.
S. FISCHER-GALATI, 400(MLN):DEC70-938
DUUS, P. FEUDALISM IN JAPAN.
C.J. KILEY, 293(JAST):AUG70-940
DUUS, P. PARTY RIVALRY AND POLITICAL
CHANGE IN TAISHŌ JAPAN.*
N.R. BENNETT, 302:JUL69-278
A. IRIYE, 244(HJAS):VOL29-305
A.E. TIEDEMANN, 293(JAST):NOV69-170
DUVAL, J. CAHIERS.
J. BOREL, 98:MAR69-280
DUVIOLS, P. LA LUTTE CONTRE LES RELIG-
IONS AUTOCHTONES DANS LE PÉROU COLON-
IAL.
617(TLS):18AUG72-972
DÜWEL, K. RUNENKUNDE.*
W.L. WARDALE & S.H. PALSSON, 220
(GL&L):JUL71-380
VAN DUYN, R. MESSAGE OF A WISE KABOUTER.
617(TLS):19MAY72-585
DVINOV, B. OT LEGAL'NOSTI K PODPOL'YU
(1921-1922).
B.C. KIRKHAM, 587:APR69-556
DVONČ, L. BIBLIOGRAFIA SLOVENSKEJ
JAZYKOVEDY ZA ROKY 1961-1965.
W. BROWNE, 574(SEEJ):WINTER71-526
DVORÁK, M. IDEALISM AND NATURALISM IN
GOTHIC ART.
J. BECKWITH, 39:SEP69-267
DVORNIK, F. BYZANTINE MISSIONS AMONG THE
SLAVS.*
G.P. MAJESKA, 32:DEC71-876
DWIGHT, T. TRAVELS IN NEW ENGLAND AND
NEW YORK. (B.M. SOLOMON, ED)
I.B. HOLLEY, JR., 579(SAQ):WINTER71-
115
L. HOWARD, 656(WMQ):JUL70-487
T.E. JOHNSTON, JR., 432(NEQ):JUN70-
344
DWYER, D. & D. SMITH. AN INTRODUCTION TO
WEST AFRICAN PIDGIN ENGLISH.
R.B. LE PAGE, 315(JAL):VOL7PT3-220
DYCE, A. THE REMINISCENCES OF ALEXANDER
DYCE. (R.J. SCHRADER, ED)
617(TLS):15SEP72-1070
DYCK, H.L. WEIMAR GERMANY AND SOVIET
RUSSIA, 1926-1933.
H.W. HELD, 497(POLR):WINTER68-106
DYCK, J. TICHT-KUNST.
H-J. LANGE, 52:BAND4HEFT2-207

DYCK, J.W. NIETZSCHE.
G.E. CONDOYANNIS, 564:SPRING69-75
DYE, L. BLOWOUT AT PLATFORM A.
G. MARINE, 441:9JAN72-18
DYEN, I. A LEXICOSTATISTICAL CLASSIFICA-
TION OF THE AUSTRONESIAN LANGUAGES.
A. HEALEY, 353:SEP69-111
DYKEMAN, W. THE FAR FAMILY.
R. DRAKE, 219(GAR):SPRING69-114
DYMENT, C. COLLECTED POEMS.*
L. CLARK, 493:WINTER70/71-370
DYNAMIUS & FAUSTUS DE RIEZ. DINAMII,
"VITA SANCTI MAXIMI EPISCOPI REIENSIS,"
ET FAVSTI REIENSIS, "SERMO DE SANCTO
MAXIMO EPISCOPO ET ABBATE." (S. GEN-
NARO, ED)
J. ANDRÉ, 555:VOL44FASC1-163
DYNNIK, A. A.I. KUPRIN.
L.G. LEIGHTON, 574(SEEJ):SUMMER71-226
A.M. SHANE, 32:SEP71-705
DYSON, A.E. BETWEEN TWO WORLDS.
J. CAREY, 362:1JUN72-725
617(TLS):4FEB72-123
DYSON, A.E., ED. DICKENS.
E. ROSENBERG, 155:SEP69-187
DYSON, A.E., ED. DICKENS: "BLEAK HOUSE."
T. BLOUNT, 155:JAN70-57
DYSON, A.E. THE INIMITABLE DICKENS.
A.B., 155:SEP70-244
DZIEWANOWSKI, M.K. JOSEPH PIŁSUDSKI.*
L. BLIT, 575(SEER):APR71-311
J. ROTHSCHILD, 104:SPRING71-135
P.S. WANDYCZ, 550(RUSR):JUL70-344

EAMES, E.R. BERTRAND RUSSELL'S THEORY
OF KNOWLEDGE.
N. GRIFFIN, 393(MIND):JUL70-466
A. PHILLIPS, 518:JAN70-5
EARL, L. RISK.
G. ROPER, 627(UTQ):JUL70-343
EARLE, P. THE LIFE AND TIMES OF HENRY V.
617(TLS):14JUL72-799
EARLEY, T. THE SAD MOUNTAIN.
W.H. PRITCHARD, 491:DEC71-159
"EARLY AMERICAN FURNITURE-MAKING HAND-
BOOK."
B. GLADSTONE, 441:3DEC72-99
EARNEST, E. EXPATRIATES AND PATRIOTS.
R.E. KNOLL, 502(PRS):SUMMER69-230
EASON, E.A. - SEE LOPE DE VEGA
EASSON, A. - SEE DICKENS, C.
EAST, R.M. STORIES OF OLD ADAMAWA.
A.H.M. KIRK-GREENE, 69:JUL69-319
EASTLAKE, W. THE BAMBOO BED.*
639(VQR):SPRING70-XLI
EASTMAN, L.E. THRONE AND MANDARIN.
J.J. GERSON, 302:JAN69-126
EASTWOOD, J. HENRY IN A SILVER FRAME.
N. CALLENDAR, 441:9JUL72-30
442(NY):2SEP72-71
617(TLS):28APR72-500
EATON, C.B. THE NAMING.
K.B. HARDER, 424:MAR68-64
EATON, L.K. TWO CHICAGO ARCHITECTS AND
THEIR CLIENTS.
639(VQR):SPRING70-LXXI
EAVES, T.C.D. & B.D. KIMPEL. SAMUEL
RICHARDSON.*
E. MOERS, 453:10FEB72-27
EAYRS, J. DIPLOMACY AND ITS DISCONTENTS.
J.L. GRANATSTEIN, 99:SEP72-16
EBEL, R.E. COMMUNIST TRADE IN OIL AND
GAS.
M. BORNSTEIN, 550(RUSR):OCT70-477
R. CAMPBELL, 32:JUN71-437

EBELING, D.G. WORT UND GLAUBE. (VOL 2)
  G. PHILIPS, 182:VOL23#1/2-17
EBER, D., ED. PITSEOLAK.
  G. SWINTON, 99:MAY72-65
EBERHART, M.G. TWO LITTLE RICH GIRLS.
  N. CALLENDAR, 441:23JAN72-28
  H. FRANKEL, 561(SATR):26FEB72-71
  T. LASK, 441:1JAN72-17
EBERHART, R. SHIFTS OF BEING.*
  R.H.W. DILLARD, 340(KR):1969/3-425
EBERSOLE, A.E., ED. CINCO CUENTISTAS
  CONTEMPORÁNEOS.
  C.W. BUTLER, 238:MAY70-353
EBERSOLE, F.B. THINGS WE KNOW.
  G.M., 477:SPRING69-289
ECCLES, M., ED. THE MACRO PLAYS.
  S.J. KAHRL, 589:JAN71-144
ECKARDT, A.R. ELDER AND YOUNGER BROTH-
  ERS.
  M.H., 477:SUMMER69-404
ECKARDT, L. LOVE APPLES.
  T.L. WEPPLER, 99:JUL-AUG72-46
ECKAUS, R.S. & K.S. PARIKH. PLANNING FOR
  GROWTH.
  E. MUELLER, 293(JAST):MAY70-665
ECKERT, W.P. ERASMUS VON ROTTERDAM.
  (VOL 2)
  H. MEYLAN, 182:VOL23#3-65
ECKSCHMITT, W. DIE KONTROVERSE UM LINEAR
  B.
  A.M. DAVIES, 123:DEC71-431
ECKSTEIN, A., W. GALENSON & T-C. LIU,
  EDS. ECONOMIC TRENDS IN COMMUNIST
  CHINA.*
  A. DONNITHORNE, 293(JAST):NOV69-150
ECKSTEIN, F. ANATHĒMATA.
  A.E. RAUBITSCHEK, 182:VOL23#6-292
ECKSTEIN, J. THE PLATONIC METHOD.*
  N. GULLEY, 123:MAR71-127
ECO, U. LE FORME DEL CONTENUTO.
  617(TLS):8DEC72-1510
"ECONOMIC DEVELOPMENTS IN COUNTRIES OF
  EASTERN EUROPE."
  C. MARFELS, 104:WINTER71-588
"AN ECONOMIC PROFILE OF MAINLAND CHINA."
  R.M. FIELD, 293(JAST):NOV69-157
EDDINS, D. YEATS.
  617(TLS):17MAR72-311
EDDIS, W. LETTERS FROM AMERICA. (A.C.
  LAND, ED)
  D.W. JORDAN, 656(WMQ):JUL70-508
EDEL, E. & OTHERS. DAS SONNENHEILIGTUM
  DES KÖNIGS USERKAF. (VOL 2)
  T.G.H. JAMES, 182:VOL23#4-176
EDEL, L. HENRY JAMES.* (VOL 4: THE
  TREACHEROUS YEARS: 1895-1901.)
  H. FRIEDL, 72:BAND208HEFT4/6-408
EDEL, L. HENRY JAMES. (VOL 5: THE
  MASTER 1901-1916.)
  J.W. ALDRIDGE, 561(SATR):12FEB72-65
  N. BLIVEN, 442(NY):29APR72-137
  J. EPSTEIN, 440:6FEB72-1
  H. KRAMER, 441:6FEB72-1
  C. LEHMANN-HAUPT, 441:14FEB72-31
  P. RAHV, 453:10FEB72-18
  F. WYNDHAM, 362:17AUG72-213
  617(TLS):18AUG72-957
EDELMAN, M. DISRAELI IN LOVE.
  D.A.N. JONES, 362:6JUL72-22
  M. LEVIN, 441:9JUL72-28
  617(TLS):7JUL72-765
EDEN, D. BRIDE BY CANDLELIGHT.
  H. FRANKEL, 561(SATR):26FEB72-71
EDEN, M. THE GILT-EDGED TRAITOR.
  N. CALLENDAR, 441:25JUN72-30

EDER, W. DAS VORSULLANISCHE REPETUNDEN-
  VERFAHREN.
  E.S. GRUEN, 24:APR71-372
  S.I. OOST, 122:APR71-140
EDGAR, F. HAUSA READINGS, SELECTIONS
  FROM EDGAR'S "TATSUNIYOYI." (N. SKIN-
  NER, ED)
  C. GOUFFÉ, 315(JAL):VOL8PT1-64
EDGAR, K. END AND THE BEGINNING.
  M. LEVIN, 441:19NOV72-62
EDGERTON, F. THE BEGINNINGS OF INDIAN
  PHILOSOPHY.
  W.H. MAURER, 485(PE&W):JUL68-229
EDGERTON, M.F., JR., ED. SIGHT AND
  SOUND.
  E. HOCKING, 207(FR):FEB70-537
  J.M. TOLMAN, 238:MAY70-350
  G.M. TORKELSON, 399(MLJ):APR70-278
EDGERTON, W.B. - SEE LESKOV, N.
EDGEWORTH, M. MARIA EDGEWORTH: LETTERS
  FROM ENGLAND 1813-1844.* (C. COLVIN,
  ED)
  617(TLS):14JAN72-39
EDGLEY, R. REASON IN THEORY AND PRAC-
  TICE.
  D. POLE, 483:OCT70-333
  K. WARD, 518:OCT70-3
EDIE, J.M. & OTHERS, EDS. RUSSIAN
  PHILOSOPHY.*
  E. KAMENKA, 587:JAN69-401
EDINGER, H.G. - SEE CICERO
"LES ÉDITIONS DE CORRESPONDANCES."
  C.P. COURTNEY, 208(FS):APR71-247
EDKINS, A. & D. HARRIS, EDS. THE POETRY
  OF LUIS CERNUDA.
  617(TLS):7JUL72-769
EDMONSON, M.S. - SEE "THE BOOK OF COUN-
  SEL"
EDSALL, N.C. THE ANTI-POOR LAW MOVEMENT
  1834-44.
  617(TLS):31MAR72-367
EDSMAN, C-M., ED. STUDIES IN SHAMANISM.
  E. HABERLAND, 182:VOL23#3-122
EDSON, J.S. ORGAN-PRELUDES.
  W. EMERY, 415:JUL70-713
EDSTRÖM, V. & P-A. HENRICSON, EDS.
  NOVELLANALYSER.
  E. SELLIN, 563(SS):AUTUMN71-448
EDWARDES, M. EAST-WEST PASSAGE.
  H. LOMAS, 364:JUN/JUL71-139
EDWARDES, M. GLORIOUS SAHIBS.
  A.J. GREENBERGER, 293(JAST):MAY70-718
EDWARDS, A. FLAWED WORDS AND STUBBORN
  SOUNDS.
  V. THOMSON, 453:31AUG72-19
EDWARDS, C.D. CONRAD RICHTER'S OHIO
  TRILOGY.
  G.H. ORIANS, 27(AL):NOV71-475
EDWARDS, D.L. LEADERS OF THE CHURCH OF
  ENGLAND 1828-1944.
  617(TLS):28JAN72-106
EDWARDS, D.L. RELIGION AND CHANGE.
  C.P.S., 543:DEC69-344
EDWARDS, D.L. WHAT IS REAL IN CHRIST-
  IANITY?
  617(TLS):13OCT72-1234
EDWARDS, F. THE MARVELLOUS CHANCE.
  A. CRAWFORD, 325:OCT69-589
EDWARDS, G. - SEE CALDERÓN DE LA BARCA,
  P.
EDWARDS, I., ED. A HUMANIST VIEW.
  G.W. LEEPER, 381:VOL29#4-530
EDWARDS, J. LAS MÁSCARAS.
  270:VOL20#3-61
EDWARDS, J. THE WORKS OF JONATHAN
  EDWARDS. (VOL 3) (C.A. HOLBROOK, ED)
  N.S. GRABO, 27(AL):MAY71-286
EDWARDS, L.F. - SEE NENADOVIĆ, M.

89

EDWARDS, M. A STAGE IN OUR PAST.
 R. DAVIES, 627(UTQ):JUL69-402
EDWARDS, M.G. MANY-COLOURED GLASS.
 J. SMITH, 493:SPRING70-89
EDWARDS, M.H. HAZARDOUS TO YOUR HEALTH.
 M.G. MICHAELSON, 441:9JUL72-5
EDWARDS, O.D. - SEE RYAN, D.
EDWARDS, P., ED-IN-CHIEF. ENCYCLOPEDIA
 OF PHILOSOPHY.*
 F.C. COPLESTON, 543:DEC69-301
 A. DONAGAN, 482(PHR):JAN70-83
 S. KÖRNER, 536:DEC70-189
 L. LINSKY, 185:JUL70-322
EDWARDS, P. SHAKESPEARE AND THE CONFINES
 OF ART.*
 W.C. FERGUSON, 529(QQ):SPRING70-131
 S.G. PUTT, 175:SPRING69-30
EDWARDS, P. & H. PÁLSSON - SEE "ARROW-
 ODD: A MEDIEVAL NOVEL"
EDWARDS, R.D. A NEW HISTORY OF IRELAND.
 617(TLS):11AUG72-949
EDWARDS, R.S. & R.D.V. ROBERTS. STATUS,
 PRODUCTIVITY AND PAY.
 617(TLS):28JAN72-109
EDWARDS, S. GEORGE SAND.
 A. BALAKIAN, 561(SATR):29JUL72-61
 J. WEIGHTMAN, 440:28MAY72-7
EDWARDS, T. THE CANONS OF CRITICISM AND
 GLOSSARY.
 617(TLS):18FEB72-178
EDWARDS, T.J. REGIMENTAL BADGES.
 617(TLS):21APR72-457
EDWARDS, T.R. IMAGINATION AND POWER.
 M. DICKSTEIN, 441:16JAN72-6
 R. FULLER, 362:9MAR72-316
VAN EEGHEN, I.H. DE AMSTERDAMSE BOEK-
 HANDEL 1680-1725. (VOLS 3&4)
 H. CARTER, 354:MAR69-68
EELLS, G. HEDDA AND LOUELLA.
 N. EPHRON, 441:23APR72-7
 L. SMITH, 440:2APR72-4
EFFINGER, G.A. WHAT ENTROPY MEANS TO ME.
 T. STURGEON, 441:3SEP72-20
EFRON, E. THE NEWS TWISTERS.
 N.W. POLSBY, 231:MAR72-88
EGAN, L. MALICIOUS MISCHIEF.
 N. CALLENDAR, 441:6FEB72-38
 H. FRANKEL, 561(SATR):29JAN72-73
EGAN, L. PAPER CHASE.
 N. CALLENDAR, 441:27AUG72-14
EGAN, M., ED. IBSEN: THE CRITICAL HERI-
 TAGE.
 617(TLS):26MAY72-601
EGAN, M. HENRY JAMES: THE IBSEN YEARS.
 617(TLS):18AUG72-957
EGBERT, V.W. THE MEDIEVAL ARTIST AT
 WORK.*
 J. BECKWITH, 39:SEP69-267
 M.S. FRINTA, 54:SEP69-292
EGERTON, C. - SEE "THE GOLDEN LOTUS (CHIN
 P'ING MEI)"
EGGERS, R. COLDITZ.
 617(TLS):1DEC72-1469
EGGLESTON, W. WHILE I STILL REMEMBER.*
 W.H. KESTERTON, 627(UTQ):JUL69-398
EGLETON, C. THE JUDAS MANDATE.
 N. CALLENDAR, 441:16APR72-29
EGLINTON, J.Z. GREEK LOVE.
 617(TLS):25FEB72-224
EHLE, J. THE JOURNEY OF AUGUST KING.
 P. ADAMS, 61:JAN72-97
EHLERS, B. EINE VORPLATONISCHE DEUTUNG
 DES SOKRATISCHEN EROS.*
 J.S. MORRISON, 123:JUN71-292
EHLERS, W.W. UNTERSUCHUNGEN ZUR HAND-
 SCHRIFTLICHEN ÜBERLIEFERUNG DER ARGO-
 NAUTIKA DES C. VALERIUS FLACCUS.
 F. LASSERRE, 182:VOL23#11/12-627

EHMER, H.K., ED. VISUELLE KOMMUNIKATION.
 617(TLS):16JUN72-691
EHRARD, J. MONTESQUIEU CRITIQUE D'ART.
 A. BROOKNER, 90:JUN69-397
EHRARD, J. - SEE MONTESQUIEU
EHRENBERG, V. FROM SOLON TO SOCRATES.*
 C.D. HAMILTON, 122:JUL71-216
 R.J. HOPPER, 123:DEC71-412
EHRENBERG, V. THE GREEK STATE. (2ND ED)
 P.A. BRUNT, 123:JUN71-297
EHRENFELD, D. CONSERVING LIFE ON EARTH.
 S.B. SHEPARD, 441:19NOV72-52
EHRENKREUTZ, A.S. - SEE GRENVILLE, H.
EHRENPREIS, A.H. - SEE SMITH, C.
EHRENPREIS, I. SWIFT.* (VOL 2)
 P.K. ELKIN, 67:MAY71-102
 P. HARTH, 405(MP):FEB70-273
EHRLE, F. GESAMMELTE AUFSÄTZE ZUR ENG-
 LISCHEN SCHOLASTIK. (F. PELSTER, ED)
 N. HARING, 382(MAE):1971/2-213
EHRMAN, J. THE YOUNGER PITT.
 W.B. HAMILTON, 579(SAQ):WINTER71-116
 639(VQR):SUMMER70-CV
EHRMAN, M. THE MEANINGS OF THE MODALS
 IN PRESENT-DAY AMERICAN ENGLISH.
 R. HUDDLESTON, 361:VOL23#2-165
EHRSAM, T.G., COMP. A BIBLIOGRAPHY OF
 JOSEPH CONRAD.
 E.W. SAID, 637(VS):JUN70-429
EIBL-EIBESFELDT, I. LOVE AND HATE.
 S. MARCUS, 441:23APR72-2
 617(TLS):3MAR72-238
VON EICHENDORFF, J. GEDICHTE. (M.L.
 KASCHNITZ, ED)
 T.T. KARST, 221(GQ):NOV70-828
VON EICHENDORFF, J. - SEE UNDER VON AR-
 NIM, L.A.
EICHHORN, W. HELDENSAGEN AUS DEM UNTEREN
 YANGTSE-TAL (WU-YÜEH CH'UN-CH'IU).
 E.G. PULLEYBLANK, 182:VOL23#6-274
EICHLER, W. JAN VAN RUUSBROECS "BRU-
 LOCHT" IN OBERDEUTSCHER ÜBERLIEFERUNG.*
 H.B. WILLSON, 402(MLR):APR71-443
EICHNER, H. - SEE SCHLEGEL, F.
EICHSTÄDT, H. ŽUKOVSKIJ ALS ÜBERSETZER.
 K.H. OBER, 574(SEEJ):WINTER71-501
 W. SCHAMSCHULA, 32:DEC71-907
EIDELBERG, P. THE PHILOSOPHY OF THE
 AMERICAN CONSTITUTION.
 J.A. SCHWANDT, 613:WINTER69-626
EIFLER, G. DIE ETHISCHEN ANSCHAUUNGEN
 IN "FREIDANKS BESCHEIDENHEIT."
 D.H. GREEN, 402(MLR):APR71-440
EIGELDINGER, J-J., ED. CHOPIN VU PAR
 SES ÉLÈVES.
 H.F., 410(M&L):APR71-180
EIGELDINGER, M. LA MYTHOLOGIE SOLAIRE
 DANS L'OEUVRE DE RACINE.
 R.C. KNIGHT, 208(FS):JAN71-74
EIKHENBAUM, B.M. O. HENRY AND THE THEORY
 OF THE SHORT STORY.
 G.M. ERAMIAN, 104:SUMMER71-274
EILHART VON OBERG. TRISTRANT. (H. BUSS-
 MANN, ED)
 D.H. GREEN, 402(MLR):JUL71-701
EINAUDI, M. THE EARLY ROUSSEAU.
 M.B. ELLIS, 546(RR):OCT70-225
 B.C. FINK, 399(MLJ):OCT70-445
EINBOND, B.L. SAMUEL JOHNSON'S ALLEGORY.
 E.A. BLOOM, 677:VOL2-287
EIS, H. ZUR REZEPTION DER KANONISCHEN
 VERWANDTSCHAFTSBÄUME JOHANNES ANDREAES.
 W. SCHMITT, 597(SN):VOL41#1-169
EISELE, A. ALMOST TO THE PRESIDENCY.
 L.W. KOENIG, 561(SATR):3JUN72-62
EISELEY, L. THE INVISIBLE PYRAMID.*
 H. CARRUTH, 249(HUDR):SPRING71-153
 D. TERRILL, 396(MODA):SUMMER71-317

EISENHOWER, D.D. DEAR GENERAL.* (J.P. HOBBS, ED)
617(TLS):7JAN72-11

EISENHOWER, D.D. THE PAPERS OF DWIGHT DAVID EISENHOWER: THE WAR YEARS.* (A.D. CHANDLER, JR. & S.E. AMBROSE, EDS)
E.P. HAMILTON, 432(NEQ):DEC70-677

EISENSTADT, S.N., R. BAR YOSEF & C. ADLER, EDS. INTEGRATION AND DEVELOPMENT IN ISRAEL.
617(TLS):19MAY72-580

EISINGER, C.E. FICTION OF THE FORTIES.
R.L. DRAIN, 179(ES):OCT70-467

EISNER, S. THE TRISTAN LEGEND.
E.M. KENNEDY, 382(MAE):1971/3-284
J. MITCHELL, 301(JEGP):JAN71-146
W.E. RICHMOND, 292(JAF):JUL-SEP70-360

EISSLER, K.R. TALENT AND GENIUS.
617(TLS):28APR72-499

EITNER, L., ED. NEOCLASSICISM AND ROMANTICISM, 1750-1850.
J. MOFFITT, 127:SPRING71-324

EIZENHÖFER, L. & H. KNAUS, EDS. DIE LITURGISCHEN HANDSCHRIFTEN DER HESSISCHEN LANDES- UND HOCHSCHULBIBLIOTHEK DARMSTADT.
R. RUDOLF, 182:VOL23#8-385

VAN EK, J.A. FOUR COMPLEMENTARY STRUCTURES OF PREDICATION IN CONTEMPORARY BRITISH ENGLISH.*
B. CARSTENSEN, 38:BAND87HEFT3/4-434
G.N. LEECH, 597(SN):VOL41#1-230

EKELÖF, G. SELECTED POEMS.
J. SYMONS, 364:FEB/MAR72-160

EKELUND, E. FINLANDS SVENSKA LITTERATUR 2.
G.C. SCHOOLFIELD, 563(SS):SPRING71-213

EKLUND, T. - SEE STRINDBERG, A.

EKMANN, B. GESELLSCHAFT UND GEWISSEN.
J. FUEGI, 301(JEGP):APR71-342
B.A. WOODS, 222(GR):JAN70-61

EKNER, R. GUNNAR EKELÖF - EN BIBLIOGRAFI.
L. SJÖBERG, 563(SS):SPRING71-210

EKSCHMITT, W. DIE KONTROVERSE UM LINEAR B.
F. BADER, 555:VOL44FASC2-299
E.L. BENNETT, JR., 124:NOV70-88

ELBERT, J. DRUNK IN MADRID.
M. LEVIN, 441:1OCT72-42

ELBERT, J. GETTING RID OF RICHARD.
M. LEVIN, 441:23APR72-41

ELBERT, S.H. & T. MONBERG. FROM THE TWO CANOES.
B.F. KIRTLEY, 650(WF):APR68-132

ELDER, M.J. NATHANIEL HAWTHORNE.
M. BELL, 27(AL):MAY71-287

ELDERSHAW, M.B. TOMORROW AND TOMORROW.
R. BURNS, 381:VOL29#3-320

ELEMA, H. IMAGINÄRES ZENTRUM.
U. WEISSTEIN, 221(GQ):MAR70-246

ELERT, C-C. LJUD OCH ORD I SVENSKAN.
K. NILSSON, 563(SS):SUMMER71-293

ELEVITCH, M.D. GRIPS.
M. LEVIN, 441:20AUG72-26

ELGAR, E. A FUTURE FOR ENGLISH MUSIC. (P.M. YOUNG, ED)
A.E.F. DICKINSON, 607:SUMMER68-41

ELIADE, M. MYTHS, DREAMS AND MYSTERIES.
G.M., 477:SUMMER69-423

ELIADE, M. THE QUEST.
F.J.N., 543:MAR70-555

ELIADE, M. TWO TALES OF THE OCCULT.
M. MUDRICK, 249(HUDR):SPRING71-185

ELIADE, M. & M. NICULESCU. FANTASTIC TALES.
C. BLAYLOCK, 574(SEEJ):SUMMER71-236
G. CAMPBELL, 575(SEER):JAN71-167

ELIAS, C. FLEECING THE LAMBS.*
G. WHEELER, 440:6FEB72-7

ELÍAS, J.T. - SEE UNDER TORRAS ELÍAS, J.

ELIOT, A. A CONCISE HISTORY OF GREECE.
617(TLS):17NOV72-1405

ELIOT, T.S. ELIZABETHAN DRAMATISTS.
R. GILL, 179(ES):OCT70-455

ELIOT, T.S. THE WASTE LAND.* (V. ELIOT, ED)
F. KERMODE, 61:JAN72-89
J. KORG, 659:AUTUMN72-535
G. STEINER, 442(NY):22APR72-134

ELIOVSON, S. GARDENING THE JAPANESE WAY.
617(TLS):5MAY72-524

ELISSEEFF, N. LA DESCRIPTION DE DAMAS D'IBN 'ASĀKIR.
H.K. SHERWANI, 273(IC):JUL69-239

ELIZONDO, S. EL HIPOGEO SECRETO.
G.R. MC MURRAY, 238:MAY70-330

ELKIN, S. THE DICK GIBSON SHOW.*
W.H. PRITCHARD, 249(HUDR):SUMMER71-357

ELLEDGE, W.P. BYRON AND THE DYNAMICS OF METAPHOR.*
E.E.B., 191(ELN):SEP69(SUPP)-28
B. BEATTY, 447(N&Q):MAY70-197
J.J. DUFFY, 399(MLJ):JAN70-41
R.F. GLECKNER, 141:WINTER70-70
J.D. JUMP, 541(RES):FEB70-112
J.J. MC GANN, 405(MP):NOV69-203

ELLENIUS, A. KAROLINSKA BILDIDÉER.
J. MONTAGU, 90:AUG69-524

ELLIN, S. MIRROR, MIRROR, ON THE WALL.
O.L. BAILEY, 561(SATR):26AUG72-62
N. CALLENDAR, 441:24SEP72-39

ELLING, R., ED. NATIONAL HEALTH CARE.
R. BAZELL, 453:2NOV72-38

ELLIOT, G. TWENTIETH CENTURY BOOK OF THE DEAD.
617(TLS):29SEP72-1157

ELLIOT, R. MYTHE ET LÉGENDE DANS LE THÉÂTRE DE RACINE.
H.T. BARNWELL, 402(MLR):OCT71-898

ELLIOT, R.S.P. & J. HICKIE. ULSTER.*
617(TLS):17MAR72-297

ELLIOTT, A. - SEE EURIPIDES

ELLIOTT, C. - SEE HENRYSON, R.

ELLIOTT, D.W. LISTEN TO THE SILENCE.
639(VQR):WINTER70-VIII

ELLIOTT, G.P. CONVERSIONS.*
D.J. GORDON, 441:6FEB72-28
L. GRAVER, 561(SATR):15JAN72-43

ELLIOTT, G.P. MURIEL.
B. BERNSTEIN, 561(SATR):8APR72-74
R. SALE, 453:4MAY72-3
G. WOLFF, 441:16APR72-5

ELLIOTT, J. ANGELS FALLING.
F.P.W. MC DOWELL, 659:SUMMER72-361
B. WRIGHT, 619(TC):VOL177#1042-57

ELLIOTT, J. THE KINDLING.
F.P.W. MC DOWELL, 659:SUMMER72-361

ELLIOTT, J. PRIVATE LIFE.
J.G. FARRELL, 362:2NOV72-611
617(TLS):3NOV72-1305

ELLIOTT, J. A STATE OF PEACE.*
F.P.W. MC DOWELL, 659:SUMMER72-361

ELLIOTT, P. THE MAKING OF A TELEVISION SERIES.
G.W. GOLDIE, 362:19OCT72-517
617(TLS):24NOV72-1425

ELLIOTT, P. THE SOCIOLOGY OF THE PROFESSIONS.
617(TLS):1DEC72-1456

ELLIOTT, R.C. THE SHAPE OF UTOPIA.*
676(YR):WINTER71-XXX
ELLIOTT, S.L. EDENS LOST.
639(VQR):WINTER70-VIII
ELLIOTT, S.L. THE MAN WHO GOT AWAY.
S. BLACKBURN, 441:15OCT72-2
C. LEHMANN-HAUPT, 441:18OCT72-49
ELLIOTT, W.R. MONEMVASIA.
617(TLS):3MAR72-245
ELLIS, C.H. THE LORE OF THE TRAIN.
617(TLS):16JUN72-697
ELLIS, F.H., ED. POEMS ON AFFAIRS OF
STATE.* (VOL 6)
C.J. RAWSON, 677:VOL2-274
ELLIS, J.M. KLEIST'S "PRINZ FRIEDRICH
VON HOMBURG."
W. HOFFMEISTER, 406:SUMMER71-163
C.E. PASSAGE, 301(JEGP):JAN71-120
ELLIS, J.M. SCHILLER'S "KALLIASBRIEFE"
AND THE STUDY OF HIS AESTHETIC THEORY.
H.B. NISBET, 402(MLR):APR71-457
ELLIS, M. THIS MYSTERIOUS RIVER.
A. HISLOP, 440:21MAY72-5
ELLIS, M.B. ROUSSEAU'S VENETIAN STORY.
V.W. TOPAZIO, 593:SPRING71-84
ELLIS, P.B. A HISTORY OF THE IRISH WORK-
ING CLASS.
617(TLS):14APR72-416
ELLIS, R.A., S.K. THOMSON & J. WEISS.
NIL: A STUDY OF UNFILLED INTERLIBRARY
LOAN REQUESTS IN THE NYSILL SYSTEM.
A. MC ANALLY, 356:OCT71-331
ELLIS, R.E. THE JEFFERSONIAN CRISIS.
617(TLS):7JAN72-11
ELLIS-FERMOR, U. THE IRISH DRAMATIC
MOVEMENT.
W. TYDEMAN, 148:SPRING70-92
ELLISON, H., ED. AGAIN, DANGEROUS
VISIONS.
T. STURGEON, 441:3SEP72-20
ELLISON, J.W. THE SUMMER AFTER THE WAR.
L.J. DAVIS, 441:19NOV72-60
ELLISON, R.Y. & A. RAFFANEL. PROFIL DE
LA FRANCE NOUVELLE.
R. MERKER, 399(MLJ):NOV70-551
ELLMAN, M. SOVIET PLANNING TODAY.
617(TLS):11FEB72-164
ELLMANN, R. EMINENT DOMAIN.
H. SERGEANT, 175:SPRING69-33
ELLMANN, R. ULYSSES ON THE LIFFEY.
C.G. ANDERSON, 440:21MAY72-6
B. DE MOTT, 561(SATR):13MAY72-67
J. GROSS, 441:14MAY72-5
S. HEANEY, 362:2MAR72-281
C. LEHMANN-HAUPT, 441:17MAY72-49
617(TLS):17MAR72-310
ELLMANN, R., ED. OSCAR WILDE.
J.B. GORDON, 340(KR):1970/1-152
ELLMANN, R. - SEE JOYCE, J.
ELLMANN, R. - SEE WILDE, O.
ELLRICH, R.J. ROUSSEAU AND HIS READER.
M.L. PERKINS, 399(MLJ):NOV70-539
ELLSBERG, D. PAPERS ON THE WAR.
M. KEMPTON, 441:23JUL72-1
J. MIRSKY, 561(SATR):19AUG72-54
442(NY):5AUG72-83
ELLUL, J. AUTOPSY OF REVOLUTION.
R. SCHICKEL, 231:APR72-96
ELLUL, J. LE VOULOIR ET LE FAIRE.
V-A. DEMANT, 182:VOL23#7-338
ELMAN, R., ED. THE GREAT AMERICAN SHOOT-
ING PRINTS.
E. WEEKS, 61:DEC72-143
442(NY):9DEC72-180
ELMAN, R.M. AN EDUCATION IN BLOOD.*
J.M. MORSE, 249(HUDR):AUTUMN71-535

ELMAN, R.M. FREDI & SHIRL & THE KIDS.
P. WEST, 441:25JUN72-4
442(NY):5AUG72-82
ELRINGTON, C.R. & N.M. HERBERT, EDS.
THE VICTORIA HISTORY OF THE COUNTIES
OF ENGLAND: A HISTORY OF THE COUNTY OF
GLOUCESTER. (VOL 10)
617(TLS):30JUN72-752
ELSCHEK, O. & D. STOCKMANN, EDS. METHO-
DEN DER KLASSIFIKATION VON VOLKSLIED-
WEISEN.
B. NETTL, 187:MAY72-288
ELSCHEK, O., E. STOCKMANN & I. MAČÁK -
SEE "MUSIKETHNOLOGISCHE JAHRESBIBLIO-
GRAPHIE EUROPAS"
ELTON, A. - SEE KLINGENDER, F.D.
ELTON, G.R. "THE BODY OF THE WHOLE
REALM."
J.C. RAINBOLT, 656(WMQ):APR70-334
ELTON, G.R. POLICY AND POLICE.
617(TLS):17MAR72-296
ELTON, W.R. KING LEAR AND THE GODS.
E.A. LANGHANS, 570(SQ):WINTER69-99
ELTON, W.R., ED. SRO: SHAKESPEAREAN
RESEARCH OPPORTUNITIES.
H.W. DONNER, 597(SN):VOL41#2-431
ELVIN, L. ORGAN BLOWING.*
P. WILLIAMS, 415:SEP71-864
ELWERT, W.T. ITALIENISCHE METRIK.
J. MOESTRUP, 462(OL):VOL24#3-225
R. STEFANINI, 545(RPH):NOV69-259
ELWERT, W.T. LA POESIA LIRICA ITALIANA
DEL SEICENTO.
G. COSTA, 545(RPH):FEB70-369
ELWERT, W.T. TRAITÉ DE VERSIFICATION
FRANÇAISE DES ORIGINES À NOS JOURS.
F. DELOFFRE, 545(RPH):AUG69-135
ELY, D. WALKING DAVIS.
A. BROYARD, 441:6NOV72-43
442(NY):18NOV72-245
EMBERTON, W. LOVE LOYALTY.
617(TLS):10NOV72-1377
EMBLER, W. METAPHOR AND MEANING.*
R.J. REILLY, 613:SUMMER68-298
EMECHETA, B. IN THE DITCH.
617(TLS):11AUG72-936
EMERICK, K.F. WAR RESISTERS CANADA.
453:4MAY72-40
EMERSON, E.H. ENGLISH PURITANISM FROM
JOHN HOOPER TO JOHN MILTON.
J. WEBBER, 191(ELN):DEC69-141
EMERSON, E.H. CAPTAIN JOHN SMITH.
R. BAIN, 578:SPRING72-107
EMERSON, R.W. ESSAYS AND JOURNALS. (L.
MUMFORD, ED)
S.O.H., 543:DEC69-345
EMERSON, R.W. THE JOURNALS AND MISCEL-
LANEOUS NOTEBOOKS OF RALPH WALDO
EMERSON.* (VOL 7) (A.W. PLUMSTEAD &
H. HAYFORD, EDS)
L. BUELL, 432(NEQ):MAR70-145
E.J. ROSE, 150(DR):SPRING70-133
639(VQR):WINTER70-XIV
EMERSON, R.W. THE JOURNALS AND MISCEL-
LANEOUS NOTEBOOKS OF RALPH WALDO
EMERSON. (VOL 9) (R.H. ORTH & A.R.
FERGUSON, EDS)
617(TLS):17NOV72-1403
EMERSON, T.I. THE SYSTEM OF FREEDOM OF
EXPRESSION.
C.H. PRITCHETT, 639(VQR):AUTUMN70-650
EMERY, C. THE WORLD OF DYLAN THOMAS.*
P. DICKINSON, 364:OCT/NOV71-136
EMERY, F.B. THE VIOLIN CONCERTO.
R. ANDERSON, 415:AUG70-808
EMILIANI, A. LA PINACOTECA NAZIONALE DI
BOLOGNA.
D. POSNER, 90:MAY69-308

EMMERICK, R.E., ED & TRANS. THE BOOK
OF ZAMBASTA.
A. WAYMAN, 293(JAST):NOV69-151
EMMERSON, J.K. THE JAPANESE DILEMMA.
H.S. STOKES, 441:9APR72-6
EMMONS, M. DEEP LIKE THE RIVERS.
C.Y. RICH, 582(SFQ):DEC69-376
EMMONS, T. THE RUSSIAN LANDED GENTRY
AND THE PEASANT EMANCIPATION OF 1861.*
J.S. CURTISS, 550(RUSR):APR70-222
EMPSON, W. & D. PIRIE - SEE COLERIDGE,
S.T.
EMRICH, D. FOLKLORE ON THE AMERICAN
LAND.
P. ADAMS, 61:APR72-128
T. LASK, 441:25MAR72-33
"EN AVANT."
E.H. BOURQUE, 207(FR):MAR70-708
"ENCICLOPEDIA FILOSOFICA." (2ND ED)
F.C. COPLESTON, 483:OCT70-348
M. DEL PRA, 548(RCSF):OCT-DEC69-459
ENDACOTT, G.W. WOODWORKING AND FURNITURE
MAKING FOR THE HOME.
B. GLADSTONE, 441:3DEC72-99
ENDO, S. THE SEA AND POISON.
617(TLS):14JUL72-793
ENGBERG, H. BRECHT PÅ FYN.
B. EKMANN, 462(OL):VOL23#3-251
ENGEL, F. DIE MECKLENBURGISCHEN KAISER-
BEDEREGISTER VON 1496.
P. BRIGHTWELL, 182:VOL23#7-377
ENGEL, H. MUSIK IN THÜRINGEN.
S. DEAS, 182:VOL23#9-486
ENGEL, J.E. HANDBUCH DER DEUTSCHEN LIT-
ERATURGESCHICHTE.* (VOL 4)
M.L. BAEUMER, 406:SPRING71-66
J-U. FECHNER, 402(MLR):JAN71-212
ENGEL, L. WORDS WITH MUSIC.
E. WELTY, 441:28MAY72-7
442(NY):3JUN72-112
ENGEL, M. THE HONEYMAN FESTIVAL.
A. GOTTLIEB, 441:10CT72-40
ENGEL, M. NO CLOUDS OF GLORY.
G. ROPER, 627(UTQ):JUL69-358
ENGELS-MARX. LA SACRA FAMIGLIA. (A.
ZANARDO, ED)
C. CESA, 548(RCSF):JUL-SEP68-356
ENGLAND, M.W. GARRICK'S JUBILEE.
L. FOX, 570(SQ):WINTER68-99
ENGLEKIRK, J.E. & OTHERS, EDS. AN
ANTHOLOGY OF SPANISH AMERICAN LITERA-
TURE. (2ND ED)
R.J. CALLAN, 238:MAY70-352
ENGLEKIRK, J.E. & M.M. RAMOS. LA NARRA-
TIVA URUGUAYA.
B.G. CARTER, 240(HR):JUL70-341
ENGLER, R. LEXIQUE DE LA TERMINOLOGIE
SAUSSURIENNE.
K. CONNORS, 545(RPH):NOV69-201
E.F.K. KOERNER, 350:JUN71-447
ENGLER, R. - SEE DE SAUSSURE, F.
ENGLERT, S. ISLAND AT THE CENTRE OF THE
WORLD.
617(TLS):29DEC72-1586
ENGUÍDANOS, M. - SEE BORGES, J.L.
ENKVIST, N.E. BRITISH AND AMERICAN LIT-
ERARY LETTERS IN SCANDINAVIAN PUBLIC
COLLECTIONS.
P.M. MITCHELL, 462(OL):VOL23#4-331
ENKVIST, N.E. GEOFFREY CHAUCER.
H. PILCH, 38:BAND87HEFT3/4-451
ENNIS, R.H. LOGIC IN TEACHING.
N.G.E. HARRIS, 479(PHQ):OCT70-407
ENNIUS. QVINTO ENNIO, "I FRAMMENTI DEGLI
ANNALI." (R. ARGENIO, ED & TRANS)
J. ANDRÉ, 555:VOL44FASC2-343
ENQUIST, P.O. SEKONDEN.
617(TLS):2JUN72-622

ENRIGHT, D.J. DAUGHTERS OF EARTH.
P.N. FURBANK, 362:21SEP72-374
617(TLS):9JUN72-651
ENRIGHT, D.J. MAN IS AN ONION.
617(TLS):1DEC72-1454
ENRIGHT, D.J. THE TYPEWRITER REVOLUTION.
S. MILLER, 441:13FEB72-6
ENROTH, R.M., E.E. ERICSON, JR. & C.B.
PETERS. THE JESUS PEOPLE.
D. POLING, 561(SATR):22JUL72-57
VON ENSE, R.V. - SEE UNDER VARNHAGEN VON
ENSE, R.
ENSLIN, T. FORMS. (PT 1)
G. BURNS, 584(SWR):SPRING71-207
ENTENZA, P. NO HAY ACERAS.
E.L. RIVERS, 400(MLN):MAR70-321
K. SCHWARTZ, 238:MAY70-346
"ENTERING THE PATH OF ENLIGHTENMENT."
(M.L. MATICS, TRANS)
617(TLS):26MAY72-608
"ENTRETIENS SUR L'ANTIQUITÉ CLASSIQUE."
(VOL 15: LUCAIN.) (O. REVERDIN, ED)
F. LASSERRE, 182:VOL23#17/18-812
EOFF, S.H. & N. RAMÍREZ. COMPOSICIÓN-
CONVERSACIÓN.
R.W. HATTON, 238:MAR70-177
EPICURUS. ÉPICURE. (P. BOYANCÉ, ED &
TRANS)
C. MUGLER, 555:VOL44FASC2-327
EPINEY-BURGARD, G. GÉRARD GROTE (1340-
84) ET LES DÉBUTS DE LA DÉVOTION MOD-
ERNE.
J-M. AUBERT, 182:VOL23#17/18-782
EPPERLEIN, S. HERRSCHAFT UND VOLK IM
KAROLINGISCHEN IMPERIUM.
K.F. DREW, 589:JAN71-148
EPPERT, F. DEUTSCHE WORTSCHATZÜBUNGEN.
H. BROCKHAUS, 221(GQ):JAN70-133
EPPSTEIN, J. HAS THE CATHOLIC CHURCH
GONE MAD?*
441:13FEB72-16
EPSTEIN, E. THE ORDEAL OF STEPHEN
DEDALUS.
M. SHECHNER, 329(JJQ):WINTER71-280
EPSTEIN, J. THE GREAT CONSPIRACY TRIAL.
617(TLS):18FEB72-186
EPSTEIN, M., ED & TRANS. TALES OF SENDE-
BAR.*
J.R. JONES, 582(SFQ):MAR69-64
EPTON, N. VICTORIA AND HER DAUGHTERS.*
442(NY):29JAN72-95
ERASMUS. THE COLLOQUIES OF ERASMUS.
(C.R. THOMPSON, TRANS)
D.F.S. THOMSON, 627(UTQ):JAN70-181
ERASMUS. DILUTIO EORUM QUAE IODOCUS
CLITHOVEUS SCRIPSIT ADVERSUS DECLAMA-
TIONEM DES. ERASMI ROTERODAMI SUASORIAM
MATRIMONII. (É.V. TELLE, ED)
E. SURTZ, 481(PQ):APR70-269
ERASMUS. ERASMUS VON ROTTERDAM: "EIN
KLAG DES FRYDENS." (A.M. HAAS & U.
HERZOG, EDS)
R.H. BAINTON, 182:VOL23#6-310
ERASMUS. NATIONALE ERASMUS-HERDENKING.
A. NOVOTNY, 182:VOL23#11/12-577
ERBSE, H., ED. SCHOLIA GRAECA IN HOMERI
ILIADEM.* (VOL 1)
F.M. COMBELLACK, 122:JAN71-43
S. WEST, 123:MAR71-65
ERDMAN, D.V. BLAKE: PROPHET AGAINST
EMPIRE.* (REV)
I.H.C., 191(ELN):SEP70(SUPP)-22
ERDMAN, D.V., ED. A CONCORDANCE TO THE
WRITINGS OF WILLIAM BLAKE.
F.W. BATESON, 354:JUN69-170
G.E. BENTLEY, JR., 627(UTQ):APR70-274
I.H.C., 191(ELN):SEP69(SUPP)-21

ERDMAN, D.V. & E.G. VOGEL, EDS. EVIDENCE
FOR AUTHORSHIP.
  R.W. DENT, 570(SQ):WINTER69-99
  C. SCHAAR, 597(SN):VOL40#1-261
ERDMANN, K. SEVEN HUNDRED YEARS OF ORI-
ENTAL CARPETS. (GERMAN TITLE: SIEBEN-
HUNDERT JAHRE ORIENTTEPPICH.)
  C.G. ELLIS, 57:VOL31#2/3-232
  90:NOV70-774
ERDMANN, K.D. GESCHICHTE, POLITIK UND
PÄDAGOGIK.
  C.E. MC CLELLAND, 182:VOL23#23/24-
  1003
"EREC." (2ND ED) (C.E. PICKFORD, ED)
  G.J. HALLIGAN, 402(MLR):JUL71-684
ERH-MIN, W. - SEE UNDER WANG ERH-MIN
ERICKSON, S.A. LANGUAGE AND BEING.
  J.G. GRAY, 319:JAN72-114
ERIGENA [ERIUGENA], J.S. JEAN SCOT:
"HOMÉLIE SUR LE PROLOGUE DE JEAN.
(É. JEAUNEAU, ED & TRANS)
  P.G. WALSH, 123:DEC71-468
ERIKSEN, S. LOUIS DELANOIS, MENUISIER
EN SIÈGES (1731-1792).
  F.J.B. WATSON, 90:JUL69-463
ERIKSEN, S. THE JAMES DE ROTHSCHILD COL-
LECTION AT WADDESDON MANOR; SÈVRES
PORCELAIN.
  F.J.B. WATSON, 39:JUN69-485
ERIKSON, E.H. GANDHI'S TRUTH.*
  D.A. RUSTOW, 639(VQR):WINTER70-153
ERIUGENA, J.S. - SEE UNDER ERIGENA, J.S.
ERLER, A. AEGIDIUS ALBORNOZ ALS GESETZ-
GEBER DES KIRCHENSTAATES.
  W. ULLMANN, 382(MAE):1971/3-290
ERLICH, V. GOGOL.*
  N.M. KOLB-SELETSKI, 32:JUN71-438
  Y. LOURIA, 104:SUMMER71-261
  A.C. WRIGHT, 529(QQ):AUTUMN70-460
  639(VQR):SPRING70-LXVI
ERLINGER, H.D. SPRACHWISSENSCHAFT UND
SCHULGRAMMATIK.
  E.H. YARRILL, 182:VOL23#13/14-664
ERMOLAEV, H. - SEE GORKY, M.
ERNST, J. DIE ESCHATOLOGISCHEN GEGEN-
SPIELER IN DEN SCHRIFTEN DES NEUEN
TESTAMENTS.
  F.F. BRUCE, 182:VOL23#8-396
ERNST, R. RUFUS KING.
  J.M. BANNER, JR., 656(WMQ):APR70-331
ERNY, P. L'ENFANT ET SON MILIEU EN
AFRIQUE NOIRE.
  617(TLS):22SEP72-1094
ERRINGTON, R.M. THE DAWN OF EMPIRE.
  617(TLS):31MAR72-375
ERRINGTON, R.M. PHILOPOEMEN.*
  J. BRISCOE, 313:VOL60-208
  J.A.O. LARSEN, 487:SPRING70-86
  S.I. OOST, 122:APR71-134
ÉRTAVY-BARÁTH, J.M. - SEE ADY, E.
ERTZ, S. SUMMER'S LEASE.
  M. LEVIN, 441:9JUL72-28
ERVINE, S. BERNARD SHAW.
  C. JAMES, 362:27JUL72-114
  617(TLS):1SEP72-1017
ERWITT, E. PHOTOGRAPHS AND ANTI-PHOTO-
GRAPHS.
  S. SCHWARTZ, 441:3DEC72-16
ESCREET, P.K. INTRODUCTION TO THE ANGLO-
AMERICAN CATALOGUING RULES.
  617(TLS):7JAN72-21
ESHLEMAN, C. ALTARS.
  H. CARRUTH, 441:13FEB72-7
ESHLEMAN, C. CANTALOUPS & SPLENDOR.
INDIANA.*
  R. BROTHERSON, 661:FALL/WINTER69-105

ESHLEMAN, C., ED. A CATERPILLAR ANTHOL-
OGY.
  H. CARRUTH, 441:13FEB72-7
ESKENAZI, G. A THINKING MAN'S GUIDE TO
PRO HOCKEY.
  J. DURSO, 441:3DEC72-40
ESPMARK, K. HARRY MARTINSON ERÖVRAR SITT
SPRÅK.
  W.A. BERENDSOHN, 182:VOL23#10-551
ESSAME, H. THE BATTLE FOR EUROPE 1918.
  441:15OCT72-40
  617(TLS):27OCT72-1294
ESSELBORN, K.G. HOFMANNSTHAL UND DER
ANTIKE MYTHOS.
  E.M. WEBER, 301(JEGP):APR71-347
ESSER, H.P. UNTERSUCHUNGEN ZU GEBET UND
GOTTESVEREHRUNG DER NEUPLATONIKER.
  H.J. BLUMENTHAL, 123:MAR71-130
ESSLIN, M. BERTOLT BRECHT.
  E. SPEIDEL, 447(N&Q):JUN70-238
ESSLIN, M. HAROLD PINTER.
  R. COHN, 397(MD):DEC68-338
  K. TETZELI VON ROSADOR, 72:BAND208
  HEFT1-49
ESTES, W.M. A STREETFUL OF PEOPLE.
  M. LEVIN, 441:16APR72-30
ESTIENNE, H. [H. STEPHANUS] FRANCOFORD-
IENSE EMPORIUM.
  R.A. SAYCE, 354:DEC69-348
ESTRADA, F.L. - SEE UNDER LÓPEZ ESTRADA,
F.
"ESTUDIOS DEDICADOS A JAMES HOMER HER-
RIOTT."
  A. DEYERMOND, 545(RPH):AUG70-147
ETHEREGE, G. THE POEMS OF SIR GEORGE
ETHEREGE. (J. THORPE, ED)
  D.R.M. WILKINSON, 179(ES):DEC69-612
ETIEMBLE, R. LE SONNET DES VOYELLES.
  E.H. RHODES, 207(FR):DEC69-341
ETIENNE, G. LES CHANCES DE L'INDE.
  617(TLS):15SEP72-1066
ÉTIENNE, R. LA VIE QUOTIDIENNE À POMPÉI.
  J-C. DUMONT, 555:VOL44FASC1-167
ETMEKJIAN, J. & R.J. CAEFER. LE FRANÇAIS
COURANT II.
  J. HELLERMANN, 207(FR):OCT69-150
"ÉTUDES D'HISTOIRE LITTÉRAIRE ET DOC-
TRINALE." (4TH SER)
  L. MOSER, 182:VOL23#5-199
"ETUDES LITTÉRAIRES." [FACULTÉ DES
LETTRES DE L'UNIVERSITÉ LAVAL]
  W.T. BANDY, 399(MLJ):APR70-290
"ÉTUDES PHONOLOGIQUES DÉDIÉES À LA
MÉMOIRE DE M. LE PRINCE TRUBETZKOY."
  F. SALTER, 104:WINTER71-567
"ÉTUDES PORTUGAISES ET BRÉSILIENNES."
[FACULTÉ DES LETTRES ET SCIENCES HU-
MAINES DE L'UNIVERSITÉ DE RENNES]
  O. FERNÁNDEZ, 399(MLJ):NOV70-540
"ÉTUDES RABELAISIENNES." (VOL 8)
  D. COLEMAN, 208(FS):JAN71-66
"ETUDES SUR LE CURÉ MESLIER."
  G. BESSE, 542:JUL-DEC69-464
EUCHERII. DE LAUDE EREMI. (S. PRICOCO,
ED)
  P. LANGLOIS, 555:VOL44FASC2-354
EUDES, D. THE KAPETANIOS.* (FRENCH
TITLE: LES KAPETANIOS.)
  617(TLS):10NOV72-1377
"THE EUING COLLECTION OF ENGLISH BROAD-
SIDE BALLADS."
  617(TLS):26MAY72-612
EULER, L. & T. MAYER. THE EULER-MAYER
CORRESPONDENCE (1751-1755). (E.G.
FORBES, ED & TRANS)
  617(TLS):23JUN72-708

EULOGIO DE LA VIRGEN DEL CARMIN, P. SAN
JUAN DE LA CRUZ Y SUS ESCRITOS.
  J.O. VALENCIA, 238:SEP70-570
EURICH, N. SCIENCE IN UTOPIA.
  M.E. PRIOR, 405(MP):NOV69-187
EURIPIDES. EURIPIDE, "ALCESTI." (G.
PADUANO, ED)
  S.A. BARLOW, 123:DEC71-449
EURIPIDES. HELENA. (R. KANNICHT, ED)
  T.V. BUTTREY, 124:DEC70-122
EURIPIDES. MEDEA. (A. ELLIOTT, ED)
  B.F. DICK, 124:DEC70-122
EURIPIDES. NOVA FRAGMENTA EURIPIDEA IN
PAPYRIS REPERTA.* (C. AUSTIN, ED)
  B.E. DONOVAN, 303:VOL90-205
EURIPIDES. ORESTES AND OTHER PLAYS.
(P. VELLACOTT, ED & TRANS)
  617(TLS):21JUL72-853
EURIPIDES. PHAETHON. (J. DIGGLE, ED)
  H. LLOYD-JONES, 123:DEC71-341
"THE EUROPA YEAR BOOK 1972."
  617(TLS):21JUL72-853
EUSTIS, A., ED. SEVENTEENTH-CENTURY
FRENCH LITERATURE, POETRY-THEATER-
NOVEL.
  D.L. RUBIN, 399(MLJ):OCT70-469
  W. WRAGE, 207(FR):DEC69-386
EVANS, A.H. COLLECTED POEMS.
  S.F. MORSE, 385(MQR):FALL72-297
EVANS, A.R., JR., ED. ON FOUR MODERN
HUMANISTS.
  M.W. BLOOMFIELD, 545(RPH):FEB71-506
EVANS, D. TOMMY JOHNSON.
  M. HARRISON, 415:SEP71-864
EVANS, D.E. GAULISH PERSONAL NAMES.*
  E.C. SMITH, 424:SEP68-302
EVANS, E. THE REMINISCENCES OF EDMUND
EVANS. (R. MC LEAN, ED)
  K. ROBERTS, 90:OCT70-703
  G.W., 503:SPRING68-42
EVANS, E.C. PHYSIOGNOMICS IN THE ANCIENT
WORLD.*
  P. DE LACY, 24:JUL71-508
EVANS, G.E. THE FARM AND THE VILLAGE.
  H. GLASSIE, 292(JAF):JUL-SEP70-371
EVANS, G.E. & D. THOMSON. THE LEAPING
HARE.
  S. HEANEY, 362:21DEC72-869
EVANS, G.N.D. UNCOMMON OBDURATE.
  D.B. LITTLE, 432(NEQ):SEP70-510
  W.S. MAC NUTT, 656(WMQ):JUL70-515
EVANS, H. EDITING AND DESIGN. (BK 1)
  617(TLS):4FEB72-118
EVANS, J. MONASTIC ICONOGRAPHY IN FRANCE
FROM THE RENAISSANCE TO THE REVOLUTION.
  F. AMES-LEWIS, 89(BJA):SPRING71-210
EVANS, J. SMALL-RIVER FLY FISHING FOR
TROUT AND GRAYLING.
  617(TLS):19MAY72-585
EVANS, J.M. "PARADISE LOST" AND THE
GENESIS TRADITION.*
  G. BULLOUGH, 175:SPRING69-28
EVANS, J.X. - SEE WILLIAMS, R.
EVANS, L. CHESS QUESTIONS ANSWERED.
  617(TLS):4AUG72-926
EVANS, M. SPENSER'S ANATOMY OF HEROISM.
  K. WILLIAMS, 301(JEGP):OCT71-656
EVANS, M.G. THE PHYSICAL PHILOSOPHY OF
ARISTOTLE.*
  J.D.M., 477:SPRING69-289
EVANS, P. THE EARLY TROPE REPERTORY OF
SAINT MARTIAL DE LIMOGES.*
  I.D. BENT, 415:NOV70-1113
EVANS, R., JR. & R.D. NOVAK. NIXON IN
THE WHITE HOUSE.*
  W.A. WILLIAMS, 453:24FEB72-7

EVANS, W. PHOTOGRAPHS. (J. SZARKOWSKI,
ED)
  617(TLS):29DEC72-1589
EVANS, W.M. TO DIE GAME.
  617(TLS):21JUL72-829
EVENSON, N. CHANDIGARH.
  M. BESSET, 576:MAY68-148
EVENSON, N. LE CORBUSIER.
  R.G. HOWES, 363:MAY70-105
EVERITT, A. THE PATTERN OF RURAL DIS-
SENT: THE NINETEENTH CENTURY.
  617(TLS):6OCT72-1205
EVERITT, B. A COLD FRONT.
  617(TLS):14APR72-427
EVERITT, E.B. & R.L. ARMSTRONG. SIX
EARLY PLAYS RELATED TO THE SHAKESPEARE
CANON.
  W.A. ARMSTRONG, 179(ES):DEC70-556
EVERS, H-D., ED. LOOSELY STRUCTURED
SOCIAL SYSTEMS.
  J.N. ANDERSON, 293(JAST):FEB70-417
  C.F. KEYES, 293(JAST):FEB70-415
EVERSON, R.G. SELECTED POEMS 1920/1970.
  W. DICKEY, 249(HUDR):SPRING71-159
  D. FETHERLING, 606(TAMR):#57-80
  R. GUSTAFSON, 102(CANL):SUMMER71-65
  C. MOLESWORTH, 491:MAY72-107
EWALD, K. TERMINOLOGIE EINER FRANZÖ-
SISCHEN GESCHÄFTS- UND KANZLEISPRACHE
VOM 13. BIS 16. JAHRHUNDERT (AUF GRUND
DES "CARTULAIRE DE L'ABBAYE DE FLINES").
  T.D. HEMMING, 208(FS):JAN71-63
EWART, G. THE GAVIN EWART SHOW.
  617(TLS):21APR72-441
EWEN, D. THE WORLD OF TWENTIETH CENTURY
MUSIC.
  A. JACOBS, 415:FEB70-160
EWERT, A. - SEE BÉROUL
EWING, A.C. NON-LINGUISTIC PHILOSOPHY.
  E.J. FURLONG, 393(MIND):JUL70-473
EYRE, F. BRITISH CHILDREN'S BOOKS IN THE
TWENTIETH CENTURY.
  617(TLS):28APR72-473
EYTAN, S., ED. COUNCIL ON THE TEACHING
OF HEBREW. (BULLETIN NO. 1)
  J.B. ZELDIS, 399(MLJ):APR70-285

FABER, T. NEW DANISH ARCHITECTURE.
  J.M.R., 46:JUL69-84
VON FABER DU FAUR, C. GERMAN BAROQUE
LITERATURE.*
  K.F. OTTO, JR., 221(GQ):JAN70-142
FABIAN, J. A CHEMICAL ROMANCE.
  617(TLS):23JUN72-705
FABRE, J.H. THE LIFE OF THE SPIDER.
  H. MOSS, 442(NY):27MAY72-109
FABRE-LUCE, A. L'ANNIVERSAIRE.
  617(TLS):29SEP72-1134
FABRICIUS, F. LEISTUNGSSTÖRUNGEN IM
ARBEITSVERHÄLTNIS.
  P. PADIS, 182:VOL23#13/14-655
FABRICIUS-BJERRE, C. CARL NIELSEN.
  R. LAYTON, 415:JAN70-45
FABUN, D., WITH K. HYLAND & R. CONOVER.
DIMENSIONS OF CHANGE.
  617(TLS):23JUN72-730
FACETTI, G. & A. FLETCHER. IDENTITY
KITS.
  617(TLS):30JUN72-740
FACKENHEIM, E.L. THE RELIGIOUS DIMENSION
IN HEGEL'S THOUGHT.*
  A. BERNDTSON, 484(PPR):SEP69-148
  N. ROTENSTREICH, 328:FALL69-508
FACOS, J. THE SILVER LADY.
  M. LEVIN, 441:23APR72-41

95

FADINGER, V. DIE BEGRÜNDUNG DES PRINZI-
PATS.
S.I. OOST, 122:JUL71-208
M. WOLOCH, 124:JAN71-168
FAGG, W., ED. THE LIVING ARTS OF NI-
GERIA.
617(TLS):16JUN72-694
FAHEY, J. CHARLEY PATTON.
M. HARRISON, 415:FEB71-141
FAHLIN, C. - SEE BENOIT
FAIDIT, U. THE "DONATZ PROENSALS" OF
UC FAIDIT.* (J.H. MARSHALL, ED)
L.T. TOPSFIELD, 208(FS):OCT71-448
FAIN, H. BETWEEN PHILOSOPHY AND HISTORY.
W. SUCHTING, 63:MAY71-120
R.H. WEINGARTNER, 311(JP):20APR72-227
FAIR, C. FROM THE JAWS OF VICTORY.*
617(TLS):24NOV72-1413
FAIR, R. WE CAN'T BREATHE.
G. DAVIS, 441:6FEB72-6
L. FLEISCHER, 561(SATR):19FEB72-74
442(NY):5FEB72-103
FAIRBANK, J.K. CHINA: THE PEOPLE'S MID-
DLE KINGDOM AND THE USA.
O. LATTIMORE, 587:APR68-598
FAIRBANK, J.K., ED. CHINESE THOUGHT AND
INSTITUTIONS.
C-Y. CHENG, 485(PE&W):OCT69-457
FAIRBANK, J.K. THE UNITED STATES AND
CHINA.* (3RD ED)
R. STEEL, 440:9APR72-1
FAIRCHILD, H.N. RELIGIOUS TRENDS IN ENG-
LISH POETRY.* (VOL 6)
F.P.W. MC DOWELL, 481(PQ):APR70-273
FAIRFAX, J. BRITANNIA.
617(TLS):2JUN72-639
FAIRFIELD, J. DAVID JOHNSON PASSED
THROUGH HERE.
D-K. MANO, 441:16APR72-4
FAIRHALL, D. RUSSIA LOOKS TO THE SEA.
617(TLS):31MAR72-358
FAJEN, F. ÜBERLIEFERUNGSGESCHICHTLICHE
UNTERSUCHUNGEN ZU DEN HALIEUTIKA DES
OPPIAN.
J.M. HUNT, 124:DEC70-124
N.G. WILSON, 123:DEC71-450
FAKHRY, M. A HISTORY OF ISLAMIC PHIL-
OSOPHY.*
R.E. ABU SHANAB, 319:APR72-222
FALK, E.H. TYPES OF THEMATIC STRUCTURE.*
G. BRÉE, 397(MD):SEP69-211
J.H. MATTHEWS, 593:SPRING71-90
FALKENSTEIN, L. DER "LATERAN" DER KARO-
LINGISCHEN PFALZ ZU AACHEN.
E. MEUTHEN, 182:VOL23#11/12-622
FALKUS, C. THE LIFE AND TIMES OF CHARLES
II.
617(TLS):12MAY72-536
FALL, T. THE ORDEAL OF RUNNING STANDING.
617(TLS):13OCT72-1235
FALLACI, O. NOTHING, AND SO BE IT.
(BRITISH TITLE: NOTHING AND AMEN.)
M. PARTON, 561(SATR):18MAR72-75
617(TLS):11AUG72-936
FALSAFI, A.N. CHAND MAQALAI TARIKHI-I-WA
ADABI.
273(IC):APR69-163
FAN, I. - SEE UNDER I FAN
FANELLI, G. ARCHITETTURA MODERNA IN
OLANDA.
N.P., 46:APR69-308
FANN, K.T., ED. SYMPOSIUM ON J.L.
AUSTIN.
R.J.B., 543:JUN70-756
A. PHILLIPS, 518:OCT70-5
A.R. WHITE, 479(PHQ):APR70-181

FANN, K.T. WITTGENSTEIN'S CONCEPTION OF
PHILOSOPHY.*
R. BAMBROUGH, 518:OCT70-8
J. BURNHEIM, 63:MAY71-119
FANOUDH-SIEFER, L. LE MYTHE DU NÈGRE ET
DE L'AFRIQUE NOIRE DANS LA LITTÉRATURE
FRANÇAISE (DE 1800 À LA 2E GUERRE MON-
DIALE).
M.S. WHITNEY, 207(FR):FEB70-508
FANTEL, H. JOHANN STRAUSS.
617(TLS):4FEB72-137
AL-FĀRĀBĪ - SEE FILED UNDER A
FARADAY, A. DREAM POWER.
T. ROSZAK, 440:26MAR72-1
617(TLS):24MAR72-340
FARADAY, M. THE SELECTED CORRESPONDENCE
OF MICHAEL FARADAY. (L.P. WILLIAMS,
ED)
617(TLS):3NOV72-1301
FARAGO, L. THE GAME OF THE FOXES.
R. HANSER, 440:16JAN72-12
C. LEHMANN-HAUPT, 441:17JAN72-33
R. LEWIN, 362:8JUN72-767
H.H. RANSOM, 561(SATR):26FEB72-74
A.J.P. TAYLOR, 453:10FEB72-14
H. TREVOR-ROPER, 441:30JAN72-1
442(NY):29JAN72-94
617(TLS):12MAY72-538
FARBER, M. - SEE MELCHERT, N.P.
FARBER, M. - SEE RIEPE, D.
FARDOULIS-LAGRANGE, M. MEMORABILIA.
J. PRUNIER, 98:JUN69-575
FARGA, F. VIOLINS & VIOLINISTS.
M. PETERSON, 470:NOV69-51
FARGEAUD, M. BALZAC ET LA RECHERCHE DE
L'ABSOLU.
C. AFFRON, 207(FR):DEC69-348
C-C., 191(ELN):SEP69(SUPP)-55
FARIS, J.C. NUBA PERSONAL ART.
E.H. GOMBRICH, 453:4MAY72-35
617(TLS):2JUN72-620
FARLEY, J. FIGURE AND FIELD.
N. SULLIVAN, 491:NOV71-107
FARLEY-HILLS, D., ED. ROCHESTER: THE
CRITICAL HERITAGE.
617(TLS):24MAR72-332
FARMAN, C. THE GENERAL STRIKE.
617(TLS):3NOV72-1347
FARMER, F. WILL THERE REALLY BE A
MORNING?
441:20AUG72-20
FARMER, P. A CASTLE OF BONE.
J. HUNTER, 362:29JUN72-874
FARMER, P.J. TARZAN ALIVE.
C. LEHMANN-HAUPT, 441:27APR72-45
FARNEWORTH, E. - SEE MACHIAVELLI, N.
FARR, F. FDR.
617(TLS):3NOV72-1312
FARRELL, K. CONY-CATCHING.*
M. CAVELL, 473(PR):1971/1-117
W.H. PRITCHARD, 249(HUDR):SUMMER71-
357
FARRELL, R.B. THE MAKING OF CANADIAN
FOREIGN POLICY.
P.V. LYON, 529(QQ):AUTUMN70-466
FARREN, M. WATCH OUT KIDS.
617(TLS):22SEP72-1104
FARRER, A. FAITH AND SPECULATION.
R.E. SANTONI, 258:MAR69-146
N. SMART, 479(PHQ):JAN70-93
FARRIER, D. COUNTRY VET.
617(TLS):15SEP72-1071
FARRINGTON, B. SCIENCE IN ANTIQUITY.
C. MUGLER, 555:VOL44FASC2-334
FARRINGTON, F. THE STRANGERS IN 7-A.
N. CALLENDAR, 441:13FEB72-34
FARSON, D. JACK THE RIPPER.
617(TLS):17NOV72-1402

FARSON, D. MARIE LLOYD AND MUSIC HALL.
617(TLS):22DEC72-1566
AL-FARUQI, I.R. CHRISTIAN ETHICS.
M.H., 477:SUMMER69-424
FARWELL, B. QUEEN VICTORIA'S LITTLE
WARS.
N. ANNAN, 453:30NOV72-12
FASSÒ, G. STORIA DELLA FILOSOFIA DEL
DIRITTO. CRISTIANESIMO E SOCIETÀ.
(2ND ED)
A.H. CAMPBELL, 483:APR70-158
FAST, H. THE HESSIAN.
M. LEVIN, 441:10SEP72-41
FAUCHEREAU, S. THÉOPHILE GAUTIER.
617(TLS):29DEC72-1578
FAULK, O.B. THE GERONIMO CAMPAIGN.*
617(TLS):21JUL72-829
FAULKNER, R. & E. ZIEGFELD. ART TODAY.
R.J. CARIOLA, 363:NOV69-27
DU FAUR, C.V. - SEE UNDER VON FABER DU
FAUR, C.
FAURE, E. THE HEART OF THE BATTLE.
617(TLS):8DEC72-1476
FAURE, E. LE ÉLÉMENTS DU RYTHME
POÉTIQUE EN ANGLAIS MODERNE.
T. HAWKES, 402(MLR):OCT71-885
FAUST, C.H. & J. FEINGOLD, EDS. APPROA-
CHES TO EDUCATION FOR CHARACTER.*
S.O.H., 543:DEC69-361
FAUST, I. THE FILE ON STANLEY PATTON
BUCHTA.
639(VQR):AUTUMN70-CXXIX
FAUST, M. DIE ANTIKEN EINWOHNERNAMEN
UND VÖLKERNAMEN AUF -ITANI, -ETANI.
J. ANDRÉ, 555:VOL44FASC1-144
FAVIER, J. LES CONTRIBUABLES PARISIENS
À LA FIN DE LA GUERRE DE CENT ANS.
J.B. HENNEMAN, 589:OCT71-736
FAVRE, A. KIRCHBERGER ET L'ILLUMINISME
DU DIX-HUITIÈME SIÈCLE.
M.J.V., 543:SEP69-129
FAX, E.C. GARVEY.
E. FONER, 561(SATR):1JUL72-52
J.R. WILLIS, 441:20AUG72-5
FAY, S., L. CHESTER & M. LINKLATER. HOAX.
A. FAIRLEY, 362:13JUL72-55
C. LEHMANN-HAUPT, 441:15MAY72-37
T. MEEHAN, 561(SATR):1JUL72-56
J. SEELYE, 441:25JUN72-2
617(TLS):4AUG72-911
FAYER, M.H. BASIC RUSSIAN.* (BK 1) (2ND
ED)
G.M. ERAMIAN, 104:FALL71-421
FAYOLLE, R. SAINTE-BEUVE ET LE XVIIIE
SIÈCLE, OU COMMENT LES RÉVOLUTIONS
ARRIVENT.
617(TLS):16JUN72-682
FAZAN, E.A.C. CINQUE PORTS BATTALION.
617(TLS):7JAN72-22
FEARNLEY, B. CHILD PHOTOGRAPHY.
617(TLS):2JUN72-641
FEATHER, L. THE ENCYCLOPEDIA OF JAZZ IN
THE SIXTIES.
J.E. DUCKWORTH, 650(WF):OCT69-287
FEATHERSTONE, D. MACDONALD OF THE 42ND.
617(TLS):4FEB72-132
FEAVER, G. FROM STATUS TO CONTRACT.
J.R.Y. KING, 325:OCT70-159
FECHNER, J-U. DER ANTIPETRARKISMUS.*
R. HESS, 72:BAND208HEFT4/6-446
FECHNER, J-U., ED. DAS DEUTSCHE SONETT
- DICHTUNGEN, GATTUNGSPOETIK, DOKU-
MENTE.
L. BORNSCHEUER, 406:SPRING71-77
R.K., 221(GQ):JAN70-142
E. STOPP, 402(MLR):APR71-450
FECHNER, J-U. - SEE OPITZ, M.
FECHNER, J-U. - SEE WAGNER, H.L.

FEDER, N. AMERICAN INDIAN ART.*
P. ADAMS, 61:MAR72-110
FEDERMAN, R. DOUBLE OR NOTHING.
R. SCHOLES, 561(SATR):22JAN72-67
R. SUKENICK, 441:10OCT72-40
FEDORENKO, N.P., ED. EKONOMICHESKAIA
SEMIOTIKA.
L. SMOLINSKI, 32:DEC71-903
FÉDOU, R. LE TERRIER DE JEAN JOSSARD,
COSEIGNEUR DE CHÂTILLON-D'AZERGUES,
1430-1463.
J.B. HENNEMAN, 589:JAN71-149
FEELEY, K. FLANNERY O'CONNOR.
P.K. CUNEO, 561(SATR):26FEB72-79
F. SWEENEY, 441:13FEB72-30
FEENSTRA, R., ED. REPERTORIUM BIBLIOGRA-
PHICUM INSTITUTORUM ET SODALITATUM
IURIS HISTORIAE.
P. PADIS, 182:VOL23#11/12-602
FEHÉR, F. & Z. KENYERES - SEE LUKÁCS, G.
FEHLING, D. DIE WIEDERHOLUNGSFIGUREN
UND IHR GEBRAUCH BEI DEN GRIECHEN VOR
GORGIAS.
G. NAGY, 24:OCT71-730
S. USHER, 303:VOL90-231
FEIFER, G. THE GIRL FROM PETROVKA.*
S. BLACKBURN, 440:9APR72-8
J. HENDIN, 441:23APR72-42
L.E. SISSMAN, 442(NY):5AUG72-78
FEIFFER, J. CARNAL KNOWLEDGE.
617(TLS):14JAN72-35
FEIL, E. & R. WETH, EDS. DISKUSSION ZUR
"THEOLOGIE DER REVOLUTION."
J-M. AUBERT, 182:VOL23#3-79
FEIN, A. FREDERICK LAW OLMSTED AND THE
AMERICAN ENVIRONMENTAL TRADITION.
T. LASK, 441:2SEP72-19
FEINBERG, B. - SEE RUSSELL, B.
FEINBERG, B. & R. KASRILS, EDS. DEAR
BERTRAND RUSSELL.
R. DUNSTAN, 619(TC):VOL177#1042-58
FEINBERG, J. DOING AND DESERVING.
V. HAKSAR, 518:OCT71-7
FEINENGER, A. BASIC COLOUR PHOTOGRAPHY.
617(TLS):27OCT72-1297
FEINER, J. & M. LÖHRER, EDS. MYSTERIUM
SALUTIS. (VOLS 1-3)
J-M. AUBERT, 182:VOL23#17/18-783
FEINSTEIN, E. THE AMBERSTONE EXIT.
D.A.N. JONES, 362:10AUG72-184
617(TLS):11AUG72-935
FEINSTEIN, E. THE MAGIC APPLE TREE.
N. RENNIE, 364:AUG/SEP71-120
FEIRING, E. GOD AND THE SEVEN SPIRITS.
J.J. STOUDT, 319:JUL72-379
FEIX, I. & E. SCHLANT. GESPRÄCHE, DIS-
KUSSIONEN, AUFSÄTZE.
R. BOECKLIN, 399(MLJ):MAY70-378
FEKETE, I. TIME ELSEWHERE.
617(TLS):28JAN72-94
FELCZAK, W. UGODA WĘGIERSKO-CHORWACKA
1868 ROKU.
H. WERESZYCKI, 575(SEER):JAN71-157
FELD, E.S., W. SCHUMANN & E. VON NARD-
ROFF. ANFANG UND FORTSCHRITT.
E.K. NEUSE, 221(GQ):JAN70-127
FELDKAMP, P. & F. THE GOOD LIFE...OR
WHAT'S LEFT OF IT.
A. KISSELGOFF, 441:30AUG72-35
R.A. SOKOLOV, 441:3SEP72-16
442(NY):23SEP72-134
FELDMAN, D.M. & W.D. KLINE. SPANISH:
CONTEMPORARY METHODOLOGY.
H.J. FREY, 351(LL):DEC70-269
T.A. SEWARD, 238:SEP70-587
P. STANDISH, 86(BHS):JUL71-255
FELDMAN, H. FROM CRISIS TO CRISIS.
617(TLS):30JUN72-736

FELDMAN, I. MAGIC PAPERS AND OTHER
POEMS.
S. MOORE, 385(MQR):SUMMER72-217
W.H. PRITCHARD, 491:DEC71-159
FELDMAN, J.M. & N. KETAY. NEW YORK ON
$10 A DAY.
C. SIMMONS, 441:4JUN72-7
FELDMAN, S., ED. THE STORY TELLING
STONE.
G.S. NICKERSON, 650(WF):JAN68-66
FELDMAN, S.D. THE MORALITY-PATTERNED
COMEDY OF THE RENAISSANCE.
617(TLS):4FEB72-134
FELLER, R. GESCHICHTE BERNS. (VOL 4)
J.M.J. ROGISTER, 182:VOL23#17/18-823
FELLOWES, E.H. ENGLISH CATHEDRAL MUSIC.*
(REV BY J.A. WESTRUP)
N. TEMPERLEY, 415:JUL70-712
FELLOWES-GORDON, I. THE MAGIC WAR.
441:30APR72-28
FELLOWS, O. & D. GUIRAGOSSIAN, EDS. DID-
EROT STUDIES XII.
R. NIKLAUS, 208(FS):JAN71-88
FELMAN, S. LA "FOLIE" DANS L'OEUVRE
ROMANESQUE DE STENDHAL.
617(TLS):25FEB72-226
FELMINGHAM, M. & R. GRAHAM. RUINS.
617(TLS):21JUL72-853
FELS, A. THE BRITISH PRICES AND INCOMES
BOARD.
617(TLS):2JUN72-638
FELSTEIN, I. SNAKES AND LADDERS.
617(TLS):7JUL72-768
FELSTINER, J. THE LIES OF ART.
N. BALAKIAN, 441:10JUL72-33
FELTON, D., R. GREEN & D. DALTON. MIND-
FUCKERS. (D. FELTON, ED)
J. KANON, 561(SATR):11NOV72-67
FENBY, E. DELIUS.
C. PALMER, 415:OCT71-965
FENG-HAN, L. - SEE UNDER LIU FENG-HAN
FENIK, B. TYPICAL BATTLE SCENES IN THE
"ILIAD."
P. CHANTRAINE, 555:VOL44FASC1-122
FENNELL, J. & D. OBOLENSKY, EDS. A HIS-
TORICAL RUSSIAN READER.*
S.P. HILL, 399(MLJ):OCT70-444
FENNELLY, C. LIFE IN AN OLD NEW ENGLAND
COUNTRY VILLAGE.
L.D. GELLER, 432(NEQ):MAR70-160
FENTON, J. TERMINAL MORAINE.
617(TLS):26MAY72-607
FENWICK, H. THE AULD ALLIANCE.
617(TLS):14APR72-429
FERENCZI, S. SCHRIFTEN ZUR PSYCHOANA-
LYSE. (M. BALINT & J. DUPONT, EDS)
617(TLS):29DEC72-1579
FERGUSON, J. LIBRARIES IN FRANCE.
R.K. GARDNER, 356:OCT71-349
FERGUSON, J. THE RELIGIONS OF THE ROMAN
EMPIRE.*
R. MELLOR, 124:APR71-272
FERGUSON, S. THE POETRY OF RANDALL
JARRELL.
R. WEISBERG, 441:17SEP72-46
FERGUSON, W.K. IL RINASCIMENTO NELLA
CRITICA STORICA.
M.A. DEL TORRE, 548(RCSF):JUL/SEP69-
329
FERGUSSON, A. THE LOST EMBASSY.
617(TLS):26MAY72-595
FERGUSSON, B. CAPTAIN JOHN NIVEN.
D.A.N. JONES, 362:11MAY72-628
FERGUSSON, J. THE DECLARATION OF ARBRO-
ATH.*
G.W.S. BARROW, 595(SCS):VOL15PT2-158

FERLINGHETTI, L. THE SECRET MEANING OF
THINGS.
J. MC GAHEY, 661:FALL/WINTER69-102
FERLOSIO, R.S. - SEE UNDER SÁNCHEZ FER-
LOSIO, R.
FERNANDEZ, D. L'ARBRE JUSQU'AUX RACINES.
617(TLS):14JUL72-817
FERNÁNDEZ, F.D. - SEE UNDER DE ASÍS FER-
NÁNDEZ, F.
FERNÁNDEZ, O. A PRELIMINARY LISTING OF
FOREIGN PERIODICAL HOLDINGS IN THE
UNITED STATES AND CANADA WHICH GIVE
COVERAGE TO PORTUGUESE AND BRAZILIAN
LANGUAGE AND LITERATURE.
F.P. ELLISON, 399(MLJ):JAN70-58
FERNÁNDEZ DE CÓRDOVA, F. MIS MEMORIAS
ÍNTIMAS. (M. ARTOLA GALLEGO, ED)
191(ELN):SEP69(SUPP)-142
FERNÁNDEZ DE LIZARDI, J.J. OBRAS.* (VOL
3) (M.R. PALAZÓN & J. CHENCINSKY, EDS)
B.G. CARTER, 238:DEC70-1025
FERNÁNDEZ DE LIZARDI, J.J. OBRAS. (VOL
4)
617(TLS):8DEC72-1503
FERNÁNDEZ GONZÁLEZ, Á.R. EL HABLA Y LA
CULTURA POPULAR DE OSEJA DE SAJAMBRE.
L.V. FAINBERG & L.S. LEFKOWITZ,
545(RPH):AUG70-189
FERNÁNDEZ MARTÍNEZ, F. DICCIONARIO DE
PROVERBIOS Y REFRANES.
M. VALLDEPERES, 263:JAN-MAR71-73
FERNÁNDEZ SANTOS, J. EL HOMBRE DE LOS
SANTOS.
J.W. DÍAZ, 238:MAY70-340
FERRARI, L. CONGETTURE STESICHOREE.
H. LLOYD-JONES, 123:DEC70-398
FERRARI, L. I DRAMMI PERDUTI DI ESCHILO.
H. LLOYD-JONES, 123:DEC70-294
FERRARI, L. REALTÀ E FANTASIA NELLA
GEOGRAFIA DELL'ODISSEA.
J.B. HAINSWORTH, 123:DEC70-396
FERRARI, O. & G. SCAVIZZI. LUCA GIORDANO.
W. VITZTHUM, 90:APR70-239
FERRARS, E. FOOT IN THE GRAVE.
617(TLS):29DEC72-1588
FERRARS, E.X. BREATH OF SUSPICION.
N. CALLENDAR, 441:3SEP72-22
FERRATER MORA, J. OBRAS SELECTAS.
A.M., 543:DEC69-345
FERREIRA, A. BOM SENSO E BOM GOSTO.
191(ELN):SEP69(SUPP)-132
FERRERO, G. HISTOIRE ET POLITIQUE AU
XXE SIÈCLE. (L. SALVATORELLI & OTHERS,
EDS)
G. SERBAT, 555:VOL44FASC1-175
FERRIS, P. THE HOUSE OF NORTHCLIFFE.*
442(NY):29APR72-142
FERRIS, W. BLUES FROM THE DELTA.
M. HARRISON, 415:SEP71-864
FERRO, M. THE RUSSIAN REVOLUTION OF
FEBRUARY, 1917.* (FRENCH TITLE: LA
RÉVOLUTION DE 1917.)
617(TLS):22DEC72-1553
FERRON, J. TALES FROM THE UNCERTAIN
COUNTRY.
P. SOCKEN, 99:JUN72-41
FERRY, A.D. MILTON AND THE MILTONIC
DRYDEN.
E. MACKENZIE, 541(RES):FEB70-82
E. MINER, 173(ECS):WINTER69-296
FERRY, W.H. THE BUILDINGS OF DETROIT.
L.K. EATON, 54:DEC69-403
FEST, J.C. THE FACE OF THE THIRD REICH.*
639(VQR):AUTUMN70-CXLVI
FESTUGIERE, A.J. GEORGE HERBERT, POETE,
SAINT, ANGLICAN.
617(TLS):22SEP72-1099

FETHERLING, D. THE UNITED STATES OF
HEAVEN/GWENDOLYN PAPERS/THAT CHAIN-
LETTER HIWAY.*
   H. MAC CALLUM, 627(UTQ):JUL69-351
FETSCHER, I. - SEE KOLLONTAI, A.
FEUCHTWANGER, E.J. DISRAELI, DEMOCRACY
AND THE TORY PARTY.
   R. BULLEN, 325:APR70-82
   L.C., 619(TC):1968/3-57
   T.J. SPINNER, JR., 637(VS):DEC69-225
FEUERBACH, L. KLEINE SCHRIFTEN.
   E. RAMBALDI, 548(RCSF):JAN-MAR68-114
FEUERBACH, L. LECTURES ON THE ESSENCE
OF RELIGION. THE ESSENCE OF FAITH
ACCORDING TO LUTHER.
   J. GLASSE, 319:JAN72-101
FEUERLICHT, I. THOMAS MANN.*
   K.W. JONAS, 399(MLJ):FEB70-144
   H. LEHNERT, 221(GQ):MAR70-290
FEUERWERKER, A. THE CHINESE ECONOMY, CA.
1770-1911. THE CHINESE ECONOMY, 1912-
1949.
   R. MYERS, 293(JAST):AUG70-897
FEUERWERKER, A., R. MURPHEY & M.C. WRIGHT,
EDS. APPROACHES TO MODERN CHINESE HIS-
TORY.
   P. CAVENDISH, 587:JUL69-123
FEUILLATRE, E. ÉTUDES SUR LES ÉTHIO-
PIQUES D'HÉLIODORE.
   H.H.O. CHALK, 123:MAR71-131
FFRENCH BLAKE, R.L.V. THE CRIMEAN WAR.
   617(TLS):28APR72-501
FIBER, A. THE COMPLETE GUIDE TO RETAIL
MANAGEMENT.
   617(TLS):14APR72-429
FICHTE, H. DIE PALETTE.
   T. WEYR, 19(AGR):VOL35#4-31
FICHTNER, E.G. - SEE FÜETRER, U.
FICK, C. THE DANZIGER TRANSCRIPT.
   H. FRANKEL, 561(SATR):29JAN72-73
   442(NY):1JAN72-64
FICKELSON, M. DOD.
   V. CUNNINGHAM, 362:9NOV72-643
   617(TLS):27OCT72-1274
FIDO, M. CHARLES DICKENS.
   A.B., 155:SEP70-244
   R.L. PATTEN, 155:MAY69-124
   W.D. SCHAEFER, 445(NCF):SEP69-249
FIEDLER, F. ENGLISCHER SPRACHGEBRAUCH
UND ENGLISCHE SCHULGRAMMATIK.
   J. BOURKE, 38:BAND87HEFT3/4-427
FIEDLER, L.A. THE COLLECTED ESSAYS OF
LESLIE FIEDLER.*
   W.H. PRITCHARD, 249(HUDR):WINTER
71/72-706
FIEDLER, L.A. THE STRANGER IN SHAKE-
SPEARE.
   F. KERMODE, 441:10DEC72-35
   C. LEHMANN-HAUPT, 441:30JUN72-37
   442(NY):5AUG72-83
FIEDLER, W. & OTHERS - SEE GRZIMEK, B.
FIELD, A. THE COMPLECTION OF RUSSIAN
LITERATURE.*
   P.D. RAYFIELD, 575(SEER):OCT71-614
FIELD, E. VARIETY PHOTOPLAYS.*
   S. COOPERMAN, 502(PRS):FALL68-266
FIELD, G.C. THE PHILOSOPHY OF PLATO.
   R.K. SPRAGUE, 122:JAN71-53
FIELD, G.C. PLATO AND HIS CONTEMPOR-
ARIES.
   E.A.R., 543:SEP69-129
FIELD, G.W. HERMANN HESSE.
   J. MILECK, 406:WINTER71-396
FIELD, G.W. - SEE FONTANE, T.
FIELD, J. ENGLISH FIELD NAMES.
   617(TLS):29DEC72-1590

FIELD, J.A., JR. AMERICA AND THE
MEDITERRANEAN WORLD, 1776-1882.
   S.S. HAYDEN, 432(NEQ):JUN70-348
   W. STINCHCOMBE, 656(WMQ):JAN70-163
FIELD, R.S. FIFTEENTH CENTURY WOODCUTS
AND METALCUTS FROM THE NATIONAL GALLERY
OF ART.
   J. SNYDER, 90:MAR69-160
FIELD, T.W. AN ESSAY TOWARDS AN INDIAN
BIBLIOGRAPHY.
   A.L. CAMPA, 582(SFQ):JUN69-130
FIELDEN, C. CRYING AS SHE RAN.
   A. THOMAS, 102(CANL):SPRING71-84
FIELDING, G. NEW QUEENS FOR OLD.
   A. BROYARD, 441:7SEP72-45
   D.A.N. JONES, 362:6JUL72-22
   617(TLS):1SEP72-1013
FIELDING, H. JOSEPH ANDREWS. (M.C.
BATTESTIN, ED)
   H.W. DRESCHER, 38:BAND87HEFT1-101
   N.J. SKYDSGAARD, 179(ES):AUG69-409
FIELDING, H. THE GRUB STREET OPERA.
(E.V. ROBERTS, ED)
   R.H. DAMMERS, 568(SCN):WINTER71-72
   A. SHERBO, 402(MLR):OCT71-867
FIELDING, J. THE BEST OF FRIENDS.
   M. LEVIN, 441:13AUG72-32
FIELDING, R. THE AMERICAN NEWSREEL,
1911-1967.
   M.A. JACKSON, 441:6AUG72-4
FIELDING, T. FIELDING'S TRAVEL GUIDE.
   C.W. CASEWIT, 440:30APR72-4
FIELDS, B. REALITY'S DARK DREAM.
   K.T.A., 191(ELN):SEP69(SUPP)-31
   M.J.D., 477:SUMMER69-413
   L. LERNER, 184(EIC):JAN70-89
   R. WELLS, 447(N&Q):MAY70-191
FIELDS, J. & D. SOUTH PACIFIC.
   561(SATR):7OCT72-100
FIELDS, W.C. FIELDS FOR PRESIDENT.
   G. MILLAR, 362:1JUN72-726
   617(TLS):26MAY72-600
FIFOOT, C.H.S. FREDERIC WILLIAM MAIT-
LAND.
   617(TLS):2JUN72-627
FIFOOT, R. A BIBLIOGRAPHY OF EDITH,
OSBERT AND SACHEVERELL SITWELL.
   617(TLS):18FEB72-188
"50 YEARS BAUHAUS."
   R. BOYD, 44:MAR69-76
FIGES, E. B.
   E. MORGAN, 362:23MAR72-393
   617(TLS):31MAR72-353
FIGGE, U. DIE ROMANISCHE ANLAUTSONORI-
SATION.
   C. BLAYLOCK, 545(RPH):FEB70-345
FIGUEROA, J., ED. CARIBBEAN VOICES.
   617(TLS):28JAN72-94
"THE FIHRIST OF AL-NADÎM."* (B. DODGE,
ED & TRANS)
   L.E. GOODMAN, 319:OCT72-478
   617(TLS):14JAN72-46
FILDES, L.V. LUKE FILDES, R.A., A VIC-
TORIAN PAINTER.*
   G. REYNOLDS, 592:MAR68-160
   K. ROBERTS, 90:OCT70-707
FILESI, T. CHINA AND AFRICA IN THE
MIDDLE AGES.
   617(TLS):13OCT72-1236
FILEY, M. TORONTO.
   102(CANL):SPRING71-120
FILHO, A. MEMORIES OF LAZARUS.
   37:OCT69-43
FINAS, L. LE MEURTRION.
   J-N. VUARNET, 98:MAY69-422
FINCH, C. POP ART; OBJECT AND IMAGE.
   E. LUCIE-SMITH, 46:APR69-308
   J. MASHECK, 592:NOV68-217

FINCH, R. & E. JOLIAT, EDS. FRENCH
INDIVIDUALIST POETRY 1686-1760.
617(TLS):17NOV72-1398
"FINDING THE CENTER." (D. TEDLOCK,
TRANS)
W. KITTREDGE, 231:NOV72-120
A. MAC INTYRE, 441:24DEC72-4
FINDLATER, R. - SEE GRIMALDI, J.
FINDLAY, J.N. AXIOLOGICAL ETHICS.
B. MAYO, 518:MAY71-5
FINE, W. THEIR FAMILY.
L. GRAVER, 441:2JUL72-6
"FINE BINDINGS 1500-1700 FROM OXFORD
LIBRARIES."
A.R.A. HOBSON, 354:SEP69-257
FINEGAN, J. THE ARCHEOLOGY OF THE NEW
TESTAMENT.
639(VQR):SUMMER70-CXV
FINEMAN, D.A. - SEE MORGANN, M.
FINGARD, J. THE ANGLICAN DESIGN IN
LOYALIST NOVA SCOTIA 1783-1816.
617(TLS):3MAR72-258
FINGARETTE, H. SELF DECEPTION.
S.A.M. BURNS, 483:JAN70-72
J.P. FELL, 479(PHQ):JUL70-290
C.M. TYLEE, 518:MAY70-6
FINGERHUT, M. RACINE IN DEUTSCHEN
ÜBERSETZUNGEN DES NEUNZEHNTEN UND
ZWANZIGSTEN JAHRHUNDERTS.
R. KLESCZEWSKI, 72:BAND208HEFT1-42
FINKE, U., ED. FRENCH NINETEENTH CENTURY
PAINTING AND LITERATURE.
617(TLS):14JUL72-821
FINKEL, D. THE GARBAGE WARS.*
M.L. ROSENTHAL, 491:NOV71-99
FINKELPEARL, P.J. JOHN MARSTON OF THE
MIDDLE TEMPLE.*
A. CAPUTI, 551(RENQ):SPRING70-91
B.N. DE LUNA, 191(ELN):DEC70-149
G.K. HUNTER, 401(MLQ):SEP70-375
FINKENSTAEDT, T., E. LEISI & D. WOLFF.
A CHRONOLOGICAL ENGLISH DICTIONARY.
S.I. TUCKER, 677:VOL2-226
FINLAY, I.H. THE DANCERS INHERIT THE
PARTY.
A. OSTRIKER, 473(PR):1971/2-218
FINLAY, J.C. THE LIBERAL WHO FAILED.
J.N. MOODY, 613:SUMMER69-317
FINLEY, J.H., JR. FOUR STAGES OF GREEK
THOUGHT.*
M.G. DORE, 548(RCSF):JAN-MAR68-87
FINLEY, M.I. EARLY GREECE.
J. BOARDMAN, 123:DEC71-460
C.G. STARR, 124:DEC70-128
FINLEY, M.I. A HISTORY OF SICILY.*
(VOL 1)
S. HUGHES, 613:AUTUMN69-476
FINNERAN, R.J. - SEE YEATS, W.B.
FINNIGAN, J. ENTRANCE TO THE GREEN-
HOUSE.*
H. MAC CALLUM, 627(UTQ):JUL69-350
T. MARSHALL, 529(QQ):SUMMER70-294
FINNIGAN, J. IN THE BROWN COTTAGE ON
LOUGHBOROUGH LAKE.
B.D. BARRIE, 198:SPRING72-102
FINNIGAN, J. IT WAS WARM AND SUNNY WHEN
WE SET OUT.
D. BARBOUR, 150(DR):AUTUMN70-433
E. WOODS, 606(TAMR):#55-79
FIORE, P.A., ED. JUST SO MUCH HONOR.
617(TLS):29DEC72-1581
FIORI, G. ANTONIO GRAMSCI.
617(TLS):28APR72-493
FIRBAS, J., WITH J. HLADKÝ, EDS. CHARIS-
TERIA IOSEPHO VACHEK SEXAGENARIO OB-
LATA.
A.A. HILL, 350:JUN71-451

FIRE, J. & R. ERDOES. LAME DEER, SEEKER
OF VISIONS.
W. KITTREDGE, 231:NOV72-120
FIRESTONE, R., ED. GETTING BUSTED.
441:9JAN72-28
FIRESTONE, S. THE DIALECTIC OF SEX.*
R. SENNETT, 453:20APR72-22
FIRKINS, P. THE AUSTRALIANS IN NINE
WARS.
617(TLS):16JUN72-690
FIRPO, L. - SEE CAMPANELLA, T.
FIRST, R., J. STEELE & C. GURNEY. THE
SOUTH AFRICAN CONNECTION.
J. VAIZEY, 362:19OCT72-509
617(TLS):1DEC72-1451
FIRTH, F. - SEE PIRANDELLO, L.
FIRTH, J.R. SELECTED PAPERS OF J.R.
FIRTH, 1952-59. (F.L. PALMER, ED)
D.T. LANGENDOEN, 350:MAR71-180
FIRTH, R. RANK AND RELIGION IN TIKOPIA.
617(TLS):7JAN72-7
FISCHEL, W.J. IBN KHALDŪN IN EGYPT.*
H.K. SHERWANI, 273(IC):APR69-164
FISCHER, E., WITH F. MAREK. LENIN IN
HIS OWN WORDS.
617(TLS):17MAR72-298
FISCHER, F. GERMANY'S AIMS IN THE FIRST
WORLD WAR.
N.A. PETERSEN, 497(POLR):SUMMER68-86
FISCHER, G.B. BEDROHT - BEWAHRT.
H. LEHNERT, 400(MLN):APR70-411
FISCHER, H. GNU SOUP.
L. BOOTH, 529(QQ):SUMMER70-295
M. DOYLE, 491:MAR72-356
FISCHER, H. JUDENTUM, STAAT UND HEER IN
PREUSSEN IM FRÜHEN 19. JAHRHUNDERT.
G.M. KREN, 182:VOL23#4-185
FISCHER, H. STUDIEN ZUR DEUTSCHEN MÄREN-
DICHTUNG DES 15. JAHRHUNDERTS.*
E.G. FICHTNER, 221(GQ):MAR70-260
FISCHER, H.C. & L. BESCH. THE LIFE OF
MOZART.
S. SADIE, 415:MAR70-278
FISCHER, H-D. PARTEIEN UND PRESSE IN
DEUTSCHLAND SEIT 1945.
617(TLS):26MAY72-596
FISCHER, J.L. THE CASE OF SOCRATES.
G. HEILBRUNN, 124:MAY71-316
FISCHER, L. GEBUNDENE REDE.
R.G. WARNOCK, 221(GQ):NOV70-807
FISCHER, L. RUSSIA'S ROAD FROM PEACE TO
WAR.*
J.C. CAMPBELL, 550(RUSR):APR70-213
FISCHER, W.G. MÖBLIERTE ZIMMER.
617(TLS):21JUL72-851
FISCHER-GALAŢI, S. TWENTIETH CENTURY
RUMANIA.
K. HITCHINS, 32:MAR71-187
FISCHER-LAMBERG, H. - SEE VON GOETHE,
J.W.
FISH, R.L. THE TRICKS OF THE TRADE.
N. CALLENDAR, 441:12MAR72-40
H. FRANKEL, 561(SATR):25MAR72-104
FISH, S.E. SURPRISED BY SIN.*
E. MINER, 173(ECS):WINTER69-296
FISHEL, W.R., ED. VIETNAM.
C. HOBBS, 293(JAST):NOV69-207
FISHER, A. & N. MARSHALL. GARDEN OF
INNOCENTS.
C. LEHMANN-HAUPT, 441:22AUG72-45
441:24SEP72-52
FISHER, A.W. THE RUSSIAN ANNEXATION OF
THE CRIMEA, 1772-1783.
H.H. KAPLAN, 32:JUN71-392
FISHER, E.M. & M.C. BASSIOUNI. STORM
OVER THE ARAB WORLD.
T. LASK, 441:25AUG72-33

FISHER, F.J., ED. CALENDAR OF THE MANU-
SCRIPTS OF THE RIGHT HONOURABLE LORD
SACKVILLE OF KNOLE. (VOL 2)
R.B. OUTHWAITE, 325:APR69-505
FISHER, J.H. JOHN GOWER.
J. RICHARDSON, 179(ES):DEC70-547
FISHER, M. THE VOYAGER.
617(TLS):5MAY72-526
FISHER, M. - SEE HORNE, R.H.
FISHER, M.F.K. - SEE BRILLAT-SAVARIN,
J.A.
FISHER, R. DEAR ISRAELIS, DEAR ARABS.
T. LASK, 441:25AUG72-33
FISHER, S. THE FEMALE ORGASM.
I. SINGER, 453:30NOV72-29
FISHER, S.G. MEN, WOMEN & MANNERS IN
COLONIAL TIMES.
J.C. SEARLES, 568(SCN):SUMMER/AUTUMN
71-50
FISHER, S.T. AN ENGINEER LOOKS AT SHAKE-
SPEARE.
L.F. BALL, 570(SQ):AUTUMN69-477
FISHLOCK, T. WALES AND THE WELSH.
617(TLS):18AUG72-965
FISHMAN, J.A. & OTHERS. LANGUAGE LOYALTY
IN THE UNITED STATES.*
K. LUBBERS, 38:BAND87HEFT3/4-441
FISHWICK, M. THE HERO, AMERICAN STYLE.
W. TILLSON, 292(JAF):JUL-SEP70-371
FISKE, R. BEETHOVEN CONCERTOS AND OVER-
TURES.*
E. SAMS, 415:MAR71-245
FITCH, M., ED. INDEX TO TESTAMENTARY
RECORDS IN THE COMMISSARY COURT OF
LONDON (LONDON DIVISION). (VOL 1)
I. DARLINGTON, 325:OCT70-151
FITCH, R.E. SHAKESPEARE: THE PERSPEC-
TIVE OF VALUE.
R.M. FRYE, 402(MLR):JUL71-660
FITCHEN, J. THE NEW WORLD DUTCH BARN.
W.J. MURTAGH, 505:JUL69-174
FITTER, R.S.R. FINDING WILD FLOWERS.
617(TLS):30JUN72-754
FITTSCHEN, K. UNTERSUCHUNGEN ZUM BEGINN
DER SAGENDARSTELLUNGEN BEI DEN GRIECH-
EN.
M.L. THOMPSON, 124:JAN71-162
FITZGERALD, A.E. THE HIGH PRIESTS OF
WASTE.
P. ADAMS, 61:NOV72-131
W. BEECHER, 441:19NOV72-54
FITZGERALD, C.P. THE SOUTHERN EXPANSION
OF THE CHINESE PEOPLE.
617(TLS):16JUN72-681
FITZ GERALD, F. FIRE IN THE LAKE.
M. BERNAL, 453:5OCT72-24
S. HOFFMANN, 441:27AUG72-1
C. LEHMANN-HAUPT, 441:17AUG72-37
J. MIRSKY, 561(SATR):19AUG72-54
FITZGERALD, F.S. F. SCOTT FITZGERALD IN
HIS OWN TIME.* (M. BRUCCOLI & J.
BRYER, EDS)
R.M. ADAMS, 453:27JAN72-26
FITZGERALD, F.S. & H. OBER. AS EVER,
SCOTT FITZ. (M.J. BRUCCOLI, WITH J.M.
ATKINSON, EDS)
E. WEEKS, 61:MAY72-110
A. WHITMAN, 561(SATR):8JUL72-60
FITZGERALD, F.S. & M. PERKINS. DEAR
SCOTT/DEAR MAX.* (J. KUEHL & J.R.
BRYER, EDS)
R.M. ADAMS, 453:27JAN72-26
E. WEEKS, 61:JAN72-95
441:23APR72-10
FITZ GERALD, G. TOWARDS A NEW IRELAND.
C.C. O'BRIEN, 362:23NOV72-712

FITZGERALD, G.E., ED. THE CONSTITUTIONS
OF LATIN AMERICA.
R.H. FITZGIBBON, 263:APR-JUN71-213
FITZGERALD, R. SPRING SHADE.
R. LATTIMORE, 249(HUDR):AUTUMN71-499
A. WILLIAMSON, 491:FEB72-296
FITZGERALD, R. - SEE AGEE, J.
FITZGERALD, S. CHINA AND THE OVERSEAS
CHINESE.
617(TLS):17NOV72-1386
FITZGERALD, S. & R. - SEE O'CONNOR, F.
FITZ GIBBON, C. RED HAND.*
P. BROGAN, 440:23APR72-9
O.D. EDWARDS, 441:9APR72-7
617(TLS):17MAR72-297
FITZPATRICK, H. THE HORN AND HORN-
PLAYING AND THE AUSTRO-BOHEMIAN TRA-
DITION FROM 1680 TO 1830.*
A.C.B., 410(M&L):OCT71-438
R. MORLEY-PEGGE, 415:FEB71-137
FITZPATRICK, S. THE COMMISSARIAT OF
ENLIGHTENMENT.*
H.R. HOLTER, 32:DEC71-887
H. MUCHNIC, 453:23MAR72-37
FITZSIMMONS, T. - SEE "JAPANESE POETRY
NOW"
FITZ SIMONS, L. THE KENNEDY DOCTRINE.
S. SCHLESINGER, 561(SATR):15JUL72-56
D. SCHOENBRUN, 441:19MAR72-6
R. STEEL, 453:19OCT72-43
FLACELIÈRE, R. & É. CHAMBRY - SEE PLU-
TARCH
FLACH, D. DAS LITERARISCHE VERHÄLTNIS
VON HORAZ UND PROPERZ.
R.G.M. NISBET, 123:MAR71-57
FLAHERTY, D.H., ED. ESSAYS IN THE HIS-
TORY OF EARLY AMERICAN LAW.
M. CANTOR, 656(WMQ):JAN70-146
639(VQR):WINTER70-XXIII
FLAKE, O. DIE VERURTEILUNG DES SOKRATES.
617(TLS):14JAN72-44
FLAKOLL, D.J. & C. ALEGRIA. CENIZAS DE
IZALCO.
A. ADELL, 270:VOL20#3-78
FLAM, L. PASSÉ ET AVENIR DE LA PHILOSO-
PHIE.
W. HALBFASS, 182:VOL23#17/18-769
FLANAGAN, P. THE BALLINAMORE AND BALLY-
CONNELL CANAL.
617(TLS):1SEP72-1034
FLANAGAN, R. BODY.
M. DOYLE, 491:MAR72-356
150(DR):AUTUMN70-427
FLANNER, J. PARIS WAS YESTERDAY: 1925-
1939. (I. DRUTMAN, ED)
A. BROYARD, 441:11JUL72-37
J. STAFFORD, 453:10AUG72-22
A. SZOGYI, 561(SATR):29JUL72-56
E. WEEKS, 61:OCT72-133
FLASCHE, H., ED. AUFSÄTZE ZUR PORTUGIES-
ISCHEN KULTURGESCHICHTE. (VOL 6)
E. GLASER, 240(HR):OCT70-451
FLASCHE, H., ED. LITTERAE HISPANAE ET
LUSITANAE.
R.S. SAYERS, 546(RR):APR70-126
FLASHAR, H. DER EPITAPHIOS DES PERIKLES.
J. DAY, 124:DEC70-125
F.M. WASSERMANN, 121(CJ):APR-MAY71-
368
FLAUBERT, G. FLAUBERT IN EGYPT. (F.
STEEGMULLER, ED & TRANS)
G. GRIGSON, 362:23NOV72-715
617(TLS):29SEP72-1156
FLAUBERT, G. L'ÉDUCATION SENTIMENTALE.
(J. SUFFEL, ED)
A. FAIRLIE, 208(FS):JAN71-98

FLAUBERT, G. MADAME BOVARY: EXTRAITS.
(C. BOUTON, ED)
R. MERKER, 399(MLJ):DEC70-616
FLEEMAN, J.D. A PRELIMINARY HANDLIST OF
DOCUMENTS & MANUSCRIPTS OF SAMUEL
JOHNSON.
J.T. BOULTON, 354:MAR69-70
FLEET, B. BULLETS AND CATHEDRALS.
C. SPRAY, 198:WINTER72-114
T.L. WEPPLER, 99:JUL-AUG72-46
FLEET, B. CATCHING THE SUN'S FIRE.
M. DOYLE, 491:MAR72-356
FLEETWOOD, H. A PAINTER OF FLOWERS.
M. LEVIN, 441:24SEP72-40
E. MORGAN, 362:23MAR72-393
617(TLS):31MAR72-353
FLEISCHER, M. - SEE HUSSERL, E.
FLEISCHMANN, W.B., GENERAL ED. ENCYCLO-
PEDIA OF WORLD LITERATURE IN THE 20TH
CENTURY. (VOL 1)
G.A. PANICHAS, 399(MLJ):APR70-297
FLEISHMAN, A. CONRAD'S POLITICS.
E.W. SAID, 637(VS):JUN70-429
W.D. SCHAEFER, 445(NCF):SEP68-248
N. SHERRY, 541(RES):AUG70-373
FLEISHMAN, A. A READING OF "MANSFIELD
PARK."*
L.W. BROWN, 173(ECS):FALL69-145
J.E.J., 191(ELN):SEP69(SUPP)-18
M.A. MUELLERLEILE, 405(MP):NOV69-201
FLEISSNER, O.S. & E.M. DEUTSCHES LITER-
ATURLESEBUCH.
A. CLAESGES, 399(MLJ):FEB70-130
FLEMING, D.F. AMERICA'S ROLE IN ASIA.
N.H. CHI, 529(QQ):SPRING70-138
W.C. JOHNSTONE, 639(VQR):SPRING70-352
FLEMING, J. BE A GOOD BOY.
N. CALLENDAR, 441:5MAR72-34
FLEMING, J.M. ESSAYS IN INTERNATIONAL
ECONOMICS.
617(TLS):21APR72-457
LE FLEMING, L.S.K. - SEE CHEKHOV, A.P.
FLEMING, T. THE MAN FROM MONTICELLO.
J.A. BEAR, JR., 656(WMQ):JUL70-518
FLEMING, T. - SEE "BENJAMIN FRANKLIN"
FLEMING, W.G. ONTARIO'S EDUCATIVE SOCI-
ETY.
W. PITMAN, 99:OCT/NOV72-62
FLEMMING, W. GOETHE UND DAS THEATER
SEINER ZEIT.
J. ANNABLE, 402(MLR):JAN71-217
FLEMMING, W. ANDREAS GRYPHIUS.
G. HAY, 462(OL):VOL23#4-332
FLESCH-BRUNNINGEN, H. DIE TEILE UND DAS
GANZE.
G. FISCHER, 270:VOL20#1-11
FLETCHER, G. DICKENS' LONDON.
L.C.S., 155:SEP69-190
FLETCHER, G. THE LONDON DICKENS KNEW.
A.B., 155:SEP70-244
FLETCHER, I., ED. MEREDITH NOW.
617(TLS):21JAN72-59
FLETCHER, J. NEW DIRECTIONS IN LITERA-
TURE.
J.S., 619(TC):1968/3-54
FLETCHER, J.B. DANTE.
N.J. PERELLA, 545(RPH):FEB71-560
FLETCHER, J.W. A MENACE TO SOCIETY.
617(TLS):14JUL72-825
FLETCHER, N.M. THE SEPARATION OF SINGA-
PORE FROM MALAYSIA.
J. SILVERSTEIN, 293(JAST):AUG70-990
FLETCHER, R. THE POEMS AND TRANSLATIONS
OF ROBERT FLETCHER. (D.H. WOODWARD,
ED)
568(SCN):SUMMER/AUTUMN71-41
FLETCHER, R. - SEE MILL, J.S.

FLETCHER, W.C. NIKOLAI.
M. KLIMENKO, 32:JUN71-403
DE FLEURY, A. VITA GAUZLINI, ABBATIS
FLORIACENSIS MONASTERII. (R-H.
BAUTIER & G. LABORY, EDS & TRANS)
I. MÜLLER, 182:VOL23#11/12-633
FLEW, A. AN INTRODUCTION TO WESTERN
PHILOSOPHY.*
T.E. JESSOP, 319:APR72-246
FLEXNER, E. MARY WOLLSTONECRAFT.
S. BROWNMILLER, 441:8OCT72-4
V.S. PRITCHETT, 453:2NOV72-8
FLEXNER, J.T. GEORGE WASHINGTON. (VOL
4)
G. DANGERFIELD, 441:19NOV72-2
T. LASK, 441:24NOV72-40
FLINT, R.W. - SEE MARINETTI, F.T.
FLINT, T. RECOLLECTIONS OF THE LAST TEN
YEARS.
B. CRESAP, 9(ALAR):JAN69-75
FLOECK, W. "LAS MOCEDADES DEL CID" VON
GUILLÉN DE CASTRO UND "LE CID" VON
PIERRE CORNEILLE.*
K.A. OTT, 72:BAND208HEFT3-230
P.J. YARROW, 208(FS):JAN71-72
FLOOD, C.B. TROUBLE AT THE TOP.
N. CALLENDAR, 441:7MAY72-34
FLORES, E. CONTRIBUTI DI FILOLOGIA
MANILIANA.
J. SOUBIRAN, 555:VOL44FASC2-345
FLORES, J. POETRY IN EAST GERMANY.*
H.M. WAIDSON, 301(JEGP):OCT71-746
FLORES CABALLERO, R. LA CONTRA-REVOLU-
CIÓN EN LA INDEPENDENCIA.
M.P. COSTELOE, 86(BHS):OCT71-366
FLORESCU, F.B. DAS SIEGESDENKMAL VON
ADAMKLISSI (TROPAEUM TRAIANI).
A. HUS, 555:VOL44FASC1-169
FLOREY, G. BISCHÖFE, KETZER, EMIGRANTEN.
Q. BREEN, 182:VOL23#9-505
FLORIOT, R. WHEN JUSTICE FALTERS.
617(TLS):14APR72-410
FLOTZINGER, R. DER DISCANTUSSATZ IM
MAGNUS LIBER UND SEINER NACHFOLGE.
I.D.B., 410(M&L):JAN71-80
FLOWER, J.E. INTENTION AND ACHIEVEMENT.*
V. MINOGUE, 402(MLR):JAN71-195
FLOWER, R. NAPOLEON TO NASSER.
617(TLS):15DEC72-1522
FLYGT, S.G. FRIEDRICH HEBBEL.*
T.C. DUNHAM, 399(MLJ):NOV70-531
F.M. FOWLER, 402(MLR):JAN71-226
W. WITTKOWSKI, 221(GQ):MAY70-517
FLYS, M.J. LA POESIA EXISTENCIAL DE
DÁMASO ALONSO.*
J.F. CIRRE, 238:SEP70-577
FOAKES, R.A. SHAKESPEARE: THE DARK
COMEDIES TO THE LAST PLAYS.
617(TLS):30JUN72-739
FOAKES, R.A. - SEE SHAKESPEARE, W.
FOAKES, R.A. & R.T. RICKERT - SEE HENS-
LOWE, P.
FODOR, I. THE PROBLEMS IN THE CLASSIFI-
CATION OF THE AFRICAN LANGUAGES.*
J. & T. BYNON, 315(JAL):VOL7PT3-219
VON FOERSTER, H. & J.W. BEAUCHAMP, EDS.
MUSIC BY COMPUTERS.
S. ARNOLD, 607:AUTUMN69-39
FOGELIN, R.J. EVIDENCE AND MEANING.*
J. HARRISON, 479(PHQ):JUL70-307
FOGG, H.G.W. DICTIONARY OF ANNUAL
PLANTS.
617(TLS):7APR72-402
FOGLE, F. - SEE MILTON, J.
FOKKEMA, D.W. REPORT FROM PEKING.
617(TLS):24MAR72-324

FOLEY, D.J. THE COMPLETE BOOK OF GARDEN
ORNAMENTS, COMPLEMENTS, AND ACCESSOR-
IES.
    J. SAVERCOOL, 441:3DEC72-92
FOLEY, M., ED. THE BEST AMERICAN SHORT
STORIES 1972.
    C.D.B. BRYAN, 441:15OCT72-31
FOLEY, R. SLEEP WITHOUT MORNING.
    N. CALLENDAR, 441:7MAY72-34
"FOLIO 21."
    D. CHAMBERS, 503:SPRING69-39
FOLIOT, G. THE LETTERS AND CHARTERS OF
GILBERT FOLIOT.* (Z.N. BROOKE, WITH
A. MOREY & C.N.L. BROOKE, EDS)
    M.A.F. BORRIE, 325:OCT69-586
FOLSOM, K.E. FRIENDS, GUESTS, AND COL-
LEAGUES.*
    T.A. METZGER, 244(HJAS):VOL29-315
FOLSOM, R.S. HANDBOOK OF GREEK POTTERY.*
    M. ROBERTSON, 90:MAR69-160
FOLTIN, H.F., I-M. GREVERUS & J. SCHWEBE,
EDS. KONTAKTE UND GRENZEN.
    B. GUNDA, 292(JAF):OCT-DEC70-469
FOLTIN, L.B. & K. HEINEN, EDS. PATHS TO
GERMAN POETRY.
    E. KRISPYN, 221(GQ):NOV70-823
FOLTINEK, H. VORSTUFEN ZUM VIKTORIAN-
ISCHEN REALISMUS.*
    I-S. EWBANK, 541(RES):MAY70-231
    H. REINHOLD, 155:MAY69-123
FONE, B.R.S. - SEE CIBBER, C.
FONER, E. FREE SOIL, FREE LABOR, FREE
MEN.*
    V.J. VOEGELI, 676(YR):SPRING71-449
    639(VQR):AUTUMN70-CXLVIII
FONSECA, C.D. MEDIOEVO CANONICALE.
    G. CONSTABLE, 589:JAN71-151
FONTAINE, J. ASPECTS ET PROBLÈMES DE LA
PROSE D'ART LATINE AU IIIE SIÈCLE.
    A. ERNOUT, 555:VOL44FASC2-352
    L.J. SWIFT, 24:APR71-367
FONTAINE, P. BASIC FORMAL STRUCTURES IN
MUSIC.
    J.D. WHITE, 308:WINTER67-285
FONTAINE, P.H. PROFICIENCY IN COUNTER-
POINT.
    C. WHITTENBERG, 308:SPRING68-112
FONTANA, M.J. L'ATHENAION POLITEIA DEL
V SECOLO A. C.
    D.M. LEWIS, 123:MAR71-126
FONTANE, T. IRRUNGEN WIRRUNGEN. (G.W.
FIELD, ED)
    F. OPPENHEIMER, 399(MLJ):OCT70-470
FONTANIER, P. FIGURES DU DISCOURS.
(EDITION PRESENTEE PAR G. GENETTE)
    M. DEGUY, 98:OCT69-841
FOORD, B. - SEE MORE, T.
FOOTE, P.G. & D.M. WILSON. THE VIKING
ACHIEVEMENT.
    D.W. EVANS, 402(MLR):JAN71-235
FOOTMAN, D. RED PRELUDE. (2ND ED)
    P. AVRICH, 587:JAN69-397
FORBES, B. THE DISTANT LAUGHTER.
    V. CUNNINGHAM, 362:27APR72-564
    M. LEVIN, 441:17SEP72-42
    617(TLS):19MAY72-565
FORBES, C. THE PALERMO AFFAIR.
    M. LEVIN, 441:25JUN72-26
FORBES, E.G. - SEE EULER, L. & T. MAYER
FORBES, S. A DEADLY KIND OF LONELY.
    N. CALLENDAR, 441:23JAN72-28
FORCE, R.W. & M. THE FULLER COLLECTION
OF PACIFIC ARTIFACTS.
    617(TLS):19MAY72-582
FORCIONE, A.K. CERVANTES, ARISTOTLE AND
THE "PERSILES."
    617(TLS):29SEP72-1167

FORCIONE, A.K. CERVANTES' CHRISTIAN
ROMANCE.
    617(TLS):1DEC72-1445
FORD, B.J. NONSCIENCE...OR HOW TO RULE
THE WORLD.
    617(TLS):21JAN72-78
FORD, C. BERKELEY JOURNAL.
    D. POLING, 561(SATR):22JUL72-57
FORD, C. DONOVAN OF OSS.
    617(TLS):14JAN72-30
FORD, F.M. THE BODLEY HEAD FORD MADOX
FORD. (VOL 5) (M. KILLIGREW, ED)
SELECTED POEMS. (B. BUNTING, ED)
    617(TLS):5MAY72-519
FORD, F.M. RETURN TO YESTERDAY.
    A. BROYARD, 441:13OCT72-41
FORD, F.M. YOUR MIRROR TO MY TIMES.*
(M. KILLIGREW, ED)
    G. CORE, 598(SOR):AUTUMN72-956
    G. STEINER, 442(NY):12FEB72-97
FORD, G.B. A DEGREE OF DIFFERENCE.
    J.P. ASCHERL, 363:MAY70-101
FORD, G.B., JR., ED & TRANS. THE OLD
LITHUANIAN CATECHISM OF BALTRAMIEJUS
VILENTAS (1579).
    W.R. SCHMALSTIEG, 574(SEEJ):SPRING71-
    105
FORD, G.B., JR., ED. OLD LITHUANIAN
TEXTS OF THE SIXTEENTH AND SEVENTEENTH
CENTURIES.
    H. LEEMING, 575(SEER):JAN71-134
    D.F. ROBINSON, 574(SEEJ):SPRING71-109
FORD, G.B., JR. - SEE ST. ISIDORE OF
SEVILLE
FORD, G.B., JR. - SEE MAŽVYDAS, M.
FORD, G.B., JR. - SEE "THE RUODLIEB"
FORD, J. THE CHRONICLE HISTORY OF PERKIN
WARBECK.* (P. URE, ED)
    R. GILL, 541(RES):MAY70-204
FORD, R.A.D. THE SOLITARY CITY.
    M. WADDINGTON, 102(CANL):SPRING71-68
FORDE, D. & P.M. KABERRY, EDS. WEST
AFRICAN KINGDOMS IN THE NINETEENTH
CENTURY.
    J.D. FAGE, 69:JAN69-79
FORDER, A. - SEE "PENELOPE HALL'S SOCIAL
SERVICES OF ENGLAND AND WALES"
FORDHAM, P. INSIDE THE UNDERWORLD.
    617(TLS):20OCT72-1250
FOREMAN, J.B., GENERAL ED. COLLINS GEM
DICTIONARY OF FIRST NAMES.
    M.M. BRYANT, 424:JUN69-164
FORER, M. THE HUMBACK.
    M. LAURENCE, 606(TAMR):#55-77
    R. WIEBE, 102(CANL):SPRING71-86
FORMAN, D. MOZART'S CONCERTO FORM.
    617(TLS):14JAN72-36
FORMAN, H.C. EARLY NANTUCKET AND ITS
WHALE HOUSES.
    R.W. BRUNSKILL, 576:DEC68-306
FORMAN, J. THE MAKING OF BLACK REVOLU-
TIONARIES.
    B. DE MOTT, 441:17SEP72-32
    T. LASK, 441:19AUG72-21
FORMAN, W. & C.A. BURLAND. MARCO POLO.
    617(TLS):4FEB72-137
FORMIGARI, L. L'ESTETICA DEL GUSTO NEL
SETTECENTO INGLESE.
    P. THOMSON & P. DIXON, 179(ES):DEC70-
    565
FORREST, J.F. - SEE BUNYAN, J.
FORREST, W.G. THE EMERGENCE OF GREEK
DEMOCRACY.
    S. NODDER, JR., 124:JAN71-162
FORRESTER, J.W. WORLD DYNAMICS. URBAN
DYNAMICS.
    P. PASSELL, M. ROBERTS & L. ROSS,
    441:2APR72-1

"FORSCHUNGEN ZUR OSTEUROPÄISCHEN GE-
SCHICHTE." (VOL 14)
W. KIRCHNER, 32:JUN71-384
"FORSCHUNGEN ZUR OSTEUROPÄISCHEN GE-
SCHICHTE." (VOL 15) (M. BERNATH, H.
JABLONOWSKI & W. PHILIPP, EDS)
M. RAEFF, 32:JUN71-385
FORSTER, E.M. THE LIFE TO COME.
617(TLS):13OCT72-1215
FORSTER, E.M. MAURICE.*
E. FEINSTEIN, 364:DEC71/JAN72-154
FORSTER, K.W. JACOPO DA PONTORMO.
A. WERNER, 56:SPRING69-91
FORSTER, L. JANUS GRUTER'S ENGLISH
YEARS.*
H. DYSERINCK, 52:BAND4HEFT3-314
N.E. OSSELTON, 179(ES):AUG70-354
C.K. POTT, 551(RENQ):AUTUMN70-316
FORSTER, L. THE ICY FIRE.
J.L. LIEVSAY, 551(RENQ):WINTER70-438
G.A. STRINGER, 568(SCN):SUMMER/AUTUMN
71-37
639(VQR):SUMMER70-C
FORSTER, L. THE POET'S TONGUES.*
P.M. MITCHELL, 301(JEGP):OCT71-748
FORSTER, R. & E., EDS. EUROPEAN SOCIETY
IN THE EIGHTEENTH CENTURY.
D.G., 173(ECS):SPRING70-422
FORSTER, U. DER VERFALLSPROZESS DER
ALTHOCHDEUTSCHEN VERBALENDUNGEN.
H. PENZL, 353:MAY69-117
FORSYTH, F. THE ODESSA FILE.
P. ADAMS, 61:DEC72-144
R.P. BRICKNER, 441:5NOV72-5
M. CRICHTON, 561(SATR):9DEC72-68
C. LEHMANN-HAUPT, 441:24OCT72-45
F. RAPHAEL, 362:28SEP72-416
FORSYTH, J. A GRAMMAR OF ASPECT.
S. LOJKINE, 67:NOV71-269
S. MORRIS, 574(SEEJ):SUMMER71-237
FORSYTH, W.D. GOVERNOR ARTHUR'S CONVICT
SYSTEM.
617(TLS):11FEB72-153
FORSYTHE, K. INSIDE ME.
M. DOYLE, 491:MAR72-356
FORTES, M., ED. MARRIAGE IN TRIBAL SOCI-
ETIES.
617(TLS):21APR72-445
FORTIER, J., ED. LE MYTHE ET LES CONTES
DE SOU EN PAYS MBAÏ-MOÏSSALA.
A.N.T., 69:JAN69-98
FORTMAN, E.J. THE TRIUNE GOD.
617(TLS):30JUN72-753
FOSBROOKE, H. NGORONGORO - THE EIGHTH
WONDER.
617(TLS):1DEC72-1466
FOSCOLO, U. ULTIME LETTERE DI JACOPO
ORTIS. (A. BALDUINO, ED)
W.T.S., 191(ELN):SEP70(SUPP)-134
FOSDICK, R.B. EUROPEAN POLICE SYSTEMS.
AMERICAN POLICE SYSTEMS.
617(TLS):18FEB72-191
FOSKETT, D. A DICTIONARY OF BRITISH
MINIATURE PAINTERS.
617(TLS):24MAR72-338
FOSS, A. MAJORCA.
617(TLS):21JUL72-846
FOSS, M. THE AGE OF PATRONAGE.
442(NY):19FEB72-116
617(TLS):10MAR72-282
FOSSI, M. BARTOLOMEO AMMANNATI, ARCHI-
TETTO.
C. DAVIS, 576:DEC69-302
FOSTER, C. POLITICS, FINANCE AND THE
ROLE OF ECONOMICS.
617(TLS):2JUN72-637

FOSTER, D.W. THE MYTH OF PARAGUAY IN THE
FICTION OF AUGUSTO ROA BASTOS.
G. BROTHERSTON, 86(BHS):JUL71-285
L.F. LYDAY, 238:SEP70-585
M.E. VENIER, 400(MLN):MAR70-319
FOSTER, D.W. & V.R., COMPS. MANUAL OF
HISPANIC BIBLIOGRAPHY.
H.C. WOODBRIDGE, 517(PBSA):JUL-SEP71-
329
FOSTER, J. DISCOVERY LEARNING IN THE
PRIMARY SCHOOL.
617(TLS):20OCT72-1264
FOSTER, J. D.H. LAWRENCE IN TAOS.
M. SCHORER, 441:16JAN72-36
617(TLS):10MAR72-280
FOSTER, L. & J.W. SWANSON, EDS. THEORY
AND EXPERIENCE.
R.E. GRANDY, 311(JP):18MAY72-282
FOSTER, L.A., COMP. BIBLIOGRAFIIA RUS-
SKOI ZARUBEZHNOI LITERATURY, 1918-1968.
S. YAKOBSON, 32:JUN71-456
FOSTER, M. JOYCE CARY.*
R.D. RODGERS, 627(UTQ):JUL69-392
FOSTER, M.B. ANTHEMS AND ANTHEM COMPOS-
ERS.
N. TEMPERLEY, 415:MAR71-243
FOSTER, R., ED. SIX AMERICAN NOVELISTS
OF THE NINETEENTH CENTURY.
R. LEHAN, 445(NCF):DEC68-373
L.L.R., 502(PRS):SUMMER69-234
FOTHERGILL, B. SIR WILLIAM HAMILTON.
D. UNDERDOWN, 639(VQR):SPRING70-361
F.J.B. WATSON, 39:DEC69-547
FOTINE, L. THEORY AND TECHNIQUES OF
TWELVE-TONE COMPOSITION.
P. STANDFORD, 415:JAN71-36
FOUCAULT, M. THE ARCHAEOLOGY OF KNOW-
LEDGE. (FRENCH TITLE: L'ARCHÉOLOGIE
DU SAVOIR.)
P. CAWS, 441:22OCT72-6
G. DELEDALLE, 319:OCT72-495
617(TLS):9JUN72-663
DE FOUCHÉCOUR, C-H. LA DESCRIPTION DE LA
NATURE DANS LA POÉSIE LYRIQUE PERSANE
DU XIE SIÈCLE.
M.B. LORAINE, 182:VOL23#23/24-979
FOUET, G. LA VILLA GALLO-ROMAINE DE
MONTMAURIN.
A.L.F. RIVET, 313:VOL60-249
DU FOUILLOUX, J. LA VÉNERIE ET L'ADOL-
ESCENCE. (G. TILANDER, ED)
M.D. LEGGE, 208(FS):APR71-189
M. THIEBAUX, 589:JUL71-511
FOULKES, A.P. THE RELUCTANT PESSIMIST.*
M. PASLEY, 220(GL&L):APR71-288
FOULKES, A.P. & E. LOHNER, EDS. DEUTSCHE
NOVELLEN VON TIECK BIS HAUPTMANN.
U.H. GERLACH, 221(GQ):JAN70-136
FOUQUET, J. THE HOURS OF ETIENNE CHEV-
ALIER.*
617(TLS):21APR72-452
FOUREL, M. DIX CONTES CHOISIS.
G. BRÉE, 207(FR):OCT69-155
FOURQUET, J. PROLEGOMENA ZU EINER
DEUTSCHEN GRAMMATIK.
G.L. TRACY, 406:FALL71-299
FOUST, C.M. MUSCOVITE AND MANDARIN.
G.A. LENSEN, 293(JAST):AUG70-919
639(VQR):SUMMER70-CIX
FOWLER, A. TRIUMPHAL FORMS.*
J. DAALDER, 67:MAY71-93
FOWLER, A. - SEE LEWIS, C.S.
FOWLER, D.C. A LITERARY HISTORY OF THE
POPULAR BALLAD.*
B.H. BRONSON, 650(WF):OCT69-280
E. FOWKE, 292(JAF):JAN-MAR70-90
L.H. HORNSTEIN, 191(ELN):SEP69-73
B.A. ROSENBERG, 405(MP):FEB70-301

FOWLER, F.G. & H.W. THE POCKET OXFORD
DICTIONARY OF CURRENT ENGLISH.* (5TH
ED REV BY E. MC INTOSH)
C.L. BARNHART, 447(N&Q):FEB70-67
FOWLER, H.W. & F.G., EDS. THE CONCISE
OXFORD DICTIONARY OF CURRENT ENGLISH.
(REV BY E. MC INTOSH & G.W.S. FRIED-
RICHSEN)
617(TLS):13OCT72-1209
FOWLES, A. DUPE NEGATIVE.
N. CALLENDAR, 441:2JUL72-15
FOWLES, J. THE FRENCH LIEUTENANT'S
WOMAN.
P. EVARTS, JR., 145(CRIT):VOL13#3-57
42(AR):WINTER69/70-587
639(VQR):SPRING70-XL
FOWLIE, W. CLIMATE OF VIOLENCE.*
L. LE SAGE, 546(RR):FEB70-68
FOWLIE, W. THE FRENCH CRITIC, 1549-
1967.*
A. GLAUSER, 207(FR):OCT69-199
FOWLIE, W. RIMBAUD.
R.T. DONOMMÉ, 569(SR):AUTUMN71-637
N. WING, 400(MLN):MAY70-623
FOWLIE, W. STENDHAL.
639(VQR):WINTER70-XIX
FOWLIE, W. - SEE RIMBAUD, A.
FOX, C. THE DOLL.
E. DE LA IGLESIA, 441:3DEC72-94
FOX, C. THE GREAT RACING CARS AND DRIV-
ERS.
J. DURSO, 441:3DEC72-7
FOX, D. - SEE HENRYSON, R.
FOX, E.I. - SEE MARTÍNEZ RUIZ, J.
FOX, E.W. HISTORY IN GEOGRAPHIC PERSPEC-
TIVE.
C.B.A. BEHRENS, 453:27JAN72-29
"FONTAINE FOX'S TOONERVILLE TROLLEY."
(H. GALEWITZ & D. WINSLOW, COMPS)
S.D. SMITH, 441:3SEP72-15
FOX, G. DANGEROUS SEASON.
D. BARBOUR, 102(CANL):SPRING71-70
E. WOODS, 606(TAMR):#55-79
FOX, J. THE LYRIC POETRY OF CHARLES
D'ORLÉANS.*
M. IVENS, 619(TC):1969/2-48
FOX, M. BEHAVIOUR OF WOLVES, DOGS AND
RELATED CANIDS.
S.K. OBERBECK, 440:21MAY72-8
FOX, M. UNDERSTANDING YOUR DOG.
441:16APR72-20
FOX, P. THE WESTERN COAST.
T.R. EDWARDS, 453:5OCT72-21
V. GORNICK, 441:8OCT72-5
T. LASK, 441:22SEP72-46
442(NY):28OCT72-158
FOX, R. THE CALORIC THEORY OF GASES FROM
LAVOISIER TO REGNAULT.
617(TLS):4FEB72-133
FOX, S.R. THE GUARDIAN OF BOSTON.
J. STUART, 432(NEQ):DEC70-684
FOXELL, N. CARNIVAL.*
G. ROPER, 627(UTQ):JUL69-359
FRAENKEL, E. LESEPROBEN AUS REDEN
CICEROS UND CATOS.
E. LAUGHTON, 313:VOL60-188
FRAENKEL, E. & OTHERS, EDS. JAHRBUCH FÜR
AMERIKASTUDIEN IM AUFTRAG DER DEUT-
SCHEN GESELLSCHAFT FÜR AMERIKASTUDIEN.
(VOLS 8-11)
J.A. WOODS, 179(ES):OCT70-473
FRAISSE, J-C. - SEE ST. AUGUSTINE
FRAME, D.M. MONTAIGNE'S ESSAIS.
F.S. BROWN, 207(FR):DEC69-354
FRAME, J. DAUGHTER BUFFALO.
J. HENDIN, 441:27AUG72-3
442(NY):30SEP72-125

FRAME, J. THE RAINBIRDS.
P. EVANS, 368:JUN69-189
FRANCE, P. RHETORIC AND TRUTH IN FRANCE.
617(TLS):21JUL72-849
FRANCH, J.A. - SEE UNDER ALCINA FRANCH,
J.
FRANCHÈRE, G. THE JOURNAL OF GABRIEL
FRANCHÈRE. (W.K. LAMB, ED)
J.S. ERSKINE, 150(DR):AUTUMN70-412
DE FRANCIA, P. LEGER'S "THE GREAT PAR-
ADE."
D. SUTTON, 39:JUN69-414
FRANCILLON, R.J. AMERICAN FIGHTERS OF
WORLD WAR TWO. (VOL 2)
617(TLS):28JUL72-900
FRANCIS, A.D. THE WINE TRADE.
617(TLS):8DEC72-1513
FRANCIS, D. BONECRACK.
P. ADAMS, 61:JUN72-112
N. CALLENDAR, 441:21MAY72-30
R. FREEDMAN, 440:30APR72-6
442(NY):22JUL72-80
FRANCIS, D. SMOKESCREEN.
617(TLS):1DEC72-1467
FRANCIS, E., WITH T. MORIARTY. THE SEC-
RETS OF WINNING HOCKEY.
J. DURSO, 441:3DEC72-40
FRANCIS, P. - SEE PALMA, R.
FRANCIS, R. THE TROUBLE WITH FRANCIS.*
D. JUNKINS, 231:OCT72-128
FRANCIS, R. - SEE FROST, R.
FRANCIS, S., ED. LIBRARIES IN THE USSR.
617(TLS):21JAN72-78
FRANCO, J. AN INTRODUCTION TO SPANISH-
AMERICAN LITERATURE.*
J.M. FLINT, 86(BHS):APR71-179
FRANCO, L. MEMORIA DE LOS DÍAS.
R. SQUIRRU, 37:JUN69-39
FRANÇON, M. - SEE DE MONTAIGNE, M.
FRÄNGSMYR, T. GEOLOGI OCH SKAPELSETRO.
A.F., 566:AUTUMN70-7
FRANK, G. AN AMERICAN DEATH.
F.J. COOK, 561(SATR):8APR72-62
G.W. JOHNSON, 440:16APR72-4
C. LEHMANN-HAUPT, 441:11APR72-43
P. WHITEHEAD, 362:14SEP72-343
442(NY):22APR72-143
FRANK, J.D. SANITY AND SURVIVAL. (GER-
MAN TITLE: MUSS KRIEG SEIN?)
H. WINDISCHER, 182:VOL23#6-257
FRANK, R. THE LINES OF MY HAND.
S. SCHWARTZ, 441:3DEC72-5
FRANK, R.I. SCHOLAE PALATINAE.*
J.K. ANDERSON, 122:JAN71-53
W. GOFFART, 487:WINTER70-361
A.H.M. JONES, 313:VOL60-227
M. WOLOCH, 24:APR71-345
FRANKE, D. & H. SAFE PLACES.
M. KITMAN, 441:4JUN72-6
FRANKE, W. CHINA AND THE WEST.
O. LATTIMORE, 587:APR68-598
FRANKE, W. AN INTRODUCTION TO THE
SOURCES OF MING HISTORY.
J.W. DARDESS, 293(JAST):MAY70-687
FRANKEL, C. EDUCATION AND THE BARRI-
CADES.
S.O.H., 543:DEC69-346
FRANKEL, C. HIGH ON FOGGY BOTTOM.
E.V. ROSTOW, 639(VQR):SPRING70-335
FRANKEL, C. A STUBBORN CASE.
M. LEVIN, 441:1OCT72-42
FRANKEL, F.R. INDIA'S GREEN REVOLUTION.
N. MAXWELL, 453:23MAR72-8
FRÄNKEL, H. NOTEN ZU DEN ARGONAUTIKA
DES APOLLONIOS.*
G. GIANGRANDE, 303:VOL90-212
FRANKEL, J. - SEE AKIMOV, V.

FRANKEL, L. & G. THE BICYCLE BOOK.
  H.C. GARDNER, 441:4JUN72-8
FRANKEL, S. BEYOND A REASONABLE DOUBT.
  P. WALL, 441:23JAN72-4
  442(NY):11MAR72-126
FRANKENSTEIN, A. & OTHERS. THE WORLD OF
  COPLEY 1738-1815.
  N. HARRIS, 432(NEQ):DEC70-664
FRANKFURT, H.G. DEMONS, DREAMERS, AND
  MADMEN.
  T. KEEFE, 518:JAN71-6
  C. PARSONS, 311(JP):27JAN72-38
FRANKFURTER, G. BANEFUL DOMINATION.
  J.E. TRENT, 99:JAN-FEB72-68
FRANKLIN, B. THE PAPERS OF BENJAMIN
  FRANKLIN. (VOL 13) (L.W. LABAREE, ED)
  S.E. MORISON, 432(NEQ):DEC70-646
  639(VQR):SUMMER70-CIV
FRANKLIN, B. THE PAPERS OF BENJAMIN
  FRANKLIN. (VOL 14) (L.W. LABAREE, ED)
  S.E. MORISON, 432(NEQ):DEC70-646
FRANKLIN, B. THE PAPERS OF BENJAMIN
  FRANKLIN. (VOL 15) (W.B. WILLCOX &
  OTHERS, EDS)
  617(TLS):22SEP72-1117
"BENJAMIN FRANKLIN: A BIOGRAPHY IN HIS
  OWN WORDS." (T. FLEMING, ED)
  442(NY):25NOV72-200
FRANKLIN, C. THE PRIVATE PRESSES.
  R. CAVE, 503:SUMMER69-86
FRANKLIN, D. BASSO CANTANTE.*
  A. BLYTH, 415:JAN70-45
FRANKLIN, E. THE MONEY MURDERS.
  N. CALLENDAR, 441:23JUL72-22
FRANKLIN, P. SHOW THYSELF A MAN.
  W.L. HEDGES, 165:FALL72-202
FRANKLIN, R.W. THE EDITING OF EMILY
  DICKINSON.
  P. URE, 447(N&Q):SEP70-359
FRANKLIN, S. THE CHICKENS IN THE AIR-
  SHAFT.
  N. CALLENDAR, 441:13AUG72-20
FRANKLIN, S. KNOWLEDGE PARK.
  J.R. SORFLEET, 296:FALL72-106
FRANKLIN, S. LEACOCK.
  102(CANL):WINTER71-107
FRANSEN, G., ED. SUMMA "ELEGANTIUS IN
  IURE DIUINO" SEU COLONIENSIS.
  J. GILCHRIST, 589:OCT71-738
FRANTZ, R.W. THE ENGLISH TRAVELLER AND
  THE MOVEMENT OF IDEAS, 1660-1732.
  R.S., 502(PRS):SUMMER68-185
VON FRANZ, M-L. ZAHL UND ZEIT.
  A. MERCIER, 182:VOL23#23/24-970
FRASER, A. THE BULL.
  617(TLS):13OCT72-1237
FRASER, D. & H.M. COLE, EDS. AFRICAN ART
  AND LEADERSHIP.
  617(TLS):16JUN72-694
FRASER, D., H. HIBBARD & M.J. LEWINE,
  EDS. ESSAYS IN THE HISTORY OF ART PRE-
  SENTED TO RUDOLF WITTKOWER. ESSAYS IN
  THE HISTORY OF ARCHITECTURE PRESENTED
  TO RUDOLF WITTKOWER.
  J. SUMMERSON, 90:JUL69-459
FRASER, G.M. FLASH FOR FREEDOM.*
  T. LASK, 441:28APR72-41
  T. SEVERIN, 440:14MAY72-3
FRASER, G.M. THE STEEL BONNETS.
  B. FARWELL, 440:23APR72-1
  T. LASK, 441:28APR72-41
  442(NY):1JUL72-75
  617(TLS):7APR72-396
FRASER, G.S. LAWRENCE DURRELL.*
  H. SERGEANT, 175:SPRING69-33
FRASER, P.M. - SEE MEYNELL, A.

FRASER, R. IN HIDING.
  P. ADAMS, 61:AUG72-92
  G. BRENAN, 453:10AUG72-21
  S. KOVEN, 561(SATR):2SEP72-52
  R.R. LINGEMAN, 441:1JUL72-19
  A. MILLER, 441:9JUL72-1
  442(NY):29JUL72-79
  617(TLS):17NOV72-1390
FRASER, R. THE WAR AGAINST POETRY.
  D.C. ALLEN, 301(JEGP):OCT71-654
  L. FEDER, 385(MQR):SPRING72-138
  R.H. WEST, 579(SAQ):AUTUMN71-611
FRASER, R.S., ED. ESSAYS ON THE ROS-
  SETTIS.
  617(TLS):17NOV72-1404
FRASER, S. PANDORA.
  H. PORTER, 296:FALL72-92
FRASER, T.M., JR. CULTURE AND CHANGE IN
  INDIA.
  H.M. CHOLDIN, 293(JAST):AUG70-965
FRASER, W.R. REFORMS AND RESTRAINTS IN
  MODERN FRENCH EDUCATION.
  617(TLS):14JAN72-49
FRAYNE, J.P. - SEE YEATS, W.B.
FRAZEE, C.A. THE ORTHODOX CHURCH AND
  INDEPENDENT GREECE 1821-1852.*
  P. SHERRARD, 575(SEER):JUL71-472
FRAZER, W.D. LOVE AS DEATH IN "THE ICE-
  MAN COMETH."
  C. DAY, 397(MD):FEB69-449
FRAZIER, A.M., ED. READINGS IN EASTERN
  RELIGIOUS THOUGHT. (VOLS 1&2)
  L. ROCHER, 318(JAOS):APR-JUN70-409
FREDE, D. ARISTOTELES UND DIE "SEE-
  SCHLACHT."
  J.R. CASSIDY, 124:JAN71-161
FRÉDÉRIC, L. DAILY LIFE IN JAPAN AT THE
  TIME OF THE SAMURAI, 1185-1603.
  617(TLS):22DEC72-1561
FREDERIC, L. JAPAN'S ART AND CIVILIZA-
  TION.
  617(TLS):5MAY72-524
FREDERICK, J.T. THE DARKENED SKY.
  M.E. RUCKER, 50(ARQ):WINTER69-369
FREDOUILLE, J-C. DICTIONNAIRE DE LA
  CIVILISATION ROMAINE.
  J. ANDRÉ, 555:VOL44FASC2-370
FREDRICKSON, O.A., WITH B. EAST. THE
  SILENCE OF THE NORTH.
  A. BROYARD, 441:25JUL72-35
FREDRO, A. THE MAJOR COMEDIES OF ALEXAN-
  DER FREDRO.* (H.B. SEGEL, ED & TRANS)
  M. GIERGIELEWICZ, 497(POLR):AUTUMN69-
  92
FREE, C. CARBON COPY.
  D.A.N. JONES, 362:10AUG72-184
  617(TLS):22SEP72-1122
FREE, W.J. "THE COLUMBIAN MAGAZINE" AND
  AMERICAN LITERARY NATIONALISM.
  C.R. DOLMETSCH, 656(WMQ):JUL70-490
FREEDBERG, S.J. PAINTING IN ITALY 1500-
  1600.*
  H. ZERNER, 453:31AUG72-25
FREEDMAN, M. - SEE UNDER HARRIS, M.
FREEDMAN, R. & J.Y. TAKESHITA. FAMILY
  PLANNING IN TAIWAN.
  D.W. VARLEY, 293(JAST):AUG70-937
FREELAND, J.M. THE MAKING OF A PROFES-
  SION.
  617(TLS):28JAN72-109
FREELAND, R.M. THE TRUMAN DOCTRINE AND
  THE ORIGINS OF MC CARTHYISM.
  S.E. AMBROSE, 440:30JAN72-5
  R. GRIFFITH, 561(SATR):22APR72-75
  C. LEHMANN-HAUPT, 441:21JAN72-45
  W.V. SHANNON, 441:16JAN72-3

FREELING, N. AUPRÈS DE MA BLONDE.
O.L. BAILEY, 561(SATR):26AUG72-61
A. BROYARD, 441:19JUL72-39
N. CALLENDAR, 441:6AUG72-24
442(NY):2SEP72-72
FREELING, N. A LONG SILENCE.
617(TLS):7JUL72-783
FREEMAN, A. ASSAYS OF BIAS.
R.B. SHAW, 491:MAR72-342
FREEMAN, A. THOMAS KYD.
R. LEVIN, 405(MP):FEB70-282
R.W. VAN FOSSEN, 191(ELN):MAR70-217
FREEMAN, L. THE DREAM.*
N. CALLENDAR, 441:9JAN72-33
FREEMAN, R. ENGLISH EMBLEM BOOKS.
B. VICKERS, 148:WINTER70-382
FREEMAN, S.T. NEIGHBORS.
617(TLS):19MAY72-580
FREER, C. MUSIC FOR A KING.
617(TLS):22SEP72-1099
FRÉGAULT, G. LE XVIIIE SIÈCLE CANADIEN.
J-C. BONENFANT, 627(UTQ):JUL69-454
FREGE, G. KLEINE SCHRIFTEN. (I. ANGEL-
ELLI, ED)
M.D. RESNIK, 486:DEC68-424
FREI, G. WALSERDEUTSCH IN SALEY.
E.H. YARRILL, 182:VOL23#7-351
FREIBERG, M., ED. JOURNALS OF THE HOUSE
OF REPRESENTATIVES OF MASSACHUSETTS,
1761, 1762 AND 1762-1763. (VOLS 38 &
39)
J.A. SCHUTZ, 432(NEQ):JUN70-340
FREIDIN, S.K. A SENSE OF THE SENATE.
T. LASK, 441:4JUL72-15
442(NY):12AUG72-78
FREIRE, P. PEDAGOGY OF THE OPPRESSED.
E. SHORRIS, 231:DEC72-119
FREMLIN, C. APPOINTMENT WITH YESTERDAY.
N. CALLENDAR, 441:1OCT72-43
617(TLS):28APR72-500
FRÉMONT, J.C. THE EXPEDITIONS OF JOHN
CHARLES FRÉMONT. (VOL 1) (D. JACKSON &
M.L. SPENCE, EDS)
J.F. BANNON, 377:JUL71-114
FRENCH, A. GONE FOR A SOLDIER.
617(TLS):13OCT72-1236
FRENCH, A. THE POETS OF PRAGUE.*
E.J. CZERWINSKI, 32:DEC71-915
R.B. PYNSENT, 575(SEER):JAN71-143
FRENCH, F-J. A BIBLIOGRAPHY OF THE ABBEY
THEATRE SERIES OF PLAYS.
J. COTTON, 503:AUTUMN69-131
FRENCH, P.J. JOHN DEE.
617(TLS):19MAY72-579
FREND, W.H.C. MARTYRDOM AND PERSECUTION
IN THE EARLY CHURCH.*
W.A.J., 543:SEP69-129
G.M., 477:SUMMER69-411
FRENKEL, V. IMAGE SPACES.
T.L. WEPPLER, 99:JUL-AUG72-46
FRÈRE, É. & R. LABORDE. QUELQUES JOUR-
NÉES FRANÇAISES.
H.L. ROBINSON, 399(MLJ):NOV70-530
FRERE, S. & OTHERS. VERULAMIUM EXCAVA-
TIONS. (VOL 1)
617(TLS):26MAY72-599
FREUD, A. THE WRITINGS OF ANNA FREUD.
R. COLES, 442(NY):23SEP72-124
R.S. STEWART, 441:23JAN72-1
FREUD, A. & OTHERS, EDS. THE PSYCHOANA-
LYTIC STUDY OF THE CHILD. (VOL 25)
617(TLS):14APR72-425
FREUD, H.H. PALISSOT AND "LES PHILOSO-
PHES."*
J.N. PAPPAS, 546(RR):APR70-143
FREUDMANN, F.R. - SEE RACINE, J.

FREUND, F. PRÄPOSITIONALE UND KASUELLE
ZEITANGABEN AUF DIE FRAGE "WANN" IM
GEGENWÄRTIGEN DEUTSCH.
J. EICHHOFF, 406:WINTER71-417
FREUND, J. L'ESSENCE DU POLITIQUE.
C. SCHUWER, 542:JUL-DEC69-454
FREUND, P.A., ED. EXPERIMENTATION WITH
HUMAN SUBJECTS.
617(TLS):17NOV72-1395
FREY, F. & W. HUGELSHOFER. THE BÜRGEN-
STOCK.
R. ELVIN, 39:NOV69-445
FREY, J.R. GERMAN LITERATURE.
I.C., 191(ELN):SEP70(SUPP)-92
FREY, O-H. DIE ENTSTEHUNG DER SITULEN-
KUNST.
J. BOARDMAN, 313:VOL60-266
FREY-ROHN, L. VON FREUD ZU JUNG.
V. VON DER HEYDT, 182:VOL23#8-394
FREYTAG, H. KOMMENTAR ZUR FRÜHMITTEL-
HOCHDEUTSCHEN SUMMA THEOLOGIAE.*
D.H. GREEN, 402(MLR):JUL71-702
FRIDH, A. LE PROBLÈME DE LA PASSION DES
SAINTES PERPÉTUE ET FÉLICITÉ.
P. LANGLOIS, 555:VOL44FASC2-357
FRIEDBERG, M. - SEE TROTSKY, L.
FRIEDLAENDER, W. NICOLAS POUSSIN.
R.W. LEE, 54:SEP69-298
FRIEDLANDER, A.H. LEO BAECK.
H.W. BRANN, 328:SPRING69-251
FRIEDLÄNDER, M.J. EARLY NETHERLANDISH
PAINTING.* (VOLS 1&2) (NEW ED)
T.P. GRANGE, 90:JUL69-460
FRIEDLÄNDER, P. PLATO 2.
R. BAMBROUGH, 123:JUN71-289
FRIEDLÄNDER, P. PLATO 3.
R. BAMBROUGH, 123:JUN71-289
D.W. HAMLYN, 518:MAY70-8
R.G. HOERBER, 122:JUL71-192
A.R. LACEY, 483:JUL70-261
FRIEDLÄNDER, P. STUDIEN ZUR ANTIKEN LIT-
ERATUR UND KUNST.*
H. LLOYD-JONES, 123:DEC71-409
FRIEDMAN, A. HERMAPHRODEITY.
L.J. DAVIS, 440:12MAR72-10
W. HJORTSBERG, 441:19MAR72-4
J. HUNTER, 362:27JUL72-118
R. SALE, 453:4MAY72-3
617(TLS):4AUG72-909
FRIEDMAN, A.B. & N.T. HARRINGTON - SEE
"YWAIN AND GAWAIN"
FRIEDMAN, B.H. JACKSON POLLOCK.
D. HICKEY, 561(SATR):9SEP72-80
H. KRAMER, 441:8OCT72-7
FRIEDMAN, D.M. MARVELL'S PASTORAL ART.*
R.J. BAUER, 568(SCN):SUMMER/AUTUMN71-
43
M. SHAPIRO, 301(JEGP):OCT71-665
FRIEDMAN, L. & F.L. ISRAEL, EDS. THE
JUSTICES OF THE UNITED STATES SUPREME
COURT, 1789-1969.
R.K. NEWMYER, 656(WMQ):OCT70-680
FRIEDMAN, M. TO DENY OUR NOTHINGNESS.*
L.B. CEBIK, 219(GAR):FALL69-397
FRIEDMAN, M.J., ED. SAMUEL BECKETT NOW.
R. PEARCE, 295:VOL2#3-442
FRIEDMAN, M.J. & J.B. VICKERY, EDS. THE
SHAKEN REALIST.
G.M. PERKINS, 295:VOL2#1-133
FRIEDMAN, R. THE INSURRECTION OF HIPPO-
LYTUS BRANDENBERG.
D. MARTIN, 381:VOL29#1-128
FRIEDMANN, G. LEIBNIZ ET SPINOZA.
L. PRENANT, 542:JUL-SEP68-410
FRIEDRICH, C.J. TRADITION AND AUTHORITY.
617(TLS):13OCT72-1221
FRIEDRICH, H., ED. MAN AND ANIMAL.
617(TLS):16JUN72-694

FRIEDRICH, H. MONTAIGNE.
  I.D. MC FARLANE, 208(FS):JUL71-326
FRIEDRICH, H-V. - SEE THESSALUS OF
  TRALLES
FRIEDRICH, O. BEFORE THE DELUGE.
  P. ADAMS, 61:JUN72-112
  C. LEHMANN-HAUPT, 441:5MAY72-43
  442(NY):12AUG72-80
FRIEDRICH, O. DECLINE AND FALL.
  W. HARDCASTLE, 362:20APR72-523
  617(TLS):26MAY72-596
FRIEDRICH, P. PROTO-INDO-EUROPEAN TREES.
  F.J. OINAS, 574(SEEJ):SUMMER71-239
FRIEDRICH, W. MODERNE DEUTSCHE IDIO-
  MATIK.
  A.L. LLOYD, 221(GQ):MAR70-257
FRIEL, G. MR. ALFRED MA.
  V. CUNNINGHAM, 362:2MAR72-283
  617(TLS):10MAR72-265
FRIESE, W. NORDISCHE BAROCKDICHTUNG.*
  F. PAUL, 462(OL):VOL25#1/2-214
  P. RIES, 220(GL&L):JUL71-392
FRINGS, M.S., ED. HEIDEGGER AND THE
  QUEST FOR TRUTH.
  Q. LAUER, 613:WINTER69-623
FRINTA, M.S. THE GENIUS OF ROBERT CAM-
  PIN.
  T.P. GRANGE, 90:JUL69-460
FRISCH, M. TAGEBUCH 1966-1971.
  617(TLS):29SEP72-1144
FRISCH, O.R. THE NATURE OF MATTER.
  617(TLS):14JUL72-798
FRISCH, P. DIE TRÄUME BEI HERODOT.*
  H.C. AVERY, 24:JUL71-510
FRISCHAUER, W. DAVID FROST.
  W. HARDCASTLE, 362:24FEB72-250
  617(TLS):7APR72-402
FRISK, H. GRIECHISCHES ETYMOLOGISCHES
  WÖRTERBUCH. (PTS 13-22)
  W.F. WYATT, 124:MAR71-240
FRISK, H. KLEINE SCHRIFTEN ZUR INDOGER-
  MANISTIK UND ZUR GRIECHISCHEN WORT-
  KUNDE.
  D.M. JONES, 123:JUN71-242
FRISTEDT, S.L. THE WYCLIFFE BIBLE.*
  (PT 2)
  A. HUDSON, 382(MAE):1971/2-204
FRITZ, H. LITERARISCHER JUGENDSTIL UND
  EXPRESSIONISMUS.
  I.K. MC GILL, 67:NOV71-260
VON FRITZ, K. PLATON IN SIZILIEN UND DAS
  PROBLEM DER PHILOSOPHENHERRSCHAFT.*
  P. LOUIS, 555:VOL44FASC1-128
  G.R. MORROW, 487:SPRING70-79
  J.B. SKEMP, 123:MAR71-26
  F.M. WASSERMANN, 121(CJ):DEC70-JAN71-
  188
FRIZELL, B. THE GRAND DEFIANCE.
  A. BROYARD, 441:9MAR72-43
  M. LEVIN, 441:26MAR72-43
FRODSHAM, J.D. THE MURMURING STREAM.
  W.J•F. JENNER, 447(N&Q):JUL70-279
FRÖHLICH, H.J. ENGELS KOPF.
  617(TLS):5MAY72-526
FRÖHLICH, K. - SEE CULLMANN, O.
FROHOCK, W.M., ED. IMAGE AND THEME.
  V. MINOGUE, 402(MLR):JAN71-197
FRÖLICH, P. ROSA LUXEMBURG.
  617(TLS):24NOV72-1433
FROMM, E. THE CRISIS OF PSYCHOLANALYSIS.
  617(TLS):28APR72-499
FROMM, H. BERNARD SHAW AND THE THEATER
  IN THE NINETIES.
  T.F. EVANS, 571:SPRING-SUMMER68-20
  F.P.W. MC DOWELL, 397(MD):DEC68-341
FROST, D.L. THE SCHOOL OF SHAKESPEARE.
  C. LEECH, 570(SQ):AUTUMN69-474
  M. MINCOFF, 179(ES):DEC70-554

FROST, H. THE MORTAR WRECK IN MELLIEHA
  BAY.
  R.W. HUTCHINSON, 303:VOL90-262
FROST, L. NEW HAMPSHIRE'S CHILD. (L.
  THOMPSON & A. GRADE, EDS)
  P.L. NICOLOFF, 432(NEQ):MAR70-165
FROST, R. FROST: A TIME TO TALK. (R.
  FRANCIS, ED)
  P. DAVISON, 441:10DEC72-5
  D. JUNKINS, 231:OCT72-128
FROST, R. THE POETRY OF ROBERT FROST.*
  (E.C. LATHEM, ED)
  F. BIDART, 473(PR):1971/3-350
  G. BURNS, 584(SWR):SUMMER71-295
FROST, R. & E. FAMILY LETTERS OF ROBERT
  AND ELINOR FROST. (A. GRADE, ED)
  P. DAVISON, 441:10DEC72-5
FROTHINGHAM, A.W. TILE PANELS OF SPAIN
  1500-1650.
  R.C. SMITH, 90:OCT70-708
FROUD, N. SOME OF OUR BEST RECIPES ARE
  JEWISH.
  617(TLS):29DEC72-1591
FROUD, N. & J. HANLEY - SEE CHALIAPIN,
  F.I.
FRUCHTER, N. SINGLE FILE.*
  M. MIRSKY, 473(PR):WINTER71/72-480
"DER FRÜHE REALISMUS IN DEUTSCHLAND
  1800-1850."
  H. HUTH, 54:MAR69-98
FRÜHWALD, W. - SEE BRENTANO, C.
FRUMAN, N. COLERIDGE, THE DAMAGED
  ARCHANGEL.*
  G.H. HARTMAN, 441:12MAR72-1
  L.C. KNIGHTS, 453:4MAY72-25
  H. ORMSBY-LENNON, 31(ASCH):SUMMER72-
  468
  R. PARK, 362:14DEC72-836
  C. RICKS, 561(SATR):15JAN72-31
  617(TLS):1DEC72-1463
FRUMKIN, G. ARCHAEOLOGY IN SOVIET CEN-
  TRAL ASIA.
  C.C. LAMBERG-KARLOVSKY, 32:SEP71-656
FRY, A. COME A LONG JOURNEY.*
  S. ATHERTON, 296:SPRING72-82
FRY, A. HOW A PEOPLE DIE.*
  P. BARCLAY, 102(CANL):AUTUMN71-94
FRY, D.K. "BEOWULF" AND "THE FIGHT AT
  FINNSBURH."*
  F.C. ROBINSON, 589:APR71-367
  639(VQR):SUMMER70-XCVIII
FRY, D.K., ED. THE BEOWULF POET.
  J. TORRINGA, 179(ES):DEC69-603
FRY, E.F. DAVID SMITH.*
  G. BARO, 592:NOV69-197
FRY, R. LETTERS OF ROGER FRY. (D. SUT-
  TON, ED)
  P.N. FURBANK, 362:5OCT72-444
  617(TLS):1DEC72-1457
FRYE, N. THE CRITICAL PATH.
  P.C. NOEL-BENTLEY, 296:SUMMER72-78
FRYE, N. FOOLS OF TIME.
  R.M. FRYE, 570(SQ):WINTER69-101
FRYE, N. THE STUBBORN STRUCTURE.*
  W. JACKSON, 579(SAQ):SUMMER71-418
  676(YR):SPRING71-VI
FRYE, N. A STUDY OF ENGLISH ROMANTICISM.
  J.J. DUFFY, 399(MLJ):FEB70-131
  R.G. WOODMAN, 627(UTQ):JUL69-371
FRYKENBERG, R.E., ED. LAND CONTROL AND
  SOCIAL STRUCTURE IN INDIAN HISTORY.
  R.I. CRANE, 293(JAST):AUG70-951
  J.D.M. DERRETT, 318(JOAS):OCT-DEC70-
  596
FRYKMAN, E. W.E. AYTOUN, PIONEER PROFES-
  SOR OF ENGLISH AT EDINBURGH.
  H.H. MEIER, 179(ES):OCT70-461

FU, L-S. A DOCUMENTARY CHRONICLE OF
SINO-WESTERN RELATIONS (1644-1820).
J. SPENCE, 318(JAOS):OCT-DEC70-626
FUBINI, M. MÉTRICA Y POESÍA.
M. ARIZMENDI, 202(FMOD):NOV69-100
FUCHS, A. VOM MORGEN IN DIE NACHT.
T. WEYR, 19(AGR):VOL35#3-33
FUCHS, E. & R.J. HAVIGHURST. TO LIVE ON
THIS EARTH.
M. ROGIN, 441:24DEC72-4
FUCHS, G. ARCHITEKTURDARSTELLUNGEN AUF
RÖMISCHEN MÜNZEN DER REPUBLIK UND DER
FRÜHER KAISERZEIT.
J.M.C. TOYNBEE, 123:MAR71-122
FUCHS, G.B., ED. DIE MEISENGEIGE.
J.C. MIDDLETON, 220(GL&L):OCT70-108
FUCHS, H. DAS KLAGELIED DER SULPICIA
ÜBER DIE GEWALTHERRSCHAFT DES KAISERS
DOMITIAN.
J. ANDRÉ, 555:VOL44FASC2-349
FUCHS, R.H. REMBRANDT IN AMSTERDAM.
A. WERNER, 340(KR):1970/1-121
FUCHS, V. THE ART OF SINGING AND VOICE
TECHNIQUE. (REV)
A. BLYTH, 415:FEB70-164
FÜCHTNER, J. DIE BÜNDNISSE DER BODEN-
SEESTÄDTE BIS ZUM JAHRE 1390.
R. FOLZ, 182:VOL23#19/20-886
S.W. ROWAN, 589:OCT71-740
DE FUENTES, Â.G. - SEE UNDER GALMÉS DE
FUENTES, Â.
FUENTES, C. LA NUEVA NOVELA HISPANO-
AMERICANA.
R.M. REEVE, 238:MAY70-347
FUENTES, C., J. DONOSO & S. SARDUY.
TRIPLE CROSS.
P. ADAMS, 61:OCT72-135
E. RODRÍGUEZ MONEGAL, 441:24DEC72-6
FÜETRER, U. DER TROJANERKRIEG. (E.G.
FICHTNER, ED)
W.H. JACKSON, 402(MLR):JAN71-211
FUGARD, S. THE CASTAWAYS.
617(TLS):10NOV72-1375
FUHRMANN, M. DIE ANTIKE UND IHRE VER-
MITTLER.
H. LLOYD-JONES, 123:DEC70-384
FUKUTAKE, T. JAPANESE RURAL SOCIETY.
E.H. JOHNSON, 293(JAST):MAY70-703
FUKUZAWA YUKICHI. AN ENCOURAGEMENT OF
LEARNING. (D.A. DILWORTH & UMEYO
HIRANO, TRANS)
K.B. PYLE, 293(JAST):AUG70-941
FULFORD, R. CRISIS AT THE VICTORY BUR-
LESQUE.*
J.M. ROBSON, 627(UTQ):JUL69-425
FULFORD, R., D. GODFREY & A. ROTSTEIN.
READ CANADIAN.
R. COOK, 99:JUN72-32
FULLARD, H., ED. PHILIPS' CONCORDE
WORLD ATLAS.
617(TLS):22DEC72-1562
FULLER, J. CANNIBALS AND MISSIONARIES.
P.N. FURBANK, 362:21SEP72-374
617(TLS):26MAY72-607
FULLER, J. A READER'S GUIDE TO W.H.
AUDEN.*
G.L. BRUNS, 590:WINTER71-37
FULLER, J.O. SHELLEY.
K.N.C., 191(ELN):SEP69(SUPP)-41
FULLER, J.O. SWINBURNE.
J. BAIRD, 541(RES):MAY70-235
A. TIBBLE, 175:SUMMER69-69
J.R. WATSON, 148:AUTUMN70-287
FULLER, R. NEW POEMS.
W·P·T·, 619(TC):1968/3-58
FULLER, R. OWLS AND ARTIFICERS.*
B. JONES, 364:OCT/NOV71-140

FULLER, R.B. INTUITION.
E. CAPOUYA, 561(SATR):24JUN72-67
FULLER, R.H. THE FORMATION OF THE
RESURRECTION NARRATIVES.
617(TLS):17NOV72-1399
FULLERTON, B. & A.F. WILLIAMS. SCANDI-
NAVIA.
617(TLS):2JUN72-626
FUMAGALLI, M.T-B-B. - SEE UNDER BEONIO-
BROCCHIERI FUMAGALLI, M.T.
FUNT, D. DIDEROT AND THE ESTHETICS OF
THE ENLIGHTENMENT.*
D.G. CREIGHTON, 207(FR):OCT69-185
FURBANK, P.N. REFLECTIONS ON THE WORD
"IMAGE."*
J. LEES, 89(BJA):SPRING71-206
FURBANK, P.N. - SEE DICKENS, C.
FURBERG, M. SAYING AND MEANING.
617(TLS):21JAN72-61
FURHAMMAR, L. & F. ISAKSSON. POLITICS
AND FILM.
B. BARNEY, 99:JUL-AUG72-40
FURLEY, D.J. TWO STUDIES IN THE GREEK
ATOMISTS.*
J.L. ACKRILL, 393(MIND):APR70-307
FURLEY, D.J. & R.E. ALLEN, EDS. STUDIES
IN PRESOCRATIC PHILOSOPHY.* (VOL 1)
A.J. BOYLE, 63:DEC71-329
R.W. HALL, 124:MAY71-317
FURLONG, G. JOSÉ TORRE REVELLO, "A
SELF-MADE MAN."
E. DE GANDÍA, 263:OCT-DEC71-462
"FURNITURE HISTORY." (VOL 7)
617(TLS):7JAN72-8
"FURNITURE YOU CAN MAKE."
B. GLADSTONE, 441:3DEC72-99
FURST, L.R. ROMANTICISM IN PERSPECTIVE.
T·P· SAINE, 406:SUMMER71-177
E. SHAFFER, 402(MLR):JAN71-172
G. THOMAS, 175:SUMMER69-70
FÜRSTENWALD, M. ANDREAS GRYPHIUS: DIS-
SERTATIONES FUNEBRES.*
F.W. WENTZLAFF-EGGEBERT, 406:FALL71-
278
FURTH, C. TING WEN-CHIANG.
M. BERNAL, 453:23MAR72-31
FUSERO, C. THE BORGIAS.
617(TLS):10NOV72-1360
FUSSELL, P. SAMUEL JOHNSON AND THE LIFE
OF WRITING.*
617(TLS):20OCT72-1241
FUTUTAKE, T., T. ŌUCHI & C. NAKANE. THE
SOCIO-ECONOMIC STRUCTURE OF THE INDIAN
VILLAGE.
D.M. SPENCER, 318(JAOS):APR-JUN70-363
FUZŪLĪ. LEYLA AND MEJNŪN. (S. HURI,
TRANS; A. BOMBACI, ED)
617(TLS):3MAR72-257

GABAŁÓWNA, L. ZE STUDIÓW NAD GRUPĄ
BRZESKOKUJAWSKĄ KULTURY LENDZIELSKIEJ.
K. TACKENBERG, 182:VOL23#21/22-940
GABEL, J. LA FAUSSE CONSCIENCE.
J. PIQUEMAL, 542:JAN-MAR68-136
GABINSKIJ, M.A. VOZNIKNOVENIE INFINITIVA
KAK VTORIČNYJ BALKANSKIJ JAZYKOVOJ
PROCESS.
J.S. KOLSTI, 574(SEEJ):SUMMER71-247
GABOR, D. THE MATURE SOCIETY.
S. HAMPSHIRE, 453:21SEP72-12
617(TLS):23JUN72-714
GABOR, M. THE PIN-UP.
561(SATR):23DEC72-61

GABORIT-CHOPIN, D. LA DÉCORATION DES
MANUSCRITS À SAINT-MARTIAL DE LIMOGES
ET EN LIMOUSIN DU IXE AU XIIE SIÈCLE.
J.J.G. ALEXANDER, 382(MAE):1971/2-210
GABRIEL, A.L. GARLANDIA.
J.A.W.B., 382(MAE):1971/1-90
GABRIELI, V. - SEE DIGBY, K.
GÁBRY, G. OLD MUSICAL INSTRUMENTS.
G. OLDHAM, 415:APR70-393
GABUS, J. ART NÈGRE.
G.I. JONES, 69:APR69-191
GAD, T. & K. WEBER - SEE ANDERSEN, H.C.
GADAMER, H-G. KLEINE SCHRIFTEN.
L. WELCH, 290(JAAC):SUMMER70-545
GADAMER, H-G. & OTHERS. IDEE UND ZAHL.*
N. GULLEY, 123:MAR71-30
GADD, C.J. THE CAMBRIDGE ANCIENT HIS-
TORY. (REV) (VOL 2, CHAPTER 18)
D.B. WEISBERG, 318(JAOS):APR-JUN70-
330
GADDIS, J.L. THE UNITED STATES AND THE
ORIGINS OF THE COLD WAR 1941-1947.
C.S. MAIER, 441:10SEP72-6
DI GADDO, B. LE FONTANE DI ROMA.
N. MILLER, 54:MAR69-96
GADEA, H. ERNESTO.
R. SEAVER, 561(SATR):2SEP72-56
GADNEY, R. SOMEWHERE IN ENGLAND.
N. CALLENDAR, 441:19MAR72-41
H. FRANKEL, 561(SATR):13MAY72-86
GADOFFRE, G. CLAUDEL ET L'UNIVERS
CHINOIS.
E. BEAUMONT, 208(FS):JAN71-104
H. WATERS, 207(FR):MAR70-684
GADOL, J. LEON BATTISTA ALBERTI.
L.V.R., 568(SCN):SPRING71-30
GAEFFKE, P. UNTERSUCHUNGEN ZUR SYNTAX
DES HINDI.*
L.A. SCHWARZSCHILD, 318(JAOS):APR-
JUN70-359
GAENG, P.A. AN INQUIRY INTO LOCAL VARI-
ATIONS IN VULGAR LATIN, AS REFLECTED
IN THE VOCALISM OF CHRISTIAN INSCRIP-
TIONS.
L. ROMEO, 545(RPH):FEB71-516
GAENG, P.A. AN INQUIRY INTO THE INFLU-
ENCES OF THE GERMANIC SUPERSTRATUM ON
THE VOCABULARY AND PHONETIC STRUCTURE
OF GALLO-ROMANCE.
P.M. LLOYD, 545(RPH):NOV70-363
GAFURIUS, F. THE "PRACTICA MUSICAE" OF
FRANCHINUS GAFURIUS.* (I. YOUNG, ED &
TRANS)
L. GUSHEE, 308:SPRING70-127
GAGE, J. COLOUR IN TURNER.
M. BUTLIN, 592:NOV69-185
GAGE, J. LIFE IN ITALY AT THE TIME OF
THE MEDICI.
C.H. CLOUGH, 39:OCT69-353
GAGE, J. TURNER: RAIN, STEAM AND SPEED.
617(TLS):11AUG72-940
GAGE, N. THE MAFIA IS NOT AN EQUAL
OPPORTUNITY EMPLOYER.*
W. SHEED, 453:20JUL72-23
GAGE, N., ED. MAFIA, U.S.A.
J. CONAWAY, 561(SATR):18NOV72-86
GAHLEN, B. DIE ÜBERPRÜFUNG PRODUKTIONS-
THEORETISCHER HYPOTHESEN FÜR DEUTSCH-
LAND (1830 BIS 1913).
A. HÜFNER, 182:VOL23#4-150
DE GAIFFIER, B. & OTHERS. RELIGION,
ERUDITION ET CRITIQUE À LA FIN DU
XVIIE SIÈCLE ET AU DÉBUT DU XVIIIE.
B.E. SCHWARZBACH, 546(RR):OCT70-223
GAIL, A. BHAKTI IM BHĀGAVATAPURĀṆA.*
O. VON HINÜBER, 182:VOL23#13/14-647
GAILEY, A. IRISH FOLK DRAMA.
M. EMSLIE, 595(SCS):VOL15PT1-83

GAILEY, A. & A. FENTON, EDS. THE SPADE
IN NORTHERN AND ATLANTIC EUROPE.
M.J. STANLEY, 595(SCS):VOL15PT1-75
GAILEY, H.A. THE ROAD TO ABA.
617(TLS):10MAR72-268
GAINER, B. THE ALIEN INVASION.
617(TLS):15DEC72-1526
GAINES, C. STAY HUNGRY.
M. LEVIN, 441:13AUG72-31
A. PRYCE-JONES, 617(TLS):1SEP72-1022
E. WEEKS, 61:AUG72-90
GAINHAM, S. TAKEOVER BID.
M. LEVIN, 441:9JAN72-32
442(NY):22JAN72-99
GAJECKY, G. & A. BARAN. THE COSSACKS IN
THE THIRTY YEARS WAR. (VOL 1)
P. LONGWORTH, 575(SEER):JUL71-471
GAL, G. & S. BROWN - SEE OCKHAM, WILLIAM
OF
GALAAL, M.H.I. THE TERMINOLOGY AND PRAC-
TICE OF SOMALI WEATHER LORE, ASTRONOMY
AND ASTROLOGY.
B.W. ANDRZEJEWSKI, 315(JAL):VOL7PT3-
223
GALANOY, T. TONIGHT!
R. LASSON, 441:24DEC72-12
GALARZA, E. BARRIO BOY.
J. WOMACK, JR., 453:31AUG72-12
GALAVARIS, G. BREAD AND THE LITURGY.
J.D. BRECKENRIDGE, 589:JAN71-152
GALBRAITH, J.K. AMBASSADOR'S JOURNAL.
639(VQR):SPRING70-LXVII
GALBRAITH, J.K. ECONOMICS, PEACE AND
LAUGHTER.* (A.D. WILLIAMS, ED)
P. OPPENHEIMER, 362:6JAN72-23
GALBRAITH, J.K. THE NEW INDUSTRIAL
STATE.* (2ND ED)
L. ROSS, 453:27JAN72-25
GALE, G.R. - SEE DE CÓRDOBA, S.
GALE, J. TRAVELS WITH A SON.
617(TLS):10MAR72-272
GALE, R.L. PLOTS AND CHARACTERS IN THE
FICTION AND SKETCHES OF NATHANIEL HAW-
THORNE.
S.J. KRAUSE, 432(NEQ):MAR70-152
GALEA, J. BIBLIOGRAPHY OF THE GREAT
SIEGE OF MALTA, 1565-1965.
H. ALKER, 182:VOL23#5-193
GALEN. ON THE USEFULNESS OF THE PARTS
OF THE BODY.* (M.T. MAY, ED & TRANS)
F. SOLMSEN, 122:OCT71-267
GALEWITZ, H. & D. WINSLOW - SEE "FONTAINE
FOX'S TOONERVILLE TROLLEY"
GALIANI, F. DIALOGUES ENTRE M. MARQUIS
DE ROQUEMAURE, ET MS. LE CHEVALIER
ZANOBI.* (P. KOCH, ED)
J. ROGERS, 400(MLN):MAY70-613
A.M. WILSON, 399(MLJ):JAN70-50
W. WRAGE, 207(FR):DEC69-350
GALIANO, A.A. - SEE UNDER ALCALÁ GALIANO,
A.
GALINSKY, G.K. AENEAS, SICILY, AND
ROME.*
R.R. HOLLOWAY & M.C.J. PUTNAM, 122:
OCT71-280
R.M. OGILVIE, 123:JUN71-218
639(VQR):SPRING70-LX
GALINSKY, G.K. THE HERAKLES THEME.
617(TLS):3NOV72-1344
GALLAGHER, P. THE LIFE AND WORKS OF
GARCI SÁNCHEZ DE BADAJOZ.
E.L. RIVERS, 400(MLN):MAR70-291
GALLAGHER, S. MEDIEVAL ART.
A. KUHN, 58:SEP/OCT69-14
GALLARATI SCOTTI, T. LA GIOVINEZZA DEL
MANZONI.
O.R., 191(ELN):SEP70(SUPP)-139

GALLAS, H. MARXISTISCHE LITERATUR-
THEORIE.
617(TLS):29SEP72-1169
GALLEGLY, J. FROM ALAMO PLAZA TO JACK
HARRIS'S SALOON.
W. GARD, 584(SWR):SUMMER71-V
GALLEGO, M.A. - SEE UNDER ARTOLA GALLEGO,
M.
GALLEGO MORELL, A. GARCILASO DE LA VEGA
Y SUS COMENTARISTAS.
A. ESPANTOSO-FOLEY, 240(HR):JAN70-88
GALLER, M. & H.E. MARQUESS. SOVIET
PRISON CAMP SPEECH.
617(TLS):21JUL72-838
GALLERY, D.V. THE PUEBLO INCIDENT.
J.E. DORNAN, JR., 396(MODA):SPRING71-
197
GALLET, M. DEMEURES PARISIENNES.
L.C. LANGE, 576:OCT69-230
GALLET, M. PARIS DOMESTIC ARCHITECTURE
OF THE 18TH CENTURY.
617(TLS):25AUG72-989
GALLETIER, É., WITH J. FONTAINE - SEE
AMMIANUS
GALLIE, W.B. PEIRCE AND PRAGMATISM.
A. MONTI, 548(RCSF):JUL/SEP69-336
GALLO, M. HISTOIRE DE L'ESPAGNE FRAN-
QUISTE.
R.A.H. ROBINSON, 86(BHS):OCT71-358
GALLO, M. THE NIGHT OF THE LONG KNIVES.
P. ADAMS, 61:AUG72-92
GALLOWAY, D. & J. WHITLEY, EDS. TEN
MODERN AMERICAN SHORT STORIES.
J.D. HAINSWORTH, 67:MAY71-124
GALLUP, D. WHERE I HANG MY HAT.
D. LEHMAN, 491:JAN72-224
GALMÉS DE FUENTES, Á. EL LIBRO DE LAS
BATALLAS (NARRACIONES CABALLERESCAS
ALJAMIADO-MORISCAS).
C. LÓPEZ-MORILLAS, 545(RPH):MAY70-607
J.M. SOLÁ-SOLÉ, 240(HR):JUL70-320
GALPERIN, I.R., ED. BOLSHOI ANGLO-
RUSSKII SLOVAR.
617(TLS):13OCT72-1230
GALPIN, F.W. THE MUSIC OF THE SUMERIANS,
BABYLONIANS AND ASSYRIANS.
R. ANDERSON, 415:NOV70-1116
GALSWORTHY, J. JOHN GALSWORTHY'S LETTERS
TO LEON LION. (A.B. WILSON, ED)
D.W. EVANS, 402(MLR):JUL71-681
GALT, J. THE ENTAIL. (I.A. GORDON, ED)
P. FAULKNER, 677:VOL2-292
GAMBER, K. DIE AUTORSCHAFT VON DE SACRA-
MENTIS.
E. KÄHLER, 182:VOL23#9-467
GAMBER, K. MISSA ROMENSIS.
O. LANG, 182:VOL23#10-525
GAMBERALE, L. LA TRADUZIONE IN GELLIO.
W.T. AVERY, 124:NOV70-94
GAMIO, M. THE LIFE STORY OF THE MEXICAN
IMMIGRANT.
J. WOMACK, JR., 453:31AUG72-12
GAMMOND, P., ED. BEST MUSIC HALL AND
VARIETY SONGS.
617(TLS):3NOV72-1349
GANDHI, I. WIT AND WISDOM OF INDIRA
GANDHI, THE UNCROWNED QUEEN OF INDIA.
(N.B. SEN, ED)
617(TLS):23JUN72-729
GANDHI, M. SELECTED WRITINGS OF MAHATMA
GANDHI. (R. DUNCAN, ED)
617(TLS):31MAR72-351
GANDOLFO, M. POEMA DE LA NUEVE LUNAS.
V.L.E., 37:NOV-DEC69-53
GANDON, J., JR. & T.J. MULVANY. THE LIFE
OF JAMES GANDON.
90:APR70-264

GANGULY, S. LOGICAL POSITIVISM AS A
THEORY OF MEANING.
E.J. QUIGLEY, 485(PE&W):OCT68-336
GANIVET, Á. CORRESPONDENCIA FAMILIAR
(CARTAS INÉDITAS) (1888-1897). (J.
HERRERO, ED)
M. NOZICK, 240(HR):APR70-229
G. RIBBANS, 86(BHS):JAN71-77
GANN, L.H. & P. DUIGNAN, EDS. COLONIAL-
ISM IN AFRICA 1870-1960. (VOL 1)
H. STOECKER, 182:VOL23#5-248
GANSHOF, F.L. THE CAROLINGIANS AND THE
FRANKISH MONARCHY.
617(TLS):20OCT72-1255
GANTMAN, V.I. & S.A. MIKOYAN. S.SH.A.:
GOSUDARSTVO, POLITIKA, VYBORY.
K.W. RYAVEC, 32:JUN71-366
GANZ, P.F. & W. SCHRÖDER, EDS. PROBLEME
MITTELALTERLICHER ÜBERLIEFERUNG UND
TEXTKRITIK.
R. SCHRÖDER, 462(OL):VOL25#4-363
GANZ, P.L. DIE BASLER GLASMALER DER
SPÄTRENAISSANCE UND DER BAROCKZEIT.
J.F.H., 90:MAY69-309
GANZEL, D. MARK TWAIN ABROAD.
R.L. HOUGH, 502(PRS):WINTER68/69-360
R. LEHAN, 445(NCF):DEC69-377
B. POLI, 402(MLR):OCT71-882
GARAB, A.M. BEYOND BYZANTIUM.
J.L. ALLEN, JR., 295:VOL2#1-148
GARAMVÖLGYI, J. AUS DEN ANFÄNGEN SOWJET-
ISCHER AUSSENPOLITIK/DAS BRITISCH-SOW-
JETRUSSISCHE HANDELSABKOMMEN VON 1921.
L. KOCHAN, 587:APR69-565
GARAS, K. EIGHTEENTH CENTURY VENETIAN
PAINTINGS.
F.J.B. WATSON, 39:JUL69-82
GARAS, K. SELECTED PAINTINGS FROM THE
BUDAPEST MUSEUM OF FINE ARTS.
90:OCT70-716
GARAUDY, R. THE CRISIS IN COMMUNISM.
R.O. PAXTON, 441:24SEP72-46
GARAUDY, R. MARXISM IN THE TWENTIETH
CENTURY.
J.P. SCANLAN, 32:MAR71-162
GARBELL, I. THE JEWISH NEO-ARAMAIC DIA-
LECTS OF PERSIAN AZERBAIJAN.
J.C. GREENFIELD, 318(JAOS):APR-JUN70-
293
J. KRÁMSKÝ, 353:SEP69-95
GARBER, F. WORDSWORTH AND THE POETRY
OF ENCOUNTER.
617(TLS):6OCT72-1186
GARBER, L. GARBER'S TALES FROM THE QUAR-
TER.*
G. ROPER, 627(UTQ):JUL70-342
GARCÍA, A.R. - SEE UNDER REGALADO GARCÍA,
A.
GARCÍA, M. FRANCO'S PRISONER.
617(TLS):17NOV72-1390
GARCÍA BERRIO, A. ESPAÑA E ITALIA ANTE
EL CONCEPTISMO.
R. HESS, 72:BAND208HEFT4/6-446
GARCÍA MÁRQUEZ, G. LA INCREIBLE Y TRISTE
HISTORIA DE LA CÁNDIDA ERÉNDIRA Y DE SU
ABUELA DESALMADA.
617(TLS):29SEP72-1140
GARCÍA MÁRQUEZ, G. LEAF STORM AND OTHER
STORIES.
A. KAZIN, 441:20FEB72-1
R. LOCKE, 441:17MAR72-43
E. SHORRIS, 231:FEB72-102
P. THEROUX, 440:20FEB72-3
M. WOOD, 453:6APR72-25
J. YGLESIAS, 61:AUG72-86
442(NY):11MAR72-125

111

GARCÍA MÁRQUEZ, G. NO ONE WRITES TO THE
   COLONEL.*
     E. SHORRIS, 231:FEB72-98
     V.M. VALENZUELA, 263:JAN-MAR71-74
     I. WEDDE, 364:OCT/NOV71-149
GARCÍA MÁRQUEZ, G. ONE HUNDRED YEARS OF
   SOLITUDE.* (SPANISH TITLE: CIEN AÑOS
   DE SOLEDAD.)
     P.E. GRAY, 676(YR):AUTUMN70-101
     E. SHORRIS, 231:FEB72-99
     J. UPDIKE, 442(NY):29JAN72-93
GARCILASO DE LA VEGA. OBRAS COMPLETAS.
   (E.L. RIVERS, ED) (2ND ED)
     A.L. KOUVEL, 400(MLN):MAR70-289
GARD, R., ED. HENRY JAMES.
     D.C. GERVAIS, 97(CQ):AUTUMN/WINTER
       69/70-412
     K. GRAHAM, 541(RES):FEB70-100
GARD, R.E., M. BALCH & P. TEMKIN.
   THEATRE IN AMERICA.
     S. FALK, 397(MD):FEB70-432
GARD, R.M. & J.R. HARTLEY, COMPS. RAIL-
   WAYS IN THE MAKING.
     W.B. STEPHENS, 325:APR70-83
GARDE, P. L'ACCENT.
     E. PULGRAM, 361:VOL23#4-372
GARDER, M. A HISTORY OF THE SOVIET ARMY.
     R.S. FELDMAN, 587:JUL69-116
GARDINER, C.H. WILLIAM HICKLING PRES-
   COTT.*
     G. LOHMANN VILLENA, 263:APR-JUN71-210
     H. SCHWARTZ, 432(NEQ):JUN70-304
GARDINER, J. A GUIDE TO GOOD SINGING.
     A. BLYTH, 415:FEB70-164
GARDINER, M. - SEE "THE WOLF-MAN: HIS
   MEMOIRS"
GARDNER, B. THE EAST INDIA COMPANY.
     G.M. FRASER, 440:30JAN72-12
     T. LASK, 441:8JAN72-31
     C. MILLER, 561(SATR):22JAN72-65
GARDNER, E.S. THE CASE OF THE BEAUTIFUL
   BEGGAR.
     617(TLS):14APR72-427
GARDNER, H., ED. A BOOK OF RELIGIOUS
   VERSE. (BRITISH TITLE: THE FABER BOOK
   OF RELIGIOUS VERSE.)
     H. VENDLER, 441:15OCT72-3
     617(TLS):1SEP72-1020
GARDNER, H. KING LEAR.
     L.F. BALL, 570(SQ):AUTUMN69-478
GARDNER, H., ED. THE NEW OXFORD BOOK OF
   ENGLISH VERSE 1250-1950.
     P. BEER, 362:23NOV72-720
     T. LASK, 441:27OCT72-41
     H. VENDLER, 441:15OCT72-3
GARDNER, H. A READING OF "PARADISE
   LOST."
     W.M. BECKETT, 180(ESA):SEP70-419
GARDNER, H. - SEE WILSON, F.P.
GARDNER, J. GRENDEL.*
     J. HUNTER, 362:29JUN72-874
     617(TLS):14JUL72-793
GARDNER, J. THE SUNLIGHT DIALOGUES.
     T.R. EDWARDS, 441:10DEC72-1
     C. LEHMANN-HAUPT, 441:15DEC72-49
     M. WOOD, 453:19OCT72-33
GARDNER, J. THE WRECKAGE OF AGATHON.
     D.J. GORDON, 676(YR):SPRING71-428
GARDNER, J.W. THE RECOVERY OF CONFI-
   DENCE.
     J.J. CORSON, 639(VQR):AUTUMN70-656
GARDNER, L. FAT CITY.*
     42(AR):FALL69-443
     639(VQR):WINTER70-VIII
GARDNER, L.C. ARCHITECTS OF ILLUSION.*
     639(VQR):SUMMER70-CXII
GARDNER, R. GRITO!
     J. WOMACK, JR., 453:31AUG72-12

GARDNER, S. BLAKE.
     J.B. BEER, 402(MLR):OCT71-872
     D.V.E., 191(ELN):SEP69(SUPP)-22
     D.W. HARDING, 447(N&Q):MAR70-120
     W.H. STEVENSON, 184(EIC):APR70-251
GARFIELD, B. DEATH WISH.
     N. CALLENDAR, 441:8OCT72-46
     T. LASK, 441:14JUL72-33
GARFIELD, B. RELENTLESS.
     N. CALLENDAR, 441:14MAY72-35
GARFORTH, F.W. THE SCOPE OF PHILOSOPHY.
     617(TLS):25FEB72-230
GARGAN, W. WHY ME?
     A.H. WITHAM, 200:AUG-SEP69-427
GARGANI, A.G. HOBBES E LA SCIENZA.
     H.W. SCHNEIDER, 319:JUL72-360
GARGANI, A.G. LINGUAGGIO ED ESPERIENZA
   IN LUDWIG WITTGENSTEIN.
     M. FERRIANI, 548(RCSF):JAN/MAR69-101
GARGANIGO, J.F. & W. RELA, EDS. ANTOLO-
   GÍA DE LA LITERATURA GAUCHESCA Y CRI-
   OLLISTA.
     M.I. LICHTBLAU, 240(HR):APR70-236
GARGI, B. FOLK THEATRE OF INDIA.*
     W. TILLSON, 650(WF):OCT68-284
GARLAND, H.B. SCHILLER: THE DRAMATIC
   WRITER.*
     A. CLOSS, 402(MLR):JAN71-215
GARLAND, M. KLEIST'S "PRINZ FRIEDRICH
   VON HOMBURG."*
     J.M. ELLIS, 221(GQ):NOV70-781
     E. SCHWARZ, 220(GL&L):JUL71-390
     J.T., 191(ELN):SEP70(SUPP)-121
GARMONSWAY, G.N., J. SIMPSON & H.E.
   DAVIDSON. "BEOWULF" AND ITS ANALOGUES.
     R.M. WILSON, 175:SPRING69-27
GARNEAU, H.S-D. OEUVRES. (J. BRAULT &
   B. LACROIX, EDS)
     617(TLS):7APR72-399
GARNER, F.H., ED. MODERN BRITISH FARMING
   SYSTEMS.
     617(TLS):29SEP72-1176
GARNER, H. CABBAGETOWN.*
     G. ROPER, 627(UTQ):JUL69-357
GARNER, H. A NICE PLACE TO VISIT.*
     M. WADDINGTON, 102(CANL):AUTUMN71-72
GARNER, H. VIOLATION OF THE VIRGINS.
     H. KIRKWOOD, 99:APR72-53
     J. PARR, 296:WINTER72-85
GARNETT, C.B., JR. TASTE.
     E.H. DUNCAN, 290(JAAC):WINTER69-258
     A.W. MUNK, 484(PPR):JUN70-626
GARNETT, C.B., JR. THE WORLD OF SILENCE.
     A.W. MUNK, 484(PPR):JUN70-626
GARNETT, D. THE SONS OF THE FALCON.
     J. HUNTER, 362:9MAR72-317
     617(TLS):21APR72-438
GARNHAM, B.G. - SEE ROBBE-GRILLET, A.
GARNSEY, P. SOCIAL STATUS AND LEGAL
   PRIVILEGE IN THE ROMAN EMPIRE.
     F. LASSERRE, 182:VOL23#6-298
     A.A. SCHILLER, 124:MAR71-242
GARRARD, J.G. MIXAIL ČULKOV.
     J. RICE, 574(SEEJ):WINTER71-495
GARRAD, L.S. THE NATURALIST IN THE ISLE
   OF MAN.
     617(TLS):1SEP72-1028
GARRARD, L.S., WITH OTHERS. THE INDUS-
   TRIAL ARCHAEOLOGY OF THE ISLE OF MAN.
     617(TLS):14JUL72-822
GARRATY, J. & P. GAY, EDS. THE COLUMBIA
   HISTORY OF THE WORLD.
     J.H. PLUMB, 440:30APR72-3
GARRATY, J.A., W. ADAMS & C.J.H. TAYLOR.
   THE NEW GUIDE TO STUDY ABROAD.
     J.R. STAMM, 399(MLJ):NOV70-547

GARRETT, J. ROGER WILLIAMS.
C.E. CLARK, JR., 109:FALL/WINTER
71/72-138
L. ZIFF, 27(AL):MAY71-285
GARRETT, P.K. SCENE AND SYMBOL FROM
GEORGE ELIOT TO JAMES JOYCE.*
R.M. ADAMS, 445(NCF):SEP69-236
J.S. PHILLIPSON, 136:FALL69-117
R. SCHMIDT-VON BARDELEBEN, 182:
VOL23#6-275
R. VIDÁN MELÉNDEZ, 202(FMOD):NOV69-97
GARRETT, R. RUN DOWN.
N. CALLENDAR, 441:27FEB72-50
GARRETT, R. SPIRAL.
N. CALLENDAR, 441:13AUG72-20
GARRETT, W.D. & OTHERS. THE ARTS IN
AMERICA: THE NINETEENTH CENTURY.*
N. HARRIS, 432(NEQ):SEP70-506
GARRIGUE, J. CHARTRES AND PROSE POEMS.
V. YOUNG, 249(HUDR):WINTER71/72-678
GARRIGUES, E. THE ONENESS OF THE AMERI-
CAS.
J.H. PARRY, 263:JAN-MAR71-70
GARROD, J.W. - SEE DICKENS, C.
GARSIDE, W.R. THE DURHAM MINERS 1919-
1960.
617(TLS):28JAN72-88
GARTNER, A., M. KOHLER & F. RIESSMAN.
CHILDREN TEACH CHILDREN.
J.S. BRUNER, 561(SATR):15JAN72-62
GARVE, A. THE CASE OF ROBERT QUARRY.
N. CALLENDAR, 441:21MAY72-30
442(NY):13MAY72-148
GARVEY, G. ENERGY, ECOLOGY, ECONOMY.
S.B. SHEPARD, 441:19NOV72-52
GARVIE, A.F. AESCHYLUS' "SUPPLICES."*
A.P. BURNETT, 122:JAN71-54
R. WEIL, 555:VOL44FASC2-310
E.W. WHITTLE, 123:DEC70-296
GARY, R. EUROPA.
617(TLS):16JUN72-677
GASAWAY, E.B. GREY WOLF, GREY SEA.
617(TLS):7JUL72-785
GASCOIGNE, B. MURGATREUD'S EMPIRE.
J. HUNTER, 362:4MAY72-596
M. LEVIN, 441:17SEP72-42
617(TLS):19MAY72-565
GASH, N. SIR ROBERT PEEL. (VOL 2)
R. MITCHISON, 362:7DEC72-798
617(TLS):3NOV72-1312
GASIOROWSKA, X. WOMEN IN SOVIET FICTION,
1917-1964.*
S.J.M. LIPPERT, 219(GAR):SUMMER69-259
L.B. TURKEVICH, 550(RUSR):JUL70-345
GASKELL, E. CRANFORD. (E.P. WATSON, ED)
617(TLS):30JUN72-741
GASKELL, E.C.S. THE LETTERS OF MRS. GAS-
KELL. (J.A.V. CHAPPLE & A. POLLARD,
EDS)
K.J. FIELDING, 445(NCF):SEP68-243
GASKELL, J. SUMMER COMING.
V. CUNNINGHAM, 362:12OCT72-482
GASKELL, P. A NEW INTRODUCTION TO BIB-
LIOGRAPHY.
617(TLS):6OCT72-1204
GASKELL, P. & R. ROBSON. THE LIBRARY OF
TRINITY COLLEGE, CAMBRIDGE.
617(TLS):21JAN72-76
GASKELL, R. DRAMA AND REALITY.
617(TLS):30JUN72-739
GASMAN, D. THE SCIENTIFIC ORIGINS OF
NATIONAL SOCIALISM.*
G. BARRACLOUGH, 453:19OCT72-37
GASPAR, L. SOL ABSOLU.
617(TLS):22SEP72-1092
GASPARINI, L. CUTTY SARK.*
L.T. CORNELIUS, 102(CANL):SUMMER71-95
GASPARINI, L. - SEE WARR, B.

GASS, W. OMENSETTER'S LUCK.
R.V. CASSILL, 340(KR):SEP66-562
GASS, W.H. WILLIE MASTERS' LONESOME
WIFE.*
M. WOOD, 453:14DEC72-12
GASSET, J.O. - SEE UNDER ORTEGA Y GASSET,
J.
GASSIER, P. & J. WILSON. THE LIFE AND
COMPLETE WORK OF FRANCISCO GOYA.*
(BRITISH TITLE: GOYA.) (F. LACHENAL,
ED)
617(TLS):28JAN72-97
GASSIOT-TALABOT, G. ROMAN AND PALAEO-
CHRISTIAN PAINTING.
G. SCAGLIA, 124:OCT70-61
GASSTER, M. CHINESE INTELLECTUALS AND
THE REVOLUTION OF 1911.
Y.C. WANG, 293(JAST):MAY70-691
GASTON, P.M. THE NEW SOUTH CREED.
G.B. TINDALL, 639(VQR):SUMMER70-506
P. WATTERS, 676(YR):AUTUMN70-114
GATELL, F.O., P. GOODMAN & A. WEINSTEIN,
EDS. THE GROWTH OF AMERICAN POLITICS.
617(TLS):15DEC72-1529
GATES, R.J., ED. THE AWNTYRS OFF ARTHURE
AT THE TERNE WATHELYNE.
D. FOX, 589:JAN71-154
GATHERCOLE, P.M., ED. LAURENT DE PRE-
MIERFAIT'S "DES CAS DES NOBLES HOMMES
ET FEMMES."*
R. O'GORMAN, 399(MLJ):MAY70-381
F.W. VOGLER, 207(FR):APR70-847
GATHORNE-HARDY, G.M., ED & TRANS. THE
NORSE DISCOVERES OF AMERICA.
102(CANL):WINTER71-107
GATHORNE-HARDY, J. THE RISE AND FALL OF
THE BRITISH NANNY.
P. NAPIER, 362:28SEP72-412
617(TLS):1SEP72-1019
GATHORNE-HARDY, R. & W.P. WILLIAMS. A
BIBLIOGRAPHY OF THE WRITINGS OF JEREMY
TAYLOR TO 1700.
617(TLS):10MAR72-284
GATT, G. MAX ERNST.
617(TLS):7JAN72-18
GATZEMEIER, M. DIE NATURPHILOSOPHIE DES
STRATON VON LAMPSAKOS.
F. LASSERRE, 182:VOL23#8-430
GAUCHHWAL, B.S. THE CONCEPT OF PERFEC-
TION IN THE TEACHINGS OF KANT AND THE
GITA.
W. GRIFFIS, 485(PE&W):OCT68-335
GAUDIO, A. ALLAL EL FASSI OU L'HISTOIRE
DE L'ISTIQLAL.
617(TLS):29SEP72-1172
GAUDON, J. LE TEMPS DE LA CONTEMPLATION.
J-B. BARRÈRE, 208(FS):APR71-218
P.J. YARROW, 182:VOL23#4-167
GAULD, A. THE FOUNDERS OF PSYCHICAL
RESEARCH.
R.K. DONOVAN, 637(VS):DEC69-234
GAULDIE, W.S. THE APPRECIATION OF THE
ARTS: ARCHITECTURE.*
639(VQR):SPRING70-LXXIV
DE GAULLE, C. MEMOIRS OF HOPE.* (VOL 2)
(FRENCH TITLE: MÉMOIRES D'ESPOIR.)
J. ARDAGH, 440:6FEB72-8
A. BROYARD, 441:3FEB72-35
J. CHACE, 441:30JAN72-4
S. HOFFMANN, 453:24FEB72-23
D. SCHOENBRUN, 561(SATR):5FEB72-60
442(NY):11MAR72-126
GAULMIER, J. MICHELET.
J.S.P., 191(ELN):SEP70(SUPP)-75
GAUNT, W. THE RESTLESS CENTURY.
J. CANADAY, 441:3DEC72-90
617(TLS):22DEC72-1550

DE GAURY, G. TRAVELLING GENT.
617(TLS):10NOV72-1358
GAUS, J. CARLO MARCHIONNI.
A. BLUNT, 90:MAR69-162
GAUTHIER, D.P. THE LOGIC OF "LEVIATHAN."
K.R. MINOGUE, 518:OCT70-10
W.J. REES, 479(PHQ):JUL70-271
GAUTHIER, J.D. DOUZE VOIX FRANÇAISES
1900-1960.
H.L. ROBINSON, 399(MLJ):OCT70-463
W. WRAGE, 207(FR):DEC69-381
GAUTIER DE COINCI. "LES MIRACLES DE
NOSTRE DAME" PAR GAUTIER DE COINCI.
(VOL 3) (F.V. KOENIG, ED)
G. BIANCIOTTO, 545(RPH):MAY71-656
GAUTIER, J-M. - SEE DE CHATEAUBRIAND,
F-R.
GAUTIER, T. EMAUX ET CAMÉES. (M. COT-
TIN, ED)
R. MERKER, 207(FR):DEC69-345
GAUTIER, T. & C. BAUDELAIRE. HASHISH
WINE OPIUM.
617(TLS):3MAR72-257
GAWRECKI, D. COMPACT LIBRARY SHELVING.
I.P. COLLIS, 325:OCT70-163
GAY, J. THE BEGGAR'S OPERA. (E.V.
ROBERTS, ED)
J.B. KERN, 481(PQ):JUL70-351
C. PHILLABAUM, 399(MLJ):JAN70-38
A. SHERBO, 402(MLR):OCT71-867
568(SCN):SPRING71-26
GAY, P. THE ENLIGHTENMENT. (VOL 2)
A.J. BINGHAM, 149:MAR71-81
A.J. BINGHAM, 402(MLR):JAN71-169
G.R. HEALY, 656(WMQ):JUL70-477
A. SEDGWICK, 639(VQR):SPRING70-356
42(AR):WINTER69/70-588
566:AUTUMN70-28
GAY, P. A LOSS OF MASTERY.
P. CARROLL, 656(WMQ):APR70-324
GAY, P. WEIMAR CULTURE.
A. BEICHMAN, 19(AGR):VOL35#3-30
K. BULLIVANT, 220(GL&L):APR71-286
M. JAY, 390:FEB69-68
GAY-CROSIER, R. LES ENVERS D'UN ÉCHEC.*
G. JOYAUX, 207(FR):OCT69-168
GAY-LUSSAC, B. DIALOGUE AVEC UNE OMBRE.
617(TLS):29SEP72-1174
GAYLIN, W. IN THE SERVICE OF THEIR
COUNTRY.
639(VQR):AUTUMN70-CLII
GEACH, P.T. GOD AND THE SOUL.
A. FLEW, 479(PHQ):APR70-189
R.H.K., 543:JUN70-741
K. WARD, 518:JAN70-8
GEACH, P.T. & A.J.P. KENNY - SEE PRIOR,
A.N.
GEAREY, J. HEINRICH VON KLEIST.*
J.C. BRUCE, 405(MP):FEB70-289
GEBHARD, D. SCHINDLER.
617(TLS):11FEB72-161
GEBHARDT, P. A.W. SCHLEGELS SHAKESPEARE-
ÜBERSETZUNG.
H. VON HOFE, 301(JEGP):OCT71-729
GECAN, M., ED. SEEN THROUGH OUR EYES.
J.D. O'HARA, 561(SATR):22JUL72-58
GECK, L.H.A. ÜBER DAS EINDRINGEN DES
WORTES "SOZIAL" IN DIE DEUTSCHE
SPRACHE.
B.F.O. HILDEBRANDT, 353:MAY69-123
GECK, M. DIE BILDNISSE RICHARD WAGNERS.
J.W.D., 410(M&L):JAN71-69
GEDDES, C.F. PATIÑO THE TIN KING.
617(TLS):18AUG72-962
GEDDES, G., ED. FIFTEEN CANADIAN POETS.
G. WOODCOCK, 102(CANL):AUTUMN71-4
GEDULD, H., ED. AUTHORS ON FILM.
D. BROMWICH, 441:17DEC72-2

GEDULD, H.M. PRINCE OF PUBLISHERS.*
J.D. FLEEMAN, 447(N&Q):MAR70-105
J. FREEHAFER, 566:AUTUMN70-32
D.P. VARMA, 150(DR):WINTER70/71-571
GEERING, K., ED. IT'S WORLD THAT MAKES
THE LOVE GO ROUND.
M. RICHARDS, 381:VOL29#1-122
GEFVERT, C.J. EDWARD TAYLOR.
D.E. STANFORD, 165:FALL72-200
GEHLEN, M.P. THE COMMUNIST PARTY OF THE
SOVIET UNION.
R.R. POPE, 550(RUSR):JUL70-353
GEHLEN, R. THE SERVICE. (GERMAN TITLE:
DER DIENST. BRITISH TITLE: THE GEHLEN
MEMOIRS.)
N. ASCHERSON, 453:1JUN72-3
R.G. DEINDORFER, 561(SATR):24JUN72-61
S. DELMER, 362:7SEP72-311
617(TLS):14JAN72-30
617(TLS):22DEC72-1566
GEIB, K. ALEKSEJ MICHAJLOVIČ REMIZOV.
M.E. SHAW, 575(SEER):JUL71-466
AF GEIJERSTAM, R. - SEE DE HEREDIA, J.F.
GEIRINGER, K., WITH I. GEIRINGER. JOHANN
SEBASTIAN BACH.
J.F. OHL, 414(MQ):JAN69-120
GEISMAR, M. HENRY JAMES AND HIS CULT.
P. MICHEL, 179(ES):AUG70-375
GEISMAR, M. MARK TWAIN.*
R. BONAZZI, 584(SWR):SPRING71-202
L.J. BUDD, 579(SAQ):SUMMER71-426
J.C. GERBER, 27(AL):MAY71-296
L.D. RUBIN, JR., 569(SR):SUMMER71-426
L.P. SIMPSON, 578:SPRING72-93
GEISSLER, R. BOUREAU-DESLANDES.
P.H. MEYER, 546(RR):APR70-138
GEIST, J.F. PASSAGEN.*
N. PEVSNER, 90:JUL70-475
GEIST, S. BRANCUSI.
A. BOWNESS, 592:NOV68-223
A.T. SPEAR, 90:MAR69-154
GELDNER, F. DIE DEUTSCHEN INKUNABEL-
DRUCKER. (VOL 1)
V. SCHOLDERER, 354:SEP69-259
GELLER, R. IOWA.
D. BARBOUR, 102(CANL):SPRING71-70
GELLINEK, C. "KÖNIG ROTHER."*
E.S. COLEMAN, 221(GQ):MAR70-262
F.G. GENTRY, 399(MLJ):JAN70-38
W.T.H. JACKSON, 222(GR):MAY70-229
GELLINEK, C. PROGRAMMED GERMAN DICTION-
ARY.
K. BUNG, 220(GL&L):JUL71-371
GELLING, M., W.F.H. NICOLAISEN & M.
RICHARDS, COMPS. THE NAMES OF TOWNS
AND CITIES IN BRITAIN. (W.F.H. NIC-
OLAISEN, ED)
I. FRASER, 595(SCS):VOL15PT1-82
G.F. JENSEN, 447(N&Q):NOV70-425
GELLIUS. A GELLII "NOCTES ATTICAE."*
(P.K. MARSHALL, ED) AULU-GELLE, "LES
NUITS ATTIQUES." (VOL 1) (R. MARACHE,
ED & TRANS)
F.R.D. GOODYEAR, 123:DEC71-385
GELLNER, J. CANADA IN NATO.
I.M. ABELLA, 529(QQ):WINTER70-640
GELMAN, B., ED. THE WOOD ENGRAVINGS OF
WINSLOW HOMER.
W.D. ALLEN, 58:MAR70-12
GELZER, M. CICERO UND CAESAR.
R. SEAGER, 313:VOL60-213
GEMMETT, R.J., ED. SALE CATALOGUES OF
LIBRARIES OF EMINENT PERSONS. (VOL 3:
WILLIAM BECKFORD)
617(TLS):29SEP72-1175
GENDERS, R. COLLECTING ANTIQUE PLANTS.
617(TLS):16JUN72-697

114

GENDERS, R. SCENTED WILD FLOWERS OF
BRITAIN.
617(TLS):30JUN72-754
GENDZIER, S.J., ED & TRANS. THE ENCYCLO-
PEDIA: SELECTIONS.
S. WERNER, 546(RR):FEB70-62
GENETTE, G. FIGURES III.
617(TLS):22DEC72-1560
GENETTE, G. - SEE FONTANIER, P.
GENGENBACH, P. DIE TOTENFRESSER. (J.
SCHMIDT, ED)
R.K., 221(GQ):JAN70-143
GENJI, K. - SEE UNDER KEITA GENJI
GENNARO, S. - SEE DYNAMIUS & FAUSTUS DE
RIEZ
GENOV, K. ROMANTIZMUT V BŬLGARSKATA
LITERATURA.
C.A. MOSER, 32:MAR71-219
GENOVÉS, S. IS PEACE INEVITABLE?
617(TLS):17NOV72-1401
GENOVESE, E.D. IN RED AND BLACK.*
L.C. MILAZZO, 584(SWR):AUTUMN71-385
LE GENTIL, P. THE CHANSON DE ROLAND.
(F.F. BEER, TRANS)
D.M. DOUGHERTY, 207(FR):OCT69-197
F. WHITEHEAD, 208(FS):OCT71-442
GENTILE, G. GENESIS AND STRUCTURE OF
SOCIETY.
R. PARENTI, 548(RCSF):JUL-SEP68-364
GENTILI, V. - SEE SIDNEY, P.
GENTILLET, I. ANTI-MACHIAVEL. (C.E.
RATHÉ, ED)
R.C. LA CHARITÉ, 207(FR):DEC69-355
GENTLEMAN, D. DESIGN IN MINIATURE.
617(TLS):5MAY72-529
GEOFFREY OF VINSAUF. THE POETRIA NOVA OF
GEOFFREY OF VINSAUF.* (M.F. NIMS,
TRANS)
H. GRABES, 38:BAND87HEFT3/4-449
D.R. MURDOCH, 597(SN):VOL41#2-424
GEORGANO, G.N., ED. A HISTORY OF TRANS-
PORT.
617(TLS):15DEC72-1528
GEORGE III. THE LATER CORRESPONDENCE OF
GEORGE III. (VOL 5) (A. ASPINALL, ED)
W.B. HAMILTON, 579(SAQ):AUTUMN71-612
G. NIEDHART, 182:VOL23#4-180
GEORGE IV. THE CORRESPONDENCE OF GEORGE,
PRINCE OF WALES, 1770-1812. (VOLS 4&5)
(A. ASPINALL, ED)
D.V.E., 191(ELN):SEP69(SUPP)-11
GEORGE IV. THE CORRESPONDENCE OF GEORGE,
PRINCE OF WALES 1770-1812. (VOL 8)
(A. ASPINALL, ED)
617(TLS):7APR72-393
GEORGE, A., D. HALL & W. SIMONS. THE
LIMITS OF COERCIVE DIPLOMACY.*
R. STEEL, 453:19OCT72-43
GEORGE, G. TONALITY AND MUSICAL STRUC-
TURE.*
E. SAMS, 415:NOV70-1111
GEORGE, M.D. HOGARTH TO CRUIKSHANK.
H. DANIEL, 592:MAR68-158
J.R. HARVEY, 97(CQ):SPRING68-176
GEORGE, T. THE DEADLY HOMECOMING.
N. CALLENDAR, 441:31DEC72-18
GEORGE, T. THE MURDERS ON THE SQUARE.
N. CALLENDAR, 441:9JAN72-33
GEORGE, V. & P. WILDING. MOTHERLESS
FAMILIES.
617(TLS):1DEC72-1456
GEORGI, A. DAS LATEINISCHE UND DEUTSCHE
PREISGEDICHT DES MITTELALTERS IN DER
NACHFOLGE DES GENUS DEMONSTRATIVUM.
F.H. BÄUML, 406:FALL71-303
B. NAUMANN, 382(MAE):1971/2-189
R. RUDOLF, 182:VOL23#7-355

GEORGIEV, V. OSNOVNI PROBLEMI NA SLAV-
JANSKATA DIAXRONNA MORFOLOGIJA.
H. ANDERSEN, 350:DEC71-949
GEORGIEV, V.I. INTRODUZIONE ALLA STORIA
DELLE LINGUE INDEUROPEE.
V. PISANI, 361:VOL23#2-177
GERALD, J.B. CONVENTIONAL WISDOM.
J. DECK, 441:18JUN72-6
442(NY):3JUN72-110
GÉRARD, A. LES TAMBOURS DU NÉANT.
B.H. GELFANT, 27(AL):MAR71-147
GÉRARD, A.S. ENGLISH ROMANTIC POETRY.*
J.A. APPLEYARD, 613:SUMMER69-297
E. SHAFFER, 402(MLR):OCT71-874
GERARD, J. GERARD'S HERBALL. (REV BY M.
WOODWARD)
617(TLS):18FEB72-199
GÉRARD, Y. THEMATIC, BIBLIOGRAPHICAL AND
CRITICAL CATALOGUE OF THE WORKS OF
LUIGI BOCCHERINI.*
E. AMSTERDAM, 317:SPRING71-131
S. SADIE, 415:MAR70-279
412:NOV71-363
GERASSI, J., ED. TOWARDS REVOLUTION.*
N. FOUNTAIN, 364:JUN/JUL71-143
GERBER, D. THE REVENANT.
S. MOORE, 385(MQR):SUMMER72-217
GERBER, D.E. A BIBLIOGRAPHY OF PINDAR,
1513-1966.
M.M. WILLCOCK, 123:MAR71-16
GERBER, H.E. - SEE MOORE, G.
GERBER, R.J. & P.D. MC ANANY, EDS. CON-
TEMPORARY PUNISHMENT.
617(TLS):6OCT72-1202
GERBER, W. THE MIND OF INDIA.*
J. ERICKSON, 485(PE&W):OCT68-342
GERBOD, P. LA VIE QUOTIDIENNE DANS LES
LYCÉES ET COLLÈGES AU XIXE SIÈCLE.
R. MERKER, 207(FR):MAY70-948
GERBOTH, W. AN INDEX TO MUSICAL FEST-
SCHRIFTEN AND OTHER SIMILAR PUBLICA-
TIONS.
S. SADIE, 415:OCT70-1004
GERBRANDS, A.A. WOW-IPITS.
E. FISCHER, 182:VOL23#21/22-956
GERHARD, H.P. THE WORLD OF ICONS.
617(TLS):31MAR72-368
GERHARDT, D. GOGOL' UND DOSTOJEVSKIJ IN
IHREM KÜNSTLERISCHEN VERHÄLTNIS.
A.B. MC MILLIN, 575(SEER):APR71-319
GERHARDT, P. GEDICHTE. (A. GOES, ED)
T.T. KARST, 221(GQ):NOV70-828
GÉRIN, W. CHARLOTTE BRONTË.
E. HARDWICK, 453:4MAY72-11
B. HARDY, 445(NCF):SEP68-240
GÉRIN, W. EMILY BRONTË.*
E. HARDWICK, 453:4MAY72-11
GERKE, E-O. DER ESSAY ALS KUNSTFORM BEI
HUGO VON HOFMANNSTHAL.
P. GOFF, 301(JEGP):OCT71-739
GERLINGHOFF, P. BIBLIOGRAPHISCHE EIN-
FÜHRUNG IN DAS STUDIUM DER NEUEREN
BULGARISCHEN LITERATUR (1850-1950).
M. PUNDEFF, 104:WINTER71-569
GERLO, A. & H.D.L. VERVLIET. INVENTAIRE
DE LA CORRESPONDANCE DE JUSTE LIPSE,
1564-1606.
E. ARMSTRONG, 354:SEP69-266
G. GÜLDNER, 182:VOL23#3-110
GERMER, H. THE GERMAN NOVEL OF EDUCA-
TION 1792-1805.*
D. VAN ABBE, 220(GL&L):JUL71-393
GERMER, R. T.S. ELIOTS ANFÄNGE ALS
LYRIKER (1905-1915).*
J. WESTLAKE, 402(MLR):JAN71-181
GERNET, J. ANCIENT CHINA.
A. LONSDALE, 447(N&Q):JUL70-276

GERNET, L. ANTHROPOLOGIE DE LA GRÈCE
ANTIQUE.
    P. CHANTRAINE, 555:VOL44FASC2-296
    S.C. HUMPHREYS, 303:VOL90-247
GERSCHENKRON, A. CONTINUITY IN HISTORY
AND OTHER ESSAYS.*
    R. BEERMAN, 587:OCT69-237
GERSCHENKRON, A. EUROPE IN THE RUSSIAN
MIRROR.
    H.L. ROBERTS, 32:SEP71-659
GERSHMAN, H.S. A BIBLIOGRAPHY OF THE
SURREALIST REVOLUTION IN FRANCE.
    R.S. SHORT, 208(FS):JUL71-351
GERSHMAN, H.S. THE SURREALIST REVOLUTION
IN FRANCE.*
    W.V. HOFFMAN, 400(MLN):MAY70-626
    M. POPS, 141:FALL69-389
    R.S. SHORT, 208(FS):JUL71-351
GERSHON, K. LEGACIES & ENCOUNTERS.
    617(TLS):29SEP72-1146
GERSON, H. REMBRANDT.
    G. MARTIN, 39:SEP69-266
GERSON, H. REMBRANDT PAINTINGS.
    A. DORN, 58:DEC69/JAN70-16
    B.A. RIFKIN, 55:MAY69-26
    A. WERNER, 340(KR):1970/1-121
GERSON, H. - SEE BREDIUS, A.
GERSON, N.B. LILLIE LANGTRY.
    617(TLS):11AUG72-954
GERSON, N.B. TEMPTATION TO STEAL.
    N. CALLENDAR, 441:13FEB72-34
GERSON, S. SOUND AND SYMBOL IN THE DIA-
LOGUE OF THE WORKS OF CHARLES DICKENS.
    S. JACOBSON, 597(SN):VOL41#1-221
GERSTEIN, L. NIKOLAI STRAKHOV.
    617(TLS):14JAN72-44
GERSTENBERG, K. & H. DOMKE. LE GOTHIQUE.
    P. GUERRE, 98:MAR69-265
GERTEL, Z. BORGES Y SU RETORNO A LA PO-
ESÍA.
    R.S. MILLS, 86(BHS):JUL71-286
GERVAIS, C.H. OTHER MARRIAGE VOWS.
    D. BARBOUR, 150(DR):AUTUMN70-433
GESCHE, H. DIE VERGOTTUNG CAESARS.
    A. ALFÖLDI, 487:SUMMER70-166
    J-C. RICHARD, 555:VOL44FASC2-364
GESNER, C. SHAKESPEARE AND THE GREEK
ROMANCE.
    S. WELLS, 677:VOL2-257
GESUALDI, M. - SEE MILANI, L.
GETZLER, I. MARTOV.*
    S.H. BARON, 587:OCT68-259
GEYER, G.A. THE NEW 100 YEARS WAR.
    441:16JUL72-14
GEYL, P. PENNESTRIJD OVER STAAT EN
HISTORIE.
    617(TLS):11AUG72-944
GHAI, D.P. & Y.P., EDS. PORTRAIT OF A
MINORITY.
    617(TLS):1SEP72-1029
GHISELIN, B. COUNTRY OF THE MINOTAUR.*
    K. RAINE, 569(SR):SPRING71-288
    R.B. SHAW, 491:MAR72-342
    H. TAYLOR, 651(WHR):AUTUMN71-367
GHOSE, Z. THE INCREDIBLE BRAZILIAN.
    J.R. FRAKES, 441:12NOV72-64
GHOSE, Z. THE VIOLENT WEST.
    617(TLS):28JUL72-873
GHOSH, A., ED. AJANTA MURALS.
    S. KRAMRISCH, 57:VOL31#4-329
GHOSH, K.K. THE INDIAN NATIONAL ARMY.
    J.C. LEBRA, 293(JAST):FEB70-476
GHURYE, G.S. TWO BRAHMANICAL INSTITU-
TIONS.
    617(TLS):29SEP72-1176
GIACOMAN, H.F. - SEE CALDERÓN DE LA
BARCA, P.

GIAMATTI, A.B. THE EARTHLY PARADISE AND
THE RENAISSANCE EPIC.*
    A.A., 477:SUMMER69-416
GIANNANTONI, G. - SEE PLATO
GIANNONE, R. MUSIC IN WILLA CATHER'S
FICTION.
    J.E. HARDY, 340(KR):1969/1-143
GIANTURCO, E. A SELECTIVE BIBLIOGRAPHY
OF VICO SCHOLARSHIP (1948-1968).
    A. ILLIANO, 131(CL):SPRING71-182
GIARDINA, I.C. - SEE CICERO
GIAVERI, M.T. L'ALBUM DE VERS ANCIENS
DI PAUL VALÉRY.
    N. SUCKLING, 208(FS):APR71-233
GIBB, H.A.R. - SEE IBN BATTŪTA
GIBBON, E. MEMOIRS OF MY LIFE.* (G.A.
BONNARD, ED)
    P. DANCHIN, 179(ES):DEC70-567
GIBBONS, S. EUROPE 1.
    617(TLS):21APR72-458
GIBBONS, S. EUROPE 2.
    617(TLS):18AUG72-978
GIBBS, A.M. - SEE DAVENANT, W.
GIBIAN, G. - SEE TOLSTOY, L.
GIBIAN, G., WITH R. BASS - SEE MASARYK,
T.G.
GIBRAN, K. & M. HASKELL. BELOVED PRO-
PHET. (V. HILU, ED)
    N.W. ROSS, 561(SATR):15APR72-68
    617(TLS):25AUG72-986
GIBSON, A.B. MUSE AND THINKER.
    M. WEITZ, 393(MIND):JUL70-472
GIBSON, A.B. THEISM AND EMPIRICISM.
    A.J. WATT, 63:AUG71-216
    F.H. YOUNG, 319:APR72-241
GIBSON, A.M. THE CHICKASAWS.*
    W. GARD, 584(SWR):AUTUMN71-VI
GIBSON, D.B. THE FICTION OF STEPHEN
CRANE.
    K. JOHNSON, 330(MASJ):FALL69-82
    R.E. PECK, 219(GAR):WINTER69-545
GIBSON, G. FIVE LEGS.*
    G. ROPER, 627(UTQ):JUL70-339
GIBSON, I. LA REPRESIÓN NACIONALISTA
EN GRANADA EN 1936 Y LA MUERTE DE
FEDERICO GARCÍA LORCA.
    617(TLS):10MAR72-267
GIBSON, J. FILE ON HELEN MORGAN.
    G. ROPER, 627(UTQ):JUL69-360
GIBSON, J.J. THE SENSES CONSIDERED AS
PERCEPTUAL SYSTEMS.
    T.R. MILES, 393(MIND):JAN70-145
GIBSON, J.R. FEEDING THE RUSSIAN FUR
TRADE.*
    G.A. LENSEN, 293(JAST):AUG70-919
    D.S.M. WILLIAMS, 575(SEER):JAN71-150
GIBSON, R. AFRICAN LIBERATION MOVEMENTS.
    617(TLS):26MAY72-598
GIBSON, R. - SEE ALAIN-FOURNIER
GIBSON, W.M. - SEE TWAIN, M.
GICOVATE, B. ENSAYOS SOBRE POESÍA HIS-
PANICA.
    A.P. DEBICKI, 240(HR):JAN70-103
GIDDENS, A. - SEE DURKHEIM, E.
GIDDINGS, R.W., COMP. YAQUI MYTHS AND
LEGENDS. (H. BEHN, ED)
    T.B. UNTHANK, 582(SFQ):JUN69-133
    292(JAF):JUL-SEP70-362
GIDE, A. THE NOTEBOOKS OF ANDRÉ WALTER.
(W. BASKIN, TRANS)
    A.M. BEICHMAN, 399(MLJ):JAN70-59
    C. SAVAGE, 219(GAR):SUMMER69-258
GIDION, H. ZUR DARSTELLUNGSWEISE VON
GOETHES "WILHELM MEISTERS WANDERJAHRE."
    D.G. LITTLE, 402(MLR):APR71-459
GIELGUD, J. DISTINGUISHED COMPANY.
    617(TLS):8DEC72-1482

GIERDEN, K. DAS ALTFRANZÖSISCHE ALEXIUS-
LIED DER HANDSCHRIFT L.
  K.D. UITTI, 545(RPH):AUG70-128
GIERGIELEWICZ, M. INTRODUCTION TO POLISH
VERSIFICATION.
  J. PETERKIEWICZ, 575(SEER):JUL71-463
  D. WELSH, 104:FALL71-424
GIERGIELEWICZ, M. HENRYK SIENKIEWICZ.
  J. MAURER, 497(POLR):AUTUMN69-104
GIEROW, P.G. SAN GIOVENALE: THE TOMBS
OF FOSSO DEL PIETRISCO AND VALLE VESCA.
  R.M. OGILVIE, 123:DEC71-463
GIL, A. - SEE BRUNER, J.S.
GILBERT, A. MURDER'S A WAITING GAME.
  N. CALLENDAR, 441:2JUL72-15
  442(NY):15JUL72-84
GILBERT, C. CHANGE IN PIERO DELLA FRAN-
CESCA.
  P. HENDY, 90:JUL70-469
  S. PFEIFFENBERGER, 551(RENQ):AUTUMN
  70-283
GILBERT, C., COMP. THOMAS CHIPPENDALE
AND HIS PATRONS IN THE NORTH.
  R. EDWARDS, 39:AUG69-160
GILBERT, E. CONNECTICUT CIRCLE.
  M. LEVIN, 441:24DEC72-14
GILBERT, J.G. UMBRELLA STEPS.
  M. LEVIN, 441:7MAY72-32
GILBERT, M. THE BODY OF A GIRL.
  N. CALLENDAR, 441:5MAR72-34
  H. FRANKEL, 561(SATR):25MAR72-104
  442(NY):1APR72-108
  617(TLS):28APR72-500
GILBERT, M. CLOSE QUARTERS.
  617(TLS):28APR72-500
GILBERT, M. RUSSIAN HISTORY ATLAS.
  617(TLS):2JUN72-641
GILBERT, R. & B. PARK. PLAYING HOCKEY
THE PROFESSIONAL WAY.
  J. DURSO, 441:3DEC72-40
GILBERT, W.S. GILBERT BEFORE SULLIVAN.
(J.W. STEDMAN, ED)
  B.H., 502(PRS):SUMMER68-186
GILBOA, Y. THE BLACK YEARS OF SOVIET
JEWRY.*
  R.N. LEVY, 441:9JAN72-4
GILDEA, W. & K. TURAN. THE FUTURE IS
NOW.
  J. DURSO, 441:3DEC72-44
GILDON, C. THE LIFE OF MR. THOMAS BET-
TERTON [TOGETHER WITH] BETTERTON, T.
THE AMOROUS WIDOW.
  617(TLS):18FEB72-178
GILIO, M.E. THE TUPAMAROS.* (SPANISH
TITLE: LA GUERILLA TUPAMARA.)
  617(TLS):4AUG72-915
GILL, B. TALLULAH.
  P. ANDREWS, 441:24DEC72-13
  J. KANON, 561(SATR):16DEC72-58
GILL, H.S. & H.A. GLEASON, JR. A START
IN PANJABI.
  V. MILTNER, 353:SEP69-88
GILL, J. THE LISTENER.
  N. CALLENDAR, 441:23JUL72-22
GILL, J. THE TENANT.
  617(TLS):25AUG72-1005
GILL, J.A., ED. PHILOSOPHY AND RELIGION.
  S.O.H., 543:DEC69-366
GILL, J.H., ED. ESSAYS ON KIERKEGAARD.
  R.J.B., 543:DEC69-364
GILL, M.L. MIND-WALLS.
  T.L. WEPPLER, 99:JUL-AUG72-46
GILLEL'SON, M.I. P.A. VJAZEMSKIJ.
  L.G. LEIGHTON, 104:SPRING71-118
  J.M. MEIJER, 574(SEEJ):SUMMER71-219
GILLES, D. CHEKHOV.*
  42(AR):WINTER69/70-589

GILLESPIE, J. ONE OF THE FAMILY.
  D.A.N. JONES, 362:10AUG72-184
GILLETT, C. THE SOUND OF THE CITY.*
  N. FOUNTAIN, 364:FEB/MAR72-141
GILLETT, J.D. MOSQUITOS.
  617(TLS):4FEB72-135
GILLETTE, A.S. AN INTRODUCTION TO SCENIC
DESIGN.
  L. RIDDLE, 583:SPRING69-236
GILLETTE, P. THE VASECTOMY INFORMATION
MANUAL.
  453:6APR72-34
GILLIATT, P. NOBODY'S BUSINESS.
  N. BALAKIAN, 441:5SEP72-39
  A. BURGESS, 441:10SEP72-4
  J.G. FARRELL, 362:5OCT72-447
  J. KANON, 561(SATR):9SEP72-73
  617(TLS):22SEP72-1087
GILLIES, A. A HEBRIDEAN IN GOETHE'S
WEIMAR.
  W.H. BRUFORD, 402(MLR):JAN71-218
GILLIES, A. - SEE VON HERDER, J.G.
GILLIS, F. THE HITCH HIKER.
  M. DOYLE, 491:MAR72-356
GILLIS, J.R. THE PRUSSIAN BUREAUCRACY
IN CRISIS, 1840-1860.
  617(TLS):7JUL72-771
GILLISPIE, C.C. LAZARE CARNOT, SAVANT.
  617(TLS):4FEB72-133
GILLON, A., ED. POEMS OF THE GHETTO.
  M. FRIEDBERG, 32:MAR71-220
GILLON, A. - SEE TUWIM, J.
GILMAN, D. THE ELUSIVE MRS. POLLIFAX.*
  T. LASK, 441:1JAN72-17
GILMAN, D. UPSTATE.
  D. ALLEN, 491:JUL72-235
GILMAN, L. EDWARD MAC DOWELL.
  M. PETERSON, 470:JAN70-45
GILMAN, S. THE TOWER AS EMBLEM.
  J.C. ALCIATORE, 546(RR):FEB70-66
GILMORE, T.B., JR. THE EIGHTEENTH-CEN-
TURY CONTROVERSY OVER RIDICULE AS A
TEST OF TRUTH.
  566:AUTUMN70-30
GILMOUR, J.S.L. - SEE JOHNSON, T.
GILPIN, L. THE ENDURING NAVAHO.
  F. GILLMOR, 50(ARQ):WINTER69-364
GIMPEL, J. CONTRE L'ART ET LES ARTISTES.
  V.M. AMES, 290(JAAC):FALL69-114
GINER DE LOS RÍOS, G. & L. DE LOS RÍOS
DE GARCÍA LORCA. ESQUEMA HISTÓRICO DE
LA CIVILIZACIÓN ESPAÑOLA.
  D. JAÉN, 238:MAR70-175
GINESTIER, P. LA PENSÉE DE BACHELARD.
  J.G. CLARK, 208(FS):JAN71-115
GINSBERG, A. AIRPLANE DREAMS.
  R. DURGNAT, 493:WINTER70/71-366
GINSBERG, R., ED. THE CRITIQUE OF WAR.
  A.C. EWING, 483:APR70-165
GINSBURG, M., ED & TRANS. THE MASTER OF
THE WINDS AND OTHER TALES FROM SIBERIA.
  W. EBERHART, 574(SEEJ):SUMMER71-232
GINSBURG, M. - SEE ZAMYATIN, Y.
GINZBURG, N. TI HO SPOSATO PER ALLEGRIA
E ALTRE COMMEDIE.
  G.S. PANOFSKY, 276:WINTER70-445
GIOBBI, E. ITALIAN FAMILY COOKING.
  N. MAGID, 440:13FEB72-12
GIONO, J. OEUVRES ROMANESQUES COMPLÈTES.
(VOL 1) (R. RICATTE, ED) LES RÉCITS DE
LA DEMI-BRIGADE.
  617(TLS):30JUN72-738
GIONO, J. OEUVRES ROMANESQUES COMPLÈTES.
(VOL 2) (R. RICATTE, ED)
  617(TLS):29DEC72-1578
GIORCELLI, C. HENRY JAMES E L'ITALIA.
  J-P. BARRICELLI, 275(IQ):FALL69-81
  L. EDEL, 131(CL):SUMMER71-284

GIORGETTI, P. & J. NORMAN. ITALIAN
PHRASE BOOK.
M. BORELLI, 399(MLJ):APR70-288
GIORNO, J. BALLING BUDDHA.
D. LEHMAN, 491:JAN72-224
GIOURTSI, A. PÄDAGOGISCHE ANTHROPOLOGIE
BEI JEAN PAUL.
R.M., 191(ELN):SEP70(SUPP)-118
GIOVANNI, N. GEMINI.
J.H. BRYANT, 561(SATR):15JAN72-34
J. JORDAN, 441:13FEB72-6
DI GIOVANNI, N.T. - SEE BORGES, J.L.
DI GIOVANNI, N.T. - SEE BORGES, J.L.,
WITH M. GUERRERO
DI GIOVANNI, N.T., WITH J.L. BORGES -
SEE BORGES, J.L.
GIOVANNINI, A. ÉTUDE HISTORIQUE SUR
LES ORIGINES DU CATALOGUE DES VAIS-
SEAUX.
F.M. COMBELLACK, 122:JAN71-45
J.B. HAINSWORTH, 123:DEC71-448
GIPPER, H. & H. SCHWARZ. BIBLIOGRAPHIS-
CHES HANDBUCH ZUR SPRACHINHALTSFOR-
SCHUNG. (PT 1)
J. ANDRÉ, 555:VOL44FASC1-143
J. ANDRÉ, 555:VOL44FASC2-369
GIRALDI, G. - SEE CARRARA, G.M.A.
GIRARD, A. LE JOURNAL INTIME.
M. CHASTAING, 542:JAN-MAR68-142
GIRARD, R. LENZ, 1751-1792.
M. CARTWRIGHT, 207(FR):MAR70-692
GIRARDI, J. & J-F. SIX, EDS. L'ATHÉISME
DANS LA PHILOSOPHIE CONTEMPORAINE.
N. FEHRINGER, 182:VOL23#11/12-581
GIRAUDOUX, J. LYING WOMAN.
T. BISHOP, 561(SATR):5FEB72-59
V. CUNNINGHAM, 362:9NOV72-643
A. FOOTE, 440:5MAR72-7
M. GALLANT, 441:30JAN72-7
442(NY):12FEB72-103
617(TLS):15DEC72-1521
GIRAULT DE COURSAC, P. L'EDUCATION D'UN
ROI: LOUIS XVI.
617(TLS):21JUL72-837
GIRDLESTONE, C. POÉSIE, POLITIQUE,
PYRÉNÉES.
N. SUCKLING, 208(FS):APR71-209
GIRDLESTONE, C. JEAN-PHILIPPE RAMEAU.
(NEW ED)
S. SADIE, 415:OCT70-1003
GIRKE, W. STUDIEN ZUR SPRACHE N.S.
LESKOVS.
S.S. LOTTRIDGE, 574(SEEJ):SUMMER71-
220
GIROD DE L'AIN, G. BERNADOTTE.
H. ROUSSEAU, 98:NOV69-1028
GIRODIAS, M., ED. THE OBSCENITY REPORT.
617(TLS):22SEP72-1083
GIROUARD, M. ROBERT SMYTHSON AND THE
ARCHITECTURE OF THE ELIZABETHAN AGE.
D. STILLMAN, 576:MAY68-156
GIROUARD, M. THE VICTORIAN COUNTRY
HOUSE.*
N. ANNAN, 453:18MAY72-22
GIRRI, A. COSMOPOLITISMO Y DISENSIÓN.
G. FIGUEIRA, 263:APR-JUN71-218
GIRVAN, W.D. HISTORIC BUILDINGS, GROUPS
OF BUILDINGS, AREAS OF ARCHITECTURAL
IMPORTANCE IN NORTH ANTRIM, INCLUDING
THE TOWNS OF PORTRUSH, BALLYMONEY AND
BUSHMILLS.
617(TLS):15SEP72-1050
GISH, L., WITH A. PINCHOT. THE MOVIES,
MR. GRIFFITH AND ME.
H.H., 200:AUG-SEP69-430

GISOLFI, A.M. THE ESSENTIAL MATILDE
SERAO.
L.C. BORELLI, 399(MLJ):MAY70-383
V. LUCIANI, 276:SUMMER70-220
GISSING, G. ISABEL CLARENDON. (P. COUS-
TILLAS, ED) NOTES ON SOCIAL DEMOCRACY.
(J. KORG, ED)
P.J. KEATING, 637(VS):JUN70-393
GISSING, G. ESSAYS AND FICTION.* (P.
COUSTILLAS, ED)
P.J. KEATING, 637(VS):JUN70-393
G.J. WORTH, 301(JEGP):APR71-326
A. WRIGHT, 677:VOL2-322
GITTELSON, N. THE EROTIC LIFE OF THE
AMERICAN WIFE.
R. JAFFE, 441:13AUG72-5
GITTINGS, J. THE ROLE OF THE CHINESE
ARMY.
R.E. GILLESPIE, 293(JAST):AUG70-930
GITTINGS, J., ED. SURVEY OF THE SINO-
SOVIET DISPUTE.*
U. LEE, 293(JAST):NOV69-152
GITTINGS, R. AMERICAN JOURNEY.
617(TLS):4AUG72-910
GITTINGS, R. JOHN KEATS.*
I.H.C., 191(ELN):SEP69(SUPP)-36
K. MC SWEENEY, 529(QQ):SPRING70-125
GITTLEMAN, E. JONES VERY.
F. GADO, 597(SN):VOL41#1-197
G.E.W., 502(PRS):SUMMER68-187
GITTLEMAN, S. FRANK WEDEKIND.
R.A. JONES, 221(GQ):NOV70-780
GIUDICI, G. O BEATRICE.
617(TLS):21JUL72-839
GIUSEPPI, M.S. & G.D. OWEN, EDS. CALEN-
DAR OF THE MANUSCRIPTS OF THE MARQUESS
OF SALISBURY, PRESERVED AT HATFIELD
HOUSE. (PT 20)
A.G.R. SMITH, 325:OCT70-153
GIUSTA, M. I DOSSOGRAFI DI ETICA. (VOL
2)
G.B. KERFERD, 123:DEC71-371
GLADIGOW, B. SOPHIA UND KOSMOS.
A.W.H. ADKINS, 123:DEC71-391
GLADSTONE, W.E. AUTOBIOGRAPHICA. (J.
BROOKE & M. SORENSEN, EDS)
617(TLS):7APR72-388
GLADT, K. STAMMBUCHBLÄTTER AUS WIEN.
R.K., 221(GQ):MAY70-526
LORD GLADWYN. THE MEMOIRS OF LORD GLAD-
WYN.
442(NY):11NOV72-190
617(TLS):2JUN72-619
GLANVILL, J. THE VANITY OF DOGMATIZING.
J.W. YOLTON, 319:JUL72-359
GLANVILLE, B. A CRY OF CRICKETS.*
F.P.W. MC DOWELL, 659:SUMMER72-361
GLANVILLE, B. THE FINANCIERS.
V. CUNNINGHAM, 362:12OCT72-482
617(TLS):6OCT72-1185
GLASER, E., ED. THE CANCIONERO "MANUEL
DE FARIA."
E.M. WILSON, 240(HR):OCT70-455
GLASER, E. - SEE PINTO, H.
GLASS, D.V. & R. REVELLE, EDS. POPULA-
TION AND SOCIAL CHANGE.
617(TLS):29DEC72-1585
GLASS, N. - SEE DE NERVAL, G.
GLASSCO, J. MEMOIRS OF MONTPARNASSE.*
M. LAURENCE, 606(TAMR):#54-77
GLASSCO, J., ED. POETRY OF FRENCH CANADA
IN TRANSLATION.*
P. STRATFORD, 102(CANL):SUMMER71-88
GLASSCOTE, R.M. & OTHERS. THE TREATMENT
OF DRUG ABUSE.
J.M. MARKHAM, 441:21MAY72-33

GLASSER, R. TIME IN FRENCH LIFE AND
THOUGHT.
617(TLS):22SEP72-1100
GLASSER, R.J. 365 DAYS.*
L. SIMPSON, 362:1JUN72-735
617(TLS):16JUN72-676
GLASSIE, H. PATTERN IN THE MATERIAL FOLK
CULTURE OF THE EASTERN UNITED STATES.
P.O. WACKER, 292(JAF):JAN-MAR70-92
GLATZER, N., ED. THE DIMENSIONS OF JOB.
F.J.N., 543:MAR70-572
GLATZER, N.N. - SEE KAFKA, F.
GLATZER, N.N. - SEE ZUNZ, L.
GLAUSER, A. LE POÈME-SYMBOLE DE SCÈVE
À VALÉRY.
B. WEINBERG, 401(MLQ):SEP70-373
GLAZIER, L. VOICES OF THE DEAD.
E.M. BRONER, 398:VOL3#1-45
GLEASON, H.A. INTRODUCTION À LA LIN-
GUISTIQUE.
F. BADER, 555:VOL44FASC1-112
GLEASON, J.H. THE JUSTICES OF THE PEACE
IN ENGLAND 1558-1640.
J.R.Y. KING, 325:APR70-73
GLEASON, R.W. SITUATIONAL MORALITY.
W.A.J., 543:DEC69-346
GLECKNER, R.F. BYRON AND THE RUINS OF
PARADISE.*
T. BECKET, 613:SPRING69-133
J.J. MC GANN, 405(MP):NOV69-203
GLEIM, J.W.L. GEDICHTE.* (J. STENZEL,
ED)
M.K. TORBRUEGGE, 221(GQ):MAR70-313
GLEN, R.S. THE TWO MUSES.*
H.C. BALDRY, 123:MAR71-139
GLICK, G.W. THE REALITY OF CHRISTIANITY.
M.H., 477:SUMMER69-428
GLICK, W., ED. THE RECOGNITION OF HENRY
DAVID THOREAU.
J.R. MC ELRATH, JR., 577(SHR):FALL70-
377
GLIGORIC, S. & R.G. WADE. THE WORLD
CHESS CHAMPIONSHIP. (PT 1)
617(TLS):8DEC72-1513
GLIMCHER, A. LOUISE NEVELSON.
D.L. SHIREY, 441:10DEC72-47
442(NY):23DEC72-80
GLOAG, J. CAESAR OF THE NARROW SEAS.
R. PAYNE, 561(SATR):8APR72-72
GLOVER, M. BRITANNIA SICKENS.
617(TLS):4FEB72-132
GLOVER, M. LEGACY OF GLORY.
442(NY):15JAN72-92
GLOVER, R. THE WINE AND THE GARLIC.
A. RODDICK, 368:MAR69-84
GŁOWIŃSKI, M. PORZĄDEK, CHAOS, ZNAC-
ZENIE.
J.T. BAER, 497(POLR):SPRING69-119
GLÜCK, L. FIRSTBORN.*
R. HOWARD, 340(KR):1970/1-130
J. SMITH, 493(AUTUMN70-243
GLUCKMAN, M., ED. THE ALLOCATION OF
RESPONSIBILITY.
617(TLS):28JUL72-874
GLUECK, N. THE RIVER JORDAN.
J. VAN SETERS, 318(JAOS):OCT-DEC70-
540
GLYNN GRYLLS, R. - SEE KINGSLEY, M.
GNAROWSKI, M. THE GENTLEMEN ARE ALSO
LEXICOGRAPHERS.*
M. HORNYANSKY, 627(UTQ):JUL70-332
GNAROWSKI, M. ARCHIBALD LAMPMAN.
M.J. EDWARDS, 102(CANL):AUTUMN71-85
D.O. SPETTIGUE, 529(QQ):WINTER70-638
"GO ASK ALICE."
617(TLS):1SEP72-1012

DE GOBINEAU, J.A. GOBINEAU: SELECTED
POLITICAL WRITINGS. (M. BIDDIS, ED)
J. DUNN, 362:10FEB72-186
GOCHBERG, H.S. STAGE OF DREAMS.
S.A. ROTHSCHILD, 546(RR):APR70-152
GODARD, J-L. GODARD ON GODARD. (J. NAR-
BONI & T. MILNE, EDS)
R. LOCKE, 441:21JUN72-45
617(TLS):17NOV72-1392
GODARD, J-L. WEEKEND [AND] WIND FROM THE
EAST.
617(TLS):17NOV72-1392
GODBOUT, J. D'AMOUR, P.Q.
617(TLS):20OCT72-1245
GODBOUT, J. HAIL GALARNEAU!
H. MC PHERSON, 606(TAMR):#57-84
J. WARWICK, 102(CANL):SUMMER71-87
GODDARD, D. BLIMEY! ANOTHER BOOK ABOUT
LONDON.
A. BURGESS, 441:13AUG72-4
T. LASK, 441:16JUN72-39
GODDEN, G.A. JEWITT'S CERAMIC ART OF
GREAT BRITAIN 1800-1900.
617(TLS):28JUL72-900
GODDEN, J. MRS. STARR LIVES ALONE.
442(NY):19AUG72-79
GODDEN, J. & R. SHIVA'S PIGEON'S.
T. LASK, 441:26AUG72-23
617(TLS):8DEC72-1508
GODDEN, R. THE TALE OF THE TALES.
441:9APR72-34
617(TLS):12MAY72-557
GODECHOT, J. THE COUNTER-REVOLUTION.
C.B.A. BEHRENS, 453:27JAN72-29
J.H. PLUMB, 441:21MAY72-6
617(TLS):11AUG72-949
GODEL, R. LES SOURCES MANUSCRITES DU
"COURS DE LINGUISTIQUE GÉNÉRALE" DE F.
DE SAUSSURE.
K. CONNORS, 545(RPH):NOV69-201
GODEY, J. THE THREE WORLDS OF JOHNNY
HANDSOME.
N. CALLENDAR, 441:21MAY72-30
GODFREY, D. E.M. FORSTER'S OTHER KING-
DOM.
T. ROGERS, 175:SUMMER69-73
S.P. ROSENBAUM, 627(UTQ):JUL69-374
GODFREY, D. THE NEW ANCESTORS.*
A. THOMAS, 102(CANL):SUMMER71-78
GODIN, J-C. HENRI BOSCO.
R.G. MARSHALL, 207(FR):DEC69-330
F.W. SAUNDERS, 208(FS):JAN71-108
GODIN, M. UNE DENT CONTRE DIEU.
R. ROBIDOUX, 627(UTQ):JUL70-440
GODINHO, V.M. - SEE UNDER MAGALHÃES GOD-
INHO, V.
"GODISHNIK NA SOFIĬSKIĬA UNIVERSITET:
FILOLOGICHESKI FAKULTET." (VOLS 59,
60, 61)
P.F. DEMBOWSKI, 545(RPH):NOV69-249
GODLOVITCH, S. & R. AND J. HARRIS, EDS.
ANIMALS, MEN AND MORALS.*
617(TLS):25FEB72-217
GODWIN, G. GLASS PEOPLE.
S. BLACKBURN, 441:15OCT72-2
A. BROYARD, 441:21SEP72-45
G. STUTTAFORD, 561(SATR):28OCT72-83
442(NY):7OCT72-159
GOEBEL, J., JR. - SEE HAMILTON, A.
GOEDSCHE, C.R. & M. SPANN. GERMAN REVIEW
AND PRACTICE.
K. BAHNICK, 221(GQ):MAR70-304
GOEHRKE, C. DIE WÜSTUNGEN IN DER MOSKAU-
ER RUS'.*
R.E.F. SMITH, 32:MAR71-139
GOERDT, W., ED. DIE SOWJETPHILOSOPHE.
E. KAMENKA, 587:JAN69-401

GOES, A. ALBRECHT GOES: DAS LÖFFELCHEN.
(C.E. SCHWEITZER, ED)
H.L. STOUT, 221(GQ):JAN70-141
GOES, A. - SEE GERHARDT, P.
VON GOETHE, J.W. HERMANN UND DOROTHEA.
(K. SPALDING, ED)
'W.H. BRUFORD, 220(GL&L):APR71-279
VON GOETHE, J.W. DER JUNGE GOETHE.*
(VOL 4) (H. FISCHER-LAMBERG, ED)
D.F.S. SCOTT, 220(GL&L):APR71-281
VON GOETHE, J.W. RETURN FROM ITALY. (K.
MÜLLER-VOLLMER, ED)
R. GRIMM, 406:FALL71-280
VON GOETHE, J.W. SATIREN, FARCEN UND
HANSWURSTIADEN. (M. STERN, ED)
G.E. GRISHAM, 221(GQ):MAR70-314
VON GOETHE, J.W. THE SUFFERINGS OF YOUNG
WERTHER. (H. STEINHAUER, TRANS)
J.L. GREENWAY, 406:SUMMER71-200
GOFF, B.L. SYMBOLS OF PREHISTORIC MESO-
POTAMIA.
R. HENSHAW, 318(JAOS):APR-JUN70-322
GOFF, F.R. THE PERMANENCE OF JOHANN
GUTENBERG.
617(TLS):10MAR72-284
GOFF, M. VICTORIAN AND EDWARDIAN SURREY
FROM OLD PHOTOGRAPHS.
617(TLS):29DEC72-1590
GOFF, P. WILHELMINISCHES ZEITALTER.
H.G. HERMANN, 406:WINTER71-408
GOFFMAN, E. INTERACTION RITUAL.
E. LEACH, 362:20APR72-520
GOFFMAN, E. RELATIONS IN PUBLIC.*
M. BERMAN, 441:27FEB72-1
GOGARTY, O.S. MANY LINES TO THEE. (J.F.
CARENS, ED)
617(TLS):21JUL72-836
GOGGIN, D.T., COMP. PRELIMINARY INVEN-
TORY (NO. 170) OF RECORDS RELATING TO
INTERNATIONAL BOUNDARIES (RECORD GROUP
76).
H.J. DEUTSCH, 14:OCT69-386
VAN GOGH, V. VINCENT VAN GOGH IN ENG-
LAND. (V.W. VAN GOGH, COMP)
H. CASSON, 46:NOV69-402
GOGOL, N. SELECTED PASSAGES FROM COR-
RESPONDENCE WITH FRIENDS.* (J. ZELDIN,
TRANS)
Y. LOURIA, 104:SUMMER71-259
R. SHELDON, 550(RUSR):JAN70-109
R.L. STRONG, JR., 574(SEEJ):SPRING71-
113
GOH CHENG TEIK. THE MAY THIRTEENTH INCI-
DENT AND DEMOCRACY IN MALAYSIA.
617(TLS):22DEC72-1565
GOHDES, C. LITERATURE AND THEATER OF THE
STATES AND REGIONS OF THE U.S.A.*
R.R. MASHBURN, 583:SUMMER69-325
E. MOTTRAM, 354:MAR69-78
GOHEEN, J.D. & J.L. MOTHERSHEAD, JR. -
SEE LEWIS, C.I.
GOITEIN, S.D. STUDIES IN ISLAMIC HISTORY
AND INSTITUTIONS.
J. KRITZECK, 318(JAOS):APR-JUN70-285
GOLAN, G. THE CZECHOSLOVAK REFORM MOVE-
MENT.
N. ASCHERSON, 453:10AUG72-16
617(TLS):14JAN72-41
GOLD, H. THE GREAT AMERICAN JACKPOT.*
639(VQR):SUMMER70-LXXXIX
GOLD, H. MY LAST TWO THOUSAND YEARS.
W. ABRAHAMS, 561(SATR):11NOV72-69
T.R. EDWARDS, 441:15OCT72-4
R.R. LINGEMAN, 441:20OCT72-44
442(NY):14OCT72-182
GOLDBERG, G.J. 126 DAYS OF CONTINUOUS
SUNSHINE.
M. LEVIN, 441:19NOV72-62

GOLDBERG, H. THE ART OF "JOSEPH AN-
DREWS."*
H. ANDERSON, 481(PQ):JUL70-349
A. SHERBO, 173(ECS):SUMMER70-560
GOLDBERG, M. THE KARAMANOV EQUATIONS.
N. CALLENDAR, 441:2APR72-22
GOLDBERG, M.A. THE POETICS OF ROMANTI-
CISM.
I.H.C., 191(ELN):SEP70(SUPP)-38
42(AR):SUMMER69-266
GOLDBERG, T. & OTHERS. L'ORFÈVRERIE ET
LA BIJOUTERIE RUSSES AUX XV-XX SIÈCLES.
C. OMAN, 90:FEB69-93
GOLDEN, A. - SEE WHITMAN, W.
"THE GOLDEN LOTUS (CHIN P'ING MEI)."
(C. EGERTON, TRANS)
617(TLS):27OCT72-1274
GOLDENBERG, G. THE AMHARIC TENSE-
SYSTEM.* [IN HEBREW]
A.K. IRVINE, 315(JAL):VOL7PT3-218
GOLDFARB, S. MESSAGES.*
D. ALLEN, 491:JUL72-235
GOLDIN, F. "THE MIRROR OF NARCISSUS" IN
THE COURTLY LOVE LYRIC.*
A. FOULET, 546(RR):FEB70-45
GOLDIN, M.G. SPANISH CASE AND FUNCTION.*
K. TOGEBY, 545(RPH):NOV70-364
GOLDING, J. CUBISM. (FRENCH TITLE: LE
CUBISME.)
P. DUFOUR, 98:AUG-SEP69-809
Y. YAPOU, 39:MAY69-406
GOLDING, W. THE SCORPION GOD.*
P. ADAMS, 61:FEB72-109
E. FEINSTEIN, 364:FEB/MAR72-177
D.J. GORDON, 561(SATR):5FEB72-72
E. HOAGLAND, 441:6FEB72-6
F. KERMODE, 61:JUL72-87
V.S. PRITCHETT, 453:24FEB72-12
P. WEST, 440:23JAN72-4
442(NY):29JAN72-94
GOLDMAN, A. JAMES JOYCE.
P. RECONDO, 202(FMOD):APR/AUG69-299
GOLDMAN, A. & E. SPRINCHORN - SEE WAG-
NER, R.
GOLDMAN, A.I. A THEORY OF HUMAN ACTION.
M. BRAND, 311(JP):4MAY72-249
GOLDMAN, M. AT THE EDGE.
P. COOPER, 340(KR):1970/1-143
GOLDMANN, H. & OTHERS. DANTE ALIGHIERI,
1265-1321.
R. BRÄNDLI, 545(RPH):NOV69-258
GOLDMANN, L. IMMANUEL KANT.
617(TLS):31MAR72-359
GOLDMANN, L. SITUATION DE LA CRITIQUE
RACINIENNE.
617(TLS):7APR72-399
GOLDSCHMIDT, L. & H. SCHIMMEL - SEE DE
TOULOUSE-LAUTREC, H.
GOLDSMITH, J. HAMBLEDON.
617(TLS):28JAN72-109
GOLDSMITH, M.E. THE MODE AND MEANING OF
"BEOWULF."
N.E. ELIASON, 301(JEGP):APR71-283
K. MALONE, 589:APR71-369
T.A. SHIPPEY, 402(MLR):JUL71-655
GOLDSMITH, V.F. A SHORT TITLE CATALOGUE
OF FRENCH BOOKS 1601-1700 IN THE LIB-
RARY OF THE BRITISH MUSEUM.* (FASC 1)
P. KREISS, 517(PBSA):JAN-MAR71-80
GOLDSMITH, V.F. A SHORT TITLE CATALOGUE
OF FRENCH BOOKS 1601-1700 IN THE LIB-
RARY OF THE BRITISH MUSEUM. (FASC 4&5)
617(TLS):14JAN72-48
GOLDSTEIN, A. A PERSON SHOULDN'T DIE
LIKE THAT.
N. CALLENDAR, 441:26MAR72-42

GOLDSTEIN, B.R. THE ARABIC VERSION OF
PTOLEMY'S PLANETARY HYPOTHESES.
G.J. TOOMER, 318(JAOS):APR-JUN70-296
GOLDSTEIN, J.A. THE LETTERS OF DEMOS-
THENES.*
D.M. MACDOWELL, 123:DEC70-322
L. PEARSON, 487:AUTUMN70-265
GOLDSTEIN, R. GOLDSTEIN'S GREATEST
HITS.*
L. BERKMAN, 418(MR):SPRING71-360
GOLDSTON, R. THE COMING OF THE CIVIL
WAR.
E. & N. FONER, 453:20APR72-39
GOLDSTON, R. THE RUSSIAN REVOLUTION.
L. KOCHAN, 587:OCT68-272
GOLDSTROM, J.M., ED. EDUCATION.
617(TLS):19MAY72-584
GOLDWATER, B. THE CONSCIENCE OF A MAJOR-
ITY.
C.P. IVES, 396(MODA):SPRING71-193
GOLDWATER, R. ART OF OCEANIA, AFRICA
AND THE AMERICAS FROM THE MUSEUM OF
PRIMITIVE ART.
W.L. HOMMEL, 127:WINTER70/71-220
GOLDWATER, R. SPACE AND DREAM.
A. BOWNESS, 592:MAR69-155
GOLDZIHER, I. MUSLIM STUDIES. (S.M.
STERN, ED)
617(TLS):4FEB72-130
GOLINO, C.L., ED. GALILEO REAPPRAISED.
A. PACCHI, 548(RCSF):JAN/MAR69-110
GOLINO, C.L. & F. FRANCK. TUTTE LE
STRADE PORTANO A ROMA.
C.J. GALLANT, 399(MLJ):OCT70-471
GOLL, C. TRAUMTÄNZERIN.
617(TLS):4FEB72-120
GOLLWITZER, H. THE CHRISTIAN FAITH AND
THE MARXIST CRITICISM OF RELIGION.*
J.P. SCANLAN, 32:MAR71-162
GOMBIN, R. LES ORIGINES DU GAUCHISME.
617(TLS):3MAR72-236
GOMBRICH, E.H. NORM AND FORM.*
S. HOWARD, 54:JUN69-184
GOMBRICH, E.H. SYMBOLIC IMAGES.
A. BROYARD, 441:1JUN72-45
A. FORGE, 362:27APR72-561
617(TLS):20OCT72-1248
GOMBROWICZ, W. DZIELA ZEBRANE. (VOLS
1-6)
617(TLS):11FEB72-155
GÓMEZ, A. LOS GRANDES.
J.C. TORCHIA-ESTRADA, 37:JAN69-40
GÓMEZ, C.B. - SEE UNDER BANDERA GÓMEZ, C.
GÓMEZ DE IVASHEVSKY, A. LENGUAJE COLO-
QUIAL VENEZOLANO.
H. SCHNEIDER, 72:BAND208HEFT4/6-437
GOMME, A. & D. WALKER. ARCHITECTURE OF
GLASGOW.
A.A. TAIT, 90:DEC69-768
GOMME, A.H., ED. JACOBEAN TRAGEDIES.
R.J. LORDI, 568(SCN):SUMMER/AUTUMN71-
47
J.C. MAXWELL, 447(N&Q):JUN70-232
GOMPERTZ, G.S.M. KOREAN POTTERY AND POR-
CELAIN OF THE YI PERIOD.*
G. HENDERSON, 57:VOL31#4-323
J. RAWSON, 90:MAY69-308
GOMRINGER, E. JOSEF ALBERS.
D. SEWELL, 127:FALL70-120
617(TLS):11AUG72-940
DE GONCOURT, E. PARIS UNDER SIEGE, 1870-
1871. (G.J. BECKER, ED & TRANS)
J.T. JOUGHIN, 399(MLJ):DEC70-620
GONDA, J. CHANGE AND CONTINUITY IN
INDIAN RELIGION.
L. ROCHER, 318(JAOS):APR-JUN70-343

GONDA, J. A CONCISE ELEMENTARY GRAMMAR
OF THE SANSKRIT LANGUAGE.
J-L. PERPILLOU, 555:VOL44FASC2-294
GONZÁLEZ, Á.R.F. - SEE UNDER FERNÁNDEZ
GONZÁLEZ, Á.R.
GONZÁLEZ, J.C. - SEE UNDER CASO GONZÁLEZ,
J.
GONZÁLEZ LEÓN, A. PAÍS PORTÁTIL.
E. ECHEVARRÍA, 263:JAN-MAR71-75
GONZÁLEZ PEÑA, C. HISTORY OF MEXICAN
LITERATURE.* (3RD ED)
W.P. SCOTT, 219(GAR):SUMMER69-261
GOOCH, A. DIMINUTIVE, AUGMENTATIVE AND
PEJORATIVE SUFFIXES IN MODERN SPANISH.
F. GONZÁLEZ-OLLÉ, 240(HR):APR70-208
GOOCH, P.H. IDEAS FOR ART TEACHERS.
617(TLS):11AUG72-954
GOODALL, J.L. AN INTRODUCTION TO THE
PHILOSOPHY OF RELIGION.
W.A.J., 543:DEC69-346
GOODALL, N. ECUMENICAL PROGRESS.
617(TLS):29SEP72-1173
GOODHEART, E. THE UTOPIAN VISION OF D.H.
LAWRENCE.
R.L. DRAIN, 179(ES):OCT70-465
GOODLAD, J.S.R. A SOCIOLOGY OF POPULAR
DRAMA.
617(TLS):4AUG72-911
LORD GOODMAN. NOT FOR THE RECORD.
F. KERMODE, 362:4MAY72-591
617(TLS):19MAY72-572
GOODMAN, A. THE LOYAL CONSPIRACY.
617(TLS):2JUN72-636
GOODMAN, E.J. THE TENANT SURVIVAL BOOK.
A.R. BENTLEY, 441:19NOV72-44
GOODMAN, F.D. SPEAKING IN TONGUES.
617(TLS):1DEC72-1468
GOODMAN, N. HOLLANDS LEAGUER. (D.S.
BARNARD, JR., ED)
E.D. PENDRY, 677:VOL2-264
GOODMAN, N. LANGUAGES OF ART.*
F.N. SIBLEY, 518:MAY71-9
GOODMAN, P. HOMESPUN OF OATMEAL GRAY.
D. ALLEN, 491:JUL72-236
GOODMAN, P. LITTLE PRAYERS AND FINITE
EXPERIENCE.
J.M. CAMERON, 453:30NOV72-18
442(NY):18NOV72-246
GOODMAN, P. SPEAKING AND LANGUAGE.
R.L. CHAPMAN, 561(SATR):15JAN72-44
E.W. SAID, 441:20FEB72-21
GOODMAN, P. TRAGEDY & COMEDY.
M.L. ROSENTHAL, 491:NOV71-99
GOODMAN, R. AFTER THE PLANNERS.
G. ALPEROVITZ, 441:6FEB72-4
GOODOVITCH, I.M. ARCHITECTUROLOGY.
C. JENCKS, 46:JUN69-470
GOODRICH, L. WINSLOW HOMER'S AMERICA.
W.D. ALLEN, 58:MAR70-12
GOODRICH, L. EDWARD HOPPER.*
442(NY):11MAR72-126
GOODRICH, N.L. CHARLES OF ORLÉANS.*
C.C. WILLARD, 545(RPH):NOV70-353
GOODSTEIN, R.L. DEVELOPMENT OF MATHE-
MATICAL LOGIC.
617(TLS):30JUN72-757
GOODWIN, K.L. THE INFLUENCE OF EZRA
POUND.*
F.K. SANDERS, 569(SR):SUMMER71-433
GOODWIN, K.L., ED. NATIONAL IDENTITY.
L.T. HERGENHAN, 71(ALS):OCT72-441
GOODWIN, L. DO THE POOR WANT TO WORK?
D. KEARNS, 441:17SEP72-4
GOODY, J. LITERACY IN TRADITIONAL SOCI-
ETIES.
W.W. ELMENDORF, 293(JAST):AUG70-907
GOODY, J. THE MYTH OF THE BAGRE.
617(TLS):21JUL72-848

GOODYEAR, F.R.D. - SEE TACITUS
GOOSSENS, J. STRUKTURELLE SPRACHGEOG-
RAPHIE.
H. BURGER, 72:BAND208HEFT4/6-370
P. IVIĆ, 350:SEP71-685
GOPAL, S. BRITISH POLICY IN INDIA, 1858-
1905.
L.R. WRIGHT, 302:JAN69-124
GOPI KRISHNA, WITH C.F. VON WEIZSÄCKER.
THE YOGI AND THE PHYSICIST.
W.I. THOMPSON, 231:NOV72-124
GORBANEVSKAYA, N. RED SQUARE AT NOON.
S. HOOD, 362:24FEB72-248
441:30JUL72-21
453:15JUN72-35
617(TLS):26MAY72-589
GORBANEVSKAYA, N. SELECTED POEMS. (D.
WEISSBORT, ED & TRANS)
S. HOOD, 362:24FEB72-248
617(TLS):26MAY72-589
GORDAN, J.D. ARNOLD BENNETT, THE CEN-
TENARY OF HIS BIRTH.
D. BALL, 447(N&Q):FEB70-76
GORDIMER, N. A GUEST OF HONOUR.*
D.J. GORDON, 676(YR):SPRING71-428
F.P.W. MC DOWELL, 659:SUMMER72-361
F. MC GUINNESS, 364:AUG/SEP71-143
GORDIMER, N. LIVINGSTONE'S COMPANIONS.*
V. CUNNINGHAM, 362:25MAY72-693
617(TLS):26MAY72-595
GORDON, C.H. BEFORE COLUMBUS.*
617(TLS):8DEC72-1504
GORDON, C.H. HOMER AND THE BIBLE.
S.D. WALTERS, 318(JAOS):APR-JUN70-407
GORDON, D.E. ERNST LUDWIG KIRCHNER.
F. WHITFORD, 592:NOV69-192
GORDON, D.J. D.H. LAWRENCE AS A LIT-
ERARY CRITIC.
M. ALLOTT, 677:VOL2-327
GORDON, E. FREEDOM IS A WORD.
441:9APR72-34
617(TLS):14JAN72-38
GORDON, E. NEPAL, SIKKIM AND BHUTAN.
617(TLS):10NOV72-1377
GORDON, G. ABOUT A MARRIAGE.
J. HUNTER, 362:29JUN72-874
M. LEVIN, 441:13AUG72-32
617(TLS):28JUL72-865
GORDON, H.J., JR. HITLER AND THE BEER
HALL PUTSCH.
G. BARRACLOUGH, 453:2NOV72-32
R. GRUNBERGER, 441:29OCT72-54
GORDON, I.A. THE MOVEMENT OF ENGLISH
PROSE.
F. MONTESER, 577(SHR):SUMMER70-280
GORDON, I.A. - SEE GALT, J.
GORDON, I.L. THE DOUBLE SORROW OF
TROILUS.
D. BIGGINS, 67:MAY71-81
J.M. COWEN, 677:VOL2-243
GORDON, L.G. STRATAGEMS TO UNCOVER
NAKEDNESS.
A.P. HINCHLIFFE, 148:SPRING70-95
GORDON, M.H.G. SHERRY.
617(TLS):22SEP72-1124
GORDON, R.C. UNDER WHICH KING?
R. BARTEL, 131(CL):SPRING71-179
K.C., 191(ELN):SEP70(SUPP)-42
GORDON, W.A. WRITER AND CRITIC.
P. CORWIN, 448:SUMMER70-132
GORDON WALKER, P. THE CABINET.
617(TLS):14APR72-413
GORE, A. LET THE GLORY OUT.
C.V. WOODWARD, 453:14DEC72-37
GÓRECKI, J. DIVORCE IN POLAND.
K. GRZYBOWSKI, 32:SEP71-695
GORER, R. CHOOSING YOUR GARDEN PLANTS.
617(TLS):21JUL72-853

GORES, J. DEAD SKIP.
O.L. BAILEY, 561(SATR):25NOV72-70
N. CALLENDAR, 441:12NOV72-67
GOREY, E. AMPHIGOREY.
P. ADAMS, 61:DEC72-146
E. JANEWAY, 441:29OCT72-6
GOREY, E. THE AWDREY-GORE LEGACY.
O.L. BAILEY, 561(SATR):30SEP72-79
GORKY, M. FRAGMENTS FROM MY DIARY. (M.
BUDBERG, TRANS)
442(NY):4NOV72-196
GORKY, M. THE LIFE OF A USELESS MAN.*
(M. BUDBERG, TRANS)
D.J. ENRIGHT, 362:3AUG72-153
H. MUCHNIC, 453:23MAR72-37
GORKY, M. UNTIMELY THOUGHTS.* (H. ERMO-
LAEV, ED & TRANS)
K. FITZLYON, 364:AUG/SEP71-132
GORMAN, J.B. KEFAUVER.*
R. GRIFFITH, 561(SATR):1JAN72-29
617(TLS):10MAR72-264
GORNICK, V. & B.K. MORAN, EDS. WOMAN IN
SEXIST SOCIETY.*
M.J. LUPTON, 31(ASCH):SPRING72-330
GORODETSKY, B.P., ED. ISTORIIA RUSSKOI
POEZII.
O. RAEVSKY-HUGHES, 32:SEP71-701
GOROSCH, M., B. POTTIER & D.C. RIDDY.
MODERN LANGUAGES IN EUROPE. (VOL 3)
I.D. MC FARLANE, 208(FS):JUL71-375
GOSDEN, P.H.J.H. THE EVOLUTION OF A
PROFESSION.
617(TLS):20OCT72-1264
GOSLICH, S. MUSIK IM RUNDFUNK.
J.S.W., 410(M&L):OCT71-436
GOSLING, J.C.B. PLEASURE AND DESIRE.
C.C.W. TAYLOR, 518:OCT70-12
GOSSETT, L.Y. VIOLENCE IN RECENT SOUTH-
ERN FICTION.
J.T. FLANAGAN, 179(ES):1969SUPP-XCII
GOSSMAN, L. MEDIEVALISM AND THE IDEOLO-
GIES OF THE ENLIGHTENMENT.
S.C. ASTON, 382(MAE):1971/1-91
R. BIRN, 131(CL):FALL71-372
R. O'GORMAN, 377:JUL71-108
R. SHACKLETON, 400(MLN):MAY70-609
A. VARTANIAN, 399(MLJ):JAN70-36
GOTLIEB, P. ORDINARY, MOVING.*
M. HORNYANSKY, 627(UTQ):JUL70-334
J. RAPOPORT, 606(TAMR):#54-85
GOTLIEB, P. PASSAGE OF SUMMER.
M. HORNYANSKY, 627(UTQ):JUL70-334
GOTLIEB, P. WHY SHOULD I HAVE ALL THE
GRIEF?*
J. RAPOPORT, 606(TAMR):#54-87
G. ROPER, 627(UTQ):JUL70-342
GOTTESMAN, L., H. OBENZINGER & A.
SENAUKE, EDS. A CINCH.
K. MC SWEENEY, 529(QQ):SUMMER70-286
GOTTESMAN, R. & S. BENNETT, EDS. ART AND
ERROR.*
J.C. MAXWELL, 402(MLR):OCT71-843
GOTTEWALD, C. DIE HANDSCHRIFTEN DER WURT-
TEMBERGISCHEN LANDESBIBLIOTHEK, STUTT-
GART. (1ST SER, VOL 1; 2ND SER, VOL 6)
J.A.W., 410(M&L):OCT71-443
GOTTFRIED VON STRASSBURG. TRISTAN.*
(K. MAROLD, ED)
P. SALMON, 402(MLR):JUL71-700
GOTTSCHALCH, W., F. KARRENBERG & F.J.
STEGMANN. GESCHICHTE DER SOZIALEN
IDEEN IN DEUTSCHLAND. (H. GREBING, ED)
A. LASSERRE, 182:VOL23#1/2-54
GOTTSCHED, J.C. AUSGEWÄHLTE WERKE.
(VOLS 2&3) (J. BIRKE, ED)
H. EICHNER, 301(JEGP):APR71-360
GOTWALS, V. & P. KEPPLER - SEE BRAHMS, J.

GOTZ, W. ZENTRALBAU UND ZENTRALBAUTEN-
DENZ IN DER GOTISCHEN ARCHITEKTUR.
N.P., 46:APR69-308
GOUBERT, P. L'ANCIEN RÉGIME. (VOL 1)
W. WRAGE, 207(FR):MAY70-946
GOUDRIAAN, T. KĀŚYAPA'S BOOK OF WISDOM
(KĀŚYAPA-JÑĀNAKĀṆḌAḤ).
L. ROCHER, 318(JAOS):APR-JUN70-344
GOUGENHEIM, G., WITH OTHERS, EDS. PROB-
LÈMES DE LA TRADUCTION AUTOMATIQUE.
H.W. BRANN, 207(FR):FEB70-552
GOUGH, B.M. THE ROYAL NAVY AND THE
NORTHWEST COAST OF NORTH AMERICA, 1810-
1914.
617(TLS):7JAN72-22
GOULART, R. WHAT'S BECOME OF SCREW-
LOOSE?*
617(TLS):14APR72-427
GOULD, C. THE DRAPED FIGURE.
617(TLS):10NOV72-1377
GOULD, J. & LORD CRAIGMYLE, EDS. YOUR
DEATH WARRANT?
617(TLS):21JAN72-75
GOULD, J. & L. HICKOK. WALTER REUTHER.
441:30JUL72-21
GOULD, J.W. THE UNITED STATES AND
MALAYSIA.
K. MULLINER, 293(JAST):MAY70-735
GOULD, L. NECESSARY OBJECTS.
S. BLACKBURN, 441:15OCT72-2
A. BROYARD, 441:19SEP72-61
G. STUTTAFORD, 561(SATR):14OCT72-83
GOULD, S.B. TODAY'S ACADEMIC CONDITION.
C.P. IVES, 396(MODA):WINTER71-96
GOULD, T. & J. KENYON, COMPS. STORIES
FROM THE DOLE QUEUE.
617(TLS):16JUN72-697
GOULDEN, J.C. MEANY.
W.C. MC WILLIAMS, 441:22OCT72-2
A.H. RASKIN, 441:23OCT72-33
GOULDEN, J.C. THE SUPERLAWYERS.
G. COWAN, 441:28MAY72-1
453:4MAY72-40
GOULEMOT, J-M. - SEE MARQUIS DE SADE
GOUNOD, C.F. MOZART'S DON GIOVANNI.
S. SADIE, 415:FEB71-140
GOURLAY, E. MOTIONS DREAMS & ABERRA-
TIONS.*
D. BARBOUR, 150(DR):SPRING70-112
GOVE, P.B. - SEE "WEBSTER'S THIRD NEW
INTERNATIONAL DICTIONARY OF THE ENGLISH
LANGUAGE"
GOVENDER, R. THE MARTYRDOM OF PATRICE
LUMUMBA.
617(TLS):15SEP72-1046
GOW, A.S.F. & D.L. PAGE, EDS & TRANS.
THE GREEK ANTHOLOGY.*
A.H. GRIFFITHS, 303:VOL90-216
GOWER, H. - SEE HAUN, M.
GOYTISOLO, J. EL FURGÓN DE COLA.
J.W. SCHWEITZER, 238:MAR70-151
GRABAND, G. DIE ENTWICKLUNG DER FRÜH-
NEUENGLISCHEN NOMINALFLEXION.
B. SUNDBY, 179(ES):JUN69-305
GRABAR, A. CHRISTIAN ICONOGRAPHY.*
A.W. GODFREY, 363:FEB70-76
J.M.C. TOYNBEE, 123:DEC70-380
639(VQR):WINTER70-XXVII
GRABAR, A. THE GOLDEN AGE OF JUSTINIAN.
G.M.A. HANFMANN, 124:SEP70-28
GRABAR, A. L'EMPEREUR DANS L'ART BYZAN-
TIN.
617(TLS):18FEB72-182
GRACIÁN, B. AGUDEZA Y ARTE DE INGENIO.
(E. CORREA CALDERÓN, ED)
H. ETTINGHAUSEN, 86(BHS):APR71-163

GRACIÁN DANTISCO, L. GALATEO ESPAÑOL.*
(M. MORREALE, ED)
P. DESCOUZIS, 238:SEP70-570
J.J. REYNOLDS, 551(RENQ):AUTUMN70-309
GRADE, A. - SEE FROST, R. & E.
GRAESER, A. PROBLEME DER PLATONISCHEN
SEELENTEILUNGSLEHRE.
N. GULLEY, 123:DEC71-451
F. LASSERRE, 182:VOL23#7-374
J.M. RIST, 124:SEP70-21
GRAF, L.P. & R.W. HASKINS - SEE JOHNSON,
A.
GRAHAM, A. ANDREW GRAHAM'S OBSERVATIONS
ON HUDSON'S BAY, 1767-1791. (G. WIL-
LIAMS, ED)
J.S. ERSKINE, 150(DR):SPRING70-147
GRAHAM, C. PORTRAIT OF ABERDEEN AND
DEESIDE.
617(TLS):13OCT72-1236
GRAHAM, C. & B. CURLING. THE GRAND
NATIONAL.
G.F.T. RYALL, 441:3DEC72-28
GRAHAM, G.S. GREAT BRITAIN IN THE
INDIAN OCEAN.
W.D. MC INTYRE, 637(VS):JUN70-455
GRAHAM, H. PASSPORT TO EARTH.
H. WILLIAMS, 364:FEB/MAR72-155
GRAHAM, H.D., ED. VIOLENCE.
K.E. MEYER, 440:12MAR72-6
GRAHAM, L.R. SCIENCE AND PHILOSOPHY IN
THE SOVIET UNION.
M.W. WARTOFSKY, 441:5MAR72-27
GRAHAM, L.R. THE SOVIET ACADEMY OF SCI-
ENCES AND THE COMMUNIST PARTY 1927-32.
S. FITZPATRICK, 587:JAN69-390
GRAHAM, S. A STATE OF HEAT.
N. EPHRON, 441:23APR72-7
GRAHAM, V. - SEE PERNETTE DU GUILLET
GRAHAM, W. THE SPANISH ARMADAS.
617(TLS):29SEP72-1171
GRAHAM, W.S. MALCOLM MOONEY'S LAND.*
R. BOTTRALL, 493:AUTUMN70-247
GRAINGER, J.H. CHARACTER AND STYLE IN
ENGLISH POLITICS.
T.J. SPINNER, JR., 637(VS):DEC69-225
DE GRAMONT, S. THE FRENCH.
H. PEYRE, 207(FR):FEB70-533
GRAMSCI, A. PRISON NOTEBOOKS. (Q.
HOARE & G.N. SMITH, EDS & TRANS)
617(TLS):28APR72-493
GRANA, G. MALAPARTE.
A. TRALDI, 276:SPRING70-101
GRANAT, R. REGENESIS.
M. LEVIN, 441:26NOV72-38
GRANATSTEIN, J.L. MARLBOROUGH MARATHON.
N. & D. NOWLAN, 99:MAY72-45
DE GRANDA GUTIÉRREZ, G. LA ESTRUCTURA
SILÁBICA Y SU INFLUENCIA EN LA EVOLU-
CIÓN FONÉTICA DEL DOMINIO IBERO-
ROMÁNICO.
O.T. MYERS, 545(RPH):AUG70-176
A. NOUGUÉ, 182:VOL23#4-161
"THE GRANDES HEURES OF JEAN, DUKE OF
BERRY."* (BRITISH TITLE: "LES GRANDES
HEURES DE JEAN DUC DE BERRY.") (M.
THOMAS, ED)
617(TLS):14JAN72-48
"GRANDES VILLES ET PETITES VILLES."
P. VOSSELER, 182:VOL23#13/14-699
DE GRANDPRÉ, P., ED. HISTOIRE DE LA
LITTÉRATURE FRANÇAISE DU QUÉBEC.
J-L. MAJOR, 627(UTQ):JUL70-424
GRANE, L. PETER ABELARD.
J.F. BENTON, 589:APR71-371
GRANEL, G. LE SENS DU TEMPS ET DE LA
PERCEPTION CHEZ E. HUSSERL.
M. RICHIR, 98:AUG-SEP69-778

GRANESE, A. IL GIOVANE DEWEY (DALLO
SPIRITUALISMO AL NATURALISMO).
E. BECCHI, 548(RCSF):JAN-MAR68-116
GRANGER, L. OUATE DE PHOQUE.
R. ROBIDOUX, 627(UTQ):JUL70-435
GRANJARD, H. & A. ZVIGUILSKY, WITH D.
PEROVIĆ - SEE TURGENEV, I.
GRANSDEN, K.W., ED. TUDOR VERSE SATIRE.*
P. THOMSON, 677:VOL2-248
GRANT, D. NATIONALISM AND THE LITERATURE
OF THE UNITED STATES.
A.D. HOOK, 447(N&Q):MAR70-117
GRANT, D. REALISM.
C. LYAS, 89(BJA):SUMMER71-293
GRANT, D. - SEE MATURIN, C.R.
GRANT, E. - SEE ORESME, N.
GRANT, E.M. EMILE ZOLA.
R.J. NIESS, 207(FR):OCT69-178
GRANT, G. TECHNOLOGY AND EMPIRE.*
D. HELWIG, 529(QQ):AUTUMN70-464
GRANT, J. HAROLD MONRO AND THE POETRY
BOOKSHOP.
M. THORPE, 179(ES):JUN70-269
GRANT, M. THE ANCIENT HISTORIANS.*
F.C. BOURNE, 124:FEB71-202
GRANT, M. THE ANCIENT MEDITERRANEAN.*
W.G. EAST, 303:VOL90-243
GRANT, M. JULIUS CAESAR.*
J.S. RICHARDSON, 313:VOL60-263
GRANT, M. NERO.*
T.J. LUCE, 124:APR71-276
GRANT, M. ROMAN MYTHS.
D. WENDER, 440:9APR72-6
617(TLS):21JAN72-58
GRANT, M.A. FOLKTALE AND HERO-TALE
MOTIFS IN THE ODES OF PINDAR.*
G.S. KIRK, 303:VOL90-202
GRANT, R.B. THE PERILOUS QUEST.*
F. BASSAN, 207(FR):DEC69-345
A.G.E., 191(ELN):SEP69(SUPP)-72
GRANT, R.M. AUGUSTUS TO CONSTANTINE.*
H. MUSURILLO, 124:JAN71-172
GRANT, U.S. THE PAPERS OF ULYSSES S.
GRANT. (VOL 4) (J.Y. SIMON, ED)
617(TLS):22SEP72-1117
GRANT, V.W. GREAT ABNORMALS.*
R. LEHAN, 445(NCF):DEC68-371
GRANT, W. & D.D. MURISON, EDS. THE
SCOTTISH NATIONAL DICTIONARY. (A-T)
617(TLS):13OCT72-1209
GRANT, W. & D.D. MURISON, EDS. THE SCOT-
TISH NATIONAL DICTIONARY. (VOL 7, PTS
1&2)
K. WITTIG, 38:BAND87HEFT3/4-414
GRANT, W.L. NEO-LATIN LITERATURE AND THE
PASTORAL.
A.D. SCAGLIONE, 545(RPH):NOV69-244
GRANVILLE, A.B. SPAS OF ENGLAND AND
PRINCIPAL SEA-BATHING PLACES. (VOL 2)
617(TLS):18FEB72-196
GRAS, C. ALFRED ROSMER ET LE MOUVEMENT
RÉVOLUTIONNAIRE INTERNATIONAL.
617(TLS):5MAY72-511
GRASS, F. STUDIEN ZUR SAKRALKULTUR UND
KIRCHLICHEN RECHTSHISTORIE ÖSTERREICHS.
L. KRETZENBACHER, 182:VOL23#1/2-56
GRASS, G. AUS DEM TAGEBUCH EINER
SCHNECKE. GÜNTER GRASS - DOKUMENTE
ZUR POLITISCHEN WIRKUNG. (H.L. ARNOLD
& F.J. GORTZ, EDS)
617(TLS):22DEC72-1549
GRASS, G. KATZ UND MAUS. (E. LOHNER,
ED)
K. GUDDAT, 399(MLJ):DEC70-619
GRASS, G. LOCAL ANESTHETIC.* (GERMAN
TITLE: ÖRTLICH BETAUBT.)
P.E. GRAY, 676(YR):AUTUMN70-101

GRASS, G. NEW POEMS.
R.H.W. DILLARD, 340(KR):1969/3-425
GRASSI, C. PROBLEMI DI SINTASSI LATINA.*
H. PINKSTER, 361:VOL24#1-33
GRASSI, G. - SEE ASCOLI, G.I.
GRASSMUCK, G., L.W. ADAMEC & F.H. IRWIN,
EDS. AFGHANISTAN - SOME NEW APPROA-
CHES.
R.L. CANFIELD, 293(JAST):MAY70-731
GRATE, P., ED. TREASURES OF SWEDISH
ART.
J. BECKWITH, 39:SEP69-267
GRAUR, A. NUME DE PERSOANE.
E. HAMP, 424:MAR68-59
GRAUR, A. THE ROMANCE CHARACTER OF
ROMANIAN.
E. PULGRAM, 353:NOV69-116
GRAVER, L. CONRAD'S SHORT FICTION.*
F.P.W. MC DOWELL, 136:FALL69-113
E.W. SAID, 637(VS):JUN70-429
W.F. WRIGHT, 445(NCF):DEC69-370
GRAVES, J. GOODBYE TO A RIVER.
M.E. BRADFORD, 598(SOR):AUTUMN72-949
GRAVES, J.C. THE CONCEPTUAL FOUNDATIONS
OF CONTEMPORARY RELATIVITY THEORY.
J. EARMAN, 311(JP):26OCT72-634
H. STEIN, 311(JP):26OCT72-621
GRAVES, R. LARS PORSENA.
617(TLS):31MAR72-360
GRAVES, R. ON POETRY.
J. DOLLAR, 590:SPRING70-39
GRAVES, R. POEMS, 1965-1968.*
E.J., 619(TC):1968/3-52
"ROBERT GRAVES' POEMS ABOUT LOVE."*
J. DOLLAR, 590:SPRING70-39
J. HEADLAM, 493:SPRING70-91
GRAY, B. STYLE.
S.R. LEVIN, 350:DEC71-1000
M. MINCOFF, 402(MLR):JAN71-162
GRAY, C. ARMAND GUILLAUMIN.
D.L. SHIREY, 441:10DEC72-46
GRAY, C. - SEE "DAVID SMITH BY DAVID
SMITH"
GRAY, C.M. - SEE HALE, M.
GRAY, D. LITTLE UN'S BOOK.
J. HOPPER, 661:SPRING69-105
GRAY, D. THEMES AND IMAGES IN THE MEDI-
EVAL ENGLISH RELIGIOUS LYRIC.
617(TLS):1SEP72-1020
GRAY, D.J. - SEE CARROLL, L.
GRAY, G.Z. THE CHILDREN'S CRUSADE.
V. CRONIN, 440:9APR72-5
GRAY, H. - SEE BAZIN, A.
GRAY, J. JOHNSON'S SERMONS.
617(TLS):20OCT72-1241
GRAY, J., ED. MODERN CHINA'S SEARCH FOR
A POLITICAL FORM.
M. GASSTER, 293(JAST):FEB70-434
GRAY, J.A. THE PSYCHOLOGY OF FEAR AND
STRESS.
617(TLS):24MAR72-340
GRAY, J.G. ON UNDERSTANDING VIOLENCE
PHILOSOPHICALLY, AND OTHER ESSAYS.
S. GENDIN, 311(JP):6APR72-186
GRAY, J.M. MAN AND MYTH IN VICTORIAN
ENGLAND.*
P. TURNER, 447(N&Q):JUL70-274
GRAY, J.W., ED. PERSPECTIVES ON ORAL
INTERPRETATION.
R.G. ANDERSON, 583:WINTER69-185
GRAY, M., WITH M. GALLO. FOR THOSE I
LOVED.
442(NY):30DEC72-72
561(SATR):23DEC72-69
GRAY, R. GOETHE: A CRITICAL INTRODUC-
TION.*
F. RADANDT, 405(MP):AUG69-72
P. SALM, 400(MLN):APR70-403

124

GRAY, R. INTROSPECT, RETROSPECT.
J. TULIP, 581:1971/1-72
GRAY, T. THE ORANGE ORDER.
617(TLS):24NOV72-1428
GRAY, T., W. COLLINS & O. GOLDSMITH.
THE POEMS OF THOMAS GRAY, WILLIAM COL-
LINS, AND OLIVER GOLDSMITH. (R. LONS-
DALE, ED)
C. PRICE, 541(RES):NOV70-506
GRAYMONT, B. THE IROQUOIS IN THE AMERI-
CAN REVOLUTION.
A.M. JOSEPHY, JR., 561(SATR):19FEB72-
71
GREAN, S. SHAFTESBURY'S PHILOSOPHY OF
RELIGION AND ETHICS.
G.M., 477:SUMMER69-403
"GREAT HOUSES OF ITALY."
H. ACTON, 39:AUG69-161
"GREAT STORIES OF AMERICAN BUSINESSMEN."
561(SATR):16DEC72-68
"THE GREAT TOURNAMENT ROLL OF WESTMIN-
STER."* (NOTES BY S. ANGLO)
J. BROMLEY, 325:APR70-72
R. STRONG, 90:DEC70-835
"GREAT WESTERN PROGRESS, 1835-1935."
617(TLS):22SEP72-1124
GREAVES, C.D. THE IRISH CRISIS.
617(TLS):16JUN72-697
GREAVES, R.L. THE PURITAN REVOLUTION
AND EDUCATIONAL THOUGHT.*
R. MIDDLEKAUFF, 656(WMQ):OCT70-666
GREBANIER, B. THE UNINHIBITED BYRON.*
579(SAQ):SUMMER71-437
GREBE, P., ED. GRAMMATIK DER DEUTSCHEN
GEGENWARTSSPRACHE. (2ND ED)
H. MAYER, 564:SPRING68-67
GREBE, P. & W. MÜLLER, COMPS. DUDEN-
LANGENSCHEIDT: DEUTSCHER WORTSCHATZ -
DEUTSCH ERKLÄRT.
U. THOMAS, 406:FALL71-290
GREBING, H. - SEE GOTTSCHALCH, W., F.
KARRENBERG & F.J. STEGMANN
GREBLER, L., J.W. MOORE & R.C. GUZMAN.
THE MEXICAN-AMERICAN PEOPLE.
J. WOMACK, JR., 453:31AUG72-12
GRECHKO, A.A. BITVA ZA KAVKAZ.
M. PARRISH, 587:OCT69-251
GREELEY, A.M. COME BLOW YOUR MIND WITH
ME.*
J.O. MEANY, 142:FALL71-468
GREELEY, A.M. PRIESTS IN THE UNITED
STATES.
R. NEUHAUS, 440:26MAR72-11
C. SIMMONS, 441:13MAR72-37
F. SWEENEY, 441:2APR72-5
GREELEY, A.M. UNSECULAR MAN.
P.L. BERGER, 441:19NOV72-22
A. BROYARD, 441:4DEC72-41 [& CONTIN-
UED IN] 441:6DEC72-49
GREEN, E. ELY: TOO BLACK, TOO WHITE.
(E.N. & A.B. CHITTY, EDS)
F.A. GREEN, 569(SR):AUTUMN71-641
GREEN, G. BLOCKBUSTER.
M. LEVIN, 441:11JUN72-34
GREEN, G.F. THE POWER OF SERGEANT
STREATER.
617(TLS):21JUL72-835
GREEN, H. THE DEAD OF THE HOUSE.
P. ADAMS, 61:MAY72-112
J. CATINELLA, 561(SATR):27MAY72-68
L.J. DAVIS, 440:27FEB72-4
R. ELMAN, 441:13FEB72-5
T. LASK, 441:12FEB72-31
GREEN, H. THE KING'S OWN ROYAL REGIMENT.
617(TLS):28JUL72-900
GREEN, J. CE QUI RESTE DU JOUR. OEUVRES
COMPLETES. (VOL 1) (J. PETIT, ED)
617(TLS):21JUL72-836

GREEN, M. CITIES OF LIGHT AND SONS OF
MORNING.
T. GITLIN, 561(SATR):16DEC72-64
T. LASK, 441:12MAY72-42
GREEN, M.J., WITH B.C. MOORE, JR. & B.
WASSERSTEIN. THE CLOSED ENTERPRISE
SYSTEM.
P. ADAMS, 61:MAY72-112
A.A. LEFF, 441:30APR72-4
GREEN, M.M. & G.E. IGWE. A DESCRIPTIVE
GRAMMAR OF IGBO.
J. KNAPPERT, 353:SEP69-101
GREEN, O.H. THE LITERARY MIND OF MEDI-
EVAL AND RENAISSANCE SPAIN. (J.E.
KELLER, ED)
K. WHINNOM, 86(BHS):OCT71-350
GREEN, P. ALEXANDER THE GREAT.
R.D. MILNS, 67:NOV71-219
GREEN, P. XERXES AT SALAMIS.*
F.J. FROST, 122:OCT71-264
GREEN, P. THE YEAR OF SALAMIS.
J.R. ELLIS, 67:NOV71-217
GREEN, P. & S. LEVINSON, EDS. POWER AND
COMMUNITY.
617(TLS):4FEB72-115
GREEN, T. THE UNIVERSAL EYE.
617(TLS):2JUN72-628
GREEN, W.M. AVERY'S FORTUNE.
N. CALLENDAR, 441:22OCT72-47
GREENAN, R.H. THE QUEEN OF AMERICA.
N. CALLENDAR, 441:9APR72-40
J.R. FRAKES, 440:28MAY72-6
H. FRANKEL, 561(SATR):13MAY72-86
GREENAWAY, P.V. JUDAS!
D.A.N. JONES, 362:8JUN72-768
GREENAWAY, P.V. THE JUDAS GOSPEL.
N. CALLENDAR, 441:17SEP72-45
GREENBAUM, S. VERB-INTENSIFIER COLLOCA-
TIONS IN ENGLISH.
H.V. KING, 350:DEC71-936
GREENBERG, A. THE METAPHYSICAL GIRAFFE.
J. HOPPER, 661:SPRING69-102
GREENBERG, C. AVANT-GARDE ATTITUDES.
C.R. BRIGHTON, 89(BJA):WINTER71-105
GREENBERG, D. & J. KENNEDY. THE HITCH-
HIKER'S ROADBOOK.
C.W. CASEWIT, 440:30APR72-4
GREENBERG, J. RITES OF PASSAGE.
T. LASK, 441:18MAR72-29
J.C. OATES, 440:19MAR72-3
R. SALE, 453:4MAY72-3
442(NY):15APR72-147
GREENBERG, J.A. FIRE IN AUGUST.
F. MORAMARCO, 651(WHR):WINTER71-98
GREENBERG, J-H., ED. UNIVERSALS IN LAN-
GUAGE. (2ND ED)
R. POSNER, 545(RPH):FEB70-336
GREENBERG, M. THE TERROR OF ART.*
C. SINGER, 222(GR):JAN70-70
GREENBERG, R.A. - SEE SWIFT, J.
GREENBERGER, A.J. THE BRITISH IMAGE OF
INDIA.
J. BUTLER, 637(VS):JUN70-418
R.A. CALLAHAN, 318(JAOS):OCT-DEC70-
599
D. SCHURMAN, 529(QQ):AUTUMN70-460
S. WOLPERT, 293(JAST):AUG70-956
GREENBERGER, E.B. ARTHUR HUGH CLOUGH.*
M. TIMKO, 301(JEGP):OCT71-688
GREENBLATT, S.J. THREE MODERN SATIRISTS.
K. SCHLÜTER, 38:BAND87HEFT3/4-473
GREENBURG, D. SCORING.
H. FRANKEL, 561(SATR):20MAY72-77
L.L. KING, 441:18JUN72-26
R. LASSON, 440:16APR72-8
C. LEHMANN-HAUPT, 441:2JUN72-39
GREENE, A. FORBIDDEN VOICE.
L. RICOU, 296:SUMMER72-84

GREENE, A.C. THE LAST CAPTIVE.
  W. BRANDON, 561(SATR):1JUL72-50
GREENE, A.C. THE SANTA CLAUS BANK ROB-
  BERY.
  P. ADAMS, 61:SEP72-110
  442(NY):16SEP72-127
GREENE, D. THE AGE OF EXUBERANCE.
  G.W. STONE, JR., 566:AUTUMN70-28
GREENE, G. COLLECTED ESSAYS.
  R.D., 619(TC):1968/4&1969/1-92
  G. WEALES, 340(KR):1969/4-554
  639(VQR):WINTER70-XV
GREENE, G. COLLECTED STORIES.
  617(TLS):20OCT72-1245
GREENE, G. GRAHAM GREENE ON FILM.
  N. SAYRE, 441:17DEC72-3
GREENE, G. A SORT OF LIFE.*
  R. FULLER, 364:OCT/NOV71-143
  K. MILLER, 453:20JUL72-12
GREENE, G. TRAVELS WITH MY AUNT.*
  F.P.W. MC DOWELL, 659:SUMMER72-361
GREENE, H. THE FUTURE OF BROADCASTING IN
  BRITAIN.
  617(TLS):15DEC72-1541
GREENE, R., ED. SICK DOCTORS.
  H. MILLER, 362:23NOV72-707
GREENE, R.L., ED. A SELECTION OF ENGLISH
  CAROLS.
  D.S. BREWER, 179(ES):FEB70-60
GREENE, R.W. THE POETIC THEORY OF PIERRE
  REVERDY.
  R. FEDERMAN, 131(CL):WINTER71-74
  C.H. WAKE, 208(FS):APR71-239
GREENE, T.M. RABELAIS.
  R. COOPER, 402(MLR):OCT71-895
GREENE, T.P. AMERICA'S HEROES.
  L.C. MILAZZO, 584(SWR):WINTER71-105
  617(TLS):28APR72-469
GREENFELD, J. A CHILD CALLED NOAH.
  A. BROYARD, 441:9JUN72-39
  S. KANFER, 231:SEP72-108
  D.K. MANO, 441:11JUN72-7
  C.C. PARK, 440:21MAY72-1
GREENFIELD, E. JOAN SUTHERLAND.
  617(TLS):8DEC72-1513
GREENFIELD, S.B. A CRITICAL HISTORY OF
  OLD ENGLISH LITERATURE.
  J.E. CROSS, 179(ES):JUN70-245
GREENFIELD, S.B. THE INTERPRETATION OF
  OLD ENGLISH POEMS.
  617(TLS):24NOV72-1439
GREENFIELD, T.N. THE INDUCTION IN ELIZA-
  BETHAN DRAMA.
  R. HAPGOOD, 131(CL):FALL71-359
  S. HOMAN, 301(JEGP):APR71-292
GREENHILL, B. & A. GIFFARD. TRAVELLING
  BY SEA IN THE NINETEENTH CENTURY.
  617(TLS):15DEC72-1541
GREENHILL, R. & V.B. BLAKE. RURAL
  ONTARIO.
  T. EMERY, 627(UTQ):JUL70-383
GREENHILL, R. & T.D. MAHONEY. NIAGARA.
  T. EMERY, 627(UTQ):JUL70-383
GREENSLADE, M.W., ED. A HISTORY OF THE
  COUNTY OF STAFFORD. (VOL 3)
  C.R. YOUNG, 589:OCT71-742
GREENWAY, D.E., ED. CHARTERS OF THE
  HONOUR OF MOWBRAY 1107-1191.
  617(TLS):1DEC72-1469
GREENWOOD, C. FIREARMS CONTROL.
  617(TLS):8DEC72-1507
GREENWOOD, J. & H. BARROW. THE WRITINGS
  OF JOHN GREENWOOD AND HENRY BARROW,
  1591-1593. (L.H. CARLSON, ED)
  T.G.A. NELSON, 67:NOV71-232
GREER, C. THE GREAT SCHOOL LEGEND.
  J. CALAM, 561(SATR):29APR72-52

GREET, A.H. JACQUES PRÉVERT'S WORD
  GAMES.
  R.R. HUBERT, 399(MLJ):NOV70-532
GREG, W.W. THE COLLECTED PAPERS OF SIR
  WALTER W. GREG. (J.C. MAXWELL, ED)
  G.W. WILLIAMS, 570(SQ):WINTER69-103
GRÉGOIRE DE NYSSE. TRAITÉ DE LA VIRGIN-
  ITÉ. (M. AUBINEAU, ED & TRANS)
  J. IRIGOIN, 555:VOL44FASC1-101
GREGOR, A. SELECTED POEMS.*
  V. YOUNG, 249(HUDR):WINTER71/72-677
GREGOR, D.B. STRALCI.
  J.A. TURSI, 399(MLJ):FEB70-135
DI GREGORIO, L. LE SCENE D'ANNUNCIO
  NELLA TRAGEDIA GRECA.
  S.A. BARLOW, 303:VOL90-202
  F. JOUAN, 555:VOL44FASC2-309
GREGOROVICH, A. CANADIAN ETHNIC GROUPS
  BIBLIOGRAPHY.
  H. TROPER, 99:JUL-AUG72-39
GREGOROVICH, J., ED. A UKRAINIAN CANAD-
  IAN IN PARLIAMENT.
  C.H. ANDRUSYSHEN, 627(UTQ):JUL69-493
LADY GREGORY. COOLE. (C. SMYTHE, ED)
  617(TLS):17MAR72-310
LADY GREGORY. THE KILTARTAN BOOKS.
  617(TLS):11AUG72-946
GREGORY, D. DICK GREGORY'S POLITICAL
  PRIMER. (J.R. MC GRAW, ED)
  V.S. NAVASKY, 441:6FEB72-5
GREGORY, J.S. GREAT BRITAIN AND THE
  TAIPINGS.
  E. BOARDMAN, 293(JAST):MAY70-689
  P.A. KUHN, 637(VS):MAR70-367
GREGORY, P. SOCIALIST AND NONSOCIALIST
  INDUSTRIALIZATION PATTERNS.
  M. BORNSTEIN, 32:DEC71-900
GREGORY, R.G. INDIA AND EAST AFRICA.
  617(TLS):1SEP72-1029
GREGSON, H. A HISTORY OF VICTORIA.
  G.W., 102(CANL):WINTER71-108
GREIDER, J. HU SHIH AND THE CHINESE
  RENAISSANCE.
  M. BERNAL, 453:23MAR72-31
GREIFENHAGEN, A. FRÜHLUKANISCHER KOL-
  ONETTENKRATER MIT DARSTELLUNG DER
  HERAKLIDEN.
  R.M. COOK, 123:DEC71-465
GREIFENHAGEN, A. DAS VESTARELIEF AUS
  WILTON HOUSE.
  D.E. STRONG, 123:JUN71-304
GREIG, C. IVY COMPTON-BURNETT.
  617(TLS):19MAY72-566
GREIMAS, A.J. DICTIONNAIRE DE L'ANCIEN
  FRANÇAIS JUSQU'AU MILIEU DU XIVE
  SIÈCLE.
  J. ANDRÉ, 555:VOL44FASC1-96
  F. KOENIG, 207(FR):MAR70-725
GREIMAS, A-J. SÉMANTIQUE STRUCTURALE.*
  K. SEKVENT, 597(SN):VOL40#2-427
GREINER, D.J. & E.B. - SEE CRANE, S.
GREINER, W.F., ED. ENGLISH THEORIES OF
  THE NOVEL. (VOL 2)
  A. WRIGHT, 677:VOL2-276
GREIVE, A. ETYMOLOGISCHE UNTERSUCHUNGEN
  ZUM FRANZÖSISCHEN "H" ASPIRÉ.
  H. STIMM, 72:BAND208HEFT2-143
GRENE, M. - SEE POLANYI, M.
GRENVILLE, H. OBSERVATIONS SUR L'ÉTAT
  ACTUEL DE L'EMPIRE OTTOMAN. (A.S.
  EHRENKREUTZ, ED)
  R.H. DAVISON, 318(JAOS):APR-JUN70-282
GRESCHAT, H-J. & H. JUNGRAITHMAYR, EDS.
  WORT UND RELIGION: KALIMA NA DINI.
  B. HEINE, 315(JAL):VOL8PT2-131
GREVEN, J. - SEE WALSER, R.

GREVEN, P.J., JR. FOUR GENERATIONS.
J.H. CASSEDY, 432(NEQ):SEP70-514
J.J. WATERS, 656(WMQ):OCT70-657
639(VQR):SUMMER70-CVI
GREVILLE, F. FULKE GREVILLE, LORD
BROOKE: THE REMAINS. (G.A. WILKES, ED)
G. BULLOUGH, 179(ES):AUG70-357
GREVILLE, F. SELECTED POEMS OF FULKE
GREVILLE.* (T. GUNN, ED)
C. WILLIAMSON, 541(RES):NOV70-529
42(AR):SUMMER69-266
GRÉVISSE, M. PROBLÈMES DE LANGAGE.
D.R. BRODIN, 207(FR):MAY70-951
GREY, A. A MAN ALONE.
E. MORGAN, 362:23MAR72-393
GREY, H. TALES FROM THE MOHAVES.
W. GARD, 584(SWR):SPRING71-199
GREY, I. THE FIRST FIFTY YEARS.
W.V. WALLACE, 587:OCT68-270
GREY OWL. THE MEN OF THE LAST FRONTIER.
TALES OF AN EMPTY CABIN.
G. STOW, 296:SUMMER72-82
GRIBBLE, L. MORE FAMOUS HISTORICAL MYS-
TERIES.
617(TLS):8DEC72-1513
GRIDLEY, R.E. BROWNING.
617(TLS):24NOV72-1420
GRIECO, A. VIAGEM EM TORNO A MACHADO DE
ASSIS.
H.M., 191(ELN):SEP70(SUPP)-145
GRIER, E. SELECTED POEMS: 1955-1970.
L. GASPARINI, 102(CANL):AUTUMN71-79
GRIERSON, E. THE DEATH OF THE IMPERIAL
DREAM.
442(NY):2SEP72-72
GRIERSON, E. THE IMPERIAL DREAM.
617(TLS):28APR72-467
GRIEST, G.L. MUDIE'S CIRCULATING LIB-
RARY AND THE VICTORIAN NOVEL.*
P.D. HERRING, 356:APR71-177
GRIEVE, M. & A. SCOTT - SEE MAC DIARMID,
H.
GRIFFEN, R.A. - SEE TOPONCE, A.
GRIFFITH, E. THE MORALITY OF SHAKE-
SPEARE'S DRAMA ILLUSTRATED.
617(TLS):18FEB72-178
GRIFFITH, G. ARTISTRY IN SINGING.
A. BLYTH, 415:FEB70-164
GRIFFITH, L. - SEE ROYALL, A.N.
GRIFFITH, P. MY STILLNESS.
L.J. DAVIS, 441:19NOV72-59
GRIFFITHS, P. EMPIRE INTO COMMONWEALTH.
B. PORTER, 637(VS):JUN70-444
GRIFFITHS, P.J. VIETNAM INC.
J. MORGAN, 362:2MAR72-283
GRIFFITHS, R., ED. CLAUDEL.
M-F. GUYARD, 208(FS):JAN71-103
GRIFFITHS, R. THE DRAMATIC TECHNIQUE OF
ANTOINE DE MONTCHRÉSTIEN.
K.M. HALL, 402(MLR):JUL71-686
G. JONDORF, 208(FS):APR71-192
GRIFFITHS, R. PÉTAIN.*
A. HARTLEY, 440:16APR72-7
R.O. PAXTON, 441:14MAY72-28
GRIFFO, P. & L. VON MATT. GELA.*
C.C. VERMEULE, 55:JAN69-49
GRIGGS, E.L. - SEE COLERIDGE, S.T.
GRIGORIEV, A. APOLLON GRIGOR'EV: SOCHI-
NENIIA. (VOL 1) (V.S. KRUPITSCH, ED)
V. TERRAS, 32:SEP71-703
GRIGSBY, J.L., ED. THE MIDDLE FRENCH
LIBER FORTUNAE.
G. MERMIER, 207(FR):OCT69-194
GRIGSON, G. DISCOVERIES OF BONES AND
STONES.*
I. WEDDE, 364:DEC71/JAN72-118

GRIGSON, G., ED. THE FABER BOOK OF POPU-
LAR VERSE. UNRESPECTABLE VERSE.
D.A.N. JONES, 362:9NOV72-643
617(TLS):4FEB72-123
GRIGSON, G., ED. RAINBOWS, FLEAS AND
FLOWERS.
D.A.N. JONES, 362:9NOV72-643
GRIGSON, J. GOOD THINGS.
N. MAGID, 440:13FEB72-12
617(TLS):23JUN72-730
GRILLÈS, D. CHEKHOV.
M. VALENCY, 397(MD):FEB70-435
GRILLONE, A. IL SOGNO NELL' EPICA LAT-
INA.*
S. VIARRE, 555:VOL44FASC1-148
GRILLPARZER, F. DER TRAUM EIN LEBEN.
(W.E. YATES, ED)
T.C. DUNHAM, 399(MLJ):OCT70-464
I.V. MORRIS, 220(GL&L):APR71-285
"FRANZ GRILLPARZER." (K. PÖRNBACHER, ED)
W. PAULSEN, 301(JEGP):APR71-337
"GRILLPARZER-FORUM FORCHTENSTEIN."
A.C. KIRKNESS, 67:MAY71-135
G.W. REINHARDT, 222(GR):MAY70-254
GRIMAL, P. LES JARDINS ROMAINS. (2ND
ED)
D.E. EICHHOLZ, 123:MAR71-112
GRIMAL, P., ED. L. ANNAEI SENECAE OPERUM
MORALIUM CONCORDANTIA. (VOLS 4&5)
123:DEC70-402
GRIMAL, P. - SEE CICERO
GRIMALDI, J. MEMOIRS OF JOSEPH GRIMALDI;
EDITED BY "BOZ." (R. FINDLATER, ED)
K.J. WORTH, 155:JAN69-46
GRIMBLE, A. MIGRATIONS, MYTH AND MAGIC
FROM THE GILBERT ISLANDS. (R. GRIMBLE,
ED)
617(TLS):4AUG72-923
GRIMES, M. TURNIP GREENS AND SERGEANT
STRIPES.
441:15OCT72-40
GRIMM, R., ED. DEUTSCHE ROMANTHEORIEN.*
L.W. KAHN, 222(GR):MAY70-234
E. MC INNES, 220(GL&L):OCT70-112
GRIMM, R. & C. WIEDEMANN, EDS. LITERATUR
UND GEISTESGESCHICHTE.
I.C., 191(ELN):SEP69(SUPP)-94
VON GRIMMELSHAUSEN, H.J.C. DER ABEN-
THEURLICHE SIMPLICISSIMUS TEUTSCH UND
CONTINUATIO DES ABENTHEURLICHEN SIM-
PLICISSIMI. DIETWALTS UND AMELINDEN
ANMUTHIGE LIEB- UND LEIDS-BESCHREIBUNG.
LEBENSBESCHREIBUNG DER ERTZBETRÜGERIN
UND LANDSTÖRTZERIN COURASCHE. DES
DURCHLEUCHTIGEN PRINTZEN PROXIMI UND
SEINER OHNVERGLEICHLICHEN LYMPIDAE
LIEBS-GESCHICHT-ERZEHLUNG. DES VOR-
TREFFLICH KEUSCHEN JOSEPHS IN EGYPTEN
LEBENSBESCHREIBUNG SAMT DES MUSAI
LEBENS-LAUFF. SIMPLICIANISCHER ZWEY-
KÖPFFIGER RATIO STATUS. (ALL ED BY R.
TAROT, WITH W. BENDER & F.G. SIEVEKE)
K. NEGUS, 221(GQ):MAR70-268
GRIMMINGER, R. POETIK DES FRÜHEN MINNE-
SANGS.*
V. GÜNTHER, 182:VOL23#17/18-798
O. SAYCE, 402(MLR):APR71-438
GRIMSLEY, R. - SEE ROUSSEAU, J-J.
GRIMSTED, D. MELODRAMA UNVEILED.
J.W.R., 502(PRS):SUMMER69-234
GRIMSTED, P.K. THE FOREIGN MINISTERS OF
ALEXANDER I.*
H. RAGSDALE, 550(RUSR):JUL70-336
GRISÉ, C.M. - SEE L'HERMITE, F.T.

127

GRITTNER, F.M. TEACHING FOREIGN LAN-
GUAGES.
    H.J. FREY, 238:MAR70-168
    J.B. PANE, 399(MLJ):MAY70-360
    L.R. SCHUB, 207(FR):APR70-855
GROBOVSKY, A.N. THE "CHOSEN COUNCIL" OF
IVAN IV.
    N. ANDREYEV, 32:MAR71-136
    S.A. ZENKOVSKY, 550(RUSR):JUL70-354
DE GROCHEO, J. CONCERNING MUSIC (DE
MUSICA). (A. SEAY, TRANS)
    A. CLARKSON, 308:WINTER68-281
GROENNINGS, S. SCANDINAVIA IN SOCIAL
SCIENCE LITERATURE.
    G.G. GAGE, 563(SS):AUTUMN71-442
GROGAN, D. MORE CASE STUDIES IN REFER-
ENCE WORK.
    617(TLS):16JUN72-697
GROGAN, E. RINGOLEVIO.
    J. FLAHERTY, 441:11JUN72-7
    C. LEHMANN-HAUPT, 441:26MAY72-37
    J.D. O'HARA, 561(SATR):15JUL72-54
    442(NY):10JUN72-130
GROHMANN, W. PAUL KLEE.
    M. MORÉ, 98:JUL69-639
GRONER, A. & OTHERS. THE AMERICAN HERI-
TAGE HISTORY OF AMERICAN BUSINESS AND
INDUSTRY.
    561(SATR):16DEC72-68
VAN GRONINGEN, B.A. & A. WARTELLE - SEE
ARISTOTLE
GRONOWICZ, A. AN ORANGE FULL OF DREAMS.
    M. LEVIN, 441:27FEB72-52
    D. STEWART, 561(SATR):19FEB72-72
    M. WOOD, 453:6APR72-25
GROOMBRIDGE, B. TELEVISION AND THE
PEOPLE.
    J. CRAWLEY, 362:27APR72-533
    617(TLS):2JUN72-628
GROPIUS, W. APOLLO IN THE DEMOCRACY.
    P. COLLINS, 505:APR69-156
GROSE, F. A CLASSICAL DICTIONARY OF THE
VULGAR TONGUE. (E. PARTRIDGE, ED)
    N.E. OSSELTON, 179(ES):1969SUPP-XCIII
GROSS, H. THE CONTRIVED CORRIDOR.
    617(TLS):2JUN72-634
GROSS, J., ED. THE AGE OF KIPLING.
    P. ADAMS, 61:DEC72-144
    E. MORISON, 441:17DEC72-17
GROSS, J. BUBBLE'S SHADOW.
    M. MUDRICK, 249(HUDR):SPRING71-185
GROSS, J., ED. RUDYARD KIPLING.
    J. BAYLEY, 362:14SEP72-342
GROSS, J. THE RISE AND FALL OF THE MAN
OF LETTERS.*
    M. LIGHTFOOT, 184(EIC):JUL70-359
    A.D. MOODY, 97(CQ):SUMMER69-285
GROSS, M. QUATTLEBAUM'S TRUTH.*
    F. SONTAG, 142:FALL71-475
GROSS, M., ED. THE WORLD OF GEORGE
ORWELL.*
    P. THEROUX, 440:19MAR72-5
    442(NY):18MAR72-156
GROSS, T.L. & S. WERTHEIM. HAWTHORNE,
MELVILLE, STEPHEN CRANE.
    617(TLS):14JUL72-824
GROSSER, A. GERMANY IN OUR TIME.*
(FRENCH TITLE: L'ALLEMAGNE DE NOTRE
TEMPS.)
    N. ASCHERSON, 453:20APR72-26
    G. BARRACLOUGH, 453:2NOV72-32
GROSSER, M. PAINTER'S PROGRESS.
    J. FLANNER, 442(NY):24JUN72-92
GROSSETESTE, R. THE MIDDLE ENGLISH
TRANSLATIONS OF ROBERT GROSSETESTE'S
"CHÂTEAU D'AMOUR."* (K. SAJAVAARA, ED)
    R.W. ACKERMAN, 545(RPH):NOV69-255
    T.P. DUNNING, 597(SN):VOL41#2-463

GROSSMAN, A.R. POETIC KNOWLEDGE IN THE
EARLY YEATS.*
    J.R. MULRYNE, 402(MLR):JUL71-680
GROSSMAN, M.L. DADA.
    D. SCHIER, 109:FALL/WINTER71/72-129
    R. SHATTUCK, 453:1JUN72-22
GROSSMAN, V. FOREVER FLOWING.
    I. HOWE, 441:26MAR72-1
    T. LASK, 441:1APR72-21
    442(NY):13MAY72-144
GROSSMANN, R. GESCHICHTE UND PROBLEME
DER LATEINAMERIKANISCHEN LITERATUR.*
    S. KARSEN, 263:OCT-DEC71-443
GROSSVOGEL, D.I. LIMITS OF THE NOVEL.
    D.E.S. MAXWELL, 402(MLR):APR71-402
    R. REID, 405(MP):MAY70-402
GROSUL, I.S. & OTHERS, EDS. ISTORIČESKIE
SVJAZI NARODOV SSSR I RUMYNII V XV-
NAČALE XVIII V. (VOL 2)
    D. DVOICHENKO-MARKOV, 104:SUMMER71-
282
GROTZFELD, H. DAS BAD IM ARABISCH-
ISLAMISCHEN MITTELALTER.
    J. VAN ESS, 182:VOL23#6-311
GROVE, J.W. GOVERNMENT AND INDUSTRY IN
BRITAIN.
    617(TLS):2JUN72-637
GROVES, N.J., ED. A.Y.'S CANADA.*
    A. EMERY, 627(UTQ):JUL69-405
GROZDIĆ, O. SERBO-CROATIAN GRAMMAR AND
READER.
    C.C. MILLS, 575(SEER):JAN71-136
GRUBB, G.W. THE GRUBBS OF TIPPERARY.
    617(TLS):13OCT72-1236
GRUBER, H. INTERNATIONAL COMMUNISM IN
THE ERA OF LENIN.
    H. TICKTIN, 587:APR69-562
GRUDER, V.R. THE ROYAL PROVINCIAL IN-
TENDANTS.
    J. LOUGH, 208(FS):JAN71-81
GRUEN, E.S., ED. IMPERIALISM IN THE
ROMAN REPUBLIC.
    T.E. GREGORY, 124:APR71-272
GRUEN, E.S. ROMAN POLITICS AND THE
CRIMINAL COURTS, 149-78 B.C.*
    B.M. LEVICK, 123:MAR71-86
    T.P. WISEMAN, 313:VOL60-212
GRUEN, J. THE PARTY'S OVER NOW.
    R. DREXLER, 441:13FEB72-10
GRUFFYDD, P. THE SHIVERING SEED.
    617(TLS):21APR72-441
GRUN, B. GOLD AND SILVER.
    A. LAMB, 415:AUG70-807
GRUN, B. - SEE BERG, A.
GRÜNBAUM, A. GEOMETRY AND CHRONOMETRY
IN PHILOSOPHICAL PERSPECTIVE.
    R.H.K., 543:SEP69-130
    V-F. LENZEN, 484(PPR):SEP69-151
    J. NORTH, 479(PHQ):JUL70-296
GRÜNBAUM, A. MODERN SCIENCE AND ZENO'S
PARADOXES.
    P. CAWS, 486:MAR69-106
    J. NORTH, 479(PHQ):JUL70-296
    W.C. SALMON, 536:DEC70-178
GRÜNBAUM, A. PHILOSOPHICAL PROBLEMS OF
SPACE AND TIME.
    B.R. GRUNSTRA, 486:DEC69-429
GRÜNBERG, M. THE WEST-SAXON GOSPELS.
    E.G. STANLEY, 72:BAND208HEFT2-135
GRUNBERGER, R. THE TWELVE-YEAR REICH.*
(BRITISH TITLE: A SOCIAL HISTORY OF
THE THIRD REICH.)
    G. BARRACLOUGH, 453:2NOV72-32
GRUNDMANN, S. - SEE HECKEL, J.
VON GRUNEBAUM, G.E. & R. CAILLOIS, EDS.
THE DREAM AND HUMAN SOCIETIES.
    O. GRABAR, 318(JAOS):APR-JUN70-404

GRUNFELD, F.V.   THE ART AND TIMES OF THE
  GUITAR.
    T.F. HECK, 317:SUMMER71-310
GRUNWALD, S., ED. OSTEN UND WESTEN.
    G. REIMER, 221(GQ):NOV70-826
GRYAZNOV, M. SOUTH SIBERIA.
    C.S. CHARD, 293(JAST):MAY70-713
GRYLLS, R.G. - SEE UNDER GLYNN GRYLLS, R.
GRYPHIUS, A. HERR PETER SQUENTZ. (H.
  POWELL, ED)
    P. SKRINE, 402(MLR):APR71-447
GRZIMEK, B. GRZIMEK'S ANIMAL LIFE ENCY-
  CLOPEDIA. (VOL 10: MAMMALS 1) (W.
  FIEDLER & OTHERS, EDS)
    617(TLS):23JUN72-729
GRZYBOWSKI, K. POLAND IN THE COLLECTIONS
  OF THE LIBRARY OF CONGRESS.
    L.R. LEWITTER, 575(SEER):APR71-303
GRZYBOWSKI, K. SOVIET PUBLIC INTERNA-
  TIONAL LAW.
    J.N. HAZARD, 32:JUN71-428
GUAGLIANONE, A. - SEE PHAEDRUS
GUARDINI, R. PASCAL FOR OUR TIME.
    J. WEBER, 613:SPRING68-140
GUDIOL Y RICART, J. GOYA.
    617(TLS):28JAN72-97
GUDSCHINSKY, S.C. HOW TO LEARN AN UNWRIT-
  TEN LANGUAGE.
    W.J. SAMARIN, 315(JAL):VOL8PT1-46
GUENTHER, H.V., ED & TRANS. THE ROYAL
  SONG OF SARAHA.
    P.J.H., 543:MAR70-556
    639(VQR):WINTER70-XXVII
VON GUENTHER, J. EIN LEBEN IM OSTWIND -
  ZWISCHEN PETERSBURG UND MÜNCHEN.
    H.A. STAMMLER, 104:SPRING71-123
GUERIN, M. L'OEUVRE GRAVE DE MANET.
    S. SPECTOR, 58:MAY70-10
GUERINOT, J.V. PAMPHLET ATTACKS ON ALEX-
  ANDER POPE 1711-1744.
    J.W. PERRY, 180(ESA):SEP70-411
    C.J. RAWSON, 402(MLR):APR71-396
    481(PQ):JUL70-370
GUERRA, T. EQUILIBRIUM.
    I. WEDDE, 364:OCT/NOV71-149
GUEST, J., ED. THE EARTH AND ITS SATEL-
  LITE.
    617(TLS):4FEB72-133
GUEVARA, E.C. BOLIVIAN DIARY.
    A. SINCLAIR, 619(TC):1968/3-46
GUEVARA, E.C. THE COMPLETE BOLIVIAN
  DIARIES OF CHE GUEVARA. (D. JAMES, ED)
    J. CARMICHAEL, 390:JAN69-143
GUEVARA, J.S. - SEE UNDER SILES GUEVARA,
  J.
DE GUEVARA, J.V. - SEE UNDER VÉLEZ DE
  GUEVARA, J.
GUÈVREMONT, G. LE SURVENANT. (A.S.
  MOLLICA & G.P. DESLAURIERS, EDS)
    A. HULL, 207(FR):MAY70-954
GUFFEY, G.R., ED. AFTER "THE TEMPEST."*
    C.A. ZIMANSKY, 481(PQ):JUL70-313
GUGGISBERG, C.A.W. CROCODILES.
    617(TLS):30JUN72-754
GUGLIELMINETTI, M. STRUTTURA E SINTASSI
  DEL ROMANZO ITALIANO DEL PRIMO NOVE-
  CENTO.
    A. ILLIANO, 131(CL):WINTER71-80
GUICHARD, L. - SEE BERLIOZ, H.
GUILBERT, L. LA FORMATION DU VOCABULAIRE
  DE L'AVIATION.
    J. DARBELNET, 207(FR):DEC69-374
GUILES, F.L. MARION DAVIES.
    N. JOHNSON, 441:24SEP72-7
    J. KANON, 561(SATR):16DEC72-58
GUILES, F.L. NORMA JEAN.
    E.H. NASH, 200:AUG-SEP69-429

GUILLAIN, R. JAPON TROISIÈME GRAND.
    EBATA KIYOSHI, 285(JAPQ):APR-JUN70-
    213
GUILLAUME DE CONCHES. GLOSAE SUPER
  PLATONEM. (É. JEAUNEAU, ED)
    J. TROUILLARD, 542:APR-JUN68-288
GUILLAUME, G. LEÇONS DE LINGUISTIQUE
  1948-1949.
    617(TLS):1SEP72-1030
GUILLAUME, J. - SEE DE NERVAL, G.
GUILLEMINAULT, G., ED. LE ROMAN VRAI DE
  LA IIIE RÉPUBLIQUE.
    J.A. GREEN, 207(FR):MAY70-947
GUILLÉN, J. AFFIRMATION. (J. PALLEY,
  ED & TRANS)
    M.A. SALGADO, 399(MLJ):NOV70-551
GUILLERMIT, L. - SEE SPINOZA, B.
DU GUILLET, P. - SEE UNDER PERNETTE DU
  GUILLET
GUILLEVIC. VILLE.
    M. NAUDIN, 207(FR):APR70-865
GUIMOND, J. THE ART OF WILLIAM CARLOS
  WILLIAMS.*
    R. EBERHART, 340(KR):1969/3-415
GUINN, J.P. SHELLEY'S POLITICAL
  THOUGHT.*
    K.N.C., 191(ELN):SEP70(SUPP)-43
GUINNESS, D. & W. RYAN. IRISH HOUSES AND
  CASTLES.*
    442(NY):26FEB72-103
    617(TLS):11FEB72-161
GULDESCU, S. THE CROATIAN-SLAVONIAN
  KINGDOM, 1526-1792.
    G.E. ROTHENBERG, 32:SEP71-689
VAN GULIK, R.H. HSI K'ANG AND HIS POETI-
  CAL ESSAY ON THE LUTE. (2ND ED)
    FUKUNAGA MITSUJI, 285(JAPQ):APR-JUN
    70-216
GÜLKE, C. MYTHOS UND ZEITGESCHICHTE BEI
  AISCHYLOS.*
    A.G. MC KAY, 24:OCT71-754
GULLANS, C.B., WITH J.J. ESPEY, COMPS.
  A CHECKLIST OF TRADE BINDINGS DESIGNED
  BY MARGARET ARMSTRONG.
    D.T. RODGER, 78(BC):WINTER70-539
GULLASON, T.A. - SEE CRANE, S.
GULLEY, N. THE PHILOSOPHY OF SOCRATES.*
    W. CHARLTON, 393(MIND):JAN70-149
    I.M. CROMBIE, 123:DEC70-355
    J.M. ROBINSON, 482(PHR):OCT70-565
    E. TELFER, 479(PHQ):JAN70-77
GULLICK, J.M. MALAYSIA.
    C.A. LOCKARD, 293(JAST):MAY70-734
GULLIVER, L. A NEW VOYAGE TO THE COUNTRY
  OF THE HOUYHNHNMS.* (BRITISH TITLE: A
  VOYAGE TO THE COUNTRY OF THE HOUYHNHNMS
  BEING THE FIFTH PART OF THE TRAVELS
  INTO SEVERAL REMOTE PARTS OF THE
  WORLD.) (M. HODGART, ED)
    J.R. CLARK, 385(MQR):SPRING72-147
    R.D. HUME, 566:AUTUMN70-23
    J.M. LALLEY, 396(MODA):WINTER71-90
GULLÓN, R. LA INVENCIÓN DEL 98 Y OTROS
  ENSAYOS.*
    F. IBARRA, 238:SEP70-574
GULLÓN, R. EL ÚLTIMO JUAN RAMÓN.
    B.B. APONTE, 238:MAY70-337
GUMUCIO, M.B. - SEE UNDER BAPTISTA GUMU-
  CIO, M.
GUN-SAM, L. - SEE UNDER LEE GUN-SAM
GUNDEL, W. DEKANE UND DEKANSTERNBILDER.
  (2ND ED)
    J.G. GRIFFITHS, 123:JUN71-306
GUNDERSHEIMER, W.L., ED. FRENCH HUMAN-
  ISM 1470-1600.
    C.N. SMITH, 208(FS):OCT71-451

GUNDOLF, F. FRIEDRICH GUNDOLF: BRIEF-
WECHSEL MIT HERBERT STEINER UND ERNST
ROBERT CURTIUS. GUNDOLF BRIEFE, NEUE
FOLGE. (BOTH ED BY L. HELBING & C.V.
BOCK)
D. JOST, 182:VOL23#15/16-744
GUNDY, H.P. THE SPREAD OF PRINTING:
WESTERN HEMISPHERE, CANADA.
617(TLS):24NOV72-1440
GUNN, J.A.W., COMP. FACTIONS NO MORE.
617(TLS):23JUN72-706
GUNN, P. MY DEAREST AUGUSTA.
E.E.B., 191(ELN):SEP69(SUPP)-28
GUNN, T. MOLY.*
N. RENNIE, 364:JUN/JUL71-129
GUNN, T. TOUCH.*
G. GILDNER, 448:WINTER70-129
J. MC MICHAEL, 598(SOR):WINTER72-213
GUNN, T. - SEE GREVILLE, F.
GUNNELL, J.G. POLITICAL PHILOSOPHY AND
TIME.*
A.G. ROBSON, 121(CJ):DEC70-JAN71-182
GUNSTON, B. TRANSPORT TECHNOLOGY.
617(TLS):9JUN72-667
GÜNTER, H., ED. TRANSNATIONAL INDUSTRIAL
RELATIONS.
617(TLS):7APR72-401
GÜNTHER, A. WILLIAM SHAKESPEARE: KOMÖ-
DIEN. WILLIAM SHAKESPEARE: TRAGÖDIEN
UND HISTORIEN.
K. TETZELI VON ROSADOR, 72:BAND208
HEFT1-49
GUNTHER, E. ART IN THE LIFE OF THE
NORTHWEST COAST INDIANS.
D.J. CROWLEY, 290(JAAC):FALL69-104
GUNTHER, J. & W.H. FORBIS. INSIDE AUS-
TRALIA AND NEW ZEALAND.
617(TLS):13OCT72-1236
GUPTE, R.S. THE ART AND ARCHITECTURE OF
AIHOLE.
H. GOETZ, 318(JAOS):OCT-DEC70-590
GURR, A. THE SHAKESPEAREAN STAGE 1574-
1642.*
J.J. JORGENS, 568(SCN):SUMMER/
AUTUMN71-46
GURR, T.R. WHY MEN REBEL.
639(VQR):SUMMER70-CXII
GURVIN, O., ED. NORSK FOLKEMUSIKK.
(VOLS 2-4/5)
A. FLEISCHMANN, 182:VOL23#1/2-34
GUSDORF, G. DIEU, LA NATURE, L'HOMME AU
SIÈCLE DES LUMIÈRES.
617(TLS):24NOV72-1412
GUSDORF, G. LES SCIENCES HUMAINES ET LA
PENSÉE OCCIDENTALE. (VOL 2)
P. LOUIS, 555:VOL44FASC1-109
GUSSOW, A. A SENSE OF PLACE.
P. ADAMS, 61:AUG72-92
A. BROYARD, 441:1MAR72-41
L.E. SISSMAN, 442(NY):16SEP72-123
GUSSOW, M. ZANUCK.
617(TLS):2JUN72-635
GUSTAFSON, R. IXION'S WHEEL.*
M. HORNYANSKY, 627(UTQ):JUL70-327
A. MOTYER, 529(QQ):SPRING70-129
GUSTAFSSON, L. LE POÈTE MASQUÉ ET DÉ-
MASQUÉ.
J. FARROW, 290(JAAC):WINTER69-251
GUSTIN, M. TONALITY.
I. KEMP, 607:AUTUMN69-41
GUTERSOHN, H. GEOGRAPHIE DER SCHWEIZ IN
3 BÄNDEN.
J.P. MOREAU, 182:VOL23#3-125
GUTH, K. GUIBERT VON NOGENT UND DIE
HOCHMITTELALTERLICHE KRITIK AN DER
RELIQUIENVEREHRUNG.
J.F. BENTON, 589:OCT71-743

GUTHKE, K.S. MODERN TRAGICOMEDY.
F.S.K., 477:SUMMER69-398
GUTHKE, K.S. WEGE ZUR LITERATUR.*
M.B. BENN, 402(MLR):OCT71-942
GUTHRIE, A.B., JR. ARFIVE.*
J. HUNTER, 362:10FEB72-188
GUTHRIE, G.M., ED. SIX PERSPECTIVES ON
THE PHILIPPINES.
A.A. YENGOYAN, 293(JAST):NOV69-209
GUTHRIE, R. MAXIMUM SECURITY WARD.*
S.F. MORSE, 385(MQR):FALL72-297
W.H. PRITCHARD, 491:DEC71-159
GUTHRIE, W. AN ESSAY UPON ENGLISH TRAG-
EDY [TOGETHER WITH] HOLT, J. AN
ATTEMPTE TO RESCUE THAT AUNCIENTE ENG-
LISH POET AND PLAYWRIGHTE MAISTER WIL-
LIAUME SHAKESPERE FROM THE MANEY
ERROURS, FAULSELY CHARGED ON HIM, BY
CERTAINE NEW-FANGLED WITTES.
617(TLS):18FEB72-178
GUTHRIE, W.K.C. A HISTORY OF GREEK
PHILOSOPHY.* (VOL 3)
H.D. RANKIN, 63:AUG71-219
R.K. SPRAGUE, 122:APR71-117
G. TREASH, 150(DR):SUMMER70-262
A. WASSERSTEIN, 518:OCT71-9
L. WOODBURY, 487:WINTER70-348
GUTIÉRREZ, G.D. - SEE UNDER DE GRANDA
GUTIÉRREZ, G.
GUTIÉRREZ-GIRARDOT, R. POESÍA Y PROSA
EN ANTONIO MACHADO.
G.D. CARRILLO, 238:DEC70-1023
GUTKIND, E.A. INTERNATIONAL HISTORY OF
CITY DEVELOPMENT. (VOL 1)
S. LANG, 576:MAY69-148
GUTKIND, E.A. URBAN DEVELOPMENT IN
SOUTHERN EUROPE.
639(VQR):SPRING70-LXXIV
GUTNOV, A. & OTHERS. THE IDEAL COMMUN-
IST CITY.
A.J. SCHMIDT, 32:SEP71-696
GUTTERIDGE, D. RIEL: A POEM FOR VOICES.
H. MAC CALLUM, 627(UTQ):JUL69-352
GUTTMANN, A. THE CONSERVATIVE TRADITION
IN AMERICA.*
F.X. DUGGAN, 613:SPRING69-157
GUTWIRTH, M. MOLIÈRE, OU L'INVENTION
COMIQUE.
W.G. MOORE, 402(MLR):JUL71-689
GUY DE BAZOCHES. LIBER EPISTULARUM
GUIDONIS DE BASOCHIA. (H. ADOLFSSON,
ED)
A.B. SCOTT, 382(MAE):1971/2-187
GUY DE CHAULIAC. THE MIDDLE ENGLISH
TRANSLATION OF GUY DE CHAULIAC'S
TREATISE ON FRACTURES AND DISLOCATIONS.
(B. WALLNER, ED)
E.J. FREEMAN, 597(SN):VOL41#2-474
M.S. OGDEN, 541(RES):AUG70-381
"GUY OF WARWICK." (W.B. TODD, ED)
A. HEISERMAN, 405(MP):NOV69-184
GUYARD, M-F. - SEE DE CHATEAUBRIAND,
F-R.
GUYARD, M.F. - SEE HUGO, V.
GUYOT, C. DE ROUSSEAU À MARCEL PROUST.
N. SUCKLING, 208(FS):JAN71-116
AP GWILYM, D. NINE THORNY THICKETS.
H. MORRIS, 569(SR):SPRING71-301
GYBBON-MONYPENNY, G.B., ED. "LIBRO DE
BUEN AMOR" STUDIES.
E.M. WILSON, 382(MAE):1971/1-80
GYSIN, B. THE PROCESS.
K.J. ATCHITY, 340(KR):1969/5-675

H.D. HERMETIC DEFINITION.
  H. KENNER, 441:10DEC72-55
HAACKE, R. - SEE RUPERT VON DEUTZ
HAAGEN, V.B. ALABAMA.
  W.S. HOOLE, 9(ALAR):OCT69-290
HAAK, B. REMBRANDT.
  A. DORN, 58:DEC69/JAN70-16
  G. MARTIN, 39:SEP69-266
  A. WERNER, 340(KR):1970/1-121
HAAS, A. - SEE ABRAHAM À SANCTA CLARA
HAAS, A.M. & U. HERZOG - SEE ERASMUS
HAAS, B. THE CHANDLER HERITAGE.
  M. LEVIN, 441:13FEB72-32
HAAS, E. THE CREATION.*
  617(TLS):28JAN72-109
HAAS, G. ESSAY.
  H.T. BETTERIDGE, 402(MLR):JUL71-709
  W. EMMERICH, 406:SUMMER71-168
HAAS, G. STUDIEN ZUR FORM DES ESSAYS
  UND ZU SEINEN VORFORMEN IM ROMAN.
  H. KOOPMANN, 52:BAND4HEFT1-112
HABAKKUK, H.J. POPULATION GROWTH AND
  ECONOMIC DEVELOPMENT SINCE 1750.
  617(TLS):24MAR72-321
HABER, T.B. THE MAKING OF "A SHROPSHIRE
  LAD."
  B. FABIAN, 182:VOL23#6-278
HABERLAND, W. ART OF THE WORLD: NORTH
  AMERICA.
  M.S. YOUNG, 39:APR69-330
HABERMAN, A.M. ATERET RENAMIN.
  A.S. CITRON, 399(MLJ):APR70-297
HABERMAN, D. THE PLAYS OF THORNTON WIL-
  DER.*
  S. FALK, 397(MD):FEB68-436
HABERMAS, J. KNOWLEDGE AND HUMAN INTER-
  ESTS.
  617(TLS):11FEB72-151
HABIBULLAH, A.B.M. DESCRIPTIVE CATALOGUE
  OF THE PERSIAN, URDU AND ARABIC MANU-
  SCRIPTS IN THE DACCA UNIVERSITY LIB-
  RARY.* (VOL 1)
  M. ASHRAF, 273(IC):JAN69-69
HABICHT, C. ALTERTÜMER VON PERGAMON.
  (VOL 8, PT 3)
  D.M. LEWIS, 123:DEC70-406
HABICHT, W., ED. ENGLISH AND AMERICAN
  STUDIES IN GERMAN.* (1968 & 1969)
  W. WEISS, 72:BAND208HEFT3-220
HABICHT, W. STUDIEN ZUR DRAMENFORM VOR
  SHAKESPEARE.
  T. STEMMLER, 72:BAND208HEFT1-51
HABRAKEN, N.J. SUPPORTS.
  617(TLS):24NOV72-1441
VON HABSBURG, O. CHARLES V.
  639(VQR):AUTUMN70-CXLIII
HACHMANN, R. DIE GOTEN UND SKANDINAVIEN.
  T.M. ANDERSSON, 589:APR71-373
HACK, B. & M. KLEISS - SEE "HERMANN
  BROCH - DANIEL BRODY: BRIEFWECHSEL
  1930-1951"
HACKER, A. THE END OF THE AMERICAN ERA.*
  C. MAECHLING, JR., 639(VQR):AUTUMN70-
  653
HACKER, P.M.S. INSIGHT AND ILLUSION.
  617(TLS):29SEP72-1153
HACKETT, C.A. AUTOUR DE RIMBAUD.
  E.J. AHEARN, 207(FR):FEB70-515
  E.J. AHEARN, 399(MLJ):FEB70-145
HACKETT, M.B. THE ORIGINAL STATUTES OF
  CAMBRIDGE UNIVERSITY.*
  J.A. WEISHEIPL, 382(MAE):1971/1-85
HACKETT, W.M. LA LANGUE DE GIRART DE
  ROUSSILLON.
  P. RICKARD, 382(MAE):1971/3-277
HACKNEY, S. POPULISM TO PROGRESSIVISM
  IN ALABAMA.
  639(VQR):SUMMER70-CVIII

HADDING, W. DER BEREICHERUNGSAUSGLEICH
  BEIM VERTRAG ZU RECHTEN DRITTER.
  P. PADIS, 182:VOL23#9-471
HADDOX, J.H. VASCONCELOS OF MEXICO.
  H.B., 543:SEP69-130
  G. DE BEER, 263:JAN-MAR71-82
  A. DONOSO, 258:JUN69-303
HADFIELD, C. THE CANALS OF YORKSHIRE
  AND NORTH EAST ENGLAND.
  617(TLS):22DEC72-1566
HADFIELD, J., ED. THE SATURDAY BOOK.
  617(TLS):3NOV72-1349
HADLEY, E.M. ANTITRUST IN JAPAN.
  K. YAMAMURA, 293(JAST):AUG70-944
HADLEY, L. FIELDING'S GUIDE TO TRAVELING
  WITH CHILDREN.
  C.W. CASEWIT, 440:30APR72-4
HADOT, P. PORPHYRE ET VICTORINUS.
  J.M. RIST, 303:VOL90-242
HAEDRICH, M. COCO CHANEL.
  P. ADAMS, 61:JUL72-96
  M. MC LAUGHLIN, 561(SATR):15JUL72-53
  J. STAFFORD, 453:10AUG72-22
  617(TLS):22DEC72-1554
HAENDEL, I. WOMAN WITH VIOLIN.
  R. ANDERSON, 415:JAN71-34
DE HAES, F. IMAGES DE LAUTRÉAMONT.*
  G. DÜRR, 72:BAND208HEFT4/6-463
HAFTMANN, W. & OTHERS. ABSTRACT ART
  SINCE 1945.
  617(TLS):19MAY72-568
HAGEDORN, U. & D. AND L.C. & H.C. YOUTIE.
  DAS ARCHIV DES PETAUS (P. PETAUS).
  J.D. THOMAS, 123:JUN71-196
HAGELMAN, C.W., JR., & R.J. BARNES, EDS.
  A CONCORDANCE TO BYRON'S "DON JUAN."
  J.J. MC GANN, 405(MP):NOV69-203
HAGEN, O.A. WHO DONE IT?
  W.B. STEVENSON, 355:NOV69-345
VON HAGEN, V.W. THE ROADS THAT LED TO
  ROME.*
  R. HIGGINS, 39:AUG69-162
HAGENDAHL, H. AUGUSTINE AND THE LATIN
  CLASSICS.*
  M-J. RONDEAU, 555:VOL44FASC1-158
HAGER, F-P., ED. METAPHYSIK UND THEO-
  LOGIE DES ARISTOTELES.
  P.M. HUBY, 123:DEC71-452
HAGER, R.E. LÉON BLOY ET L'ÉVOLUTION DU
  CONTE CRUEL.*
  A. VIATTE, 207(FR):OCT69-176
HAGGARD, W. THE PROTECTORS.
  617(TLS):29SEP72-1174
HAGGARD, W. TOO MANY ENEMIES.
  A. BROYARD, 441:14JAN72-35
  N. CALLENDAR, 441:23APR72-43
HAGGIS, D.R. C-F. RAMUZ, OUVRIER DU
  LANGAGE.
  D.L. PARRIS, 402(MLR):JAN71-193
HAGGIS, D.R. & OTHERS, EDS. THE FRENCH
  RENAISSANCE AND ITS HERITAGE.
  A.E. CREORE, 551(RENQ):SUMMER70-184
  D.M. FRAME, 546(RR):APR70-132
  M.A. SCREECH, 447(N&Q):JAN70-40
HAGIWARA, M.P. & R.L. POLITZER. CONTINU-
  ONS À PARLER.
  R.C. KELLY, 207(FR):OCT69-152
HAGOPIAN, J.V. J.F. POWERS.*
  L. CUNNINGHAM, 613:SPRING69-132
HAGSTRUM, J.H. SAMUEL JOHNSON'S LITERARY
  CRITICISM.
  H.W. DONNER, 597(SN):VOL41#1-194
HAHLWEG, W., ED. DER FRIEDE VON BREST-
  LITOVSK.
  617(TLS):19MAY72-581
HAHN, F.H. THE SHARE OF WAGES IN THE
  NATIONAL INCOME.
  617(TLS):4AUG72-920

131

HAIDU, P. AESTHETIC DISTANCE IN CHRÉ-
TIEN DE TROYES.
    A.M. COLBY, 589:JUL71-514
    N.J. LACY, 399(MLJ):MAY70-385
HAIG, A. FLIGHT FROM MONTEGO BAY.
    N. CALLENDAR, 441:24DEC72-14
HAIGHT, G.S. GEORGE ELIOT.*
    A.O.J. COCKSHUT, 541(RES):FEB70-94
    B. HARDY, 445(NCF):DEC69-366
    G. THOMAS, 175:SPRING69-31
    42(AR):SPRING69-112
HAIGHT, M.V.J. EUROPEAN POWERS AND
SOUTH-EAST AFRICA.
    W.D. MC INTYRE, 637(VS):JUN70-455
HAILE, H.G. THE HISTORY OF DOCTOR JOHANN
FAUSTUS.
    A.P. FOULKES, 564:SPRING69-72
HAINES, C. IMMORTALS OF LITERATURE:
CHARLES DICKENS.
    A.B., 155:SEP70-244
HAINES, F. THE BUFFALO.*
    639(VQR):SUMMER70-CIX
HAINES, F. HORSES IN AMERICA.
    W. GARD, 584(SWR):SUMMER71-V
HAINES, J. THE STONE HARP.*
    J.R. CARPENTER, 491:JUN72-164
    H. CARRUTH, 249(HUDR):SUMMER71-323
    S. MOORE, 385(MQR):SUMMER72-217
    H. TAYLOR, 651(WHR):AUTUMN71-369
HAINES, J. TWENTY POEMS.
    C. MOLESWORTH, 491:MAY72-107
HAINSWORTH, J.B. THE FLEXIBILITY OF THE
HOMERIC FORMULA.*
    P. CHANTRAINE, 555:VOL44FASC2-304
HAIR, P.E.H. THE EARLY STUDY OF NIGERIAN
LANGUAGES.*
    E.C. ROWLANDS, 315(JAL):VOL8PT1-45
AL-HAJJI, A.R.A. - SEE AL-BAKRI, A.'U.
HAJNAL, J. THE STUDENT TRAP.
    617(TLS):4AUG72-922
HÅKANSON, L. STATIUS' "SILVAE."
    E.J. KENNEY, 123:JUN71-210
    D.W.T.C. VESSEY, 122:OCT71-273
HAKIMA, A.M.A. - SEE UNDER ABU HAKIMA,
A.M.
HAKUIN. THE ZEN MASTER HAKUIN: SELECTED
WRITINGS. (P.B. YAMPOLSKY, TRANS)
    617(TLS):24MAR72-342
HALACY, D.S., JR. THE GEOMETRY OF HUN-
GER.
    E. EDELSON, 440:23APR72-4
HALBERSTAM, D. THE BEST AND THE BRIGHT-
EST.
    J.M. GAVIN, 231:DEC72-104
    C. LEHMANN-HAUPT, 441:14NOV72-49
    V.S. NAVASKY, 441:12NOV72-1
HALBERSTAM, M. THE PILLS IN YOUR LIFE.
    441:30APR72-28
HALBFASS, W. DESCARTES' FRAGE NACH DER
EXISTENZ DER WELT.
    W. KNEALE, 479(PHQ):JAN70-79
HALDANE, A.R.B. THREE CENTURIES OF
SCOTTISH POSTS.
    617(TLS):17MAR72-317
HALDANE, S. THE OCEAN EVERYWHERE.
    D. FETHERLING, 606(TAMR):#57-80
HALE, B.M. THE SUBJECT BIBLIOGRAPHY OF
THE SOCIAL SCIENCES AND HUMANITIES.
    R.C. ELLSWORTH, 356:JAN71-76
HALE, C.A. MEXICAN LIBERALISM IN THE AGE
OF MORA, 1821-1853.
    617(TLS):8DEC72-1503
HALE, J.R. RENAISSANCE EXPLORATION.
    442(NY):15JUL72-83
HALE, L. BONNEY'S PLACE.
    M. LEVIN, 441:7MAY72-32

HALE, M. THE HISTORY OF THE COMMON LAW
OF ENGLAND. (C.M. GRAY, ED)
    617(TLS):18FEB72-175
HALE, N.G., JR. FREUD AND THE AMERI-
CANS.*
    617(TLS):8DEC72-1484
HALE, N.G., JR. - SEE PUTNAM, J.J.
HALES, F.D. - SEE KROEBER, T. & R.F.
HEIZER
HALEWOOD, W.H. THE POETRY OF GRACE.
    V.R. MOLLENKOTT, 568(SCN):SUMMER/
    AUTUMN71-40
HALEY, A.H. THE CRAWLEY AFFAIR.
    617(TLS):7APR72-402
HALEY, K.H.D. THE DUTCH IN THE SEVEN-
TEENTH CENTURY.
    617(TLS):26MAY72-610
HALKETT, J.G. MILTON AND THE IDEA OF
MATRIMONY.*
    D. MC COLLEY, 301(JEGP):APR71-308
HALL, A.R. & M.B. - SEE OLDENBURG, H.
HALL, D. THE ALLIGATOR BRIDE.*
    G.S. FRASER, 473(PR):WINTER71/72-469
    639(VQR):SPRING70-XLIV
HALL, D. THE YELLOW ROOM.*
    P. PETTINGELL, 491:JAN72-234
HALL, D. - SEE WHITMAN, W.
HALL, D.K. ON THE WAY TO THE SKY.
    M. LEVIN, 441:12MAR72-42
HALL, D.K. & S.G. CLARK. ROCK - A WORLD
BOLD AS LOVE.
    L. BERKMAN, 418(MR):SPRING71-366
HALL, E.T. THE HIDDEN DIMENSION.
    A. HUMPHREY-REEVE, 619(TC):VOL177
    #1042-57
HALL, J. THE LUNATIC GIANT IN THE DRAW-
ING ROOM.
    A.D. HOOK, 447(N&Q):MAR70-117
HALL, J. STAFFORDSHIRE PORTRAIT FIGURES.
    617(TLS):21APR72-457
HALL, J.B. MAYO SERGEANT.*
    A. DRAKE, 448:WINTER70-131
HALL, J.B. - SEE CLAUDIAN
HALL, J.W. & M.B. JANSEN, EDS. STUDIES
IN THE INSTITUTIONAL HISTORY OF EARLY
MODERN JAPAN.
    H.P. VARLEY, 244(HJAS):VOL29-324
HALL, N.J. - SEE TROLLOPE, A.
HALL, O. REPORT FROM BEAU HARBOR.*
    S. BLACKBURN, 440:2JAN72-2
"PENELOPE HALL'S SOCIAL SERVICES OF
ENGLAND AND WALES." (A. FORDER, ED)
    617(TLS):14JAN72-47
HALL, R. HEAVEN, IN A WAY.
    J. TULIP, 581:1971/1-72
HALL, R. LONG GEORGE ALLEY.
    J. CAREW, 441:10SEP72-47
HALL, R.A., JR. AN ESSAY ON LANGUAGE.*
    A.A. HILL, 361:VOL24#3-295
    M.S. RUBIN, 350:DEC71-913
HALL, R.A., JR. PIDGIN AND CREOLE LAN-
GUAGES.
    H. HELMCKE, 38:BAND87HEFT1-66
    T. KAUFMAN, 545(RPH):AUG69-104
HALL, S. & P. WHANNEL. THE POPULAR ARTS.
    W.L. BURKE, 186(ETC.):JUN69-245
HALLADE, M. GANDHĀRAN ART OF NORTH
INDIA AND THE GRAECO-BUDDHIST TRADITION
IN INDIA, PERSIA AND CENTRAL ASIA.
    S. KRAMRISCH, 57:VOL31#4-329
HALLANDER, L-G. OLD ENGLISH VERBS IN
-SIAN.*
    C.J.E. BALL, 541(RES):MAY70-187
HALLÉ, C. THE AUTOBIOGRAPHY OF CHARLES
HALLÉ. (M. KENNEDY, ED)
    617(TLS):15DEC72-1538
HALLE, L.J. THE IDEOLOGICAL IMAGINATION.
    617(TLS):18FEB72-185

HALLE, L.J. THE STORM PETREL AND THE OWL
OF ATHENA.
S. BARR, 639(VQR):AUTUMN70-677
H. CARRUTH, 249(HUDR):SPRING71-153
617(TLS):5MAY72-516
HALLER, H. DIE STEUERN.
P.M. GAUDEMET, 182:VOL23#4-152
HALLETT, G. WITTGENSTEIN'S DEFINITION OF
MEANING AS USE.
J.H. GILL, 613:WINTER68-632
HALLIDAY, F.E. THOMAS HARDY.
617(TLS):6OCT72-1193
HALLIDAY, F.E. WORDSWORTH AND HIS WORLD.
639(VQR):AUTUMN70-CXLIII
HALLIDAY, J. SIRK ON SIRK.
617(TLS):4FEB72-125
HALLIDAY, M.A.K. INTONATION AND GRAMMAR
IN BRITISH ENGLISH.
A. CRUTTENDEN, 297(JL):OCT69-309
W.R. LEE, 361:VOL24#1-62
HALLIDAY, M.A.K., A. MC INTOSH & P.
STREVENS. THE LINGUISTIC SCIENCES
AND LANGUAGE TEACHING.
W.P. LEHMANN, 545(RPH):AUG69-130
G. NICKEL, 72:BAND208HEFT3-199
HALLIG, R. SPRACHERLEBNIS UND SPRACHFOR-
SCHUNG.
K.D. SCHNEIDER, 72:BAND208HEFT4/6-425
HALLPIKE, C.R. THE KONSO OF ETHIOPIA.
617(TLS):21JUL72-848
HALPERT, H. & G.M. STORY, EDS. CHRISTMAS
MUMMING IN NEWFOUNDLAND.
E. ANDREWS, 529(QQ):SUMMER70-291
L.S. THOMPSON, 582(SFQ):DEC69-368
HALSEY, A.H., ED. TRENDS IN BRITISH
SOCIETY SINCE 1900.
617(TLS):20OCT72-1260
HALSTEAD, B. & J. MIDDLETON. BARE BONES.
617(TLS):29DEC72-1590
HAMANN, J.G. BRIEFWECHSEL. (A. HENKEL,
ED) HAMANN'S SOCRATIC MEMORABILIA.*
(J.C. O'FLAHERTY, ED & TRANS)
H. VON HOFE, 182:VOL23#1/2-29
HAMANN, J.G. BRIEFWECHSEL. (W. ZIESEMER
& A. HENKEL, EDS)
S-A. JØRGENSEN, 462(OL):VOL24#3-229
HAMANN, J.G. JOHANN GEORG HAMANNS
HAUPTSCHRIFTEN ERKLÄRT. (VOL 4)
S-A. JØRGENSEN, 462(OL):VOL24#3-231
HAMBLET, E.C. MARCEL DUBÉ AND FRENCH-
CANADIAN DRAMA.
L.C. KEATING, 399(MLJ):OCT70-472
HAMBLIN, C.L. FALLACIES.
M. CLARK, 518:JAN71-11
P. THOM, 63:MAY71-106
HAMBLY, G., ED. CENTRAL ASIA.
S.A.M. ADSHEAD, 67:MAY71-143
HAMBURGER, A., A. SUDMANN & B. MOLDE -
SEE "SPRÅK I NORDEN 1970"
HAMBURGER, K. DIE LOGIK DER DICHTUNG.
(2ND ED)
D. COHN, 222(GR):JAN70-65
W.D. WILLIAMS, 220(GL&L):APR71-278
HAMBURGER, K. PHILOSOPHIE DER DICHTER.
P. PÜTZ, 490:APR68-272
HAMBURGER, M., ED. EAST GERMAN POETRY.
617(TLS):15DEC72-1524
HAMBURGER, M. TRAVELLING.*
E. HOMBERGER, 111:8MAY70-167
HAMBURGER, M. THE TRUTH OF POETRY.*
E. HOMBERGER, 111:8MAY70-167
M.L. ROSENTHAL, 491:NOV71-99
HAMELINK, J. RANONKEL.
A. DIXON, 270:VOL20#1-17
HAMER, D.A. LIBERAL POLITICS IN THE AGE
OF GLADSTONE AND ROSEBERY.
617(TLS):11AUG72-949

HAMER, D.A. JOHN MORLEY.
P. STANSKY, 637(VS):SEP69-105
HAMER, R., ED & TRANS. A CHOICE OF
ANGLO-SAXON VERSE.
T.A. SHIPPEY, 677:VOL2-231
HAMEROW, T.S. THE SOCIAL FOUNDATIONS OF
GERMAN UNIFICATION 1858-1871.
617(TLS):29DEC72-1576
HAMILTON, A. THE APPEAL OF FASCISM.*
K. FITZLYON, 364:AUG/SEP71-132
HAMILTON, A., ED. THE INFAMOUS ESSAY ON
WOMAN.
617(TLS):15DEC72-1532
HAMILTON, A. THE LAW PRACTICE OF ALEX-
ANDER HAMILTON. (J. GOEBEL, JR., ED)
639(VQR):AUTUMN70-CXLVII
HAMILTON, A. & K. THE ELEMENTS OF JOHN
UPDIKE.*
639(VQR):SUMMER70-C
HAMILTON, A.C. THE EARLY SHAKESPEARE.
E. JONES, 541(RES):AUG70-348
HAMILTON, B. THE LIGHT WENT OUT.
B. BROPHY, 362:13JUL72-54
617(TLS):14JUL72-796
HAMILTON, D. & A. ROBBE-GRILLET. DREAMS
OF A YOUNG GIRL.* (BRITISH TITLE:
DREAMS OF YOUNG GIRLS.)
617(TLS):7APR72-391
HAMILTON, E. THE BACKSTAIRS DRAGON.
W.A. SPECK, 566:AUTUMN70-25
HAMILTON, E. HÉLOÏSE.*
H. MAGARET, 613:AUTUMN68-471
HAMILTON, E. WILLIAM'S MARY.
617(TLS):21JUL72-850
HAMILTON, E.W. THE DIARY OF SIR EDWARD
WALTER HAMILTON. (VOLS 1&2) (D.W.R.
BAHLMAN, ED)
617(TLS):25AUG72-999
HAMILTON, G.H. PAINTING AND SCULPTURE
IN EUROPE, 1880-1940.*
A. ELSEN, 90:DEC69-766
HAMILTON, G.H. RAYMOND DUCHAMP VILLON.
A. BOWNESS, 592:MAR69-155
HAMILTON, H.W. DOCTOR SYNTAX.
P. DANCHIN, 179(ES):APR70-165
R.E. KELLEY, 481(PQ):JUL70-334
HAMILTON, I. THE VISIT.*
R. BOTTRALL, 493:AUTUMN70-247
HAMILTON, J.R. PLUTARCH, "ALEXANDER."*
T.S. BROWN, 24:APR71-352
A.J. GOSSAGE, 123:MAR71-37
HAMILTON, K.G. THE TWO HARMONIES.
R.P. DRAPER, 179(ES):AUG70-361
HAMILTON, P. HANGOVER SQUARE. THE
SLAVES OF SOLITUDE.
B. BROPHY, 362:13JUL72-54
617(TLS):14JUL72-796
HAMILTON, S. EARLY AMERICAN BOOK ILLUS-
TRATORS AND WOOD ENGRAVERS 1670-1870.
(VOL 2)
P.H. MUIR, 78(BC):SUMMER70-252
HAMILTON, V.V. HUGO BLACK.
441:20AUG72-20
HAMILTON-EDWARDS, G. IN SEARCH OF SCOT-
TISH ANCESTRY.
617(TLS):8DEC72-1483
HAMILTON-PATERSON, J. A VERY PERSONAL
WAR.
617(TLS):10MAR72-264
HAMLIN, F.R., P.T. RICKETTS & J. HATHA-
WAY, EDS. INTRODUCTION À L'ÉTUDE DE
L'ANCIEN PROVENÇAL.*
F.M. CHAMBERS, 545(RPH):NOV70-339
J.M. FERRANTE, 546(RR):APR70-123
HAMMACHER, A.M. THE EVOLUTION OF MODERN
SCULPTURE.
B. BETTINSON, 363:AUG70-135

HAMMACHER, A.M.   BARBARA HEPWORTH.
   B.M. REISE, 592:JUL/AUG68-56
HAMMACHER, A.M.   LE MONDE DE HENRY VAN DE
   VELDE.
   L.K. EATON, 505:MAY68-186
HAMMARSTRÖM, G.   LINGUISTISCHE EINHEITEN
   IM RAHMEN DER MODERNEN SPRACHWISSEN-
   SCHAFT.*
   E. LANG & W.U. WURZEL, 353:DEC69-89
HAMMER, K., ED.   DRAMATURGISCHE SCHRIFTEN
   DES 18. JAHRHUNDERTS.
   R. GRIMM, 406:SPRING71-70
HAMMERICH, L.L. & OTHERS - SEE "TÖNNIES
   FENNE'S LOW GERMAN MANUAL OF SPOKEN
   RUSSIAN, PSKOV 1607"
HAMMOND, A.L.   IDEAS ABOUT SUBSTANCE.
   W. CHARLTON, 123:DEC71-457
HAMMOND, B.   SOVEREIGNTY AND AN EMPTY
   PURSE.
   676(YR):SPRING71-XX
HAMMOND, J.   A VOICE, A LIFE.
   A. BLYTH, 415:DEC70-1227
HAMMOND, N.   THE WHITE HORSE COUNTRY.
   617(TLS):2JUN72-641
HAMMOND, N.G.L.   A HISTORY OF GREECE TO
   322 B.C.   (2ND ED)
   R.J. HOPPER, 123:MAR71-95
HAMMOND, N.G.L. & H.H. SCULLARD, EDS.
   OXFORD CLASSICAL DICTIONARY.   (NEW ED)
   M.L. CLARKE, 123:MAR71-124
HAMNETT, B.R.   POLITICS AND TRADE IN
   SOUTHERN MEXICO 1750-1821.
   617(TLS):7JUL72-782
HAMPDEN, J., ED.   FRANCIS DRAKE, PRIVA-
   TEER.
   617(TLS):29SEP72-1171
HAMPE, R.   KRETISCHE LÖWENSCHALE DES
   SIEBTEN JAHRHUNDERTS V. CHR.*
   J. BOARDMAN, 123:JUN71-301
HAMSHERE, C.   THE BRITISH IN THE CARIB-
   BEAN.
   617(TLS):29DEC72-1584
HAMSÍK, D.   WRITERS AGAINST RULERS.*
   E. OSERS, 364:AUG/SEP71-110
HAMSUN, K.   THE CULTURAL LIFE OF MODERN
   AMERICA.*   (B.G. MORGRIDGE, ED & TRANS)
   D.J. ENRIGHT, 453:24FEB72-42
   A. LIEN, 149:DEC71-357
HAMSUN, K.   MYSTERIES.*
   D.J. ENRIGHT, 453:24FEB72-42
   J.D. O'HARA, 440:16JAN72-10
HAMSUN, K.   PAN.   VICTORIA.   HUNGER.
   D.J. ENRIGHT, 453:24FEB72-42
HAN SUYIN.   THE MORNING DELUGE.
   J.K. FAIRBANK, 453:19OCT72-9
   A. PRAGER, 561(SATR):18NOV72-91
   442(NY):4NOV72-195
   617(TLS):17NOV72-1386
HAN, Y.F.   THE CHINESE KINSHIP SYSTEM.
   M. TOPLEY, 302:JAN69-116
HANAK, H.   SOVIET FOREIGN POLICY SINCE
   THE DEATH OF STALIN.
   617(TLS):5MAY72-511
HANCHETT, W.   IRISH.
   M. RICKELS, 27(AL):MAY71-292
HANCOCK, L.   THERE'S A SEAL IN MY SLEEP-
   ING BAG.
   J.E. BRODY, 441:14AUG72-29
HANCOCK, W.K.   DISCOVERING MONARO.
   617(TLS):28JUL72-872
HANDKE, P.   THE GOALIE'S ANXIETY AT THE
   PENALTY KICK.
   F. CONROY, 441:21MAY72-5
   R. LOCKE, 441:8JUN72-49
   R. SEAVER, 561(SATR):10JUN72-64
   442(NY):24JUN72-93

HANDKE, P.   DER KURZE BRIEF ZUM LANGEN
   ABSCHIED.
   617(TLS):21APR72-438
HANDKE, P.   WUNSCHLOSES UNGLÜCK.
   617(TLS):1DEC72-1449
HANDLER, H.   THE SPANISH RIDING SCHOOL.
   G.F.T. RYALL, 441:3DEC72-28
HANDLER, J.F.   REFORMING THE POOR.
   D. KEARNS, 441:17SEP72-4
HANDLER, P., ED.   BIOLOGY AND THE FUTURE
   OF MAN.*
   639(VQR):SUMMER70-CXV
HANDLEY-TAYLOR, G., ED.   YORKSHIRE
   AUTHORS TODAY.
   617(TLS):16JUN72-697
HANDLIN, O. & M.F.   FACING LIFE.*
   M. DUBERMAN, 441:2APR72-4
   C. LASCH, 453:10FEB72-25
HANDS, A.R.   CHARITIES AND SOCIAL AID IN
   GREECE AND ROME.*
   R.M. ERRINGTON, 303:VOL90-254
   O. MURRAY, 123:DEC71-397
HANDSCHUH, D. & OTHERS, EDS.   SPRACHATLAS
   DER DEUTSCHEN SCHWEIZ.   (VOL 4)
   W.G. MOULTON, 301(JEGP):APR71-365
HANDY, R.   VALUE THEORY AND THE BEHAVIOR-
   AL SCIENCES.
   D.H. DEGROOD, 484(PPR):DEC69-303
HANDY, R.T.   A CHRISTIAN AMERICA.
   441:6FEB72-40
HANES, D.G.   THE FIRST BRITISH WORKMEN'S
   COMPENSATION ACT, 1897.
   P. STANSKY, 637(VS):DEC69-227
HANFORD, J.H.   MILTON.
   F.S.K., 477:SPRING69-299
HANFORD, J.H. & J.G. TAAFE.   A MILTON
   HANDBOOK.   (5TH ED)
   J.H. SIMS, 568(SCN):WINTER71-62
HANHAM, H.J. - SEE BUCKLE, H.T.
HANKINS, J.E.   SOURCE AND MEANING IN
   SPENSER'S ALLEGORY.
   617(TLS):22DEC72-1559
HANKINSON, A.   THE FIRST TIGERS.
   617(TLS):29DEC72-1589
HANKS, K.   FALK.
   J. HUNTER, 362:21SEP72-376
   617(TLS):29SEP72-1138
HANKS, L.   BUFFON AVANT L'"HISTOIRE
   NATURELLE."
   G. SOLINAS, 548(RCSF):JUL-SEP68-347
HANKS, P., ED.   ENCYCLOPEDIC WORLD DIC-
   TIONARY.
   617(TLS):13OCT72-1209
HANLEY, G.   WARRIORS AND STRANGERS.*
   A. BROYARD, 441:11SEP72-39
HANLEY, J.   ANOTHER WORLD.
   A. BROYARD, 441:27JUN72-43
   D.A.N. JONES, 362:8JUN72-768
   D.K. MANO, 441:27AUG72-2
   617(TLS):9JUN72-649
HANNA, A.J. & K.A.   NAPOLEON III AND
   MEXICO.
   617(TLS):8DEC72-1503
HANNA, H.M.   THE PHRASE STRUCTURE OF
   EGYPTIAN COLLOQUIAL ARABIC.
   L. DROZDÍK, 353:APR69-119
HANNA, S.A. & N. GREIS.   INTRODUCING LIT-
   ERARY ARABIC.
   A.D. CORRÉ, 399(MLJ):OCT70-447
HANNAH, B.   GERONIMO REX.
   J. HARRISON, 441:14MAY72-4
   J. UPDIKE, 442(NY):9SEP72-121
HANNEBORG, K.   THE STUDY OF LITERATURE.
   C.M.R., 543:SEP69-131
   L.P. RØMHILD, 462(OL):VOL23#4-334
   D.T. WIECK, 290(JAAC):SPRING70-401

HANNIGAN, P. LAUGHING.
   J. KOETHE, 491:APR72-49
   F. MORAMARCO, 651(WHR):WINTER71-99
HANOUZ, S. GRAMMAIRE BERBÈRE.
   T.G. PENCHOEN, 350:MAR71-228
HANSEL, J. BÜCHERKUNDE FÜR GERMANISTEN:
   STUDIENAUSGABE. (5TH ED)
   R.K., 221(GQ):MAR70-315
   L. NEWMAN, 220(GL&L):JAN71-216
HANSEL, J. PERSONALBIBLIOGRAPHIE ZUR
   DEUTSCHEN LITERATURGESCHICHTE.
   J-U. FECHNER, 220(GL&L):JAN71-217
HANSEN, B. DEN MARXISTISKE LITTERATUR-
   KRITIK.
   J.L. SAMMONS, 563(SS):WINTER71-97
HANSEN, B.J. COOKING CALIFORNIA STYLE.
   N. MAGID, 440:20FEB72-8
HANSEN, C. WITCHCRAFT AT SALEM.*
   S. BERCOVITCH, 656(WMQ):OCT70-670
   J.T. FLANAGAN, 292(JAF):JUL-SEP70-370
HANSEN, S. & J. JENSEN, WITH W. ROBERTS.
   THE LITTLE RED SCHOOLBOOK.*
   G. CHANNON, 561(SATR):5FEB72-56
HANSEN, W. THE PEACOCK THRONE.
   441:31DEC72-19
HANSFORD, S.H. CHINESE CARVED JADES.
   H.M. GARNER, 39:MAR69-242
   J.M. HARTMAN, 57:VOL31#2/3-220
HANSLICK, E. AUS MEINEM LEBEN. THE COL-
   LECTED MUSICAL CRITICISM. CONCERTE,
   COMPONISTEN UND VIRTUOSEN. GESCHICHTE
   DES CONCERTWESENS IN WIEN.
   617(TLS):18FEB72-193
HANSON, A.C. JACOPO DELLA QUERCIA'S
   FONTE GAIA.
   R.W. LIGHTBOWN, 90:JAN69-38
HANSON, L. RENOIR.
   E.R. DE ZURKO, 219(GAR):SUMMER69-261
HANSON, N.R. OBSERVATION AND EXPLANA-
   TION.
   617(TLS):21JAN72-61
HANSON, R.M. VIRGINIA PLACE NAMES.
   P.B. ROGERS, 424:DEC69-306
HARADA KUMAO. FRAGILE VICTORY. (T.F.
   MAYER-OAKES, TRANS)
   B-A. SHILLONY, 293(JAST):NOV69-173
HARARI, M. MEMOIRS: 1906-1969.
   617(TLS):27OCT72-1278
HARBOTTLE, M. THE BLUE BERETS.
   617(TLS):17MAR72-312
HARDEN, A.R., ED. LA VIE DE SEINT AU-
   BAN.*
   F. KOENIG, 545(RPH):FEB71-558
   M-D. LEGGE, 208(FS):JAN71-58
HARDEN, O.E.M. MARIA EDGEWORTH'S ART OF
   PROSE FICTION.
   617(TLS):14JAN72-39
HARDER, H-B. SCHILLER IN RUSSLAND.
   E. KOSTKA, 574(SEEJ):SPRING71-83
   V. TERRAS, 222(GR):MAY70-251
HARDER, P.O. HARMONIC MATERIALS IN TONAL
   MUSIC.
   C. WHITTENBERG, 308:SPRING68-115
HARDGRAVE, R.L., JR. THE NADARS OF
   TAMILNAD.
   E.F. IRSCHICK, 293(JAST):FEB70-485
HARDIE, M. PAINTING IN BRITAIN. (VOL 1)
   H. GEORGE, 56:SUMMER69-197
HARDIE, M. WATERCOLOUR PAINTING IN BRIT-
   AIN.* (VOL 3) (D. SNELGROVE, WITH J.
   MAYNE & B. TAYLOR, EDS)
   T. CROMBIE, 39:DEC69-545
   L. HERRMANN, 90:APR70-255
   J. MAAS, 592:JUL/AUG69-48
HARDIE, W.F.R. ARISTOTLE'S ETHICAL
   THEORY.*
   N. COOPER, 479(PHQ):OCT70-397
   C. KIRWAN, 393(MIND):JUL70-445 [CONT]

[CONTINUING]
   F.E. SPARSHOTT, 487:SPRING70-84
   W. WICK, 185:OCT69-76
HARDING, D.P. THE CLUB OF HERCULES.
   M-S. RØSTVIG, 179(ES):JUN70-258
HARDING, D.W. THE IRON AGE IN THE UPPER
   THAMES BASIN.
   617(TLS):5MAY72-523
HARDING, G. THE SKYTRAP.
   617(TLS):29DEC72-1588
HARDING, J. SACHA GUITRY, THE LAST
   BOULEVARDIER.
   D. KNOWLES, 208(FS):JAN71-109
HARDING, J. MASSENET.*
   R. CRICHTON, 415:FEB71-132
HARDING, J. THE OX ON THE ROOF.
   617(TLS):7JUL72-770
HARDING, M.E. WOMAN'S MYSTERIES.
   A. LAHR, 561(SATR):6MAY72-85
HARDING, R.E.M., COMP. A THEMATIC CATA-
   LOGUE OF THE WORKS OF MATTHEW LOCKE.
   617(TLS):7APR72-387
HARDING, W. EMERSON'S LIBRARY.
   E. MOTTRAM, 354:MAR69-78
HARDINGE, G. CHALMERIANA [TOGETHER WITH]
   STEEVENS, G. MR. IRELAND'S VINDICATION
   OF HIS CONDUCT.
   617(TLS):18FEB72-178
HARDISON, O.B., JR. CHRISTIAN RITE AND
   CHRISTIAN DRAMA IN THE MIDDLE AGES.*
   H-J. DILLER, 179(ES):AUG70-352
   T.A. KIRBY, 570(SQ):WINTER68-86
HARDISON, O.B., JR. - SEE ARISTOTLE
HARDRÉ, J. LA FRANCE ET SA CIVILISATION.
   T. GREENE, 207(FR):MAY70-952
   L.C. KEATING, 399(MLJ):OCT70-458
HARDT, J.P. & OTHERS, EDS. MATHEMATICS
   AND COMPUTERS IN SOVIET ECONOMIC PLAN-
   NING.
   L. SMOLINSKI, 32:DEC71-903
HARDWICK, M. MRS. DIZZY.
   617(TLS):25AUG72-986
HARDWICK, M. THE OSPREY GUIDE TO GILBERT
   AND SULLIVAN.
   617(TLS):22DEC72-1550
HARDWICK, M. & M. AS THEY SAW HIM -
   CHARLES DICKENS. DICKENS'S ENGLAND.
   A.B., 155:SEP70-244
HARDY, B. CHARLES DICKENS: THE LATER
   NOVELS.
   W.W. ROBSON, 155:MAY69-114
HARDY, B. THE EXPOSURE OF LUXURY.
   617(TLS):6OCT72-1198
HARDY, B., ED. MIDDLEMARCH.
   W.C. BOOTH, 445(NCF):MAR69-478
   J.C. MAXWELL, 447(N&Q):OCT70-398
HARDY, B. THE MORAL ART OF DICKENS.
   F.N. LEES, 89(BJA):SUMMER71-310
HARDY, G.H. BERTRAND RUSSELL AND TRIN-
   ITY.
   639(VQR):AUTUMN70-CLII
HARDY, T. ONE RARE FAIR WOMAN. (E.
   HARDY & F.B. PINION, EDS)
   617(TLS):16JUN72-687
HARDY, W.J., ED. A SYMPOSIUM ON FORMAL-
   IST CRITICISM.
   A. RODWAY, 447(N&Q):JUL70-269
HARE, J., ED. CONTES ET NOUVELLES DU
   CANADA FRANÇAIS 1778-1859. (VOL 1)
   617(TLS):7APR72-399
HARE, P.H. & E.H. MADDEN. EVIL AND THE
   CONCEPT OF GOD.
   W.A.J., 543:MAR70-556
HARE, R.M. FREEDOM AND REASON.
   M.G. SINGER, 482(PHR):APR70-253
LORD HAREWOOD - SEE "KOBBÉ'S COMPLETE
   OPERA BOOK"

HARGREAVES, D.H. INTERPERSONAL RELATIONS
AND EDUCATION.
    617(TLS):2JUN72-621
HARGREAVES, E. THE FAIR GREEN WEED.
    617(TLS):29SEP72-1174
HARGREAVES-MAWDSLEY, W.N. THE ENGLISH
DELLA CRUSCANS AND THEIR TIME, 1783-
1828.*
    A.F. FALCONER, 541(RES):FEB70-88
HARINGTON, D. SOME OTHER PLACE. THE
RIGHT PLACE.
    J.R. FRAKES, 441:12NOV72-65
HARKABI, Y. ARAB ATTITUDES TO ISRAEL.
    M. HALPERN, 561(SATR):10JUN72-60
HARKER, H. GOLDENROD.
    C. LEHMANN-HAUPT, 441:15AUG72-37
    R. MACDONALD, 441:11JUN72-6
    E. THOMPSON, 296:FALL72-103
HARKINS, W.E., ED. AMERICAN CONTRIBU-
TIONS TO THE SIXTH INTERNATIONAL CON-
GRESS OF SLAVISTS. (VOL 2)
    H.E. BOWMAN, 574(SEEJ):SPRING71-66
    G. IVASK, 550(RUSR):APR70-224
HARLAN, R.D. JOHN HENRY NASH.
    H.R. ARCHER, 356:JUL71-267
HARLEY, N. RUSSIAN TALES.
    W. JASZCZUN, 574(SEEJ):SPRING71-129
HARLOW, G. & J. REDMOND, EDS. THE YEAR'S
WORK IN ENGLISH STUDIES.* (VOL 49:
1968)
    568(SCN):SUMMER/AUTUMN71-44
HARMAN, J. & H.E. 3D. HARMAN'S OFFICIAL
GUIDE TO CRUISE SHIPS.
    C.W. CASEWIT, 440:30APR72-4
HARMAN, R.A. A CATALOGUE OF THE PRINTED
MUSIC AND BOOKS ON MUSIC IN DURHAM
CATHEDRAL LIBRARY.
    D.W. KRUMMEL, 354:JUN69-164
HARMON, J. & D.F. GLUT. THE GREAT MOVIE
SERIALS.
    441:24SEP72-52
HARMON, M., ED. J.M. SYNGE: CENTENARY
PAPERS 1971.
    617(TLS):22SEP72-1112
HARMON, W. TREASURY HOLIDAY.
    R.B. SHAW, 491:MAR72-342
    J. VERNON, 651(WHR):SPRING71-194
DE HARO, A.S. - SEE UNDER SERRANO DE
HARO, A.
HARPAZ, E. L'ECOLE LIBÉRALE SOUS LA
RESTAURATION.*
    F. BASSAN, 207(FR):OCT69-184
HARPER, J.R. EARLY PAINTERS AND ENGRAV-
ERS IN CANADA.
    617(TLS):24MAR72-345
HARPER, J.R. PAINTING IN CANADA.*
    W. TOWNSEND, 592:MAR68-152
HARPER, M. DEAR JOHN, DEAR COLTRANE.
    639(VQR):AUTUMN70-CXXXIV
HARPER, P. THE STORY OF A GARDEN.
    617(TLS):6OCT72-1205
HARPNER, S., H.C.R. LANDON & C.H. SHER-
MAN, EDS. THE HAYDN YEARBOOK. (VOL 7)
    J.A.W., 410(M&L):JUL71-332
HARRÉ, R. THE PHILOSOPHIES OF SCIENCE.
    617(TLS):10MAR72-263
HARRÉ, R. THE PRINCIPLES OF SCIENTIFIC
THINKING.
    N. GRIFFIN, 518:OCT71-13
HARRÉ, R. & P.F. SECORD. THE EXPLANATION
OF SOCIAL BEHAVIOUR.
    617(TLS):27OCT72-1282
HARRIES, K. THE MEANING OF MODERN ART.
    E.H. DUNCAN, 290(JAAC):SPRING70-403
HARRINGTON, A. PSYCHOPATHS.
    A. BROYARD, 441:7JUN72-47
HARRINGTON, A. THE SECRET SWINGER.
    R. GOVER, 340(KR):SEP66-565

HARRINGTON, M. SOCIALISM.
    P. CLECAK, 561(SATR):13MAY72-77
    C. LASCH, 453:20JUL72-15
    C. LEHMANN-HAUPT, 441:1MAY72-35
    R. TERRILL, 61:OCT72-120
    G. WILLS, 441:30APR72-1
    442(NY):12AUG72-80
HARRIOTT, R. POETRY AND CRITICISM BEFORE
PLATO.*
    K.J. DOVER, 303:VOL90-230
    L. GOLDEN, 122:JAN71-73
    M.R. LEFKOWITZ, 121(CJ):FEB-MAR71-269
    É. DES PLACES, 555:VOL44FASC1-127
    S.E. SMETHURST, 529(QQ):AUTUMN70-457
HARRIS, B. CONFESSIONS OF CHERUBINO.
    S. BLACKBURN, 440:26MAR72-6
    442(NY):8APR72-130
HARRIS, B.S. WHO IS JULIA?
    T. LASK, 441:12AUG72-21
HARRIS, C.D. CITIES OF THE SOVIET
UNION.
    R.A. FRENCH, 575(SEER):JUL71-476
    D. HOOSON, 32:JUN71-431
HARRIS, D. - SEE CERNUDA, L.
HARRIS, D.P. TESTING ENGLISH AS A SECOND
LANGUAGE.
    J.A. UPSHUR, 351(LL):DEC70-265
    R.M. VALETTE, 399(MLJ):APR70-300
HARRIS, E.E. FUNDAMENTALS OF PHILOSOPHY.
    M.A. STEWART, 479(PHQ):APR70-184
HARRIS, G.W. HIGH TIMES AND HARD TIMES.
    (M.T. INGE, ED)
    E. CURRENT-CARGIA, 9(ALAR):JAN69-72
HARRIS, H. THE ROYAL IRISH FUSILIERS.
    617(TLS):7APR72-402
HARRIS, H. & M. ELLIS. THE BLUE CANAL.
    617(TLS):1SEP72-1034
HARRIS, H.A. SPORT IN GREECE AND ROME.
    617(TLS):22DEC72-1564
HARRIS, H.S. HEGEL'S DEVELOPMENT.
    617(TLS):28APR72-466
HARRIS, J. THE BITTER FIGHT.
    617(TLS):28JAN72-88
HARRIS, J. SIR WILLIAM CHAMBERS.*
    J. EMERSON, 362:24AUG72-249
    N. PEVSNER, 362:12OCT72-466
HARRIS, J. A KIND OF COURAGE.
    617(TLS):15DEC72-1521
"JULIE HARRIS TALKS TO YOUNG ACTORS."
    (B. TARSHIS, ED)
    G. WEALES, 441:11JUN72-8
"LAWREN HARRIS." (B. HARRIS & R.G.P.
COLGROVE, EDS)
    T. EMERY, 627(UTQ):JUL70-382
    M. WADDINGTON, 96:APR70-63
HARRIS, M. POEMS FROM RITUAL [TOGETHER
WITH] FREEDMAN, M. THROUGH THE TEL-
EMETER.
    H. MAC CALLUM, 627(UTQ):JUL69-353
HARRIS, M. TEXT FOR NAUSIKAA.
    S. SCOBIE, 102(CANL):AUTUMN71-75
HARRIS, M. - SEE "THE CORNISH ORDINALIA"
HARRIS, R.W. REASON AND NATURE IN 18TH
CENTURY THOUGHT.
    566:AUTUMN70-28
HARRIS, R.W. ROMANTICISM AND THE SOCIAL
ORDER 1780-1830.
    D.V.E., 191(ELN):SEP70(SUPP)-12
HARRIS, S.H. PAUL CUFFE.
    J.R. WILLIS, 441:20AUG72-5
HARRIS, T. GOYA, ENGRAVINGS AND LITHO-
GRAPHS.
    J.C. SLOANE, 54:JUN69-193
HARRIS, T.F. PEARL S. BUCK. (VOL 2)
    617(TLS):28JUL72-868
HARRIS, W.C. - SEE LYNCH, J.R.
HARRIS, W.V. ROME IN ETRURIA AND UMBRIA.
    617(TLS):11FEB72-158

HARRISON, A.R.W. THE LAW OF ATHENS: PRO-
CEDURE. (D.M. MAC DOWELL, ED)
617(TLS):21JAN72-58
HARRISON, A.R.W. THE LAW OF ATHENS: THE
FAMILY AND PROPERTY.*
G.E.M. DE STE. CROIX, 123:DEC70-387
HARRISON, G. RAGE OF SAND.
617(TLS):4FEB72-138
HARRISON, G.A. & A.J. BOYCE, EDS. THE
STRUCTURE OF HUMAN POPULATIONS.
617(TLS):18AUG72-963
HARRISON, H. MONTEZUMA'S REVENGE.
O.L. BAILEY, 561(SATR):25NOV72-70
N. CALLENDAR, 441:15OCT72-42
HARRISON, H. & T.J. GORDON, EDS. AHEAD
OF TIME.
T. STURGEON, 441:3SEP72-20
HARRISON, H. & L. STOVER. STONEHENGE.
M. LEVIN, 441:12NOV72-67
HARRISON, J. OUTLYER & GHAZALS.*
V. YOUNG, 249(HUDR):WINTER71/72-669
HARRISON, J.F.C. QUEST FOR THE NEW MORAL
WORLD.
E. YEO, 637(VS):JUN70-463
HARRISON, J.F.C., ED. UTOPIANISM AND
EDUCATION.
B. SIMON, 637(VS):JUN70-403
HARRISON, K. SONGS FROM THE DRIFTING
HOUSE.
617(TLS):28JUL72-873
HARRISON, L.H. JOHN BRECKINRIDGE, JEFF-
ERSONIAN REPUBLICAN.
G.H. CLARFIELD, 656(WMQ):JAN70-158
HARRISON, M. CLARENCE.
617(TLS):17NOV72-1402
HARRISON, M. THE LIEDER OF BRAHMS.
617(TLS):16JUN72-684
HARRISON, M. THE LONDON OF SHERLOCK
HOLMES.
617(TLS):7APR72-391
HARRISON, M. PEOPLE AND FURNITURE.
617(TLS):7JAN72-8
HARRISON, R. SAMUEL BECKETT'S "MURPHY."
P.F. HERRING, 219(GAR):FALL69-421
HARRISON, R.K. THE ANCIENT WORLD.
617(TLS):28JAN72-109
HARRISON, T. THE LOINERS.*
W.H. PRITCHARD, 491:DEC71-159
HARRISON, T.P. & OTHERS, EDS. STUDIES IN
HONOR OF DE WITT T. STARNES.
G.R. HIBBARD, 447(N&Q):JUN70-231
A.R. HUMPHREYS, 570(SQ):AUTUMN68-395
HARROD, J. TRADE UNION FOREIGN POLICY.
617(TLS):29DEC72-1584
HARROD, R. TOWARDS A NEW ECONOMIC POLI-
CY.
J.B. KNIGHT, 97(CQ):SPRING68-194
HARSDÖRFER, G.P. FRAUENZIMMER GESPRÄCH-
SPIELE. (I. BÖTTCHER, ED)
K.F. OTTO, JR., 221(GQ):MAR70-313
HARSENT, D. A VIOLENT COUNTRY.*
639(VQR):SPRING70-L
HARSH, G. LONESOME ROAD.
617(TLS):24MAR72-345
HART, C. THE DREAM OF FLIGHT.
617(TLS):21JUL72-853
HART, C., ED. JAMES JOYCE'S "DUBLINERS."
F.L. WALZL, 399(MLJ):MAY70-372
HART, E.L. - SEE NICHOLS, J.
HART, H.H. MARCO POLO.
D. SINOR, 318(JAOS):APR-JUN70-405
HART, H.L.A. PUNISHMENT AND RESPONSI-
BILITY.
W.D. HUDSON, 483:APR70-162
HART, W.H. - SEE BLOOMFIELD, R.
HART-DAVIS, D. SPIDER IN THE MORNING.
N. CALLENDAR, 441:13FEB72-34

HART-DAVIS, R., COMP. A CATALOGUE OF
THE CARICATURES OF MAX BEERBOHM.
617(TLS):15SEP72-1043
HART-DAVIS, R. - SEE BEERBOHM, M.
HARTE, N.B., ED. THE STUDY OF ECONOMIC
HISTORY.
617(TLS):7JUL72-772
HARTH, P. CONTEXTS OF DRYDEN'S THOUGHT.
P.K. ELKIN, 67:NOV71-210
E. LEHMANN, 72:BAND208HEFT3-216
H. TROWBRIDGE, 405(MP):MAY70-382
502(PRS):WINTER69/70-426
HARTLEY, A. GAULLISM.*
617(TLS):29SEP72-1134
HARTLEY, L. & G. CORE, EDS. KATHERINE
ANNE PORTER.*
B. CHENEY, 577(SHR):FALL70-385
HARTLEY, L.P. THE COLLECTIONS.
D.A.N. JONES, 362:28SEP72-418
617(TLS):29SEP72-1138
HARTLEY, L.P. MRS. CARTERET RECEIVES AND
OTHER STORIES.*
G. EWART, 364:OCT/NOV71-159
HARTLEY, L.P. MY SISTER'S KEEPER.
F.P.W. MC DOWELL, 659:SUMMER72-361
HÄRTLING, P. NIEMBSCH OU L'IMMOBILITÉ.
IANEK, PORTRAIT D'UN SOUVENIR. DAS
FAMILIENFEST ODER DAS ENDE DER GE-
SCHICHTE.
J-C. SCHNEIDER, 98:DEC69-1055
HARTLING, P. - SEE SCHUBART, C.F.D.
HARTMAN, G.H. BEYOND FORMALISM.*
R.H. FOGLE, 676(YR):SUMMER71-618
M. LEBOWITZ, 598(SOR):SUMMER72-696
R. SMITH, 150(DR):WINTER70/71-561
HARTMAN, G.H. WORDSWORTH'S POETRY 1787-
1814.
H. SCHNYDER, 179(ES):JUN70-263
HARTMANN, D. GOTTFRIED VON EINEM.
N. O'LOUGHLIN, 607:SPRING69-67
HARTNELL, N. ROYAL COURTS OF FASHION.
617(TLS):14JAN72-48
HARTNER, W. DIE GOLDHÖRNER VON GALLE-
HUS.*
R.W.V. ELLIOTT, 382(MAE):1971/2-176
E.A. PHILIPPSON, 301(JEGP):JAN71-102
HARTNETT, M. TAO.
617(TLS):28JUL72-873
HARTNOLL, P. A CONCISE HISTORY OF THE
THEATRE.
S.G. PUTT, 175:SPRING69-30
N.D. SHERGOLD, 447(N&Q):JUN70-229
HARTNOLL, P., ED. THE OXFORD COMPANION
TO THE THEATRE.
R. COHN, 397(MD):MAY69-102
HARTNOLL, P. WINTER WAR.
H. SERGEANT, 175:SPRING69-33
DE HARTOG, J. THE PEACEABLE KINGDOM.
J.R. FRAKES, 440:9JAN72-2
J. HAVERSTICK, 561(SATR):11MAR72-77
T. LASK, 441:7JAN72-34
M. TUCKER, 441:16JAN72-32
HARTSHORNE, C. CREATIVE SYNTHESIS AND
PHILOSOPHIC METHOD.
A.B. GIBSON, 63:MAY71-125
HARTSHORNE, C. A NATURAL THEOLOGY FOR
OUR TIME.
P.G. KUNTZ, 477:SUMMER69-393
HARTT, F., G. CORTI & C. KENNEDY. THE
CHAPEL OF THE CARDINAL OF PORTUGAL
1434-1459 AT SAN MINIATO IN FLORENCE.
R.W. LIGHTBOWN, 90:JAN69-38
HARTT, J. A CHRISTIAN CRITIQUE OF AMERI-
CAN CULTURE.
W.A.J., 543:MAR70-556
HARTWELL, R.M. THE INDUSTRIAL REVOLUTION
AND ECONOMIC GROWTH.
617(TLS):24MAR72-321

HARTWIG, J. SHAKESPEARE'S TRAGICOMIC
VISION.
617(TLS):13OCT72-1216
HARVEY, J. THE MASTER BUILDERS.
617(TLS):11FEB72-165
HARVEY, J.H. - SEE WORCESTRE, W.
HARVEY, L.E. SAMUEL BECKETT.
E. KERN, 659:AUTUMN72-530
R. PEARCE, 295:VOL2#3-442
HARVEY, W.J. & R. GRAVIL, EDS. WORDS-
WORTH: THE PRELUDE.
617(TLS):20OCT72-1262
HARWEG, R. PRONOMINA UND TEXTKONSTITU-
TION.
H-H. BAUMANN, 361:VOL23#3-274
"HARY'S 'WALLACE'."* (VOL 1) (M.P.
MC DIARMID, ED)
K. WITTIG, 38:BAND87HEFT3/4-454
"HARY'S 'WALLACE'."* (VOL 2) (M.P.
MC DIARMID, ED)
J. NORTON-SMITH, 541(RES):AUG70-382
VON HASE, M. BIBLIOGRAPHIE DER ERFURTER
DRUCKE VON 1501-1550. (3RD ED)
A.F. JOHNSON, 354:SEP69-261
HASELBACH, I. AUFSTIEG UND HERRSCHAFT
DER KARLINGER IN DER DARSTELLUNG DER
SOG. ANNALES METTENSES PRIORES.
U. NONN, 182:VOL23#10-563
HASENCLEVER, W. IRRTUM UND LEIDENSCHAFT.
W. PAULSEN, 221(GQ):MAR70-292
HASKELL, A. BALLETOMANE AT LARGE.
617(TLS):22DEC72-1550
HASKELL, A. & M. LEWIS. INFANTILIA.
617(TLS):21JAN72-77
HASKELL, F. AN ITALIAN PATRON OF FRENCH
NEO-CLASSIC ART.
617(TLS):15DEC72-1520
HASLINGER, A. EPISCHE FORMEN IM HÖFIS-
CHEN BAROCKROMAN.
K.F. OTTO, JR., 301(JEGP):JUL71-499
HASLIP, J. THE CROWN OF MEXICO.
E. WEEKS, 61:MAY72-111
442(NY):13MAY72-146
HASLIP, J. IMPERIAL ADVENTURER.
617(TLS):8DEC72-1503
HASSALL, W.O. HISTORY THROUGH SURNAMES.
H. CARLSON, 424:JUN69-159
HASSAN, I. THE DISMEMBERMENT OF OR-
PHEUS.*
M. MUDRICK, 249(HUDR):AUTUMN71-519
HASSAN, I., ED. LIBERATIONS.*
M. MUDRICK, 249(HUDR):AUTUMN71-519
J. VERNON, 651(WHR):AUTUMN71-365
HASSAN, I. THE LITERATURE OF SILENCE.
E. KERN, 131(CL):WINTER71-68
HASSLER, K.W. THE GLASS CAGE.
617(TLS):13OCT72-1235
HASTINGS, M. JESUIT CHILD.*
P.P. READ, 441:18JUN72-4
HASTINGS, P., ED. PAPUA/NEW GUINEA.
617(TLS):4AUG72-923
HASTINGS, P. RAILROADS.
617(TLS):7APR72-402
HASTINGS, T. A DISSERTATION ON MUSICAL
TASTE.
N. TEMPERLEY, 415:DEC70-1226
HASTON, D. IN HIGH PLACES.
P. GILLMAN, 362:30NOV72-759
HASWELL, J. JAMES II.
617(TLS):28JUL72-898
HATCH, B.L. A CHECK LIST OF THE PUBLICA-
TIONS OF THOMAS BIRD MOSHER OF PORTLAND,
MAINE, MDCCCXCI-MDCCCCXXIII.
S. NOWELL-SMITH, 354:MAR69-75
HATCH, J. NIGERIA.
617(TLS):10MAR72-268

HATFIELD, G.W. HENRY FIELDING AND THE
LANGUAGE OF IRONY.*
A. SHERBO, 173(ECS):SUMMER70-560
P. STEVICK, 141:WINTER70-76
HATFIELD, H. CRISIS AND CONTINUITY IN
MODERN GERMAN FICTION.
R. GRIMM, 406:SUMMER71-194
H. MEYER, 399(MLJ):MAY70-371
HATTA, M. PORTRAIT OF A PATRIOT.
617(TLS):8DEC72-1513
HATTON, R. - SEE LUND, E., M. PIHL & J.
SLOK
HATZFELD, H. INITIATION À L'EXPLICATION
DE TEXTES FRANÇAIS. (3RD ED)
E.L. DUTHIE, 208(FS):JUL71-372
HATZFELD, H.A. SAGGI DI STILISTICA
ROMANZA.
S. ULLMANN, 545(RPH):AUG70-173
HAUCK, R.B. A CHEERFUL NIHILISM.
W. THORP, 27(AL):NOV71-492
HAUDRICOURT, A.G. & J.M-C. THOMAS. LA
NOTATION DES LANGUES.
A.N.T., 69:JAN69-97
HAUG, H. ERKENNTNISEKEL.
A. VON GRONICKA, 222(GR):MAR70-134
T.J. REED, 402(MLR):APR71-471
HAUG, W. & OTHERS. WERK - TYP - SITUA-
TION.
D.H. GREEN, 402(MLR):OCT71-923
HAUG, W.F. KRITIK DER WARENÄSTHETIK.
617(TLS):16JUN72-691
HAUGAARD, W.P. ELIZABETH AND THE ENGLISH
REFORMATION.
L.H. CARLSON, 551(RENQ):SUMMER70-195
HAUGEN, E., ED & TRANS. FIRST GRAMMATI-
CAL TREATISE.
617(TLS):29SEP72-1164
HAUGEN, E. LANGUAGE CONFLICT AND LAN-
GUAGE PLANNING.*
B.H. JERNUDD, 350:JUN71-490
HAUN, M. THE HAWK'S DONE GONE AND OTHER
STORIES.* (H. GOWER, ED)
J.L. DAVIS, 582(SFQ):DEC69-371
B.A. ROSENBERG, 219(GAR):SUMMER69-254
HAUPT, G., ED. BUREAU SOCIALISTE INTER-
NATIONAL.* (VOL 1)
A. LASSERRE, 182:VOL23#15/16-756
HAUPT, G. SOCIALISM AND THE GREAT WAR.
617(TLS):5MAY72-514
HAURY, A. - SEE CICERO
HÄUSLER, F. DAS EMMENTAL IM STAATE BERN
BIS 1798.
H.S. OFFLER, 182:VOL23#7-379
HAUSMAN, A. & F. WILSON. CARNAP AND
GOODMAN.
M.S. GRAM, 486:SEP69-327
HAUSMANN, R. AM ANFANG WAR DADA. (K.
RIHA & G. KÄMPF, EDS)
617(TLS):27OCT72-1277
HAUSMANN, U., ED. ALLGEMEINE GRUNDLAGEN
DER ARCHÄOLOGIE.
J.M. COOK, 123:DEC71-429
R. SCRANTON, 122:OCT71-270
HAUSTEIN, U. SOZIALISMUS UND NATIONALE
FRAGE IN POLEN.
I. GETZLER, 32:JUN71-410
HAVARD, W.C., ED. THE CHANGING POLITICS
OF THE SOUTH.
C.V. WOODWARD, 453:14DEC72-37
441:17SEP72-44
HAVEL, V. THE INCREASED DIFFICULTY OF
CONCENTRATION.
617(TLS):10MAR72-267
HAVELOCK, E.A. PROMETHEUS, WITH A TRANS-
LATION OF AESCHYLUS' "PROMETHEUS
BOUND."
H. LLOYD-JONES, 123:JUN71-288

HAVEN, R. PATTERNS OF CONSCIOUSNESS.
I.H.C., 191(ELN):SEP70(SUPP)-32
HAVENS, G.R. - SEE DE VOLTAIRE, F.M.A.
HAWES, H.B. A LAND CALLED CRETE.
R.F. WILLETTS, 303:VOL90-245
HAWKE, D.F. BENJAMIN RUSH.
L.H. BUTTERFIELD, 441:2JAN72-15
HAWKE, D.F. - SEE OLMSTED, F.L.
HAWKES, J. THE BLOOD ORANGES.*
C. MORAN, 418(MR):AUTUMN71-840
G. WEALES, 249(HUDR):WINTER71/72-716
HAWKES, J. LUNAR LANDSCAPES.
W. HEATH, 340(KR):1970/1-186
HAWKES, N. THE COMPUTER REVOLUTION.
617(TLS):11FEB72-166
HAWKINS, A. COOK IT QUICK.
N. MAGID, 440:20FEB72-8
HAWKINS, H. BETWEEN HARVARD AND AMERICA.
J.A. GARRATY, 441:19NOV72-64
HAWKINS, W. THE GIFT OF SPACE.
C. LEVENSON, 99:JUN72-43
HAWLEY, D. THE TRUCIAL STATES.
617(TLS):21JAN72-56
HAWORTH, L. THE GOOD CITY.
H.L. PARSONS, 486:JUN68-198
HAWTHORN, A. ART OF THE KWAKIUTL INDIANS
AND OTHER NORTHWEST COAST TRIBES.*
B.M. REISE, 592:NOV68-220
HAWTHORN, J.R. - SEE SALLUST
HAWTHORNE, J. NATHANIEL HAWTHORNE AND
HIS WIFE. HAWTHORNE AND HIS CIRCLE.
R. LEHAN, 445(NCF):JUN69-123
HAWTHORNE, N. OUR OLD HOME.
B. JONES, 27(AL):MAY71-287
HAY, D. & J. NO STAR AT THE POLE.
617(TLS):10MAR72-285
HAY, J. IN DEFENSE OF NATURE.
639(VQR):WINTER70-XXVIII
HAYAKAWA, S.I. SEMANTIK. VOM UMGANG MIT
SICH UND ANDEREN.
W. SCHÄFER, 182:VOL23#19/20-847
HAYAKAWA, S.I., ED. WORT UND WIRKLICH-
KEIT.
W. SCHÄFER, 182:VOL23#19/20-847
HAYAKAWA, S.I. & OTHERS, EDS. THE MODERN
GUIDE TO SYNONYMS AND RELATED WORDS.
R.E. LEOPOLD, 186(ETC.):MAR69-79
HAYASHI, T. ROBERT GREENE CRITICISM.
S. WELLS, 677:VOL2-256
HAYASHIYA, S. & G. HASEBE. CHINESE CER-
AMICS.
L. KATZ, 57:VOL31#2/3-218
HAYDEN, J.O., ED. ROMANTIC BARDS AND
BRITISH REVIEWERS.
617(TLS):19MAY72-573
HAYDEN, J.O. THE ROMANTIC REVIEWERS,
1802-1824.*
I.H.C., 191(ELN):SEP70(SUPP)-16
R.G. COX, 447(N&Q):JUL70-277
K. KROEBER, 191(ELN):JUN70-311
N. TEICH, 141:SUMMER70-255
HAYDEN, J.O., ED. SCOTT: THE CRITICAL
HERITAGE.*
J. KINSLEY, 402(MLR):JUL71-672
HAYDN, H. IL CONTRORINASCIMENTO.
R. PARENTI, 548(RCSF):JUL-SEP68-343
VON HAYEK, F.A. FREIBURGER STUDIEN.
A. HÜFNER, 182:VOL23#15/16-725
HAYES, B. THE BLACK AMERICAN TRAVEL
GUIDE.
441:6FEB72-40
HAYES, C. RENOIR.
P. POOL, 39:DEC69-542
HAYES, D. A PLAYER'S HIDE.
617(TLS):24MAR72-326
HAYES, D. THE WAR OF '39.* TOMORROW THE
APRICOTS.*
F.P.W. MC DOWELL, 659:SUMMER72-361

HAYES, H. & A. LOOS. TWICE OVER LIGHTLY.
K. SIMON, 441:1OCT72-26
442(NY):23SEP72-134
561(SATR):7OCT72-108
HAYES, J. ROWLANDSON.
617(TLS):8DEC72-1473
HAYES, P.M. QUISLING.
441:30JUL72-21
617(TLS):21JAN72-70
HAYES, R.M. & J. BECKER. HANDBOOK OF
DATA PROCESSING FOR LIBRARIES.
R. BREGZIS, 356:OCT71-345
HAYFORD, H., H. PARKER & G.T. TANSELLE -
SEE MELVILLE, H.
HAYIT, B. DIE WIRTSCHAFTSPROBLEME
TURKESTANS.
D.S.M. WILLIAMS, 575(SEER):JAN71-170
HAYMAN, R. EUGÈNE IONESCO.
617(TLS):9JUN72-662
HAYN, A. RAPUNZEL.
T.L. WEPPLER, 99:JUL-AUG72-46
HAYS, D.G. INTRODUCTION TO COMPUTATIONAL
LINGUISTICS.*
M.F. BOTT, 297(JL):APR69-190
HAYTER, A. HORATIO'S VERSION.
D.J. ENRIGHT, 362:23MAR72-385
HAYTER, A. OPIUM AND THE ROMANTIC IMAG-
INATION.*
G. THOMAS, 175:SUMMER69-70
HAYTER, T. HAYTER OF THE BOURGEOISIE.
M. DRABBLE, 362:17FEB72-220
617(TLS):18FEB72-172
HAYWARD, C.H. ENGLISH PERIOD FURNITURE.
617(TLS):7JAN72-8
HAYWARD, M. & W.C. FLETCHER, EDS. RELI-
GION AND THE SOVIET STATE.
J.P. SCANLAN, 550(RUSR):OCT70-466
HAYWOOD, C., ED. FOLK SONGS OF THE
WORLD.
C.M. SIMPSON, JR., 650(WF):APR68-136
HAYWOOD, R.M. THE BEGINNING OF RAILWAY
DEVELOPMENT IN RUSSIA IN THE REIGN OF
NICHOLAS I, 1835-1842.*
B. HOLLINGSWORTH, 575(SEER):JAN71-152
M.S. MIRSKI, 550(RUSR):APR70-223
HAZARD, C.C. CONFESSIONS OF A WALL
STREET INSIDER.
K. KOYEN, 441:1OCT72-10
HAZARD, J., I. SHAPIRO & P.B. MAGGS, EDS.
THE SOVIET LEGAL SYSTEM.* (REV)
A. KIRALFY, 575(SEER):JAN71-169
HAZARI. UNTOUCHABLE.
R.S. SIMMONS, 293(JAST):FEB70-467
HAZEN, A.T. A CATALOGUE OF HORACE WAL-
POLE'S LIBRARY.*
C.A. ZIMANSKY, 481(PQ):JUL70-389
HAZEN, E.P., G. MILNE & P.H. HEMINGSON -
SEE "AMERICAN BOOK-PRICES CURRENT"
HAZLITT, M. THE JOURNAL OF MARGARET
HAZLITT. (E.J. MOYNE, ED)
J.E.J., 191(ELN):SEP69(SUPP)-34
HAZLITT, W.C. ENGLISH PROVERBS AND PRO-
VERBIAL PHRASES.
E.G. STANLEY, 447(N&Q):MAY70-187
HAZZARD, S. THE BAY OF NOON.*
M. CAVELL, 473(PR):1971/1-117
HEAD, C. JUSTINIAN II OF BYZANTIUM.
617(TLS):17MAR72-317
HEAD, F.B. A NARRATIVE. (S.F. WISE, ED)
102(CANL):SPRING71-120
HEAD, S. BROADCASTING IN AMERICA.
K. ADAM, 362:25MAY72-691
HEADLAM-MORLEY, J. A MEMOIR OF THE PARIS
PEACE CONFERENCE 1919. (A. HEADLAM-
MORLEY, R. BRYANT & A. CIENCIALA, EDS)
617(TLS):27OCT72-1271

HEADLEY, J.M., ED. MEDIEVAL AND RENAIS-
SANCE STUDIES. [1967]
G.B. PARKS, 551(RENQ):SPRING70-54
HEALEY, B. THE VESPUCCI PAPERS.
N. CALLENDAR, 441:18JUN72-31
HEALY, J. THE JUST WAGE, 1750-1890.
O. SCHAFFNER, 182:VOL23#5-208
HEALY, T.S. - SEE DONNE, J.
HEANEY, S. DOOR INTO THE DARK.*
E. JENNINGS, 619(TC):1969/2-44
HEANEY, S. WINTERING OUT.
P. BEER, 362:7DEC72-795
617(TLS):15DEC72-1524
HEARD, N.C. TO REACH A DREAM.
M. WATKINS, 441:14JUL72-32
HEARTZ, D. PIERRE ATTAINGNANT, ROYAL
PRINTER OF MUSIC.*
H.M. BROWN, 317:SPRING71-125
L. LOCKWOOD, 415:FEB71-135
HEATH, P. THE ENGLISH PARISH CLERGY ON
THE EVE OF THE REFORMATION.
J.W. MC KENNA, 589:JUL71-517
HEATH-STUBBS, J. THE VERSE SATIRE.
566:SPRING71-71
HEATH-STUBBS, J. - SEE POPE, A.
HEATON, P. MAKE SAIL.
617(TLS):2JUN72-639
HEBDEN, M. A KILLER FOR THE CHAIRMAN.
N. CALLENDAR, 441:28MAY72-25
617(TLS):28APR72-500
HEBER, R. BISHOP HEBER IN NORTHERN
INDIA. (M.A. LAIRD, ED)
617(TLS):23JUN72-729
HECHT, W. - SEE BRECHT, B.
HECHT, W. - SEE SCHOTTELIUS, J.G.
HECKEL, J. DAS BLINDE, UNDEUTLICHE WORT
"KIRCHE." (S. GRUNDMANN, ED)
D.W. JELLEMA, 182:VOL23#13/14-649
HEDBERG, S. CONTAMINATION AND INTERPOLA-
TION.*
J. ANDRÉ, 555:VOL44FASC2-346
HEDBERG, S. - SEE COLUMELLA
HÉDELIN, F. "LA PRATIQUE DU THÉÂTRE" UND
ANDERE SCHRIFTEN ZUR "DOCTRINE CLAS-
SIQUE."
W. FLOECK, 72:BAND208HEFT4/6-460
HEDGECOE, J. & H. MOORE. HENRY MOORE.*
S.R. LEVITT, 592:NOV68-226
HEDGES, D. & F. MAYER. HORSES AND
COURSES.
G.F.T. RYALL, 441:3DEC72-28
617(TLS):29DEC72-1589
HEDGES, J.B. THE BROWNS OF PROVIDENCE
PLANTATIONS.
S. BRUCHEY, 656(WMQ):JAN70-153
HEDLEY, O. ROYAL PALACES.
617(TLS):25AUG72-1006
HEENAN, J.C. NOT THE WHOLE TRUTH.*
617(TLS):10MAR72-283
HEENEY, B. MISSION TO THE MIDDLE CLASS.
B. SIMON, 637(VS):JUN70-403
HEER, N.W. POLITICS AND HISTORY IN THE
SOVIET UNION.*
L.R. TILLETT, 32:DEC71-896
HEFFERNAN, J.A.W. WORDSWORTH'S THEORY
OF POETRY.*
K.K., 191(ELN):SEP70(SUPP)-48
R.D MC GHEE, 577(SHR):FALL70-374
E.J. SCHULZE, 385(MQR):SPRING72-144
HEFTING, V. JONGKIND D'APRÈS SA CORRES-
PONDANCE.
M. HUGGLER, 182:VOL23#5-233
HEGEL, G.W.F. GESAMMELTE WERKE. (VOL 4)
(H. BUCHNER & O. PÖGGELER, EDS)
H.W. BRANN, 258:DEC69-631
E. WEIL, 98:NOV69-1024

HEGEL, G.W.F. HEGEL'S PHILOSOPHY OF
NATURE.* (A.V. MILLER, TRANS)
R.J.B., 543:JUN70-741
HEGEL, G.W.F. JENAER KRITISCHE SCHRIF-
TEN. (H. BUCHNER & O. PÖGGELER, EDS)
M. DAL PRA, 548(RCSF):JUL/SEP69-343
HEGEL, G.W.F. SCIENCE OF LOGIC. (A.V.
MILLER, TRANS)
R.J.B., 543:DEC69-346
M.J. PETRY, 479(PHQ):JUL70-273
HEGELE, W. GRABBES DRAMENFORM.*
H.J. SCHMIDT, 406:SPRING71-78
HEGER, H. DIE MELANCHOLIE BEI DEN FRAN-
ZÖSISCHEN LYRIKERN DES SPÄTMITTELAL-
TERS.
W. CALIN, 545(RPH):FEB71-527
HEGER, K., ED. DIE BIBEL IN DER ROMANIA:
MATTHÄUS 6, 5-13.
L.J. FRIEDMAN, 545(RPH):AUG69-136
HEGGOY, A.A. INSURGENCY AND COUNTERIN-
SURGENCY IN ALGERIA.
617(TLS):1SEP72-1021
HEIBER, H. GOEBBELS.
R. GRUNBERGER, 441:29OCT72-54
HEIBERG, P.A. & V. KUHR, WITH N. THUL-
STRUP - SEE "SÖREN KIERKEGAARDS PAP-
IRER"
ZUR HEIDE, K.G. DEEP SOUTH PIANO.
M. HARRISON, 415:FEB71-141
HEIDEGGER, M. THE ESSENCE OF REASONS.*
(T. MALICK, TRANS) IDENTITY AND DIF-
FERENCE. (J. STAMBAUGH, TRANS)
J.D.C., 543:JUN70-742
HEIDEGGER, M. WEGMARKEN.
J.D.C., 543:DEC69-347
HEIDEGGER, M. ZUR SACHE DES DENKENS.
J.D.C., 543:JUN70-743
HEIDEMANN, I. DER BEGRIFF DES SPIELES.
D.B. KUSPIT, 484(PPR):MAR70-472
HEIDENREICH, H., ED. THE LIBRARIES OF
DANIEL DEFOE AND PHILLIPS FAREWELL.*
L.S. HORSLEY, 402(MLR):JUL71-665
HEIDSIECK, A. DAS GROTESKE UND DAS
ABSURDE IM MODERNEN DRAMA.*
H. DENKLER, 222(GR):NOV70-302
HEIDSIECK, F. PLAISIR ET TEMPÉRANCE.
R. VIOLETTE, 542:OCT-DEC68-496
VAN HEIJENOORT, J., ED. FROM FREGE TO
GÖDEL.
M.D. RESNIK, 486:MAR68-72
VAN HEIJENOORT, J. - SEE HERBRAND, J.
HEIKAL, M. NASSER.
617(TLS):15DEC72-1522
HEILBRONER, R.L. BETWEEN CAPITALISM AND
SOCIALISM.*
W. LEONTIEF, 453:20JUL72-30
HEILBRONER, R.L. & OTHERS. IN THE NAME
OF PROFIT.
N. BLIVEN, 442(NY):8JUL72-73
L.L.L. GOLDEN, 561(SATR):27MAY72-70
R. TOWNSEND, 441:30APR72-5
HEILMAN, R.B. TRAGEDY AND MELODRAMA.
A. BONGIORNO, 50(ARQ):SUMMER69-174
L.F. DEAN, 131(CL):WINTER71-86
W.N. KING, 397(MD):DEC69-327
I. RIBNER, 141:SUMMER69-305
E.M. WAITH, 402(MLR):JAN71-165
HEIM, M. ASWAN!
P. ADAMS, 61:SEP72-110
O.L. BAILEY, 561(SATR):30SEP72-79
M. LEVIN, 441:27AUG72-26
HEIMBECK, R.S. THEOLOGY AND MEANING.
A. FLEW, 518:MAY70-10
HEIMRICH, B. FIKTION UND FIKTIONSIRONIE
IN THEORIE UND DICHTUNG DER DEUTSCHEN
ROMANTIK.
E. MARSCH, 490:OCT68-567

141

HEMLOW, J., WITH J.M. BURGESS & A. DOUG-
LAS. A CATALOGUE OF THE BURNEY FAMILY
CORRESPONDENCE 1749-1878.
617(TLS):14APR72-428
HEMLOW, J., C.D. CECIL & A. DOUGLAS -
SEE BURNEY, F.
HEMMING, J. THE CONQUEST OF THE INCAS.
676(YR):WINTER71-VIII
HEMMINGS, F.W.J. CULTURE AND SOCIETY IN
FRANCE 1848-1898.
617(TLS):14JAN72-43
HEMMINGS, R. FIFTY YEARS OF FREEDOM.
617(TLS):22DEC72-1552
HÉMON, L. LETTRES À SA FAMILLE. (N.
DESCHAMPS, ED)
P.M. GATHERCOLE, 207(FR):OCT69-174
R.J. HATHORN, 402(MLR):APR71-415
HEMPHILL, W.E. - SEE CALHOUN, J.C.
HENCKEN, H. TARQUINIA, VILLANOVANS AND
EARLY ETRUSCANS.* TARQUINIA AND
ETRUSCAN ORIGINS.*
J. CLOSE-BROOKS, 313:VOL60-238
HENDEL, S. & R.L. BRAHAM, EDS. THE
U.S.S.R. AFTER 50 YEARS.
W.V. WALLACE, 587:OCT68-270
HENDEL, S.C. BIKES.
H.C. GARDNER, 441:4JUN72-8
HENDERSON, C.P., JR. THE NIXON THEOLOGY.
M.E. MARTY, 441:6AUG72-7
HENDERSON, D. DITCH VALLEY.
M. LEVIN, 441:15OCT72-43
HENDERSON, D.F. THE CONSTITUTION OF
JAPAN.
T. MC NELLY, 293(JAST):FEB70-453
HENDERSON, G. EARLY MEDIEVAL.
617(TLS):18AUG72-966
HENDERSON, G. GOTHIC.*
J. BECKWITH, 39:SEP69-267
HENDERSON, J.A. THE FIRST AVANT-GARDE,
1887-1894.
617(TLS):3MAR72-253
HENDERSON, J.L.S. JOHN STRACHAN, 1778-
1868.*
M. ANGUS, 529(QQ):SPRING70-124
W.L. MORTON, 331:NOV69-46
HENDERSON, L. CAGE UNTIL TAME.
N. CALLENDAR, 441:24SEP72-41
617(TLS):26MAY72-612
HENDERSON, L. SITTING TARGET.
N. CALLENDAR, 441:20AUG72-27
HENDERSON, L. WITH INTENT.
N. CALLENDAR, 441:9JUL72-30
HENDERSON, N. OUT OF THE CURTAINED
WORLD.
F. SWEENEY, 441:2APR72-5
HENDERSON, P. WILLIAM MORRIS.*
D.J. GORDON, 592:MAR68-156
B.J. INMAN, 50(ARQ):SPRING69-90
HENDERSON, R.B. MAURY MAVERICK.
W. GARD, 584(SWR):WINTER71-91
HENDERSON, R.M. D.W. GRIFFITH.
J. LEYDA, 561(SATR):1APR72-71
W. MARKFIELD, 441:23APR72-6
H.L. WEGNER, 651(WHR):WINTER71-89
HENDIN, J. THE WORLD OF FLANNERY O'CON-
NOR.
W. SULLIVAN, 27(AL):MAR71-146
HENDON, R.S., ED & TRANS. SIX INDONESIAN
SHORT STORIES.
A.M. STEVENS, 293(JAST):FEB70-490
M. VISICK, 302:JAN70-249
HENDRICKS, G. THE PHOTOGRAPHS OF THOMAS
EAKINS.
L. MUMFORD, 453:21SEP72-3
HENDRICKS, G.D. MIRRORS, MICE, AND MUS-
TACHES.
H. TROYER, 650(WF):OCT68-282

HENDRIX, W. & W. MEIDEN. BEGINNING
FRENCH. (4TH ED)
M. WALTER, 399(MLJ):DEC70-616
HENDY, P. PIERO DELLA FRANCESCA AND THE
EARLY RENAISSANCE.*
C. GILBERT, 290(JAAC):SPRING70-397
HENFREY, N. - SEE SANTAYANA, G.
HENKEL, A. - SEE HAMANN, J.G.
HENKEL, A. & A. SCHÖNE, EDS. EMBLEMATA.
W.S. HECKSCHER & C.F. BUNKER, 551
(RENQ):SPRING70-59
HENLE, J. & K. PFEUFER. DER BRIEFWECHSEL
ZWISCHEN JAKOB HENLE UND KARL PFEUFER
1843-69. (H. HOEPKE, ED)
F. GRASS, 182:VOL23#15/16-705
HENN, T.R. THE LIVING IMAGE.
617(TLS):5MAY72-517
HENNESSEY, R.A.S. THE ELECTRIC REVOLU-
TION.
617(TLS):26MAY72-609
HENNESSY, J.P. - SEE UNDER POPE HENNESSY,
J.
HENNING, H. & S. SEIFERT, EDS. INTERNA-
TIONALE BIBLIOGRAPHIE ZUR DEUTSCHEN
KLASSIK, 1750-1850.
K.L. BERGHAHN, 406:SUMMER71-157
HENRI, A. AUTOBIOGRAPHY.
J. FULLER, 362:24FEB72-251
H. WILLIAMS, 364:FEB/MAR72-155
HENRY, A. C'ÉTAIT "IL Y A" DES LUNES.
P.A. GAENG, 207(FR):DEC69-368
N.C.W. SPENCE, 208(FS):JAN71-118
HENRY, D.P. THE LOGIC OF SAINT ANSELM.*
E.A. MOODY, 482(PHR):APR70-274
HENRY, D.P. MEDIEVAL LOGIC AND META-
PHYSICS.
617(TLS):24NOV72-1439
HENRY, J. PATHWAYS TO MADNESS.
H. HENDIN, 441:26MAR72-5
A. STORR, 440:9JAN72-12
617(TLS):28JUL72-894
HENRY, L. DÉMOGRAPHIE.
617(TLS):29DEC72-1585
HENRY, M.R. A FARMHOUSE IN PROVENCE.
A. SANOUILLET, 207(FR):APR70-850
HENRY, R. - SEE PHOTIUS
HENRYSON, R. POEMS. (C. ELLIOTT, ED)
A.J. AITKEN, 597(SN):VOL41#2-427
HENRYSON, R. THE TESTAMENT OF CRESSEID.
(D. FOX, ED)
T.A. STROUD, 405(MP):NOV69-182
HENSEL, G. SAMUEL BECKETT.
K. TETZELI VON ROSADOR, 72:BAND208
HEFT1-49
HENSEL, K.P. & OTHERS. DIE SOZIALIST-
ISCHE MARKTWIRTSCHAFT IN DER TSCHE-
CHOSLOWAKEI.
V. HOLEŠOVSKÝ, 32:MAR71-195
HENSLEY, C.S. THE LATER CAREER OF GEORGE
WITHER.
M. ECCLES, 551(RENQ):AUTUMN70-338
J. GRUNDY, 541(RES):AUG70-354
C. HILL, 447(N&Q):JUL70-267
P. PALMER, 677:VOL2-262
HENSLEY, J. LEGISLATIVE BODY.
O.L. BAILEY, 561(SATR):9SEP72-75
HENSLOWE, P. HENSLOWE'S DIARY. (R.A.
FOAKES & R.T. RICKERT, EDS)
N. SANDERS, 179(ES):FEB70-64
HENSMAN, B. & M. KWOK-PING, EDS & TRANS.
HONG KONG TALE-SPINNERS.*
J.L.B., 244(HJAS):VOL29-334
HENZO D'ALESSIO, R. LOS MUÑECOS DE
PAJA.
R. SQUIRRU, 37:JUL69-40
HEPBURN, J. THE AUTHOR'S EMPTY PURSE AND
THE RISE OF THE LITERARY AGENT.
W.D. SCHAEFER, 445(NCF):MAR69-491

HEPP, N. - SEE PELLISSON, P. & C. FLEURY
HEPPENSTALL, R. BLUEBEARD AND AFTER.
617(TLS):7APR72-402
HEPWORTH, P. VICTORIAN AND EDWARDIAN
NORFOLK FROM OLD PHOTOGRAPHS.
617(TLS):29DEC72-1590
VON HERBERSTEIN, S. DESCRIPTION OF MOS-
COW AND MUSCOVY, 1557. (B. PICARD, ED)
A.E. ALEXANDER, 574(SEEJ):SPRING71-
141
B. UROFF, 32:MAR71-138
HERBERT, D. SECOND SON.
617(TLS):13OCT72-1227
HERBERT, J. BIBLIOGRAPHIE DU SHINTŌ ET
DES SECTES SHINTOÏSTES.
H.B. EARHART, 293(JAST):NOV69-171
HERBERT, R.L. J.L. DAVID: BRUTUS.
617(TLS):22DEC72-1550
HERBERT, Z. SELECTED POEMS.*
J.J. MACIUSZKO, 574(SEEJ):SPRING71-
125
HERBIG, R. GÖTTER UND DÄMONEN DER
ETRUSKER. (2ND ED)
R.M. OGILVIE, 123:MAR71-148
HERBRAND, J. ECRITS LOGIQUES. (J. VAN
HEIJENOORT, ED)
W.D. GOLDFARB, 482(PHR):OCT70-576
HERDEG, K. FORMAL STRUCTURE IN INDIAN
ARCHITECTURE.
W. KIDNEY, 505:AUG68-182
HERDEG, W., ED. PHOTOGRAPHIS '72.
617(TLS):14JUL72-826
VON HERDER, J.G. HERDER ON SOCIAL AND
POLITICAL CULTURE. (F.M. BARNARD, ED &
TRANS)
F. GRIES, 406:WINTER71-410
VON HERDER, J.G. ÜBER DIE NEUERE DEUT-
SCHE LITERATUR. (ED & ABRIDGED BY A.
GILLIES)
W.H. BRUFORD, 402(MLR):OCT71-943
DE HEREDIA, J.F. LA GRANT CRONICA DE
ESPANYA LIBROS I-II. (R. AF GEIJER-
STAM, ED)
S.G. ARMISTEAD, 545(RPH):MAY71-648
HERES, G. DIE PUNISCHEN UND GRIECHISCHEN
TONLAMPEN DER STAATLICHEN MUSEEN ZU
BERLIN.
J. RUSSELL, 124:DEC70-128
HERGENHAN, L.T. - SEE MEREDITH, G.
HERHAUS, E. HOMBURGISCHE HOCHZEIT.
ROMAN EINES BUERGERS.
T. WEYR, 19(AGR):VOL35#4-31
HERING, C. FRIEDRICH MAXIMILIAN KLINGER.*
R. VAN DUSEN, 564:FALL69-149
HERINGTON, C.J. THE AUTHOR OF THE PROM-
ETHEUS BOUND.
H. MUSURILLO, 124:FEB71-198
HERLIHY, D. MEDIEVAL AND RENAISSANCE
PISTOIA.
E. WELCH, 325:APR69-504
HERLIHY, J.L. THE SEASON OF THE WITCH.*
J.M. MORSE, 249(HUDR):AUTUMN71-527
HERLING, J. RIGHT TO CHALLENGE.
A.H. RASKIN, 441:20FEB72-6
453:9MAR72-34
HERMAN, G. THE WHO.
N. FOUNTAIN, 364:FEB/MAR72-141
HERMAND, J. SYNTHETISCHES INTERPRETIER-
EN.*
G. REBING, 52:BAND4HEFT3-306
J.L. SAMMONS, 221(GQ):JAN70-98
HERMAND, J. VON MAINZ NACH WEIMAR (1793-
1919).*
P.U. HOHENDAHL, 221(GQ):NOV70-798
M. ZUTSHI, 402(MLR):OCT71-949
HERMAND, J. - SEE HOLZ, A.

HERMANN, P. & K.Z. POLATKAN. DAS TESTA-
MENT DES EPIKRATES UND ANDERE NEUE IN-
SCHRIFTEN AUS DEM MUSEUM VON MANISA.
D.M. LEWIS, 123:DEC71-466
HERMANNS, M. DIE RELIGIÖS-MAGISCHE
WELTANSCHAUUNG DER PRIMITIVSTÄMME
INDIENS.
R.N. DANDEKAR, 182:VOL23#1/2-58
HERNÁNDEZ, J. THE GAUCHO MARTÍN FIERRO.
(C.E. WARD, TRANS)
F. DEMARÍA, 37:JAN69-39
HERNÁNDEZ, L.R. - SEE UNDER RUIZ HERNÁN-
DEZ, L.
HERNÁNDEZ MILLARES, J. & A. CARRILLO
ESCRIBANO. ATLAS PORRÚA DE LA RE-
PÚBLICA MEXICANA.
J.A. DABBS, 399(MLJ):MAR70-198
HERNDL, G.C. THE HIGH DESIGN.
C.E. BAIN, 568(SCN):SUMMER/AUTUMN71-
45
R. SOELLNER, 579(SAQ):SUMMER71-423
HERNDON, J. HOW TO SURVIVE IN YOUR
NATIVE LAND.*
N. HENTOFF, 442(NY):5FEB72-99
HERNER, S. A BRIEF GUIDE TO SOURCES OF
SCIENTIFIC AND TECHNICAL INFORMATION.
T.J. WHITBY, 356:JAN71-74
HERODAS. MIMIAMBI. (I.C. CUNNINGHAM,
ED)
617(TLS):31MAR72-374
HERODIAN. HISTORY. (LOEB, VOL 1, BKS
1-4) (C.R. WHITTAKER, TRANS)
T.F. CARNEY, 123:JUN71-194
HEROLD, C.P. THE MORPHOLOGY OF KING
ALFRED'S TRANSLATION OF THE "OROSIUS."
E.M. LIGGINS, 382(MAE):1971/3-266
HERRENSCHMIDT, O. LE CYCLE DE LINGAL.
D.M. SPENCER, 318(JAOS):APR-JUN70-361
HERRERO, J. - SEE GANIVET, Á.
DE LOS HERREROS, M.B. - SEE UNDER BRETÓN
DE LOS HERREROS, M.
HERRESHOFF, D. AMERICAN DISCIPLES OF
MARX.
G.W. BARGER, 330(MASJ):FALL69-84
HERRICK, F.H. AUDUBON THE NATURALIST.
W. BLUNT, 90:JUN69-398
M.S. YOUNG, 39:APR69-328
HERRIG, L., H. MELLER & R. SÜHNEL, EDS.
BRITISH AND AMERICAN CLASSICAL POEMS.
F.W. SCHULZE, 38:BAND87HEFT2-257
HERRIOT, J. ALL CREATURES GREAT AND
SMALL.
A. BROYARD, 441:14DEC72-49
HERRMANN, F., ED. THE ENGLISH AS COL-
LECTORS.
617(TLS):4AUG72-905
HERRMANN, H-V. DIE KESSEL DER ORIENTAL-
ISIERENDEN ZEIT. (PT 1)
G. ROUX, 555:VOL44FASC1-114
HERRMANN, L. CHRESTOS.
J.E. SEAVER, 124:JAN71-172
HERRMANN, L. RUSKIN AND TURNER.*
M. BUTLIN, 90:APR70-251
T. HILTON, 592:MAR69-152
HERRMANN, P. DER RÖMISCHE KAISEREID.*
J. BRISCOE, 123:JUN71-260
F. LASSERRE, 182:VOL23#5-239
E.M. SMALLWOOD, 313:VOL60-231
HERRMANN, R-D. KÜNSTLER UND INTERPRET.
V.M. AMES, 290(JAAC):FALL69-114
HERRMANN, W. YARIH UND NIKKAL UND DER
PREIS DER KUTARAT-GÖTINNEN.
A.F. RAINEY, 318(JAOS):OCT-DEC70-533
HERRNSTADT, R.L. - SEE ALCOTT, A.B.
HERRON, I.H. THE SMALL TOWN IN AMERICAN
DRAMA.*
F.M. LITTO, 432(NEQ):MAR70-149

HERRON, S.   THROUGH THE DARK AND HAIRY
WOOD.
   N. CALLENDAR, 441:10SEP72-40
HERSEY, G.L.   HIGH VICTORIAN GOTHIC.
   617(TLS):10NOV72-1365.
HERSEY, J.   THE CONSPIRACY.
   L.J. DAVIS, 440:26MAR72-4
   B.F. DICK, 561(SATR):18MAR72-74
   J. HENDIN, 441:2APR72-6
   D.A.N. JONES, 362:11MAY72-628
   C. LEHMANN-HAUPT, 441:24MAR72-43
   E. WEEKS, 61:MAR72-106
   617(TLS):16JUN72-677
HERSH, B.   THE EDUCATION OF EDWARD KEN-
NEDY.
   C. KILPATRICK, 561(SATR):13MAY72-79
   R.R. LINGEMAN, 441:4JUN72-1
   M.F. NOLAN, 441:9JUL72-4
   R.J. WALTON, 440:28MAY72-1
HERSH, S.M.   COVER-UP.
   R. HAMMER, 441:26MAR72-3
   A. PRAGER, 561(SATR):1APR72-81
   R. SHERRILL, 440:2APR72-1
HERTLING, G.H.   WANDLUNG DER WERTE IM
DICHTERISCHEN WERKE DER RICARDA HUCH.
   A.E. RATZ, 564:FALL68-167
HERTZMAN, L., J. WARNOCK & T. HOCKIN.
ALLIANCES & ILLUSIONS.
   D. SCHURMAN, 529(QQ):SPRING70-136
HERWIG, W. - SEE VON BIEDERMANN, F.
HERZ, M.F.   BEGINNINGS OF THE COLD WAR.
   H.B. MOULTON, 461:SPRING68-326
HERZFELD, E.   THE PERSIAN EMPIRE.   (G.
WALSER, ED)
   A.R. BURN, 303:VOL90-246
HERZOG, U.   JAKOB GRETSERS "UDO VON
MAGDEBURG" 1598.
   W.F. MICHAEL, 301(JEGP):APR71-362
HESELTINE, H.   VANCE PALMER.*
   A.A. PHILLIPS, 381:VOL29#4-523
HESKETH, P.   RIVINGTON.
   617(TLS):1DEC72-1469
HESLA, D.H.   THE SHAPE OF CHAOS.
   C. RICKS, 453:14DEC72-42
HESS, T.B. & J. ASHBERY, EDS.   ART NEWS
ANNUAL XXXVI: NARRATIVE ART.
   J. O'SULLIVAN, 127:SPRING71-324
HESSE, E., ED.   NEW APPROACHES TO EZRA
POUND.*
   D. BARBOUR, 529(QQ):AUTUMN70-470
   W.M. CHACE, 598(SOR):WINTER72-225
   F.K. SANDERS, 569(SR):SUMMER71-433
   639(VQR):SPRING70-LVI
HESSE, E.W.   CALDERÓN DE LA BARCA.
   P.N. DUNN, 240(HR):APR70-223
HESSE, H.   AUTOBIOGRAPHICAL WRITINGS.
   E.Z. FRIEDENBERG, 231:JUL72-88
HESSEL, V.   LE TEMPS DES PARENTS.
   M.G. ROSE, 207(FR):APR70-866
HESTER, M.B.   THE MEANING OF POETIC META-
PHOR.
   D.T. WIECK, 290(JAAC):SPRING70-400
HESTER, R.M., ED.   TEACHING A LIVING LAN-
GUAGE.
   J.D. WORKMAN, 406:SPRING71-90
HETTICH, D.W. & W.C. MILLER.   FUNDAMEN-
TALS OF ENGLISH.
   M. GRADY, 353:JUL69-101
HETZRON, R.   THE VERBAL SYSTEM OF SOUTH-
ERN AGAW.*
   B.W. ANDRZEJEWSKI, 315(JAL):VOL8PT2-
124
HEUBNER, H.   P. CORNELIUS TACITUS, "DIE
HISTORIEN:" KOMMENTAR.   (VOL 2)
   R.H. MARTIN, 123:DEC71-381
HEURGON, J.   ROME ET LA MÉDITERRANÉE
OCCIDENTALE JUSQU'AUX GUERRES PUNIQUES.
   A. ERNOUT, 555:VOL44FASC1-94

DE HEUSCH, L.   POURQUOI L'ÉPOUSER?
   617(TLS):21APR72-445
HEUSLER, A.   KLEINE SCHRIFTEN.   (VOLS
1&2) (H. REUSCHEL & S. SONDEREGGER,
EDS)   SCHRIFTEN ZUM ALEMANNISCHEN.
(S. SONDEREGGER, ED)
   M. SZADROWSKY, 182:VOL23#4-164
HEUSSLER, R.   THE BRITISH IN NORTHERN
NIGERIA.
   P.C. LLOYD, 69:JUL69-320
HEWITT, D.   THE APPROACH TO FICTION.
   617(TLS):17NOV72-1392
HEWITT, G.   WAKING UP STILL PICKLED.
   W. WITHERUP, 502(PRS):WINTER69/70-422
HEWITT, H. - SEE PETRUCCI, O.
HEWITT, J., ED.   EYE WITNESSES TO NEL-
SON'S BATTLES.
   617(TLS):16JUN72-697
HEWITT, J., ED.   EYE-WITNESSES TO THE
INDIAN MUTINY.
   617(TLS):1SEP72-1033
HEWITT, J.   THE NEW YORK TIMES HERITAGE
COOKBOOK.
   N. HAZELTON, 441:3DEC72-96
HEWITT, J.   THE NEW YORK TIMES LARGE TYPE
COOKBOOK.   (REV)
   N. MAGID, 440:13FEB72-5
HEWLETT, D.   A LIFE OF JOHN KEATS.   (3RD
ED)
   N. ROGERS, 677:VOL2-302
HEXTER, J.H.   DOING HISTORY.
   617(TLS):15SEP72-1047
HEXTER, J.H.   THE HISTORY PRIMER.
   617(TLS):24NOV72-1437
VON HEYDEBRAND, R.   DIE REFLEXIONEN
ULRICHS IN ROBERT MUSILS ROMAN "DER
MANN OHNE EIGENSCHAFTEN."
   G. MÜLLER, 597(SN):VOL40#2-476
VON HEYDEBRAND, R. & K.G. JUST.   WISSEN-
SCHAFT ALS DIALOG.*
   W. PAULSEN, 222(GR):MAY70-242
   W. VAN DER WILL, 402(MLR):APR71-475
HEYER, A.H., COMP.   HISTORICAL SETS, COL-
LECTED EDITIONS, AND MONUMENTS OF
MUSIC.*   (2ND ED)
   L. CORAL, 317:SUMMER71-308
HEYN, L.L.   CHALLENGE TO BECOME A DOCTOR.
   E. & N. FONER, 453:20APR72-39
HEYWORTH, P. - SEE NEWMAN, E.
HEYWORTH, P.L., ED.   "JACK UPLAND,"
"FRIAR DAW'S REPLY" AND "UPLAND'S
REJOINDER."*
   A. BRUTEN, 541(RES):MAY70-194
   R.H. ROBBINS, 447(N&Q):JUL70-266
HIBBARD, G.R. - SEE SHAKESPEARE, W.
HIBBERT, C.   GEORGE IV.
   617(TLS):17NOV72-1388
HIBBERT, C.   THE PERSONAL HISTORY OF
SAMUEL JOHNSON.*
   P. CRUTTWELL, 440:13FEB72-4
HIBBS, B., ED.   WHITE HOUSE SERMONS.
   M.E. MARTY, 441:6AUG72-7
HICKEY, D. & G. SMITH.   A PALER SHADE OF
GREEN.
   617(TLS):29SEP72-1148
HICKS, G., WITH J.A. ROBBINS.   LITERARY
HORIZONS.*
   I. MALIN, 651(WHR):AUTUMN71-363
HICKS, J.   A THEORY OF ECONOMIC HISTORY.
   639(VQR):SUMMER70-CX
HIEBLE, J., ED.   DIE WELT VON HEUTE UND
MORGEN.
   G.E. CONDOYANNIS, 399(MLJ):APR70-302
   C.P. HOMBERGER, 221(GQ):MAR70-310
HIELSCHER, K.   A.S. PUŠKINS VERSEPIK.
   J.P. PAULS, 574(SEEJ):WINTER71-503
HIENER, W.   WILLIAM STREET.
   J. TULIP, 581:1971/1-72

HIGGINBOTHAM, D. THE WAR OF AMERICAN
INDEPENDENCE.*
    617(TLS):1SEP72-1031
HIGGINBOTHAM, J., ED. GREEK AND LATIN
LITERATURE.*
    M.L. CLARKE, 123:MAR71-75
    G.S. ROUSSEAU, 121(CJ):FEB-MAR71-262
    E. TIFFOU, 487:WINTER70-363
HIGGINBOTHAM, J. - SEE CICERO
HIGGINS, A. BALCONY OF EUROPE.
    D.A.N. JONES, 362:28SEP72-418
    617(TLS):6OCT72-1185
HIGGINS, G.V. THE FRIENDS OF EDDIE
COYLE.
    P. ADAMS, 61:MAR72-108
    H. FRANKEL, 561(SATR):26FEB72-71
    C. LEHMANN-HAUPT, 441:25JAN72-37
    J. MC GINNISS, 441:6FEB72-7
    442(NY):4MAR72-113
    617(TLS):7JUL72-783
HIGGINS, H. & J. MYERS. TO BE A MATADOR.
    617(TLS):15SEP72-1071
HIGGINS, J. THE LAST PLACE GOD MADE.
    M. LEVIN, 441:2APR72-23
HIGGINS, J. THE SAVAGE DAY.
    N. CALLENDAR, 441:12NOV72-67
HIGGINS, J. TRAVELS IN THE BALKANS.
    617(TLS):30JUN72-752
HIGGINS, J.A. F. SCOTT FITZGERALD.
    H.D. PIPER, 27(AL):NOV71-468
HIGGINS, J.J. MERTON'S THEOLOGY OF
PRAYER.
    617(TLS):5MAY72-527
HIGGINS, R.A. GREEK TERRACOTTAS.*
    D. WHITE, 56:AUTUMN69-316
HIGH, D.M. LANGUAGE, PERSONS, AND
BELIEF.
    L. GRIFFITHS, 483:JUL70-257
HIGH, D.M., ED. NEW ESSAYS ON RELIGIOUS
LANGUAGE.
    S.O.H., 543:SEP69-144
HIGHAM, C. ZIEGFELD.
    N. TEITEL, 561(SATR):4NOV72-84
HIGHAM, J. WRITING AMERICAN HISTORY.
    H.V.S. OGDEN, 385(MQR):WINTER72-68
HIGHAM, R. AIR POWER.
    617(TLS):3NOV72-1308
HIGHAM, R., ED. A GUIDE TO THE SOURCES
OF BRITISH MILITARY HISTORY.
    617(TLS):21JUL72-850
HIGHFIELD, R., ED. SPAIN IN THE FIF-
TEENTH CENTURY 1369-1516.
    617(TLS):10MAR72-285
HIGHSMITH, P. A DOG'S RANSOM.
    B. BROPHY, 362:11MAY72-627
    N. CALLENDAR, 441:3SEP72-22
    442(NY):16SEP72-128
    617(TLS):12MAY72-537
HIGMAN, F.M. THE STYLE OF JOHN CALVIN
IN HIS FRENCH POLEMICAL TREATISES.
    C.E. RATHÉ, 207(FR):APR70-845
HILCZERÓWNA, Z. DORZECZE GÓRNEJ I ŚROD-
KOWEJ OBRY OD VI DO POCZĄTKÓW XI WIEKU.
    K. TACKENBERG, 182:VOL23#23/24-996
HILDEBRANDT, D., W. HUDER & T. KRISCHKE
- SEE VON HORVÁTH, Ö.
HILKA, A. - SEE CHRÉTIEN DE TROYES
HILL, A., ED. DATA.
    A. GRIEVE, 592:MAR69-151
HILL, B.H. MEDIEVAL MONARCHY IN ACTION.
    617(TLS):11AUG72-954
HILL, C. ANTICHRIST IN SEVENTEENTH-
CENTURY ENGLAND.*
    I. GENTLES, 99:JUN72-37
HILL, C. GOD'S ENGLISHMAN.
    T. HAYES, 568(SCN):WINTER71-78
HILL, C., ED. KÄSTNER FÜR STUDENTEN.
    J. WINKELMAN, 221(GQ):MAY70-528

HILL, C. THE WORLD TURNED UPSIDE DOWN.
    J. DUNN, 362:3AUG72-151
    K. THOMAS, 453:30NOV72-26
    617(TLS):18AUG72-969
HILL, C.W. SCOTLAND IN STAMPS.
    617(TLS):25AUG72-1006
HILL, E. QUIETLY CRUSH THE LIZARD.
    M. LEVIN, 441:10DEC72-57
HILL, E.B. MODERN FRENCH MUSIC.
    R. CRICHTON, 415:FEB71-132
HILL, G. KING LOG.
    W.P.T., 619(TC):1968/3-58
HILL, G. MERCIAN HYMNS.*
    M. SCHMIDT, 491:JUN72-170
    I. WEDDE, 364:DEC71/JAN72-118
HILL, H. - SEE TWAIN, M.
HILL, J. HYPOCHONDRIASIS.
    P.C. RITTERBUSH, 481(PQ):JUL70-305
HILL, P. RURAL HAUSA.
    617(TLS):23JUN72-715
HILL, R. AN ADVANCEMENT OF LEARNING.
    617(TLS):4FEB72-135
HILL, R. A FAIRLY DANGEROUS THING.
    617(TLS):10NOV72-1375
HILL, S. THE BIRD OF NIGHT.
    V. CUNNINGHAM, 362:14SEP72-344
    617(TLS):15SEP72-1041
HILL, S. STRANGE MEETING.*
    G. EWART, 364:FEB/MAR72-180
    442(NY):15APR72-146
HILL, W. JEFFERSON MC GRAW.
    M. LEVIN, 441:13FEB72-32
HILLABY, J. A WALK THROUGH EUROPE.
    (BRITISH TITLE: JOURNEY THROUGH EUROPE)
    R. BLYTHE, 362:13JUL72-55
    A. BROYARD, 441:9OCT72-33
    441:10DEC72-48
    617(TLS):25AUG72-993
HILLEBRAND, H., ED. GRAPHIC DESIGNERS IN
EUROPE. (VOL 1) GRAPHIC DESIGNERS IN
THE USA. (VOLS 1&2)
    617(TLS):30JUN72-740
HILLEN, W. BLACKWATER RIVER.
    P. ADAMS, 61:FEB72-109
HILLGARTH, J.N., ED. THE CONVERSION OF
WESTERN EUROPE, 350-750.
    D.E. GROH, 124:MAY71-311
HILLGARTH, J.N. RAMÓN LULL AND LULLISM
IN FOURTEENTH-CENTURY FRANCE.
    617(TLS):2JUN72-631
HILLIARD, N. A NIGHT AT GREEN RIVER.
    R.A. COPLAND, 368:DEC69-401
HILLIER, B. ART DECO OF THE 20S AND 30S.
    J. MASHECK, 592:NOV68-229
HILLIER, B. POTTERY AND PORCELAIN 1700-
1914.*
    G. WILLS, 39:OCT69-352
HILLIER, C. DIALOGUE ON AN ISLAND.
    617(TLS):28JUL72-865
HILLIER, J. HOKUSAI DRAWINGS.
    P. HARDIE, 39:APR69-325
HILLMAN, J. INSEARCH.
    G.M., 477:SUMMER69-405
HILLMAN, R. GUSTAVIANSK RETORIK.
    E. ALKER, 182:VOL23#5-218
HILLS, L.D. GROW YOUR OWN FRUIT AND
VEGETABLES.
    617(TLS):30JUN72-757
HILLS, L.R. HOW TO DO THINGS RIGHT.
    N. EPHRON, 441:16JUL72-3
    C. LEHMANN-HAUPT, 441:16JUN72-41
HILLS, R.J.T. THE LIFE GUARDS.
    617(TLS):28JAN72-109
HILSCH, P. DIE BISCHÖFE VON PRAG IN DER
FRÜHEN STAUFERZEIT.
    G.H. FICK, 589:JUL71-518
    H. KAMINSKY, 32:MAR71-130

HILTON, R., ED. THE SCIENTIFIC INSTITU-
TIONS OF LATIN AMERICA.
R.P. ATCON, 263:JUL-SEP71-351
HILU, V. - SEE GIBRAN, K. & M. HASKELL
HIMES, C. THE QUALITY OF HURT.
R.H. GAINES, 561(SATR):15APR72-69
A. GINGRICH, 440:26MAR72-12
N.I. HUGGINS, 441:12MAR72-5
C. LEHMANN-HAUPT, 441:8MAR72-45
442(NY):18MAR72-155
HINCHLIFFE, A.P. HAROLD PINTER.
F.S.K., 477:SUMMER69-426
A. WALKER, 397(MD):FEB69-448
HINDE, T. GENERALLY A VIRGIN.
D.A.N. JONES, 362:8JUN72-768
617(TLS):9JUN72-649
HINDERMANN, W.F. WIEDERGEWONNENE SCHWES-
TERWERKE DER BRANDENBURGISCHEN KONZERTE
JOHANN SEBASTIAN BACHS.
W. EMERY, 415:OCT71-969
HINDLEY, G. - SEE "LAROUSSE ENCYCLOPEDIA
OF MUSIC"
HINDUS, M., ED. WALT WHITMAN: THE CRITI-
CAL HERITAGE.
617(TLS):28JAN72-95
HINE, D. MINUTES.*
H. MAC CALLUM, 627(UTQ):JUL69-344
J. WESTON, 50(ARQ):AUTUMN69-276
HINE, R.V. BARTLETT'S WEST.
M.S. YOUNG, 39:APR69-328
HINES, B. FIRST SIGNS.
E. MORGAN, 362:24FEB72-252
HINES, R.S., ED. THE ORCHESTRAL COM-
POSER'S POINT OF VIEW.
P. DICKINSON, 415:SEP71-862
A. PAYNE, 607:AUTUMN70-35
HINGLEY, R. A CONCISE HISTORY OF RUSSIA.
617(TLS):31MAR72-358
HINGLEY, R. RUSSIAN WRITERS AND SOCIETY,
1825-1904.
M. DEWHIRST, 587:APR68-597
HINNELLS, J.R. & E.J. SHARPE, EDS. HIN-
DUISM.
617(TLS):25AUG72-1002
HINTIKKA, J. MODELS AND MODALITIES.
R.H.K., 543:JUN70-743
R.C. STALNAKER, 311(JP):17AUG72-456
HINTIKKA, J. & P. SUPPES, EDS. ASPECTS
OF INDUCTIVE LOGIC.
L.J. COHEN, 479(PHQ):JUL70-293
HINTON, D.A. OXFORD BUILDINGS FROM MEDI-
EVAL TO MODERN.
617(TLS):6OCT72-1205
HINZ, S., ED. CASPAR DAVID FRIEDRICH IN
BRIEFEN UND BEKENNTNISSEN.
I.C., 191(ELN):SEP70(SUPP)-93
HIPOLITO, J. & W.E. MC NELLY, EDS. MARS,
WE LOVE YOU.
T. STURGEON, 441:14MAY72-34
HIPPOCRATES. KITĀB BUQRĀT FI'L-AMRĀD
AL-BILĀDIYYA/ON ENDEMIC DISEASES (AIR,
WATERS AND PLACES). (J.N. MATTOCK &
M.C. LYONS, EDS & TRANS)
F.E. PETERS, 124:OCT70-59
HIPPOCRATES. KITĀB TADBĪR AL-AMRĀD AL-
HĀDDA LI-BUQRĀT/REGIMEN IN ACUTE DIS-
EASES. (M.C. LYONS, ED & TRANS) KITĀB
BUQRĀT 'ALĀ HABL/ON SUPERFOETATION.
(J.N. MATTOCK & M.C. LYONS, EDS &
TRANS) KITĀB BUQRĀT FĪ TABĪ'AT AL-
INSĀN/ON THE NATURE OF MAN. (J.N.
MATTOCK & M.C. LYONS, EDS & TRANS)
F.E. PETERS, 124:OCT70-58
LE HIR, Y. - SEE MARTIAL D'AUVERGNE
HIRSCH, E.F. DAMIÃO DE GOIS.
E. GLASER, 240(HR):JAN70-111

HIRSCH, H. ROSA LUXEMBURG IN SELBST-
ZEUGNISSEN UND BILDDOKUMENTEN.
K.J. HERRMANN, 104:SPRING71-138
HIRSCH, H. - SEE "EDUARD BERNSTEINS
BRIEFWECHSEL MIT FRIEDRICH ENGELS"
HIRSCHFELD, B. FATHER PIG.
N. CALLENDAR, 441:28MAY72-25
HIRTLE, W.H. THE SIMPLE AND PROGRESSIVE
FORMS.
R.A. HALL, JR., 545(RPH):NOV69-230
"THE HISTORY OF REYNARD THE FOX."* (W.
CAXTON, TRANS; N.F. BLAKE, ED)
A.C. CAWLEY, 447(N&Q):DEC70-472
R.M. WILSON, 402(MLR):OCT71-846
R.W. ZANDVOORT, 382(MAE):1971/1-83
"HISTORY, SOCIOLOGY AND EDUCATION."
617(TLS):28JAN72-109
HITCHCOCK, G. THE DOLPHIN WITH THE
REVOLVER IN ITS TEETH.*
R. BROTHERSON, 661:FALL/WINTER69-109
HITCHCOCK, H-R. GERMAN ROCOCO: THE
ZIMMERMANN BROTHERS.
S.L. FAISON, JR., 39:NOV69-442
HITCHCOCK, H-R. ROCOCO ARCHITECTURE IN
SOUTHERN GERMANY.
S.L. FAISON, JR., 39:NOV69-442
A. MURRAY, 19(AGR):VOL36#4-15
HITCHCOCK, H-R. & OTHERS. THE RISE OF
AN AMERICAN ARCHITECTURE. (E. KAUF-
MANN, JR., ED)
W.J. MALARCHER, 363:AUG70-136
HITCHCOCK, H.W. MUSIC IN THE UNITED
STATES.
M. PETERSON, 470:JAN70-45
HITCHINS, K. THE RUMANIAN NATIONAL MOVE-
MENT IN TRANSYLVANIA, 1780-1849.*
J.M. KITCH, 575(SEER):APR71-300
HITCHINS, K. & L. MAIOR - SEE RAŢIU, I.
HITIER, E. L'OMBRE PERDUE.
I.C., 191(ELN):SEP69(SUPP)-100
HITOSHI, A., S. KAZUKO & T. SHUNTARO -
SEE ANZAI HITOSHI, SHIRAISHI KAZUKO &
TANIKAWA SHUNTARO
HIXSON, W.B., JR. MOORFIELD STOREY AND
THE ABOLITIONIST TRADITION.
617(TLS):1SEP72-1031
HJELMSLEV, L. LANGUAGE.
J. KLAUSENBURGER, 399(MLJ):DEC70-621
HÔ, A.N.N. - SEE MUS, P.
HO, P-T. STUDIES ON THE POPULATION OF
CHINA, 1368-1953.
J. WONG, 302:JUL69-284
HO, P-T. & T. TSOU, EDS. CHINA IN CRI-
SIS. (VOL 1, BKS 1&2)
R. CROZIER, 293(JAST):NOV69-153
HOA, N.D. READ VIETNAMESE.
R.L. WATSON, 318(JAOS):APR-JUN70-400
HOA, N.D. VIETNAMESE-ENGLISH DICTIONARY.
R.L. WATSON, 318(JAOS):APR-JUN70-402
HOAGLAND, E. THE COURAGE OF TURTLES.*
N. MILLS, 676(YR):SUMMER71-609
HOAGLAND, J. SOUTH AFRICA.
442(NY):11NOV72-190
HOAR, V. MORLEY CALLAGHAN.*
D. CAMERON, 529(QQ):SUMMER70-282
S.E. MC MULLIN, 150(DR):SUMMER70-291
HOARE, Q. & G.N. SMITH - SEE GRAMSCI, A.
HOBBES, T. A DIALOGUE BETWEEN A PHILOSO-
PHER AND A STUDENT OF THE COMMON LAWS
OF ENGLAND. (J. CROPSEY, ED)
T. WALDMAN, 319:JAN72-90
HOBBES, T. ELEMENTI DI LEGGE NATURALE E
POLITICA. (A. PACCHI, ED & TRANS)
R. PARENTI, 548(RCSF):JUL-SEP68-361
HOBBS, J.P. - SEE EISENHOWER, D.D.
HOBHOUSE, C. A WELL-TOLD LIE.
617(TLS):10NOV72-1375

HOBHOUSE, H. LOST LONDON.
    G. ANNAN, 362:6JAN72-24
    C. HIBBERT, 440:14MAY72-5
    T. LASK, 441:16JUN72-39
    617(TLS):4FEB72-116
HOBSBAUM, P. A THEORY OF COMMUNICATION.*
    J. KILLHAM, 89(BJA):SPRING71-200
HOBSBAUM, P. WOMEN AND ANIMALS.
    617(TLS):20OCT72-1249
HOBSBAWM, E. & G. RUDÉ. CAPTAIN SWING.
    D.V.E., 191(ELN):SEP70(SUPP)-12
HOBSBAWM, E.J. INDUSTRY AND EMPIRE.
    J. VINCENT, 637(VS):JUN70-440
HOBSON, A. FULL CIRCLE.
    617(TLS):10MAR72-270
HOBSON, B. CATALOGUE OF SCANDINAVIAN
    COINS SINCE 1534.
    617(TLS):1DEC72-1469
HOBSON, H., P. KNIGHTLEY & L. RUSSELL.
    THE PEARL OF DAYS.
    W. HARDCASTLE, 362:23NOV72-723
    617(TLS):27OCT72-1287
HOCHMAN, B. ANOTHER EGO.
    P.L. WILEY, 659:SPRING72-249
HOCHMAN, S. EARTHWORKS.
    J. KOETHE, 491:APR72-49
    617(TLS):26MAY72-607
HOCKETT, C.F. THE STATE OF THE ART.
    J. NIST, 577(SHR):SPRING70-183
HOCKETT, C.F. - SEE BLOOMFIELD, L.
HOCKING, M. FAMILY CIRCLE.
    J. HUNTER, 362:19OCT72-513
    617(TLS):8DEC72-1477
HOCTOR, T.M. - SEE ARNOLD, M.
HODGART, M. SATIRE.
    J.R. CLARK, 385(MQR):SPRING72-146
    571:WINTER69/70-76
HODGART, M. - SEE GULLIVER, L.
HODGE, J.A. ONLY A NOVEL. (BRITISH
    TITLE: THE DOUBLE LIFE OF JANE AUSTEN.)
    442(NY):5AUG72-84
    617(TLS):23JUN72-704
HODGES, C.W. THE GLOBE RESTORED.
    W.C. FERGUSON, 529(QQ):SPRING70-131
HODGES, G. MEMOIRS OF AN OLD BALLOON-
    ATIC.
    617(TLS):16JUN72-697
HODGETTS, A.B. WHAT CULTURE? WHAT HERI-
    TAGE?
    R.C. ELLSWORTH, 529(QQ):SUMMER70-294
HODGSON, H.W., COMP. A BIBLIOGRAPHY OF
    THE HISTORY AND TOPOGRAPHY OF CUMBER-
    LAND AND WESTMORLAND.
    J.D. MARSHALL, 325:OCT70-162
HODGSON, P. - SEE CHAUCER, G.
HODGSON, S. NEGOTIATIONS.
    D.A.N. JONES, 362:16MAR72-348
HODIN, J.P. MANESSIER.
    617(TLS):28JUL72-888
HODIN, J.P. EDVARD MUNCH.
    P. GAY, 31(ASCH):AUTUMN72-660
HODIN, J.P. ZUR PROBLEMATIK UNSERES
    ZEITALTERS.
    S.S. PRAWER, 220(GL&L):APR71-287
HODIN, J.P. RUSZKOWSKI, LIFE AND WORK.
    D. HALL, 39:DEC69-547
HODIN, J.P. & OTHERS. FIGURATIVE ART
    SINCE 1945.
    617(TLS):19MAY72-568
HODLER, W. BERNDEUTSCHE SYNTAX.
    R.E. KELLER, 402(MLR):OCT71-915
    B.J. KOEKKOEK, 301(JEGP):APR71-368
    M. SZADROWSKY, 182:VOL23#17/18-791
HODSON, D. PRINTED MAPS OF HERTFORD-
    SHIRE. (PT 1)
    R. HYDE, 325:OCT70-154

"HODSON'S BOOKSELLERS, PUBLISHERS AND
    STATIONERS DIRECTORY 1855." (G. POL-
    LARD, ED)
    617(TLS):16JUN72-696
HOEFERT, S. DAS DRAMA DES NATURALISMUS.
    D. FOGG, 402(MLR):JUL71-712
    J. OSBORNE, 220(GL&L):APR71-285
HOENIGER, F.D. & J.F.M. THE DEVELOPMENT
    OF NATURAL HISTORY IN TUDOR ENGLAND.
    THE GROWTH OF NATURAL HISTORY IN STUART
    ENGLAND FROM GERARD TO THE ROYAL SOCI-
    ETY.
    R.G. FRANK, JR., 627(UTQ):JUL70-371
HOEPKE, H. - SEE HENLE, J. & K. PFEUFER
HOF, W. PESSIMISTISCH-NIHILISTISCHE
    STRÖMUNGEN IN DER DEUTSCHEN LITERATUR
    VOM STURM UND DRANG BIS ZUM JUNGEN
    DEUTSCHLAND.
    M.B. BENN, 402(MLR):OCT71-947
HOFER, P. EDWARD LEAR AS A LANDSCAPE
    DRAUGHTSMAN.*
    E.D.H. JOHNSON, 637(VS):SEP69-102
    K. ROBERTS, 90:OCT70-706
HOFER, V. DIE BEDEUTUNG DES BERICHTES
    GENERAL GUISANS ÜBER DEN AKTIVDIENST
    1939-45 FÜR DIE GESTALTUNG DES SCHWEI-
    ZERISCHEN WEHRWESENS.
    O. SCHEITLIN, 182:VOL23#15/16-758
HOFF, A. WILHELM LEHMBRUCK.
    A. WERNER, 58:DEC69/JAN70-12
HOFF, B.J. THE CARIB LANGUAGE.
    D. TAYLOR, 361:VOL24#3-299
HOFF, U. & M. DAVIES. THE NATIONAL GAL-
    LERY OF VICTORIA, MELBOURNE.
    617(TLS):12MAY72-542
HOFFMAN, A.W. JOHN DRYDEN'S IMAGERY.
    P. DIXON, 179(ES):AUG70-363
HOFFMAN, D. BARBAROUS KNOWLEDGE.*
    J.D. BOULGER, 613:SPRING68-128
    R.S. KINSMAN, 650(WF):JAN69-63
HOFFMAN, D. BROKEN LAWS.*
    M. BORROFF, 676(YR):WINTER71-277
    T. HARRISON, 364:APR/MAY71-163
    E. NELSON, 590:WINTER71-41
HOFFMAN, D. POE POE POE POE POE POE POE.
    J. HOLLANDER, 441:13FEB72-7
    C. LEHMANN-HAUPT, 441:27JAN72-39
    R.W.B. LEWIS, 31(ASCH):AUTUMN72-680
    R.D. SPECTOR, 561(SATR):15APR72-73
    617(TLS):23JUN72-710
HOFFMAN, F.J. THE ART OF SOUTHERN FIC-
    TION.
    L. CASPER, 613:WINTER68-612
    K. KING, 399(MLJ):JAN70-51
HOFFMAN, R. LANGUAGE, MINDS AND KNOW-
    LEDGE.
    F.C. JACKSON, 63:DEC71-318
    D. MC QUEEN, 518:OCT71-16
HOFFMAN, S.D. COMEDY AND FORM IN THE
    FICTION OF JOSEPH CONRAD.
    J. FEASTER, 136:FALL69-121
    J. FEASTER, 295:VOL2#3-417
    G. MORGAN, 627(UTQ):JUL70-361
    C.T. WATTS, 541(RES):NOV70-519
HOFFMANN, B., WITH H. DUKAS. ALBERT
    EINSTEIN.
    M.J. KLEIN & R.K. MERTON, 441:5NOV72-
    3
    T. LASK, 441:4NOV72-31
    561(SATR):28OCT72-82
HOFFMANN, D. - SEE ROOT, J.W.
HOFFMANN, E.T.A. E.T.A. HOFFMANNS BRIEF-
    WECHSEL. (VOLS 2&3) (F. SCHNAPP, ED)
    R.M., 191(ELN):SEP70(SUPP)-114
HOFFMANN, E.T.A. DER SANDMANN. (M.
    WACKER, ED)
    R.M., 191(ELN):SEP70(SUPP)-115

HOFFMANN, H-C. DIE THEATERBAUTEN VON
FELLNER UND HELMER.*
    R. CARTER, 576:DEC68-304
HOFFMANN, K. & F. DEUCHLER, EDS. THE
YEAR 1200.
    78(BC):SUMMER70-164
HOFFMANN, L. IMPORTSUBSTITUTION UND
WIRTSCHAFTLICHES WACHSTUM IN ENTWICK-
LUNGSLÄNDERN.
    J. VALARCHÉ, 182:VOL23#10-539
HOFFMANN, L-F. LA PESTE À BARCELONE.
    L. ALLEN, 208(FS):APR71-214
HOFFMANN, U. - SEE WEIGAND, H.J.
HOFMANN, J.B. LATEINISCHE GRAMMATIK.
(VOL 2, PT 3) (REV BY A. SZANTYR)
    D.M. JONES, 123:DEC70-364
HOFMANN, W. GUSTAV KLIMT.
    P. ADAMS, 61:JUL72-97
    D.L. SHIREY, 441:10DEC72-46
HOFMANN, W. DER MALER WALTER DEXEL.
    617(TLS):28JUL72-888
HOFMANN, W. TURNING POINTS IN TWENTIETH-
CENTURY ART: 1890-1917.
    C. NEMSER, 58:SEP/OCT69-14
    592:NOV69-198
HOFMANN, W.J. SCHLOSS POMMERSFELDEN
GESCHICHTE SEINER ENTSTEHUNG.
    A. VON SCHUCKMANN, 39:NOV69-444
VON HOFMANNSTHAL, H. & L. VON ANDRIAN.
BRIEFWECHSEL. (W.H. PERL, ED)
    H. LEHNERT, 400(MLN):APR70-405
VON HOFMANNSTHAL, H. & C.J. BURCKHARDT.
BRIEFWECHSEL HUGO VON HOFMANNSTHAL/CARL
JACOB BURCKHARDT. (C.J. BURCKHARDT,
ED)
    F.G. CRONHEIM, 402(MLR):APR71-470
HOFSTADTER, R. AMERICA AT 1750.*
    617(TLS):24NOV72-1419
HOFSTADTER, R. THE IDEA OF A PARTY SYS-
TEM.
    M. KAMMEN, 432(NEQ):JUN70-311
    J.W. WARD, 639(VQR):WINTER70-173
HOFSTATTER, H.H. GOTHIQUE.
    P. GUERRE, 98:MAR69-265
HOGAN, R. ARTHUR MILLER.
    S. FALK, 397(MD):DEC67-318
HOGAN, R. & J. KILROY, EDS. LOST PLAYS
OF THE IRISH RENAISSANCE.
    617(TLS):17MAR72-306
HOGARTH, J. SENTENCING AS A HUMAN PRO-
CESS.
    P. RUSSELL, 99:APR72-6
HOGGART, R. ONLY CONNECT.
    C. RICKS, 362:6JUL72-19
    617(TLS):21JUL72-832
HOGGART, R. SPEAKING TO EACH OTHER.*
    D. BARBOUR, 150(DR):AUTUMN70-410
    A. BEAR, 381:VOL29#3-370
HOGROGIAN, R. THE ARMENIAN COOKBOOK.
    N. MAGID, 440:13FEB72-12
HOGSTRAND, O. ON THE PRIME MINISTER'S
ACCOUNT.
    O.L. BAILEY, 561(SATR):5AUG72-56
    N. CALLENDAR, 441:21MAY72-30
HOHENBALKEN, P. - SEE VON LÜTZOW, H.
HOHN, G.K. THE BLEAK STRAND.
    N. CALLENDAR, 441:9JUL72-30
HÖHNE, H. CODEWORD: DIREKTOR.
    C.C. DAVIS, 441:16APR72-40
    J. MANDER, 440:9JAN72-3
    H.H. RANSOM, 561(SATR):26FEB72-74
    A.J.P. TAYLOR, 453:10FEB72-14
    617(TLS):14JAN72-30
HÖHNE, H. & H. ZOLLING. THE GENERAL WAS
A SPY.
    N. ASCHERSON, 453:1JUN72-3
    R.G. DEINDORFER, 561(SATR):24JUN72-61
                            [CONTINUED]

[CONTINUING]
    C. FELIX, 441:16APR72-3
    442(NY):13MAY72-147
HÖHNE, H. & H. ZOLLING. NETWORK.
    R. LEWIN, 362:8JUN72-767
    617(TLS):12MAY72-538
HOLADAY, A. - SEE CHAPMAN, G.
HOLAN, V. SELECTED POEMS. (I. MILNER,
ED)
    I. WEDDE, 364:FEB/MAR72-148
    617(TLS):25AUG72-984
HOLAS, B. CRAFTS AND CULTURE IN THE
IVORY COAST.
    G.I. JONES, 69:APR69-191
HOLBORN, H. A HISTORY OF MODERN GERMANY,
1840-1945.
    G. BARRACLOUGH, 453:19OCT72-37
    G. BARRACLOUGH, 453:2NOV72-32
HOLBORN, H., ED. REPUBLIC TO REICH.
    G. BARRACLOUGH, 453:2NOV72-32
HOLBROOK, C.A. - SEE EDWARDS, J.
HOLBROOK, D., ED. THE CASE AGAINST POR-
NOGRAPHY.
    617(TLS):3NOV72-1346
HOLBROOK, D. OLD WORLD NEW WORLD.*
    R. DURGNAT, 493:SPRING70-81
HOLBROOK, D. THE PSEUDO-REVOLUTION.
    617(TLS):3NOV72-1346
HOLCROFT, M.H. RELUCTANT EDITOR.
    D. MC ELDOWNEY, 368:DEC69-394
HOLDEN, D. GREECE WITHOUT COLUMNS.
    N. GAGE, 441:1OCT72-34
    617(TLS):19MAY72-564
HOLDEN, D. WHISTLER LANDSCAPES AND SEA-
SCAPES.
    S. SPECTOR, 58:MAY70-14
HOLDEN, D. AIR AND CHILL EARTH.
    J. FULLER, 362:24FEB72-251
    617(TLS):28JAN72-94
HÖLDERLIN, F. OEUVRES. (P. JACCOTTET,
ED)
    I.C., 191(ELN):SEP70(SUPP)-109
HÖLDERLIN, F. SÄMTLICHE WERKE.* (VOL 7,
PT 1) (A. BECK, ED)
    P. PROCHNIK, 182:VOL23#7-364
HOLDHEIM, W.W. THEORY AND PRACTICE OF
THE NOVEL.
    A.H. PASCO, 405(MP):MAY70-390
HOLGATE, D. NEW HALL AND ITS IMITATORS.
    617(TLS):7JAN72-8
HOLINSHED, R. SHAKESPEARE'S HOLINSHED.*
(R. HOSLEY, ED)
    T. HAWKES, 570(SQ):AUTUMN69-473
    K. MAGAREY, 67:MAY71-88
HOLL, O. DER ROMAN ALS FUNKTION UND ALS
ÜBERWINDUNG DER ZEIT.*
    L.W. KAHN, 222(GR):MAY70-234
HOLLAENDER, A.E.J. & W. KELLAWAY, EDS.
STUDIES IN LONDON HISTORY.
    E. WELCH, 325:OCT70-161
HOLLAND, A.J. SHIPS OF BRITISH OAK.
    617(TLS):7APR72-398
HOLLAND, C. HAMMER FOR PRINCES.
    617(TLS):7APR72-385
HOLLAND, D.F. STEAM LOCOMOTIVES OF THE
SOUTH AFRICAN RAILWAYS. (VOL 1)
    617(TLS):21APR72-458
HOLLAND, F.R., JR. AMERICA'S LIGHT-
HOUSES.
    M. OLMERT, 440:14MAY72-8
HOLLAND, N.N. THE DYNAMICS OF LITERARY
RESPONSE.*
    D. BURKE, 613:SPRING69-125
    A.D. NUTTALL, 541(RES):MAY70-242
    G. STADE, 340(KR):1969/4-573
HOLLAND, N.N. PSYCHOANALYSIS AND SHAKE-
SPEARE.
    M. CHARNEY, 570(SQ):AUTUMN68-401

HOLLANDER, J.   THE NIGHT MIRROR.*
   R. HOWARD, 491:AUG72-296
   V. YOUNG, 249(HUDR):WINTER71/72-679
HOLLANDER, J.   TYPES OF SHAPE.
   H. MORRIS, 569(SR):SPRING71-301
HOLLANDER, R.   ALLEGORY IN DANTE'S "COM-
MEDIA."
   T.G. BERGIN, 589:APR71-380
   D.J. DONNO, 551(RENQ):WINTER70-434
   639(VQR):WINTER70-XIX
HOLLANDER, X., WITH R. MOORE & Y. DUN-
LEAVY.   THE HAPPY HOOKER.
   A. WHITMAN, 231:MAY72-102
HOLLENWEGER, W.J.   THE PENTECOSTALS.
   617(TLS):31MAR72-377
HÖLLHUBER, I.   GESCHICHTE DER ITALIEN-
ISCHEN PHILOSOPHIE VON DEN ANFÄNGEN DES
19. JAHRHUNDERTS BIS ZUR GEGENWART.
   M. JUNGO, 182:VOL23#9-459
HOLLI, M.G.   REFORM IN DETROIT.
   639(VQR):AUTUMN70-CXLVIII
HOLLIDAY, V.L.   POMPEY IN CICERO'S "COR-
RESPONDENCE" AND LUCAN'S "CIVIL WAR."*
   M. MORFORD, 121(CJ):FEB-MAR71-268
HOLLINGSWORTH, T.H.   HISTORICAL DEMOG-
RAPHY.
   R.V. WELLS, 656(WMQ):JUL70-492
HOLLIS, A.S. - SEE OVID
HOLLIS, J.R.   HAROLD PINTER.
   J.R. BROWN, 402(MLR):JUL71-683
HOLLIS, M.   THE SIGNIFICANCE OF SOUTH
INDIA.
   K.W.B., 477:SUMMER69-420
HOLLOWAY, J.   BLAKE: THE LYRIC POETRY.
   D.V.E., 191(ELN):SEP70(SUPP)-23
HOLMAN, C.H. & S.F. ROSS - SEE WOLFE, T.
HOLMAN-HUNT, D.   MY GRANDFATHER, HIS
WIVES AND LOVES.
   K. ROBERTS, 90:OCT70-707
HOLMBERG, O.   TANKAR I EN HUSVAGN.
   270:VOL20#2-43
HOLME, T.   CHELSEA.
   617(TLS):28JAN72-86
HOLMER, N.M.   AN ATTEMPT TOWARDS A COM-
PARATIVE GRAMMAR OF TWO AUSTRALIAN
LANGUAGES.*
   V. KRUPA, 353:SEP69-126
HOLMES, B. & D.G. SCANLON, EDS.   HIGHER
EDUCATION IN A CHANGING WORLD.
   617(TLS):21JAN72-77
HOLMES, C.S.   THE CLOCKS OF COLUMBUS.
   W. HOGAN, 561(SATR):21OCT72-74
   C. LEHMANN-HAUPT, 441:21NOV72-45
   E. WEEKS, 61:NOV72-128
HOLMES, D.M.   THE ART OF THOMAS MIDDLE-
TON.*
   M.P. JACKSON, 67:NOV71-227
HOLMES, J.D.L. - SEE BAILY, F.
HOLMES, P.   3 SECTIONS OF POEMS.
   617(TLS):28JUL72-873
HOLOTÍK, L., ED.   L'UDOVÍT ŠTÚR UND DIE
SLAWISCHE WECHSELSEITIGKEIT.*
   R.J.W. EVANS, 575(SEER):JAN71-153
HOLROYD, M.   LYTTON STRACHEY.* (VOL 1)
   42(AR):SPRING69-112
HOLROYD, M.   LYTTON STRACHEY.* (VOL 2)
   C.E. BARON, 97(CQ):SUMMER68-274
   42(AR):SPRING69-112
HOLROYDE, P.   INDIAN MUSIC.
   617(TLS):29SEP72-1163
HÖLSCHER, U.   ANFÄNGLICHES FRAGEN.*
   G.B. KERFERD, 123:DEC70-353
HOLSCHNEIDER, A.   DIE ORGANA VON WINCHES-
TER.
   E.H. SANDERS, 317:SPRING71-121
HOLST, I.   BRITTEN. (NEW ED)
   S. SADIE, 415:OCT70-1004

HOLST, I.   GUSTAV HOLST. THE MUSIC OF
GUSTAV HOLST.
   A.E.F. DICKINSON, 607:WINTER69/70-43
HOLT, C., WITH B.R.O. ANDERSON & J.
SIEGEL, EDS.   CULTURE AND POLITICS IN
INDONESIA.
   617(TLS):11AUG72-941
HOLT, J.   FREEDOM AND BEYOND.
   N. HENTOFF, 561(SATR):8JUL72-64
HOLT, J. - SEE UNDER GUTHRIE, W.
HOLT, P.M., A.K.S. LAMBTON & B. LEWIS,
EDS.   THE CAMBRIDGE HISTORY OF ISLAM.*
   617(TLS):4FEB72-130
HOLTON, L.   THE MIRROR OF HELL.
   N. CALLENDAR, 441:2APR72-22
HOLTORF, G.W.   HONG KONG - WORLD OF CON-
TRASTS.
   617(TLS):27OCT72-1297
HOLTZ, W.V.   IMAGE AND IMMORTALITY.
   A.H. CASH, 677:VOL2-289
   J. STEDMOND, 529(QQ):WINTER70-645
HOLUB, M.   ALTHOUGH.
   617(TLS):25AUG72-984
HOLUBAR, J.   THE SENSE OF TIME.
   R.H.K., 543:JUN70-744
HOLZ, A.   ARNO HOLZ: PHANTASUS. (J.
HERMAND, ED)
   S. PRAWER, 220(GL&L):JUL71-388
HOLZHAUER, H.   WILLENSFREIHEIT UND
STRAFE.
   F. GILLIARD, 182:VOL23#19/20-846
HOLZHEID, S.   DIE NOMINALKOMPOSITA IN DER
ILIASÜBERSETZUNG VON N.I. GNEDIČ.
   G.H. WORTH, 574(SEEJ):WINTER71-518
HOLZHEY, H.   KANTS ERFAHRUNGSBEGRIFF.
   W.H. WERKMEISTER, 319:JAN72-99
HÖLZL, N.   THEATERGESCHICHTE DES ÖST-
LICHEN TIROL VOM MITTELALTER BIS ZUR
GEGENWART. (PT 2)
   W.F. MICHAEL, 221(GQ):MAR70-265
HOMANN-WEDEKING, E.   THE ART OF ARCHAIC
GREECE.*
   D.E. STRONG, 39:MAR69-246
HOMANS, P., ED.   THE DIALOGUE BETWEEN
THEOLOGY AND PSYCHOLOGY.
   S.O.H., 543:DEC69-363
HOMBERGER, C.P.   RÜCKSCHAU UND FORT-
SCHRITT.
   H. BROCKHAUS, 221(GQ):JAN70-130
"HOMENAJE A RODRÍGUEZ-MOÑINO."
   M.E. BARRICK, 240(HR):APR70-198
HOMER.   THE ILIAD OF HOMER.* (A. POPE,
TRANS; R.A. BROWER & W.H. BOND, EDS)
   J.C. BRYCE, 123:DEC70-395
HOMER.   THE ILIAD OF HOMER.* THE ODYSSEY
OF HOMER.* (BOTH TRANS BY A. POPE & ED
BY M. MACK)
   R.A. BROWER, 405(MP):NOV69-192
   J.C. BRYCE, 123:DEC70-395
HOMER.   THE ODYSSEY. (R. FITZGERALD,
TRANS)
   R. BAGG, 5:SPRING69-51
HOMER.   OMERO: "ODISSEA." (CANTO 23)
(G. MAINA, ED)
   J.B. HAINSWORTH, 123:DEC70-397
HOMER, W.I., WITH V. ORGAN.   ROBERT HENRI
AND HIS CIRCLE.
   D.M. SOKOL, 127:FALL70-120
   S. SPECTOR, 58:MAR70-12
"THE HOMERIC HYMNS." (C. BOER, TRANS)
   M. AUGEN, 385(MQR):SUMMER72-223
   R. LATTIMORE, 249(HUDR):AUTUMN71-508
HOMEYER, H.   DIE ANTIKEN BERICHTE ÜBER
DEN TOD CICEROS UND IHRE QUELLEN.
   P. LANGLOIS, 555:VOL44FASC2-334
HOMEYER, H. - SEE HROTSVITHA OF GANDER-
SHEIM

HOMMEL, C.U. CHIFFER UND DOGMA.
B. WELTE, 182:VOL23#4-132
HONAN, P. BROWNING'S CHARACTERS.
P. TURNER, 179(ES):APR70-168
HONAN, W.H. TED KENNEDY.
C. KILPATRICK, 561(SATR):13MAY72-79
R.R. LINGEMAN, 441:4JUN72-1
M.F. NOLAN, 441:9JUL72-4
HONDA, H.H. - SEE "KOKIN WAKA-SHŪ"
HONDERICH, T. PUNISHMENT.
R.S. DOWNIE, 483:OCT70-341
J.D. MABBOTT, 393(MIND):OCT70-624
R. SQUIRES, 479(PHQ):JUL70-302
HONE, J. THE PRIVATE SECTOR.*
N. CALLENDAR, 441:18JUN72-31
HONEYCOMBE, G. DRAGON UNDER THE HILL.
617(TLS):1DEC72-1449
HONIG, L. FOR YOUR EYES ONLY: READ AND
DESTROY.
N. CALLENDAR, 441:24DEC72-14
HÖNLE, A. OLYMPIA IN DER POLITIK DER
GRIECHISCHEN STAATENWELT (VON 776 BIS
ZUM ENDE DES 5. JAHRHUNDERTS).
S.I. OOST, 122:APR71-135
HONOUR, H. NEO-CLASSICISM.*
D. IRWIN, 39:APR69-324
R.G. SAISSELIN, 290(JAAC):SPRING70-
395
HOOD, H. THE FRUIT MAN, THE MEAT MAN &
THE MANAGER.
H. KIRKWOOD, 99:APR72-53
K. THOMPSON, 198:WINTER72-116
HOOD, R., WITH K.W. ELLIOTT & E. SHIRLEY.
SENTENCING THE MOTORING OFFENDER.
617(TLS):27OCT72-1282
HOOGASIAN-VILLA, S., ED. 100 ARMENIAN
TALES AND THEIR FOLKLORISTIC RELE-
VANCE.*
E.W. BAUGHMAN, 650(WF):OCT68-279
HOOK, S. ACADEMIC FREEDOM AND ACADEMIC
ANARCHY.
C.P. IVES, 396(MODA):WINTER71-96
HOOK, S., ED. LANGUAGE AND PHILOSOPHY.*
P.W. ROGERS, 529(QQ):WINTER70-653
HOOK, S. & OTHERS. HUMAN VALUES AND
ECONOMIC POLICY.
B. CAZES, 98:APR69-359
HOOKER, R. M.A.S.H. GOES TO MAINE.
M. LEVIN, 441:5MAR72-15
HOOPER, W. - SEE LEWIS, C.S.
HOOPES, D.F. WINSLOW HOMER WATERCOLORS.
W.D. ALLEN, 58:MAR70-12
HOOYKAAS, R. RELIGION AND THE RISE OF
MODERN SCIENCE.
617(TLS):6OCT72-1200
HOPE, A.D. DUNCIAD MINOR.*
D. GREEN, 381:VOL29#4-424
HOPE, A. A MIDSUMMER EVE'S DREAM.*
A.M. KINGHORN, 677:VOL2-246
J. KINSLEY, 382(MAE):1971/1-87
C.J. WATSON, 381:VOL29#4-430
HOPE, M. YOUTH AGAINST THE WORLD.
676(YR):AUTUMN70-XII
HOPKINS, A. TALKING ABOUT SONATAS.
617(TLS):14JAN72-36
HOPKINS, J. ELVIS.*
N. SMITH, 362:27JUL72-123
617(TLS):29SEP72-1163
HOPKINS, J. TANGIER BUZZLESS FLIES.
J.R. FRAKES, 440:26MAR72-3
J. HARRISON, 441:14MAY72-4
442(NY):15APR72-147
617(TLS):18AUG72-961
HOPKINS, J.H. OROZCO.
M.S. YOUNG, 39:APR69-331
HOPKINS, M.W. MASS MEDIA IN THE SOVIET
UNION.
L. GRULIOW, 32:JUN71-434

HOPKINS, R.A. THE LONG MARCH.
J.P. LOVEKIN, 529(QQ):AUTUMN70-458
HOPKINS, R.H. THE TRUE GENIUS OF OLIVER
GOLDSMITH.*
R.M. DYER, 481(PQ):JUL70-353
A. SHERBO, 401(MLQ):MAR70-121
S.H. WOODS, JR., 191(ELN):SEP70-56
HOPPE, H. KANTS THEORIE DER PHYSIK.
W. SCHWARZ, 484(PPR):MAR70-471
HOPPEN, K.T. THE COMMON SCIENTIST IN
THE SEVENTEENTH CENTURY.*
566:SPRING71-75
HOPPER, S.R. & D.L. MILLER, EDS. INTER-
PRETATION.
A.A., 477:SPRING69-295
HOPWOOD, D. THE RUSSIAN PRESENCE IN
SYRIA AND PALESTINE, 1843-1914.
F. KAZEMZADEH, 32:DEC71-884
P. ROLLINS, 550(RUSR):JUL70-354
HORACE. ORAZIO, LE OPERE. (A. LA PENNA,
ED)
M.L. CLARKE, 123:MAR71-52
HORACE. THE THIRD BOOK OF HORACE'S
"ODES."* (G. WILLIAMS, ED & TRANS)
H.H. HUXLEY, 313:VOL60-257
K.J. RECKFORD, 24:JAN71-116
HORAK, S.M., COMP. JUNIOR SLAVICA.
R.A. KARLOWICH, 32:JUN71-455
HORÁNYI, M. & T. KLANICZAY, EDS. ITALIA
ED UNGHERIA.
O. RAGUSA, 149:JUN71-179
HORECKY, P.L., ED. EAST CENTRAL EUROPE.
SOUTHEASTERN EUROPE.
J.M. KITCH, 575(SEER):JUL71-477
S.D. SPECTOR, 32:JUN71-457
HORGAN, P. ENCOUNTERS WITH STRAVINSKY.
S. KARLINSKY, 441:2JUL72-1
H. KELLER, 362:26OCT72-547
R. PHELPS, 561(SATR):29JUL72-60
442(NY):15JUL72-82
617(TLS):22DEC72-1557
HORGAN, P. WHITEWATER.*
W. GARD, 584(SWR):WINTER71-91
HORN, D.D. SING TO ME OF HEAVEN.
F. HOWES, 415:MAY71-445
HORN, J.S. AWAY WITH ALL PESTS.*
R. BAZELL, 453:2NOV72-38
HORN-ONCKEN, A. ÜBER DAS SCHICKLICHE.*
W. HERRMANN, 576:MAY69-143
HORNBY, A.S., E.V. GATENBY AND H. WAKE-
FIELD, EDS. THE ADVANCED LEARNER'S
DICTIONARY OF CURRENT ENGLISH.
617(TLS):13OCT72-1209
HORNE, A. SMALL EARTHQUAKE IN CHILE.
M. DEAS, 362:23NOV72-722
HORNE, A. TO LOSE A BATTLE.
F. BUSI, 207(FR):APR70-851
HORNE, R.H. MEMOIRS OF A LONDON DOLL
WRITTEN BY HERSELF. (M. FISHER, ED)
K. TILLOTSON, 155:JAN69-42
HORNE, T.H. AN INTRODUCTION TO THE
STUDY OF BIBLIOGRAPHY.
J.D. FLEEMAN, 503:AUTUMN69-127
HORNER, A. SIRIUS, DOG STAR.
617(TLS):15SEP72-1071
HORNSBY, R.A. PATTERNS OF ACTION IN "THE
AENEID."
M.C.J. PUTNAM, 124:FEB71-204
HORNUNG, C.P., ED. TREASURY OF AMERICAN
DESIGN.
H. KRAMER, 441:3DEC72-4
HORNUNG, E.W. RAFFLES.
D.A.N. JONES, 362:31AUG72-280
HOROVITZ, M., ED. CHILDREN OF ALBION.
E. LUCIE-SMITH, 493:SPRING70-77
M. RICHARDS, 381:VOL29#1-122
HOROVITZ, M. THE WOLVERHAMPTON WANDERER.
J. FULLER, 362:24FEB72-251

HOROWITZ, D. EMPIRE AND REVOLUTION.
J. SCHIEBEL, 32:DEC71-883
HOROWITZ, I.L. PROFESSING SOCIOLOGY.
D.C. HODGES, 484(PPR):MAR70-465
HORSBURGH, H.J.N. MAHATMA GANDHI.
617(TLS):21APR72-457
HORSBURGH, H.J.N. NON-VIOLENCE AND
AGGRESSION.
M. PITTOCK, 97(CQ):SUMMER68-287
HORSFALL, J. THE IRON MASTER OF PENNS,
1720-1970.
617(TLS):25FEB72-229
HORSFIELD, B. & P.B. STONE. THE GREAT
OCEAN BUSINESS.
D. MC KENZIE, 362:27JAN72-119
617(TLS):30JUN72-754
HORSLEY, I. FUGUE.
G. LEFKOFF, 308:SPRING67-152
HORST, L. PRE-CLASSIC DANCE FORMS.
J. DE LABAN, 290(JAAC):SUMMER70-556
HORTENBACH, J.C. FREIHEITSSTREBEN UND
DESTRUKTIVITÄT.
W.A. BERENDSOHN, 462(OL):VOL23#4-327
B. LIDE, 400(MLN):OCT70-761
HORTON, J. MENDELSSOHN CHAMBER MUSIC.
617(TLS):21JUL72-853
VON HORVÁTH, Ö. GESAMMELTE WERKE. (D.
HILDEBRANDT, W. HUDER & T. KRISCHKE,
EDS)
617(TLS):30JUN72-756
HORVATH, T. CARITAS EST IN RATIONE.
P. SCHMITZ, 589:APR71-382
HORVATH, V.M. ANDRÉ MALRAUX.*
W.G. LANGLOIS, 399(MLJ):DEC70-615
HORWOOD, H. NEWFOUNDLAND.*
G.M. STORY, 627(UTQ):JUL70-379
HORWOOD, H. WHITE ESKIMOS.
M. LEVIN, 441:5NOV72-40
HOSEGOOD, L. THE MINOTAUR GARDEN.
J. HUNTER, 362:1JUN72-736
M. LEVIN, 441:29OCT72-58
HOSLEY, R. - SEE HOLINSHED, R.
HOSLEY, R., A.C. KIRSCH & J.W. VELZ - SEE
MC MANAWAY, J.G.
HOTCHNER, A.E. KING OF THE HILL.
M. LEVIN, 441:13AUG72-31
442(NY):9SEP72-124
HOTZENKÖCHERLE, R., ED. SPRACHATLAS DER
DEUTSCHEN SCHWEIZ. (VOL 4)
R.E. KELLER, 402(MLR):APR71-424
HOUGH, G. STYLE AND STYLISTICS.
F.W. BATESON, 184(EIC):APR70-264
HOUGH, J.F. THE SOVIET PREFECTS.*
M. MC CAULEY, 575(SEER):JAN71-165
HOUGH, R. THE BLIND HORN'S HATE.*
442(NY):15JAN72-92
HOUGHTON, H. OPERATION PORTLAND.
617(TLS):28JUL72-866
"THE HOUGHTON LIBRARY, 1942-1967."
D.F. FOXON, 354:SEP69-255
HOURANI, A.H. & S.M. STERN, EDS. THE
ISLAMIC CITY.
R.W. BULLIET, 589:APR71-385
HOURD, M.L. RELATIONSHIP IN LEARNING.
617(TLS):13OCT72-1236
HOUSBY, T. THE RUBBY-DUBBY TRAIL.
617(TLS):28JUL72-900
HOUSE, M. & G. STOREY - SEE DICKENS, C.
HOUSEHOLD, G. THE THREE SENTINELS.
A. BROYARD, 441:12MAY72-43
M. LEVIN, 441:18JUN72-30
617(TLS):8DEC72-1507
HOUSEMAN, J. RUN-THROUGH.
W. KERR, 441:19MAR72-1
C. LEHMANN-HAUPT, 441:6MAR72-35
N.R. TEITEL, 561(SATR):11MAR72-61
V. THOMSON, 453:4MAY72-38

HOUSMAN, A.E. THE CONFINES OF CRITICISM.
(J. CARTER, ED)
J. COLMER, 67:MAY71-118
G.P. GOOLD, 487:WINTER70-369
A.S.F. GOW, 123:DEC70-394
639(VQR):SPRING70-LX
HOUSMAN, A.E. THE LETTERS OF A.E. HOUS-
MAN.* (H. MAAS, ED)
W.H. AUDEN, 442(NY):19FEB72-111
W. WHITE, 70(ANQ):JAN72-78
HOUSSAYE, A. MAN ABOUT PARIS. (H.
KNEPLER, ED & TRANS)
617(TLS):25FEB72-211
HOUSTON, C.O., ED. PROCEEDINGS OF THE
FIRST NATIONAL COLLOQUIUM ON THE PHILI-
PPINES.
R.W. LIEBAN, 293(JAST):AUG70-992
HOUSTON, J.P. THE DEMONIC IMAGINATION.
A.J. WRIGHT, JR., 207(FR):FEB70-517
"HOW TO MAKE YOUR HOME MORE CONVENIENT."
B. GLADSTONE, 441:3DEC72-98
HOWARD, C.H.D. SPLENDID ISOLATION.*
R.L. TIGNOR, 637(VS):JUN70-421
HOWARD, D. - SEE LUXEMBURG, R.
HOWARD, D.F. - SEE BUTLER, S.
HOWARD, D.R. THE THREE TEMPTATIONS.*
H. NEWSTEAD, 545(RPH):NOV70-349
HOWARD, D.R. - SEE POPE INNOCENT III
HOWARD, D.R. & C.K. ZACHER, EDS. CRITI-
CAL STUDIES OF SIR GAWAIN AND THE
GREEN KNIGHT.
S.S. HUSSEY, 447(N&Q):DEC70-471
HOWARD, E.J. ODD GIRL OUT.
A. BROYARD, 441:11FEB72-39
M. ELLMANN, 362:30MAR72-428
H. KEYISHIAN, 440:30JAN72-10
M. LEVIN, 441:30JAN72-26
442(NY):26FEB72-102
617(TLS):24MAR72-326
HOWARD, F. & B. GUNSTON. THE CONQUEST
OF THE AIR.
617(TLS):6OCT72-1205
HOWARD, J.W. MR. JUSTICE MURPHY.
F.H. HELLER, 330(MASJ):FALL69-85
HOWARD, M. THE CONTINENTAL COMMITMENT.
E. YOUNG, 362:1JUN72-732
617(TLS):30JUN72-733
HOWARD, M. GRAND STRATEGY. (VOL 4)
617(TLS):25FEB72-205
HOWARD, O.O. MY LIFE AND EXPERIENCES
AMONG OUR HOSTILE INDIANS.
M. ROGIN, 441:24DEC72-4
HOWARD, P. THE OPERAS OF BENJAMIN BRIT-
TEN.*
M. PETERSON, 470:NOV69-51
S. WALSH, 607:SUMMER69-35
HOWARD, R. ALONE WITH AMERICA.*
F. MORAMARCO, 651(WHR):WINTER71-95
42(AR):WINTER69/70-591
639(VQR):AUTUMN70-CXXXVI
HOWARD, R. FINDINGS.*
H. CARRUTH, 249(HUDR):SUMMER71-329
R.B. SHAW, 491:MAR72-342
HOWARD, R. UNTITLED SUBJECTS.*
G.S. FRASER, 473(PR):WINTER71/72-469
HOWARD, R. - SEE BUTOR, M.
HOWARD, T. THE DEAR RUIN.
M. LEVIN, 441:8OCT72-42
HOWARD-HILL, T.H. BIBLIOGRAPHY OF BRIT-
ISH LITERARY BIBLIOGRAPHIES.
L.M. HARRISON, 355:MAY69-164
G. WAKEMAN, 503:SUMMER69-88
HOWARD-HILL, T.H., ED. OXFORD SHAKE-
SPEARE CONCORDANCES: CORIOLANUS;
TROILUS AND CRESSIDA; ROMEO AND JULIET;
TITUS ANDRONICUS; ANTONY AND CLEOPATRA;
PERICLES; OTHELLO; MACBETH; KING LEAR;
[CONTINUED]

151

[CONTINUING]
   JULIUS CAESAR; TIMON OF ATHENS.
      617(TLS):14APR72-412
HOWARD-HILL, T.H., ED. OXFORD SHAKE-
   SPEARE CONCORDANCES: THE TEMPEST AND
   THE TWO GENTLEMEN OF VERONA.
      A.C. PARTRIDGE, 180(ESA):SEP70-411
HOWARTH, D. TRAFALGAR.
      D. UNDERDOWN, 639(VQR):SPRING70-361
HOWARTH, W.L. - SEE STOWELL, R.F.
HOWAT, J.K. THE HUDSON RIVER AND ITS
   PAINTERS.
      T. LASK, 441:8SEP72-36
      J. SEELYE, 441:30JUL72-6
      E. WEEKS, 61:SEP72-108
HOWE, B. ARBITER OF ELEGANCE.
      E. MOERS, 637(VS):MAR70-370
HOWE, E. THE MAGICIANS OF THE GOLDEN
   DAWN.
      617(TLS):10NOV72-1370
HOWE, I. DECLINE OF THE NEW.*
      E. THOMAS, 364:JUN/JUL71-158
HOWE, I., ED. THE WORLD OF THE BLUE-
   COLLAR WORKER.
      N. BIRNBAUM, 441:26NOV72-2
HOWE, I. & E. GREENBERG, EDS. VOICES
   FROM THE YIDDISH.
      441:16JUL72-14
HOWE, Q. ASHES OF VICTORY.
      J. TOLAND, 441:10SEP72-6
      442(NY):23SEP72-133
HOWE, R. REGIONAL ITALIAN COOKERY.
      617(TLS):15DEC72-1541
HOWELL, A. IMRUIL.
      P. LESTER, 493:AUTUMN70-250
HOWELL, G. A HISTORY OF THE WORKING
   MEN'S ASSOCIATION FROM 1836 TO 1850.
   (D.J. ROWE, ED)
      617(TLS):9JUN72-667
HOWELLS, W.D. THE RISE OF SILAS LAPHAM.
   (W.J. MESERVE, ED) A CHANCE ACQUAINT-
   ANCE. (J. THOMAS & D.J. NORDLOH, EDS)
      J. SCHIFFMAN, 27(AL):JAN72-663
HOWELLS, W.D. THE SON OF ROYAL LANG-
   BRITH.* (D. BURROWS, WITH R. GOTTES-
   MAN & D.J. NORDLOH, EDS) THE SHADOW
   OF A DREAM [AND] AN IMPERATIVE DUTY.*
   (M. BANTA, WITH R. GOTTESMAN & D.J.
   NORDLOH, EDS)
      C.L. ANDERSON, 579(SAQ):WINTER71-128
HOWELLS, W.D. THEIR WEDDING JOURNEY.
   (J.K. REEVES, ED)
      B. HARDY, 447(N&Q):NOV70-440
HOWES, F. FOLK MUSIC OF BRITAIN - AND
   BEYOND.*
      J. RIMMER, 415:MAY70-505
HOWES, F. OXFORD CONCERTS.
      A. PORTER, 415:MAR70-281
HOWES, R.C., ED & TRANS. THE TESTAMENTS
   OF THE GRAND PRINCES OF MOSCOW.
      O.P. BACKUS 3D, 575(SEER):APR71-297
HOWITH, H. FRAGMENTS OF THE DANCE.
      D. BARBOUR, 150(DR):SPRING70-112
      A. SHUCARD, 102(CANL):SPRING71-80
HOWSON, G. THIEF-TAKER GENERAL.
      566:SPRING71-71
HOY, P. CAMUS IN ENGLISH.
      I.H. WALKER, 208(FS):JAN71-112
HOYEM, A. ARTICLES.
      R.B. SHAW, 491:MAR72-342
HOYER, L.G. ENCHANTMENT.*
      W.H. PRITCHARD, 249(HUDR):SUMMER71-
      359
HOYLE, F. THE NEW FACE OF SCIENCE.
      E. EDELSON, 440:16JAN72-5
HOYLES, J. THE WANING OF THE RENAISSANCE
   1640-1740.
      A.O. ALDRIDGE, 319:JUL72-361

HOYT, E.P. THE NIXONS.
      P. ADAMS, 61:JUL72-96
      R.R. LINGEMAN, 441:4JUN72-1
HROTSVITHA OF GANDERSHEIM. HROTSVITHAE
   OPERA.* (H. HOMEYER, ED)
      P. DRONKE, 382(MAE):1971/2-185
      L.B. WARREN, 124:DEC70-135
HSIA, A. D.H. LAWRENCE.
      M. ALLOTT, 677:VOL2-327
HSIA, C.T. THE CLASSIC CHINESE NOVEL.
      H.C. CHUANG, 141:SPRING69-206
      P. HANAN, 244(HJAS):VOL29-294
HSIA, C.T., WITH J.S.M. LAU, EDS. TWEN-
   TIETH-CENTURY CHINESE STORIES.
      617(TLS):19MAY72-573
HSIA, T-A. THE GATE OF DARKNESS.
      M. GOLDMAN, 293(JAST):NOV69-155
      L.O. LEE, 244(HJAS):VOL29-309
      I. LO, 141:WINTER70-68
HSIAO, T-L. THE LAND REVOLUTION IN
   CHINA, 1930-1934.
      W. KLATT, 293(JAST):AUG70-923
HSÜ, I.C.Y. THE RISE OF MODERN CHINA.*
      639(VQR):AUTUMN70-CL
HTIN AUNG, M., ED & TRANS. EPISTLES
   WRITTEN ON THE EVE OF THE ANGLO-BURMESE
   WAR.
      J. OKELL, 318(JAOS):APR-JUN70-397
HTIN AUNG, M. A HISTORY OF BURMA.
      J.F. CADY, 318(JAOS):APR-JUN70-396
HUAN, M. - SEE UNDER MA HUAN
HUART, P. LE VOCABULAIRE DE L'ANALYSE
   PSYCHOLOGIQUE DANS L'OEUVRE DE THUCY-
   DIDE.
      A. PARRY, 124:JAN71-158
      F.M. WASSERMANN, 121(CJ):FEB-MAR71-
      282
      R. WEIL, 555:VOL44FASC2-316
      H.D. WESTLAKE, 123:DEC70-307
HUBAY, I. INCUNABULA EICHSTÄTTER BIBLIO-
   THEKEN.
      V. SCHOLDERER, 354:JUN69-165
HUBBARD, P.M. THE WHISPER IN THE GLEN.
      N. CALLENDAR, 441:7MAY72-34
HUBBARD, R.H. RIDEAU HALL.
      J.C. FREEMAN, 576:MAY68-154
HUBBELL, J.B. WHO ARE THE MAJOR AMERICAN
   WRITERS?
      C. LEHMANN-HAUPT, 441:30MAR72-39
HUBER, P., ED. ATHOS.
      E. VON IVÁNKA, 182:VOL23#3-66
HUBER, R.M. THE AMERICAN IDEA OF SUC-
   CESS.
      441:23APR72-10
HUBERT, J., J. PORCHER & W.F. VOLBACH.
   THE CAROLINGIAN RENAISSANCE.
      J.G. PLANTE, 363:AUG70-134
HUBMANN, F. THE HABSBURG EMPIRE.
      617(TLS):21APR72-458
HÜBNER, G.E. KIRCHENLIEDREZEPTION UND
   REZEPTIONSWEGFORSCHUNG.
      J.S. ANDREWS, 220(GL&L):JUL71-388
HUBSCHMID, J. THESAURUS PRAEROMANICUS.
   (FASC 1&2)
      Y. MALKIEL, 350:JUN71-465
HUCHEL, P. GEZÄHLTE TAGE.
      617(TLS):29DEC72-1572
HUCKABY, G. CITY, UNCITY.
      J.A. BORRECA, 363:FEB70-74
HUCKER, C.O. CHINESE GOVERNMENT IN MING
   TIMES.
      R.B. CRAWFORD, 293(JAST):AUG70-917
HUDDLESTON, R.D. THE SENTENCE IN WRITTEN
   ENGLISH.
      617(TLS):7JAN72-21
HUDSON, B. 150 CAREERS IN PHOTOGRAPHY.
      617(TLS):8DEC72-1513

HUDSON, D. MUNBY.
  W.H. AUDEN, 453:19OCT72-6
  J. CAREY, 362:6APR72-455
  J. CLIVE, 441:29OCT72-7
  617(TLS):7APR72-388
HUDSON, G.W. PARADISE LOST: A CONCOR-
  DANCE.
  J.M.P., 568(SCN):WINTER71-64
HUDSON, K. PATRIOTISM WITH PROFIT.
  617(TLS):29DEC71-1590
HUDSON, L. THE CULT OF THE FACT.
  M. WARNOCK, 362:6JUL72-20
  617(TLS):11AUG72-939
HUDSON, R.A. ENGLISH COMPLEX SENTENCES.
  617(TLS):7JAN72-21
HUDSON, W.D. REASON AND RIGHT.
  P. JONES, 518:MAY71-12
HUEBENER, T. THE LITERATURE OF EAST
  GERMANY.*
  L.H. LEGTERS, 32:JUN71-453
HUEBNER, K. ÜBER DAS SCHÖNE UND DAS
  DEFORMIERTE.
  K. MITCHELLS, 89(BJA):WINTER71-97
HUESMANN, H. SHAKESPEARE-INSZENIERUNGEN
  UNTER GOETHE IN WEIMAR.
  W.H. BRUFORD, 220(GL&L):OCT70-116
  J. WESTLAKE, 402(MLR):APR71-389
HUET, P.D. TRAITÉ DE L'ORIGINE DES
  ROMANS (1670).
  K.G. KNIGHT, 220(GL&L):OCT70-111
HUFF, M.N. ROBERT PENN WARREN: A BIBLI-
  OGRAPHY.
  J. GRIMSHAW, 517(PBSA):APR-JUN71-188
HUFNAGL, E., WITH A. CRAIG-BENNETT. LIB-
  YAN MAMMALS.
  617(TLS):24MAR72-345
HÜFNER, A. BRECHT IN FRANKREICH, 1930-
  1963.
  S. STERNLICHT, 131(CL):SPRING71-185
  A. SUBIOTTO, 220(GL&L):APR71-289
HUGGETT, F.E. HOW IT HAPPENED.
  617(TLS):14JAN72-49
HUGGETT, F.E. THE MODERN NETHERLANDS.
  617(TLS):11AUG72-941
HUGGINS, N.I. HARLEM RENAISSANCE.
  G.E. KENT, 441:2JAN72-4
  617(TLS):9JUN72-656
HUGHES, G. NEIGHBOURS.*
  P. LESTER, 493:AUTUMN70-250
HUGHES, G. REST THE POOR STRUGGLER.
  617(TLS):20OCT72-1249
HUGHES, G. SIDELIGHTS ON A CENTURY OF
  MUSIC (1825-1924).*
  G. ABRAHAM, 415:JAN70-46
HUGHES, L., ED. NEW NEGRO POETS: USA.
  N. JACOBS, 447(N&Q):DEC70-476
HUGHES, M.R. - SEE MUMFORD, L. & F.J.
  OSBORN
HUGHES, P.L. & J.F. LARKIN, EDS. TUDOR
  ROYAL PROCLAMATIONS. (VOLS 2&3)
  P. CHRISTIANSON, 529(QQ):AUTUMN70-471
HUGHES, R. BEETHOVEN.
  S. SADIE, 415:DEC70-1225
HUGHES, R. FOREIGN DEVIL.
  617(TLS):20OCT72-1244
HUGHES, R. HEAVEN AND HELL IN WESTERN
  ART.
  R.W. LIGHTBOWN, 39:OCT69-355
  592:NOV68-232
HUGHES, S. THE ART OF COARSE ENTERTAIN-
  ING.
  617(TLS):15DEC72-1541
HUGHES, T. CROW.*
  H. CARRUTH, 249(HUDR):SUMMER71-327
  G.S. FRASER, 473(PR):WINTER71/72-469
  C. KIZER, 491:FEB72-291
HUGHES, T. WODWO.*
  R. MARIELS, 448:SUMMER68-125

HUGHES, T. & B. ENGLISH PAINTED ENAMELS.
  G. WILLS, 39:JUN69-488
HUGHEY, R. JOHN HARINGTON OF STEPNEY.
  617(TLS):14APR72-417
HUGO, L. BERNARD SHAW.
  617(TLS):4AUG72-917
HUGO, R. GOOD LUCK IN CRACKED ITALIAN.
  R. HOWARD, 491:OCT71-34
  E.L. MAYO, 448:SUMMER70-115
HUGO, V. LES MISÉRABLES. (M.F. GUYARD,
  ED) LA LÉGENDE DES SIÈCLES. (J. TRU-
  CHET, ED)
  J-P. RICHARD, 98:MAY69-387
"HUGO'S WHEN IN ITALY."
  M. BORELLI, 399(MLJ):OCT70-472
HUIZINGA, J. LA CIVILTÀ OLANDESE DEL
  SEICENTO.
  F. DE MICHELIS, 548(RCSF):APR-JUN68-
  234
HUIZINGA, J. HOMO LUDENS.
  J. EHRMANN, 98:JUL69-579
HULCOOP, J. THREE RING CIRCUS SONGS.
  H. MAC CALLUM, 627(UTQ):JUL69-348
HULLEY, K.K. & S.T. VANDERSALL - SEE OVID
HULTBERG, H. SEMANTISK LITTERATURBE-
  TRAGTNING.
  J.L. SAMMONS, 563(SS):SPRING71-196
"THE HUMAN AGENT."
  A.P. GRIFFITHS, 479(PHQ):JAN70-87
"HUMANISME ACTIF: MÉLANGES D'ART ET DE
  LITTÉRATURE OFFERTS À JULIEN CAIN."
  R.A. SAYCE, 354:SEP69-253
HUMBERT-DROZ, J. DIX ANS DE LUTTE ANTI-
  FASCISTE 1931-1941.
  617(TLS):29SEP72-1158
DE HUMBOLDT, G. DE L'ORIGINE DES FORMES
  GRAMMATICALES, SUIVI DE LETTRE À M.
  ABEL RÉMUSAT.
  N.C.W. SPENCE, 208(FS):OCT71-503
HUME, B. DEATH AND THE MINES.*
  K.W. CLAWSON, 440:23JAN72-4
  T. GOLDWASSER, 561(SATR):1APR72-82
HUME, I.N. A GUIDE TO ARTIFACTS OF
  COLONIAL AMERICA.
  C. CARSON, 656(WMQ):OCT70-684
HUME, R.D. DRYDEN'S CRITICISM.*
  J.R. CLARK, 568(SCN):WINTER71-73
  P.K. ELKIN, 67:NOV71-210
HUMMEL, A. EMINENT CHINESE OF THE CH'ING
  PERIOD.
  M. BERNAL, 453:23MAR72-31
"DORIS HUMPHREY: AN ARTIST FIRST." (ED &
  COMPLETED BY S.J. COHEN)
  T. LASK, 441:9DEC72-37
HUMPHREY, J. ARGUMENT FOR LOVE.
  J. NAIDEN, 491:MAY72-116
HUMPHREYS, C. THE BUDDHIST WAY OF LIFE.
  P.J.H., 543:DEC69-348
HUMPHREYS, C. A WESTERN APPROACH TO ZEN.
  617(TLS):14JUL72-823
HUMPHRIES, C. & W.C. SMITH. MUSIC PUB-
  LISHING IN THE BRITISH ISLES. (2ND ED)
  S. SADIE, 415:AUG70-807
HUMPHRY, D., WITH G. JOHN. POLICE POWER
  AND BLACK PEOPLE.
  617(TLS):20OCT72-1260
HUNEBELLE, D. DEAR HENRY.
  R.R. LINGEMAN, 441:16JUL72-3
  I.F. STONE, 453:19OCT72-12
HUNGER, H. & O. KRESTEN. ÖSTERREICHISCHE
  NATIONALBIBLIOTHEK: KATALOG DER GRIECH-
  ISCHEN HANDSCHRIFTEN. (VOL 2)
  N.G. WILSON, 303:VOL90-238
HUNKEMÖLLER, J. W.A. MOZARTS FRÜHE
  SONATEN FÜR VIOLINE UND KLAVIER.
  A.H. KING, 182:VOL23#23/24-993
HUNKIN, H. THERE IS NO FINALITY.
  J. MURRAY, 99:MAY72-66

153

HUNNISETT, R.F. INDEXING FOR EDITORS.
617(TLS):22SEP72-1124
HUNT, H.D. HANNIBAL HAMLIN OF MAINE.
K.B. SHOVER, 432(NEQ):JUN70-307
HUNT, J.D., ED. POPE: "THE RAPE OF THE
LOCK."
566:SPRING71-71
HUNT, J.D. THE PRE-RAPHAELITE IMAGINA-
TION, 1848-1900.*
J.B. GORDON, 637(VS):MAR70-358
T. HILTON, 592:MAR69-152
L. STEVENSON, 191(ELN):SEP70-63
R.G. THOMAS, 541(RES):NOV70-530
J.R. WATSON, 148:AUTUMN70-287
HUNT, L. TWENTY-ONE SQUADRONS.
617(TLS):15DEC72-1541
HUNT, M. THE MUGGING.
L.J. DAVIS, 440:21MAY72-4
G.V. HIGGINS, 441:21MAY72-3
S. KLEIN, 561(SATR):1JUL72-54
442(NY):15JUL72-83
HUNT, N., ED. CLUNIAC MONASTICISM IN THE
CENTRAL MIDDLE AGES.
617(TLS):26MAY72-608
HUNT, R. THE SHADOWLESS LAMP.
617(TLS):14JAN72-49
HUNTER, A.C. LEXIQUE DE LA LANGUE DE
JEAN CHAPELAIN.
A. FOULET, 545(RPH):FEB71-559
HUNTER, E. EVERY LITTLE CROOK AND NANNY.
M. LEVIN, 441:16APR72-30
617(TLS):14JUL72-793
HUNTER, E. LAST SUMMER.
J. WESTON, 50(ARQ):SPRING69-81
HUNTER, E. SEVEN.
J. HUNTER, 362:27JUL72-118
HUNTER, G.K. - SEE SHAKESPEARE, W.
HUNTER, G.K. - SEE WILSON, F.P.
HUNTER, H. SOVIET TRANSPORT EXPERIENCE.*
M. BORNSTEIN, 550(RUSR):APR70-231
HUNTER, J.P. THE RELUCTANT PILGRIM.
F. WÖLCKEN, 38:BAND87HEFT1-97
HUNTER, R. EREBUS.*
K.J. ATCHITY, 340(KR):1969/5-675
G. ROPER, 627(UTQ):JUL69-359
HUNTER, R.G. SHAKESPEARE AND THE COMEDY
OF FORGIVENESS.
R.F. HILL, 570(SQ):WINTER68-93
M. MINCOFF, 179(ES):FEB70-61
HUNTER, W.B., C.A. PATRIDES & J.H. ADAM-
SON. BRIGHT ESSENCE.
P. SHERIDAN, 109:SPRING/SUMMER72-147
HUNTFORD, R. THE NEW TOTALITARIANS.
P.B. AUSTIN, 441:27FEB72-6
617(TLS):2JUN72-626
HUNTLEY, F.L. JEREMY TAYLOR AND THE
GREAT REBELLION.
K.S. DAVIS, 385(MQR):SPRING72-143
K. KOLLAR, 568(SCN):WINTER71-76
HUNTLEY, H.R. THE ALIEN PROTAGONIST OF
FORD MADOX FORD.*
G. CORE, 598(SOR):AUTUMN72-956
J. FEASTER, 295:VOL2#3-417
HUOT, J-L. PERSIA I.*
E. PORADA, 57:VOL31#1-95
HUPPÉ, B.F. THE WEB OF WORDS.
A. CAMERON, 589:APR71-383
HURD, D. THE ARROW WAR.
P.A. KUHN, 637(VS):MAR70-367
HURD, D. TRUTH GAME.
N. CALLENDAR, 441:17DEC72-23
617(TLS):25AUG72-1005
HURD, M. MENDELSSOHN.
M.J.E. BROWN, 415:NOV70-1109
HURD, M. VAUGHAN WILLIAMS.
H. OTTAWAY, 415:MAY70-505

HUREWITZ, J.C., ED. SOVIET-AMERICAN
RIVALRY IN THE MIDDLE EAST.*
G. RENTZ, 550(RUSR):APR70-232
HURLIMANN, B. PICTURE-BOOK WORLD.
F.P.P., 503:AUTUMN69-126
HURST, M. JOSEPH CHAMBERLAIN AND LIBERAL
REUNION.
G.R. SEARLE, 637(VS):DEC69-235
HURSTFIELD, J. & A.G.R. SMITH, EDS.
ELIZABETHAN PEOPLE.
617(TLS):22SEP72-1124
HURWITZ, A.B. & A. GODDARD. GAMES TO
IMPROVE YOUR CHILD'S ENGLISH.
617(TLS):14JUL72-825
HURWOOD, B.J. PASSPORT TO THE SUPERNAT-
URAL.
T. STURGEON, 441:3SEP72-20
HUSÁK, G. SVEDECTVO O SLOVENSKOM NÁROD-
NOM POVSTANÍ. (2ND ED)
V.S. MAMATEY, 32:SEP71-681
HUSSAIN, F. LE JUGEMENT ESTHÉTIQUES.
V.M. AMES, 290(JAAC):SUMMER70-559
HUSSERL, E. LOGICAL INVESTIGATIONS.*
W.V. DONIELA, 63:AUG71-227
D.M. LEVIN, 311(JP):13JUL72-384
W. MAYS, 518:JAN71-13
HUSSERL, E. ZUR PHÄNOMENOLOGIE DES
INNEREN ZEITBEWUSSTSEINS (1893-1917).
(R. BOEHM, ED) ANALYSEN ZUR PASSIVEN
SYNTHESIS (1918-1926). (M. FLEISCHER,
ED) LEÇONS POUR UNE PHÉNOMÉNOLOGIE DE
LA CONSCIENCE INTIME DU TEMPS.
M. RICHIR, 98:AUG-SEP69-778
HUSSEY, C. ENGLISH GARDENS AND LAND-
SCAPES 1700-1750.
G.B. TATUM, 54:SEP69-304
HUSSEY, J.M., WITH D.M. NICOL & G. COWAN,
EDS. THE CAMBRIDGE MEDIEVAL HISTORY.*
(VOL 4, PTS 1&2)
P.J. ALEXANDER, 32:SEP71-635
J. MEYENDORFF, 32:SEP71-619
I. ŠEVČENKO, 32:SEP71-624
HUSSEY, M., ED. CHAUCER'S WORLD.
P.M. VERMEER, 179(ES):DEC69-607
HUSSEY, M. THE WORLD OF SHAKESPEARE AND
HIS CONTEMPORARIES.
617(TLS):4FEB72-137
HUSSEY, R.F. MURDERER SCOT-FREE.
617(TLS):11FEB72-165
HUSSEY, S.S., ED. PIERS PLOWMAN.
J. LAWLOR, 677:VOL2-237
HUSSON, G. - SEE LUCIAN
HUTCHESON, F. ILLUSTRATIONS ON THE MORAL
SENSE. (B. PEACH, ED)
D.F. NORTON, 319:JAN72-96
HUTCHINGS, R.J. DICKENS ON AN ISLAND.
A.B., 155:SEP70-244
HUTCHINS, M. TYPOGRAPHICS.
D.A. HARROP, 355:JUL69-226
HUTCHINS, T. AN HISTORICAL NARRATIVE AND
TOPOGRAPHICAL DESCRIPTION OF LOUISIANA
AND WEST-FLORIDA.
R.R. REA, 9(ALAR):OCT69-289
HUTCHINSON, C.A. FRONTIER SETTLEMENT IN
MEXICAN CALIFORNIA.
639(VQR):WINTER70-XXII
HUTCHINSON, J. BRITISH WILD FLOWERS.
617(TLS):2JUN72-641
HUTCHINSON, R. - SEE BRADSTREET, A.
HUTCHINSON, W.T. & W.M.E. RACHAL - SEE
MADISON, J.
HUTCHISON, H.H. EDWARD II.
442(NY):29APR72-141
HUTCHISON, S.C. HISTORY OF THE ROYAL
ACADEMY 1768-1968.*
I. DUNLOP, 592:JUL/AUG68-54
HUTH, A. VIRGINIA FLY IS DROWNING.
J.G. FARRELL, 362:7SEP72-312

HUTT, A. FOURNIER.
617(TLS):3NOV72-1348
HUTTER, I. EARLY CHRISTIAN AND BYZANTINE
ART.
W.C. LOERKE, 32:SEP71-658
HUTTON, H. THE TECHNIQUE OF COLLAGE.
J. BRODY, 139:JAN-FEB69-9
HUTTON, J.B. THE GREAT ILLUSION.
617(TLS):30JUN72-757
HUTTON, J.B. THE SUBVERTERS OF LIBERTY.
617(TLS):2JUN72-641
HUXLEY, A. THE COLLECTED POETRY OF
ALDOUS HUXLEY.* (D. WATT, ED)
P. MURRAY, 491:JUL72-230
HUXLEY, F. THE INVISIBLES.
639(VQR):SPRING70-LXXI
HUXLEY, G.L. GREEK EPIC POETRY FROM
EUMELOS TO PANYASSIS.
C.R. BEYE, 124:NOV70-86
W. MC LEOD, 487:AUTUMN70-261
M.L. WEST, 123:MAR71-67
HUXLEY, H.H., ED. COROLLA CAMENAE.
J.F. GUMMERE, 124:NOV70-94
J.I.J., 568(SCN):SUMMER/AUTUMN71-58
E.J. KENNEY, 123:MAR71-74
HUYBRECHTS, A. TRANSPORTS ET STRUCTURES
DE DÉVELOPPEMENT AU CONGO.
J. COMTE, 182:VOL23#13/14-659
HUYSSEN, A. DIE FRÜHROMANTISCHE KONZEP-
TION VON ÜBERSETZUNG UND ANEIGNUNG.
R. IMMERWAHR, 301(JEGP):APR71-350
N.H. SMITH, 182:VOL23#23/24-982
HWANG SUN-WON. DESCENDANTS OF CAIN.
270:VOL20#4-97
HYAM, R. ELGIN AND CHURCHILL AT THE
COLONIAL OFFICE, 1905-1908.
B. PORTER, 637(VS):JUN70-444
HYAMS, E. ANIMALS IN THE SERVICE OF MAN.
617(TLS):2JUN72-641
HYAMS, E. PLANTS IN THE SERVICE OF MAN.
617(TLS):4FEB72-137
HYAMS, J. BOGIE.
617(TLS):2JUN72-635
HYDE, H.M. HENRY JAMES AT HOME.*
639(VQR):WINTER70-XX
HYDE, H.M. STALIN.*
R.C. TUCKER, 441:19MAR72-35
442(NY):15JAN72-91
HYDE, R. THE GODWITS FLY. (G. RAWLIN-
SON, ED)
K.L. GOODWIN, 67:MAY71-122
HYDE-THOMPSON, R. THE ALTERNATIVE.
617(TLS):28JAN72-85
HYDER, C.K. - SEE SWINBURNE, A.C.
HYMAN, A. THE RISE AND FALL OF HORATIO
BOTTOMLEY.
617(TLS):21APR72-435
HYMAN, L. THE JEWS OF IRELAND.
617(TLS):15DEC72-1526
HYMAN, L.W. ANDREW MARVELL.
M.S. RØSTVIG, 179(ES):OCT70-458
HYMAN, R. DISPUTES PROCEDURE IN ACTION.
617(TLS):23JUN72-724
HYMAN, R. STRIKES.
K. HINDELL, 362:21SEP72-375
617(TLS):15SEP72-1051
HYMAN, S.E. IAGO.*
M. LEBOWITZ, 598(SOR):SUMMER72-696
HYMANS, J.L. LÉOPOLD SÉDAR SENGHOR.
617(TLS):3NOV72-1313
HYMES, D.H., WITH W.E. BITTLE, EDS.
STUDIES IN SOUTHWESTERN ETHNOLINGUIS-
TICS.
D.A. BARTHOLOMEW, 361:VOL23#1-66
HYNEK, J.A. THE UFO EXPERIENCE.
617(TLS):17NOV72-1401
HYNES, S. EDWARDIAN OCCASIONS.
617(TLS):10NOV72-1362

HYNES, S. THE EDWARDIAN TURN OF MIND.*
B. BERGONZI, 191(ELN):SEP69-68
HYNES, S. - SEE CAUDWELL, C.
HYPSICLES. HYPSIKLES: DIE AUFGANGSZEITEN
DER GESTIRNE. (V. DE FALCO & M.
KRAUSE, EDS & TRANS)
G.J. TOOMER, 318(JAOS):APR-JUN70-298
HYSLOP, L.B., ED. BAUDELAIRE AS A LOVE
POET, AND OTHER ESSAYS.
A. FAIRLIE, 208(FS):OCT71-477
G.D. SAUNDERS, 402(MLR):JAN71-192

I FAN. COMMUNIST CHINESE ECONOMY UNDER
THE CULTURAL REVOLUTION.
N. SUN, 293(JAST):FEB70-440
IAKOVLEV, N.N. FRANKLIN RUSVEL'T. (2ND
ED)
K.W. RYAVEC, 32:JUN71-366
IANNI, F.A.J. A FAMILY BUSINESS.
F. FERRETTI, 441:16JUL72-7
IANNUZZI, J.N. SICILIAN DEFENSE.
N. CALLENDAR, 441:2JUL72-15
IBN 'ARABĪ. SUFIS OF ANDALUSIA.
617(TLS):28JAN72-92
IBN KHALDUN. DISCOURS SUR L'HISTOIRE
UNIVERSELLE (AL-MUQADDIMA). (V. MON-
TEIL, TRANS) VOYAGES D'IBN BATTÛTA.
(C. DEFRÉMERY, B.R. SANGUINETTI & V.
MONTEIL, EDS & TRANS)
A. MIQUEL, 98:AUG-SEP69-826
IBSEN, H. THE OXFORD IBSEN. (VOL 3)
(J.W. MC FARLANE, ED)
617(TLS):1SEP72-1014
IBUSE, M. BLACK RAIN.*
I. WEDDE, 364:OCT/NOV71-149
ICHIKAWA, S. & OTHERS, EDS. THE KENKY-
USHA DICTIONARY OF CURRENT ENGLISH
IDIOMS.
N.E. OSSELTON, 179(ES):JUN70-282
ICHON, A. LA RELIGION DES TOTONAQUES
DE LA SIERRA.
R. FREISE, 182:VOL23#10-571
IGLESIA, R. COLUMBUS, CORTÉS, AND OTHER
ESSAYS. (L.B. SIMPSON, ED & TRANS)
G.J. WALKER, 86(BHS):JUL71-284
IGLESIAS DÍAZ, J. LA SICOLOGÍA FRANCESA
A TRAVÉS DEL LENGUAJE.
M.M.G. SANDMANN, 545(RPH):AUG69-132
IGNATOW, D. POEMS 1934-1969.*
L. GOLDSTEIN, 385(MQR):SUMMER72-214
J. VERNON, 651(WHR):SPRING71-196
IGNATOW, D. RESCUE THE DEAD.
R. MORAN, 598(SOR):WINTER72-243
IGNOTUS, P. HUNGARY.
617(TLS):25FEB72-210
IGNYATOVICH, D. LYUBEN KARAVELOV I
SR'BSKOTO OBSHTESTVO.
C.C. MILLS, 575(SEER):JAN71-167
"VOM IGORLIED BIS ZUM 'STILLEN DON'."
D. TSCHIŽEWSKIJ, 72:BAND208HEFT4/6-
466
IJSEWIJN, J., ED. HUMANISTICA LOVANIEN-
SIA. (VOL 17)
L.M. KAISER, 551(RENQ):AUTUMN70-302
IKIN, C.W. - SEE CAMPBELL, D.A.
ILCHMAN, W.F. & N.T. UPHOFF. THE POLITI-
CAL ECONOMY OF CHANGE.*
L.A. FALLERS, 293(JAST):AUG70-908
IL'F, I. & E. PETROV. KAK SOZDAVAL'SJA
ROBINZON I DRUGIJE RASSKAZY. (A.V.
KNOWLES, ED)
W.H. BENNETT, 574(SEEJ):SUMMER71-235
ILIE, P., ED. DOCUMENTS OF THE SPANISH
VANGUARD.
J.W. SCHWEITZER, 238:DEC70-1022
A. TERRY, 86(BHS):APR71-171

IRELAND, W.H. VORTIGERN [AND] HENRY THE
SECOND [TOGETHER WITH] AN AUTHENTIC
ACCOUNT OF THE SHAKESPEARE MANUSCRIPTS.
617(TLS):18FEB72-178
IRESON, J.C., I.D. MC FARLANE & G. REES,
EDS. STUDIES IN FRENCH LITERATURE
PRESENTED TO H.W. LAWTON.
G.B. DANIEL, 399(MLJ):MAR70-207
L.J. FRIEDMAN, 545(RPH):FEB71-553
"IRISH LITERARY PORTRAITS."
617(TLS):29SEP72-1148
IRONSIDE, E. HIGH ROAD TO COMMAND.
(LORD IRONSIDE, ED)
617(TLS):4AUG72-921
IRSCHICK, E.F. POLITICS AND SOCIAL CON-
FLICT IN SOUTH INDIA.
P.D. REEVES, 293(JAST):FEB70-484
IRVIN, E. THEATRE COMES TO AUSTRALIA.
W. STONE, 71(ALS):OCT72-437
IRVINE, D. WRITING ABOUT MUSIC.
S. SADIE, 415:JAN70-46
IRVINE, D. - SEE MOLDENHAUR, H.
IRVING, E.B., JR. A READING OF "BEO-
WULF."*
H.D. CHICKERING, JR., 191(ELN):DEC69-
134
N.E. ELIASON, 405(MP):AUG69-80
D.A.H. EVANS, 597(SN):VOL41#2-450
J. KLEGRAF, 72:BAND208HEFT2-126
H.L. ROGERS, 67:MAY71-79
R.M. WILSON, 175:SPRING69-27
IRVING, J. THE WATER-METHOD MAN.
J. CAREW, 441:10SEP72-46
442(NY):22JUL72-78
IRVING, R.M. & G.B. PRIDDLE, EDS. CRI-
SIS.
617(TLS):31MAR72-372
IRVING, W. THE COMPLETE WORKS OF WASH-
INGTON IRVING.* (VOL 1) (N. WRIGHT,
ED)
E. WAGENKNECHT, 432(NEQ):MAR70-147
IRVING, W. THE COMPLETE WORKS OF WASH-
INGTON IRVING. (VOL 3) (W.A. REICHART,
ED)
L.J. BUDD, 579(SAQ):SUMMER71-433
IRVING, W. MAHOMET AND HIS SUCCESSORS.
(H.A. POCHMANN & E.N. FELTSKOG, EDS)
L.J. BUDD, 579(SAQ):SUMMER71-433
B.H. MC CLARY, 27(AL):NOV71-449
IRWIN, D. - SEE WINCKELMANN, J.J.
IRWIN, G. SAMUEL JOHNSON.
617(TLS):20OCT72-1241
IRWIN, I.H. THE STORY OF THE WOMAN'S
PARTY.
617(TLS):18FEB72-180
IRWIN, J. & M. HALL. INDIAN PAINTED AND
PRINTED FABRICS.
617(TLS):8DEC72-1508
IRWIN, R.W. DANIEL D. TOMPKINS.
R.E. ELLIS, 656(WMQ):JUL70-503
ISAACS, B. SELECTED STORIES.
I.T. NAAMANI, 287:JUL/AUG69-27
ISAACS, K. MILITARY AIRCRAFT OF AUS-
TRALIA 1909-1918.
617(TLS):22SEP72-1124
ISAACS, N.D. STRUCTURAL PRINCIPLES IN
OLD ENGLISH POETRY.*
J. TURVILLE-PETRE, 597(SN):VOL41#2-
454
ISAACS, N.D. & R.A. ZIMBARDO, EDS. TOL-
KIEN AND THE CRITICS.
D. BARBOUR, 529(QQ):WINTER70-651
ISAACSON, J. MONET: LE DÉJEUNER SUR
L'HERBE.
617(TLS):11AUG72-940
ISAKSSON, F. & L. FURHAMMAR. POLITICS
AND FILM.
617(TLS):21APR72-433

ISELLA, D. - SEE VITTORINI, E.
"SIR THOMAS ISHAM: AN ENGLISH COLLECTOR
IN ROME, 1677-78."
M. ALLENTUCK, 481(PQ):JUL70-301
ISHERWOOD, C. KATHLEEN AND FRANK.*
W.H. AUDEN, 453:27JAN72-19
R. BLYTHE, 441:23JAN72-3
J. CATINELLA, 561(SATR):22JAN72-66
R. CONSTABLE, 440:23JAN72-5
T. LASK, 441:21JAN72-43
442(NY):22JAN72-100
ISHIKAWA JUN'ICHIRŌ, ED. KAPPA HI YARŌ.
F.H. MAYER, 293(JAST):MAY70-702
ST. ISIDORE OF SEVILLE. THE LETTERS OF
ST. ISIDORE OF SEVILLE. (2ND ED)
(G.B. FORD, JR., ED & TRANS)
J.W. BINNS, 402(MLR):OCT71-845
"ISIS CUMULATIVE BIBLIOGRAPHY." (VOL 1,
PT 1; VOL 2, PTS 1&2) (M. WHITROW, ED)
617(TLS):23JUN72-722
ISLE, W. EXPERIMENTS IN FORM.
L.B. HOLLAND, 445(NCF):DEC68-361
ISLER, H.P. ACHELOOS.
F. BROMMER, 182:VOL23#23/24-999
ISRAEL, L. MISS TALLULAH BANKHEAD.
J.K. HUTCHENS, 440:12MAR72-3
"ISTORIA TOU ELLINIKOU ETHNOUS." (VOL 2)
617(TLS):31MAR72-363
ITA, N.O. BIBLIOGRAPHY OF NIGERIA.
617(TLS):16JUN72-696
"ITALIAN, GRADES 11, 12 & 13." [ONTARIO
BOARD OF EDUCATION]
J.A. TURSI, 399(MLJ):APR70-287
"ITALIAN PAINTINGS AND DRAWINGS AT 56
PRINCES GATE, LONDON, SW7; ADDENDA."
(VOL 5)
C. GOULD, 90:NOV70-764
ITOH, T. THE ESSENTIAL JAPANESE HOUSE.
E. GALANTAY, 505:FEB68-164
ITZKOWITZ, N. & M. MOTE - SEE REPNIN,
N.V. & A. PASHA
VON IVÁNKA, E. RHOMÄERREICH UND GOTTES-
VOLK.*
J. MEYENDORFF, 32:MAR71-129
IVANOV, A.S. & OTHERS, EDS. CHELOVEK,
OBSHCHESTVO, RELIGIIA.
Z. KATZ, 32:DEC71-870
IVANOV, V.V. ISTORIČESKAJA FONOLOGIJA
RUSSKOGO JAZYKA.
S.G. THOMASON, 574(SEEJ):WINTER71-519
IVANOV, Y. CAUTION, ZIONISM!
M. AGURSKY, 453:16NOV72-19
DE IVASHEVSKY, A.G. - SEE UNDER GÓMEZ DE
IVASHEVSKY, A.
IVASK, I., ED. FIRST CONFERENCE ON
BALTIC STUDIES.
H. KUKK, 550(RUSR):JUL70-355
IVASK, I. & J. MARICHAL. LUMINOUS
REALITY.*
J.F. CIRRE, 238:SEP70-577
IVASK, J. ZOLUŠKA.
V. TERRAS, 574(SEEJ):WINTER71-511
IVENS, M. PRIVATE AND PUBLIC.
W.P.T., 619(TC):1968/48 1969/1-90
IVERSEN, A.N. & A.V. CAROZZI - SEE
RASPE, R.E.
IVES, B., ED. MORE BURL IVES SONGS.
E.A. WIENANDT, 650(WF):JAN69-66
IVES, C. ESSAYS BEFORE A SONATA AND
OTHER WRITINGS.* (H. BOATWRIGHT, ED)
T. SOUSTER, 607:SUMMER69-34
IVINS, W.M., JR. PRINTS AND VISUAL COM-
MUNICATION.
A.H. MAYOR, 90:MAY70-316
IYENGAR, K.R.S. SHAKESPEARE, HIS WORLD
AND HIS ART.
M. MINCOFF, 179(ES):FEB70-91

IZARD, B. & C. HIERONYMUS. REQUIEM FOR
A NUN.
G. SMITH, 579(SAQ):SUMMER71-431
IZENBERG, J. HOW MANY MILES TO CAMELOT?
441:15OCT72-41
"THE IZUMI SHIKIBU DIARY." (E. CRANSTON,
TRANS)
I. MORRIS, 293(JAST):MAY70-671
639(VQR):WINTER70-XIII

JACANO, F.L. GROWING UP IN A PHILIPPINE
BARRIO.
D.V. HART, 293(JAST):FEB70-502
JACCOTTET, P. LA SEMAISON.
617(TLS):11FEB72-146
JACCOTTET, P. - SEE HÖLDERLIN, F.
JACK, I. - SEE BROWNING, R.
JACK-HINTON, C. THE SEARCH FOR THE
ISLANDS OF SOLOMON 1567-1838.
R.C. GREEN, 293(JAST):AUG70-997
J.L. HOWGEGO, 325:APR70-80
JÄCKEL, E. HITLER'S WELTANSCHAUUNG.
G. BARRACLOUGH, 453:2NOV72-32
JACKSON, B., ED. FOLKLORE AND SOCIETY.
W.E. SIMEONE, 650(WF):JAN69-51
JACKSON, B., ED. THE NEGRO AND HIS FOLK-
LORE IN NINETEENTH-CENTURY PERIODICALS.
W.H. JANSEN, 582(SFQ):MAR69-54
JACKSON, B. WAKE UP DEAD MAN.
N. BLIVEN, 442(NY):8JUL72-74
JACKSON, C.J. ENGLISH GOLDSMITHS AND
THEIR MARKS.
C. OMAN, 39:DEC69-546
JACKSON, D. & M.L. SPENCE - SEE FRÉMONT,
J.C.
JACKSON, E.R. L'ÉVOLUTION DE LA MÉMOIRE
INVOLONTAIRE DANS L'OEUVRE DE MARCEL
PROUST.
R.M. BIRN, 131(CL):WINTER71-77
JACKSON, G. HISTORIAN'S QUEST.
639(VQR):WINTER70-XXI
JACKSON, G. HULL IN THE EIGHTEENTH CEN-
TURY.
617(TLS):7APR72-391
JACKSON, G. LINES.
A. RODDICK, 368:MAR69-84
JACKSON, G. THE MAKING OF MEDIEVAL
SPAIN.
617(TLS):25FEB72-214
JACKSON, G. SOLEDAD BROTHER.*
N.C. MILLS, 676(YR):SPRING71-440
JACKSON, G.B. VISION AND JUDGMENT IN
BEN JONSON'S DRAMA.*
R. LEVIN, 401(MLQ):SEP70-377
JACKSON, G.B. - SEE JONSON, B.
JACKSON, G.L. BLOOD IN MY EYE.
S.A. BOSWORTH, 561(SATR):26FEB72-62
D. CAUTE, 362:18MAY72-659
D. LEWIS, 441:16APR72-32
617(TLS):7JUL72-763
JACKSON, J.A. THE CENTENNIAL HISTORY OF
MANITOBA.
102(CANL):WINTER71-106
JACKSON, J.A., ED. MIGRATION.
J. HENNINGSEN, 182:VOL23#4-156
JACKSON, J.A., ED. ROLE.
617(TLS):10MAR72-278
JACKSON, J.C. SARAWAK.
J.A. HAFNER, 293(JAST):MAY70-739
JACKSON, J.R.D., ED. COLERIDGE: THE
CRITICAL HERITAGE.
J. COLMER, 677:VOL2-296
JACKSON, J.R.D. METHOD AND IMAGINATION
IN COLERIDGE'S CRITICISM.
D.V.E., 191(ELN):SEP70(SUPP)-32
L. LERNER, 184(EIC):JAN70-89 [CONT]

[CONTINUING]
T. MC FARLAND, 191(ELN):MAR71-231
W.J.B. OWEN, 541(RES):AUG70-370
G. THOMAS, 175:SUMMER69-70
JACKSON, K.H. THE GODODDIN.*
G.W. DUNLEAVY, 399(MLJ):MAR70-201
JACKSON, R. BEFORE THE STORM.
617(TLS):28APR72-501
JACKSON, R.L., ED. CHEKHOV.
W. TYDEMAN, 148:SPRING70-92
T.G. WINNER, 32:MAR71-205
JACKSON, R.S. JOHN DONNE'S CHRISTIAN
VOCATION.
E.B. BATSON, 568(SCN):WINTER71-71
JACKSON, S. CARUSO.
M. DAVENPORT, 441:29OCT72-6
JACKSON, T.H. THE EARLY POETRY OF EZRA
POUND.
D. BARBOUR, 529(QQ):SUMMER70-285
H.N. SCHNEIDAU, 405(MP):FEB70-297
J. SCHWARTZ, 590:SUMMER70-42
H. SERGEANT, 175:SUMMER69-71
JACKSON, W.A. RECORDS OF A BIBLIOGRAPH-
ER. (W.H. BOND, ED)
N. BARKER, 354:DEC69-347
JACKSON, W.A.D., ED. AGRARIAN POLICIES
AND PROBLEMS IN COMMUNIST AND NON-
COMMUNIST COUNTRIES.
617(TLS):3MAR72-250
JACKSON, W.H.T. THE ANATOMY OF LOVE.
617(TLS):21APR72-452
JACOB, A. TEMPS ET LANGAGE.
A.K. MARIETTI, 98:DEC69-1114
JACOB, E.F. - SEE CRASTER, E.
JACOB, J.M. INTRODUCTION TO CAMBODIAN.
P.N. JENNER, 318(JAOS):OCT-DEC70-629
H-J. PINNOW, 361:VOL24#1-96
JACOBS, J. WIELANDS ROMANE.*
W.E. YUILL, 402(MLR):APR71-456
JACOBS, J.R. & G. TUCKER. THE WAR OF
1812.
V. SAPIO, 656(WMQ):OCT70-685
JACOBS, R.A. & P.S. ROSENBAUM. ENGLISH
TRANSFORMATIONAL GRAMMAR.
F.J. NEWMEYER, 399(MLJ):NOV70-530
JACOBS, R.D. POE: JOURNALIST AND CRIT-
IC.*
J. SALZBERG, 191(ELN):JUN70-312
639(VQR):SPRING70-LXIV
JACOBS, S. ON STAGE.
G. WEALES, 441:11JUN72-8
JACOBS, W.D. FRUNZE, THE SOVIET CLAUSE-
WITZ (1885-1925).
E. HONEGGER, 182:VOL23#23/24-1007
K.R. WHITING, 32:DEC71-889
JACOBS, W.R. DISPOSSESSING THE AMERICAN
INDIAN.
RARIHOKWATS, 561(SATR):8JUL72-70
M. ROGIN, 441:24DEC72-4
JACOBSEN, J. & W.R. MUELLER. IONESCO
AND GENET.
H.E. STEWART, 207(FR):OCT69-164
JACOBSON, D. THE RAPE OF TAMAR.*
D.J. GORDON, 676(YR):SPRING71-428
F.P.W. MC DOWELL, 659:SUMMER72-361
JACOBSON, M.F. EATER'S DIGEST.
441:24SEP72-52
JACOBY, E.H. & C.F. MAN AND LAND.
617(TLS):15SEP72-1066
JACOBY, F.R. VAN DEN VOS REINAERDE.
N.F. BLAKE, 382(MAE):1971/1-70
JACOBY, S. MOSCOW CONVERSATIONS.
561(SATR):7OCT72-108
JACQUOT, J., WITH M. ODDON, EDS. LES
TRAGÉDIES DE SÉNÈQUE ET LE THÉÂTRE DE
LA RENAISSANCE.
G.K. HUNTER, 179(ES):1969SUPP-LXXXII

JAEGER, W. FIVE ESSAYS.
  J.S. MORRISON, 123:JUN71-309
JAEGGI, U. LITERATUR UND POLITIK.
  617(TLS):7APR72-399
JAEHRLING, J. DIE PHILOSOPHISCHE TERMIN-
  OLOGIE NOTKERS DES DEUTSCHEN IN SEINER
  ÜBERSETZUNG DER ARISTOTELISCHEN "KATE-
  GORIEN."*
  E.S. FIRCHOW, 406:WINTER71-402
  J. MARGETTS, 402(MLR):OCT71-919
  K. OSTBERG, 382(MAE):1971/3-272
JAFFA, H.C. KENNETH SLESSOR.*
  D. STEWART, 581:1971/4-316
JAFFE, A. THE PROCESS OF KAFKA'S
  "TRIAL."
  K.J. ATCHITY, 613:SUMMER69-299
  R. HARRISON, 219(GAR):SUMMER69-251
  H. LEHNERT, 149:JUN71-174
JAFFE, D. DAN FREEMAN.
  S.J. SACKETT, 650(WF):JUL69-219
JAFFE, H.L. PICASSO.
  617(TLS):7JAN72-18
JAFFÉ, H.L.C. VORDEMBERGE-GILDEWART.
  617(TLS):25FEB72-222
JAFFÉ, M. VAN DYCK'S ANTWERP SKETCHBOOK.
  C. WHITE, 90:JUL69-459
JAFFE, R. THE OTHER WOMAN.
  G. DAVIS, 441:29OCT72-57
JAFFIN, D. CONFORMED TO STONE.
  S. MOORE, 385(MQR):SUMMER72-217
JÄGER, G. "NUS" IN PLATONS DIALOGEN.*
  A.A. LONG, 123:JUN71-184
JÄGERSKIÖLD, S. FRÅN JAKTSLOTTET TILL
  LANDSFLYKTEN.
  C.L. ANDERSON, 563(SS):AUTUMN71-450
JÄGERSKIÖLD, S. VALTIONHOITAJA MANNER-
  HEIM.
  M. RINTALA, 550(RUSR):APR70-233
JAHĀNGĪR. THE TUZUK-I-JĀHĀNGĪRĪ. (A.
  ROGERS, TRANS; H. BEVERIDGE, ED)
  S.A. AKBAR, 273(IC):APR69-166
JAHODA, M., P.F. LAZARSFELD & H. ZEISEL.
  MARIENTHAL.
  617(TLS):6OCT72-1205
"JAHRBUCH FÜR WIRTSCHAFTSGESCHICHTE."
  (VOLS 1, 3 & 4)
  R.J. BAZILLION, 104:WINTER71-581
JAIMES-FREYRE, M. MODERNISMO Y 98 A
  TRAVÉS DE RICARDO JAIMES FREYRE.*
  S.H. TILLES, 238:SEP70-581
JAIN, S.C. INDIAN MANAGER.
  617(TLS):31MAR72-378
JAIRAZBHOY, N.A. THE RĀGS OF NORTH
  INDIAN MUSIC.*
  R. MASSEY, 415:DEC71-1175
JAKOBOVITS, L.A. FOREIGN LANGUAGE LEARN-
  ING.
  D.L. WOLFE, 351(LL):DEC70-278
JAKOBSON, M. FINNISH NEUTRALITY.*
  G.G. GAGE, 563(SS):SPRING71-190
JALABERT, J. LE DIEU DE LEIBNIZ.
  L. PRENANT, 542:JUL-SEP68-412
JALABERT, J. - SEE LEIBNIZ, G.W.
JALAL, F. THE ROLE OF GOVERNMENT IN THE
  INDUSTRIALIZATION OF IRAQ, 1950-1965.
  617(TLS):1SEP72-1028
JAMAL, H.A. FROM THE DEAD LEVEL.*
  C.C. WARE, 561(SATR):1JUL72-52
JAMES, B. BRAHMS.
  617(TLS):18AUG72-964
JAMES, C. THE IMPERIAL HOTEL.
  H.A. BROOKS, 505:JUL69-150
JAMES, D. - SEE GUEVARA, E.C.
JAMES, D.G. MATTHEW ARNOLD AND THE
  DECLINE OF ENGLISH ROMANTICISM.
  P. TURNER, 179(ES):JUN70-266
JAMES, D.N. HAWKER.
  617(TLS):17NOV72-1405

JAMES, E.T., WITH J.W. JAMES & P.S.
  BOYER, EDS. NOTABLE AMERICAN WOMEN
  1607-1950.
  H. VENDLER, 441:17SEP72-1
  617(TLS):7JUL72-767
JAMES, H. THE BODLEY HEAD HENRY JAMES.
  (VOL 10)
  617(TLS):18AUG72-957
JAMES, H. THE PAINTER'S EYE.
  K. ROBERTS, 90:OCT70-707
JAMES, J.W., ED & TRANS. RHIGYFARCH'S
  LIFE OF ST. DAVID.
  P.G. WALSH, 123:MAR71-138
JAMES, M.K. STUDIES IN THE MEDIEVAL WINE
  TRADE. (E.M. VEALE, ED)
  617(TLS):11FEB72-165
JAMES, P. EARLY KEYBOARD INSTRUMENTS.*
  G. OLDHAM, 415:MAR71-244
JAMES, P.D. SHROUD FOR A NIGHTINGALE.*
  N. CALLENDAR, 441:16JAN72-42
JAMES, P.D. AN UNSUITABLE JOB FOR A
  WOMAN.
  617(TLS):8DEC72-1507
JAMES, R.R. AMBITION AND REALITIES.
  617(TLS):9JUN72-648
JAMES, R.R. - SEE CHANNON, H.
JAMES, W. THE MORAL PHILOSOPHY OF WIL-
  LIAM JAMES. (J.K. ROTH, ED)
  H.A. LARRABEE, 432(NEQ):JUN70-298
JAMMES, F. MÉMOIRES.
  617(TLS):5MAY72-509
JANES, P. HOUSE OF HATE.
  G. WOODCOCK, 102(CANL):WINTER71-88
JANEWAY, E. MAN'S WORLD, WOMAN'S PLACE.*
  617(TLS):30JUN72-742
JANIK, D. GESCHICHTE DER ODE UND DER
  "STANCES" VON RONSARD BIS BOILEAU.
  R. HESS, 72:BAND208HEFT4/6-446
JANIN, J. LES AMOURS DE JULES JANIN ET
  "LE MARIAGE DU CRITIQUE." (MERGIER-
  BOURDEIX, ED)
  J.S.P., 191(ELN):SEP70(SUPP)-72
JANIS, H. & R. BLESH. COLLAGE. (REV)
  H. THUBRON, 592:JUL/AUG68-54
JANKOVIČ, M., Z. PEŠAT & F. VODIČKA, EDS.
  STRUKTURA A SMYSL LITERÁRNÍHO DÍLA.
  W. & H. SCHMID, 490:JAN68-134
JANKUHN, H. DIE PASSIVE BEDEUTUNG MEDI-
  ALER FORMEN UNTERSUCHT AN DER SPRACHE
  HOMERS.
  J.B. HAINSWORTH, 123:DEC71-333
  J.W. POULTNEY, 124:DEC70-121
JANOV, A. THE PRIMAL REVOLUTION.
  A. STORR, 441:5NOV72-8
JANSEN, F.J.B. & P.M. MITCHELL, EDS.
  ANTHOLOGY OF DANISH LITERATURE.
  617(TLS):7JUL72-785
JANSSEN, K-H., ED. DIE GRAUE EXZELLENZ.
  617(TLS):7JUL72-771
JANSSON, S.B.F. SWEDISH VIKINGS IN
  ENGLAND.
  H. BECK, 72:BAND208HEFT3-196
JANTSCH, E. TECHNOLOGICAL PLANNING AND
  SOCIAL FUTURES.
  617(TLS):26MAY72-609
JANTZ, H. THE MOTHERS IN "FAUST."*
  L. DIECKMANN, 401(MLQ):SEP70-391
  H. MEYER, 399(MLJ):JAN70-34
"JAPANESE POETRY NOW." (T. FITZSIMMONS,
  TRANS)
  617(TLS):4AUG72-910
JARDEN, D., ED. SEFUNEI SHIRA.
  A.S. CITRON, 399(MLJ):MAY70-368
JARDIN, P. LA GUERRE À NEUF ANS.
  617(TLS):9JUN72-664
JARMAN, C. ATLAS OF ANIMAL MIGRATION.
  561(SATR):23DEC72-69
  617(TLS):10NOV72-1376

JARMAN, R.H. WE SPEAK NO TREASON.*
E. WEEKS, 61:JAN72-96
JARRELL, R. THE COMPLETE POEMS.
J. FULLER, 362:24FEB72-251
H. NEMEROV, 340(KR):1969/4-570
617(TLS):31MAR72-360
JARRELL, R. JEROME.
R. WEISBERG, 441:17SEP72-46
JARRETT-KERR, M. PATTERNS OF CHRISTIAN
ACCEPTANCE.
617(TLS):30JUN72-753
JARRY, A. OEUVRES COMPLÈTES. (VOL 1)
(M. ARRIVÉ, ED)
617(TLS):1SEP72-1014
JARRY, M. THE CARPETS OF AUBUSSON.
G. DE BELLAIGUE, 90:MAY70-320
JÄRV, H. STRINDBERGSFEJDEN.
E. POULENARD, 462(OL):VOL24#3-221
JARVIE, I.C. CONCEPTS AND SOCIETY.
617(TLS):1SEP72-1026
JARVIE, I.C. & J. AGASSI, EDS. HONG
KONG.
B. BOXER, 293(JAST):FEB70-437
JARVIS, R.C. COLLECTED PAPERS ON THE
JACOBITE RISINGS.
617(TLS):23JUN72-706
JASINSKI, B.W. L'ENGAGEMENT DE BENJAMIN
CONSTANT.
617(TLS):14JAN72-44
JASINSKI, R. DEUX ACCÈS À LA BRUYÈRE.
617(TLS):4FEB72-134
JASNY, N. SOVIET ECONOMISTS OF THE
TWENTIES.
617(TLS):16JUN72-683
JAUHARI, R.C. FIROZ TUGHLUQ.
H.K. SHERWANI, 273(IC):JUL69-240
JAUSLIN, C. TENNESSEE WILLIAMS.
K. TETZELI VON ROSADOR, 72:BAND208
HEFT1-49
JAUSS, H.R. LITERATURGESCHICHTE ALS
PROVOKATION DER LITERATURWISSENSCHAFT.
L.J. FRIEDMAN, 545(RPH):FEB71-548
JAUSS, H.R., ED. DIE NICHT MEHR SCHÖNEN
KÜNSTE.
L. WELCH, 290(JAAC):SUMMER70-548
JAUSS, H.R. PERCHÉ LA STORIA DELLA LET-
TERATURA? (A. VARVARO, ED)
G. COSTA, 545(RPH):FEB71-549
JAUSS, H.R. & J. BEYER. LA LITTÉRATURE
DIDACTIQUE, ALLÉGORIQUE ET SATIRIQUE.*
(VOL 1)
F. WHITEHEAD, 208(FS):JAN71-55
JAUSSEN, T. GRAMMAIRE ET DICTIONNAIRE
DE LA LANGUE TAHITIENNE. (5TH ED REV
BY P. MAZÉ & R.P.H. COPPENRATH)
H. KÄHLER, 182:VOL23#5-212
JAWORSKA, W. GAUGUIN AND THE PONT-AVEN
SCHOOL.
J. CANADAY, 441:3DEC72-90
P. GAY, 31(ASCH):AUTUMN72-660
JAY, A. CORPORATION MAN.*
K. ADAM, 362:13APR72-491
441:5MAR72-12
617(TLS):7APR72-383
JAYATILLEKE, K.N. EARLY BUDDHIST THEORY
OF KNOWLEDGE.
R.H. ROBINSON, 485(PE&W):JAN69-69
"JAZZFORSCHUNG I."
M. HARRISON, 415:MAR71-246
JEAN, M. - SEE ARP, J.
JEAN, R. LA VIVE.
J. CARDUNER, 207(FR):OCT69-161
JEAUNEAU, É. - SEE ERIGENA, J.S.
JEAUNEAU, É. - SEE GUILLAUME DE CONCHES
JEDRUSZCZAK, H. & T. OSTATNIE LATA
DRUGIEJ RZECZYPOSPOLITEJ (1935-1939).
A.M. CIENCIALA, 32:DEC71-914
JEDRZEJEWICZ, W. - SEE LIPSKI, J.

JEDRZEJEWICZ, W. - SEE ŁUKASIEWICZ, J.
JEFFARES, A.N. THE CIRCUS ANIMALS.*
L. PERRINE, 584(SWR):SPRING71-211
JEFFARES, A.N. A COMMENTARY ON THE COL-
LECTED POEMS OF WILLIAM BUTLER YEATS.
M. BOWEN, 405(MP):FEB70-294
R.H. LASS, 141:FALL69-391
JEFFERSON, A. DELIUS.
617(TLS):17MAR72-294
JEFFERSON, T. THE PAPERS OF THOMAS JEF-
FERSON. (VOL 18) (J.P. BOYD, ED)
617(TLS):17NOV72-1388
JEFFERY, B. FRENCH RENAISSANCE COMEDY,
1552-1630.*
H.G. HALL, 402(MLR):JAN71-184
JEFFREYS, J.G. THE THIEFTAKER.
N. CALLENDAR, 441:31DEC72-18
JEFFREYS, M.V.C. EDUCATION.
617(TLS):28JAN72-109
JEHLIČKA, M. VYPRÁVEČSKÉ UMĚNÍ LVA
TOLSTÉHO.
G. GIBIAN, 574(SEEJ):FALL71-378
JELAVICH, B. THE HABSBURG EMPIRE IN
EUROPEAN AFFAIRS, 1814-1918.
R.A. KANN, 32:MAR71-130
B.K. KIRÁLY, 104:FALL71-443
JELAVICH, C., ED. LANGUAGE AND AREA
STUDIES.
R. BANCROFT, 575(SEER):JUL71-480
K. HITCHINS, 574(SEEJ):SUMMER71-255
S.D. SPECTOR, 32:JUN71-457
JELEN, C. LA PURGE.
617(TLS):15SEP72-1068
JELENSKI, C. & D. DE ROUX, EDS. GOM-
BROWICZ.
617(TLS):11FEB72-155
JELINEK, E. MICHAEL.
617(TLS):29SEP72-1140
JELINEK, H. LES BÊTES N'AIMENT PAS
L'AMOUR DES HOMMES.
617(TLS):15DEC72-1521
JELLICOE, G.A. STUDIES IN LANDSCAPE
DESIGN. (VOL 3)
H. ROSEMAN, 89(BJA):SPRING71-209
JELLISON, C.A. ETHAN ALLEN.
G.A. BILLIAS, 432(NEQ):MAR70-161
D.G. LEVY, 656(WMQ):JUL70-484
JENCKS, C. & OTHERS. INEQUALITY.
H.M. LEVIN, 561(SATR):11NOV72-49
G. LEVINE, 441:26NOV72-3
JENCKS, C. & G. BAIRD, EDS. MEANING IN
ARCHITECTURE.*
H. SWAIN, 111:29MAY70-201
JENCKS, C. & D. RIESMAN. THE ACADEMIC
REVOLUTION.
F.C. WARD, 185:OCT69-74
JENKINS, C. - SEE SWIFT, J.
JENKINS, D. SEMI-TOUGH.
D. HALBERSTAM, 441:17SEP72-2
R.R. LINGEMAN, 441:6OCT72-44
J. SPENCER, 561(SATR):14OCT72-80
JENKINS, E. DR. GULLY.
E. MORGAN, 362:20APR72-524
617(TLS):24MAR72-326
JENKINS, E. DR. GULLY'S STORY.
L.J. DAVIS, 440:13FEB72-4
T. LASK, 441:25FEB72-39
JENKINS, G. THE HOLLOW SEA.
M. LEVIN, 441:26MAR72-43
JENKINS, J., ED. ETHNIC MUSICAL INSTRU-
MENTS.
G. OLDHAM, 415:JAN71-34
JENKINS, J.G., ED. THE WOOL TEXTILE
INDUSTRY IN GREAT BRITAIN.
617(TLS):14JUL72-822
JENKINS, J.L. MUSICAL INSTRUMENTS,
HORNIMAN MUSEUM, LONDON.
G. OLDHAM, 415:MAR71-245

JENKINS, R. AFTERNOON ON THE POTOMAC?
617(TLS):23JUN72-703
JENKINS, R. A TOAST TO THE LORD.
617(TLS):11AUG72-935
JENKINS, R. WHAT MATTERS NOW.
617(TLS):6OCT72-1192
JENKINS, R.J.H. STUDIES ON BYZANTINE
HISTORY OF THE 9TH AND 10TH CENTURIES.
617(TLS):18FEB72-182
JENNINGS, J.M. THE LIBRARY OF THE COL-
LEGE OF WILLIAM AND MARY IN VIRGINIA,
1693-1793.
M.A. MC CORISON, 656(WMQ):JAN70-169
JENNISON, P.S. & R.N. SHERIDAN, EDS.
THE FUTURE OF GENERAL ADULT BOOKS AND
READING IN AMERICA.
H.W. WINGER, 356:OCT71-333
JENSEN, H. SIGN, SYMBOL AND SCRIPT.
J. DUNSTON, 67:MAY71-69
JENSEN, H.J. A GLOSSARY OF JOHN DRYDEN'S
CRITICAL TERMS.*
J.M. ADEN, 481(PQ):JUL70-343
W. FROST, 301(JEGP):APR71-310
JENSEN, M. THE FOUNDING OF A NATION.
W.W. ABBOT, 656(WMQ):JAN70-148
J.R. FRESE, 613:SUMMER69-319
JENTZSCH, P., M. BRAUNECK & E.E. STARKE.
DAS 17. JAHRHUNDERT IN NEUER SICHT.
P. SKRINE, 402(MLR):APR71-446
JEPHSON, A.J.M. THE DIARY OF A.J.
MOUNTENEY JEPHSON. (D. MIDDLETON, ED)
A.R. TAYLOR, 637(VS):JUN70-385
JEPPESEN, K. THE STYLE OF PALESTRINA
AND THE DISSONANCE.
P. RADCLIFFE, 415:JUN71-558
ST. JEROME. THE FIRST DESERT HERO.*
(I.S. KOZIK, ED) [SHOWN IN PREV UNDER
ED]
P.G. WALSH, 123:MAR71-135
JEROME, J. THE DEATH OF THE AUTOMOBILE.
J. CANADAY, 441:20NOV72-39
441:10DEC72-48
JERSTAD, L.G. MANI-RIMDU.
M. SLOBIN, 293(JAST):MAY70-712
639(VQR):AUTUMN70-CLVI
JESPERSEN, O. ESSENTIALS OF ENGLISH
GRAMMAR.
J. NIST, 353:MAY69-104
JESSOP, T.E. - SEE BERKELEY, G.
JESTAZ, B. LE "VOYAGE D'ITALIE" DE
ROBERT DE COTTE.
P. REUTERSWÄRD, 90:JUN69-394
JETTMAR, K. ART OF THE STEPPES.
R.D. BARNETT, 39:OCT69-353
JEUNE, S. POÉSIE ET SYSTÈME.
O. DE MOURGUES, 208(FS):OCT71-478
F. SCHALK, 182:VOL23#1/2-32
P.A. WADSWORTH, 207(FR):APR70-840
JEVONS, W.S. PAPERS AND CORRESPONDENCE
OF WILLIAM STANLEY JEVONS. (VOL 1)
(R.D.C. BLACK & R. KONEKAMP, EDS)
617(TLS):29DEC72-1590
JEZIORKOWSKI, K. - SEE "GOTTFRIED KELLER"
JHA, D.C. INDO-PAKISTAN RELATIONS.
617(TLS):15DEC72-1541
JHABVALA, R.P. AN EXPERIENCE OF INDIA.
D.A.N. JONES, 362:20JAN72-90
442(NY):3JUN72-110
JIMÉNEZ PATÓN, B. EPÍTOME DE LA ORTOGRA-
FÍA LATINA Y CASTELLANA. (A. QUILIS &
J.M. ROZAS, EDS)
Á. GALMÉS DE FUENTES, 545(RPH):FEB71-
522
JINGORŌ, U. - SEE UNDER USUDA JINGORŌ
JOACHIM, H-E. DIE HUNSRÜCK-EIFEL-KULTUR
AM MITTELRHEIN.
A. HAFNER, 182:VOL23#9-491

JOANS, T. BLACK POW-WOW.*
H. TAYLOR, 651(WHR):AUTUMN71-371
JOEL, I. INDEX OF ARTICLES ON JEWISH
STUDIES. (NO. 1)
S.R. BRUNSWICK, 356:JUL71-269
JOHANNESSON, E.O. THE NOVELS OF AUGUST
STRINDBERG.*
T. STENSTRÖM, 149:SEP71-280
JOHANNSEN, R.L., R. TRICKLAND & R.T.
EUBANKS - SEE WEAVER, R.M.
JOHN, DUKE OF BEDORD, WITH G. MIKES - SEE
UNDER LORD BEDFORD, WITH G. MIKES
ST. JOHN DAMASCENE. BARLAAM AND IOASAPH.
(G.R. WOODWARD & H. MATTINGLY, TRANS)
M. AUBINEAU, 555:VOL44FASC1-137
JOHN, D.A.S. - SEE CAESAR
JOHN, M., ED. MUSIC DRAMA IN SCHOOLS.
H. COLE, 415:NOV71-1072
617(TLS):30JUN72-757
JOHN, O. THE SHADOW IN THE SEA.
N. CALLENDAR, 441:31DEC72-18
JOHN, O. TWICE THROUGH THE LINES.
K. ROBSON, 362:3AUG72-152
617(TLS):28JUL72-866
JOHNPOLL, B.K. THE POLITICS OF FUTIL-
ITY.*
L. BLIT, 587:JAN68-450
JOHNS, F.A. THE STRATEGIST.
E. LUCIE-SMITH, 503:SPRING69-35
JOHNSON, A. THE PAPERS OF ANDREW JOHN-
SON. (VOL 1) (L.P. GRAF & R.W. HAS-
KINS, EDS)
C.B. DEW, 330(MASJ):SPRING69-90
JOHNSON, B. CONRAD'S MODELS OF MIND.
J. FEASTER, 295:VOL2#3-417
JOHNSON, B., ED. NEW WRITING IN YUGO-
SLAVIA.*
V.D. MIHAILOVICH, 574(SEEJ):FALL71-
397
JOHNSON, B.S. POEMS TWO.
617(TLS):9JUN72-651
JOHNSON, C., ED. CHANGE IN COMMUNIST
SYSTEMS.
B. HARASYMIW, 104:WINTER71-585
JOHNSON, D. FRANCE.
N. HAMPSON, 208(FS):JUL71-366
JOHNSON, D. LESSER LIVES.
441:31DEC72-19
442(NY):16DEC72-150
JOHNSON, D. MUSIC AND SOCIETY IN LOWLAND
SCOTLAND IN THE EIGHTEENTH CENTURY.
617(TLS):27OCT72-1292
JOHNSON, D. THE TRUE HISTORY OF THE
FIRST MRS. MEREDITH AND OTHER LESSER
LIVES.
P. ADAMS, 61:NOV72-130
V.S. PRITCHETT, 453:2NOV72-8
JOHNSON, D.B. TRANSFORMATIONS AND THEIR
USE IN THE RESOLUTION OF SYNTACTIC
HOMOMORPHY.
F.Y. GLADNEY, 574(SEEJ):FALL71-364
JOHNSON, D.C. A GUIDE TO REFERENCE MAT-
ERIALS ON SOUTHEAST ASIA.
R.C. ELLSWORTH, 356:JAN71-70
R.C. ELLSWORTH, 529(QQ):WINTER70-656
JOHNSON, D.N. INSTRUCTION BOOK FOR
BEGINNING ORGANISTS.
J. DALTON, 415:JUL70-713
JOHNSON, E. SIR WALTER SCOTT.*
F.R. HART, 639(VQR):AUTUMN70-680
JOHNSON, E.D.H. CHARLES DICKENS.
R.D. ALTICK, 155:JAN70-59
W.D. SCHAEFER, 445(NCF):SEP69-249
JOHNSON, E.L. AN INTRODUCTION TO THE
SOVIET LEGAL SYSTEM.
R.J. JOHNSON, 32:DEC71-896
JOHNSON, E.R. CASE LOAD - MAXIMUM.
N. CALLENDAR, 441:16JAN72-42

161

JOHNSON, G.W., JR. THE EMERGENCE OF
BLACK POLITICS IN SENEGAL.
617(TLS):3NOV72-1313
JOHNSON, H. & G.C. WILSON. ARMY IN AN-
GUISH.
R.J. BARNET, 453:16NOV72-14
JOHNSON, H.G. THE ECONOMIC APPROACH TO
SOCIAL QUESTIONS.
J. CORINA, 97(CQ):SUMMER68-294
JOHNSON, J.K. & C.B. STELMACK - SEE
MACDONALD, J.A.
JOHNSON, L.B. THE VANTAGE POINT.*
R. DWORKIN, 362:20JAN72-88
G. WILLS, 231:JAN72-92
617(TLS):21JAN72-55
JOHNSON, O. THE MORAL LIFE.
E. TELFER, 518:OCT70-14
JOHNSON, P. THE OFFSHORE ISLANDERS.
C.B. MACPHERSON, 362:28SEP72-415
617(TLS):15SEP72-1052
JOHNSON, P.H. THE HOLIDAY FRIEND.
D.A.N. JONES, 362:26OCT72-557
617(TLS):27OCT72-1274
JOHNSON, P.H. THE HONOURS BOARD.
F.P.W. MC DOWELL, 659:SUMMER72-361
JOHNSON, R. THE FRENCH COMMUNIST PARTY
VERSUS THE STUDENT.
R.O. PAXTON, 441:24SEP72-46
JOHNSON, R.B. HENRY DE MONTHERLANT.
J. CRUICKSHANK, 208(FS):APR71-239
G. MORREALE, 207(FR):DEC69-331
K.S. WHITE, 399(MLJ):JAN70-62
JOHNSON, R.F. THE ROYAL GEORGE.
617(TLS):3MAR72-257
JOHNSON, R.O. AN INDEX TO LITERATURE IN
THE NEW YORKER, VOLS I-XV, 1925-1940.
R.C. ELLSWORTH, 529(QQ):SUMMER70-288
JOHNSON, R.S. MORE'S "UTOPIA."
L.C. KHANNA, 551(RENQ):WINTER70-465
L. MILES, 402(MLR):APR71-386
JOHNSON, S. THE GREEN REVOLUTION.
617(TLS):31MAR72-372
JOHNSON, S. JOHNSON ON SHAKESPEARE.
(A. SHERBO, ED)
J.D. FLEEMAN, 447(N&Q):NOV70-435
J.H. HAGSTRUM, 597(SN):VOL41#2-435
J. HARDY, 541(RES):FEB70-86
S.W. JOHNSTON, 173(ECS):SPRING70-404
JOHNSON, S. A JOURNEY TO THE WESTERN
ISLANDS OF SCOTLAND.* (M. LASCELLES,
ED)
617(TLS):20OCT72-1241
JOHNSON, S. LIFE OF SAVAGE.* (C. TRACY,
ED)
E.A. BLOOM, 677:VOL2-284
JOHNSON, S. THE RAMBLER.* (W.J. BATE &
A.B. STRAUSS, EDS)
J.T. BOULTON, 402(MLR):OCT71-870
O.M. BRACK, JR., 481(PQ):JUL70-358
639(VQR):SPRING70-LX
JOHNSON, S. SELECTED ESSAYS FROM THE
"RAMBLER," "ADVENTURER," AND "IDLER."*
(W.J. BATE, ED)
J.C. MAXWELL, 447(N&Q):MAR70-105
173(ECS):FALL69-154
JOHNSON, T. BOTANICAL JOURNEYS IN KENT
AND HAMPSTEAD. (J.S.L. GILMOUR, ED)
617(TLS):22SEP72-1124
JOHNSON, T.H. - SEE DICKINSON, E.
JOHNSON, U., ED. DAS NEUE FENSTER.
N.H. BINGER, 399(MLJ):MAY70-368
JOHNSON, W., WITH C. EVANS - SEE STEVEN-
SON, A.E.
JOHNSON, W.O., JR. SUPER SPECTATOR AND
THE ELECTRIC LILLIPUTIANS.*
E. SEGAL, 676(YR):SUMMER71-605

JOHNSON, W.S. GERARD MANLEY HOPKINS.
R. BRINLEE, 577(SHR):FALL70-375
F.N. LEES, 637(VS):JUN70-451
N.H. MAC KENZIE, 401(MLQ):JUN70-236
A. ORZA, 191(ELN):SEP69-65
J. PICK, 141:SUMMER69-302
JOHNSON, W.S. THE VOICES OF MATTHEW
ARNOLD.
P. TURNER, 179(ES):JUN70-266
JOHNSTON, C. THE BRINK OF JORDAN.
617(TLS):21JUL72-834
JOHNSTON, E. FORMAL PENMANSHIP AND OTHER
PAPERS. (H. CHILD, ED)
617(TLS):25FEB72-219
JOHNSTON, G. ANNALS OF AUSTRALIAN LIT-
ERATURE.
S.J. ROUTH, 381:VOL29#4-555
JOHNSTON, H.A.S. THE FULANI EMPIRE OF
SOKOTO.
M.G. SMITH, 69:JAN69-78
JOHNSTON, H.J.M. BRITISH EMIGRATION POL-
ICY 1815-1830.
617(TLS):22SEP72-1096
JOHNSTON, J. THE CAPTAINS AND THE KINGS.
E. MORGAN, 362:27JAN72-120
617(TLS):18FEB72-173
JOHNSTON, J. THE HEART THAT WOULD NOT
HOLD.*
H.A. POCHMANN, 27(AL):NOV71-448
JOHNSTON, R. PARADISE SMITH.
M. LEVIN, 441:24SEP72-40
JOHNSTON, V. THE MOURNING TREES.
N. CALLENDAR, 441:9APR72-41
H. FRANKEL, 561(SATR):26FEB72-71
JOHNSTON, W. THE STILL POINT.
A.W. SADLER, 142:WINTER71-117
JOLY, H.L. LEGEND IN JAPANESE ART.
A.C. SOPER, 57:VOL31#2/3-222
JOLY, R. LE VOCABULAIRE CHRÉTIEN DE
L'AMOUR EST-IL ORIGINAL?
P. CHANTRAINE, 555:VOL44FASC2-331
JONARĀJA. RĀJATARAṄGIṆĪ OF JONARĀJA.
(S. KAUL, ED)
L. STERNBACH, 318(JAOS):APR-JUN70-411
JONAS, G. THE HAPPY HUNGRY MAN.*
M. DOYLE, 491:MAR72-356
150(DR):AUTUMN70-427
JONAS, G. ON DOING GOOD.
441:30APR72-28
JONAS, I.B. THOMAS MANN UND ITALIEN.
T.J. REED, 402(MLR):OCT71-958
JONAS, K.W. & I.B. THOMAS MANN STUDIES.*
(VOL 2)
K. HASSELBACH, 399(MLJ):FEB70-133
A.W. RILEY, 564:FALL68-172
JONDORF, G. ROBERT GARNIER AND THE
THEMES OF POLITICAL TRAGEDY IN THE SIX-
TEENTH CENTURY.*
F.S. BROWN, 207(FR):FEB70-527
V.E. GRAHAM, 401(MLQ):JUN70-248
JONES, A. THE POLITICS OF REFORM 1884.
617(TLS):25AUG72-999
JONES, A.E. THE WAR AGAINST CRIME.
617(TLS):28APR72-501
JONES, A.H.M. THE CRIMINAL COURTS OF THE
ROMAN REPUBLIC AND PRINCIPATE.
617(TLS):31MAR72-376
JONES, A.H.M. A HISTORY OF ROME THROUGH
THE FIFTH CENTURY. (VOL 1)
J. BRISCOE, 123:DEC70-405
JONES, A.I. AN OUTLINE WORD PHONOLOGY
FOR AUSTRALIAN ENGLISH.
H.E. KIJLSTRA, 353:JUL69-119
JONES, A.R. & W. TYDEMAN, EDS. WORDS-
WORTH: LYRICAL BALLADS.
617(TLS):20OCT72-1262
JONES, B.L. ROBERT WILLIAMS PARRY.
617(TLS):15SEP72-1048

JONES, C.M. & C.A.E. JENSEN, EDS. LES
LETTRES EN FRANCE.
  A. SZOGYI, 207(FR):OCT69-156
JONES, C.P. PLUTARCH AND ROME.
  617(TLS):21JAN72-58
JONES, D. THE TRIBUNE'S VISITATION.*
  J. HEATH-STUBBS, 493:SUMMER70-168
JONES, D. & D. WARD. THE PHONETICS OF
RUSSIAN.*
  W.W. DERBYSHIRE, 32:MAR71-214
  T. WAIGHT, 575(SEER):APR71-276
JONES, D.G. BUTTERFLY ON ROCK.*
  D. BARBOUR, 150(DR):AUTUMN70-417
  W.H. NEW, 102(CANL):WINTER71-94
JONES, E. SCENIC FORM IN SHAKESPEARE.
  617(TLS):30JUN72-739
JONES, E.D. VICTORIAN AND EDWARDIAN
WALES FROM OLD PHOTOGRAPHS.
  617(TLS):29DEC72-1590
JONES, F.A. - SEE ASHER, R.
JONES, G. A HISTORY OF THE VIKINGS.
  J.F. POWERS, 613:AUTUMN69-473
JONES, G. KINGS, BEASTS AND HEROES.
  P. ADAMS, 61:OCT72-135
  617(TLS):6OCT72-1190
JONES, G.F. WALTHER VON DER VOGELWEIDE.*
  W.H. JACKSON, 402(MLR):APR71-437
  E.H. ZEYDEL, 221(GQ):MAY70-506
JONES, G.S. OUTCAST LONDON.
  P. WHITEHEAD, 362:6APR72-455
  617(TLS):28JAN72-86
JONES, G.S. TREATMENT OR TORTURE.
  F. CIOFFI, 479(PHQ):JAN70-88
JONES, H.M. BELIEF AND DISBELIEF IN
AMERICAN LITERATURE.*
  M. MILLGATE, 447(N&Q):FEB70-75
JONES, J. JOHN KEATS'S DREAM OF TRUTH.
  M. BOTTRALL, 148:AUTUMN70-286
  R.H. FOGLE, 579(SAQ):WINTER71-125
JONES, J. THE MERRY MERRY MONTH OF MAY.*
  W.H. PRITCHARD, 249(HUDR):SUMMER71-
360
JONES, J.A. POPE'S COUPLET ART.*
  R. PARKIN, 173(ECS):SPRING70-419
  C.E. RAMSEY, 481(PQ):JUL70-370
  C. TRACY, 529(QQ):SPRING70-140
JONES, J.R. & J.E. KELLER - SEE ALFONSO,
P.
JONES, K., ED. THE YEAR BOOK OF SOCIAL
POLICY IN BRITAIN 1971.
  617(TLS):13OCT72-1237
JONES, K.S. AUTOMATIC KEYWORD CLASSIFI-
CATION FOR INFORMATION RETRIEVAL.
  E. SVENONIUS, 356:OCT71-338
JONES, L. EUROLENGO.
  617(TLS):9JUN72-661
JONES, L. - SEE UNDER BARAKA, I.A.
JONES, M. A CRY OF ABSENCE.*
  J.G. FARRELL, 362:13JUL72-57
  617(TLS):21JUL72-835
JONES, M. DUCAL BRITTANY, 1364-1399.*
  R. VAUGHAN, 382(MAE):1971/3-315
JONES, M. LIFE ON THE DOLE.
  617(TLS):16JUN72-697
JONES, M.E.W. THE LITERARY WORLD OF ANA
MARÍA MATUTE.
  L. HICKEY, 86(BHS):OCT71-363
JONES, P. THE PEACE & THE HOOK.
  617(TLS):29SEP72-1146
JONES, P.F. RICHMOND PARK.
  617(TLS):6OCT72-1205
JONES, R. THE RESCUE OF EMIN PASHA.
  617(TLS):8DEC72-1478
JONES, R.B., ED. ANATOMY OF WALES.
  617(TLS):3NOV72-1349

JONES, R.E. PANORAMA DE LA NOUVELLE
CRITIQUE EN FRANCE, DE GASTON BACHELARD
À JEAN-PAUL WEBER.
  R. CHAMPIGNY, 207(FR):MAR70-679
JONES, R.H. THE ROADS TO RUSSIA.*
  M.L. HARVEY, 550(RUSR):JAN70-81
JONES, R.O. THE GOLDEN AGE.
  617(TLS):14APR72-419
JONES, S. THE MAN WITH THE TALENTS.
  J.G., 502(PRS):WINTER68/69-364
JONES, T. WHITEHALL DIARY. (VOL 1) (K.
MIDDLEMAS, ED)
  I. BULMER-THOMAS, 619(TC):1969/2-54
JONES, W. THE LETTERS OF SIR WILLIAM
JONES.* (G. CANNON, ED)
  R.W. BAILEY, 385(MQR):SUMMER72-210
  M.B. EMENEAU, 350:DEC71-959
  F.W. HILLES, 676(YR):WINTER71-259
  E. SHAFFER, 677:VOL2-291
  P.M. SPACKS, 301(JEGP):APR71-321
JONES, W.G. DENMARK.
  J.R. CHRISTIANSON, 563(SS):WINTER71-
96
JONES, W.I. THE SCIENCES AND THE HUMANI-
TIES.
  J.A. WINNIE, 485(PE&W):APR69-202
JONES, W.J. POLITICS AND THE BENCH.
  617(TLS):10MAR72-266
JONES, W.K. BEHIND SPANISH AMERICAN
FOOTLIGHTS.
  R.J. BARNES, 397(MD):DEC67-321
JONES-DAVIES, M-T. INIGO JONES, BEN
JONSON ET LE MASQUE.
  W.A. ARMSTRONG, 551(RENQ):AUTUMN70-
333
JONG, E. FRUITS & VEGETABLES.*
  A. WILLIAMSON, 491:FEB72-296
DE JONG, E. HERMAN HEIJERMANS EN DE
VERNIEUWING VAN HET EUROPESE DRAMA.
  C-O. JELLEMA, 52:BAND4HEFT3-326
DE JONG, J.W. BUDDHA'S WORD IN CHINA.
  L. HURVITZ, 318(JAOS):OCT-DEC70-617
JONKE, G.F. DIE VERMEHRUNG DER LEUCHT-
TÜRME.
  617(TLS):4FEB72-135
JONSON, B. EVERY MAN IN HIS HUMOR.
(G.B. JACKSON, ED)
  N.W. BAWCUTT, 677:VOL2-255
JONSON, B. EVERY MAN IN HIS HUMOUR.
  617(TLS):26MAY72-613
JONSON, B. BEN JONSON: THE COMPLETE
MASQUES. (S. ORGEL, ED)
  I. DONALDSON, 541(RES):AUG70-352
  K.M. LEA, 447(N&Q):JUN70-234
JONSON, B. BEN JONSON: SELECTED MASQUES.
(S. ORGEL, ED)
  R.J. LORDI, 568(SCN):WINTER71-71
JOOST, N. & A. SULLIVAN. D.H. LAWRENCE
AND "THE DIAL."*
  M. ALLOTT, 677:VOL2-327
JOPLIN, S. THE COLLECTED WORKS OF SCOTT
JOPLIN. (V.B. LAWRENCE, ED)
  617(TLS):30JUN72-755
JORAVSKY, D. THE LYSENKO AFFAIR.*
  B.M. COHEN, 104:WINTER71-581
  M.W. MIKULAK, 32:DEC71-898
JORAVSKY, D. & G. HAUPT - SEE MEDVEDEV,
R.A.
JORDAN, A.C. THE WRITER'S MANUAL.
  K.J. FRANKLIN, 353:JUL69-103
JORDAN, D.P. GIBBON AND HIS ROMAN EM-
PIRE.
  617(TLS):14APR72-422
JORDAN, E.L. - SEE SEALSFIELD, C.
JORDAN, M. - SEE OLEŠA, J.
JORDAN, R. THANKSGIVING.
  617(TLS):23JUN72-705

JORDAN, R.F. LE CORBUSIER.
    617(TLS):17NOV72-1389
JORDAN, R.F. VICTORIAN ARCHITECTURE.*
    D. GEBHARD, 576:DEC69-306
JORDAN, R.M. CHAUCER AND THE SHAPE OF
CREATION.*
    B.F. HUPPÉ, 141:WINTER69-94
    S.A. WEBER, 613:WINTER69-608
JORDAN, W.K. EDWARD VI: THE YOUNG KING.
    J. BOSSY, 551(RENQ):AUTUMN70-312
    J.B. HIBBITTS, 150(DR):SUMMER70-267
JØRGENSEN, A. H.C. ANDERSEN-LITTERATUREN
1875-1968.
    E. BREDSDORFF, 301(JEGP):APR71-377
    F.J. MARKER, 563(SS):AUTUMN71-444
JORIS, S. THE QUIDDITY OF SETOFIM.
    V. CUNNINGHAM, 362:6APR72-458
JOSEPH, G. TENNYSONIAN LOVE.*
    A. DANZIG, 637(VS):MAR70-372
JOSEPH, M.K. THE HOLE IN THE ZERO.
    P.J. DOWNEY, 368:MAR69-88
JOSEPHS, H. DIDEROT'S DIALOGUE OF GES-
TURE AND LANGUAGE.
    P. FRANCE, 402(MLR):JAN71-185
JOSEPHSON, M. THE MONEY LORDS.
    J. BROOKS, 441:5NOV72-34
JOSEY, A. LEE KUAN YEW. LEE KUAN YEW
AND THE COMMONWEALTH.
    W. LEVI, 293(JAST):MAY70-737
JOSEY, E.J., ED. THE BLACK LIBRARIAN IN
AMERICA.
    C.S. JONES, 356:JUL71-265
JOSHUA, W. & S.P. GILBERT. ARMS FOR THE
THIRD WORLD.
    D.R. NORLAND, 550(RUSR):OCT70-470
    B. WHALEY, 32:MAR71-157
JOSIPOVICI, G. THE WORLD AND THE BOOK.
    617(TLS):25FEB72-216
JOST, F. ESSAIS DE LITTÉRATURE COMPARÉE.
(VOL 2)
    T.E.D. BRAUN, 399(MLJ):JAN70-42
    L.R. FURST, 208(FS):APR71-250
JOTTRAND, M. PORCELAINES DE TOURNAI DU
XVIII SIÈCLE.
    J.V.G. MALLET, 39:OCT69-355
JOUANNY, R.A. JEAN MORÉAS, ÉCRIVAIN
FRANÇAIS.
    J.A. DUNCAN, 208(FS):APR71-227
JOUANNY, R.A. - SEE MORÉAS, J.
JOUFFROY, A. - SEE "SAINT-POL-ROUX"
JOUHANDEAU, M. AZAËL. AUX CENT ACTES
DIVERS. GÉMONIES. LETTRES D'UNE MÈRE
À SON FILS.
    617(TLS):22SEP72-1116
JOUKOVSKY, F. LA GLOIRE DANS LA POÉSIE
FRANÇAISE ET NÉO-LATINE DU XVIE SIÈCLE.
    J.I.J., 568(SCN):SUMMER/AUTUMN71-56
    I.D. MC FARLANE, 208(FS):JUL71-321
    D.B. WILSON, 182:VOL23#3-92
JOUKOWSKY, F. ORPHÉE ET SES DISCIPLES
DANS LA POÉSIE FRANÇAISE ET NÉO-LATINE
DU XVIE SIÈCLE.
    M. JEANNERET, 208(FS):JUL71-322
    F. WAGNER, 182:VOL23#9-475
JOÜON DES LONGRAIS, F. TASHI.
    W. MC CULLOUGH, 318(JAOS):APR-JUN70-
    367
JOVAIŠAS, A. LIUDVIKAS RĖZA.
    V. MACIŪNAS, 574(SEEJ):SPRING71-138
JOVICEVICH, A. - SEE DE LA HARPE, J-F.
JOYAUX, G.J. & A. TUKEY, EDS. SI NOUS
COMMENCIONS À LIRE.
    L.C. KEATING, 399(MLJ):JAN70-62
JOYCE, J. EXILES.
    617(TLS):12MAY72-541
JOYCE, J. GIACOMO JOYCE.* (R. ELLMANN,
ED)
    P. RECONDO, 202(FMOD):NOV69-104

JOYNES, E.S. - SEE SCHILLER, F.
JUDAH, J. THE HISTORY AND PHILOSOPHY OF
THE METAPHYSICAL MOVEMENTS IN AMERICA.
    S.A.S., 543:DEC69-348
JUDD, D. BALFOUR AND THE BRITISH EMPIRE.
    S.H. ZEBEL, 637(VS):SEP69-107
JUDD, N.M. MEN MET ALONG THE TRAIL.
    C.L. TANNER, 50(ARQ):SUMMER69-186
JUDEN, B. TRADITIONS ORPHIQUES ET TEN-
DANCES MYSTIQUES DANS LE ROMANTISME
FRANÇAIS (1800-1855).
    617(TLS):12MAY72-554
JUDGE, A. A MAN APART.
    617(TLS):8DEC72-1507
JUHÁSZ, F. THE BOY CHANGED INTO A STAG.*
    J. ATLAS, 491:OCT71-45
JUHÁSZ, G. MAGYARORSZÁG KÜLPOLITIKÁJA,
1919-1945.
    M.D. FENYO, 32:MAR71-184
JUILLAND, A., P.M.H. EDWARDS & I. JUIL-
LAND. FREQUENCY DICTIONARY OF RUMANIAN
WORDS.
    W. NOOMEN, 361:VOL23#2-202
JUILLAND, A. & H.H. LIEB. "KLASSE" UND
KLASSIFIKATION IN DER SPRACHWISSEN-
SCHAFT.
    L. NEBESKÝ & P. PIŤHA, 361:VOL24#2-
    201
JULIEN, C. AMERICA'S EMPIRE.*
    P. PASSELL, 441:23JAN72-23
JULIEN, C-A. L'AFRIQUE DU NORD EN
MARCHE.
    617(TLS):29SEP72-1172
JULLIAN, P. DREAMERS OF DECADENCE.*
    F. BROWN, 441:2JAN72-6
    P. GAY, 31(ASCH):AUTUMN72-660
JUMP, J., ED. SHAKESPEARE: "HAMLET."
    A.L. FRENCH, 184(EIC):JAN70-98
JUMP, J.D. BYRON.
    617(TLS):17NOV72-1398
JUNG, C.G. FREUD UND DIE PSYCHOANALYSE.
(F. RIKLIN, L. JUNG-MERKER & E. RÜF,
EDS)
    V. VON DER HEYDT, 182:VOL23#8-394
JUNG, C.G., K. KERÉNYI & P. RADIN. DER
GÖTTLICHE SCHELM.
    J. STAROBINSKI, 98:DEC69-1033
JUNG-EN, L. - SEE UNDER LIU JUNG-EN
JUN'ICHI, N. - SEE UNDER NOMURA JUN'ICHI
JUN'ICHIRŌ, I. - SEE UNDER ISHIKAWA
JUN'ICHIRŌ
JUREWICZ, O. - SEE KUMANIECKI, C.F.
JURGENS, M. DOCUMENTS DU MINUTIER CEN-
TRAL CONCERNANT L'HISTOIRE DE LA
MUSIQUE (1600-1650). (VOL 1)
    M.D. FENYO, 14:APR69-163
JURGENSEN, M., GENERAL ED. STUDIES IN
SWISS LITERATURE.
    E.W. HERD, 67:NOV71-263
JURGONS, R. DIE HÜTTENSTANDORTE DÜN-
KIRCHEN, IJMUIDEN, BREMEN UND LÜBECK.
    J. COMTE, 182:VOL23#1/2-63
JURT, J. LES ATTITUDES POLITIQUES DE
GEORGES BERNANOS JUSQU'EN 1931.
    E. BEAUMONT, 208(FS):JAN71-110
JUST, W. MILITARY MEN.*
    617(TLS):10MAR72-264
JÜTHNER, J. DIE ATHLETISCHEN LEIBESÜB-
UNGEN DER GRIECHEN. (1ST HALF OF PT 2)
(F. BREIN, ED)
    H.A. HARRIS, 123:MAR71-84
JUVENAL. JUVÉNAL, "EXTRAITS DES
SATIRES." (J. HELLEGOUARC'H, ED &
TRANS)
    J. ANDRÉ, 555:VOL44FASC1-151
JUZL, M. DAS WESEN DES AESTHETISCHEN
ERFASSENS DER REALITÄT.
    M. RIESER, 290(JAAC):WINTER69-247

KABLE, W.S., ED. WILLIAM HILL BROWN.
  C.H. CHAPMAN, 432(NEQ):DEC70-666
KACHRU, B.B. A REFERENCE GRAMMAR OF
  KASHMIRI.
  R.E. ASHER, 293(JAST):AUG70-977
KACZEROWSKY, K. BÜRGERLICHE ROMANKUNST
  IM ZEITALTER DES BAROCK.
  K.F. OTTO, JR., 301(JEGP):JAN71-111
KADIĆ, A. FROM CROATIAN RENAISSANCE TO
  YUGOSLAV SOCIALISM.
  E.D. GOY, 575(SEER):APR71-289
  R.E. KANET, 32:JUN71-412
  A.M. MLIKOTIN, 574(SEEJ):SPRING71-85
DE KADT, E., ED. PATTERNS OF FOREIGN
  INFLUENCE IN THE CARIBBEAN.
  617(TLS):30JUN72-745
KAEGI, W. WAS IST ELEKTRONISCHE MUSIK.
  W.M. STROH, 513:FALL-WINTER68-145
KAEL, P. THE CITIZEN KANE BOOK.*
  C. JAMES, 362:3FEB72-155
KAEMPFER, H.M. & W.O.G. SICKINGHE, EDS.
  THE FASCINATING WORLD OF THE JAPANESE
  ARTIST.
  617(TLS):24MAR72-345
KAESTLI, J-D. L'ESCHATOLOGIE DANS
  L'OEUVRE DE LUC.
  F.F. BRUCE, 182:VOL23#13/14-650
KAFKA, F. BRIEFE AN FELICE.* (E. HELLER
  & J. BORN, EDS)
  H. LEHNERT, 400(MLN):APR70-407
KAFKA, F. FRANZ KAFKA: THE COMPLETE
  STORIES.* (N.N. GLATZER, ED)
  G. STEINER, 442(NY):15JUL72-75
"FRANZ KAFKA." (E. HELLER & J. BEUG,
  EDS)
  J.C. BRUCE, 406:SUMMER71-167
  A.P. FOULKES, 301(JEGP):APR71-339
KAGAN, D. THE OUTBREAK OF THE PELOPON-
  NESIAN WAR.*
  H.D. WESTLAKE, 123:JUN71-248
KAGANOVICH, A.L. ARTS OF RUSSIA: 17TH
  AND 18TH CENTURIES.
  R.M. QUINN, 50(ARQ):SPRING69-85
KAHANE, A., L.M. THREIPLAND & J. WARD-
  PERKINS. THE AGER VEIENTANUS, NORTH
  AND EAST OF ROME.
  R.M. OGILVIE, 123:DEC71-438
KAHANE, H. LOGIC AND PHILOSOPHY.
  D. EDGINGTON, 479(PHQ):OCT70-406
KAHANE, M. NEVER AGAIN!
  R.J. MILCH, 561(SATR):8JAN72-32
KAHL, J. THE MISERY OF CHRISTIANITY.
  617(TLS):28JAN72-104
KAHL-FURTHMANN, G. WANN LEBTE HOMER?*
  E.C. REINKE, 121(CJ):DEC70-JAN71-171
KAHLE, G. MILITÄR UND STAATSBILDUNG IN
  DEN ANFÄNGEN DER UNABHÄNGIGKEIT MEX-
  IKOS.
  W. HAHLWEG, 182:VOL23#4-187
KAHLER, E. THE ORBIT OF THOMAS MANN.*
  T.J. REED, 402(MLR):APR71-473
KAHMEN, V. EROTIC ART TODAY.
  P. ADAMS, 61:DEC72-146
KAHN, E.J., JR. THE FIRST DECADE.
  442(NY):6MAY72-146
KAHN, H. & B. BRUCE-BRIGGS. THINGS TO
  COME.
  P. ADAMS, 61:JUN72-112
  442(NY):19AUG72-80
KAHN, R. THE BOYS OF SUMMER.
  H.H. BROUN, 440:27FEB72-4
  J.K. HUTCHENS, 561(SATR):11MAR72-67
  C. LEHMANN-HAUPT, 441:25FEB72-41
  G. LICHTENSTEIN, 441:5MAR72-32
  E. WEEKS, 61:APR72-124
KAHNWEILER, D-H. LA MONTÉE DU CUBISME.
  JUAN GRIS.
  P. DUFOUR, 98:AUG-SEP69-809

KAHNWEILER, D-H., WITH F. CRÉMIEUX. MY
  GALLERIES AND PAINTERS.*
  R. DOWNES, 441:31DEC72-7
KAHRMANN, B. DIE IDYLLISCHE SZENE IM
  ZEITGENÖSSISCHEN ENGLISCHEN ROMAN.
  J. WESTLAKE, 677:VOL2-339
KAILASAPATHY, K. TAMIL HEROIC POETRY.
  B.E.F. BECK & K.V. ZVELEBIL, 293
  (JAST):NOV69-184
KAIMIO, M. THE CHORUS OF GREEK DRAMA
  WITHIN THE LIGHT OF THE PERSON AND NUM-
  BER USED.
  F. LASSERRE, 182:VOL23#11/12-629
KAIN, R.M. DUBLIN.
  617(TLS):17MAR72-302
KAINEN, J. THE ETCHINGS OF CANALETTO.*
  39:JUL69-84
KAISER, G. BEITRÄGE ZU DEN LIEDERN DES
  MINNESÄNGERS RUBIN.
  J.W. THOMAS, 222(GR):MAY70-255
KAISER, G., ED. DIE DRAMEN DES ANDREAS
  GRYPHIUS.
  G. HILLEN, 221(GQ):MAY70-507
  H. POWELL, 220(GL&L):OCT70-115
KAISER, G. DIE KORALLE. (B.J. KENWOR-
  THY, ED)
  J.M. BURNS, 399(MLJ):MAY70-362
KAISER, J. GREAT PIANISTS OF OUR TIME.*
  F. DAWES, 415:NOV71-1072
KAISER, K., ED. BRITAIN AND WEST GER-
  MANY.*
  N. ASCHERSON, 453:20APR72-26
KAJANTO, I. ON THE PROBLEM OF THE
  AVERAGE DURATION OF LIFE IN THE ROMAN
  EMPIRE.
  J. ANDRÉ, 555:VOL44FASC2-366
KAJANTO, I. ONOMASTIC STUDIES IN THE
  EARLY CHRISTIAN INSCRIPTIONS OF ROME
  AND CARTHAGE. SUPERNOMINA. THE LATIN
  COGNOMINA.
  D.J. GEORGACAS, 424:MAR69-91
KALADZE, K. STIKHOTVORENIYA I POEMY.
  617(TLS):31MAR72-360
KALB, M. & E. ABEL. ROOTS OF INVOLVE-
  MENT.*
  617(TLS):21APR72-436
KALENSKY, V.G. POLITICHESKAIA NAUKA V
  S.SH.A.
  K.W. RYAVEC, 32:JUN71-366
KÄLLBERG, S. OFF THE MIDDLE WAY.
  N. BIRNBAUM, 441:24SEP72-50
  442(NY):9SEP72-127
KALLEN, H.M. LIBERTY, LAUGHTER, AND
  TEARS.*
  V.M. AMES, 290(JAAC):WINTER69-262
  Y.H. KRIKORIAN, 484(PPR):MAR70-466
KALLICH, M., ED. A LETTER FROM A CLERGY-
  MAN TO HIS FRIEND, WITH AN ACCOUNT OF
  THE TRAVELS OF CAPTAIN LEMUEL GULLIVER.
  566:SPRING71-70
KALLICH, M. THE OTHER END OF THE EGG.
  R. QUINTANA, 566:AUTUMN70-25
KALLICH, M.I. HEAV'N'S FIRST LAW.
  J.M. ADEN, 219(GAR):SPRING69-107
KALLIR, O. EGON SCHIELE.*
  W. FISCHER, 90:OCT69-621
KALLMAN, C. THE SENSE OF OCCASION.
  W.H. AUDEN, 231:MAR72-92
  R. MAZZOCCO, 453:15JUN72-31
  M. MESIC, 491:APR72-47
KALLMANN, H. A HISTORY OF MUSIC IN
  CANADA, 1534-1914.
  W. MELLERS, 415:JUL70-710
KALMYKOW, A.D. MEMOIRS OF A RUSSIAN
  DIPLOMAT. (A. KALMYKOW, ED)
  617(TLS):7APR72-384
KALYANARAMAN, A. ARYATARANGINI.
  J.P. SHARMA, 293(JAST):AUG70-998

KAMANIN, N.P. - SEE RIABCHIKOV, E.
KAMBER, G. MAX JACOB AND THE POETICS OF
  CUBISM.
    R. SHATTUCK, 453:1JUN72-25
KAMEN, H. THE IRON CENTURY.
    617(TLS):24MAR72-329
KAMEN, H. THE WAR OF SUCCESSION IN
  SPAIN 1700-15.
    P. ILIE, 86(BHS):JAN71-71
    639(VQR):SUMMER70-CVI
KAMENKA, E. MARXISM AND ETHICS.*
    C.P.S., 543:SEP69-131
    A.J. SKILLEN, 393(MIND):OCT70-633
KAMENKA, E., ED. PARADIGM FOR REVOLU-
  TION?
    617(TLS):23JUN72-706
KAMERBEEK, J., JR. DE POËZIE VAN J.C.
  BLOEM IN EUROPEES PERSPECTIEF.
    P.J.H. VERMEEREN, 52:BAND4HEFT3-328
KAMINSKY, A.R. GEORGE HENRY LEWES AS
  LITERARY CRITIC.
    C.M. FULMER, 677:VOL2-316
    W. MYERS, 637(VS):DEC69-229
    W.D. SCHAEFER, 445(NCF):SEP69-246
KAMM, J. INDICATIVE PAST.
    617(TLS):10MAR72-278
KAMMAN, M. THE MAKING OF A COOK.
    N. MAGID, 440:13FEB72-12
KAMMEN, M. DEPUTYES & LIBERTYES.
    R.D. BROWN, 432(NEQ):DEC70-656
    S.S. WEBB, 656(WMQ):OCT70-686
KAMMEN, M. EMPIRE AND INTEREST.
    R.E. BROWN, 432(NEQ):SEP70-511
KAMMEN, M. PEOPLE OF PARADOX.
    M. CUNLIFFE, 441:1OCT72-4
KAMMEN, M.G. A ROPE OF SAND.
    B.W. LABAREE, 656(WMQ):JAN70-150
KAMPF, L. ON MODERNISM.*
    L.G. GORDON, 330(MASJ):SPRING69-91
KAMPF, L. & P. LAUTER, EDS. THE POLITICS
  OF LITERATURE.
    T. LASK, 441:2JUN72-38
    E. SHORRIS, 231:DEC72-119
KAMPMANN, L. THE WORLD OF PUPPETS.
    617(TLS):4AUG72-926
KAMSHAD, H. MODERN PERSIAN PROSE LITERA-
  TURE.
    M.A. JAZAYERY, 318(JAOS):APR-JUN70-
      257
KAMSHAD, H., ED. A MODERN PERSIAN PROSE
  READER.*
    M.B. LORAINE, 399(MLJ):FEB70-136
KANE, H. THE VIRILITY FACTOR.
    M. LEVIN, 441:19MAR72-40
KANE, L.M., COMP. GUIDE TO THE PUBLIC
  AFFAIRS COLLECTION OF THE MINNESOTA
  HISTORICAL SOCIETY.
    R.W. RICHMOND, 14:APR69-163
KANE, P. WANDERINGS OF AN ARTIST.
    M.S. YOUNG, 39:APR70-330
KANIN, G. TRACY AND HEPBURN.*
    R. HECTOR, 561(SATR):8JAN72-29
    G. MILLAR, 362:1JUN72-726
    617(TLS):2JUN72-635
KANIUK, Y. ADAM RESURRECTED.*
    D.A.N. JONES, 362:17FEB72-221
    617(TLS):10MAR72-265
KANNICHT, R. - SEE EURIPIDES
KANT, H. DAS IMPRESSUM.
    617(TLS):22SEP72-1088
KANT, I. GESAMMELTE SCHRIFTEN. (PT 4,
  VOL 1)
    C. CESA, 548(RCSF):JUL/SEP69-342
KANT, I. KANT'S POLITICAL WRITINGS. (H.
  REISS, ED)
    J. DAY, 518:OCT71-25

KANT, I. PHILOSOPHICAL CORRESPONDENCE
  1759-99. (A. ZWEIG, ED & TRANS)
    J. FANG, 393(MIND):JUL70-470
KANTOR, M. I LOVE YOU, IRENE.
    M. LEVIN, 441:26NOV72-38
KANZA, T. CONFLICT IN THE CONGO.
    617(TLS):16JUN72-676
KAPEŁUŚ, H. & J. KRZYŻANOWSKIEGO, EDS.
  DZIEJE FOLKLORYSTYKI POLSKIEJ, 1800-63.
    H. RÖSEL, 182:VOL23#3-120
KAPITSA, P. PETER KAPITSA ON LIFE AND
  SCIENCE. (A. PARRY, ED & TRANS)
    A. VUCINICH, 550(RUSR):JAN70-111
KAPLAN, A. PAPER AIRPLANE.
    V. YOUNG, 249(HUDR):WINTER71/72-669
KAPLAN, L.S. COLONIES INTO NATION.
    T. LASK, 441:26MAY72-35
KAPP, Y. ELEANOR MARX. (VOL 1)
    E. HOBSBAWM, 362:7SEP72-309
    617(TLS):7JUL72-766
KAPPLER, C.J., ED. INDIAN TREATIES
  1778-1883.
    M. ROGIN, 441:24DEC72-4
KAPRALIK, C.I. REPORT ON THE WORK OF THE
  JEWISH TRUST CORPORATION FOR GERMANY.
    617(TLS):15SEP72-1068
KAPROW, A. ASSEMBLAGES, ENVIRONMENTS AND
  HAPPENINGS.*
    M. BENEDIKT, 55:OCT69-22
    A. BERLEANT, 186(ETC.):MAR69-89
KAPS, H.K. MORAL PERSPECTIVE IN "LA
  PRINCESSE DE CLÈVES."*
    G. HAINSWORTH, 208(FS):APR71-196
    E. REICHEL, 72:BAND208HEFT2-154
    W.V. WORTLEY, 131(CL):SPRING71-183
KARADJORDJEVIĆ, D. ISTINA O MOME ŽIVOTU.
    R.M. SUSEL, 104:SPRING71-136
KARADŽIĆ, V. DELA.
    M. MATEJIĆ, 574(SEEJ):SPRING71-88
KARAGEORGHIS, V. THE ANCIENT CIVILIZA-
  TION OF CYPRUS.
    G.E. KADISH, 124:APR71-274
KARAGEORGHIS, V. SALAMIS IN CYPRUS,
  HOMERIC, HELLENISTIC AND ROMAN.
    T.B. MITFORD, 123:DEC71-436
KARAMZIN, N.M. THE SELECTED PROSE OF
  N.M. KARAMZIN.* (H.M. NEBEL, JR.,
  TRANS)
    J. FIZER, 399(MLJ):FEB70-126
    J.G. GARRARD, 550(RUSR):APR70-233
KARANDIKAR, M.A. ISLAM IN INDIA'S TRAN-
  SITION TO MODERNITY.
    T.P. WRIGHT, JR., 293(JAST):AUG70-955
KARANIKAS, A. TILLERS OF A MYTH.
    A. GUTTMANN, 340(KR):SEP66-548
    G.A.M. JANSSENS, 179(ES):DEC69-618
KARANIKAS, A. & H. ELIAS VENEZIS.
    C.M. PROUSSIS, 574(SEEJ):FALL71-399
KARÁTSON, A. LE SYMBOLISME EN HONGRIE.
    G.F. CUSHING, 575(SEER):JAN71-141
KARLSSON, H. STUDIER ÖVER BÅTNAMN,
  SÄRSKILT NAMN PÅ BACKEBÅTAR OCH BANK-
  SKUTOR FRÅN 1700-TALETS BOHUSLÄN.
    G. FRANZÉN, 563(SS):SUMMER71-292
KARMI, H.S. AL-MANAR AN ENGLISH-ARABIC
  DICTIONARY.
    617(TLS):21APR72-455
KARNEIN, A. DE AMORE DEUTSCH.
    K. LANGOSCH, 182:VOL23#15/16-730
    H.B. WILLSON, 402(MLR):OCT71-928
KÄRNELL, K-Å. STRINDBERGS BILDSPRÅK.
    E. POULENARD, 462(OL):VOL23#4-325
KARNICK, M. "WILHELM MEISTERS WANDER-
  JAHRE" ODER DIE KUNST DES MITTELBAREN.*
    D.G. LITTLE, 402(MLR):APR71-459
    H.R. VAGET, 222(GR):MAY70-247
KARNOW, S. MAO AND CHINA.
    J. PECK, 441:29OCT72-2

KAROLIDES, N.J. THE PIONEER IN THE
AMERICAN NOVEL, 1900-1950.
D.J. MC MILLAN, 650(WF):JAN69-56
KARP, A.J., ED. THE JEWISH EXPERIENCE IN
AMERICA.
M. FREIBERG, 432(NEQ):SEP70-502
KARPELES, M. FOLK SONGS FROM NEWFOUND-
LAND.*
E. FOWKE, 99:APR72-53
KARPELES, M. CECIL SHARP.*
B.H. BRONSON, 650(WF):JUL68-200
E. FOWKE, 582(SFQ):SEP68-269
KARSH, Y. FACES OF OUR TIME.
617(TLS):24MAR72-345
KARTODIRDJO, S. - SEE UNDER SARTONO
KARTODIRDJO
KARUNADASA, Y. BUDDHIST ANALYSIS OF
MATTER.
A. WAYMAN, 293(JAST):FEB70-460
KARVE, I. MAHARASHTRA - LAND AND ITS
PEOPLE.*
J.E. SCHWARTZBERG, 293(JAST):AUG70-
970
KARVE, I. YUGANTA.
E. BENDER, 318(JAOS):APR-JUN70-348
KARYAKIN, Y. RE-READING DOSTOYEVSKY...
(S. KOTLOBYE & L. TETSKAYA, EDS)
617(TLS):4FEB72-138
KASCHNITZ, M.L. ZWISCHEN IMMER UND NIE.
617(TLS):14JAN72-44
KASCHNITZ, M.L. - SEE VON EICHENDORFF, J.
KASER, D. BOOK PIRATING IN TAIWAN.
R.N. TANG, 293(JAST):AUG70-938
KASER, D., ED. BOOKS IN AMERICA'S PAST.*
E. MOTTRAM, 354:MAR69-78
KASER, M. SOVIET ECONOMICS.
M. BORNSTEIN, 32:DEC71-900
KASHOKI, M.E. A PHONEMIC ANALYSIS OF
BEMBA.
W.M. MANN, 69:OCT69-441
KASSÁK, L. ÖSSZES VERSEI.
G. RÓNAY, 270:VOL20#3-68
KASTLE, H. MILLIONAIRES.
M. LEVIN, 441:14MAY72-37
"KATALOG DER TONBANDAUFNAHMEN B 7001 -
B 10 000 DES PHONOGRAMMARCHIVES DER
ÖSTERREICHISCHEN AKADEMIE DER WISSEN-
SCHAFTEN IN WIEN."
A. BRIEGLEB, 187:SEP72-547
"KATALOG DER TONBANDAUFNAHMEN M 1 -
M 2000 DER MUSIKETHNOLOGISCHEN ABTEIL-
UNG, MUSEUM FÜR VÖLKERKUNDE BERLIN."
(D. CHRISTENSEN, WITH H-J. JORDAN, EDS)
A. BRIEGLEB, 187:SEP72-547
KATAYEV, V. THE GRASS OF OBLIVION.
639(VQR):AUTUMN70-CXLIII
KATES, G.N. CHINESE HOUSEHOLD FURNITURE.
P. HARDIE, 39:APR69-325
J.A. PRESCOTT, 302:JUL70-410
KATKOV, G. RUSSIA 1917.
W.E. MOSSE, 587:JAN68-430
P.C. ROBERTS, 396(MODA):SUMMER71-328
N.D. ROODKOWSKY, 613:AUTUMN68-475
KATKOV, G. THE TRIAL OF BUKHARIN.
A. WALKER, 575(SEER):APR71-322
KATRIS, J.A. EYEWITNESS IN GREECE.
G. ANASTAPLO, 561(SATR):12FEB72-79
KATZ, E. ARMED LOVE.
H.L. VAN BRUNT, 561(SATR):22JAN72-78
617(TLS):1SEP72-1012
KATZ, F. THE ANCIENT AMERICAN CIVILISA-
TIONS.
617(TLS):15DEC72-1529
KATZ, H. SHADOW ON THE ALAMO.
M. WALDRON, 441:10SEP72-2
KATZ, J., ED. PROOF. (VOL 1)
617(TLS):2JUN72-640
KATZ, J. - SEE CRANE, S.

KATZ, J.J. THE PHILOSOPHY OF LANGUAGE.*
H.E. BREKLE, 38:BAND87HEFT2-236
J. NARVESON, 486:JUN68-195
KATZ, M. CLASS, BUREAUCRACY, AND
SCHOOLS.
J. CALAM, 561(SATR):29APR72-52
KATZ, P. & W. JACKSON, EDS. ART NOW:
NEW YORK.
B. REISE, 592:NOV69-186
KATZ, S. SAW.
M. LEVIN, 441:1OCT72-42
KATZ, S.N. WHEN PARENTS FAIL.
H.D. KRAUSE, 441:27FEB72-44
KATZ, W.L. TEACHERS' GUIDE TO AFRICAN
HISTORY.
N. WEYL, 396(MODA):SPRING71-217
KATZMAN, A. OUR TIME.
441:9APR72-34
KAUFFMANN, S., WITH B. HENSTELL, EDS.
AMERICAN FILM CRITICISM.
D. BROMWICH, 441:17DEC72-2
KAUFMAN, P. THE COMMUNITY LIBRARY.
P. MORGAN, 354:MAR69-74
KAUFMANN, D.L. NORMAN MAILER.*
R. FOSTER, 141:SPRING70-164
M.F. SCHULZ, 659:SPRING72-243
KAUFMANN, E. L'ARCHITECTURE AU SIÈCLE
DES LUMIÈRES.
P. GUERRE, 98:NOV69-978
KAUFMANN, E., JR. - SEE HITCHCOCK, H-R. &
OTHERS
KAUFMANN, G. WIE SAG ICH'S AUF DEUTSCH?
H. BROCKHAUS, 221(GQ):JAN70-133
KAUFMANN, H. ERNST FÖRSTEMANN: ALT-
DEUTSCHE PERSONENNAMEN: ERGÄNZUNGSBAND.
R.E. KELLER, 402(MLR):JAN71-208
KAUFMANN, H. HEINRICH HEINE.
J.L.S., 191(ELN):SEP69(SUPP)-103
KAUFMANN, H. UNTERSUCHUNGEN ZU ALT-
DEUTSCHEN RUFNAMEN.
C. ROTHRAUFF, 424:MAR68-65
KAUFMANN, P. L'EXPÉRIENCE ÉMOTIONNELLE
DE L'ESPACE.
Y. BRÈS, 542:JAN-MAR68-129
KAUFMANN, W. NIETZSCHE. (3RD ED)
S.O.H., 543:MAR70-557
KAUFMANN, W. THE RAGAS OF NORTH INDIA.
M.J. CURTISS, 318(JAOS):OCT-DEC70-593
KAUFMANN, W. TRAGEDY AND PHILOSOPHY.*
J.P. ANTON, 149:JUN71-188
H.C. BALDRY, 123:DEC71-393
E.H. DUNCAN, 290(JAAC):SPRING70-404
J.M. HEMS, 484(PPR):DEC69-307
C.R. LYONS, 397(MD):DEC69-325
KAUFMANN-ROCHARD, J. ORIGINES D'UNE
BOURGEOISIE RUSSE, XVIE ET XVIIE
SIÈCLES.
S.H. BARON, 32:SEP71-660
KAUL, A.N. THE ACTION OF ENGLISH COMEDY.
T. HAWKES, 676(YR):AUTUMN70-130
J.R. KINCAID, 301(JEGP):APR71-299
KAUL, S. - SEE JONARĀJA
KAULBACH, F. PHILOSOPHIE DER BESCHREI-
BUNG.
J. FANG, 319:APR72-243
KAUSHIK, D. THE INDIAN OCEAN.
617(TLS):13OCT72-1237
KAVALER, L. FREEZING POINT.
617(TLS):29SEP72-1136
KAVAN, A. ASYLUM PIECE.
E. FEINSTEIN, 364:FEB/MAR72-177
617(TLS):28JAN72-85
KAVANAGH, D. POLITICAL CULTURE.
617(TLS):9JUN72-666
KAVANAGH, P. THE GREEN FOOL.
S. HEANEY, 362:13JAN72-55
KAVANAGH, P.J. ABOUT TIME.*
P. LESTER, 493:AUTUMN70-250

KAVANAGH, P.J. A HAPPY MAN.
  V. CUNNINGHAM, 362:24AUG72-248
  617(TLS):15SEP72-1042
KAVANAUGH, J. THERE ARE MEN TOO GENTLE
  TO LIVE AMONG WOLVES.
  R.B. SHAW, 491:MAR72-342
KAWABATA, Y. HOUSE OF THE SLEEPING BEAU-
  TIES.
  A.G. KIMBALL, 145(CRIT):VOL13#1-19
KAWABATA, Y. THE MASTER OF GO.
  A. FRIEDMAN, 441:22OCT72-4
  M. MADDOCKS, 61:OCT72-126
KAWABATA, Y. THE SOUND OF THE MOUNTAIN.*
  P. BAILEY, 364:DEC71/JAN72-157
  639(VQR):AUTUMN70-CXXIX
KAY, J. A HISTORY OF COUNTY CRICKET:
  LANCASHIRE.
  617(TLS):13OCT72-1237
KAY, N. SHOSTAKOVITCH.
  617(TLS):28JAN72-87
KAY-ROBINSON, D. HARDY'S WESSEX REAP-
  PRAISED.
  617(TLS):13OCT72-1237
KAYE, E. A HISTORY OF QUEEN'S COLLEGE,
  LONDON, 1848-1972.
  617(TLS):1DEC72-1453
KAYE, E. - SEE MARMIER, X.
KAYE, E. - SEE"MARIE MATTEI: LETTRES À
  THÉOPHILE GAUTIER ET À LOUIS DE COR-
  MENIN"
KAYSING, B. THE EX-URBANITE'S COMPLETE
  AND ILLUSTRATED EASY-DOES-IT FIRST-TIME
  FARMER'S GUIDE.
  M. OLMERT, 440:2JAN72-6
KAZAN, E. THE ASSASSINS.
  G. HICKS, 441:5MAR72-6
  W. KENNEDY, 561(SATR):1APR72-75
  C. LEHMANN-HAUPT, 441:16FEB72-41
  442(NY):26FEB72-101
  617(TLS):10NOV72-1357
KAZANTZAKIS, H.N. NIKOS KAZANTZAKIS.
  42(AR):SPRING69-112
KAZANTZAKIS, N. ENGLAND.
  617(TLS):25FEB72-212
KAZEMZADEH, F. RUSSIA AND BRITAIN IN
  PERSIA, 1864-1914.
  R.L. TIGNOR, 637(VS):JUN70-421
KEALEY, E.J. ROGER OF SALISBURY.
  617(TLS):24NOV72-1439
KEAN, P.M. CHAUCER AND THE MAKING OF
  ENGLISH POETRY.
  617(TLS):29SEP72-1152
KEAREY, C. LAST PLANE FROM ULI.
  M. LEVIN, 441:1OCT72-42
KEARNEY, H. SCIENCE AND CHANGE 1500-
  1700.
  617(TLS):14JAN72-37
KEARNEY, H.F. SCHOLARS AND GENTLEMEN.*
  K. CHARLTON, 402(MLR):APR71-385
  J. CONNELL, 356:JUL71-264
KEARNS, D. WORLD WANDERER.
  617(TLS):14APR72-429
KEARNS, J. BY THE LIGHT OF THE SILVERY
  MC LUNE.*
  M. DOYLE, 491:MAR72-356
KEARNS, L. POINTING.
  R. SOMMER, 448:SUMMER68-107
KEATING, H.R.F. INSPECTOR GHOTE GOES BY
  TRAIN.*
  O.L. BAILEY, 561(SATR):28OCT72-89
  N. CALLENDAR, 441:16JUL72-32
KEATING, H.R.F. INSPECTOR GHOTE TRUSTS
  THE HEART.
  617(TLS):1DEC72-1467
KEATING, L.C. ANDRÉ MAUROIS.*
  J. KOLBERT, 207(FR):DEC69-332
  M.I. MORAUD, 399(MLJ):MAR70-208

KEATS, J. HOWARD HUGHES. (REV)
  J. SEELYE, 441:25JUN72-2
KEATS, J. THE POEMS OF JOHN KEATS.*
  (M. ALLOTT, ED)
  J-C. SALLÉ, 677:VOL2-301
KEDDIE, N.R. AN ISLAMIC RESPONSE TO
  IMPERIALISM.*
  J.B. KELLY, 293(JAST):AUG70-980
KEDOURIE, E., ED. NATIONALISM IN ASIA
  AND AFRICA.*
  617(TLS):28JAN72-90
KEE, A. THE WAY OF TRANSCENDENCE.
  617(TLS):28JAN72-105
KEE, R. THE GREEN FLAG.
  P. ADAMS, 61:OCT72-135
  D. O'MALLEY, 362:4MAY72-592
  617(TLS):26MAY72-597
KEELER, W. WALKING ON THE GREENHOUSE
  ROOF.
  S. SCOBIE, 102(CANL):AUTUMN71-75
KEELING, D. MANAGEMENT IN GOVERNMENT.
  617(TLS):5MAY72-507
KEELING, W. & T. BONNER. THE EAST INDIA
  COMPANY JOURNALS OF CAPTAIN WILLIAM
  KEELING AND MASTER THOMAS BONNER, 1615-
  1617. (M. STRACHAN & B. PENROSE, EDS)
  617(TLS):24NOV72-1424
KEEN, S. APOLOGY FOR WONDER.
  W.A.J., 543:DEC69-348
KEETON, G.W. SHAKESPEARE'S LEGAL AND
  POLITICAL BACKGROUND.
  J.E. PHILLIPS, 570(SQ):WINTER69-101
KEEVIL, A. THE STORY OF FITCH LOVELL.
  617(TLS):17NOV72-1405
KEIL, G. & OTHERS, EDS. FACHLITERATUR
  DES MITTELALTERS.
  J.L. FLOOD, 220(GL&L):APR71-273
KEITA GENJI. THE OGRE.
  617(TLS):22SEP72-1122
KEITH, A. A THOUSAND YEARS OF ABERDEEN.
  617(TLS):13OCT72-1236
KEITH, A.N. BELOVED EXILES.
  M. LEVIN, 441:26MAR72-44
KEITH, H. NEW ZEALAND ART: PAINTING
  1827-1890.
  W. CURNOW, 368:JUN69-186
KEITH, W.J. CHARLES G.D. ROBERTS.*
  D. CAMERON, 529(QQ):SUMMER70-282
KEITHLEY, G. THE DONNER PARTY.
  J. DICKEY, 441:6FEB72-7
  D. JUNKINS, 61:MAR72-95
  T. LASK, 441:11MAR72-27
  N. ROSTEN, 561(SATR):11MAR72-81
KELEMEN, P. ART OF THE AMERICAS.
  639(VQR):SPRING70-LXXV
KELEMEN, P. BAROQUE AND ROCOCO IN LATIN
  AMERICA.*
  J.B., 90:OCT69-624
"GOTTFRIED KELLER." (K. JEZIORKOWSKI,
  ED)
  S. MEWS, 301(JEGP):APR71-338
  H.W. REICHERT, 406:SPRING71-73
KELLER, H. TIZIANS POESIE FÜR KÖNIG
  PHILIPP II. VON SPANIEN.
  R. JULLIAN, 182:VOL23#21/22-938
KELLER, J.E. ALFONSO X, EL SABIO.
  A.I. BAGBY, JR., 240(HR):JUL70-322
  R.I. BURNS, 589:JAN71-157
KELLER, J.E. - SEE GREEN, O.H.
KELLER, J.E. & R.W. LINKER, EDS. EL
  LIBRO DE CALILA E DIGNA.
  T. MONTGOMERY, 240(HR):OCT70-425
  582(SFQ):MAR68-69
KELLER, W. DIASPORA.
  617(TLS):17NOV72-1399
KELLETT, A. - SEE DE MAUPASSANT, G.

KELLETT, J.R. THE IMPACT OF RAILWAYS ON
VICTORIAN CITIES.
D.J. OLSEN, 637(VS):DEC69-217
KELLEY, D.M. WHY CONSERVATIVE CHURCHES
ARE GROWING.
E. WRIGHT, 441:6AUG72-6
KELLEY, E.S. WEEDS.
442(NY):9DEC72-177
KELLEY, P. & R. HUDSON - SEE BROWNING,
E.B.
KELLEY, R. THE TRANSATLANTIC PERSUASION.
D.P. CROOK, 637(VS):MAR70-360
KELLEY, W.M. DEM.
D. JAFFE, 502(PRS):SPRING68-83
KELLGREN, R., ED. KVINNOR I POLITIKEN.
I. CAMERINI, 563(SS):AUTUMN71-457
KELLOGG, C.F. NAACP. (VOL 1)
E.V. TOY, JR., 330(MASJ):SPRING69-91
KELLOGG, M. LIKE THE LION'S TOOTH.
J. HENDIN, 441:5NOV72-4
C. LEHMANN-HAUPT, 441:18OCT72-49
G. STUTTAFORD, 561(SATR):14OCT72-83
E. WEEKS, 61:NOV72-129
KELLOGG, M. TELL ME THAT YOU LOVE ME,
JUNIE MOON.
42(AR):SPRING69-109
KELLY, D. ALL HERE TOGETHER.
J. TIPTON, 661:SUMMER70-120
KELLY, F.D. "SENS" AND "CONJOINTURE" IN
THE "CHEVALIER DE LA CHARRETTE."
J.N. CARMAN, 545(RPH):AUG69-123
KELLY, G.A. IDEALISM, POLITICS AND
HISTORY.*
T. BODAMMER, 182:VOL23#7-329
C.J. HUGHES, 518:OCT70-15
KELLY, H.A. DIVINE PROVIDENCE IN THE
ENGLAND OF SHAKESPEARE'S HISTORIES.
J.W. VELZ, 301(JEGP):OCT71-659
KELLY, L. THE MARVELLOUS BOY.
617(TLS):25AUG72-988
KELLY, M. THE TWENTY-FIFTH HOUR.
442(NY):11MAR72-125
KELLY, R. THE COMMON SHORE.*
N. MARTIEN, 473(PR):1971/1-122
KELLY, R. FLESH:DREAM:BOOK.
V. YOUNG, 249(HUDR):WINTER71/72-669
KELMAN, S. PUSH COMES TO SHOVE.
D.J. LEAB, 432(NEQ):DEC70-672
KELSALL, M.M. - SEE CONGREVE, W.
KELSALL, R.K., A. POOLE & A. KUHN. GRAD-
UATES.
617(TLS):7JUL72-768
KELSEY, H. FRONTIER CAPITALIST.
W.B. FAHERTY, 377:JUL71-118
KELVIN, N. A TROUBLED EDEN.
G. THOMAS, 175:SPRING69-31
KEMBLE, J.P. MACBETH AND KING RICHARD
THE THIRD.
617(TLS):18FEB72-178
KEMELMAN, H. MONDAY THE RABBI TOOK OFF.
N. CALLENDAR, 441:19MAR72-41
H. FRANKEL, 561(SATR):13MAY72-86
617(TLS):13OCT72-1235
KEMP, A. EAT OF ME, I AM THE SAVIOR.
R. SALE, 453:29JUN72-28
M. WATKINS, 441:8JUL72-23
442(NY):22JUL72-78
KEMP, F. - SEE VARNHAGEN VON ENSE, R.
KEMP, F. - SEE VARNHAGEN VON ENSE, R. &
A.
KEMP, I. HINDEMITH.
P. EVANS, 415:APR71-343
KEMP, J. ETHICAL NATURALISM.
C.L. TEN, 63:MAY71-114
KEMP, J.A. - SEE WALLIS, J.
KEMPER, H-G. GEORG TRAKLS ENTWÜRFE.
R.D. SCHIER, 301(JEGP):APR71-343

KEMPF, B. SUFFRAGETTE FOR PEACE.
617(TLS):24NOV72-1433
KEMPF, R. SUR LE CORPS ROMANESQUE.*
W. WRAGE, 399(MLJ):FEB70-138
KEMPLEY, W. THE PROBABILITY FACTOR.
N. CALLENDAR, 441:29OCT72-58
KENDALL, A. THEIR FINEST HOUR.
617(TLS):24NOV72-1441
KENDALL, W. & G.W. CAREY. THE BASIC
SYMBOLS OF THE AMERICAN POLITICAL TRA-
DITION.
L.P.S. DE ALVAREZ, 396(MODA):SUMMER
71-323
KENEALLY, T. THE CHANT OF JIMMIE BLACK-
SMITH.
V. CUNNINGHAM, 362:14SEP72-344
T. LASK, 441:9SEP72-21
A. THWAITE, 441:27AUG72-3
617(TLS):15SEP72-1041
KENISTON, K. YOUTH AND DISSENT.*
M. DUBERMAN, 441:2APR72-4
KENNA, V.E.G. THE CRETAN TALISMANIC
STONE IN THE LATE MINOAN AGE.
E. VERMEULE, 124:DEC70-128
KENNAN, G.F. THE MARQUIS DE CUSTINE AND
HIS "RUSSIA IN 1839."*
J. BAYLEY, 362:23MAR72-381
W.N. VICKERY, 574(SEEJ):WINTER71-527
617(TLS):14APR72-423
KENNAN, G.F. FROM PRAGUE AFTER MUNICH.*
W.J. MILLER, 377:MAR71-48
A. POLONSKY, 587:JAN69-392
KENNAN, G.F. MEMOIRS: 1950-1963.
J.K. GALBRAITH, 441:8OCT72-1
A. KAZIN, 453:2NOV72-3
T. LASK, 441:16SEP72-29
H.E. SALISBURY, 561(SATR):23SEP72-71
442(NY):30SEP72-125
KENNAN, K.W. TECHNIQUE OF ORCHESTRATION.
(2ND ED)
P. STANDFORD, 415:JAN71-35
KENNAWAY, J. SILENCE.
617(TLS):15SEP72-1042
KENNEDY, D. THE CUISINES OF MEXICO.
N. HAZELTON, 441:3DEC72-96
KENNEDY, D. RECOLLECTIONS OF AN ASSINI-
BOINE CHIEF. (J.R. STEVENS, ED)
L. RICOU, 296:SUMMER72-84
KENNEDY, E. THE BIG LOSER.
N. CALLENDAR, 441:17DEC72-23
KENNEDY, E.C. IN THE SPIRIT, IN THE
FLESH.
441:5MAR72-10
KENNEDY, E.C. THE NEW SEXUALITY.
R. JAFFE, 441:13AUG72-5
KENNEDY, E.M. IN CRITICAL CONDITION.
R. BAZELL, 453:2NOV72-38
M.G. MICHAELSON, 441:9JUL72-5
KENNEDY, G. QUINTILIAN.*
E.B. HOLTSMARK, 121(CJ):APR-MAY71-371
M.H. MC CALL, JR., 24:APR71-330
M. WINTERBOTTOM, 313:VOL60-267
KENNEDY, J.M. - SEE MONTEMAYOR, G. & G.
POLO
KENNEDY, M. BARBIROLLI.
617(TLS):21JAN72-65
KENNEDY, M. ELGAR ORCHESTRAL MUSIC.
R. ANDERSON, 415:NOV70-1111
KENNEDY, M. THE HISTORY OF THE ROYAL
MANCHESTER COLLEGE OF MUSIC 1893-1972.*
B. RAINBOW, 415:SEP71-863
KENNEDY, M. PORTRAIT OF ELGAR.
A.E.F. DICKINSON, 607:SUMMER68-41
R. FREEDMAN, 340(KR):1969/2-264
N. TEMPERLEY, 637(VS):SEP69-110
KENNEDY, M. - SEE HALLÉ, C.

KENNEDY, M.D. THE ESTRANGEMENT OF GREAT
BRITAIN AND JAPAN - 1917-35.
D.B. RAMSDELL, 293(JAST):MAY70-705
KENNEDY, R. A BOY AT THE HOGARTH PRESS.
N.'ANNAN, 362:15JUN72-794
617(TLS):27OCT72-1278
KENNEDY, R. GOOD NIGHT, JUPITER.*
639(VQR):SUMMER70-LXXXVIII
KENNEDY, R.S. & P. REEVES - SEE WOLFE, T.
KENNEDY, X.J. BREAKING AND ENTERING.*
J. FULLER, 362:24FEB72-251
KENNEDY, X.J. GROWING INTO LOVE.*
P. COOPER, 340(KR):1970/1-143
P. COOPER, 577(SHR):SPRING70-178
S. TUDOR, 590:SPRING70-36
639(VQR):WINTER70-XII
KENNER, C.L. A HISTORY OF NEW MEXICAN-
PLAINS INDIAN RELATIONS.
B.L. FONTANA, 50(ARQ):WINTER69-377
KENNER, G.C. THE REVOLUTION IN ETHICAL
THEORY.*
S.A.S., 543:DEC69-349
KENNER, H. THE POUND ERA.
D. DONOGHUE, 362:23NOV72-718
C.D. HEYMANN, 561(SATR):13MAY72-71
C. LEHMANN-HAUPT, 441:28MAR72-45
M. ROSENTHAL, 441:26MAR72-7
617(TLS):15SEP72-1049
KENNET, W. PRESERVATION.
617(TLS):5MAY72-516
KENNEY, A.P. THE GANSEVOORTS OF ALBANY.
C.S. CRARY, 656(WMQ):APR70-341
KENNINGTON, D. THE LITERATURE OF JAZZ.*
M. HARRISON, 415:JUN71-559
KENNY, A. THE FIVE WAYS.
P.T. GEACH, 479(PHQ):JUL70-311
J. HICK, 393(MIND):JUL70-467
T. MC PHERSON, 518:JAN70-10
J.J.R., 543:MAR70-557
KENNY, A. - SEE DESCARTES, R.
KENRICK, D. & G. PUXON. THE DESTINY OF
EUROPE'S GYPSIES.
617(TLS):17NOV72-1400
KENRICK, T. A TOUGH ONE TO LOSE.
O.L. BAILEY, 561(SATR):9SEP72-80
N. CALLENDAR, 441:15OCT72-42
KENT, A. SLOOP OF WAR.
M. LEVIN, 441:15OCT72-43
KENT, J.A. ONE OF THE FEW.
617(TLS):14JAN72-49
KENT, L.J. THE SUBCONSCIOUS IN GOGOL
AND DOSTOEVSKIJ, AND ITS ANTECEDENTS.*
J.G. GARRARD, 550(RUSR):OCT70-478
B.H. MONTER, 32:SEP71-703
KENWORTHY, B.J. - SEE KAISER, G.
KENYON, F.W. PASSIONATE REBEL.
617(TLS):28APR72-501
KENYON, J. THE POPISH PLOT.
617(TLS):1SEP72-1018
KENYON, K. ROYAL CITIES OF THE OLD
TESTAMENT.
617(TLS):28JAN72-102
KEOGH, J. PRESIDENT NIXON AND THE PRESS.
E.M. YODER, JR., 440:28MAY72-4
KEOHANE, R.O. & J.S. NYE, JR., EDS.
TRANSNATIONAL RELATIONS AND WORLD POLI-
TICS.
S. BROWN, 561(SATR):20MAY72-64
KER, N.R. RECORDS OF ALL SOULS COLLEGE
LIBRARY 1437-1600.
617(TLS):21JAN72-76
KERBLAY, B.H. LES MARCHÉS PAYSANS EN
U.R.S.S.
E. CLAYTON, 32:MAR71-167
KERÉNYI, K. OPUSCULA.
J. POLLARD, 303:VOL90-263

KERKHOF, J. STUDIES IN THE LANGUAGE OF
GEOFFREY CHAUCER.
K.C. PHILLIPPS, 179(ES):APR70-153
KERMAN, J. - SEE "LUDWIG VAN BEETHOVEN"
KERMODE, F. CONTINUITIES.
R. BERMAN, 340(KR):1969/3-378
KERMODE, F., ED. FOUR CENTURIES OF
SHAKESPEARIAN CRITICISM.
R.H. GOLDSMITH, 570(SQ):WINTER68-94
KERMODE, F. THE SENSE OF AN ENDING.*
L. CASPER, 613:AUTUMN68-443
R. COHEN, 445(NCF):JUN68-104
D. NEWTON-DE MOLINA, 148:WINTER70-352
KERMODE, F. SHAKESPEARE, SPENSER,
DONNE.*
J. CREASER, 364:OCT/NOV71-146
L.C. KNIGHTS, 453:15OCT72-3
KERN, A., ED. DIE HANDSCHRIFTEN DER
UNIVERSITÄTSBIBLIOTHEK GRAZ. (VOL 3)
J. BACKHOUSE, 354:SEP69-256
KERN, E. EXISTENTIAL THOUGHT AND FIC-
TIONAL TECHNIQUE.
H. LINDENBERGER, 131(CL):FALL71-376
KERN, P. TRINITÄT, MARIA, INKARNATION.
R. RUDOLF, 182:VOL23#19/20-864
KERNER, G.C. THE REVOLUTION IN ETHICAL
THEORY.*
T. HONDERICH, 393(MIND):APR70-294
E. MIGLIORINI, 548(RCSF):APR/JUN69-
221
KERR, C. MARSHALL, MARX AND MODERN
TIMES.*
H.B., 543:JUN70-744
M. KRANZBERG, 639(VQR):SPRING70-342
KERR, J. NO DEADLY DRUG.
M. LEVIN, 441:23APR72-41
KERR, W. HAROLD PINTER.
I. BLAKE, 447(N&Q):FEB70-77
J. FUEGI, 399(MLJ):JAN70-32
A. WALKER, 397(MD):DEC68-345
KERRIGAN, A. - SEE BORGES, J.L.
KERSHAW, J. THE PRESENT STAGE.
M. PAGE, 397(MD):DEC67-325
"ANDRÉ KERTÉSZ: SIXTY YEARS OF PHOTOGRA-
PHY, 1912-72." (N. DUCROT, ED)
S. SCHWARTZ, 441:3DEC72-4
442(NY):9DEC72-179
617(TLS):29DEC72-1589
KESEY, K. ONE FLEW OVER THE CUCKOO'S
NEST.
617(TLS):25FEB72-209
KESSLER, C.S. MAX BECKMANN'S TRIPTYCHS.
C. EUBANKS, JR., 19(AGR):VOL36#5-24
A. WERNER, 579(SAQ):WINTER71-116
639(VQR):AUTUMN70-CLIV
KESSLER, E. IMAGES OF WALLACE STEVENS.
G.P. GARRETT, 31(ASCH):SUMMER72-466
KESSLER, H. IN THE TWENTIES.*
W.H. AUDEN, 453:31AUG72-4
N. BLIVEN, 442(NY):15JAN72-87
KESSLER, H.L. - SEE WEITZMANN, K.
KESTERS, H. KÉRYGMES DE SOCRATE.
W.E-W.S. CHARLTON, 123:JUN71-292
KETCHAM, C.H. - SEE WORDSWORTH, J.
KETCHAM, R. JAMES MADISON.*
L.C. MILAZZO, 584(SWR):SUMMER71-291
KETCHUM, A. COLETTE OU LA NAISSANCE DU
JOUR.
M.W. HERZ, 399(MLJ):MAR70-210
KETTLER, D. MARXISMUS UND KULTUR.
Z. TAR, 32:JUN71-426
KETTON-CREMER, R.W. NORFOLK IN THE
CIVIL WAR.
W. KEUTSCH, 182:VOL23#6-313
KEYES, M.N. NINETEENTH CENTURY HOME
ARCHITECTURE OF IOWA CITY.
M.E. HINSHAW, 576:OCT69-232

KEYNES, G. A BIBLIOGRAPHY OF SIR THOMAS
BROWNE, KT., M.D.* (2ND ED)
J. HORDEN, 354:DEC69-350
J.H.P. PAFFORD, 447(N&Q):NOV70-433
KEYNES, G. A BIBLIOGRAPHY OF SIR WILIAM
PETTY, F.R.S. AND OF OBSERVATIONS ON
THE BILLS OF MORTALITY BY JOHN GRAUNT,
F.R.S.
617(TLS):7JAN72-20
KEYNES, G. WILLIAM PICKERING PUBLISHER.
(REV)
N. BARKER, 78(BC):AUTUMN70-390
KEYNES, G. - SEE BLAKE, W.
KEYNES, G. - SEE BROWNE, T.
KEYNES, J.M. THE COLLECTED WRITINGS OF
JOHN MAYNARD KEYNES. (VOLS 3-6)
617(TLS):11FEB72-164
KEYNES, J.M. THE COLLECTED WRITINGS OF
JOHN MAYNARD KEYNES. (VOLS 9&10)
617(TLS):22SEP72-1095
KEYSAAR, A. MELVILLE'S "ISRAEL POTTER."
W. BEZANSON, 27(AL):MAR71-133
639(VQR):SUMMER70-C
IBN KHALDUN - SEE FILED UNDER IBN
KHALEIF, F. A STUDY ON FAKHR AL-DIN AL-
RAZI AND HIS CONTROVERSIES IN TRANS-
OXIANA.
S.A. AKBARABADI, 273(IC):JUL69-241
KHAN, M.A. - SEE UNDER AYUB KHAN, M.
KHAN, M.A.W. A MONOGRAPH ON THE DISCOV-
ERY OF MURAL PAINTINGS OF KALYANI
CHALUKYAS AT ALLADURG.
S. KRAMRISCH, 57:VOL31#2/3-229
KHAN, M.Z. - SEE UNDER ZAFRULLA KHAN, M.
KHARE, R.S. THE CHANGING BRAHMANS.
617(TLS):22SEP72-1119
KHAYYÁM, O. - SEE UNDER OMAR KHAYYÁM
KHJAPKINA, N.S. POLITIKA RUSSKOGO
SAMODERŽAVIJA V OBLASTI PROMYŠLENNOSTI
(20-50E GODY XIX V.)
A.J. RIEBER, 104:SUMMER71-286
KHOURY, P. PAUL D'ANTIOCHE, ÉVÊQUE MEL-
KITE DE SIDON (XIIE S.).
J. KRITZECK, 318(JAOS):APR-JUN70-287
KHUSRO, A.M. A SURVEY OF LIVING AND
WORKING CONDITIONS OF STUDENTS OF THE
UNIVERSITY OF DELHI.
L. DUSHKIN, 293(JAST):NOV69-186
KIDDER, J.E. EARLY BUDDHIST JAPAN.
617(TLS):22DEC72-1561
KIDEL, B. A FLAWED ESCAPE.
617(TLS):14JAN72-31
KIEFER, F. MATHEMATICAL LINGUISTICS IN
EASTERN EUROPE.
J.F. HENDRY, 104:SUMMER71-267
P. SGALL, 361:VOL23#2-188
KIEFER, F. ON EMPHASIS AND WORD ORDER
IN HUNGARIAN.
I. BÁTORI, 361:VOL24#1-89
KIEFER, W. THE LINGALA CODE.
O.L. BAILEY, 561(SATR):26AUG72-61
N. CALLENDAR, 441:24SEP72-41
KIEFT, D.O. BELGIUM'S RETURN TO NEU-
TRALITY.
617(TLS):11AUG72-951
KIELY, B. DOGS ENJOY THE MORNING.
J.W. FOSTER, 448:SUMMER72-113
KIEMLE, M. AESTHETISCHE PROBLEME DER
ARCHITEKTUR UNTER DEM ASPEKT DER
INFORMATIONSAESTHETIK.
R. ARNHEIM, 290(JAAC):SUMMER70-551
KIENIEWICZ, S. THE EMANCIPATION OF THE
POLISH PEASANTRY.
J. GOLDBERG, 575(SEER):OCT71-622
R.F. LESLIE, 104:SPRING71-133
C. MORLEY, 32:JUN71-409

KIERKEGAARD, S. L'ÉCOLE DU CHRISTIAN-
ISME.
L. JERPHAGNON, 542:JAN-MAR69-117
"KIERKEGAARDIANA VI." (N. THULSTRUP, ED)
A.C., 462(OL):VOL23#4-323
"SÖREN KIERKEGAARDS PAPIRER." (VOL 4)
(P.A. HEIBERG & V. KUHR, WITH N. THUL-
STRUP, EDS)
N. VIALLANEIX, 98:OCT69-895
KIERNAN, B. IMAGES OF SOCIETY AND
NATURE.
B. ELLIOTT, 71(ALS):MAY72-333
KILBOURN, W., ED. CANADA.*
A. APPENZELL, 102(CANL):AUTUMN71-95
KILBY, K. THE COOPER AND HIS TRADE.
617(TLS):31MAR72-378
KILCHENMANN, R.J. DIE KURZGESCHICHTE.
G. BAUMGAERTEL, 131(CL):SUMMER71-282
H-M. GERRESHEIM, 52:BAND4HEFT3-308
KILCHENMANN, R.J. PANORAMA.
C. ZIEGLER, 399(MLJ):MAY70-383
KILGALLIN, T., ED. THE CANADIAN SHORT
STORY.
J.G. MOSS, 296:WINTER72-79
KILLAM, G.D. THE NOVELS OF CHINUA
ACHEBE.
J. DALE, 529(QQ):WINTER70-646
M. LAURENCE, 627(UTQ):JUL70-362
KILLENS, J.O. GREAT GETTIN' UP MORNING.
E. & N. FONER, 453:20APR72-39
KILLICK, B. THE NANNIES.
E. MORGAN, 362:24FEB72-252
617(TLS):3MAR72-239
KILLIGREW, M. - SEE FORD, F.M.
KILLY, W. ELEMENTE DER LYRIK.
617(TLS):7JUL72-769
KILLY, W. & H. SZKLENAR - SEE TRAKL, G.
KILMINSTER, C. THE NATURE OF THE UNI-
VERSE.
617(TLS):21JAN72-77
KIM, C.I.E. & C. CHEE, EDS. ASPECTS OF
SOCIAL CHANGE IN KOREA.
Y.H. LEE, 293(JAST):FEB70-454
KIM IL SUNG. JUCHE! (LI YUK-SA, ED)
R. HALLORAN, 561(SATR):18MAR72-78
KIM, J-Y. & C-S. HANKUK KONGSAN-JU'ŬI
UNDONG-SA, JE-IL-KWON. (VOLS 1&2)
H.C. KIM, 293(JAST):AUG70-947
KIM KWANG-SOB. SONGBUKTONG DOVES.
270:VOL20#4-98
KIM, R.E. LOST NAMES.
639(VQR):AUTUMN70-CXXVIII
KIM SU-YONG. GAME IN THE MOON COUNTRY.
270:VOL20#4-101
KIMBALL, E. THE MAN IN THE PANAMA HAT.
D. CAMERON, 102(CANL):WINTER71-102
KIMBALL, F., ED. THOMAS JEFFERSON,
ARCHITECT.
S. ABERCROMBIE, 505:MAY69-172
T.J. MC CORMICK, 39:AUG69-160
KIMBALL, N. NELL KIMBALL. (S. LONG-
STREET, ED)
A. WHITMAN, 231:MAY72-102
KIMBALL, R., ED. COLE.*
P. ADAMS, 61:JAN72-96
P. BAILEY, 362:28SEP72-413
R. MAZZOCCO, 453:27JAN72-3
442(NY):12FEB72-104
617(TLS):8DEC72-1482
KIMBALL, W.F. THE MOST UNSORDID ACT.
M.L. HARVEY, 550(RUSR):JAN70-81
KIMBROUGH, R. - SEE SIDNEY, P.
KIMMICH, C.M. THE FREE CITY.
H. HANAK, 575(SEER):JAN71-160
KINDERLEHRER, J. CONFESSIONS OF A SNEAKY
ORGANIC COOK.
N. MAGID, 440:13FEB72-5
KINDINGER, R. - SEE MEINONG, A.

171

KINDLEBERGER, C.P., ED. THE INTERNATION-
AL CORPORATION.
P. PASSELL, 441:23JAN72-23
KING, A. THE MAGIC TORTOISE RANCH.
M. LEVIN, 441:6FEB72-36
KING, A. & H. NORTH - SEE CAPLAN, H.
KING, A.H. MOZART.
S. SADIE, 415:DEC70-1225
KING, A.H. MOZART IN RETROSPECT.
S. SADIE, 415:FEB71-140
KING, B., ED. INTRODUCTION TO NIGERIAN
LITERATURE.
D.A.N. JONES, 362:30MAR72-426
KING, C. THE CECIL KING DIARY 1965-1970.
R. CROSSMAN, 362:16NOV72-680
617(TLS):1DEC72-1461
KING, C.R. - SEE COLEMAN, A.R.
KING, E.L. THE DEATH OF THE ARMY.
P. BARNES, 441:20AUG72-3
KING, H. RICHARD BOURKE.
617(TLS):4AUG72-923
KING, H. THE POEMS OF HENRY KING. (M.
CRUM, ED)
T.A. BIRRELL, 179(ES):DEC70-559
KING, J.C., W.K. LEGNER & F.A. RAVEN,
EDS. GERMANIC STUDIES IN HONOR OF
EDWARD HENRY SEHRT.
G.J. METCALF, 221(GQ):JAN70-105
KING, L.T. & J.S. WEXLER. THE MARTHA'S
VINEYARD COOKBOOK.
N. MAGID, 440:20FEB72-8
KING, P. & B.C. PAREKH, EDS. POLITICS
AND EXPERIENCE.
R.S. DOWNIE, 479(PHQ):JUL70-299
KING, R.A., JR. THE FOCUSING ARTIFICE.*
M. HANCHER, 677:VOL2-312
W.D. SHAW, 627(UTQ):APR70-289
M.G. WIEBE, 529(QQ):WINTER70-649
KING, R.A., JR. & OTHERS - SEE BROWNING,
R.
KING, R.D. HISTORICAL LINGUISTICS AND
GENERATIVE GRAMMAR.
L. CAMPBELL, 350:MAR71-191
KING, S.B. GEORGIA VOICES.
K. COLEMAN, 219(GAR):SPRING69-111
KING, W.L.M. THE MACKENZIE KING RECORD.
(VOL 2) (J.W. PICKERSGILL & D.F. FOR-
STER, EDS)
R. GRAHAM, 219(GAR):WINTER69-560
KING, W.L.M. THE MACKENZIE KING RECORD.*
(VOLS 3&4) (J.W. PICKERSGILL & D.F.
FORSTER, EDS)
102(CANL):WINTER71-107
KING-HELE, D. - SEE DARWIN, E.
KINGSFORD, R.J.L. THE PUBLISHERS ASSOCI-
ATION, 1896-1946.
D. LACY, 356:APR71-179
KINGSLAND, G. FROM THE WHORES OF MONTE-
ZUMA.
617(TLS):13OCT72-1214
KINGSLEY, M. TRAVELS IN WEST AFRICA.
(ABRIDGED BY R. GLYNN GRYLLS)
617(TLS):25AUG72-993
KINGSTON, C. IT DON'T SEEM A DAY TOO
MUCH.
617(TLS):26MAY72-600
KININMONTH, C. THE TRAVELLERS' GUIDE
TO MOROCCO.
C.W. CASEWIT, 440:30APR72-15
617(TLS):10MAR72-285
KINKEAD-WEEKES, M. & I. GREGOR. WILLIAM
GOLDING.
J.R. BAKER, 50(ARQ):SPRING69-77
KINNELL, G. BODY RAGS.*
T. BLACKBURN, 493:SPRING70-85

KINNELL, G. THE BOOK OF NIGHTMARES.*
P. DAVISON, 61:FEB72-104
R. HOWARD, 473(PR):WINTER71/72-484
R. LATTIMORE, 249(HUDR):AUTUMN71-501
J.T. MC DONNELL, 109:SPRING/SUMMER72-
153
KINOSHITA, N. PILLAR OF FIRE.
617(TLS):5MAY72-526
KINSELLA, T. NIGHTWALKER AND OTHER
POEMS.*
H. SERGEANT, 175:SPRING69-33
KINSELLA, T. A SELECTED LIFE.
617(TLS):8DEC72-1481
KINSEY, T.E. - SEE CICERO
KINSLEY, J., ED. THE OXFORD BOOK OF
BALLADS.*
D. HAMER, 541(RES):NOV70-482
J.H.P. PAFFORD, 402(MLR):APR71-382
KINSLEY, J. - SEE BURNS, R.
KINSLEY, J. & R.S. SMITH, EDS. RENAIS-
SANCE AND MODERN STUDIES XII.
E. JONES, 447(N&Q):NOV70-428
KINSMAN, R.S. - SEE SKELTON, J.
KINTNER, E. - SEE BROWNING, R. & E.B.
BARRETT
KINTNER, W.L. & J.R. KELLER. THE SIBYL.
P. DAMON, 545(RPH):NOV69-234
KINZEL, P.F. LEXICAL AND GRAMMATICAL
INTERFERENCE IN THE SPEECH OF A BI-
LINGUAL CHILD.
L.A. GYURKO, 545(RPH):MAY71-635
KINZL, K. MILTIADES-FORSCHUNGEN.
R. DREWS, 24:OCT71-756
N.G.L. HAMMOND, 123:MAR71-141
E. WILL, 555:VOL44FASC2-314
KIRBY, E.S. THE SOVIET FAR EAST.
617(TLS):30JUN72-744
KIRBY, I.M., COMP. DIOCESE OF GLOUCESTER:
A CATALOGUE OF THE RECORDS OF THE BISH-
OP AND ARCHDEACONS.
E. WELCH, 325:OCT69-588
KIRBY, I.M. DIOCESE OF GLOUCESTER: A
CATALOGUE OF THE RECORDS OF THE DEAN
AND CHAPTER INCLUDING THE FORMER ST.
PETER'S ABBEY.
E. WELCH, 325:APR70-77
KIRBY, M. THE ART OF TIME.
J. ANDERSON, 151:SEP69-25
"KIRCHENMUSIK IN ÖKUMENISCHER SCHAU."
B. BUJIC, 182:VOL23#1/2-37
KIRCHHOFF, G., ED. DEUTSCHE GEGENWART.
G. GILLESPIE, 221(GQ):NOV70-791
KIRFEL, E-A. UNTERSUCHUNGEN ZUR BRIEF-
FORM DER "HEROIDES" OVIDS.*
W.C. SCOTT, 122:JUL71-205
KIRILOV, N. & F. KIRK, EDS. INTRODUCTION
TO MODERN BULGARIAN LITERATURE.
J-F. CLARKE, 574(SEEJ):SUMMER71-230
KIRK, D. WIDER WAR.*
617(TLS):11FEB72-143
KIRK, G.S. MYTH, ITS MEANING AND FUNC-
TIONS IN ANCIENT AND OTHER CULTURES.*
J. CULLER, 676(YR):AUTUMN70-108
S. LIEBERMAN, 124:DEC70-128
J. SEZNEC, 208(FS):APR71-243
KIRK, R. ELIOT AND HIS AGE.
F. KERMODE, 441:26MAR72-6
P. THEROUX, 440:12MAR72-5
KIRK-GREENE, A.H.M. HAUSA BA DABO BA NE.
N. SKINNER, 69:JUL69-318
KIRKBRIDE, A. AN AWAKENING.
617(TLS):3MAR72-237
KIRKENDALE, U. ANTONIO CALDARA.
P.H.L., 414(MQ):JAN68-118
KIRKER, H. THE ARCHITECTURE OF CHARLES
BULFINCH.
W.M. WHITEHILL, 432(NEQ):MAR70-139
639(VQR):SPRING70-LXXIV

KIRKHAM, M. THE POETRY OF ROBERT
  GRAVES.*
    R. BATES, 627(UTQ):JUL70-348
    J. DOLLAR, 590:SPRING70-39
    H. SERGEANT, 175:AUTUMN69-111
    R. SMITH, 150(DR):SUMMER70-273
    J. WALSH, 541(RES):NOV70-523
KIRKLAND, E.C. A BIBLIOGRAPHY OF SOUTH
  ASIAN FOLKLORE.*
    K. LUOMALA, 650(WF):OCT68-282
KIRKUP, J. THE BODY SERVANT.
    I. WEDDE, 364:FEB/MAR72-148
    617(TLS):7JAN72-6
KIRKUP, J. WHITE SHADOWS, BLACK SHADOWS.
    A. IRELAND, 285(JAPQ):OCT-DEC70-481
    J. SMITH, 493:WINTER70/71-363
KIRKWOOD, J. P.S. YOUR CAT IS DEAD!
    N. CALLENDAR, 441:26NOV72-36
KIRSCHBAUM, J. SLOVAKS IN CANADA.*
    C.H. ANDRUSYSHEN, 627(UTQ):JUL69-494
KIRSCHENMANN, P.P. INFORMATION AND
  REFLECTION.
    D.V. SCHWARTZ, 32:SEP71-695
KIRSCHNER, P. CONRAD.
    E.K. HAY, 136:FALL69-107
    R. RAPIN, 136:WINTER69/70-129
    E.W. SAID, 637(VS):JUN70-429
    C.T. WATTS, 541(RES):FEB70-101
KIRST, H.H. HERO IN THE TOWER.
    V. CUNNINGHAM, 362:22JUN72-841
    T. MORRISON, 441:10CT72-41
KIRSTEIN, L. DANCE.
    J. ANDERSON, 151:NOV69-21
    J. DE LABAN, 290(JAAC):SUMMER70-556
KIRSTEIN, L. MOVEMENT AND METAPHOR.*
    617(TLS):4FEB72-125
KISELEVA, L.A. & OTHERS. A PRACTICAL
  HANDBOOK OF RUSSIAN STYLE.
    K.A. KLEIN, 574(SEEJ):SPRING71-134
KISSAM, E. THE SHAM FLYERS.
    J. SMITH, 493:AUTUMN70-243
KITAGAWA, J.M., ED. THE HISTORY OF
  RELIGIONS.
    G.M., 477:SUMMER69-414
KITAGAWA, J.M., ED. UNDERSTANDING MODERN
  CHINA.
    O.H. SHAO, 293(JAST):MAY70-690
KITCHEN, P. PARADISE.
    E. MORGAN, 362:18MAY72-660
    617(TLS):7JUL72-783
KITMAN, M., ED. GEORGE WASHINGTON'S
  EXPENSE ACCOUNT.
    639(VQR):AUTUMN70-CLIII
KITSON, F. LOW INTENSITY OPERATIONS.
    I. SMART, 362:3AUG72-129
    617(TLS):11FEB72-144
KITSON, M. THE AGE OF BAROQUE.
    M. LEVEY, 592:MAR68-155
KITTRIE, N.N. THE RIGHT TO BE DIFFERENT.
    A. STORR, 440:2JAN72-3
KIZER, C. MIDNIGHT WAS MY CRY.
    R. HOWARD, 491:AUG72-296
KLAPPENBACH, R. & H. MALIGE-KLAPPENBACH,
  EDS. WÖRTERBUCH DER DEUTSCHEN GEGEN-
  WARTSSPRACHE. (PTS 18-25)
    R.W. JUMPELT, 75:2/1969-114
KLAPPENBACH, R. & W. STEINITZ, EDS. WÖR-
  TERBUCH DER DEUTSCHEN GEGENWARTS-
  SPRACHE. (PTS REVIEWED UNKNOWN)
    M.Å. HOLMBERG, 597(SN):VOL40#2-473
KLAPPERT, P. LUGGING VEGETABLES TO NAN-
  TUCKET.
    A. BROYARD, 441:9FEB72-41
    A. PRYCE-JONES, 617(TLS):19MAY72-574
KLARE, M. WAR WITHOUT END.
    R.J. BARNET, 453:16NOV72-14
KLARMANN, A.D. - SEE WERFEL, F.

KLASS, P.J. SECRET SENTRIES IN SPACE.*
    441:12MAR72-39
KLEBERG, T. & OTHERS, EDS. I BOKENS
  TJÄNST.
    K.W. SODERLAND, 356:APR71-189
KLECZYNSKI, J. FREDERIC CHOPIN [TOGETHER
  WITH] RIPOLL, L. CHOPIN'S PIANOS.
    M.J.E. BROWN, 415:OCT71-966
KLEE, F. PAUL KLEE PAR LUI-MÊME ET PAR
  SON FILS.
    M. MORÉ, 98:JUL69-639
KLEE, P. JOURNAL. (P. KLOSSOWSKI,
  TRANS)
    M. MORÉ, 98:JUL69-639
KLEIN, A., ED. DISSENT, POWER, AND CON-
  FRONTATION.
    C. LEHMANN-HAUPT, 441:24FEB72-41
KLEIN, D.W. & A.B. CLARK, EDS. BIOGRAPH-
  IC DICTIONARY OF CHINESE COMMUNISM,
  1921-1965.
    M. BERNAL, 453:23MAR72-31
    617(TLS):28JAN72-90
KLEIN, E., ED. A COMPREHENSIVE ETYMOLO-
  GICAL DICTIONARY OF THE ENGLISH LANG-
  UAGE.
    617(TLS):13OCT72-1209
KLEIN, J. A COMMENTARY ON PLATO'S
  "MENO."
    F. ADORNO, 548(RCSF):JAN-MAR68-104
    I.M. CROMBIE, 479(PHQ):JAN70-78
KLEIN, J. GREEK MATHEMATICAL THOUGHT AND
  THE ORIGIN OF ALGEBRA.
    R.H.K., 543:SEP69-132
KLEIN, N. LOVE AND OTHER EUPHEMISMS.*
    C.D.B. BRYAN, 441:15OCT72-31
KLEIN, P.W. MODAL AUXILIARIES IN SPAN-
  ISH.*
    D. BOLINGER, 545(RPH):MAY70-572
    R.L. HADLICH, 240(HR):OCT70-420
"KLEINE BIBLIOGRAPHIE DER WERKE KARL
  HEINRICH WAGGERLS ZUM 70. GEBURTSTAG
  DES DICHTERS."
    L. NEWMAN, 220(GL&L):JAN71-215
KLEINEIDAM, H., ED. LI VER DE COULOIGNE,
  DI BON ANGE ET DU MAUVÉS, UN ENSEINGE-
  MENT.
    J. CHAURAND, 545(RPH):FEB70-367
VON KLEIST, H. DAS BETTELWEIB VON
  LOCARNO - DER ZWEIKAMPF. (D.H. CROSBY,
  ED)
    J.M. ELLIS, 221(GQ):MAR70-309
    R. MOLLENAUER, 399(MLJ):MAY70-373
"HEINRICH VON KLEIST." (H. SEMBDNER, ED)
    P. HORWATH, 406:SUMMER71-185
    J.M. MC GLATHERY, 301(JEGP):APR71-336
    J.T., 191(ELN):SEP70(SUPP)-123
KLEMKE, E.D. THE EPISTEMOLOGY OF G.E.
  MOORE.*
    J.J.E., 543:MAR70-558
    A.R. WHITE, 518:JAN70-12
KLEMKE, E.D., ED. ESSAYS ON FREGE.
    H.D. SLUGA, 483:JAN70-75
    R. TRAGESSER, 484(PPR):MAR70-463
KLESSMANN, R. THE BERLIN GALLERY.
    617(TLS):25FEB72-222
KLIBANOV, A., ED. KONKRETNYE ISSLEDOV-
  ANIIA SOVREMENNYKH RELIGIOZNYKH VERO-
  VANIIA.
    Z. KATZ, 32:DEC71-870
KLIBANOV, A.I. RELIGIOZNOE SEKTANTSTVO
  I SOVREMENNOST' (SOTSIOLOGICHESKIE I
  ISTORICHESKIE OCHERKI).
    E. DUNN, 32:JUN71-406
KLIBANSKY, R., ED. CONTEMPORARY PHILOSO-
  PHY (LA PHILOSOPHIE CONTEMPORAINE).
  (VOL 1)
    N.G.E. HARRIS, 479(PHQ):APR70-183
    R.H.K., 543:MAR70-570

KLIBANSKY, R., ED. CONTEMPORARY PHILOSO-
PHY (LA PHILOSOPHIE CONTEMPORAINE).
(VOL 2)
    M. FERRIANI, 548(RCSF):APR/JUN69-235
    R.H.K., 543:MAR70-571
KLIEMAN, A.S. SOVIET RUSSIA AND THE
MIDDLE EAST.
    W. LAQUEUR, 32:SEP71-673
KLIMOV, G.A. DIE KAUKASISCHEN SPRACHEN.
    H.I. ARONSON, 350:MAR71-232
"GUSTAV KLIMT."
    P. ADAMS, 61:JUL72-97
KLINCK, R. DIE LATEINISCHE ETYMOLOGIE
DES MITTELALTERS.*
    M.L. COLKER, 589:APR71-385
    P.F. GANZ, 382(MAE):1971/1-84
    U. KINDERMANN, 182:VOL23#15/16-734
KLINE, G.L. RELIGIOUS AND ANTI-RELIGIOUS
THOUGHT IN RUSSIA.*
    T.D.Z., 543:SEP69-132
KLING, J.W. & L.A. RIGGS - SEE WOODWORTH,
R.S. & H. SCHLOSBERG
KLINGENDER, F. ANIMALS IN ART AND
THOUGHT TO THE END OF THE MIDDLE AGES.
(E. ANTAL & J. HARTHAN, EDS)
    J. GARDNER, 441:9APR72-27
    617(TLS):18AUG72-966
KLINGENDER, F.D. ART AND THE INDUSTRIAL
REVOLUTION. (A. ELTON, ED)
    T. CROMBIE, 39:APR69-331
    617(TLS):29DEC72-1577
KLINK, J.L. YOUR CHILD AND RELIGION.
    617(TLS):15SEP72-1064
KLIVAR, M. TECHNIKE VYTVARNICTVO A JEHO
ESTETIKA.
    M. RIESER, 290(JAAC):SPRING70-406
KLOPFENSTEIN, E. ERZÄHLER UND LESER BEI
WILHELM RAABE.
    E.V.K. BRILL, 402(MLR):APR71-469
KLOTZBÜCHER, A. FORMEN DER INTEGRATION
UND ZENTRALISATION DER WISSENSCHAFT-
LICHEN STADTBIBLIOTHEK UND DER ÖFFENT-
LICHEN BÜCHEREI.
    G. STEVENSON, 356:APR71-186
KLUCKHOHN, P., ED. LUSTSPIELE.
    R-K., 221(GQ):JAN70-146
KLUGE, G. - SEE VON ARNIM, L.A.
KLUTH, R. GRUNDRISS DER BIBLIOTHEKS-
LEHRE.
    R.E. CAZDEN, 182:VOL23#13/14-644
    J.P. DANTON, 356:APR71-172
KLYMASZ, R.B., COMP. A BIBLIOGRAPHY OF
UKRAINIAN FOLKLORE IN CANADA, 1902-64.
    J.B. RUDNYCKYJ, 292(JAF):OCT-DEC70-
    470
KLYMASZ, R.B. AN INTRODUCTION TO THE
UKRAINIAN-CANADIAN IMMIGRANT FOLKSONG
CYCLE. THE UKRAINIAN WINTER FOLKSONG
CYCLE IN CANADA.
    N. MC LEOD, 187:MAY72-289
KNAAK, L. TROTZ/PROTEST/REBELLION.
    F. BRUNNER, 182:VOL23#15/16-713
KNACHEL, P.A. - SEE NEDHAM, M.
KNAPP, B.L. ANTONIN ARTAUD.
    A. AMOIA, 207(FR):MAR70-683
    R.J. DOAN, 399(MLJ):JAN70-37
KNAPP, B.L. JEAN GENET.*
    A. AMOIA, 207(FR):OCT69-165
    R. NUGENT, 399(MLJ):FEB70-144
KNAPP, G. MENSCH UND KRANKHEIT.
    W. KURTH, 182:VOL23#15/16-715
KNAPP, L.M. - SEE SMOLLETT, T.
KNAPP, P. THE BERENGARIA EXCHANGE.
    441:20FEB72-24
KNAPP, W.I. LIFE, WRITINGS AND CORRES-
PONDENCE OF GEORGE BORROW.
    A. EASSON, 447(N&Q):JUL70-273

KNAPPERT, J. TRADITIONAL SWAHILI POETRY.
    G.S.P. FREEMAN-GRENVILLE, 315(JAL):
    VOL8PT1-41
KNAUF, D., ED. PAPERS IN DRAMATIC THEORY
AND CRITICISM.
    J.W. KIRK, 583:SUMMER70-361
KNEBEL, F. DARK HORSE.
    M. LEVIN, 441:23JUL72-21
KNEISSL, P. DIE SIEGESTITULATUR DER
RÖMISCHEN KAISER.
    M. HAMMOND, 124:JAN71-169
    F. LASSERRE, 182:VOL23#5-242
KNEPLER, H. - SEE HOUSSAYE, A.
KNESSL, L. ERNST KRENEK.*
    N. O'LOUGHLIN, 607:SPRING69-67
KNEVET, R. THE SHORTER POEMS OF RALPH
KNEVET. (A.M. CHARLES, ED)
    K.J. HÖLTGEN, 38:BAND87HEFT1-90
KNEZ, E.I. & C-S. SWANSON. A SELECTED
AND ANNOTATED BIBLIOGRAPHY OF KOREAN
ANTHROPOLOGY.
    F. MOOS, 293(JAST):MAY70-708
"KNIGA: ISSLEDOVANIYA I MATERIALY."
(VOLS 17-19)
    J.S.G. SIMMONS, 78(BC):SPRING70-104
"KNIGA: ISSLEDOVANIYA I MATERIALY."
(VOL 20)
    J.S.G. SIMMONS, 78(BC):WINTER70-536
KNIGHT, D. THE ARMY DOES NOT GO AWAY.
    D. BARBOUR, 150(DR):SPRING70-112
    M. HORNYANSKY, 627(UTQ):JUL70-336
KNIGHT, D. FARQUHARSON'S PHYSIQUE AND
WHAT IT DID TO HIS MIND.*
    M. LAURENCE, 296:WINTER72-77
KNIGHT, D., ED. A POCKETFUL OF STARS.
    617(TLS):13OCT72-1235
KNIGHT, G.W. NEGLECTED POWERS.*
    F.F. CANNAN, 677:VOL2-325
KNIGHT, I.F. THE GEOMETRIC SPIRIT.
    P.D. JIMACK, 208(FS):JUL71-336
KNIGHT, J. & N. BAXTER-MOORE. NORTHERN
IRELAND: THE ELECTIONS OF THE TWENTIES.
    617(TLS):16JUN72-697
KNIGHT, K.G. DEUTSCHE ROMANE DER BAROCK-
ZEIT.*
    P. SKRINE, 402(MLR):APR71-448
KNIGHT, R.C., ED. RACINE.
    I. BARKO, 67:MAY71-58
    H.T. BARNWELL, 208(FS):JAN71-73
KNIGHT, S. THE STRUCTURE OF SIR THOMAS
MALORY'S ARTHURIAD.*
    R.W. ACKERMAN, 589:JAN71-158
    R.T. DAVIES, 382(MAE):1971/3-303
    D. PEARSALL, 402(MLR):JUL71-656
KNIGHT, W.F.J. ELYSION.
    F. LASSERRE, 182:VOL23#13/14-677
    E. PHINNEY, JR., 124:MAY71-310
KNIGHT, W.F.J. MANY-SIDED HOMER. (J.D.
CHRISTIE, ED)
    F.M. COMBELLACK, 122:JAN71-51
    J.C. WILLIAMS, 124:OCT70-58
KNIGHTS, L.C. PUBLIC VOICES.
    617(TLS):5MAY72-517
KNJAZEVSKAJA, O.A., V.G. DEMJANOV & M.V.
LJAPON, EDS. USPENSKIJ SBORNIK DES
XII.-XIII. JAHRHUNDERTS.
    B. CONRAD, 72:BAND208HEFT4/6-468
KNOBLOCH, E. BEYOND THE OXUS.
    617(TLS):28JUL72-887
KNOEPFLE, J. THE INTRICATE LAND.
    J. NAIDEN, 491:MAY72-116
KNOEPFLMACHER, U.C. GEORGE ELIOT'S
EARLY NOVELS.*
    I. ADAM, 529(QQ):SPRING70-139
    T. PINNEY, 445(NCF):JUN69-120
KNOLL, E. & J.N. MC FADDEN, EDS. WAR
CRIMES AND THE AMERICAN CONSCIENCE.*
    G.C. ZAHN, 142:WINTER71-120

KNOLL, R.E. CHRISTOPHER MARLOWE.
C.G. MASINTON, 551(RENQ):AUTUMN70-320
KNOTT, B. NIGHTS OF NAOMI (PLUS 2
SONGS).
C. MOLESWORTH, 491:MAY72-107
KNOTT, J.R., JR. MILTON'S PASTORAL
VISION.
617(TLS):18FEB72-184
"KNOWLEDGE AND NECESSITY."
D. MC QUEEN, 518:JAN71-29
KNOWLER, J. TRUST AN ENGLISHMAN.
617(TLS):20OCT72-1259
KNOWLES, A.V. - SEE IL'F, I. & E. PETROV
KNOWLES, D. FRENCH DRAMA OF THE INTER-
WAR YEARS: 1918-39.
H.M. BLOCK, 397(MD):MAY69-100
KNOWLES, D. - SEE SAINT AUGUSTINE
KNOWLES, D., C.N.L. BROOKE & V.C.M. LON-
DON, EDS. THE HEADS OF RELIGIOUS
HOUSES: ENGLAND AND WALES, 940-1216.
617(TLS):28JUL72-897
KNOWLES, D. & R.N. HADCOCK. MEDIEVAL
RELIGIOUS HOUSES. (NEW ED)
617(TLS):28JAN72-103
KNOWLES, D., WITH D. OBOLENSKY. THE
MIDDLE AGES.
A.G. BIGGS, 589:JAN71-160
KNOWLES, J. PHINEAS.
J.P. DEGNAN, 340(KR):1969/2-272
KNOX, A. NIGHT OF THE WHITE BEAR.*
S. BLACKBURN, 440:2JAN72-2
KNOX, B. TO KILL A WITCH.*
N. CALLENDAR, 441:2APR72-22
KNOX, M. ACTION.
R. TAYLOR, 479(PHQ):JUL70-305
KNOX, M. A LAYMAN'S QUEST.
A.C. EWING, 479(PHQ):OCT70-410
KNUTSON, H.C. THE IRONIC GAME.
J. DOOLITTLE, 593:SPRING71-82
KNUTTER, H-H. DIE JUDEN UND DIE DEUTSCHE
LINKE IN DER WEIMARER REPUBLIK.
617(TLS):28JAN72-81
KOBATA, A. & M. MATSUDA. RYUKYUAN RELA-
TIONS WITH KOREA AND SOUTH SEA COUN-
TRIES.
S. SAKAMAKI, 293(JAST):FEB70-443
KOBAYASHI, E. THE VERB FORMS OF THE
SOUTH ENGLISH LEGENDARY.
K.R. BROOKS, 179(ES):OCT70-448
"KOBBÉ'S COMPLETE OPERA BOOK." (8TH ED)
(LORD HAREWOOD, ED)
S. SADIE, 415:AUG70-808
KOBEL, E. HUGO VON HOFMANNSTHAL.*
R.C. NORTON, 301(JEGP):OCT71-738
KOBLER, J. CAPONE.*
617(TLS):31MAR72-357
KOCH, F. GOETHES GEDANKENFORM.*
F. RADANDT, 405(MP):AUG69-72
KOCH, G.F. DIE KUNSTAUSTELLUNG.
H. HUTH, 54:JUN69-198
KOCH, K. THE PLEASURES OF PEACE.
P. CARROLL, 491:NOV71-104
KOCH, K. POEMS FROM 1952 AND 1953.
SLEEPING WITH WOMEN.
R. BROTHERSON, 661:FALL/WINTER69-105
KOCH, P. - SEE GALIANI, F.
KOCH, R. & C. EDUCATIONAL COMMUNE.
E-Z. FRIEDENBERG, 453:16NOV72-35
KOCH, R.A. JOACHIM PATINIR.*
C.D. CUTTLER, 56:WINTER69-431
KOCH, S. NIGHT WATCH.
K.J. ATCHITY, 340(KR):1969/5-675
KOCH, W.A. VOM MORPHEM ZUM TEXTEM (FROM
MORPHEME TO TEXTEME).
K. TOGEBY, 545(RPH):FEB71-545
KOCHAN, M. & L., EDS. RUSSIAN THEMES.
W.V. WALLACE, 587:OCT68-270

KOCHANEK, S.A. THE CONGRESS PARTY OF
INDIA.
B.D. GRAHAM, 293(JAST):NOV69-187
KOCHER, P.H. MASTER OF MIDDLE-EARTH.
J.A. SMITH, 453:14DEC72-19
KOCHNO, B. DIAGHILEV AND THE BALLETS
RUSSES.*
B.H. HAGGIN, 249(HUDR):SUMMER71-312
KODÁLY, Z. FOLK MUSIC OF HUNGARY. (2ND
ED REV BY L. VARGYAS)
617(TLS):26MAY72-613
KOEHLER, L. ANTON ANTONOVIČ DEL'VIG.
A.B. MC MILLIN, 575(SEER):OCT71-615
KOELLE, S.W. AFRICAN NATIVE LITERATURE.
A.H.M. KIRK-GREENE, 69:JUL69-317
KOEMAN, I.C., ED. ATLANTES NEERLANDICI.
N. BARKER, 78(BC):SUMMER70-246
KOENIG, F.V. - SEE GAUTIER DE COINCI
KOEPER, F. ILLINOIS ARCHITECTURE.
J. MAASS, 576:OCT69-232
KOERNER, J.D. THE PARSONS COLLEGE BUB-
BLE.
C.P. IVES, 396(MODA):WINTER71-96
KOESTERMANN, E. - SEE TACITUS
KOESTLER, A. THE CALL-GIRLS.
R. FULLER, 362:26OCT72-556
617(TLS):27OCT72-1274
KOESTLER, A. THE CASE OF THE MIDWIFE
TOAD.*
P. ADAMS, 61:APR72-128
R. CLAIBORNE, 441:2APR72-17
E. EDELSON, 440:2APR72-5
D. JORAVSKY, 453:21SEP72-23
J. LEAR, 561(SATR):1APR72-63
442(NY):8APR72-131
KOESTLER, A. THE ROOTS OF COINCIDENCE.
P. ADAMS, 61:SEP72-110
N. BLIVEN, 442(NY):12AUG72-75
E. FREMONT-SMITH, 561(SATR):30SEP72-
72
D. JORAVSKY, 453:21SEP72-23
C. LEHMANN-HAUPT, 441:11AUG72-29
J. MADDOX, 362:10FEB72-187
617(TLS):19MAY72-569
KOH, B.C. THE FOREIGN POLICY OF NORTH
KOREA.
S-W. LEE, 293(JAST):MAY70-709
KOHÁK, E.V. - SEE MASARYK, T.G.
KÖHLER, E. "CONSEIL DES BARONS" UND
"JUGEMENT DES BARONS."
W.M. HACKETT, 545(RPH):FEB71-556
F. WHITEHEAD, 208(FS):JUL71-314
KOHLER, F.D. UNDERSTANDING THE RUSSIANS.
T. SHABAD, 32:DEC71-899
KÖHLER, K-H. & G. HERRE, WITH P. PÖTSCH-
NER - SEE VAN BEETHOVEN, L.
KOHLHAUSSEN, H. NÜRNBERGER GOLDSCHMIEDE-
KUNST DES MITTELALTERS UND DER DÜRER-
ZEIT, 1240 BIS 1540.
C. OMAN, 90:JAN70-56
KOHLSCHMIDT, W. DICHTER, TRADITION UND
ZEITGEIST.
L. SPULER, 400(MLN):APR70-396
KOHLSCHMIDT, W. GESCHICHTE DER DEUTSCHEN
LITERATUR VOM BAROCK BIS ZUR KLASSIK.
L.L. ALBERTSEN, 462(OL):VOL23#3-247
KÖHN, L. VIELDEUTIGE WELT.
K.N., 191(ELN):SEP69(SUPP)-108
KOHOUT, P. FROM THE DIARY OF A COUNTER-
REVOLUTIONARY.* (FRENCH TITLE: JOURNAL
D'UN CONTRE-RÉVOLUTIONNAIRE.)
S. DE GRAMONT, 561(SATR):29JUL72-62
KOJECKÝ, R. T.S. ELIOT'S SOCIAL CRITI-
CISM.
F. KERMODE, 441:26MAR72-6
617(TLS):4FEB72-123

KOJÈVE, A. ESSAI D'UNE HISTOIRE RAISON-
NÉE DE LA PHILOSOPHIE PAÏENNE. (VOL 1)
J-M. REY, 98:MAY69-437
KOJÈVE, A. INTRODUCTION TO THE READING
OF HEGEL. (A. BLOOM, ED)
R.J.B., 543:DEC69-349
"KOJIKI." (D.L. PHILIPPI, TRANS)
R. HUNTSBERRY, 244(HJAS):VOL29-300
R.A. MILLER, 293(JAST):FEB70-441
KOJIRO, Y. FORMS IN JAPAN.
C. HEIMSATH, 363:FEB70-70
"KOKIN WAKA-SHŪ." (H.H. HONDA, TRANS)
M. BROCK, 285(JAPQ):JUL-SEP70-336
KOKOLAKIS, M.M. HO ISOKRATOYS "EYAGORAS"
KAI Ē CHRONOLOGĒSIS TŌN KYPRIAKŌN
LOGŌN.
D.M. MAC DOWELL, 123:DEC71-451
KOKOSCHKA, O. LONDON VIEWS, BRITISH
LANDSCAPES.
617(TLS):15DEC72-1541
KOLAKOWSKI, L. THE ALIENATION OF REASON.
W.T. BLACKSTONE, 219(GAR):FALL69-402
KOLAKOWSKI, L. POSITIVIST PHILOSOPHY.
617(TLS):5MAY72-513
KOLATCH, A.J. THE NAME DICTIONARY.
E.C. SMITH, 424:MAR68-51
KOLB, H.H., JR. THE ILLUSION OF LIFE.*
P.C. WERMUTH, 432(NEQ):SEP70-492
KOLB, P. & L.B. PRICE - SEE PROUST, M.
KOLBE, J., ED. ANSICHTEN EINER KÜNFTIGEN
GERMANISTIK. (2ND ED)
M.L. BAEUMER, 406:SPRING71-69
KOLBE, J. GOETHES WAHLVERWANDTSCHAFTEN
UND DER ROMAN DES 19. JAHRHUNDERTS.
H. REISS, 220(GL&L):OCT70-106
KOLINSKI, M., ED. STUDIES IN ETHNOMUSI-
COLOGY. (VOL 2)
D.P. MC ALLESTER, 650(WF):APR68-134
KOLINSKY, E. ENGAGIERTER EXPRESSIONIS-
MUS.
M. ADAMS, 67:NOV71-262
VAN DER KOLK, H. DAS HILDEBRANDLIED.
H. HOMANN, 400(MLN):OCT70-747
KOLKO, J. & G. THE LIMITS OF POWER.
G. SMITH, 441:27FEB72-31
KOLKOWICZ, R. THE SOVIET MILITARY AND
THE COMMUNIST PARTY.
M. MACKINTOSH, 587:APR69-548
KØLLN, H. OPPOSITIONS OF VOICE IN GREEK,
SLAVIC, AND BALTIC.
F. BADER, 555:VOL44FASC2-285
KOLLONTAI, A. THE AUTOBIOGRAPHY OF A
SEXUALLY EMANCIPATED WOMAN. (I. FET-
SCHER, ED)
M. DRABBLE, 362:17FEB72-220
617(TLS):18FEB72-172
KÖLMEL, W. REGIMEN CHRISTIANUM.
W. ULLMANN, 382(MAE):1971/3-288
KOLNEDER, W. ANTONIO VIVALDI.*
M.T., 410(M&L):JUL71-314
M. TALBOT, 415:MAY71-445
KOLNEDER, W. ANTON WEBERN.
J. MEKEEL, 513:SPRING-SUMMER69-172
S. WALSH, 607:WINTER68/69-40
KOLODIN, I. THE CONTINUITY OF MUSIC.
R. FREEDMAN, 340(KR):1969/4-560
KOMISAR, L. THE NEW FEMINISM.
617(TLS):4FEB72-138
KONDO, I. THE 36 VIEWS OF MT. FUJI BY
HOKUSAI.
P. HARDIE, 39:APR69-326
KÖNIG, H. LENIN UND DER ITALIENISCHE
SOZIALISMUS 1915-1921.
N. MC INNES, 587:OCT68-267
KONIGSBERG, I. SAMUEL RICHARDSON AND
THE DRAMATIC NOVEL.*
A. SHERBO, 173(ECS):SUMMER70-560
KONONOV, I.F. - SEE MAKSAKOV, V.V.

KONOVALOV, S. & D.J. RICHARDS, EDS. RUS-
SIAN CRITICAL ESSAYS. (XIXTH CENTURY)
617(TLS):13OCT72-1237
KONRÁD, G. A LÁTOGATÓ.
G. WALKÓ, 270:VOL20#3-72
KONRAD, M. HÖLDERLINS PHILOSOPHIE IM
GRUNDRISS.
I.C., 191(ELN):SEP70(SUPP)-110
KONSTANTINOVIĆ, R.D. VERCORS - ECRIVAIN
ET DESSINATEUR.
R.D. COTTRELL, 207(FR):FEB70-512
J. KOLBERT, 399(MLJ):MAY70-366
KONUŠ, J.J., COMP. SLOVAK-ENGLISH
PHRASEOLOGICAL DICTIONARY.
A. ISAČENKO, 32:DEC71-918
S.E. MANN, 575(SEER):JUL71-481
KONWICKI, T. ZWIERZOCZŁEKOUPIÓR.
D.C. WILLIAMSON, 270:VOL20#1-3
KOONCE, B.G. CHAUCER AND THE TRADITION
OF FAME.
H. NEWSTEAD, 545(RPH):NOV70-349
KOOSER, T. OFFICIAL ENTRY BLANK.
W. GAFFNEY, 502(PRS):WINTER69/70-420
KOPAL, Z. MAN AND HIS UNIVERSE.
617(TLS):24MAR72-345
KÖPECZI, B., ED. A RÁKÓCZI-SZABADSÁGHARC
ÉS EURÓPA.
B.S. KIRÁLY, 32:SEP71-682
KOPF, D. BRITISH ORIENTALISM AND THE
BENGAL RENAISSANCE.
A.T. EMBREE, 293(JAST):FEB70-473
KOPP, R. - SEE BAUDELAIRE, C.
KOPP, R.L. MARCEL PROUST AS A SOCIAL
CRITIC.
441:16APR72-20
KOPP, W.L. GERMAN LITERATURE IN THE
UNITED STATES 1945-1960.*
L. NEWMAN, 220(GL&L):JAN71-216
KOPS, B. BY THE WATERS OF WHITECHAPEL.
F.P.W. MC DOWELL, 659:SUMMER72-361
KOPS, B. FOR THE RECORD.*
G. EWART, 364:JUN/JUL71-132
KOPS, B. THE PASSIONATE PAST OF GLORIA
GAYE.*
S. BLACKBURN, 440:9APR72-8
T. LASK, 441:22APR72-35
KORFF, F.W. DIASTOLE UND SYSTOLE.*
H.R. KLIENEBERGER, 402(MLR):JAN71-226
R.M., 191(ELN):SEP70(SUPP)-119
KORG, J., ED. TWENTIETH CENTURY INTER-
PRETATIONS OF "BLEAK HOUSE."
T. BLOUNT, 155:JAN70-57
KORG, J. - SEE GISSING, G.
KÖRNER, K-H. DIE "AKTIONSGEMEINSCHAFT
FINITES VERB + INFINITIV" IM SPANISCHEN
FORMENSYSTEM.
M. SANDMANN, 545(RPH):FEB70-364
KÖRNER, S. EXPERIENCE AND THEORY.*
P. BUTCHVAROV, 486:SEP68-292
KÖRNER, S. WHAT IS PHILOSOPHY?
R.F.D., 543:MAR70-558
R.J. HIRST, 518:MAY70-12
C.H. WHITELEY, 393(MIND):APR70-310
KORNWOLF, J.D. M.H. BAILLIE SCOTT AND
THE ARTS AND CRAFTS MOVEMENT.
617(TLS):28JUL72-892
KOROLENKO, V.G. THE HISTORY OF MY CON-
TEMPORARY. (TRANS & ABRIDGED BY N.
PARSONS)
617(TLS):14APR72-423
KORSAKAS, K., ED. LIETUVIŲ LITERATŪR-
INIAI RYŠIAI IR SĄVEIKOS.
R. ŠILBAJORIS, 574(SEEJ):WINTER71-513
KORSHIN, P.J., ED. PROCEEDINGS OF THE
MODERN LANGUAGE ASSOCIATION NEOCLASS-
ICISM CONFERENCES 1967-1968.
566:SPRING71-72

KORTH, E.H. SPANISH POLICY IN COLONIAL
CHILE.
J. LOCKHART, 377:MAR71-45
KORTSEN, B. CONTEMPORARY NORWEGIAN
ORCHESTRAL MUSIC.
R. LAYTON, 415:JAN70-45
KORTSEN, B. TONALITY AND FORM IN NOR-
WEGIAN SPRINGLEIKS.
F. HOWES, 415:MAY70-506
KOSAMBI, D.D. ANCIENT INDIA.
P.B. CALKINS, 293(JAST):NOV69-188
KOSCH, W., COMP. DEUTSCHES LITERATUR-
LEXIKON. (VOL 1) (3RD ED) (B. BERGER
& H. RUPP, EDS)
J.G. KUNSTMANN, 221(GQ):JAN70-94
KOSCH, W., COMP. DEUTSCHES LITERATUR-
LEXIKON. (VOL 2) (3RD ED) (B. BERGER &
H. RUPP, EDS)
P.M. MITCHELL, 301(JEGP):JAN71-138
V. NOLLENDORFS, 406:SUMMER71-184
KOSEGARTEN, A. & P. TIGLER, EDS. FEST-
SCHRIFT ULRICH MIDDELDORF.
J.C. SLOANE, 54:MAR69-91
KOSINSKI, J. BEING THERE.*
J.M. MORSE, 249(HUDR):AUTUMN71-539
I. WEDDE, 364:OCT/NOV71-149
KOSKIMIES, R. DER NORDISCHE DEKADENT.*
P.M. MITCHELL, 149:JUN71-183
KOSSMAN, R.R. HENRY JAMES: DRAMATIST.*
Q. ANDERSON, 27(AL):MAY71-294
KOSSOFF, D. THE BOOK OF WITNESSES.
617(TLS):21JUL72-853
KOSTARAS, G.P. DER BEGRIFF DES LEBENS
BEI PLOTIN.
J.M. RIST, 124:DEC70-125
KOSTELANETZ, R., ED. JOHN CAGE.
P. DICKINSON, 415:OCT71-967
617(TLS):18FEB72-193
KÖSTER, R., ED. ULLSTEIN LEXIKON DER
DEUTSCHEN SPRACHE.
K.E.H. LIEDTKE, 399(MLJ):NOV70-543
KOSTER, R.M. THE PRINCE.
J. CATINELLA, 561(SATR):27MAY72-68
C. LEHMANN-HAUPT, 441:22FEB72-39
P. RAND, 441:5MAR72-6
P. THEROUX, 440:13FEB72-6
KOSTER, S. ANTIKE EPOSTHEORIEN.
F. LASSERRE, 182:VOL23#17/18-810
KOSTOF, S.K. THE ORTHODOX BAPTISTERY OF
RAVENNA.
M. HEUSER, 576:OCT69-226
KOTEL'NIKOVA, L.A. ITALIANSKOE KRESTIAN-
STVO I GOROD V XI-XIV VV.
B. KREKIĆ, 589:APR71-386
KOTHARI, K.S. INDIAN FOLK MUSICAL IN-
STRUMENTS.
V.P. VATUK, 292(JAF):OCT-DEC70-480
KOTHARI, R., ED. CASTE IN INDIAN POLI-
TICS.
617(TLS):22SEP72-1119
KOTKER, Z. BODIES IN MOTION.
J. CATINELLA, 561(SATR):27MAY72-68
J. DECK, 441:18JUN72-6
T. LASK, 441:14JUL72-33
442(NY):1JUL72-74
KOTLER, M. NEIGHBORHOOD GOVERNMENT.
H. KOHL, 453:23MAR72-39
KOTLOBYE, S. & L. TETSKAYA - SEE KARYA-
KIN, Y.
KOTLOWITZ, R. SOMEWHERE ELSE.
P. ADAMS, 61:DEC72-144
J. HENDIN, 441:5NOV72-4
T. LASK, 441:18NOV72-39
442(NY):23DEC72-78
KOTT, J. THEATRE NOTEBOOK: 1947-67.
S.J.M. LIPPERT, 219(GAR):SUMMER69-256
C.R. LYONS, 397(MD):SEP69-210

KOTZWINKLE, W. HERMES 3000.
M. OWEN-FEKETE, 296:SUMMER72-86
KOURMOULIS, G.J. ANTISTROPHON LEXIKON
TĒS NEAS HELLĒNIKĒS.
C.N. TSIRPANLIS, 121(CJ):APR-MAY71-
364
KOUTSOUDAS, A. WRITING TRANSFORMATIONAL
GRAMMARS.*
W.O. DINGWALL, 361:VOL23#2-149
G. NICKEL, 72:BAND208HEFT3-208
P.A.M. SEUREN, 297(JL):APR69-188
KOVAČIĆ, I. SMIJ I SUZE STAREGA SPLITA.
R. DUNATOV, 574(SEEJ):SUMMER71-245
KOVAL'ČENKO, I.D. RUSSKOE KREPOSTNOE
KREST"JANSTVO V PERVOJ POLOVINE XIX
VEKA.
E. NIEDERHAUSER, 104:SUMMER71-284
KOVALEV, V.A., ED. TVORCHESTVO LEONIDA
LEONOVA.
R.D.B. THOMSON, 32:JUN71-442
KOVNA, A. & N. SACHS. SELECTED POEMS.
J. SYMONS, 364:FEB/MAR72-160
KOVNER, A. & N. SACHS. SELECTED POEMS.
617(TLS):11FEB72-166
KOWALENKO, L. NASHA NE SVOYA ZEMLIA.
C.H. ANDRUSYSHEN, 627(UTQ):JUL70-448
KOWZAN, T. LITTÉRATURE ET SPECTACLE DANS
LEURS RAPPORTS ESTHÉTIQUES THÉMATIQUES
ET SEMIOLOGIQUES.
F. HALL, 89(BJA):SPRING71-206
KOYRÉ, A. & I.B. COHEN, WITH A. WHITMAN
- SEE NEWTON, I.
KOYRMOYLĒ, G.I. HANTISTROPHON LEXIKON
TĒS NEAS ELLĒNICHĒS.
K. KAZAZIS, 361:VOL24#1-86
KOZIK, I.S. - SEE ST. JEROME
KOZINTSEV, G. NASH SOVREMENNIK VILJAM
SHEKSPIR.
A. GLASSE, 570(SQ):WINTER68-97
KOZINTSEV, G. SHAKESPEARE - TIME AND
CONSCIENCE.
R. SPEAIGHT, 570(SQ):WINTER68-90
KOZIOL, H. GRUNDZÜGE DER ENGLISCHEN
SEMANTIK.*
K. BALDINGER, 38:BAND87HEFT2-243
KOZLOFF, M. JASPER JOHNS.
J. MASHECK, 592:NOV69-193
KOZŁOWSKA, H. FORMENNEUTRALISIERUNG IM
NOMINALEN BEREICH DER DEUTSCHEN
SPRACHE.
H.L. KUFNER, 350:MAR71-217
KOZOL, J. FREE SCHOOLS.
T. LASK, 441:7APR72-36
R. POIRIER, 441:5MAR72-5
442(NY):15APR72-148
KRAAK, A. & W.G. KLOOSTER. SYNTAXIS.
J.G. KOOIJ, 361:VOL24#1-65
KRAFFT, F. DYNAMISCHE UND STATISCHE
BETRACHTUNGSWEISE IN DER ANTIKEN MECH-
ANIK.
W. BURKERT, 182:VOL23#19/20-876
KRAFT, H. - SEE SCHILLER, F.
KRAFT, J. THE EARLY TALES OF HENRY
JAMES.*
Q. ANDERSON, 27(AL):MAY71-294
639(VQR):AUTUMN70-CXXXVI
KRAFT, K. DER GOLDEN KRANZ CAESARS UND
DER KAMPF UM DIE ENTLARVUNG DES
"TYRANNEN." (2ND ED)
B.M. LEVICK, 123:DEC71-460
KRAFT, L. A NEW APPROACH TO EAR TRAIN-
ING.
S. ANDERSON, 308:SPRING69-152
KRAFT, M. STUDIEN ZUR THEMATIK VON MAX
FRISCHS ROMAN "MEIN NAME SEI GANTEN-
BEIN."
M.E. COCK, 402(MLR):JUL71-717

KRAGGERUD, E. AENEISSTUDIEN.*
J. HELLEGOUARC'H, 555:VOL44FASC2-337
KRAILSHEIMER, A.J., ED. THE CONTINENTAL
RENAISSANCE 1500-1600.
617(TLS):7JAN72-16
KRÄMER, J., ED. PFÄLZISCHES WÖRTERBUCH.
(VOL 1)
V. GÜNTHER, 182:VOL23#5-213
KRAMER, P. & R.E. MC NICOLL, EDS. LATIN
AMERICAN PANORAMA.
D. HERNANDEZ, 50(ARQ):WINTER69-371
KRAMER-LAUFF, D. TANZ UND TÄNZERISCHES
IN RILKES LYRIK.
B.L. BRADLEY, 406:SPRING71-60
KRAMNICK, I. BOLINGBROKE AND HIS CIRCLE.
R.I. COOK, 191(ELN):DEC69-143
KRANES, D. MARGINS.
M. LEVIN, 441:19NOV72-62
KRANOWSKI, N. PARIS DANS LES ROMANS
D'EMILE ZOLA.
P. BRADY, 207(FR):FEB70-514
KRANZ, G. EUROPAS CHRISTLICHE LITERA-
TUR.* (VOLS 1&2) (VOL 2 IS 2ND ED)
[TITLE SHOWN IN PREV IS VOL 1]
E. STOPP, 402(MLR):JAN71-167
KRAPF, G. ORGAN IMPROVISATION.
J. DALTON, 415:JUL70-713
KRATZ, H. FRÜHES MITTELALTER.
K.J. NORTHCOTT, 406:SUMMER71-162
KRATZSCH, K. - SEE VON ARNIM, A.
KRAUS, A.L. THE NEW YORK TIMES GUIDE TO
BUSINESS AND FINANCE.
K. KOYEN, 441:10CT72-10
KRAUS, H. THE LIVING THEATRE OF MEDIEVAL
ART.*
J. BECKWITH, 39:SEP69-267
T.W. LYMAN, 54:SEP69-290
KRAUSE, S.J. MARK TWAIN AS CRITIC.*
C.A. BROWN, 613:AUTUMN68-445
R. LEHAN, 445(NCF):DEC69-377
B. POLI, 402(MLR):OCT71-881
J.R. WELSH, 219(GAR):SUMMER69-244
KRAUSE, W. RUNEN.
C.W. THOMPSON, 563(SS):AUTUMN71-437
KRAUSS, P.G., ED. DEUTSCHE LEKTÜRE.
H. BLANCHARD, 399(MLJ):MAY70-370
KRAUSS, R.E. TERMINAL IRON WORKS.
K. BAKER, 441:30APR72-6
KRAUSS, W., ED. EST-IL UTILE DE TROMPER
LE PEUPLE? IST DER VOLKSBETRUG VON
NUTZEN?
A.D. HYTIER, 546(RR):APR70-145
KRAUSS, W. FONTENELLE UND DIE AUFKLÄR-
UNG.
D. MEAKIN, 208(FS):OCT71-458
KRAUSS, W., ED. DIE FRANZÖSISCHE AUF-
KLÄRUNG IM SPIEGEL DER DEUTSCHEN LIT-
ERATUR DES 18. JAHRHUNDERTS.
R. GIRARD, 182:VOL23#5-219
KRAUSSER, P. KRITIK DER ENDLICHEN VER-
NUNFT.
R.A. MAKKREEL, 319:APR72-232
KRAUTH, L. DIE PHILOSOPHIE CARNAPS.
N. FEHRINGER, 182:VOL23#10-513
KRAUTHEIMER, R. GHIBERTI'S BRONZE DOORS.
617(TLS):2JUN72-620
KRAUTHEIMER, R. STUDIES IN EARLY CHRIS-
TIAN, MEDIEVAL AND RENAISSANCE ART.*
R. CORMACK, 89(BJA):SUMMER71-309
KREBS, S.D. SOVIET COMPOSERS AND THE
DEVELOPMENT OF SOVIET MUSIC.
M.H. BROWN, 32:SEP71-699
R. MC ALLISTER, 415:FEB71-133
KREISEL, G. & J.L. KRIVINE. ELEMENTS OF
MATHEMATICAL LOGIC.*
J.C. SHEPHERDSON, 536:JUN70-93

KREISEL, H. DIE KUNST DES DEUTSCHEN
MÖBELS. (VOL 1)
H. HUTH, 54:SEP69-308
P. THORNTON, 90:AUG70-544
F.J.B. WATSON, 39:NOV69-445
KRENTS, H. TO RACE THE WIND.
441:30JUL72-20
KRESS, F. & H.A. MAIER - SEE BROCH, H.
KRESS, H. GUĐMUNDUR KAMBAN.
R. BECK, 563(SS):WINTER71-95
KRESTIĆ, V. HRVATSKO-UGARSKA NAGODBA
1868. GODINE.
G. STOKES, 32:MAR71-190
KRETZMANN, N. - SEE WILLIAM OF SHERWOOD
KREUTZBERGER, M., WITH I. FOERG, EDS.
LEO BAECK INSTITUTE NEW YORK: BIBLIO-
THEK UND ARCHIV. (VOL 1)
P.U. HOHENDAHL, 221(GQ):NOV70-817
KREUTZER, E. SPRACHE UND SPIEL IM
"ULYSSES" VON JAMES JOYCE.
M. JAHN, 72:BAND208HEFT4/6-413
KREUZER, H. DIE BOHEME.*
G. LOOSE, 401(MLQ):DEC70-514
KREUZER, H. & R. GUNZENHÄUSER, EDS.
MATHEMATIK UND DICHTUNG.*
G.F. PROBST, 133:1969/3-344
KRIARAS, E. LEXIKO TĒS MESAIŌNIKĒS
ELLĒNIKĒS DĒMŌDOYS GRAMMATEIAS 1100-
1669.
K. MITSAKIS, 303:VOL90-267
KRIEGEL, A. THE FRENCH COMMUNISTS.
R.O. PAXTON, 441:24SEP72-46
KRIEGEL, A. LES GRANDS PROCÈS DANS LES
SYSTÈMES COMMUNISTES.
617(TLS):5MAY72-511
KRIEGEL, L. EDMUND WILSON.
T. LASK, 441:19FEB72-33
KRIEGEL, L. WORKING THROUGH.
M. DICKSTEIN, 441:19NOV72-65
561(SATR):25NOV72-72
KRIEGER, L. THE POLITICS OF DISCRETION.
F.P. DE MICHELIS, 548(RCSF):JAN/MAR
69-91
KRIEGER, M., ED. NORTHROP FRYE IN MODERN
CRITICISM.
D. MURDOCH, 597(SN):VOL40#1-258
KRIEGER, M. THE PLAY AND PLACE OF CRITI-
CISM.
D. BURKE, 613:SPRING68-127
D.T. WIECK, 290(JAAC):WINTER69-250
KRIEGHBAUM, H. PRESSURES ON THE PRESS.
B.H. BAGDIKIAN, 441:11JUN72-2
KRIELE, C. UNTERSUCHUNGEN ZUR ALEXIUS-
LEGENDE DES "TOMBEL DE CHARTROSE."
K.D. UITTI, 545(RPH):AUG70-128
KRIM, S. SHAKE IT FOR THE WORLD, SMART-
ASS.* (BRITISH TITLE: SHAKE IT FOR
THE WORLD.)
M. BRADBURY, 364:DEC71/JAN72-149
KRIPALANI, K. MODERN INDIAN LITERATURE.
C. COPPOLA, 293(JAST):FEB70-471
KRISCHKE, T., ED. MATERIALIEN ZU ÖDON
VON HORVÁTH.
617(TLS):30JUN72-756
KRISHNA, G., WITH C.F. VON WEIZSÄCKER -
SEE UNDER GOPI KRISHNA, WITH C.F. VON
WEIZSÄCKER
KRISHNAMOORTHY, K. THE DHVANYĀLOKA AND
ITS CRITICS.
D. LORENZEN, 293(JAST):NOV69-189
KRISHNAMOORTHY, K. - SEE SĀYAŅA
KRISTENSSON, G. STUDIES ON MIDDLE
ENGLISH TOPOGRAPHICAL TERMS.
M. GELLING, 677:VOL2-232

178

KRISTENSSON, G. A SURVEY OF MIDDLE ENG-
LISH DIALECTS 1290-1350: THE SIX NORTH-
ERN COUNTIES AND LINCOLNSHIRE.*
  H.E. KIJLSTRA, 353:NOV69-113
  B. SELTÉN, 179(ES):OCT70-445
  A. ZETTERSTEN, 597(SN):VOL41#1-218
KRISTOL, I. ON THE DEMOCRATIC IDEA IN
AMERICA.
  A. BROYARD, 441:10MAY72-49
  Y. ROGAT, 453:21SEP72-6
KRITZECK, J., ED. ANTHOLOGY OF ISLAMIC
LITERATURE.
  A.A.A. FYZEE, 273(IC):OCT69-307
KRIVATSY, P., COMP. A CATALOGUE OF IN-
CUNABULA AND SIXTEENTH CENTURY PRINTED
BOOKS.
  617(TLS):18AUG72-978
KRLEŽA, M. THE RETURN OF PHILIP LATINO-
VICZ.
  J. SUHADOLC, 574(SEEJ):SPRING71-87
KROEBER, K. STYLES IN FICTIONAL STRUC-
TURE.*
  B.G. HORNBACK, 301(JEGP):OCT71-680
KROEBER, T. & R.F. HEIZER. ALMOST
ANCESTORS. (F.D. HALES, ED)
  F.L. PHELPS, 37:FEB69-41
KROETSCH, R. ALBERTA.*
  E. MANDEL, 627(UTQ):JUL69-401
KROETSCH, R. THE STUDHORSE MAN.*
  G. ROPER, 627(UTQ):JUL70-344
KROLOW, K. POEMS AGAINST DEATH.
  L.B. FOLTIN, 221(GQ):NOV70-788
KRÖMER, W. ZUR WELTANSCHAUUNG, ÄSTHETIK
UND POETIK DES NEOKLASSIZISMUS UND DER
ROMANTIK.
  W. KRAUSS, 72:BAND208HEFT1-79
KRONENBERGER, L. ANIMAL, VEGETABLE,
MINERAL.
  P. ADAMS, 61:MAR72-110
  R. LASSON, 440:20FEB72-4
KRONENBERGER, L., WITH E.M. BECK, EDS.
ATLANTIC BRIEF LIVES.*
  N. BALAKIAN, 441:28JAN72-42
KROOK, D. ELEMENTS OF TRAGEDY.
  M.R. HAIGHT, 89(BJA):WINTER71-102
  C. LEECH, 191(ELN):JUN71-306
KROPOTKIN, P. THE CONQUEST OF BREAD.
MUTUAL AID. (BOTH ED BY P. AVRICH)
  617(TLS):18AUG72-974
KRUGER, P. THE BRONZE CLAW.
  N. CALLENDAR, 441:2APR72-22
KRUGER, P. THE COLD ONES.
  N. CALLENDAR, 441:17SEP72-45
KRUMMACHER, F.A. & H. LANGE. KRIEG UND
FRIEDEN.
  A. WAHL, 182:VOL23#17/18-826
KRUPITSCH, V.S. - SEE GRIGORIEV, A.
KRUUK, H. THE SPOTTED HYENA.
  G. STADE, 441:3DEC72-6
KUBE, J. "TECHNĒ" UND "ARETĒ."
  J.B. SKEMP, 123:MAR71-28
KUBIŃSKA, J. LES MONUMENTS FUNÉRAIRES
DANS LES INSCRIPTIONS GRECQUES DE
L'ASIE MINEURE.
  A.G. WOODHEAD, 123:MAR71-146
KUBLER, G. - SEE DA COSTA, F.
KUBOTA, A. HIGHER CIVIL SERVANTS IN
POSTWAR JAPAN.
  A.B. CLUBOK, 293(JAST):FEB70-449
KUČERA, H. & W.N. FRANCIS. COMPUTATIONAL
ANALYSIS OF PRESENT-DAY AMERICAN ENG-
LISH.
  G.V. MAVERICK, 269(IJAL):JAN69-71
KUČERA, H. & G.K. MONROE. A COMPARATIVE
QUANTITATIVE PHONOLOGY OF RUSSIAN,
CZECH, AND GERMAN.*
  J.F. HENDRY, 104:SUMMER71-268
  J. KRAUS, 182:VOL23#8-412

KUCZYNSKI, M. & R.L. MEEK. QUESNAY'S
TABLEAU ÉCONOMIQUE.
  617(TLS):3MAR72-257
KUDSZUS, W. SPRACHVERLUST UND SINNWAN-
DEL.*
  M.B. BENN, 402(MLR):APR71-463
  C. HAMLIN, 222(GR):NOV70-310
KUEHL, J. & J.R. BRYER - SEE FITZGERALD,
F.S. & M. PERKINS
KUEHL, W.F. SEEKING WORLD ORDER.
  639(VQR):SUMMER70-CVIII
KUEHN, R.E., ED. TWENTIETH CENTURY IN-
TERPRETATIONS OF "LORD JIM."
  D.D. ZINK, 136:SPRING70-148
KUHLMAN, A.F. A GUIDE TO MATERIAL ON
CRIME AND CRIMINAL JUSTICE.
  617(TLS):18FEB72-191
KUHLMANN, Q. AUS DEM KÜHLPSALTER. (W.
VORTRIEDE, ED)
  R.L. BEARE, 220(GL&L):JAN71-208
KÜHLWEIN, W. MODELL EINER OPERATIONELLEN
LEXIKOLOGISCHEN ANALYSE: ALTENGLISCH
"BLUT."
  H. BECKERS, 72:BAND208HEFT2-122
KÜHLWEIN, W. DIE VERWENDUNG DER FEIND-
SELIGKEITSBEZEICHNUNGEN IN DER ALTENG-
LISCHEN DICHTERSPRACHE.
  N.E. ENKVIST & H. RINGBOM, 597(SN):
    VOL41#2-457
  E. STANDOP, 38:BAND87HEFT1-73
KUHN, D. LA POÉTIQUE DE FRANÇOIS VILLON.
  J. PALERMO, 546(RR):APR70-124
KUHN, D., ED. REISEBILDER AUS ITALIEN.
  I.C., 191(ELN):SEP70(SUPP)-94
KUHN, D., A. HOFMANN & A. KUHN, EDS.
AUCH ICH IN ARCADIEN.
  I.C., 191(ELN):SEP69(SUPP)-95
KUHN, D. & F. RUSSIA ON OUR MINDS.
  T. SHABAD, 32:DEC71-899
KUHN, S.M. - SEE "THE VESPASIAN PSALTER"
KUHN-FOELIX, A. VOM WESEN DES GENIALEN
MENSCHEN.
  V. VON DER HEYDT, 182:VOL23#10-524
KÜHNEL, E. THE MINOR ARTS OF ISLAM.
  M. KREK, 356:OCT71-340
KUHNS, W. THE POST-INDUSTRIAL PROPHETS.
  V. RAKOFF, 99:JUN72-6
KUKENHEIM, L. GRAMMAIRE HISTORIQUE DE LA
LANGUE FRANÇAISE.*
  F. SIGURET, 320(CJL):FALL69-32
  K. TOGEBY, 361:VOL23#4-400
KUKULSKI, L. - SEE MORSZTYN, J.A.
KULKE, H. CIDAMBARAMĀHĀTMYA.
  O. VON HINUBER, 182:VOL23#8-397
KULTERMANN, U. ART AND LIFE.
  D. YOUNG, 99:OCT/NOV72-85
KULTERMANN, U. NEW DIMENSIONS IN SCULP-
TURE.
  R. KUDIELKA, 592:MAR68-160
KULTERMANN, U. NEW JAPANESE ARCHITEC-
TURE. (REV)
  H.H. WAECHTER, 505:AUG68-176
KUMANIECKI, C.F. SCRIPTA MINORA. (O.
JUREWICZ, ED)
  A.C. DIONISOTTI, 182:VOL23#9-496
KUMAO, H. - SEE UNDER HARADA KUMAO
KUMAR, S.K. - SEE DEFOE, D.
KUMIN, M. UP COUNTRY.
  J.C. OATES, 441:19NOV72-7
KUNA, F. T.S. ELIOT.
  K. TETZELI VON ROSADOR, 72:BAND208
    HEFT1-49
KUNER, M.C. THORNTON WILDER.
  G. WEALES, 441:11JUN72-8
KUNERT, G. - SEE LENAU, N.
KUNG, D. THE CONTEMPORARY ARTIST IN
JAPAN.
  P. HARDIE, 39:APR69-326

KÜNG, H. INFALLIBLE?*
  B.L. MARTHALER, 142:FALL71-481
KÜNG, H. MENSCHWERDUNG GOTTES.
  P. MÜLLER, 182:VOL23#17/18-771
KÜNG, H. WHY PRIESTS?
  441:17SEP72-44
KUNISCH, H. KLEINE SCHRIFTEN.*
  E. STOPP, 402(MLR):APR71-452
KUNNAS, T. DRIEU LA ROCHELLE, CÉLINE,
  BRASILLACH ET LA TENTATION FASCISTE.
  617(TLS):13OCT72-1221
KUNST, A.E. LAFCADIO HEARN.
  B.C. YU, 149:DEC71-358
KÜNSTLER, G. ROMANESQUE ART IN EUROPE.
  A. KUHN, 58:SEP/OCT69-14
KUNTZ, P.G., ED. THE CONCEPT OF ORDER.
  S.O.H., 543:DEC69-363
  A. SHIELDS, 290(JAAC):WINTER69-248
KUNZ, J. DIE DEUTSCHE NOVELLE IM 19.
  JAHRHUNDERT.
  N.H. SMITH, 182:VOL23#23/24-985
KUNZ, J. DIE DEUTSCHE NOVELLE ZWISCHEN
  KLASSIK UND ROMANTIK.
  J.T., 191(ELN):SEP69(SUPP)-95
KUNZ, J., ED. NOVELLE.
  I.C., 191(ELN):SEP70(SUPP)-94
KUNZE, K. STUDIEN ZUR LEGENDE DER HEILI-
  GEN MARIA AEGYPTIACA IM DEUTSCHEN
  SPRACHGEBIET.
  F.H. BÄUML, 406:FALL71-302
  L. MORTIMER, 382(MAE):1971/2-197
  R. RUDOLF, 182:VOL23#7-357
KUPFERBERG, H. THE MENDELSSOHNS.
  P. ADAMS, 61:APR72-128
  441:20AUG72-20
  617(TLS):27OCT72-1276
KUPFERBERG, H. THOSE FABULOUS PHILADEL-
  PHIANS.
  K. SPENCE, 415:SEP70-897
KÜPPER, P. - SEE MILCH, W.
KUPPUSWAMY, B. SOCIAL CHANGE IN INDIA.
  617(TLS):29DEC72-1591
KURATH, G., WITH A. GARCIA. MUSIC AND
  DANCE OF THE TEWA PUEBLOS.
  D.P. MC ALLESTER, 187:SEP72-546
KURATH, H. & S.M. KUHN, EDS. MIDDLE
  ENGLISH DICTIONARY. (A-L2)
  617(TLS):13OCT72-1209
DE KURLAT, F.W. - SEE SÁNCHEZ DE BADAJOZ,
  D.
KURMAN, M.V. & I.V. LEBEDINSKY. NASE-
  LENIE BOL'SHOGO SOTSIALISTICHESKOGO
  GORODA.
  F.A. LEEDY, 32:JUN71-432
KURODA, S-Y. YAWELMANI PHONOLOGY.
  L.A. RICE, 269(IJAL):JUL69-274
KURSCHAT, A. LITAUISCH-DEUTSCHES WÖRTER-
  BUCH. (VOL 1) (W. WISSMANN & E. HOF-
  MANN, EDS)
  V. RŪĶE-DRAVIŅA, 182:VOL23#1/2-18
KURTÉN, B. THE AGE OF MAMMALS.
  617(TLS):25FEB72-217
KURTÉN, B. NOT FROM THE APES.
  P. ADAMS, 61:FEB72-109
  D. PILBEAM, 561(SATR):4MAR72-78
  617(TLS):30JUN72-751
KURTZ, D.C. & J. BOARDMAN. GREEK BURIAL
  CUSTOMS.
  617(TLS):21JAN72-58
KURTZ, P., ED. SIDNEY HOOK AND THE CON-
  TEMPORARY WORLD.
  D.S. ROBINSON, 484(PPR):DEC69-306
KURTZ, P., ED. MORAL PROBLEMS IN CON-
  TEMPORARY SOCIETY.*
  S.O.H., 543:DEC69-365
  H.M. KALLEN, 484(PPR):JUN70-621
  42(AR):WINTER69/70-592

KURTZMAN, J. CROWN OF FLOWERS.
  639(VQR):SUMMER70-LXXXIX
KURVINEN, A., ED. THE SIEGE OF JERUSALEM
  IN PROSE.
  V.J. SCATTERGOOD, 402(MLR):APR71-384
KURZ, O. FAKES. (2ND ED)
  J.S.G., 90:MAY69-328
KURZE, D. PFARRERWAHLEN IM MITTELALTER.
  A. GERLICH, 182:VOL23#5-250
KURZMAN, D. GENESIS 1948.
  617(TLS):13OCT72-1222
KURZOVÁ, H. ZUR SYNTAKTISCHEN STRUKTUR
  DES GRIECHISCHEN.
  L. ZGUSTA, 350:SEP71-733
KUSHNIR, S. THE VILLAGE BUILDER.
  L. BEYRACK-COHEN, 287:MAR69-21
KUSPIT, D.B. THE PHILOSOPHICAL LIFE OF
  THE SENSES.
  F. SONTAG, 484(PPR):MAR70-470
KUZMA, G. SITTING AROUND.*
  J. TIPTON, 661:SUMMER70-120
KUZNEC, M.D. & J.M. SKREBNEV. STILISTIK
  DER ENGLISCHEN SPRACHE.
  A. WOLLMANN, 38:BAND87HEFT3/4-430
KUZNETSOV, A. [A. ANATOLI] BABI YAR.*
  (RUSSIAN TITLE: BABIJ JAR.)
  W.H. PRITCHARD, 249(HUDR):SUMMER71-
  362
  I. WEIL, 574(SEEJ):WINTER71-509
KUZNETSOV, B. EINSTEIN AND DOSTOYEVSKY.
  617(TLS):27OCT72-1288
KWANG-SOB, K. - SEE UNDER KIM KWANG-SOB
KWANT, R.C. CRITIQUE.
  M.H., 477:SUMMER69-400
KWANT, R.C. PHENOMENOLOGY OF EXPRESSION.
  J. ASHMORE, 484(PPR):MAR70-469
KWOK, D.W.Y. SCIENTISM IN CHINESE
  THOUGHT, 1900-1950.
  S-H. LIU, 485(PE&W):JUL68-224
KYBURG, H.E., JR. PHILOSOPHY OF SCI-
  ENCE.*
  J.R. CAMERON, 479(PHQ):JUL70-294
  A.C. MICHALOS, 486:SEP69-326
KYD, T. THE SPANISH TRAGEDY. (J.R.
  MULRYNE, ED)
  N.W. BAWCUTT, 677:VOL2-255
KYES, R.L., ED. THE OLD LOW FRANCONIAN
  PSALMS AND GLOSSES.
  E.A. EBBINGHAUS, 221(GQ):MAR70-258
  B. MURDOCH, 402(MLR):APR71-435
KYLE, D. FLIGHT INTO FEAR.
  O.L. BAILEY, 561(SATR):9SEP72-80
KYLE, E. THE SCENT OF DANGER.
  N. CALLENDAR, 441:30APR72-36
KYROU, A. LUIS BUÑUEL.
  C. HODIN, 98:JUN69-512

LM [I. BAKER]. KATHERINE MANSFIELD: THE
  MEMORIES OF LM.*
  442(NY):9SEP72-127
LAAGE, K.E., ED. SCHRIFTEN DER THEODOR-
  STORM-GESELLSCHAFT. (1968)
  E.A. MC CORMICK, 221(GQ):MAY70-518
LABALME, P.H. BERNARDO GIUSTINIANI.
  G. COZZI, 551(RENQ):WINTER70-441
LABAREE, L.W. - SEE FRANKLIN, B.
LA BARRE, W. THE GHOST DANCE.
  617(TLS):10NOV72-1374
LABLENIE, E. MONTAIGNE AUTEUR DE MAX-
  IMES.
  L. VAN DELFT, 207(FR):FEB70-526
LABORDE, A.M. L'OEUVRE DE MADAME DE
  GENLIS.
  P. BEVIER, 593:SPRING71-85
"THE LABOUR ANNUAL 1895."
  617(TLS):18FEB72-172

LABRIOLA, A. L'UNIVERSITÀ E LA LIBERTÀ
DELLA SCIENZA.
  G. OLDRINI, 548(RCSF):APR/JUN69-233
DE LABRIOLLE, M-R. LE "POUR ET CONTRE"
ET SON TEMPS.
  J.L. WALDAUER, 546(RR):APR70-141
LABROUSSE, A. L'EXPÉRIENCE CHILIENNE.
LES TUPAMAROS.
  617(TLS):4AUG72-915
LABUDA, G., ED. HISTORIA POMORZA. (VOL
1)
  P.W. KNOLL, 32:MAR71-179
LA CAPRA, D. EMILE DURKHEIM.
  617(TLS):28JUL72-876
LACARRA, J.M., WITH A.J. MARTÍN DUQUE.
FUEROS DERIVADOS DE JACA. (VOL 1:
ESTELLA - SAN SEBASTIÁN.)
  F.J. OROZ, 72:BAND208HEFT2-148
LACENAIRE. MEMOIRES, POEMES ET LETTRES.
(M. LEBAILLY, ED)
  R. PASSERON, 98:FEB69-160
LACEY, R. THE LIFE AND TIMES OF HENRY
VIII.
  617(TLS):11AUG72-949
LACEY, W.K. & B.W.J.G. WILSON, EDS &
TRANS. RES PUBLICA.
  W.C. MC DERMOTT, 124:APR71-272
LACH, D.F. ASIA IN THE MAKING OF EUROPE.
(VOL 1)
  H. NAKAMURA, 322(JHI):JUL-SEP69-451
LA CHARITÉ, R.C. THE CONCEPT OF JUDGMENT
IN MONTAIGNE.
  I.D. MC FARLANE, 208(FS):JUL71-325
LA CHARITÉ, V.A. THE POETICS AND THE
POETRY OF RENÉ CHAR.
  L.C. BREUNIG, 207(FR):OCT69-167
  J.H. MATTHEWS, 546(RR):OCT70-236
  Y. SCALZITTI, 405(MP):MAY70-398
LACHENAL, F. - SEE GASSIER, P. & J. WIL-
SON
LACHIVER, M. LA POPULATION DE MEULAN DU
XVIIE AU XIX SIÈCLE.
  617(TLS):3MAR72-243
LACHMUND, C.V. MEIN LEBEN MIT FRANZ
LISZT.
  A.H. KING, 182:VOL23#9-487
LACHS, J. MARXIST PHILOSOPHY.
  J.H. MILLER, 587:JAN70-388
LACHS, J. THE TIES OF TIME.
  S. SCOBIE, 102(CANL):AUTUMN71-75
LACIS, A. REVOLUTIONÄR IM BERUF. (H.
BRENNER, ED)
  617(TLS):25FEB72-212
LACKÓ, M. ARROW-CROSS MEN.*
  I. DEÁK, 32:MAR71-185
LACKO, M. SLOVAK BIBLIOGRAPHY ABROAD,
1945-1965.
  S.E. MANN, 575(SEER):OCT71-631
LACKSTROM, J.E. PRO-FORMS IN THE SPANISH
NOUN PHRASE.
  R.L. HADLICH, 240(HR):JAN70-82
LA COUR, T. & H. MOGENSEN. THE MURDER
BOOK.
  617(TLS):11FEB72-165
LACY, A.D. GREEK POTTERY IN THE BRONZE
AGE.*
  C. HOPKINS, 56:SUMMER69-202
LACY, D. THE WHITE USE OF BLACKS IN
AMERICA.
  442(NY):8APR72-131
LADEN, A. THE GEORGE BERNARD SHAW
VEGETARIAN COOK BOOK.
  617(TLS):20OCT72-1264
LADO, R. LANGUAGE TESTING.
  M.M. HEISER, 399(MLJ):JAN70-43
LADO, R. & OTHERS. TESORO HISPÁNICO.
  A.B. HENKIN, 399(MLJ):MAR70-207

LAFFOUCREIÈRE, O. LA DESTIN DE LA PENSÉE
ET "LA MORT DE DIEU" SELON HEIDEGGER.
  J.D.C., 543:MAR70-559
LAFFRANQUE, M. POSEIDONIOS D'APAMÉE.
  J-P. DUMONT, 542:APR-JUN69-278
LAFORE, L. THE END OF GLORY.
  B.H. SMITH, 396(MODA):WINTER71-105
LAFORGUE, R. L'ÉCHEC DE BAUDELAIRE.
  C. BARDET, 542:JAN-MAR68-147
LAGARDE, A. & L. MICHARD. LES GRANDS
AUTEURS FRANÇAIS.
  617(TLS):12MAY72-544
LAGARDE, F. JOHN WEBSTER.
  R.G. HOWARTH, 677:VOL2-258
DE LAGE, G.R. - SEE UNDER RAYNAUD DE
LAGE, G.
DE LA GENIÈRE, J. RECHERCHES SUR L'ÂGE
DU FER EN ITALIE MÉRIDIONALE: SALA
CONSILINA.
  D. RIDGWAY, 313:VOL60-241
LAGERCRANTZ, O. VERSUCH ÜBER DIE LYRIK
DER NELLY SACHS.*
  W.H. MC CLAIN, 400(MLN):APR70-412
LA GUMA, A. IN THE FOG OF A SEASON'S
END.
  J. HUNTER, 362:19OCT72-513
  617(TLS):20OCT72-1245
DE LA HARPE, J-F. CORRESPONDANCE INÉD-
ITE. (A. JOVICEVICH, ED)
  A.W. HUNWICK, 402(MLR):JAN71-187
LAHR, J. ACTING OUT AMERICA.
  617(TLS):1DEC72-1454
LAIDLAW, J.C., ED. THE FUTURE OF THE
MODERN HUMANITIES.
  W.G. MOORE, 208(FS):JUL71-356
DE LA IGLESIA, M.E. THE CATALOGUE OF
CATALOGUES.
  L. TANNER, 441:10DEC72-50
  561(SATR):7OCT72-103
DE L'AIN, G.G. - SEE UNDER GIROD DE L'AIN,
G.
LAÍN, M. LA PALABRA EN UNAMUNO.
  C.P. OTERO, 545(RPH):NOV70-301
LAING, D. BUDDY HOLLY.
  N. FOUNTAIN, 364:FEB/MAR72-141
LAING, D. THE SOUND OF OUR TIME.
  L. BERKMAN, 418(MR):SPRING71-362
LAING, E.J. CHINESE PAINTINGS IN
CHINESE PUBLICATIONS, 1956-1968.
  293(JAST):MAY70-744
LAING, M. EDWARD HEATH: PRIME MINISTER.
  R. CROSSMAN, 362:12OCT72-479
  617(TLS):27OCT72-1286
LAING, R.D. KNOTS.*
  J.C. OATES, 398:VOL3#3-141
  J. VERNON, 651(WHR):SPRING71-190
LAIRD, M.A. MISSIONARIES AND EDUCATION
IN BENGAL, 1793-1837.
  617(TLS):28APR72-501
LAIRD, M.A. - SEE HEBER, R.
LAIRD, R.D. & B.A. SOVIET COMMUNISM AND
AGRARIAN REVOLUTION.
  N. NIMITZ, 32:MAR71-166
LAKATOS, I., ED. THE PROBLEM OF INDUC-
TIVE LOGIC.
  D.H. MELLOR, 479(PHQ):OCT70-405
LAKATOS, I., ED. PROBLEMS IN THE PHIL-
OSOPHY OF MATHEMATICS.
  J. CLEAVE, 536:DEC70-155
LALIC, I.V. FIRE GARDENS.
  J.R. LINDROTH, 590:SUMMER70-40
LAMANTIA, P. THE BLOOD OF THE AIR.
  J.R. CARPENTER, 491:JUN72-164
DE LAMARTINE, A.M.L.D. MÉDITATIONS.
(F. LETESSIER, ED)
  J.S.P., 191(ELN):SEP69(SUPP)-74
  A.J. STEELE, 208(FS):OCT71-469

LAMB, B.P. INDIA. (3RD ED)
   R.L. PARK, 293(JAST):FEB70-504
LAMB, H.H. CLIMATE. (VOL 1)
   617(TLS):23JUN72-726
LAMB, J.W. THE ARCHBISHOPRIC OF CANTER-
BURY.
   617(TLS):28JAN72-106
LAMB, W.K. - SEE FRANCHÈRE, G.
LAMBERT, B. BIBLIOTHECA HIERONYMIANA
MANUSCRIPTA.
   D.F. HEIMANN, 377:JUL71-100
LAMBERT, D. THE RED HOUSE.
   442(NY):3JUN72-110
LAMBERT, G. THE GOODBY PEOPLE.
   D.A.N. JONES, 362:17FEB72-221
   617(TLS):3MAR72-239
LAMBERT, G. ON CUKOR.
   C. HIGHAM, 441:24SEP72-6
   J. KANON, 561(SATR):16DEC72-58
LAMBERT, K., ED. THE LOGICAL WAY OF
DOING THINGS.
   R.H.K., 543:JUN70-753
LAMBRICK, H.T., ED & TRANS. THE TERROR-
IST.
   617(TLS):29DEC72-1591
LAMÉRAND, R. SYNTAXE TRANSFORMATIONNELLE
DES PROPOSITIONS HYPOTHÉTIQUES DU FRAN-
ÇAIS PARLÉ.
   R.W. LANGACKER, 350:SEP71-716
LAMÉRAND, R. THÉORIES D'ENSEIGNEMENT
PROGRAMMÉ ET LABORATOIRES DE LANGUES.
   N. GABRIEL, 67:NOV71-272
LAMMING, G. NATIVES OF MY PERSON.
   J. CAREW, 441:27FEB72-4
   T.R. EDWARDS, 453:9MAR72-19
   T. LASK, 441:15JAN72-33
   P. THEROUX, 440:23JAN72-2
   442(NY):29APR72-140
   617(TLS):15DEC72-1521
LAMMING, G. WATER WITH BERRIES.
   G. DAVIS, 441:15OCT72-32
   617(TLS):11FEB72-145
LANCASTER, J.C. GODIVA OF COVENTRY.*
   R. VIRGOE, 325:OCT69-584
LANCASTER-GAYE, D., ED. PERSONAL RELA-
TIONSHIPS, THE HANDICAPPED AND THE
COMMUNITY.
   617(TLS):10NOV72-1377
LAND, A.C. - SEE EDDIS, W.
LANDA, L. - SEE DEFOE, D.
LANDA, L.A. - SEE SWIFT, J.
LANDAU, D. KISSINGER.
   J. CHACE, 441:10DEC72-2
   C. LEHMANN-HAUPT, 441:10OCT72-47
   I.F. STONE, 453:19OCT72-12
   I.F. STONE, 453:2NOV72-21
   442(NY):21OCT72-167
LANDAU, J. IT'S TOO LATE TO STOP NOW.
   G. HOENIG, 441:29OCT72-34
LANDAU, J.M., ED. MAN, STATE, AND SOCI-
ETY IN THE CONTEMPORARY MIDDLE EAST.
   617(TLS):13OCT72-1222
LANDAUER, C. GERMANY.
   O.J. HALE, 639(VQR):SPRING70-349
LANDEN, R.G. OMAN SINCE 1856.
   G. RENTZ, 318(JAOS):OCT-DEC70-581
LANDGREBE, L. PHÄNOMENOLOGIE UND GE-
SCHICHTE.
   S.L. HART, 484(PPR):SEP69-155
LANDINO, C. DE VERA NOBILITATE. (M.T.
LIACI, ED)
   L.V.R., 568(SCN):SPRING71-29
LANDMANN, G.P. - SEE BRASCH, H.
LANDOLFI, T. CANCERQUEEN.*
   G. WEALES, 249(HUDR):WINTER71/72-716
LANDON, F. AN EXILE FROM CANADA.
   102(CANL):WINTER71-107

LANDON, H.C.R., ED. BEETHOVEN.*
   A. TYSON, 415:OCT70-999
LANDON, H.C.R. ESSAYS ON THE VIENNESE
CLASSICAL STYLE.
   S. SADIE, 415:AUG70-804
   412:FEB71-77
LANDON, H.C.R. & R.E. CHAPMAN, EDS.
STUDIES IN EIGHTEENTH-CENTURY MUSIC.
   M. TILMOUTH, 415:FEB71-136
   R.W., 410(M&L):APR71-201
   412:MAY71-181
LANDON, M. THE TRIUMPH OF THE LAWYERS,
THEIR ROLE IN ENGLISH POLITICS, 1678-
1689.
   R.W. LINKER, 568(SCN):SPRING71-17
LANDOR, W.S. SELECTED IMAGINARY CONVER-
SATIONS OF LITERARY MEN AND STATESMEN.
(C.L. PROUDFIT, ED)
   K.C., 191(ELN):SEP70(SUPP)-40
LANDWEHR, J. EMBLEM BOOKS IN THE LOW
COUNTRIES 1554-1949.
   D.L. FARREN, 356:OCT71-347
   E. ZIMMERMANN, 182:VOL23#23/24-961
   617(TLS):7JAN72-20
LANDWEHR, J. GERMAN EMBLEM BOOKS 1531-
1888.
   617(TLS):3NOV72-1348
LANDY, E.E., COMP. THE UNDERGROUND DIC-
TIONARY.
   617(TLS):26MAY72-605
LANE, A.J., ED. THE DEBATE OVER SLAVERY.
   617(TLS):17MAR72-296
LANE, B.M. ARCHITECTURE AND POLITICS IN
GERMANY 1918-1945.
   P. COLLINS, 505:DEC69-112
LANE, D. THE ROOTS OF RUSSIAN COMMUNISM.
   A. WILDMAN, 550(RUSR):APR70-215
LANE, M. FRANCES WRIGHT AND THE "GREAT
EXPERIMENT."
   617(TLS):17MAR72-300
LANE, M.T. AN INCH OR SO OF GARDEN.
   M. HORNYANSKY, 627(UTQ):JUL70-333
LANE, P. THE INDUSTRIAL REVOLUTION 1750-
1830. THE VICTORIAN AGE 1830-1914.
THE TWENTIETH CENTURY 1914-1970.
   617(TLS):6OCT72-1205
LANE, P. THE UPPER CLASS.
   617(TLS):17NOV72-1405
LANE, R. COLLECTED POEMS OF RED LANE.*
   H. MAC CALLUM, 627(UTQ):JUL69-351
LANE, R. SEPARATIONS.
   D. BARBOUR, 102(CANL):SPRING71-70
LANE, R.E. THE LIBERTIES OF WIT.
   C. LYAS, 89(BJA):SUMMER71-294
LANE, W.G. RICHARD HARRIS BARHAM.
   N. BURGIS, 155:MAY69-116
LANG, G. THE CUISINE OF HUNGARY.
   N. MAGID, 440:13FEB72-12
LANG, M.L. THE PALACE OF NESTOR AT
PYLOS IN WESTERN MESSENIA.* (VOL 2)
   J. BOARDMAN, 123:JUN71-301
   R.S. STROUD, 121(CJ):OCT-NOV70-81
LANG, P.H. CRITIC AT THE OPERA.*
   W. SARGEANT, 442(NY):24JAN72-59
LANGAN, T. MERLEAU-PONTY'S CRITIQUE OF
REASON.
   R.T. MURPHY, 613:SPRING68-153
LANGBAUM, R. THE MODERN SPIRIT.*
   M. COOKE, 676(YR):WINTER71-294
   G.H. HARTMAN, 31(ASCH):WINTER71/72-
146
   M. LEBOWITZ, 598(SOR):SUMMER72-696
   L. STEVENSON, 579(SAQ):WINTER71-132
LANGE, J. BINARY.
   O.L. BAILEY, 561(SATR):30SEP72-80
   N. CALLENDAR, 441:20AUG72-26
LANGE, J. - SEE LEWIS, C.I.

LANGE, K-P. THEORETIKER DES LITERARIS-
CHEN MANIERISMUS.
R. HESS, 72:BAND208HEFT4/6-446
LANGE, U. UNTERSUCHUNGEN ZU BODINS
DEMONOMANIE.
A. BUCK, 72:BAND208HEFT1-71
LANGE, V., ED. GOETHE.*
J.W. DYCK, 399(MLJ):OCT70-448
LANGE, V., ED. MODERN LITERATURE.
(VOL 2)
A. DEMAITRE, 399(MLJ):JAN70-60
J.G. FUCILLA, 276:WINTER70-433
LANGELLIER, A. & S.N. LEVY. CHEZ LES
FRANÇAIS.
P. ARSENAULT, 207(FR):APR70-861
LANGENDOEN, D.T. THE STUDY OF SYNTAX.
F.W. HOUSEHOLDER, 350:JUN71-453
"LANGENSCHEIDT'S STANDARD DICTIONARY OF
THE FRENCH AND ENGLISH LANGUAGES."
(K. URWIN, ED)
H.W. BRANN, 207(FR):DEC69-393
VON LANGENSTEIN, H. ERCHANTNUZZ DER
SUND. (P.R. RUDOLF, ED)
D. BLAMIRES, 402(MLR):JUL71-706
LANGER, S. MIND. (VOL 1)
P.A. BERTOCCI, 543:MAR70-527
LANGER, W.C. THE MIND OF ADOLF HITLER.
R.J. LIFTON, 441:31DEC72-2
LANGIULLI, N. - SEE ABBAGNANO, N.
LANGLEY, M. THE EAST SURREY REGIMENT.
617(TLS):22DEC72-1555
LANGLEY, M. WHEN THE POLE STAR SHONE.
617(TLS):2JUN72-641
LANGLOIS, W.G. ANDRÉ MALRAUX: L'AVENTURE
INDOCHINOISE.
J. CARDUNER, 207(FR):DEC69-326
LANGLOTZ, E. THE ART OF MAGNA GRAECIA.
N.R. OAKESHOTT, 303:VOL90-260
LANGMAID, K. THE BLIND EYE.
617(TLS):12MAY72-536
LANGRIDGE, D. YOUR JAZZ COLLECTION.
M. HARRISON, 415:MAR71-246
"LANGUAGE IN EDUCATION."
617(TLS):13OCT72-1230
"A LANGUAGE-TEACHING BIBLIOGRAPHY."*
F.B. NOSTRAND, 399(MLJ):JAN70-39
LANGWILL, L.G. & N. BOSTON. CHURCH AND
CHAMBER BARREL-ORGANS. (2ND ED)
P. WILLIAMS, 415:JUL70-714
LANIER, V. ESSAYS IN ART EDUCATION.
H.J. MC WHINNIE, 89(BJA):AUTUMN71-415
LANNOIS, G., ED. PAGES FRANÇAISES.
A.M. BEICHMAN, 399(MLJ):NOV70-542
LANNOY, R. THE SPEAKING TREE.
617(TLS):22SEP72-1119
LANSBURY, C. ARCADY IN AUSTRALIA.
P.D. EDWARDS & L.T. HERGENHAN,
71(ALS):MAY72-328
LANSDALE, E.G. IN THE MIDST OF WARS.
P. ARNETT, 441:9APR72-2
S. DICKERMAN, 440:19MAR72-4
J. MIRSKY, 561(SATR):1APR72-76
LAO SHE. CAT COUNTRY.
639(VQR):AUTUMN70-CXXIX
LA PENNA, A. ORAZIO E LA MORALE MONDANA
EUROPEA.
M.L. CLARKE, 123:MAR71-52
F.A. SULLIVAN, 122:JAN71-65
LA PENNA, A. SALLUSTIO E LA "RIVOLU-
ZIONE" ROMANA.
E. BADIAN, 24:JAN71-103
S.E. SMETHURST, 124:OCT70-63
LA PENNA, A. - SEE HORACE
LAPENNA, I. SOVIET PENAL POLICY.*
P.B. TAYLOR, 550(RUSR):APR70-234

LAPESA, R. DE LA EDAD MEDIA A NUESTROS
DÍAS.
E.S. MORBY, 545(RPH):AUG70-155
K. SCHWARTZ, 546(RR):FEB70-50
LAPESA, R. & M. SOLEDAD DE ANDRÉS - SEE
MENENDEZ PIDAL, R.
LAPIERRE, J.W. ESSAI SUR LE FONDEMENT
DU POUVOIR POLITIQUE.
P. CLASTRES, 98:NOV69-1000
LAPP, J.C. - SEE DE TYARD, P.
LAQUEUR, W. A HISTORY OF ZIONISM.
H. GOLD, 561(SATR):28OCT72-80
H.M. SACHAR, 441:12NOV72-39
LAQUEUR, W. OUT OF THE RUINS OF EUROPE.*
617(TLS):22DEC72-1554
LAQUEUR, W. THE STRUGGLE FOR THE MIDDLE
EAST.
G. RENTZ, 550(RUSR):OCT70-479
LARGE, B. SMETANA.*
J.C., 410(M&L):APR71-177
E.V. GARRETT, 32:DEC71-917
A. SIMPSON, 415:FEB71-132
LARKIN, P. ALL WHAT JAZZ.*
N. BRYCE, 607:SUMMER70-39
W. MELLERS, 415:MAY70-507
LARMOTH, J. MURDER ON THE MENU.
O.L. BAILEY, 561(SATR):25NOV72-70
LARNER, J. CULTURE AND SOCIETY IN ITALY,
1290-1420.*
617(TLS):14JAN72-37
DE LA ROCHEFOUCAULD, F. MAXIMES. (J.
TRUCHET, ED)
L. VAN DELFT, 207(FR):OCT69-189
"LAROUSSE ENCYCLOPEDIA OF MUSIC." (G.
HINDLEY, ED)
617(TLS):4FEB72-131
LARSEN, C. THE GOOD FIGHT.
441:16JUL72-14
LARSEN, J.A.O. GREEK FEDERAL STATES.*
P. GAUTHIER, 555:VOL44FASC1-108
LARSEN, K. FREDERIK ROSTGAARD OG
BØGERNE.
L.S. THOMPSON, 356:APR71-190
LARSON, C.R. THE EMERGENCE OF AFRICAN
FICTION.
617(TLS):29DEC72-1573
LARSON, G.J. CLASSICAL SAMKHYA.
K.H. POTTER, 293(JAST):AUG70-949
LARSON, J.L. REASON AND EXPERIENCE.
617(TLS):31MAR72-371
LARSON, R.C. URBAN POLICE PATROL ANALY-
SIS.
J.M. CHAIKEN, 441:29OCT72-52
LARSSON, L.O. ADRIAN DE VRIES.
C. AVERY, 90:JAN69-39
LARSSON, R. THEORIES OF REVOLUTION.*
H.L. ROBERTS, 32:DEC71-882
LA RUE, J. GUIDELINES FOR STYLE ANALY-
SIS.
R. JACKSON, 317:FALL71-489
LASCELLES, M. - SEE JOHNSON, S.
LASER, S. ARCHAEOLOGIA HOMERICA.* (VOL
P: HAUSRAT.)
P. CHANTRAINE, 555:VOL44FASC2-303
LASH, J.P. ELEANOR: THE YEARS ALONE.
B. DE MOTT, 561(SATR):19AUG72-56
T. LASK, 441:4AUG72-31
J-P. ROCHE, 441:30JUL72-3
E. WEEKS, 61:SEP72-104
442(NY):19AUG72-80
LASH, J. ELEANOR AND FRANKLIN.*
P. WHITEHEAD, 362:8JUN72-766
617(TLS):25AUG72-995
LASKER-SCHÜLER, E. EIN BUCH ZUM 100
GEBURTSTAG DER DICHTERIN.
H. WALZ, 202(FMOD):NOV69-105
LASKO, P. THE KINGDOM OF THE FRANKS.
617(TLS):11FEB72-165

LASLETT, P., W.G. RUNCIMAN & Q. SKINNER, EDS. PHILOSOPHY, POLITICS AND SOCIETY. (4TH SER)
  617(TLS):22DEC72-1552
LASSERRE, F. - SEE STRABO
LASSITER, W.L. SHAKER ARCHITECTURE.
  R.W. BRUNSKILL, 576:DEC68-306
LASSO DE LA VEGA, J.S. IDEALES DE LA FORMACIÓN GRIEGA.
  A.W.H. ADKINS, 123:JUN71-294
LASSO DE LA VEGA, J.S. SINTAXIS GRIEGA. (VOL 1)
  A.G. WAY, 303:VOL90-234
LASSWITZ, K. TWO PLANETS.
  T. STURGEON, 441:14MAY72-33
"THE LAST WHOLE EARTH CATALOG."* (S. BRAND, ED)
  M. OLMERT, 440:2JAN72-6
LASZLO, E. BEYOND SCEPTICISM AND REALISM.
  W. KUBICEK, 182:VOL23#9-460
LASZLO, E. & J.B. WILBUR, EDS. HUMAN VALUES AND NATURAL SCIENCE.
  T. MAUTNER, 63:DEC71-322
LATAKOS, I., ED. PROBLEMS IN THE PHILOSOPHY OF MATHEMATICS.
  E.A. MAZIARZ, 486:SEP69-324
LATHAM, A. CRAZY SUNDAYS.*
  R.M. ADAMS, 453:27JAN72-26
  J.R. BRYER, 27(AL):JAN72-667
  617(TLS):6OCT72-1193
LATHAM, J. THE PLEASURE OF YOUR COMPANY.
  617(TLS):4AUG72-926
LATHAM, R. & W. MATTHEWS - SEE PEPYS, S.
LATHEM, E.C. - SEE FROST, R.
LATHEN, E. THE LONGER THE THREAD.
  N. CALLENDAR, 441:26MAR72-42
  T. LASK, 441:1JAN72-17
  442(NY):29APR72-144
LATHEN, E. MURDER WITHOUT ICING.
  N. CALLENDAR, 441:26NOV72-36
  T. LASK, 441:30DEC72-19
LATTIMORE, R. POEMS FROM THREE DECADES.
  J.M. BRINNIN, 441:19NOV72-6
LAUCH, A. WISSENSCHAFT UND KULTURELLE BEZIEHUNGEN IN DER RUSSISCHEN AUFKLÄRUNG.
  M. RAEFF, 104:FALL71-435
LAUDE, J. LA PEINTURE FRANÇAISE (1905-1914) ET "L'ART NÈGRE."
  V.M. AMES, 290(JAAC):SUMMER70-560
  P. DUFOUR, 98:AUG-SEP69-809
LAUFHÜTTE, H. WIRKLICHKEIT UND KUNST IN GOTTFRIED KELLERS ROMAN "DER GRÜNE HEINRICH."
  H.W. REICHERT, 406:SUMMER71-186
LAUGESEN, A.T. MIDDELALDERLITTERATUREN: EN ORIENTERING.
  W. SAYERS, 597(SN):VOL40#2-457
LAUGHTON, B. PHILIP WILSON STEER 1860-1942.
  617(TLS):26MAY72-603
LAUGIER, J-L. TACITE.*
  N.P. MILLER, 123:MAR71-63
  P. WHITE, 122:APR71-142
  H.B. WOLMAN, 124:NOV70-93
LAUMER, K. ASSIGNMENT IN NOWHERE.
  617(TLS):13OCT72-1235
LAUMER, K. DEADFALL.
  N. CALLENDAR, 441:30JAN72-24
LAUNOIR, R. CLEFS POUR LA 'PATAPHYSIQUE.
  M. RYBALKA, 207(FR):MAY70-933
LAURENCE, D.H. - SEE SHAW, G.B.
LAURENCE, M. THE FIRE-DWELLERS.*
  G. ROPER, 627(UTQ):JUL70-344
LAURENCE, M. JASON'S QUEST.
  C. THOMAS, 102(CANL):AUTUMN71-88

LAURENCE, M. THE TOMORROW-TAMER AND OTHER STORIES.* A BIRD IN THE HOUSE.*
  H. KREISEL, 606(TAMR):#55-91
LAURENCE, M. A TREE FOR POVERTY.
  M. MUGO, 296:SPRING72-86
LAURENSON, D. & A. SWINGEWOOD. THE SOCIOLOGY OF LITERATURE.
  617(TLS):4AUG72-911
LAURENT, V. LE CORPUS DES SCEAUX DE L'EMPIRE BYZANTIN. (VOL 5)
  A. BRYER, 182:VOL23#1/2-48
LAURENTS, A. THE WAY WE WERE.
  R.A. SOKOLOV, 441:16APR72-31
LAURIDSEN, H.V. - SEE ANDERSEN, H.C.
LAUSBERG, M. UNTERSUCHUNGEN ZU SENECAS FRAGMENTEN.
  W.M. CALDER 3D, 124:MAR71-240
  F. LASSERRE, 182:VOL23#10-559
COMTE DE LAUTRÉAMONT. ISIDORE DUCASSE, COMTE DE LAUTRÉAMONT: OEUVRES COMPLÈTES (LES CHANTS DE MALDOROR, POÉSIES, LETTRES). (M. BONNET, ED)
  S.I. LOCKERBIE, 208(FS):OCT71-481
COMTE DE LAUTRÉAMONT. LAUTRÉAMONT'S "MALDOROR."* (A. LYKIARD, TRANS)
  T. LASK, 441:15SEP72-40
LAUTS, J. JEAN-BAPTISTE OUDRY.
  H.N. OPPERMAN, 90:OCT69-623
LA VALLEY, A.J. CARLYLE AND THE IDEA OF THE MODERN.*
  G. AHRENDS, 72:BAND208HEFT4/6-398
  D.V.E., 191(ELN):SEP69(SUPP)-7
  P. MUDFORD, 597(SN):VOL41#2-441
  G.B. TENNYSON, 141:SPRING69-212
  R. TRICKETT, 447(N&Q):OCT70-389
LAVALLEYE, J. BRUEGEL AND LUCAS VAN LEYDEN.
  J.K. ROWLANDS, 90:DEC70-834
LAVER, J. THE AGE OF ILLUSION.
  T. LASK, 441:26FEB72-31
  442(NY):22APR72-144
  617(TLS):9JUN72-652
LAVER, J. MODESTY IN DRESS.
  639(VQR):SPRING70-LXXVI
LAVER, J. & L. DE VRIES. VICTORIAN ADVERTISEMENTS.
  M. VICINUS, 637(VS):JUN70-433
LAVERS, A. - SEE BARTHES, R.
LAVERYCHEV, V.I. PO TU STORONU BARRIKAD.*
  M.F. HAMM, 32:JUN71-397
LA VEY, A.S. THE COMPLEAT WITCH.
  C.M. MAHON, 651(WHR):SUMMER71-273
LAVIN, I. BERNINI AND THE CROSSING OF ST. PETER'S.
  J. LEES-MILNE, 39:SEP69-270
LAVIN, M. COLLECTED STORIES.*
  J.M. MORSE, 249(HUDR):AUTUMN71-540
LAVIN, M. A MEMORY.
  617(TLS):29DEC72-1573
LAVIN, M.A. PIERO DELLA FRANCESCA: THE FLAGELLATION.
  617(TLS):11AUG72-940
LAWALL, S.N. CRITICS OF CONSCIOUSNESS.
  J.G. CLARK, 208(FS):JUL71-363
  E. COLEMAN, 340(KR):1969/2-283
  F.C. ST. AUBYN, 207(FR):APR70-836
VAN LAWICK-GOODALL, J. IN THE SHADOW OF MAN.*
  G. STADE, 441:3DEC72-6
LAWLER, J.R. THE LANGUAGE OF FRENCH SYMBOLISM.*
  M. FÖRDE, 402(MLR):APR71-413
  V-A. LA CHARITÉ, 399(MLJ):OCT70-449
LAWLER, J.R. - SEE VALÉRY, P.
LAWRENCE, B. THE ADMINISTRATION OF EDUCATION IN BRITAIN.
  617(TLS):15SEP72-1071

LAWRENCE, B. SIX PRESIDENTS, TOO MANY
WARS.
G.W. JOHNSON, 441:1OCT72-36
LAWRENCE, D.H. THE COMPLETE POEMS OF
D.H. LAWRENCE. (3RD ED) (V. DE SOLA
PINTO & W. ROBERTS, EDS)
617(TLS):1DEC72-1469
LAWRENCE, D.H. THE FIRST LADY CHATTER-
LEY.
D. DONOGHUE, 362:14SEP72-342
LAWRENCE, D.H. LAWRENCE IN LOVE.* (J.T.
BOULTON, ED)
M. ALLOTT, 677:VOL2-327
M. GREEN, 340(KR):1969/3-411
LAWRENCE, D.H. MOVEMENTS IN EUROPEAN
HISTORY.
617(TLS):1OMAR72-280
LAWRENCE, D.H. THE QUEST FOR RANANIM.
(G.J. ZYTARUK, ED)
M. ALLOTT, 677:VOL2-327
A. ALPERS, 529(QQ):SUMMER70-297
LAWRENCE, D.H. SELECTED POEMS. (K.
SAGAR, ED)
617(TLS):25AUG72-1006
LAWRENCE, D.H. JOHN THOMAS AND LADY
JANE.
D. DONOGHUE, 362:14SEP72-342
H.T. MOORE, 441:27AUG72-7
LAWRENCE, F.L. MOLIÈRE.
G.R. DANNER, 399(MLJ):APR70-288
LAWRENCE, J. ALL THE YEARS OF HER LIFE.
M. LEVIN, 441:22OCT72-46
LAWRENCE, M. SHADOW ON THE WALL.
V. CUNNINGHAM, 362:24AUG72-248
LAWRENCE, P. & M.J. MEGGITT, EDS. GODS,
GHOSTS AND MEN IN MELANESIA.
E.A. COOK, 318(JAOS):APR-JUN70-364
LAWRENCE, R. A RAGE FOR OPERA.
W. SARGEANT, 442(NY):1JAN72-59
LAWRENCE, R.D. CRY WILD.
J. ARNASON, 296:SUMMER72-89
LAWRENCE, V.B. - SEE JOPLIN, S.
LAWRENSON, T.E. - SEE LESAGE, A-R.
LAWRENSON, T.E., F.E. SUTCLIFFE & G.F.A.
GADOFFRE, EDS. MODERN MISCELLANY PRE-
SENTED TO EUGÈNE VINAVER BY PUPILS,
COLLEAGUES, AND FRIENDS.*
D.R. HAGGIS, 402(MLR):OCT71-888
LAWRY, J.S. THE SHADOW OF HEAVEN.*
H. RUSCHE, 141:SPRING70-157
LAWSON, G. SURGEON IN THE CRIMEA. (V.
BONHAM-CARTER, ED)
R.L. BLANCO, 637(VS):JUN70-448
LAWSON, R.A. THE FAILURE OF INDEPENDENT
LIBERALISM, 1930-1941.
617(TLS):25AUG72-995
LAWSON, T.S.J. PATRIOTIC POEMS OF AMER-
IKKKA.
H. TAYLOR, 651(WHR):AUTUMN71-371
LAYE, C. THE DARK CHILD.
639(VQR):SPRING70-LXX
LAYMON, C.M., ED. THE INTERPRETER'S
ONE-VOLUME COMMENTARY ON THE BIBLE.
617(TLS):13OCT72-1234
LAYTON, I. THE COLLECTED POEMS OF IRVING
LAYTON.
R. GIBBS, 198:SUMMER72-129
F.W. WATT, 99:SEP72-38
LAYTON, I. SELECTED POETRY (1945-67).
M. HORNYANSKY, 627(UTQ):JUL70-329
LAYTON, I. THE SHATTERED PLINTHS.*
H. MAC CALLUM, 627(UTQ):JUL69-346
LAYTON, I. THE WHOLE BLOODY BIRD.*
M. HORNYANSKY, 627(UTQ):JUL70-328
LAYTON, R. SIBELIUS AND HIS WORLD.
J.H., 410(M&L):JAN71-77
A. PAYNE, 415:SEP70-896
LAZAR, M. - SEE ALMERICH

LAZAR, M. - SEE BERNARD DE VENTADOUR
LAZAREV, L.N. NOVGORODIAN ICON PAINTING.
T.T. RICE, 90:JAN70-54
LAZAREV, V.N. STORIA DELLA PITTURA BIZ-
ANTINA.
D.T. RICE, 90:FEB69-93
LAZAREV, V.N. THEOPHANES DER GRIECHE,
UND SEINE SCHULE.
D.T. RICE, 90:SEP69-569
LAZARUS, A.L. ENTERTAINMENTS AND VALE-
DICTIONS.
S. MOORE, 385(MQR):SUMMER72-217
LAZEROWITZ, M. PHILOSOPHY AND ILLUSION.
V.C. ALDRICH, 484(PPR):DEC69-302
M.B.M., 543:SEP69-133
"TOM LEA: A PORTFOLIO OF SIX PAINTINGS."
M.S. YOUNG, 39:APR69-328
LEACH, J. BRIGHT PARTICULAR STAR.*
S. WELLS, 402(MLR):JUL71-677
LEACH, M. & H. GLASSIE. A GUIDE FOR COL-
LECTORS OF ORAL TRADITIONS AND FOLK
CULTURAL MATERIAL IN PENNSYLVANIA.
B. TOELKEN, 292(JAF):JAN-MAR70-93
LEACOCK, S. FEAST OF STEPHEN.* (R.
DAVIES, ED)
D. CAMERON, 150(DR):WINTER70/71-554
LEADER, N.A.M. HUNGARIAN CLASSICAL BAL-
LADS AND THEIR FOLKLORE.*
L. DÉGH, 292(JAF):OCT-DEC70-472
B. KRADER, 32:MAR71-215
LEAKE, J.A. THE GEATS OF "BEOWULF."*
A.D. MILLS, 447(N&Q):FEB70-68
LEAKEY, M.D. OLDUVAI GORGE. (VOL 3)
617(TLS):3MAR72-241
LEAL, L. PANORAMA DE LA LITERATURA MEXI-
CANA ACTUAL.
A.J. CARLOS, 238:SEP70-583
LEAMER, L. THE PAPER REVOLUTIONARIES.
N. SCHREIBER, 561(SATR):2SEP72-58
LEARDI, M. LA POESIA DI HENRY VAUGHAN.
J.D. SIMMONDS, 179(ES):1969SUPP-
LXXXIX
LEARMONTH, N. & A. REGIONAL LANDSCAPES
OF AUSTRALIA.
617(TLS):18AUG72-977
LEARY, L. NORMAN DOUGLAS.
H.T. MASON, 447(N&Q):OCT70-394
LEARY, L. SOUTHERN EXCURSIONS.
J-R. WELSH, 578:SPRING72-128
LEARY, L. - SEE TWAIN, M. & H.H. ROGERS
LEARY, L., WITH C. BARTHOLET & C. ROTH.
ARTICLES ON AMERICAN LITERATURE, 1950-
1967.
J.A. ROBBINS, 517(PBSA):OCT-DEC71-417
LEASE, G. WITNESS TO THE FAITH.
617(TLS):14JUL72-823
LEASKA, M.A. VIRGINIA WOOLF'S LIGHT-
HOUSE.
R.Z. TEMPLE, 295:VOL2#3-421
LEAVIS, F.R. "ANNA KARENINA" AND OTHER
ESSAYS.*
J.M. NEWTON, 97(CQ):AUTUMN68-354
LEAVIS, F.R. ENGLISH LITERATURE IN OUR
TIME AND THE UNIVERSITY.*
G. STEINER, 111:30JAN70-69
LEAVIS, F.R. NOR SHALL MY SWORD.
J. BAYLEY, 362:20JUL72-86
617(TLS):21JUL72-832
LEAVIS, F.R. & Q.D. DICKENS THE NOVEL-
IST.*
M. MUDRICK, 249(HUDR):SUMMER71-346
LEAVITT, T.W., ED. THE HOLLINGWORTH LET-
TERS.
R. BERTHOFF, 432(NEQ):DEC70-660
LEBAILLY, M. - SEE LACENAIRE

185

LEBEER, L. BRUEGEL: LE STAMPE. CATA-
LOGUE RAISONNÉ DES ESTAMPES DE PIERRE
BRUEGEL L'ANCIEN.
  J.K. ROWLANDS, 90:DEC70-834
LEBEUF, J-P. & P-F. LACROIX. DEVINETTES
PEULES.
  617(TLS):10NOV72-1374
LEBJAOUI, M. BATAILLE D'ALGER OU BAT-
AILLE D'ALGÉRIE?
  617(TLS):1SEP72-1021
LEBLON, J. - SEE PEREC, G.
LEBOWITZ, A. PROGRESS INTO SILENCE.
  H. COHEN, 27(AL):NOV71-453
  617(TLS):21JAN72-53
LEBRA, J.C. CHANDRA BOSE TO NIHON.
  Y. AKASHI, 293(JAST):NOV69-146
LEBRUN, Y. ANATOMIE ET PHYSIOLOGIE DE
L'APPAREIL PHONATOIRE.*
  A.W. GRUNDSTROM, 207(FR):APR70-857
LECALDANO, P. THE COMPLETE PAINTINGS OF
PICASSO: BLUE AND ROSE PERIODS.
  617(TLS):7APR72-386
LECAT, J. - SEE DE MONTAIGNE, M.
LE CHÊNE, E. MAUTHAUSEN.
  617(TLS):21JAN72-64
LECKE, B. - SEE "FRIEDRICH SCHILLER"
LECKIE, R. WARFARE.
  639(VQR):AUTUMN70-CLIII
LECLERC, G. ANTHROPOLOGIE ET COLONIAL-
ISME.
  617(TLS):12MAY72-540
LE CLÉZIO, J.M.G. THE BOOK OF FLIGHTS.
  P. BROOKS, 441:30JAN72-6
  T.R. EDWARDS, 453:9MAR72-19
  J.R. FRAKES, 440:9JAN72-2
  D.A.N. JONES, 362:20JAN72-90
  R. SCHOLES, 561(SATR):22JAN72-67
  617(TLS):17MAR72-295
LE CORBUSIER. THE RADIANT CITY.*
  T. CROSBY, 592:JAN68-52
LE CORBUSIER, A. OZENFANT & P. DERMÉE,
EDS. L'ESPRIT NOUVEAU.
  B.T., 44:APR69-67
LEDERER, H. GERMAN GRAMMAR SIMPLIFIED.
  W.L. CUNNINGHAM, 221(GQ):JAN70-129
LEDERER, H. REFERENCE GRAMMAR OF THE
GERMAN LANGUAGE.*
  E.H. ANTONSEN, 301(JEGP):JAN71-135
  J.A. PFEFFER, 221(GQ):NOV70-819
LEDERER, H. - SEE SCHNITZLER, A.
LEDNICKI, W. REMINISCENCES.
  617(TLS):25AUG72-987
LEDUC, V. MAD IN PURSUIT.* (FRENCH
TITLE: LA FOLIE EN TÊTE.)
  N. BLIVEN, 442(NY):4MAR72-111
LEDUC, V. THE TAXI.* (FRENCH TITLE: LE
TAXI.)
  A. BROYARD, 441:31JUL72-25
  M. WOOD, 453:10AUG72-14
  P. ZWEIG, 441:9JUL72-6
LEDYARD, G. THE DUTCH COME TO KOREA.
  L. ASH, 70(ANQ):NOV71-45
LEE, A. GOERING.
  617(TLS):8DEC72-1513
LEE, A.A. JAMES REANEY.*
  E. MANDEL, 627(UTQ):JUL69-394
LEE, C.N. THE NOVELS OF MARK ALEKSANDRO-
VIČ ALDANOV.*
  E.K. BEAUJOUR, 574(SEEJ):SPRING71-77
  G. STRUVE, 32:MAR71-208
LEE, D. CIVIL ELEGIES.
  H. MAC CALLUM, 627(UTQ):JUL69-347
LEE, D.A. THE WORKS OF CHRISTOPH NICHEL-
MANN.
  P. DRUMMOND, 415:NOV71-1073
LEE GUN-SAM. THE 18TH REPUBLIC.
  CHA BUM-SUCK, 270:VOL20#4-102

LEE, L.T. CHINA AND INTERNATIONAL AGREE-
MENTS.
  O. SVARLIEN, 293(JAST):AUG70-935
LEE, M. DR. BLOCK AND THE HUMAN CONDI-
TION.
  M. LEVIN, 441:5MAR72-35
LEE, M.O. WORD, SOUND, AND IMAGE IN THE
ODES OF HORACE.*
  M.L. CLARKE, 123:MAR71-53
  D. HENRY, 122:APR71-120
  J.M. HUNT, 121(CJ):DEC70-JAN71-184
  P.L. SMITH, 487:AUTUMN70-279
LEE, P. LIVES OF EMINENT KOREAN MONKS.
  C.S. KIM, 293(JAST):MAY70-707
LEE, R.A. ORWELL'S FICTION.
  A.W. FRIEDMAN, 191(ELN):SEP70-66
  G. WOODCOCK, 401(MLQ):SEP70-394
LEE, R.E. THE LONDON JOURNAL OF GENERAL
RAYMOND E. LEE 1940-1941.* (BRITISH
TITLE: THE LONDON OBSERVER.) (J.
LEUTZE, ED)
  A.J.P. TAYLOR, 453:10FEB72-14
  617(TLS):30JUN72-748
LEE, R.F. CONRAD'S COLONIALISM.*
  E.W. SAID, 637(VS):JUN70-429
LEE, W.L.M. A HISTORY OF THE POLICE IN
ENGLAND.
  617(TLS):18FEB72-191
LEECH, C. - SEE SHAKESPEARE, W.
LEECH, G.N. A LINGUISTIC GUIDE TO
ENGLISH POETRY.
  J. DAALDER, 67:MAY71-115
LEEDS, B.H. THE STRUCTURED VISION OF
NORMAN MAILER.*
  M.F. SCHULZ, 659:SPRING72-243
LEES, D. ZODIAC.
  617(TLS):26MAY72-612
LEES, F.N. GERARD MANLEY HOPKINS.
  J. BRYSON, 597(SN):VOL40#1-253
LEES, R. POLITICS AND SOCIAL WORK.
  617(TLS):29DEC72-1591
LEESON, F. A GUIDE TO THE RECORDS OF THE
BRITISH STATE TONTINES AND LIFE ANNU-
ITIES OF THE SEVENTEENTH AND EIGHTEENTH
CENTURIES.
  A.C. CARTER, 325:OCT70-153
LEETE, H.M., ED. THE BEST OF BICYCLING!
  H.C. GARDNER, 441:4JUN72-8
VAN LEEUWEN, A.T. CRITIQUE OF HEAVEN.
  617(TLS):1DEC72-1468
LEFCOURT, R., ED. LAW AGAINST THE
PEOPLE.
  M. MELTSNER, 441:5MAR72-44
LE FEVOUR, E. WESTERN ENTERPRISE IN LATE
CH'ING CHINA.
  S-H. CHOU, 318(JAOS):OCT-DEC70-616
LEFÈVRE, E. DIE EXPOSITIONSTECHNIK IN
DEN KOMÖDIEN DES TERENZ.
  G.F. OSMUN, 124:OCT70-62
LEFKOFF, G., ED. COMPUTER APPLICATIONS
IN MUSIC.
  A.W. SLAWSON, 308:SPRING68-105
LEFORT, C. - SEE MERLEAU-PONTY, M.
LE FORT, P. LES STRUCTURES DE L'ÉGLISE
MILITANTE SELON SAINT JEAN.
  F.F. BRUCE, 182:VOL23#13/14-653
LEFRANC, P. SIR WALTER RALEGH ÉCRIVAIN.*
  W. OAKESHOTT, 551(RENQ):AUTUMN70-329
  D.B. QUINN, 656(WMQ):APR70-322
LEGGE, J.D. SUKARNO.
  617(TLS):13OCT72-1232
LEGKAJA, I. POPUTNYJ VETER 1962-1967.
  V. TERRAS, 574(SEEJ):SPRING71-81
LEGMAN, G. RATIONALE OF THE DIRTY JOKE.
  R.E. BUEHLER, 292(JAF):JAN-MAR70-87
LEGOUIS, E. & L. CAZAMIAN, WITH R. LAS
VERGNAS. A HISTORY OF ENGLISH LITERA-
TURE.
  617(TLS):18FEB72-194

LEGOUIS, P. ANDREW MARVELL. (2ND ED)
M-S. RØSTVIG, 179(ES):JUN69-310
LEGOUIS, P., WITH E.E. DUNCAN-JONES - SEE
MARVELL, A.
LEGROS, G.V. FABRE, POET OF SCIENCE.
H. MOSS, 442(NY):27MAY72-109
LE GUILLOU, L. LES "DISCUSSIONS CRI-
TIQUES."
F.P. BOWMAN, 546(RR):APR70-153
LE GUIN, U.K. THE LATHE OF HEAVEN.*
T. STURGEON, 441:14MAY72-33
617(TLS):23JUN72-705
LEGVOLD, R. SOVIET POLICY IN WEST
AFRICA.
B.C. ODUM, 32:SEP71-674
LEHMAN, F.K. THE STRUCTURE OF CHIN
SOCIETY.
H. MANNDORFF, 182:VOL23#13/14-700
LEHMANN, J. IN MY OWN TIME.
A. WRIGHT, 340(KR):1969/5-699
LEHMANN, J. A NEST OF TIGERS.
G. GERSH, 502(PRS):SPRING69-138
A.S. JOHNSON, 50(ARQ):WINTER69-365
LEHMANN, J. & D. PARKER - SEE SITWELL, E.
LEHMANN, J.H. THE FIRST BOER WAR.
617(TLS):13OCT72-1228
LEHMANN, L. EIGHTEEN SONG CYCLES.
P.J.P., 412:NOV71-361
E. SAMS, 415:NOV71-1072
617(TLS):21JAN72-65
LEHMANN, P.W. & OTHERS. SAMOTHRACE.*
(PT 3: THE HIERON.)
J.M. COOK, 123:JUN71-272
LEHMANN, W.P. & Y. MALKIEL, EDS. DIREC-
TIONS FOR HISTORICAL LINGUISTICS.*
R. POSNER, 545(RPH):NOV69-143
LEHMANN, W.R. - SEE BÜCHNER, G.
LEHMANN-HAUPT, H. GUTENBERG AND THE
MASTER OF THE PLAYING CARDS.
R.W. LIGHTBOWN, 39:NOV69-447
LEHNERT, M. MORPHEM, WORT UND SATZ IM
ENGLISCHEN.
J. MEY, 350:MAR71-185
LEHNING, A. - SEE BAKUNIN, M.
LE HURAY, P. MUSIC AND THE REFORMATION
IN ENGLAND 1549-1660.
F.J. GUENTNER, 377:MAR71-43
LEIBHOLZ-BONHOEFFER, S. THE BONHOEFFERS.
617(TLS):28JAN72-103
LEIBNIZ, G.W. ESSAI DE THÉODICÉE. (J.
JALABERT, ED)
L. PRENANT, 542:JUL-SEP68-401
LEIBNIZ, G.W. GENERAL INVESTIGATIONS
CONCERNING THE ANALYSIS OF CONCEPTS
AND TRUTHS.* (W.H. O'BRIANT, ED &
TRANS)
R.H.K., 543:MAR70-559
LEIBNIZ, G.W. THE POLITICAL WRITINGS OF
LEIBNIZ. (P. RILEY, ED & TRANS)
617(TLS):7JUL72-785
LEIBNIZ, G.W. SÄMTLICHE SCHRIFTEN UND
BRIEFE. (1ST SER, VOL 8) (K. MÜLLER,
G. SCHEEL & G. GERBER, EDS)
L.E. LOEMKER, 319:APR72-227
LEIBNIZ, G.W. WRORZEC DOWODÓW POLITYCZ-
NYCH.
D. STONE, 104:WINTER71-575
LEIBOWITZ, H.A. HART CRANE.
G. BJORNSON, 597(SN):VOL41#2-443
J.B. CHAMBERS, 541(RES):AUG70-375
J. MAZZARO, 141:WINTER69-104
G. VAN CROMPHOUT, 179(ES):JUN70-272
LEIBOWITZ, H.A. - SEE ROSENFELD, P.
LEIBOWITZ, R. SCHOENBERG AND HIS SCHOOL.
P. EVANS, 415:MAY71-443
412:MAY71-188

LEIDERER, R., ED. WILHALM VON ORLENS.
J.R. ASHCROFT, 402(MLR):OCT71-935
M.C. PHINNEY, 301(JEGP):JAN71-110
LEIGH, J. YOUNG PEOPLE AND LEISURE.
617(TLS):3MAR72-250
LEIGH, R.A. - SEE ROUSSEAU, J-J.
LEIGHTON, A. EARLY AMERICAN GARDENS.
R.D. ARNER, 568(SCN):SPRING71-19
G.H. PRIDE, 432(NEQ):DEC70-654
639(VQR):SUMMER70-CXV
LEIGHTON, A.C. TRANSPORT AND COMMUNICA-
TION IN EARLY MEDIEVAL EUROPE AD 500-
1100.
617(TLS):6OCT72-1205
LEISHMAN, J.B. MILTON'S MINOR POEMS.
R.E.C. HOUGHTON, 447(N&Q):NOV70-428
LEISS, W. THE DOMINATION OF NATURE.
C. LEHMANN-HAUPT, 441:7AUG72-29
LEITCH, D.B. RAILWAYS OF NEW ZEALAND.
617(TLS):9JUN72-667
LEITES, N. THE RULES OF THE GAME IN
PARIS.*
M. ROSS, 399(MLJ):MAY70-369
LEJEUNE, R. & J. STIENNON. THE LEGEND OF
ROLAND IN THE MIDDLE AGES.
617(TLS):3MAR72-240
LELAND, C.G. LEGENDS OF FLORENCE.
J.E. KELLER, 582(SFQ):DEC69-360
LELAND, J. THE TOWER.
617(TLS):26MAY72-595
LEMAÎTRE, G. JEAN GIRAUDOUX.
T. BISHOP, 561(SATR):5FEB72-59
M. GALLANT, 441:30JAN72-7
LEMARCHAND, E. CYANIDE WITH COMPLIMENTS.
617(TLS):28APR72-500
LEMARIÉ, J. & H. TARDIF - SEE CHROMATIUS
LEMIEUX, L. L'ETABLISSEMENT DE LA
PREMIÈRE PROVINCE ECCLÉSIASTIQUE AU
CANADA 1783-1844.
J-C. BONENFANT, 627(UTQ):JUL69-451
LEMIRE, E.D. - SEE MORRIS, W.
LEMIRE, M. LES GRANDS THÈMES NATIONA-
LISTES DU ROMAN HISTORIQUE CANADIEN-
FRANÇAIS.
R. LE MOINE, 102(CANL):SUMMER71-85
LEMMER, M. - SEE BRANT, S.
LEMMON, E.J. INTRODUCTION TO AXIOMATIC
SET THEORY.
A. SLOMSON, 479(PHQ):JAN70-82
LENAGHAN, J.O. A COMMENTARY ON CICERO'S
ORATION "DE HARUSPICUM RESPONSO."
D. STOCKTON, 123:DEC71-453
LENARD, Y. - SEE PAUWELS, L. & J. BER-
GIER
LENAU, N. GEDICHTE. (G. KUNERT, ED)
I.C., 191(ELN):SEP70(SUPP)-124
T.T. KARST, 221(GQ):NOV70-828
LENDVAI, P. ANTI-SEMITISM IN EASTERN
EUROPE.
617(TLS):15SEP72-1068
LE NESTOUR, P. THE MYSTERY OF THINGS.
P. ADAMS, 61:MAY72-113
L'ENGLE, M. A CIRCLE OF QUIET.
P. LONGSWORTH, 441:13FEB72-28
LENGYEL, J. SZEMBESITÉS.
617(TLS):28APR72-465
LENIN, V.I. LENIN ON THE UNITED STATES.
A. PARRY, 550(RUSR):OCT70-457
LENK, K. & F. NEUMANN, EDS. THEORIE UND
SOZIOLOGIE DER POLITISCHEN PARTEIEN.
E. GRUNER, 182:VOL23#10-541
LENNAM, T.N.S. - SEE MERBURY, F.
LENNEBERG, E.H. BIOLOGICAL FOUNDATIONS
OF LANGUAGE.
L. PAP, 186(ETC.):DEC69-490
M.M. VIHMAN, 269(IJAL):JAN69-75

LENNOX, C. THE FEMALE QUIXOTE. (M. DALZIEL, ED)
    P. FAULKNER, 677:VOL2-292
LENS, S. THE FORGING OF THE AMERICAN EMPIRE.
    A. SCHLESINGER, JR., 561(SATR): 5FEB72-71
    R.J. WALTON, 440:30JAN72-9
    441:20FEB72-24
LENSCHEN, W. GLIEDERUNGSMITTEL UND IHRE ERZÄHLERISCHEN FUNKTIONEN IM "WILLEHALM VON ORLENS" DES RUDOLF VON EMS.
    E. SPIELMANN, 221(GQ):NOV70-813
LENSEN, G.A. JAPANESE RECOGNITION OF THE U.S.S.R.
    T. HASEGAWA, 32:JUN71-399
LENSEN, G.A. THE RUSSO-CHINESE WAR.
    W. LEVI, 32:MAR71-148
LENTIN, A. - SEE SHCHERBATOV, M.M.
LENTON, H.T. BRITISH BATTLESHIPS AND AIRCRAFT CARRIERS. BRITISH SUBMARINES.
    617(TLS):22SEP72-1124
LENTRICCHIA, F. THE GAIETY OF LANGUAGE.
    R. BUTTEL, 295:VOL2#3-431
    P. LE BRUN, 541(RES):MAY70-239
LENZ, F.W. OVID, DIE LIEBESKUNST.
    F. LASSERRE, 182:VOL23#7-376
LENZ, F.W. - SEE OVID
LENZ, J.M.R. GESAMMELTE WERKE IN VIER BÄNDEN.* (VOL 1) (R. DAUNICHT, ED)
    R. PASCAL, 220(GL&L):APR71-280
LENZ, S. THE GERMAN LESSON.* (GERMAN TITLE: DEUTSCHSTUNDE.)
    P. ADAMS, 61:FEB72-110
    J.M. BERNSTEIN, 19(AGR):VOL35#6-24
    D.J. ENRIGHT, 362:9MAR72-314
    M. HAMBURGER, 561(SATR):18MAR72-71
    D. JOHNSON, 440:7MAY72-8
    C. LEHMANN-HAUPT, 441:5APR72-47
    E. PAWEL, 441:9APR72-5
LEODHAS, S.N. TWELVE GREAT BLACK CATS.
    V. CUNNINGHAM, 362:9NOV72-643
LEÓN, A.G. - SEE UNDER GONZÁLEZ LEÓN, A.
DE LEÓN, J.L.S.P. - SEE UNDER PONCE DE LEÓN, J.L.S.
LEÓN, P. PRONONCIATION DU FRANÇAIS STANDARD.
    R.R. NUNN, 207(FR):OCT69-143
LEONARD, C. THE OTHER MARITHA.
    N. CALLENDAR, 441:9APR72-40
LEONARD, F. BOX 100.
    N. CALLENDAR, 441:2APR72-22
    S. KROLL, 440:19MAR72-7
LEONARD, G.B. EDUCATION AND ECSTASY.
    S.O.H., 543:SEP69-133
LEONARD, K., ED. A REGISTER OF BIRTHS AND BAPTISMS, DEATHS AND BURIALS - 1788-1812 AND OF BAPTISMS AND BURIALS - 1813-1837 IN THE PARISH OF HAWKS-HEAD, LANCASHIRE.
    617(TLS):7JAN72-21
LEONARD, O.E. THE ROLE OF THE LAND GRANT IN THE SOCIAL ORGANIZATION AND SOCIAL PROCESSES OF A SPANISH-AMERICAN VILLAGE IN NEW MEXICO.
    W. GARD, 584(SWR):SPRING71-199
LEONHARD, K., ED. PICASSO: GRAPHIC WORK. (VOL 2)
    D. HALL, 39:MAY69-404
LEONHARDI, A. ENGLISH WORDS AS THEY ARE USED.
    75:3/1969-185
LEONT'EV, K. MOJA LITRATURNAJA SUD"BA.
    S. LUKASHEVICH, 104:SUMMER71-277
LEONTJEV, A.A. & T.V. RJABOVA, EDS. VOPROSY POROŽDENIJA REČI I OBUČENIJA JAZYKU.
    J. PRŮCHA, 353:JUL69-123

LEOPARDI, G. CANTI. (J.H. WHITFIELD, ED)
    R. HASTINGS, 402(MLR):JAN71-202
LEOPARDI, G. CANTI, PARALIPOMENI, POESIE VARIE, TRADUZIONI POETICHE E VERSI PUERILI. (C. MUSCETTA & G. SAVOCA, EDS)
    J.W., 191(ELN):SEP70(SUPP)-137
LEOPARDI, G. SCRITTI FILOLOGICI (1817-1832). (G. PACELLA & S. TIMPANARO, EDS)
    N.G. WILSON, 123:JUN71-307
"LEOPARDI E L'OTTOCENTO."
    617(TLS):21JAN72-60
LEOPOLD, J.H. THE ALMANUS MANUSCRIPT.
    617(TLS):25AUG72-1005
"L'ÉPIGRAMME GRECQUE."
    K.V. HARTIGAN, 122:JAN71-75
    F.M. WASSERMANN, 121(CJ):DEC70-JAN71-181
LERMAN, L. THE MUSEUM.
    P. RUSSELL, 96:FEB70-60
LERNER, A. FLATION.
    M. BENDER, 441:10AUG72-37
LERNER, A. FOLLOW-UP.
    R.B.K., 477:SPRING69-292
LERNER, G., ED. BLACK WOMEN IN WHITE AMERICA.
    J. JENKINS, 561(SATR):6MAY72-80
LERNER, G. THE GRIMKÉ SISTERS FROM SOUTH CAROLINA.
    442(NY):25MAR72-132
LERNER, L. THE TRUTHTELLERS.*
    I. ARMSTRONG, 541(RES):MAY70-240
LERNER, L. THE USES OF NOSTALGIA.
    617(TLS):6OCT72-1186
LERNER, M-P. LA NOTION DE FINALITÉ CHEZ ARISTOTE.
    P.M. HUBY, 123:MAR71-36
LERNER, R.E. THE HERESY OF THE FREE SPIRIT IN THE LATER MIDDLE AGES.
    617(TLS):27OCT72-1295
LERNER, W. KARL RADEK.*
    R.K. DEBO, 104:FALL71-438
LEROUX, É. 18/44.
    442(NY):22JUL72-78
LE ROY, J.A. & J.E. STEVENS. THE PHILIPPINES CIRCA 1900. (BKS 1&2)
    J.N. ANDERSON, 293(JAST):NOV69-210
LESAGE, A-R. TURCARET. (T.E. LAWRENSON, ED)
    M.H. WADDICOR, 208(FS):JUL71-335
LESAGE, L. & A. YON. DICTIONNAIRE DES CRITIQUES LITTÉRAIRES.
    J.G. CLARK, 208(FS):OCT71-498
LE SENNE, R. INTRODUCTION À LA PHILOSOPHIE. (5TH ED) (E. MOROT-SIR & P. LEVERT, EDS)
    H.W. SCHNEIDER, 319:OCT72-490
LESKOV, N. SATIRICAL STORIES OF NIKOLAI LESKOV.* (W.B. EDGERTON, ED & TRANS)
    S.A. ZENKOVSKY, 550(RUSR):APR70-225
LESLAU, W. AMHARIC TEXTBOOK.
    R. HETZRON, 318(JAOS):OCT-DEC70-559
    A.K. IRVINE, 315(JAL):VOL8PT1-47
LESLAU, W. AN ANNOTATED BIBLIOGRAPHY OF THE SEMITIC LANGUAGES OF ETHIOPIA.
    R. HETZRON, 353:SEP69-99
LESLAU, W. ETHIOPIAN ARGOTS.
    R. HETZRON, 318(JAOS):APR-JUN70-405
    R. HETZRON, 353:SEP69-100
LESLAU, W., ED. ETHIOPIANS SPEAK.* (VOL 1)
    A.J. SHELTON, 650(WF):APR68-133
LESLAU, W. ETHIOPIANS SPEAK. (VOL 3)
    R. HETZRON, 318(JAOS):OCT-DEC70-561
LESLIE, A. EDWARDIANS IN LOVE.
    617(TLS):15DEC72-1541

LESSING, D. BRIEFING FOR A DESCENT INTO
HELL.*
  F.P.W. MC DOWELL, 659:SUMMER72-361
  W.H. PRITCHARD, 249(HUDR):SUMMER71-
  366
LESSING, D. THE STORY OF A NON-MARRYING
MAN.
  J. HUNTER, 362:21SEP72-376
  617(TLS):22SEP72-1087
LESSING, D. THE TEMPTATION OF JACK ORK-
NEY AND OTHER STORIES.
  P. ADAMS, 61:DEC72-144
  L. GRAVER, 441:29OCT72-4
  R. LOCKE, 441:21OCT72-35
LESSING, F.D. & A. WAYMAN, EDS & TRANS.
MKHAS GRUB RJE'S FUNDAMENTALS OF THE
BUDDHIST TANTRAS.*
  P.J.H., 543:MAR70-560
LESTER, J. TO BE A SLAVE. LONG JOURNEY
HOME.
  E. & N. FONER, 453:20APR72-39
LESTER, J. TWO LOVE STORIES.
  A. BROYARD, 441:11OCT72-41
LESTER, J. - SEE DU BOIS, W.E.B.
LESTER, J. & P. SEEGER. THE 12-STRING
GUITAR AS PLAYED BY LEADBELLY.
  D. MURPHY, 650(WF):OCT68-277
LESTER, J.A., JR. JOURNEY THROUGH
DESPAIR, 1880-1914.
  H. AUSTER, 445(NCF):JUN69-109
  R.J. KAUFMANN, 637(VS):SEP69-112
LESTER, M., ED. READINGS IN APPLIED
TRANSFORMATIONAL GRAMMAR.
  P.C. HAUPTMAN, 351(LL):DEC70-284
LESURE, F. - SEE DEBUSSY, C.
LETESSIER, F. - SEE DE LAMARTINE,
A.M.L.D.
"LET'S GO: THE STUDENT GUIDE TO EUROPE."
(NEW ED)
  C.W. CASEWIT, 440:30APR72-4
LETTERS, F. PEOPLE OF SHIVA.
  617(TLS):31MAR72-378
LEUBE, E. FORTUNA IN KARTHAGO.
  V.J. CLEARY, 124:NOV70-93
  P. WALEY, 86(BHS):APR71-156
LEUTZE, J. - SEE LEE, R.E.
LEVAILLANT, J. LES AVENTURES DU SCEP-
TICISME.
  D. BRESKY, 131(CL):SUMMER71-273
LEVARIE, S. GUILLAUME DE MACHAUT.
  A.F.L.T., 412:MAY71-190
LEVAS, S. SIBELIUS.
  617(TLS):26MAY72-613
LEVENSON, C. STILLS.
  617(TLS):21APR72-441
LEVENSON, J.R. CONFUCIAN CHINA AND ITS
MODERN FATE. (VOL 3)
  M. GASSTER, 485(PE&W):JUL68-205
LEVENSON, J.R. LIANG CH'I-CH'AO AND THE
THE MIND OF MODERN CHINA.
  D.W.Y. KWOK, 485(PE&W):OCT69-450
LEVENSON, J.R. & F. SCHURMANN. CHINA.
  A.F.P. HULSEWÉ, 293(JAST):MAY70-685
LEVENSON, S. & W. KENDRICK, EDS. READ-
INGS IN FOREIGN LANGUAGES FOR THE
ELEMENTARY SCHOOL.
  G.C. LIPTON, 207(FR):FEB70-539
LÉVÊQUE, P. LE MONDE HELLÉNISTIQUE.
  O. MURRAY, 303:VOL90-250
LEVER, T. CLAYTON OF TOC H.
  617(TLS):21APR72-450
LEVERTOV, D. RELEARNING THE ALPHABET.*
  G.S. FRASER, 473(PR):WINTER71/72-469
  T. HARRISON, 364:APR/MAY71-163
  E. NELSON, 590:FALL70-42

LEVEY, M. THE LIFE AND DEATH OF MOZART.*
  D. HENAHAN, 441:12MAR72-6
  C. ROSEN, 453:18MAY72-15
  617(TLS):14JAN72-36
LEVEY, M. THE NUDE.
  617(TLS):10NOV72-1377
LEVI, A. IL PROBLEMA DELL'ERRORE NELLA
METAFISICA E NELLA GNOSEOLOGIA DI
PLATONE. (G. REALE, ED)
  V. TEJERA, 319:OCT72-474
LEVI, A. STORIA DELLA SOFISTICA. (D.
PESCE, ED)
  M. BUCCELLATO, 548(RCSF):APR-JUN68-
  225
LEVI, A. & M. ITINERARIA PICTA.
  A.L.F. RIVET, 313:VOL60-242
LÉVI, E. ELIPHAS LÉVI, VISIONNAIRE
ROMANTIQUE. (F.P. BOWMAN, ED)
  B. JUDEN, 208(FS):OCT71-472
LEVI, M.A. COMMENTO STORICO ALLA RES-
PUBLICA ATHENIENSIUM DI ARISTOTELE.
  P.J. RHODES, 303:VOL90-211
LEVI, P. THE LIGHT GARDEN OF THE ANGEL
KING.
  617(TLS):10NOV72-1358
LEVI, W. THE CHALLENGE OF WORLD POLITICS
IN SOUTH AND SOUTHEAST ASIA.
  C-J. LEE, 293(JAST):FEB70-487
LÉVI-STRAUSS, C. L'HOMME NU.
  617(TLS):7APR72-381
LÉVI-STRAUSS, C. THE RAW AND THE COOKED.
  H.J. MULLER, 639(VQR):WINTER70-150
LEVIANT, C., ED & TRANS. KING ARTUS.*
  M. EPSTEIN, 589:JAN71-162
LEVICK, B. ROMAN COLONIES IN SOUTHERN
ASIA MINOR.*
  E.L. BOWIE, 313:VOL60-202
LEVIN, D., ED. JONATHAN EDWARDS.
  R.A. DELATTRE, 432(NEQ):MAR70-169
LEVIN, D.M. REASON AND EVIDENCE IN
HUSSERL'S PHENOMENOLOGY.
  W. MAYS, 518:MAY71-14
LEVIN, H. THE MYTH OF THE GOLDEN AGE IN
THE RENAISSANCE.*
  A.O. ALDRIDGE, 399(MLJ):OCT70-444
  J.L. LIEVSAY, 191(ELN):JUN71-312
  E. SPIVAKOVSKY, 551(RENQ):AUTUMN70-
  278
LEVIN, I. THE STEPFORD WIVES.
  P. ADAMS, 61:NOV72-130
  M. LEVIN, 441:15OCT72-43
  W. SCHOTT, 561(SATR):7OCT72-98
  617(TLS):24NOV72-1415
LEVIN, J. THE CHARTER CONTROVERSY IN
THE CITY OF LONDON, 1660-1688, AND ITS
CONSEQUENCES.
  568(SCN):SPRING71-18
LEVIN, M. NOEL COWARD.
  J.H. ADLER, 397(MD):FEB70-429
LEVIN, M. GORE & IGOR.
  J. GREENFIELD, 287:APR69-29
LEVIN, M. THE SETTLERS.
  G. HICKS, 441:23APR72-30
LEVIN, M.B. POLITICAL HYSTERIA IN
AMERICA.
  R. GRIFFITH, 561(SATR):22APR72-75
LEVIN, N.G. WOODROW WILSON AND WORLD
POLITICS.
  A. RAPPAPORT, 340(KR):1969/2-277
LEVIN, R. THE MULTIPLE PLOT IN ENGLISH
RENAISSANCE DRAMA.*
  W.G. MC COLLOM, 301(JEGP):OCT71-663
  A.C. SPRAGUE, 677:VOL2-254
LEVINE, B. THE DISSOLVING IMAGE.*
  J.L. ALLEN, JR., 295:VOL2#1-148

LEVINE, G. THE BOUNDARIES OF FICTION.*
    D.P. DENEAU, 577(SHR):FALL70-381
    M.P. SCOFIELD, 541(RES):MAY70-229
    J. SUDRANN, 637(VS):SEP69-101
    G.B. TENNYSON, 445(NCF):JUN69-112
LEVINE, G. & W. MADDEN, EDS. THE ART
OF VICTORIAN PROSE.*
    I. FLETCHER, 541(RES):FEB70-98
LEVINE, J.P. CREATION AND CRITICISM.
    617(TLS):31MAR72-354
LEVINE, N. I DON'T WANT TO KNOW ANYONE
TOO WELL.*
    J. METCALF, 99:JUN72-39
LEVINE, P. NOT THIS PIG.
    J. MC MICHAEL, 598(SOR):WINTER72-213
LEVINE, P. PILI'S WALL.
    D. ALLEN, 491:JUL72-235
LEVINE, P. THEY FEED THEY LION.
    W.H. PRITCHARD, 441:16JUL72-4
    R.D. SPECTOR, 561(SATR):11MAR72-80
LEVINE, R.A. BENJAMIN DISRAELI.
    J.D. MERRITT, 637(VS):JUN70-454
LEVINSON, C. INTERNATIONAL TRADE UNION-
ISM.
    617(TLS):1DEC72-1464
LEVIS, J.H. FOUNDATIONS OF CHINESE
MUSICAL ART.
    F. LIEBERMAN, 293(JAST):AUG70-912
LEVITAN, S.A. & B. HETRICK. BIG BROTH-
ER'S INDIAN PROGRAMS - WITH RESERVA-
TIONS.
    M. ROGIN, 441:24DEC72-4
LEVITT, J. THE "GRAMMAIRE DES GRAMMAIRES"
OF GIRAULT-DUVIVIER.
    O. DUCROT, 361:VOL24#1-98
    P.A. GAENG, 207(FR):OCT69-202
LEVITT, L. THE LONG WAY ROUND.
    M. LEVIN, 441:24SEP72-40
LEVY, D.N.L. SVETOZAR GLIGORIC'S CHESS
CAREER, 1945-1970.
    617(TLS):1DEC72-1469
LEVY, J.D. NATURE'S CHILDREN.
    M. OLMERT, 440:2JAN72-6
LEVY, L.W. ORIGINS OF THE FIFTH AMEND-
MENT.
    J.F. COSTANZO, 613:AUTUMN69-467
LÉVY, M. LE ROMAN "GOTHIQUE" ANGLAIS,
1764-1824.
    J.M.S. TOMPKINS, 541(RES):AUG70-367
LEVY, P. - SEE STRACHEY, L.
LEWALD, H.E. ARGENTINA.
    I.A. LEONARD, 238:SEP70-580
LEWALSKI, B.K. MILTON'S BRIEF EPIC.
    D. MEHL, 38:BAND87HEFT2-261
    E. MINER, 173(ECS):WINTER69-296
LEWICKA, H. LA LANGUE ET LE STYLE DU
THÉÂTRE COMIQUE FRANÇAIS DES XVE ET
XVIE SIÈCLES.*
    J.A. RAMSEY, 207(FR):DEC69-357
LEWIN, L.C. TRIAGE.
    W. HJORSTBERG, 441:2JUL72-9
LEWIN, M. LENIN'S LAST STRUGGLE.
    A. PARRY, 550(RUSR):OCT70-457
LEWIN, M.Z. ASK THE RIGHT QUESTION.*
    617(TLS):26MAY72-612
LEWIN, R. HORMONES.
    617(TLS):9JUN72-667
LEWIS, A. THE LANGUAGE OF PURCELL.
    412:FEB71-85
LEWIS, A.A. & C. WOODWORTH. MISS ELIZA-
BETH ARDEN.
    M. MC LAUGHLIN, 561(SATR):4NOV72-86
    K. PERUTZ, 441:22OCT72-44
LEWIS, A.H. CHILDREN'S PARTY.
    N. CALLENDAR, 441:29OCT72-59
LEWIS, C.D. - SEE UNDER DAY LEWIS, C.

LEWIS, C.I. COLLECTED PAPERS OF CLARENCE
IRVING LEWIS. (J.D. GOHEEN & J.L.
MOTHERSHEAD, JR., EDS)
    W. MAYS, 518:MAY71-7
LEWIS, C.I. VALUES AND IMPERATIVES.*
(J. LANGE, ED)
    M.B.M., 543:MAR70-560
LEWIS, C.S. SELECTED LITERARY ESSAYS.
(W. HOOPER, ED)
    R.A. NEALE, 67:MAY71-117
    W.D. TAYLOR, 399(MLJ):NOV70-546
LEWIS, C.S. SPENSER'S IMAGES OF LIFE.
(A. FOWLER, ED)
    S.K. HENINGER, JR., 551(RENQ):
    SPRING70-89
LEWIS, D.K. CONVENTION.
    R. KIRK, 518:MAY70-14
    J.E. LLEWELYN, 479(PHQ):JUL70-286
LEWIS, D.L. KING.
    H.A. LARRABEE, 432(NEQ):DEC70-638
LEWIS, G. LIFE IN REVOLUTIONARY FRANCE.
    617(TLS):25FEB72-214
LEWIS, G.L. TURKISH GRAMMAR.
    W.G. ANDREWS, 318(JAOS):OCT-DEC70-578
LEWIS, H.D. THE ELUSIVE MIND.
    A.C. EWING, 393(MIND):OCT70-629
    E. HINDESS, 518:OCT70-16
    J. TROYER, 311(JP):23MAR72-168
LEWIS, J. THE LEFT BOOK CLUB.
    G.B. NEAVILL, 356:APR71-173
LEWIS, J. & B. TOWERS. NAKED APE OR HOMO
SAPIENS?
    N. BRAYBROOKE, 619(TC):VOL177#1042-55
LEWIS, J.W., ED. PARTY LEADERSHIP AND
REVOLUTIONARY POWER IN CHINA.*
    P.K.T. SIH, 396(MODA):WINTER71-103
LEWIS, M. SPITHEAD.
    617(TLS):4AUG72-920
LEWIS, M.B. SENTENCE ANALYSIS IN MODERN
MALAY.
    A. HALIM, 293(JAST):MAY70-736
LEWIS, N. FLIGHT FROM A DARK EQUATOR.
    M. LEVIN, 441:8OCT72-42
    617(TLS):7APR72-385
LEWIS, N. INVENTORY OF COMPULSORY SER-
VICES IN PTOLEMAIC AND ROMAN EGYPT.
    J.D. THOMAS, 313:VOL60-236
LEWIS, R. A WOLF BY THE EARS.
    N. CALLENDAR, 441:5NOV72-44
LEWIS, R.S. THE NUCLEAR-POWER REBELLION.
    S.B. SHEPARD, 441:29OCT72-50
LEWIS, R.W.B. THE POETRY OF HART CRANE.*
    L. CASPER, 613:WINTER68-613
    K. JOHNSON, 330(MASJ):FALL69-82
LEWIS, S.R., JR. PAKISTAN.
    617(TLS):15SEP72-1066
LEWIS, W.C., JR. - SEE SMITH, M.C.
LEWIS, W.S. & OTHERS - SEE WALPOLE, H.
"WYNDHAM LEWIS ON ART."* (W. MICHEL &
C.J. FOX, EDS)
    N.H. FRASER, 58:MAY70-14
    617(TLS):7APR72-386
"WYNDHAM LEWIS: PAINTINGS AND DRAWINGS."*
(W. MICHEL, ED)
    617(TLS):7APR72-386
LEY, F. BERNARDIN DE SAINT-PIERRE, MAD-
AME DE STAËL.
    C.F. COATES, 207(FR):MAR70-691
LEY-PISCATOR, M. THE PISCATOR EXPERI-
MENT.
    D.B. WILMETH, 397(MD):FEB69-451
LEYBURN, E.D. STRANGE ALLOY.
    L.B. HOLLAND, 445(NCF):DEC68-361
LEYDA, J. & S. BERTENSSON, EDS & TRANS.
THE MUSORGSKY READER.
    G. ABRAHAM, 415:DEC70-1227

190

VON LEYDEN, W. SEVENTEENTH-CENTURY META-
PHYSICS.*
G.A.J. ROGERS, 518:JAN70-13
J.W. YOLTON, 393(MIND):APR70-304
LEYMARIE, J. THE GRAPHIC WORKS OF THE
IMPRESSIONISTS.
D.L. SHIREY, 441:10DEC72-44
LEYMARIE, J. IMPRESSIONIST DRAWINGS
FROM MANET TO RENOIR.
R. LEBOWITZ, 58:APR70-14
LEYMARIE, J. PICASSO DRAWINGS.
V.H. MIESEL, 56:SPRING69-101
LEYMARIE, J. PICASSO: MÉTAMORPHOSES ET
UNITÉ.
617(TLS):21JUL72-840
LEYMARIE, J. PICASSO, THE ARTIST OF THE
CENTURY.
D.L. SHIREY, 441:10DEC72-47
LEYVRAZ, J-P. PHÉNOMÉNOLOGIE DE L'EX-
PÉRIENCE.
A. MERCIER, 182:VOL23#11/12-586
L'HERMITE, F.T. LES VERS HÉROÏQUES.
(C.M. GRISÉ, ED)
J. PEDERSEN, 462(OL):VOL24#3-228
L'HEUREUX, J. THE CLANG BIRDS.
P. ADAMS, 61:NOV72-130
M. LEVIN, 441:8OCT72-42
L'HEUREUX, J. NO PLACE FOR HIDING.
J. KOETHE, 491:APR72-49
L'HEUREUX, J. TIGHT WHITE COLLAR.
J.W. HUGHES, 561(SATR):13MAY72-84
M. LEVIN, 441:9APR72-42
LI, T-Y. CHINESE FICTION.
244(HJAS):VOL29-332
LI YUK-SA - SEE KIM IL SUNG
LI YU-SHU. CHUNG-JIH ERH-SHIH-I T'IAO
CHIAO-SHE. (VOL 1)
T.K. TONG, 293(JAST):NOV69-158
LIACI, M.T. - SEE LANDINO, C.
LIANG, C-T. THE SINISTER FACE OF THE
MUKDEN INCIDENT.*
P. HYER, 293(JAST):AUG70-942
LIBANIUS. SELECTED WORKS. (VOL 1) (A.F.
NORMAN, ED & TRANS)
W. LIEBESCHUETZ, 303:VOL90-221
LIBBY, B. & S. HAYWOOD. STAND UP FOR
SOMETHING.
J. DURSO, 441:3DEC72-44
"THE LIBERAL YEAR BOOK 1887."
617(TLS):18FEB72-172
LIBERMAN, A. & I.C. LOVE. GREECE, GODS
AND ART.*
C.C. VERMEULE, 55:JAN69-49
LIBMAN, L. AND MUSIC AT THE CLOSE.
H. KELLER, 362:26OCT72-547
M. STEINBERG, 441:8OCT72-6
617(TLS):22DEC72-1557
"LA LIBRAIRIE DE CHARLES V."
S.C. ASTON, 208(FS):OCT71-449
"LIBROS VIRUMQUE CANO, GAUDEAMUS."
M.A. MC CORISON, 432(NEQ):DEC70-676
LICHEM, K. PHONETIK UND PHONOLOGIE DES
HEUTIGEN ITALIENISCH.
R.J. DI PIETRO, 276:AUTUMN70-327
I. RONCA, 72:BAND208HEFT3-222
LICHTENBERG, G.C. HOGARTH ON HIGH LIFE.
(A.S. WENSINGER & W.B. COLEY, EDS &
TRANS)
W. JACKSON, 566:AUTUMN70-26
M. PRICE, 676(YR):SPRING71-425
LICHTENBERG, G.C. SCHRIFTEN UND BRIEFE.
(VOLS 1&2) (W. PROMIES, ED)
617(TLS):16JUN72-682
LICHTHEIM, G. EUROPE IN THE TWENTIETH
CENTURY.
D. CAUTE, 362:7DEC72-796
617(TLS):25AUG72-991

LICHTHEIM, G. GEORGE LUKACS.
E.J. BROWN, 574(SEEJ):WINTER71-514
LICHTHEIM, G. A SHORT HISTORY OF SOCIAL-
ISM.
N. LOBKOWICZ, 32:SEP71-691
A. WALKER, 575(SEER):APR71-307
639(VQR):AUTUMN70-CLI
LID, R.W., ED. GROOVING THE SYMBOL.
J.D.A. OGILVY, 191(ELN):SEP70-74
LIDDY, J. BLUE MOUNTAIN.
W.H. PRITCHARD, 491:DEC71-159
LIE, H. NORSK VERSLAERE.
M. BRØNDSTED, 462(OL):VOL23#4-332
LIEB, M. THE DIALECTICS OF CREATION.
V.R. MOLLENKOTT, 568(SCN):SUMMER/
AUTUMN71-33
LIEBENOW, P.K., ED. DAS KÜNZELSAUER
FRONLEICHNAMSPIEL.*
W.F. MICHAEL, 221(GQ):NOV70-802
LIEBER, J. TWO-WAY TRAFFIC.
L. DUBERSTEIN, 561(SATR):22JAN72-68
M. LEVIN, 441:27FEB72-52
LIEBERG, G. PUELLA DIVINA.
A. MICHEL, 555:VOL44FASC1-146
LIEBERMAN, H. CRAWLSPACE.*
J. HUNTER, 362:13APR72-493
617(TLS):21APR72-439
LIEBERMAN, J.K. HOW THE GOVERNMENT
BREAKS THE LAW.
P. ADAMS, 61:AUG72-92
G. COWAN, 441:20AUG72-2
LIEBERMAN, M. CREATIVE COUNTERPOINT.
C. SCHACHTER, 308:SPRING67-169
"ROLF LIEBERMANN ZUM 60 GEBURTSTAG."
M. CARNER, 415:JAN71-33
LIEBESCHUETZ, J.H.W.G. ANTIOCH.
617(TLS):31MAR72-376
LIEBNER, J. MOZART ON THE STAGE.
617(TLS):25AUG72-1003
VON LIECHTENSTEIN, U. - SEE UNDER ULRICH
VON LIECHTENSTEIN
LIEF, R.A. HOMAGE TO OCEANIA.
D. RANKIN, 399(MLJ):OCT70-446
LIEHM, A.J. THE POLITICS OF CULTURE.
N. ASCHERSON, 453:10AUG72-16
"LIETUVIŲ KALBOS MORFOLOGINĖ SANDARA IR
JOS RAIDA."
V. RŪĶE-DRAVIŅA, 353:APR69-104
"LIETUVIŲ KALBOS ŽODYNAS." (VOL 2)
G.B. FORD, JR., 574(SEEJ):SPRING71-
110
LIEUWEN, E. MEXICAN MILITARISM.
T. WOLFF, 50(ARQ):SUMMER69-184
LIEVSAY, J.L. THE ENGLISHMAN'S ITALIAN
BOOKS 1550-1700.*
C. SPERONI, 551(RENQ):WINTER70-459
LIEVSAY, J.L., ED. MEDIEVAL AND RENAIS-
SANCE STUDIES. [1966]
G.B. PARKS, 551(RENQ):SPRING70-54
LIFSHIN, L. WHY IS THE HOUSE DISSOLVING?
J. HOPPER, 661:SPRING69-97
LIFTON, B.J. & T.C. FOX. CHILDREN OF
VIETNAM.
C. LEHMANN-HAUPT, 441:1DEC72-41
LIFTON, R.J. HISTORY AND HUMAN SURVIVAL.
ITŌ TAKESHI, 285(JAPQ):JUL-SEP70-334
LIKHTENSHTEĬN, E.S. & A.A. SIDOROV, EDS.
PYAT'SOT LET POSLE GUTENBERGA, 1468-
1968.
J.S.G. SIMMONS, 78(BC):SUMMER70-256
LILAR, S. LE MALENTENDU DU DEUXIÈME
SEXE.
C. RADFORD, 208(FS):OCT71-490
LILIENTHAL, D.E. THE JOURNALS OF DAVID
E. LILIENTHAL.* (VOL 5)
441:30JAN72-33

191

LILJA, S. ON THE STYLE OF THE EARLIEST
GREEK PROSE.*
P. CHANTRAINE, 555:VOL44FASC2-315
H.L. HUDSON-WILLIAMS, 123:MAR71-73
LILLARD, P.P. MONTESSORI.
A. TROWBRIDGE, 561(SATR):4MAR72-57
LILLO, G. FATAL CURIOSITY. (W.H.
MC BURNEY, ED)
M.R.M., 477:SPRING69-298
LILLY, J.C. THE CENTER OF THE CYCLONE.
J.S. GORDON, 441:26MAR72-4
LILLY, M. SICKERT.
617(TLS):11FEB72-150
LILLYWHITE, B., COMP. LONDON SIGNS.
617(TLS):25AUG72-1005
LIMA, F. UNDERGROUND WITH THE ORIOLE.
S. MOORE, 385(MQR):SUMMER72-217
LIMBOUR, G. SOLEILS BAS.
617(TLS):22SEP72-1092
LIMENTANI, U., ED. THE MIND OF DANTE.*
N.J. PERELLA, 545(RPH):AUG70-237
LINCK, W. WENCESLAUS LINCK'S REPORTS AND
LETTERS 1762-1778. (E.J. BURRUS, ED &
TRANS)
J.F. BANNON, 377:MAR71-46
LINCOLN, H.B., ED. THE COMPUTER AND
MUSIC.
D.C.H., 410(M&L):JAN71-86
M. HERNDON, 187:MAY72-290
412:MAY71-184
617(TLS):7APR72-387
LINCOLN, H.B., ED. THE MADRIGAL COLLEC-
TION L'AMOROSA ERO (BRESCIA, 1588).
M. PICKER, 414(MQ):OCT68-553
"MARY TODD LINCOLN: HER LIFE AND LET-
TERS." (J.G. & L.L. TURNER, EDS)
T.H. WILLIAMS, 441:24SEP72-3
LIND, J. COUNTING MY STEPS.*
E. PAWEL, 390:NOV69-74
LIND, J. NUMBERS.
E. PAWEL, 441:11JUN72-6
P. WEST, 440:21MAY72-12
LIND, L.R. PROBLEMATA VARIA ANATOMICA:
MS. 1165.
H.M. HOWE, 121(CJ):DEC70-JAN71-170
LINDBERG, C., ED. MS. BODLEY 959.* (VOL
5)
P. GRADON, 382(MAE):1971/2-201
LINDBERGH, A.M. BRING ME A UNICORN.
H. BEVINGTON, 441:27FEB72-3
G. CULLIGAN, 561(SATR):4MAR72-72
J. STAFFORD, 440:20FEB72-1
442(NY):1APR72-108
617(TLS):11AUG72-936
LINDBERGH, C.A. THE WARTIME JOURNALS OF
CHARLES A. LINDBERGH.*
H.M. ADAMS, 396(MODA):SPRING71-200
LINDEMAN, F.O., WITH C.H. BORGSTRØM.
EINFÜHRUNG IN DIE LARYNGALTHEORIE.
R. AUTY, 402(MLR):JUL71-720
LINDOP, A.E. JOURNEY INTO STONE.
O.L. BAILEY, 561(SATR):25NOV72-70
N. CALLENDAR, 441:5NOV72-44
LINDOW, W. INSIDE THE MONEY MARKET.
K. KOYEN, 441:1OCT72-10
LINDSAY, J. THE ANCIENT WORLD.*
R.J. HOPPER, 123:DEC71-401
LINDSAY, J. CÉZANNE.
R.W. RATCLIFFE, 592:JUL/AUG69-41
42(AR):FALL69-447
LINDSAY, J. THE ORIGINS OF ALCHEMY IN
GRAECO-ROMAN EGYPT.
E. ROSEN, 124:JAN71-173
LINDSAY, M. PORTRAIT OF GLASGOW.
617(TLS):13OCT72-1236
LINDT, A. - SEE BELL, G. & A. KOECHLIN
"L'INFALLIBILITA."
B.L. MARTHALER, 142:FALL71-481

LING, K. THE REVENGE OF HEAVEN. (I. &
M. LONDON, EDS)
J.K. FAIRBANK, 453:24FEB72-3
R. STEEL, 440:9APR72-1
442(NY):26FEB72-102
LINGAT, R. LES SOURCES DU DROIT DANS LE
SYSTÈME TRADITIONNEL DE L'INDE.
J.D.M. DERRETT, 318(JAOS):APR-JUN70-
346
LINGENFELTER, R.E., R.A. DWYER & D.
COHEN, EDS. SONGS OF THE AMERICAN
WEST.*
J. GREENWAY, 650(WF):JAN69-68
"LINGUISTIQUE APPLIQUÉE."
G. FRANCESCATO, 361:VOL23#1-105
LINHARTOVÁ, V. ANTONI TÀPIES.
617(TLS):29DEC72-1590
LINK, A.S. - SEE WILSON, W.
LINK, F.M. - SEE DRYDEN, J.
LINKE, H. EPISCHE STRUKTUREN IN DER
DICHTUNG HARTMANNS VON AUE.*
M. CURSCHMANN, 221(GQ):JAN70-109
LINKE, H.G. DEUTSCH-SOWJETISCHE BEZIE-
HUNGEN BIS RAPALLO.
G.L. WEINBERG, 32:JUN71-398
LINKS, J.G. TOWNSCAPE PAINTING AND DRAW-
ING.
617(TLS):21APR72-443
LINN, J.G. THE THEATER IN THE FICTION OF
MARCEL PROUST.
L. LE SAGE, 397(MD):DEC67-324
LINNÉR, S. DOSTOEVSKIJ ON REALISM.*
J. WEISGERBER, 149:JUN71-182
LINSCHOTEN, H. ON THE WAY TOWARD A
PHENOMENOLOGICAL PSYCHOLOGY.
J.M. EDIE, 543:MAR70-481
LINTON, R.M. TERRACIDE.*
639(VQR):AUTUMN70-CLV
LINTOTT, A.W. VIOLENCE IN REPUBLICAN
ROME.*
R.T. SCOTT, 121(CJ):APR-MAY71-372
G.V. SUMNER, 487:SPRING70-88
LIOU, B. PRAETORES ETRURIAE XV POPULOR-
UM.
M. HAMMOND, 124:NOV70-95
LIPCHITZ, J., WITH H.H. ARNASON. MY LIFE
IN SCULPTURE.
R. DOWNES, 441:31DEC72-7
LIPKING, L. THE ORDERING OF THE ARTS IN
EIGHTEENTH-CENTURY ENGLAND.
L. NELSON, JR., 676(YR):WINTER71-289
P. THORPE, 566:SPRING71-67
617(TLS):14APR72-405
LIPMAN, J., WITH N. FOOTE, EDS. CALDER'S
CIRCUS.
B. MELSON, 441:23JUL72-3
LIPMANN, T., JR. SPIRO AGNEW'S AMERICA.
W. JACOBSON, 440:14MAY72-1
441:21MAY72-28
LIPP, S. THREE ARGENTINE THINKERS.
H.B., 543:DEC69-349
M.S. HARRIS, 484(PPR):MAR70-470
M.S. STABB, 238:MAY70-344
LIPP, S. & S.E. HISPANOAMÉRICA VISTA POR
SUS ENSAYISTAS.
R.J. MORRIS, 238:SEP70-587
LIPPARD, L.R., ED. SURREALISTS ON ART.
DADAS ON ART.
R. SHATTUCK, 453:1JUN72-23
LIPPMANN, F. VINCENZO BELLINI UND DIE
ITALIENISCHE OPERA SERIA SEINER ZEIT.*
P. GOSSETT, 317:SUMMER71-301
LIPSET, S.M. REBELLION IN THE UNIVER-
SITY.
617(TLS):17NOV72-1385
LIPSET, S.M. & G.M. SCHAFLANDER. PASSION
AND POLITICS.
R.S. BERMAN, 5..(ASCH):SPRING72-296

LIPSKI, J. DIPLOMAT IN BERLIN, 1933-
1939.* (W. JEDRZEJEWICZ, ED)
N.E. EVANS, 325:OCT69-591
LIPSKY, E. MALPRACTICE.
M. LEVIN, 441:21MAY72-31
LIPTÁK, L. SLOVENSKO V 20. STOROČÍ.
Y. JELINEK, 32:MAR71-176
LIPTZIN, S. THE MATURING OF YIDDISH
LITERATURE.
B. MURDOCH, 402(MLR):OCT71-959
LISCANO, J. RÓMULO GALLEGOS Y SU TIEMPO.
(2ND ED)
D. MILIANI, 263:OCT-DEC71-468
LISSITZKY, L. EL LISSITSKY: LIFE, LET-
TERS, TEXTS.
S. CUNNINGHAM, 505:JUN69-146
LISSITZKY, L. RUSSIA: AN ARCHITECTURE
FOR WORLD REVOLUTION.*
A.J. SCHMIDT, 32:SEP71-696
LISSITZKY-KÜPPERS, S. EL LISSITZKY.
M. LAST, 55:OCT69-20
N. LYNTON, 592:NOV68-222
LIST, G. & J. ORREGO-SALAS, EDS. MUSIC
IN THE AMERICAS.*
A. REYES-SCHRAMM, 187:SEP72-550
LIST, S.S. DID YOU LOVE DADDY WHEN I
WAS BORN?
A. BROYARD, 441:10APR72-37
W. GOYEN, 441:30APR72-32
LISTER, F.C. & R.H. EARL MORRIS AND
SOUTHWESTERN ARCHAEOLOGY.*
W.A. LONGACRE, 50(ARQ):SPRING69-95
LISTER, M. COSTUMES OF EVERYDAY LIFE.
617(TLS):12MAY72-557
LISTER, R. WILLIAM BLAKE.*
D.V.E., 191(ELN):SEP69(SUPP)-24
P. MALEKIN, 541(RES):MAY70-249
LISTER, R. SAMUEL PALMER AND HIS ETCH-
INGS.
L. HERRMANN, 90:NOV70-765
J.K. HOBHOUSE, 58:SUMMER70-12
LISTOWEL, W.H. MODERN AESTHETICS. (NEW
ED)
E.H. DUNCAN, 290(JAAC):FALL69-113
"LISTS OF GIFTS AND DEPOSITS IN THE
SCOTTISH RECORD OFFICE." (VOL 1)
617(TLS):11FEB72-165
"L'ITALIANISME EN FRANCE AU XVIIe
SIÈCLE."
I.D. MC FARLANE, 208(FS):JUL71-319
LITTAUER, R. & N. UPHOFF, EDS. THE AIR
WAR IN INDOCHINA. (REV)
R. KLEIMAN, 441:13AUG72-1
"LITTÉRATURE HONGROISE, LITTÉRATURE EURO-
PÉENNE."
B. NORRETRANDERS, 462(OL):VOL23#3-251
LITTLE, B. ENGLISH CATHEDRALS.
617(TLS):7JUL72-785
LITTLE, D.P. AN INTRODUCTION TO MAMLŪK
HISTORIOGRAPHY.
J. VAN ESS, 182:VOL23#15/16-761
LITTLE, I., T. SCITOVSKY & M. SCOTT.
INDUSTRY AND TRADE IN SOME DEVELOPING
COUNTRIES.
617(TLS):15SEP72-1066
LITTLE, S.W. OFF-BROADWAY.
R. HORWICH, 561(SATR):24JUN72-72
442(NY):29APR72-142
LITTLE, W., H.W. FOWLER & J. COULSON,
EDS. THE SHORTER OXFORD ENGLISH
DICTIONARY ON HISTORICAL PRINCIPLES.
(REV BY C.T. ONIONS)
617(TLS):13OCT72-1209
LITTLEJOHN, D. THE PATRIOTIC TRAITORS.
617(TLS):4AUG72-921
LITTLETON, B.J., ED. CLYOMON AND
CLAMYDES.
G.R. PROUDFOOT, 541(RES):FEB70-76

LITTO, F.M. AMERICAN DISSERTATIONS ON
THE DRAMA AND THEATRE.
J. MATES, 432(NEQ):SEP70-508
"THE LITURGY OF THE HOURS." (COMMENTARY
BY A.M. ROGUET)
617(TLS):14APR72-426
LITVINOFF, E. JOURNEY THROUGH A SMALL
PLANET.
617(TLS):17NOV72-1390
LITVINOV, P. THE DEMONSTRATION IN PUSH-
KIN SQUARE.
B.R. BOCIURKIW, 550(RUSR):JUL70-328
I. LAPENNA, 32:MAR71-161
L.M. TIKOS, 418(MR):SPRING71-352
LITWAK, L. & H. WILNER. COLLEGE DAYS IN
EARTHQUAKE COUNTRY.
E. SHORRIS, 231:DEC72-119
LIU FENG-HAN. HSIN-CHIEN LU-CHUN.
J.T. CHEN, 293(JAST):NOV69-159
LIU JUNG-EN - SEE "SIX YÜAN PLAYS"
LIU, J.J.Y. THE POETRY OF LI SHANG-YIN.
Y-T. WANG, 293(JAST):FEB70-423
LIU, J.T.C. OU-YANG HSIU.*
C-Y. CHENG, 485(PE&W):JAN-APR68-101
LIU SHAO-CH'I. THE COLLECTED WORKS OF
LIU SHAO-CH'I, 1945-1957.
H.C. HINTON, 293(JAST):MAY70-694
LIU, S.S., ED & TRANS. ONE HUNDRED AND
ONE CHINESE POEMS.
R.C. MIAO, 318(JAOS):APR-JUN70-390
LIVERMORE, H.V. THE ORIGINS OF SPAIN AND
PORTUGAL.
617(TLS):25FEB72-214
LIVESAY, D. DISASTERS OF THE SUN.
R. GIBBS, 198:SUMMER72-129
LIVESAY, D. THE DOCUMENTARIES.*
H. MAC CALLUM, 627(UTQ):JUL69-349
LIVESAY, D., ED. 40 WOMEN POETS OF
CANADA.
N. BAUER, 198:SUMMER72-125
LIVESAY, D. PLAINSONGS.
M. DOYLE, 491:MAR72-356
"LIVING IN THE SEVENTIES."
A. APPENZELL, 102(CANL):AUTUMN71-96
LIVINGSTONE, L. - SEE CLARÍN
LIVINGSTONE, R. - SEE MARX, K. & F.
ENGELS
LIVREA, E. - SEE COLLUTHUS
DE LIZARDI, J.J.F. - SEE UNDER FERNÁNDEZ
DE LIZARDI, J.J.
LLEWELLYN, A. THE DECADE OF REFORM.
617(TLS):21APR72-451
LLEWELLYN, R. THE NIGHT IS A CHILD.
N. CALLENDAR, 441:5MAR72-34
LLOBERA, J. ALIVE TO ART.
617(TLS):14JUL72-821
LLORENS, J.M. LE OPERE MUSICALI DELLA
CAPPELLA GIULIA. (VOL 1)
J.A.W., 410(M&L):OCT71-443
LLORENS, V. LITERATURA, HISTORIA, POLÍ-
TICA.
R.P. SEBOLD, 240(HR):JAN70-98
LLORENS, V. - SEE ALCALÁ GALIANO, A.
LLOSA, M.V. - SEE UNDER VARGAS LLOSA, M.
LLOYD, A. THE WICKEDEST AGE.
617(TLS):9JUN72-652
LLOYD, A.L. FOLK SONG IN ENGLAND.
W.H. JANSEN, 582(SFQ):MAR69-58
LLOYD, A.L., ED. DER MÜNCHENER PSALTER
DES 14. JAHRHUNDERTS.
R. RUDOLF, 182:VOL23#21/22-932
LLOYD, A.L. & I. ARETZ DE RAMÓN Y RIVERA,
EDS. FOLK SONGS OF THE AMERICAS.
F. GILLMOR, 650(WF):APR68-139

193

LLOYD, G.E.R. ARISTOTLE: THE GROWTH AND
STRUCTURE OF HIS THOUGHT.*
A.R.C. DUNCAN, 529(QQ):SUMMER70-298
G.B. KERFERD, 123:DEC70-313
J. OWENS, 258:JUN69-299
LLOYD, G.E.R. POLARITY AND ANALOGY.
J.B., 542:APR-JUN69-275
LLOYD, J.B. AFRICAN ANIMALS IN RENAIS-
SANCE LITERATURE AND ART.
617(TLS):19MAY72-568
LLOYD-JONES, D.M. PREACHING AND PREACH-
ERS.
617(TLS):28JAN72-101
LLOYD-JONES, H. THE JUSTICE OF ZEUS.
617(TLS):31MAR72-365
LO, K.H.C. PEKING COOKING.
617(TLS):14JAN72-49
LÖB, L. MENSCH UND GESELLSCHAFT BEI
J.B. PRIESTLEY.
J. RAITH, 182:VOL23#5-221
LOBKOWICZ, N. THEORY AND PRACTICE.
Z.A. JORDAN, 483:JAN70-75
LOCHER, K.T. GOTTFRIED KELLER.*
S. MEWS, 301(JEGP):JAN71-126
LOCHHEAD, D. A & B & C &.
D. BARBOUR, 102(CANL):SPRING71-70
LOCHHEAD, D. & R. SOUSTER, EDS. MADE IN
CANADA.*
M. DOYLE, 102(CANL):AUTUMN71-99
M. DOYLE, 491:MAR72-356
LOCHMAN, J.M. CHURCH IN A MARXIST SOCI-
ETY.*
J.P. SCANLAN, 32:MAR71-162
LOCK, C.B.M. GEOGRAPHY. (2ND ED)
617(TLS):15SEP72-1071
LOCK, P.W. - SEE DE BALZAC, H.
LOCKE, D. PERCEPTION AND OUR KNOWLEDGE
OF THE EXTERNAL WORLD.
H. HEIDELBERGER, 482(PHR):APR70-284
LOCKE, J. THE EDUCATIONAL WRITINGS OF
JOHN LOCKE. (J.L. AXTELL, ED)
J.J. JENKINS, 483:JUL70-244
LOCKERT, L., ED & TRANS. MORE PLAYS BY
RIVALS OF CORNEILLE AND RACINE.
J. LOUGH, 447(N&Q):APR70-156
LOCKHART, J. SPANISH PERU, 1532-1560.*
R.E. CRIST, 37:MAR69-40
LOCKRIDGE, K.A. A NEW ENGLAND TOWN, THE
FIRST HUNDRED YEARS.
B.E. STEINER, 432(NEQ):SEP70-482
J.J. WATERS, 656(WMQ):OCT70-657
LOCKRIDGE, R. DEATH IN A SUNNY PLACE.
N. CALLENDAR, 441:30JAN72-24
H. FRANKEL, 561(SATR):29JAN72-73
LOCKRIDGE, R. SOMETHING UP A SLEEVE.
N. CALLENDAR, 441:2JUL72-15
442(NY):22JUL72-80
LOCKRIDGE, R. WRITE MURDER DOWN.
T. LASK, 441:30DEC72-19
LOCKWOOD, L. THE COUNTER-REFORMATION AND
THE MASSES OF VINCENZO RUFFO.
D. ARNOLD, 415:MAR71-240
J.A.C., 410(M&L):JUL71-318
LOCKWOOD, W.B. HISTORICAL GERMAN SYNTAX.
G.S. LANE, 221(GQ):MAR70-252
LOCKWOOD, W.B. INDO-EUROPEAN PHILOLOGY.*
A.M. DAVIES, 402(MLR):OCT71-841
LODGE, D. LANGUAGE OF FICTION.*
R. COHEN, 445(NCF):JUN68-104
E. JACQUES, 98:JUL69-648
LODGE, D. THE NOVELIST AT THE CROSS-
ROADS.
617(TLS):3MAR72-252
LOEB, O.W. & T. PRITTIE. MOSELLE.
617(TLS):24NOV72-1441
LOEBL, E. CONVERSATIONS WITH THE BEWIL-
DERED.
617(TLS):29SEP72-1170

LOEBL, E. STALINISM IN PRAGUE.* (H.
STAROBIN, ED)
R. LUZA, 32:MAR71-177
LOEHR, M. CHINESE LANDSCAPE WOODCUTS.
R. BARNHART, 57:VOL31#2/3-210
M. SULLIVAN, 39:FEB69-158
LOERKE, O. DER BÜCHERKARREN.
D. VAN ABBÉ, 182:VOL23#11/12-620
LOEWEN, J.W. THE MISSISSIPPI CHINESE.
R. COLES, 442(NY):20MAY72-135
LOEWENBERG, B.J. AMERICAN HISTORY IN
AMERICAN THOUGHT.
G.D. LILLIBRIDGE, 31(ASCH):AUTUMN72-
677
LOEWINSOHN, R. MEAT AIR.*
J. ATLAS, 491:OCT71-45
LOFMARK, C. RENNEWART IN WOLFRAM'S
"WILLEHALM."
617(TLS):27OCT72-1296
LÖFSTEDT, L. LES EXPRESSIONS DU COM-
MANDEMENT ET DE LA DÉFENSE EN LATIN ET
LEUR SURVIE DANS LES LANGUES ROMANES.
P.F. DEMBOWSKI, 545(RPH):NOV70-337
LOFTUS, T., WITH OTHERS, EDS. THE ATLAS
OF THE EARTH.
617(TLS):23JUN72-727
LOGAN, J. THE ZIG-ZAG WALK.*
G.S. FRASER, 473(PR):WINTER71/72-469
J. MAZZARO, 340(KR):1970/1-163
639(VQR):SUMMER70-XCV
LOGAN, O. CULTURE AND SOCIETY IN VENICE
1470-1790.
617(TLS):6OCT72-1201
LOGAN, R.W., ED. W.E.B. DU BOIS.
H.W. CRUSE & C. GIPSON, 453:30NOV72-
22
LOGAN, R.W. HAITI AND THE DOMINICAN RE-
PUBLIC.
R.M. MALEK, 263:JAN-MAR71-71
LOGUE, C. NEW NUMBERS.
G. BURNS, 584(SWR):WINTER71-100
LOGUINE, T., ED. GONTCHAROVA ET LARION-
OV.
617(TLS):26MAY72-611
LOHF, K.A., COMP. THE LITERARY MANU-
SCRIPTS OF HART CRANE.
C. BUSH, 447(N&Q):FEB70-72
LOHNER, E. - SEE "GOTTFRIED BENN"
LOHNER, E. - SEE GRASS, G.
LOHNES, W.F.W. & F.W. STROTHMANN. GER-
MAN.
C. GELLINEK, 221(GQ):MAR70-302
LOHRMANN, D. DAS REGISTER PAPST JOHAN-
NES' VIII (872-882).
W. GOFFART, 589:JAN71-164
LOHSE, B. ASKESE UND MÖNCHTUM IN DER
ANTIKE UND IN DER ALTEN KIRCHE.
A. KEMMER, 182:VOL23#4-144
R.D. SIDER, 124:NOV70-97
LOIS, G., WITH B. PITTS. GEORGE, BE
CAREFUL.
441:1OCT72-38
561(SATR):4NOV72-87
LOMAX, A. FOLK SONG STYLE AND CULTURE.
J. DE LABAN, 290(JAAC):FALL69-106
LOMAX, A., W. GUTHRIE & P. SEEGER. HARD-
HITTING SONGS FOR HARD-HIT PEOPLE.
D.K. WILGUS, 650(WF):JUL69-219
LOMBARD, M. L'ISLAM DANS SA PREMIÈRE
GRANDEUR (VIIIE-XIE SIÈCLE).
A.R. LEWIS, 589:OCT71-744
LOMBARDO, A. LETTURA DEL MACBETH.
J. TORBARINA, 447(N&Q):APR70-154
LOMBARDO, A. RITRATTO DI ENOBARBO.
617(TLS):11FEB72-162
LOMIENTO, G. L'ESEGESI ORIGENIANA DEL
VANGELO DI LUCA.
H. SAVON, 555:VOL44FASC1-135

194

LONDON, A. & B.K. BISHOV, EDS. THE COM-
PLETE JEWISH COOKBOOK.
617(TLS):29DEC72-1591
LONDON, I. & M. - SEE LING, K.
LONDON, J. & H. ANDERSON. SO SHALL YE
REAP.
J. WOMACK, JR., 453:31AUG72-12
"THE LONDON OF CHARLES DICKENS."
A.B., 155:SEP70-244
LONG, A.A., ED. PROBLEMS IN STOICISM.
H.K. HUNT, 63:DEC71-334
LONG, C.C. THE ROLE OF NEMESIS IN THE
STRUCTURE OF SELECTED PLAYS BY EUGENE
O'NEILL.
D. ALEXANDER, 397(MD):MAY69-108
LONG, E.B., WITH B. LONG. THE CIVIL WAR
DAY BY DAY.
441:6FEB72-40
LONG, J. & A. NORTON. SETTING UP THE NEW
AUTHORITIES.
617(TLS):18AUG72-977
LONG, J.H., ED. MUSIC IN ENGLISH
RENAISSANCE DRAMA.*
J.P. CUTTS, 141:SPRING69-201
F.W. STERNFELD, 541(RES):FEB70-111
LONG, J.H. SHAKESPEARE'S USE OF MUSIC.
617(TLS):28JUL72-867
LONG, K.R. THE MUSIC OF THE ENGLISH
CHURCH.
617(TLS):1DEC72-1462
LONG, M. AT THE PIANO WITH DEBUSSY.
617(TLS):24MAR72-333
LONG, N. HARMONY AND STYLE.
R. JESSON, 415:JAN70-47
DE LONGCHAMPS, J. THE WISHING ANIMAL.
N. SULLIVAN, 491:NOV71-107
LONGEGA, G. ARSINOE II.*
J. BRISCOE, 123:MAR71-99
LONGFORD, E. WELLINGTON: PILLAR OF
STATE.
J. VINCENT, 362:2NOV72-607
617(TLS):17NOV72-1388
LONGFORD, E. WELLINGTON: THE YEARS OF
THE SWORD.
D.V.E., 191(ELN):SEP70(SUPP)-12
LONGGOOD, W. THE DARKENING LAND.
P. ADAMS, 61:OCT72-135
S.B. SHEPARD, 441:19NOV72-52
LONGHI, R. "ME PINXIT" E QUESITI CARA-
VAGGESCHI.
90:AUG70-557
LONGHURST, H. MY LIFE AND SOFT TIMES.
617(TLS):2JUN72-639
LONGINUS. "LIBELLUS DE SUBLIMITATE"
DIONYSIO LONGINO "FERE ADSCRIPTUS."
(D.A. RUSSELL, ED)
P. CHANTRAINE, 555:VOL44FASC1-134
LONGMATE, N. IF BRITAIN HAD FALLEN.
617(TLS):27OCT72-1294
LONGO, V. ARETALOGIE NEL MONDO GRECO.
(VOL 1)
K.J. RIGSBY, 24:OCT71-741
LONGOBARDI, F. MORAVIA.
G. CARSANIGA, 270:VOL20#3-75
DES LONGRAIS, F.J. - SEE UNDER JOÜON DES
LONGRAIS, F.
LONGRIGG, R. THE DESPERATE CRIMINALS.*
F.P.W. MC DOWELL, 659:SUMMER72-361
LONGRIGG, R. THE HISTORY OF HORSE RAC-
ING.
G.F.T. RYALL, 441:3DEC72-7
617(TLS):29DEC72-1589
LONGSTREET, S. WAR CRIES ON HORSEBACK.
617(TLS):21JUL72-829
LONGSTREET, S. WE ALL WENT TO PARIS.
A. BROYARD, 441:12APR72-47
441:23APR72-10
442(NY):29APR72-143

LONGSTREET, S. - SEE KIMBALL, N.
LONGWORTH, P. THE COSSACKS.*
P. AVRICH, 550(RUSR):OCT70-479
LONGWORTH, P. THE THREE EMPRESSES.
617(TLS):22DEC72-1553
LONGYEAR, R.M. SCHILLER AND MUSIC.
I.A. LEVITSKY, 564:SPRING68-72
LÖNNROT, E., COMP. THE OLD KALEVALA AND
CERTAIN ANTECEDENTS.
R.T. HARMS, 32:JUN71-452
F.J. OINAS, 574(SEEJ):SPRING71-128
G.C. SCHOOLFIELD, 563(SS):SPRING71-
219
LONSDALE, R. - SEE BECKFORD, W.
LONSDALE, R. - SEE GRAY, T., W. COLLINS &
O. GOLDSMITH
LONTEEN, J.A. INTERPRETACIÓN DE UNA
AMISTAD INTELECTUAL Y SU PRODUCTO LIT-
ERARIO.
M.E. VENIER, 400(MLN):MAR70-320
LOOCK, H-D. QUISLING, ROSENBERG, UND
TERBOVEN.
617(TLS):21JAN72-70
LOOKER, R. - SEE LUXEMBURG, R.
"LOOKING INTO ORGANISMS."
617(TLS):30JUN72-754
LOOMIS, S. THE FATAL FRIENDSHIP.
S. DE GRAMONT, 441:16APR72-10
B. LEVY, 561(SATR):12FEB72-80
J.H. PLUMB, 440:6FEB72-4
442(NY):6MAY72-147
VAN LOON, G.W. THE STORY OF HENDRIK
WILLEM VAN LOON.
A. WHITMAN, 561(SATR):20MAY72-73
LOOS, B. MYTHOS, ZEIT UND TOD.
617(TLS):25FEB72-226
LOOSE, G. FRANZ KAFKA UND AMERIKA.
W. KUDSZUS, 52:BAND4HEFT3-322
I. SEIDLER, 149:JUN71-173
LOOZE, H.J. ALEXANDER HAMILTON AND THE
BRITISH ORIENTATION OF AMERICAN FOR-
EIGN POLICY, 1783-1803.
W.G. MORGAN, 432(NEQ):JUN70-337
J.L. NEEL, 656(WMQ):JUL70-513
LOPE BLANCH, J.M. EL ESPAÑOL DE AMÉRICA.
D.N. CÁRDENAS, 238:MAY70-343
LOPE BLANCH, J.M. - SEE DE VALDÉS, J.
LOPE DE VEGA. EL CABALLERO DE OLMEDO.
(F. RICO, ED)
A.S. TRUEBLOOD, 400(MLN):MAR70-308
LOPE DE VEGA. EL DUQUE DE VISEO. (E.A.
EASON, ED)
V. DIXON, 86(BHS):OCT71-353
LOPE DE VEGA. EL SUFRIMIENTO PREMIADO.*
(V. DIXON, ED)
A.G. REICHENBERGER, 240(HR):JAN70-92
LOPE DE VEGA & C. DE MONROY. FUENTE
OVEJUNA (DOS COMEDIAS). (F. LOPEZ
ESTRADA, ED)
V. DIXON, 86(BHS):OCT71-354
LÖPELMANN, M. ETYMOLOGISCHES WÖRTERBUCH
DER BASKISCHEN SPRACHE.
M.R. HARRIS, 240(HR):JUL70-315
LOPEZ, C.L. ALEXANDER POPE.
G.S. ROUSSEAU, 566:SPRING71-69
LOPEZ, F.P. - SEE UNDER PEREZ LOPEZ, F.
LÓPEZ, M.L. PROBLEMAS Y MÉTODOS EN EL
ANÁLISIS DE PREPOSICIONES.
A. GOOCH, 86(BHS):OCT71-346
M. SANDMANN, 72:BAND208HEFT4/6-433
LÓPEZ-REY, J. VELAZQUEZ' WORK AND WORLD.
T. CROMBIE, 39:NOV69-447
A. DORN, 58:FEB70-12
J.D. HOAG, 551(RENQ):AUTUMN70-289
LÓPEZ ESTRADA, F. MÉTRICA ESPAÑOLA DEL
SIGLO XX.
D.R. HARRIS, 86(BHS):APR71-170

LÓPEZ ESTRADA, F. - SEE LOPE DE VEGA &
C. DE MONROY
LÓPEZ MORALES, H. POESÍA CUBANA CONTEM-
PORÁNEA.
M-L. GAZARIAN, 238:MAR70-159
LÓPEZ MORALES, H. TRADICIÓN Y CREACIÓN
EN LOS ORÍGENES DEL TEATRO CASTELLANO.
M.J. RUGGERIO, 545(RPH):FEB71-541
E.J. WEBBER, 405(MP):MAY70-373
LÓPEZ MUÑOZ, J.L., ED. NARRACIONES
POSTGUERRA U.S.A.
L. MATEO, 202(FMOD):APR/AUG69-299
L'ORANGE, H.P. ART FORMS AND CIVIC LIFE
IN THE LATE ROMAN EMPIRE.*
J.E. GAEHDE, 576:MAR68-79
LORANGER, F. DOUBLE JEU.
R. ROBIDOUX, 627(UTQ):JUL70-441
LORANT, A. LES PARENTS PAUVRES D'HONORE
DE BALZAC.
C.C., 191(ELN):SEP69(SUPP)-57
LORAS, O. RENCONTRE AVEC HENRI MICHAUX
AU PLUS PROFOND DES GOUFFRES.
V.A. LA CHARITÉ, 207(FR):OCT69-167
LORCH, F.W. THE TROUBLE BEGINS AT EIGHT.
F.R. HOROWITZ, 330(MASJ):FALL69-82
R. LEHAN, 445(NCF):DEC69-377
LORD, G.D. - SEE MARVELL, A.
LORD, G.D. & OTHERS, EDS. POEMS ON
AFFAIRS OF STATE. (VOLS 1-4)
R. BERMAN, 340(KR):1969/5-708
LORD, J. THE MAHARAJAHS.*
617(TLS):25AUG72-1006
LORD, P.J. - SEE SIMPSON, C.
LORD, R. DOSTOYEVSKY.
R.L. BELKNAP, 574(SEEJ):SUMMER71-217
M.V. JONES, 575(SEER):OCT71-616
639(VQR):AUTUMN70-CXXXVII
LORD, R. RUSSIAN AND SOVIET LITERATURE.
617(TLS):8DEC72-1509
LORD, W. THE DAWN'S EARLY LIGHT.
G. DANGERFIELD, 441:23JUL72-5
E. WEEKS, 61:JUL72-94
442(NY):15JUL72-82
LORDE, A. CABLES TO RAGE.
M. DOYLE, 491:MAR72-356
LORENZ, K. STUDIES IN ANIMAL AND HUMAN
BEHAVIOR. (VOL 1)
R.A. HINDE, 440:30JAN72-8
LORENZ, K. STUDIES IN ANIMAL AND HUMAN
BEHAVIOUR. (VOL 2)
R.A. HINDE, 440:30JAN72-8
617(TLS):3MAR72-238
LORENZ, R. ANFÄNGE DER BOLSCHEWISTISCHEN
INDUSTRIEPOLITIK.
N. SPULBER, 587:JUL69-107
LORENZO-RIVERO, L. LARRA Y SARMIENTO.
191(ELN):SEP70(SUPP)-157
LORIAN, A. L'ORDRE DES PROPOSITIONS DANS
LA PHRASE FRANÇAISE CONTEMPORAINE - LA
CAUSE.
P.F. DEMBOWSKI, 545(RPH):AUG70-208
LORIAUX, R., ED & TRANS. LE PHÉDON DE
PLATON. (VOL 1)
M. BROWN, 24:OCT71-752
LOSCHÜTZ, G., ED. VON BUCH ZU BUCH.
I. TIESLER, 221(GQ):MAR70-300
LOSFELD, G. LE LIVRE DES RENCONTRES.
P. GINESTIER, 208(FS):OCT71-499
LOSHAK, D. PAKISTAN CRISIS.*
A. CAMPBELL, 561(SATR):4MAR72-69
N. MAXWELL, 453:23MAR72-8
LOSSKY [LOSSKII], N.O. VOSPOMINANIIA.*
S. LEVITZKY, 550(RUSR):APR70-226
LOTMAN, J. STRUKTUR DES KÜNSTLERISCHEN
TEXTES.
D. TSCHIŽEWSKIJ, 72:BAND208HEFT4/6-
471

"LORENZO LOTTO: IL 'LIBRO DI SPESE DI-
VERSE' (1538-1556)." (P. ZAMPETTI, ED)
C. GOULD, 90:OCT70-708
LOTZ, J. NORTHERN REALITIES.*
102(CANL):WINTER71-108
LOUGH, J. ESSAYS ON THE "ENCYCLOPÉDIE"
OF DIDEROT AND D'ALEMBERT.*
A.M. WILSON, 173(ECS):SPRING70-411
LOUIS, P. - SEE ARISTOTLE
LOUIS, V.E. & J.M. A MOTORIST'S GUIDE TO
THE SOVIET UNION.
L. VLADIMIROV, 587:APR69-550
LOUIS, W.R. & J. STENGERS. E.D. MOREL'S
HISTORY OF THE CONGO REFORM MOVEMENT.
N.R. BENNETT, 637(VS):DEC69-223
LOUSLEY, J.E. FLORA OF THE ISLES OF
SCILLY.
617(TLS):16JUN72-697
LOVE, G.A. & M. PAYNE, EDS. CONTEMPORARY
ESSAYS ON STYLE.
F.W. BATESON, 184(EIC):APR70-264
LOVE, H., ED. RESTORATION LITERATURE.
617(TLS):13OCT72-1216
LOVE, J.O. WORLDS IN CONSCIOUSNESS.*
R.Z. TEMPLE, 295:VOL2#3-421
LOVE, K. SUEZ.*
R.P. MITCHELL, 385(MQR):WINTER72-66
LOVEJOY, D.S. THE GLORIOUS REVOLUTION IN
AMERICA.
M. KAMMEN, 441:12NOV72-5
LOVEJOY, D.S., ED. RELIGIOUS ENTHUSIASM
AND THE GREAT AWAKENING.
E.S. GAUSTAD, 432(NEQ):JUN70-328
LOVELL, E.J., JR. - SEE LADY BLESSINGTON
LOVELL, M. A PRESENCE IN THE HOUSE.
N. CALLENDAR, 441:30JUL72-22
LOVELOCK, W. A STUDENT'S DICTIONARY OF
MUSIC.
A. JACOBS, 415:NOV70-1115
LOVESEY, P. ABRACADAVER.
O.L. BAILEY, 561(SATR):28OCT72-89
N. CALLENDAR, 441:15OCT72-42
617(TLS):7JUL72-783
LOVINS, A. ERYRI, THE MOUNTAINS OF LONG-
ING.
617(TLS):22DEC72-1562
LOVSKY, F. LA DÉCHIRURE DE L'ABSENCE.
617(TLS):25FEB72-225
LOW, A. AUGUSTINE BAKER.*
T.A. BIRRELL, 677:VOL2-259
LOW, D.A., ED. SOUNDINGS IN MODERN SOUTH
ASIAN HISTORY.
F.J. CORLEY, 613:SPRING69-152
R.L. HARDGRAVE, JR., 318(JAOS):OCT-
DEC70-600
LOW, D.A., J.O. ILTIS & M.D. WAINWRIGHT,
EDS. GOVERNMENT ARCHIVES IN SOUTH
ASIA.
M.H. CASE, 293(JAST):FEB70-459
LOWBURY, E., T. SALTER & A. YOUNG. THOM-
AS CAMPION.
D.C-B., 412:MAY71-191
LOWE, A. THE BARRIER AND THE BRIDGE.
442(NY):22JUL72-79
LOWE, C.J. & M.L. DOCKRILL. THE MIRAGE
OF POWER.
617(TLS):7APR72-398
LOWE, G-R. THE GROWTH OF PERSONALITY.
617(TLS):18AUG72-978
LOWE, N. THE LANCASHIRE TEXTILE INDUSTRY
IN THE SIXTEENTH CENTURY.
617(TLS):14JUL72-822
LOWELL, J.R. DAUGHTER OF DARKNESS.
N. CALLENDAR, 441:29OCT72-59

LOWELL, R. NOTEBOOK.* (NEW ED)
G. BURNS, 584(SWR):SPRING71-207
W. DICKEY, 249(HUDR):SPRING71-159
L.L. MARTZ, 676(YR):SPRING71-403
W.H. PRITCHARD, 491:DEC71-159
LOWELL, R. NOTEBOOK 1967-68.*
P. SCHWABER, 651(WHR):AUTUMN71-348
LOWENFELS, W., ED. THE WRITING ON THE
WALL.
42(AR):FALL69-448
LOWENFELS, W. - SEE WHITMAN, W.
LOWENSTEIN, C. A FESTIVAL OF JEWISH
COOKING.
N. MAGID, 440:20FEB72-8
617(TLS):16JUN72-697
LOWERY, B. WEREWOLF.
M. LEVIN, 441:30APR72-38
LOWI, T.J. THE END OF LIBERALISM.
R. GOEDECKE, 185:JAN70-170
LOWINSKY, E.E., ED. THE MEDICI CODEX OF
1518.
L.L. PERKINS, 414(MQ):APR69-255
LÖWITH, K. DIO, UOMO E MONDO DA CARTESIO
A NIETZSCHE.
E. RAMBALDI, 548(RCSF):JUL-SEP68-354
LOWITT, R. GEORGE W. NORRIS. (VOL 2)
441:21MAY72-28
LOWMAN, E.W., WITH R. O'DONNELL. THE
HOW-NOT-TO-MISS-THE-COCKTAIL-HOUR COOK-
BOOK.
N. MAGID, 440:13FEB72-5
LOWRY, M. DARK AS THE GRAVE WHEREIN MY
FRIEND IS LAID.* (D. DAY & M. LOWRY,
EDS)
G. ROPER, 627(UTQ):JUL69-356
LOWRY, M. OCTOBER FERRY TO GABRIOLA.*
(M. LOWRY, ED)
M. CORRIGAN, 102(CANL):SPRING71-74
F.P.W. MC DOWELL, 659:SUMMER72-361
LOWTHER, P. THIS DIFFICULT FLOWRING.
H. MAC CALLUM, 627(UTQ):JUL69-352
LOY, J.R. MONTESQUIEU.
C.P. COURTNEY, 208(FS):JAN71-86
R.B. HOLTMAN, 577(SHR):WINTER70-97
R. SHACKLETON, 546(RR):APR70-139
LOZANO, C. RUBÉN DARÍO Y EL MODERNISMO
EN ESPAÑA 1888-1920.*
A. PAGÉS LARRAYA, 131(CL):SPRING71-
177
ŁOZIŃSKI, J.Z. & A. MIŁOBĘDZKI. GUIDE TO
ARCHITECTURE IN POLAND.
W.C. LEEDY, 576:MAY69-152
LUARD, E., ED. THE INTERNATIONAL REGULA-
TION OF CIVIL WARS.
617(TLS):14APR72-407
DE LUBAC, H. LES ÉGLISES PARTICULIÈRES
DANS L'EGLISE UNIVERSELLE.
617(TLS):9JUN72-665
LUBBERS, K. EMILY DICKINSON.
R.E. PECK, 219(GAR):WINTER69-550
LÜBBREN, R. ARTHUR MILLER.
K. TETZELI VON ROSADOR, 72:BAND208
HEFT1-49
LUBENOW, W.C. THE POLITICS OF GOVERNMENT
GROWTH.
617(TLS):7JAN72-10
LUBOS, A. GESCHICHTE DER LITERATUR
SCHLESIENS.
H. BOESCHENSTEIN, 182:VOL23#4-169
LUCAS, A. HUGH MAC LENNAN.
D. BARBOUR, 102(CANL):SUMMER71-75
LUCAS, D.D. EMILY DICKINSON AND RIDDLE.*
G.W. ALLEN, 27(AL):MAR71-135
LUCAS, J., ED. LITERATURE AND POLITICS
IN THE NINETEENTH CENTURY.*
S.M. SMITH, 677:VOL2-304
LUCAS, J.R. THE FREEDOM OF THE WILL.*
D.C. DENNETT, 311(JP):21SEP72-527

LUCE, D. & J. SOMMER. VIETNAM.
F. FITZ GERALD, 293(JAST):FEB70-498
LUCE, G.G. BODY TIME.*
617(TLS):29DEC72-1590
LUCE, J.V. LOST ATLANTIS.*
639(VQR):WINTER70-XXVII
LUCIAN. LUCIEN, "LE NAVIRE OU LES SOU-
HAITS." (G. HUSSON, ED & TRANS)
B. BALDWIN, 124:MAY71-315
"LUCIAN." (LOEB, VOL 8) (M.D. MACLEOD,
ED & TRANS)
J. BOMPAIRE, 303:VOL90-219
LUCID, R.F., ED. NORMAN MAILER.*
T.R. EDWARDS, 453:15JUN72-21
LUCID, R.F. - SEE MAILER, N.
LUCIE-SMITH, E. A CONCISE HISTORY OF
FRENCH PAINTING.
617(TLS):7JAN72-18
LUCIE-SMITH, E. MOVEMENTS IN ART SINCE
1945.
R. RUMNEY, 592:NOV69-193
LUCIE-SMITH, E. THINKING ABOUT ART.
N. TRESILIAN, 592:JUL/AUG68-50
LUCIE-SMITH, E. TOWARDS SILENCE.
H. SERGEANT, 175:SPRING69-33
LUCIE-SMITH, E. & P. WHITE. ART IN BRIT-
AIN 1969-70.
90:SEP70-652
LUCINI, G.P. SCRITTI CRITICI. (L. MAR-
TINELLI, ED)
617(TLS):24MAR72-341
LUCK, G. THE LATIN LOVE ELEGY. (2ND ED)
E.J. KENNEY, 123:DEC71-456
LUCK, G. UNTERSUCHUNGEN ZUR TEXTGES-
CHICHTE OVIDS.
M.P. CUNNINGHAM, 124:SEP70-27
M. WINTERBOTTOM, 123:JUN71-208
LUCK, G.M. & OTHERS. PATIENTS, HOSPITALS
AND OPERATIONAL RESEARCH.
617(TLS):10MAR72-278
LUCKETT, R. THE WHITE GENERALS.*
617(TLS):27OCT72-1295
LUCRETIUS. ON THE NATURE OF THINGS.
(M.F. SMITH, TRANS)
J.M. SNYDER, 124:NOV70-90
LUCRETIUS. THE WAY THINGS ARE.* (R.
HUMPHRIES, TRANS; NOTES BY G.K. STRO-
DACH)
P.M. BROWN, 123:DEC70-400
P. CRUTTWELL, 5:SPRING69-121
LUDAT, H. DEUTSCH-SLAWISCHE FRÜHZEIT UND
MODERNES POLNISCHES GESCHICHTSBEWUSST-
SEIN.
O. HALECKI, 182:VOL23#13/14-688
LUDECKE, H. ALBRECHT DÜRER.
442(NY):23DEC72-80
LUDWIG, E.W. & J. SANTIBANEZ, EDS. THE
CHICANOS.
J. WOMACK, JR., 453:31AUG72-12
LUDWIG, J. ABOVE GROUND.*
G. ROPER, 627(UTQ):JUL69-356
LUDWIG, J. & A. WAINWRIGHT, EDS. SOUND-
INGS.*
R.L. RAYMOND, 150(DR):WINTER70/71-557
LUHMANN, N. ZWECKBEGRIFF UND SYSTEM-
RATIONALITÄT.
T. RAISER, 182:VOL23#4-157
LUISELLI, B. - SEE TERTULLIAN
LUKÁCS, G. ESSAYS ÜBER REALISMUS.
617(TLS):29SEP72-1169
LUKÁCS, G. HISTORY AND CLASS CONSCIOUS-
NESS.*
W.A. SUCHTING, 63:DEC71-338
LUKÁCS, G. MAGYAR IRODALOM - MAGYAR KUL-
TÚRA. (F. FEHÉR & Z. KENYERES, EDS)
L. CZIGÁNY, 32:SEP71-688

LUKACS, J. THE PASSING OF THE MODERN
AGE.
J. HELLMAN, 142:SPRING71-232
LUKAS, R.C. EAGLES EAST.
R.L. GARTHOFF, 32:DEC71-895
ŁUKASIEWICZ, J. DIPLOMAT IN PARIS, 1936-
1939. (W. JĘDRZEJEWICZ, ED)
Z.J. GĄSIOROWSKI, 32:JUN71-411
LUKE, P. SISYPHUS AND REILLY.
M. SULLIVAN, 362:28DEC72-902
617(TLS):29SEP72-1133
LUKIĆ, S. CONTEMPORARY YUGOSLAV LITERA-
TURE.
N. ASCHERSON, 453:30NOV72-15
LUKONIN, W. PERSIA II.*
E. PORADA, 57:VOL31#1-95
LULL, R. [R. LULLUS] QUATTUOR LIBRI
PRINCIPIORUM.
617(TLS):2JUN72-631
LUMBY, E.W.R., ED. POLICY AND OPERATIONS
IN THE MEDITERRANEAN 1912-1914.
617(TLS):7APR72-398
LUMIANSKY, R.M. & H. BAKER, EDS. CRITI-
CAL APPROACHES TO SIX MAJOR ENGLISH
WORKS.
R.M. WILSON, 175:AUTUMN69-106
DE LUMLEY-WOODYEAR, H. LE PALÉOLITHIQUE
INFÉRIEUR ET MOYEN DU MIDI MÉDITER-
RANÉEN DANS SON CADRE GÉOLOGIQUE.
(VOL 1)
R. PITTIONI, 182:VOL23#7-371
LUMSDEN, I., ED. CLOSE THE 49TH PARALLEL
ETC.
R.C. ELLSWORTH, 529(QQ):SUMMER70-288
DE LUNA, B.N. THE QUEEN DECLINED.
G.B. HARRISON, 191(ELN):JUN71-315
DE LUNA, F.A. THE FRENCH REPUBLIC UNDER
CAVAIGNAC 1848.*
L.C. JENNINGS, 207(FR):MAR70-723
J.M. ROBERTS, 208(FS):OCT71-474
LUNACHARSKY, A.V. SOBRANIE SOCHINENII.
(VOLS 7&8) OB IZOBRAZITEL'NOM ISKUS-
STVE. (I.A. SATS, ED) VOSPOMINANIYA I
VPECHATLENIYA. (N.A. TRIFONOV, ED)
S. FITZPATRICK, 587:APR69-527
LUND, E., M. PIHL & J. SLOK. A HISTORY
OF EUROPEAN IDEAS. (R. HATTON, ED)
617(TLS):29SEP72-1137
LUNDWALL, S.J. SCIENCE FICTION.
T. STURGEON, 441:5MAR72-36
LUNENFELD, M. THE COUNCIL OF THE SANTA
HERMANDAD.
J.L. SHNEIDMAN, 589:OCT71-746
LUNN, J.E. & U. VAUGHAN WILLIAMS. RALPH
VAUGHAN WILLIAMS.
617(TLS):4FEB72-131
LUNT, H.G., ED. HARVARD SLAVIC STUDIES.
(VOL 5)
V.D. MIHAILOVICH, 574(SEEJ):FALL71-
379
LURIE, L. THE RUNNING OF RICHARD NIXON.
M.F. NOLAN, 441:27AUG72-5
LUSCOMBE, D.E. THE SCHOOL OF PETER
ABELARD.
J.A. BRUNDAGE, 121(CJ):FEB-MAR71-274
M.M. MC LAUGHLIN, 589:JUL71-523
LUTTWAK, E. COUP D'ETAT.
S.H. BARNES, 639(VQR):WINTER70-164
LUTYENS, M. MILLAIS AND THE RUSKINS.
P. GROSSKURTH, 637(VS):DEC69-219
LUTYENS, M. THE RUSKINS AND THE GRAYS.
617(TLS):10NOV72-1354
LUTZ, A. CRUSADE FOR FREEDOM.
H.D. WOODMAN, 330(MASJ):FALL69-83
VON LÜTZOW, H. IM DIPLOMATISCHEN DIENST
DER K.U.K. MONARCHIE. (P. HOHENBALKEN,
ED)
617(TLS):4AUG72-912

LUXEMBURG, R. SELECTED POLITICAL WRIT-
INGS. (R. LOOKER, ED) SELECTED POL-
ITICAL WRITINGS OF ROSA LUXEMBURG.
(D. HOWARD, ED)
617(TLS):18FEB72-172
LYALL, G. BLAME THE DEAD.
617(TLS):1DEC72-1467
"LYBEAUS DESCONUS."* (M. MILLS, ED)
G.C. BRITTON, 447(N&Q):OCT70-385
V.J. SCATTERGOOD, 677:VOL2-236
LYCURGUS. LYCURGI ORATIO IN LEOCRATEM
CUM CETERARUM LYCURGI ORATIONUM FRAG-
MENTIS. (N.C. CONOMIS, ED)
W.R. CONNOR, 124:JAN71-161
LYDON, J.F. THE LORDSHIP OF IRELAND IN
THE MIDDLE AGES.
617(TLS):7JUL72-778
LYNAM, R., ED. PARIS FASHION.
617(TLS):8DEC72-1505
LYNCH, J. SPAIN UNDER THE HABSBURGS.*
(VOL 2)
639(VQR):WINTER70-XXIV
LYNCH, J.R. THE FACTS OF RECONSTRUCTION.
(W.C. HARRIS, ED)
R.H. WOODY, 579(SAQ):WINTER71-114
LYNN, K.S. WILLIAM DEAN HOWELLS.*
G. ARMS, 27(AL):JAN72-665
LYNN, R. AN INTRODUCTION TO THE STUDY
OF PERSONALITY.
617(TLS):28JAN72-109
LYNNE, J.B. THE WEDNESDAY VISITORS.
502(PRS):WINTER68/69-366
LYNSKEY, W., ED. READING MODERN FICTION.
D.E.S. MAXWELL, 402(MLR):APR71-402
LYNTON, N. LANDMARKS OF THE WORLD'S ART:
THE MODERN WORLD.
P. OVERY, 592:JUL/AUG68-52
LYON, J.S. THOMAS DE QUINCEY.
J.E.J., 191(ELN):SEP70(SUPP)-36
LYON, M. SYMBOL AND IDEA IN HENRY
ADAMS.*
P. SHAW, 301(JEGP):JUL71-574
639(VQR):AUTUMN70-CXXXVII
LYONS, A. THE SECOND COMING.
C.M. MAHON, 651(WHR):SUMMER71-273
LYONS, J. NOAM CHOMSKY.*
J.M.E. MORAVCSIK, 473(PR):1971/3-336
LYONS, J. INTRODUCTION TO THEORETICAL
LINGUISTICS.
S. STAROSTA, 350:JUN71-429
LYONS, J. & R.J. WALES, EDS. PSYCHOLIN-
GUISTICS PAPERS.*
J. PRŮCHA, 353:OCT69-123
LYONS, L.M. NEWSPAPER STORY.
T.M. BERNSTEIN, 441:27FEB72-35
617(TLS):26MAY72-596
LYONS, M.C. - SEE HIPPOCRATES
ŁYSOHORSKY, O. SELECTED POEMS. (E.
OSERS, ED)
J. SYMONS, 364:FEB/MAR72-160
617(TLS):10MAR72-273

"M." A YEAR IS EIGHT MONTHS.*
R. LUZA, 32:MAR71-177
MA HUAN. YING-YAI SHENG-LAN. (J.V.G.
MILLS, ED & TRANS)
617(TLS):16JUN72-681
MAAS, H. - SEE HOUSMAN, A.E.
MAAS, H., J.L. DUNCAN & W.G. GOOD - SEE
BEARDSLEY, A.
MAAS, J. VICTORIAN PAINTERS.*
T. HILTON, 592:NOV69-190
K. ROBERTS, 90:OCT70-705
MABBOTT, T.O. - SEE POE, E.A.
MABEY, R. FOOD FOR FREE.
617(TLS):15DEC72-1541

MACADAM, I., ED. THE ANNUAL REGISTER.
(1971 ED)
617(TLS):18AUG72-971
MAC ADAMS, L., JR. THE POETRY ROOM.
J. KOETHE, 491:APR72-49
MC AFEE, T. I'LL BE HOME LATE TONIGHT.
R.H.W. DILLARD, 340(KR):1969/3-425
MC ALEER, J.J. THEODORE DREISER.*
J.L. MAHONEY, 613:SPRING69-131
MC ALISTER, J.T., JR. & P. MUS. THE
VIETNAMESE AND THEIR REVOLUTION.*
639(VQR):SUMMER70-CXIV
MAC ANDREW, M-C. & G.W. NUTTER - SEE
ZALESKI, E.
MACARTNEY, C.A. MARIA THERESA AND THE
HOUSE OF AUSTRIA.
F.L. CARSTEN, 575(SEER):JAN71-151
MACAULAY, T.B. SELECTED WRITINGS. (J.
CLIVE & T. PINNEY, EDS)
617(TLS):20OCT72-1258
MC BAIN, E. HAIL, HAIL, THE GANG'S ALL
HERE!*
617(TLS):7JAN72-17
MC BAIN, E. SADIE WHEN SHE DIED.
O.L. BAILEY, 561(SATR):9SEP72-80
N. CALLENDAR, 441:10DEC72-56
617(TLS):1DEC72-1467
MACBEATH, I. THE TIMES GUIDE TO THE
INDUSTRIAL RELATIONS ACT.
617(TLS):28JAN72-88
MAC BETH, G. THE BURNING CONE.*
P. LESTER, 493:AUTUMN70-250
MAC BETH, G. COLLECTED POEMS, 1958-
1970.*
P.J. CALLAHAN, 561(SATR):15APR72-71
T. LASK, 441:7JUL72-32
M. SCHMIDT, 491:JUN72-170
MAC BETH, G. THE NIGHT OF STONES.*
H. MORRIS, 569(SR):SPRING71-301
H. SERGEANT, 175:SPRING69-33
MAC BETH, G. THE ORLANDO POEMS.
J. FULLER, 362:24FEB72-251
617(TLS):14JAN72-32
MAC BETH, G. A WAR QUARTET.*
R. DURGNAT, 493:SPRING70-81
MACBETH, N. DARWIN RETRIED.
D. JORAVSKY, 453:21SEP72-23
MC BURNEY, W.H. - SEE LILLO, G.
MC CABE, P. & R.D. SCHONFELD. APPLE TO
THE CORE.
D. HECKMAN, 441:8AUG72-35
MC CAFFREY, L.J. THE IRISH QUESTION,
1800-1922.
D.W. MILLER, 637(VS):JUN70-417
MAC CAFFREY, W.T. - SEE CAMDEN, W.
MAC CAIG, N. A MAN IN MY POSITION.*
C. KIZER, 491:FEB72-291
MC CALL, A. THE FRENCH BOY.
R.H. BAYES, 50(ARQ):WINTER69-373
MC CALL, A. THE MISTRESS.
617(TLS):18AUG72-961
MC CALL, D. THE EXAMPLE OF RICHARD
WRIGHT.
K. KINNAMON, 301(JEGP):JAN71-180
MC CALL, D.K. THE THEATRE OF JEAN-PAUL
SARTRE.*
R. CHAMPIGNY, 659:SPRING72-261
639(VQR):AUTUMN70-CXL
MC CALL, E.B. OLD PHILADELPHIA HOUSES
ON SOCIETY HILL, 1750-1840.
R.W. BRUNSKILL, 576:DEC68-306
MC CALL, M.H., JR. ANCIENT RHETORICAL
THEORIES OF SIMILE AND COMPARISON.
P. DE LACY, 24:APR71-360
G.M.A. GRUBE, 124:DEC70-138

MC CANN, A.M. THE PORTRAITS OF SEPTIMIUS
SEVERUS (A.D. 193-211).
M.A.R. COLLEDGE, 313:VOL60-244
A.G. MC KAY, 124:JAN71-170
MC CANN, S. THE FIGHTING IRISH.
617(TLS):21JUL72-853
MC CARRY, C. CITIZEN NADER.
E. DREW, 441:19MAR72-7
R. EISNER, 561(SATR):1APR72-73
MC CARTHY, A. PRIVATE FACES/PUBLIC
PLACES.
E. JANEWAY, 441:2JUL72-4
R.R. LINGEMAN, 441:23JUN72-38
442(NY):5AUG72-84
MC CARTHY, E. OTHER THINGS AND THE AARD-
VARK.*
L.L. MARTZ, 676(YR):SPRING71-403
MAC CARTHY, F. ALL THINGS BRIGHT AND
BEAUTIFUL.
617(TLS):30JUN72-740
MC CARTHY, M. BIRDS OF AMERICA.*
E. FEINSTEIN, 364:FEB/MAR72-177
J.M. MORSE, 249(HUDR):AUTUMN71-527
MC CARTHY, M. ELECTIONS FOR SALE.
L.L.L. GOLDEN, 561(SATR):15APR72-67
W. PINCUS, 440:21MAY72-11
MC CARTHY, M. MEDINA.
G. EMERSON, 441:13AUG72-21
F.S. FRIEDMAN, 561(SATR):15JUL72-55
B.T. PAQUET, 453:21SEP72-35
MC CARTHY, W.E.J., ED. TRADE UNIONS.
617(TLS):23JUN72-724
MC CARUS, E.N. A KURDISH-ENGLISH DIC-
TIONARY, DIALECT OF SULAIMANIA, IRAQ.
E.R. ONEY, 318(JAOS):APR-JUN70-295
MC CAUGHEY, G. & M. LEGRIS, EDS. OF
SEVERAL BRANCHES.
W. BLISSETT, 627(UTQ):JUL69-397
MC CHESNEY, D. A HOPKINS COMMENTARY.*
F.N. LEES, 637(VS):JUN70-451
N.H. MAC KENZIE, 401(MLQ):JUN70-236
MACCHI, V., GENERAL ED. SANSONI-HARRAP
STANDARD ITALIAN AND ENGLISH DICTION-
ARY. (PT 1, VOL 1) (I. MC GILVRAY &
OTHERS, COMPS)
617(TLS):13OCT72-1231
MC CLAIN, F.M. MAURICE.
617(TLS):23JUN72-717
MC CLARY, J.M. A PORTION FOR FOXES.
M. LEVIN, 441:18JUN72-30
MC CLEAN, R.J. A BOOK OF SWEDISH VERSE.
C. LOFMARK, 220(GL&L):APR71-275
MC CLELLAN, E. TWO JAPANESE NOVELISTS.
639(VQR):SPRING70-LXVI
MC CLELLAND, I.L. BENITO JERÓNIMO
FEIJÓO.
G.E. MAZZEO, 238:MAY70-336
MC CLELLAND, J.S., ED. THE FRENCH RIGHT
FROM DE MAISTRE TO MAURRAS.*
J. DUNN, 362:10FEB72-186
MC CLOSKEY, D.N., ED. ESSAYS ON A
MATURE ECONOMY.
617(TLS):24MAR72-321
MC CLOSKEY, H.J. META-ETHICS AND NORMA-
TIVE ETHICS.*
A. PHILLIPS, 518:MAY70-15
A.L. THOMAS, 479(PHQ):OCT70-408
MC CLOSKEY, P.N., JR. TRUTH AND UNTRUTH.
L.L.L. GOLDEN, 561(SATR):12FEB72-72
G. WILLS, 440:5MAR72-4
MC CLOSKEY, R.G. - SEE WILSON, J.
MC CLURE, J. THE CATERPILLAR COP.
617(TLS):13OCT72-1235
MC CLURE, J. THE STEAM PIG.*
O.L. BAILEY, 561(SATR):28OCT72-89
N. CALLENDAR, 441:22OCT72-47
MC CLURE, R. RAWLINS.
M. LEVIN, 441:23APR72-41

MAC COLLA, F. THE ALBANNACH.
  E. MORGAN, 362:20APR72-524
MC CONICA, J.K. ENGLISH HUMANISTS AND
  REFORMATION POLITICS UNDER HENRY VIII
  AND EDWARD VI.
  D.F.S. THOMSON, 627(UTQ):JAN70-181
MC CONKEY, J. A JOURNEY TO SAHALIN.*
  V. CUNNINGHAM, 362:22JUN72-841
  J.M. MORSE, 249(HUDR):AUTUMN71-527
MC CONNELL, A. TSAR ALEXANDER I.
  J.C. ZACEK, 32:JUN71-392
MC CORD, N. & D.J. ROWE. NORTHUMBERLAND
  AND DURHAM.
  617(TLS):25FEB72-230
MC CORKELL, E.J. HENRY CARR - REVOLU-
  TIONARY.
  R.S. HARRIS, 627(UTQ):JUL70-401
  D.V. WADE, 627(UTQ):JUL70-393
MC CORMACK, E. WOULD YOU BELIEVE LOVE?*
  617(TLS):12MAY72-537
MC CORMACK, M.H. THE WORLD OF PROFES-
  SIONAL GOLF.
  617(TLS):2JUN72-639
MAC CORMICK, D. HEBRIDEAN FOLKSONGS.*
  (J.L. CAMPBELL, ED)
  E. FOWKE, 292(JAF):JUL-SEP70-368
MC CORMICK, D. ONE MAN'S WARS.
  617(TLS):2JUN72-641
MC COURT, E. SASKATCHEWAN.
  E. MANDEL, 627(UTQ):JUL69-400
MC COURT, E. THE YUKON AND NORTHWEST
  TERRITORIES.
  R.A.J. PHILLIPS, 627(UTQ):JUL70-380
MC COY, A.W., WITH C.B. READ & L.P. ADAMS
  2D. THE POLITICS OF HEROIN IN SOUTH-
  EAST ASIA.
  E. HYMOFF, 561(SATR):23SEP72-72
  T. LASK, 441:31AUG72-35
  F. LEWIS, 61:NOV72-112
  J.M. MARKHAM, 441:3SEP72-1
  442(NY):30SEP72-126
MC COY, E. CRAIG ELWOOD - ARCHITECTURE.
  D. LOHAN, 44:DEC69-61
MC CUBBIN, C. AUSTRALIAN BUTTERFLIES.
  617(TLS):18AUG72-975
MC CULLERS, C. THE MORTGAGED HEART.*
  (M.G. SMITH, ED)
  N. BALAKIAN, 441:3JAN72-29
  D. MADDEN, 578:FALL72-137
MC CULLIN, D. THE DESTRUCTION BUSINESS.
  617(TLS):7APR72-391
MC CULLOUGH, D. THE GREAT BRIDGE.
  N. BLIVEN, 442(NY):11NOV72-187
  J. KAPLAN, 561(SATR):30SEP72-70
  C. LEHMANN-HAUPT, 441:4OCT72-49
  G. CARSON, 441:15OCT72-7
MC CULLOUGH, H.C., ED & TRANS. TALES OF
  ISE.*
  O.G. LIDIN, 462(OL):VOL24#3-227
  L.M. ZOLBROD, 293(JAST):AUG70-939
MAC CURDY, R.R. FRANCISCO DE ROJAS ZOR-
  RILLA.
  V. DIXON, 86(BHS):JUL71-274
  E. RUIZ-FORNELLS, 238:DEC70-1022
MAC CURTAIN, M. TUDOR AND STUART IRE-
  LAND.
  617(TLS):21JUL72-850
MC CUTCHEON, H. RED SKY AT NIGHT.
  N. CALLENDAR, 441:31DEC72-18
MAC DERMOT, V. THE CULT OF THE SEER IN
  THE ANCIENT MIDDLE EAST.
  J-J. D'AOUST & R.F. FLEISSNER,
  70(ANQ):JUN72-159
MC DERMOTT, G. LEADER LOST.*
  J. GRIGG, 362:6APR72-457
  617(TLS):14APR72-413
MC DERMOTT, J.J. - SEE ROYCE, J.

MAC DIARMID, H. A DRUNK MAN LOOKS AT THE
  THISTLE.* (J.C. WESTON, ED)
  H. CARRUTH, 249(HUDR):SUMMER71-333
MAC DIARMID, H. A LAP OF HONOUR.
  G. BURNS, 584(SWR):WINTER71-100
MAC DIARMID, H. LUCKY POET.
  617(TLS):18AUG72-962
MAC DIARMID, H. THE HUGH MAC DIARMID
  ANTHOLOGY. (M. GRIEVE & A. SCOTT, EDS)
  617(TLS):3NOV72-1304
MC DIARMID, M.P. - SEE "HARY'S 'WALLACE'"
MAC DONAGH, D. A WARNING TO CONQUERORS.
  H. SERGEANT, 175:SPRING69-33
MACDONALD, A.M. - SEE "CHAMBERS TWENTIETH
  CENTURY DICTIONARY"
MACDONALD, C. - SEE CICERO
MACDONALD, H. BERLIOZ' ORCHESTRAL MUSIC.
  A.F.L.T., 412:AUG71-275
MACDONALD, J.A. THE PAPERS OF THE PRIME
  MINISTERS. (VOL 2: THE LETTERS OF SIR
  JOHN A. MACDONALD, 1858-1861.) (J.K.
  JOHNSON & C.B. STELMACK, EDS)
  P.B. WAITE, 150(DR):AUTUMN70-423
MC DONALD, K. THE WRECK DETECTIVES.
  617(TLS):17NOV72-1405
MC DONALD, L. ICE CREAM, SHERBET, AND
  ICES.
  N. MAGID, 440:20FEB72-8
MC DONALD, M. THE HOMING ELEPHANT AND
  CUCUMBER PROPHESY PARTY.
  J. HOPPER, 661:SPRING69-105
MAC DONALD, M. TITANS AND OTHERS.
  617(TLS):3MAR72-236
MACDONALD, R. THE UNDERGROUND MAN.*
  G. HARTMAN, 453:18MAY72-31
  617(TLS):7JAN72-17
MAC DONALD, R.H., ED. THE LIBRARY OF
  DRUMMOND OF HAWTHORNDEN.*
  P. MORGAN, 677:VOL2-260
MACDONALD, S. THE HISTORY AND PHILOSOPHY
  OF ART EDUCATION.*
  S. ROUVE, 89(BJA):SUMMER71-314
MAC DOWELL, D.M. - SEE HARRISON, A.R.W.
MAC DOWELL, E. CRITICAL AND HISTORICAL
  ESSAYS. (W.J. BALTZELL, ED)
  M. PETERSON, 470:JAN70-45
MC DOWELL, W.L., JR., ED. DOCUMENTS
  RELATING TO INDIAN AFFAIRS 1754-1765.
  617(TLS):21JUL72-829
MAČEK, V. IN THE STRUGGLE FOR FREEDOM.
  R.E. KANET, 32:SEP71-690
MC ELROY, D.D. SCOTLAND'S AGE OF IM-
  PROVEMENT.
  566:SPRING71-74
MACENKO, P. NARYSY DO ISTORIYI UKRAIN-
  SKOYI TSERKOVNOYI MUZYKY.
  C.H. ANDRUSYSHEN, 627(UTQ):JUL69-492
MAC EWEN, G. THE ARMIES OF THE MOON.
  J. SHERMAN, 198:SUMMER72-118
MAC EWEN, G. KING OF EGYPT, KING OF
  DREAMS.
  H. JACKSON, 99:JAN-FEB72-76
  E. WATERSTON, 296:SUMMER72-76
MAC EWEN, G. THE SHADOW MAKER.
  D. BARBOUR, 150(DR):SPRING70-112
  M. HORNYANSKY, 627(UTQ):JUL70-333
MC EWEN, G.D. THE ORACLE OF THE COFFEE
  HOUSE.
  617(TLS):18AUG72-977
MACEY, S.L., ED. A LEARNED DISSERTATION
  ON DUMPLING (1726) [AND] PUDDING AND
  DUMPLING BURNT TO POT (1727).
  566:SPRING71-70
MC FADDEN, D. INTENSE PLEASURE.
  J. SHERMAN, 198:SUMMER72-118
MC FADDEN, D. LETTERS FROM THE EARTH
  TO THE EARTH.
  D. BARBOUR, 150(DR):SPRING70-112

MC FADDEN, D. & G. CURNOE. THE GREAT
CANADIAN SONNET. (PT 1)
D. PRINGLE, 96:AUG70-71
MC FADDEN, R. THE GARRYOWEN.
617(TLS):28JAN72-94
MC FARLAND, T. COLERIDGE AND THE PAN-
THEIST TRADITION.*
J.R. BARTH, 141:FALL70-353
D.V.E., 191(ELN):SEP70(SUPP)-32
W.J.B. OWEN, 541(RES):NOV70-507
MACFARLANE, A. THE FAMILY LIFE OF RALPH
JOSSELIN, A SEVENTEENTH-CENTURY CLERGY-
MAN.
568(SCN):SPRING71-16
MC FARLANE, I.D. - SEE D'AUBIGNÉ, A.
MC FARLANE, J.W. - SEE IBSEN, H.
MC FARLANE, K.B. HANS MEMLING. (E.
WIND, WITH G.L. HARRISS, EDS)
G. MARTIN, 362:9MAR72-314
617(TLS):17MAR72-294
MACFARLANE, L.J. POLITICAL DISOBEDIENCE.
617(TLS):9JUN72-666
MAC FARQUHAR, R., ED. SINO-AMERICAN
RELATIONS.
617(TLS):17NOV72-1386
MC GAHERN, J. THE DARK.
T. MAC INTYRE, 340(KR):SEP66-560
MC GAHERN, J. NIGHTLINES.*
W.H. PRITCHARD, 249(HUDR):SUMMER71-
365
MC GANN, J.J. FIERY DUST.*
E.E.B., 191(ELN):SEP69(SUPP)-29
A.H. ELLIOTT, 541(RES):MAY70-227
R.F. GLECKNER, 141:WINTER70-70
K. OTTEN, 182:VOL23#15/16-747
MC GANN, M.J. STUDIES IN HORACE'S FIRST
BOOK OF EPISTLES.
N. RUDD, 123:MAR71-55
G. WILLIAMS, 313:VOL60-258
MC GARRY, K.J. & T.W. BURRELL. SEMANTICS
IN THE ORGANIZATION OF KNOWLEDGE.
LOGIC IN THE ORGANIZATION OF KNOW-
LEDGE.
617(TLS):1SEP72-1033
MC GILL, V.G. THE IDEA OF HAPPINESS.
C.M.R., 543:SEP69-134
MC GILVRAY, I. & OTHERS - SEE MACCHI, V.
MC GINNISS, J. THE DREAM TEAM.
J. FLAHERTY, 441:30APR72-34
C. LEHMANN-HAUPT, 441:9MAY72-43
MC GINNISS, J. THE SELLING OF THE PRESI-
DENT 1968.
639(VQR):WINTER70-XXVIII
MC GIVERN, W.P. CAPRIFOIL.
O.L. BAILEY, 561(SATR):30SEP72-79
N. CALLENDAR, 441:3SEP72-22
442(NY):14OCT72-182
MC GLYNN, P. LEXICON TERENTIANUM.*
(VOL 2) [LISTING IN PREV WAS OF VOLS
1&2]
J. ANDRÉ, 555:VOL44FASC1-146
MC GOUGH, R. AFTER THE MERRYMAKING.
H. WILLIAMS, 364:FEB/MAR72-155
MC GOVERN, G.S. & L.F. GUTTRIDGE. THE
GREAT COALFIELD WAR.
H.M. CAUDILL, 453:21SEP72-38
C. LYDON, 441:9JUL72-4
442(NY):3JUN72-111
MC GOVERN, R. & R. SNYDER, EDS. 60 ON
THE 60'S.
R. JANUSKO, 590:WINTER71-40
MC GOWAN, M.M. - SEE RACINE, J.
MC GRADY, D. MATEO ALEMÁN.*
E. GLASER, 551(RENQ):SUMMER70-181
MC GRATH, E. THE CLAY GREW TALL.
M. LEVIN, 441:7MAY72-32

MC GRATH, T. LETTER TO AN IMAGINARY
FRIEND, PARTS I & II.
J. ATLAS, 491:OCT71-45
J. BERNARDIN, 493:AUTUMN70-254
MC GRAW, J.R. - SEE GREGORY, D.
"MC GRAW-HILL DICTIONARY OF ART."
A. WERNER, 58:SEP/OCT69-12
"MC GRAW-HILL ENCYCLOPEDIA OF WORLD
DRAMA."
M. KIRBY, 441:26NOV72-46
MAC GREGOR, G. THE SENSE OF ABSENCE.
E.G., 477:SPRING69-303
W.A.J., 543:SEP69-133
MC GREGOR, R.S. THE LANGUAGE OF INDRAJIT
OF ORCHĀ.*
R.K. BARZ, 293(JAST):NOV69-191
R. LORD, 302:JAN69-111
MC GREGOR, R.S. OUTLINE OF HINDI GRAM-
MAR.
617(TLS):19MAY72-584
MAC GREGOR-HASTIE, R., ED & TRANS. AN-
THOLOGY OF CONTEMPORARY ROMANIAN
POETRY.
C.C. POPESCU, 399(MLJ):NOV70-550
MC GUANE, T. THE BUSHWHACKED PIANO.*
W.H. PRITCHARD, 249(HUDR):SUMMER71-
357
MC GUINNESS, A.E. HENRY HOME, LORD
KAMES.
D.D. RAPHAEL, 677:VOL2-282
MC GUINNESS, B.F., T. NYBERT & G.H. VON
WRIGHT - SEE WITTGENSTEIN, L.
MC GUINNESS, R. ENGLISH COURT ODES 1660-
1820.
617(TLS):4FEB72-131
MC GUIRE, T. THE TOOTH TRIP.
441:15OCT72-41
561(SATR):25NOV72-74
MC HALE, T. FARRAGAN'S RETREAT.*
W.H. PRITCHARD, 249(HUDR):SUMMER71-
357
MAC HARDY, C. THE ICE MIRROR.
M. LEVIN, 441:10DEC72-57
MACHIAVELLI, N. THE ART OF WAR. (E.
FARNEWORTH, ED & TRANS)
E. NAMER, 542:JUL-DEC69-492
MACHIAVELLI, N. THE FIRST DECENNALE.
D. HAY, 447(N&Q):NOV70-433
MÄCHLER, R. - SEE WALSER, R.
MACHLIN, M. THE SEARCH FOR MICHAEL
ROCKEFELLER.
A. BROYARD, 441:23FEB72-43
MACIEJEWSKI, B.M. KAROL SZYMANOWSKI.
D. COX, 607:WINTER67/68-32
MC ILVANNEY, W. THE LONGSHIPS IN HAR-
BOUR.
L. CLARK, 493:WINTER70/71-370
MAC INNES, C. THE LONDON NOVELS OF COLIN
MAC INNES.
M. GREEN, 340(KR):1969/2-255
MAC INNES, C. WESTWARD TO LAUGHTER.*
THREE YEARS TO PLAY.
F.P.W. MC DOWELL, 659:SUMMER72-361
MC INNES, E. & A.J. HARPER. GERMAN
TODAY.
W.P. HANSON, 220(GL&L):JAN71-215
MAC INNES, H. MESSAGE FROM MÁLAGA.*
617(TLS):14APR72-427
MC INTOSH, A. & M.A.K. HALLIDAY. PAT-
TERNS OF LANGUAGE.
G. NICKEL, 72:BAND208HEFT3-204
MC INTOSH, E. - SEE FOWLER, F.G. & H.W.
MC INTOSH, E. & G.W.S. FRIEDRICHSEN - SEE
FOWLER, H.W. & F.G.
MAC INTOSH, J.J. & S.C. COVAL, EDS. THE
BUSINESS OF REASON.
G.J. WARNOCK, 479(PHQ):JUL70-281

MAC INTYRE, A. AGAINST THE SELF-IMAGES
OF THE AGE.*
G. GERSH, 99:SEP72-33
617(TLS):28APR72-466
MAC INTYRE, A. HERBERT MARCUSE.
E. VIVAS, 396(MODA):WINTER71-80
MC INTYRE, B. THE BIKE BOOK.
561(SATR):7OCT72-108
MACK, J.E. NIGHTMARES AND HUMAN CON-
FLICT.
R. COLES, 442(NY):1JUL72-70
MACK, M. THE GARDEN AND THE CITY.*
B. BOYCE, 481(PQ):JUL70-372
R.L. BRETT, 148:SPRING70-93
A.R. HUMPHREYS, 677:VOL2-279
R. PITMAN, 184(EIC):OCT70-472
E. TUVESON, 191(ELN):MAR71-228
MACK, M. - SEE HOMER
MACK, M. & I. GREGOR, EDS. IMAGINED
WORLDS.
M.S., 155:SEP69-180
MACK SMITH, D. A HISTORY OF SICILY.*
(VOLS 2&3)
S. HUGHES, 613:AUTUMN69-476
MACK SMITH, D., ED. THE MAKING OF ITALY
1796-1866.
617(TLS):16JUN72-673
MACK SMITH, D. VICTOR EMANUEL, CAVOUR,
AND THE RISORGIMENTO.
L. BARZINI, 453:5OCT72-16
R. MITCHISON, 362:31AUG72-278
617(TLS):16JUN72-673
MACK SMITH, D. VITTORIO EMANUELE II.
L. BARZINI, 453:5OCT72-16
MC KAY, A.G. & D.M. SHEPHERD - SEE CATUL-
LUS & HORACE
MAC KAY, A.R. - SEE DE MAGNY, O.
MC KAY, J.P. PIONEERS FOR PROFIT.
W.L. BLACKWELL, 32:JUN71-396
617(TLS):21APR72-453
MACKAY, M. THE VIOLENT FRIEND.
B.H., 502(PRS):FALL68-279
MAC KENDRICK, P. THE ATHENIAN ARISTOC-
RACY, 399 TO 31 B.C.*
F.W. MITCHEL, 24:JAN71-111
S.I. OOST, 122:APR71-139
639(VQR):WINTER70-XXV
MAC KENDRICK, P. THE IBERIAN STONES
SPEAK.*
D. HENRY, 122:OCT71-284
MAC KENDRICK, P. ROMANS ON THE RHINE.
J.J. POLLITT, 124:JAN71-170
MC KENNA, J.B. A SPANIARD IN THE PORTU-
GUESE INDIES.
E. GLASER, 240(HR):JUL70-347
MACKENZIE, B. & F. SINGERS OF AUSTRALIA
FROM MELBA TO SUTHERLAND.
A. BLYTH, 415:MAR70-282
MC KENZIE, G. THE LITERARY CHARACTER OF
WALTER PATER.
D.L. HILL, 445(NCF):JUN68-109
MACKENZIE, G. MARYLEBONE.
617(TLS):22DEC72-1562
MACKENZIE, H. LETTERS TO ELIZABETH ROSE
OF KILRAVOCK. (H.W. DRESCHER, ED)
K. STEWART, 405(MP):NOV69-197
MAC KENZIE, W.J.M. THE STUDY OF POLITI-
CAL SCIENCE TODAY.
617(TLS):9JUN72-666
MC KERN, S. & T. TRACKING FOSSIL MAN.
617(TLS):31MAR72-371
MACKERRAS, C. THE UIGHUR EMPIRE (744-
840) ACCORDING TO THE T'ANG DYNASTIC
HISTORIES.
E.H. SCHAFER, 318(JAOS):OCT-DEC70-623
MC KIMMEY, J. THE MAN WITH THE GLOVED
HAND.
N. CALLENDAR, 441:3SEP72-22

MC KINLEY, G. FOLLOW THE RUNNING GRASS.*
639(VQR):SPRING70-XLI
MC KINNON, A. FALSIFICATION AND BELIEF.
S.C. BROWN, 518:MAY71-16
MACKINNON, D.M. BORDERLANDS OF THEOLOGY.
R. WALLACE, 483:OCT70-343
MAC KINNON, S. SKYDECK.
T. MARSHALL, 99:MAY72-69
MAC KINNON, S. THE WELDER'S ARC.
D. BARBOUR, 150(DR):SPRING70-112
MC KINNON, W.T. APOLLO'S BLENDED DREAM.
P. DICKINSON, 364:OCT/NOV71-136
MACKINTOSH, M. JUGGERNAUT.
R.S. FELDMAN, 587:JAN70-379
MC KINTY, A. THE FATHER OF BRITISH AIR-
SHIPS.
617(TLS):16JUN72-697
MC KISSICK, F. THREE-FIFTHS OF A MAN.
H.A. LARRABEE, 432(NEQ):DEC70-638
MACKLEM, M. GOD HAVE MERCY.
M. CUDDIHY, 613:AUTUMN68-472
MACKSEY, K. TANK WARFARE.
617(TLS):3MAR72-258
MC KUEN, R. IN SOMEONE'S SHADOW.
42(AR):WINTER69/70-591
MC LACHLAN, D. NO CASE FOR THE CROWN.
617(TLS):7JUL72-783
MC LACHLAN, G., ED. CHALLENGES FOR
CHANGE.
617(TLS):10MAR72-278
MC LACHLAN, G., ED. PATIENT DOCTOR
SOCIETY.
H. MILLER, 362:30MAR72-421
617(TLS):7APR72-400
MC LACHLAN, G., ED. PROBLEMS AND PROG-
RESS IN MEDICAL CARE.
617(TLS):16JUN72-694
MC LACHLAN, N. - SEE VAUX, J.H.
MC LAREN, M. BONNIE PRINCE CHARLIE.
617(TLS):20OCT72-1247
MC LAREN, M. SIR WALTER SCOTT.*
I. CAMPBELL, 595(SCS):VOL15PT2-163
MC LAUGHLIN, J.C. ASPECTS OF THE HISTORY
OF ENGLISH.
J.A. JOHNSON, 350:SEP71-703
MC LAUGHLIN, J.C. A GRAPHEMIC PHONEMIC
STUDY OF A MIDDLE-ENGLISH MANUSCRIPT.
J. CRAWFORD, 179(ES):1969SUPP-LXXIX
MC LAUGHLIN, T. MUSIC AND COMMUNICA-
TION.*
F.H., 410(M&L):JUL71-329
E. SAMS, 415:MAR71-239
MAC LEAN, A. CAPTAIN COOK.
442(NY):14OCT72-182
MC LEAN, A. HUMANISM AND THE RISE OF
SCIENCE IN TUDOR ENGLAND.
617(TLS):15SEP72-1057
MACLEAN, A.D., ED. WINTER'S TALES 18.
V. CUNNINGHAM, 362:9NOV72-643
617(TLS):29DEC72-1573
MC LEAN, A.F., JR. AMERICAN VAUDEVILLE
AS RITUAL.
R. TRACY, 650(WF):APR68-144
MACLEAN, C. ISLAND ON THE EDGE OF THE
WORLD.
617(TLS):1SEP72-1028
MAC LEAN, J., F. KRIEGEL & H. HARTMAN-
SHENN. 2000 JAHRE DEUTSCHES LEBEN.
H. FISCHER, 564:SPRING69-74
MC LEAN, R. MAGAZINE DESIGN.
592:JUL/AUG69-54
639(VQR):WINTER70-XXVII
MC LEAN, R. VICTORIAN BOOK DESIGN AND
COLOUR PRINTING.
617(TLS):15DEC72-1540
MC LEAN, R. - SEE EVANS, E.
MAC LEISH, A. THE HUMAN SEASON.
J.M. BRINNIN, 441:19NOV72-6

MC LEISH, D. THE TRAITOR GAME.*
    G. ROPER, 627(UTQ):JUL69-361
MC LELLAN, D. MARX BEFORE MARXISM.
    J. HELLMAN, 142:SPRING71-233
    N. LOBKOWICZ, 32:JUN71-425
MC LELLAN, D. THE THOUGHT OF KARL MARX.
    617(TLS):18FEB72-185
MC LELLAN, D. THE YOUNG HEGELIANS AND
    KARL MARX.*
    R.J.B., 543:SEP69-135
MC LELLAN, D. - SEE MARX, K.
MC LEMORE, M.T. THE MIAMI DOLPHINS.
    J. DURSO, 441:3DEC72-44
MAC LENNAN, T. 1 WALKED OUT OF 2 AND
    FORGOT IT.
    T. LASK, 441:15SEP72-40
MAC LEOD, D. THE GARDENER'S LONDON.
    617(TLS):8DEC72-1513
MACLEOD, M.D. - SEE "LUCIAN"
MAC LEOD, R. A KILLING IN MALTA.
    617(TLS):14APR72-427
MACLEOD, R. CHARLES RENNIE MACKINTOSH.*
    S. BLUTMAN, 505:OCT69-236
    D. IRWIN, 90:NOV69-692
MAC LEOD, R. PATH OF GHOSTS.
    N. CALLENDAR, 441:2JAN72-16
    H. FRANKEL, 561(SATR):29JAN72-73
MC LEOD, W.H. GURU NANAK AND THE SIKH
    RELIGION.
    K. SINGH, 293(JAST):NOV69-192
MAC LIAMMÓIR, M. ALL FOR HECUBA.
    R. HOGAN, 397(MD):DEC68-339
MC LOGHLEN, D. THE LAST HEADLANDS.
    617(TLS):4AUG72-910
MC LOUGHLIN, W.G. NEW ENGLAND DISSENT,
    1630-1833.
    617(TLS):16JUN72-695
MAC LOW, J. STANZAS FOR IRIS LEZAK.
    T. LASK, 441:15SEP72-40
MC LUHAN, M. THE GUTENBERG GALAXY.
    J.D. BEACH, 363:NOV69-22
MC LUHAN, M. THE INTERIOR LANDSCAPE.
    (E. MC NAMARA, ED)
    N. COMPTON, 102(CANL):WINTER71-91
    W.J. ONG, 141:SUMMER70-244
    639(VQR):SUMMER70-C
MC LUHAN, M., WITH H. PARKER. COUNTER-
    BLAST.*
    N. COMPTON, 102(CANL):WINTER71-91
MC LUHAN, M., WITH H. PARKER. THROUGH
    THE VANISHING POINT.
    P-Y. PÉTILLON, 98:JUN69-504
MC LUHAN, T.C., COMP. TOUCH THE EARTH.*
    W. KITTREDGE, 231:NOV72-120
    H. ROBERTSON, 99:APR72-54
MACLURE, M. - SEE MARLOWE, C.
MC MAHON, J.H. HUMANS BEING.*
    R. CHAMPIGNY, 659:SPRING72-261
MC MAHON, T. PRINCIPLES OF AMERICAN
    NUCLEAR CHEMISTRY: A NOVEL.* (BRITISH
    TITLE: A RANDOM STATE.)
    639(VQR):AUTUMN70-CXXVIII
MC MAHON, T.P. & B.P. CORNERED AT SIX.
    N. CALLENDAR, 441:5NOV72-44
MC MANAWAY, J.G. STUDIES IN SHAKESPEARE,
    BIBLIOGRAPHY, AND THEATER.* (R. HOS-
    LEY, A.C. KIRSCH & J.W. VELZ, EDS)
    J.C. MAXWELL, 447(N&Q):APR70-154
MC MASTER, J. THACKERAY.
    617(TLS):14JUL72-794
MAC MASTER, R.E. DANILEVSKY.
    E. LAMPERT, 587:JAN68-449
    N.D. ROODKOWSKY, 613:SPRING69-142
MC MENAMIN, T.J. A CIRCLE OF HANDS.
    617(TLS):25FEB72-209
MACMILLAN, D. ENGLISH AT CHAPEL HILL,
    1795-1969.
    L. PATTON, 579(SAQ):WINTER71-118

MACMILLAN, H. POINTING THE WAY 1959-
    1961.
    J. CHACE, 441:8OCT72-2
    E. POWELL, 362:8JUN72-765
    617(TLS):9JUN72-648
MC MILLAN, M.C. THE LAND CALLED ALABAMA.
    H.C. BAILEY, 9(ALAR):JUL69-239
MC MILLEN, H. THE MANY MANSIONS OF SAM
    PEEPLES.
    J. CATINELLA, 561(SATR):27MAY72-68
    M. LEVIN, 441:27FEB72-52
MAC MULLEN, R. CONSTANTINE.*
    F. MILLAR, 313:VOL60-216
    S.I. OOST, 122:APR71-136
MC MURTRY, L. ALL OF MY FRIENDS ARE
    GOING TO BE STRANGERS.
    J. HARRISON, 441:19MAR72-5
    C. LEHMANN-HAUPT, 441:24MAR72-43
    442(NY):1APR72-106
MAC NAB, J. THE EDUCATION OF A DOCTOR.
    E. CRAY, 441:23JAN72-4
MACNAGHTEN, A. MORE DIFFERENT THAN
    OTHERS.
    617(TLS):14JAN72-49
MC NALLY, R.T. - SEE CHAADAEV, P.Y.
MC NALLY, R.T. & R. FLORESCU. IN SEARCH
    OF DRACULA.
    P. ADAMS, 61:NOV72-130
MC NAMARA, B. THE AMERICAN PLAYHOUSE IN
    THE EIGHTEENTH CENTURY.
    J. MATES, 656(WMQ):JAN70-160
MC NAMARA, E. OUTERINGS.*
    S. SCOBIE, 102(CANL):AUTUMN71-75
MC NAMARA, E. - SEE MC LUHAN, M.
MAC NAMARA, J.J., JR. THE MONEY MAKER.
    M. LEVIN, 441:29OCT72-59
MC NAMEE, L. NINETY-NINE YEARS OF ENG-
    LISH DISSERTATIONS.
    J.D. PICKLES, 677:VOL2-225
    W. WEISS, 72:BAND208HEFT3-220
MC NAMEE, S. SEVEN FOR THE ROAD.
    G. ROPER, 627(UTQ):JUL69-362
MC NEAL, R.H. BRIDE OF THE REVOLUTION.
    C. SIMMONS, 441:19JUN72-35
MC NEAL, R.H., ED. RUSSIA IN TRANSITION
    1905-1914.
    M. MC CAULEY, 575(SEER):JUL71-478
MC NEAL, R.H. - SEE STALIN, I.V.
MAC NEILL, D.H. THE HISTORICAL SCOTTISH
    CONSTITUTION.
    617(TLS):14JUL72-826
MC NEILLY, F.S. THE ANATOMY OF "LEVIA-
    THAN."
    H.J. JOHNSON, 185:APR70-243
MC NEIR, W.F., ED. STUDIES IN COMPARA-
    TIVE LITERATURE.
    C. DE DEUGD, 179(ES):JUN70-273
MC NEIR, W.F. & T.N. GREENFIELD, EDS.
    PACIFIC COAST STUDIES IN SHAKESPEARE.*
    H.W. DONNER, 597(SN):VOL40#1-245
MC NIECE, G. SHELLEY AND THE REVOLUTION-
    ARY IDEA.*
    K.N.C., 191(ELN):SEP70(SUPP)-45
    639(VQR):SUMMER70-XCVI
MAC NIOCAILL, G. IRELAND BEFORE THE
    VIKINGS.
    617(TLS):21JUL72-850
MC NULTY, R. - SEE ARIOSTO, L.
MACPHAIL, I., COMP. ALCHEMY AND THE
    OCCULT.
    E. HOWE, 78(BC):AUTUMN70-389
MC PHEE, J. THE CROFTER AND THE LAIRD.
    617(TLS):20OCT72-1259
MC PHEETERS, D.W. CAMILO JOSÉ CELA.
    R. KIRSNER, 238:SEP70-578
MC PHERSON, B. CHARLES DICKENS 1812-
    1870. (REV BY M.A. RONNIE)
    155:SEP70-253

203

MC PHERSON, H. A POLITICAL EDUCATION.
A. BROYARD, 441:5JUN72-35
R. DUGGER, 441:30JUL72-18
442(NY):8JUL72-75
MACPHERSON, J. THE BOATMAN AND OTHER
POEMS.
H. MAC CALLUM, 627(UTQ):JUL69-343
T. MARSHALL, 529(QQ):SUMMER70-294
MC PHERSON, T. THE ARGUMENT FROM DESIGN.
617(TLS):13OCT72-1234
MC PHERSON, T. POLITICAL OBLIGATION.
T. HONDERICH, 393(MIND):APR70-313
MACQUARRIE, J. EXISTENTIALISM.
617(TLS):9JUN72-663
MACQUARRIE, J. THE FAITH OF THE PEOPLE
OF GOD.
C.E. SIMCOX, 441:29OCT72-42
617(TLS):20OCT72-1261
MACQUARRIE, J. GOD-TALK.
G.M., 477:SUMMER69-410
MACQUARRIE, J. MARTIN HEIDEGGER.
J.D.C., 543:SEP69-134
MACQUARRIE, J. PATHS IN SPIRITUALITY.
N.K. BURGER, 441:27AUG72-22
617(TLS):29SEP72-1173
MACQUARRIE, J. STUDIES IN CHRISTIAN
EXISTENTIALISM.
S.A.S., 543:DEC69-350
MC QUEEN, H. A NEW BRITANNIA.
N. MC LACHLAN, 381:VOL29#4-547
MAC QUEEN, J., ED. BALLATIS OF LUVE.
J. KINSLEY, 402(MLR):OCT71-853
MACROBIUS. THE SATURNALIA. (P.V.
DAVIES, TRANS)
J. ANDRÉ, 555:VOL44FASC2-348
A. BENJAMIN, 124:NOV70-94
M.J. CARTON, 377:MAR71-32
J.W. HALPORN, 121(CJ):OCT-NOV70-76
MACROBIUS. AMBROSII THEODOSII MACROBII:
"SATURNALIA." AMBROSII THEODOSII
MACROBII: "COMMENTARII IN SOMNIUM
SCIPIONIS." (I. WILLIS, ED OF BOTH)
G. SERBAT, 182:VOL23#5-244
MACRORY, P. - SEE LADY SALE
MAC SHANE, F., ED. FORD MADOX FORD: THE
CRITICAL HERITAGE.
617(TLS):15SEP72-1045
MC SHANE, M. SEANCE FOR TWO.
N. CALLENDAR, 441:17DEC72-23
MC SHEA, R.J. THE POLITICAL PHILOSOPHY
OF SPINOZA.
A.G. WERNHAM, 479(PHQ):JUL70-272
MC SHERRY, J.E. STALIN, HITLER, AND
EUROPE.* (VOL 2)
G.L. WEINBERG, 32:SEP71-668
MAC SWEENEY, B. OUR MUTUAL SCARLET
BOULEVARD.
H. WILLIAMS, 364:FEB/MAR72-155
617(TLS):14JAN72-32
MARQUIS MAC SWINEY OF MASHANAGLASS. SIX
CAME FLYING.
P. ADAMS, 61:APR72-129
S.K. OBERBECK, 440:21MAY72-8
MACŮREK, J. & V. ŽÁČEK, EDS. ČEŠI A
POLÁCI V MINULOSTI.
S.Z. PECH, 497(POLR):WINTER68-100
MC VICKER, C.D. & O.N. SOTO - SEE ARCIN-
IEGAS, G.
MC WHIRTER, G. CATALAN POEMS.
T. MARSHALL, 99:MAY72-69
MC WILLIAMS, C. NORTH FROM MEXICO.
J. WOMACK, JR., 453:31AUG72-12
MADAULE, J. CLAUDEL ET LE LANGAGE.
E. BEAUMONT, 208(FS):APR71-230
MADDEN, D. CASSANDRA SINGING.*
639(VQR):SPRING70-XLIV

MADDEN, E.H. CIVIL DISOBEDIENCE AND
MORAL LAW IN NINETEENTH-CENTURY AMERI-
CAN PHILOSOPHY.
L.B. HOLLAND, 141:WINTER69-109
MADDEN, W.A. MATTHEW ARNOLD.
J-C. ROJAHN, 38:BAND87HEFT3/4-466
MADDISON, A. ECONOMIC GROWTH IN JAPAN
AND THE USSR.
M. BORNSTEIN, 32:DEC71-900
M. ELLMAN, 587:JAN70-387
MADDOX, B. BEYOND BABEL.
P. WHITEHEAD, 362:29JUN72-851
617(TLS):4AUG72-911
MADDOX, J. THE DOOMSDAY SYNDROME.
B. DE MOTT, 561(SATR):28OCT72-77
A. MANNING, 362:1JUN72-731
617(TLS):23JUN72-727
MADDOX, L.G. ADDRESSES OF LESTER GAR-
FIELD MADDOX, 1967-1971.
M. FRADY, 453:6APR72-13
MADDOX, R.J. WILLIAM E. BORAH AND AMERI-
CAN FOREIGN POLICY.
639(VQR):SUMMER70-CX
MADDUX, R., S. SILLIPHANT & N.D. ISAACS.
FICTION INTO FILM.
N. SILVERSTEIN, 295:VOL2#1-154
MADISON, C.A. YIDDISH LITERATURE.
B. MURDOCH, 402(MLR):JAN71-236
MADISON, J. THE PAPERS OF JAMES MADISON.
(VOL 7) (W.T. HUTCHINSON & W.M.E.
RACHAL, EDS)
617(TLS):18AUG72-977
MADSEN, C.K. & C.H., JR. EXPERIMENTAL
RESEARCH IN MUSIC.
E. SAMS, 415:MAY71-447
MADSEN, W.G. FROM SHADOWY TYPES TO
TRUTH.
E. MINER, 173(ECS):WINTER69-296
K. WILLIAMSON, 597(SN):VOL41#2-432
MADUELL, C.R., JR. THE ROMANCE OF
SPANISH SURNAMES.
D.P. HINKLE, 424:JUN68-189
MAEHLER, H., ED. AEGYPTISCHE URKUNDEN
AUS DEN STAATLICHEN MUSEEN, BERLIN.
J.F. OATES, 24:OCT71-725
MAENZ, P. & G. DE VRIES, EDS. ART AND
LANGUAGE/TEXTE ZUM PHÄNOMEN KUNST UND
SPRACHE.
617(TLS):11AUG72-940
MAES, V. VOCABULAIRE FRANÇAIS-NGBAKA.
A.N. TUCKER, 69:OCT69-439
MAGALANER, M. THE FICTION OF KATHERINE
MANSFIELD.
T. LASK, 441:19FEB72-33
MAGALHÃES GODINHO, V. A ESTRUTURA DA
ANTIGA SOCIEDADE PORTUGUESA.
617(TLS):21JAN72-62
MAGEE, B., ED. MODERN BRITISH PHILOSO-
PHY.*
M. COHEN, 362:27JAN72-116
MAGER, W. ZUR ENTSTEHUNG DES MODERNEN
STAATSBEGRIFFS.
G. STRAUSS, 182:VOL23#9-507
MAGIDOFF, R. & OTHERS, EDS. STUDIES IN
SLAVIC LINGUISTICS AND POETICS IN HONOR
OF BORIS O. UNBEGAUN.
A. SENN, 32:MAR71-198
MAGIS, C.H. LA LÍRICA POPULAR CONTEM-
PORÁNEA.
D. BRIESEMEISTER, 182:VOL23#9-476
MAGNAN, A. - SEE DE VOLTAIRE, F.M.A.
MAGNAN, J-M. ESSAI SUR JEAN GENET.
A. CISMARU, 399(MLJ):MAY70-364
MAGNER, J.E., JR. JOHN CROWE RANSOM.
J.H. JUSTUS, 27(AL):JAN72-669

MAGNER, T.F. THE STUDENT'S DICTIONARY OF
SERBO-CROATIAN.
Y. BURNS, 575(SEER):OCT71-611
T.J. BUTLER, 574(SEEJ):SUMMER71-245
MAGNER, T.F. A ZAGREB KAJKAVIAN DIALECT.
M. SURDUCKI, 104:WINTER71-554
DE MAGNY, O. OLIVIER DE MAGNY: LES
GAYETEZ.* (A.R. MAC KAY, ED)
C. GRISÉ, 627(UTQ):JUL69-383
M.S. WHITNEY, 546(RR):OCT70-220
MAGOULIAS, H.J. BYZANTINE CHRISTIANITY.
P. CHARANIS, 32:JUN71-378
MAGOUN, F.P., JR. A CHAUCER GAZETTEER.
K.B. HARDER, 424:MAR68-66
MAGRO, H.S. & P. DE PAULA. PORTUGUÊS.
O. FERNÁNDEZ, 399(MLJ):FEB70-128
MAH, F-H. THE FOREIGN TRADE OF MAINLAND
CHINA.
617(TLS):10NOV72-1361
MAHDI, M. - SEE AL-FĀRĀBĪ
MAHER, J.T. - SEE WILDER, A.
MAHER, R. THE BLIND BOY AND THE LOON AND
OTHER ESKIMO MYTHS.
S.J. SACKETT, 651(WHR):WINTER71-88
MAHESHWARI, S. THE ADMINISTRATIVE RE-
FORMS COMMISSION.
617(TLS):1SEP72-1033
MAHESHWARI, S. GOVERNMENT THROUGH CON-
SULTATION.
617(TLS):13OCT72-1236
MAHLER, R. A HISTORY OF MODERN JEWRY
1780-1815.
617(TLS):14JAN72-46
MAHON, D. LIVES.
P.N. FURBANK, 362:21SEP72-374
617(TLS):9JUN72-651
MAHR, J. ÜBERGANG ZUM ENDLICHEN.
A. HUYSSEN, 406:SPRING71-86
J. PURVER, 402(MLR):APR71-460
MAI, J. DAS DEUTSCHE KAPITAL IN RUSS-
LAND, 1850-1894.
J.P. MC KAY, 32:DEC71-885
W.M. STERN, 575(SEER):JUL71-473
MAIER, B. ITALO SVEVO. (2ND ED)
E. SACCONE, 400(MLN):JAN70-104
MAIER, P. FROM RESISTANCE TO REVOLUTION.
T. LASK, 441:26MAY72-35
G.S. WOOD, 441:21MAY72-6
MAIER, W. LEBEN, TAT UND REFLEXION.
J.L.S., 191(ELN):SEP70(SUPP)-103
MAILER, N. EXISTENTIAL ERRANDS.
C. BUCHANAN, 441:16APR72-27
T.R. EDWARDS, 453:15JUN72-21
T. LASK, 441:5MAY72-42
S.K. OBERBECK, 440:30APR72-5
442(NY):17JUN72-103
MAILER, N. THE LONG PATROL.* (R.F.
LUCID, ED)
T.R. EDWARDS, 453:15JUN72-21
MAILER, N. THE PRISONER OF SEX.*
H. LOMAS, 364:DEC71/JAN72-143
MAILER, N. ST. GEORGE AND THE GODFATHER.
C. LEHMANN-HAUPT, 441:16OCT72-39
G. WILLS, 441:15OCT72-1
442(NY):28OCT72-158
561(SATR):21OCT72-80
MAINA, G. - SEE HOMER
MAINUSCH, H. ROMANTISCHE ÄSTHETIK.
K. MITCHELLS, 89(BJA):WINTER71-97
MAIR, L. MARRIAGE.
617(TLS):21APR72-445
MAIRE, G. LES INSTANTS PRIVILÉGIÉS.
M. BARTHÉLEMY-MADAULE, 542:OCT-DEC68-
499
MAIRE, G. PLATON.
P. SOMVILLE, 542:APR-JUN68-287
MAJORINO, G. EQUILIBRIO IN PEZZI.
617(TLS):29SEP72-1166

MAJUMDAR, B. HEROINES OF TAGORE.
R.R. VAN METER, 293(JAST):NOV69-190
MAKA-DE SCHEPPER, M. LE THÈME DE LA
PYTHIE CHEZ PAUL VALÉRY.
C-M. CROW, 208(FS):OCT71-487
MAKKONEN, O. ANCIENT FORESTRY.* (PTS
1&2)
R. MEIGGS, 123:DEC71-446
MAKSAKOV, V.V. ISTORIIA I ORGANIZATSIIA
ARKHIVNOGO DELA V SSSR (1917-1945 GG.).
(I.F. KONONOV, ED)
P.K. GRIMSTED, 32:JUN71-407
MALAGOLI, L. L'ANTI-OTTOCENTO.
617(TLS):18AUG72-967
MALAMAT, A. PROPHECY IN THE MARI DOCU-
MENTS AND THE BIBLE.
Z. GARBER, 318(JAOS):OCT-DEC70-532
MALAMUD, B. PICTURES OF FIDELMAN.*
A.H. ROSENFELD, 328:FALL69-504
MALAMUD, B. THE TENANTS.*
G. WEALES, 249(HUDR):WINTER71/72-716
F. WYNDHAM, 362:23MAR72-390
617(TLS):24MAR72-325
MALAND, D. CULTURE AND SOCIETY IN
SEVENTEENTH-CENTURY FRANCE.*
F.K. DAWSON, 402(MLR):OCT71-897
MALANGA, G. CHIC DEATH / POEMS.
D. LEHMAN, 491:JAN72-224
MALANGA, G. 3 POEMS FOR BENEDETTA BAR-
ZINI.
J. HOPPER, 661:SPRING69-107
MALAQUAIS, J. SÖREN KIERKEGAARD.
617(TLS):4AUG72-924
MALAY, A.J. OCCUPIED PHILIPPINES.
G.E. TAYLOR, 293(JAST):NOV69-212
MALCLÈS, L-N. MANUEL DE BIBLIOGRAPHIE.
(2ND ED)
D.E. COLE, 356:JAN71-77
MALCOLM, A. A TREATISE OF MUSICK.
M. TILMOUTH, 415:MAR71-241
J.A.W., 410(M&L):APR71-207
MALCOLMSON, A., ED. WILLIAM BLAKE.
G.E. BENTLEY, JR., 627(UTQ):APR70-274
MALE, D.J. RUSSIAN PEASANT ORGANISATION
BEFORE COLLECTIVISATION.*
M. MC CAULEY, 575(SEER):OCT71-624
R.G. WESSON, 32:SEP71-668
MALEVICH, K.S. ESSAYS ON ART 1915-1933.*
(T. ANDERSEN, ED)
C. ABRAMSKY, 592:NOV68-226
MALGONKAR, M. THE DEVIL'S WIND.
V. CUNNINGHAM, 362:14SEP72-344
M. LEVIN, 441:14MAY72-37
MALHERBE, V.C. EMINENT VICTORIANS IN
SOUTH AFRICA.
617(TLS):8DEC72-1513
MALIN, I. SAUL BELLOW'S FICTION.*
E.L. RODRIGUES, 27(AL):NOV71-482
MALINA, J. THE ENORMOUS DESPAIR.
A. LAHR, 561(SATR):24JUN72-72
D. RADER, 441:22OCT72-49
MALINGREY, A-M. - SEE CHRYSOSTOM, J.
MALINS, E. SAMUEL PALMER'S ITALIAN HON-
EYMOON.
L. HERRMANN, 90:OCT69-624
M. WEBSTER, 39:NOV69-448
MALIS, J.C. THE OFFICE COOKBOOK.
N. MAGID, 440:20FEB72-8
MALKIEL, Y. ESSAYS ON LINGUISTIC
THEMES.*
K. TOGEBY, 597(SN):VOL41#1-166
M.G. WORTHINGTON, 545(RPH):AUG69-65
MALKIEL, Y. PATTERNS OF DERIVATIONAL
AFFIXATION IN THE CABRANIEGO DIALECT
OF EAST-CENTRAL ASTURIAN.*
W.H. HAVERKATE, 182:VOL23#15/16-738
MALKO, G. SCIENTOLOGY.
617(TLS):12MAY72-545

MALKOFF, K. MURIEL SPARK.
F. MC COMBIE, 447(N&Q):DEC70-475
MALLABY, G. EACH IN HIS OFFICE.
617(TLS):14APR72-418
MALLARMÉ, S. DOCUMENTS STÉPHANE MALLAR-
MÉ. (C.P. BARBIER, ED)
E. SOUFFRIN, 208(FS):APR71-226
MALLEA, E. GABRIEL ANDARAL.
617(TLS):4FEB72-117
MALLET-JORIS, F. THE WITCHES.
639(VQR):SPRING70-LXXI
MALLETT, M.E. THE FLORENTINE GALLEYS IN
THE FIFTEENTH CENTURY WITH THE DIARY OF
LUCA DI MASO DEGLI ALBIZZI, CAPTAIN OF
THE GALLEYS, 1429-1430.
F.E. DE ROOVER, 551(RENQ):SPRING70-52
MALLIN, T. DODECAHEDRON.
M. LEVIN, 441:31DEC72-18
MALLIN, T. EROWINA.
617(TLS):3NOV72-1306
DE MALLMANN, M-T. LES ENSEIGNEMENTS
ICONOGRAPHIQUES DE L'AGNI-PURĀNA.
A. BHARATI, 57:VOL31#1-92
MALLO, J. & J. RODRÍGUEZ-CASTELLANO.
ESPAÑA. (2ND ED)
E. MORO DE FERNÁNDEZ, 238:SEP70-588
MALMBERG, B., ED. MANUAL OF PHONETICS.
A. MALÉCOT, 361:VOL24#3-286
MALONE, B.C. COUNTRY MUSIC, U.S.A.
N. COHEN, 292(JAF):JUL-SEP70-366
MALONE, D. JEFFERSON THE PRESIDENT:
FIRST TERM, 1801-1805.*
R.B. MORRIS, 639(VQR):SUMMER70-496
MALONE, E. AN INQUIRY INTO THE AUTHEN-
TICITY OF CERTAIN MISCELLANEOUS PAPERS
AND LEGAL INSTRUMENTS.
617(TLS):18FEB72-178
MALONE, E. - SEE UNDER RITSON, J.
MALONE, K., ED. THE NOWELL CODEX.
G. STORMS, 179(ES):DEC69-598
MALONEY, R. THE NIXON RECESSION CAPER.
N. CALLENDAR, 441:5MAR72-34
H. FRANKEL, 561(SATR):25MAR72-104
A. HISLOP, 440:2APR72-8
C. LEHMANN-HAUPT, 441:2MAR72-41
E. WEEKS, 61:MAR72-107
MALORY, T. SIR THOMAS MALORY, "LE MORTE
D'ARTHUR." (J. COWEN, ED)
S.S. HUSSEY, 447(N&Q):AUG70-319
MALORY, T. THE WORKS OF SIR THOMAS
MALORY.* (2ND ED) (E. VINAVER, ED)
J.A.W. BENNETT, 541(RES):MAY70-192
P.J.C. FIELD, 597(SN):VOL41#1-180
MALRAUX, A. FALLEN OAKS.* (FRENCH
TITLE: LE CHÊNES QU'ON ABAT...)
S. HOFFMANN, 453:24FEB72-23
M. KEMPTON, 441:23APR72-1
442(NY):27MAY72-115
617(TLS):7APR72-395
MALRAUX, A. ORAISONS FUNÈBRES.
617(TLS):25FEB72-207
MALSON, L. WOLF CHILDREN.
L. HUDSON, 362:25MAY72-690
MAMAN, A. & OTHERS. LA FRANCE.
M.M. CELLER, 207(FR):DEC69-382
DE MAN, P. BLINDNESS AND INSIGHT.
R.M. ADAMS, 249(HUDR):WINTER71/72-687
G.H. HARTMAN, 31(ASCH):WINTER71/72-
146
"MAN AND HIS ENVIRONMENT."
617(TLS):30JUN72-754
MANACORDA, M.A. LA PAIDEIA DI ACHILLE.
617(TLS):25AUG72-992
MANDEL, D. CHANGING ART, CHANGING MAN.
E.H. DUNCAN, 290(JAAC):SPRING70-402
MANDEL, E., ED. CONTEXTS OF CANADIAN
CRITICISM.
A. LUCAS, 296:SUMMER72-93

MANDEL, E., ED. POETS OF CONTEMPORARY
CANADA: 1960-1970.
J.R. SORFLEET, 296:SPRING72-92
MANDEL, J. & B.A. ROSENBERG, EDS. MEDIE-
VAL LITERATURE AND FOLKLORE STUDIES.
R.M. WILSON, 677:VOL2-233
MANDELBAUM, D.G. SOCIETY IN INDIA.
617(TLS):22SEP72-1119
MANDELBAUM, M. PHILOSOPHY, SCIENCE AND
SENSE PERCEPTION.
A. NARVESON, 486:JUN68-198
MANDELKAU, J. HARMONY FARM.
617(TLS):7JUL72-765
MANDELL, M. BEING SAFE.
B. GLADSTONE, 441:3DEC72-98
MANDELL, R.D. THE NAZI OLYMPICS.*
E. SEGAL, 676(YR):SUMMER71-605
MANDELSTAM, N. HOPE AGAINST HOPE.*
G. IVASK, 32:SEP71-706
S. KARLINSKY, 574(SEEJ):FALL71-385
M. MALIA, 453:27JAN72-34
V. YOUNG, 249(HUDR):SUMMER71-337
MANDELSTAM [MANDELSHTAM], N. VOSPOMINAN-
IIA.
G. IVASK, 32:SEP71-706
S. KARLINSKY, 574(SEEJ):FALL71-385
MANDELSTAM [MANDEL'ŠTAM], O. SOBRANIE
SOČINENIJ V TREX TOMAX. (VOL 3) (G.P.
STRUVE & B.A. FILIPPOVA, EDS)
I. CHINNOV, 574(SEEJ):SPRING71-75
MANDER, G. GEORGE BERNARD SHAW. SHAKE-
SPEARES ZEITGENOSSEN.
K. TETZELI VON ROSADOR, 72:BAND208
HEFT1-49
DE MANDIARGUES, A.P. LE CADRAN LUNAIRE.
617(TLS):15DEC72-1537
DE MANDIARGUES, A.P. MASCARETS. BLAZE
OF EMBERS. TROISIÈME BELVÉDÈRE.
BONA: L'AMOUR ET LA PEINTURE.
617(TLS):14JAN72-44
MANDOUZE, A. SAINT AUGUSTIN.
T. VAN BAVEL, 182:VOL23#7-342
MANGA, J. HUNGARIAN FOLK SONG AND FOLK
INSTRUMENTS.
G. OLDHAM, 415:MAR70-281
MANGAT, J.S. A HISTORY OF THE ASIANS
IN EAST AFRICA C. 1886 TO 1945.
A. BHARATI, 293(JAST):MAY70-678
MANGINI, N. & V. BRANCA, EDS. STUDI
GOLDONIANI.
P. ROSSI, 546(RR):OCT70-227
MANGIONE, J. THE DREAM AND THE DEAL.
C. LEHMANN-HAUPT, 441:22SEP72-43
MANGO, A. DISCOVERING TURKEY.
617(TLS):21APR72-455
MANGO, C. MATERIALS FOR THE STUDY OF THE
MOSAICS OF ST. SOPHIA AT ISTANBUL.
C. BERTELLI, 54:SEP69-293
MANIK, L. DAS ARABISCHE TONSYSTEM IM
MITTELALTER.
H.H. TOUMA, 187:JAN72-140
MANKIEWICZ, J.L. MORE ABOUT ALL ABOUT
EVE.
J. KANON, 561(SATR):16DEC72-58
MANN, G. WALLENSTEIN.
617(TLS):14APR72-417
MANN, J. MRS. KNOX'S PROFESSION.
N. CALLENDAR, 441:17DEC72-23
617(TLS):25AUG72-1005
MANN, J.D. THE CLOTH INDUSTRY IN THE
WEST OF ENGLAND FROM 1640 TO 1880.
617(TLS):21APR72-451
MANN, O., ED. CHRISTLICHE DICHTER IM
20. JAHRHUNDERT. (2ND ED)
E. STOPP, 402(MLR):JAN71-167

MANN, T. THE LETTERS OF THOMAS MANN, 1889-1955.* (R. & C. WINSTON, EDS & TRANS)
    P. BAILEY, 364:APR/MAY71-180
MANN, T. & H. THOMAS MANN - HEINRICH MANN, BRIEFWECHSEL 1900-1949. (H. WYSLING, ED)
    H.F. GARTEN, 270:VOL20#2-36
MANN, U. THEOGONISCHE TAGE.
    F.F. BRUCE, 182:VOL23#5-210
MANN, W.E., ED. THE UNDERSIDE OF TORONTO.
    R.M. PIKE, 529(QQ):WINTER70-655
MANNACK, E. ANDREAS GRYPHIUS.
    P. SKRINE, 402(MLR):JAN71-213
MANNERS, A. POOR COUSINS.
    R. LASSON, 440:23JAN72-6
    C. LEHMANN-HAUPT, 441:10FEB72-45
    R.J. MILCH, 561(SATR):22JAN72-73
MANNES, M. OUT OF MY TIME.*
    617(TLS):7JUL72-767
MANNES, M. THEY.
    R.H. BAYES, 50(ARQ):WINTER69-373
MANNIN, E. ENGLAND MY ADVENTURE.
    617(TLS):25AUG72-1006
MANNONI, M. THE CHILD, HIS "ILLNESS" AND THE OTHERS.
    617(TLS):14APR72-425
MANO, D.K. BISHOP'S PROGRESS.
    502(PRS):WINTER68/69-365
MANO, D.K. THE DEATH AND LIFE OF HARRY GOTH.*
    W.H. PRITCHARD, 249(HUDR):SUMMER71-357
MANO, D.K. THE PROSELYTIZER.
    B.H. LEEDS, 561(SATR):15JUL72-58
    G. WOLFF, 441:23APR72-4
    442(NY):8APR72-130
MANOLIKAKI, I.G. - SEE VENIZELOS, E.
MANOOGIAN, H.P. THE FILM-MAKER'S ART.
    M.J. MC KEE, 397(MD):SEP67-219
MANOS, C. A GREEK PORTFOLIO.
    617(TLS):29DEC72-1589
MANSER, A. SARTRE.*
    D.R. BELL, 479(PHQ):JUL70-277
MANSERGH, N., WITH E.W.R. LUMBY, EDS. CONSTITUTIONAL RELATIONS BETWEEN BRITAIN AND INDIA; THE TRANSFER OF POWER 1942-47.* (VOL 1)
    G. NIEDHART, 182:VOL23#15/16-764
MANSERGH, N., WITH E.W.R. LUMBY, EDS. CONSTITUTIONAL RELATIONS BETWEEN BRITAIN AND INDIA; THE TRANSFER OF POWER 1942-7. (VOL 3)
    617(TLS):31MAR72-351
MANSFIELD, P. THE BRITISH IN EGYPT.*
    T. LASK, 441:17JUN72-27
    617(TLS):21JAN72-56
MANSUY, M. GASTON BACHELARD ET LES ÉLÉMENTS.
    J. BELLEMIN-NOEL, 98:NOV69-937
MANTE, A., ED. PARIS UND VIENNA.
    G. KORLÉN, 597(SN):VOL40#2-467
MANTE, H. COLOR DESIGN IN PHOTOGRAPHY.
    617(TLS):22DEC72-1566
VON MANTEUFFEL, C.Z. DIE BILDHAUERFAMILIE ZÜRN 1606-1666.
    M. BAXANDALL, 90:NOV70-764
MANUEL, F.E. FREEDOM FROM HISTORY.
    617(TLS):24NOV72-1437
MANUEL, F.E. SHAPES OF PHILOSOPHICAL HISTORY.
    F. DE MICHELIS, 548(RCSF):JAN-MAR68-101
MANUPPELLA, G., ED. ESTÊVÃO RODRIGUES DE CASTRO.
    E. GLASER, 240(HR):JAN70-115

"MANUSCRIPTS AND MEN."
    R.C. JARVIS, 325:OCT70-160
MANUUD, A.G., ED. BROWN HERITAGE.
    J.V. LANDY, 613:SPRING69-127
MANVELL, R. ELLEN TERRY.
    A.S. DOWNER, 572:JAN69-30
    F. GLENDENNING, 571:WINTER68/69-29
MANYPENNY, G.W. OUR INDIAN WARDS.
    M. ROGIN, 441:24DEC72-4
MANZI, P. ANNALI DELLA STAMPERIA STIGLIOLA A PORTA REALE IN NAPOLI (1593-1606).
    D.E. RHODES, 354:DEC69-349
MAO TSE-TUNG. THE POEMS OF MAO TSE-TUNG. (W. BARNSTONE, ED & TRANS)
    D. LATTIMORE, 441:13AUG72-7
    J.D. O'HARA, 440:7MAY72-7
MARABOTTINI, A. POLIDORO DA CARAVAGGIO.
    E. LANGMUIR, 90:JUL70-471
MARACHE, R. - SEE GELLIUS
MARAINI, D. MEMORIE DI UNA LADRA.
    617(TLS):1SEP72-1013
MARAINI, F. JAPAN.
    617(TLS):22DEC72-1561
MARAIS, E. THE SOUL OF THE APE.
    639(VQR):SPRING70-LXXI
MARAIS, G. KWAME NKRUMAH AS I KNEW HIM.
    617(TLS):15SEP72-1046
MARAMBAUD, P. WILLIAM BYRD OF WESTOVER, 1674-1744.
    G. CORE, 578:SPRING72-117
    R.B. DAVIS, 27(AL):JAN72-655
    L.P. SIMPSON, 165:FALL72-187
MARANA, G.P. LETTERS WRIT BY A TURKISH SPY. (A.J. WEITZMAN, ED)
    R.A. DAY, 568(SCN):SPRING71-7
    P.J. KORSHIN, 566:SPRING71-73
MARANDA, P., ED. MYTHOLOGY.
    617(TLS):21JUL72-848
MARCH, M.E. FORMA E IDEA DE LOS ESPERPENTOS DE VALLE-INCLÁN.
    J.L. BROOKS, 86(BHS):JUL71-278
MARC'HADOUR, G. THE BIBLE IN THE WORKS OF ST. THOMAS MORE. (PT 1) THOMAS MORE ET LA BIBLE.
    W. ALLEN, 551(RENQ):WINTER70-468
MARCHAND, H. THE CATEGORIES AND TYPES OF PRESENT-DAY ENGLISH WORD-FORMATION. (2ND ED)
    D.T. LANGENDOEN, 350:SEP71-708
MARCHENKO, A. MOI POKAZANIIA.
    B.R. BOCIURKIW, 550(RUSR):JUL70-328
MARCILLET-JAUBERT, J. LES INSCRIPTIONS D'ALTAVA.
    J.C. MANN, 313:VOL60-234
MARCKWARDT, A.H. LINGUISTICS AND THE TEACHING OF ENGLISH.
    W.S. CHISHOLM, 353:MAY69-111
MARCO, J. POESÍA POPULAR POLÍTICA DEL SEGLE XIX.
    191(ELN):SEP70(SUPP)-150
MARCOS, M.B. - SEE UNDER BERMEJO MARCOS, M.
MARCOTTE, G. LE TEMPS DES POÈTES.
    J-L. MAJOR, 627(UTQ):JUL70-422
MARCOVICH, M. HERACLITUS.
    G.B. KERFERD, 123:DEC70-305
MARCU, E. RÉPERTOIRE DES IDÉES DE MONTAIGNE.
    E. SPANG-HANSSEN, 462(OL):VOL23#4-328
MARCUS, D., ED. TEARS OF THE SHAMROCK.
    617(TLS):1SEP72-1013
MARCUS, G.J. THE AGE OF NELSON.*
    441:5MAR72-10
MARCUS, R.D. GRAND OLD PARTY.*
    617(TLS):14APR72-410

MARCUSE, H. COUNTERREVOLUTION AND RE-
VOLT.
B.M. BERGER, 441:9JUL72-3
S. DE GRAMONT, 561(SATR):3JUN72-58
617(TLS):1DEC72-1450
MARCUSE, H. AN ESSAY ON LIBERATION.
S.O.H., 543:MAR70-561
MARCUSE, H. FIVE LECTURES.*
E. VIVAS, 396(MODA):WINTER71-80
MARCUSE, H. NEGATIONS.
R.J.B., 543:JUN70-745
MARCUSE, H. STUDIES IN CRITICAL PHILOSO-
PHY.
617(TLS):25AUG72-998
MARDER, A. WINSTON IS BACK.
617(TLS):20OCT72-1246
MARDER, H. FEMINISM AND ART.
B. HARDY, 541(RES):AUG70-377
G. THOMAS, 175:SPRING69-31
DE LA MARE, A., COMP. CATALOGUE OF THE
COLLECTION OF MEDIEVAL MANUSCRIPTS
BEQUEATHED TO THE BODLEIAN LIBRARY,
OXFORD, BY JAMES P.R. LYELL.
617(TLS):3NOV72-1348
DE MARÉ, P.B. PERSPECTIVES IN GROUP
PSYCHOTHERAPY.
617(TLS):2JUN72-621
DE LA MARE, W. THE COMPLETE POEMS OF
WALTER DE LA MARE.
J. HEADLAM, 493:SPRING70-91
MARÉCHAL, J. A MARÉCHAL READER. (J.
DONCEEL, ED & TRANS)
G.A. MC COOL, 613:AUTUMN69-465
MAREK, F. PHILOSOPHY OF WORLD REVOLU-
TION.
H.B., 543:MAR70-561
MARES, F.H. - SEE CAREY, R.
MARETT, R. MEXICO.
617(TLS):21JAN72-62
MARETZEK, M. REVELATIONS OF AN OPERA
MANAGER IN 19TH-CENTURY AMERICA.*
K. SPENCE, 415:MAY71-448
MARGARITO, M.C. - SEE UNDER CAPEL MAR-
GARITO, M.
MARGESON, J.M.R. THE ORIGINS OF ENGLISH
TRAGEDY.
N.W. BAWCUTT, 447(N&Q):JUN70-229
P. EDWARDS, 541(RES):FEB70-109
MARGETSON, S. REGENCY LONDON.
T. LASK, 441:16JUN72-39
617(TLS):7JAN72-22
MARGOLIES, D. THE FUNCTION OF LITERA-
TURE.
R. FULLER, 362:6JAN72-21
MARGOLIES, E. NATIVE SONS.
R. WELBURN, 50(ARQ):SUMMER69-182
MARGOLIN, J.C. RECHERCHES ÉRASMIENNES.
A. HYMA, 551(RENQ):SPRING70-57
MARGOLIOUTH, H.M. - SEE MARVELL, A.
MARGOLIS, J., ED. FACT AND EXISTENCE.
R.H.K., 543:JUN70-751
L. STEVENSON, 479(PHQ):JUL70-285
MARGOLIS, J. & M. GUITTON, EDS. PUBLIC
ECONOMICS.*
617(TLS):2JUN72-637
MARGOLIS, J.D. T.S. ELIOT'S INTELLECTUAL
DEVELOPMENT.
F. KERMODE, 441:26MAR72-6
MARGUERON, C. RECHERCHES SUR GUITTONE
D'AREZZO, SA VIE, SON ÉPOQUE, SA CUL-
TURE.
F.B. AGENO, 545(RPH):MAY71-644
MARGULIES, S.R. THE PILGRIMAGE TO
RUSSIA.
R.P. BROWDER, 550(RUSR):JUL70-356
J. MILLER, 587:JAN69-400
MARIA, LADY CALLCOTT - SEE UNDER LADY
CALLCOTT

MARIACHER, G. PALMA IL VECCHIO.
C. GOULD, 90:MAR70-183
MARÍAS, J. MIGUEL DE UNAMUNO.*
M.J. VALDES, 627(UTQ):JAN69-207
MARICA, G.E. & OTHERS. IDEOLOGIA GENER-
AŢIEI ROMÂNE DE LA 1848 DIN TRANSIL-
VANIA.
K. HITCHINS, 32:MAR71-185
DE MARICHAL, S.S. - SEE UNDER SALINAS DE
MARICHAL, S.
MARIJNISSEN, R-H. DÉGRADATION, CONSERVA-
TION ET RESTAURATION DE L'OEUVRE D'ART.
S.R. JONES, 90:AUG69-525
MARIN, L. - SEE PASCAL, B.
MARINE, G. & J. VAN ALLEN. FOOD POLLU-
TION.
441:13FEB72-16
MARINETTI, F.T. MARINETTI: SELECTED
WRITINGS. (R.W. FLINT, ED)
M. KIRBY, 441:26NOV72-6
H. KRAMER, 441:16NOV72-49
617(TLS):29DEC72-1578
MARINI, L. IL MEZZOGIORNO D'ITALIA DI
FRONTE A VIENNA E A ROMA E ALTRI STUDI
DI STORIA MERIDIONALE.
H. BENEDIKT, 182:VOL23#17/18-827
MARININ, S.B. S.SH.A.: POLITIKA I UPRAV-
LENIE (FEDERAL'NYI PRAVITEL'STVENNYI
APPARAT).
K.W. RYAVEC, 32:JUN71-366
MARINKOVIĆ, R. SRPSKA ALEKSANDRIDA.
W.F. RYAN, 575(SEER):JUL71-461
MARINO, G. ADONIS. (H.M. PRIEST, TRANS)
J.V. MIROLLO, 546(RR):APR70-137
MARIÑO, M.B. - SEE UNDER BREY MARIÑO, M.
MARION, F. OFF WITH THEIR HEADS!
C. HIGHAM, 441:24SEP72-6
MARIOTTI, I. ARISTONE D'ALESSANDRIA.
F.D. CAIZZI, 548(RCSF):JAN/MAR69-105
MARISSEL, A. CHOIX DE POÈMES (1957-
1968).
C. FRANCOIS, 207(FR):FEB70-529
MARISSEL, A. POÈTES VIVANTS.
C. FRANÇOIS, 207(FR):FEB70-509
MARIUS, R. THE COMING OF RAIN.
639(VQR):WINTER70-VIII
DE MARIVAUX, P.C.D. JOURNAUX ET OEUVRES
DIVERSES. (F. DELOFFRE & M. GILOT,
EDS)
H.T. MASON, 208(FS):APR71-202
DE MARIVAUX, P.C.D. THÉÂTRE COMPLET.
(F. DELOFFRE, ED)
F.J. CARMODY, 207(FR):OCT69-186
H.T. MASON, 208(FS):JAN71-82
MARK, T. - SEE VERCORS
MARKEL, L., ED. THE NEW YORK TIMES/RAND
MC NALLY WORLD IN REVIEW.
441:6AUG72-20
MARKEL, L. WHAT YOU DON'T KNOW CAN HURT
YOU.
B.H. BAGDIKIAN, 441:11JUN72-2
MARKELS, J. THE PILLAR OF THE WORLD.*
J.B. ARNOLD, 141:WINTER70-73
MARKER, F.J. HANS CHRISTIAN ANDERSEN AND
THE ROMANTIC THEATRE.
617(TLS):11AUG72-946
MARKFIELD, W. TEITLEBAUM'S WINDOW.
M. MIRSKY, 473(PR):WINTER71/72-480
M. MUDRICK, 249(HUDR):SPRING71-185
MARKMAN, S.D. COLONIAL ARCHITECTURE OF
ANTIGUA GUATEMALA.
J. LUJÁN MUÑOZ, 576:MAR68-88
MARKOOSIE. HARPOON OF THE HUNTER.*
A.R. BEVAN, 150(DR):WINTER70/71-556
MARKS, C. FROM THE SKETCHBOOKS OF THE
GREAT ARTISTS.
T. LASK, 441:8SEP72-36

MARKS, C.L. & G.R. GUFFEY - SEE TRAHERNE, T.

MARKS, F.R., WITH K. LESWING & B.A. FORTINSKY. THE LAWYER, THE PUBLIC, AND PROFESSIONAL RESPONSIBILITY.
   J.R. WALTZ, 440:21MAY72-9

MARKS, J. RELATIVITY.
   617(TLS):9JUN72-667

MARKS, L.J. THEMATIC DESIGN IN THE NOVELS OF JOHN STEINBECK.*
   C.W.E. BIGSBY, 677:VOL2-335

MARKS, P. COLLECTOR'S CHOICE.
   N. CALLENDAR, 441:23APR72-43
   617(TLS):8DEC72-1507

MARKS, R.W. THE MEANING OF MARCUSE.
   E. VIVAS, 396(MODA):WINTER71-80

MARKSON, D. GOING DOWN.
   639(VQR):SUMMER70-LXXXVIII

MARLATT, D. FRAMES.
   H. MAC CALLUM, 627(UTQ):JUL69-351
   T. MARSHALL, 529(QQ):SUMMER70-294

MARLOW, J. THE TOLPUDDLE MARTYRS.
   S. RAVEN, 362:9MAR72-316
   617(TLS):14APR72-416

MARLOW, L. WELSH AMBASSADORS.
   617(TLS):24MAR72-328

MARLOWE, C. DIDO QUEEN OF CARTHAGE [AND] THE MASSACRE AT PARIS.* (H.J. OLIVER, ED)
   D. MEHL, 72:BAND208HEFT1-52

MARLOWE, C. CHRISTOPHER MARLOWE: THE JEW OF MALTA 1633.
   C.J. SUMMERS, 568(SCN):SUMMER/AUTUMN 71-46

MARLOWE, C. THE POEMS OF CHRISTOPHER MARLOWE. (M. MACLURE, ED)
   R. GILL, 541(RES):AUG70-346

MARLOWE, D. DO YOU REMEMBER ENGLAND?
   O.L. BAILEY, 561(SATR):5AUG72-56
   A. BROYARD, 441:29JUN72-41
   M. LEVIN, 441:11JUN72-34
   E.S. TURNER, 362:22JUN72-840
   442(NY):15JUL72-81

MARLOWE, J. THE GOLDEN AGE OF ALEXANDRIA.
   617(TLS):30JUN72-757

MARLOWE, J. PERFIDIOUS ALBION.
   617(TLS):26MAY72-610

MARMIER, X. XAVIER MARMIER: JOURNAL (1848-1890). (E. KAYE, ED)
   A.G. ENGSTROM, 207(FR):FEB70-515
   A. MONCHOUX, 546(RR):APR70-155

MARMONTEL, J-F. MÉMOIRES. (J. RENWICK, ED)
   617(TLS):1SEP72-1011

MAROIS, R. THE TELEPHONE POLE.
   G. ROPER, 627(UTQ):JUL70-339

MAROLD, K. - SEE GOTTFRIED VON STRASSBURG

MAROT, C. LES ÉPIGRAMMES. (C.A. MAYER, ED)
   H.W. LAWTON, 208(FS):APR71-190

MARPLES, M. WICKED UNCLES IN LOVE.
   617(TLS):24NOV72-1441

MARQUARD, L. A FEDERATION OF SOUTHERN AFRICA.
   617(TLS):28JAN72-90

MARQUARDT, H. HENRY CRABB ROBINSON UND SEINE DEUTSCHEN FREUNDE. (VOL 1)
   I.C., 191(ELN):SEP69(SUPP)-39
   W.D. ROBSON-SCOTT, 179(ES):OCT70-459

MARQUARDT, H. HENRY CRABB ROBINSON UND SEINE DEUTSCHEN FREUNDE.* (VOL 2)
   I.C., 191(ELN):SEP69(SUPP)-39

MARQUE, J.N. LÉON DAUDET.
   617(TLS):25AUG72-991

MÁRQUEZ, G.G. - SEE UNDER GARCÍA MÁRQUEZ, G.

MARR, D.G. VIETNAMESE ANTICOLONIALISM 1885-1925.
   F. FITZ GERALD, 453:19OCT72-21

MARRIAN, F.J.M. SHAKESPEARE AT GRAY'S INN.
   L.F. BALL, 570(SQ):AUTUMN69-477

MARRIC, J.J. GIDEON'S ART.*
   H. FRANKEL, 561(SATR):29JAN72-73

MARRIOTT, A. & C.K. RACHLIN. PEYOTE.*
   W. GARD, 584(SWR):SUMMER71-V

MARRS, E.W., JR. - SEE CARLYLE, T.

MARRUS, M.R. THE POLITICS OF ASSIMILATION.
   617(TLS):28APR72-498

MARS, A. BRITISH SUBMARINES AT WAR: 1939-1945.
   617(TLS):9JUN72-667

MARS, F.L. ANGE GOUDAR, CET INCONNU (1708-1791).
   B. GUY, 207(FR):DEC69-353

MARSDEN, E.W. GREEK AND ROMAN ARTILLERY.
   R.W. DAVIES, 313:VOL60-225
   A.M. SNODGRASS, 123:MAR71-106
   F.E. WINTER, 487:AUTUMN70-268

MARSDEN, K. THE POEMS OF THOMAS HARDY.
   J.O. BAILEY, 191(ELN):MAR70-230

MARSELLA, E.M. THE QUEST FOR EDEN.
   F. ZEMAN, 318(JAOS):APR-JUN70-318

MARSH, A.I., E.O. EVANS & P. GARCIA. WORKPLACE INDUSTRIAL RELATIONS IN ENGINEERING.
   617(TLS):14APR72-429

MARSH, J.J. THE PEKING SWITCH.
   N. CALLENDAR, 441:19NOV72-61

MARSH, N. TIED UP IN TINSEL.
   N. CALLENDAR, 441:25JUN72-30
   T. LASK, 441:22JUL72-25
   442(NY):27MAY72-116
   617(TLS):28APR72-500

MARSHACK, A. THE ROOTS OF CIVILIZATION.
   442(NY):1JUL72-74

MARSHAK, S. AT LIFE'S BEGINNING.
   L. BERNHARDT, 550(RUSR):APR70-235

MARSHALL, D. THE LIFE AND TIMES OF VICTORIA.
   M. DRABBLE, 362:26OCT72-546
   617(TLS):24NOV72-1433

MARSHALL, J. THE LANCASHIRE AND YORKSHIRE RAILWAY. (VOL 3)
   617(TLS):7APR72-402

MARSHALL, J.D. OLD LAKELAND.
   617(TLS):3MAR72-245

MARSHALL, J.F. - SEE MADAME DE STAËL & P-S. DU PONT DE NEMOURS

MARSHALL, J.H., ED. THE "RAZOS DE TROBAR" OF RAIMON VIDAL AND ASSOCIATED TEXTS.
   617(TLS):28JUL72-884

MARSHALL, J.H. - SEE FAIDIT, U.

MARSHALL, P.J., ED. THE BRITISH DISCOVERY OF HINDUISM IN THE EIGHTEENTH CENTURY.
   566:SPRING71-73

MARSHALL, P.J. & J.A. WOODS - SEE BURKE, E.

MARSHALL, P.K. - SEE GELLIUS

MARSHALL, S. FENLAND CHRONICLE.
   T.B. UNTHANK, 582(SFQ):DEC69-373

MARSHALL, T., ED. A.M. KLEIN.
   D.O. SPETTIGUE, 529(QQ):WINTER70-638

MARSHALL, T. MAGIC WATER.
   M. DAGG, 198:SPRING72-112
   D. HELWIG, 99:JAN-FEB72-82

MARSHALL, T. THE PSYCHIC MARINER.*
   P. THOMAS, 651(WHR):SPRING71-181
   G. WOODCOCK, 102(CANL):SUMMER71-67

MARSHALL, T. THE SILENCES OF FIRE.
  D. BARBOUR, 150(DR):SPRING70-112
  M. HORNYANSKY, 627(UTQ):JUL70-336
  D. LEE, 606(TAMR):#54-81
MARSHALL, W.H. THE WORLD OF THE VICTOR-
IAN NOVEL.
  B. HARDY, 155:JAN69-44
  B.R.M., 477:SPRING69-300
  R.W. RADER, 445(NCF):DEC68-347
MARSHALL-CORNWALL, J. FOCH AS MILITARY
COMMANDER.
  617(TLS):13OCT72-1236
MARSOLAIS, G. LA CARAVELLE INCENDIÉE.
  J-L. MAJOR, 627(UTQ):JUL69-480
MARTEL, B. LA PSYCHOLOGIE DE GONSALVE
D'ESPAGNE.*
  L. SWEENEY, 589:JAN71-166
MARTEL, S. SURRÉAL 3000. (H.C. STEELE,
ED)
  L.D. NEWMAN, 207(FR):DEC69-379
MARTENS, W. DIE BOTSCHAFT DER TUGEND.*
  P.U. HOHENDAHL, 221(GQ):MAR70-276
  G. MÜLLER, 597(SN):VOL41#2-418
MARTENS, W., ED. DER PATRIOT.
  W.H. BRUFORD, 402(MLR):APR71-449
MARTI, K. REPUBLIKANISCHE GEDICHTE.
  617(TLS):7JAN72-6
MARTÍ-IBÁÑEZ, F. THE MIRROR OF SOULS
AND OTHER ESSAYS.
  442(NY):30DEC72-72
MARTIAL. EPIGRAMS FROM MARTIAL.* (B.
MILLS, TRANS)
  G. ROBERTS, 121(CJ):FEB-MAR71-266
MARTIAL D'AUVERGNE. MATINES DE LA
VIERGE. (Y. LE HIR, ED)
  K. CHESNEY, 382(MAE):1971/3-285
MARTIN, B. DEUTSCHLAND UND JAPAN IM 2.
WELTKRIEG.
  F.W. IKLÉ, 293(JAST):AUG70-943
MARTIN, B. - SEE SHESTOV, L.
MARTIN, F.D. ART AND THE RELIGIOUS EX-
PERIENCE.
  617(TLS):1SEP72-1033
MARTIN, G. CAUSES AND CONFLICTS.
  639(VQR):AUTUMN70-CL
MARTIN, G. ROMA SANCTA. (G.B. PARKS,
ED)
  G. ANSTRUTHER, 677:VOL2-250
MARTIN, G.D., ED. ANTHOLOGY OF CONTEM-
PORARY FRENCH POETRY.
  617(TLS):31MAR72-360
MARTIN, H-J. LIVRE, POUVOIRS ET SOCIÉTÉ
À PARIS AU XVIIe SIÈCLE (1598-1701).
  78(BC):AUTUMN70-303
MARTIN, J. AMERICA DANCING.
  J. DE LABAN, 290(JAAC):FALL69-112
MARTIN, J., ED. A COLLECTION OF CRITICAL
ESSAYS ON "THE WASTE LAND."
  D. HOLBROOK, 619(TC):1968/2-56
MARTIN, J. HARVESTS OF CHANGE.
  R. NARVESON, 502(PRS):SPRING69-135
MARTIN, J. THE NAME ON THE WHITE HOUSE
FLOOR.
  441:8OCT72-38
MARTIN, J. NATHANAEL WEST.*
  C. BEDIENT, 473(PR):1971/3-345
  F. GADO, 27(AL):MAY71-298
MARTIN, J.R. CORPUS RUBENIANUM LUDWIG
BURCHARD. (VOL 1)
  G. MARTIN, 90:AUG70-543
MARTIN, K. EDITOR.
  H. COLLINS, 571:WINTER68/69-25
MARTIN, L. & L. MARCH, EDS. URBAN SPACE
AND STRUCTURES.
  617(TLS):1DEC72-1469
MARTIN, M. THREE POPES AND THE CARDINAL.
  W. ARNOLD, 561(SATR):8APR72-57
  F. SWEENEY, 441:2APR72-5

MARTIN, M.W. FUTURIST ART AND THEORY.
  J. GOLDING, 90:JUN69-386
  V. SPATE, 592:NOV68-222
MARTIN, M.W. WAS SHAKESPEARE SHAKE-
SPEARE?
  W.T. HASTINGS, 570(SQ):SPRING68-185
MARTIN, P. SHAKESPEARE'S SONNETS.
  617(TLS):24NOV72-1420
MARTIN, R.G. JENNIE.* [BRITISH TITLE:
LADY RANDOLPH CHURCHILL.] (VOL 2: THE
DRAMATIC YEARS, 1895-1921.)
  C. HAZLEHURST, 440:2JAN72-9
  V.G. KIERNAN, 362:7DEC72-803
MARTIN, R.L., ED. THE PARADOX OF THE
LIAR.
  J. HIGGINBOTHAM, 311(JP):13JUL72-398
MARTIN, S.E., Y.H. LEE & S-U. CHANG. A
KOREAN-ENGLISH DICTIONARY.
  J.C. JAMIESON, 318(JAOS):APR-JUN70-
  395
MARTIN, S.E. & Y-S.C. LEE. BEGINNING
KOREAN.
  S.C. SONG, 399(MLJ):DEC70-611
  E.S. YU, 293(JAST):AUG70-945
MARTIN, W.K. SKETCHES FOR THE FLORA.
  617(TLS):17MAR72-317
MARTINA, A., ED. SOLON, TESTIMONIA
VETERUM.
  A.E. RAUBITSCHEK, 124:JAN71-158
MARTINELLI, L. - SEE LUCINI, G.P.
MARTINENGO, A. QUEVEDO E IL SIMBOLO
ALCHIMISTICO.
  J.O. CROSBY, 240(HR):JUL70-330
  G. SOBEJANO, 546(RR):APR70-128
MARTINET, A. LE FRANÇAIS SANS FARD.
  P. RICKARD, 208(FS):JUL71-371
MARTINET, A., ED. LE LANGAGE.
  N.C.W. SPENCE, 208(FS):JUL71-376
MARTÍNEZ, F.F. - SEE UNDER FERNÁNDEZ MAR-
TÍNEZ, F.
MARTÍNEZ ALBIACH, A. RELIGIOSIDAD HIS-
PAÑA Y SOCIEDAD BORBÓNICA.
  191(ELN):SEP70(SUPP)-150
MARTÍNEZ RUIZ, J. LA VOLUNTAD. (E.I.
FOX, ED)
  J. DÍAZ, 241:JAN71-75
MARTINI, M. DOMITIUS PALLADIUS SORANUS
POETA (CONTRIBUTO ALLA STORIA DELL'
UMANESIMO).
  G. TOURNOY-THOEN, 568(SCN):WINTER71-
  84
MARTINO, A. STORIA DELLE TEORIE DRAM-
MATISCHE NELLA GERMANIA DEL SETTECENTO
(1730-1780). (VOL 1)
  H. DIECKMANN, 221(GQ):MAY70-510
  A. SUBIOTTO, 220(GL&L):JUL71-389
DE MARTINO, F. STORIA DELLA COSTITUZ-
IONE ROMANA. (VOL 5)
  M.A.R. COLLEDGE, 123:JUN71-253
MARTINS, E. STUDIEN ZUR FRAGE DER LIN-
GUISTISCHEN INTERFERENZ.
  M.D. BIRNBAUM, 574(SEEJ):SUMMER71-251
MARTON, E. THE FORBIDDEN SKY.
  S·S· ROSENFELD, 561(SATR):1JAN72-27
MARTY, F. ACTIVE FRENCH SERIES.
  J. GREENLEE, 207(FR):OCT69-148
MARTY, M.E. PROTESTANTISM.
  E.B. FISKE, 441:8DEC72-47
MARTZ, L.L. THE WIT OF LOVE.*
  J. FORD, 191(ELN):MAR71-221
  H. TOLIVER, 401(MLQ):SEP70-380
MARTZ, L.L. & R.S. SYLVESTER - SEE
"THOMAS MORE'S PRAYER BOOK"
MARVELL, A. ANDREW MARVELL: THE COMPLETE
POEMS. (E.S. DONNO, ED)
  617(TLS):15DEC72-1524

MARVELL, A. ANDREW MARVELL: COMPLETE
  POETRY. (G.D. LORD, ED)
    M. WILDING, 402(MLR):JUL71-664
MARVELL, A. THE POEMS AND LETTERS OF
  ANDREW MARVELL. (H.M. MARGOLIOUTH, ED;
  3RD ED REV BY P. LEGOUIS, WITH E.E.
  DUNCAN-JONES)
    617(TLS):7JUL72-769
MARX, A. SON OF GROUCHO.
  D. ADLER, 441:24DEC72-12
MARX, K. CRITIQUE OF HEGEL'S "PHILOSOPHY
  OF RIGHT."* (J. O'MALLEY, ED)
    G.H.R. PARKINSON, 518:OCT71-20
    W. SUCHTING, 63:MAY71-122
MARX, K. EARLY TEXTS.* (D. MC LELLAN,
  ED & TRANS)
    W. SUCHTING, 63:MAY71-122
MARX, K. ON REVOLUTION. (S.K. PADOVER,
  ED & TRANS)
    S.M. LIPSET, 561(SATR):3JUN72-53
MARX, K. THEORIES OF SURPLUS VALUE.
  (PT 3)
    617(TLS):10MAR72-285
MARX, K. & F. ENGELS. THE COLOGNE COM-
  MUNIST TRIAL. (R. LIVINGSTONE, ED &
  TRANS)
    617(TLS):11FEB72-151
MARX, K. & J. THE UNKNOWN KARL MARX.
  (R. PAYNE, ED)
    617(TLS):19MAY72-578
MARX, O. STEFAN GEORGE IN SEINEN ÜBER-
  TRAGUNGEN ENGLISCHER DICHTUNG.
    F.G. CRONHEIM, 402(MLR):OCT71-956
MARX, W. HEIDEGGER UND DIE TRADITION.
  J. GRANIER, 542:JAN-MAR69-109
MARX-WEBER, M. KATALOG DER MUSIKHAND-
  SCHRIFTEN IM BESITZ DES MUSIKWISSEN-
  SCHAFTLICHEN SEMINARS DER RHEINISCHEN
  FRIEDRICH-WILHELMS-UNIVERSITÄT ZU BONN.
    J.A.W., 410(M&L):OCT71-443
MASARYK, T.G. MASARYK ON MARX. (E.V.
  KOHÁK, ED & TRANS)
    617(TLS):1DEC72-1450
MASARYK, T.G. THE SPIRIT OF RUSSIA.
  (VOL 3) (G. GIBIAN, WITH R. BASS, EDS)
    R.T. MC NALLY, 32:MAR71-201
    J. RABINOWITCH, 587:JUL69-110
MASARYK, T.G. SUICIDE AND THE MEANING
  OF CIVILIZATION.
    L.J. SHEIN, 104:FALL71-444
MASCALL, E.L. WOMEN PRIESTS?
    617(TLS):17NOV72-1399
MASCARENHAS, A. THE RAPE OF BANGLA DESH.
    617(TLS):28JAN72-90
MASEFIELD, G.B. A HISTORY OF THE COL-
  ONIAL AGRICULTURAL SERVICE.
    617(TLS):1DEC72-1469
MASEFIELD, J. IN GLAD THANKSGIVING.
    J.W.R., 502(PRS):SUMMER68-185
MA'SHAR, A. - SEE UNDER ABŪ MA'SHAR
MASHKOVA, M.V. ISTORIIA RUSSKOI BIBLIO-
  GRAFII NACHALA XX VEKA (DO OKTIABRIA
  1917 GODA).
    J.S.G. SIMMONS, 32:MAR71-144
MASINI, L.V. BRAQUE. GAUDÍ.
    617(TLS):7JAN72-18
MASLOW, A.H. THE FARTHER REACHES OF
  HUMAN NATURE.*
    J.C. OATES, 561(SATR):26AUG72-53
MASON, E.C. GOETHE'S "FAUST."*
    A.P. FOULKES, 131(CL):WINTER71-86
    S. STEFFENSEN, 462(OL):VOL25#3-275
MASON, H.T. PIERRE BAYLE AND VOLTAIRE.
    E.R. LABROUSSE, 542:JUL-DEC69-490
MASON, M. 71 HOURS.
    N. CALLENDAR, 441:9APR72-41
MASON, P. THE FEMALE PLEASURE HUNT.
    R. JAFFE, 441:13AUG72-5

MASON, P., ED. INDIA AND CEYLON.
    M. DEMBO, 318(JAOS):OCT-DEC70-601
MASON, P. PATTERNS OF DOMINANCE.
    639(VQR):SUMMER70-CXII
MASON, R.H.P. JAPAN'S FIRST GENERAL
  ELECTION.
    R. SMETHURST, 293(JAST):NOV69-172
MASSA, J-M. LA JEUNESSE DE MACHADO DE
  ASSIS (1839-1870).
    H.M., 191(ELN):SEP70(SUPP)-146
MASSER, A. BIBEL, APOKRYPHEN UND LEGEN-
  DEN.*
    B. MURDOCH, 402(MLR):OCT71-920
    W. VEIT, 67:NOV71-251
MASSEY, H., ED. THE CANADIAN MILITARY.
    J.L. GRANATSTEIN, 99:SEP72-16
MASSEY, I. - SEE SHELLEY, P.B.
MASSEY, L.R., COMP. WILLIAM FAULKNER:
  "MAN WORKING," 1919-1962.*
    T.L. MC HANEY, 219(GAR):FALL69-416
MASSINGHAM, H. FROST-GODS.*
    J. SYMONS, 364:DEC71/JAN72-128
MASSON, É. RECHERCHES SUR LES PLUS
  ANCIENS EMPRUNTS SÉMITIQUES EN GREC.
    F. ROSENTHAL, 318(JAOS):APR-JUN70-338
MASSON, V.M. & V.I. SARIANIDI. CENTRAL
  ASIA. (R. TRINGHAM, ED & TRANS)
    617(TLS):28JUL72-887
MASSU, J. LA VRAIE BATAILLE D'ALGER.
    617(TLS):28APR72-464
MASTERMAN, J.C. THE DOUBLE-CROSS SYSTEM
  IN THE WAR OF 1939 TO 1945.
    L.B. KIRKPATRICK, JR., 561(SATR):
    19FEB72-68
    T. LASK, 441:11FEB72-38
    R. LEWIN, 362:17FEB72-219
    M. MUGGERIDGE, 440:13FEB72-1
    A.J.P. TAYLOR, 453:10FEB72-14
    H. TREVOR-ROPER, 441:30JAN72-1
    E. WEEKS, 61:FEB72-108
    442(NY):18MAR72-155
    617(TLS):18FEB72-171
MASTERMAN, N. THE FORERUNNER.
    617(TLS):15DEC72-1522
MASTERS, A. THE NATURAL HISTORY OF THE
  VAMPIRE.
    P. ADAMS, 61:NOV72-131
MASTERS, B.R. & E. RALPH, EDS. THE
  CHURCH BOOK OF ST. EWEN'S, BRISTOL
  1454-1584.
    E. WELCH, 325:OCT69-588
MASTERS, G.M. RABELAISIAN DIALECTIC AND
  THE PLATONIC-HERMETIC TRADITION.
    D. COLEMAN, 551(RENQ):AUTUMN70-296
    R. COOPER, 402(MLR):APR71-407
    T.M.G., 543:MAR70-562
    A.J. KRAILSHEIMER, 208(FS):JAN71-68
MASTERS, J. THE RAVI LANCERS.
    J. HUNTER, 362:21SEP72-376
    M. LEVIN, 441:12NOV72-66
MASTERS, R.D. THE POLITICAL PHILOSOPHY
  OF ROUSSEAU.
    R. GRIMSLEY, 208(FS):APR71-207
MASTERSON, W. WHY SHE CRIES I DO NOT
  KNOW.
    N. CALLENDAR, 441:15OCT72-42
MASUI, M. THE STRUCTURE OF CHAUCER'S
  RIME WORDS.
    T.A. KIRBY, 179(ES):OCT70-450
MATA, G.H. SOBRE MONTALVO O DEMISTIFI-
  CACIÓN DE UN MIXTIFICADOR.*
    P. RODRÍGUEZ-PERALTA, 238:SEP70-583
MATEŠIĆ, J. DER WORTAKZENT IN DER SERBO-
  KROATISCHEN SCHRIFTSPRACHE.
    W. BROWNE, 574(SEEJ):FALL71-351
MATHAUSER, Z. DIE KUNST DER POESIE.
    J. HOLTHUSEN, 490:OCT68-571

MATHER, B. THE TERMINATORS.
N. CALLENDAR, 441:6FEB72-38
MATHER, C. SELECTED LETTERS OF COTTON
MATHER. (K. SILVERMAN, ED)
D. LEVIN, 165:FALL72-196
MATHERS, P. TRAP.*
R. BURNS, 381:VOL29#1-95
MATHESON, P. CARDINAL CONTARINI AT
REGENSBURG.
617(TLS):7APR72-397
MATHEW, D. LADY JANE GREY.
617(TLS):11AUG72-949
MATHEWS, J. FORD STRIKE.
R. HYMAN, 362:25MAY72-692
MATHEWS, J.D. THE FEDERAL THEATRE, 1935-
1939.*
J.T. FLANAGAN, 397(MD):SEP68-217
MATHEWS, M.M. HENRY OSSAWA TANNER,
AMERICAN ARTIST.
D. CLIVE, 58:MAY70-12
MATHEWS, M.V. & OTHERS. THE TECHNOLOGY
OF COMPUTER MUSIC.
S. ARNOLD, 607:SPRING70-41
W. SLAWSON, 308:SPRING69-148
MATHEWS, R. THIS COLD FIST.
D. BARBOUR, 102(CANL):SPRING71-70
MATHEWS, R. & J. STEELE, EDS. THE STRUG-
GLE FOR CANADIAN UNIVERSITIES.
W.P. IRVINE, 529(QQ):SPRING70-135
MATHIAS, P., ED. SCIENCE AND SOCIETY
1600-1900.
617(TLS):15SEP72-1057
MATHUR, M.V. & I. NARAIN, EDS. PANCHAY-
ATI RAJ.
P. ZWICK, 293(JAST):AUG70-962
MATICS, M.L. - SEE "ENTERING THE PATH OF
ENLIGHTENMENT"
MATLAW, M. MODERN WORLD DRAMA.
617(TLS):22DEC72-1550
MATLEY, I.M. ROMANIA.
F. KELLOGG, 32:SEP71-691
G. TORREY, 574(SEEJ):FALL71-400
MATSUMOTO, K. ON THE VOWEL SYSTEM OF
IONIC-ATTIC.
C.J. RUIJGH, 361:VOL24#1-82
"MARIE MATTEI: LETTRES À THÉOPHILE
GAUTIER ET À LOUIS DE CORMENIN." (E.
KAYE, ED)
617(TLS):4AUG72-925
MATTENKLOTT, G. MELANCHOLIE IN DER
DRAMATIK DES STURM UND DRANG.
J. OSBORNE, 402(MLR):JAN71-214
T.K. THAYER, 221(GQ):MAR70-282
MATTHEWS, C.M. HOW SURNAMES BEGAN.
E.C. SMITH, 424:JUN69-163
MATTHEWS, C.M. PLACE-NAMES OF THE
ENGLISH-SPEAKING WORLD.
617(TLS):24NOV72-1430
MATTHEWS, C.N. ENGLISH SURNAMES.
E.C. SMITH, 424:JUN68-184
MATTHEWS, D., ED. KEYBOARD MUSIC.
617(TLS):30JUN72-755
MATTHEWS, E.N. COLONIAL ORGANS AND
ORGANBUILDERS.
P. WILLIAMS, 415:AUG70-806
MATTHEWS, G.M., ED. KEATS: THE CRITICAL
HERITAGE.
617(TLS):19MAY72-573
MATTHEWS, H. THE HARD JOURNEY.*
H. SERGEANT, 175:SUMMER69-71
MATTHEWS, H.L. A WORLD IN REVOLUTION.
G.A. CRAIG, 441:9APR72-26
T. LASK, 441:17MAR72-42
MATTHEWS, J. BEYOND THE BRIDGE.
639(VQR):SPRING70-XLI
MATTHEWS, J. THE CHARISMA CAMPAIGNS.
A. HISLOP, 440:2APR72-8
M. LEVIN, 441:19MAR72-41

MATTHEWS, J. - SEE VALÉRY, P.
MATTHEWS, J.H., ED. AN ANTHOLOGY OF
FRENCH SURREALIST POETRY.
R.L. ADMUSSEN, 207(FR):OCT69-158
M. BEAUJOUR, 546(RR):FEB70-72
MATTHEWS, J.H. SURREALISM AND FILM.
R. SHATTUCK, 453:1JUN72-24
MATTHEWS, J.H. SURREALIST POETRY IN
FRANCE.*
S. LAWALL, 418(MR):SPRING71-354
MATTHEWS, K. MEMORIES OF A MOUNTAIN WAR.
617(TLS):22DEC72-1555
MATTHEWS, M. CLASS AND SOCIETY IN SOVIET
RUSSIA.
617(TLS):15DEC72-1534
MATTHEWS, M.M., ED. A DICTIONARY OF
AMERICANISMS ON HISTORICAL PRINCIPLES.
617(TLS):13OCT72-1209
MATTHEWS, W. BROKEN SYLLABLES.
J. TIPTON, 661:SUMMER70-120
MATTHEWS, W., ED. MEDIEVAL SECULAR LIT-
ERATURE.
L.J. FRIEDMAN, 545(RPH):FEB70-348
MATTHEWS, W. RUINING THE NEW ROAD.*
639(VQR):AUTUMN70-CXXXIV
MATTHIAS, J. BUCYRUS.
S. MOORE, 385(MQR):SUMMER72-217
MATTHIAS, K. THOMAS MANN UND SKANDINAV-
IEN.
G.C. SCHOOLFIELD, 563(SS):AUTUMN71-
460
MATTHIESSEN, P. SAL SI PUEDES (ESCAPE
IF YOU CAN).
J. WOMACK, JR., 453:31AUG72-12
MATTHIESSEN, P. & E. PORTER. THE TREE
WHERE MAN WAS BORN.
A. BROYARD, 441:17OCT72-43
P. SHEPARD, 441:26NOV72-31
E. WEEKS, 61:NOV72-125
561(SATR):28OCT72-78
MATTOCK, J.N. - SEE ARISTOTLE
MATTOCK, J.N. & M.C. LYONS - SEE HIPPO-
CRATES
MATTSSON, G. SÅ RULLA VÅRA ÖDEN.
G.C. SCHOOLFIELD, 563(SS):AUTUMN71-
457
MATURIN, C.R. MELMOTH THE WANDERER.
(D. GRANT, ED)
P. FAULKNER, 677:VOL2-292
MATUTE, A.M. LA TRAMPA.
M.E.W. JONES, 238:MAY70-339
MATZ, F. & H. BIESANTZ. CORPUS DER
MINOISCHEN UND MYKENISCHEN SIEGEL.
(VOL 7, PT 2)
J.H. BETTS, 303:VOL90-258
MAUCH, U. GESCHEHEN "AN SICH" UND VOR-
GANG OHNE URHEBERBEZUG IM MODERNEN
FRANZÖSISCH.
E.H. YARRILL, 182:VOL23#3-82
MAUD, R. DYLAN THOMAS IN PRINT.
E.W. MELLOWN, 579(SAQ):SUMMER71-432
617(TLS):3MAR72-254
MAUGER, G. GRAMMAIRE PRATIQUE DU FRAN-
ÇAIS D'AUJOURD'HUI.
J. CASAGRANDE, 399(MLJ):MAR70-202
MAUGHAM, R. ESCAPE FROM THE SHADOWS.
T. DRIBERG, 362:5OCT72-447
617(TLS):20OCT72-1259
MAUGHAM, R. THE LAST ENCOUNTER.
V. CUNNINGHAM, 362:6APR72-458
617(TLS):14APR72-409
MAULDIN, B. THE BRASS RING.*
M. OLMERT, 440:16JAN72-12
441:20FEB72-24
MAULE, H. THE GREAT BATTLES OF WORLD WAR
II.
617(TLS):1DEC72-1469

MAUNG, M. BURMA AND GENERAL NE WIN.
J. BADGLEY, 293(JAST):AUG70-987
DE MAUPASSANT, G. CONTES DU SURNATUREL.
(A. KELLETT, ED)
D. FREIMANIS, 399(MLJ):MAY70-374
MAURER, R.K. HEGEL UND DAS ENDE DER
GESCHICHTE.
M.J.V., 543:DEC69-350
MAURIAC, F. UN ADOLESCENT D'AUTREFOIS.
J. CARDUNER, 207(FR):OCT69-162
MAURIAC, F. MALTAVERNE.
617(TLS):30JUN72-738
MAURIAC, J. MORT DU GÉNÉRAL DE GAULLE.
617(TLS):29SEP72-1134
MAURICE, F., ED. THE LIFE OF FREDERICK
DENISON MAURICE.
617(TLS):23JUN72-717
MAURICE, N., ED. THE MAURICE CASE.
617(TLS):22DEC72-1555
DU MAURIER, D. RULE BRITANNIA.
D.A.N. JONES, 362:26OCT72-557
DE MAURO, T. LUDWIG WITTGENSTEIN.
G. NUCHELMANS, 361:VOL23#3-310
MAUROIS, A. LES ILLUSIONS.
J. KOLBERT, 207(FR):DEC69-333
MAUSS, M. A GENERAL THEORY OF MAGIC.
617(TLS):10NOV72-1374
MAUTNER, F.H. LICHTENBERG, GESCHICHTE
SEINES GEISTES.
P. GAY, 222(GR):MAR70-138
MAUTNER, F.H. - SEE NESTROY, J.
MAVRODES, G.I. & S.C. HACKETT, EDS.
PROBLEMS AND PERSPECTIVES IN THE PHIL-
OSOPHY OF RELIGION.
W.A.J., 543:DEC69-366
MAVRODIN, V.V. & S.B. OKUN'. ISTORIJA
LENINGRADSKOGO UNIVERSITETA, 1819-
1969.
W.L. MATHES, 104:SUMMER71-287
MAW, B. - SEE UNDER BA MAW
MAX, S. LES MÉTAMORPHOSES DE LA GRANDE
VILLE DANS LES ROUGON-MACQUART.
R.J. NIESS, 207(FR):OCT69-179
MAXTONE-GRAHAM, J. THE ONLY WAY TO
CROSS.
C. AMORY, 441:19NOV72-50
MAXWELL, D.E.S. AMERICAN FICTION.
R.L. DRAIN, 179(ES):AUG70-372
MAXWELL, D.E.S. POETS OF THE THIRTIES.*
H. SERGEANT, 175:AUTUMN69-111
MAXWELL, J.C. - SEE GREG, W.W.
MAXWELL-HYSLOP, K.R. WESTERN ASIATIC
JEWELLERY C. 3000-612 B.C.
617(TLS):21JAN72-72
MAY, D. THE PROFESSIONALS.
K.J. ATCHITY, 340(KR):1969/5-675
MAY, E. SIGNAL CORPORAL.
617(TLS):22DEC72-1555
MAY, G. MADAME ROLAND AND THE AGE OF
REVOLUTION.
639(VQR):AUTUMN70-CXLVI
MAY, K.M. ALDOUS HUXLEY.
617(TLS):17NOV72-1405
MAY, M.T. - SEE GALEN
MAY, R. POWER AND INNOCENCE.
A. BROYARD, 441:2NOV72-45
P.A. ROBINSON, 441:10DEC72-6
442(NY):16DEC72-149
561(SATR):25NOV72-72
MAY, W. REPORTS.
N. ROSTEN, 561(SATR):12AUG72-58
MAYAKOVSKY, V. HOW ARE VERSES MADE?*
(G.M. HYDE, TRANS)
617(TLS):14JAN72-49
MAYER, C.A. - SEE MAROT, C.
MAYER, M. ABOUT TELEVISION.
R.D. HEFFNER, 561(SATR):26AUG72-62
R.R. LINGEMAN, 441:12JUL72-43

MAYER, R. CHRISTUSWIRKLICHKEIT.
F.F. BRUCE, 182:VOL23#3-81
"TOBIAS MAYER'S 'OPERA INEDITA'." (E.G
FORBES, TRANS)
617(TLS):23JUN72-708
MAYERHÖFER, J. & W. RITZER, WITH M. RAZU-
MOVSKY, EDS. FESTSCHRIFT JOSEF STUMM-
VOLL.
F. REICHMANN, 356:OCT71-334
MAYEROFF, M. ON CARING.
E. SHIRK, 311(JP):24FEB72-114
MAYERSON, H. VINH LONG.
639(VQR):SUMMER70-CXIV
MAYFIELD, S. EXILES FROM PARADISE.*
R.M. ADAMS, 453:27JAN72-26
MAYHEW, G.P. RAGE OR RAILLERY.
J. KINSLEY, 354:MAR69-69
MAYNE, F. THE WIT AND SATIRE OF BERNARD
SHAW.
F.P.W. MC DOWELL, 397(MD):DEC68-341
MAYNE, R., ED. EUROPE TOMORROW.
C. SERPELL, 362:20JAN72-89
MAYNE, R. THE EUROPEANS.
617(TLS):28JUL72-861
MAYNE, R.C. FOUR YEARS IN BRITISH
COLUMBIA AND VANCOUVER ISLAND.
102(CANL):WINTER71-108
MAYNE, S. FACE.
R. GIBBS, 198:SUMMER72-129
MAYO, A.P. - SEE UNDER PORQUERAS MAYO, A.
MAYO, R.S. HERDER AND THE BEGINNINGS OF
COMPARATIVE LITERATURE.*
H.B. NISBET, 402(MLR):APR71-457
MAYR-HARTING, H. THE COMING OF CHRIS-
TIANITY TO ANGLO-SAXON ENGLAND.
617(TLS):22SEP72-1121
MAYRHOFER, M. DIE REKONSTRUKTION DES
MEDISCHEN.
R. ROCHER, 318(JAOS):APR-JUN70-407
MAYRHOFER, M., WITH F. LOCHNER-HÜTTENBACH
& H. SCHMEJA, EDS. STUDIEN ZUR SPRACH-
WISSENSCHAFT UND KULTURKUNDE.
G. LIEBERT, 596(SL):VOL23#2-132
MAYRÖCKER, F. FANTOM FAN.
617(TLS):14JAN72-32
MAYS, J.B., ED. JUVENILE DELINQUENCY,
THE FAMILY AND THE SOCIAL GROUP.
617(TLS):19MAY72-585
MAYS, W. & S.C. BROWN, EDS. LINGUISTIC
ANALYSIS AND PHENOMENOLOGY.
617(TLS):5MAY72-513
MAZAR, B., ED. THE WORLD HISTORY OF THE
JEWISH PEOPLE. (VOL 2)
617(TLS):14JAN72-46
MAZAR, B., ED. THE WORLD HISTORY OF THE
JEWISH PEOPLE. (VOL 3)
617(TLS):27OCT72-1295
MAZÉ, P. & R.P.H. COPPENRATH - SEE
JAUSSEN, T.
MAZIARZ, E.A. & T. GREENWOOD. GREEK
MATHEMATICAL PHILOSOPHY.
C. EISELE, 124:OCT70-59
I. MUELLER, 482(PHR):JUL70-427
MAZLAKH, S. & V. SHAKHRAI. ON THE CUR-
RENT SITUATION IN THE UKRAINE. (P.J.
POTICHNYJ, ED)
I.L. RUDNYTSKY, 104:WINTER71-536
MAZLISH, B. IN SEARCH OF NIXON.
J. DEMOS, 441:4JUN72-37
C. LEHMANN-HAUPT, 441:11MAY72-47
R.R. LINGEMAN, 441:4JUN72-1
G. STRICKER, 561(SATR):29APR72-68
MAZMANIAN, A. THE STRUCTURE OF PRAISE.
D.J. COOLIDGE, 432(NEQ):DEC70-650
MAZOUR, A.G. THE WRITING OF HISTORY IN
THE SOVIET UNION.
617(TLS):21APR72-453

MAZRUI, A.A. THE TRIAL OF CHRISTOPHER OKIGBO.
G. DAVIS, 441:17SEP72-48
D.A.N. JONES, 362:30MAR72-426
617(TLS):3MAR72-247
MAŽVYDAS, M. THE OLD LITHUANIAN CATE-CHISM OF MARTYNAS MAŽVYDAS (1547).
(G.B. FORD, JR., ED & TRANS)
W.R. SCHMALSTIEG, 574(SEEJ):FALL71-368
A. SENN, 32:SEP71-709
MEACHAM, S. - SEE BULWER-LYTTON, E.
MEACOCK, N. THINKING GIRL.
D. LEVINSON, 441:13FEB72-4
R.R. LINGEMAN, 441:26JAN72-39
P. THEROUX, 440:23JAN72-2
MEAD, M. THE ADMINISTRATION OF THINGS.
J. SMITH, 493:AUTUMN70-243
MEAD, M. BLACKBERRY WINTER.
C. BIRD, 561(SATR):25NOV72-64
J. HOWARD, 441:12NOV72-49
442(NY):25NOV72-200
MEAD, M. CULTURE AND COMMITMENT.*
K.E. BOULDING, 639(VQR):SPRING70-339
MEAD, S. FREE THE MALE MAN!
P. ADAMS, 61:APR72-129
MEAD, W.R. & W. HALL. SCANDINAVIA.
617(TLS):2JUN72-626
MEADE, E. INDIAN ROCK CARVINGS OF THE PACIFIC NORTHWEST.
G.W., 102(CANL):AUTUMN71-102
MEADE, R.D. PATRICK HENRY.
D.E. BENSON, 656(WMQ):JUL70-496
MEADOWS, A.J. SCIENCE AND CONTROVERSY.
561(SATR):23DEC72-68
617(TLS):3NOV72-1301
MEADOWS, D. HISTORIC PLACE NAMES IN ORANGE COUNTY.
M.A. MOOK, 424:JUN68-187
MEADOWS, D.H. & OTHERS. THE LIMITS TO GROWTH.
L.R. BROWN, 561(SATR):22APR72-65
E. EDELSON, 440:26MAR72-13
P. PASSELL, M. ROBERTS & L. ROSS, 441:2APR72-1
MEAKER, M. SHOCKPROOF SYDNEY SKATE.
P. THEROUX, 440:16APR72-9
MECH, L.D. THE WOLF.
617(TLS):26MAY72-611
MECKLING, I. DIE AUSSENPOLITIK DES GRAFEN CZERNIN.
617(TLS):11FEB72-152
MEDAWAR, P.B. THE HOPE OF PROGRESS.
E. LEACH, 362:3AUG72-150
617(TLS):23JUN72-701
MEDEIROS, W.D. HIPPONACTEA.
M.L. WEST, 123:MAR71-12
"MEDIEVAL LATIN LYRICS." (B. STOCK, TRANS)
617(TLS):28JUL72-884
DE MEDINA, F.D. - SEE UNDER DIEZ DE MEDINA, F.
THE DUCHESS OF MEDINA SIDONIA. MY PRISON.
A. BROYARD, 441:30CT72-47
MEDLEY, R. RUBEN'S "THE ASCENT TO CAL-VARY."
D. SUTTON, 39:JUN69-414
MEDLICOTT, W.N. BRITISH FOREIGN POLICY SINCE VERSAILLES 1919-1963.
L.C., 619(TC):1968/4&1969/1-93
MEDLICOTT, W.N., D. DAKIN & M.E. LAMBERT, EDS. DOCUMENTS ON BRITISH FOREIGN POLICY 1919-1939. (SER 1, VOL 18)
617(TLS):23JUN72-713

MEDLICOTT, W.N., D. DAKIN & M.E. LAMBERT, EDS. DOCUMENTS ON BRITISH FOREIGN POLICY 1919-1939. (SER 1A, VOL 4)
617(TLS):11FEB72-151
MEDLICOTT, W.N., D. DAKIN & M.E. LAMBERT, EDS. DOCUMENTS ON BRITISH FOREIGN POLICY 1919-1939. (2ND SER, VOL 12)
617(TLS):22DEC72-1547
MEDLIN, D.M. THE VERBAL ART OF JEAN-FRANÇOIS REGNARD.
A. CALAME, 207(FR):FEB70-523
MEDVEDEV, R.A. LET HISTORY JUDGE.* (D. JORAVSKY & G. HAUPT, EDS)
M. FAINSOD, 440:2JAN72-4
I.F. STONE, 453:10FEB72-7 [& CONT IN] 453:24FEB72-14
R.C. TUCKER, 561(SATR):8JAN72-25
617(TLS):26MAY72-589
MEDVEDEV, Z.A. THE MEDVEDEV PAPERS.*
617(TLS):7JAN72-15
MEDVEDEV, Z.A. THE RISE AND FALL OF T.D. LYSENKO.*
B.M. COHEN, 104:SPRING71-133
MEDVEDEV, Z.A. & R.A. A QUESTION OF MADNESS.*
I.F. STONE, 453:10FEB72-7
617(TLS):7JAN72-15
MEE, C.L., JR. WHITE ROBE, BLACK ROBE.
V. CRONIN, 440:28MAY72-6
MEE, M. FLOWERS OF THE BRAZILIAN FOR-ESTS.
T. CROMBIE, 39:FEB69-160
MEEBELO, H.S. REACTION TO COLONIALISM.
617(TLS):4FEB72-138
MEEKINGS, C.A.F. & P. SHEARMAN, EDS. FITZNELLS CARTULARY.
C.N.L. BROOKE, 325:OCT69-587
MEEN, V.B. & A.D. TUSHINGHAM. CROWN JEWELS OF IRAN.
A. EMERY, 627(UTQ):JUL69-406
VAN DER MEER, F. EARLY CHRISTIAN ART.*
A. FRAZER, 576:DEC69-301
MEGGYSEY, D. OUT OF THEIR LEAGUE.*
T.R. EDWARDS, 473(PR):1971/3-330
MEHL, D. THE MIDDLE ENGLISH ROMANCES OF THE THIRTEENTH AND FOURTEENTH CENTUR-IES.* (GERMAN TITLE: DIE MITTELENGLIS-CHEN ROMANZEN DES 13. UND 14. JAHR-HUNDERTS.)
G.C. BRITTON, 447(N&Q):JUN70-226
M. MILLS, 382(MAE):1971/3-291
R.M. WILSON, 175:AUTUMN69-106
MEHLINGER, H.D. & J.M. THOMPSON. COUNT WITTE AND THE TSARIST GOVERNMENT IN THE 1905 REVOLUTION.
617(TLS):18AUG72-972
MEHNERT, K. CHINA RETURNS.
J.K. FAIRBANK, 453:24FEB72-3
S.R. SCHRAM, 441:7MAY72-2
R. STEEL, 440:9APR72-1
MEHNERT, K. CHINA TODAY.
617(TLS):21APR72-436
MEHNERT, K. PEKING AND THE NEW LEFT.
H.G. CALLIS, 293(JAST):MAY70-693
MEHRA, P. THE YOUNGHUSBAND EXPEDITION.
R.P. GATES, 293(JAST):AUG70-958
MEHROTRA, S.R. THE EMERGENCE OF THE INDIAN NATIONAL CONGRESS.
617(TLS):7APR72-402
MEHTA, V. DADDYJI.
A. BROYARD, 441:8MAY72-39
P.K.S. RAJAN, 561(SATR):20MAY72-72
MEIER, H., ED. FÜNF MADRIGALE VENEZIAN-ISCHER KOMPONISTEN UM ADRIAN WILLAERT.
412:NOV71-365
MEIER, H.K. FRIENDSHIP UNDER STRESS.
H.R. GUGGISBERG, 182:VOL23#17/18-829

MEIER, M.S. & F. RIVERA. THE CHICANOS.
J. WOMACK, JR., 453:31AUG72-12
MEIGGS, R. THE ATHENIAN EMPIRE.
M.I. FINLEY, 362:19OCT72-495
MEIGGS, R. & D. LEWIS, EDS. A SELECTION
OF GREEK HISTORICAL INSCRIPTIONS TO THE
END OF THE FIFTH CENTURY B.C.*
R. FLACELIÈRE, 555:VOL44FASC2-311
M.F. MC GREGOR, 487:SUMMER70-176
MEIJER, R.P. LITERATURE OF THE LOW
COUNTRIES.
617(TLS):11AUG72-938
MEIL, K. & M. ARNDT. ABC DER SCHWACHEN
VERBEN.
H. BROCKHAUS, 221(GQ):JAN70-133
MEILAND, J.W. THE NATURE OF INTENTION.*
A.R. WHITE, 518:OCT70-18
T.E. WILKERSON, 479(PHQ):OCT70-402
MEILAND, J.W. SKEPTICISM AND HISTORICAL
KNOWLEDGE.*
J.J. LEACH, 486:SEP68-294
MEILAND, J.W. TALKING ABOUT PARTICULARS.
D. HOLDCROFT, 518:MAY71-18
MEILLASSOUX, C., L. DOUCOURÉ & D. SIMAGHA.
LÉGENDE DE LA DISPERSION DES KUSA (ÉPO-
PÉE SONINKÉ).
R. MURRAY, 315(JAL):VOL8PT1-43
MEILLET, A. THE INDO-EUROPEAN DIALECTS.
V.J. ZEPS, 574(SEEJ):SUMMER71-244
MEINECKE, F. COSMOPOLITANISM AND THE
NATIONAL STATE.*
E.H. GLAS, 396(MODA):WINTER71-110
MEINECKE, F. HISTORISM.
617(TLS):15SEP72-1047
MEINERS, I. SCHELM UND DÜMMLING IN
ERZÄHLUNGEN DES DEUTSCHEN MITTELALTERS.
G. PAULINE, 182:VOL23#5-223
MEINHARD, H. GERMAN WINES.
617(TLS):21JAN72-78
MEININGER, T.A. IGNATIEV AND THE ESTAB-
LISHMENT OF THE BULGARIAN EXARCHATE,
1864-1872.
P.W. SCHROEDER, 32:JUN71-421
MEINONG, A. GESAMTAUSGABE. (VOL 3) (R.
KINDINGER, ED)
J.N. FINDLAY, 479(PHQ):OCT70-400
MEISE, E. UNTERSUCHUNGEN ZUR GESCHICHTE
DER JULISCH-CLAUDISCHEN DYNASTIE.*
M. SWAN, 24:OCT71-739
MEISEL, J. A MATTER OF ENDURANCE.
M.C. BROMAGE, 385(MQR):WINTER72-69
MEISEL, P. THOMAS HARDY.
617(TLS):16JUN72-687
MEISNER, M. LI TA-CHAO AND THE ORIGINS
OF CHINESE MARXISM.
J. CH'EN, 302:JUL69-280
D.W.Y. KWOK, 485(PE&W):OCT69-449
MEISS, M. FRENCH PAINTING IN THE TIME OF
JEAN DE BERRY.*
M.S. FRINTA, 127:FALL70-106
R.E. SPEAR, 207(FR):FEB70-536
E.P. SPENCER, 90:APR69-226
MEISS, M., WITH K. MORAND & E.W. KIRSCH.
THE BOUCICAUT MASTER.
E.P. SPENCER, 90:APR69-226
MEISSNER, B., ED. DAS SELBSTBESTIMMUNGS-
RECHT DER VÖLKER IN OSTEUROPA UND
CHINA.*
H.F. FIRESIDE, 104:SUMMER71-293
MEISSNER, E. FÜRSTBISCHOF ANTON IGNAZ
FUGGER (1711-87).
H.S. OFFLER, 182:VOL23#23/24-1012
MEISTER, J. THE SOVIET NAVY. (VOLS 1&2)
617(TLS):12MAY72-557
MEJÍA SANCHEZ, E. LAS CASAS EN MÉXICO.
J. AMOR Y VÁZQUEZ, 240(HR):JAN70-108

MELADA, I. THE CAPTAIN OF INDUSTRY IN
ENGLISH FICTION, 1821-1871.
S.M. SMITH, 677:VOL2-308
G.J. WORTH, 301(JEGP):OCT71-685
"MÉLANGES D'ARCHÉOLOGIE, D'ÉPIGRAPHIE ET
D'HISTOIRE OFFERTS À JÉRÔME CARCOPINO."
A. ERNOUT, 555:VOL44FASC1-140
"MÉLANGES D'ARCHÉOLOGIE ET D'HISTOIRE
OFFERTS À ANDRÉ PIGANIOL."
A. ERNOUT, 555:VOL44FASC1-140
"MÉLANGES DE LITTÉRATURE COMPARÉE ET DE
PHILOLOGIE À MIECZYSŁAW BRAHMER."
U. WEISSTEIN, 52:BAND4HEFT2-202
"MÉLANGES DE PHILOLOGIE ET DE LINGUIS-
TIQUE OFFERTS À TAUNO NURMELA."
B. FOSTER, 208(FS):JAN71-117
MELCHER, D., WITH M. SAUL. MELCHER ON
ACQUISITION.
R.C. MILLER, 356:OCT71-332
MELCHERT, N.P. REALISM, MATERIALISM,
AND THE MIND. (M. FARBER, ED)
G. TREASH, 150(DR):SPRING70-128
W.P. WARREN, 484(PPR):SEP69-140
MELCHIOR, I. ORDER OF BATTLE.
M. LEVIN, 441:19NOV72-62
MELCHIORI, B. BROWNING'S POETRY OF
RETICENCE.*
P.F. MATTHEISEN, 637(VS):SEP69-108
MÉLÈSE, P. BECKETT.
L. PRONKO, 397(MD):DEC67-320
MELLANBY, K. THE MOLE.
617(TLS):14JAN72-45
MELLEN, P. JEAN CLOUET.
617(TLS):4FEB72-124
MELLEN, P. THE GROUP OF SEVEN.
J. MURRAY, 99:MAY72-66
MELLER, H. & H-J. ZIMMERMANN, EDS. LEB-
ENDE ANTIKE.*
J. KLEINSTÜCK, 52:BAND4HEFT2-204
E.N. TIGERSTEDT, 597(SN):VOL40#1-238
MELLERIO, A. ODILON REDON.*
R. PICKVANCE, 90:SEP69-570
MELLERS, W. HARMONIOUS MEETING.
E.K. WOLF, 317:FALL71-486
MELLERT-HOFFMANN, G. UNTERSUCHUNGEN ZUR
"IPHIGENIE IN AULIS" DES EURIPIDES.
J. DIGGLE, 123:JUN71-178
J. PETROFF, 124:FEB71-199
MELLON, M.T. EARLY AMERICAN VIEWS ON
NEGRO SLAVERY FROM THE LETTERS AND
PAPERS OF THE FOUNDERS OF THE REPUBLIC.
F.N. BONEY, 219(GAR):FALL69-409
MELLOR, J.W. & OTHERS. DEVELOPING RURAL
INDIA.
E. MUELLER, 293(JAST):MAY70-665
MELLOWN, E.W. A DESCRIPTIVE CATALOGUE OF
THE BIBLIOGRAPHIES OF 20TH CENTURY
BRITISH WRITERS.
617(TLS):6OCT72-1204
MELLUISH, T.W. A.R.L.T. LATIN PROSE
COMPOSITIONS.
D.S. COLMAN, 123:MAR71-149
MELVILLE, H. THE WRITINGS OF HERMAN MEL-
VILLE. (VOL 1: TYPEE.) (H. HAYFORD, H.
PARKER & G.T. TANSELLE, EDS)
V.A. DEARING, 445(NCF):MAR69-482
MELVILLE, H. THE WRITINGS OF HERMAN
MELVILLE. (VOL 3: MARDI: AND A VOYAGE
THITHER.) (H. HAYFORD, H. PARKER & G.T.
TANSELLE, EDS)
L. THOMPSON, 27(AL):NOV71-450
617(TLS):21JAN72-53
MELVILLE, H. THE WRITINGS OF HERMAN
MELVILLE.* (VOL 4: REDBURN: HIS FIRST
VOYAGE.) (H. HAYFORD, H. PARKER & G.T.
TANSELLE, EDS)
617(TLS):21JAN72-53

MELVILLE, H. THE WRITINGS OF HERMAN
MELVILLE. (VOL 5: WHITE-JACKET: OR,
THE WORLD IN A MAN-OF-WAR.) (H. HAY-
FORD, H. PARKER & G.T. TANSELLE, EDS)
   H.P. VINCENT, 27(AL):MAY71-292
  617(TLS):21JAN72-53
MELVILLE, J. IRONWOOD.
   N. CALLENDAR, 441:20AUG72-27
  617(TLS):7JUL72-783
MELVILLE, J. THE SUMMER ASSASSIN.
  617(TLS):7JAN72-17
MELVILLE, S. LETTERS FROM ATTICA.
   F. FERRETTI, 440:27FEB72-8
MELVILLE, T. & M. GUATEMALA - ANOTHER
VIETNAM?
  617(TLS):4AUG72-915
MÉNAGE, V.L. NESHRĪ'S HISTORY OF THE
OTTOMANS.
   J. STEWART-ROBINSON, 318(JAOS):APR-
   JUN70-274
MENANDER. MENANDRI "ASPIS" ET "SAMIA."*
(VOL 1) (C. AUSTIN, ED)
   E.G. TURNER, 123:DEC71-351
   T.B.L. WEBSTER, 124:MAR71-238
MENANDER. MENANDRI "ASPIS" ET "SAMIA."
(VOL 2) (C. AUSTIN, ED)
   T.B.L. WEBSTER, 124:MAR71-238
MÉNARD, J. XAVIER MARMIER ET LE CANADA.
   R.J. HATHORN, 402(MLR):JUL71-693
MÉNARD, J. LA VIE LITTÉRAIRE AU CANADA
FRANÇAIS.
  617(TLS):7APR72-399
MÉNARD, P. MANUEL D'ANCIEN FRANÇAIS.
(FASC 3)
   F.J. BARNETT, 208(FS):JUL71-369
MÉNARD, P. LE RIRE ET LE SOURIRE DANS
LE ROMAN COURTOIS EN FRANCE AU MOYEN
ÂGE (1150-1250).
   R.J. CORMIER, 589:JAN71-168
   J.C. GILLIS, 402(MLR):APR71-403
   D.D.R. OWEN, 208(FS):OCT71-444
MENDE, F. HEINRICH HEINE.
   J.A. KRUSE, 182:VOL23#6-281
   S.S. PRAWER, 402(MLR):APR71-465
  617(TLS):7JUL72-784
MENDE, F. & K.H. HAHN - SEE HEINE, H.
MENDEL, A.P. - SEE ANNENKOV, P.V.
MENDEL, A.P. - SEE MILIUKOV, P.
MENDEL, D. THE POLITICS OF FORMOSAN
NATIONALISM.
   E.I-T. CHEN, 293(JAST):AUG70-936
MENDELL, C.W. LATIN POETRY.*
   E.J. KENNEY, 123:DEC71-456
MENDELSOHN, E. LETTERS OF AN ARCHITECT.
(O. BEYER, ED)
   L.K. EATON, 505:FEB69-146
MENDELSON, D. LE VERRE ET LES OBJETS DE
VERRE DANS L'UNIVERS IMAGINAIRE DE
MARCEL PROUST.
   R.M. BIRN, 131(CL):WINTER71-77
   M. MEIN, 208(FS):JAN71-105
   W.A. STRAUSS, 207(FR):MAY70-936
MENDILOW, A.A. & A. SHALVI. THE WORLD
AND ART OF SHAKESPEARE.
   H. HOWARTH, 570(SQ):SPRING69-234
MENEN, A. THE SPACE WITHIN THE HEART.*
   M. WIMSATT, 676(YR):AUTUMN70-138
MENENDEZ PIDAL, R. CRESTOMATĪA DEL ES-
PAÑOL MEDIEVAL. (VOL 1) (REV BY R.
LAPESA & M. SOLEDAD DE ANDRÉS)
   R.S. WILLIS, 240(HR):JAN70-83
DE MENEZES, R. DICIONÁRIO LITERÁRIO
BRASILEIRO ILUSTRADO.
   H.M., 191(ELN):SEP70(SUPP)-141
MENGE, U. DIE DIALEKTISCHE STRUKTUR DER
KURZGESCHICHTEN DOÑA EMILIA PARDO
BAZÁNS.
   J. CANO BALLESTA, 240(HR):APR70-232

MENGEL, R.M., COMP. A CATALOGUE OF THE
ELLIS COLLECTION OF ORNITHOLOGICAL
BOOKS IN THE UNIVERSITY OF KANSAS LIB-
RARIES. (VOL 1)
  617(TLS):24NOV72-1440
MENGES, K. KRITISCHE STUDIEN ZUR WERT-
PHILOSOPHIE HERMANN BROCHS.
   P.M. LÜTZELER, 406:FALL71-291
MENICHETTI, A. - SEE CHIARO DAVANZATI
MENNINGER, K. NUMBER WORDS AND NUMBER
SYMBOLS.
   I.L. KALDOR, 356:JAN71-65
MENON, K.P.S. THE INDO-SOVIET TREATY.
  617(TLS):24MAR72-345
MENUHIN, Y. THEME AND VARIATIONS.
   T. LASK, 441:27MAY72-27
   D. NOAKES, 441:28MAY72-6
  617(TLS):28JUL72-893
MENUHIN, Y. VIOLIN.
   A. GINGRICH, 440:16JAN72-4
MENZEL, B. GOLDGEWICHTE AUS GHANA.
   V.L. GROTTANELLI, 69:JUL69-312
MÉRAS, P. FIRST SPRING.
   A. BROYARD, 441:5JUL72-41
MERBURY, F. THE MARRIAGE BETWEEN WIT AND
WISDOM. (T.N.S. LENNAM, ED)
  617(TLS):26MAY72-613
MERCADIER, G. - SEE DE TORRES VILLARROEL,
D.
MERCER, E. ENGLISH ART, 1553-1625.
   D. STILLMAN, 576:MAY68-156
MERCER, P. SYMPATHY AND ETHICS.
  617(TLS):9JUN72-667
MERCER, V. JOHN ARNOLD & SON, CHRONO-
METER MAKERS, 1762-1843.
  617(TLS):25AUG72-1005
MERCHANT, L. "...AND EVERY DAY YOU TAKE
ANOTHER BITE."*
   J. FLAHERTY, 440:2JAN72-11
MERCHANT, W.M. - SEE SHAKESPEARE, W.
MERCIÉ, J-L. VICTOR HUGO ET JULIE CHE-
NAY.
   R.B. GRANT, 207(FR):OCT69-181
MEREDITH, G. THE ADVENTURES OF HARRY
RICHMOND. (L.T. HERGENHAN, ED)
   P.D. EDWARDS, 67:MAY71-108
   M. HARRIS, 581:1971/1-79
MEREDITH, G. THE LETTERS OF GEORGE
MEREDITH. (C.L. CLINE, ED)
   P.D. EDWARDS, 67:NOV71-241
   W.F. WRIGHT, 301(JEGP):OCT71-686
MEREDITH, W. EARTH WALK AND SELECTED
POEMS.*
   M. BORROFF, 676(YR):WINTER71-277
   G.S. FRASER, 473(PR):WINTER71/72-469
   R. MAZZOCCO, 453:15JUN72-31
MEREGALLI, F. "PAROLE NEL TEMPO."
   J. ALBERICH, 86(BHS):JAN71-81
MERENTITES, C.J. HO HĒSIODOS PARA
PLATŌNI.
   J.E. REXINE, 121(CJ):DEC70-JAN71-179
   P. WALCOT, 303:VOL90-202
MERETSKOV, K.A. NA SLUZHBE NARODU.
   M. PARRISH, 587:OCT69-251
MERGIER-BOURDEIX - SEE JANIN, J.
MÉRIMÉE, P. ROMANS ET NOUVELLES. (M.
PARTURIER, ED)
   J.S.P., 191(ELN):SEP69(SUPP)-78
MERITT, H.D. SOME OF THE HARDEST GLOSSES
IN OLD ENGLISH.*
   S.M. KUHN, 301(JEGP):OCT71-651
MERIVALE, P. PAN THE GOAT-GOD.*
   H. BERGHOLZ, 149:SEP71-267
   I. FLETCHER, 402(MLR):JAN71-173
   W.J. KEITH, 627(UTQ):JUL70-363
   W.D. PADEN, 191(ELN):SEP70-72

MERIWETHER, L. DADDY WAS A NUMBER RUN-
NER.
617(TLS):21JAN72-57
MERKELBACH, R. & H. VAN THIEL. LATEIN-
ISCHES LESEHEFT ZUR EINFÜHRUNG IN
PALÄOGRAPHIE UND TEXTKRITIK.
J. ANDRÉ, 555:VOL44FASC2-369
MERLE, R. BEHIND THE GLASS.* (FRENCH
TITLE: DERRIÈRE LA VITRE.)
M. LEVIN, 441:13AUG72-31
MERLE, R. MALEVIL.
617(TLS):2JUN72-623
MERLEAU-PONTY, M. HUMANISM AND TERROR.*
(J. O'NEILL, ED & TRANS)
T.J. BLAKELEY, 550(RUSR):JUL70-356
MERLEAU-PONTY, M. THE VISIBLE AND THE
INVISIBLE. (C. LEFORT, ED)
B. FALK, 479(PHQ):JUL70-278
MERLO, J.C. - SEE INÉS DE LA CRUZ, S.J.
MERRIAM, A.P. ETHNOMUSICOLOGY OF THE
FLATHEAD INDIANS.*
D.P. MC ALLESTER, 292(JAF):OCT-DEC70-
481
MERRILEES, B.S. - SEE "LE PETIT PLET"
MERRILL, J. BRAVING THE ELEMENTS.
H. VENDLER, 441:24SEP72-5
MERRILL, J. THE FIRE SCREEN.*
M. BORROFF, 676(YR):WINTER71-277
T. HARRISON, 364:APR/MAY71-163
42(AR):WINTER69/70-591
MERRILL, J. TWO POEMS.
617(TLS):29SEP72-1146
MERTEN, E.W. ZWEI HERRSCHERFESTE IN DER
HISTORIA AUGUSTA.
T.D. BARNES, 313:VOL60-268
MERTNER, E. & H. MAINUSCH. PORNOTOPIA.
H. TUCKER, JR., 406:SUMMER71-175
MERTON, T. CONTEMPLATION IN A WORLD OF
ACTION.*
617(TLS):5MAY72-527
MERTON, T. & J.H. GRIFFIN. A HIDDEN
WHOLENESS.
R. BONAZZI, 584(SWR):WINTER71-VII
MERWIN, W.S. THE CARRIER OF LADDERS.*
G.S. FRASER, 473(PR):WINTER71/72-469
J. VERNON, 651(WHR):SPRING71-187
MERWIN, W.S. THE LICE.*
S. COOPERMAN, 502(PRS):FALL68-266
MERWIN, W.S. THE MINER'S PALE CHILDREN.*
G.S. FRASER, 473(PR):WINTER71/72-469
J. VERNON, 651(WHR):SPRING71-188
676(YR):AUTUMN70-XXXIV
MERWIN, W.S. SELECTED TRANSLATIONS 1948-
1968.
R. MITCHELL, 399(MLJ):MAR70-216
MÉRY, M. LA CRITIQUE DU CHRISTIANISME
CHEZ RENOUVIER.
R. BALMÈS, 542:JUL-DEC69-431
MESCHONNIC, H. DÉDICACES PROVERBES.
617(TLS):21APR72-441
MESEROLE, H.T. & OTHERS, COMPS. 1969
MLA INTERNATIONAL BIBLIOGRAPHY OF BOOKS
AND ARTICLES ON THE MODERN LANGUAGES
AND LITERATURES. (VOL 3: LINGUISTICS)
E.F.K. KOERNER, 350:DEC71-915
MESEROLE, H.T., W. SUTTON & B. WEBER,
EDS. AMERICAN LITERATURE. (VOL 1)
F. SHUFFELTON, 165:SPRING72-93
MESERVE, W.J., ED. DISCUSSIONS OF AMERI-
CAN DRAMA.
J.T. FLANAGAN, 397(MD):SEP67-216
MESERVE, W.J. ROBERT E. SHERWOOD.
T.F. MARSHALL, 27(AL):NOV71-471
MESERVE, W.J. - SEE HOWELLS, W.D.
MESONERO ROMANOS, R. OBRAS. (C. SECO
SERRANO, ED)
191(ELN):SEP69(SUPP)-156

MESSÉGUÉ, M. OF MEN AND PLANTS.
617(TLS):25AUG72-1000
MÉSZÁROS, I., ED. ASPECTS OF HISTORY AND
CLASS CONSCIOUSNESS.*
W.A. SUCHTING, 63:DEC71-338
MÉSZÁROS, I. MARX'S THEORY OF ALIENA-
TION.
W.A. SUCHTING, 63:DEC71-338
METCALF, J., ED. KALEIDOSCOPE.
D. ROLLINS, 296:FALL72-104
METCALF, J. THE LADY WHO SOLD FURNITURE.
H. ROSENGARTEN, 102(CANL):WINTER71-
101
L. WOODS, 606(TAMR):#56-85
METCALF, J., ED. THE NARRATIVE VOICE.
G. PURNELL, 99:JUN72-91
D. ROLLINS, 296:FALL72-104
METCALF, J., ED. SIXTEEN BY TWELVE.
J.G. MOSS, 296:WINTER72-79
METCALF, P. PATAGONI.
T. LASK, 441:15SEP72-40
METCALF, P. VICTORIAN LONDON.
617(TLS):1DEC72-1453
METCALF, T.R., ED. MODERN INDIA.
617(TLS):22SEP72-1119
METSCHIES, M. ZITAT UND ZITIERKUNST IN
MONTAIGNES "ESSAIS."*
P.M. SCHON, 52:BAND4HEFT2-205
METZ, C. ESSAIS SUR LA SIGNIFICATION AU
CINÉMA.
N. SILVERSTEIN, 295:VOL2#1-154
M. ZÉRAFFA, 98:APR69-380
METZGER, H.P. THE ATOMIC ESTABLISHMENT.
S.B. SHEPARD, 441:29OCT72-50
METZGER, I.R. DIE HELLENISTISCHE KERAMIK
IN ERETRIA.
A.H. ASHMEAD, 124:OCT70-62
MEWSHAW, M. WAKING SLOW.
L.J. DAVIS, 440:12MAR72-10
MEY, H. FIELD-THEORY.
617(TLS):28APR72-471
MEYER, B.C. JOSEPH CONRAD.*
P. GOETSCH, 38:BAND87HEFT3/4-469
L.A. RUFF, 613:AUTUMN68-450
W.D. SCHAEFER, 445(NCF):SEP68-248
MEYER, E. HEINRICH SCHLIEMANN.*
J.M. COOK, 123:DEC70-390
MEYER, E.H., ED. MUSA-MENS-MUSICI.
G. ABRAHAM, 415:NOV70-1114
F.W.S., 410(M&L):JUL71-322
MEYER, H. DAS COROLLARIUM DE TEMPORE DES
SIMPLIKIOS UND DIE APORIEN DES ARIS-
TOTELES ZUR ZEIT.
P.J.W. MILLER, 319:OCT72-476
MEYER, L.B. MUSIC, THE ARTS, AND IDEAS.*
L. PLANTINGA, 308:SPRING69-141
MEYER, M. IBSEN.*
B. GILL, 442(NY):8APR72-126
MEYER, R. ZUR MORPHOLOGIE UND SPRACH-
GEOGRAPHIE DES ARTIKELS IM SCHWEIZER-
DEUTSCHEN.
S.E. BELLAMY, 400(MLN):APR70-399
W.G. MOULTON, 350:DEC71-938
MEYER, R.W. HISTORY OF THE SANTEE SIOUX.
H.E. FRITZ, 330(MASJ):FALL69-80
MEYER, S. AN INTERPRETATION OF EDMUND
SPENSER'S "COLIN CLOUT."*
B.E.C. DAVIS, 541(RES):NOV70-486
MEYER-BAER, K. MUSIC OF THE SPHERES AND
THE DANCE OF DEATH.
M.W. BLOOMFIELD, 589:JAN71-172
G. OLDHAM, 415:OCT71-967
617(TLS):15DEC72-1538
MEYER-DOHM, P., ED. DAS WISSENSCHAFT-
LICHE BUCH.
I. IBEN, 356:APR71-188
MEYER-ECKHARDT, V. WANDERFAHRTEN.
D. VAN ABBÉ, 182:VOL23#11/12-620

MEYER-LEVINÉ, R. LEVINÉ.
617(TLS):24NOV72-1433
MEYERBEER, G. BRIEFWECHSEL UND TAGE-
BÜCHER.
A.H. KING, 182:VOL23#9-489
MEYERHOFF, W., ED. 50 JAHRE GÖTTINGER
HÄNDEL-FESTSPIELE.
W.D., 410(M&L):APR71-186
MEYERHOLD, V.E. MEYERHOLD ON THEATRE.
(E. BRAUN, ED & TRANS)
S.P. HILL, 104:FALL71-428
M.L. HOOVER, 574(SEEJ):SPRING71-119
MEYLAN, J-P. LA REVUE DE GENÈVE.
H. GODIN, 208(FS):JUL71-348
MEYNELL, A. THE WARES OF AUTOLYCUS.
(P.M. FRASER, ED)
P. DANCHIN, 179(ES):AUG70-371
MEYNELL, F. MY LIVES.*
A. PRYCE-JONES, 440:16JAN72-10
MEYNELL, L. DEATH BY ARRANGEMENT.
N. CALLENDAR, 441:12NOV72-67
DE MÉZIÈRES, P. LE SONGE DU VIEIL PÈL-
ERIN.* (G.W. COOPLAND, ED)
U.T. HOLMES, 207(FR):MAY70-941
MEZU, S.O. BEHIND THE RISING SUN.
617(TLS):3MAR72-247
MEZU, S.O. LÉOPOLD SÉDAR SENGHOR ET LA
DÉFENSE ET ILLUSTRATION DE LA CIVILISA-
TION NOIRE.
E.A. JONES, 207(FR):FEB70-534
MICHA, A. - SEE DE MONTAIGNE, M.
MICHAEL, H.N. - SEE OKLADNIKOV, A.P.
MICHAEL, I. ENGLISH GRAMMATICAL CATE-
GORIES AND THE TRADITION TO 1800.*
G.L. BROOK, 677:VOL2-230
MICHAEL, I. THE TREATMENT OF CLASSICAL
MATERIAL IN THE "LIBRO DE ALEXANDRE."
L.P. HARVEY, 382(MAE):1971/3-279
J.E. KELLER, 589:JUL71-527
N.J. WARE, 86(BHS):OCT71-351
MICHAEL, R., ED. THE ABZ OF PORNOGRAPHY.
617(TLS):3NOV72-1346
MICHAELIDES, C.E. HYDRA.*
F. HERMAN, 576:MAR69-76
W. KIDNEY, 505:OCT68-286
MICHAELS, L. GOING PLACES.*
E.L. GILBERT, 340(KR):1969/3-422
MICHALOWSKI, K. KARNAK. PALMYRA.
A.T. HODGE, 124:FEB71-206
MICHAUX, H. SELECTED WRITINGS.
L.E. AULD, 399(MLJ):OCT70-456
MICHEL, H. LA DRÔLE DE GUERRE.
617(TLS):14APR72-424
MICHEL, H. LA SECONDE GUERRE MONDIALE.
617(TLS):17MAR72-298
MICHEL, L. THE THING CONTAINED.
E. QUINN, 191(ELN):JUN71-310
MICHEL, P. MONTAIGNE.
I.D. MC FARLANE, 208(FS):JUL71-326
MICHEL, W. - SEE "WYNDHAM LEWIS: PAINT-
INGS AND DRAWINGS"
MICHEL, W. & C.J. FOX - SEE "WYNDHAM
LEWIS ON ART"
MICHELS, A.K. THE CALENDAR OF THE ROMAN
REPUBLIC.*
J-C. DUMONT, 555:VOL44FASC1-165
MICHIELS, I. ORCHIS MILITARIS.
270:VOL20#3-64
MICHON, J. LA MUSIQUE ANGLAISE.
C. CUDWORTH, 415:APR71-347
MICLĂU, P. LE SIGNE LINGUISTIQUE.
H.G. SCHOGT, 320(CJL):SPRING70-150
"THE MIDDLE EAST AND NORTH AFRICA 1972-
73."
617(TLS):13OCT72-1222
MIDDLEBROOK, M. FIRST DAY ON THE SOMME.*
441:6FEB72-40

MIDDLEKAUFF, R. THE MATHERS.*
A.O. ALDRIDGE, 377:JUL71-119
MIDDLEMAS, K. DIPLOMACY OF ILLUSION.
617(TLS):23JUN72-713
MIDDLEMAS, K. THE LIFE AND TIMES OF
EDWARD VII.
617(TLS):14JUL72-799
MIDDLEMAS, K. - SEE JONES, T.
MIDDLETON, C. OUR FLOWERS AND NICE
BONES.*
R. DURGNAT, 493:SUMMER70-162
MIDDLETON, D. - SEE JEPHSON, A.J.M.
MIDDLETON, S. APPLE OF THE EYE. BRAZEN
PRISON.*
F.P.W. MC DOWELL, 659:SUMMER72-361
MIDDLETON, S. COLD GRADATIONS.
V. CUNNINGHAM, 362:6APR72-458
617(TLS):31MAR72-352
MIDDLETON, W.E.K. THE EXPERIMENTERS.
617(TLS):28JUL72-871
MIDWINTER, E.C. SOCIAL ADMINISTRATION
IN LANCASHIRE, 1830-1860.
D.C. MOORE, 637(VS):JUN70-438
MIÈGE, J-L. DOCUMENTS D'HISTOIRE ÉCONO-
MIQUE ET SOCIALE MAROCAINE AU XIXE
SIÈCLE.
P. SALMON, 182:VOL23#23/24-1014
MIEL, J. PASCAL AND THEOLOGY.
H. DAVIES, 402(MLR):OCT71-897
MIGEL, P. THE BALLERINAS.
D. HARRIS, 561(SATR):7OCT72-95
MIGNOT, X. LES VERBES DÉNOMINATIFS
LATINS.
A. ERNOUT, 555:VOL44FASC2-351
G. SELIGSON, 124:NOV70-94
G.J. ZEBIAN, 24:JUL71-511
MIGNUCCI, M. - SEE ARISTOTLE
MIHAILOVIĆ, L. THE PHONEMIC ELEMENTS OF
MODERN ENGLISH.
A. WOLLMANN, 38:BAND87HEFT3/4-421
MIKES, G. ANY SOUVENIRS?
561(SATR):7OCT72-101
MIKHAIL, E.H. A BIBLIOGRAPHY OF MODERN
IRISH DRAMA 1899-1970.
617(TLS):22SEP72-1112
MIKKOLA, E. DIE ABSTRAKTION.
G. NUCHELMANS, 361:VOL24#2-203
MIKKOLA, E. DIE KONZESSIVITÄT DES ALT-
LATEINS IM BEREICH DES SATZGANZEN.
J. ANDRÉ, 555:VOL44FASC1-143
VON MIKLOS, J. THE ILLUSTRATED GUIDE TO
PERSONAL GARDENING.
J. SAVERCOOL, 441:3DEC72-92
MIKO, S.J. TOWARD "WOMEN IN LOVE."
617(TLS):10MAR72-280
MILANI, L. LETTERE. (M. GESUALDI, ED)
617(TLS):21APR72-454
MILANO, P. - SEE DANTE ALIGHIERI
MILCH, W. DIE JUNGE BETTINE 1785-1811.*
(P. KÜPPER, ED)
L.R. FURST, 220(GL&L):APR71-283
H.R. LIEDKE, 222(GR):NOV70-314
MILES, J. KINDS OF AFFECTION.*
J. MC MICHAEL, 598(SOR):WINTER72-213
S. MC PHERSON, 448:SUMMER68-104
H.Z., 502(PRS):FALL69-328
MILES, T.R. RELIGIOUS EXPERIENCE.
617(TLS):13OCT72-1234
MILFORD, N. ZELDA.* (BRITISH TITLE:
ZELDA FITZGERALD.)
P. OWEN, 606(TAMR):#55-85
MILGATE, W. - SEE BALD, R.C.
MILGATE, W. - SEE DONNE, J.
MILHAVEN, J.G. TOWARD A NEW CATHOLIC
MORALITY.
J.J. MAWHINNEY, 142:SPRING71-235
MILIO, N. 9226 KERCHEVAL.
H. KOHL, 453:23MAR72-39

MILIS, L., ED. CONSTITUTIONES CANONICOR-
UM REGULARIUM ORDINIS ARROASIENSIS.
G. CONSTABLE, 589:JUL71-530
MILIS, L. L'ORDRE DES CHANOINES RÉGU-
LIERS D'ARROUAISE.
G. CONSTABLE, 589:JUL71-530
"MILITARY CAMPAIGNS IN CHINA: 1924-1950."
(W.W. WHITSON, P. YANG & P. LAI, TRANS)
293(JAST):MAY70-744
MILIUKOV, P. POLITICAL MEMOIRS 1905-
1917. (A.P. MENDEL, ED)
H.W. DEWEY, 385(MQR):WINTER72-61
MILIUKOV, P. & OTHERS. HISTORY OF RUS-
SIA.
S. MONAS, 550(RUSR):APR70-211
MILL, J.S. COLLECTED WORKS OF JOHN
STUART MILL. (VOL 10) (J.M. ROBSON,
F.E.L. PRIESTLEY & D.P. DRYER, EDS)
K. BRITTON, 483:JUL70-252
J.C. HALL, 518:OCT70-28
MILL, J.S. ESSAYS ON ETHICS, RELIGION
AND SOCIETY. (J.M. ROBSON, ED)
C.J. MYERS, 150(DR):WINTER70/71-559
MILL, J.S. A LOGICAL CRITIQUE OF SOCIOL-
OGY. (R. FLETCHER, ED)
617(TLS):14JAN72-49
"JAMES MILL ON EDUCATION." (W.H. BUR-
STON, ED)
B. SIMON, 637(VS):JUN70-403
MILLAR, B. THE DRIFTERS.
N. FOUNTAIN, 364:FEB/MAR72-141
"THE ERIC GEORGE MILLAR BEQUEST OF MANU-
SCRIPTS AND DRAWINGS 1967."
A.G. WATSON, 325:OCT69-589
MILLAR, F., ED. THE ROMAN EMPIRE AND
ITS NEIGHBOURS.*
D. FISHWICK, 24:JAN71-114
MILLAR, O., ED. THE INVENTORIES AND
VALUATIONS OF THE KING'S GOODS 1649-
1651.
617(TLS):4AUG72-905
MILLAR, O. ZOFFANY AND HIS TRIBUNA.*
R. PAULSON, 173(ECS):WINTER69-278
MILLAR, R. THE PILTDOWN MEN.
617(TLS):29SEP72-1136
MILLAR, T.B. - SEE CASEY, R.G.
MILLARD, O. A MISSING PERSON.
N. CALLENDAR, 441:6AUG72-24
MILLARES, J.H. & A. CARRILLO ESCRIBANO -
SEE UNDER HERNÁNDEZ MILLARES, J. &
A. CARRILLO ESCRIBANO
MILLARES CARLO, A. RAFAEL MARÍA BARALT
(1810-1860).
J.L. HELGUERA, 263:JUL-SEP71-334
MILLER, A., WITH N.L. BROWNING. MILLER'S
HIGH LIFE.
J. KANON, 561(SATR):16DEC72-58
MILLER, A.R. THE ASSAULT ON PRIVACY.*
J. LAX, 385(MQR):SUMMER72-208
D. TERRILL, 396(MODA):FALL71-435
MILLER, B. FERTILIZED BRAINS.
J. HOPPER, 661:SPRING69-97
MILLER, C. THE LUNATIC EXPRESS.*
617(TLS):28APR72-467
MILLER, D.C. & W.S. LIEBERMAN. THE NEW
JAPANESE PAINTING AND SCULPTURE.
P. HARDIE, 39:APR69-326
MILLER, E.H., ED. A CENTURY OF WHITMAN
CRITICISM.
S. GILL, 447(N&Q):JUL70-272
MILLER, E.H. WALT WHITMAN'S POETRY.
R. ROGERS, 191(ELN):SEP70-61
G.M. WHITE, 646(WWR):MAR69-61
MILLER, E.H. - SEE WHITMAN, W.
MILLER, F.P. MAN FROM THE VALLEY.
C. PHILLIPS, 441:27FEB72-40

MILLER, G. THE BOURNEMOUTH SYMPHONY
ORCHESTRA.
K. SPENCE, 415:APR71-347
MILLER, H. MY LIFE AND TIMES.*
A. BURGESS, 441:2JAN72-1
617(TLS):14APR72-408
MILLER, H. SEXUS.*
W. ROWE, 619(TC):1969/2-48
MILLER, H.H. GREECE THROUGH THE AGES.
617(TLS):7JUL72-785
MILLER, H.K., E. ROTHSTEIN & G.S. ROUS-
SEAU, EDS. THE AUGUSTAN MILIEU.
B. BOYCE, 579(SAQ):SUMMER71-432
M. PRICE, 566:SPRING71-64
MILLER, I. PATIENCE AND SARAH.
R.A. WEYR, 441:23APR72-40
MILLER, J. CENSORSHIP AND THE LIMITS OF
PERMISSION.
617(TLS):22SEP72-1083
MILLER, J., ED. FREUD.
M. INGRAM, 362:19OCT72-511
MILLER, J. LIFE IN RUSSIA TODAY.
G.G. MORGAN, 32:MAR71-161
MILLER, J.E., JR. & P.F. HERRING, EDS.
THE ARTS AND THE PUBLIC.*
F. KERMODE, 597(SN):VOL41#1-208
A. RODWAY, 447(N&Q):JUL70-269
A. SHIELDS, 290(JAAC):WINTER69-257
MILLER, J.H. THE FORM OF VICTORIAN
FICTION.
B. HARDY, 155:SEP69-184
E.D.H. JOHNSON, 445(NCF):JUN69-106
G. LEVINE, 637(VS):JUN70-427
MILLER, J.H. THOMAS HARDY.
B.G. HORNBACK, 141:FALL70-356
J.F. SCOTT, 301(JEGP):APR71-332
L. STEVENSON, 676(YR):AUTUMN70-126
MILLER, J.H., ED. WILLIAM CARLOS WIL-
LIAMS.
M.M., 502(PRS):SUMMER69-232
MILLER, J.I. THE SPICE TRADE OF THE
ROMAN EMPIRE, 29 B.C.-A.D. 641.*
E.W. GRAY, 313:VOL60-222
L.D. JOHNSTON, 121(CJ):FEB-MAR71-280
P. WHEATLEY, 293(JAST):MAY70-677
MILLER, M. THE KINGS HAVE DONNED THEIR
FINAL MASK.
D. BARBOUR, 102(CANL):SPRING71-70
MILLER, M. THE SICILIAN COLONY DATES.
C.G. STARR, 124:APR71-275
MILLER, M. WHAT HAPPENED.
M. LEVIN, 441:20AUG72-24
MILLER, P. JAMES.
617(TLS):3MAR72-242
MILLER, P. & L.G. LOST HERITAGE OF
ALASKA.
D.J. CROWLEY, 290(JAAC):FALL69-104
MILLER, R. THE POETRY OF EMILY DICKIN-
SON.
D. PORTER, 141:WINTER69-97
MILLER, R.A. - SEE "BERNARD BLOCH ON
JAPANESE"
MILLER, R.F. ONE HUNDRED THOUSAND TRAC-
TORS.
R.D. LAIRD, 32:MAR71-165
M. MC CAULEY, 575(SEER):APR71-316
MILLER, R.L. & R.M. WILLIAMS. THE NEW
ECONOMICS OF RICHARD NIXON.
H.G. JOHNSON, 441:27AUG72-4
MILLER, S.C. THE UNWELCOME IMMIGRANT.
J.P. O'KEEFE, 293(JAST):AUG70-922
MILLER, T. HENRI IV OF CASTILE.
617(TLS):22SEP72-1114
MILLER, W.C. AN ARMED AMERICA.
M. MILLGATE, 27(AL):NOV71-487
MILLER, W.D. A HARSH AND DREADFUL LOVE.
W.H. AUDEN, 453:14DEC72-3

MILLET, L. LE SYMBOLISME DANS LA PHIL-
OSOPHIE DE LACHELIER.
F. KAPLAN, 542:JAN-MAR68-131
MILLETT, K. SEXUAL POLITICS.*
M. ELLMANN, 676(YR):SUMMER71-590
H., LOMAS, 364:DEC71/JAN72-143
MILLGATE, M. THOMAS HARDY.*
T. SLADE, 67:NOV71-242
MILLHAUSER, S. EDWIN MULLHOUSE.
W. HJORTSBERG, 441:17SEP72-2
J. KANON, 561(SATR):30SEP72-73
MILLHISER, M. MICHAEL'S WIFE.
N. CALLENDAR, 441:26NOV72-36
MILLIGAN, S. THE GOON SHOW SCRIPTS.
617(TLS):24NOV72-1425
MILLOT, B. DIVINE THUNDER.
617(TLS):25FEB72-230
MILLS, H. PEACOCK.
F. BURWICK, 445(NCF):SEP69-240
D. GALLON, 97(CQ):SUMMER69-313
J.E.J., 191(ELN):SEP70(SUPP)-40
L. MADDEN, 637(VS):JUN70-435
G. THOMAS, 175:SUMMER69-70
A. WELSH, 191(ELN):MAR70-225
MILLS, H. - SEE CRABBE, G.
MILLS, J. REPORT TO THE COMMISSIONER.
P. ADAMS, 61:AUG72-92
S. ELLIN, 441:16JUL72-4
I.P. HELDMAN, 561(SATR):12AUG72-57
J. HUNTER, 362:21DEC72-869
T. LASK, 441:18JUL72-35
617(TLS):10NOV72-1375
MILLS, J.A. LANGUAGE AND LAUGHTER.*
F.P.W. MC DOWELL, 572:SEP69-122
MILLS, J.V.G. - SEE MA HUAN
MILLS, M. - SEE "LYBEAUS DESCONUS"
MILLS, R.J., JR. - SEE ROETHKE, T.
MILLWARD, R. & A. ROBINSON. CUMBRIA.
617(TLS):27OCT72-1297
MILNE, A.J.M. FREEDOM AND RIGHTS.
J. DAY, 518:JAN70-14
MILNER, I. THE STRUCTURE OF VALUES IN
GEORGE ELIOT.*
J.C. MAXWELL, 447(N&Q):APR70-160
G.W. SPENCE, 67:MAY71-107
MILNER, I. - SEE HOLAN, V.
MILNER, M. GEORGES BERNANOS.
G.R. BLUMENTHAL, 207(FR):MAY70-933
MILNS, R.D. ALEXANDER THE GREAT.*
E.A. FREDRICKSMEYER, 124:DEC70-129
MILOBENSKI, E. DER NEID IN DER GRIECHIS-
CHEN PHILOSOPHIE.
A.W.H. ADKINS, 123:JUN71-293
MILSON, F. SEX AND A PASTOR.
617(TLS):29SEP72-1173
MILSON, F. YOUTH IN A CHANGING SOCIETY.
617(TLS):24MAR72-345
MILTON, J. COMPLETE PROSE WORKS OF JOHN
MILTON. (VOL 5, PT 1) (F. FOGLE, ED)
G.B. PARKS, 568(SCN):SUMMER/AUTUMN71-
33
MILTON, J. COMPLETE PROSE WORKS OF JOHN
MILTON. (VOL 5, PT 2) (J.M. PATRICK,
ED)
W.B. HUNTER, JR., 568(SCN):WINTER71-
61
MILTON, J. THE POEMS OF JOHN MILTON.*
(J. CAREY & A. FOWLER, EDS)
R.W. FRENCH, 150(DR):AUTUMN70-406
MILTON, J. A VARIORUM COMMENTARY ON THE
POEMS OF JOHN MILTON - SEE UNDER BUSH,
D., J.E. SHAW & A.B. GIAMATII
MILTON, J.R. - SEE WATERS, F.
MILTON, R. THE ENGLISH CEREMONIAL BOOK.
617(TLS):23JUN72-730
MILWARD, A.S. THE FASCIST ECONOMY IN
NORWAY.
617(TLS):16JUN72-692

MILWARD, P. A COMMENTARY ON G.M. HOP-
KINS' "THE WRECK OF THE DEUTSCHLAND."
N.H. MAC KENZIE, 401(MLQ):JUN70-236
R.V. SCHODER, 613:AUTUMN69-469
MILWARD, P. A COMMENTARY ON THE SONNETS
OF G.M. HOPKINS.
N.H. MAC KENZIE, 401(MLQ):JUN70-236
MINADEO, R. THE LYRE OF SCIENCE.*
P.M. BROWN, 123:DEC70-409
MINEAR, R.H. VICTOR'S JUSTICE.
617(TLS):1SEP72-1029
MINER, E. THE CAVALIER MODE FROM JONSON
TO COTTON.
617(TLS):2JUN72-634
MINER, E. AN INTRODUCTION TO JAPANESE
COURT POETRY.
R.L. BACKUS, 318(JAOS):OCT-DEC70-605
MINER, E. JAPANESE POETIC DIARIES.
K. YASUDA, 293(JAST):FEB70-443
MINER, E. THE METAPHYSICAL MODE FROM
DONNE TO COWLEY.*
A. LOW, 568(SCN):SPRING71-12
J. WEBBER, 401(MLQ):DEC70-506
MINER, E., ED. RESTORATION DRAMATISTS.
R.T. BARBER, JR., 583:SUMMER69-325
MINER, E. & OTHERS - SEE DRYDEN, J.
MINH, D.V. VIETNAM.
P. WHEATLEY, 293(JAST):NOV69-206
MINIO-PALUELLO, L. & B.G. DOD. ARISTO-
TELES LATINUS. (VOL 4, PTS 1-4)
P.M. HUBY, 123:DEC70-319
MINKOWSKI, E. TRAITÉ DE PSYCHOPATHOLO-
GIE.
V. RÜFNER, 182:VOL23#3-68
MINNEY, R.J., ED. THE GEORGE BERNARD
SHAW VEGETARIAN COOK BOOK.
B. BROPHY, 362:28SEP72-410
MINOR, A.C. & B. MITCHELL, EDS. A REN-
AISSANCE ENTERTAINMENT.
B. CORRIGAN, 276:WINTER70-437
MINTER, D.L. THE INTERPRETED DESIGN AS
A STRUCTURAL PRINCIPLE IN AMERICAN
PROSE.*
639(VQR):SPRING70-LII
MINTZ, R., ED. MODERN HEBREW POETRY.
A.I. KATSH, 399(MLJ):MAY70-365
MIQUEL, A. LA GÉOGRAPHIE HUMAINE DU
MONDE MUSULMAN JUSQU' AU MILIEU DE 11E
SIÈCLE.
S.D. GOITEIN, 318(JAOS):OCT-DEC70-
551
MIRABELLI, E. NO RESTING PLACE.
J. CAREW, 441:10SEP72-47
MIRALLES, C. LA NOVELA EN LA ANTIGÜEDAD
CLÁSICA.
B.P. REARDON, 123:MAR71-134
B.P. REARDON, 487:AUTUMN70-274
"AUSTIN MIRES: AN INDEXED REGISTER OF
HIS PAPERS, 1872-1936."
J.P. BUTLER, 14:JAN69-36
MIROIU, M. & M. SPARIOSU - SEE STERNE,
L.
MIRSKY, M. BLUE HILL AVENUE.
G. WOLFF, 441:5NOV72-38
"MISCELLANY ONE." [EDINBURGH STAIR
SOCIETY]
617(TLS):14APR72-429
MISCHEL, T., ED. HUMAN ACTION.
R.J.B., 543:SEP69-143
MISH, C.C., ED. RESTORATION PROSE FIC-
TION, 1666-1700.
R.A. DAY, 568(SCN):SUMMER/AUTUMN71-47
MISHIMA, Y. AI NO KAWAKI.
R.L. BROWN, 270:VOL20#2-42
MISHIMA, Y. SPRING SNOW.
H. CALISHER, 441:12NOV72-56
J.G. FARRELL, 362:2NOV72-611
D. KEENE, 561(SATR):10JUN72-57 [CONT]

MISHIMA, Y. SPRING SNOW. [CONTINUED]
   T. LASK, 441:6JUL72-39
   D. RICHIE, 231:SEP72-105
   442(NY):29JUL72-78
   617(TLS):10NOV72-1357
MISHIMA, Y. SUN AND STEEL.*
   H. CALISHER, 441:12NOV72-56
MISHIMA, Y. THIRST FOR LOVE.
   639(VQR):WINTER70-XII
MISHRA, D.P. STUDIES IN THE PROTO-
  HISTORY OF INDIA.
   617(TLS):7JAN72-21
MISKAWAYH. THE REFINEMENT OF CHARACTER
  (TAHDHĪB AL-AKHLĀQ). (C.K. ZURAYK,
  TRANS)
   G.M. WICKENS, 318(JAOS):OCT-DEC70-552
MISKAWAYH [MISKAWAIH]. TAHDHĪB AL-AKHLĀQ.
  (C.K. ZURAYK, ED)
   M.S. KHAN, 273(IC):JUL69-242
MISKAWAYH. TRAITÉ D'ÉTHIQUE (TAHDHĪB AL-
  'AHLĀQ WA TATHĪR AL-'A'RĀQ). (M.
  ARKOUN, ED & TRANS)
   J. VAN ESS, 182:VOL23#15/16-709
MISKIMIN, A. - SEE "SUSANNAH"
MISKIMIN, H.A. THE ECONOMY OF EARLY
  RENAISSANCE EUROPE 1300-1460.
   S.L. THRUPP, 589:JAN71-174
MISRA, A. THE FINANCING OF INDIAN EDU-
  CATION.
   W.H. HILL, 293(JAST):NOV69-193
MISRA, B.B. THE ADMINISTRATIVE HISTORY
  OF INDIA.
   617(TLS):21APR72-458
MISRA, V.N. THE DESCRIPTIVE TECHNIQUE
  OF PĀNINI.
   R. ROCHER, 318(JAOS):APR-JUN70-357
"MISS READ." EMILY DAVIS.
   M. LEVIN, 441:13FEB72-32
MISTRAL, G. SELECTED POEMS OF GABRIELA
  MISTRAL.* (D. DANA, ED & TRANS)
   G. DAVENPORT, 249(HUDR):WINTER71/72-
   699
MITCHELL, A. RIDE THE NIGHTMARE.*
   I. WEDDE, 364:DEC71/JAN72-118
MITCHELL, G. BLOW MY BLUES AWAY.
   441:12MAR72-38
MITCHELL, H.H. BLACK PREACHING.
   J. MC DONNELL, 142:FALL71-469
MITCHELL, J. THOMAS HOCCLEVE.*
   J.S. KANTROWITZ, 405(MP):AUG69-81
   G. KINNEAVY, 191(ELN):SEP69-58
   G. REINECKE, 219(GAR):FALL69-410
   A.N. WAWN, 402(MLR):OCT71-851
   R.M. WILSON, 175:SPRING69-27
MITCHELL, J. THE NATIONAL BOARD FOR
  PRICES AND INCOMES.
   617(TLS):1DEC72-1464
MITCHELL, J. A RED FILE FOR CALLAN.
   N. CALLENDAR, 441:2JAN72-16
MITCHELL, J. REMINISCENCES OF MY LIFE
  IN THE HIGHLANDS 1884. (VOL 2)
   617(TLS):21APR72-450
MITCHELL, J. WOMEN'S ESTATE.*
   E. JANEWAY, 440:30JAN72-6
   R. SENNETT, 453:20APR72-22
MITCHELL, R.H. THE KOREAN MINORITY IN
  JAPAN.
   C.I.E. KIM, 293(JAST):MAY70-709
MITCHELL, W.S., COMP. CATALOGUE OF THE
  INCUNABULA IN ABERDEEN UNIVERSITY
  LIBRARY.*
   A.G. RIGG, 447(N&Q):MAR70-101
MITCHISON, N. CLEOPATRA'S PEOPLE.
   D.A.N. JONES, 362:6JUL72-22
MITCHISON, R. A HISTORY OF SCOTLAND.*
   E. CREGEEN, 595(SCS):VOL15PT1-73

MITGANG, H. GET THESE MEN OUT OF THE HOT
  SUN.
   A. COOPER, 561(SATR):8APR72-73
   F. TRIPPETT, 441:26MAR72-40
MITTINS, W.H. A GRAMMAR OF MODERN ENG-
  LISH.
   W.A. KOCH, 38:BAND87HEFT3/4-425
MITTON, R. & E. MORRISON. A COMMUNITY
  PROJECT IN NOTTING DALE.
   617(TLS):23JUN72-724
MIYAGAWA, T. MODERN JAPANESE PAINTING.
   P. HARDIE, 39:APR69-327
MIZENER, A. SCOTT FITZGERALD AND HIS
  WORLD.
   617(TLS):3NOV72-1349
MIZENER, A. THE SADDEST STORY.*
   G. CORE, 598(SOR):AUTUMN72-956
   C. JAMES, 362:18MAY72-656
   R. SALE, 249(HUDR):AUTUMN71-511
   617(TLS):5MAY72-519
MŇAČKO, L. THE SEVENTH NIGHT.*
   A. PRAVDA, 447(N&Q):FEB70-77
MOAKLEY, G. THE TAROT CARDS PAINTED BY
  BONIFACIO BEMBO FOR THE VISCONTI-SFORZA
  FAMILY.*
   K.T. STEINITZ, 54:JUN69-188
MOBERLY, W. THE ETHICS OF PUNISHMENT.
   D.N. MAC CORMICK, 479(PHQ):JUL70-301
MODDIE, A.D. THE BRAHMANICAL CULTURE AND
  MODERNITY.
   R.G. FOX, 293(JAST):NOV69-194
MODELSKI, G. PRINCIPLES OF WORLD POLI-
  TICS.
   617(TLS):8DEC72-1476
"MODERN POETRY IN TRANSLATION." (NO. 6)
   J. BERNARDIN, 493:AUTUMN70-254
MODIANO, P. LES BOULEVARDS DE CEINTURE.
   617(TLS):15DEC72-1521
MODIANO, P. NIGHT ROUNDS.*
   V. CUNNINGHAM, 362:2MAR72-283
MOERMAN, M. AGRICULTURAL CHANGE AND
  PEASANT CHOICE IN A THAI VILLAGE.
   W.F. VELLA, 318(JAOS):OCT-DEC70-627
MOERS, E. TWO DREISERS.*
   42(AR):FALL69-446
MOFFETT, T. THE PARTICIPATION PUT-ON.
   S. SCHLESINGER, 561(SATR):1JAN72-31
MOGAN, J.J., JR. CHAUCER AND THE THEME
  OF MUTABILITY.
   E. REISS, 589:JAN71-175
MOHAN, G.B. THE RESPONSE TO POETRY.
   V.M. AMES, 290(JAAC):SUMMER70-559
MOHANTY, J. GANGEŚA'S THEORY OF TRUTH.
   B.K. MATILAL, 485(PE&W):OCT68-321
MOHL, R. JOHN MILTON AND HIS "COMMON-
  PLACE BOOK."*
   R.W. AYERS, 551(RENQ):WINTER70-489
MOHOLY-NAGY, S. THE MATRIX OF MAN.
   E. GALANTAY, 505:MAR69-158
   P. GOODMAN, 45:MAR69-147
   J.M. JOHANSEN, 44:MAY69-84
MOHRT, M. L'OURS DES ADIRONDACKS.
   R. MERKER, 207(FR):FEB70-530
MOIGNET, G. LE PRONOM PERSONNEL FRAN-
  ÇAIS.
   E. GARCÍA, 545(RPH):AUG69-110
MOIGNET, G. - SEE "LA CHANSON DE ROLAND"
MOIR, D.W. - SEE BANCES CANDAMO, F.
MOISAN, C. L'ÂGE DE LA LITTÉRATURE
  CANADIENNE.
   B.T. GODARD, 102(CANL):SPRING71-94
MOK, Q.I.M. CONTRIBUTION À L'ÉTUDE DES
  CATÉGORIES MORPHOLOGIQUES DU GENRE ET
  DU NOMBRE DANS LE FRANÇAIS PARLÉ
  ACTUEL.*
   W. ZWANENBURG, 361:VOL24#4-395
MOK-WOL, P. - SEE UNDER PAK MOK-WOL

MOLAJOLI, B. FLORENCE.
  561(SATR):7OCT72-108
MOLDENHAUR, H., COMP. ANTON VON WEBERN:
  PERSPECTIVES. (D. IRVINE, ED)
  B.C. CANNON, 308:WINTER67-292
MOLER, K.L. JANE AUSTEN'S ART OF ALLU-
  SION.*
  L.W. BROWN, 173(ECS):FALL69-145
  W.D. SCHAEFER, 445(NCF):SEP69-247
MOLES, A. INFORMATION THEORY AND ESTHET-
  IC PERCEPTION.
  D. KRAEHENBUEHL, 308:SPRING67-149
MOLESWORTH, H.D. & J. KENWORTHY-BROWNE.
  THREE CENTURIES OF FURNITURE IN COLOUR.
  617(TLS):22DEC72-1566
MOLHO, A. FLORENTINE PUBLIC FINANCES IN
  THE EARLY RENAISSANCE, 1400-1433.
  617(TLS):27OCT72-1296
MOLHO, M. LINGUISTIQUES ET LANGUAGE.
  R.G. KEIGHTLEY, 86(BHS):APR71-151
  N.C.W. SPENCE, 208(FS):OCT71-503
MOLHO, M. & J.F. REILLE - SEE "ROMANS
  PICARESQUES ESPAGNOLS"
MOLIÈRE, J.B.P. THE SCHOOL FOR WIVES.
  (R. WILBUR, TRANS)
  P. MURRAY, 491:JUL72-230
MOLINA, F.R., ED. THE SOURCES OF EXIS-
  TENTIALISM AS PHILOSOPHY.
  W.A.J., 543:MAR70-573
DE MOLINA, T. - SEE UNDER TIRSO DE MOLINA
MOLINARD, B. VIENS.
  H. MICHOT-DIETRICH, 207(FR):APR70-867
MOLLICA, A.S. & G.P. DESLAURIERS - SEE
  GUÈVREMONT, G.
MOLLOY, H. OEDIPUS IN DISNEYLAND.
  617(TLS):1SEP72-1031
MOLNÁR, E. VÁLOGATOTT TANULMÁNYOK.
  A. KADARKAY, 182:VOL23#23/24-1014
MOLNÁR, M. BUDAPEST 1956.
  617(TLS):20OCT72-1258
MOMADAY, N.S. THE WAY TO RAINY MOUNTAIN.*
  B.L. FONTANA, 50(ARQ):WINTER69-377
MOMBELLO, G. LA TRADIZIONE MANOSCRITTA
  DELL' "EPISTRE OTHEA" DI CHRISTINE DE
  PIZAN.
  K. VARTY, 208(FS):JAN71-60
MOMBERT, A. BRIEFE AN VASANTA, 1922-37.
  (B.J. MORSE, ED)
  D. VAN ABBÉ, 182:VOL23#11/12-620
MOMIGLIANO, A. THE DEVELOPMENT OF GREEK
  BIOGRAPHY.
  617(TLS):24NOV72-1418
MOMIGLIANO, A. QUARTO CONTRIBUTO ALLA
  STORIA DEGLI STUDI CLASSICI E DEL MONDO
  ANTICO.
  P.A. BRUNT, 123:JUN71-280
MOMMSEN, K. NATUR- UND FABELREICH IN
  FAUST II.*
  H. REHDER, 301(JEGP):JAN71-117
  J.W. SMEED, 220(GL&L):OCT70-113
MOMMSEN, W.J. DIE GESCHICHTSWISSENSCHAFT
  JENSEITS DES HISTORISMUS.
  617(TLS):15SEP72-1047
MON, F. TEXTE ÜBER TEXTE.
  617(TLS):22SEP72-1085
MONAN, J.D. MORAL KNOWLEDGE AND ITS
  METHODOLOGY IN ARISTOTLE.*
  W. WICK, 185:OCT69-76
MONDRAGÓN, M. PORQUE ME DA LA GANA!
  (J. SARNACKI, ED)
  A.B. HENKIN, 399(MLJ):NOV70-530
MONÉSI, I. VIE D'UNE BÊTE.
  617(TLS):29SEP72-1140
MONET, J. THE LAST CANNON SHOT.
  G.F.G. STANLEY, 529(QQ):AUTUMN70-440
DE MONFRED, A.H. THE NDM PRINCIPLE OF
  RELATIVE MUSIC.
  N. O'LOUGHLIN, 415:AUG71-761

MONGRÉDIEN, G. DICTIONNAIRE BIOGRAPHIQUE
  DES COMÉDIENS FRANÇAIS DU XVIIe SIÈCLE.
  E.T. DUBOIS, 182:VOL23#19/20-868
MONGRÉDIEN, G. RECUEIL DES TEXTES ET DES
  DOCUMENTS DU XVIIe SIÈCLE RELATIFS À
  MOLIÈRE.
  J. LOUGH, 182:VOL23#17/18-801
MONGUIÓ, L. DON JOSÉ JOAQUÍN DE MORA Y
  EL PERÚ DEL OCHOCIENTOS.*
  191(ELN):SEP69(SUPP)-157
MONK, S.H., WITH A.E.W. MAURER - SEE
  DRYDEN, J.
MONKHOUSE, F. & J. WILLIAMS. CLIMBER AND
  FELL WALKER IN LAKELAND.
  617(TLS):14JUL72-826
DE LA MONNERAYE, J. & R-A. WEIGERT.
  PARIS.
  617(TLS):25FEB72-230
MONOD, J. CHANCE AND NECESSITY.*
  (FRENCH TITLE: LE HASARD ET LA NÉCES-
  SITÉ.)
  N. BLIVEN, 442(NY):12AUG72-75
  617(TLS):2JUN72-629
MONOD, M. MANUEL D'APPLICATION DU TEST
  DU VILLAGE (MATÉRIEL MABILLE).
  V. RÜFNER, 182:VOL23#6-258
MONOD, S. DICKENS THE NOVELIST.
  T.J. CRIBB, 541(RES):MAY70-251
  K.J. FIELDING, 155:JAN69-49
  R.D. MC MASTER, 445(NCF):DEC68-359
MONRO, D.H. EMPIRICISM AND ETHICS.*
  R.L. ARRIGON, 613:SPRING69-154
MONROE, H.M., JR. & J.T. MC INTOSH - SEE
  DAVIS, J.
MONSMAN, G.C. PATER'S PORTRAITS.
  R.A. BELLAS, 613:AUTUMN68-449
  D.L. HILL, 445(NCF):JUN68-109
MONSONÉGO, S. ÉTUDE STYLO-STATISTIQUE DU
  VOCABULAIRE DES VERS ET DE LA PROSE
  DANS LA CHANTEFABLE "AUCASSIN ET NICO-
  LETTE."
  J.J. DUGGAN, 545(RPH):NOV69-253
MONTAGU, A. THE ELEPHANT MAN.*
  617(TLS):9JUN72-655
MONTAGU, A. TOUCHING.*
  617(TLS):11FEB72-149
MONTAGU, E. AN ESSAY ON THE WRITINGS AND
  GENIUS OF SHAKESPEAR.
  617(TLS):18FEB72-178
MONTAGUE, J. TIDES.
  R. LATTIMORE, 249(HUDR):AUTUMN71-502
MONTAGUE, M.F.A., ED. MAN AND AGGRES-
  SION.
  S.O.H., 543:DEC69-364
DE MONTAIGNE, M. ESSAIS. (2ND ED) (M.
  FRANÇON, ED) ESSAIS. (A. MICHA, ED)
  I.D. MC FARLANE, 208(FS):JUL71-326
DE MONTAIGNE, M. ESSAIS. (J. LECAT, ED)
  M-C. WRAGE, 399(MLJ):OCT70-469
MONTALE, E. POÉSIES. (P. ANGELINI &
  OTHERS, TRANS)
  L. REBAY, 131(CL):SPRING71-173
MONTALE, E. PROVISIONAL CONCLUSIONS.
  XENIA.* THE BUTTERFLY OF DINARD.*
  S. SPENDER, 453:1JUN72-29
MONTANER, C.A. PÓKER DE BRUJAS.
  L. FERNÁNDEZ-MARCANÉ, 263:APR-JUN71-
  220
DE MONTCLOS, J-P.P. - SEE UNDER PÉROUSE
  DE MONTCLOS, J-P.
MONTEIL, P. - SEE THEOCRITUS
MONTEMAYOR, G. & G. POLO. A CRITICAL
  EDITION OF YONG'S TRANSLATION OF GEORGE
  OF MONTEMAYOR'S "DIANA" AND GIL POLO'S
  "ENAMOURED DIANA." (J.M. KENNEDY, ED)
  K. DUNCAN-JONES, 541(RES):FEB70-108
  R. GRAZIANI, 627(UTQ):JUL69-365

MONTESQUIEU. CONSIDÉRATIONS SUR LES
CAUSES DE LA GRANDEUR DES ROMAINS ET
DE LEUR DÉCADENCE. (J. EHRARD, ED)
J.H. BROOME, 208(FS):JAN71-87
MONTESQUIEU. ESSAI SUR LE GOÛT.* (C-J.
BEYER, ED)
R.F. O'REILLY, 593:FALL71-312
R.G. SAISSELIN, 546(RR):FEB70-60
MONTGOMERIE, J. THE QUIET GAME.
617(TLS):9JUN72-667
LORD MONTGOMERY. A HISTORY OF WARFARE.
J.E. TALMADGE, 219(GAR):FALL69-405
MONTGOMERY, C.C. HEMINGWAY IN MICHIGAN.
H. KLAPPER, 502(PRS):SPRING68-84
MONTGOMERY, C.F. AMERICAN FURNITURE:
THE FEDERAL PERIOD.*
G. HOOD, 56:AUTUMN69-318
F.J.B. WATSON, 39:FEB69-159
MONTGOMERY, M. THE GULL AND OTHER GEOR-
GIA SCENES.
S. MOORE, 385(MQR):SUMMER72-217
MONTGOMERY, S. CIRCE.
R. DURGNAT, 493:SPRING70-81
MONTONERI, L. IL PROBLEMA DEL MALE
NELLA FILOSOFIA DI PLATONE.
W.E. CHARLTON, 123:MAR71-128
MONTOTO, S. FERNÁN CABALLERO (ALGO MAS
QUE UNA BIOGRAFÍA).
191(ELN):SEP70(SUPP)-155
MOODY, J.N. THE CHURCH AS ENEMY.
C.C., 191(ELN):SEP70(SUPP)-56
H.S. GERSHMAN, 207(FR):OCT69-158
MOODY, R. LILLIAN HELLMAN.
P. ADAMS, 61:JUL72-97
C.T. SAMUELS, 441:18JUN72-2
MOOG, V. EM BUSCA DE LINCOLN.*
V. VALDÉS-RODRÍGUEZ, 37:MAY69-42
MOOKERJEE, G.K. THE INDIAN IMAGE OF
NINETEENTH-CENTURY EUROPE.
S.N. MUKHERJEE, 293(JAST):FEB70-505
MOONEY, H.J., JR. JAMES GOULD COZZENS.
H. STRAUMANN, 179(ES):APR69-221
MOONEY, H.J., JR. & T.F. STALEY, EDS.
THE SHAPELESS GOD.
R.J. THOMPSON, 613:WINTER69-602
MOONEY, M.M. THE HINDENBURG.
J.G. VAETH, 441:19MAR72-18
E. WEEKS, 61:APR72-126
442(NY):15APR72-148
MOORCOCK, M. AN ALIEN HEAT.
617(TLS):27OCT72-1273
MOORCOCK, M. THE ENGLISH ASSASSIN.
BREAKFAST IN THE RUINS.
617(TLS):29SEP72-1174
MOORCRAFT, C. MUST THE SEAS DIE?
617(TLS):3NOV72-1302
MOORE, B. CATHOLICS.
D. MAHON, 362:2NOV72-610
617(TLS):10NOV72-1357
MOORE, B. FERGUS.*
D.J. GORDON, 676(YR):SPRING71-428
G. WOODCOCK, 102(CANL):SUMMER71-81
MOORE, B. I AM MARY DUNNE.
G. ROPER, 627(UTQ):JUL69-354
MOORE, B. THE LUCK OF GINGER COFFEY.
J.R. SORFLEET, 296:SPRING72-92
MOORE, B. THE REVOLUTION SCRIPT.*
D. ARNASON, 296:WINTER72-86
D.A.N. JONES, 362:20JAN72-90
C.I. MILLER, 99:JAN-FEB72-74
P. NADEAU, 561(SATR):12FEB72-77
617(TLS):21JAN72-57
MOORE, B., JR. REFLECTIONS ON THE
CAUSES OF HUMAN MISERY AND UPON CER-
TAIN PROPOSALS TO ELIMINATE THEM.
R.L. HEILBRONER, 453:5OCT72-19
R. TERRILL, 61:OCT72-120
617(TLS):1DEC72-1450

MOORE, C.A., ED. THE JAPANESE MIND.
G.A. DE VOS, 318(JAOS):OCT-DEC70-608
MOORE, C.A., WITH A.V. MORRIS, EDS. THE
STATUS OF THE INDIVIDUAL IN EAST AND
WEST.
S. LAMBERT, 319:JAN72-108
MOORE, D.B. THE POETRY OF LOUIS
MAC NEICE.
617(TLS):25AUG72-984
MOORE, F.C.T. THE PSYCHOLOGY OF MAINE
DE BIRAN.*
R.B. ROSTHAL, 311(JP):27JAN72-29
MOORE, F.D. TRANSPLANT.
W.A. NOLEN, 441:5MAR72-38
MOORE, G. THE CHOSEN TONGUE.
E. WRIGHT, 315(JAL):VOL8PT1-69
MOORE, G. GEORGE MOORE IN TRANSITION.*
(H.E. GERBER, ED)
C. BURKHART, 445(NCF):DEC68-365
F.H. MEGALLY, 541(RES):FEB70-97
L. ORMOND, 677:VOL2-323
MOORE, G. WOLE SOYINKA.
D.A.N. JONES, 362:30MAR72-426
MOORE, H.T., ED. D.H. LAWRENCE.
A. RUDRUM, 529(QQ):AUTUMN70-454
MOORE, J.N. ELGAR.
617(TLS):27OCT72-1289
MOORE, J.W., WITH A. CUÉLLAR. MEXICAN
AMERICANS.
J. WOMACK, JR., 453:31AUG72-12
MOORE, L. ARTISTS OF THE DANCE.
J. DE LABAN, 290(JAAC):SUMMER70-556
MOORE, L.H., JR. ROBERT PENN WARREN AND
HISTORY.
J.E. HARDY, 27(AL):NOV71-481
MOORE, M. THE COMPLETE POEMS OF MARIANNE
MOORE.*
H. SERGEANT, 175:SPRING69-33
MOORE, P. CAN YOU SPEAK VENUSIAN?
617(TLS):20OCT72-1264
MOORE, P., ED. 1973 YEARBOOK OF ASTRON-
OMY.
617(TLS):1DEC72-1469
MOORE, P. THE SKY AT NIGHT 4.
617(TLS):3NOV72-1349
MOORE, P. & D.A. HARDY. CHALLENGE OF THE
STARS.
617(TLS):7JUL72-785
MOORE, R. LIZZIE AND CAROLINE.
M. LEVIN, 441:23JUL72-20
MOORE, T.I. SOCIAL PATTERNS IN AUSTRAL-
IAN LITERATURE.
J. COLMER, 71(ALS):MAY72-323
MOORE, V. SCOTTSVILLE ON THE JAMES.
639(VQR):SPRING70-LXXIV
MOORE, W.G. FRENCH ACHIEVEMENT IN LIT-
ERATURE.
R.C. REARDON, 207(FR):MAR70-703
M.G. WORTHINGTON, 545(RPH):FEB71-552
MOORE, W.G. LA ROCHEFOUCAULD.*
J. DOOLITTLE, 401(MLQ):SEP70-382
D. SECRETAN, 402(MLR):JUL71-690
MOORE, W.L. - SEE WHITMAN, W.
MOOREY, P.R.S. CATALOGUE OF THE ANCIENT
PERSIAN BRONZES IN THE ASHMOLEAN MUS-
EUM.
617(TLS):21JAN72-72
MOORHEAD, A. MORGANSTALL.
T.L. WEPPLER, 99:JUL-AUG72-46
MOORHOUSE, G. CALCUTTA.
T. LASK, 441:18FEB72-36
J.A. LUKAS, 441:13FEB72-3
N. MAXWELL, 453:23MAR72-8
B.D. NOSSITER, 440:12MAR72-1
617(TLS):5MAY72-524
MOORMAN, C. A KNYGHT THERE WAS.*
L.M. SKLUTE, 545(RPH):MAY71-640

223

MOORMAN, M. WILLIAM WORDSWORTH. (VOL 1:
THE EARLY YEARS 1770-1803.)
J.C. MAXWELL, 447(N&Q):MAY70-189
MOORMAN, M. WILLIAM WORDSWORTH.* (VOL
2: THE LATER YEARS, 1803-1850.)
J.C. MAXWELL, 447(N&Q):MAY70-189
H. SCHNYDER, 179(ES):JUN70-263
MOORMAN, M. - SEE WORDSWORTH, W. & D.
MOORMAN, M. & A.G. HILL - SEE WORDSWORTH,
W. & D.
MOORTGAT, A. THE ART OF ANCIENT MESOPO-
TAMIA.
M. MALLOWAN, 90:JUN70-406
O.W. MUSCARELLA, 58:APR70-10
MORA, J.F. - SEE FERRATER MORA, J.
DE MORAES, R.B. BIBLIOGRAFIA BRASILEIRA
DO PERÍODO COLONIAL.
H.M., 191(ELN):SEP70(SUPP)-142
MORALES, H.L. - SEE UNDER LÓPEZ MORALES,
H.
MORAN, G. THE NEW COMMUNITY.
R. BRADLEY, 142:WINTER71-113
MORAN, J. THE COMPOSITION OF READING
MATTER.
N. BARKER, 354:MAR69-77
MORAN, J. STANLEY MORISON.*
R. STONE, 362:17AUG72-214
MORANTI, L. L'ARTE TIPOGRAFICA IN
URBINO (1493-1800) CON APPENDICE DI
DOCUMENTE E ANNALI.
J.M. POTTER, 78(BC):SPRING70-107
D.E. RHODES, 354:MAR69-61
MORAVIA, A. PARADISE AND OTHER STORIES.*
(ITALIAN TITLE: IL PARADISO.)
G. EWART, 364:OCT/NOV71-159
617(TLS):5MAY72-509
MORAVIA, A. TWO.
A. BROYARD, 441:2MAY72-45
L. FIEDLER, 441:30APR72-2
K. MILLER, 453:20APR72-19
P. WOOD, 561(SATR):29APR72-76
442(NY):29APR72-141
MORAVIA, A. THE TWO OF US.
J. HUNTER, 362:4MAY72-596
617(TLS):5MAY72-509
MORAVIA, S. LA RAGIONE NASCOSTA.
E. GIANTURCO, 131(CL):FALL71-360
MORAZÉ, C. LE GÉNÉRAL DE GAULLE ET LA
RÉPUBLIQUE.
617(TLS):29SEP72-1134
MORE, T. CONSCIENCE DECIDES. (B. FOORD,
ED)
617(TLS):9JUN72-667
"THOMAS MORE'S PRAYER BOOK."* (L.L.
MARTZ & R.S. SYLVESTER, EDS)
W. ALLEN, 551(RENQ):WINTER70-468
J.M. HEADLEY, 577(SHR):SUMMER70-282
MOREA, P.C. GUIDANCE, SELECTION AND
TRAINING.
617(TLS):18AUG72-978
MORÉAS, J. CENT SOIXANTE-TREIZE LETTRES
DE JEAN MORÉAS. (R.A. JOUANNY, ED)
J.A. DUNCAN, 208(FS):APR71-227
MOREAU, J. LES SENS DU PLATONISME.
P. LOUIS, 555:VOL44FASC2-321
MOREHOUSE, W., ED. SCIENCE AND THE HUMAN
CONDITION IN INDIA AND PAKISTAN.
R.S. ANDERSON, 293(JAST):MAY70-720
MOREL, J. JEAN ROTROU, DRAMATURE DE
L'AMBIGUÏTÉ.*
R.C. KNIGHT, 208(FS):JAN71-70
R.W. TOBIN, 546(RR):OCT70-222
MORELL, A.G. - SEE UNDER GALLEGO MORELL,
A.
MORELLA, J., E.Z. EPSTEIN & E. CLARK.
THOSE GREAT MOVIE ADS.
J. KANON, 561(SATR):16DEC72-58

DE MORELOS, L.C. & A. LAFORA - SEE CAR-
BONELL, R.
MORESCHINI, C. STUDI SUL "DE DOGMATE
PLATONIS" DI APULEIO.
R.E. WITT, 123:JUN71-213
MORESCHINI, C. - SEE PLATO
MORETO Y CAVAÑA, A. A CRITICAL EDITION
OF MORETO'S "EL PODER DE LA AMISTAD."*
(D.E. DEDRICK, ED)
E. RUIZ-FORNELLS, 238:SEP70-572
MORETTI, L., ED. INSCRIPTIONES GRAECAE
URBIS ROMAE. (FASC 1)
V. NUTTON, 303:VOL90-236
MORETTI, M. NEW MONUMENTS OF ETRUSCAN
PAINTING.
617(TLS):24MAR72-338
MORETTI, M. TRE ANNI E UN GIORNO.
617(TLS):22SEP72-1092
MORGAN, A. THE WHOLE WORLD IS WATCHING.
M. LEVIN, 441:27AUG72-26
MORGAN, E. THE DESCENT OF WOMAN.
P. ADAMS, 61:JUN72-112
G. GORER, 362:26OCT72-554
C. LEHMANN-HAUPT, 441:31MAY72-43
J. PFEIFFER, 441:25JUN72-6
A. STORR, 440:7MAY72-3
442(NY):20MAY72-139
MORGAN, E.S. ROGER WILLIAMS.
S.V. JAMES, 656(WMQ):APR70-326
MORGAN, G., ED. CONTEMPORARY THEATRE.
M. PAGE, 397(MD):SEP69-214
MORGAN, H.M. - SEE TRUMBULL, H. & M.
MORGAN, H.W. UNITY AND CULTURE.
617(TLS):14APR72-410
MORGAN, M.M. THE SHAVIAN PLAYGROUND.
S. WEINTRAUB, 441:5NOV72-36
617(TLS):4AUG72-917
MORGAN, R. MONSTER.
M. SWENSON, 441:19NOV72-7
MORGAN, R., ED. THE STUDY OF INTERNA-
TIONAL AFFAIRS.
617(TLS):7JUL72-763
MORGAN, R. WEST EUROPEAN POLITICS SINCE
1945.
617(TLS):8DEC72-1476
MORGAN, R. ZIRCONIA POEMS.
639(VQR):SPRING70-L
MORGAN, T. & N. SPOELSTRA, EDS. ECONOMIC
INTERDEPENDENCE IN SOUTHEAST ASIA.
E. VAN ROY, 293(JAST):AUG70-984
MORGANN, M. SHAKESPEARIAN CRITICISM.
(D.A. FINEMAN, ED)
617(TLS):28JUL72-867
MORGENBESSER, S., P. SUPPES & M. WHITE,
EDS. PHILOSOPHY, SCIENCE AND METHOD.
R.H.K., 543:JUN70-755
MORGENSTERN, C. GALLOWS SONGS. (W.D.
SNODGRASS & L. SEGAL, TRANS)
P.R. GRAHAM, 220(GL&L):OCT70-120
MORGRIDGE, B.G. - SEE HAMSUN, K.
MORIN, L. L'IL D'ELLE.
J-L. MAJOR, 627(UTQ):JUL69-484
MORISON, S. LETTER FORMS, TYPOGRAPHIC
AND SCRIPTORIAL.
H. CARTER, 354:JUN69-158
D. CHAMBERS, 503:AUTUMN69-134
MORISON, S. POLITICS AND SCRIPT. (ED &
COMPLETED BY N. BARKER)
R. STONE, 362:17AUG72-214
617(TLS):1SEP72-1032
MORISON, S., WITH H. CARTER. JOHN FELL
AND THE UNIVERSITY PRESS AND THE "FELL"
TYPES.
J. MILES, 592:APR68-231
MORISON, S.E. SAMUEL DE CHAMPLAIN.
C. LEHMANN-HAUPT, 441:20JUN72-41
L.B. WRIGHT, 441:16JUL72-23
442(NY):24JUN72-94

MORISON, S.E., F. MERK & F. FREIDEL.
DISSENT IN THREE AMERICAN WARS.
R.E. WELCH, JR., 432(NEQ):SEP70-494
639(VQR):AUTUMN70-CXLVII
MORIZE, A. - SEE DE VOLTAIRE, F.M.A.
MORLEY, A.F. THE HARRAP OPERA GUIDE.*
L. SALTER, 415:FEB71-138
MORLEY, F. THE LONG ROAD WEST.*
J.M. LALLEY, 396(MODA):SUMMER71-306
MORLEY, J. DEATH, HEAVEN AND THE VICTOR-
IANS.*
A. WHITMAN, 440:30APR72-13
MORLEY, J. NINETEENTH-CENTURY ESSAYS.
(P. STANSKY, ED)
617(TLS):18FEB72-175
MÖRNER, M. LA CORONA ESPAÑOLA Y LOS
FORÁNEOS EN LOS PUEBLOS DE INDIOS DE
AMERICA.
617(TLS):25AUG72-1001
MORNY, C., ED. A WINE AND FOOD BEDSIDE
BOOK.
617(TLS):1DEC72-1469
MOROT-SIR, E. LA PENSÉE FRANÇAISE
D'AUJOURD'HUI.
H. PEYRE, 319:OCT72-493
MOROT-SIR, E. & P. LEVERT - SEE LE SENNE,
R.
MORPURGO, J.E. BARNES WALLIS.
H. STOPES-ROE, 362:29JUN72-872
617(TLS):11FEB72-153
MORRALL, J.B. THE MEDIEVAL IMPRINT.*
D. GRAY, 382(MAE):1971/1-89
MORREALE, M. - SEE GRACIÁN DANTISCO, L.
MORRELL, D. FIRST BLOOD.
J. CATINELLA, 561(SATR):27MAY72-68
J. DECK, 441:18JUN72-6
617(TLS):10NOV72-1375
MORRELL, M.C. A MANUAL OF OLD ENGLISH
BIBLICAL MATERIALS.
H. GNEUSS, 38:BAND87HEFT2-249
MORRIS, A. & A. BUTLER. NO FEET TO DRAG.
617(TLS):15DEC72-1527
MORRIS, B., ED. CHRISTOPHER MARLOWE.*
E.A.J. HONIGMANN, 447(N&Q):APR70-148
MORRIS, B. & E. WITHINGTON - SEE CLEVE-
LAND, J.
MORRIS, C. THE PRAGMATIC MOVEMENT IN
AMERICAN PHILOSOPHY.
H.A. LARRABEE, 432(NEQ):DEC70-668
MORRIS, C. SIGNIFICATION AND SIGNIFI-
CANCE.
H.L. PARSONS, 486:MAR68-72
MORRIS, C.B. A GENERATION OF SPANISH
POETS, 1920-1936.
H.F. GRANT, 86(BHS):JAN71-83
R. GULLÓN, 401(MLQ):DEC70-516
H. RHEINFELDER, 182:VOL23#4-171
MORRIS, D. DAILY TELEGRAPH GUIDE TO THE
PLEASURES OF WINE.
617(TLS):29DEC72-1589
MORRIS, D. INTIMATE BEHAVIOUR.*
P. ADAMS, 61:APR72-128
A. BROYARD, 441:3MAR72-41
A. COMFORT, 440:27FEB72-1
M. RICHLER, 441:5MAR72-3
B.J. SIEGEL, 561(SATR):4MAR72-77
MORRIS, H. RICHARD BARNFIELD COLIN'S
CHILD.
W. BLISSETT, 179(ES):1969SUPP-
LXXXVIII
MORRIS, H. THE MASKED CITADEL.
J.C. ALCIATORE, 546(RR):FEB70-66
S. GILMAN, 399(MLJ):APR70-301
J.S.P., 191(ELN):SEP69(SUPP)-89
R.J. SEALY, 207(FR):DEC69-349
MORRIS, I. FOUL PLAY AND OTHER PUZZLES.
617(TLS):1DEC72-1469

MORRIS, I. SHAKESPEARE'S GOD.
617(TLS):15DEC72-1537
MORRIS, I. - SEE "AS I CROSSED A BRIDGE
OF DREAMS"
MORRIS, I. - SEE SHŌNAGON, S.
MORRIS, J. CORRESPONDENCE OF JOHN MORRIS
WITH JOHANNES DE LAET (1634-1649).
(J.A.F. BEKKERS, ED)
J.W. BINNS, 677:VOL2-267
568(SCN):SPRING71-16
MORRIS, J. PAX BRITANNICA.
B. PORTER, 637(VS):JUN70-444
MORRIS, J. PLACES.
617(TLS):29DEC72-1586
MORRIS, J.N. GREEN BUSINESS.*
R. HOWARD, 491:OCT71-34
MORRIS, R.B. THE EMERGING NATIONS AND
THE AMERICAN REVOLUTION.
639(VQR):AUTUMN70-CXLVI
MORRIS, R.K. THE NOVELS OF ANTHONY
POWELL.
M.W. MILLS, 141:WINTER69-111
MORRIS, T. THE WALK OF THE CONSCIOUS
ANTS.
A. BROYARD, 441:28APR72-43
MORRIS, W. FIRE SERMON.*
W. CARVER, 109:FALL/WINTER71/72-151
G. WEALES, 249(HUDR):WINTER71/72-716
MORRIS, W. GREEN GRASS, BLUE SKY, WHITE
HOUSE.
M. MUDRICK, 249(HUDR):SPRING71-185
MORRIS, W. LOVE AFFAIR - A VENETIAN
JOURNAL.
442(NY):11NOV72-191
561(SATR):7OCT72-108
MORRIS, W. THE UNPUBLISHED LECTURES OF
WILLIAM MORRIS.* (E.D. LEMIRE, ED)
R.C. ELLSWORTH, 529(QQ):AUTUMN70-461
R.M. STINGLE, 627(UTQ):JUL70-346
MORRIS, W. - SEE "THE AMERICAN HERITAGE
DICTIONARY OF THE ENGLISH LANGUAGE"
MORRIS, W. & E. MAGNÚSSON. THE STORY OF
KORMAK, THE SON OF OGMUND.
617(TLS):25FEB72-230
MORRIS-JONES, W.H. THE GOVERNMENT AND
POLITICS OF INDIA.
N. MAXWELL, 453:23MAR72-8
MORRISH, I. THE SOCIOLOGY OF EDUCATION.
617(TLS):9JUN72-667
MORRISON, C. LES CROISADES.
J.H. HILL, 589:JAN71-176
MORRISON, C.C. FREUD AND THE CRITIC.
H.S. ABRAM, 219(GAR):WINTER69-561
MORRISON, J. TREEHOUSE.
M. LEVIN, 441:23JUL72-19
MORRISON, J.C. MEANING AND TRUTH IN
WITTGENSTEIN'S "TRACTATUS."
G. NUCHELMANS, 361:VOL23#3-310
E. STENIUS, 482(PHR):OCT70-573
MORRISON, J.L. GOVERNOR O. MAX GARDNER.
617(TLS):10MAR72-264
MORRISON, N.B. KING'S QUIVER.
617(TLS):15DEC72-1541
MORSE, B.J. - SEE MOMBERT, A.
MORSE, D. MOTOWN.
N. FOUNTAIN, 364:FEB/MAR72-141
MORSE, E.R., ED. DALI.
M. LAST, 55:OCT69-20
MORSE, E.S. JAPANESE HOMES AND THEIR
SURROUNDINGS.
J.A. PRESCOTT, 302:JUL70-413
MORSE, J.M. THE IRRELEVANT ENGLISH
TEACHER.
C. LEHMANN-HAUPT, 441:18SEP72-23
MORSE, S.F. WALLACE STEVENS.
R. BUTTEL, 295:VOL2#3-431
R.H. PEARCE, 27(AL):JAN72-671

MORSY, Z. D'UN SOLEIL RÉTICENT.
  D. GROJNOWSKI, 98:NOV69-1026
MORSZTYN, J.A. GESAMMELTE WERKE (UTWORY
  ZEBRANE). (L. KUKULSKI, ED)
    D. TSCHIŽEWSKIJ, 72:BAND208HEFT4/6-
    473
MORTIER, R. CLARTÉS ET OMBRES DU SIÈCLE
  DES LUMIÈRES.
    J.H. DAVIS, JR., 207(FR):APR70-842
    N. SUCKLING, 208(FS):APR71-199
MORTIMER, J.E. TRADE UNIONS AND TECHNO-
  LOGICAL CHANGE.
    617(TLS):12MAY72-549
MORTIMER, P. THE HOME.*
    E. FEINSTEIN, 364:DEC71/JAN72-154
    S. KROLL, 440:19MAR72-6
    M. LEVIN, 441:27FEB72-52
    K. MILLER, 453:20APR72-19
    442(NY):18MAR72-153
MORTIMER, R. & P. WILLETT. MORE GREAT
  RACEHORSES OF THE WORLD.
    617(TLS):22DEC72-1566
MORTLOCK, B. THE INSIDE OF DIVORCE.
    617(TLS):23JUN72-724
MORTON, A. THE BARON GOES FAST.
    T. LASK, 441:22JUL72-25
MORTON, B.N. - SEE DE BEAUMARCHAIS,
  P.A.C.
MORTON, C. & H. MUNTZ, EDS. THE "CARMEN
  DE HASTINGAE PROELIO" OF GUY BISHOP OF
  AMIENS.
    617(TLS):4AUG72-912
MORTON, H.V. THE WATERS OF ROME.
    N. MILLER, 54:MAR69-96
MORTON, J. MAN, SCIENCE AND GOD.
    617(TLS):4FEB72-138
MORTON, J. THREE GENERATIONS IN A FAMILY
  TEXTILE FIRM.
    617(TLS):28JAN72-88
MORTON, R.S. SEXUAL FREEDOM AND VEN-
  EREAL DISEASE.
    617(TLS):3MAR72-258
MORTON, W.E. U.S. BUREAU OF THE CENSUS
  LIST OF SPANISH SURNAMES.
    K.B. HARDER, 424:DEC69-311
MOSCATO, A. INTENZIONALITÀ E DIALETTICA.
    M. RIESER, 319:OCT72-489
MOSELEY, V. JOYCE AND THE BIBLE.*
    A. MAC GILLIVRAY, 613:AUTUMN68-452
MOSER, C.A. PISEMSKY.*
    639(VQR):SPRING70-LXVI
MOSER, H., ED. SATZ UND WORT IM HEUTIGEN
  DEUTSCH.
    M.G. CLYNE, 564:SPRING69-69
MOSER, H., ED. SPRACHE DER GEGENWART.
  (VOL 1)
    C.V.J. RUSS, 402(MLR):JAN71-207
MOSER, H. & OTHERS, EDS. SPRACHNORM,
  SPRACHPFLEGE, SPRACHKRITIK.
    G.G. GILBERT, 350:DEC71-984
MOSLEY, N. THE ASSASSINATION OF TROTSKY.
    617(TLS):11AUG72-933
MOSLEY, N. NATALIE NATALIA.*
    P. BAILEY, 364:DEC71/JAN72-157
    F.P.W. MC DOWELL, 659:SUMMER72-361
    442(NY):15JAN72-91
MOSLEY, O. MY LIFE.
    N. ANNAN, 453:31AUG72-22
    K. ROSE, 440:12MAR72-4
    P. STANSKY, 441:12MAR72-2
    R. WINEGARTEN, 390:MAR69-69
    442(NY):5FEB72-103
MOSS, H. SELECTED POEMS.*
    R. LATTIMORE, 249(HUDR):AUTUMN71-499
MOSS, L. ARTHUR MILLER.
    C-W. TROWBRIDGE, 397(MD):DEC67-329
MOSS, R. URBAN GUERRILLAS.
    617(TLS):17MAR72-293

MOSS, S. THE WRONG ANGEL.*
    J. SMITH, 493:AUTUMN70-243
MOSS, S.P. POE'S MAJOR CRISIS.*
    M. ALLEN, 677:VOL2-309
    H. BRADDY, 301(JEGP):JUL71-569
    W. GOLDHURST, 31(ASCH):SPRING72-298
    D.J. YANNELLA, JR., 399(MLJ):NOV70-
    541
    639(VQR):AUTUMN70-CXLII
MOSSÉ, C. THE ANCIENT WORLD AT WORK.
    P.N. LOCKHART, 124:DEC70-137
    K.D. WHITE, 123:DEC71-467
MOSSÉ, C. LES INSTITUTIONS POLITIQUES
  GRECQUES À L'ÉPOQUE CLASSIQUE.*
    P. GAUTHIER, 555:VOL44FASC1-107
MOSSÉ, C. LA TYRANNIE DANS LA GRÈCE
  ANTIQUE.
    S.I. OOST, 122:APR71-133
MOSSE, G.L. GERMANS AND JEWS.*
    H.M. ADAMS, 396(MODA):WINTER71-108
MOSSE, W.E., WITH A. PAUCKER, EDS. DEUT-
  SCHES JUDENTUM IN KRIEG UND REVOLUTION.
    617(TLS):28JAN72-81
MOSSMAN, D. THE STONES OF SUMMER.
    T. LASK, 441:19MAY72-39
    J. SEELYE, 441:21MAY72-4
MOSSNER, E.C. THE LIFE OF DAVID HUME.
    D.S. GALLAGHER, 67:NOV71-236
"MOSTRA DEI CODICI GONZAGHESCHI."
    N. BARKER, 78(BC):AUTUMN70-398
MOTTRAM, E. - SEE REXROTH, K.
MOTTRAM, E., M. BRADBURY & J. FRANCO,
  EDS. THE PENGUIN COMPANION TO LITERA-
  TURE: USA AND LATIN AMERICA.
    617(TLS):7JUL72-780
MOULIN, J. LA PIERRE À FEUX.
    M. CRANSTON, 207(FR):OCT69-163
MOULTON, E.C. LORD NORTHBROOK'S INDIAN
  ADMINISTRATION: 1872-1876.
    G.W. SPENCER, 293(JAST):AUG70-957
MOULTON, J.L. THE ROYAL MARINES.
    617(TLS):28JUL72-900
MOULSDALE, J.R.B. THE KING'S SHROPSHIRE
  LIGHT INFANTRY.
    617(TLS):22DEC72-1555
MOUNIN, G. HISTOIRE DE LA LINGUISTIQUE
  DES ORIGINES AU XXE SIÈCLE.
    G.L. BURSILL-HALL, 320(CJL):SPRING70-
    143
MOUNIN, G. MACHIAVEL, SA VIE, SON
  OEUVRE AVEC UN EXPOSÉ DE SA PHILOSO-
  PHIE.
    E. NAMER, 542:JUL-DEC69-491
MOUNIN, G. SAUSSURE OU LE STRUCTURALISTE
  SANS LE SAVOIR.
    E.F.K. KOERNER, 320(CJL):FALL69-27
MOUNT, F. THE THEATRE OF POLITICS.
    617(TLS):8DEC72-1476
MOUNTFORD, A.R. THE ILLUSTRATED GUIDE TO
  STAFFORDSHIRE SALTGLAZED STONEWARE.
    617(TLS):7JAN72-8
MOUNTFORD, J. KEELE.
    617(TLS):4AUG72-922
MOUNTJOY, A.B., ED. DEVELOPING THE
  UNDERDEVELOPED COUNTRIES.
    617(TLS):15SEP72-1066
MOUNTZOURES, H.L. THE BRIDGE.
    M. LEVIN, 441:18JUN72-30
    442(NY):17JUN72-102
MOURELATOS, A.P.D. THE ROUTE OF PAR-
  MENIDES.
    P. BICKNELL, 63:AUG71-226
    R.K. SPRAGUE, 124:JAN71-160
MOUSNIER, R. EIN KÖNIGSMORD IN FRANK-
  REICH.
    W. FLOECK, 72:BAND208HEFT1-74

MOUSSY, C. RECHERCHES SUR TREPHŌ ET LES
VERBES GRECS SIGNIFIANT "NOURRIR."
A.C. MOORHOUSE, 123:MAR71-90
J-L. PERPILLOU, 555:VOL44FASC2-281
MOUSTIERS, P. LA PAROI.
H.W. BRANN, 207(FR):MAY70-944
MOUTON, J. PROUST.
R.M. BIRN, 131(CL):WINTER71-77
M. MEIN, 208(FS):JAN71-105
MOUTOTE, D., ED. ENTRETIENS SUR PAUL
VALÉRY.
617(TLS):29SEP72-1143
MOUTOTE, D. LE JOURNAL DE GIDE ET LES
PROBLÈMES DU MOI (1889-1925).
R. THEIS, 72:BAND208HEFT2-157
MOVIA, G. ANIMA E INTELLETTO.
W.E. CHARLTON, 123:DEC70-413
MOWAT, C.L. GREAT BRITAIN SINCE 1914.*
C.F. MULLETT, 356:OCT71-350
MOWAT, F. THE BOAT WHO WOULDN'T FLOAT.*
J.M. ROBSON, 627(UTQ):JUL70-385
MOWAT, F. A WHALE FOR THE KILLING.
561(SATR):21OCT72-80
MOWAT, F. & J. DE VISSER. THIS ROCK
WITHIN THE SEA.*
A. EMERY, 627(UTQ):JUL69-408
MOWATT, D.G. & H. SACKER. THE NIBELUN-
GENLIED.*
J.R. ASHCROFT, 402(MLR):APR71-432
M.E. GIBBS, 220(GL&L):JUL71-375
MOYNE, E.J. - SEE HAZLITT, W.
MOYSE-BARTLETT, H. LOUIS EDWARD NOLAN
AND HIS INFLUENCE ON THE BRITISH CAVAL-
RY.
617(TLS):4FEB72-132
MOZART, W.A. LE NOZZE DI FIGARO; COSÌ
FAN TUTTE.* DIE ZAUBERFLÖTE; DIE ENT-
FÜHRUNG AUS DEM SERAIL. DON GIOVANNI;
IDOMENEO.* (ALL TRANS BY L. SALTER)
617(TLS):30JUN72-757
MPHAHLELE, E. VOICES IN THE WHIRLWIND.
J. LESTER, 441:22OCT72-50
MPHAHLELE, E. THE WANDERERS.*
D.A.N. JONES, 362:30MAR72-426
617(TLS):10MAR72-265
MRABET, M. THE LEMON. (P. BOWLES, ED
& TRANS)
442(NY):23DEC72-78
MRAZEK, J.E. THE FALL OF EBEN EMAEL.
617(TLS):10NOV72-1377
MUCHNIC, H. RUSSIAN WRITERS.*
R.E. MATLAW, 574(SEEJ):FALL71-381
MUCK, O. THE TRANSCENDENTAL METHOD.
J. DISTER, 613:SUMMER69-312
MUDRICK, M. ON CULTURE AND LITERATURE.*
I. MALIN, 651(WHR):SPRING71-183
MUECKE, D.C. THE COMPASS OF IRONY.
G.D. JOSIPOVICI, 541(RES):NOV70-526
MUEHSAM, G., ED. FRENCH PAINTERS AND
PAINTINGS FROM THE FOURTEENTH CENTURY
TO POST-IMPRESSIONISM.
90:OCT70-716
MUELLER, R.E. THE SCIENCE OF ART.
A. SHIELDS, 290(JAAC):SPRING70-399
MUELLER, T.H., E.N. MAYER & H. NIEDZIEL-
SKI. HANDBOOK OF FRENCH STRUCTURE.
W.N. FELT, 399(MLJ):FEB70-141
R.W. NEWMAN, 207(FR):OCT69-153
MUES, W. VOM LAUT ZUM SATZ.
J.A. CZOCHRALSKI, 353:NOV69-115
MUGGERIDGE, K. & R. ADAM. BEATRICE WEBB.
571:SPRING-SUMMER68-25
MUGGERIDGE, M. CHRONICLES OF WASTED
TIME. (VOL 1)
C. RICKS, 362:28SEP72-414
617(TLS):29SEP72-1133

MUGGERIDGE, M. & A. VIDLER. PAUL.
C.E. SIMCOX, 441:7MAY72-7
617(TLS):31MAR72-377
MUIR, E. & W. - SEE BURCKHARDT, C.J.
MUIR, J. STRANGER, TREAD LIGHT.
N. CALLENDAR, 441:2JAN72-16
MUIR, K., ED. SHAKESPEARE SURVEY 20.
K. MAGAREY, 67:MAY71-87
MUIR, K., ED. SHAKESPEARE SURVEY 21.*
K. MAGAREY, 67:MAY71-87
M. MINCOFF, 447(N&Q):APR70-150
MUIR, K., ED. SHAKESPEARE SURVEY 22.
K. MAGAREY, 67:MAY71-88
D. MEHL, 72:BAND208HEFT1-55
W.F. SODINI, 517(PBSA):JAN-MAR71-79
MUIR, K., ED. SHAKESPEARE SURVEY 23.*
D.M. BERGERON, 517(PBSA):JUL-SEP71-
322
MUIR, K. & P. THOMSON - SEE WYATT, T.
MUIRHEAD, J.H. THE PLATONIC TRADITION IN
ANGLO-SAXON PHILOSOPHY.
F. RESTAINO, 548(RCSF):JAN-MAR68-89
MUKHERJEE, B. THE TIGER'S DAUGHTER.
J.R. FRAKES, 440:9JAN72-2
J. HITREC, 561(SATR):11MAR72-76
M. LEVIN, 441:2JAN72-16
C. RICKS, 453:9MAR72-23
MUKHERJEE, S. PASSAGE TO AMERICA.
S.N. HAY, 293(JAST):AUG70-972
MUKHERJEE, S. & D.V.K. RAGHAVACHARYULU,
EDS. INDIAN ESSAYS IN AMERICAN LITERA-
TURE.
A.C. KERN, 651(WHR):WINTER71-91
MULHAUSER, R.E. SAINTE-BEUVE AND GRECO-
ROMAN ANTIQUITY.*
R.T. BRUÈRE, 122:JAN71-68
W.G. MOORE, 402(MLR):JUL71-691
MÜLLENBROCK, H-J. LITERATUR UND ZEITGE-
SCHICHTE IN ENGLAND ZWISCHEN DEM ENDE
DES 19. JAHRHUNDERTS UND DEM AUSBRUCH
DES ERSTEN WELTKRIEGES.
D. ENGLÄNDER, 72:BAND208HEFT3-219
J. LEJE, 597(SN):VOL41#1-200
MULLER, C. INITIATION À LA STATISTIQUE
LINGUISTIQUE.
K-J. DANELL, 597(SN):VOL41#2-412
MÜLLER, G. - SEE SOPHOCLES
MULLER, G.H. NIGHTMARES AND VISIONS.
441:1OCT72-38
MULLER, H.J. IN PURSUIT OF RELEVANCE.
442(NY):1JAN72-64
MÜLLER, K., G. SCHEEL & G. GERBER - SEE
LEIBNIZ, G.W.
MÜLLER, K-D. DIE FUNKTION DER GESCHICHTE
IM WERK BERTOLT BRECHTS.
B.A. WOODS, 222(GR):JAN70-61
MÜLLER, U. "DICHTUNG" UND "WAHRHEIT" IN
DEN LIEDERN OSWALDS VON WOLKENSTEIN.
J.L. FLOOD, 220(GL&L):APR71-272
G.F. JONES, 400(MLN):OCT70-749
MÜLLER, U., ED. KREUZZUGSDICHTUNG.*
J.R. ASHCROFT, 402(MLR):JUL71-707
R.K., 221(GQ):MAY70-532
MÜLLER-LAUTER, W. NIETZSCHE.
H. NEUMANN, 319:JUL72-371
MÜLLER-SCHWEFE, G. EINFÜHRUNG IN DAS
STUDIUM DER ENGLISCHEN PHILOLOGIE.
(2ND ED)
H. GNEUSS, 38:BAND87HEFT3/4-404
MÜLLER-SEIDEL, W., ED. HEINRICH VON
KLEIST: AUFSÄTZE UND ESSAYS.
J.T., 191(ELN):SEP70(SUPP)-122
MÜLLER-SEIDEL, W. - SEE DAVID, C., W.
WITTKOWSKI & L. RYAN
MÜLLER-VOLMER, K. POESIE UND EINBIL-
DUNGSKRAFT.*
I.C., 191(ELN):SEP69(SUPP)-96
R. NOVAK, 400(MLN):OCT70-752

MÜLLER-VOLLMER, K. - SEE VON GOETHE, J.W.
MULRYNE, J.R. - SEE KYD, T.
MULVANEY, D.J. THE PREHISTORY OF AUS-
TRALIA.
   T.G. HARDING, 318(JAOS):OCT-DEC70-630
MULVIHILL, W. NIGHT OF THE AXE.
   S. KROLL, 440:19MAR72-7
   T. LASK, 441:11MAR72-27
   M. LEVIN, 441:5MAR72-35
MUMFORD, L. THE MYTH OF THE MACHINE.
   R.E. SPILLER, 27(AL):JAN72-675
MUMFORD, L. - SEE EMERSON, R.W.
MUMFORD, L. & F.J. OSBORN. THE LETTERS
OF LEWIS MUMFORD AND FREDERIC J. OS-
BORN. (M.R. HUGHES, ED)
   A. WHITMAN, 440:27FEB72-6
   617(TLS):11FEB72-161
MUNBY, A.N.L. CONNOISSEURS AND MEDIEVAL
MINIATURES 1750-1850.
   617(TLS):24NOV72-1414
MUNBY, A.N.L., ED. POETS AND MEN OF
LETTERS. (VOLS 1&2)
   617(TLS):18FEB72-200
MUNBY, A.N.L. PORTRAIT OF AN OBSESSION.
   R.C., 503:SPRING68-40
MUNBY, A.N.L. & L.W. TOWNER. THE FLOW
OF BOOKS AND MANUSCRIPTS.
   F. RANGER, 325:OCT70-147
MUNCH, P. CRISIS IN UTOPIA.
   617(TLS):10MAR72-278
MUNDLE, C.W.K. A CRITIQUE OF LINGUISTIC
PHILOSOPHY.*
   A.R. WHITE, 518:MAY71-20
MUNDT, M. STURLA ÞÓRÐARSON UND DIE LAX-
DAELA SAGA.
   P. SCHACH, 563(SS):WINTER71-91
MUNGO, R. TOTAL LOSS FARM.*
   N. MILLS, 676(YR):SUMMER71-609
MUNGO, R. TROPICAL DETECTIVE STORY.
   P. ADAMS, 61:AUG72-92
MUNHALL, E. MASTERPIECES OF THE FRICK
COLLECTION.
   S. FRANK, 58:SUMMER70-12
MUNITZ, M.K., ED. IDENTITY AND INDIVIDU-
ATION.
   W.V. QUINE, 311(JP):7SEP72-488
MUNN-RANKIN, J.M. THE CAMBRIDGE ANCIENT
HISTORY. (REV) (VOL 2, CHAPTER 25)
   D.B. WEISBERG, 318(JAOS):APR-JUN70-
   330
MUÑOZ, J.L.L. - SEE UNDER LÓPEZ MUÑOZ,
J.L.
MUÑOZ, R.J. EL CÍRCULO DE LOS 3 SOLES.
   R. SQUIRRU, 37:JUL69-40
MUNRO, A. DANCE OF THE HAPPY SHADES.*
   D. HELWIG, 529(QQ):SPRING70-127
   G. ROPER, 627(UTQ):JUL69-363
MUNRO, A. LIVES OF GIRLS AND WOMEN.
   H. JACKSON, 99:JAN-FEB72-76
   C. THOMAS, 296:FALL72-95
MUNRO, A.K. AUTOBIOGRAPHY OF A THIEF.
   617(TLS):26MAY72-613
MUNRO, D.A. ENGLISH-EDO WORDLIST.*
   R.W. WESCOTT, 315(JAL):VOL8PT2-133
MUNRO, D.J. THE CONCEPT OF MAN IN EARLY
CHINA.
   D. BODDE, 293(JAST):NOV69-160
   B.E. WALLACKER, 318(JAOS):OCT-DEC70-
   615
MUNSON, K. AIRCRAFT OF WORLD WAR II.
(2ND ED)
   617(TLS):22DEC72-1566
MÜNZEL, F. STRAFRECHT IM ALTEN CHINA
NACH DEN STRAFRECHTSKAPITELN IN DEN
MING-ANNALEN.
   W. EBERHARD, 293(JAST):FEB70-425

MÜNZEL, M. MEDIZINMANNWESEN UND GEISTER-
VORSTELLUNGEN BEI DEN KAMAYURÁ (ALTO
XINGÚ, BRASILIEN).
   R. BASTIDE, 182:VOL23#23/24-1018
MURATO, M. CARPACCIO.
   A. MARTINDALE, 90:JAN69-39
MURDOCH, I. AN ACCIDENTAL MAN.*
   A. BROYARD, 441:18JAN72-33
   F. KERMODE, 61:JUL72-87
   F.P.W. MC DOWELL, 659:SUMMER72-361
   G. MALLET, 561(SATR):29JAN72-68
   K. MILLER, 453:20APR72-19
   J.C. OATES, 440:23JAN72-3
   N. SAYRE, 441:23JAN72-7
   442(NY):12FEB72-102
MURDOCH, I. BRUNO'S DREAM.*
   M.I., 619(TC):1968/4&1969/1-93
MURDOCH, I. A FAIRLY HONOURABLE DEFEEAT.*
   P.E. GRAY, 676(YR):AUTUMN70-101
   F.P.W. MC DOWELL, 659:SUMMER72-361
MURDOCH, I. THE SOVEREIGNTY OF GOOD.*
   J. KLEINIG, 63:MAY71-112
   C. TYLEE, 518:OCT71-18
MURENA, H.A. EPITALÁMICA.
   G.R. MC MURRAY, 238:SEP70-581
MURILLO, L.A. THE CYCLICAL NIGHT.
   R. CHRIST, 613:AUTUMN69-472
   J. FLETCHER, 402(MLR):JAN71-198
MURISON, W.J. THE PUBLIC LIBRARY. (NEW
ED)
   617(TLS):28APR72-501
MURPHY, F., ED. WALT WHITMAN.
   S. GILL, 447(N&Q):JUL70-272
MURPHY, J. THE EDUCATION ACT 1870.
   617(TLS):17MAR72-317
MURPHY, J.J., ED. THREE MEDIEVAL RHE-
TORICAL ARTS.
   B. ROWLAND, 70(ANQ):JAN72-77
MURPHY, M. GOLF IN THE KINGDOM.
   C. LEHMANN-HAUPT, 441:27NOV72-37
   J. UPDIKE, 442(NY):29JUL72-76
   N. WEBER, 441:22OCT72-36
MURPHY, P.L. THE CONSTITUTION IN CRISIS
TIMES: 1918-1969.
   E.M. YODER, JR., 440:23JAN72-1
MURPHY, R. THE BATTLE OF AUGHRIM.
   H. SERGEANT, 175:SPRING69-33
MURPHY, R.F. THE DIALECTICS OF SOCIAL
LIFE.*
   617(TLS):1SEP72-1026
MURPHY, R.W. & OTHERS. THE WORLD OF
CÉZANNE.
   617(TLS):21JUL72-853
MURPHY, W.P.D., ED. THE EARL OF HERT-
FORD'S LIEUTENANCY PAPERS, 1603-1612.
   J.C. SAINTY, 325:APR70-75
MURRAY, A. SOUTH TO A VERY OLD PLACE.*
   A. BROYARD, 441:4APR72-45
   E.Z. FRIEDENBERG, 453:24FEB72-30
   R.A. GROSS, 561(SATR):22JAN72-72
   T. MORRISON, 441:2JAN72-5
   442(NY):8JAN72-84
MURRAY, D.S. WHY A NATIONAL HEALTH
SERVICE?
   617(TLS):7APR72-400
MURRAY, E. ARTHUR MILLER, DRAMATIST.
   C.W. TROWBRIDGE, 397(MD):DEC67-329
MURRAY, H. SELECTED LETTERS OF HUBERT
MURRAY. (F. WEST, ED)
   617(TLS):4AUG72-923
MURRAY, J. THE FIRST EUROPEAN AGRICUL-
TURE.
   617(TLS):7JAN72-17
MURRAY, J. - SEE BERNANOS, G.
MURRAY, J.A.H. & OTHERS - SEE "THE OXFORD
ENGLISH DICTIONARY"

MURRAY, J.J. AMSTERDAM IN THE AGE OF
REMBRANDT.
A. WERNER, 340(KR):1970/1-121
617(TLS):11AUG72-941
MURRAY, J.J. ANTWERP IN THE AGE OF
PLANTIN AND BRUEGHEL.
617(TLS):11AUG72-941
MURRAY, P. PIRANESI AND THE GRANDEUR OF
ANCIENT ROME.
617(TLS):21APR72-443
MURRAY, P. THE SHAKESPEAREAN SCENE.
T. HAWKES, 676(YR):AUTUMN70-130
MURRAY, P.B. THOMAS KYD.
J.R. MULRYNE, 402(MLR):JUL71-659
MURRAY, P.B. A STUDY OF JOHN WEBSTER.
B. MORRIS, 402(MLR):APR71-391
MURRAY, R.N. WORDSWORTH'S STYLE.
B.R.M., 477:SPRING69-300
MURRAY-BROWN, J. KENYATTA.
617(TLS):15DEC72-1522
MURRAY-OLIVER, A. AUGUSTUS EARLE IN NEW
ZEALAND.
R. FRASER, 368:MAR69-70
MURRIN, M. THE VEIL OF ALLEGORY.
M.C. BRADBROOK, 551(RENQ):WINTER70-
474
SISTER M. JOSEPH, 191(ELN):SEP70-53
J. MAZZARO, 141:SPRING70-155
K. WILLIAMS, 301(JEGP):JUL71-533
639(VQR):WINTER70-XVIII
MURRY, C. PRIVATE VIEW.
617(TLS):7JUL72-783
MURSIA, U. - SEE CONRAD, J.
MURTAGH, W.J. MORAVIAN ARCHITECTURE AND
TOWN PLANNING.
J.J. BISHOP, 576:DEC69-299
MURTONEN, A. EARLY SEMITIC.
R. HETZRON, 353:APR69-109
MURTY, K.S., ED. READINGS IN INDIAN
HISTORY, POLITICS AND PHILOSOPHY.
S.N. MAHAJAN, 485(PE&W):OCT69-461
MUS, P. HO CHI MINH, LE VIETNAM, L'ASIE.
(A.N.N. HÔ, ED)
F. FITZ GERALD, 453:19OCT72-21
617(TLS):21APR72-436
MUSCETTA, C. & G. SAVOCA - SEE LEOPARDI,
G.
"DIE MUSEN."
617(TLS):18FEB72-194
MUSES, C. & A.M. YOUNG, EDS. CONSCIOUS-
NESS AND REALITY.
T. STURGEON, 441:3SEP72-20
MUSGRAVE, B. & J. WHEELER-BENNETT, EDS.
WOMEN AT WORK.
617(TLS):27OCT72-1297
MUSGRAVE, S. SONGS OF THE SEA WITCH.*
E. WOODS, 606(TAMR):#55-79
150(DR):AUTUMN70-431
"MUSIC AND TECHNOLOGY: STOCKHOLM MEETING,
8-12 JUNE 1970."
D.C.H., 410(M&L):OCT71-442
"MUSIC AND THE YOUNG SCHOOL-LEAVER."
P. STANDFORD, 415:SEP71-863
"MUSICAL EDUCATION IN HUNGARY."
P. STANDFORD, 415:SEP70-897
"MUSIKETHNOLOGISCHE JAHRESBIBLIOGRAPHIE
EUROPAS." (VOLS 1-3) (O. ELSCHEK, E.
STOCKMANN & I. MAČÁK, EDS)
F.J. GILLIS, 187:JAN72-138
MUSPER, H.T., ED. DER ANTICHRIST UND DIE
FÜNFZEHN ZEICHEN.*
H. LEHMANN-HAUPT, 517(PBSA):JUL-SEP
71-331
MUSSET, L. INTRODUCTION À LA RUNOLOGIE.
R. DEROLEZ, 179(ES):DEC70-572

MÜSSIGGANG, A. DIE SOZIALE FRAGE IN DER
HISTORISCHEN SCHULE DER DEUTSCHEN
NATIONALÖKONOMIE.
L. NEUMANN, 182:VOL23#13/14-661
MUSSON, A.E., ED. SCIENCE, TECHNOLOGY,
AND ECONOMIC GROWTH IN THE EIGHTEENTH
CENTURY.
617(TLS):7APR72-401
MUSURILLO, H. THE LIGHT AND THE DARK-
NESS.*
D. HENRY, 122:APR71-122
MUTAFČIEVA, V. I KLIO E MUZA.
P. SHASHKO, 104:WINTER71-576
AL-MUTANABBĪ, A.T.A.H. POEMS FROM THE
DIWAN OF ABŪ TAYYIB AHMAD IBN HUSAIN
AL-MUTANABBĪ. (A. WORMHOUDT, ED &
TRANS)
M.A.M. KHAN, 273(IC):OCT69-309
AL-MUTANABBĪ, A.T.A.H. POEMS OF AL-MUT-
ANABBĪ. (A.J. ARBERRY, ED & TRANS)
T. LE GASSICK, 318(JAOS):APR-JUN70-
292
MUUS, B.J. FRESHWATER FISH OF BRITAIN
AND EUROPE. (A. WHEELER, ED)
617(TLS):14APR72-429
MWASE, G.S. STRIKE A BLOW AND DIE.
(R.I. ROTBERG, ED)
T. PRICE, 69:APR69-194
MYERS & COPPLESTONE, EDS. ART TREASURES
IN THE BRITISH ISLES.
J.H. HOBHOUSE, 58:MAR70-14
MYERS, D.H. THE THURSDAY EVENING ART
WORLD.
H.F. GAUGH, 127:SPRING71-326
MYERS, G. A HISTORY OF CANADIAN WEALTH.
(VOL 1)
H.C. PENTLAND, 99:SEP72-6
MYERS, G.E. SELF.
D. LOCKE, 479(PHQ):JUL70-291
MYERS, J.B., ED. THE POETS OF THE NEW
YORK SCHOOL.
F.D. REEVE, 491:OCT71-39
MYERS, N. THE LONG AFRICAN DAY.
P. SHEPARD, 441:26NOV72-31
MYERS, R. EMMANUEL CHABRIER AND HIS
CIRCLE.*
R. CRICHTON, 415:MAR70-277
MYERS, R. MODERN FRENCH MUSIC.
617(TLS):14JAN72-36
MYERS, R.H., ED. TWENTIETH-CENTURY
MUSIC.* (REV)
M. PETERSON, 470:NOV69-51
S. WALSH, 607:SPRING69-63
MYERS, R.M., ED. THE CHILDREN OF PRIDE.
E.D. GENOVESE, 453:21SEP72-16
M. JONES, 441:7MAY72-1
617(TLS):9JUN72-656
MYINT, H. ECONOMIC THEORY AND THE UNDER-
DEVELOPED COUNTRIES.
617(TLS):15SEP72-1066
MYLONAS, G.E. MYCENAE'S LAST CENTURY OF
GREATNESS.
J. BOARDMAN, 123:DEC70-413
MYNORS, R.A.B. - SEE VERGIL
MYRDAL, G. ASIAN DRAMA.
J. ROBINSON, 97(CQ):AUTUMN68-381
MYRDAL, G. THE CHALLENGE OF WORLD POV-
ERTY.
G.E. TAYLOR, 639(VQR):AUTUMN70-660
MYRDAL, J. & G. KESSLE. GATES TO ASIA.
A. PRYCE-JONES, 440:2APR72-7
617(TLS):28JUL72-887
MYRUS, D. BALLADS, BLUES, AND THE BIG
BEAT.
D.R. BARNES, 650(WF):OCT68-281

NAAMAN, A., ED. GUIDE BIBLIOGRAPHIQUE
DES THÈSES LITTÉRAIRES CANADIENNES DE
1921 À 1969.
   W.N., 102(CANL):SUMMER71-98
NABARRO, G. STEAM NOSTALGIA.
   617(TLS):10NOV72-1377
NABERT, J. ELEMENTS FOR AN ETHIC.
   F.A. OLAFSON, 311(JP):15JUN72-336
NABOKOV, V. ADA.*
   42(AR):SUMMER69-261
   639(VQR):WINTER70-IX
NABOKOV, V. THE ANNOTATED "LOLITA."*
(A. APPEL, JR., ED)
   617(TLS):25FEB72-213
NABOKOV, V. GLORY.*
   B. BROPHY, 362:27APR72-552
   H. CALISHER, 441:9JAN72-1
   C. LEHMANN-HAUPT, 441:11JAN72-39
   J.D. O'HARA, 561(SATR):15JAN72-36
   V.S. PRITCHETT, 453:24FEB72-12
   A. PRYCE-JONES, 440:2JAN72-3
   J. UPDIKE, 442(NY):26FEB72-96
   617(TLS):24MAR72-325
NABOKOV, V. KING, QUEEN, KNAVE.*
   M.K.M., 502(PRS):WINTER68/69-363
NABOKOV, V. MARY.*
   D.J. GORDON, 676(YR):SPRING71-428
NABOKOV, V. POEMS AND PROBLEMS.*
   R. LATTIMORE, 249(HUDR):AUTUMN71-506
   F. WYNDHAM, 362:27JUL72-116
   617(TLS):25AUG72-984
NABOKOV, V. TRANSPARENT THINGS.
   R. ALTER, 561(SATR):11NOV72-72
   M. GALLANT, 441:19NOV72-1
   C. LEHMANN-HAUPT, 441:13NOV72-39
   J. UPDIKE, 442(NY):18NOV72-242
   E. WEEKS, 61:DEC72-141
   M. WOOD, 453:16NOV72-12
NACHOD, O., H. PRAESENT & W. HAENISCH.
BIBLIOGRAPHIE VON JAPAN, 1906-1937.
   S.E. THOMPSON, 517(PBSA):OCT-DEC71-
429
NADAUS, R. MAISON EN PAROLES.
   R.R. HUBERT, 207(FR):MAR70-730
NADEAU, M. GUSTAVE FLAUBERT ÉCRIVAIN.
   C. CARLUT, 400(MLN):MAY70-621
NADEAU, M. THE GREATNESS OF FLAUBERT.
   J. WEIGHTMAN, 453:6APR72-10
NADELSON, R. WHO IS ANGELA DAVIS?
   P. ADAMS, 61:OCT72-135
   T. MORRISON, 441:29OCT72-48
NAEF, H. LES ORIGINES DE LA RÉFORME À
GENÈVE. (VOL 2)
   R.D. LINDER, 551(RENQ):SUMMER70-191
NAEF, W.J. BEHIND THE GREAT WALL OF
CHINA.
   S. SCHWARTZ, 441:3DEC72-20
NAERT, É. LEIBNIZ ET LA QUERELLE DU
PUR AMOUR.
   L. PRENANT, 542:JUL-SEP68-416
NAERT, É. MÉMOIRE ET CONSCIENCE DE SOI
SELON LEIBNIZ.
   L. PRENANT, 542:JUL-DEC69-459
NAERT, É. LA PENSÉE POLITIQUE DE LEIB-
NIZ.
   A. DE LATTRE, 542:JUL-DEC69-464
NAESS, A. SCEPTICISM.
   A. FLEW, 479(PHQ):JAN70-85
   T. GREENWOOD, 483:APR70-165
   M.B.M., 543:MAR70-562
   W.W. MELLOR, 393(MIND):JUL70-461
NAESS, H.S. KNUT HAMSUN OG AMERIKA.
   G. THURSON, 563(SS):SPRING71-205
NAGAR, M.L. PUBLIC LIBRARY MOVEMENT IN
BARODA, 1901-1949.
   N. TIWANA, 356:OCT71-348

NAGAVAJARA, C. AUGUST WILHELM SCHLEGEL
IN FRANKREICH.
   R. BAUER, 52:BAND4HEFT1-100
NAGEL, O. KATHE KOLLWITZ.
   D.L. SHIREY, 441:10DEC72-44
NAGEL, T. THE POSSIBILITY OF ALTRUISM.*
   B. GERT, 311(JP):15JUN72-340
   B. MAYO, 518:OCT70-19
NAGLER, B. BROWN BOMBER.
   453:18MAY72-37
NAGY, G. GREEK DIALECTS AND THE TRANS-
FORMATION OF AN INDO-EUROPEAN PROCESS.
   L.J. HEIRMAN, 124:OCT70-60
   J.W. POULTNEY, 24:OCT71-721
NAGY-TALAVERA, N.M. THE GREEN SHIRTS AND
THE OTHERS.
   G. KLINGENSTEIN, 32:JUN71-420
NAHM, M.C., ED. SELECTIONS FROM EARLY
GREEK PHILOSOPHY. (4TH ED)
   542:APR-JUN69-267
NAIK, M.K., S.K. DESAI & S.T. KALLAPUR,
EDS. THE IMAGE OF INDIA IN WESTERN
CREATIVE WRITING.
   617(TLS):4FEB72-138
NAIPAUL, S. FIREFLIES.*
   F.P.W. MC DOWELL, 659:SUMMER72-361
   W.H. PRITCHARD, 249(HUDR):SUMMER71-
364
NAIPAUL, V.S. IN A FREE STATE.*
   F.P.W. MC DOWELL, 659:SUMMER72-361
   F. MC GUINNESS, 364:OCT/NOV71-156
NAIPAUL, V.S. THE OVERCROWDED BARRACOON.
   R. BRYDEN, 362:9NOV72-641
   617(TLS):17NOV72-1391
NAJARIAN, P. VOYAGES.*
   J.M. MORSE, 249(HUDR):AUTUMN71-540
NAJITA, T. HARA KEI IN THE POLITICS OF
COMPROMISE, 1905-1915.
   L. OLSON, 244(HJAS):VOL29-321
NALDEN, C. FUGAL ANSWER.
   R.F.T.B., 410(M&L):OCT71-430
   P. RADCLIFFE, 415:JUN71-558
NAMIER, J. LEWIS NAMIER.*
   G. STEINER, 442(NY):1JAN72-61
NANCE, W.L. THE WORLDS OF TRUMAN
CAPOTE.*
   C.H. HOLMAN, 27(AL):MAY71-307
NANDA, B.R., ED. SOCIALISM IN INDIA.
   617(TLS):4AUG72-926
NANTON, P. ARCTIC BREAKTHROUGH.
   102(CANL):SPRING71-120
NAPOLI, M. LA TOMBA DEL TUFFATORE.
   617(TLS):24MAR72-338
NAPOLITAN, J. THE ELECTION GAME AND HOW
TO WIN IT.
   J. GREENFIELD, 441:4JUN72-40
   A. SCHLESINGER, JR., 440:16APR72-3
NAQVI, H.K. URBAN CENTRES OF INDUSTRIES
IN UPPER INDIA.
   S.M. ALAM, 273(IC):OCT69-307
NARASIMHAN, V.K. KASTURI SRINIVASAN.
   A.B. FRANKLIN, 293(JAST):AUG70-974
NARAYAN, S. MEMOIRS.
   617(TLS):1SEP72-1029
NARBONI, J. & T. MILNE - SEE GODARD, J-L.
NARCISSOV, B. POD"EM.
   V. TERRAS, 574(SEEJ):SPRING71-81
NARDI, B. SAGGI DI FILOSOFIA DANTESCA.
(NEW ED)
   R. PARENTI, 548(RCSF):APR-JUN68-244
NARKIEWICZ, O.A. THE MAKING OF THE
SOVIET STATE APPARATUS.*
   M. MC CAULEY, 575(SEER):APR71-321
NASATIR, A.P. SPANISH WAR VESSELS ON THE
MISSISSIPPI, 1792-1796.*
   G.H. CLARFIELD, 330(MASJ):SPRING69-92
NASH, O. THE OLD DOG BARKS BACKWARDS.
   561(SATR):4NOV72-88

NASH, R. MULTILINGUAL LEXICON OF LIN-
GUISTICS AND PHILOLOGY.*
R.C. HOLLOW, JR., 545(RPH):FEB71-511
H. PENZL, 221(GQ):MAR70-251
NATAN, A. & B. KEITH-SMITH, EDS. GERMAN
MEN OF LETTERS. (VOL 6)
617(TLS):28APR72-468
NATHANSON, L. THE STRATEGY OF TRUTH.
T. HERRING, 67:MAY71-121
V.D. PINTO, 175:AUTUMN69-108
C.F. WILLIAMSON, 597(SN):VOL41#1-190
NATHANSON, M. - SEE STRAUS, E.W., M.
NATHANSON & H. EY
"NATIONAL SECURITY STUDY MEMORANDUM NO.
1: THE SITUATION IN VIETNAM."
I.F. STONE, 453:1JUN72-11
"THE NATIONAL UNION CATALOG OF MANUSCRIPT
COLLECTIONS, 1965; 1966; 1967."*
L. RAPPORT, 14:JUL69-273
NATSUME SŌSEKI - SEE UNDER SŌSEKI, N.
NAUDEAU, O. LA PENSÉE DE MONTAIGNE ET LA
COMPOSITION DES ESSAIS.
617(TLS):22SEP72-1100
NAUMANN, W. TRAUM UND TRADITION IN DER
DEUTSCHEN LYRIK.
H. LEHNERT, 400(MLN):APR70-400
NAUMOV, N. DIKENS KOD SRBA I HRVATA.
E. ROSENBERG, 155:JAN70-52
NAUMOV, Y. SERGEY YESENIN.
G. MC VAY, 575(SEER):JAN71-145
NAVARRO, T. REPERTORIO DE ESTROFAS
ESPAÑOLAS.*
G.W. ANDRIAN, 238:SEP70-579
O.T. MYERS, 545(RPH):MAY71-647
NAVASKY, V.S. KENNEDY JUSTICE.*
M.E. TIGAR & M.R. LEVY, 453:29JUN72-
25
NAVILLE, P. D'HOLBACH ET LA PHILOSOPHIE
SCIENTIFIQUE AU XVIIIE SIÈCLE. (NEW
ED)
G. SOLINAS, 548(RCSF):APR/JUN69-231
NAYAGAM, X.S.T. - SEE UNDER THANI NAYA-
GAM, X.S.
NAYAR, P.K.B. LEADERSHIP, BUREAUCRACY
AND PLANNING IN INDIA.
617(TLS):22SEP72-1119
NAYLOR, E. AN ELIZABETHAN VIRGINAL BOOK.
R. MARLOW, 415:MAR71-243
NAYMAN, J. ATLAS OF WILDLIFE.
561(SATR):23DEC72-69
617(TLS):10NOV72-1376
NEAL, C.V. HOW TO KEEP WHAT YOU HAVE,
OR, WHAT YOUR BROKER NEVER TOLD YOU.
M. BENDER, 441:10AUG72-37
NEALE-SILVA, E. & D.A. NELSON. LENGUA
HISPÁNICA MODERNA.
P. GIL CASADO, 399(MLJ):JAN70-37
NEARING, H. & S. LIVING THE GOOD LIFE.
N. MILLS, 676(YR):SUMMER71-609
NEAVE, A. THE FLAMES OF CALAIS.
617(TLS):22DEC72-1555
NECK, R., ED. ÖSTERREICH IM JAHRE 1918.
F. L'HUILLIER, 182:VOL23#3-111
NEDERGAARD-HANSEN, L. BAYLE'S OG LEIBNIZ'
DRØFTELSE AF THEODICÉ-PROBLEMET.
S. HOLM, 462(OL):VOL24#3-228
NEDERVEEN, C.J. ACOUSTICAL ASPECTS OF
WOODWIND INSTRUMENTS.*
N. O'LOUGHLIN, 415:JAN70-47
NEDHAM, M. MARCHAMOUNT NEDHAM: THE CASE
OF THE COMMONWEALTH OF ENGLAND, STATED.
(P.A. KNACHEL, ED)
E. EMERSON, 568(SCN):SPRING71-17
NÉDONCELLE, M. LOVE AND THE PERSON.
B. GILLIGAN, 613:SPRING68-152

NEEDHAM, C.D., WITH E. HERMAN, EDS. THE
STUDY OF SUBJECT BIBLIOGRAPHY WITH
SPECIAL REFERENCE TO THE SOCIAL SCI-
ENCES.
W.L. WILLIAMSON, 356:APR71-175
NEEDHAM, J., WITH WANG LING & LU GWEI-
DJEN. SCIENCE AND CIVILISATION IN
CHINA.* (VOL 4, PT 3)
617(TLS):7JAN72-1
NEEDHAM, R. A FRIEND IN NEEDHAM.
J.M. ROBSON, 627(UTQ):JUL70-385
NEEDHAM, R., ED. RETHINKING KINSHIP AND
MARRIAGE.
617(TLS):9JUN72-653
NEEDHAM, R.J. THE GARDEN OF NEEDHAM.
J.M. ROBSON, 627(UTQ):JUL69-424
NEEDLEMAN, J. THE NEW RELIGIONS.
617(TLS):25AUG72-1002
NEELY, R. THE JAPANESE MISTRESS.
T. LASK, 441:30DEC72-19
NEF, E. DER ZUFALL IN DER ERZÄHLKUNST.
C.A. BERND, 406:FALL71-309
J.M. MC GLATHERY, 301(JEGP):JUL71-521
NEIDER, C., ED. ANTARCTICA.
P. ADAMS, 61:MAY72-112
D.S. ROBERTS, 440:7MAY72-4
NEIDERMAN, A. SISTERS.
M. LEVIN, 441:23JAN72-36
NEIHARDT, J.G. ALL IS BUT A BEGINNING.
441:10DEC72-48
NEILL, A.S. NEILL! NEILL! ORANGE PEEL!
B. DE MOTT, 561(SATR):16SEP72-97
C. LEHMANN-HAUPT, 441:3AUG72-35
NEIMAN, F. MATTHEW ARNOLD.
E. ALEXANDER, 637(VS):DEC69-230
NEKRICH, A. L'ARMÉE ROUGE ASSASSINÉE.
A. PARRY, 550(RUSR):APR70-235
NELLIST, J.B. BRITISH ARCHITECTURE AND
ITS BACKGROUND.
S. BLUTMAN, 505:AUG68-158
NELSON, B. ARTHUR MILLER.*
T.F. MARSHALL, 27(AL):MAY71-306
NELSON, B.J. THE LAST STATION.
M. LEVIN, 441:1OCT72-42
NELSON, C.E. & D.K. POLLOCK, EDS. COM-
MUNICATION AMONG SCIENTISTS AND EN-
GINEERS.
A. BOOKSTEIN, 356:JUL71-258
NELSON, G. CHANGES OF HEART.*
G.L. BRUNS, 590:WINTER71-37
NELSON, G.B. TEN VERSIONS OF AMERICA.
441:21MAY72-29
NELSON, J. - SEE CHRÉTIEN DE TROYES
NELSON, J. & R.J. OSTROW. THE FBI AND
THE BERRIGANS.
G. WILLS, 441:12NOV72-44
NELSON, J.K. HARRY BERTOIA, SCULPTOR.
A. WERNER, 127:SPRING71-334
NELSON, L., ED. CERVANTES: A COLLECTION
OF CRITICAL ESSAYS.
R.L. PREDMORE, 238:DEC70-1020
NELSON, R.K. HUNTERS OF THE NORTHERN
ICE.
639(VQR):WINTER70-XXVIII
NELSON, S.M. THE VIOLIN AND VIOLA.
617(TLS):1DEC72-1462
NEMIRO, B.A. THE BUSY PEOPLE'S COOKBOOK.
N. MAGID, 440:13FEB72-5
NENADOVIĆ, M. THE MEMOIRS OF PROTA
MATIJA NENADOVIĆ. (L.F. EDWARDS, ED &
TRANS)
T.J. BUTLER, 574(SEEJ):SPRING71-136
P.F. SUGAR, 32:MAR71-188
NEPOS, C. VIES D'HANNIBAL, DE CATON ET
D'ATTICUS. (M. RUCH, ED)
H. OPPERMANN, 182:VOL23#10-559

NERHOOD, J.H., ED. THE RUSSIA AND RE-
TURN.*
   A.J. SCHMIDT, 550(RUSR):JUL70-357
NERSOYAN, H.J. ANDRÉ GIDE.
   J.C. MC LAREN, 207(FR):MAR70-682
NERUDA, P. EXTRAVAGARIA.
   617(TLS):21JUL72-839
NERUDA, P. SELECTED POEMS. (N. TARN,
ED)
   J. BERNARDIN, 493:AUTUMN70-254
   A. COLEMAN, 441:7MAY72-4
NERUDA, P. SPLENDOR AND DEATH OF JOAQUIN
MURIETA.
   P. ADAMS, 61:SEP72-110
NERUDA, P. TWENTY LOVE POEMS AND A SONG
OF DESPAIR.
   P. MURRAY, 491:AUG72-304
NERUDA, P. & C. VALLEJO. NERUDA AND
VALLEJO: SELECTED POEMS. (R. BLY, ED)
   A. COLEMAN, 441:7MAY72-4
   P. MURRAY, 491:AUG72-304
   V. YOUNG, 249(HUDR):WINTER71/72-673
DE NERVAL, G. JOURNEY TO THE ORIENT.
(N. GLASS, ED & TRANS)
   617(TLS):7JUL72-784
DE NERVAL, G. PANDORA.* (J. GUILLAUME,
ED)
   F. BASSAN, 207(FR):FEB70-518
NERVI, P.L. AESTHETICS AND TECHNOLOGY IN
BUILDING.
   S. ANDERSON, 576:MAR68-82
NESKE, F. & I. DTV-WÖRTERBUCH ENGLISCHER
UND AMERIKANISCHER AUSDRÜCKE IN DER
DEUTSCHEN SPRACHE.
   A.W. STANFORTH, 406:SUMMER71-165
NESSELROTH, P.W. LAUTRÉAMONT'S IMAGERY.
   H.A. GRUBBS, 399(MLJ):MAY70-377
   S.I. LOCKERBIE, 208(FS):OCT71-482
NESTROY, J. JOHANN NESTROY, KOMÖDIEN.
(F.H. MAUTNER, ED)
   W.E. YATES, 402(MLR):OCT71-952
NETTL, B. FOLK AND TRADITIONAL MUSIC OF
THE WESTERN CONTINENTS.
   G. LIST, 650(WF):JUL69-221
NETTL, P. MOZART AND MASONRY.
   S. SADIE, 415:FEB71-140
NEUBERG, V.E., ED. LITERACY AND SOCIETY.
   617(TLS):14APR72-428
NEUBURG, P. THE HERO'S CHILDREN.
   D. CAUTE, 362:30NOV72-759
   617(TLS):29DEC72-1575
NEUFFER, C.H., ED. NAMES IN SOUTH CARO-
LINA.
   K.B. HARDER, 424:JUN68-194
NEUMANN, G., COMP. DEUTSCHE EPIGRAMME.
   E. STOPP, 402(MLR):APR71-450
NEUMANN, G. & J. MÜLLER, EDS. DER NACH-
LASS ARTHUR SCHNITZLERS.*
   W.G. CUNLIFFE, 406:SPRING71-91
   M.W. SWALES, 402(MLR):APR71-469
NEUMANN, P.H. ZUR LYRIK PAUL CELANS.
   S.S. PRAWER, 220(GL&L):OCT70-100
NEUMANN, W. BACH. (REV)
   S. SADIE, 415:OCT70-1003
NEUMEYER, P.F., ED. TWENTIETH CENTURY
INTERPRETATIONS OF "THE CASTLE."
   C.B. EVANS, 399(MLJ):MAR70-218
NEVEU, B. SÉBASTIEN JOSEPH DU CAMBOUT DE
PONTCHÂTEAU (1634-1690) ET SES MISSIONS
À ROME.
   H.G. JUDGE, 208(FS):JUL71-331
NEVILLE, D.E. HENRY DE MONTHERLANT AND
HIS CRITICS.
   J. CRUICKSHANK, 208(FS):APR71-239
NEVIN, D. MUSKIE OF MAINE.
   L.W. KOENIG, 561(SATR):3JUN72-62
   R.R. LINGEMAN, 441:4JUN72-1

NEVIUS, B. IVY COMPTON-BURNETT.
   R. LIDDELL, 402(MLR):OCT71-887
NEW, A.S.B. THE OBSERVER'S BOOK OF
CATHEDRALS.
   617(TLS):7JUL72-785
NEW, M. LAURENCE STERNE AS SATIRIST.*
   H. ANDERSON, 481(PQ):JUL70-381
   J-C. SALLÉ, 402(MLR):JUL71-669
   J.L. THOMPSON, 529(QQ):AUTUMN70-455
   566:AUTUMN70-33
NEW, W.H. MALCOLM LOWRY.
   F. COGSWELL, 296:SUMMER72-92
"NEW AMERICAN REVIEW NUMBER 13." (T.
SOLOTAROFF, ED)
   P. THEROUX, 440:6FEB72-9
"THE NEW ENGLISH BIBLE, WITH THE APOCRY-
PHA."*
   J.P. HYATT, 639(VQR):SUMMER70-514
"NEW YORK CITY." [MICHELIN GUIDE]
   C. SIMMONS, 441:4JUN72-7
"NEW YORK CITY FOREIGN LANGUAGE PROGRAM
FOR SECONDARY SCHOOLS: FRENCH, LEVELS
I-V."
   B. EBLING, 207(FR):MAR70-707
"NEW YORK CITY GUIDE." [FEDERAL WRITERS'
PROJECT]
   C. SIMMONS, 441:4JUN72-7
"NEW YORK CITY: NAGEL'S ENCYCLOPEDIA-
GUIDE."
   C. SIMMONS, 441:4JUN72-7
"NEW YORK IN FLASHMAPS."
   C. SIMMONS, 441:4JUN72-7
"THE NEW YORKER BOOK OF POEMS."*
   42(AR):WINTER69/70-590
   639(VQR):SUMMER70-XCV
NEWBOLD, E.B. PORTRAIT OF COVENTRY.
   617(TLS):9JUN72-667
NEWBOLD, T.J. POLITICAL AND STATISTICAL
ACCOUNT OF THE BRITISH SETTLEMENTS IN
THE STRAITS OF MALACCA.
   617(TLS):22DEC72-1565
NEWBY, E. WHEN THE SNOW COMES, THEY WILL
TAKE YOU AWAY.*
   L.E. SISSMAN, 442(NY):3JUN72-108
NEWCOMB, F.J. NAVAHO FOLK TALES.
   B. TOELKEN, 292(JAF):JUL-SEP70-361
NEWELL, R.W. THE CONCEPT OF PHILOSOPHY.
   R. BAMBROUGH, 483:JUL70-255
   E. TELFER, 393(MIND):JAN70-147
NEWELS, M. - SEE ARISTOTLE
NEWFIELD, J. & J. GREENFIELD. A POPULIST
MANIFESTO.
   E. DREW, 441:4JUN72-3
   R. JELLINEK, 441:3MAR72-40
   J. KRAFT, 441:12MAR72-3
   C. LASCH, 453:20JUL72-15
   S. SCHLESINGER, 561(SATR):18MAR72-78
   442(NY):22JUL72-79
NEWHOUSE, J., WITH OTHERS. U.S. TROOPS
IN EUROPE.
   617(TLS):30JUN72-733
NEWLOVE, J. BLACK NIGHT WINDOW.*
   H. MAC CALLUM, 627(UTQ):JUL69-346
NEWLOVE, J. THE CAVE.
   A.W. PURDY, 102(CANL):SPRING71-91
NEWMAN, A. THE STANHOPES OF CHEVENING.
   D. SPRING, 637(VS):JUN70-453
NEWMAN, C., ED. THE ART OF SYLVIA
PLATH.*
   E.M. AIRD, 148:SPRING70-94
NEWMAN, C. THE PROMISEKEEPER.*
   J.M. MORSE, 249(HUDR):AUTUMN71-539
NEWMAN, D. A PROCESSION OF FRIENDS.
   441:26MAR72-36
NEWMAN, E. BERLIOZ, ROMANTIC AND CLAS-
SIC. (P. HEYWORTH, ED)
   617(TLS):17MAR72-294

NEWMAN, E. THE MAN LISZT.
R. ANDERSON, 415:FEB70-160
NEWMAN, F.X., ED. THE MEANING OF COURTLY
LOVE.*
C. MUSCATINE, 589:OCT71-747
L.T. TOPSFIELD, 208(FS):APR71-187
NEWMAN, J.H. APOLOGIA PRO VITA SUA.
(M.J. SVAGLIC, ED)
A.D. CULLER, 405(MP):AUG69-97
NEWMAN, J.H. THE LETTERS AND DIARIES OF
JOHN HENRY NEWMAN.* (VOLS 17 & 18)
(C.S. DESSAIN, ED)
M.J. SVAGLIC, 637(VS):SEP69-98
NEWMAN, J.H. THE LETTERS AND DIARIES OF
JOHN HENRY NEWMAN. (VOL 22) (C.S.
DESSAIN, ED)
617(TLS):2JUN72-627
NEWMAN, S. RELATIVISM IN LANGUAGE AND
CULTURE.
W.P. LEHMANN, 545(RPH):FEB71-510
NEWMAN, W.S. PERFORMANCE PRACTICES IN
BEETHOVEN'S PIANO SONATAS.
617(TLS):28JUL72-893
NEWMAN, W.S. THE SONATA SINCE BEETHO-
VEN.*
F.E. KIRBY, 317:SPRING71-133
J. WARRACK, 415:JUL70-708
NEWMAN-GORDON, P. HÉLÈNE DE SPARTE, LA
FORTUNE DU MYTHE EN FRANCE.
S. MAX, 207(FR):MAR70-701
NEWPORT, W. STAMPS AND POSTAL HISTORY OF
THE CHANNEL ISLANDS.
617(TLS):5MAY72-529
NEWTON, H.P. TO DIE FOR THE PEOPLE.
C.C. WARE, 561(SATR):1JUL72-52
NEWTON, I. THE MATHEMATICAL PAPERS OF
ISAAC NEWTON. (VOL 4) (D.T. WHITESIDE,
ED)
617(TLS):23JUN72-723
NEWTON, I. PHILOSOPHIAE NATURALIS PRIN-
CIPIA MATHEMATICA. (A. KOYRÉ & I.B.
COHEN, WITH A. WHITMAN, EDS)
617(TLS):13OCT72-1212
NEWTON, R. VICTORIAN EXETER, 1837-1914.
H.J. HANHAM, 637(VS):DEC69-231
NEWTON, R.R. MEDIEVAL CHRONICLES AND
THE ROTATION OF THE EARTH.
617(TLS):22SEP72-1124
NGUGI WA THIONG'O. HOMECOMING.
617(TLS):3NOV72-1344
NIBBI, A. THE TYRRHENIANS.*
R.M. OGILVIE, 123:DEC71-459
NIČEV, A. L'ÉNIGME DE LA CATHARSIS
TRAGIQUE DANS ARISTOTE.
F. LASSERRE, 182:VOL23#9-498
NICHOL, B.P., ED. THE COSMIC CHEF.*
M. DOYLE, 491:MAR72-356
E. WOODS, 606(TAMR):#55-79
NICHOL, B.P. STILL WATER.
G. WOODCOCK, 102(CANL):AUTUMN71-15
NICHOL, B.P. TWO NOVELS [IN ONE]: ANDY
[AND] FOR LUNATICK JESUS.
P.M. BATES, 96:APR70-64
NICHOLLS, C.S. THE SWAHILI COAST.
617(TLS):1SEP72-1029
NICHOLLS, K. GAELIC AND GAELICISED IRE-
LAND IN THE MIDDLE AGES.
617(TLS):21JUL72-850
NICHOLLS, R.A. THE DRAMAS OF CHRISTIAN
DIETRICH GRABBE.*
R.C. COWEN, 222(GR):MAY70-253
D. JOST, 182:VOL23#13/14-672
NICHOLS, B. FATHER FIGURE.
P. ADAMS, 61:OCT72-135
G. ANNAN, 362:2MAR72-282
G. DAVENPORT, 441:8OCT72-2
617(TLS):10MAR72-272

NICHOLS, J. LITERARY ANECDOTES OF THE
EIGHTEENTH CENTURY. (C. CLAIR, ED)
G.M., 477:SUMMER69-423
NICHOLS, J. MINOR LIVES. (E.L. HART,
ED)
617(TLS):21APR72-450
NICHOLS, J.G. THE POETRY OF BEN JONSON.*
B. BABINGTON, 447(N&Q):NOV70-431
NICHOLS, R. CEREMONY OF INNOCENCE.
G. WOODCOCK, 102(CANL):WINTER71-88
"BEN NICHOLSON: DRAWINGS, PAINTINGS AND
RELIEFS, 1911-68."
C. FOX, 592:JUL/AUG69-52
C. LICHTBLAU, 58:NOV69-16
NICHOLSON, N. A LOCAL HABITATION.
S. HEANEY, 362:26OCT72-549
617(TLS):20OCT72-1249
NICKEL, G. DIE EXPANDED FORM IM ALTENG-
LISCHEN.*
H. KOZIOL, 179(ES):AUG70-349
NICKISCH, R.M.G. DIE STILPRINZIPIEN IN
DEN DEUTSCHEN BRIEFSTELLERN DES 17.
UND 18. JAHRHUNDERTS.
F. JOST, 301(JEGP):JUL71-507
NICKL, T. & H. SCHNITZLER - SEE SCHNITZ-
LER, A.
NICKLAUS, F. CUT OF NOON.
V. YOUNG, 249(HUDR):WINTER71/72-684
NICOD, M. DU RÉALISME À LA RÉALITÉ.
D.R. HAGGIS, 208(FS):APR71-237
NICOL, C.W. FROM THE ROOF OF AFRICA.
P. ADAMS, 61:FEB72-109
A. BROYARD, 441:10JAN72-31
A. WHITMAN, 440:2JAN72-8
441:13FEB72-14
NICOL, E. A SCAR IS BORN.
J.M. ROBSON, 627(UTQ):JUL69-424
NICOLAI, H., ED. STURM UND DRANG.
617(TLS):22SEP72-1109
NICOLAIDES, K. THE NATURAL WAY TO DRAW.
617(TLS):9JUN72-667
NICOLAISEN, W.F.H. - SEE GELLING, M.,
W.F.H. NICOLAISEN & M. RICHARDS
NICOLAOU, K. ANCIENT MONUMENTS OF
CYPRUS.
J. BOARDMAN, 123:DEC70-408
"NICOLÁS DE CUSA EN EL V CENTENARIO DE
SU MUERTE (1464-1964)." (VOL 1)
G. SANTINELLO, 548(RCSF):JAN/MAR69-
107
NICOLET, C. LES GRACQUES, CRISE AGRAIRE
ET RÉVOLUTION À ROME.
D. EARL, 313:VOL60-209
NICOLL, A. ENGLISH DRAMA.
M.D. FABER, 397(MD):SEP69-215
NICOLL, A. MASKS, MIMES AND MIRACLES.
(NEW ED) THE WORLD OF HARLEQUIN.
J. STAROBINSKI, 98:DEC69-1033
NICOLSON, B. JOSEPH WRIGHT OF DERBY.*
D. CLIFFORD, 592:MAR69-154
J. GAGE, 90:MAY69-304
G. GRIGSON, 39:JAN69-78
A. NEUMEYER, 127(WINTER70/71-216
R. PAULSON, 173(ECS):WINTER69-278
NICOLSON, J.R. SHETLAND.
617(TLS):1SEP72-1028
NICOLSON, M. & G.S. ROUSSEAU. "THIS LONG
DISEASE, MY LIFE."
R. HARRÉ, 541(RES):MAY70-219
L.C. MC HENRY, JR., 173(ECS):FALL69-
136
R. PARKIN, 173(ECS):FALL69-139
NICOSIA, S. TEOCRITO E L'ARTE FIGURATA.
W. BERG, 24:APR71-383
T. BREITENSTEIN, 303:VOL90-215
C. MEILLIER, 555:VOL44FASC2-328

NIEBUHR, R.R. SCHLEIERMACHER ON CHRIST
AND RELIGION.
J.M.S., 543:DEC69-351
NIEDECKER, L. COLLECTED POEMS 1968: MY
LIFE BY WATER.
T. HARRISON, 364:APR/MAY71-163
J. NAIDEN, 491:MAY72-115
NIEDERAUER, D.J. - SEE DE RÉGNIER, H.
NIELSEN, C. LIVING MUSIC.
R. LAYTON, 415:JAN70-45
NIELSEN, W.A. THE BIG FOUNDATIONS.
T. LASK, 441:11NOV72-35
P. STEINFELS, 441:26NOV72-2
NIEMEYER, G. BETWEEN NOTHINGNESS AND
PARADISE.
F.G. WILSON, 396(MODA):FALL71-433
NIESS, R.J. ZOLA, CÉZANNE, AND MANET.
P. BRADY, 400(MLN):DEC70-931
C.S. BROWN, 219(GAR):SUMMER69-266
R.T. DENOMMÉ, 207(FR):DEC69-339
NIETO, M.C. - SEE UNDER CASADO NIETO, M.
NIEWYK, D.L. SOCIALIST, ANTI-SEMITE AND
JEW.*
617(TLS):28JAN72-81
TE NIJENHUIS, E. DATTILAM.
N.A. JAIRAZBHOY, 187:MAY72-292
NIJLAND-VERWEY, M. - SEE WOLFSKEHL, K. &
A. VERWEY
NIKAM, N.A. SENSE, UNDERSTANDING AND
REASON.
A. BORGMANN, 485(PE&W):JUL68-217
NIKI, T. FIFTY PAINTERS OF JAPAN.
P. HARDIE, 39:APR69-326
NIKLAUS, R. A LITERARY HISTORY OF
FRANCE: THE EIGHTEENTH CENTURY 1715-
1789.*
J.H. BRUMFITT, 208(FS):JAN71-80
NILSSON, E. LES TERMES RELATIFS ET LES
PROPOSITIONS RELATIVES EN ROUMAIN
MODERNE.*
H.A. HURREN, 402(MLR):JAN71-205
NILSSON, N.Å. THE RUSSIAN IMAGINISTS.
E. BRISTOL, 574(SEEJ):WINTER71-506
NILSSON, N.Å. STUDIES IN ČECHOV'S NAR-
RATIVE TECHNIQUE.*
P. ROSSBACHER, 550(RUSR):JAN70-112
NILSSON, S. EUROPEAN ARCHITECTURE IN
INDIA.
L. BRETT, 46:AUG69-156
NIMETZ, M. HUMOR IN GALDÓS.*
S. BESER, 546(RR):OCT70-232
NIMS, J.F., ED & TRANS. SAPPHO TO
VALÉRY.
P. MURRAY, 491:AUG72-304
NIN, A. THE DIARY OF ANAÏS NIN 1944-
1947.* (BRITISH TITLE: THE JOURNALS OF
ANAÏS NIN 1944-1947.) (G. STUHLMANN,
ED)
A. BALAKIAN, 441:16JAN72-28
E.J. HINZ, 659:SPRING72-255
617(TLS):12MAY72-553
NIN, A. THE NOVEL OF THE FUTURE.
W. ROWE, 619(TC):1969/2-48
NINIOVS'KYJ, V. UKRAINIAN REVERSE DIC-
TIONARY.
G.Y. SHEVELOV, 574(SEEJ):FALL71-356
NISBET, H.B. HERDER AND THE PHILOSOPHY
AND HISTORY OF SCIENCE.* HERDER AND
SCIENTIFIC THOUGHT.*
J-J. DAETWYLER, 182:VOL23#17/18-775
E.B. GASKING, 67:NOV71-253
NISBET, R. THE DEGRADATION OF THE ACA-
DEMIC DOGMA.*
617(TLS):14JAN72-47
NISBET, R.A. SOCIAL CHANGE AND HISTORY.*
R.J.B., 543:DEC69-352

NISBET, R.G.M. & M. HUBBARD. A COMMEN-
TARY ON HORACE: "ODES" BOOK I.*
M.L. CLARKE, 123:JUN71-203
E.T. SILK, 24(JUL71-488
T.A. SUITS, 124:JAN71-166
F.A. SULLIVAN, 122:APR71-116
NISH, C. LES BOURGEOIS-GENTILSHOMMES
DE LA NOUVELLE-FRANCE, 1729-1748.
J-C. BONENFANT, 627(UTQ):JUL69-452
F. OUELLET, 331:AUG69-57
Y.F. ZOLTVANY, 656(WMQ):APR70-338
NISHIKAWA YASUSHI, ED. SAIAN HIRIN.
A.C. SOPER, 57:VOL31#1-88
NISSENSON, H. IN THE REIGN OF PEACE.
T. LASK, 441:18MAR72-29
C. OZICK, 441:19MAR72-4
NITCHIE, G.W. MARIANNE MOORE.*
M.B. QUINN, 191(ELN):MAR71-240
NIVEN, D. THE MOON'S A BALLOON.
G.M. FRASER, 440:16JAN72-4
D. GODDARD, 441:30JAN72-30
C. LEHMANN-HAUPT, 441:13JAN72-43
NIVER, K.R. THE FIRST TWENTY YEARS.
(B. BERGSTEN, ED)
R. GIROUX, 200:MAR69-176
NIXON, A. THE ATTACK ON VIENNA.
N. CALLENDAR, 441:18JUN72-32
NIXON, E. MARY WOLLSTONECRAFT.*
617(TLS):7APR72-388
NIXON, I.G. THE RISE OF THE DORIANS.*
P. MAC KENDRICK, 121(CJ):OCT-NOV70-80
NIXON, R.F., ED. THE GUELPH PAPERS.
I.M. ABELLA, 529(QQ):WINTER70-640
NIZAMI, K.A., ED. MEDIEVAL INDIA. (VOL
2)
617(TLS):27OCT72-1296
NIZAN, P. PAUL NIZAN, INTELLECTUEL COM-
MUNISTE, 1926-1940. (J-J. BROCHIER,
ED)
S.M. SULEIMAN, 546(RR):OCT70-237
NIZAN, P. THE WATCHDOGS.
M. CRANSTON, 440:23APR72-5
617(TLS):25AUG72-998
NOAKES, V. EDWARD LEAR.*
E.D.H. JOHNSON, 637(VS):SEP69-102
K. ROBERTS, 90:OCT70-706
M. WEBSTER, 39:NOV69-448
NOBLE, D.W. THE ETERNAL ADAM AND THE NEW
WORLD GARDEN.*
R. LEHAN, 445(NCF):JUN68-117
NOBLE, F. THE SHELL BOOK OF OFFA'S DYKE
PATH.
617(TLS):20OCT72-1264
NOBLE, J.R., ED. RECOLLECTIONS OF VIR-
GINIA WOOLF.
N. ANNAN, 362:15JUN72-794
617(TLS):5MAY72-509
NOCHLIN, L. REALISM.
617(TLS):11FEB72-150
NOCK, A.D. ESSAYS ON RELIGION AND THE
ANCIENT WORLD. (Z. STEWART, ED)
617(TLS):15SEP72-1064
NOEHLES, K. ROMA L'ANNO 1663 DI GIOV.
BATT. MOLA.
J. MONTAGU, 90:FEB69-96
NOËL, M. NOTES FOR MYSELF.
J. HARDRÉ, 399(MLJ):MAR70-206
NØJGAARD, M. LA FABLE ANTIQUE.* (VOL 2)
E.D. PHILLIPS, 123:JUN71-214
NOLAN, P.T., ED. PROVINCIAL DRAMA IN
AMERICA, 1870-1916.
W.L. FRAZER, 397(MD):FEB69-452
NOMURA JUN'ICHI, ED. FUEFUKI MUKO.
F.H. MAYER, 293(JAST):MAY70-702
NOONAN, J.T., JR. POWER TO DISSOLVE.
F.X. MURPHY, 441:17SEP72-40
NOONE, R. RAPE OF THE DREAM PEOPLE.
617(TLS):27OCT72-1281

NOONE, R., WITH D. HOLMAN. IN SEARCH OF
THE DREAM PEOPLE.
    A. BROYARD, 441:22NOV72-37
NORBERG-SCHULZ, C. INTENTIONS IN ARCHI-
TECTURE.
    P. ZUCKER, 290(JAAC):SPRING70-405
NORDENFALK, C. DIE SPÄTANTIKEN ZIERBUCH-
STABEN.
    H. KNAUS, 182:VOL23#21/22-897
NORDENSTAM, T. SUDANESE ETHICS.
    H.J.N. HORSBURGH, 479(PHQ):JUL70-309
NORDSTRÖM, C-O. THE DUKE OF ALBA'S
CASTILIAN BIBLE.
    J. GUTMANN, 54:MAR69-91
NORMAN, A.F. - SEE LIBANIUS
NORMAN, B. REQUIEM FOR A SPANISH VIL-
LAGE.
    A. BROYARD, 441:20DEC72-45
    442(NY):30DEC72-71
NORMAN, C. EZRA POUND. (REV)
    F.K. SANDERS, 569(SR):SUMMER71-433
    J. SCHWARTZ, 590:SUMMER70-42
NORMAN, F. THE LIVES OF FRANK NORMAN.
    617(TLS):26MAY72-594
NORMAN, G. DIVINE RIGHT'S TRIP.
    J. DECK, 441:2JUL72-17
    J. UPDIKE, 442(NY):9SEP72-115
NORMAN, K.R., ED & TRANS. THE ELDERS'
VERSES I: THERAGATHA.
    J. DHIRASEKERA, 318(JAOS):OCT-DEC70-
    587
NORMAN, L. & R.B. COOTE. THE FARM BUSI-
NESS.
    617(TLS):5MAY72-529
NORMAN, M. BIKE RIDING IN LOS ANGELES.
    J.R. FRAKES, 441:12NOV72-64
NORMAN, P. WILD THING.
    J. HUNTER, 362:21DEC72-869
    617(TLS):22DEC72-1549
NORMAN, V. THE MEDIEVAL SOLDIER.
    617(TLS):21APR72-458
NORMAND, J. NATHANIEL HAWTHORNE.
    N. BAYM, 301(JEGP):OCT71-696
NÖRR, D. IMPERIUM UND POLIS IN DER
HOHEN PRINZIPATSZEIT.*
    B.M. LEVICK, 123:JUN71-257
NORRIS, H. IT'S NOT FAR BUT I DON'T
KNOW THE WAY.
    639(VQR):SPRING70-XLI
NORRIS, J.A. THE FIRST AFGHAN WAR,
1838-1842.
    W.D. MC INTYRE, 637(VS):JUN70-455
NORRIS, L. RANSOMS.
    C. MOLESWORTH, 491:MAY72-107
NORTH, E. SUMMER SOLSTICE.
    J. CATINELLA, 561(SATR):27MAY72-68
    A. HISLOP, 440:21MAY72-5
    M. LEVIN, 441:30APR72-38
NORTH, G. SERGEANT CLUFF RINGS TRUE.
    617(TLS):25AUG72-1005
"NORTH AMERICAN BICYCLE ATLAS."
    H.C. GARDNER, 441:4JUN72-8
NORTON, F.J. PRINTING IN SPAIN - 1501-
1520.
    A. RODRÍGUEZ-MOÑINO, 551(RENQ):
    SUMMER70-179
NORTON, F.J. & E.M. WILSON. TWO SPANISH
VERSE CHAP-BOOKS.*
    B. GICOVATE, 238:MAR70-147
    J.J. REYNOLDS, 551(RENQ):AUTUMN70-309
    M.E. SIMMONS, 292(JAF):OCT-DEC70-479
    C. STERN, 545(RPH):AUG70-221
NORTON, L. - SEE DUC DE SAINT-SIMON
NORTON, M.B. THE BRITISH-AMERICANS.
    W.M. WALLACE, 441:12NOV72-4
NORWICH, J.J. THE KINGDOM IN THE SUN.*
    676(YR):WINTER71-XXIV

NOSEK, J. CONTRIBUTIONS TO THE SYNTAX OF
THE NEW ENGLISH COMPLEX SENTENCE.
    K. AIJMER, 597(SN):VOL41#1-227
NOSSITER, B.D. SOFT STATE.
    N. MAXWELL, 453:23MAR72-8
NOSSITER, T.J., A.H. HANSON & S. ROKKAN,
EDS. IMAGINATION AND PRECISION IN THE
SOCIAL SCIENCES.
    617(TLS):13OCT72-1220
NOSWORTHY, J.M. - SEE VEVER, R.
NOUGÉ, P. NOTES SUR LES ÉCHECS.
    H.S. GERSHMAN, 207(FR):MAR70-731
NOULET, E., ED. ENTRETIENS SUR PAUL
VALÉRY.
    J.C. MC LAREN, 207(FR):MAY70-934
"NOUS LES TUPAMAROS."
    617(TLS):4AUG72-915
"NOUVELLES ÉTUDES D'HISTOIRE, PUBLIÉES À
L'OCCASION DU XIIIE CONGRÈS DES SCI-
ENCES HISTORIQUES, MOSCOU, 1970."
    J.C. CAMPBELL, 104:WINTER71-580
NOVA, C. TURKEY HASH.
    J.G. BOWLES, 561(SATR):23DEC72-62
    M. LEVIN, 441:29OCT72-58
NOVAK, B. AMERICAN PAINTING IN THE NINE-
TEENTH CENTURY.
    R. FRIEDMAN, 58:MAR70-14
NOVAK, B.C. TRIESTE, 1941-1954.
    J.B. DUROSELLE, 32:DEC71-919
NOVAK, M. THE RISE OF THE UNMELTABLE
ETHNICS.
    T. LASK, 441:29APR72-33
    B.A. WEISBERGER, 440:14MAY72-6
    G. WILLS, 441:23APR72-27
NOVAK, M.E. & G.R. GUFFEY - SEE DRYDEN,
J.
NOVALIS. NOVALIS SCHRIFTEN. (VOL 3)
(R. SAMUEL, WITH H-J. MÄHL & G. SCHULZ,
EDS)
    E. STOPP, 402(MLR):JAN71-220
NOVALIS. NOVALIS WERKE. (G. SCHULZ, ED)
    M.L. BAEUMER, 406:SPRING71-67
NOVE, A. AN ECONOMIC HISTORY OF THE
USSR.*
    G. GROSSMAN, 550(RUSR):JUL70-338
NOVE, A. & D.M. NUTI, EDS. SOCIALIST
ECONOMICS.
    617(TLS):17NOV72-1405
NOVOTNY, A. STRANGERS AT THE DOOR.
    441:23APR72-10
NOWAKOWSKI, T. ALEJA DOBRYCH ZNAJOMYCH.
    D.C.W., 270:VOL20#3-77
NOWELL-SMITH, S. INTERNATIONAL COPYRIGHT
LAW AND THE PUBLISHER IN THE REIGN OF
QUEEN VICTORIA.*
    J.D. JUMP, 447(N&Q):SEP70-360
NOWIKOWA, I. EINE ANONYME RUSSISCHE
HANDSCHRIFT DES 17. JAHRHUNDERTS.
    V.A. TUMINS, 574(SEEJ):SPRING71-111
NOWLAN, A. BETWEEN TEARS AND LAUGHTER.
    P. PACEY, 198:SPRING72-114
NOWLAN, A. THE MYSTERIOUS NAKED MAN.*
    M. HORNYANSKY, 627(UTQ):JUL70-335
    150(DR):AUTUMN70-424
NOWLAN, A. PLAYING THE JESUS GAME.
    M. DOYLE, 491:MAR72-356
NOYES, R. WORDSWORTH AND THE ART OF
LANDSCAPE.*
    D.S. BLAND, 447(N&Q):MAY70-191
    J.A.W. HEFFERNAN, 179(ES):AUG70-365
    K.K., 191(ELN):SEP69(SUPP)-48
NUNES, C. BREVES ESTUDOS DE LITERATURA
BRASILEIRA.
    O. FERNÁNDEZ, 399(MLJ):OCT70-461
NUNES, M. & D. WHITE. THE LACE GHETTO.
    M. HARRIS, 99:SEP72-35

NÚÑEZ, Á. LA OBRA NARRATIVA DE ROBERTO
ARLT.
H.E. LEWALD, 238:MAR70-156
NUNNERLEY, D. PRESIDENT KENNEDY AND
BRITAIN.
617(TLS):20OCT72-1244
NURMELA, T. - SEE BOCCACCIO, G.
NURSE, P.H., ED. THE ART OF CRITICISM.
E.L. DUTHIE, 208(FS):JUL71-373
NUTTALL, A.D. TWO CONCEPTS OF ALLEGORY.
W. ROSEN, 141:WINTER69-106
NUTTALL, J. POEMS: 1962-69.
C. MOLESWORTH, 491:MAY72-107
NUTTER, G.W. THE STRANGE WORLD OF IVAN
IVANOV.
R. LANE, 550(RUSR):JUL70-357
NUTTING, A. NASSER.
M. COPELAND, 441:6AUG72-17
P. MANSFIELD, 362:15JUN72-795
442(NY):9SEP72-126
617(TLS):16JUN72-676
NYE, R. DOUBTFIRE.
P.H. POROSKY, 448:SUMMER68-100
NYE, R. - SEE RALEIGH, W.
NYE, R.B. AMERICAN LITERARY HISTORY:
1607-1830.
T. HORNBERGER, 165:FALL72-200
L. LEARY, 27(AL):MAY71-309
NYGREN, A. MEANING AND METHOD.
617(TLS):24NOV72-1434
NYKROG, P. LA PENSÉE DE BALZAC DANS LA
"COMÉDIE HUMAINE."
J-H. DONNARD, 597(SN):VOL40#2-461
NYLUND, M. & M. POLKINEN, EDS. LYRIK I
FINLAND NU.
G.C. SCHOOLFIELD, 563(SS):SUMMER71-
311
DE NYSSE, G. - SEE UNDER GRÉGOIRE DE
NYSSE

"O LITERÁRNEJ AVANTGARDE."
W. & H. SCHMID, 490:JAN68-134
OAKESHOTT, W. THE MOSAICS OF ROME.*
J. BECKWITH, 90:MAR70-176
OAKESHOTT, W. SIGENA.
617(TLS):10NOV72-1356
OAKLEY, A. SEX, GENDER AND SOCIETY.
617(TLS):3MAR72-235
OAKLEY, S. THE STORY OF DENMARK.
617(TLS):24NOV72-1423
OATES, J.C. ANONYMOUS SINS AND OTHER
POEMS.*
639(VQR):WINTER70-XIII
OATES, J.C. THE EDGE OF IMPOSSIBILITY.
P. ADAMS, 61:MAY72-112
N. BALAKIAN, 441:12JUN72-37
C.C. PARK, 440:23APR72-8
R. SALE, 441:9JUL72-23
B. WEBER, 561(SATR):10JUN72-63
OATES, J.C. EXPENSIVE PEOPLE.
42(AR):SPRING69-109
OATES, J.C. MARRIAGES AND INFIDELITIES.
W. ABRAHAMS, 561(SATR):23SEP72-76
M. WOOD, 441:1OCT72-6
OATES, J.C. THEM.*
639(VQR):SPRING70-XL
OATES, J.C. WONDERLAND.*
J.G. FARRELL, 362:15JUN72-797
617(TLS):7JUL72-765
OATES, J.C.T. SHANDYISM AND SENTIMENT,
1760-1800.
R. LONSDALE, 354:DEC69-352
OATLEY, K. BRAIN MECHANISMS AND MIND.
617(TLS):8DEC72-1484
OATRIDGE, N.C. BERNARD SHAW'S GOD.
R.J. CLAPP, 571:SPRING-SUMMER68-24

OBA OSAMU. EDO JIDAI NI OKERAI TŌSEN
NOSHIWATORI SHO NO KENKYU.
D.F. HENDERSON, 293(JAST):MAY70-700
O'BALLANCE, E. THE THIRD ARAB-ISRAELI
WAR.
617(TLS):13OCT72-1222
OBERG, E. - SEE AMPHILOCHIUS
VON OBERG, E. - SEE UNDER EILHART VON
OBERG
OBERKOFLER, G. DIE GESCHICHTLICHEN
FÄCHER AN DER PHILOSOPHISCHEN FAKULTÄT
DER UNIVERSITÄT INNSBRUCK 1850-1945.
W. ULLMANN, 182:VOL23#8-387
OBERMAYER-MARNACH, E. & L. SANTIFALLER,
EDS. ÖSTERREICHISCHES BIOGRAPHISCHES
LEXIKON 1815 BIS 1950. (VOL 1 THRU VOL
5, PT 1)
E. ALKER, 182:VOL23#11/12-579
OBERTELLO, L. JOHN LOCKE E PORT-ROYAL.
F. DE MICHELIS, 548(RCSF):JAN-MAR68-
109
OBEYD-I-ZAKANI. GORBY AND THE RATS.
617(TLS):13OCT72-1217
OBOLENSKY, D. THE BYZANTINE COMMON-
WEALTH.*
S. RUNCIMAN, 362:1JUN72-728
OBOLENSKY, D. BYZANTIUM AND THE SLAVS:
COLLECTED STUDIES.
617(TLS):18FEB72-182
O'BRIANT, W.H. - SEE LEIBNIZ, G.W.
O'BRIEN, B.T. SUMMER OF THE BLACK SUN.*
G. ROPER, 627(UTQ):JUL70-340
O'BRIEN, C.C. ALBERT CAMUS OF EUROPE
AND AFRICA.
K.J. HARROW, 295:VOL2#1-143
O'BRIEN, C.C. STATES OF IRELAND.
K. KYLE, 362:12OCT72-480
617(TLS):10NOV72-1355
O'BRIEN, C.C. THE SUSPECTING GLANCE.
M.I. FINLEY, 362:1JUN72-723
617(TLS):7JUL72-764
O'BRIEN, D. THE CONSCIENCE OF JAMES
JOYCE.
T.E. CONNOLLY, 405(MP):AUG69-102
T. ROGERS, 175:SUMMER69-73
O'BRIEN, D. EMPEDOCLES' COSMIC CYCLE.*
G.B. KERFERD, 123:JUN71-176
A-A. LONG, 303:VOL90-238
C. MUGLER, 555:VOL44FASC1-125
J.J.R., 543:MAR70-563
O'BRIEN, D.P. - SEE LORD OVERSTONE
O'BRIEN, E. NIGHT.
A. BROYARD, 441:28DEC72-29
J.G. FARRELL, 362:5OCT72-447
617(TLS):6OCT72-1184
O'BRIEN, J.A., ED. WHY PRIESTS LEAVE.
J-M. PETULLA, 142:WINTER71-121
O'BRIEN, K. & G.I. BRACHFELD & M.C. THOMP-
SON. FRENCH 3.
R. WALDINGER, 207(FR):MAR70-710
O'BRIEN, K., M.S. LAFRANCE & G. BRACH-
FELD. FRENCH 2.
R. WALDINGER, 207(FR):MAR70-710
O'BRIEN, K. & OTHERS. FRENCH 1.
R. WALDINGER, 207(FR):MAR70-710
O'BRIEN, M. & C.C. A CONCISE HISTORY OF
IRELAND.
617(TLS):21JUL72-850
O'BRIEN, M.J. THE SOCRATIC PARADOXES AND
THE GREEK MIND.*
W.E. CHARLTON, 123:MAR71-31
O'BRIEN, M.J., ED. TWENTIETH CENTURY
INTERPRETATIONS OF "OEDIPUS REX."*
H. LLOYD-JONES, 123:DEC70-398
O'BRIEN, R.C. A REPORT FROM GROUP 17.
N. CALLENDAR, 441:9APR72-41
S. KROLL, 440:19MAR72-7
C. LEHMANN-HAUPT, 441:16MAR72-49

O'BRIEN, R.C. WHITE SOCIETY IN BLACK
AFRICA.
R. WEST, 362:17FEB72-220
617(TLS):3NOV72-1313
Ó BROIN, L. THE PRIME INFORMER.*
617(TLS):25FEB72-227
"OBSERVER." MESSAGE FROM MOSCOW.
B.R. BOCIURKIW, 550(RUSR):JUL70-328
J.C. MC CLELLAND, 32:MAR71-159
O'CALLAGHAN, J. THE SAGA OF THE STEAM
SHIP "GREAT BRITAIN."
617(TLS):12MAY72-557
O'CASEY, E. SEAN.* (J.C. TREWIN, ED)
P. ADAMS, 61:FEB72-109
A. ALVAREZ, 561(SATR):29JAN72-57
D.H. GREENE, 440:6FEB72-5
V.S. PRITCHETT, 441:12MAR72-5
O'CASEY, S. THE SEAN O'CASEY READER.
(B. ATKINSON, ED)
R. HOGAN, 397(MD):MAY69-107
OCHMAŃSKI, J. HISTORIA LITWY.
J.P. SLAVENAS, 32:JUN71-408
OCHS, I. WOLFRAMS "WILLEHALM"-EINGANG
IM LICHTE DER FRÜHMITTELHOCHDEUTSCHEN
GEISTLICHEN DICHTUNG.
V. GÜNTHER, 182:VOL23#15/16-741
OCKHAM, WILLIAM OF. PREDESTINATION,
GOD'S FOREKNOWLEDGE AND FUTURE CONTIN-
GENTS. (M.M. ADAMS & N. KRETZMANN,
EDS & TRANS)
R.H.K., 543:JUN70-745
OCKHAM, WILLIAM OF. SCRIPTUM IN LIBRUM
PRIMUM SENTENTIARUM: ORDINATIO. (VOL
1) (G. GAL & S. BROWN, EDS)
M.M. ADAMS, 482(PHR):APR70-268
O'CONNELL, M.R. THE OXFORD CONSPIRATORS.
A.R.K. WATKINSON, 637(VS):JUN70-460
O'CONNELL, R., ED. APOLLO'S DAY.
B.W. BOOTHE, 577(SHR):SUMMER70-284
O'CONNELL, R.J. ST. AUGUSTINE'S "CON-
FESSIONS."
J.D. CLOUD, 518:JAN70-17
R.A. MARKUS, 479(PHQ):JUL70-269
O'CONNELL, R.J. ST. AUGUSTINE'S EARLY
THEORY OF MAN, A.D. 386-391.
J.D. CLOUD, 518:JAN70-17
J. DILLON, 121(CJ):DEC70-JAN71-180
R.A. MARKUS, 479(PHQ):JUL70-269
O'CONNOR, D.J. AQUINAS AND NATURAL LAW.
C.L. TEN, 63:MAY71-114
O'CONNOR, D.J. JOHN LOCKE.
L. TURCO, 548(RCSF):JUL/SEP69-341
O'CONNOR, F. EVERYTHING THAT RISES MUST
CONVERGE.*
M. MONTGOMERY, 145(CRIT):VOL13#2-15
O'CONNOR, F. MYSTERY AND MANNERS.*
(S. & R. FITZGERALD, EDS)
617(TLS):25FEB72-213
O'CONNOR, F. FLANNERY O'CONNOR: THE COM-
PLETE STORIES.*
R. FREEDMAN, 440:30JAN72-11
O'CONNOR, J. HORSE AND BUGGY WEST.*
M.T. SOLVE, 50(ARQ):SUMMER69-189
O'CONNOR, J.J. "AMADIS DE GAULE" AND
ITS INFLUENCE ON ELIZABETHAN LITERA-
TURE.
E.M. WILSON, 402(MLR):JUL71-657
O'CONNOR, K. THE IRISH IN BRITAIN.
617(TLS):8DEC72-1483
O'CONNOR, P.F. OLD MORALS, SMALL CONTI-
NENTS, DARKER TIMES.*
W. EYSTER, 598(SOR):SUMMER72-689
O'CONNOR, R. THE CACTUS THRONE.*
617(TLS):8DEC72-1503
O'CONNOR, R. THE GERMAN-AMERICANS.
T. WEYR, 19(AGR):VOL35#4-28
O'CONNOR, R. O. HENRY.
E. CURRENT-GARCIA, 27(AL):MAR71-137

O'CONNOR, R. THE OIL BARONS.*
617(TLS):1DEC72-1464
O'CONNOR, R. PACIFIC DESTINY.
42(AR):WINTER69/70-590
Ó CORRÁIN, D. IRELAND BEFORE THE NOR-
MANS.
617(TLS):21JUL72-850
ODIER, D. THE JOB.
639(VQR):AUTUMN70-CXLII
ODLE, R. SALT OF OUR YOUTH.
617(TLS):7JUL72-785
ODOEVCEVA, I. NA BEREGAX NEVY.
N. GALICHENKO, 104:SUMMER71-278
ODOJEWSKIJ, W.F. RUSSISCHE NÄCHTE.
(H.A. STAMMLER, ED)
V. TERRAS, 574(SEEJ):SUMMER71-223
O'DONNELL, C.P. - SEE SIMON, Y.
O'DONNELL, L. THE PHONE CALLS.
N. CALLENDAR, 441:30JAN72-24
H. FRANKEL, 561(SATR):29JAN72-73
617(TLS):29DEC72-1588
O'DONNELL, P. THE IMPOSSIBLE VIRGIN.*
N. CALLENDAR, 441:2JAN72-16
O'DONOGHUE, M. WILD HONEY TIME.
617(TLS):13OCT72-1235
O'DONOVAN, J. SHAW AND THE CHARLATAN
GENIUS.
A.H. NETHERCOT, 397(MD):FEB68-434
O'DRISCOLL, R., ED. THEATRE AND NATION-
ALISM IN TWENTIETH-CENTURY IRELAND.
617(TLS):28JAN72-100
OELLERS, N. - SEE SCHILLER, F.
OESER, E. DIE ANTIKE DIALEKTIK IN DER
SPÄTPHILOSOPHIE SCHELLINGS.
M.J.V., 543:SEP69-135
OESER, E. BEGRIFF UND SYSTEMATIK DER
ABSTRAKTION.
S. DECLOUX, 182:VOL23#19/20-840
OESTERLEY, W.O.E. THE SACRED DANCE.
J. DE LABAN, 290(JAAC):FALL69-112
OFFNER, R. & K. STEINWEG. A CORPUS OF
FLORENTINE PAINTING: GIOVANNI DEL
BIONDO. (PT 1)
J. WHITE, 90:MAY69-308
O'FLAHERTY, J.C. - SEE HAMANN, J.G.
O'FLAHERTY, L. THE INFORMER.
D.A.N. JONES, 362:20JAN72-90
OGDEN, J. ISAAC D'ISRAELI.
R.G. COX, 447(N&Q):OCT70-387
OGDEN, P.S. PETER SKENE OGDEN'S SNAKE
COUNTRY JOURNALS. (G. WILLIAMS, ED)
617(TLS):12MAY72-536
OGDEN, S.M. THE REALITY OF GOD AND OTHER
ESSAYS.
R.C. NEVILLE, 258:DEC69-605
OGILVIE, R.M. THE ROMANS AND THEIR GODS
IN THE AGE OF AUGUSTUS.
J-C. RICHARD, 555:VOL44FASC2-361
H.C. RUTLEDGE, 124:JAN71-168
P.G. WALSH, 123:JUN71-241
OGILVY, D. FLYING LIGHT AIRCRAFT.
617(TLS):12MAY72-557
OGNEV, V. & D. RATTENBERG, COMPS. FIFTY
SOVIET POETS.
W.H. BENNETT, 574(SEEJ):SUMMER71-235
O'GORMAN, N. THE FLAG THE HAWK FLIES.
P. DALE, 561(SATR):8JUL72-57
O'GRADY, R. BLEAK NOVEMBER.*
617(TLS):7JAN72-17
O'HARA, J. AND OTHER STORIES.
J.P. DEGNAN, 340(KR):1969/2-272
O'HARA, J. THE EWINGS.
P. ADAMS, 61:MAR72-110
M. BELL, 561(SATR):4MAR72-80
L.J. DAVIS, 440:20FEB72-11
R. KIELY, 441:27FEB72-48
C. LEHMANN-HAUPT, 441:29FEB72-37

O'HARA, J. THE TIME ELEMENT AND OTHER
STORIES.
   A. BROYARD, 441:18DEC72-41
   561(SATR):16DEC72-71
O'HARA, K. THE COMPANY OF ST. GEORGE.
   617(TLS):26MAY72-612
O HEHIR, B. EXPANS'D HIEROGLYPHICKS.
HARMONY FROM DISCORDS.
   P.J. KORSHIN, 481(PQ):JUL70-338
OHLY, K. & V. SACK, EDS. INKUNABELKATA-
LOG DER STADT- UND UNIVERSITÄTSBIBLIO-
THEK UND ANDERER ÖFFENTLICHER SAMMLUN-
GEN IN FRANKFURT AM MAIN.
   V. SCHOLDERER, 354:MAR69-60
ØHRGAARD, P. C.F. MEYER.
   M. BURKHARD, 301(JEGP):JUL71-511
   G. HOFFMEISTER, 406:WINTER71-416
OIKONOMIDÈS, N., ED. ACTES DE DION-
YSIOU.*
   M. ANGOLD, 303:VOL90-269
OINAS, F.J. STUDIES IN FINNIC-SLAVIC
FOLKLORE RELATIONS.
   V. VOIGT, 574(SEEJ):SPRING71-91
OJHA, I.C. CHINESE FOREIGN POLICY IN AN
AGE OF TRANSITION.
   J.L. CRANMER-BYNG, 293(JAST):AUG70-
934
OKAMOTO, S. THE JAPANESE OLIGARCHY AND
THE RUSSO-JAPANESE WAR.
   F.W. IKLÉ, 32:DEC71-886
OKINSHEVICH, L., COMP. LATIN AMERICA IN
SOVIET WRITINGS. (R.G. CARLTON, ED)
   J.G. OSWALD, 32:MAR71-222
OKLADNIKOV, A.P. YAKUTIA BEFORE ITS
INCORPORATION INTO THE RUSSIAN STATE.
(H.N. MICHAEL, ED)
   A. FARKAS, 32:JUN71-381
OKPAKU, J., ED. NIGERIA.
   617(TLS):25AUG72-981
OKPEWHO, I. THE VICTIMS.
   J. CAREW, 441:2APR72-7
OLAFSON, F.A. PRINCIPLES AND PERSONS.*
   G.W. BARNES, 418(MR):SPRING71-367
   H.L. DREYFUS, 482(PHR):JUL70-420
   R.E. SANTONI, 258:MAR69-141
OLAVO PEREIRA, A. - SEE UNDER PEREIRA,
A.O.
OLDENBOURG, Z. THE HEIRS OF THE KING-
DOM.*
   617(TLS):3MAR72-239
OLDENBURG, C. PROPOSALS FOR MONUMENTS
AND BUILDINGS, 1965-69.*
   C. MEADMORE, 58:DEC69/JAN70-10
OLDENBURG, C. & E. WILLIAMS, EDS. STORE
DAYS.*
   A. FORGE, 592:MAR68-162
OLDENBURG, H. THE CORRESPONDENCE OF
HENRY OLDENBURG. (VOLS 7&8) (A.R. &
M.B. HALL, EDS & TRANS)
   617(TLS):14JUL72-798
OLDEROGGE, D. NEGRO ART.
   T. WATT, 592:NOV69-197
OLÉRON, P. LES ACTIVITÉS INTELLECTU-
ELLES.
   C. DURANDIN, 542:JAN-MAR68-144
OLEŠA, J. ZAVIST'. (M. JORDAN, ED)
   W.H. BENNETT, 574(SEEJ):SUMMER71-235
OLIN, J.C. THE CATHOLIC REFORMATION.
   D.S. CHAMBERS, 551(RENQ):AUTUMN70-291
OLIN, J.C., J.D. SMART & R.E. MC NALLY,
EDS. LUTHER, ERASMUS AND THE REFORMA-
TION.
   K.A. STRAND, 551(RENQ):WINTER70-453
OLIPHANT, M. RUTHERFORD: RECOLLECTIONS
OF THE CAMBRIDGE DAYS.
   617(TLS):23JUN72-723

OLIPHANT, R.T., ED. THE HARLEY LATIN-OLD
ENGLISH GLOSSARY.*
   R. DEROLEZ, 179(ES):APR70-149
OLIVA, L.J., ED. PETER THE GREAT.
   L.R. LEWITTER, 32:SEP71-661
OLIVA, L.J. RUSSIA IN THE ERA OF PETER
THE GREAT.*
   B. DMYTRYSHYN, 550(RUSR):OCT70-480
OLIVA, P.F. THE TEACHING OF FOREIGN LAN-
GUAGES.
   W.E. SWEET, 121(CJ):APR-MAY71-363
OLIVER, A. THE VICTORIAN STAFFORDSHIRE
FIGURE.
   617(TLS):7JAN72-8
OLIVER, H.J. - SEE MARLOWE, C.
OLIVER, J.H. THE CIVILIZING POWER.*
   J.H. BETTS, 122:APR71-144
OLIVER, J.H. MARCUS AURELIUS.
   G.W. BOWERSOCK, 124:APR71-276
OLIVER, P. SAVANNAH SYNCOPATORS.
   W.R. FERRIS, JR., 187:JAN72-132
   M. HARRISON, 415:SEP70-898
OLIVER, P., ED. SHELTER AND SOCIETY.
   H. SWAIN, 111:29MAY70-201
OLIVER, P. THE STORY OF THE BLUES.
   N. BRYCE, 607:SPRING70-46
   M. HARRISON, 415:JAN70-48
OLIVIER, J-P., ED & TRANS. THE MYCENAE
TABLETS IV.
   F. BADER, 555:VOL44FASC1-119
OLIVIER-LACAMP, M. LES FEUX DE LA
COLÈRE.
   M. NAUDIN, 207(FR):APR70-868
OLIVOVÁ, V. THE DOOMED DEMOCRACY.
   617(TLS):30JUN72-744
OLIVOVÁ, V. & R. KVAČEK. DĔJINY ČESKO-
SLOVENSKA. (VOL 4)
   S.B. WINTERS, 497(POLR):SPRING69-125
OLLIER, C. LA VIE SUR EPSILON.
   617(TLS):17NOV72-1387
OLLMAN, B. ALIENATION.
   R.L. HEILBRONER, 453:9MAR72-9
   617(TLS):18FEB72-185
OLMO, L. LA CAMISA. (A.K. & I.F.
ARIZA, EDS)
   E.M. DIAL, 399(MLJ):FEB70-139
OLMSTED, F.L. THE COTTON KINGDOM. (D.F.
HAWKE, ED)
   T. LASK, 441:2SEP72-19
OLNEY, J. METAPHORS OF SELF.
   453:20JUL72-33
OLSCAMP, P.J. THE MORAL PHILOSOPHY OF
GEORGE BERKELEY.
   G.J. WARNOCK, 311(JP):17AUG72-460
OLSCHAK, B.C. BHUTAN.
   617(TLS):7JAN72-22
OLSEN, A. CORCHO BLISS.
   M. LEVIN, 441:15OCT72-43
OLSEN, D.J. TOWN PLANNING IN LONDON,
THE EIGHTEENTH AND NINETEENTH CENTUR-
IES.
   H-R. HITCHCOCK, 576:MAY68-147
OLSEN, H. URBINO.
   617(TLS):3MAR72-245
OLSEN, J. THE GIRLS IN THE OFFICE.
   A. BROYARD, 441:21JUL72-33
   L.C. POGREBIN, 441:2JUL72-4
OLSHANSKY, P.N. RIZHSKII MIR.
   P.S. WANDYCZ, 32:MAR71-153
OLSON, C. ARCHAEOLOGIST OF MORNING.*
   G. BURNS, 584(SWR):SUMMER71-295
OLSON, E. THE THEORY OF COMEDY.*
   C.G. MASINTON, 397(MD):DEC69-329
OLSON, P.R. CIRCLE OF PARADOX.*
   B.B. APONTE, 240(HR):JUL70-333
   B. GICOVATE, 546(RR):FEB70-71
   T.P. WALDRON, 402(MLR):APR71-422

OLSSON, B. MEMPHIS BLUES.
   M. HARRISON, 415:FEB71-141
OLSSON, H. VINLOVSRANKA OCH HAGTORNS-
   KRANS.
   W. JOHNSON, 563(SS):SUMMER71-302
OLTEANU, Ş. & C. ŞERBAN. MEŞTEŞUGURILE
   DIN ŢARA ROMÂNEASCĂ ŞI MOLDOVA ÎN EVUL
   MEDIU.*
   K. HITCHINS, 575(SEER):JAN71-147
O'MALLEY, J. - SEE MARX, K.
O'MALLEY, J.B. SOCIOLOGY OF MEANING.
   617(TLS):20OCT72-1260
O'MALLEY, L.S.S., ED. MODERN INDIA AND
   THE WEST.
   J.H. BROOMFIELD, 293(JAST):FEB70-472
OMAN, G. L'ITTIONIMIA NEI PAESI ARABI
   DEL MEDITERRANEO.
   S.D. GOITEIN, 318(JAOS):APR-JUN70-404
O'MANIQUE, J. ENERGY IN EVOLUTION.
   N. BRAYBROOKE, 619(TC):VOL177#1042-55
OMAR KHAYYÁM. THE RUBAIYAT OF OMAR KHAY-
   YAM. (E. FITZ GERALD, TRANS)
   617(TLS):28JAN72-108
OMARI, L., S. POLLO & B. GOLEMI, EDS.
   UNIVERSITETI SHTETËROR I TIRANËS 1957-
   1967.
   E.P. HAMP, 350:JUN71-488
OMMANNEY, F.D. LOST LEVIATHAN.
   617(TLS):19MAY72-584
O MUIRITHE, D., ED. A SEAT BEHIND THE
   COACHMAN.
   617(TLS):15DEC72-1541
ONDAATJE, M. LEONARD COHEN.
   D. BARBOUR, 102(CANL):SUMMER71-75
ONDAATJE, M. THE COLLECTED WORKS OF
   BILLY THE KID.*
   D. FETHERLING, 606(TAMR):#57-80
ONDAATJE, M. THE DAINTY MONSTERS.
   D. BARBOUR, 150(DR):SPRING70-112
ONDAATJE, M. THE MAN WITH SEVEN TOES.
   D. BARBOUR, 150(DR):SPRING70-112
   M. DOYLE, 491:MAR72-356
O'NEIL, W.M. FACT AND THEORY.
   R.H.K., 543:JUN70-746
O'NEILL, C.E. CHURCH AND STATE IN FRENCH
   COLONIAL LOUISIANA.
   J.A. SCHUTZ, 613:SPRING68-144
O'NEILL, J., ED. CRITICS OF MARLOWE.
   J.C. MAXWELL, 447(N&Q):JUN70-228
O'NEILL, J., ED. CRITICS ON CHARLOTTE
   AND EMILY BRONTË.
   W.D. SCHAEFER, 445(NCF):SEP69-250
O'NEILL, J., ED. CRITICS ON KEATS.
   I.H.C., 191(ELN):SEP69(SUPP)-37
O'NEILL, J. SOCIOLOGY AS A SKIN TRADE.
   D.I. DAVIES, 99:DEC72-21
   617(TLS):28JUL72-876
O'NEILL, J. - SEE MERLEAU-PONTY, M.
O'NEILL, K. ANDRÉ GIDE AND THE "ROMAN
   D'AVENTURE."
   S. BARR, 67:MAY71-133
   R. GOLDTHORPE, 402(MLR):OCT71-902
O'NEILL, T. THE AUTOBIOGRAPHY OF TERENCE
   O'NEILL.
   617(TLS):24NOV72-1428
O'NEILL, W.L. COMING APART.*
   B.A. WEISBERGER, 440:16JAN72-6
ONIONS, C.T. - SEE LITTLE, W., H.W. FOW-
   LER & J. COULSON
ONIONS, C.T., WITH G.W.S. FRIEDRICHSEN &
   R.W. BURCHFIELD, EDS. THE OXFORD DIC-
   TIONARY OF ENGLISH ETYMOLOGY.
   M.S. BEELER, 545(RPH):FEB70-312
   617(TLS):13OCT72-1209
ONO, Y. GRAPEFRUIT.
   P. LESTER, 493:AUTUMN70-250
ONORATO, R.J. THE CHARACTER OF THE POET.
   617(TLS):11FEB72-162

ONYEAMA, D. NIGGER AT ETON.
   617(TLS):14JUL72-792
OOST, S.I. GALLA PLACIDIA AUGUSTA.*
   J.F. MATTHEWS, 313:VOL60-217
OPARIN, A.I. L'ORIGINE DE LA VIE SUR LA
   TERRE.
   G. SIMONDON, 542:JAN-MAR69-71
OPAT, J., ED. STŘEDNÍ A JIHOVÝCHODNÍ
   EVROPA VE VÁLCE A V REVOLUCI, 1939-
   1945.
   V. MASTNY, 32:MAR71-171
OPDAHL, K.M. THE NOVELS OF SAUL BELLOW.
   M. MILLGATE, 447(N&Q):FEB70-75
OPITZ, M. JUGENDSCHRIFTEN VOR 1619.
   (J-U. FECHNER, ED)
   P. SKRINE, 402(MLR):OCT71-938
OPITZ, M. MARTIN OPITZ: GESAMMELTE
   WERKE. (VOL 1) (G. SCHULZ-BEHREND, ED)
   L. FORSTER, 220(GL&L):OCT70-122
   K.F. OTTO, JR., 221(GQ):MAR70-267
OPPEL, E. OVIDS "HEROIDES."*
   W.C. SCOTT, 122:JUL71-205
OPPEL, H. DIE GERICHTSSZENE IN "KING
   LEAR."
   G.K. HUNTER, 447(N&Q):JUN70-233
OPPEL, H., ED. DAS MODERNE ENGLISCHE
   DRAMA, INTERPRETATIONEN.
   G. SORELIUS, 597(SN):VOL40#1-254
OPPEL, H., ED. DIE MODERNE ENGLISCHE
   LYRIK.
   D. MEHL, 182:VOL23#6-284
   P. MERIVALE, 447(N&Q):DEC70-473
OPPEL, H., ED. DIE MODERNE ENGLISCHE
   ROMAN.
   D. MEHL, 182:VOL23#6-284
OPPENHEIM, A.L. ANCIENT MESOPOTAMIA.
   R. BORGER, 318(JAOS):APR-JUN70-327
OPPENHEIMER, E. TEXAS IN COLOR.
   W. GARD, 584(SWR):AUTUMN71-VI
OPPENHEIMER, G. - SEE SULLIVAN, F.
"OPUSCULA ATHENIENSIA, IX."
   R.M. COOK, 123:DEC71-464
ORAISON, M. THE WOUND OF MORTALITY.
   441:5MAR72-10
ORBELL, M., ED & TRANS. MAORI FOLKTALES.
   M. HAGLER, 292(JAF):JUL-SEP70-363
ORBIN, M. KRALJEVSTVO SLOVENA.
   N.R. PRIBIĆ, 574(SEEJ):SUMMER71-252
ORDERIC VITALIS. THE ECCLESIASTICAL
   HISTORY OF ORDERIC VITALIS.* (VOL 2)
   (M. CHIBNALL, ED & TRANS)
   A.G. DYSON, 325:OCT69-585
ORDERIC VITALIS. THE ECCLESIASTICAL
   HISTORY OF ORDERIC VITALIS. (VOL 3)
   (BKS 5&6) (M. CHIBNALL, ED & TRANS)
   617(TLS):14APR72-429
ORDISH, G. THE GREAT WINE BLIGHT.
   617(TLS):18AUG72-975
ORDISH, T.F. EARLY LONDON THEATRES - IN
   THE FIELDS.
   617(TLS):18FEB72-199
OREL, H. & G.J. WORTH, EDS. THE NINE-
   TEENTH-CENTURY WRITER AND HIS AUDIENCE.
   S.M. SMITH, 402(MLR):OCT71-877
OREN, U. 99 DAYS IN DAMASCUS.
   617(TLS):11FEB72-165
ORESME, N. NICOLE ORESME AND THE KINE-
   MATICS OF CIRCULAR MOTION. (E. GRANT,
   ED & TRANS)
   617(TLS):19MAY72-579
ORESME, N. NICOLE ORESME AND THE MEDI-
   EVAL GEOMETRY OF QUALITIES AND MOTIONS.
   (M. CLAGETT, ED)
   E.D. SYLLA, 589:OCT71-728
ORESME, N. DE PROPORTIONIBUS PROPORTION-
   UM & AD PAUCA RESPICIENTES. (E. GRANT,
   ED & TRANS)
   E. RAMBALDI, 548(RCSF):JAN-MAR68-105

ORGEL, S. - SEE JONSON, B.
ORIENTI, S. THE COMPLETE PAINTINGS OF
CÉZANNE.
617(TLS):29DEC72-1590
"LES ORIGINES DE LA RÉPUBLIQUE ROMAINE."
A. DRUMMOND, 313:VOL60-199
"LE ORIGINI DELLO GNOSTICISMO, COLLOQUIO
DI MESSINA 13-18 APRILE 1966."
G. QUISPEL, 318(JAOS):APR-JUN70-321
ORIGO, I. IMAGES AND SHADOWS.*
A.M. LINDBERGH, 31(ASCH):WINTER71/72-
163
ORIGO, I., COMP. THE VAGABOND PATH.
617(TLS):15DEC72-1524
ORING, E. & J. DURHAM, EDS. PERSPECTIVES
ON FOLKLORE AND EDUCATION.
R.L. WELSCH, 292(JAF):JUL-SEP70-369
ORIOL, L. A MURDER TO MAKE YOU GROW UP
LITTLE GIRL.
N. CALLENDAR, 441:2APR72-22
H. FRANKEL, 561(SATR):13MAY72-86
ORKIN, M.M. SPEAKING CANADIAN ENGLISH.
G.L. BURSILL-HALL, 102(CANL):AUTUMN
71-69
ORLANDINI, P. IL VILLAGGIO PREISTORICO
DI MANFRIA, PRESSO GELA.
A.R. NEUMANN, 182:VOL23#11/12-625
ORLANDO, F. LETTURA FREUDIANA DELLA
"PHÈDRE."
617(TLS):28APR72-468
ORMOND, L. GEORGE DU MAURIER.
J.R. HARVEY, 97(CQ):AUTUMN/WINTER69/
70-419
E.D.H. JOHNSON, 637(VS):JUN70-461
K. ROBERTS, 90:OCT70-706
ORMSBY, W. THE EMERGENCE OF THE FEDERAL
CONCEPT IN CANADA, 1839-1845.
102(CANL):SPRING71-119
ORNATO, E. JEAN MURET ET SES AMIS
NICOLAS DE CLAMANGES ET JEAN DE MON-
TREUIL.
N. MANN, 208(FS):APR71-188
G. TOURNOY, 568(SCN):SUMMER/AUTUMN71-
55
N.P. ZACOUR, 589:JAN71-176
ORNEA, Z. SĂMĂNĂTORISMUL.
K. HITCHINS, 32:DEC71-925
O'ROURKE, W. THE HARRISBURG 7 AND THE
NEW CATHOLIC LEFT.
G. WILLS, 441:12NOV72-44
ORSINI, G.N.G. COLERIDGE AND GERMAN
IDEALISM.*
D. EMMET, 541(RES):NOV70-510
R. HAVEN, 149:MAR71-93
ORTALI, R. UN POÈTE DE LA MORT: JEAN-
BAPTISTE CHASSIGNET.*
B.L.O. RICHTER, 207(FR):APR70-846
ORTEGA, L. EL SUEÑO Y LA DISTANCIA.
C.A. MONTANER, 263:JAN-MAR71-76
ORTEGA Y GASSET, J. MEDITATIONS ON HUNT-
ING. (H.B. WESCOTT, TRANS)
P. ADAMS, 61:JUL72-96
442(NY):22JUL72-79
ORTEGA Y GASSET, J. SOME LESSONS IN
METAPHYSICS.
H.B., 543:JUN70-746
ORTEGA Y GASSET, J. VELÁZQUEZ, GOYA AND
THE DEHUMANIZATION OF ART AND OTHER
ESSAYS. (A. BROWN, TRANS)
617(TLS):20OCT72-1264
ORTH, D.J. DICTIONARY OF ALASKA PLACE
NAMES.
E.C. EHRENSPERGER, 424:JUN68-190
ORTH, R.H. & A.R. FERGUSON - SEE EMERSON,
R.W.

ORTIZ, A. & E. ZIERER. SET THEORY AND
LINGUISTICS.
L. NEBESKÝ & P. PIŤHA, 361:VOL24#2-
201
ORTIZ, A.D. - SEE UNDER DOMÍNGUEZ ORTIZ,
A.
ORTIZ ARMENGOL, P. ESPRONCEDA Y LOS
GENDARMES.
191(ELN):SEP70(SUPP)-155
ORTZEN, L. FAMOUS ARCTIC ADVENTURES.
617(TLS):23JUN72-729
ORWELL, G. THE ROAD TO WIGAN PIER.
S. SPENDER, 453:16NOV72-3
OSAMU, O. - SEE UNDER OBA OSAMU
OSBORN, J.M. YOUNG PHILIP SIDNEY 1572-
1577.
617(TLS):14JUL72-799
OSBORN, J.M. - SEE WHYTHORNE, T.
OSBORNE, C. THE COMPLETE OPERAS OF
VERDI.*
A. PORTER, 415:APR70-392
OSBORNE, C. - SEE VERDI, G.
OSBORNE, H. AESTHETICS AND ART THEORY.
E. SCHAPER, 483:JUL70-254
OSBORNE, H. THE ART OF APPRECIATION.
P. WELSH, 579(SAQ):SUMMER71-436
OSBORNE, H. MY ENEMY'S FRIEND.
N. CALLENDAR, 441:3SEP72-22
OSBORNE, H., ED. THE OXFORD COMPANION OF
ART.
L.A. REID, 89(BJA):WINTER71-106
OSBORNE, H. PAY-DAY.
617(TLS):1DEC72-1467
OSBORNE, J. THE FIRST TWO YEARS OF THE
NIXON WATCH.
W.A. WILLIAMS, 453:24FEB72-7
OSBORNE, J. THE NATURALIST DRAMA IN GER-
MANY.
617(TLS):14JUL72-825
OSBORNE, J. THE THIRD YEAR OF THE NIXON
WATCH.
M.F. NOLAN, 441:27AUG72-5
OSBORNE, J. WEST OF SUEZ.
617(TLS):29DEC72-1569
OSBORNE, M. THE STATE BARGES OF THE
STATIONERS' COMPANY, 1680-1850.
617(TLS):22DEC72-1566
OSBORNE, M.E. THE FRENCH PRESENCE IN
COCHINCHINA AND CAMBODIA.
TRUONG-BUU-LÂM, 293(JAST):AUG70-991
OSBURN, C.B. RESEARCH AND REFERENCE
GUIDE TO FRENCH STUDIES.
D.M. SUTHERLAND, 208(FS):APR71-245
OSERS, E. - SEE ŁYSOHORSKY, O.
O'SHARKEY, E.M. - SEE BERNANOS, G.
OSLEY, A.S. MERCATOR.
N. BARKER, 78(BC):SUMMER70-246
OSLEY, A.S. - SEE CRESCI, G.F.
VAN OSTAIJEN, P. PATRIOTISM, INC., AND
OTHER TALES.
J. UPDIKE, 442(NY):13MAY72-135
ÖSTENBERG, C.E. SAN GIOVENALE: THE
NECROPOLIS AT CASTELLINA CAMERATA.
R.M. OGILVIE, 123:DEC71-463
OSTERLOH, K-H. JOSEPH VON SONNENFELS
UND DIE ÖSTERREICHISCHE REFORMBEWEGUNG
IM ZEITALTER DES AUFGEKLÄRTEN ABSOLUT-
ISMUS.
G. OTRUBA, 182:VOL23#5-253
OSTERMANN, F. DIE IDEE DES SCHÖPFER-
ISCHEN IN HERDERS KALLIGONE.
F.M. WASSERMANN, 221(GQ):MAR70-281
OSTLER, G., COMP. THE LITTLE OXFORD
DICTIONARY OF CURRENT ENGLISH. (4TH
ED REV BY J. COULSON)
C.L. BARNHART, 447(N&Q):MAY70-186
OSTRIKER, A. SONGS.
H. MORRIS, 569(SR):SPRING71-301

OSTROVSKY, A.N. ARTISTES AND ADMIRERS.
N. HENLEY, 574(SEEJ):FALL71-382
OSTROVSKY, E. VOYEUR VOYANT.
N. DENNIS, 453:10FEB72-3
C. LEHMANN-HAUPT, 441:7JAN72-33
R. SEAVER, 561(SATR):5FEB72-57
P. WEST, 440:30JAN72-3
OSTRÝ, A. ČESKOSLOVENSKÝ PROBLÉM.
617(TLS):18AUG72-960
OSTWALD, M. NOMOS AND THE BEGINNINGS OF
THE ATHENIAN DEMOCRACY.*
J.K. ANDERSON, 121(CJ):APR-MAY71-369
O'SUILLEABHÁIN, S. IRISH WAKE AMUSE-
MENTS.
K. PORTER, 292(JAF):OCT-DEC70-483
O'SULLIVAN, V., ED. AN ANTHOLOGY OF
TWENTIETH CENTURY NEW ZEALAND POETRY.
H.W. RHODES, 67:NOV71-245
OSWALD, R.G. ATTICA - MY STORY. (R.
CAMPBELL, ED)
B. NELSON, 441:17DEC72-1
OSWALT, S.G. CONCISE ENCYCLOPEDIA OF
GREEK AND ROMAN MYTHOLOGY.
J. POLLARD, 303:VOL90-265
OTT, A. - SEE "RICHARD STRAUSS UND LUDWIG
THUILLE"
OTT, G.M. FRÜHE POLITISCHE ORDNUNGS-
MODELLE.
F. LASSERRE, 182:VOL23#13/14-678
OTTEN, A. VOIX ET SILENCES.
J. DECOCK, 399(MLJ):FEB70-132
OTTER, A. BEGINNING WITH ATOMS.
617(TLS):28JUL72-900
OTTO, E. GOTT UND MENSCH NACH DEN
ÄGYPTISCHEN TEMPELINSCHRIFTEN DER
GRIECHISCH-RÖMISCHEN ZEIT.
F. ZEMAN, 318(JAOS):APR-JUN70-316
OTTO, W.F. DIONYSUS, MYTH AND CULT.
A.W.H. ADKINS, 123:MAR71-147
OTTUM, B. ALL RIGHT, EVERYBODY OFF
THE PLANET!
A. COOPER, 561(SATR):19FEB72-73
L.J. DAVIS, 440:12MAR72-11
T. STURGEON, 441:3SEP72-20
Ó TUATHAIGH, G. IRELAND BEFORE THE FAM-
INE.
617(TLS):21JUL72-850
"J.B. OUDRY, FARBIGE GEMÄLDEWIEDERGABEN."
H.N. OPPERMAN, 90:OCT69-623
OUELLETTE, F. EDGARD VARÈSE.
M. PETERSON, 470:JAN69-31
V. THOMSON, 453:31AUG72-19
OUOLOGUEM, Y. LE DEVOIR DE VIOLENCE.
E. SELLIN, 207(FR):OCT69-164
OURSEL, R. LIVING ARCHITECTURE: ROMAN-
ESQUE.*
J. WASSERMAN, 576:MAR69-73
OVERATH, J., ED. SACRED MUSIC AND LITUR-
GY REFORM AFTER VATICAN II.
R. MOEVS, 363:NOV69-26
OVERDYKE, W.D. LOUISIANA PLANTATION
HOMES.
R.W. BRUNSKILL, 576:DEC68-306
LORD OVERSTONE. THE CORRESPONDENCE OF
LORD OVERSTONE. (D.P. O'BRIEN, ED)
617(TLS):19MAY72-578
OVERSTREET, C. THE BOAR HOG WOMAN.
A.C. FOOTE, 440:28MAY72-8
OVERY, P. DE STIJL.
N. LYNTON, 592:NOV69-188
OVERY, P. KANDINSKY.*
M. FIDELL, 58:APR70-14
P. VERGO, 90:OCT70-711
OVID. METAMORPHOSES VIII. (A.S. HOLLIS,
ED)
R.J. GARIEPY, JR., 124:FEB71-204

OVID. THE METAMORPHOSES OF OVID.* (W.
CAXTON, TRANS)
J. BACKHOUSE, 90:JAN70-55
OVID. OVIDE, "TRISTES."* (J. ANDRÉ,
ED & TRANS)
E.J. KENNEY, 123:DEC70-340
OVID. P. OVIDI NASONIS "ARS AMATORIA."
(F.W. LENZ, ED)
E. COURTNEY, 123:DEC71-379
T.A. SUITS, 124:DEC70-131
OVID. OVID'S "METAMORPHOSES:" SELEC-
TIONS. (C.P. WATSON & A.C. REYNELL,
EDS)
E.W. SKLAROFF, 124:NOV70-92
OVID. OVID'S "METAMORPHOSIS."* (G.
SANDYS, TRANS; K.K. HULLEY & S.T.
VANDERSALL, EDS)
D.C. ALLEN, 124:MAR71-238
"OVID'S HEROIDES." (H.C. CANNON, TRANS)
617(TLS):5MAY72-529
OVIEDO, J.M. MARIO VARGAS LLOSA.*
D.L. SHAW, 402(MLR):OCT71-913
OWEN, A.R.G. HYSTERIA, HYPNOSIS AND
HEALING.
617(TLS):21JAN72-75
OWEN, D. THE POLITICS OF DEFENCE.
E. YOUNG, 362:1JUN72-732
617(TLS):30JUN72-733
OWEN, D.D.R. THE EVOLUTION OF THE GRAIL
LEGEND.*
E.M. KENNEDY, 208(FS):OCT71-446
OWEN, D.D.R. THE VISION OF HELL.
617(TLS):21APR72-452
OWEN, D.D.R. - SEE "THE SONG OF ROLAND"
OWEN, D.M., COMP. A CATALOGUE OF LAMBETH
CHARTERS.
P.E. JONES, 325:APR69-503
OWEN, G. JOURNEY FOR JOEDEL.
W. EYSTER, 569(SR):SUMMER71-469
639(VQR):AUTUMN70-CXXVIII
OWEN, G.D., ED. CALENDAR OF THE MANU-
SCRIPTS OF THE MOST HONOURABLE THE
MARQUESS OF SALISBURY. (PT 12)
617(TLS):3MAR72-257
OWEN, G.E.L., ED. ARISTOTLE ON DIALEC-
TIC: THE "TOPICS."
J. BARNES, 482(PHR):OCT70-558
J.J.R., 543:DEC69-362
OWEN, H.P. THE CHRISTIAN KNOWLEDGE OF
GOD.
D. BASTOW, 518:MAY70-18
F. FERRÉ, 479(PHQ):OCT70-411
OWEN, P. PAINTING.
C.R. BRIGHTON, 89(BJA):SUMMER71-304
"ROBERT OWEN ON EDUCATION." (H. SILVER,
ED)
B. SIMON, 637(VS):JUN70-403
OWEN, W.J.B. WORDSWORTH AS CRITIC.*
S.K. FREIBERG, 150(DR):AUTUMN70-419
K.K., 191(ELN):SEP70(SUPP)-50
B. WILKIE, 191(ELN):SEP70-58
"THE OXFORD ENGLISH DICTIONARY." (J.A.H.
MURRAY & OTHERS, EDS)
617(TLS):13OCT72-1209
"OXFORD ILLUSTRATED DICTIONARY." (J.
COULSON & OTHERS, EDS)
617(TLS):13OCT72-1209
"OXFORD LATIN DICTIONARY." (FASC 2)
E.J. KENNEY, 123:MAR71-93
J.W. POULTNEY, 124:MAR71-241
"OXFORD LATIN DICTIONARY." (FASC 3)
617(TLS):12MAY72-557
OYINBO, J. NIGERIA.
617(TLS):25AUG72-981

OZ, A. MY MICHAEL.
R. ALTER, 441:21MAY72-5
T.R. EDWARDS, 453:50CT72-21
A.C. FOOTE, 440:28MAY72-8
R. LOCKE, 441:25MAY72-47
E. MORGAN, 362:18MAY72-660
M. RUGOFF, 561(SATR):24JUN72-60
617(TLS):21JUL72-851
OZICK, C. THE PAGAN RABBI.*
V. CUNNINGHAM, 362:22JUN72-841
J.M. MORSE, 249(HUDR):AUTUMN71-540
OZMENT, S.E. HOMO SPIRITUALIS.
J.W. O'MALLEY, 551(RENQ):AUTUMN70-292

PABST, W. LUIS DE GÓNGORA IM SPIEGEL DER
DEUTSCHEN DICHTUNG UND KRITIK.
R. HESS, 72:BAND208HEFT4/6-446
PABST, W. NOVELLENTHEORIE UND NOVELLEN-
DICHTUNG.
I.D. MC FARLANE, 208(FS):JUL71-318
PACCHI, A. - SEE HOBBES, T.
PACELLA, G. & S. TIMPANARO - SEE LEOPAR-
DI, G.
PAČESOVÁ, J. THE DEVELOPMENT OF VOCABU-
LARY IN THE CHILD.
W. KÜHLWEIN, 351(LL):JUN70-127
PACEY, D. ESSAYS IN CANADIAN CRITICISM,
1938-1968.*
C.F. KLINCK, 627(UTQ):JUL70-373
M.G. PARKS, 150(DR):SUMMER70-285
PACEY, D., ED. FREDERICK PHILIP GROVE.
D.O. SPETTIGUE, 529(QQ):WINTER70-638
PACEY, D. ETHEL WILSON.
C. KING, 627(UTQ):JUL69-396
PACHMAN, L. MODERN CHESS TACTICS.
617(TLS):21JUL72-853
PACHMUSS, T. ZINAIDA HIPPIUS.
H. MUCHNIC, 453:23MAR72-37
617(TLS):4FEB72-134
PÄCHT, O. & J.J.G. ALEXANDER. ILLUMI-
NATED MANUSCRIPTS IN THE BODLEIAN
LIBRARY, OXFORD. (VOL 2)
L.M.C. RANDALL, 589:JUL71-533
"THE PACIFIC RIVALS."
G.R. PACKARD, 441:290CT72-2
PACK, R. HOME FROM THE CEMETERY.
42(AR):FALL69-448
PACKARD, D.W. A CONCORDANCE TO LIVY.
A.H. MC DONALD, 313:VOL60-254
PACKARD, V. A NATION OF STRANGERS.
G. HICKS, 441:10SEP72-2
C. LEHMANN-HAUPT, 441:8SEP72-33
H. VAN HORNE, 561(SATR):9SEP72-71
PACOTTO, G. LA LETTERATURA IN PIEMONTESE
DALLE ORIGINI AL RISORGIMENTO. (C.
BRERO & R. GANDOLFO, EDS)
G.P. CLIVIO, 545(RPH):NOV70-359
PADGETT, R. GREAT BALLS OF FIRE.
D. LEHMAN, 491:JAN72-224
PADGETT, R. & D. SHAPIRO, EDS. AN
ANTHOLOGY OF NEW YORK POETS.
F. MORAMARCO, 651(WHR):WINTER71-96
PADMORE, G. PAN-AFRICANISM OR COMMUNISM.
M. KILSON, 441:12MAR72-27
PADOVER, S.K. - SEE MARX, K.
PADUANO, G. LA FORMAZIONE DEL MONDO
IDEOLOGICO E POETICO DI EURIPIDE.
C. WOLFF, 24:APR71-362
PADUANO, G. - SEE EURIPIDES
PAES, J.P. & M. MOISÉS, EDS. PEQUENO
DICIONÁRIO DE LITERATURA BRASILEIRA.
191(ELN):SEP69(SUPP)-130
PAFFORD, J.H.P. - SEE SHAKESPEARE, W.
PAGE, B.S. - SEE PLOTINUS
PAGE, E. FAMILY AND FRIENDS.
617(TLS):26MAY72-612

PAGE, M. THE YAM FACTOR.
J. BROOKS, 441:25JUN72-6
PAGE, R. THE BENEFITS RACKET.
A. FAIRLEY, 362:24FEB72-259
PAGETTI, C. IL SENSO DEL FUTURO.
J. WOODRESS, 27(AL):JAN72-670
"PAGINI DE VECHE ARTĂ ROMÂNEUSCĂ DE LA
ORIGINI PÎNA LA SFÎRŞITUL SECOLULUI AL
XVI-LEA."
R.A. TODD, 104:WINTER71-532
PAGLIARO, H.E., ED. MAJOR ENGLISH WRIT-
ERS OF THE EIGHTEENTH CENTURY.
D.G., 173(ECS):SPRING70-422
PAHEL, K. & M. SCHILLER, EDS. READINGS
IN CONTEMPORARY ETHICAL THEORY.
C. PARKIN, 63:MAY71-117
PAHL, J.M. & R.E. MANAGERS AND THEIR
WIVES.
617(TLS):7JUL72-768
PAIK CHULL. A HISTORY OF THE NEW LIT-
ERARY TRENDS.
270:VOL20#4-99
PAIKEDAY, T., ED. THE WINSTON DICTIONARY
OF CANADIAN ENGLISH, INTERMEDIATE EDI-
TION.
P.W. ROGERS, 529(QQ):SPRING70-111
PAK MOK-WOL. DRY LEAVES IN KYONGSANG-DO.
270:VOL20#4-96
PAK TU-JIN. WHITE WING.
270:VOL20#4-94
PAKENHAM, F. PEACE BY ORDEAL.
617(TLS):10NOV72-1355
PALA, A. ISAAC NEWTON.
G. GORI, 548(RCSF):JUL/SEP69-332
DE PALACIO, J. MARY SHELLEY DANS SON
OEUVRE.
P.H. BUTTER, 677:VOL2-300
PALADILHE, J. & J. PIERRE. GUSTAVE
MOREAU.
P. GAY, 31(ASCH):AUTUMN72-660
PALAMAS, K. THE TWELVE LAYS OF THE
GIPSY.
M.B. RAIZIS, 481(PQ):APR70-278
PALAMAS, K. THE TWELVE WORDS OF THE
GYPSY. THE KING'S FLUTE.
T.G. STAVROU, 32:JUN71-449
PALAZÓN, M.R. & J. CHENCINSKY - SEE FER-
NÁNDEZ DE LIZARDI, J.J.
PALAZZESCHI, A. VIA DELLE CENTO STELLE.
617(TLS):22DEC72-1548
PALISCA, C.V. BAROQUE MUSIC.*
M. PETERSON, 470:MAY69-32
412:FEB71-83
PALIT, D.K. THE LIGHTNING CAMPAIGN.
617(TLS):12MAY72-538
PALLABAZZER, V. SUI NOMI DELLE PIANTE
INDIGENE NEL DIALETTO DI COLLE S.
LUCIA (LIVINALLONGO).
P. VALESIO, 545(RPH):NOV70-290
PALLEY, J. - SEE GUILLÉN, J.
PALLUCCHINI, R. TIZIANO.
J. MAXON, 90:DEC70-830
PALMA, R. TRADICIONES PERUANAS. (P.
FRANCIS, ED)
J.S. CUMMINS, 86(BHS):JAN71-95
PALMADE, G.P. FRENCH CAPITALISM IN THE
NINETEENTH CENTURY.
617(TLS):26MAY72-610
PALMER, A. THE LIFE AND TIMES OF GEORGE
IV.
617(TLS):28JUL72-898
PALMER, A. METTERNICH.
I.F. STONE, 453:190CT72-12
I.F. STONE, 453:2NOV72-21
617(TLS):4AUG72-912
PALMER, D.J. & M. BRADBURY, EDS. META-
PHYSICAL POETRY.
A.L. DENEEF, 579(SAQ):WINTER71-119

PALMER, E. AN INTRODUCTION TO THE AFRI-
CAN NOVEL.
D.A.N. JONES, 362:30MAR72-426
617(TLS):29DEC72-1573
PALMER, F. GRAMMAR.
617(TLS):4FEB72-136
PALMER, F.L. - SEE FIRTH, J.R.
PALMER, F.R. A LINGUISTIC STUDY OF THE
ENGLISH VERB.*
E. CLOSS, 353:MAY69-106
PALMER, G. & N. LLOYD. A YEAR OF FESTI-
VALS.
617(TLS):26MAY72-612
PALMER, J.A. JOSEPH CONRAD'S FICTION.*
E.C. BUFKIN, 219(GAR):WINTER69-540
R.A. HAUGH, 136:FALL69-123
C.T. WATTS, 541(RES):FEB70-101
PALMER, J.A., ED. "THE NIGGER OF THE
NARCISSUS."
S. HENIG, 136:SPRING70-142
PALMER, J.J.N. ENGLAND, FRANCE AND
CHRISTENDOM, 1377-99.
617(TLS):21JUL72-850
PALMER, L.R. DESCRIPTIVE AND COMPARATIVE
LINGUISTICS.
617(TLS):24NOV72-1430
PALMER, L.R. A NEW GUIDE TO THE PALACE
OF KNOSSOS.*
J.T. HOOKER, 303:VOL90-257
P. WARREN, 123:MAR71-114
PALMER, R.E. HERMENEUTICS.*
R.J.B., 543:SEP69-136
PALMER, R.E., JR. THOMAS WHYTHORNE'S
SPEECH.
P.H. SALUS, 320(CJL):SPRING70-159
PALMER, R.E.A. THE ARCHAIC COMMUNITY OF
THE ROMANS.*
E.S. GRUEN, 124:APR71-271
F. LASSERRE, 182:VOL23#11/12-630
PALMER, S.R. A LINGUISTIC STUDY OF THE
ENGLISH VERB.
G. NICKEL, 72:BAND208HEFT3-201
DE PALOL, P. & M. HIRMER. EARLY MEDIEVAL
ART IN SPAIN.*
C.E. SELBY, 56:SPRING69-97
PALOMB, L. RÉFLEXIONS.
P. LEPAPE, 98:MAY69-476
PÁLOS, S. THE CHINESE ART OF HEALING.
E. SIMPSON, 441:30JAN72-23
PALTER, R., ED. THE ANNUS MIRABILIS OF
SIR ISAAC NEWTON: 1666-1966.
M.J. OSLER, 319:OCT72-480
PAMP, B. ORTNAMNEN I SVERIGE. (2ND ED)
N. HASSELMO, 563(SS):SPRING71-192
PANĂ, S. - SEE URMUZ
PANAGOS, C.T. LE PIRÉE.
M. AMIT, 303:VOL90-251
PANČENKO, A.M., ED. RUSSISCHE SYLLA-
BISCHE DICHTUNG XVII.-XVIII. JH.
FR. ERLENBUSCH, 72:BAND208HEFT4/6-475
PANDE, V.P. VILLAGE COMMUNITY PROJECTS
IN INDIA.
H.M. CHOLDIN, 293(JAST):MAY70-723
PANFILOV, V.Z. GRAMMAR AND LOGIC.
G. NUCHELMANS, 361:VOL23#2-197
PANGANIBAN, J.V. CONCISE ENGLISH-TAGALOG
DICTIONARY.
A.M. STEVENS, 293(JAST):FEB70-499
PANICHAS, G.A., ED. MANSIONS OF THE
SPIRIT.*
D.J. CAHILL, 613:WINTER69-601
J.P. MC INTYRE, 131(CL):SUMMER71-277
PANIKKAR, K.N. BRITISH DIPLOMACY IN
NORTH INDIA.
J.P. SHARMA, 293(JAST):FEB70-475
PANNWITZ, R. ALBERT VERWEY UND STEFAN
GEORGE.
D. VAN ABBÉ, 182:VOL23#11/12-620

PANOFSKY, E. PROBLEMS IN TITIAN, MOSTLY
ICONOGRAPHIC.
T.A. HEINRICH, 96:AUG70-71
J. MAXON, 90:DEC70-829
PANTER-BRICK, S. GANDHI AGAINST MACHIA-
VELLISM.
S.N. MAHAJAN, 485(PE&W):JAN-APR68-102
PANTER-DOWNES, M. LONDON WAR NOTES 1939-
1945.* (W. SHAWN, ED)
617(TLS):15SEP72-1065
PANTSKHAVA, I.D., ED. KONKRETNO-SOTSIOL-
OGICHESKOE IZUCHENIE SOSTOIANIIA RE-
LIGIOZNOSTI I OPYTA ATEISTICHESKOGO
VOSPITANIIA.
Z. KATZ, 32:DEC71-870
PANUNZIO, S. - SEE PERO DA PONTE
PAPADOPOULOS, S.A., ED. LIBERATED GREECE
AND THE MOREA SCIENTIFIC EXPEDITION.
617(TLS):1SEP72-1024
PAPALI, G.F. JACOB TONSON, PUBLISHER.
C.A. ZIMANSKY, 481(PQ):JUL70-293
PAPANDREOU, A.G. PATERNALISTIC CAPITAL-
ISM.
J.T. MC LEOD, 99:SEP72-24
PAPANEK, G.F. PAKISTAN'S DEVELOPMENT.
K. NAIR, 293(JAST):MAY70-730
PAPANEK, V. DESIGN FOR THE REAL WORLD.
E. EDELSON, 440:23JAN72-13
C. ENTWISTLE, 441:6FEB72-4
C. LEHMANN-HAUPT, 441:31JAN72-39
PAPANOUTSOS, E. THE FOUNDATIONS OF
KNOWLEDGE. (J.P. ANTON, ED)
D.Z. ANDRIOPOULOS, 484(PPR):SEP69-144
R.N.W. SMITH, 479(PHQ):JAN70-67
PAPE, M. GROWING UP WITH MUSIC.
P. STANDFORD, 415:SEP70-897
PAPER, H.H. - SEE RASTORGUEVA, V.S.
"PAPERMAKING - ART AND CRAFT."
G.W., 503:WINTER68-189
"PAPERS DELIVERED AT THE INDIANA UNIVER-
SITY LIBRARY DEDICATION, BLOOMINGTON
CAMPUS, OCTOBER 9-10, 1970."
D. BERGEN, 356:OCT71-341
PAPONE, A. ESISTENZA E CORPOREITÀ IN
SARTRE DALLE PRIME OPERE ALL'"ESSERE E
IL NULLA."
M. RIESER, 319:JAN72-107
X. TILLIETTE, 182:VOL23#23/24-968
PAPP, F. - SEE BOLLA, K., E. PÁLL & F.
PAPP
PARATORE, E. ANTOLOGIA LATINA DELL' ETÀ
REPUBBLICANA. ANTOLOGIA LATINA DELL'
ETÀ AUGUSTEA. LA LETTERATURA LATINA
DELL' ETÀ IMPERIALE.
A. ERNOUT, 555:VOL44FASC2-344
PARATORE, E. BIOGRAFIA E POETICA DI
PERSIO.*
C. WITKE, 24:APR71-382
PAREKH, B. & R.N. BERKI, EDS. THE MOR-
ALITY OF POLITICS.
617(TLS):7JUL72-779
PARENT, G. SHEILA LEVINE IS DEAD AND
LIVING IN NEW YORK.
M. LEVIN, 441:9JUL72-28
PARICSY, P. A NEW BIBLIOGRAPHY OF AFRI-
CAN LITERATURE.
R. BISHOP, 315(JAL):VOL8PT2-129
"A PARISIAN JOURNAL 1405-1449."* (J.
SHIRLEY, TRANS)
J.C. GILLIS, 402(MLR):OCT71-893
J.C. LAIDLAW, 208(FS):JAN71-62
PARISOT, H., ED. LEWIS CARROLL.
617(TLS):15DEC72-1525
PARKE, H.W. THE ORACLES OF ZEUS.*
A.W.H. ADKINS, 123:JUN71-235
PARKER, A. & S.G. RAYBOULD, EDS. UNIVER-
SITY STUDIES FOR ADULTS.
617(TLS):14JUL72-825

PARKER, A.A. LITERATURE AND THE DELIN-
QUENT.
G. GILLESPIE, 131(CL):SUMMER71-280
PARKER, B. A MINGLED YARN.
E. JANEWAY, 441:8OCT72-4
C. LEHMANN-HAUPT, 441:6OCT72-45
561(SATR):18NOV72-98
PARKER, B. - SEE RYGA, G.
PARKER, C. THE FISHING HANDBOOK TO END
ALL FISHING HANDBOOKS.
617(TLS):15DEC72-1541
PARKER, C.F. & P.L. GRIGAUT. INITIATION
À LA CULTURE FRANÇAISE. (3RD ED)
W.W. THOMAS, 399(MLJ):OCT70-456
PARKER, D. & J. THE COMPLEAT LOVER.
561(SATR):23DEC72-61
PARKER, F.D. TRAVELS IN CENTRAL AMERICA,
1821-1840.
C.L. STANSIFER, 263:OCT-DEC71-454
PARKER, G. THE ARMY OF FLANDERS AND THE
SPANISH ROAD 1567-1659.
617(TLS):20OCT72-1258
PARKER, G. GRAMÁTICA DEL QUECHUA AYACU-
CHANO.
M. MC CLARAN, 269(IJAL):JUL69-276
PARKER, G. THE SEATS OF THE MIGHTY.
(E. WATERSTON, ED)
C.F. KLINCK, 296:WINTER72-81
PARKER, G.J. AYACUCHO QUECHUA GRAMMAR
AND DICTIONARY.
G.D. BILLS, 350:MAR71-234
PARKER, H., ED. THE RECOGNITION OF HER-
MAN MELVILLE.
R. LEHAN, 445(NCF):JUN68-117
PARKER, J. RHODESIA.
617(TLS):30JUN72-736
PARKER, J.H. GIL VICENTE.
C. STERN, 240(HR):APR70-215
PARKER, M.E.E., ED. THE COLONIAL RECORDS
OF NORTH CAROLINA: NORTH CAROLINA
HIGHER-COURT RECORDS, 1670-1696.
F.H. ALLEN, 14:OCT69-388
PARKER, S.R. & OTHERS. THE SOCIOLOGY OF
INDUSTRY. (2ND ED)
617(TLS):1SEP72-1026
PARKER, T. IN NO MAN'S LAND.
617(TLS):30JUN72-742
PARKER, V. THE MAKING OF KING'S LYNN.
617(TLS):19MAY72-570
PARKER, W.H. AN HISTORICAL GEOGRAPHY OF
RUSSIA.
R.T. FISHER, JR., 550(RUSR):JUL70-343
PARKER, W.R. MILTON.*
G. BULLOUGH, 175:SPRING69-28
I.G. MAC CAFFREY, 551(RENQ):SUMMER70-
203
E. MINER, 173(ECS):WINTER69-296
C.A. PATRIDES, 541(RES):MAY70-212
PARKES, J. TRAVEL IN ENGLAND IN THE
SEVENTEENTH CENTURY.
G.B. PARKS, 568(SCN):SPRING71-18
PARKES, M.B. ENGLISH CURSIVE BOOK HANDS,
1250-1500.
R.J. DEAN, 589:JAN71-177
J.E. FAGG, 382(MAE):1971/2-212
PARKINSON, E.M., WITH A.E. LUMB, COMPS.
CATALOGUE OF MEDICAL BOOKS IN MAN-
CHESTER UNIVERSITY LIBRARY 1480-1700.
617(TLS):4AUG72-922
PARKINSON, G.H.R., ED. GEORG LUKÁCS.
Z. TAR, 32:JUN71-426
PARKINSON, R. PEACE FOR OUR TIME.
617(TLS):28JAN72-84
PARKINSON, S. & P. STACY. A TASTE OF THE
TROPICS.
617(TLS):3NOV72-1349
PARKS, E.W. SIDNEY LANIER.
R.F. WILSON, 219(GAR):FALL69-415

PARKS, G.B. - SEE MARTIN, G.
PARLASCA, K. MUMIENPORTRÄTS UND VER-
WANDTE DENKMÄLER.
J. LECLANT, 182:VOL23#1/2-42
PARLAVANTZA-FRIEDRICH, U. TÄUSCHUNGS-
SZENEN IN DEN TRAGÖDIEN DES SOPHOKLES.*
C. SEGAL, 121(CJ):FEB-MAR71-258
"PARMENIDES: A TEXT WITH TRANSLATION,
COMMENTARY AND CRITICAL ESSAYS." (L.
TARÁN, ED & TRANS)
C. KIRWAN, 393(MIND):APR70-308
PARMET, H.S. EISENHOWER.
T. LASK, 441:8DEC72-45
G. WILLS, 441:22OCT72-3
PARNABY, O.W. BRITAIN AND THE LABOR
TRADE IN THE SOUTHWEST PACIFIC.
A. BIRCH, 302:JUL69-287
PAROLA, R. OPTICAL ART.
M. BRUMER, 58:SEP/OCT69-16
PARPOLA, A. & OTHERS. DECIPHERMENT OF
THE PROTO-DRAVIDIAN INSCRIPTIONS OF THE
INDUS CIVILIZATION.*
T.R. TRAUTMANN, 293(JAST):MAY70-714
PARR, C.M. THE VOYAGES OF DAVID DE
VRIES, NAVIGATOR AND ADVENTURER.
A.C. LEIBY, 656(WMQ):JUL70-507
PARRA, N. EMERGENCY POEMS.
A. COLEMAN, 441:7MAY72-4
PARRA, N. POEMS AND ANTIPOEMS.
V. RUTSALA, 448:SUMMER68-112
PARRINDER, G. DICTIONARY OF NON-
CHRISTIAN RELIGIONS.
617(TLS):4FEB72-138
PARRINDER, G., ED. MAN AND HIS GODS.
617(TLS):25AUG72-1002
PARRINDER, P., ED. H.G. WELLS: THE
CRITICAL HERITAGE.
617(TLS):1DEC72-1454
PARRISH, J.A. 12, 20 & 5.
441:30JUL72-20
PARRISH, M. THE SOVIET ARMED FORCES:
BOOKS IN ENGLISH, 1950-1967.
D.E. DAVIS, 104:WINTER71-545
PARROTT, I. ELGAR.*
R. ANDERSON, 415:SEP71-858
J.B., 412:AUG71-274
J.V.C., 410(M&L):OCT71-435
PARRY, A. AMERICA LEARNS RUSSIAN.
C.L. DRAGE, 575(SEER):OCT71-634
F. DE GRAAFF, 574(SEEJ):WINTER71-517
PARRY, A., ED. YALE CLASSICAL STUDIES.
(VOL 22)
617(TLS):11AUG72-952
PARRY, A. - SEE KAPITSA, P.
PARRY, I. ANIMALS OF SILENCE.
D.J. ENRIGHT, 362:21SEP72-374
PARRY, J.H. THE SPANISH SEABORNE EMPIRE.
R.H. BOULIND, 86(BHS):JAN71-89
PARRY, J.P. THE LORD JAMES TRICYCLE.
617(TLS):15SEP72-1071
PARRY, M. THE MAKING OF HOMERIC VERSE.
(A. PARRY, ED)
G. DIMOCK, 676(YR):SUMMER71-585
H.D. RANKIN, 67:NOV71-218
PARRY-JONES, W. THE TRADE IN LUNACY.
617(TLS):10MAR72-271
PARSONS, C. A BULL CALLED MARIUS.
617(TLS):10NOV72-1377
PARSONS, N. - SEE KOROLENKO, V.G.
PARTHE, F., ED. DER GRIECHISCHE ALEXAN-
DERROMAN.
W.M. CALDER 3D, 124:NOV70-87
PARTNER, P. THE LANDS OF ST. PETER.
617(TLS):7JUL72-778
"PARTNERS IN DEVELOPMENT."
O. MEHMET, 150(DR):SPRING70-137

PARTRIDGE, A.C. THE LANGUAGE OF RENAIS-
SANCE POETRY.
617(TLS):11FEB72-162
PARTRIDGE, A.C., ED. THE TRIBE OF BEN.*
568(SCN):SUMMER/AUTUMN71-39
PARTRIDGE, A.C. TUDOR TO AUGUSTAN ENG-
LISH.
V. SALMON, 677:VOL2-247
PARTRIDGE, E. - SEE GROSE, F.
PARTURIER, M. - SEE MÉRIMÉE, P.
PASANEN, J. THE WONDERFUL WORLD OF
WOMEN'S WEAR DAILY.
P. ADAMS, 61:FEB72-110
PASCAL, B. PENSÉES. (L. MARIN, ED)
R.A. MAZZARA, 399(MLJ):FEB70-129
PASCAL, R. GERMAN LITERATURE IN THE
SIXTEENTH AND SEVENTEENTH CENTURIES.*
W.F. SCHERER, 399(MLJ):NOV70-533
E. SOBEL, 221(GQ):JAN70-101
PASCASIUS RADBERTUS. DE CORPORE ET SAN-
GUINE DOMINI CUM APPENDICE EPISTOLA AD
FREDUGARDUM. (B. PAULUS, ED)
M.E. WILLIAMS, 382(MAE):1971/3-268
PASCU, Ş. MAREA ADUNARE NAȚIONALĂ DE LA
ALBA IULIA.
S. FISCHER-GALATI, 32:JUN71-419
PASEK, J.C. DIE GOLDENE FREIHEIT DER
POLEN.* (G. WYTRZENS, ED & TRANS)
M.A.J. ŚWIĘCICKA, 497(POLR):SPRING69-
117
PASHUTO, V.T. VNESHNIAIA POLITIKA DREV-
NEI RUSI.
C.B. O'BRIEN, 32:JUN71-383
PASKE-SMITH, M. - SEE PRATT, P.
PASKE-SMITH, M. - SEE RAFFLES, S.
PASLEY, M., ED. GERMANY.
617(TLS):7JUL72-764
PASOLI, E., ED & TRANS. SCRIPTORES HIS-
TORIAE AUGUSTAE, IULIUS CAPITOLINUS:
"OPILIUS MACRINUS."*
J. ANDRÉ, 555:VOL44FASC2-350
PASOLINI, P.P. EMPIRISMO ERETICO.
617(TLS):21JUL72-833
PASQUARIELLO, A.M. - SEE SASTRE, A.
PASQUINELLI, A. LETTURE GALILEIANE.
A. PACCHI, 548(RCSF):JAN/MAR69-111
PASSERIN D'ENTRÈVES, A. LA NOTION DE
L'ETAT.
J. FREUND, 542:JUL-DEC69-465
PASSMORE, J. THE PERFECTIBILITY OF MAN.*
D.H. MONRO, 63:AUG71-211
PASTAN, L. A PERFECT CIRCLE OF SUN.
T. LASK, 441:18AUG72-31
PASTERNAK, B. THE BLIND BEAUTY.
L. BERNHARDT, 550(RUSR):JUL70-358
PATAI, R. MYTH AND MODERN MAN.
E. WILSON, JR., 561(SATR):24JUN72-68
PATAI, R. TENTS OF JACOB.
R.N. LEVY, 441:9JAN72-4
PATEL, S. THE MARXIAN MIRAGE.
617(TLS):24MAR72-345
PATEMAN, T., ED. COUNTER COURSE.
617(TLS):2JUN72-621
PATERNOST, J. FROM ENGLISH TO SLOVENIAN.
W. ARNDT, 574(SEEJ):FALL71-366
PATERSON, A.K.G. - SEE TIRSO DE MOLINA
PATEY, T. ONE MAN'S MOUNTAINS.
617(TLS):7JAN72-21
PATHAK, V.S. ANCIENT HISTORIANS OF INDIA.
S. KRAMRISCH, 57:VOL31#1-93
PATÓN, B.J. - SEE UNDER JIMÉNEZ PATÓN, B.
PATRI, A. - SEE WITTGENSTEIN, L.
PATRICK, J.M. - SEE MILTON, J.
PATRICK, J.M. & OTHERS - SEE CROLL, M.W.
PATRICK, J.M. & R.O. EVANS, WITH J.M.
WALLACE - SEE CROLL, M.W.

PATRIDES, C.A., ED. APPROACHES TO "PARA-
DISE LOST."*
R.W. AYERS, 551(RENQ):AUTUMN70-339
W.M. BECKETT, 180(ESA):SEP70-420
M. FIXLER, 541(RES):AUG70-358
J.M. STEADMAN, 402(MLR):JUL71-662
PATRIDES, C.A., ED. THE CAMBRIDGE PLAT-
ONISTS.*
J.W. BLENCH, 677:VOL2-266
PATRIDES, C.A. MILTON AND THE CHRISTIAN
TRADITION.*
E. MINER, 173(ECS):WINTER69-296
PATRUSHEV, V.D. & OTHERS, EDS. OB OSNOV-
NYKH ITOGAKH IZUCHENIIA BIUDZHETA
VREMENI ZHITELEI GOR. PSKOVA.
J. KOLAJA, 32:JUN71-433
PATTEN, B. THE IRRELEVANT SONG.
J. FULLER, 362:24FEB72-251
I. WEDDE, 364:FEB/MAR72-148
617(TLS):14JAN72-32
PATTEN, R.L. - SEE DICKENS, C.
"PATTERNS IN THE LIVING WORLD."
617(TLS):30JUN72-754
PATTERSON, A.M. HERMOGENES AND THE
RENAISSANCE.*
J.M.P., 568(SCN):SUMMER/AUTUMN71-48
PATTERSON, C.I., JR. THE DAEMONIC IN
THE POETRY OF JOHN KEATS.
M. ALLOTT, 402(MLR):JUL71-674
B. FASS, 579(SAQ):WINTER71-125
S.M. SPERRY, JR., 301(JEGP):JAN71-171
PATTERSON, E.M. THE CLOGHER VALLEY RAIL-
WAY.
617(TLS):13OCT72-1237
PATTERSON, J.G. A ZOLA DICTIONARY.
F.W.J. HEMMINGS, 208(FS):JAN71-99
PATTERSON, J.T. MR. REPUBLICAN.
W.C. MC WILLIAMS, 441:19NOV72-3
PATTERSON, O. DIE THE LONG DAY.
J. CAREW, 441:10SEP72-46
PATTISON, B. MUSIC AND POETRY OF THE
ENGLISH RENAISSANCE.
R. MARLOW, 415:MAR71-243
PATTON, L. - SEE COLERIDGE, S.T.
PATZIG, G. ARISTOTLE'S THEORY OF THE
SYLLOGISM.
P. LOUIS, 555:VOL44FASC1-128
M. MC CALL, 124:DEC70-121
J.J.R., 543:JUN70-747
PAUCKER, E.K. RELATOS DE UNAMUNO.
G.D. CARRILLO, 238:MAY70-355
PAUL, A. DOWN THE RABBIT HOLE.
617(TLS):25AUG72-985
PAUL, F. SYMBOL UND MYTHOS.
H.S. NAESS, 563(SS):SPRING71-201
PAUL, R. WHO MURDERED MARY ROGERS?*
W. GOLDHURST, 31(ASCH):SPRING72-298
PAUL, S. THE MUSIC OF SURVIVAL.
J. GUIMOND, 149:JUN71-169
PAUL, S., ED. SIX CLASSIC AMERICAN
WRITERS.
S.A. COWAN, 150(DR):WINTER70/71-575
PAULINUS. "HET EPITHALAMIUM" VAN PAUL-
INUS VAN NOLA.* (J.A. BOUMA, ED)
J. ANDRÉ, 555:VOL44FASC1-161
PAULSEN, W., ED. ASPEKTE DES EXPRESSION-
ISMUS.*
Z. KONSTANTINOVIĆ, 52:BAND4HEFT3-318
PAULSON, R. HOGARTH.*
T.R. EDWARDS, 441:2JAN72-5
L. KRONENBERGER, 61:JAN72-92
PAULSON, R. ROWLANDSON.
617(TLS):8DEC72-1473
PAULSON, R. SATIRE AND THE NOVEL IN
EIGHTEENTH CENTURY ENGLAND.*
J.L. MAHONEY, 613:WINTER68-617

PAULSON, R. & T. LOCKWOOD, EDS. HENRY
FIELDING: THE CRITICAL HERITAGE.*
T.J. CRIBB, 111:15NOV69-64
PAULUS, B. - SEE PASCASIUS RADBERTUS
PAULY, R.G. MUSIC AND THE THEATER.
L. SALTER, 415:DEC70-1224
J.A.W., 410(M&L):JUL71-330
412:MAY71-182
PAUWELS, L. & J. BERGIER. LE MATIN DES
MAGICIENS. (Y. LENARD, ED)
W. STAAKS, 207(FR):MAR70-717
PAVESE, C. SELECTED LETTERS. A MANIA
FOR SOLITUDE.
W.P. TURNER, 619(TC):VOL177#1042-56
PAVLOWITCH, S.K. YUGOSLAVIA.
617(TLS):25FEB72-210
PAWLOWSKI, C.R. TONY GARNIER ET LES DÉBUTS
DE L'URBANISME FONCTIONNEL EN FRANCE.
S.T.S., 46:JAN69-71
D. WIEBENSON, 576:DEC68-304
PAWLOWSKY, P. HELMUT KÜPPER VORMALS
GEORGE BONDI, 1895-1970.
F.G. CRONHEIM, 402(MLR):JUL71-713
PAXTON, J., ED. THE STATESMAN'S YEAR-
BOOK 1972-1973.
617(TLS):6OCT72-1192
PAXTON, N. THE DEVELOPMENT OF MALLARMÉ'S
PROSE STYLE.*
E. SOUFFRIN, 208(FS):APR71-224
D. STELAND, 182:VOL23#23/24-988
PAYEN, J-C. LE MOTIF DU REPENTIR DANS
LA LITTÉRATURE FRANÇAISE MÉDIÉVALE
(DES ORIGINES À 1230).*
L.S. CRIST, 207(FR):FEB70-528
K.D. UITTI, 400(MLN):MAY70-599
PAYEN, J.C. & J.P. CHAUVEAU. LA POÉSIE
DES ORIGINES À 1715.*
D.L. RUBIN, 207(FR):DEC69-364
PAYNE, A. SCHOENBERG.*
R. SMALLEY, 607:SUMMER68-37
412:FEB71-78
PAYNE, C.T. & R.S. MC GEE. THE UNIVER-
SITY OF CHICAGO LIBRARY BIBLIOGRAPHIC
DATA PROCESSING SYSTEM: DOCUMENTATION
AND REPORT SUPPLEMENT.
P.D.J. RAE, 356:OCT71-337
PAYNE, C.T., R.S. MC GEE & E.R. FISHER.
THE UNIVERSITY OF CHICAGO LIBRARY
BIBLIOGRAPHIC DATA PROCESSING SYSTEM:
DOCUMENTATION AND REPORT AS OF OCTOBER
31, 1969.
P.D.J. RAE, 356:OCT71-337
PAYNE, R. THE FORTRESS.
N.D. ROODKOWSKY, 613:SUMMER68-311
PAYNE, R. THE WORLD OF ART.
T. LASK, 441:28JAN72-43
PAYNE, R. - SEE MARX, K. & J.
PAYNE, S.G. THE SPANISH REVOLUTION.*
R.A.H. ROBINSON, 86(BHS):OCT71-358
PAYNE, T.R. S.L. RUBINŠTEJN AND THE
PHILOSOPHICAL FOUNDATIONS OF SOVIET
PSYCHOLOGY.
J. BROŽEK, 550(RUSR):JUL70-350
PAYNTER, J. & P. ASTON. SOUND AND
SILENCE.
K. SCHWEIZER, 182:VOL23#23/24-994
G. WINTERS, 607:SPRING70-43
PAYNTER, W. MY GENERATION.
617(TLS):19MAY72-566
PAZ, E. ILLUSTRATED FOLK GUITAR.
A.J. FIELD, 650(WF):OCT68-278
PAZ, O. CONFIGURATIONS.*
G. DAVENPORT, 249(HUDR):WINTER71/72-
698
PAZ, O. CLAUDE LÉVI-STRAUSS.
E. LEACH, 362:17FEB72-218

PAZURA, S. MARKS A KLASYCZNA ESTETYKA
NIEMIECKA.
M. RIESER, 290(JAAC):SUMMER70-550
PEACH, B. - SEE HUTCHESON, F.
PEACOCK, C. SAMUEL PALMER: SHOREHAM AND
AFTER.*
L. HERRMANN, 90:OCT69-624
M. WEBSTER, 39:NOV69-448
PEACOCK, J.L. RITES OF MODERNIZATION.
J.R. BRANDON, 397(MD):FEB70-439
V.P. VATUK, 292(JAF):JUL-SEP70-364
PEACOCKE, A.R. SCIENCE AND THE CHRISTIAN
EXPERIMENT.
617(TLS):25FEB72-217
PEAKE, M. SELECTED POEMS.
617(TLS):21APR72-441
PEARCE, C.R. THE CONFIDENT FLY FISHER.
617(TLS):14JUL72-826
PEARCE, D. PIER HEAD JUMP.
R.A. SOKOLOV, 441:16APR72-31
PEARCE, R.H. THE CONTINUITY OF AMERICAN
POETRY.
G.M. WHITE, 502(PRS):SUMMER69-224
PEARCE, R.H., ED. EXPERIENCE IN THE
NOVEL.
B. HARDY, 155:SEP69-184
PEARCE, R.H. HISTORICISM ONCE MORE.
R. LEHAN, 445(NCF):DEC69-374
J.O. MC CORMICK, 149:DEC71-363
PEARL, C. DUBLIN IN BLOOMTIME.
639(VQR):WINTER70-XXVII
PEARL, C. REBEL DOWN UNDER.
617(TLS):12MAY72-557
PEARLMAN, D.D. THE BARB OF TIME.*
W.M. CHACE, 598(SOR):WINTER72-225
F.K. SANDERS, 569(SR):SUMMER71-433
A.K. WEATHERHEAD, 141:FALL70-358
639(VQR):SPRING70-LII
PEARS, D. BERTRAND RUSSELL AND THE
BRITISH TRADITION IN PHILOSOPHY.
J. BOUVERESSE, 98:APR69-335
PEARS, D., ED. RUSSELL'S LOGICAL ATOM-
ISM.
617(TLS):14JUL72-795
PEARS, D. WHAT IS KNOWLEDGE?
P. UNGER, 311(JP):17AUG72-448
PEARS, D. LUDWIG WITTGENSTEIN.*
B. STROUD, 311(JP):13JAN72-16
PEARSALL, D. GOWER AND LYDGATE.
H. BOYD, 180(ESA):SEP70-413
PEARSALL, D. JOHN LYDGATE.
J. MITCHELL, 301(JEGP):JUL71-528
R. PRYOR, 382(MAE):1971/2-206
PEARSALL, D.A., ED. THE FLOURE AND THE
LEAFE [AND] THE ASSEMBLY OF LADIES.
R.W.V. ELLIOTT, 179(ES):FEB70-57
PEARSALL, D.A. & R.A. WALDRON, EDS. MED-
IEVAL LITERATURE AND CIVILIZATION.
J. & G. TURVILLE-PETRE, 541(RES):
NOV70-478
R.M. WILSON, 175:AUTUMN69-106
639(VQR):WINTER70-XVIII
PEARSALL, R. THE TABLE-RAPPERS.
617(TLS):16JUN72-690
PEARSALL, R. THE WORM IN THE BUD.
639(VQR):SPRING70-LXXVI
PEARSE, M.M. TRADITIONAL BRITISH COOK-
ERY.
617(TLS):15DEC72-1541
PEARSON, A. 14 POEMS.
S. SCOBIE, 102(CANL):AUTUMN71-75
PEARSON, J. THE PROFESSION OF VIOLENCE.
F. WYNDHAM, 362:30NOV72-758
617(TLS):17NOV72-1402
PEARSON, L.B. MIKE. (VOL 1)
C. SANGER, 441:31DEC72-2
PEARSON, M. THE AGE OF CONSENT.
617(TLS):3NOV72-1346

PEARSON, M. THOSE DAMNED REBELS.
J.T. FLEXNER, 441:19MAR72-34
E. WEEKS, 61:MAR72-105
617(TLS):1SEP72-1031
PEATE, I.C. TRADITION AND FOLK LIFE.
617(TLS):18AUG72-965
PECH, S.Z. THE CZECH REVOLUTION OF 1848.
639(VQR):SUMMER70-CXII
PECKETT, C.W.E. & A.R. MUNDAY. PRIN-
CIPIA. PSEUDOLUS NOSTER.
E.M.A. KOVACH, 124:NOV70-95
PECKHAM, M. ART AND PORNOGRAPHY.*
J.B. GORDON, 141:FALL70-350
PECKHAM, M. VICTORIAN REVOLUTIONARIES.*
J.L. BRADLEY, 402(MLR):OCT71-878
M. COOKE, 676(YR):WINTER71-294
PEČMAN, R., ED. COLLOQUIUM LEOŠ JANÁČEK
ET MUSICA EUROPAEA.
J.T., 410(M&L):OCT71-441
PĚDECH, P. - SEE POLYBIUS
PEDLER, K. & G. DAVIS. MUTANT 59.
C. LEHMANN-HAUPT, 441:16MAR72-49
PEDLEY, A.J.M., COMP. THE MANUSCRIPT
COLLECTIONS OF THE MARYLAND HISTORICAL
SOCIETY.
F. SHELLEY, 14:JAN69-34
PEDLEY, J.G. SARDIS IN THE AGE OF
CROESUS.*
E.L. KOHLER, 121(CJ):DEC70-JAN71-169
PEERMAN, D., ED. FRONTLINE THEOLOGY.
G.M., 477:SUMMER69-406
PEERS, F.W. THE POLITICS OF CANADIAN
BROADCASTING, 1920-1951.
G.G.E. STEELE, 529(QQ):SUMMER70-289
PEESCH, R. & W. RUDOLPH. KOLLOQUIUM
BALTICUM ETHNOGRAPHICUM 1966.
R.L. WELSCH, 292(JAF):JUL-SEP70-372
PEETERS, L. HISTORISCHE UND LITERARISCHE
STUDIEN ZUM DRITTEN TEIL DES KUDRUN-
EPOS.*
C. GELLINEK, 589:JAN71-180
PEETS, E. ON THE ART OF DESIGNING
CITIES.* (P.D. SPREIREGEN, ED)
E. COIT, 505:FEB69-154
P. ZUCKER, 290(JAAC):WINTER69-249
PEI, M. GLOSSARY OF LINGUISTIC TERMINOL-
OGY.
J. LEVITT, 207(FR):DEC69-369
R.S. MEYERSTEIN, 545(RPH):AUG69-100
PEI, M. HOW TO LEARN LANGUAGES AND WHAT
LANGUAGES TO LEARN.
M.E. GILES, 545(RPH):FEB70-362
PEIRCE, N.R. THE MEGASTATES OF AMERICA.
T. LASK, 441:24MAR72-42
441:16JUL72-14
PEKÁRY, T. UNTERSUCHUNGEN ZU DEN RÖMIS-
CHEN REICHSSTRASSEN.
E. BIRLEY, 313:VOL60-266
PELADEAU, M.B. - SEE TYLER, R.
PELC, J. "TRENY" JANA KOCHANOWSKIEGO.
D. WELSH, 104:SPRING71-127
PELFREY, W. THE BIG V.
A. HISLOP, 440:2APR72-8
M. LEVIN, 441:7MAY72-32
PELIKAN, J. THE CHRISTIAN TRADITION.*
(VOL 1: THE EMERGENCE OF THE CATHOLIC
TRADITION.) [SHOWN IN PREV UNDER SUB-
TITLE]
J.T. MOORE, 319:JUL72-358
617(TLS):11FEB72-163
PELIKAN, J. SPIRIT VERSUS STRUCTURE.
W.A.J., 543:SEP69-136
PÉLISSIER, P. LES PAYSANS DU SÉNÉGAL.
G. BRASSEUR, 69:JAN69-87
PELL, E. & OTHERS, EDS. MAXIMUM SECUR-
ITY.
J. MITFORD, 453:9MAR72-29
S.V. ROBERTS, 441:6FEB72-5

PELLEGRINI, A. NEW TENDENCIES IN ART.
D. IRWIN, 39:SEP69-271
PELLEGRINI, A.L. - SEE "DANTE STUDIES"
PELLING, H. POPULAR POLITICS AND SOCIETY
IN LATE VICTORIAN BRITAIN.
R. HARRISON, 637(VS):MAR70-364
PELLISSON, P. & C. FLEURY. DEUX AMIS
D'HOMÈRE AU XVIIE SIÈCLE. (N. HEPP,
ED)
W. ANDERSON, 124:MAR71-236
PELLOWSKI, A. THE WORLD OF CHILDREN'S
LITERATURE.
V.G. ALLEN, 399(MLJ):FEB70-130
PELSTER, F. - SEE EHRLE, F.
PELT, A. LIBYAN INDEPENDENCE AND THE
UNITED NATIONS.
617(TLS):7JAN72-4
PEMÁN, J.M. ESPRONCEDA.
191(ELN):SEP70(SUPP)-155
PEÑA, C.G. - SEE UNDER GONZÁLEZ PEÑA, C.
PEÑA, H. LA SOLEDAD Y EL DESIERTO.
S. BACIU, 263:JUL-SEP71-346
PENELHUM, T. SURVIVAL AND DISEMBODIED
EXISTENCE.
A. FLEW, 518:OCT70-21
R. PUCCETTI, 479(PHQ):OCT70-404
PENNEY, C.L. AN ALBUM OF SELECTED BOOK-
BINDINGS.
E. HELMAN, 240(HR):JUL70-314
A.R.A. HOBSON, 39:JAN69-80
PENNEY, C.L. PRINTED BOOKS 1468-1700 IN
THE HISPANIC SOCIETY OF AMERICA.*
H.C. WOODBRIDGE, 545(RPH):AUG69-141
PENNINGTON, R. CHRISTOPHER BRENNAN.
A.R. CHISHOLM, 381:VOL29#2-245
PENRICE, J. A DICTIONARY AND GLOSSARY
OF THE KOR-AN.
617(TLS):14JUL72-823
PENROSE, R. THE SCULPTURE OF PICASSO.*
V.H. MIESEL, 56:SPRING69-101
B.M.B. PETRIE, 90:MAR69-161
"THE PENTAGON PAPERS."* (N. SHEEHAN &
OTHERS, EDS) "THE PENTAGON PAPERS."*
[THE SENATOR GRAVEL EDITION]
J. MIRSKY, 561(SATR):1JAN72-23
PENTECOST, H. BIRTHDAY, DEATHDAY.
N. CALLENDAR, 441:28MAY72-25
PENTECOST, H. THE CHAMPAGNE KILLER.
O.L. BAILEY, 561(SATR):25NOV72-70
N. CALLENDAR, 441:5NOV72-44
PENTECOST, H. DON'T DROP DEAD TOMORROW.*
N. CALLENDAR, 441:16JAN72-42
442(NY):8JAN72-87
PENTIKÄINEN, J. THE NORDIC DEAD-CHILD
TRADITION.
B.H. GRANGER, 292(JAF):JAN-MAR70-94
PEÑUELAS, M.C. MR. CLARK NO TOMA POCA-
COLA. (J.M. SHARP, ED)
G. FRANKS, 238:MAY70-354
PEÑUELAS, M.C. & W.E. WILSON. INTRODUC-
CIÓN A LA LITERATURA ESPAÑOLA.
G. FLYNN, 238:MAY70-356
PENUELI, S.Y. & A. UKHMANI, COMPS.
HEBREW SHORT STORIES.
J.M. LANDAU, 399(MLJ):MAY70-363
PENZL, H. GESCHICHTLICHE DEUTSCHE
LAUTLEHRE.
J. EICHHOFF, 406:SPRING71-75
PEPPARD, M.B. NIKOLAI NEKRASOV.*
C.V. WILLIAMS, 577(SHR):SUMMER70-282
PEPPER, C.B. AN ARTIST AND THE POPE.*
E.R. DE ZURKO, 219(GAR):SUMMER69-264
PEPPER, S. HOUSING IMPROVEMENT.
617(TLS):4FEB72-137
PEPPER, S.C. CONCEPT AND QUALITY.*
D.N. MORGAN, 290(JAAC):WINTER69-243

PEPYS, S. THE DIARY OF SAMUEL PEPYS.*
(VOLS 1-3) (R. LATHAM & W. MATTHEWS,
EDS)
F. BRADY, 676(YR):WINTER71-269
E. MINER, 249(HUDR):SPRING71-171
568(SCN):SPRING71-6
PEPYS, S. THE DIARY OF SAMUEL PEPYS.*
(VOLS 4&5) (R. LATHAM & W. MATTHEWS,
EDS)
L. ASH, 70(ANQ):NOV71-47
PEPYS, S. THE DIARY OF SAMUEL PEPYS.
(VOLS 6&7) (R. LATHAM & W. MATTHEWS,
EDS)
617(TLS):8DEC72-1485
PERAZA, F. REVOLUTIONARY CUBA.
L.S. THOMPSON, 263:JAN-MAR71-65
PERCHIK, S. WHICH HAND HOLDS THE BRO-
THER.
J. HOPPER, 661:SUMMER70-123
PERCY, W. THE LAST GENTLEMAN.
P. WOLFE, 502(PRS):SUMMER68-181
PERCY, W. LOVE IN THE RUINS.*
J.M. MORSE, 249(HUDR):AUTUMN71-527
PEREC, G. LES CHOSES. (J. LEBLON, ED)
R.D. COTTRELL, 399(MLJ):NOV70-531
PEREIRA, A. SICILY.
617(TLS):29DEC72-1586
PEREIRA, A.O. MARCORÉ.* [SHOWN IN PREV
UNDER OLAVO PEREIRA, A.]
M.L. DANIEL, 399(MLJ):OCT70-465
J. PARKER, 86(BHS):OCT71-368
PEREIRA, M. THE SINGING MILLIONAIRE.
617(TLS):26MAY72-612
PERELLA, N.J. THE KISS SACRED AND PRO-
FANE.*
A.J. SMITH, 551(RENQ):AUTUMN70-279
PERELLI, L. LUCREZIO, POETA DELL'ANGOS-
CIA.
M.L. CLARKE, 123:DEC71-375
D. CLAY, 24:JAN71-119
PERELMAN, C. JUSTICE.
E.L. PINCOFFS, 482(PHR):APR70-292
PÉREZ-RIOJA, J.A. EL HELENISTA RANZ
ROMANILLOS Y LA ESPAÑA DE SU TIEMPO
(1759-1830).
191(ELN):SEP69(SUPP)-145
PEREZ LOPEZ, F. DARK AND BLOODY GROUND.
R.A. SOKOLOV, 441:16APR72-31
442(NY):3JUN72-110
PERKELL, J.S. PHYSIOLOGY OF SPEECH PRO-
DUCTION.
T.S. SMITH, 350:MAR71-237
PERKIN, H. THE ORIGINS OF MODERN ENGLISH
SOCIETY 1780-1880.
D.V.E., 191(ELN):SEP70(SUPP)-13
PERKINS, B. THE GREAT RAPPROCHEMENT.
R.A. COSGROVE, 50(ARQ):SUMMER69-172
D.P. CROOK, 637(VS):MAR70-360
B.J. DALTON, 67:NOV71-273
PERKINS, D.H., WITH OTHERS. AGRICULTURAL
DEVELOPMENT IN CHINA, 1366-1968.*
R. MYERS, 293(JAST):AUG70-897
PERKINS, J.A. THE CONCEPT OF THE SELF
IN THE FRENCH ENLIGHTENMENT.
G. MAY, 207(FR):APR70-843
J. SCHWARTZ, 400(MLN):DEC70-935
M.H. WADDICOR, 208(FS):APR71-201
PERKOWSKI, J.L. A KASHUBIAN IDIOLECT IN
THE UNITED STATES.
M.Z. BROOKS, 574(SEEJ):SPRING71-101
T.F. MAGNER, 32:JUN71-454
PERL, W.H. - SEE VON HOFMANNSTHAL, H. &
L. VON ANDRIAN
PERLBERG, M. THE BURNING FIELD.
F. MORAMARCO, 651(WHR):WINTER71-100

PERNETTE DU GUILLET. RYMES. (V. GRAHAM,
ED)
J-C. SEIGNEURET, 207(FR):MAR70-699
K. VARTY, 208(FS):JAN71-65
PERO DA PONTE. POESIE. (S. PANUNZIO,
ED)
P.E. RUSSELL, 382(MAE):1971/2-195
PÉROUSE DE MONTCLOS, J-P. ETIENNE-LOUS
BOULLÉE (1728-1799).
P. GUERRE, 98:NOV69-978
H. HONOUR, 90:AUG70-546
PEROWNE, S. DEATH OF THE ROMAN REPUB-
LIC.*
D.M. AYERS, 50(ARQ):AUTUMN69-287
PEROWNE, S. ROMAN MYTHOLOGY.
J.M. COOK, 123:DEC71-466
PEROWNE, S. & E. SMITH. ROME.
P. ADAMS, 61:APR72-129
PERRAULT, E.G. THE TWELFTH MILE.
N. CALLENDAR, 441:12MAR72-40
A. SCOTT, 296:SUMMER72-88
617(TLS):29DEC72-1588
PERRIN, R.W.E. THE ARCHITECTURE OF
WISCONSIN.
W. ANDREWS, 576:DEC69-300
PERROT, J. THE ORGAN.*
P. WILLIAMS, 415:OCT71-969
PERRY, B.E. THE ANCIENT ROMANCES.*
H.H.O. CHALK, 123:MAR71-78
PERRY, C. BOY IN THE BLITZ.
617(TLS):23JUN72-729
PERRY, G. TWO HOUSES.*
J.R. LINDROTH, 590:SPRING70-35
PERRY, H. "THEY'LL CUT OFF YOUR PROJ-
ECT."
J. KANON, 561(SATR):2SEP72-50
PERRY, H.D. A CHAIR FOR WAYNE LONERGAN.
H. FRANKEL, 561(SATR):25MAR72-104
PERRY, R. THE FALL GUY.
O.L. BAILEY, 561(SATR):30SEP72-79
N. CALLENDAR, 441:17SEP72-45
617(TLS):4FEB72-135
PERRY, T.A. ART AND MEANING IN BERCEO'S
"VIDA DE SANTA ORIA."*
C. GARIANO, 238:MAR70-145
W. METTMANN, 72:BAND208HEFT2-152
D.G. PATTISON, 447(N&Q):JUL70-275
PERSE, S-J. COLLECTED POEMS.
617(TLS):12MAY72-541
PERSIUS. A. PERSI FLACCI "SATURARUM
LIBER." (D. BO, ED)
W.S. ANDERSON, 124:DEC70-132
N. RUDD, 123:DEC71-376
"PERSPECTA 12."
P.D. EISENMAN, 44:OCT69-74
PERUSINO, F. IL TETRAMETRO GIAMBICO
CATALETTICO NELLA COMMEDIA GRECA.
A-N. MICHELINI, 24:JAN71-122
L.P.E. PARKER, 123:MAR71-71
PERUTZ, K. THE MARRIAGE FALLACY.
617(TLS):10NOV72-1359
PERUTZ, K. MARRIAGE IS HELL.
M. WATKINS, 441:18AUG72-34
PESANTE, S. CATALOGO DEGLI INCUNABULI
DELLA BIBLIOTECA CIVICA DI TRIESTE.
D.E. RHODES, 354:SEP69-261
PESCE, D. - SEE LEVI, A.
PESSOA, F. FERNANDO PESSOA: SELECTED
POEMS.* (P. RICKARD, ED & TRANS)
M. WOOD, 453:21SEP72-19
PESSOA, F. SELECTED POEMS BY FERNANDO
PESSOA. (E. HONIG, TRANS)
M. AUGEN, 385(MQR):FALL72-302
M. WOOD, 453:21SEP72-19
PETER, C.C. CHARLES MAURRAS ET L'IDÉOLO-
GIE D'ACTION FRANÇAISE.
617(TLS):25AUG72-991

PETER, H. ENTSTEHUNG UND AUSBILDUNG DER
   ITALIENISCHEN EISENBAHNTERMINOLOGIE.
   R.A. HALL, JR., 350:SEP71-730
PETER, L.J. THE PETER PRESCRIPTION.
   M. OLMERT, 441:13AUG72-4
PETERKIEWICZ, J. THE OTHER SIDE OF
   SILENCE.*
   676(YR):AUTUMN70-XVIII
PETERS, C. & T. BRANCH, EDS. BLOWING THE
   WHISTLE.
   V.S. NAVASKY, 441:30APR72-4
PETERS, E. DEATH TO THE LANDLORDS!
   N. CALLENDAR, 441:2JUL72-15
   617(TLS):28APR72-500
PETERS, F.E. ARISTOTELES ARABUS.*
   J.N. MATTOCK, 123:MAR71-129
PETERS, F.E. ARISTOTLE AND THE ARABS.*
   R.M. FRANK, 318(JAOS):OCT-DEC70-556
   M.C. LYONS, 382(MAE):1971/3-273
PETERS, J.E.C. THE DEVELOPMENT OF FARM
   BUILDINGS IN WESTERN LOWLAND STAFFORD-
   SHIRE UP TO 1880.
   A. FENTON, 595(SCS):VOL15PT1-80
PETERS, M. HENRY VIII AND HIS SIX WIVES.
   617(TLS):22SEP72-1124
PETERS, M. JEAN INGELOW.
   617(TLS):8DEC72-1487
PETERS, R. THE SOW'S HEAD AND OTHER
   POEMS.
   B.D.S., 502(PRS):FALL69-326
PETERS, V. NESTOR MAKHNO.
   D. FOOTMAN, 575(SEER):OCT71-633
   O.W. GERUS, 104:WINTER71-573
PETERSEN, C. ALBERT CAMUS.
   K.J. HARROW, 295:VOL2#1-143
PETERSEN, L. PROSOPOGRAPHIA IMPERII
   ROMANI SAEC. I. II. III. (PT 4, FASC
   3)
   M.A.R. COLLEDGE, 123:MAR71-142
PETERSON, A.D.C. THE INTERNATIONAL
   BACCALAUREATE.
   617(TLS):4AUG72-922
PETERSON, B. COALTOWN REVISITED.
   H.M. CAUDILL, 441:7MAY72-8
PETERSON, E. TRISTAN TZARA.
   R. SHATTUCK, 453:1JUN72-25
PETERSON, E.N. THE LIMITS OF HITLER'S
   POWER.
   639(VQR):SUMMER70-CIX
PETERSON, K.G. THE UNIVERSITY OF CALI-
   FORNIA LIBRARY AT BERKELEY, 1900-1945.
   M.H. HARRIS, 356:APR71-187
PETERSON, R. THE BINNACLE.
   W. WITHERUP, 502(PRS):WINTER69/70-422
PETERSON, W.S. AN APPROACH TO "PATER-
   SON."
   C.M. TAYLOR, 597(SN):VOL41#1-202
PETERSSON, R.T. THE ART OF ECSTASY.*
   J.H. HAGSTRUM, 402(MLR):JUL71-649
   L. NELSON, JR., 676(YR):SPRING71-444
PETHYBRIDGE, R. THE SPREAD OF THE RUS-
   SIAN REVOLUTION.
   617(TLS):16JUN72-683
PETIT, J. BERNANOS, BLOY, CLAUDEL,
   PÉGUY.
   617(TLS):14JUL72-794
PETIT, J. - SEE GREEN, J.
"LE PETIT PLET." (B.S. MERRILEES, ED)
   A. BELL, 382(MAE):1971/1-71
PETITFILS, P., ED. AMIS DE RIMBAUD.
   S.I. LOCKERBIE, 208(FS):JUL71-344
PETRARCH. FOUR DIALOGUES FOR SCHOLARS.*
   (C.H. RAWSKI, ED & TRANS)
   N.J. PERELLA, 551(RENQ):SUMMER70-163
PETRIE, C. A HISTORIAN LOOKS AT HIS
   WORLD.
   617(TLS):28JUL72-868

PETRIE, G. THE COMING-OUT PARTY.
   V. CUNNINGHAM, 362:22JUN72-841
PETRIE, G. A SINGULAR INIQUITY.*
   M. HAYNES, 561(SATR):1JAN72-28
PETRONIUS. CENA TRIMALCHIONIS. (T.
   CUTT, ED)
   J.C.P. COTTER, 124:FEB71-204
PETROV, V. "JUNE 22, 1941."
   A. PARRY, 550(RUSR):APR70-235
PETROV, V. MONEY AND CONQUEST.
   N. BALABKINS, 461:SPRING68-337
PETROV, V. A STUDY IN DIPLOMACY.
   P.C. DANIELS, 396(MODA):FALL71-430
PETROV, V.P. MONGOLIA.*
   N. POPPE, 32:SEP71-672
PETROVIĆ, N., ED. SVETOZAR MILETIĆ I
   NARODNA STRANKA.*
   G. STOKES, 32:MAR71-189
PETRUCCI, O. OTTAVIANO PETRUCCI, CANTI B
   NUMERO CINQUANTA. (H. HEWITT, ED)
   M. PICKER, 414(MQ):JUL68-376
PETTER, H. THE EARLY AMERICAN NOVEL.
   A. COWIE, 27(AL):NOV71-485
PETTERSSON, O. MOTHER EARTH.
   M. SMITH, 124:SEP70-25
PETTI, A. & G. LAYCOCK, EDS. THE NEW
   CATHOLIC HYMNAL.*
   617(TLS):14APR72-426
PETTIT, H. - SEE YOUNG, E.
PETTIT, P. ON THE IDEA OF PHENOMENOLOGY.
   R.C. POOLE, 483:APR70-166
PETTORUTI, E. UN PINTOR ANTE EL ESPEJO.
   R. SQUIRRU, 37:FEB69-37
PETTY, J. THE FACE.
   617(TLS):22DEC72-1554
PETZL, G. ANTIKE DISKUSSIONEN ÜBER DIE
   BEIDEN NEKYIAI.
   W.F. WYATT, JR., 124:DEC70-136
PETZOLD, K-E. STUDIEN ZUR METHODE DES
   POLYBIOS UND ZU IHRER HISTORISCHEN
   AUSWERTUNG.
   R.M. ERRINGTON, 123:DEC71-383
   J.A.O. LARSEN, 122:JAN71-66
   P.A. STADTER, 124:JAN71-162
   F.W. WALBANK, 313:VOL60-252
VAN PEURSEN, C.A. LEIBNIZ.
   G.H.R. PARKINSON, 479(PHQ):JUL70-272
VAN PEURSEN, C.A. LUDWIG WITTGENSTEIN.
   R.W. NEWELL, 479(PHQ):JUL70-275
PEUSER, G. DIE PARTIKEL "DE" IM MODERNEN
   SPANISCHEN.
   R.G. KEIGHTLEY, 86(BHS):JAN71-57
   K. TOGEBY, 545(RPH):MAY70-585
PEVSNER, N. RUSKIN AND VIOLLET-LE-DUC.*
   K. ROBERTS, 90:OCT70-706
PEVSNER, N. SOME ARCHITECTURAL WRITERS
   OF THE NINETEENTH CENTURY.
   617(TLS):24NOV72-1414
PEVSNER, N. THE SOURCES OF MODERN ARCHI-
   TECTURE AND DESIGN.
   P. COLLINS, 505:DEC68-144
   P. ZUCKER, 290(JAAC):WINTER69-259
PEVSNER, N. STUDIES IN ART, ARCHITECTURE
   AND DESIGN.*
   L.K. EATON, 505:OCT69-210
   F. HASKELL, 46:OCT69-322
   J. MASHECK, 592:MAR69-145
PEVSNER, N., WITH J. HUTCHINSON. THE
   BUILDINGS OF ENGLAND:YORKSHIRE; YORK
   AND THE EAST RIDING.
   617(TLS):15DEC72-1520
PEYRE, H. FRENCH NOVELISTS OF TODAY.*
   J. WEBER, 613:SPRING68-130
PEYRE, H. HISTORICAL AND CRITICAL
   ESSAYS.
   E. MARKS, 207(FR):DEC69-362
   M. MAURIN, 546(RR):APR70-163

PEYRE, H. JEAN-PAUL SARTRE.
  H.T. MASON, 447(N&Q):OCT70-394
PEYRE, H., ED. SIX MAÎTRES CONTEMPOR-
AINS.
  A.M. BEICHMAN, 399(MLJ):NOV70-542
PEYRE, H. - SEE VALÉRY, P.
PEYROU, M. THUNDER OF THE ROSES.
  N. CALLENDAR, 441:21MAY72-30
PFAFF, C. SCRIPTORIUM UND BIBLIOTHEK DES
KLOSTERS MONDSEE IM HOHEN MITTELALTER.
  P. MEYVAERT, 589:APR71-388
PFAFF, R.W. NEW LITURGICAL FEASTS IN
LATER MEDIEVAL ENGLAND.
  J. CREHAN, 382(MAE):1971/3-311
  M.H. SHEPHERD, JR., 589:OCT71-750
PFEFFER, J.A. GRUNDDEUTSCH.
  J. EICHHOFF, 406:SUMMER71-175
PFEFFER, J.A. INDEX OF ENGLISH EQUIVA-
LENTS FOR THE BASIC (SPOKEN) GERMAN
WORD LIST.
  R. GILL, 220(GL&L):OCT70-104
PFEFFER, M.E. EINRICHTUNGEN DER SOZIALEN
SICHERUNG IN DER GRIECHISCHEN UND
RÖMISCHEN ANTIKE.*
  A.R. HANDS, 123:MAR71-82
PFEIFFER, G. STUDIEN ZUR FRÜHPHASE DES
EUROPÄISCHEN PHILHELLENISMUS (1453-
1750).
  D.M. NICOL, 123:DEC71-468
PFNÜR, V. EINIG IN DER RECHTFERTIGUNGS-
LEHRE?
  J-D. BURGER, 182:VOL23#23/24-978
PFOHL, G. GREEK POEMS ON STONES. (VOL
1)
  P.A. HANSEN, 303:VOL90-229
PHADNIS, U. TOWARDS THE INTEGRATION OF
INDIAN STATES, 1919-1947.
  P. WALLACE, 293(JAST):NOV69-195
PHAEDRUS. PHAEDRI AUGUSTI LIBERTI LIBER
FABULARUM. (A. GUAGLIANONE, ED)
  J. VAIO, 124:DEC70-132
PHELAN, J.L. THE KINGDOM OF QUITO IN THE
SEVENTEENTH CENTURY.*
  A.B. EDWARDS, 37:OCT69-41
PHILIP, L.B. THE GHENT ALTARPIECE AND
THE ART OF JAN VAN EYCK.
  617(TLS):10NOV72-1356
PHILIPP, F. ARTHUR BOYD.
  F. LAWS, 592:MAR68-158
PHILIPP, M. PHONOLOGIE DES GRAPHIES ET
DES RIMES.
  C.V.J. RUSS, 402(MLR):APR71-445
PHILIPPEN, J. DE OUDE VLAAMSE BEDEVAART-
VAANTJES.
  S.J. SACKETT, 292(JAF):JUL-SEP70-364
PHILIPPI, D.L. - SEE "KOJIKI"
PHILIPS, J. ESCAPE A KILLER.*
  617(TLS):26MAY72-612
PHILIPS, J. THE VANISHING SENATOR.
  O.L. BAILEY, 561(SATR):9SEP72-74
  N. CALLENDAR, 441:20AUG72-26
PHILLIPS, D. WAVE.
  D. BARBOUR, 150(DR):AUTUMN70-433
PHILLIPS, D.Z. THE CONCEPT OF PRAYER.*
  R.M. ADAMS, 482(PHR):APR70-282
PHILLIPS, D.Z. DEATH AND IMMORTALITY.*
  A. FLEW, 518:MAY71-23
PHILLIPS, D.Z. FAITH AND PHILOSOPHICAL
ENQUIRY.*
  S.C. THAKUR, 63:DEC71-324
PHILLIPS, D.Z. - SEE RHEES, R.
PHILLIPS, D.Z. & H.O. MOUNCE. MORAL
PRACTICES.
  O. NELL, 311(JP):4MAY72-257
  C.M. TYLEE, 518:JAN71-17
PHILLIPS, E. THE NEW WORLD OF ENGLISH
WORDS (1658).
  V.R. MOLLENKOTT, 568(SCN):WINTER71-75

PHILLIPS, E. EDWARD PHILLIPS: THEATRUM
POETARUM OR A COMPLEAT COLLECTION OF
THE POETS (1675).
  J.M. PATRICK, 568(SCN):SPRING71-14
PHILLIPS, M.J. LIBRETTO FOR 23 POEMS.
  V.B. YOUNG, 577(SHR):WINTER70-94
PHILLIPS, M.M. THE "ADAGES" OF ERASMUS.
ERASMUS ON HIS TIMES.
  D.F.S. THOMSON, 627(UTQ):JAN70-181
PHILLIPS, O.H. SHAKESPEARE AND THE LAW-
YERS.
  617(TLS):10NOV72-1364
PHILLIPS, R., ED. ASPECTS OF ALICE.*
  J. GARDNER, 441:30JAN72-3
  W. HEYEN, 561(SATR):15JAN72-42
  617(TLS):15DEC72-1525
PHILOPON, J. COMMENTAIRE SUR LE "DE
ANIMA" D'ARISTOTE. (G. VERBEKE, ED)
  F. CORVINO, 548(RCSF):APR/JUN69-212
PHIPSON, T. LETTERS & OTHER WRITINGS OF
A NATAL SHERIFF. (R.N. CURREY, ED)
  A.R. TAYLOR, 637(VS):JUN70-385
"THE PHOENIX." (VOLS 1&2)
  R. SALE, 418(MR):WINTER71-167
  A. SULLIVAN, 295:VOL2#1-137
PHOTIUS. BIBLIOTHÈQUE. (VOL 5) (R.
HENRY, ED & TRANS)
  K. TSANTSANOGLOU, 303:VOL90-226
PHYSICK, J. DESIGNS FOR ENGLISH SCULP-
TURE 1680-1860.
  M. WHINNEY, 90:OCT70-710
PI-SUNYER, C. MIRANDA Y CASANOVA, EN-
SAYO 1.
  M.G. DE VALDÉS-RODRÍGUEZ, 37:OCT69-42
PIAGET, J. BIOLOGY AND KNOWLEDGE.
  617(TLS):17MAR72-299
PIAGET, J. INSIGHTS AND ILLUSIONS OF
PHILOSOPHY. EPISTÉMOLOGIE DES SCIENCES
DE L'HOMME.
  617(TLS):2JUN72-629
PIAGET, J. THE PRINCIPLES OF GENETIC
EPISTEMOLOGY.
  617(TLS):11AUG72-954
PIANEZZOLA, E. TRADUZIONE E IDEOLOGIA.
  S.I. OOST, 122:APR71-141
  P.G. WALSH, 123:DEC71-457
PICARD, B. - SEE VON HERBERSTEIN, S.
PICARD, G. THE ANCIENT CIVILIZATION OF
ROME.
  A.M. WARD, 124:APR71-274
PICARD, G. ROMAN PAINTING.
  617(TLS):24MAR72-338
PICASSO, P. PICASSO ON ART. (D. ASHTON,
ED)
  R. DOWNES, 441:31DEC72-6
"PICASSO: BIRTH OF A GENIUS."
  D.L. SHIREY, 441:10DEC72-47
PICCALUGA, G. LYKAON.*
  F. LASSERRE, 182:VOL23#8-432
PICCOLOMINI, A.S. SELECTED LETTERS OF
AENEAS SILVIUS PICCOLOMINI. (A.R.
BACA, TRANS)
  L.V.R., 568(SCN):SPRING71-31
PICCOTTINI, G. DIE RUNDSKULPTUREN DES
STADTGEBIETES VON VIRUNUM.*
  J.M.C. TOYNBEE, 313:VOL60-243
PICHLÍK, K. ZAHRANIČNÍ ODBOJ 1914-1918
BEZ LEGEND.
  D.H. PERMAN, 32:MAR71-173
PICHOIS, C. - SEE COLETTE
PICHOIS, C. & R. PINTARD - SEE ROUSSEAU,
J-J.
PICHOIS, C. & A-M. ROUSSEAU. LA LIT-
TÉRATURE COMPARÉE.*
  S.L. FLAXMAN, 131(CL):SPRING71-174
PICKARD, R.A.E. DICTIONARY OF 1,000
BEST FILMS.
  N. BALAKIAN, 441:5NOV72-33

PICKERING, F.P. AUGUSTINUS ODER BOE-
THIUS?*
M. WEHRLI, 182:VOL23#13/14-674
PICKERING, F.P., ED. UNIVERSITY GERMAN.
B. MOGRIDGE, 220(GL&L):JUL71-373
PICKERSGILL, J.W. & D.F. FORSTER - SEE
KING, W.L.M.
PICKFORD, C.E - SEE "EREC"
PICKNEY, P.A. PAINTING IN TEXAS.
M.S. YOUNG, 39:APR69-329
PIDAL, R.M. - SEE UNDER MENENDEZ PIDAL,
R.
PIDDUBNYJ, I. SLIDAMY ZHYTTIA.
C.H. ANDRUSYSHEN, 627(UTQ):JUL70-445
PIÉDOUE, M. LA RONDE DES AVEUGLES.
617(TLS):22SEP72-1122
PIERCE, F. & C.A. JONES, EDS. ACTAS DEL
PRIMER CONGRESO INTERNACIONAL DE HIS-
PANISTAS CELEBRADO EN OXFORD DEL 6 AL
11 DE SEPTIEMBRE DE 1962.
S.G. ARMISTEAD & J.H. SILVERMAN,
545(RPH):AUG70-138
PIERCE, N.R. THE PACIFIC STATES OF
AMERICA. THE MOUNTAIN STATES OF AMER-
ICA.
561(SATR):7OCT72-103
PIERCE, O.W. THE DEVIL'S HALF.
502(PRS):WINTER68/69-366
PIERCY, M. BREAKING CAMP.*
R. MORAN, 598(SOR):WINTER72-243
PIERCY, M. DANCE THE EAGLE TO SLEEP.*
W.H. PRITCHARD, 249(HUDR):SUMMER71-
356
PIERRARD, P. LES CHANSONS EN PATOIS DE
LILLE SOUS LE SECOND EMPIRE.
F. DELOFFRE, 545(RPH):NOV70-367
PIERRARD, P., ED. DICTIONNAIRE DE LA
IIIE RÉPUBLIQUE.
L.A. LOUBERE, 207(FR):APR70-852
PIERRE, A.J. NUCLEAR POLITICS.
617(TLS):30JUN72-733
PIERROT, R. - SEE DE BALZAC, H.
PIETERSE, C. & D. MUNRO, EDS. PROTEST
AND CONFLICT IN AFRICAN LITERATURE.
J. DALE, 529(QQ):AUTUMN70-453
PIETERSEN, L. DE FRIEZEN EN HUN TAAL.
M. CLYNE, 67:MAY71-136
PIGAFETTA, A. MAGELLAN'S VOYAGE. (R.A.
SKELTON, ED & TRANS)
S.E. MORISON, 432(NEQ):JUN70-325
PIGAFETTA, F. & D. LOPEZ. DESCRIPTION DU
ROYAUME DE CONGO ET DES CONTRÉES EN-
VIRONNANTES, PAR FILIPPO PIGAFETTA &
DUARTE LOPEZ (1591). (W. BAL, ED &
TRANS)
B.M. WOODBRIDGE, JR., 545(RPH):NOV70-
355
PIGNATTI, T. CANALETTO: SELECTED DRAW-
INGS.
90:JUN70-423
PIGNATTI, T. LONGHI.
J. CAILLEUX, 90:SEP69-567
PIGUET, J-C. - SEE ANSERMET, E.
PIIRAINEN, I.T. GRAPHEMATISCHE UNTER-
SUCHUNGEN ZUM FRÜHNEUHOCHDEUTSCHEN.*
C.V.J. RUSS, 402(MLR):JAN71-207
PIIRAINEN, I.T. TEXTBEZOGENE UNTERSUCH-
UNGEN ÜBER "KATZ UND MAUS" UND "HUNDE-
JAHRE" VON GÜNTER GRASS.*
L. FORSTER, 220(GL&L):JUL71-384
W.P. HANSON, 220(GL&L):JUL71-384
I. TIESLER, 221(GQ):MAR70-300
PIKE, A. A PHENOMENOLOGICAL ANALYSIS OF
MUSICAL EXPERIENCE AND OTHER RELATED
ESSAYS.
T. CLIFTON, 308:WINTER70-237

PIKE, E.R. HUMAN DOCUMENTS OF THE LLOYD
GEORGE ERA.
617(TLS):3NOV72-1347
PIKE, N. GOD AND TIMELESSNESS.
J. HICK, 518:JAN71-19
PIKE, R. ARISTOCRATS AND TRADERS.
617(TLS):25AUG72-1001
PIKE, R.L. THE GREMLIN'S GRANDPA.
N. CALLENDAR, 441:20FEB72-27
PILCH, H. ALTENGLISCHE GRAMMATIK. ALT-
ENGLISCHER LEHRGANG.
C.R. BARRETT, 67:NOV71-221
PILCHER, G.W. SAMUEL DAVIES.*
J.A.L. LEMAY, 27(AL):JAN72-657
S.J. STEIN, 165:SPRING72-94
PILE, J., ED. DRAWINGS OF ARCHITECTURAL
INTERIORS.
P. ANDES, 505:FEB69-170
PILKINGTON, J., JR. HENRY BLAKE FULLER.
B. GELFANT, 27(AL):NOV71-463
PILKINGTON, R. SMALL BOAT ON THE UPPER
RHINE.
617(TLS):7APR72-402
PIL'NJAK, B. BYL'Ë.
K. BROSTROM, 574(SEEJ):SUMMER71-227
PILON, J-G. SAISONS POUR LA CONTINUELLE.
J-L. MAJOR, 627(UTQ):JUL70-426
PIMSLEUR, P. & T. QUINN, EDS. THE PSY-
CHOLOGY OF SECOND LANGUAGE LEARNING.
617(TLS):14APR72-425
PIÑAL, F.A. - SEE UNDER AGUILAR PIÑAL, F.
PINCOFFS, E. THE RATIONALE OF LEGAL PUN-
ISHMENT.
J.B. MOORE, 482(PHR):JAN70-142
PINDAR. DIE ISTHMISCHEN GEDICHTE. (E.
THUMMER, ED & TRANS)
E.D. FLOYD, 24:APR71-350
G.M. KIRKWOOD, 124:SEP70-21
M.M. WILLCOCK, 123:DEC71-336
PINDAR. THE "ODES" OF PINDAR.* (C.M.
BOWRA, TRANS)
C. RUCK, 121(CJ):APR-MAY71-375
PINDAR. SELECTED ODES.* (C.A.P. RUCK &
W.H. MATHESON, EDS & TRANS)
M.M. WILLCOCK, 123:MAR71-13
PINE, L.G. THE HIGHLAND CLANS.
617(TLS):24NOV72-1441
P'ING, W. - SEE UNDER WANG P'ING
PING-FENG, C. - SEE UNDER CHI PING-FENG
PINGET, R. THE LIBERA ME DOMINE.
617(TLS):29SEP72-1167
PINGREE, D. - SEE ABŪ MA'SHAR
PINI, I. BEITRÄGE ZUR MINOISCHEN GRÄB-
ERKUNDE.
J. BOARDMAN, 123:DEC70-406
D.G. MITTEN, 182:VOL23#9-493
PINKNEY, A. THE AMERICAN WAY OF VIO-
LENCE.
P. ADAMS, 61:MAR72-108
K.E. MEYER, 440:12MAR72-6
PINKNEY, R. GHANA UNDER MILITARY RULE
1966-1969.
617(TLS):15SEP72-1046
PINKUS, B. & A.A. GREENBAUM, COMPS. RUS-
SIAN PUBLICATIONS ON JEWS AND JUDAISM
IN THE SOVIET UNION, 1917-1967. (M.
ALTSHULER, ED)
W. KOREY, 32:SEP71-711
PINSENT, J. GREEK MYTHOLOGY.
J.M. COOK, 123:DEC71-466
PINSKER, S. THE SCHLEMIEL AS METAPHOR.
A. GUTTMANN, 27(AL):NOV71-488
PINSKY, R. LANDOR'S POETRY.*
K.C., 191(ELN):SEP70(SUPP)-40
D. DAVIE, 184(EIC):OCT70-466
B. DOBRÉE, 541(RES):FEB70-111
R.H. SUPER, 405(MP):FEB70-291

251

PINTER, H. OLD TIMES.
617(TLS):29DEC72-1569
PINTNER, W.M. RUSSIAN ECONOMIC POLICY
UNDER NICHOLAS I.
P. DUKES, 587:JUL69-118
PINTO, H. IMAGEN DE LA VIDA CRISTIANA.
(E. GLASER, ED)
C. MORÓN ARROYO, 240(HR):APR70-217
PINTO, V.D. & W. ROBERTS - SEE UNDER
DE SOLA PINTO, V. & W. ROBERTS
PIONTEK, H. TOT ODER LEBENDIG.
617(TLS):7JAN72-6
PIOVANI, P. GIUSNATURALISMO ED ETICA
MODERNA.
E. NAMER, 542:JUL-DEC69-492
PIPA, A. MONTALE AND DANTE.
G. CAMBON, 275(IQ):SUMMER69-87
PIPER, H.D. - SEE COWLEY, M.
PIPER, H.W. THE ACTIVE UNIVERSE.
A. GÉRARD, 179(ES):FEB69-123
PIPER, W.B. THE HEROIC COUPLET.
P.J. KORSHIN, 481(PQ):JUL70-316
W.K. WIMSATT, 301(JEGP):APR71-312
PIPES, R. STRUVE.*
J. KEEP, 32:SEP71-666
PIPPING, E. THIS CREATURE OF FANCY.
617(TLS):16JUN72-685
PIRANDELLO, L. THREE PLAYS. (F. FIRTH,
ED)
O. RAGUSA, 276:AUTUMN70-334
PIRE, F. DE L'IMAGINATION POÉTIQUE DANS
L'OEUVRE DE GASTON BACHELARD.
J. BELLEMIN-NOEL, 98:NOV69-937
PIRENNE, M.H. OPTICS, PAINTING, & PHOT-
OGRAPHY.
B.A.R. CARTER, 89(BJA):SUMMER71-302
PIRIE, P.J. FRANK BRIDGE.
H. OTTAWAY, 415:DEC71-1174
PIRON, M. - SEE BRUNEAU, C.
DE PISAN, C. CHRISTINE DE PISAN'S
BALLADES, RONDEAUX, AND VIRELAIS. (K.
VARTY, ED)
C.C. WILLARD, 545(RPH):MAY71-664
PISAR, S. COEXISTENCE AND COMMERCE.
J.S. BERLINER, 32:JUN71-436
617(TLS):4FEB72-119
PITA ANDRADE, J.M. TREASURES OF SPAIN
FROM ALTAMIRA TO THE CATHOLIC KINGS.
C.E. SELBY, 56:SPRING69-97
PITKIN, H.F., ED. REPRESENTATION.
R.J.B., 543:DEC69-366
PITT, D.G., ED. E.J. PRATT.
D.O. SPETTIGUE, 529(QQ):WINTER70-638
PITTAU, J. POLITICAL THOUGHT IN EARLY
MEIJI JAPAN, 1868-1889.
S.N. MAHAJAN, 485(PE&W):JAN69-88
PITTER, R. COLLECTED POEMS.*
M. BORROFF, 676(YR):WINTER71-277
PITZ, E. LANDESKULTURTECHNIK, MARK-
SCHIEDE- UND VERMESSUNGSWESEN IM HER-
ZOGTUM BRAUNSCHWEIG BIS ZUM ENDE DES
18. JAHRHUNDERTS.
C.A.F. MEEKINGS, 325:APR69-506
PIWITT, H.P. ROTHSCHILDS.
617(TLS):1DEC72-1467
PIZARNIK, A. EXTRACCIÓN DE LA PIEDRA DE
LOCURA.
R. SQUIRRU, 37:JUL69-40
PIZZOLATO, L.F. LE "CONFESSIONI" DI S.
AGOSTINO.
W.H.C. FREND, 123:MAR71-136
PIZZOLATO, L.F. LA "EXPLANATIO PSALMORUM
XII."
P. LANGLOIS, 555:VOL44FASC2-359
PLACE, C.A. CHARLES BULFINCH, ARCHITECT
AND CITIZEN.
W.M. WHITEHILL, 432(NEQ):MAR70-139

PLACE, E.B., ED. AMADÍS DE GAULA. (VOL
3)
R. HAMILTON, 545(RPH):AUG69-139
PLACE, F. THE AUTOBIOGRAPHY OF FRANCIS
PLACE. (M. THALE, ED)
R. MITCHISON, 362:20APR72-522
617(TLS):19MAY72-575
DES PLACES, É. LA RELIGION GRECQUE.*
H.W. PARKE, 123:DEC71-442
M. SMITH, 124:NOV70-88
DES PLACES, É. SYNGENEIA.
A.W.H. ADKINS, 123:MAR71-148
PLAGEMANN, B. THE BOXWOOD MAZE.
M. LEVIN, 441:12NOV72-67
PLANTE, D. RELATIVES.
J.G. FARRELL, 362:15JUN72-797
617(TLS):7JUL72-783
PLANTINGA, A. GOD AND OTHER MINDS.
I.M. CROMBIE, 479(PHQ):JUL70-312
G.E. HUGHES, 482(PHR):APR70-246
PLANTY-BONJOUR, G. THE CATEGORIES OF
DIALECTICAL MATERIALISM.
A. HOLLOWAY, 479(PHQ):APR70-182
PLASCHKA, R.G. & K. MACK, EDS. DIE
AUFLÖSUNG DES HABSBURGERREICHES.
A. WAHL, 182:VOL23#9-510
PLASS, M.W. AFRICAN MINIATURES.
V.L. GROTTANELLI, 69:JUL69-312
PLATH, S. THE BELL JAR.*
J.M. MORSE, 249(HUDR):AUTUMN71-535
M.G. PERLOFF, 659:AUTUMN72-507
PLATH, S. CROSSING THE WATER.*
P. DAVISON, 61:FEB72-105
V.A. KRAMER, 398:VOL3#1-40
P. WEST, 440:9JAN72-8
PLATH, S. WINTER TREES.*
J.C. OATES, 441:19NOV72-7
R. SMITH, 398:VOL3#2-91
561(SATR):28OCT72-83
PLATNICK, K.B. GREAT MYSTERIES OF HIS-
TORY.*
617(TLS):15DEC72-1541
PLATO. PLATONE, "OPERE." (G. GIANNAN-
TONI, ED)
E.D. PHILLIPS, 123:DEC70-310
PLATO. PLATONIS "PARMENIDES, PHAEDRUS."
(C. MORESCHINI, ED)
I.G. KIDD, 123:DEC70-312
PLATO. THE "REPUBLIC" OF PLATO.* (A.
BLOOM, ED & TRANS)
N. GULLEY, 479(PHQ):JUL70-269
PLATONOV, A. THE FIERCE AND BEAUTIFUL
WORLD.*
K. FITZLYON, 364:APR/MAY71-168
PLATONOV, S.F. THE TIME OF TROUBLES.*
P. DUKES, 575(SEER):OCT71-619
LORD PLATT. PRIVATE AND CONTROVERSIAL.
617(TLS):4AUG72-926
PLATT, D.C.M. THE CINDERELLA SERVICE.
617(TLS):21JAN72-71
PLATT, D.C.M. FINANCE, TRADE, AND POLI-
TICS IN BRITISH FOREIGN POLICY, 1815-
1914.
V. CROMWELL, 325:OCT70-158
PLATT, D.C.M. LATIN AMERICA AND BRITISH
TRADE 1806-1914.
617(TLS):22DEC72-1563
PLATT, K. DEAD AS THEY COME.
N. CALLENDAR, 441:30JUL72-22
PLATZECK, E-W. RAIMUND LULL.
P. ZAMBELLI, 548(RCSF):APR-JUN68-230
PLAUTUS. AMPHITRUO. (T. CUTT, ED)
T.F. CARNEY, 124:APR71-270
PLAUTUS. ASINARIA. (F. BERTINI, ED)
F.O. COPLEY, 24:OCT71-728
PLAUTUS. MOSTELLARIA/LA FARCE DU FAN-
TÔME. (J. COLLART, ED)
H. OPPERMANN, 182:VOL23#19/20-878

PLAYER, R. OH! WHERE ARE BLOODY MARY'S
EARRINGS?
617(TLS):13OCT72-1235
PLAZA, G. LATIN AMERICA TODAY AND
TOMORROW.
L.S. THOMPSON, 263:OCT-DEC71-455
PLEASANTS, H. SERIOUS MUSIC - AND ALL
THAT JAZZ!*
R. FREEDMAN, 340(KR):1969/4-560
PLEBE, A. - SEE SHAFTESBURY, A.
PLEKHANOV, G.V. FUNDAMENTAL PROBLEMS OF
MARXISM.
H.B., 543:DEC69-352
PLESCIA, J. THE OATH AND PERJURY IN
ANCIENT GREECE.
M. OSTWALD, 124:JAN71-164
PLEUSER, C. DIE BENENNUNGEN UND DER
BEGRIFF DES LEIDES BY J. TAULER.*
C.E. REED, 221(GQ):JAN70-112
PLEYNET, M. L'ENSEIGNEMENT DE LA PEIN-
TURE.
617(TLS):19MAY72-568
PLEZIA, M., ED. LEXICON MEDIAE ET IN-
FIMAE LATINITATIS POLONORUM. (VOL 1,
FASC 4-8; VOL 2, FASC 9-18)
R. BÄCHTOLD, 182:VOL23#13/14-668
PLEZIA, M. & OTHERS, EDS. LEXICON MEDIAE
ET INFIMAE LATINITATIS POLONORUM. (VOL
2, FASC 4-8; VOL 3, FASC 1)
P.W. BLACKFORD, 551(RENQ):SUMMER70-
170
PLINY. FIFTY LETTERS OF PLINY.* (A.N.
SHERWIN-WHITE, ED)
J. ANDRÉ, 555:VOL44FASC1-152
PLINY. LETTERS [AND] PANEGYRICUS. (B.
RADICE, TRANS)
C.P. JONES, 487:AUTUMN70-270
P.G. WALSH, 123:JUN71-211
PLINY. PLINE L'ANCIEN, "HISTOIRE NAT-
URELLE." (BK 21) (J. ANDRÉ, ED &
TRANS)
R.T. BRUÈRE, 122:JUL71-193
G. STEINER, 124:DEC70-133
PLINY. PLINE L'ANCIEN: "HISTOIRE NATUR-
ELLE." (BK 22) (J. ANDRÉ, ED & TRANS)
R.T. BRUÈRE, 122:JUL71-193
PLOEBSCH, G. ALBAN BERGS "WOZZECK."
K. SCHWEIZER, 182:VOL23#9-490
PLOMER, W. CELEBRATIONS.
617(TLS):21APR72-441
PLOSS, E.E., ED. WALTHARIUS UND WALTHER-
SAGE.
D. BLAMIRES, 402(MLR):JUL71-707
PLOTINUS. THE ENNEADS. (4TH ED) (S.
MAC KENNA, TRANS; REV BY B.S. PAGE)
A.H. ARMSTRONG, 123:DEC71-453
PLUMB, J.H. IN THE LIGHT OF HISTORY.
617(TLS):24NOV72-1437
PLUMMER, J. OLD TESTAMENT MINIATURES.
L.E. BOYLE, 363:MAY70-109
A. KUHN, 58:NOV69-18
PLUMSTEAD, A.W. & H. HAYFORD - SEE EMER-
SON, R.W.
PLUNKETT, J. THE GEMS SHE WORE.
617(TLS):4AUG72-926
PLUTARCH. PLUTARCH'S MORALIA XIV. (B.
EINARSON & P.H. DE LACY, TRANS)
J. DEFRADAS, 555:VOL44FASC1-132
PLUTARCH. PLUTARQUE, "VIES." (VOL 5)
(R. FLACELIÈRE & É. CHAMBRY, EDS &
TRANS)
H. MARTIN, JR., 124:DEC70-124
POCHMANN, H.A. & E.N. FELTSKOG - SEE
IRVING, W.
POCKNEY, B.P., ED. 88 KOROTKIX RASS-
KAZOV.
W.H. BENNETT, 574(SEEJ):SUMMER71-235

POCOCK, J.G.A. POLITICS, LANGUAGE AND
TIME.
617(TLS):9JUN72-666
POE, E.A. COLLECTED WORKS OF EDGAR ALLAN
POE.* (VOL 1: POEMS.) (T.O. MABBOTT,
ED)
W. GOLDHURST, 31(ASCH):SPRING72-298
639(VQR):WINTER70-XIV
"POEMA DE MIO CID." (C. SMITH, ED)
617(TLS):22SEP72-1111
POENSGEN, T. DIE DECKENMALEREI IN
ITALIENISCHEN KIRCHEN.
E. SCHLEIER, 90:DEC70-832
"THE POETIC EDDA."* (VOL 1) (U. DRONKE,
ED & TRANS)
T.M. ANDERSSON, 589:JAN71-142
T.F. HOAD, 447(N&Q):APR70-143
A. HOLTSMARK, 402(MLR):APR71-428
"POETRY INTRODUCTION 2."
617(TLS):28JAN72-94
"A POETRY READING FOR PEACE IN VIETNAM."
R. BROTHERSON, 661:FALL/WINTER69-109
POGGI, J. THEATER IN AMERICA, THE IMPORT
OF ECONOMIC FORCES, 1870-1967.
W.J. MESERVE, 397(MD):SEP69-219
POGUE, S.F. JACQUES MODERNE, LYONS
MUSIC PRINTER OF THE SIXTEENTH CEN-
TURY.*
F. DOBBINS, 317:SPRING71-126
B.E. WILSON, 551(RENQ):WINTER70-447
POHL, C.F. MOZART UND HAYDN IN LONDON.
S. SADIE, 415:FEB71-140
POHLENZ, M. LA STOA.
R. PARENTI, 548(RCSF):APR-JUN68-244
POIGNANT, R. EDUCATION AND DEVELOPMENT
IN WESTERN EUROPE, THE UNITED STATES,
AND THE U.S.S.R.
W.H.E. JOHNSON, 32:MAR71-170
POINTON, M.R. MILTON AND ENGLISH ART.*
T.S.R. BOASE, 402(MLR):APR71-393
W. KIRKCONNELL, 150(DR):AUTUMN70-413
568(SCN):WINTER71-62
POIRIER, R. NORMAN MAILER.
R. GILMAN, 441:17DEC72-6
C. LEHMANN-HAUPT, 441:16OCT72-39
R. MAYNE, 362:6JUL72-21
617(TLS):15SEP72-1045
POIRIER, R. THE PERFORMING SELF.*
G.H. HARTMAN, 31(ASCH):WINTER71/72-
146
617(TLS):4FEB72-127
POIRIER, R. A WORLD ELSEWHERE.*
A.J. CAMERON, 613:SPRING68-133
POIRION, D. LE LEXIQUE DE CHARLES D'OR-
LÉANS DANS LES "BALLADES."
M. BANITT, 545(RPH):MAY71-666
POIRION, D. LE POÈTE ET LE PRINCE.
L.J. FRIEDMAN, 545(RPH):AUG70-230
POIS, R. - SEE ROSENBERG, A.
POIS, R.A. FRIEDRICH MEINECKE AND GERMAN
POLITICS IN THE TWENTIETH CENTURY.
617(TLS):15SEP72-1047
POKROVSKY, M.N. IZBRANNYE PROIZVEDENIIA.
(M.N. TIKHOMIROV & OTHERS, EDS)
R. SZPORLUK, 32:SEP71-649
POKROVSKY [POKROVSKII], M.N. RUSSIA IN
WORLD HISTORY.* (R. SZPORLUK, ED)
W.E. MOSSE, 575(SEER):JUL71-475
J. WATSTEIN, 385(MQR):WINTER72-63
POLANYI, M. KNOWING AND BEING. (M.
GRENE, ED)
A. MANSER, 518:MAY70-21
POLE, J.R. THE SEVENTEENTH CENTURY.
J.C. RAINBOLT, 656(WMQ):APR70-334
POLE, N., ED. ENVIRONMENTAL SOLUTIONS.
617(TLS):16JUN72-697

VON POLENZ, P. FUNKTIONSVERBEN IM HEUTI-
GEN DEUTSCH.
B.F.O. HILDEBRANDT, 353:MAY69-119
POLHEIM, K.K. THEORIE UND KRITIK DER
DEUTSCHEN NOVELLE VON WIELAND BIS
MUSIL.
D. LO CICERO, 406:SPRING71-80
POLHEMUS, R.M. THE CHANGING WORLD OF
ANTHONY TROLLOPE.*
R. AP ROBERTS, 445(NCF):DEC68-355
POLIN, R. ETHIQUE ET POLITIQUE.
J. FREUND, 542:JUL-DEC69-449
POLIŠENSKÝ, J.V. THE THIRTY YEARS WAR.
617(TLS):26MAY72-610
POLISHOOK, I.H. RHODE ISLAND AND THE
UNION: 1774-1795.
P.T. CONLEY, 432(NEQ):DEC70-678
POLITIS, L. HISTORIA TĒS NEAS HELLĒNIKĒS
LOGOTECHNIAS.
C.N. TSIRPANLIS, 121(CJ):APR-MAY71-
364
POLITZER, H. FRANZ GRILLPARZER.
617(TLS):3MAR72-254
POLITZER, R.L. BEITRAG ZUR PHONOLOGIE
DER NONSBERGER MUNDART.*
C.S. LEONARD, JR., 276:SPRING70-104
POLLAK, R. OD RENESANSU DO BAROKU.
Z. FOLEJEWSKI, 32:SEP71-710
POLLAND, M. PACKAGE TO SPAIN.*
N. CALLENDAR, 441:6FEB72-38
POLLARD, G., COMP. CATALOGUE OF [I]
TYPEFOUNDERS' SPECIMENS [II] BOOKS
PRINTED IN FOUNTS OF HISTORIC IMPOR-
TANCE AND [III] WORKS ON TYPEFOUNDING,
PRINTING AND BIBLIOGRAPHY.
617(TLS):22DEC72-1566
POLLARD, G. - SEE "HODSON'S BOOKSELLERS,
PUBLISHERS AND STATIONERS DIRECTORY
1855"
POLLARD, S. & C. HOLMES, EDS. INDUSTRIAL
POWER AND NATIONAL RIVALRY 1870-1914.
617(TLS):26MAY72-613
POLLIN, B.R. DICTIONARY OF NAMES AND
TITLES IN POE'S COLLECTED WORKS.
F. GADO, 597(SN):VOL41#1-196
K.B. HARDER, 424:JUN69-160
S.G.L., 330(MASJ):SPRING69-89
POLLIN, B.R. GODWIN CRITICISM.
D. MC CRACKEN, 405(MP):NOV69-199
POLLINI, F. GLOVER.
M. GREENBERG, 340(KR):SEP66-564
POLLINS, H. BRITAIN'S RAILWAYS.
617(TLS):21APR72-451
POLLITT, J.J. ART AND EXPERIENCE IN CLAS-
SICAL GREECE.
617(TLS):26MAY72-613
POLLOCK, N.C. STUDIES IN EMERGING
AFRICA.
617(TLS):28JAN72-109
POLLOCK, R. LOOPHOLE.
617(TLS):8DEC72-1507
POLNER, M. NO VICTORY PARADES.*
J. MORGAN, 362:2MAR72-283
POLNER, M. WHEN CAN I COME HOME?
E.G. WINDCHY, 561(SATR):22APR72-70
POLOMÉ, E.C., ED. OLD NORSE LITERATURE
AND MYTHOLOGY.
H. BEKKER-NIELSEN, 301(JEGP):APR71-
375
POLOMKA, P. INDONESIA SINCE SUKARNO.
617(TLS):11AUG72-941
PÖLÖSKEI, F. KORMÁNYZATI POLITIKA ÉS
PARLAMENTI ELLENZÉK, 1910-1914.
G. VERMES, 32:SEP71-685
POLUNIN, O., WITH R.S. WRIGHT. THE CON-
CISE FLOWERS OF EUROPE.
617(TLS):3NOV72-1349

POLYBIUS. POLYBE, "HISTOIRES." (BK 1)
(P. PÉDECH, ED & TRANS)
L.H. FELDMAN, 124:DEC70-122
F.W. WALBANK, 123:JUN71-186
POMERANTZ, E. INTO IT.
T. LASK, 441:14JUL72-33
M. LEVIN, 441:28MAY72-16
J.D. O'HARA, 561(SATR):5AUG72-52
POMEROY, W.B. DR. KINSEY AND THE INSTI-
TUTE FOR SEX RESEARCH.
P. BEER, 362:20JUL72-88
E. EDELSON, 440:5MAR72-3
N.G. HALE, JR., 441:26MAR72-4
G. KRUPP, 561(SATR):25MAR72-105
R.R. LINGEMAN, 441:4MAR72-25
P.A. ROBINSON, 61:MAY72-99
POMIAN, J. - SEE RETINGER, J.
POMORSKA, K. RUSSIAN FORMALISM AND ITS
POETIC AMBIANCE.*
R.W., 131(CL):SPRING71-167
POMPELLA, G. - SEE APOLLONIUS
POMPER, P. THE RUSSIAN REVOLUTIONARY
INTELLIGENTSIA.
A. KIMBALL, 32:DEC71-881
PONCE DE LÉON, J.L.S. EL ARTE DE LA
CONVERSACIÓN.
R.J. MIRANDA, 399(MLJ):JAN70-54
PONCEAU, A. ÉTUDES ET TÉMOIGNAGES.
P-M.S., 542:JAN-MAR68-147
PONGE, F. THINGS.* (C. CORMAN, ED &
TRANS)
J. MERRILL, 453:30NOV72-31
PONGE, F. THE VOICE OF THINGS.
J. MERRILL, 453:30NOV72-31
PONGS, H. DAS BILD IN DER DICHTUNG.
(VOL 3)
A. CLOSS, 402(MLR):APR71-454
PONNIAH, S.M. - SEE "SRI PADUKA"
PONS, G. GOTTHOLD EPHRAIM LESSING ET LE
CHRISTIANISME.
H. SCHNEIDER, 462(OL):VOL23#4-320
PONS, M. ROSA.
M. LEVIN, 441:28MAY72-16
DA PONTE, P. - SEE UNDER PERO DA PONTE
PONTUAL, R. DICIONÁRIO DAS ARTES PLÁS-
TICAS NO BRASIL.
E. WENZEL-WHITE, 127:FALL70-110
PONZOA, Á.C. - SEE UNDER CAÍÑAS PONZOA,
Á.
POOLE, H.E. - SEE BURNEY, C.
POOLE, R. TOWARDS DEEP SUBJECTIVITY.
D. CRAIG, 362:6JUL72-20
617(TLS):23JUN72-709
POOR, H.L. KURT TUCHOLSKY AND THE ORDEAL
OF GERMANY, 1914-1935.
R. HANSER, 19(AGR):VOL35#2-34
POOR, R., ED. 4 DAYS, 40 HOURS.
617(TLS):6OCT72-1202
POPE, A. SELECTED POEMS OF ALEXANDER
POPE. (J. HEATH-STUBBS, ED)
C.T.P., 566:AUTUMN70-6
POPE, A. THE SELECTED POETRY OF POPE.
(M. PRICE, ED)
566:AUTUMN70-29
POPE, D. THE GREAT GAMBLE.
617(TLS):1SEP72-1018
POPE, H., JR. VOICES FROM THE DRUG CUL-
TURE.
617(TLS):1SEP72-1012
POPE, J.A. & OTHERS. THE FREER CHINESE
BRONZES. (VOL 1)
I. MC LACHLAN, 302:JAN70-250
POPE, J.C. THE RHYTHM OF "BEOWULF."
R. FOWLER, 38:BAND87HEFT3/4-444
POPE, J.C. - SEE AELFRIC
POPE, R.G. THE HALF-WAY COVENANT.*
B.R. BURG, 432(NEQ):SEP70-500

POPE, W.H. THE ELEPHANT AND THE MOUSE.
B.W. HODGINS, 99:JAN-FEB72-69
POPE-HENNESSY, J. ESSAYS ON ITALIAN
SCULPTURE.*
A. NEUMEYER, 290(JAAC):SPRING70-397
POPE-HENNESSY, J. ITALIAN RENAISSANCE
SCULPTURE. (REV)
617(TLS):31MAR72-368
POPE-HENNESSY, J. & A.J. RADCLIFFE. THE
FRICK COLLECTION.* (VOL 3)
D. PIPER, 676(YR):SPRING71-453
POPE-HENNESSY, J., A.J. RADCLIFFE &
T.W.I. HODGKINSON. THE FRICK COLLEC-
TION.* (VOL 4)
D. PIPER, 676(YR):SPRING71-453
POPE HENNESSY, J. ANTHONY TROLLOPE.*
L. AUCHINCLOSS, 441:21MAY72-49
W.H. AUDEN, 442(NY):1APR72-102
L. EDEL, 561(SATR):8JUL72-59
T. LASK, 441:31MAR72-26
V.S. PRITCHETT, 61:MAY72-94
P. THEROUX, 440:2APR72-6
POPIVANOV, I. TVORTCHESKI PATICHTA.
N. DONTCHEV, 270:VOL20#2-36
POPOFF, G. ICH SAH DIE REVOLUTIONÄRE.
Z.A.B. ZEMAN, 587:JUL69-113
POPOVITCH, O. CATALOGUE DES PEINTURES DU
MUSÉE DES BEAUX-ARTS DE ROUEN.
J. DE CASO, 90:DEC69-767
POPPER, F. ORIGINS AND DEVELOPMENT OF
KINETIC ART.
J. BENTHALL, 592:MAR69-148
J. DANIELS, 39:DEC69-547
POPPER, K. OBJECTIVE KNOWLEDGE.
A. MACINTYRE, 362:14DEC72-835
POPPERWELL, R.G. NORWAY.
617(TLS):24NOV72-1423
POPPERWELL, R.G., ED. THE YEAR'S WORK IN
MODERN LANGUAGE STUDIES. (VOL 31,
1969)
S. ULLMANN, 208(FS):JUL71-357
POPPI, A. SAGGI SUL PENSIERO INEDITO DI
PIETRO POMPONAZZI.
A.A. DE GENNARO, 319:JAN72-88
POPS, M.L. THE MELVILLE ARCHETYPE.
J. SEELYE, 27(AL):MAY71-290
617(TLS):21JAN72-53
PORCHIA, A. VOICES.*
W. HUNT, 491:MAY72-113
PORETSKY, E.K. OUR OWN PEOPLE.
P.W. BLACKSTOCK, 550(RUSR):OCT70-481
R.F. STAAR, 32:DEC71-894
PÖRNBACHER, K. - SEE "FRANZ GRILLPARZER"
"PORNOGRAPHY: THE LONGFORD REPORT."
R. DWORKIN, 362:28SEP72-389
617(TLS):22SEP72-1083
PORQUERAS MAYO, A. EL PRÓLOGO EN EL
MANIERISMO Y BARROCO ESPAÑOLES.
R. HESS, 72:BAND208HEFT4/6-446
PORSET, C. - SEE ROUSSEAU, J-J.
PORTA, A. METROPOLIS.
617(TLS):11FEB72-146
PORTAL, E. KILLING GROUND.
G. ROPER, 627(UTQ):JUL69-361
PORTAL, R. RUSSES ET UKRAINIENS.
R. SERBYN, 104:FALL71-430
PORTAL, R. THE SLAVS.* (FRENCH TITLE:
LES SLAVES.)
N. ANDREYEV, 587:JAN70-384
N.V. RIASANOVSKY, 32:JUN71-378
639(VQR):SUMMER70-CXI
PORTCHMOUTH, J. SECONDARY SCHOOL ART.
617(TLS):30JUN72-757
PORTE, J. EMERSON AND THOREAU.
C. CROWE, 219(GAR):SPRING69-84
PORTE, J. THE ROMANCE IN AMERICA.
L. BUELL, 432(NEQ):JUN70-331
H.H. CLARK, 27(AL):MAY71-310

PORTEN, B. ARCHIVES FROM ELEPHANTINE.
J. TEIXIDOR, 318(JAOS):OCT-DEC70-543
PORTER, B., ED. THE ABERYSTWYTH PAPERS.
617(TLS):8DEC72-1476
PORTER, B. CRITICS OF EMPIRE.
J. BUTLER, 637(VS):JUN70-419
PORTER, C.A. RESTIF'S NOVELS, OR AN
AUTOBIOGRAPHY IN SEARCH OF AN AUTHOR.
E. KERN, 546(RR):OCT70-226
PORTER, D.B., COMP. THE NEGRO IN THE
UNITED STATES.
A.P. MARSHALL, 356:APR71-176
PORTER, E.W. TRINITY AND DUKE, 1892 TO
1924.
F. REDENBACHER, 182:VOL23#1/2-2
PORTER, J. A MEDDLER AND HER MURDER.
617(TLS):14APR72-427
PORTER, P. THE LAST OF ENGLAND.*
C. KIZER, 491:FEB72-291
M. SCHMIDT, 491:JUN72-170
J. SMITH, 493:WINTER70/71-363
PORTER, P., ED. NEW POEMS 1971-1972.
617(TLS):11AUG72-934
PORTER, P. PREACHING TO THE CONVERTED.
AFTER MARTIAL.
617(TLS):3NOV72-1304
PORTER, T.E. MYTH AND MODERN AMERICAN
DRAMA.*
R. COHN, 397(MD):DEC69-319
G.E. WELLWARTH, 149:SEP71-276
PORTOGHESI, P. ROMA BAROCCA.*
R. KRAUTHEIMER, 676(YR):SUMMER71-593
PORTOGHESI, P. THE ROME OF BORROMINI.
P. ZUCKER, 290(JAAC):SPRING70-406
PORTOGHESI, P. BERNARDO VITTONE.
A.A. TAIT, 90:FEB69-97
PORTUGAL, M.A.D. IL DUCA DI FOIX; ABER-
TURA. (M. DE SAMPAYO RIBEIRO, ED)
R. STEVENSON, 414(MQ):JAN68-111
PORY, J. PROCEEDINGS OF THE GENERAL
ASSEMBLY OF VIRGINIA: JULY 30-AUGUST 4,
1619. (W.J. VAN SCHREEVEN & G.H.
REESE, EDS)
J.A.L. LEMAY, 568(SCN):SPRING71-18
POSCH, S. BEOBACHTUNGEN ZUR THEOKRIT-
NACHWIRKUNG BEI VERGIL.*
E. JENKINSON, 313:VOL60-266
POSENER, J. FROM SCHINKEL TO THE BAU-
HAUS.
617(TLS):15SEP72-1044
POSGATE, H.B. MADAME DE STAËL.
C.C., 191(ELN):SEP70(SUPP)-82
"POSITIONS DE THÈSES DE TROISIÈME CYCLE
SOUTENUES DEVANT LA FACULTÉ EN 1967."
J. DECREUS, 208(FS):JUL71-367
"POSITIONS DES THÈSES DE TROISIÈME CYCLE
SOUTENUES DEVANT LA FACULTÉ EN 1968."
J. DECREUS, 208(FS):OCT71-500
POSNER, D. ANNIBALE CARRACCI.
617(TLS):22SEP72-1103
POSNER, R. - SEE IORDAN, I. & J. ORR
VAN DER POST, L. AFRICAN COOKING.
N. MAGID, 440:20FEB72-6
VAN DER POST, L. THE PRISONER AND THE
BOMB.*
R.A. MILLER, 676(YR):SUMMER71-576
VAN DER POST, L. A STORY LIKE THE WIND.
D.A.N. JONES, 362:31AUG72-280
M. LEVIN, 441:22OCT72-46
617(TLS):9JUN72-650
POSTER, C.D. THE SCHOOL AND THE COMMUN-
ITY.
617(TLS):4FEB72-138
POSTGATE, R. & G.P. WELLS - SEE WELLS,
H.G.
POSTMAN, N. & C. WEINGARTNER. LINGUIS-
TICS.
G.W. HASLAM, 186(ETC.):DEC69-488

POSTON, L. & OTHERS. CONTINUING SPANISH I AND II.
J.E. MC KINNEY, 238:MAR70-170
POTASH, R.A. THE ARMY & POLITICS IN ARGENTINA, 1928-1945.
W.H. JEFFREY, 263:JUL-SEP71-336
POTICHNYJ, P.J. - SEE MAZLAKH, S. & V. SHAKHRAI
POTOK, C. MY NAME IS ASHER LEV.
G. DAVENPORT, 441:16APR72-5
D. JOHNSON, 440:7MAY72-8
T. LASK, 441:21APR72-41
R.J. MILCH, 561(SATR):15APR72-65
442(NY):27MAY72-114
617(TLS):6OCT72-1184
POTTER, E.B. THE NAVAL ACADEMY ILLUSTRATED HISTORY OF THE UNITED STATES NAVY.
F.J. ANDERSON, 70(ANQ):DEC71-61
POTTER, J. GOING WEST.
617(TLS):10NOV72-1375
POTTIER, B. LINGÜÍSTICA MODERNA Y FILOLOGIA HISPÁNICA.
T. MONTGOMERY, 545(RPH):FEB71-513
POTTIER, B. PRÉSENTATION DE LA LINGUISTIQUE.
R.W. NEWMAN, 207(FR):MAY70-953
POTTINGER, G. MUIRFIELD AND THE HONOURABLE COMPANY.
617(TLS):2JUN72-639
POTTS, L.J. - SEE ARISTOTLE
POUGIN, A. - SEE CLÉMENT, F. & P. LAROUSSE
POUILLIART, R. LE ROMANTISME III 1869-1896.*
R. SWITZER, 399(MLJ):APR70-280
POULET, G. MESURE DE L'INSTANT.
P. DE MAN, 98:JUL69-608
A.J. STEELE, 208(FS):JUL71-364
POULET, G. METAMORPHOSEN DES KREISES IN DER DICHTUNG.
F. SCHALK, 52:BAND4HEFT1-105
POULIN, G. LES MIROIRS D'UN POÈTE.
R. FINCH, 627(UTQ):JUL70-359
POULLE, E. LA BIBLIOTHÈQUE SCIENTIFIQUE D'UN IMPRIMEUR HUMANISTE AU XVE SIÈCLE.
A. RODRÍGUEZ-MOÑINO, 545(RPH):NOV70-371
POULTON, D. JOHN DOWLAND.
D. ARNOLD, 362:15JUN72-796
617(TLS):27OCT72-1293
POULTON, R. THE PAPER TYRANT.
D. MYERS, 99:JUN72-36
POUND, E. THE CANTOS.
G. BURNS, 584(SWR):SPRING71-207
POUND, E. DRAFTS AND FRAGMENTS OF CANTOS CX-CXVII.*
D. BARBOUR, 529(QQ):AUTUMN70-470
J. SCHWARTZ, 590:SUMMER70-42
"POVERTY IN CANADA."
P. GRADY, 99:MAY72-12
POWELL, A. BOOKS DO FURNISH A ROOM.*
P. BAILEY, 364:AUG/SEP71-147
F.P.W. MC DOWELL, 659:SUMMER72-361
POWELL, A. TWO PLAYS.
A. BROYARD, 441:17FEB72-39
POWELL, E. STILL TO DECIDE.
J. VAIZEY, 362:27JUL72-115
POWELL, H. - SEE GRYPHIUS, A.
POWELL, J.E. & K. WALLIS. THE HOUSE OF LORDS IN THE MIDDLE AGES.
R. VIRGOE, 325:APR70-69
POWELL, J.R. ROBERT BLAKE.
617(TLS):1SEP72-1018
POWELL, M. MARGARET POWELL'S LONDON SEASON.
617(TLS):7JAN72-21

POWELL, W.S. THE NORTH CAROLINA GAZETTEER.
B.H. GRANGER, 424:DEC69-312
POWER, P. THIS DEADLY GRIEF.
N. CALLENDAR, 441:12MAR72-40
H. FRANKEL, 561(SATR):26FEB72-71
POWERS, D.B. DICTIONARY OF IRREGULAR RUSSIAN VERB FORMS.*
M. KANTOR, 399(MLJ):FEB70-140
POWERS, E. & J. WITT. TRAVELING WEATHERWISE IN THE U.S.A.
561(SATR):7OCT72-101
POWLEY, E.B. THE NAVAL SIDE OF KING WILLIAM'S WAR.
617(TLS):25AUG72-1001
POWYS, J.C. LETTERS TO NICHOLAS ROSS. (N. & A. ROSS, COMPS; A. UPHILL, ED)
617(TLS):24MAR72-328
POWYS, T.F. COME TO DINE [AND] TADNOL. (P. RILEY, ED)
F.G.F., 503:WINTER68-184
POYATOS, F. ESPAÑA POR DENTRO.
H.L. DOWDLE, 238:MAR70-174
POYER, J. THE BALKAN ASSIGNMENT.
N. CALLENDAR, 441:16JAN72-42
POYER, J. THE CHINESE AGENDA.
N. CALLENDAR, 441:26NOV72-36
POZO, C. FUENTES PARA LA HISTORIA DEL MÉTODO TEOLÓGICO EN LA ESCUELA DE SALAMANCA. (VOL 1)
E. BENZ, 182:VOL23#10-528
POZZA, N. LA PUTINA GRECA E ALTRE STORIE.
617(TLS):22SEP72-1086
POZZOLINI, A. ANTONIO GRAMSCI.
617(TLS):28APR72-493
PRADEL, H. & OTHERS. L'EUROPE GOTHIQUE (XIIE-XIVE SIÈCLES).
P. GUERRE, 98:MAR69-265
PRADO, C., JR. THE COLONIAL BACKGROUND OF BRAZIL.
H. BERNSTEIN, 37:APR69-38
PRANG, H., ED. BEGRIFFSBESTIMMUNG DER ROMANTIK.
I.C., 191(ELN):SEP70(SUPP)-95
L.R. FURST, 220(GL&L):APR71-284
V. LO CICERO, 221(GQ):MAY70-512
PRANINSKAS, J. TRADE NAME CREATION.
G.N. LEECH, 361:VOL24#1-53
PRASAD, B., ED. IDEAS IN HISTORY.
T.W. SIMONS, 293(JAST):AUG70-954
PRATER, D.A. EUROPEAN OF YESTERDAY.
617(TLS):28APR72-468
PRATO, C. - SEE TYRTAEUS
PRATT, A. DYLAN THOMAS' EARLY PROSE.*
J. KORG, 651(WHR):WINTER71-90
PRATT, P. HISTORY OF JAPAN. (M. PASKESMITH, ED)
617(TLS):13OCT72-1232
PRAWER, S., ED. THE ROMANTIC PERIOD IN GERMANY.
E.A. BLACKALL, 406:FALL71-304
E. SCHWARZ, 301(JEGP):OCT71-728
PRAWY, M. THE VIENNA OPERA.*
M.C., 410(M&L):APR71-180
"THE PRAYER OF THE CHURCH."
617(TLS):14APR72-426
PRAZ, M. CALEIDOSCOPIO SHAKESPEARIANO.
617(TLS):7JAN72-14
PRAZ, M. CONVERSATION PIECES.
617(TLS):7JAN72-13
PRAZ, M. MNEMOSYNE.
F.A. AMES-LEWIS, 89(BJA):WINTER71-103
R.J. BAUER, 568(SCN):SPRING71-15
J.H. HAGSTRUM, 191(ELN):JUN71-308
R.A. SMITH, 149:SEP71-266
617(TLS):7JAN72-13

PRAZ, M. ON NEO-CLASSICISM.
N. PEVSNER, 46:DEC69-482
F.J.B. WATSON, 39:MAY69-402
PRCELA, J. & S. GULDESCU, EDS. OPERATION
SLAUGHTERHOUSE.
M. MESTROVIC, 32:JUN71-413
PREBBLE, J. THE DARIEN DISASTER.
G.M. WALLER, 656(WMQ):JUL70-516
PREDMORE, R.L. THE WORLD OF DON QUIXOTE.
P.M.L., 240(HR):APR70-240
H. SIEBER, 400(MLN):MAR70-304
PRELLER, V. DIVINE SCIENCE AND THE
SCIENCE OF GOD.
A.W. WOOD, 482(PHR):APR70-279
PREMCHAND. THE GIFT OF A COW. (G.C.
ROADARMEL, TRANS)
L. ROCHER, 293(JAST):NOV69-196
PRESCOTT, O. LORDS OF ITALY.
441:8OCT72-38
PRESCOTT, P.S. SOUNDINGS.
G. STADE, 441:16JUL72-22
"PRESERVING AND RESTORING MONUMENTS AND
HISTORIC BUILDINGS."
617(TLS):13OCT72-1236
PRESS, L. BUDOWNICTWO EGEJSKIE.
R. HEIDENREICH, 182:VOL23#4-175
PRESSAT, R. DEMOGRAPHIC ANALYSIS.
617(TLS):29DEC72-1585
"DER PRESSE DER ARBEITERKLASSE UND DER
SOZIALEN BEWEGUNGEN."
R.J. BAZILLION, 104(WINTER71-551
PREST, J. LORD JOHN RUSSELL.
617(TLS):7JUL72-766
PREST, W.R. THE INNS OF COURT UNDER
ELIZABETH I AND THE EARLY STUARTS 1590-
1640.
617(TLS):28JUL72-898
PRESTIPINO, G. LAVORO E CONOSCENZA
NELL'ARTE.*
M. RIESER, 290(JAAC):SPRING70-396
PRESTON, A. & J. MAJOR. SEND A GUNBOAT!
W.D. MC INTYRE, 637(VS):JUN70-455
PRETO-RODAS, R.A. NEGRITUDE AS A THEME
IN THE POETRY OF THE PORTUGUESE-SPEAK-
ING WORLD.
J. PARKER, 86(BHS):OCT71-369
PRETZEL, U. & W. BACHOFER, EDS. BIBLIO-
GRAPHIE ZU WOLFRAM VON ESCHENBACH.
(2ND ED)
E.S. FIRCHOW, 406:SPRING71-71
S.M. JOHNSON, 221(GQ):MAR70-264
C. LOFMARK, 220(GL&L):APR71-274
PREVIN, A. & A. HOPKINS. MUSIC FACE TO
FACE.
617(TLS):14JAN72-36
PREVITALI, G. GIOTTO.
J. WHITE, 90:FEB70-114
PRICE, A. THE ALAMUT AMBUSH.*
N. CALLENDAR, 441:30JUL72-22
442(NY):23SEP72-135
PRICE, A. COLONEL BUTLER'S WOLF.
617(TLS):7JUL72-783
PRICE, G.R. THOMAS DEKKER.
M. LAWLIS, 551(RENQ):WINTER70-480
PRICE, H.H. BELIEF.
A. FLEW, 393(MIND):JUL70-454
PRICE, H.H. ESSAYS IN THE PHILOSOPHY OF
RELIGION.
617(TLS):20OCT72-1261
PRICE, J.G. THE UNFORTUNATE COMEDY.
W.W. APPLETON, 551(RENQ):SUMMER70-202
R.L. SMALLWOOD, 541(RES):MAY70-198
M. TAYLOR, 255(HAB):WINTER69-79
PRICE, M., ED. DICKENS: A COLLECTION OF
CRITICAL ESSAYS.*
E. ROSENBERG, 155:SEP69-187
PRICE, M. - SEE POPE, A.

PRICE, R. THE FRENCH SECOND REPUBLIC.
617(TLS):26MAY72-610
PRICE, R. THE HOWLING ARCTIC.
J.S. ERSKINE, 150(DR):AUTUMN70-419
PRICE, R. PERMANENT ERRORS.*
P. CRUTTWELL, 249(HUDR):SPRING71-177
PRICE, R. THINGS THEMSELVES.
S.G. NICHOLS, JR., 561(SATR):10JUN72-
62
M. WOOD, 441:18JUN72-2
PRICE, R.F. EDUCATION IN COMMUNIST
CHINA.
J. HENNINGSEN, 182:VOL23#23/24-973
PRICKETT, S. COLERIDGE AND WORDSWORTH.
J. COLMER, 402(MLR):APR71-399
J. STILLINGER, 301(JEGP):JAN71-166
PRICOCO, S. PER UNA NUOVA EDIZIONE DEL
"DE CONTEMPTU MUNDI" DI EUCHERIO DI
LIONE.
P. LANGLOIS, 555:VOL44FASC2-354
PRICOCO, S. - SEE EUCHERII
PRIESTLAND, G. FRYING TONIGHT.
C. DRIVER, 362:2NOV72-609
PRIESTLEY, J.B. OVER THE LONG HIGH WALL.
617(TLS):29SEP72-1147
PRIESTLEY, J.B. VICTORIA'S HEYDAY.
P. ADAMS, 61:AUG72-92
N. ANNAN, 453:30NOV72-12
P. STANSKY, 561(SATR):12AUG72-50
617(TLS):9JUN72-652
"PRIMERA CONFERENCIA INTERAMERICANA DE
ETNOMUSICOLOGÍA."
L.B. SPIESS, 650(WF):JAN69-64
PRIMMER, A. CICERO NUMEROSUS.
G. KENNEDY, 124:JAN71-166
PRINCE, F.T. MEMOIRS IN OXFORD.
L. CLARK, 493:WINTER70/71-370
C. KIZER, 491:FEB72-291
PRINCE, P. PLAY THINGS.
J.G. FARRELL, 362:7SEP72-312
617(TLS):22SEP72-1122
PRINGLE, J.D. ON SECOND THOUGHTS.
617(TLS):16JUN72-690
PRINS, A.A. A SYNOPSIS OF THE HISTORY OF
ENGLISH TONIC VOWELS.
E.J. DOBSON, 597(SN):VOL41#1-213
PRIOR, A.N. OBJECTS OF THOUGHT. (P.T.
GEACH & A.J.P. KENNY, EDS)
R.D. GALLIE, 518:OCT71-22
PRIOR, A.N. PAST, PRESENT AND FUTURE.*
L.J. COHEN, 479(PHQ):JAN70-83
PRIOR, M. THE LITERARY WORKS OF MATTHEW
PRIOR. (H.B. WRIGHT & M.K. SPEARS,
EDS)
617(TLS):5MAY72-528
PRIP-MØLLER, J. CHINESE BUDDHIST MONAS-
TERIES.
A.C. SOPER, 57:VOL31#1-87
PRISCHEPENKO, N.P. RUSSIAN-ENGLISH LAW
DICTIONARY.
G.G. MORGAN, 32:MAR71-169
PRITCHARD, J.B., ED. THE ANCIENT NEAR
EAST.
W.W. HALLO, 318(JAOS):OCT-DEC70-525
PRITCHARD, W. WYNDHAM LEWIS.
617(TLS):7APR72-386
PRITCHETT, V.S. MIDNIGHT OIL.*
A. ALVAREZ, 561(SATR):6MAY72-67
C. LEHMANN-HAUPT, 441:3MAY72-49
W. MAXWELL, 442(NY):17JUN72-94
K. MILLER, 453:20JUL72-12
W. SHEED, 441:30APR72-3
J. STAFFORD, 440:30APR72-1
E. WEEKS, 61:JUN72-108
PRITCHETT, W.K. STUDIES IN ANCIENT
GREEK TOPOGRAPHY.* (PT 2)
D.J. GEAGAN, 24:APR71-365

PRITT, D.N. LAW AND POLITICS AND LAW IN
THE COLONIES.
617(TLS):25FEB72-229
PRITTIE, T. KONRAD ADENAUER 1876-1967.
617(TLS):3MAR72-236
PRITTIE, T. ESHKOL.
Y. GOELL, 390:AUG/SEP69-73
PRÒ, D.F. RODOLFO MONDOLFO.* (VOL 1)
A. GRILLI, 548(RCSF):JAN/MAR69-117
"THE PROBLEM OF CHEMICAL AND BIOLOGICAL
WARFARE." (VOLS 1, 4 & 5)
617(TLS):3MAR72-235
"PROBLÈMES THÉORIQUES ACTUELS DE LA
TRADUCTION LITTÉRAIRE."
A. STRATONOVITCH, 75:1/1969-60
"PROBLEMI GUARDESCHI."
F.J.B. WATSON, 39:JUL69-79
"PROCEEDINGS OF THE ROYAL MUSICAL ASSO-
CIATION." (96TH SESSION, 1969-70)
M.T., 410(M&L):APR71-185
PROCHNAU, W.W. & R.W. LARSEN. A CERTAIN
DEMOCRAT.
L.W. KOENIG, 561(SATR):3JUN72-62
R.R. LINGEMAN, 441:4JUN72-1
PROCLUS. A COMMENTARY ON THE FIRST BOOK
OF EUCLID'S "ELEMENTS." (G.R. MORROW,
TRANS)
J.E. REXINE, 124:MAR71-236
PROCLUS. THÉOLOGIE PLATONICIENNE.* (BK
1) (H.D. SAFFREY & L.G. WESTERINK, EDS
& TRANS)
E.R. DODDS, 303:VOL90-241
É. DES PLACES, 555:VOL44FASC1-139
R.T. WALLIS, 123:DEC70-324
PROCTOR, A.P. SCULPTOR IN BUCKSKIN.
W. GARD, 584(SWR):AUTUMN71-VI
PROCTOR, T. DOSTOEVSKIJ AND THE BELIN-
SKIJ SCHOOL OF LITERARY CRITICISM.*
K.B. FEUER, 550(RUSR):JUL70-347
T. PACHMUSS, 32:MAR71-204
"ANATAŌ DE PROENÇA'S TAMIL-PORTUGUESE
DICTIONARY, A.D. 1679." (X.S. THANI
NAYAGAM, ED)
M.W.S. DE SILVA, 353:APR69-125
PROETZ, V. THE ASTONISHMENT OF WORDS.
B.H. SMEATON, 70(ANQ):OCT71-29
PROFFER, C.R. KEYS TO "LOLITA."
B. LEE, 447(N&Q):DEC70-479
PROFFER, C.R. - SEE PUSHKIN, A.S.
PROFFER, E. - SEE BULGAKOV, M.
PROFFER, E. & C.R. - SEE BULGAKOV, M.
PROFITLICH, W. EITELKEIT.
D. BERGER, 406:SPRING71-63
PROKOSCH, F. AMERICA, MY WILDERNESS.
P. ADAMS, 61:MAY72-112
A. HISLOP, 440:21MAY72-5
442(NY):10JUN72-130
617(TLS):13OCT72-1235
PROKOSCH, F. THE MISSOLONGHI MANUSCRIPT.
E.E.B., 191(ELN):SEP69(SUPP)-30
PROKUSHEV, Y.L., ED. SERGEY YESENIN.
G. MC VAY, 575(SEER):JAN71-145
PROMIES, W. - SEE LICHTENBERG, G.C.
PRONKO, L.C. THEATER EAST AND WEST.*
C. TUNG, 397(MD):MAY68-109
R.J.J. WARGO, 485(PE&W):JAN69-94
PRONZINI, B. PANIC!
N. CALLENDAR, 441:15OCT72-42
PRONZINI, B. THE SNATCH.*
N. CALLENDAR, 441:9JAN72-33
"PROPOSALS FOR TAX REFORM." [GOVERNMENT
OF CANADA]
A. DEUTSCH, 529(QQ):SPRING70-104
PROSKE, B.G. JUAN MARTÍNEZ MONTAÑÉS,
SEVILLIAN SCULPTOR.*
E. HARRIS, 90:APR69-228
H.E. WETHEY, 54:DEC69-399

PROSSER, E. HAMLET AND REVENGE.
P.N. SIEGEL, 402(MLR):JUL71-661
J. WEY, 613:SUMMER68-297
G.W. WILLIAMS, 570(SQ):AUTUMN69-475
PROU, S. THE YELLOW SUMMER.
442(NY):13MAY72-146
PROUDFIT, C.L. - SEE LANDOR, W.S.
PROUST, J. L'ENCYCLOPÉDISME DANS LE BAS-
LANGUEDOC AU XVIIIE SIÈCLE.
J. LOUGH, 208(FS):APR71-206
PROUST, M. TEXTES RETROUVÉS.* (P. KOLB
& L.B. PRICE, EDS)
M. MULLER, 207(FR):OCT69-173
W.A. STRAUSS, 399(MLJ):MAY70-379
"PROXIMA THULE."
J. WERNER, 182:VOL23#1/2-39
PRUCHA, F.P. THE SWORD OF THE REPUBLIC.
R.C. KNOPF, 656(WMQ):JAN70-173
PRÜCKNER, H. DIE LOKRISCHEN TONRELIEFS.*
J. BOARDMAN, 123:MAR71-144
PRUDHOMMEAU, G. LA DANSE GRECQUE
ANTIQUE.
F. BROMMER, 182:VOL23#6-300
PRUETT, J.W., ED. STUDIES IN MUSICOL-
OGY.*
D. ARNOLD, 415:FEB70-162
PRŮŠEK, J. THE ORIGINS AND THE AUTHORS
OF THE HUA-PEN.
J. CRUMP, 293(JAST):NOV69-162
PRYBYLA, J.S., ED. COMMUNISM AT THE
CROSSROADS.
J.H. HODGSON, 550(RUSR):JAN70-111
PRYCE-JONES, D. THE FACE OF DEFEAT.
617(TLS):1DEC72-1447
PRYCE-JONES, D. THE HUNGARIAN REVOLU-
TION.
P. KECSKEMETI, 32:SEP71-687
PRYDE, D. NUNAGA.
A. BROYARD, 441:4MAY72-47
E. WEEKS, 61:MAY72-108
PRYKE, R. PUBLIC ENTERPRISE IN PRACTICE.
617(TLS):2JUN72-637
PUCCETTI, R. PERSONS.
E. HINDESS, 518:JAN70-24
PUCCINI, D. SOR JUANA INÉS DE LA CRUZ.
I.A. LEONARD, 240(HR):APR70-225
PUDNEY, J. SPANDRELS.
W.P.T., 619(TC):1968/4&1969/1-90
PUGH, B. THE COUNTRY OF MY HEART.
617(TLS):22SEP72-1124
PUGH, M. A MURMUR OF MUTINY.
D-A.N. JONES, 362:16MAR72-348
PUGH, R.B. IMPRISONMENT IN MEDIEVAL
ENGLAND.*
H.M. WALTON, 325:OCT69-583
PUGH, T.B., ED. GLAMORGAN COUNTY HIS-
TORY. (VOL 3)
617(TLS):21APR72-451
PUIG, M. BETRAYED BY RITA HAYWORTH.*
M. WOOD, 453:6APR72-25
J. YGLESIAS, 61:AUG72-85
PUKUI, M.K. & S.H. ELBERT. PLACE NAMES
OF HAWAII.
K.B. HARDER, 424:MAR68-63
PULLAN, B. RICH AND POOR IN RENAISSANCE
VENICE.*
J. HALE, 362:27JUL72-106
PUNDEFF, M., ED. HISTORY IN THE USSR.
G. ENTEEN, 587:APR69-547
PUPI, A. LA FORMAZIONE DELLA FILOSOFIA
DI K.L. REINHOLD.
C. CESA, 548(RCSF):JUL-SEP68-361
PURCELL, H. THE FAIRY QUEEN. (B. BRIT-
TEN & I. HOLST, EDS)
H.R., 412:NOV71-365
PURCELL, J.F. THE ISSUE OF THE BISHOP'S
BLOOD.
N. CALLENDAR, 441:23APR72-43

PURCELL, S. THE HOLLY QUEEN.
617(TLS):29SEP72-1146
PURCELL, W. PORTRAIT OF SOPER.
617(TLS):8DEC72-1482
PURDY, A. SELECTED POEMS.
M. KEYES, 99:JUN72-42
J. SHERMAN, 198:SUMMER72-118
PURDY, A., ED. STORM WARNING.
G. WOODCOCK, 102(CANL):AUTUMN71-5
PURDY, A.W. LOVE IN A BURNING BUILDING.
M. ATWOOD, 102(CANL):SUMMER71-71
PURDY, A.W. WILD GRAPE WINE.*
H. MAC CALLUM, 627(UTQ):JUL69-342
PURDY, J. I AM ELIJAH THRUSH.
L. GRAVER, 441:2JUL72-7
J. HUNTER, 362:19OCT72-513
K. MEEHAN, 561(SATR):10JUN72-68
442(NY):27MAY72-114
617(TLS):3NOV72-1305
"KEN PURDY'S BOOK OF AUTOMOBILES."
J. DURSO, 441:3DEC72-7
VON PÜRKEL, J.U-S. - SEE UNDER UNGERN-
STERNBERG VON PÜRKEL, J.
PURKIS, I.E. & U.F. MATTHEWS, EDS. MEDI-
CINE IN THE UNIVERSITY AND COMMUNITY
OF THE FUTURE.
C.L. BENNET, 150(DR):SUMMER70-289
PUSHKAREV, S.G., COMP. DICTIONARY OF
RUSSIAN HISTORICAL TERMS FROM THE
ELEVENTH CENTURY TO 1917. (G. VERNAD-
SKY & R.T. FISHER, JR., EDS)
C.B. O'BRIEN, 550(RUSR):OCT70-481
W.F. RYAN, 575(SEER):APR71-281
M. SZEFTEL, 32:MAR71-134
PUSHKIN, A.S. THE CRITICAL PROSE OF
ALEXANDER PUSHKIN.* (C.R. PROFFER, ED
& TRANS)
R. GREGG, 32:MAR71-203
L.G. LEIGHTON, 104(SPRING71-120
PUSHKIN, A.S. THE LETTERS OF ALEXANDER
PUSHKIN. (J.T. SHAW, ED & TRANS)
H. GIFFORD, 447(N&Q):MAY70-194
PUSHKIN, A.S. PUSHKIN THREEFOLD. (W.
ARNDT, ED & TRANS)
617(TLS):1DEC72-1463
PUTNAM, C. FLOWERS AND TREES OF TUDOR
ENGLAND.
617(TLS):20OCT72-1264
PUTNAM, J.J. JAMES JACKSON PUTNAM AND
PSYCHOANALYSIS. (N.G. HALE, JR., ED)
617(TLS):8DEC72-1484
PUTNAM, M.C.J. VIRGIL'S PASTORAL ART.
G. LAWALL, 124:JAN71-166
639(VQR):AUTUMN70-CXL
PUTTENHAM, G. THE ARTE OF ENGLISH
POESIE. (A. WALKER & G. WILLCOCK, EDS)
B. VICKERS, 148:WINTER70-382
PUTTER, I. LA DERNIÈRE ILLUSION DE
LECONTE DE LISLE.
A. HARMS, 399(MLJ):JAN70-40
PUZO, M. THE GODFATHER.
W. SHEED, 453:20JUL72-23
PUZO, M. THE GODFATHER PAPERS AND OTHER
CONFESSIONS.
R. LASSON, 440:9APR72-5
617(TLS):13OCT72-1214
PY, A. - SEE RIMBAUD, A.
PYE, D. THE NATURE AND ART OF WORKMAN-
SHIP.
J. GLOAG, 46:MAY69-388
J. MASHECK, 592:JUL/AUG68-56
PYKE, M. TECHNOLOGICAL EATING.
617(TLS):26MAY72-609
PYLE, F. "THE WINTER'S TALE."
E. SCHANZER, 541(RES):MAY70-200
PYMAN, A. - SEE BLOK, A.

PYRITZ, H., H. NICOLAI & G. BURKHARDT,
EDS. GOETHE-BIBLIOGRAPHIE.* (VOL 2)
D.W. SCHUMANN, 301(JEGP):APR71-359

QUAMMEN, D. TO WALK THE LINE.
M. MUDRICK, 249(HUDR):SPRING71-185
QUARLES, B. BLACK ABOLITIONISTS.
639(VQR):SPRING70-LXX
QUARMBY, E. BANKNOTES AND BANKING IN THE
ISLE OF MAN 1788-1970.
617(TLS):22SEP72-1124
QUARTERMAIN, J. ROCK OF DIAMONDS.
O.L. BAILEY, 561(SATR):25NOV72-70
N. CALLENDAR, 441:24SEP72-41
617(TLS):26MAY72-612
QUAYLE, E. R.M. BALLANTYNE.
R. STOKES, 503:WINTER68-189
QUAYLE, E. THE COLLECTOR'S BOOK OF
CHILDREN'S BOOKS.*
617(TLS):28APR72-473
QUAYLE, E. THE RUIN OF SIR WALTER SCOTT.
K.C., 191(ELN):SEP70(SUPP)-42
"ELLERY QUEEN'S MYSTERY BAG."
O.L. BAILEY, 561(SATR):26AUG72-62
QUELCH, E. PERFECT DARLING.
V.G. KIERNAN, 362:7DEC72-803
QUELLET, H. LES DÉRIVÉS LATINS EN "-OR."
J.W. POULTNEY, 24:JUL71-491
QUEMADA, B., ED. P. CORNEILLE, "POLY-
EUCTE:" CONCORDANCES, INDEX ET RELEVÉS
STATISTIQUES. G. APOLLINAIRE, "CALLI-
GRAMMES:" CONCORDANCES, INDEX ET
RELEVÉS STATISTIQUES.
R.S. MEYERSTEIN, 545(RPH):FEB70-364
QUEMADA, B. LES DICTIONNAIRES DU FRAN-
ÇAIS MODERNES, 1539-1863.
J. DARBELNET, 320(CJL):SPRING70-157
W.L. WILEY, 207(FR):DEC69-394
QUENNELL, P. SAMUEL JOHNSON: HIS FRIENDS
AND ENEMIES.
617(TLS):20OCT72-1241
QUENNELL, P. ALEXANDER POPE.
R. TRICKETT, 541(RES):MAY70-221
QUENNELL, P., ED. MARCEL PROUST.*
441:16APR72-20
QUESTED, R.K.I. THE EXPANSION OF RUSSIA
IN EAST ASIA, 1857-1860.*
E.D. SOKOL, 550(RUSR):APR70-236
J.A. WHITE, 293(JAST):NOV69-163
DE QUEVEDO, F. POLÍTICA DE DIOS. (J.O.
CROSBY, ED)
A. COLLARD, 241:JAN71-73
QUIGLEY, W.G.H. & E.F.D. ROBERTS, EDS.
REGISTRUM IOHANNIS MEY.
617(TLS):22DEC72-1566
QUILICI, V., ED. L'ARCHITETTURA DEL
COSTRUTTIVISMO.*
A.C. BIRNHOLZ, 32:SEP71-697
QUILIS, A. MÉTRICA ESPAÑOLA.
D.N. CÁRDENAS, 238:MAY70-341
QUILIS, A. & J.M. ROZAS - SEE JIMÉNEZ
PATÓN, B.
QUILLET, J. LES CLEFS DU POUVOIR AU
MOYEN ÂGE.
617(TLS):2JUN72-636
QUILLIOT, R. THE SEA AND PRISONS.*
(FRENCH TITLE: LA MER ET LES PRISONS.)
K.J. HARROW, 295:VOL2#1-143
QUILTY, R. THE TENTH SESSION.
617(TLS):14APR72-427
QUIN, A. TRIPTICKS.
617(TLS):5MAY72-526
QUINE, W.V. ONTOLOGICAL RELATIVITY AND
OTHER ESSAYS.
R.H.K., 543:JUN70-747
H. LAYCOCK, 529(QQ):SUMMER70-299
42(AR):WINTER69/70-591

QUINE, W.V. SET THEORY AND ITS LOGIC.
(REV)
H.P.K., 543:MAR70-563
QUINE, W.V. WORD AND OBJECT. (2ND ED)
J. BOUVERESSE, 98:APR69-335
QUINN, A. THE ORIGINAL SIN.
P. ADAMS, 61:NOV72-130
R. BERKVIST, 441:8OCT72-41
561(SATR):21OCT72-79
QUINN, K., ED. APPROACHES TO CATULLUS.
617(TLS):11AUG72-952
QUINTANA, R. OLIVER GOLDSMITH.
R.D. STOCK, 502(PRS):SPRING68-89
QUINTUS OF SMYRNA. THE WAR AT TROY.*
(F.M. COMBELLACK, ED & TRANS)
W. ANDERSON, 149:JUN71-158
QUIRINO, C. THE YOUNG AGUINALDO FROM
KAWIT TO BIYAK-NA-BATO.
J.A. LARKIN, 293(JAST):FEB70-501
QUIRK, R. THE ENGLISH LANGUAGE AND
IMAGES OF MATTER.
617(TLS):29DEC72-1586
"THE QURAN." (M. ZAFRULLA KHAN, TRANS)
617(TLS):14JUL72-823
QVARNSTRÖM, G. THE ENCHANTED PALACE.
E.N. TIGERSTEDT, 597(SN):VOL41#1-186
QVIST, G. FREDRIKA BREMER OCH KVINNANS
EMANCIPATION.
C.L. ANDERSON, 563(SS):SPRING71-208

RA'ANAN, U. THE USSR ARMS THE THIRD
WORLD.*
R. LANE, 550(RUSR):OCT70-469
RABAN, J. THE SOCIETY OF THE POEM.*
I. WEDDE, 364:FEB/MAR72-148
RABB, T.K. & J.E. SEIGEL, EDS. ACTION
AND CONVICTION IN EARLY MODERN EUROPE.
G.C. BOYCE, 551(RENQ):WINTER70-456
A.J. LOOMIE, 613:WINTER69-627
RABINOVITZ, R. IRIS MURDOCH.
H.T. MASON, 447(N&Q):OCT70-394
RABINOVITZ, R. THE REACTION AGAINST
EXPERIMENT IN THE ENGLISH NOVEL, 1950-
1960.
E.D. PENDRY, 597(SN):VOL41#1-204
K. SCHLÜTER, 38:BAND87HEFT3/4-475
RABINOWITCH, A. PRELUDE TO REVOLUTION.*
I. GETZLER, 587:OCT69-255
RABKIN, N., ED. REINTERPRETATIONS OF
ELIZABETHAN DRAMA.*
N. SANDERS, 551(RENQ):WINTER70-476
RABOFF, E. PAUL KLEE. PABLO PICASSO.
MARC CHAGALL.
B. BETTINSON, 363:NOV69-32
RABY, P., ED. THE STRATFORD SCENE 1958-
1968.
C. LEECH, 627(UTQ):JUL69-403
RACE, J. WAR COMES TO LONG AN.
F. FITZ GERALD, 453:19OCT72-21
J.T. MC ALISTER, JR., 441:14MAY72-3
453:9MAR72-34
617(TLS):17MAR72-293
DE RACHEWILTZ, M. DISCRETIONS.*
617(TLS):21APR72-440
RACINE, J. ATHALIE. (H.P. SALOMON, ED)
D.L. RUBIN, 399(MLJ):NOV70-549
RACINE, J. BAJAZET. (M.M. MC GOWAN, ED)
H.T. BARNWELL, 208(FS):JAN71-75
RACINE, J. BRITANNICUS. (P. BUTLER, ED)
R.W. TOBIN, 207(FR):MAR70-697
RACINE, J. IPHIGÉNIE. (F.R. FREUDMANN,
ED)
C. FRANÇOIS, 399(MLJ):MAR70-201
RÁCZ, I. TREASURES OF FINNISH RENAIS-
SANCE AND BAROQUE ART.
R.V. SHAW, 127:WINTER70/71-222

RADAZA, F.D. - SEE UNDER DEMETRIO Y RA-
DAZA, F.
RADBERTUS, P. - SEE UNDER PASCASIUS RAD-
BERTUS
RADCLIFF-UMSTEAD, D. THE BIRTH OF MODERN
COMEDY IN RENAISSANCE ITALY.
B. CORRIGAN, 275(IQ):FALL69-85
J.E. ROBINSON, 141:FALL70-363
RADDALL, T. ROGER SUDDEN.
J.R. SORFLEET, 296:SPRING72-92
RADDATZ, F.J., ED. MARXISMUS UND LITERA-
TUR.
617(TLS):29SEP72-1169
RADDATZ, F.J. TRADITIONEN UND TENDENZEN.
617(TLS):14JUL72-794
RADER, M. WORDSWORTH.
B. JESSUP, 290(JAAC):SPRING70-389
RADKAU, J. DIE DEUTSCHE EMIGRATION IN
DEN USA.
617(TLS):28JAN72-81
RADKE, G., ED. CICERO.
E.S. RAMAGE, 121(CJ):FEB-MAR71-271
RADKE, G. DIE GÖTTER ALTITALIENS.
A. DRUMMOND, 123:JUN71-239
RADOSH, R. AMERICAN LABOR AND UNITED
STATES FOREIGN POLICY.
639(VQR):AUTUMN70-CXLVIII
RAE, H.C. THE SHOOTING GALLERY.
N. CALLENDAR, 441:17SEP72-45
617(TLS):29SEP72-1174
RAE, I. CHARLES CAMERON.
617(TLS):10MAR72-279
RAE, J.B. THE ROAD AND THE CAR IN AMERI-
CAN LIFE.
E. ROTHSCHILD, 453:24FEB72-40
RAEL, J.B. THE SOURCES AND DIFFUSION OF
THE MEXICAN SHEPHERDS' PLAYS.*
L.B. KIDDLE, 545(RPH):AUG70-224
RAFFAELE, P.R. & M. GAMBONE - SEE BUZ-
ZATI, D.
RAFFLES, S. REPORT ON JAPAN. (M. PASKE-
SMITH, ED)
617(TLS):13OCT72-1232
RAGONESE, G. ILLUMINISMO MANZONIANO.
W.T.S., 191(ELN):SEP69(SUPP)-127
RAHILL, F. THE WORLD OF MELODRAMA.
C.R. KRIEBEL, 290(JAAC):WINTER69-256
J.Y. MILLER, 397(MD):SEP68-219
RAHMANN, R. & G.R. ANG., EDS. DR. H.
OTLEY BEYER.
C. KAUT, 293(JAST):MAY70-742
RAHNER, K. SCHRIFTEN ZUR THEOLOGIE.
G. MAY, 182:VOL23#21/22-903
RAHNER, K. THEOLOGICAL INVESTIGATIONS.
(VOLS 7 & 9)
617(TLS):24NOV72-1434
RAHNER, K. THEOLOGICAL INVESTIGATIONS.
(VOL 8)
617(TLS):12MAY72-557
RAHNER, K., WITH C. ERNST & K. SMYTH.
SACRAMENTUM MUNDI: AN ENCYCLOPEDIA OF
THEOLOGY. (VOL 1)
E.A.R., 543:SEP69-145
RAHUL, R. MODERN BHUTAN.
617(TLS):19MAY72-585
RAIBLE, W. ARISTOTELES UND DER RAUM.
P.M. HUBY, 123:MAR71-129
RAILLARD, G. BUTOR.
E. ZANTS, 207(FR):FEB70-510
RAIMOND, J. ROBERT SOUTHEY.
K.C., 191(ELN):SEP69(SUPP)-46
RAIMOND, M. LE ROMAN DEPUIS LA REVOLU-
TION.
C.F. COATES, 207(FR):OCT69-200
RAINBOW, B. MUSIC IN THE CLASSROOM.
P. STANDFORD, 415:SEP71-863

RAINE, K. BLAKE AND TRADITION.*
  I.H.C., 191(ELN):SEP69(SUPP)-24
  D. DOUGLAS, 67:NOV71-238
  D. HIRST, 340(KR):1969/5-684
  G. KEYNES, 111:25OCT69-24
  M.D. PALEY, 191(ELN):JUN70-304
  C.M.R., 543:SEP69-137
  E.J. ROSE, 150(DR):SUMMER70-269
  D.M. SCHWEGEL, 590:WINTER71-36
  W.H. STEVENSON, 184(EIC):APR70-251
RAINE, K. THE LOST COUNTRY.
  J. SYMONS, 364:DEC71/JAN72-128
  617(TLS):7JAN72-6
RAINE, K. & G.M. HARPER - SEE TAYLOR, T.
RAINES, R. MARCELLUS LAROON.*
  R. PAULSON, 173(ECS):WINTER69-278
RAISON, J. LES VASES À INSCRIPTIONS
  PEINTES DE L'ÂGE MYCÉNIEN ET LEUR CON-
  TEXTE ARCHÉOLOGIQUE.
  J.H. BETTS, 303:VOL90-257
RAITIÈRE, A. L'ART DE L'ACTEUR SELON
  DORAT ET SAMSON.
  D.A. BONNEVILLE, 207(FR):APR70-844
RAITT, J. MADAME DE LAFAYETTE AND "LA
  PRINCESSE DE CLÈVES."
  617(TLS):28JAN72-100
RAJA, K.K. INDIAN THEORIES OF MEANING.
  J.T. KEARNS, 485(PE&W):JAN-APR68-104
RAJAN, B. THE LOFTY RHYME.
  R. DANIELLS, 102(CANL):AUTUMN71-92
  J.M. STEADMAN, 677:VOL2-268
RAJAN, B., ED. "PARADISE LOST:" A TER-
  CENTENARY TRIBUTE.*
  W. BLISSETT, 627(UTQ):JUL70-365
RAJASEKHARAIAH, T.R. THE ROOTS OF
  WHITMAN'S GRASS.
  H. BERGMAN, 27(AL):NOV71-455
RAJNAI, M. MEMBERS OF THE NORWICH SOCI-
  ETY OF ARTISTS, 1805-1833.
  F.W.H., 90:NOV70-765
RAJU, P.T. THE PHILOSOPHICAL TRADITIONS
  OF INDIA.
  617(TLS):4FEB72-138
RAKOSI, C. AMULET.
  S. COOPERMAN, 502(PRS):FALL68-266
RAKOWSKA-HARMSTONE, T. RUSSIA AND
  NATIONALISM IN CENTRAL ASIA.
  G. WHEELER, 32:MAR71-156
RALEGH, W. - SEE UNDER RALEIGH, W.
RALEIGH, J.H., ED. A COLLECTION OF CRIT-
  ICAL ESSAYS ON "THE ICEMAN COMETH."
  D. HOLBROOK, 619(TC):1968/2-56
RALEIGH, J.H. TIME, PLACE, AND IDEA.
  R. GRIMM, 406:SUMMER71-194
  R. LEHAN, 445(NCF):DEC68-369
RALEIGH, J.H. TWENTIETH CENTURY INTER-
  PRETATIONS OF "THE ICEMAN COMETH."
  J.Y. MILLER, 397(MD):MAY69-106
RALEIGH, W. A CHOICE OF SIR WALTER
  RALEGH'S VERSE. (R. NYE, ED)
  617(TLS):12MAY72-541
RALPH, E., ED. GUIDE TO THE BRISTOL
  ARCHIVES OFFICE.
  617(TLS):26MAY72-613
RAMAGE, C.T., ED & TRANS. FAMILIAR QUO-
  TATIONS FROM FRENCH AND ITALIAN AUTH-
  ORS.
  G. HAINSWORTH, 208(FS):APR71-248
RAMANAN, K.V. NĀGĀRJUNA'S PHILOSOPHY AS
  PRESENTED IN THE MAHĀ-PRAJÑĀPĀRAMITĀ-
  ŚĀSTRA.
  L. LANCASTER, 485(PE&W):JAN-APR68-97
RĀMĀNUJA. RĀMĀNUJA ON THE BHAGAVADGĪTĀ.
  (J.A.B. VAN BUITENEN, ED & TRANS)
  L. ROCHER, 318(JAOS):APR-JUN70-410
RAMANUJAN, A.K. - SEE "THE INTERIOR
  LANDSCAPE"

RAMAT, S. L'ERMETISMO.
  617(TLS):18AUG72-967
RAMAZANI, R.K. THE FOREIGN POLICY OF
  IRAN 1500-1941.
  N.R. KEDDIE, 318(JAOS):APR-JUN70-281
RAMBERT, M. QUICKSILVER.
  617(TLS):18AUG72-977
RAMCHAND, K. THE WEST INDIAN NOVEL AND
  ITS BACKGROUND.*
  A. FERNANDEZ, 584(SWR):WINTER71-103
RAMÍREZ, A. EPISTOLARIO DE JUSTO LIPSIO
  Y LOS ESPAÑOLES (1577-1606).
  P. PASCAL, 545(RPH):MAY70-589
RAMÍREZ VÁSQUEZ, P. MEXICO.
  J. SPENCER, 363:FEB70-64
RAMÓN, F.R. - SEE UNDER RUIZ RAMÓN, F.
RAMOS, P.E.D. DO BARROCCO AO MODERNISMO.
  191(ELN):SEP69(SUPP)-132
RAMPERSAD, A. MELVILLE'S "ISRAEL POT-
  TER."
  W. BEZANSON, 27(AL):MAR71-133
RAMSAY, D. A LITTLE MURDER MUSIC.
  617(TLS):4FEB72-135
RAMSDEN, H. ANGEL GANIVET'S "IDEARIUM
  ESPAÑOL."
  V. FUENTES, 546(RR):FEB70-70
  J. HERRERO, 240(HR):OCT70-434
  G. RIBBANS, 86(BHS):JAN71-77
  W.H. SHUFORD, 399(MLJ):JAN70-57
RAMSEY, M. THE CHRISTIAN PRIEST TODAY.
  617(TLS):28JUL72-897
RAMSEY, P. THE ART OF JOHN DRYDEN.*
  W. FROST, 301(JEGP):APR71-310
  A. ROPER, 481(PQ):JUL70-345
RAMSEY, P. THE PATIENT AS PERSON.*
  B.J. RANSIL, 142:SPRING71-228
RAMSEY, W., ED. JULES LAFORGUE.
  R.R. BOLGAR, 208(FS):JUL71-346
RAMSON, W.S., ED. ENGLISH TRANSPORTED.
  L.F. BROSNAHAN, 67:MAY71-137
RAMUS, P. THE LOGIKE OF PETER RAMUS.
  (R. MAC ILMAINE, TRANS; C.M. DUNN, ED)
  L.V.R., 568(SCN):SPRING71-31
RANCHETTI, M. - SEE WITTGENSTEIN, L.
RAND, E. THE SYNTAX OF MANDARIN INTER-
  ROGATIVES.
  E.S. LIU, 318(JAOS):OCT-DEC70-618
RAND, F.P. THE JONES LIBRARY IN AMHERST,
  1919-1969.
  J. ALDEN, 432(NEQ):SEP70-518
RANDAL, V. YOU GET USED TO A PLACE.
  M. LEVIN, 441:23JUL72-20
RANDALL, D.B.J. JOSEPH CONRAD AND WAR-
  RINGTON DAWSON.*
  E.W. SAID, 637(VS):JUN70-429
  W.D. SCHAEFER, 445(NCF):SEP69-248
RANDALL, J. ADAM'S DREAM.*
  P. COOPER, 340(KR):1970/1-143
  639(VQR):SPRING70-L
RANDALL, J.H., JR. ARISTOTLE. HELLENIS-
  TIC WAYS OF DELIVERANCE AND THE MAKING
  OF THE CHRISTIAN SYNTHESIS. THE
  CAREER OF PHILOSOPHY. (VOLS 1&2)
  E.J. MACHLE, 319:OCT72-459
RANDALL, J.H., JR. PLATO.
  A.R.C. DUNCAN, 529(QQ):AUTUMN70-467
  E.J. MACHLE, 319:OCT72-459
  R.K. SPRAGUE, 124:NOV70-86
  639(VQR):AUTUMN70-CXL
RANDALL, M. SO MANY ROOMS HAS A HOUSE
  BUT ONE ROOF.
  J. HOPPER, 661:SPRING69-102
RANDEL, D.M. THE RESPONSORIAL PSALM
  TONES FOR THE MOZARABIC OFFICE.
  R. STEINER, 414(MQ):OCT69-575
RANDEL, M.G. THE HISTORICAL PROSE OF
  FERNANDO DE HERRERA.
  617(TLS):14APR72-419

RANDHAWA, M.S. KANGRA PAINTINGS OF THE
BIHARI SAT SAI.
A.L. DALLAPICCOLA, 318(JAOS):OCT-DEC
70-591
RANDHAWA, M.S. & J.K. GALBRAITH. INDIAN
PAINTING.
S.J. FALK, 592:JUL/AUG69-53
RANDLE, R.F. GENEVA 1954.
639(VQR):SUMMER70-CIX
"THE RANDOM HOUSE DICTIONARY OF THE
ENGLISH LANGUAGE."* (J. STEIN, ED-IN-
CHIEF)
R. NEWTON, 219(GAR):SPRING69-90
617(TLS):13OCT72-1209
"THE RANDOM HOUSE DICTIONARY OF THE ENG-
LISH LANGUAGE: COLLEGE EDITION." (L.
URDANG, ED)
D. EAGLE, 541(RES):MAY70-244
RANHOFER, C. THE EPICUREAN.
617(TLS):18FEB72-199
RANKE, K. EUROPEAN ANECDOTES AND JESTS.
617(TLS):7JUL72-767
RANKE, K., ED. FOLKTALES OF GERMANY.*
E.W. BAUGHMAN, 650(WF):OCT68-279
RANKIN, P. IRISH BUILDING VENTURES OF
THE EARL BISHOP OF DERRY 1730-1803.
617(TLS):15SEP72-1050
RANNIE, A. THE STORY OF MUSIC AT WIN-
CHESTER COLLEGE, 1394-1969.
J. WARRACK, 415:JUN71-559
RANNIT, A. LINE.
V. TERRAS, 574(SEEJ):WINTER71-511
RANSFORD, O. THE SLAVE TRADE.
617(TLS):1SEP72-1031
RANSOM, J.C. BEATING THE BUSHES.
G. CORE, 578:FALL72-177
E.W. SAID, 441:10DEC72-4
RANSOME, M., ED. THE STATE OF THE BISH-
OPRIC OF WORCESTER, 1782-1808.
E. WELCH, 325:APR70-78
RAO, N.B. THE POLITICS OF LEADERSHIP IN
AN INDIAN STATE: ANDHRA PRADESH.
R.L. PARK, 293(JAST):FEB70-505
RAO, P.R.R. CONTEMPORARY INDIAN ART.
A. WERNER, 127:WINTER70/71-220
RAO, V.K.R.V. THE NEHRU LEGACY.
617(TLS):1SEP72-1029
RAPHAEL, F. APRIL, JUNE AND NOVEMBER.
J. HUNTER, 362:19OCT72-513
617(TLS):8DEC72-1477
RAPHAEL, F. LIKE MEN BETRAYED.* WHO
WERE YOU WITH LAST NIGHT?*
F.P.W. MC DOWELL, 659:SUMMER72-361
RAPHAEL, F. THEY GOT WHAT THEY WANTED.
M. LEVIN, 441:30APR72-38
RAPIN, R. LES RÉFLEXIONS SUR LA POÉTIQUE
DE CE TEMPS ET SUR LES OUVRAGES DES
POÈTES ANCIENS ET MODERNES.
W. FLOECK, 72:BAND208HEFT4/6-460
H. MATTAUCH, 182:VOL23#7-365
RAPOPORT, A. & A.M. CHAMMAH. PRISONER'S
DILEMMA.
A.J.M. FLOOK, 479(PHQ):JUL70-292
RAPOPORT, R. & R.N. DUAL-CAREER FAMILIES.
617(TLS):7JAN72-9
RAPP, M.A. CANAL WATER AND WHISKEY.
J.H. BRUNVAND, 650(WF):JAN68-59
RASMUSSEN, J. & O. MEYER. GAMLE TEGL-
VAERKER.
A. FENTON, 595(SCS):VOL15PT1-78
RASPE, R.E. AN INTRODUCTION TO THE
NATURAL HISTORY OF THE TERRESTRIAL
SPHERE. (A.N. IVERSEN & A.V. CAROZZI,
EDS & TRANS)
R.T. BRUÈRE, 122:OCT71-265
RASSAM, J. LA MÉTAPHYSIQUE DE SAINT
THOMAS.
M.E. REINA, 548(RCSF):APR/JUN69-229

RASTORGUEVA, V.S. A SHORT SKETCH OF
TAJIK GRAMMAR. (H.H. PAPER, ED & TRANS)
J. KRÁMSKÝ, 353:SEP69-92
RATERMANIS, J.R. - SEE DE BEAUMARCHAIS,
P.A.C.
RATH, J.R., ED. THE NATIONALITY PROBLEM
IN THE HABSBURG MONARCHY IN THE NINE-
TEENTH CENTURY.
H. HANAK, 575(SEER):APR71-304
RATHBONE, J. TRIP TRAP.
N. CALLENDAR, 441:31DEC72-18
RATHBURN, R.C. & M. STEINMANN, JR., EDS.
FROM JANE AUSTEN TO JOSEPH CONRAD.
G. SALGADO, 541(RES):FEB70-104
RATHÉ, C.E. - SEE GENTILLET, I.
RATHLESBERGER, J., ED. NIXON AND THE
ENVIRONMENT.
441:17SEP72-44
RAȚIU, I. CORESPONDENȚA LUI IOAN RAȚIU
CU GEORGE BARIȚIU (1861-1892). (K.
HITCHINS & L. MAIOR, EDS)
V. NEMOIANU, 104:WINTER71-577
RATTAN, R. GANDHI'S CONCEPT OF POLITICAL
OBLIGATION.
617(TLS):13OCT72-1237
RATYCH, J.M. INTERESSANTES AUS DEUTSCHEN
ZEITUNGEN.
H.C. VARDAMAN, 221(GQ):NOV70-824
VON RAUCH, G. A HISTORY OF SOVIET
RUSSIA. (5TH ED)
W.V. WALLACE, 587:OCT68-270
RAVÀ, A. LA FILOSOFIA EUROPEA NEL-
L'OTTOCENTO.
A. NEGRI, 548(RCSF):JAN-MAR68-114
RAVE, R. & H.J. KNÖFEL. BAUEN SEIT 1900
IN BERLIN.
N.P., 46:MAY69-388
RAVEN, D.S. GREEK METRE. (2ND ED)
L.P.E. PARKER, 123:MAR71-139
RAVEN, F.A., W.K. LEGNER & J.C. KING,
EDS. GERMANIC STUDIES IN HONOR OF
EDWARD HENRY SEHRT.*
D.H. GREEN, 400(MLN):APR70-395
B. KRATZ, 133:1969/2-264
RAVEN, S. COME LIKE SHADOWS.
R. BRYDEN, 362:30NOV72-760
617(TLS):27OCT72-1273
RAVEN, S. PLACES WHERE THEY SING.*
F.P.W. MC DOWELL, 659:SUMMER72-361
RAVEN, S. SOUND THE RETREAT.*
G. EWART, 364:FEB/MAR72-180
RAVENAL, E.C., ED. PEACE WITH CHINA?
S.S. ROSENFELD, 561(SATR):5FEB72-68
RAVENEL, B. THE YEMASSEE LANDS. (L.D.
RUBIN, JR., ED)
639(VQR):WINTER70-XIII
RAW, C., G. HODGSON & B. PAGE. "DO YOU
SINCERELY WANT TO BE RICH?"*
E.J. EPSTEIN, 442(NY):22JAN72-89
RAWICK, G.P., ED. THE AMERICAN SLAVE.
[19 VOLS]
E.D. GENOVESE, 453:21SEP72-16
RAWLINSON, D.H. THE PRACTICE OF CRITI-
CISM.*
J. COLMER, 67:MAY71-118
RAWLINSON, G. - SEE HYDE, R.
RAWLS, J. A THEORY OF JUSTICE.
M. COHEN, 441:16JUL72-1
S. HAMPSHIRE, 453:24FEB72-34
D. LYONS, 311(JP):5OCT72-535
A. RYAN, 362:22JUN72-837
M. TEITELMAN, 311(JP):5OCT72-545
617(TLS):5MAY72-505
RAWNSLEY, H.D. REMINISCENCES OF WORDS-
WORTH AMONG THE PEASANTRY OF WESTMOR-
LAND.*
J.C. MAXWELL, 447(N&Q):MAY70-189
RAWSKI, C.H. - SEE PETRARCH

RAWSON, E. THE SPARTAN TRADITION IN
EUROPEAN THOUGHT.*
J.J. FARBER, 124:NOV70-96
O. MURRAY, 123:JUN71-231
RAWSON, P. CERAMICS.
617(TLS):28JUL72-899
RAWSON, P. EROTIC ART OF THE EAST.
J. BRZOSTOSKI, 58:NOV69-14
RAWSON, P. INDIAN ART.
617(TLS):10NOV72-1356
RAY, A. ENGLISH DELFTWARE POTTERY IN
THE ROBERT HALL WARREN COLLECTION,
ASHMOLEAN MUSEUM, OXFORD.*
G. WILLS, 39:FEB69-159
RAY, D. DRAGGING THE MAIN.*
W.P.T., 619(TC):1968/4&1969/1-90
RAY, M. & K.B. LUTZ. A-LM, FRENCH,
LEVEL ONE. (2ND ED)
J.G. MIRSKY, 207(FR):APR70-859
RAY, N. AN ARTIST IN LIFE.*
S.N. HAY, 293(JAST):AUG70-972
RAY, P.C. THE SURREALIST MOVEMENT IN
ENGLAND.
R. SHATTUCK, 453:1JUN72-25
617(TLS):21APR72-442
RAY, P.S. LINGUISTIC MATRICES.
H.E. KIJLSTRA, 353:OCT69-117
RAYAN, K. SUGGESTION AND STATEMENT IN
POETRY.
617(TLS):8DEC72-1481
RAYBURN, A. GEOGRAPHICAL NAMES OF REN-
FREW COUNTY.
R.A. MOHL, 424:JUN68-193
RAYMOND, E. GENTLE GREAVES.
T. LASK, 441:16AUG72-35
M. LEVIN, 441:10OCT72-42
RAYMOND, E. OUR LATE MEMBER.
D.A.N. JONES, 362:17FEB72-221
RAYMOND, J. SIMENON IN COURT.
E.L. GALLIGAN, 399(MLJ):JAN70-47
RAYMOND, M., ED. LA POÉSIE FRANÇAISE ET
LE MANIÉRISME. (A.J. STEELE, NOTES)
617(TLS):28JAN72-100
RAYNAUD DE LAGE, G., ED. LE ROMAN DE
THÈBES. (VOL 2)
F. KOENIG, 545(RPH):FEB71-557
"MISS READ" - SEE FILED UNDER MISS
READ, G. MUSIC NOTATION.*
S. SADIE, 415:JAN70-46
READ, G. MUSIC NOTATION II.
T. SOUSTER, 607:SUMMER69-34
READ, H. ART AND ALIENATION.
H.R. WACKRILL, 39:MAR69-246
READ, P.P. MONK DAWSON.*
P. CRUTTWELL, 249(HUDR):SPRING71-177
READ, P.P. THE PROFESSOR'S DAUGHTER.*
J.R. CLARK, 561(SATR):8JAN72-34
F.P.W. MC DOWELL, 659:SUMMER72-361
F. MC GUINNESS, 364:DEC71/JAN72-159
READE, B. BEARDSLEY.*
E. HOFFMANN, 90:FEB70-118
READE, B., ED. SEXUAL HERETICS.*
L. ORMOND, 677:VOL2-319
READER, W.J. THE MIDDLE CLASSES.
617(TLS):17NOV72-1405
"READERS' GUIDE TO BOOKS ON NATURAL HIS-
TORY." (3RD ED)
617(TLS):21JAN72-78
READY, W. THE TOLKIEN RELATION.
J. REANEY, 627(UTQ):JUL69-378
"REAL ACADEMIA ESPAÑOLA, DICCIONARIO DE
LA LENGUA ESPAÑOLA, DECIMANOVENA
EDICIÓN."
A. GREIVE, 72:BAND208HEFT3-226
REALE, G. IL CONCETTO DI FILOSOFIA PRIMA
E L'UNITÀ DELLA METAFISICA DI ARISTO-
TELE.
F.D. CAIZZI, 548(RCSF):JUL/SEP69-325

REALE, G. - SEE LEVI, A.
REANEY, G. GUILLAUME DE MACHAUT.
617(TLS):3MAR72-253
REANEY, P.H. THE ORIGIN OF ENGLISH SUR-
NAMES.
O. ARNGART, 179(ES):APR70-151
K.B. HARDER, 424:SEP68-305
REAVER, J.R., COMP. AN O'NEILL CONCOR-
DANCE.
L.A. RACHOW, 70(ANQ):NOV71-46
REBER, A. STIL UND BEDEUTUNG DES GE-
SPRÄCHS IM WERKE JEREMIAS GOTTHELFS.
U. KAMBER, 133:1969/2-262
REBHOLZ, R.A. THE LIFE OF FULKE GRE-
VILLE.
617(TLS):10MAR72-270
RECH, P. INBILD DES KOSMOS.
J. DUCHESNE-GUILLEMIN, 182:VOL23
#21/22-925
RECHCÍGL, M., JR., ED. CZECHOSLOVAKIA
PAST AND PRESENT. (VOL 1)
Z.A.B. ZEMAN, 575(SEER):OCT71-633
RECHCÍGL, M., JR., ED. CZECHOSLOVAKIA
PAST AND PRESENT. (VOL 2)
M. SOUČKOVÁ, 574(SEEJ):SUMMER71-254
Z.A.B. ZEMAN, 575(SEER):OCT71-633
RECHENBACH, C.W. & OTHERS. SWAHILI-ENG-
LISH DICTIONARY.
L. HARRIES, 69:JAN69-98
RECK, A.J. THE NEW AMERICAN PHILOSOPHERS.
N. NELKIN, 330(MASJ):FALL69-84
RECK, M. EZRA POUND.
F.K. SANDERS, 569(SR):SUMMER71-433
RECK, R.D. LITERATURE AND RESPONSI-
BILITY.*
H.E. BARNES, 401(MLQ):DEC70-519
J. FLETCHER, 402(MLR):JAN71-198
J.H. MATTHEWS, 131(CL):FALL71-369
RECKERT, S. LYRA MINIMA.
J.G. CUMMINS, 86(BHS):OCT71-350
RECKERT, S. THE MATTER OF BRITAIN AND
THE PRAISE OF SPAIN (THE HISTORY OF A
PANEGYRIC).*
S.G. ARMISTEAD, 240(HR):OCT70-427
RECKFORD, K.J. HORACE.
S.P. BOVIE, 124:NOV70-91
R.S. KILPATRICK, 24:OCT71-743
M.J. MC GANN, 123:JUN71-206
RECKOW, F. DER MUSIKTRAKTAT DES ANONY-
MUS 4.* (PTS 1&2)
D.G. HUGHES, 589:JUL71-536
"THE RECORDS OF THE FOREIGN OFFICE 1782-
1939."
R. BULLEN, 325:OCT70-156
"RECUEIL DU RHODOPE." (VOL 2)
G. SOTIROFF, 104:FALL71-439
RÉDA, J. AMEN.
R. MUNIER, 98:OCT69-862
REDDAWAY, P., ED & TRANS. UNCENSORED
RUSSIA.
S.F. COHEN, 441:23JUL72-6
R. CONQUEST, 362:24FEB72-247
I.F. STONE, 453:24FEB72-14
617(TLS):26MAY72-589
REDFERN, B. HAYDN.*
S. SADIE, 415:DEC70-1225
REDFORD, D.B. HISTORY AND CHRONOLOGY OF
THE EIGHTEENTH DYNASTY OF EGYPT.
W.K. SIMPSON, 318(JAOS):APR-JUN70-314
REDGROVE, P. DR. FAUST'S SEA-SPIRAL
SPIRIT. THREE PIECES FOR VOICES.
617(TLS):11AUG72-934
REDIG DE CAMPOS, D. RAFFAELLO NELLE
STANZE.
J. MONTAGU, 54:JUN69-189
REDSTONE, L.G. ART IN ARCHITECTURE.*
J.E. ARONIN, 505:NOV68-176
W.J. MALARCHER, 363:AUG70-137

263

REED, H.H. & S. DUCKWORTH. CENTRAL PARK.
    C. SIMMONS, 441:4JUN72-52
REED, H.M. THE A.B. FROST BOOK.
    M.S. YOUNG, 39:APR69-329
REED, I. MUMBO JUMBO.
    T.R. EDWARDS, 453:5OCT72-21
    A. FRIEDMAN, 441:6AUG72-1
    A. GORDON, 561(SATR):14OCT72-76
    C. LEHMANN-HAUPT, 441:9AUG72-37
    442(NY):16SEP72-125
REED, J. SCHUBERT: THE FINAL YEARS.
    617(TLS):27OCT72-1289
REED, M.C., ED. RAILWAYS IN THE VICTOR-
    IAN ECONOMY.
    H. PARRIS, 637(VS):JUN70-423
REED, M-T.C. COMMENT DIT-ON?
    H. BRYER, 207(FR):FEB70-540
REEDY, G.E. THE TWILIGHT OF THE PRESI-
    DENCY.
    L.W. KOENIG, 639(VQR):SPRING70-331
REEMAN, D. RENDEZVOUS - SOUTH ATLANTIC.
    M. LEVIN, 441:30APR72-38
REES, B. DIMINISHING CIRCLES.*
    F.P.W. MC DOWELL, 659:SUMMER72-361
REES, G. A CHAPTER OF ACCIDENTS.
    P.N. FURBANK, 362:10FEB72-185
    P. STANSKY, 441:18JUN72-4
    617(TLS):11FEB72-141
REES, J. TITUS BRANDSMA.
    617(TLS):21JAN72-64
REES, J. SAMUEL DANIEL.*
    W. BLISSETT, 179(ES):DEC70-558
REES, J. EQUALITY.
    617(TLS):11FEB72-151
REES, R. - SEE WEIL, S.
REES, R.A. & E.N. HARBERT, EDS. FIFTEEN
    AMERICAN AUTHORS BEFORE 1900.
    617(TLS):14JUL72-825
REESE, G. FOURSCORE CLASSICS OF MUSIC
    LITERATURE.
    G. ABRAHAM, 415:DEC70-1226
REESE, J. BIG HITCH.
    M. LEVIN, 441:25JUN72-28
REESE, T.R. THE HISTORY OF THE ROYAL
    COMMONWEALTH SOCIETY, 1868-1968.
    B. PORTER, 637(VS):JUN70-444
REESING, J. MILTON'S POETIC ART.
    G. BULLOUGH, 175:SPRING69-28
    I. SIMON, 541(RES):MAY70-209
REEVE, F.A. VICTORIAN AND EDWARDIAN
    CAMBRIDGE FROM OLD PHOTOGRAPHS.*
    G. ANNAN, 362:6JAN72-24
REEVE, F.D. JUST OVER THE BORDER.*
    639(VQR):WINTER70-IX
REEVES, D. NOTES OF A PROCESSED BROTHER.
    E.Z. FRIEDENBERG, 453:4MAY72-21
    R. GROSS, 440:30JAN72-4
    441:21MAY72-28
REEVES, G.M. - SEE COINDREAU, M.E.
REEVES, J. POEMS AND PARAPHRASES.
    617(TLS):4AUG72-910
REEVES, J. & S. HALDANE, EDS. HOMAGE TO
    TRUMBULL STICKNEY.
    H. SERGEANT, 175:SPRING69-33
REEVES, J.K. - SEE HOWELLS, W.D.
REEVES, P., ED. THOMAS WOLFE AND THE
    GLASS OF TIME.
    L. FIELD, 578:FALL72-163
REEVES, P. THOMAS WOLFE'S ALBATROSS.*
    M.J. LYDE, 577(SHR):SPRING70-181
REEVES, T. & K. HESS. THE END OF THE
    DRAFT.
    M. ZUCKERT, 109:FALL/WINTER71/72-142
REGALADO GARCÍA, A. EL SIERVO Y EL
    SEÑOR.*
    D. BASDEKIS, 238:SEP70-575
REGAN, D.T. A VIEW FROM THE STREET.
    K. KOYEN, 441:1OCT72-10

REGNÉLL, H. ANCIENT VIEWS ON THE NATURE
    OF LIFE.*
    A.W.H. ADKINS, 123:DEC71-403
    M. VEGETTI, 548(RCSF):JAN/MAR69-90
DE RÉGNIER, H. LETTRES À ANDRÉ GIDE
    (1891-1911). (D.J. NIEDERAUER, ED)
    617(TLS):20OCT72-1262
REGULA, M. KURZGEFASSTE ERKLÄRENDE SATZ-
    KUNDE DES NEUHOCHDEUTSCHEN.
    B. STOLT, 597:VOL41#2-422
REGUSH, N.M. THE DRUG ADDICTION BUSI-
    NESS.
    441:12MAR72-39
REHDER, H., U. THOMAS & F. TWADDELL.
    VERSTEHEN UND SPRECHEN. (REV)
    H.C. KAYSER, 221(GQ):NOV70-820
REIBEL, D.A. & S.A. SCHANE, EDS. MODERN
    STUDIES IN ENGLISH.
    G.D. PRIDEAUX, 320(CJL):FALL69-37
REICH, C.A. THE GREENING OF AMERICA.*
    C. DERBER, 418(MR):SPRING71-336
    N. FOUNTAIN, 364:AUG/SEP71-138
    C.P. IVES, 396(MODA):SUMMER71-312
    R. SALE, 249(HUDR):SPRING71-201
    D. YERGIN, 676(YR):SPRING71-417
REICH, H. DIE ENTSTEHUNG DER ERSTEN
    FÜNF SZENEN DES GOETHESCHEN "URFAUST."
    H.R. VAGET, 222(GR):MAY70-250
REICH, S. JOHN MARIN.
    S. SPECTOR, 58:SUMMER70-14
REICH, W. CHARACTER ANALYSIS. ETHER,
    GOD AND DEVIL [AND] COSMIC SUPERIMPOS-
    ITION.
    P.A. ROBINSON, 61:DEC72-132
REICH, W. THE FUNCTION OF THE ORGASM.
    R. NEWSOM, 97(CQ):AUTUMN68-369
    P.A. ROBINSON, 61:DEC72-132
REICH, W. THE INVASION OF COMPULSORY
    SEX-MORALITY.
    A. STORR, 440:23JAN72-8
REICH, W. SCHOENBERG.*
    A. PAYNE, 415:DEC71-1172
    C. ROSEN, 441:2JAN72-3
REICH, W. ARNOLD SCHÖNBERG ODER DER
    KONSERVATIVE REVOLUTIONÄR.
    W.M. STROH, 513:FALL-WINTER68-146
REICH-RANICKI, M., ED. GESICHTETE ZEIT.
    R. GRIMM, 406:FALL71-283
    R.K., 221(GQ):MAY70-531
REICHARDT, J., ED. CYBERNETIC SERENDIP-
    ITY.
    J. YALKUT, 58:DEC69/JAN70-14
REICHART, W.A. - SEE IRVING, W.
REICHENBACH, H. AXIOMATIZATION OF THE
    THEORY OF RELATIVITY. (M. REICHENBACH,
    ED & TRANS)
    R.H.K., 543:JUN70-748
REICHMANN, E. DIE HERRSCHAFT DER ZAHL.*
    H.B. NISBET, 402(MLR):JAN71-214
    J.R. RUSSELL, 399(MLJ):FEB70-134
REICHMANN, O. DEUTSCHE WORTFORSCHUNG.
    J. EICHHOFF, 406:SPRING71-75
REICHWEIN, A. CHINA AND EUROPE.
    H.H., 90:FEB70-128
    F.J.B. WATSON, 39:OCT69-354
REID, A. ALL I CAN MANAGE, MORE THAN I
    COULD.*
    A.P. HINCHLIFFE, 148:SPRING70-95
REID, B.L. THE MAN FROM NEW YORK.
    M. MONTGOMERY, 219(GAR):WINTER69-535
REID, C. JOHN BARBIROLLI.*
    R. ANDERSON, 415:OCT71-972
    441:12MAR72-38
REID, D. A BIBLIOGRAPHY OF THE GROUP OF
    SEVEN.
    J. MURRAY, 99:MAY72-66

REID, D. THE GROUP OF SEVEN.
J. MURRAY, 99:MAY72-66
102(CANL):WINTER71-106
REID, D.A. SOLDIER-SURGEON.* (J.O. BAYLEN & A. CONWAY, EDS)
R.L. BLANCO, 637(VS):JUN70-448
REID, G.L. & K. ALLEN. NATIONALISED INDUSTRIES.*
617(TLS):2JUN72-637
REID, J. HORSES WITH BLINDFOLDS.
G. ROPER, 627(UTQ):JUL69-355
REID, J.C. BUCKS AND BRUISERS.*
I.R. MAXWELL, 67:NOV71-244
REID, M. THE SHOUTING SIGNPAINTERS.
B. SHEK, 99:DEC72-40
617(TLS):3NOV72-1307
REID, R. THE FICTION OF NATHANAEL WEST.
F. GADO, 597(SN):VOL41#1-203
B. LEE, 447(N&Q):FEB70-79
502(PRS):WINTER68/69-365
REIDA, A. FAULT LINES.
M. LEVIN, 441:28MAY72-16
REILLY, R. WEDGWOOD JASPER.
617(TLS):21APR72-457
REIMAN, D.H. PERCY BYSSHE SHELLEY.*
J.D. BONE, 447(N&Q):OCT70-388
K.N.C., 191(ELN):SEP70(SUPP)-45
REIMANN, H. KOMMUNIKATIONS-SYSTEME.
H. JACOBY, 182:VOL23#10-543
REIMER, E. SCHOOL IS DEAD.
J. FIELDS, 561(SATR):15JAN72-64
REINER, E. A LINGUISTIC ANALYSIS OF AKKADIAN.
E.E. KNUDSEN, 318(JAOS):APR-JUN70-334
REINHARD, M. NOUVELLE HISTOIRE DE PARIS: LA RÉVOLUTION, 1789-1799.
617(TLS):15DEC72-1528
REINHARDT, R. THE ASHES OF SMYRNA.*
617(TLS):3NOV72-1306
REINIG, C. - SEE VON DROSTE-HÜLSHOFF, A.
REINKRAUT-FRIEDJUNG, P. EINE DEUTSCHE KULTURGESCHICHTE.
J. RYSAN, 399(MLJ):OCT70-470
REINMUTH, H.S., JR. EARLY STUART STUDIES.
617(TLS):25FEB72-230
REISS, G. "ALLEGORISIERUNG" UND MODERNE ERZÄHLKUNST.
L. BORNSCHEUER, 406:SUMMER71-198
REISS, H. GOETHE'S NOVELS.
D.G. LITTLE, 402(MLR):OCT71-944
E.A. METZGER, 399(MLJ):MAY70-368
REISS, H. POLITISCHES DENKEN IN DER DEUTSCHEN ROMANTIK.
J.T., 191(ELN):SEP69(SUPP)-96
REISS, H. - SEE KANT, I.
REISSNER, H.G. EDUARD GANS.
E. RAMBALDI, 548(RCSF):JAN-MAR68-95
REITER, U. JAKOB VAN HODDIS.
H.G. HERMANN, 406:FALL71-295
REKERS, B. BENITO ARIAS MONTANO (1527-1598).
617(TLS):8DEC72-1485
DU RELS, A.C. - SEE UNDER COSTA DU RELS, A.
REMARQUE, E.M. SHADOWS IN PARADISE.
C. LEHMANN-HAUPT, 441:29FEB72-37
D.W. MC CULLOUGH, 561(SATR):26FEB72-78
REMINGTON, R.A. THE WARSAW PACT.
N. ASCHERSON, 453:20APR72-26
617(TLS):12MAY72-535
REMINGTON, R.A., ED. WINTER IN PRAGUE.*
Z.A.B. ZEMAN, 575(SEER):OCT71-633
REMIZOV, A. KRESTOVYE SESTRY. V ROZOVOM BLESKE.
A.M. SHANE, 574(SEEJ):FALL71-374

REMY, J-C. MADAME DE LA FAYETTE.
D.R. HALL, 207(FR):FEB70-525
RÉMY, P-J. LE SAC DU PALAIS D'ÉTÉ.
617(TLS):25FEB72-208
RÉMY, T. JEAN-GASPARD DEBURAU.
J. STAROBINSKI, 98:DEC69-1033
"RENAISSANCE AND MODERN STUDIES XIII."
B. BABINGTON, 447(N&Q):NOV70-431
RENAUD, P. LECTURE D'APOLLINAIRE.
M. DAVIES, 402(MLR):OCT71-900
RENAULT, M. FIRE FROM HEAVEN.
F.P.W. MC DOWELL, 659:SUMMER72-361
RENAULT, M. THE PERSIAN BOY.
J.G. FARRELL, 362:2NOV72-611
T. LASK, 441:23DEC72-23
E. WEEKS, 61:DEC72-142
561(SATR):9DEC72-80
617(TLS):3NOV72-1306
RENDELL, R. MURDER BEING ONCE DONE.
O.L. BAILEY, 561(SATR):25NOV72-70
N. CALLENDAR, 441:10DEC72-56
RENDELL, R. NO MORE DYING THEN.*
N. CALLENDAR, 441:2JUL72-15
RENDON, A.B. CHICANO MANIFESTO.
J. WOMACK, 453:31AUG72-12
RENEHAN, R. GREEK TEXTUAL CRITICISM.
S.G. DAITZ, 124:NOV70-88
J.M. HUNT, 122:JUL71-202
D. YOUNG, 24:JUL71-503
RENFREW, C. THE EMERGENCE OF CIVILISATION.
617(TLS):15SEP72-1054
RENN, D. MEDIEVAL CASTLES IN HERTFORD-SHIRE.
617(TLS):10MAR72-285
RENNERT, J., ED. THE POSTER ART OF TOMI UNGERER.
617(TLS):30JUN72-740
RENOIR, A. THE POETRY OF JOHN LYDGATE.*
J.A.W. BENNETT, 597(SN):VOL40#1-242
RENSCH, R. THE HARP.*
J. MARSON, 415:FEB70-162
VAN RENSSELAER, M.G. HENRY HOBSON RICHARDSON AND HIS WORKS.
W. KIDNEY, 505:JUN68-168
RENTZEL, L. WHEN ALL THE LAUGHTER DIED IN SORROW.
C. LEHMANN-HAUPT, 441:6OCT72-45
J. SPENCER, 561(SATR):14OCT72-80
RENWICK, J. LA DESTINÉE POSTHUME DE JEAN-FRANÇOIS MARMONTEL.
617(TLS):1SEP72-1011
RENWICK, J. - SEE MARMONTEL, J-F.
RENWICK, W.L. - SEE SPENSER, E.
"REPERTORIUM FONTIUM HISTORIAE MEDII AEVI." (VOL 3)
G. CONSTABLE, 589:APR71-389
REPLOGLE, J. AUDEN'S POETRY.*
G.L. BRUNS, 590:WINTER71-37
M.K. SPEARS, 676(YR):AUTUMN70-90
REPNIN, N.V. & A. PASHA. MUBADELE.*
(N. ITZKOWITZ & M. MOTE, EDS & TRANS)
B. SPULER, 32:SEP71-662
"REPORT OF THE DEPUTY KEEPER OF THE RECORDS, 1960-1965." [GOVERNMENT OF NORTHERN IRELAND, PUBLIC RECORD OFFICE]
D. CHARMAN, 325:OCT69-593
"REPORT OF THE ROYAL COMMISSION ON TAXATION." [GOVERNMENT OF CANADA]
A. DEUTSCH, 529(QQ):SPRING70-104
REPS, J.W. MONUMENTAL WASHINGTON.*
S.M. SHERMAN, 576:MAY69-145
RESCHER, N. ESSAYS IN PHILOSOPHICAL ANALYSIS.
W. HALBFASS, 182:VOL23#7-332
M.B.M., 543:DEC69-353
D. MC QUEEN, 518:MAY70-23

RESCHER, N. INTRODUCTION TO VALUE
THEORY.
M.B.M., 543:MAR70-564
RESCHER, N. THE LOGIC OF COMMANDS.*
H-N. CASTANEDA, 482(PHR):JUL70-439
RESCHER, N., ED. THE LOGIC OF DECISION
AND ACTION.
K. FINE, 479(PHQ):JUL70-287
M.B.M., 543:SEP69-143
RESCHER, N. STUDIES IN ARABIC PHILOS-
OPHY.
M.T.B. BROCCHIERI, 548(RCSF):JAN/MAR
69-106
RESCHER, N., ED. STUDIES IN LOGICAL
THEORY.
R.H.K., 543:MAR70-573
RESCHER, N. TOPICS IN PHILOSOPHICAL
LOGIC.*
R.H.K., 543:MAR70-564
RESKE, H. TRAUM UND WIRKLICHKEIT IM
WERK HEINRICH VON KLEISTS.
J.M. ELLIS, 221(GQ):NOV70-786
RESTANY, P. LES NOUVEAUX RÉALISTES.
P.W. SCHWARTZ, 592:JUL/AUG68-52
RESZKIEWICZ, A. ORDERING OF ELEMENTS IN
LATE OLD ENGLISH PROSE IN TERMS OF
THEIR SIZE AND STRUCTURAL COMPLEXITY.
K. FAISS, 353:MAY69-99
RÉTI, R. THEMATIC PATTERNS IN SONATAS OF
BEETHOVEN. (D. COOKE, ED)
M. DAWNEY, 308:WINTER68-313
RETINGER, J. MEMOIRS OF AN EMINENCE
GRISE. (J. POMIAN, ED)
617(TLS):25FEB72-207
REUSCHEL, H. & S. SONDEREGGER - SEE
HEUSLER, A.
REUTER, F.T. CATHOLIC INFLUENCE ON
AMERICAN COLONIAL POLICIES, 1898-1904.
L.E. GELFAND, 330(MASJ):SPRING69-88
REUTER, H-H. FONTANE.
A.R. ROBINSON, 220(GL&L):OCT70-97
REVANS, R.W., ED. HOSPITALS.
617(TLS):25AUG72-1000
REVEL, J-F. ON PROUST.* (FRENCH TITLE:
SUR PROUST.)
P. BROGAN, 440:30APR72-12
P.N. FURBANK, 362:11MAY72-626
617(TLS):12MAY72-554
REVEL, J-F. WITHOUT MARX OR JESUS.*
P.N. FURBANK, 362:11MAY72-626
617(TLS):7JUL72-763
REVERDIN, O. - SEE "ENTRETIENS SUR L'AN-
TIQUITÉ CLASSIQUE"
REVIE, A. THE LOST COMMAND.
617(TLS):25FEB72-230
REX, B. SAINTS AND INNOCENCE.
M. LEVIN, 441:20FEB72-26
E. WEEKS, 61:APR72-125
REXROTH, K., ED & TRANS. LOVE AND THE
TURNING YEAR.
H. CARRUTH, 249(HUDR):SUMMER71-335
REXROTH, K. THE REXROTH READER. (E.
MOTTRAM, ED)
617(TLS):16JUN72-678
DEL REY, L. PSTALEMATE.
T. STURGEON, 441:14MAY72-33
REY, W.H. ARTHUR SCHNITZLER.*
H.D. COHN, 221(GQ):MAR70-289
REYNOLDS, C.R., JR., COMP. AMERICAN
INDIAN PORTRAITS.*
P. ADAMS, 61:FEB72-109
REYNOLDS, G. A CONCISE HISTORY OF WATER-
COLOURS.
617(TLS):3MAR72-240
REYNOLDS, G. TURNER.*
639(VQR):SUMMER70-CIV
REYNOLDS, G. VICTORIAN PAINTING.
J.C. SLOANE, 54:MAR69-99

REYNOLDS, J. DISCOURSES ON ART.
E. MIGLIORINI, 548(RCSF):APR/JUN69-
230
REYNOLDS, L.D. & N.G. WILSON. SCRIBES
AND SCHOLARS.*
P.E. EASTERLING, 303:VOL90-237
J.P. ELDER, 124:DEC70-137
S. FOLLET, 555:VOL44FASC1-110
REYNOLDS, W.A. ROMANCERO DER HERNÁN COR-
TÉS (ESTUDIO Y TEXTOS DE LOS SIGLOS
XVI Y XVII).
J. AMOR Y VÁZQUEZ, 240(HR):JAN70-108
REZVANI. LIGHT YEARS.
P. RAND, 441:6FEB72-20
RHEES, R. DISCUSSIONS OF WITTGENSTEIN.*
J. BURNHEIM, 63:MAY71-119
I. DILMAN, 518:OCT70-23
RHEES, R. WITHOUT ANSWERS.* (D.Z.
PHILLIPS, ED)
R.W. NEWELL, 518:MAY70-25
RHEES, R. - SEE WITTGENSTEIN, L.
RHEIMS, M. DICTIONNAIRE DES MOTS SAU-
VAGES (ÉCRIVAINS DES XIXE ET XXE
SIÈCLES).
J. ANDRÉ, 555:VOL44FASC1-96
RHODES, A. ART TREASURES OF EASTERN
EUROPE.
617(TLS):29DEC72-1577
RHODES, D. THE LAST FAIR DEAL GOING
DOWN.
J.G. BOWLES, 561(SATR):9SEP72-73
M. LEVIN, 441:31DEC72-18
M. WOOD, 453:14DEC72-12
RHODES, G., ED. THE NEW GOVERNMENT OF
LONDON: THE FIRST FIVE YEARS.
617(TLS):29DEC72-1590
RHODES, I.S. THE PAPERS OF JOHN MAR-
SHALL: A DESCRIPTIVE CALENDAR.
H.A. JOHNSON, 432(NEQ):SEP70-498
RHYMER, J. & A. BULLEN. COMPANION TO
THE GOOD NEWS.
617(TLS):17MAR72-317
RHYS, J. AFTER LEAVING MR. MACKENZIE.
M. LEVIN, 441:27FEB72-52
V.S. NAIPAUL, 453:18MAY72-29
P. THEROUX, 440:13FEB72-6
442(NY):8APR72-130
RIABCHIKOV, E. RUSSIANS IN SPACE.*
(N.P. KAMANIN, ED)
617(TLS):17MAR72-317
RIANI, P. KENZO TANGE.
617(TLS):7JAN72-18
RIASANOVSKY, N.V. A HISTORY OF RUSSIA.*
(2ND ED)
G. LEWINSON, 575(SEER):APR71-320
RIASANOVSKY, N.V. THE TEACHING OF
CHARLES FOURIER.
W.H. HARBOLD, 32:JUN71-422
639(VQR):AUTUMN70-CXLVI
RIASANOVSKY, N.V. & G. STRUVE, EDS.
CALIFORNIA SLAVIC STUDIES. (VOL 5)
P. DEBRECZENY, 574(SEEJ):SUMMER71-229
RIBARD, J. UN MÉNESTREL DU XIVE SIÈCLE:
JEAN DE CONDÉ.
R. O'GORMAN, 589:APR71-391
RIBEIRO, M.D. - SEE UNDER DE SAMPAYO
RIBEIRO, M.
RIBERA, J. MUSIC IN ANCIENT ARABIA AND
SPAIN.
R. ANDERSON, 415:NOV70-1116
RIBIÈRE-RAVERLAT, J. THE ZOLTÁN KODÁLY
METHOD OF MUSICAL EDUCATION IN HUNGARY.
J. HORTON, 415:OCT71-971
RIBNIKAR, J. I AND YOU AND SHE.
J. HUNTER, 362:13APR72-493
RICARD, A. THÉÂTRE ET NATIONALISME.
617(TLS):12MAY72-540

RICART, J.G. - SEE UNDER GUDIOL Y RICART,
J.
RICATTE, R. - SEE GIONO, J.
RICCIARDI, M. VANISHING AFRICA.*
   617(TLS):30JUN72-757
RICCOMINI, E. IL SEICENTO FERRARESE.
   B.N., 90:JUN70-424
RICE, D.T. BYZANTINE PAINTING: THE LAST
   PHASE.*
   D.H. WRIGHT, 56:WINTER69-427
RICE, D.T. & T.T. ICONS.
   A. BRYER, 39:DEC69-545
RICE, H.C., JR. & A.S.K. BROWN, EDS &
   TRANS. THE AMERICAN CAMPAIGNS OF
   ROCHAMBEAU'S ARMY.
   B. BLIVEN, 441:12NOV72-5
   442(NY):9DEC72-177
RICE, J.M. & A.S.M. DICKINS. THE SERIES-
   HELPMATE.
   617(TLS):28JUL72-900
RICH, A. LEAFLETS.
   617(TLS):9JUN72-651
RICH, A. MUSIC.
   R. MOEVS, 363:FEB70-76
RICH, A. SNAPSHOTS OF A DAUGHTER-IN-
   LAW.*
   T. HARRISON, 364:APR/MAY71-163
RICH, A. THE WILL TO CHANGE.*
   R. HOWARD, 473(PR):WINTER71/72-484
   R. LATTIMORE, 249(HUDR):AUTUMN71-500
RICHARD, J-P. ETUDES SUR LE ROMANTISME.*
   R. CHAMBERS, 67:MAY71-131
RICHARDS, D.R. THE GERMAN BESTSELLER IN
   THE 20TH CENTURY.*
   H.D. OSTERLE, 221(GQ):NOV70-814
RICHARDS, I.A. INTERNAL COLLOQUIES.
   F. KERMODE, 362:20JUL72-87
   617(TLS):23JUN72-710
RICHARDS, J.M. A GUIDE TO FINNISH ARCHI-
   TECTURE.*
   F. GUTHEIM, 576:MAR68-86
RICHARDS, K. & P. THOMSON, EDS. THE
   EIGHTEENTH-CENTURY ENGLISH STAGE.*
   617(TLS):17NOV72-1398
RICHARDS, K. & P. THOMSON, EDS. ESSAYS
   ON NINETEENTH-CENTURY BRITISH THEATRE.*
   S. WELLS, 677:VOL2-307
RICHARDS, M.C. CENTERING.
   A.M. SULLIVAN, 363:NOV69-30
RICHARDSON, G. & W. FLETCHER. PETITES
   HISTOIRES. HISTOIRES ILLUSTRÉES.
   E. POPPER, 207(FR):FEB70-541
RICHARDSON, H.W. TOWARD AN AMERICAN
   THEOLOGY.
   P.G. KUNTZ, 477:SUMMER69-393
RICHARDSON, J. THE NEW YORK POLICE:
   COLONIAL TIMES TO 1901.
   639(VQR):AUTUMN70-CXLVII
RICHARDSON, J. LA VIE PARISIENNE 1852-
   1870.
   R. FREEDMAN, 440:20FEB72-7
   617(TLS):14JAN72-43
RICHARDSON, J.A. MODERN ART AND SCIEN-
   TIFIC THOUGHT.
   P. GAY, 31(ASCH):AUTUMN72-660
RICHARDSON, K., WITH E. HARRIS. TWENTI-
   ETH-CENTURY COVENTRY.
   617(TLS):15SEP72-1050
RICHARDSON, M. THE FASCINATION OF REP-
   TILES.
   617(TLS):10NOV72-1376
RICHARDSON, P. ISRAEL IN THE APOSTOLIC
   CHURCH.
   G. STRECKER, 182:VOL23#8-401
RICHARDSON, R. LITERATURE AND FILM.
   N. SILVERSTEIN, 295:VOL2#1-154

RICHARDSON, R.C. PURITANISM IN NORTH-
   WEST ENGLAND.
   617(TLS):25AUG72-1001
RICHETTI, J.J. POPULAR FICTION BEFORE
   RICHARDSON.*
   R.E. KELLEY, 481(PQ):JUL70-318
   N. WURZBACH, 72:BAND208HEFT4/6-389
RICHEY, M.F. ESSAYS ON MEDIAEVAL GERMAN
   POETRY.*
   R.A. AMAN, 399(MLJ):MAY70-380
   D. BLAMIRES, 402(MLR):JAN71-211
   C. GRAY, JR., 301(JEGP):APR71-363
RICHIE, D. COMPANIONS OF THE HOLIDAY.
   R.H. BAYES, 50(ARQ):AUTUMN69-273
RICHIE, D. THE INLAND SEA.
   P. ADAMS, 61:APR72-129
   N. GOSLING, 440:26MAR72-5
   441:26MAR72-37
RICHLER, M., ED. CANADIAN WRITING TODAY.
   K. FRASER, 102(CANL):SPRING71-89
RICHLER, M. COCKSURE.*
   G. ROPER, 627(UTQ):JUL69-353
RICHLER, M. ST. URBAIN'S HORSEMAN.*
   M. FELD, 364:DEC71/JAN72-162
   F.P.W. MC DOWELL, 659:SUMMER72-361
   J.M. MORSE, 249(HUDR):AUTUMN71-538
RICHLER, M. SHOVELLING TROUBLE.
   617(TLS):27OCT72-1278
RICHLER, M. THE STREET.*
   617(TLS):25FEB72-212
RICHMOND, G.C. & G.H. KIRBY, EDS. AUS-
   LESE.
   T. ALT, 221(GQ):NOV70-827
   W.H. GRILK, 399(MLJ):NOV70-537
RICHMOND, I. ROMAN ARCHAEOLOGY AND ART.*
   (P. SALWAY, ED)
   K.D. MATTHEWS, JR., 124:MAY71-309
   R.P. WRIGHT, 123:JUN71-274
RICHMOND, I. - SEE COLLINGWOOD, R.G.
RICHMOND, L. HIGH ON GOLD.
   J.R. FRAKES, 441:12NOV72-64
RICHMOND, W.K. THE LITERATURE OF EDUCA-
   TION.
   617(TLS):7JUL72-785
RICHTER, A. THE LAY ANALYST.
   M. LEVIN, 441:2JAN72-16
RICHTER, D. DIE DEUTSCHE ÜBERLIEFERUNG
   DER PREDIGTEN BERTHOLDS VON REGENS-
   BURG.*
   H.B. WILLSON, 402(MLR):APR71-443
RICHTER, G. DIE FUSSWASCHUNG IM JOHAN-
   NESEVANGELIUM.
   F.F. BRUCE, 182:VOL23#15/16-717
RICHTER, G.M.A. ENGRAVED GEMS OF THE
   GREEKS AND THE ETRUSCANS.*
   R. HIGGINS, 39:DEC69-543
RICHTER, G.M.A. A HANDBOOK OF GREEK
   ART. (6TH ED)
   J. BOARDMAN, 90:JUN70-423
RICHTER, G.M.A. KORAI.
   B. GOLDMAN, 56:AUTUMN69-316
RICHTER, G.M.A. PERSPECTIVE IN GREEK AND
   ROMAN ART.
   B.S. RIDGWAY, 124:FEB71-201
RICHTER, G.M.A. THE SCULPTURE AND SCULP-
   TORS OF THE GREEKS. (4TH ED)
   617(TLS):27OCT72-1296
RICHTER, H. VIRGINIA WOOLF.*
   R.Z. TEMPLE, 295:VOL2#3-421
RICHTER, H.W. ROSE WEISS, ROSE ROT.
   617(TLS):22SEP72-1122
RICHTER, L. DER BERLINER GASSENHAUER.
   R.T.B., 410(M&L):APR71-192
   P. BRANSCOMBE, 415:APR71-347
RICHTER, L. JEAN-PAUL SARTRE.
   R. CHAMPIGNY, 659:SPRING72-261

RICHTER, W. DIE LANDWIRTSCHAFT IM HOMER-
ISCHEN ZEITALTER.
F.M. COMBELLACK, 122:JAN71-40
RICHTER, W. & W. SCHIERING. ARCHAEOLOGIA
HOMERICA. (VOL H)
P. CHANTRAINE, 555:VOL44FASC2-302
RICKARD, P. - SEE PESSOA, F.
RICKARDS, M. WHERE THEY LIVED IN LONDON.
617(TLS):19MAY72-585
RICKER, J.C. & J.T. SAYWELL. THE STORY
OF WESTERN MAN.* (VOLS 1&2)
102(CANL):SPRING71-119
RICKETT, H.W. WILD FLOWERS OF THE UNITED
STATES.* (VOL 5)
P. ADAMS, 61:APR72-129
RICKEY, G. CONSTRUCTIVISM.
C. GRAY, 592:MAR68-164
H.H. WAECHTER, 505:JUL68-170
RICKS, C. TENNYSON.
W.H. AUDEN, 362:10AUG72-181
R.W. FLINT, 453:2NOV72-28
617(TLS):25AUG72-988
RICKS, C. - SEE TENNYSON, A.
RICO, F. LA NOVELA PICARESCA Y EL PUNTO
DE VISTA.
C.A. LONGHURST, 86(BHS):JUL71-272
RICO, F. - SEE LOPE DE VEGA
RICO, M. ENSAYO DE BIBLIOGRAFÍA PINDÁR-
ICA.
É. DES PLACES, 182:VOL23#3-102
RICOEUR, P. LE CONFLIT DES INTERPRÉTA-
TIONS. DE L'INTERPRÉTATION.
Y. BRES, 542:JUL-DEC69-425
RIDGWAY, B.S. THE SEVERE STYLE IN GREEK
SCULPTURE.*
U.W. HIESINGER, 124:FEB71-202
RIDGWAY, M.H. CHESTER GOLDSMITHS FROM
EARLY TIMES TO 1726.
C. OMAN, 39:FEB69-160
RIDGWELL, W.M. THE FORGOTTEN TRIBES OF
GUYANA.
617(TLS):11AUG72-936
RIDLER, A. SOME TIME AFTER.
617(TLS):21APR72-441
RIDLEY, J. JOHN KNOX.*
J.W. FERGUSON, 551(RENQ):SPRING70-84
G.C. TAYLOR, 325:APR70-79
RIEDEL, M. THEORIE UND PRAXIS IM DENKEN
HEGELS.
M.J.V., 543:DEC69-354
RIEDINGER, R. PSEUDO-KAISARIOS.*
J. MEYENDORFF, 589:JAN71-182
RIEDL, F. A HISTORY OF HUNGARIAN LITERA-
TURE.*
P. DEBRECZENY, 32:MAR71-216
A. DEMAITRE, 149:JUN71-175
RIEFF, P., ED. ON INTELLECTUALS.
R.J.B., 543:DEC69-365
R. GOEDECKE, 185:APR70-246
RIEGLE, D., WITH T. ARMBRISTER. O CON-
GRESS.
S. HARRINGTON, 441:2JUL72-5
442(NY):22JUL72-78
RIEMANN, H. DICTIONARY OF MUSIC. (4TH
ED)
S. SADIE, 415:FEB71-140
RIEMANN, K.A. DAS HERODOTEISCHE GE-
SCHICHTSWERK IN DER ANTIKE.
S. USHER, 303:VOL90-207
RIEPE, D. THE PHILOSOPHY OF INDIA AND
ITS IMPACT ON AMERICAN THOUGHT. (M.
FARBER, ED)
A.K. SARKAR, 319:OCT72-485
RIESE, T.A. & D. RIESNER, EDS. VERS-
DICHTUNG DER ENGLISCHEN ROMANTIK.
D. MEHL, 182:VOL23#6-284
R. TSCHUMI, 179(ES):APR69-223

RIESER, M. AN ANALYSIS OF POETIC THINK-
ING.
M.R. HAIGHT, 89(BJA):WINTER71-101
RIESS, F. THE WORD AND THE STONE.
617(TLS):22SEP72-1092
RIETH, A. MONUMENTS TO THE VICTIMS OF
TYRANNY.
C. MEADMORE, 58:DEC69/JAN70-10
RIFFATERRE, M. ESSAIS DE STYLISTIQUE
STRUCTURALE.
617(TLS):25FEB72-228
RIGG, A.G. A GLASTONBURY MISCELLANY OF
THE FIFTEENTH CENTURY.*
R. HANDS, 72:BAND208HEFT2-136
RIGLER, J. ZAČETKI SLOVENSKEGA KNJIŽNEGA
JEZIKA.
J. PATERNOST, 104:SUMMER71-275
RIGOLOT, F. LES LANGAGES DE RABELAIS.
617(TLS):7JUL72-784
RIHA, K. & G. KÄMPF - SEE HAUSMANN, R.
RIHA, T. A RUSSIAN EUROPEAN.*
G.A. HOSKING, 587:APR70-515
J.F. HUTCHINSON, 104:FALL71-436
S. MONAS, 550(RUSR):APR70-211
RIKKO, F. - SEE ROSSI, S.
RIKLIN, F., L. JUNG-MERKER & E. RÜF - SEE
JUNG, C.G.
RILEY, C.L. & OTHERS, EDS. MAN ACROSS
THE SEA.
617(TLS):21JAN72-77
RILEY, P. A BIBLIOGRAPHY OF T.F. POWYS.
F.G.F., 503:WINTER68-184
RILEY, P. - SEE LEIBNIZ, G.W.
RILEY, P. - SEE POWYS, T.F.
RILEY, R.C. THE WEST COUNTRY.
617(TLS):17MAR72-317
RIMBAUD, A. COMPLETE WORKS, SELECTED
LETTERS. (W. FOWLIE, ED & TRANS)
R.T. DENOMMÉ, 569(SR):AUTUMN71-637
RIMBAUD, A. ILLUMINATIONS. (A. PY, ED)
C.A. HACKETT, 208(FS):JAN71-102
RIMMER, J. THE IRISH HARP.
J. MARSON, 415:APR70-394
RINGBOM, H. STUDIES IN THE NARRATIVE
TECHNIQUE OF "BEOWULF" AND LAWMAN'S
"BRUT."
A.J. BLISS, 541(RES):FEB70-69
D.S. BREWER, 447(N&Q):JUN70-225
RINGBOM, S. ICON TO NARRATIVE.
C. EISLER, 54:JUN69-186
RINGEL, K.J. WILHELM RAABES ROMAN "HAS-
TENBECK."
E.V.K. BRILL, 402(MLR):OCT71-955
F.M. WASSERMANN, 406:SPRING71-82
RINGER, F.K. THE DECLINE OF THE GERMAN
MANDARINS.
G. BARRACLOUGH, 453:19OCT72-37
RINGGOLD, G. & D. BODEEN. THE FILMS OF
CECIL B. DE MILLE.
J. GROSVENOR, 200:AUG-SEP69-427
RINK, E., COMP. PRINTING IN DELAWARE,
1761-1800.
P.J. WEIMERSKIRCH, 70(ANQ):OCT71-19
RINSER, L. BAUSTELLE.
617(TLS):21APR72-450
VON RINTELEN, J. BEYOND EXISTENTIALISM.
J. GRANIER, 542:JAN-MAR69-101
DE LOS RÍOS, E. LOS JUEGOS VERDADEROS.
J.F. SAUNDERS, 238:MAY70-348
DE LOS RÍOS, G.G. & L. DE LOS RÍOS DE
GARCÍA LORCA - SEE UNDER GINER DE LOS
RÍOS, G. & L. DE LOS RÍOS DE GARCÍA
LORCA
RIOUX, J-P. LA RÉVOLUTION INDUSTRIELLE,
1780-1880.
617(TLS):28APR72-498
RIPIN, E.M., ED. KEYBOARD INSTRUMENTS.
617(TLS):27OCT72-1293

RIPLEY, J. DAVIS DOESN'T LIVE HERE ANY
MORE.
N. CALLENDAR, 441:24SEP72-41
RIPOLL, C. LA CELESTINA A TRAVÉS DEL
DECÁLOGO Y OTRAS NOTAS SOBRE LA LIT-
ERATURA DE LA EDAD DE ORO.
J.B. AVALLE-ARCE, 241:SEP71-75
R.W. TRUMAN, 86(BHS):JUL71-263
RIPOLL, C., ED. ESCRITOS DESCONOCIDOS
DE JOSÉ MARTÍ.
R. ESQUENAZI-MAYO, 263:OCT-DEC71-471
RIPOLL, C. LA GENERACIÓN DEL 23 EN CUBA
Y OTROS APUNTES SOBRE EL VANGUARDISMO.
F.S. STIMSON, 238:SEP70-582
RIPOLL, L. - SEE UNDER KLECZYNSKI, J.
RISCHBIETER, H. PETER WEISS.*
I. HILTON, 220(GL&L):JUL71-385
RISI, N. DI CERTE COSE.
617(TLS):21JUL72-839
RIST, J.M. PLOTINUS.*
A.C. LLOYD, 482(PHR):JAN70-145
RIST, J.M. STOIC PHILOSOPHY.*
D. FURLEY, 124:DEC70-136
H.S. LONG, 24:OCT71-748
H.D. RANKIN, 63:AUG71-223
RITCHESON, C.R. AFTERMATH OF REVOLU-
TION.*
J.J. HECHT, 432(NEQ):SEP70-496
W. STINCHCOMBE, 656(WMQ):OCT70-662
RITCHIE, A.D. GEORGE BERKELEY, A REAP-
PRAISAL. (G.E. DAVIE, ED)
G.M., 477:SPRING69-290
RITCHIE, G.F. CAROLINE SCHLEGEL-SCHEL-
LING IN WAHRHEIT UND DICHTUNG.
I.C., 191(ELN):SEP70(SUPP)-128
RITCHIE, J. PUNISHMENT AND PROFIT.
617(TLS):18AUG72-977
RITCHIE, J.M., ED. PERIODS IN GERMAN
LITERATURE. (VOL 2)
M.B. BENN, 402(MLR):OCT71-941
RITCHIE, T. & OTHERS. CANADA BUILDS:
1867-1967.
W.C. KIDNEY, 505:JUL68-194
RITSON, J. CURSORY CRITICISMS ON MAL-
ONE'S EDITION OF SHAKESPEARE [TOGETHER
WITH] MALONE, E. LETTER TO THE REV.
RICHARD FARMER.
617(TLS):18FEB72-178
RITSOS, Y. GESTURES AND OTHER POEMS
1968-1970.
617(TLS):10MAR72-273
RITTER, G. THE SWORD AND THE SCEPTRE.
(VOLS 1&2)
617(TLS):6OCT72-1201
RITTER, H. TŪRŌYO, DIE VOLKSSPRACHE DER
SYRISCHEN CHRISTEN DES ṬŪR 'ABDĪN.
(PT A, VOL 1)
D. COUTINHO, 353:SEP69-91
RIVAUD, A. HISTOIRE DE LA PHILOSOPHIE.
(VOL 5)
S. DANGELMAYR, 182:VOL23#5-202
DE RIVAUDEAU, A. AMAN. (K. CAMERON, ED)
W. BECK, 207(FR):MAY70-940
C.N. SMITH, 208(FS):JUL71-330
RIVELLI, C. EDUARDO MALLEA.
M. LICHTBLAU, 238:MAR70-155
RIVERA DE ÁLVAREZ, J. HISTORIA DE LA
LITERATURA PUERTORRIQUEÑA.
C.A. MONTANER, 263:JUL-SEP71-347
RIVERS, E.L. - SEE GARCILASO DE LA VEGA
RIVERS, W. TEACHING FOREIGN LANGUAGE
SKILLS.
P.B. SIMONIAN, 207(FR):OCT69-144
RIVET, A.L.F., ED. THE ROMAN VILLA IN
BRITAIN.
P. SALWAY, 123:MAR71-103

RIVKIN, E. THE SHAPING OF JEWISH HIS-
TORY.*
R. GORDIS, 441:9JAN72-5
T. LASK, 441:14JAN72-34
RIZO, T. - SEE UNDER TAKEUCHI RIZO
RIZZI, A. THE ETCHINGS OF THE TIEPOLOS.
617(TLS):31MAR72-368
RIZZO, F.P. LE FONTI PER LA STORIA DELLA
CONQUISTA POMPEIANA DELLA SIRIA.
H. OPPERMANN, 182:VOL23#19/20-879
RIZZO, S. INDEX VERBORUM AEGRITUDINIS
PERDICAE.
J. ANDRÉ, 555:VOL44FASC2-368
RIZZUTO, A. STYLE AND THEME IN REVERDY'S
"LES ARDOISES DU TOIT."
R. SHATTUCK, 453:1JUN72-25
ROAZEN, P. BROTHER ANIMAL.
639(VQR):WINTER70-XXI
ROBAK, D. LEGISLATIVE BODY.
N. CALLENDAR, 441:8OCT72-46
ROBATHAN, D.M., ED. THE PSEUDO-OVIDIAN
"DE VETULA."*
G.P. GOOLD, 124:JAN71-167
J.A. RICHMOND, 123:DEC70-343
ROBB, W.H. THE TYRIAN QUILL.
G.F.G. STANLEY, 529(QQ):SUMMER70-296
ROBBE-GRILLET, A. LA JALOUSIE. (B.G.
GARNHAM, ED)
J. CRUICKSHANK, 208(FS):JAN71-115
ROBBE-GRILLET, A. PROJECT FOR A REVOLU-
TION IN NEW YORK.
A. BROYARD, 441:16MAY72-45
R. SHATTUCK, 441:28MAY72-5
J. WEIGHTMAN, 453:1JUN72-6
ROBBINS, C., ED. TWO ENGLISH REPUBLICAN
TRACTS.
639(VQR):WINTER70-XXV
ROBE, S.L., ED. MEXICAN TALES AND LEG-
ENDS FROM LOS ALTOS.
P. DE CARVALHO-NETO, 263:JUL-SEP71-
349
LORD ROBENS. TEN YEAR STINT.
D. MOREAU, 362:23MAR72-383
617(TLS):24MAR72-336
ROBERSON, E. WHEN THY KING IS A BOY.
R.B. SHAW, 491:MAR72-342
"ROBERT DE BLOIS'S 'FLORIS ET LYRIOPÉ'."
(P. BARRETTE, ED)
N.L. CORBETT, 405(MP):FEB70-279
N.J. LACY, 399(MLJ):APR70-297
ROBERT, M. ROMAN DES ORIGINES ET ORI-
GENES DU ROMAN.
617(TLS):10NOV72-1362
ROBERT, S. - SEE UNDER SHAABAN ROBERT
ROBERTO, E. - SEE CLAUDEL, P. & A. MEYER
ROBERTS, A., ED. THE STRATEGY OF CIVIL-
IAN DEFENCE.
M. PITTOCK, 97(CQ):SPRING68-167
ROBERTS, A., ED. TANZANIA BEFORE 1900.
T.O. BEIDELMAN, 69:OCT69-442
ROBERTS, B. THE DIAMOND MAGNATES.
617(TLS):6OCT72-1193
ROBERTS, B. CECIL RHODES AND THE PRIN-
CESS.
639(VQR):SPRING70-LXVII
ROBERTS, C. SUNSHINE AND SHADOW.
617(TLS):9JUN72-647
ROBERTS, E.V. - SEE FIELDING, H.
ROBERTS, E.V. - SEE GAY, J.
ROBERTS, G.R. ENGLISH IN PRIMARY
SCHOOLS.
617(TLS):6OCT72-1205
ROBERTS, H.L. EASTERN EUROPE.
M.G. ZANINOVICH, 32:SEP71-678
ROBERTS, J.M. THE MYTHOLOGY OF THE
SECRET SOCIETIES.
R. COBB, 362:10AUG72-182
617(TLS):15DEC72-1517

ROBERTS, J.R., ED. A CRITICAL ANTHOLOGY
OF ENGLISH RECUSANT DEVOTIONAL PROSE,
1558-1603.
T.A. BIRRELL, 677:VOL2-249
ROBERTS, K. FROM SCHOOL TO WORK.
617(TLS):12MAY72-557
ROBERTS, L. MONTREAL.
102(CANL):SPRING71-119
ROBERTS, P.B. STEPHANUS DE LINGUA-
TONANTE.*
R.M. WILSON, 402(MLR):OCT71-846
ROBERTS, S., ED & TRANS. ESSAYS IN
RUSSIAN LITERATURE.
H. STAMMLER, 574(SEEJ):SPRING71-121
ROBERTS, T.A. THE HEART OF A DOG.
N. CALLENDAR, 441:26NOV72-36
ROBERTSON, A. REQUIEM.
A.E.F. DICKINSON, 607:WINTER67/68-30
ROBERTSON, D.W., JR. ABELARD AND HELO-
ISE.
V. CRONIN, 440:13FEB72-3
D. KNOWLES, 441:13FEB72-40
442(NY):12FEB72-104
ROBERTSON, D.W., JR. CHAUCER'S LONDON.*
M.M. CROW, 589:JUL71-539
P.L. HEYWORTH, 382(MAE):1971/3-309
ROBERTSON, E. THE YORKHILL STORY.
617(TLS):1SEP72-1019
ROBERTSON, G. GIOVANNI BELLINI.*
F. GIBBONS, 551(RENQ):SUMMER70-174
J. STEER, 90:FEB70-115
ROBERTSON, R.G., COMP. ENGLISH-THAI
DICTIONARY.
D.J.H. MACINTOSH, 302:JUL70-416
ROBICHEZ, J. - SEE VERLAINE, P.
ROBILLARD, R. EARLE BIRNEY.
P.C. NOEL-BENTLEY, 296:SPRING72-84
ROBIN, M. RADICAL POLITICS AND CANADIAN
LABOUR, 1880-1930.
102(CANL):SPRING71-120
ROBINS, N.S. THE PEAS BELONG ON THE EYE
LEVEL.
T. LASK, 441:18AUG72-31
ROBINS, R.H. GENERAL LINGUISTICS.*
G. NICKEL, 72:BAND208HEFT3-200
ROBINSON, D. GOSHAWK SQUADRON.*
C. LEHMANN-HAUPT, 441:19JAN72-39
M. LEVIN, 441:23JAN72-36
442(NY):12FEB72-102
ROBINSON, D.F., ED. AZTEC STUDIES I.
H.W. LAW, 350:SEP71-737
ROBINSON, D.S. ROYCE AND HOCKING.
T. HANEY, 485(PE&W):APR69-196
ROBINSON, E.A.G. & M. KIDRON, EDS. ECO-
NOMIC DEVELOPMENT IN SOUTH ASIA.
617(TLS):15SEP72-1066
ROBINSON, E.L. SLOTH AND HEATHEN FOLLY.
M. LEVIN, 441:30JUL72-23
ROBINSON, H.R. ORIENTAL ARMOUR.*
C. MILWARD, 39:MAR69-245
L. TARASSUK, 90:MAR70-176
ROBINSON, J., WITH A. DUCKETT. I NEVER
HAD IT MADE.
R. BARBER, 441:12NOV72-53
ROBINSON, J.A.T. THE DIFFERENCE IN BEING
A CHRISTIAN TODAY.
617(TLS):28JAN72-107
ROBINSON, J.O. THE PSYCHOLOGY OF VISUAL
ILLUSION.
617(TLS):29DEC72-1579
ROBINSON, M. THE LONG SONATA OF THE
DEAD.*
B. LORICH, 584(SWR):WINTER71-96
R. PEARCE, 295:VOL2#3-442
ROBINSON, R., ED. DEVELOPING THE THIRD
WORLD.
617(TLS):15SEP72-1066

ROBINSON, R. ESSAYS IN GREEK PHILOSOPHY.
D.W. HAMLYN, 518:JAN70-25
ROBINSON, R.A.H. THE ORIGINS OF FRANCO'S
SPAIN.*
R. CARR, 86(BHS):OCT71-360
ROBINSON, R.H. EARLY MADHYAMIKA IN
INDIA AND CHINA.
L. HURVITZ, 318(JAOS):APR-JUN70-384
ROBINSON, T.M. PLATO'S PSYCHOLOGY.
G. ANAGNOSTOPOULOS, 319:APR72-217
D.W. HAMLYN, 518:MAY71-25
R.G. HOERBER, 124:JAN71-158
ROBINSON, T.W., ED. THE CULTURAL REVOL-
UTION IN CHINA.
J. MATHEWS, 31(ASCH):SPRING72-304
ROBITAILLE, G. IMAGES.*
M. HORNYANSKY, 627(UTQ):JUL70-331
ROBSON, J., ED. THE YOUNG BRITISH
POETS.*
G. GRIGSON, 364:OCT/NOV71-132
ROBSON, J.M., ED. EDITING NINETEENTH-
CENTURY TEXTS.
J.C. MAXWELL, 447(N&Q):OCT70-394
ROBSON, J.M. THE IMPROVEMENT OF MANKIND.
W. ROBBINS, 627(UTQ):JUL69-411
J. STILLINGER, 191(ELN):DEC69-151
ROBSON, J.M. - SEE MILL, J.S.
ROBSON, J.M., F.E.L. PRIESTLEY & D.P.
DRYER - SEE MILL, J.S.
ROBSON, W.A. NATIONALISED INDUSTRY AND
PUBLIC OWNERSHIP.
617(TLS):2JUN72-637
ROBSON, W.W. MODERN ENGLISH LITERATURE.*
M. LEBOWITZ, 598(SOR):SUMMER72-696
A. RODWAY, 402(MLR):OCT71-885
ROCHE, J. PALESTRINA.
617(TLS):3MAR72-253
ROCHE, T.P., JR. - SEE TUVE, R.
ROCHEFORT, C. PRINTEMPS AU PARKING.
L.S. ROUDIEZ, 207(FR):APR70-869
ROCHER, R. ALEXANDER HAMILTON (1762-
1824).*
D. KOPF, 293(JAST):FEB70-464
ROCHER, R. LA THÉORIE DES VOIX DU VERBE
DANS L'ÉCOLE PĀṆINÉENNE (LE 14E
ĀHNIKA).
H. SCHARFE, 318(JAOS):OCT-DEC70-584
ROCHET, W. LES ENSEIGNEMENTS DE MAI-JUIN
1968.
P. CRANT, 207(FR):MAR70-720
ROCQ, M.M., ED. CALIFORNIA LOCAL HIS-
TORY. (2ND ED)
C. WALTON, 356:APR71-185
RODAX, Y. THE REAL AND THE IDEAL IN THE
NOVELLA OF ITALY, FRANCE AND ENGLAND.
G. COSTA, 545(RPH):AUG70-238
J. FRANK, 551(RENQ):SUMMER70-177
S.B. PURDY, 399(MLJ):APR70-291
RODDICK, A. THE EYE CORRECTS.
G. COLLIER, 368:SEP69-303
RODEN, C. A BOOK OF MIDDLE EASTERN FOOD.
N. HAZELTON, 441:3DEC72-96
RÖDER, G. GLÜCK UND GLÜCKLICHES ENDE IM
DEUTSCHEN BILDUNGSROMAN.
C.E. SCHWEITZER, 221(GQ):MAR70-284
RODGER, A. OWNERS AND NEIGHBOURS IN
ROMAN LAW.
617(TLS):22DEC72-1564
RODGERS, B. THE QUEEN'S VERNACULAR.
R.W. BURCHFIELD, 441:26NOV72-22
RODGERS, W.R. COLLECTED POEMS.
R. BLYTHE, 362:13JAN72-56
617(TLS):14JAN72-32
RODGERS, W.R. IRISH LITERARY PORTRAITS.
R. BLYTHE, 362:28SEP72-409
RODINI, R.J. ANTONFRANCESCO GRAZZINI.
M. REINTHALER, 182:VOL23#5-224

RODINSON, M. MOHAMMED.*
  L.P. ELWELL-SUTTON, 453:27JAN72-22
  442(NY):20MAY72-139
RODITI, E. NEW HIEROGLYPHIC TALES.
  A.H. ROSENFELD, 328:WINTER69-123
RODMAN, S. THE CARIBBEAN.
  V.L.E., 37:MAR69-41
RODRIGUEZ, A. A HISTORY OF MEXICAN MURAL
  PAINTING.
  B. REISE, 592:NOV69-186
RODRÍGUEZ, L. ROMANCERO HISTORIADO (AL-
  CALÁ, 1582). (A. RODRÍGUEZ-MOÑINO, ED)
  E.M. WILSON, 240(HR):JUL70-324
RODRÍGUEZ-MOÑINO, A., ED. CANCIONERO DE
  ROMANCES (ANVERS, 1550).
  E.M. WILSON, 240(HR):JUL70-324
RODRÍGUEZ-MOÑINO, A. CONSTRUCCIÓN CRÍ-
  TICA Y REALIDAD HISTÓRICA EN LA POESÍA
  ESPAÑOLA DE LOS SIGLOS XVI Y XVII.
  (2ND ED)
  M.D. TRIWEDI, 238:MAR70-148
RODRÍGUEZ-MOÑINO, A. POESÍA Y CANCION-
  EROS (SIGLO XVI).*
  E.L. RIVERS, 400(MLN):MAR70-294
  M.D. TRIWEDI, 238:DEC70-1020
RODRÍGUEZ-MOÑINO, A. - SEE RODRÍGUEZ, L.
RODRÍGUEZ-MOÑINO, A. - SEE DE SEPÚLVEDA,
  L.
RODRÍGUEZ ADRADOS, F. ILUSTRACIÓN Y
  POLÍTICA EN LA GRECIA CLÁSICA.
  F. LASSERRE, 182:VOL23#17/18-814
RODRÍGUEZ DEMORIZI, E. POETAS CONTRA
  BOLÍVAR.
  M. VALLDEPERES, 263:APR-JUN71-221
ROE, D. PREHISTORY: AN INTRODUCTION.*
  J. BOARDMAN, 123:DEC71-459
ROE, F.G. VICTORIAN CORNERS.
  A.B., 155:MAY69-120
  M. VICINUS, 637(VS):JUN70-433
ROE, I. A STYLE OF YOUR OWN.
  617(TLS):21APR72-457
ROEMING, R.F., ED. CAMUS: A BIBLIOGRA-
  PHY.*
  P.J. JOHNSON, 207(FR):OCT69-170
  I.H. WALKER, 208(FS):JAN71-112
ROESSINGH, M.P.H., COMP. GUIDE TO THE
  SOUCES IN THE NETHERLANDS FOR THE
  HISTORY OF LATIN AMERICA.
  G.S. ULIBARRI, 14:OCT69-385
ROETHEL, H.K. THE BLUE RIDER.
  617(TLS):5MAY72-508
ROETHEL, H.K. PAUL KLEE IN MÜNCHEN.
  617(TLS):31MAR72-368
ROETHKE, T. THE COLLECTED POEMS OF THEO-
  DORE ROETHKE.*
  E.J., 619(TC):1968/3-52
  H. SERGEANT, 175:SPRING69-33
ROETHKE, T. SELECTED LETTERS OF THEODORE
  ROETHKE.* (R.J. MILLS, JR., ED)
  K. JOHNSON, 330(MASJ):FALL69-81
ROETHKE, T. STRAW FOR THE FIRE. (D.
  WAGONER, ED)
  A. BROYARD, 441:7MAR72-41
  W. HEYEN, 561(SATR):11MAR72-70
  H. LEIBOWITZ, 441:9APR72-4
ROETHLISBERGER, M. CLAUDE LORRAIN: THE
  DRAWINGS.
  D. HOWARD, 90:DEC70-836
  G. MARTIN, 39:DEC69-539
ROFF, W.R. THE ORIGINS OF MALAY NATION-
  ALISM.
  L.R. WRIGHT, 302:JAN69-120
ROFFMAN, J. A BAD CONSCIENCE.
  N. CALLENDAR, 441:5MAR72-34
ROFHEART, M. FORTUNE MADE HIS SWORD.
  G. HICKS, 441:27FEB72-46
  442(NY):1APR72-105

ROGBY, O. NIEDERDEUTSCH AUF FRIESISCHEM
  SUBSTRAT.
  L-E. AHLSSON, 597(SN):VOL41#1-170
ROGER, J. LES SCIENCES DE LA VIE DANS
  LA PENSÉE FRANÇAISE DU XVIIIE SIÈCLE.
  617(TLS):3NOV72-1302
ROGERS, F.M. THE TRAVELS OF THE INFANTE
  DOM PEDRO OF PORTUGAL.
  B.M. WOODBRIDGE, JR., 545(RPH):NOV70-
  355
ROGERS, F.R. - SEE TWAIN, M.
ROGERS, M.C. - SEE "THE CHRONICLE OF FU
  CHIEN"
ROGERS, N. SHELLEY AT WORK. (2ND ED)
  R.B. WOODINGS, 597(SN):VOL41#1-195
ROGERS, N. - SEE SHELLEY, P.B.
ROGERS, P. GRUB STREET.
  617(TLS):23JUN72-710
ROGERS, R.M., W.H. SPEIDEL & A.R. WAT-
  KINS. REVIEWING GERMAN.
  R.A. AMAN, 221(GQ):MAR70-305
  G.A. DOLBERG, 399(MLJ):OCT70-443
ROGERS, T. THE CONFESSION OF A CHILD OF
  THE CENTURY.
  A. BROYARD, 441:30MAY72-39
  R. SALE, 453:29JUN72-28
  J. YARDLEY, 441:11JUN72-4
ROGERS, T. LEICESTER'S GHOST. (F.B.
  WILLIAMS, JR., ED)
  617(TLS):1DEC72-1452
ROGERS, T.J. TECHNIQUES OF SOLIPSISM.
  C.A. BERND, 301(JEGP):OCT71-736
  T.E. CARTER, 67:NOV71-256
  W.A. COUPE, 402(MLR):APR71-467
  D. JOST, 182:VOL23#9-480
ROGGE, W. ERNST KŘENEK'S OPERN.
  M. CARNER, 415:SEP71-859
ROGIER, L-J., R. AUBERT & M.D. KNOWLES,
  EDS. GESCHICHTE DER KIRCHE. (VOLS
  1, 3 & 4)
  J-D. BURGER, 182:VOL23#7-346
ROGIN, G. WHAT HAPPENS NEXT?*
  P. WOOD, 561(SATR):1JAN72-32
ROGUET, A.M. - SEE "THE LITURGY OF THE
  HOURS"
ROH, F. GERMAN ART IN THE 20TH CENTURY.
  A. WERNER, 340(KR):1969/1-137
ROHDE, G. STUDIEN UND INTERPRETATIONEN
  ZUR ANTIKEN LITERATUR, RELIGION UND
  GESCHICHTE.
  J.S. MORRISON, 123:JUN71-308
ROHDICH, H. DIE EURIPIDEISCHE TRAGÖDIE.*
  S.A. BARLOW, 123:DEC71-347
RÖHL, J.C.G., ED. ZWEI DEUTSCHE FÜRSTEN
  ZUR KRIEGSSCHULDFRAGE.
  617(TLS):9JUN72-664
ROHLFS, G. - SEE CHRÉTIEN DE TROYES
ROHNER, L. DER DEUTSCHE ESSAY.*
  H. HENNECKE, 564:FALL69-146
  G. LOOSE, 400(MLN):APR70-414
  P.M. SCHON, 52:BAND4HEFT1-108
ROHR, H. THE RADIANT UNIVERSE. (TRANS
  & REV BY A. BEER)
  617(TLS):2JUN72-641
ROHRBOUGH, M.J. THE LAND OFFICE BUSI-
  NESS.
  N.B. WILKINSON, 656(WMQ):JUL70-501
ROIPHE, A. LONG DIVISION.
  I.P. HELDMAN, 561(SATR):14OCT72-85
  C. LEHMANN-HAUPT, 441:18OCT72-49
  N. SAYRE, 441:5NOV72-5
  442(NY):4NOV72-195
ROLFE, C.D. SAINT-AMANT AND THE THEORY
  OF "UT PICTURA POESIS."
  617(TLS):1SEP72-1020
ROLFE, F. LETTERS TO JAMES WALSH. (D.
  WEEKS, ED)
  617(TLS):23JUN72-704

ROLFE, S.E. & W. DAMM, EDS. THE MULTI-
NATIONAL CORPORATION IN THE WORLD
ECONOMY.
  C.S. BURCHILL, 529(QQ):WINTER70-642
ROLI, R. DONATO CRETI.
  D.C. MILLER, 90:MAY69-306
ROLI, R. LA PALA MARMOREA DI S. FRAN-
CESCO IN BOLOGNA.
  R.W. LIGHTBOWN, 90:JUN69-389
ROLL, C.W., JR. & A.H. CANTRIL. POLLS.
  441:15OCT72-40
ROLL, R. I FREGI CENTESI DEL GUERCINO.
  D. POSNER, 54:SEP69-297
RÖLLEKE, H. - SEE VON DROSTE-HÜLSHOFF, A.
ROLO, P.J.V. ENTENTE CORDIALE.
  R. BULLEN, 325:OCT70-158
ROLOFF, H-G. - SEE WARBECK, V.
ROLOFF, H-G. - SEE WICKRAM, G.
ROMAGNESI, H. EXOTIC MUSHROOMS.
  617(TLS):7APR72-402
ROMANOS, R.M. - SEE UNDER MESONERO RO-
MANOS, R.
ROMANOV, A.I. NIGHTS ARE LONGEST THERE.
  617(TLS):15DEC72-1534
"ROMANS PICARESQUES ESPAGNOLS." (M.
MOLHO & J.F. REILLE, TRANS)
  C. ESTEBAN, 98:JAN69-27
  F.G. SALINERO, 238:MAY70-335
ROMBACH, H. SUBSTANZ SYSTEM STRUKTUR.
  M.J.V., 543:SEP69-137
ROMEO, L. THE ECONOMY OF DIPHTHONGIZA-
TION IN EARLY ROMANCE.
  N. CORBETT, 545(RPH):NOV70-273
ROMERALO, A.S. - SEE UNDER SÁNCHEZ ROMER-
ALO, A.
DE ROMILLY, J. TIME IN GREEK TRAGEDY.*
  D.J. CONACHER, 627(UTQ):JAN70-186
  J. DEFRADAS, 555:VOL44FASC2-307
  H. LLOYD-JONES, 123:DEC70-302
  D.W. LUCAS, 303:VOL90-203
ROMMEL, O. SPITTELERS "OLYMPISCHER
FRÜHLING" UND SEINE EPISCHE FORM.
  H.J. SCHUELER, 564:FALL68-169
RONAY, G. THE DRACULA MYTH.
  D.J. ENRIGHT, 362:23NOV72-713
RÓNAY, G. JEGYZETLAPOK.
  L. ILLÉS, 270:VOL20#3-73
RONCAGLIA, A. LA LINGUA DEI TROVATORI.
  F.M. CHAMBERS, 545(RPH):AUG70-205
RONNET, G. SOPHOCLE, POÈTE TRAGIQUE.
  B.M.W. KNOX, 24:OCT71-692
RONNIE, M.A. - SEE MC PHERSON, B.
DE RONSARD, P. LES OEUVRES DE PIERRE DE
RONSARD.* (VOLS 1&2) (I. SILVER, ED)
  G. CASTOR, 402(MLR):APR71-410
  R.E. HALLOWELL, 399(MLJ):MAR70-214
DE RONSARD, P. LES OEUVRES DE PIERRE DE
RONSARD.* (VOLS 3&4) (I. SILVER, ED)
  G. CASTOR, 402(MLR):APR71-410
  R.E. HALLOWELL, 399(MLJ):MAR70-214
  B.L.O. RICHTER, 207(FR):OCT69-191
  M.A. SCREECH, 447(N&Q):JAN70-39
DE RONSARD, P. LES OEUVRES DE PIERRE DE
RONSARD. (VOLS 5&6) (I. SILVER, ED)
  R.E. HALLOWELL, 399(MLJ):MAR70-214
DE RONSARD, P. POÉSIES CHOISIES.
  M. FRANÇON, 551(RENQ):SUMMER70-188
DE RONSARD, P. SONNETS POUR HELENE.
  (M. SMITH, ED)
  G. CASTOR, 208(FS):APR71-194
RONSLEY, J. YEATS'S AUTOBIOGRAPHY.
  J.R. MULRYNE, 402(MLR):JUL71-680
  A. ZWERDLING, 191(ELN):MAR70-236
ROOFF, M. A HUNDRED YEARS OF FAMILY
WELFARE.
  617(TLS):1SEP72-1019
ROOKE, B.E. - SEE COLERIDGE, S.T.

ROOKE, P. THE AGE OF DICKENS.
  A.B., 155:SEP70-244
ROOSENS, E. IMAGES AFRICAINES DE LA MÈRE
ET L'ENFANT.
  G.I. JONES, 69:APR69-191
ROOSEVELT, F.D. & W.C. BULLITT. FOR THE
PRESIDENT. (O.H. BULLITT, ED)
  K.S. DAVIS, 441:17DEC72-4
ROOT, J.W. THE MEANINGS OF ARCHITECTURE.
(D. HOFFMANN, ED)
  A.R. BUTLER, 576:DEC69-298
  F. HERMAN, 505:JUL68-174
  H-R. HITCHCOCK, 44:JAN-FEB69-82
ROOT, W. THE FOOD OF ITALY.
  N. MAGID, 440:20FEB72-8
ROOT, W.P. THE STORM AND OTHER POEMS.
  R. HOWARD, 340(KR):1970/1-130
ROOTES, N. - SEE CENDRARS, B.
ROPER, A. ARNOLD'S POETIC LANDSCAPES.
  K. ALLOTT, 191(ELN):DEC70-153
  D.J. DE LAURA, 301(JEGP):JAN71-173
  639(VQR):SUMMER70-XCVI
RÖPKE, J. PRIMITIVE WIRTSCHAFT, KULTUR-
WANDEL UND DIE DIFFUSION VON NEUER-
UNGEN.
  R. LUCCHINI, 182:VOL23#10-545
RORTY, R., ED. THE LINGUISTIC TURN.
  E.A. MAZIARZ, 486:SEP68-296
VON ROSADOR, K.T. - SEE UNDER TETZELI VON
ROSADOR, K.
ROSALES, A. TRANSZENDENZ UND DIFFERENZ.
  S. DANGELMAYR, 182:VOL23#17/18-778
ROSALES, L. PASIÓN Y MUERTE DEL CONDE
DE VILLAMEDIANA.*
  H. ZIOMEK, 238:SEP70-572
ROSBERG, R. TRIPS - WITHOUT LSD.
  D. BARBOUR, 102(CANL):SPRING71-70
ROSCOE, A.A. MOTHER IS GOLD.*
  W.P. ADAMS, 99:JUL-AUG72-41
ROSE, B. AMERICAN ART SINCE 1900.
  S. BLUTMAN, 505:JUN68-162
  M.G. COMPTON, 592:MAR68-156
ROSE, B. AMERICAN PAINTING.
  J.I.H. BAUR, 58:FEB70-10
ROSE, B. THE GOLDEN AGE OF DUTCH PAINT-
ING.
  D.F. ROWE, 363:NOV69-28
ROSE, B., ED. MODERN TRENDS IN EDUCA-
TION.
  617(TLS):14JAN72-49
ROSE, C. & M. PETERSON. THE WHOLE WHEAT
HEART OF YASHA AGINSKY.
  N. MAGID, 440:13FEB72-5
ROSE, E. & F. SEMMLER, WITH H. ROSE, EDS.
GROSSE VERGANGENHEIT.
  W. HOFFMEISTER, 221(GQ):JAN70-138
  K. MOERSCHNER, 399(MLJ):FEB70-143
ROSE, L.E. NEPAL.
  617(TLS):7JAN72-22
ROSE, M. HEROIC LOVE.*
  K. DUNCAN-JONES, 541(RES):AUG70-382
ROSE, R. GOVERNING WITHOUT CONSENSUS.*
  617(TLS):17MAR72-297
ROSEBURY, T. MICROBES AND MORALS.*
  617(TLS):25AUG72-1000
ROSEN, B., ED. WITCHCRAFT.
  D.C. GUNBY, 67:NOV71-226
  R.H. ROBBINS, 402(MLR):OCT71-860
ROSEN, C. THE CLASSICAL STYLE.*
  R.F., 410(M&L):JUL71-327
  W. SARGEANT, 442(NY):20MAY72-123
  A. TYSON, 453:15JUN72-10
  R. WEITZMAN, 364:OCT/NOV71-114
ROSEN, G. BLUES FOR A DYING NATION.
  W.C. WOODS, 441:21MAY72-51

ROSEN, K. STUDIEN ZUR DARSTELLUNGSKUNST
UND GLAUBWÜRDIGKEIT DES AMMIANUS MAR-
CELLINUS.
W.R. CHALMERS, 123:DEC70-410
ROSEN, S. PLATO'S "SYMPOSIUM."*
H.J. EASTERLING, 123:DEC71-362
T.J. SAUNDERS, 303:VOL90-209
ROSENAU, H. SOCIAL PURPOSE IN ARCHITEC-
TURE.*
J. VOELCKER, 89(BJA):AUTUMN71-417
ROSENBACH, A.S.W. EARLY AMERICAN CHILD-
REN'S BOOKS.
617(TLS):28APR72-473
ROSENBACH, M. - SEE SENECA
ROSENBAUM, P.S. THE GRAMMAR OF ENGLISH
PREDICATE COMPLEMENT CONSTRUCTIONS.*
R. HUDDLESTON, 361:VOL23#3-241
ROSENBERG, A. ALFRED ROSENBERG: SELECTED
WRITINGS.* (R. POIS, ED)
J. DUNN, 362:10FEB72-186
ROSENBERG, B. DICTIONARY FOR THE DISEN-
CHANTED.
P. ADAMS, 61:NOV72-130
ROSENBERG, H. ARTWORKS AND PACKAGES.*
G.A. PERRET, 58:FEB70-17
ROSENBERG, H. THE DE-DEFINITION OF ART.
A. BROYARD, 441:20APR72-47
D. DAVIS, 441:30APR72-6
617(TLS):3NOV72-1311
ROSENBERG, J. ON QUALITY IN ART.*
C. HARRISON, 592:JUL/AUG68-55
D.T. WIECK, 290(JAAC):WINTER69-246
ROSENBERG, M. THE MASKS OF OTHELLO. THE
MASKS OF KING LEAR.
L.C. KNIGHTS, 453:5OCT72-3
ROSENBERG, P. FRENCH MASTER DRAWINGS OF
THE 17TH AND 18TH CENTURIES IN NORTH
AMERICAN COLLECTIONS.
617(TLS):15DEC72-1520
ROSENBERGER, F.C. RECORDS OF THE COLUM-
BIA HISTORICAL SOCIETY OF WASHINGTON,
D.C., 1966-1968.
639(VQR):WINTER70-XXIV
ROSENBLAT, A. LA PRIMERA VISIÓN DE
AMÉRICA Y OTROS ESTUDIOS. (2ND ED)
M.E. GILES, 545(RPH):FEB71-547
ROSENBLATT, J. WINTER OF THE LUNA MOTH.*
H. MAC CALLUM, 627(UTQ):JUL69-351
ROSENBLATT, P. JOHN WOOLMAN.
J.W. FROST, 656(WMQ):JUL70-511
ROSENBLOOD, N., ED. SHAW: SEVEN CRITICAL
ESSAYS.*
B. BENSTOCK, 659:WINTER72-116
ROSENBLUM, R. INGRES.
M. LEVEY, 55:APR69-47
F. WHITFORD, 592:MAR69-151
ROSENBLUM, R. TRANSFORMATIONS IN LATE
EIGHTEENTH CENTURY ART.*
F. CUMMINGS, 576:MAY69-137
ROSENFELD, A.H., ED. WILLIAM BLAKE.
M. BOTTRALL, 148:AUTUMN70-286
I.H.C., 191(ELN):SEP70(SUPP)-25
ROSENFELD, P. MUSICAL IMPRESSIONS.
(H.A. LEIBOWITZ, ED)
G. LARNER, 415:JUL70-712
R.H.M., 410(M&L):JAN71-76
A.F.L.T., 412:FEB71-86
ROSENFELD, C. PARADISE OF SNAKES.*
E.D. PENDRY, 597(SN):VOL41#1-198
E.W. SAID, 637(VS):JUN70-429
W.D. SCHAEFER, 445(NCF):SEP68-248
ROSENFIELD, J.M. THE DYNASTIC ART OF THE
KUSHANS.
J.C. HARLE, 90:JUL70-471
S. KRAMRISCH, 57:VOL31#2/3-229

ROSENFIELD, L.C. FROM BEAST-MACHINE TO
MAN-MACHINE.* (NEW ED)
J. FALVEY, 208(FS):JUL71-338
Y.H. KRIKORIAN, 484(PPR):SEP69-152
H. MONOD-CASSIDY, 207(FR):MAY70-938
ROSENGREN, I. INHALT UND STRUKTUR.
D.H. GREEN, 402(MLR):APR71-431
ROSENGREN, K.E. & J. THAVENIUS, EDS.
LITTERATURSOCIOLOGI.
J.L. SAMMONS, 563(SS):SUMMER71-296
ROSENMEYER, T.G. THE GREEN CABINET.
D.N. LEVIN, 124:NOV70-87
Z. PAVLOVSKIS, 122:OCT71-291
ROSENTHAL, A. THE NEW DOCUMENTARY IN
ACTION.
617(TLS):21APR72-433
ROSENTHAL, D.B. THE LIMITED ELITE.
617(TLS):22SEP72-1119
ROSENTHAL, F. KNOWLEDGE TRIUMPHANT.
D.M. DUNLOP, 589:JUL71-542
ROSENTHAL, H. PEACE IS AN UNKNOWN CON-
TINENT.
H. MAC CALLUM, 627(UTQ):JUL69-352
ROSENTHAL, J.T. THE PURCHASE OF PARA-
DISE.
617(TLS):1SEP72-1018
ROSENTHAL, M.L. BEYOND POWER.
J. BERNARDIN, 493:AUTUMN70-254
ROSENTHAL, M.L. THE NEW MODERN POETRY.
P. CALLAHAN, 502(PRS):SPRING68-90
ROSENTHAL, M.L. THE NEW POETS.
P. CALLAHAN, 502(PRS):SPRING68-90
J.F. SCOTT, 613:SPRING68-131
ROSENTHAL, R. - SEE "ARETINO'S DIALOGUES"
ROSENZWEIG, F. THE STAR OF REDEMPTION.*
G. PEPPER, 142:FALL71-477
617(TLS):5MAY72-527
ROSETTI, A. LINGUISTICA.*
G. FRANCESCATO, 361:VOL23#1-93
W.P. LEHMANN, 545(RPH):AUG70-169
ROSIELLO, L. LINGUISTICA ILLUMINISTA.
L. CALABI, 548(RCSF):OCT-DEC68-463
ROSKILL, M.W. DOLCE'S "ARETINO" AND
VENETIAN ART THEORY OF THE CINQUECENTO.
C. GOULD, 90:FEB70-119
M. ROETHLISBERGER, 551(RENQ):SUMMER
70-172
ROSKILL, S. HANKEY. (VOL 2)
D. MARQUAND, 362:3FEB72-153
617(TLS):10MAR72-275
ROSOMAN, L. BRUEGHEL'S "MAD MEG."
D. SUTTON, 39:JUN69-414
ROSS, A. DIRECTIVES AND NORMS.*
R.H.K., 543:SEP69-138
ROSS, A. EVERYDAY LIFE OF THE PAGAN
CELTS.*
G. RITCHIE, 595(SCS):VOL15PT2-160
ROSS, A. THE LONDON ASSIGNMENT.
617(TLS):8DEC72-1507
ROSS, A., ED. LONDON MAGAZINE STORIES 7.
J.G. FARRELL, 362:5OCT72-447
617(TLS):29DEC72-1573
ROSS, A. NEW ZEALAND ASPIRATIONS IN THE
PACIFIC IN THE NINETEENTH CENTURY.
W.P. STRAUSS, 302:JUL69-286
ROSS, A.D. STUDENT UNREST IN INDIA.
C.L. GILBERT, 293(JAST):MAY70-724
ROSS, B. NASTY PLOTS.
617(TLS):3NOV72-1306
ROSS, D.O., JR. STYLE AND TRADITION IN
CATULLUS.
F.O. COPLEY, 124:SEP70-26
ROSS, E. BEYOND THE RIVER AND THE BAY.
102(CANL):WINTER71-105
ROSS, J. HERE LIES NANCY FRAIL.
N. CALLENDAR, 441:8OCT72-46
617(TLS):26MAY72-612

ROSS, J.F. PHILOSOPHICAL THEOLOGY.
  H. MEYNELL, 479(PHQ):JUL70-315
ROSS, J.J. THE APPEAL TO THE GIVEN.*
  S. CUNNEW, 483:OCT70-346
  F.C. JACKSON, 63:MAY71-104
  D. MC QUEEN, 518:JAN71-21
ROSS, L.J. - SEE TOURNEUR, C.
ROSS, M. - SEE DE VILLEFOSSE, L. & J.
  BOUISSOUNOUSE
ROSS, M.C. THE WEST OF ALFRED JACOB
  MILLER.
  M.S. YOUNG, 39:APR69-328
ROSS, N. & A. - SEE POWYS, J.C.
ROSS, R.H. THE GEORGIAN REVOLT.
  M. THORPE, 179(ES):JUN70-269
ROSS, S. THE LAMP AT NOON AND OTHER
  STORIES.
  K. FRASER, 529(QQ):SPRING70-72
  G. ROPER, 627(UTQ):JUL69-363
ROSS, S. WHIR OF GOLD.*
  D. STEPHENS, 102(CANL):SPRING71-92
ROSS, S.D. LITERATURE AND PHILOSOPHY.
  M. RADER, 290(JAAC):SUMMER70-552
ROSS, W.W.E. SHAPES AND SOUNDS. (R.
  SOUSTER & J.R. COLOMBO, EDS)
  H. MAC CALLUM, 627(UTQ):JUL69-348
ROSSELLI, H. HISTORIA DE LA PSIQUIATRÍA
  EN COLOMBIA.
  R. ARDILA, 263:APR-JUN71-223
ROSSER, R.F. AN INTRODUCTION TO SOVIET
  FOREIGN POLICY.*
  R. LANE, 550(RUSR):OCT70-469
ROSSETTI, D.G. LETTERS OF DANTE GABRIEL
  ROSSETTI. (VOLS 3&4) (O. DOUGHTY &
  R. WAHL, EDS)
  A. GERATHS, 38:BAND87HEFT3/4-461
ROSSI, G.C. ESTUDIOS SOBRE LAS LETRAS
  EN EL SIGLO XVIII.
  R.P. SEBOLD, 546(RR):OCT70-228
ROSSI, G.C. O USO DO PARÊNTESIS EM
  ALEXANDRE HERCULANO NARRADOR.
  191(ELN):SEP69(SUPP)-135
ROSSI, P. FRANCIS BACON.
  A.V. DOUGLAS, 529(QQ):SPRING70-124
  J.M.O. WHEATLEY, 191(ELN):SEP69-60
ROSSI, P.A. & D.C. HUNT. THE ART OF THE
  OLD WEST.
  E. WEEKS, 61:JAN72-95
ROSSI, S. HASHIRIM ASHER LISH'LOMO. (F.
  RIKKO, ED)
  N. ZASLAW, 414(MQ):APR69-269
ROSSI, T. TRAJAN'S COLUMN AND THE DACIAN
  WARS. (TRANS REV BY J.M.C. TOYNBEE)
  617(TLS):31MAR72-375
ROSSI, V. ANDRÉ GIDE.
  J.C. MC LAREN, 207(FR):DEC69-335
  C. SAVAGE, 399(MLJ):JAN70-32
ROSSI-LANDI, G. LA DRÔLE DE GUERRE.
  617(TLS):14APR72-424
ROSSIF, F. & M. CHAPSAL. PORTRAIT OF A
  REVOLUTION.
  T. SHABAD, 32:DEC71-899
ROSSITER, E. A MARRIAGE OF CONVENIENCE.
  M. LEVIN, 441:10SEP72-40
ROSSITER, J. A ROPE FOR GENERAL DIETZ.
  N. CALLENDAR, 441:1OCT72-43
  617(TLS):7JUL72-783
ROSSITER, S., ED. ENGLAND. (BRITISH
  TITLE: BLUE GUIDE TO ENGLAND.)
  T. LASK, 441:16JUN72-39
  617(TLS):19MAY72-570
ROSSKAM, E. ROOSEVELT, NEW JERSEY.
  G. HICKS, 441:30JUL72-7
  J. MARGOLIS, 561(SATR):19AUG72-62
  453:15JUN72-35
RÖSSLER, G. ZUR PROBLEMATIK DER STRUKTUR
  DES NORDWESTNORMANNISCHEN VOKALISMUS.
  E.H. YARRILL, 182:VOL23#7-361

ROSSMAN, M. ON LEARNING AND SOCIAL
  CHANGE.
  P. BROOKS, 441:15OCT72-4
  B. DE MOTT, 561(SATR):16SEP72-97
ROSSMAN, M. THE WEDDING WITHIN THE WAR.
  M. DUBERMAN, 441:2APR72-4
ROSSNER, J. ANY MINUTE I CAN SPLIT.
  T. LASK, 441:22DEC72-29
  M. LEVIN, 441:30JUL72-23
  J.D. O'HARA, 561(SATR):5AUG72-52
ROSSO, C. LA "MAXIME."
  A. SCAGLIONE, 208(FS):JAN71-78
ROSTAND, E. CYRANO DE BERGERAC.* (A.
  BURGESS, ED & TRANS)
  P. ADAMS, 61:JAN72-97
ROSTEN, L. THE JOYS OF YIDDISH.
  C. FAERSTEIN, 390:MAR69-75
  S. SHUNRA, 390:JAN69-78
ROSTEN, L. ROME WASN'T BURNED IN A DAY.
  441:30APR72-28
ROSTEN, N. OVER AND OUT.
  J. HENDIN, 441:5NOV72-4
  T. LASK, 441:22DEC72-29
ROSTENBERG, L. THE MINORITY PRESS AND
  THE ENGLISH CROWN.
  617(TLS):10MAR72-266
ROSTON, M. BIBLICAL DRAMA IN ENGLAND.*
  A. AVNI, 131(CL):WINTER71-71
  D. BEVINGTON, 551(RENQ):AUTUMN70-313
  A. HOLADAY, 191(ELN):DEC69-158
ROSTOW, E.V. PEACE IN THE BALANCE.
  J.L. GADDIS, 441:10DEC72-2
ROSTOW, W.W. THE DIFFUSION OF POWER.
  H.J. MORGENTHAU, 441:10DEC72-3
ROSZAK, T. WHERE THE WASTELAND ENDS.
  A. BROYARD, 441:13SEP72 [& CONTINUED
  IN] 441:14SEP72-49
  J.M. CAMERON, 453:30NOV72-18
  L. MARX, 561(SATR):23SEP72-69
  G. STADE, 441:24SEP72-1
  442(NY):30SEP72-126
ROTBERG, R.I. - SEE MWASE, G.S.
ROTBERG, R.I. & A.A. MAZRUI, EDS. PRO-
  TEST AND POWER IN BLACK AFRICA.
  639(VQR):AUTUMN70-CL
ROTENSTREICH, N. JEWISH PHILOSOPHY IN
  MODERN TIMES.
  A.A. COHEN, 390:APR69-73
ROTH, A. HEATH AND THE HEATHMEN.
  R. CROSSMAN, 362:12OCT72-479
  617(TLS):15SEP72-1046
ROTH, A. ENOCH POWELL.
  A.A. SHENFIELD, 396(MODA):SPRING71-
  190
ROTH, A. & J. KERBEY. LORD ON THE BOARD.
  617(TLS):15SEP72-1051
ROTH, E. THE BUSINESS OF MUSIC.*
  L. SALTER, 607:SUMMER69-33
ROTH, H.L. THE NATIVES OF SARAWAK AND
  BRITISH NORTH BORNEO.
  293(JAST):NOV69-212
ROTH, H.L. ORIENTAL SILVERWORK.
  P. HARDIE, 39:APR69-326
ROTH, J.K. FREEDOM AND THE MORAL LIFE.
  H.A. LARRABEE, 432(NEQ):JUN70-298
ROTH, J.K. - SEE JAMES, W.
ROTH, P. THE BREAST.
  P. ADAMS, 61:OCT72-135
  F. CREWS, 453:16NOV72-18
  E. FREMONT-SMITH, 561(SATR):23SEP72-
  80
  J. GARDNER, 441:17SEP72-3
  C. LEHMANN-HAUPT, 441:12SEP72-47
  442(NY):25NOV72-199
ROTH, P. OUR GANG.*
  P. ADAMS, 61:JAN72-97
  W. CARVER, 109:FALL/WINTER71/72-151
  M. KEMPTON, 453:27JAN72-20

ROTH, P. PORTNOY'S COMPLAINT.*
   H. WEINBERG, 328:SPRING69-241
   M. SYRKIN, 390:APR69-64
   42(AR):SPRING69-109
ROTHBARD, M.N. POWER AND MARKET.
   H.G. RESCH, 396(MODA):SPRING71-209
ROTHBERG, A. THE HEIRS OF STALIN.
   S.F. COHEN, 441:23JUL72-6
   617(TLS):26MAY72-589
ROTHBERG, A. THE STALKING HORSE.
   O.L. BAILEY, 561(SATR):28OCT72-89
   L.J. DAVIS, 441:19NOV72-60
ROTHE, W., ED. EXPRESSIONISMUS ALS
 LITERATUR.
   R.E. LORBE, 301(JEGP):APR71-345
   J.H. REID, 182:VOL23#15/16-748
ROTHENBERG, J. POEMS FOR THE GAME OF
 SILENCE 1960-1970.*
   J.R. CARPENTER, 491:JUN72-164
ROTHENBERG, J., ED. TECHNICIANS OF THE
 SACRED.*
   D. PRINGLE, 96:DEC69-48
ROTHENBERG, K-J. DAS PROBLEM DES REALIS-
 MUS BEI THOMAS MANN.*
   A. VON GRONICKA, 222(GR):MAR70-134
ROTHERMUND, I. DIE SPALTUNG DER KOMMUN-
 ISTISCHEN PARTEI INDIENS.
   T.P. THORNTON, 293(JAST):FEB70-482
ROTHERT, H. WELT, ALL, EINHEIT.
   N. FEHRINGER, 182:VOL23#10-514
ROTHERY, B. THE STORM.
   J. HUNTER, 362:21DEC72-869
   617(TLS):22DEC72-1549
ROTHMAN, E.P. THE ANGEL INSIDE WENT
 SOUR.*
   N. HENTOFF, 442(NY):5FEB72-100
   617(TLS):16JUN72-685
ROTHSCHILD, J. PIŁSUDSKI'S COUP D'ETAT.
   T.V. GROMADA, 497(POLR):SUMMER68-82
ROTHSTEIN, E. & R.N. RINGLER, EDS. LIT-
 ERARY MONOGRAPHS. (VOL 2)
   E.M. KERR, 399(MLJ):APR70-294
   F. MC COMBIE, 447(N&Q):APR70-152
ROTTMANN, H., J. BARRY & B.T. PAQUET,
 EDS. WINNING HEARTS AND MINDS.
   J. SEELYE, 441:14MAY72-2
ROUBICZEK, P. ETHICAL VALUES IN THE AGE
 OF SCIENCE.*
   H.J.N. HORSBURGH, 479(PHQ):OCT70-409
ROUCEK, J.S., ED. THE STUDY OF FOREIGN
 LANGUAGES.*
   M.E. GILES, 545(RPH):NOV69-246
ROUDAUT, J. POÈTES ET GRAMMAIRIENS AU
 XVIIIE SIÈCLE.
   617(TLS):24MAR72-341
ROUDIL, J. LES FUEROS D'ALCARAZ ET
 D'ALARCÓN.
   J.R. CRADDOCK, 545(RPH):AUG70-119
ROUDYBUSH, A. A SYBARITIC DEATH.
   N. CALLENDAR, 441:30APR72-36
ROUND, J.H. THE KING'S SERJEANTS AND
 OFFICERS OF STATE WITH THEIR CORONATION
 SERVICES. FAMILY ORIGINS AND OTHER
 STUDIES. STUDIES IN PEERAGE AND FAMILY
 HISTORY. PEERAGE AND PEDIGREE.
   617(TLS):18FEB72-190
ROUQUIER, A-L. LES LIEUX COMMUNS.
   M.G. ROSE, 207(FR):MAY70-944
ROURKE, C. CHARLES SHEELER.
   R. FRIEDMAN, 58:APR70-14
ROUSCHAUSSE, J. ERASMUS AND FISHER.
   R.C. PETRY, 551(RENQ):SUMMER70-168
ROUSE, P., JR. JAMES BLAIR OF VIRGINIA.
   R. BAIN, 578:SPRING72-107
ROUSSEAU, G.S., ED. ORGANIC FORM.
   617(TLS):23JUN72-723

ROUSSEAU, J-J. CORRESPONDANCE COMPLÈTE
 DE JEAN-JACQUES ROUSSEAU.* (VOLS 5&6)
 (R.A. LEIGH, ED)
   H. BROWN, 207(FR):MAR70-695
   L.G. CROCKER, 400(MLN):MAY70-611
ROUSSEAU, J-J. CORRESPONDANCE COMPLÈTE
 DE JEAN-JACQUES ROUSSEAU.* (VOLS 7&8)
 (R.A. LEIGH, ED)
   H. BROWN, 207(FR):MAR70-695
ROUSSEAU, J-J. ESSAI SUR L'ORIGINE DES
 LANGUES. (C. PORSET, ED)
   N. SUCKLING, 182:VOL23#4-136
   617(TLS):10NOV72-1367
ROUSSEAU, J-J. JEAN-JACQUES ENTRE SOC-
 RATE ET CATON. (C. PICHOIS & R. PIN-
 TARD, EDS) DU CONTRAT SOCIAL. (R.
 GRIMSLEY, ED)
   617(TLS):10NOV72-1367
ROUSSEL, R. IMPRESSIONS OF AFRICA.*
 LOCUS SOLUS.*
   M. MUDRICK, 249(HUDR):SPRING71-185
ROUSSET, J. L'INTÉRIEUR ET L'EXTÉRIEUR.
   H.T. BARNWELL, 208(FS):JAN71-69
ROUSSOPOULOS, D.J., ED. THE NEW LEFT IN
 CANADA.*
   I.M. ABELLA, 529(QQ):WINTER70-640
ROUSSOS, E.N. HO HĒRAKLEITOS STIS
 ENNEADES TOY PLOTINOY.
   C. MUGLER, 555:VOL44FASC1-125
   R.T. WALLIS, 123:DEC70-399
ROWE, D.J. - SEE HOWELL, G.
ROWE, V. FRENCH WINES ORDINARY AND
 EXTRAORDINARY.
   617(TLS):29DEC72-1589
ROWE, W.L. RELIGIOUS SYMBOLISM AND GOD.
   N. PIKE, 482(PHR):JUL70-424
ROWE, W.W. NABOKOV'S DECEPTIVE WORLD.*
   J.D. O'HARA, 561(SATR):15JAN72-36
ROWELL, G., ED. LATE VICTORIAN PLAYS
 1890-1914.
   J. HOPKIN, 571:WINTER68/69-23
ROWELL, G., ED. VICTORIAN DRAMATIC
 CRITICISM.*
   S. WELLS, 677:VOL2-307
ROWLAND, B. BLIND BEASTS.
   R.J. SCHOECK, 70(ANQ):FEB72-91
ROWLAND, B., ED. COMPANION TO CHAUCER
 STUDIES.*
   H. BOYD, 180(ESA):SEP70-415
   A. DAVID, 627(UTQ):JUL69-364
   H. NEWSTEAD, 545(RPH):NOV70-349
   R.M. WILSON, 175:SPRING69-27
ROWLAND, B. & F. RICE. ART IN AFGHANIS-
 TAN.
   617(TLS):12MAY72-542
ROWLAND, M.F. & P. PASTERNAK'S "DOCTOR
 ZHIVAGO."
   J. DELANEY, 613:SUMMER69-300
ROWLAND, P. THE LAST LIBERAL GOVERN-
 MENTS.
   617(TLS):18AUG72-972
ROWLANDS, P. THE FUGITIVE MIND.
   617(TLS):8DEC72-1484
"ROWLANDSON'S DRAWINGS FOR THE ENGLISH
 DANCE OF DEATH."* (R.R. WARK, ED)
   R. PAULSON, 173(ECS):SUMMER70-544
ROWLEY, D. CARPE DIEM.
   M.L. CLARKE, 123:JUN71-291
ROWLEY, T. THE SHROPSHIRE LANDSCAPE.
   617(TLS):7JUL72-785
ROWSE, A.L. THE ELIZABETHAN RENAIS-
 SANCE: THE CULTURAL ACHIEVEMENT.
   T. LASK, 441:15DEC72-42
   442(NY):23DEC72-78
   617(TLS):1DEC72-1452

ROWSE, A.L. THE ELIZABETHAN RENAIS-
SANCE: THE LIFE OF THE SOCIETY.*
J. KENYON, 440:21MAY72-10
442(NY):27MAY72-115
ROWSE, A.L. THE TOWER OF LONDON IN THE
HISTORY OF THE NATION.
617(TLS):1DEC72-1452
ROXON, L. LILLIAN ROXON'S ROCK ENCYCLO-
PEDIA.*
L. BERKMAN, 418(MR):SPRING71-366
ROY, C. NOUS.
617(TLS):21APR72-442
ROY, D. KUO MO-JO.
M. BERNAL, 453:23MAR72-31
ROY, E. CHRISTOPHER FRY.
D. GERSTENBERGER, 397(MD):SEP69-213
ROY, G. WINDFLOWER.
P. GROSSKURTH, 102(CANL):SUMMER71-83
H. MC PHERSON, 606(TAMR):#57-84
ROY, I., ED. BLAISE DE MONLUC.
617(TLS):1SEP72-1011
ROY, J. J'ACCUSE LE GÉNÉRAL MASSU.
617(TLS):28APR72-464
ROY, P., F.B. WAISANEN & E.M. ROGERS.
THE IMPACT OF COMMUNICATION ON RURAL
DEVELOPMENT.
T. POFFENBERGER, 293(JAST):AUG70-961
ROY, S.S. THE HERITAGE OF ŚAŃKARA.
S.K. SAKSENA, 485(PE&W):JAN69-93
ROYALL, A.N. LETTERS FROM ALABAMA, 1817-
1822. (L. GRIFFITH, ED)
G. BACH, 447(N&Q):OCT70-390
J.D.L. HOLMES, 656(WMQ):JUL70-509
ROYCE, J. THE BASIC WRITING OF JOSIAH
ROYCE. (J.J. MC DERMOTT, ED)
R.J.B., 543:DEC69-362
ROYCE, J. THE LETTERS OF JOSIAH ROYCE.
(J. CLENDENNING, ED)
R.J.B., 543:JUN70-752
J.G. HARRELL, 319:APR72-239
H.A. LARRABEE, 432(NEQ):SEP70-490
639(VQR):AUTUMN70-CXLII
ROYCE, K. THE MINIATURES FRAME.
N. CALLENDAR, 441:27AUG72-14
617(TLS):7JUL72-783
ROYCROFT, A.J. TEST TUBE CHESS.
617(TLS):15DEC72-1541
ROZANOV, V. DOSTOEVSKY AND THE LEGEND OF
THE GRAND INQUISITOR.
617(TLS):21JUL72-838
RÓŻEWICZ, T. FACES OF ANXIETY.*
J.J. MACIUSZKO, 574(SEEJ):SPRING71-
125
ROŽNOVSKAJA, M.G. SINTAKSIS PRILAGA-
TEL'NOGO V BOLGARSKOM LITERATURNOM
JAZYKE.
E.A. SCATTON, 574(SEEJ):FALL71-368
RUBEN, R. RUBEN, MY LIFE, MY ART.
S. SPECTOR, 58:APR70-12
RUBENSON, S. KING OF KINGS.
A.K. IRVINE, 69:OCT69-436
RUBENSTEIN, R.L. MY BROTHER PAUL.
W. ARNOLD, 441:7MAY72-6
RUBIA BARCIA, J. & M.A. ZEITLIN, EDS.
UNAMUNO.
G. RIBBANS, 402(MLR):APR71-419
RUBIN, J. & B.H. JERNUDD, EDS. CAN LAN-
GUAGE BE PLANNED?
617(TLS):7JUL72-773
RUBIN, L. LANCED IN LIGHT.*
S. COOPERMAN, 502(PRS):FALL68-266
RUBIN, L.D., JR. A BIBLIOGRAPHICAL GUIDE
TO THE STUDY OF SOUTHERN LITERATURE.*
W.J. FREE, 219(GAR):WINTER69-543
RUBIN, L.D., JR. GEORGE W. CABLE.
S.L. GROSS, 340(KR):1970/1-168

RUBIN, L.D., JR. THE CURIOUS DEATH OF
THE NOVEL.*
R. LEHAN, 445(NCF):DEC68-370
D.E.S. MAXWELL, 402(MLR):APR71-402
W.D.T., 477:SPRING69-301
RUBIN, L.D., JR. THE TELLER IN THE
TALE.*
D. HEWITT, 447(N&Q):APR70-159
RUBIN, L.D., JR. - SEE RAVENEL, B.
RUBIN, M. AN ABSENCE OF BELLS.
J.D. O'HARA, 561(SATR):20MAY72-78
P. SOURIAN, 441:5MAR72-7
RUBIN, R., ED. JEWISH FOLK SONGS IN
YIDDISH AND ENGLISH.
M.C. ASTOUR, 650(WF):APR68-138
RUBIN, W.S. DADA AND SURREALIST ART.*
R. SHATTUCK, 453:18MAY72-24
RUBIN, W.S. DADA, SURREALISM AND THEIR
HERITAGE.
A.P. CARTER, 592:NOV68-224
RUBINO, A. THANATOS, EROS, CHRONOS
NELLE OPERE GIOVANILI DI GUSTAVE FLAU-
BERT.
M.G. TILLETT, 208(FS):APR71-220
RUBINOFF, L. THE PORNOGRAPHY OF POWER.
S.O.H., 543:DEC69-354
RUBINOFF, L. - SEE COLLINGWOOD, R.G.
RUBINSTEIN, A.Z. YUGOSLAVIA AND THE NON-
ALIGNED WORLD.*
R.E. KANET, 32:JUN71-416
RUBINSTEIN, M., ED. WICKED, WICKED
LIBELS.
R.J. MARSHALL, 362:4MAY72-595
617(TLS):5MAY72-506
RUBINSTEIN, S. HISTORIANS OF LONDON.
A.N.O., 503:WINTER68-186
RUBULIS, A. BALTIC LITERATURE.
A. CĪRULE, 32:JUN71-451
R. ŠILBAJORIS, 574(SEEJ):SPRING71-92
RUCH, M. - SEE NEPOS, C.
RUCK, B. ANCESTRAL VOICES.
617(TLS):21JUL72-841
RUCK, C.A.P. & W.H. MATHESON - SEE PINDAR
RUCKER, D. THE CHICAGO PRAGMATISTS.
R.J.B., 543:SEP69-138
RUDD, N., ED. ESSAYS ON CLASSICAL LIT-
ERATURE.
617(TLS):31MAR72-362
RUDÉ, G. EUROPE IN THE EIGHTEENTH CEN-
TURY.
617(TLS):29DEC72-1576
RUDÉ, G. PARIS AND LONDON IN THE
EIGHTEENTH CENTURY.
J.H. PLUMB, 441:21MAY72-6
RUDENKO, S.I. FROZEN TOMBS OF SIBERIA.*
A. FARKAS, 32:SEP71-657
RUDENKO, S.I., ED. SOVETSKIE VOENNO-
VOZDUSHNYE SILY V VELIKOI OTECHEST-
VENNOI VOINE 1941-1945 GG.
M. PARRISH, 587:OCT69-251
RUDENSTINE, N.L. SIDNEY'S POETIC DEVEL-
OPMENT.*
M. PRAZ, 179(ES):DEC70-551
RUDNER, R. WANDERING.
561(SATR):7OCT72-101
RUDNICKIJ, K. REŽISSER MEJERXOL'D.
M.L. HOOVER, 574(SEEJ):SPRING71-117
RUDNYČKYJ, J.B. AN ETYMOLOGICAL DICTION-
ARY OF THE UKRAINIAN LANGUAGE. (PTS
6-9)
V. KIPARSKY, 574(SEEJ):SUMMER71-241
RUDOFSKY, B. STREETS FOR PEOPLE.
P. RUSSELL, 96:FEB70-60
RUDOLF, P.R. - SEE VON LANGENSTEIN, H.
RUDOLPH, W. HANDBUCH DER VOLKSTÜMLICHEN
BOOTE IM ÖSTLICHEN NIEDERDEUTSCHLAND.
292(JAF):JUL-SEP70-372

RUDORFF, R. BELLE EPOQUE.
617(TLS):10NOV72-1360
RUDORFF, R. THE DRACULA ARCHIVES.
H. FRANKEL, 561(SATR):13MAY72-86
RUDY, P., X.L. YOUHN & H.M. NEBEL, JR.
RUSSIAN.
C.L. DAWSON, 32:DEC71-912
T.F. MAGNER, 574(SEEJ):FALL71-370
RUEFF, J. THE MONETARY SIN OF THE WEST.*
(FRENCH TITLE: LE PÉCHÉ MONÉTAIRE DE
L'OCCIDENT.)
J.L. HESS, 441:26MAR72-1
RUELLE, P. LES DITS DU CLERC DE VAUDOY.
F.J. WARNE, 208(FS):OCT71-447
RUELLE, P., ED. L'ORNEMENT DES DAMES
("ORNATUS MULIERUM").*
F. KOENIG, 545(RPH):NOV70-370
RUELLO, F. LA NOTION DE VÉRITÉ CHEZ ST.
ALBERT LE GRAND ET ST. THOMAS D'AQUIN
DE 1243-54.
N. FEHRINGER, 182:VOL23#15/16-712
RUFF, M.A. - SEE BAUDELAIRE, C.
RUFFIN, E. THE DIARY OF EDMUND RUFFIN.
(VOL 1) (W.K. SCARBOROUGH, ED)
D.H. DONALD, 441:24SEP72-2
E.D. GENOVESE, 453:21SEP72-16
RUGE, H. ZUR ENSTEHUNG DER NEUGRIECH-
ISCHEN SUBSTANTIVDEKLINATION.
D.Q. ADAMS, 350:DEC71-943
RUGGIERS, P.G. THE ART OF THE CANTER-
BURY TALES.
S.W. HOLTON, 597(SN):VOL41#1-176
RUH, K., ED. ALTDEUTSCHE UND ALTNIEDER-
LÄNDISCHE MYSTIK.
M.J.V., 543:DEC69-361
RUH, K. HÖFISCHE EPIK DES DEUTSCHEN
MITTELALTERS. (PT 1)
H. BLOSEN, 462(OL):VOL24#2-158
D. MC LINTOCK, 182:VOL23#7-367
RUHE, E. UNTERSUCHUNGEN ZU DEN ALTFRAN-
ZÖSISCHEN ÜBERSETZUNGEN DER DISTICHA
CATONIS.
L.F. SOLANO, 207(FR):DEC69-364
RUHEMANN, H. THE CLEANING OF PAINTINGS.*
J.C. DELISS, 90:MAY69-311
RÜHLE, J. LITERATURE AND REVOLUTION.*
(REV) (J. STEINBERG, ED & TRANS)
S. KARLINSKY, 574(SEEJ):SPRING71-78
RUHMER, E., ED. GRUENEWALD PAINTINGS.
S. SPECTOR, 58:SUMMER70-10
RUIGH, R.E. THE PARLIAMENT OF 1624.
617(TLS):10MAR72-266
RUIJGH, C.J. ÉTUDES SUR LA GRAMMAIRE ET
LE VOCABULAIRE DU GREC MYCÉNIEN.*
D.M. JONES, 303:VOL90-232
RUIN, O., ED. SCANDINAVIAN POLITICAL
STUDIES. (VOL 4)
R.C. ELLSWORTH, 529(QQ):AUTUMN70-463
RUIZ, J. THE BOOK OF GOOD LOVE. (E.K.
KANE, TRANS)
D.G. PATTISON, 447(N&Q):JUL70-275
RUIZ, J. THE BOOK OF GOOD LOVE. (R.
MIGNANI & M.A. DI CESARE, TRANS)
E.M. WILSON, 382(MAE):1971/1-80
RUIZ, J.M. - SEE UNDER MARTÍNEZ RUIZ, J.
RUIZ HERNÁNDEZ, L. - SEE VON GOEBEN, A.
RUIZ RAMÓN, F. HISTORIA DEL TEATRO
ESPAÑOL (DESDE SUS ORÍGENES HASTA
1900).
J.H. PARKER, 240(HR):JUL70-328
RŪĶE-DRAVIŅA, V. MEHRSPRACHIGKEIT IM
VORSCHULALTER.*
A. AVRAM, 353:DEC69-109
RUKEYSER, M. THE TRACES OF THOMAS HAR-
IOT.*
617(TLS):19MAY72-579

RULAND, R., ED. A COLLECTION OF CRITICAL
ESSAYS ON "WALDEN."
D. HOLBROOK, 619(TC):1968/2-56
RULAND, R. THE REDISCOVERY OF AMERICAN
LITERATURE.
F.X. DUGGAN, 613:WINTER68-611
RULE, J. AGAINST THE SEASON.
E. NEWTON, 296:SPRING72-87
RULE, J. THIS IS NOT FOR YOU.*
K. FRASER, 102(CANL):WINTER71-104
RUMBELOW, D. I SPY BLUE.*
453:6APR72-34
RUMBUCHER, K. ANTERO DE QUENTAL.
G.M. MOSER, 546(RR):OCT70-229
RUMILLY, R. HISTOIRE DE LA PROVINCE DE
QUÉBEC. (VOL 37)
J-C. BONENFANT, 627(UTQ):JUL69-453
RUNCIMAN, S. THE GREAT CHURCH IN CAP-
TIVITY.
G. DOWNEY, 121(CJ):OCT-NOV70-85
RUNCIMAN, S. THE LAST BYZANTINE RENAIS-
SANCE.
639(VQR):AUTUMN70-CLIV
RUNCIMAN, S. THE ORTHODOX CHURCHES AND
THE SECULAR STATE.
617(TLS):1DEC72-1468
RUNCIMAN, W.G. A CRITIQUE OF MAX WEBER'S
PHILOSOPHY OF SOCIAL SCIENCE.
D. MAC RAE, 362:20APR72-521
617(TLS):24MAR72-340
RUNCIMAN, W.G. SOCIOLOGY IN ITS PLACE.*
D. MAC RAE, 362:20APR72-521
RUNDLE, B. PERCEPTION, SENSATION AND
VERIFICATION.
617(TLS):22SEP72-1101
"THE RUODLIEB." (G.B. FORD, JR., TRANS)
"THE RUODLIEB."* (G.B. FORD, JR., ED)
[2 BKS]
H. PENZL, 353:MAY69-115
RUPERT VON DEUTZ. DE VICTORIA VERBI DEI.
(R. HAACKE, ED)
I. MÜLLER, 182:VOL23#9-470
RUPP, R.H. CELEBRATION IN POSTWAR AMERI-
CAN FICTION, 1954-67.*
B.H. GELFANT, 27(AL):MAR71-147
H. HARPER, 659:AUTUMN72-523
RUPPRICH, H. VOM SPÄTEN MITTELALTER BIS
ZUM BAROCK.* (VOL 1)
D. BLAMIRES, 402(MLR):OCT71-935
RUPRECHT, E. & D. BÄNSCH, EDS. LITERAR-
ISCHE MANIFESTE DER JAHRHUNDERTWENDE
1890-1910.
617(TLS):14JUL72-825
RUSCHENBUSCH, E. UNTERSUCHUNGEN ZUR
GESCHICHTE DES ATHENISCHEN STRAF-
RECHTS.*
P.J. RHODES, 123:DEC70-358
RUSHMORE, R. THE SINGING VOICE.*
617(TLS):21JAN72-65
RUSKIN, J. THE BRANTWOOD DIARY OF JOHN
RUSKIN. (H.G. VILJOEN, ED)
J.L. BRADLEY, 677:VOL2-315
RUSKIN, J. RUSKIN IN ITALY. (H.I. SHA-
PIRO, ED) SUBLIME & INSTRUCTIVE. (V.
SURTEES, ED)
617(TLS):28JUL72-892
RUSKIN, J. THE WINNINGTON LETTERS.
(V.A. BURD, ED)
Q. BELL, 90:JUL70-476
G.P. LANDOW, 301(JEGP):APR71-324
RUSSELL, B. THE ART OF PHILOSOPHIZING
AND OTHER ESSAYS.
W.A.J., 543:DEC69-355
RUSSELL, B. THE AUTOBIOGRAPHY OF BER-
TRAND RUSSELL, 1872-1914.* THE AUTO-
BIOGRAPHY OF BERTRAND RUSSELL, 1914-
1944.*
C.E. BARON, 97(CQ):SUMMER68-274

RUSSELL, B. THE AUTOBIOGRAPHY OF BER-
TRAND RUSSELL, 1944-1969.*
639(VQR):SUMMER70-CI
RUSSELL, B. THE COLLECTED STORIES OF
BERTRAND RUSSELL. (B. FEINBERG, ED)
617(TLS):1SEP72-1013
RUSSELL, C.A. THE HISTORY OF VALENCY.
617(TLS):28JUL72-871
RUSSELL, D.A. - SEE LONGINUS
RUSSELL, D.A. & M. WINTERBOTTOM, EDS.
ANCIENT LITERARY CRITICISM.
617(TLS):10MAR72-285
RUSSELL, J. FRANCIS BACON.*
617(TLS):10MAR72-279
RUSSELL, J. HENRY MOORE.*
S.R. LEVITT, 592:NOV68-226
RUSSELL, J. NELSON AND THE HAMILTONS.
D. UNDERDOWN, 639(VQR):SPRING70-361
RUSSELL, J. & S. GABLIK. POP ART REDE-
FINED.*
E. LUCIE-SMITH, 592:JUL/AUG69-50
RUSSELL, J.C. MEDIEVAL REGIONS AND THEIR
CITIES.
617(TLS):7APR72-396
RUSSELL, J.G. THE FIELD OF THE CLOTH OF
GOLD.
J.A. EPPERSON, 551(RENQ):SUMMER70-192
RUSSELL, L. A HERITAGE OF LIGHT.
A. EMERY, 627(UTQ):JUL69-407
RUSSELL, R. GHALIB.
617(TLS):1SEP72-1033
RUSSELL, R. LOST CANALS OF ENGLAND AND
WALES.
617(TLS):7APR72-402
RUSSELL, R.W. PINE MANOR JUNIOR COLLEGE.
G.H. MERRIAM, 432(NEQ):JUN70-339
RUSSELL, T. BLACKS, WHITES AND BLUES.
W.R. FERRIS, JR., 187:JAN72-132
M. HARRISON, 415:SEP70-898
RUSSISCH-EUROPAISCHE LITERATURVERBINDUN-
GEN."
D. TSCHIŽEWSKIJ, 72:BAND208HEFT4/6-
466
"RUSSKAJA I SOVETSKAJA POĖZIJA."
W.H. BENNETT, 574(SEEJ):SUMMER71-235
RUSSOLI, F. MODIGLIANI: DRAWINGS AND
SKETCHES.
A. WERNER, 58:MAR70-10
RUSSU, I.I. ILLIRII.*
R.A. TODD, 104:WINTER71-531
RUST, E.C. SCIENCE AND FAITH.
G.M., 477:SUMMER69-409
RUSTERHOLZ, P. THEATRUM VITAE HUMANAE.
A.G. DE CAPUA, 301(JEGP):OCT71-717
RUSTOMJI, N. ENCHANTED FRONTIERS.
617(TLS):4FEB72-130
RÜTER, K. ODYSSEEINTERPRETATIONEN.*
H. CLARKE, 121(CJ):APR-MAY71-376
F.M. COMBELLACK, 122:JAN71-39
J.B. HAINSWORTH, 123:DEC71-334
F. LASSERRE, 182:VOL23#6-302
RUTGERS, A. BIRDS OF SOUTH AMERICA.
617(TLS):3NOV72-1349
RUTGERS, C.A. JAN VAN ARKEL, BISSCHOP
VAN UTRECHT.
D.W. JELLEMA, 589:OCT71-751
RUTHERFORD, A., ED. COMMONWEALTH.
J.G. MOSS, 296:FALL72-90
RUTHERFORD, D. CLEAR THE FAST LANE.*
N. CALLENDAR, 441:10SEP72-40
RUTHERFORD, J. MEXICAN SOCIETY DURING
THE REVOLUTION. AN ANNOTATED BIBLIO-
GRAPHY OF THE NOVELS OF THE MEXICAN
REVOLUTION OF 1910-1917 IN ENGLISH AND
SPANISH.
617(TLS):22SEP72-1093

RUTHERFORD, M., WITH G. ROBYNS. MARGARET
RUTHERFORD.
617(TLS):2JUN72-635
RUTHERFORD, N. SHIRLEY BAKER AND THE
KING OF TONGA.
617(TLS):18AUG72-962
RUTHVEN, K.K. A GUIDE TO EZRA POUND'S
"PERSONAE" (1926).*
W.M. CHACE, 598(SOR):WINTER72-225
F.K. SANDERS, 569(SR):SUMMER71-433
RUTKOWSKI, B. LARNAKSY EGEJSKIE.
R. HEIDENREICH, 182:VOL23#3-97
RUTLAND, W.R. THE BECOMING OF GOD.
617(TLS):28JAN72-104
RUTMAN, D.B. AMERICAN PURITANISM.
N. PETTIT, 432(NEQ):SEP70-504
RUTTER, M. MATERNAL DEPRIVATION REAS-
SESSED.
617(TLS):15DEC72-1527
RUTTKOWSKI, W.V. DAS LITERARISCHE CHAN-
SON IN DEUTSCHLAND.*
G.L. TRACY, 564:FALL69-150
RUTTKOWSKI, W.V. DIE LITERARISCHEN GAT-
TUNGEN.*
L.W. KAHN, 222(GR):MAY70-234
RUTTKOWSKI, W.V. & R.E. BLAKE. LITERA-
TURWÖRTERBUCH IN DEUTSCH, ENGLISCH UND
FRANZÖSISCH MIT GRIECHISCHEN UND LAT-
EINISCHEN ABTEILUNGEN FÜR DEN STUDENTEN
DER ALLGEMEINEN UND VERGLEICHENDEN LIT-
ERATURWISSENSCHAFT.
G. BISSAINTHE, 207(FR):APR70-849
RUWET, N. INTRODUCTION À LA GRAMMAIRE
GÉNÉRATIVE.
M. GROSS, 361:VOL24#1-46
J. LYONS, 297(JL):APR69-189
RUYER, R. LES NUISANCES IDÉOLOGIQUES.
617(TLS):9JUN72-666
RYALS, C.D. FROM THE GREAT DEEP.
R.W. RADER, 405(MP):MAY70-386
RYAN, A. JOHN STUART MILL.
K. BRITTON, 483:OCT70-338
RYAN, A. THE PHILOSOPHY OF THE SOCIAL
SCIENCES.
A.J. SKILLEN, 518:OCT71-27
RYAN, C., ED. LE QUÉBEC QUI SE FAIT.
J. LEVITT, 99:JAN-FEB72-72
RYAN, D. THE FENIAN CHIEF. (O.D. ED-
WARDS, ED)
D.W. MILLER, 637(VS):JUN70-417
RYAN, K.M. THE BETTY TREE.
M. LEVIN, 441:31DEC72-18
RYAN, N.J. THE MAKING OF MODERN MALAYA.
(2ND ED)
T.R. FENNELL, 293(JAST):FEB70-491
RYAN, W.M. WILLIAM LANGLAND.
V. EDDEN, 402(MLR):JAN71-175
RYCHNER, J. L'ARTICULATION DES PHRASES
NARRATIVES DANS LA MORT ARTU.
C.E. PICKFORD, 382(MAE):1971/2-192
RYCK, F. WOMAN HUNT.
O.L. BAILEY, 561(SATR):30SEP72-80
N. CALLENDAR, 441:27AUG72-14
617(TLS):26MAY72-612
RYDBECK, L. FACHPROSA, VERMEINTLICHE
VOLKSPROSA UND NEUES TESTAMENT.
F. LASSERRE, 182:VOL23#19/20-880
RYDBECK, L. FACHPROSA VERMEINTLICHE
VOLKSSPRACHE UND NEUES TESTAMENT.
P. CHANTRAINE, 555:VOL44FASC1-134
RYDEN, H. AMERICA'S LAST WILD HORSES.
W. GARD, 584(SWR):WINTER71-91
RYDEN, H. MUSTANGS.
G.F.T. RYALL, 441:3DEC72-30
RYDÉN, M. CO-ORDINATION OF RELATIVE
CLAUSES IN SIXTEENTH-CENTURY ENGLISH.
J. WESTLAKE, 402(MLR):OCT71-854

RYDÉN, M. RELATIVE CONSTRUCTIONS IN
EARLY SIXTEENTH CENTURY ENGLISH.*
  T. KISBYE, 179(ES):AUG69-406
  S. POTTER, 402(MLR):JAN71-176
RYDJORD, J. INDIAN PLACE-NAMES.
  V.J. VOGEL, 424:SEP69-235
RYE, J. FUTURISM.
  617(TLS):1DEC72-1448
RYGA, G. THE ECSTASY OF RITA JOE AND
OTHER PLAYS.* (B. PARKER, ED)
  H. ROBERTSON, 99:JAN-FEB72-79
  L. RUSSELL, 102(CANL):AUTUMN71-81
RYGALOFF, A. TABLES DE CONCORDANCES POUR
L'ALPHABET PHONÉTIQUE CHINOIS.
  R. HUANG, 302:JUL69-289
RYKEN, L. THE APOCALYPTIC VISION IN
"PARADISE LOST."*
  A. FERRY, 301(JEGP):APR71-306
  639(VQR):SUMMER70-XCVIII
RYPKA, J. HISTORY OF IRANIAN LITERATURE.
  M.J. DRESDEN, 318(JAOS):OCT-DEC70-577
RYSS, E. & L. RAXMANOV. DOMIK NA BOLOTE.
  C.V. CHVANY, 574(SEEJ):SPRING71-93

SAAVEDRA, M.D. - SEE UNDER DE CERVANTES
SAAVEDRA, M.
SABA, G. - SEE THÉOPHILE DE VIAU
SABATIER, R. LES ALLUMETTES SUÉDOISES.
  M. NAUDIN, 207(FR):MAY70-945
SABATIER, R. THE SAFETY MATCHES.
  M. LEVIN, 441:6FEB72-36
  P. THEROUX, 440:13FEB72-6
SABBATUCCI, D. SAGGIO SUL MISTICISMO
GRECO.
  A.W.H. ADKINS, 123:DEC71-445
EL SABIO, A. - SEE UNDER ALFONSO EL SABIO
SACCIO, P. THE COURT COMEDIES OF JOHN
LYLY.
  J.A. BARISH, 301(JEGP):JUL71-529
  M.R. BEST, 401(MLQ):JUN70-250
  M. HATTAWAY, 402(MLR):OCT71-858
  B.F. HUPPÉ, 551(RENQ):WINTER70-478
SACHS, A., ED. STUDIES IN THE DRAMA.
  C-O. GIEROW, 462(OL):VOL23#4-336
SACHS, M., ED. THE FRENCH SHORT STORY
IN THE NINETEENTH CENTURY.
  J. HELLERMANN, 207(FR):FEB70-547
  P.J. WHYTE, 208(FS):JUL71-340
SACKETT, T.A. PÉREZ GALDÓS.*
  C. OLSTAD, 50(ARQ):SUMMER69-189
  G. SMITH, 400(MLN):MAR70-312
SACKMAN, H. & N. NIE, EDS. THE INFORMA-
TION UTILITY AND SOCIAL CHOICE.
  A. BOOKSTEIN, 356:JUL71-258
SADDHATISSA, H. THE BUDDHA'S WAY.
  617(TLS):28JAN72-105
SADDLEMYER, A. J.M. SYNGE AND MODERN
COMEDY.
  F. GLENDENNING, 571:WINTER69/70-70
SADDLEMYER, A. - SEE SYNGE, J.M.
MARQUIS DE SADE. LES INFORTUNES DE LA
VERTU. (J-M. GOULEMOT, ED)
  D. WILLIAMS, 208(FS):OCT71-468
MARQUIS DE SADE. THREE PLAYS BY THE MAR-
QUIS DE SADE. (ILLUSTRATIONS BY S.
DALI)
  ATIRNOMIS, 58:NOV69-10
SADLER, M. MIRROR IMAGE.
  N. CALLENDAR, 441:14MAY72-35
SADOUL, J. ALCHEMISTS AND GOLD.
  617(TLS):28JUL72-871
AŞ-ṢAFADĪ, Ḥ.A. DAS BIOGRAPHISCHE LEXI-
KON DES ṢALAḤADDIN ḤALĪL IBN AIBAK
AŞ-ṢAFADĪ. (PT 5 ED BY S. DEDERING;
PT 7 ED BY I. ABBAS)
  J. SUBLET, 182:VOL23#9-449

SAFFREY, H.D. & L.G. WESTERINK - SEE PRO-
CLUS
SAGAN, F. DES BLEUS À L'ÂME.
  617(TLS):4AUG72-909
SAGAR, K. THE ART OF D.H. LAWRENCE.
  M. ALLOTT, 677:VOL2-327
SAGAR, K. - SEE LAWRENCE, D.H.
SAHADI, L. MIRACLE IN MIAMI.
  J. DURSO, 441:3DEC72-44
SAHAY, A. SOCIOLOGICAL ANALYSIS.
  617(TLS):1DEC72-1456
SAHAY, A., ED. MAX WEBER AND MODERN
SOCIOLOGY.
  617(TLS):24MAR72-340
SAHGAL, N. THE DAY IN SHADOW.
  M. LEVIN, 441:24SEP72-40
SA'ID, M.F. LEXICAL INNOVATION THROUGH
BORROWING IN MODERN STANDARD ARABIC.
  P.F. ABBOUD, 350:MAR71-229
SAIDY, A. THE BATTLE OF CHESS IDEAS.
  617(TLS):22DEC72-1566
SAILER, S. DIE SCHÖPFUNG. (M. STERN,
ED)
  R.K., 221(GQ):JAN70-144
ST. AUBYN, F.C. STÉPHANE MALLARMÉ.
  H.A. GRUBBS, 399(MLJ):FEB70-142
ST. CLAIR, W. THAT GREECE MIGHT STILL BE
FREE.
  M.I. FINLEY, 362:31AUG72-277
  617(TLS):1SEP72-1024
SAINT GERAUD. THE NAOMI POEMS.
  A. OSTRIKER, 473(PR):1971/2-218
ST. JOHN, D. THE COVEN.
  N. CALLENDAR, 441:6AUG72-24
ST. JOHN, P. BREATH OF LIFE.
  617(TLS):25FEB72-230
ST. JOHNS, A.R. THE HONEYCOMB.
  C. NORTH, 200:DEC69-621
DE ST. JORRE, J. THE NIGERIAN CIVIL WAR.
  R. WEST, 362:17FEB72-220
  617(TLS):25AUG72-981
SAINT LOUIS, R.A. LA PRÉSOCIOLOGIE
HAÏTIENNE OU HAÏTI ET SA VOCATION
NATIONALE.
  M.A. LUBIN, 263:APR-JUN71-224
ST. OMER, G. J--, BLACK BAM AND THE
MASQUERADERS.
  V. CUNNINGHAM, 362:20JUL72-89
  617(TLS):25AUG72-985
DE SAINT PHALLE, T. LE TOURNESOL.
  617(TLS):14APR72-427
DE SAINT-DENIS, E. - SEE COLUMELLA
"SAINT-POL-ROUX." (A. JOUFFROY, ED)
  A. WHYTE, 208(FS):JAN71-107
DUC DE SAINT-SIMON. HISTORICAL MEMOIRS
OF THE DUC DE SAINT-SIMON. (VOLS 1&2)
(L. NORTON, ED & TRANS)
  N. BLIVEN, 442(NY):30SEP72-122
  639(VQR):WINTER70-XXII
DUC DE SAINT-SIMON. HISTORICAL MEMOIRS
OF THE DUC DE SAINT-SIMON. (VOL 3)
(L. NORTON, ED & TRANS)
  N. BLIVEN, 442(NY):30SEP72-122
  M. DRABBLE, 362:27APR72-553
  617(TLS):9JUN72-652
DE STE. CROIX, G.E.M. THE ORIGINS OF THE
PELOPONNESIAN WAR.
  M.I. FINLEY, 362:19OCT72-496
SAINTSBURY, G. A HISTORY OF ENGLISH
PROSE RHYTHM.
  W. HILDICK, 340(KR):SEP66-540
SAINTY, J.C., COMP. TREASURY OFFICIALS
1660-1870.
  617(TLS):4AUG72-920
SAISSELIN, R.G. TASTE IN EIGHTEENTH
CENTURY FRANCE.
  H.D. GOLDSTEIN, 173(ECS):FALL69-148
SAJAVAARA, K. - SEE GROSSETESTE, R.

SAJÓ, G. & E. SOLTÉSZ, EDS. CATALOGUS
INCUNABULORUM QUAE IN BIBLIOTHECIS
PUBLICIS HUNGARIAE ASSERVANTUR.
C. SZABO, 356:JAN71-77
SAKELLARAKIS, J.A. & V.E.G. KENNA. COR-
PUS DER MINOISCHEN UND MYKENISCHEN
SIEGEL. (VOL 4)
J. BOARDMAN, 123:DEC71-462
SAKHAROFF, M. LE HÉROS, SA LIBERTÉ ET
SON EFFICACITÉ.
R.W. TOBIN, 546(RR):OCT70-221
SAKOL, J. I WAS NEVER THE PRINCESS.*
617(TLS):18AUG72-961
SALA, G.A. TWICE ROUND THE CLOCK, OR THE
HOURS OF THE DAY AND NIGHT IN LONDON.
617(TLS):18FEB72-181
SALAMON, G. & J.P. SPIELMAN, JR., EDS.
QUELLEN UND DARSTELLUNGEN AUS DEUTSCHER
GESCHICHTE.
E.P. DICKINS, 220(GL&L):APR71-291
E.E. HIRSHLER, 399(MLJ):APR70-303
DE SALAS, X. MIGUEL ANGEL Y EL GRECO.
E. HARRIS, 90:APR69-228
LADY SALE. THE FIRST AFGHAN WAR. (P.
MACRORY, ED)
W.D. MC INTYRE, 637(VS):JUN70-455
SALE, D. THE LOVE BITE.
617(TLS):13OCT72-1235
SALE, R.T. THE BLACKSTONE RANGERS.
W. KENNEDY, 561(SATR):8JAN72-33
SALEM, J.M. A GUIDE TO CRITICAL REVIEWS.
(PT 1)
W.J. MESERVE, 397(MD):DEC67-319
SALERNO, L. PIAZZA DI SPAGNA.
B. FORD, 90:FEB69-95
DE SALES, R.D. VIVE LA FRANCE.
J.D. GODIN, 207(FR):MAR70-714
DE SALES, R.D. - SEE DUMAS, A.
SALGADO, M.A. EL ARTE POLIFACÉTICO DE
LAS "CARICATURAS LÍRICAS" JUANRAMONI-
ANAS.
G. CONNELL, 86(BHS):JUL71-279
SALINAS, J.S. - SEE UNDER SILES SALINAS,
J.
SALINAS DE MARICHAL, S. EL MUNDO POÉTICO
DE RAFAEL ALBERTI.*
A.P. DEBICKI, 238:MAY70-339
A.P. DEBICKI, 400(MLN):MAR70-315
"LORD SALISBURY ON POLITICS." (P. SMITH,
ED)
617(TLS):7JUL72-766
SALISBURY, H.E. THE MANY AMERICAS SHALL
BE ONE.*
617(TLS):7JAN72-11
SALISBURY, H.E. THE 900 DAYS.
W.H. CHAMBERLIN, 550(RUSR):JAN70-106
SALISBURY, H.E. WAR BETWEEN RUSSIA AND
CHINA.
J.C. MC CLELLAND, 32:MAR71-159
SALK, J. MAN UNFOLDING.
C.H. WADDINGTON, 441:22OCT72-32
SALLUST. ROME AND JUGURTHA. (J.R.
HAWTHORN, ED)
R. DEN ADEL, 124:DEC70-130
SALM, P. THREE MODES OF CRITICISM.*
A. CLOSS, 402(MLR):JAN71-231
A. GALLEY, 221(GQ):MAR70-242
H. KNUST, 149:MAR71-94
L. WELCH, 290(JAAC):SPRING70-392
SALMINA-HASKELL, L. RUSSIAN PAINTINGS
AND DRAWINGS IN THE ASHMOLEAN MUSEUM.
V.B., 90:JUN70-424
SALMON, E.T. ROMAN COLONIZATION UNDER
THE REPUBLIC.*
M.H. CRAWFORD, 123:JUN71-250
SALMON, E.T. SAMNIUM AND THE SAMNITES.*
J.J. NICHOLLS, 67:MAY71-71

SALMON, P.B. INTRODUCTIONS TO GERMAN
LITERATURE.* (VOL 1)
H. HOMANN, 400(MLN):OCT70-748
SALMON, V. THE WORKS OF FRANCIS LODWICK.
617(TLS):21JUL72-849
SALOKORPI, A. MODERN ARCHITECTURE IN
FINLAND.*
K. LUNDE, 32:DEC71-913
SALOMA, J.S. 3D & F. SONTAG. PARTIES.
E. DREW, 441:4JUN72-3
SALOMON, H.P. - SEE RACINE, J.
SALONEN, A. DIE FUSSBEKLEIDUNG DER ALTEN
MESOPOTAMIER NACH SUMERISCH-AKKADISCHEN
QUELLEN.
J. BAUER, 182:VOL23#1/2-44
SALONEN, A. DIE HAUSGERÄTE DER ALTEN
MESOPOTAMIER NACH SUMERISCH-AKKADISCHEN
QUELLEN. (BK 2)
A.K. GRAYSON, 318(JAOS):OCT-DEC70-528
SALTARELLI, M. A PHONOLOGY OF ITALIAN IN
A GENERATIVE GRAMMAR.
R.J. DI PIETRO, 350:SEP71-718
SALTER, E. DAISY BATES.
A. BROYARD, 441:15FEB72-35
J. STAFFORD, 440:19MAR72-1
442(NY):17JUN72-104
SALTER, E. MEDIEVAL POETRY AND THE
FIGURAL VIEW OF REALITY.
S. BROOK, 677:VOL2-234
SALTER, K.W. THOMAS TRAHERNE.
R.E. WIEHE, 179(ES):DEC70-560
SALTMAN, B. BLUE WITH BLUE.
W. WITHERUP, 502(PRS):WINTER69/70-422
SALUS, P.H. LINGUISTICS.
W.K. PERCIVAL, 350:MAR71-181
SALVADORI, M. & M. LEVY. STRUCTURAL
DESIGN IN ARCHITECTURE.
C.W. CONDIT, 505:JAN69-178
SALVATORELLI, L. & OTHERS - SEE FERRERO,
G.
SALVUCCI, P. LA FILOSOFIA POLITICA DI
ADAM SMITH.
L. CALABI, 548(RCSF):JAN-MAR68-111
E. NAMER, 542:JUL-DEC69-459
SALWAY, P. - SEE RICHMOND, I.
SALZER, F. & C. SCHACHTER. COUNTERPOINT
IN COMPOSITION.
J. ROTHGEB, 308:WINTER69-307
SALZMAN, L.F. BUILDING IN ENGLAND DOWN
TO 1540. (2ND ED)
C.F. BARNES, JR., 54:SEP69-303
SALZMAN, L.F. EDWARD I.*
L.R. SHELBY, 589:APR71-395
SALZMANN, W. MOLIÈRE UND DIE LATEINISCHE
KOMÖDIE.
R. HESS, 72:BAND208HEFT4/6-446
W.G. MOORE, 402(MLR):JUL71-689
C.N. SMITH, 208(FS):OCT71-455
SAMARAN, C. & R. MARICHAL. CATALOGUE DES
MANUSCRITS EN ÉCRITURE LATINE PORTANT
DES INDICATIONS DE DATE, DE LIEU OU DE
COPISTE. (VOL 6)
J. ANDRÉ, 555:VOL44FASC2-371
SAMARIN, W.J. FIELD LINGUISTICS.*
K.J. FRANKLIN, 353:MAY69-125
SAMARTHA, S.J. INTRODUCTION TO RADHA-
KRISHNAN.
T.M. BOVAIRD, 485(PE&W):OCT68-340
SAMMONS, J.L. HEINRICH HEINE.*
H.S. SCHULTZ, 221(GQ):MAY70-514
SAMMONS, J.L. ANGELUS SILESIUS.*
R.L. HILLER, 221(GQ):MAR70-274
DE SAMPAYO RIBEIRO, M. - SEE PORTUGAL,
M.A.D.
SAMPSON, A. THE NEW ANATOMY OF BRITAIN.*
B. WEINRAUB, 441:18JUN72-1
SAMS, E. BRAHMS SONGS.
617(TLS):25AUG72-1003

SAMSONOV, A.M., ED. STALINGRADSKAYA
EPOPEYA.
M. PARRISH, 587:OCT69-251
SAMUEL, C. PROKOFIEV.
617(TLS):28JAN72-87
SAMUEL, R., WITH H-J. MÄHL & G. SCHULZ -
SEE NOVALIS
SAMUELS, C.T. THE AMBIGUITY OF HENRY
JAMES.
P.M. WEINSTEIN, 31(ASCH):SPRING72-310
617(TLS):18AUG72-957
SAMUELS, M.L. LINGUISTIC EVOLUTION.
617(TLS):29DEC72-1586
SANBORN, P.F. EXISTENTIALISM.
T.D.Z., 543:DEC69-355
SANCHEZ, E.M. - SEE UNDER MEJÍA SANCHEZ,
E.
SÁNCHEZ, L.A. TESTIMONIO PERSONAL.
S. LIPP, 263:OCT-DEC71-472
SÁNCHEZ, N. SIBERIA BLUES.
617(TLS):22SEP72-1122
SÁNCHEZ, R.D. - SEE UNDER DÍAZ SÁNCHEZ,
R.
SÁNCHEZ-BOUDY, J. LA TEMÁTICA NOVELÍS-
TICA DE ALEJO CARPENTIER.
J. HIGGINS, 86(BHS):JAN71-96
SÁNCHEZ BARBUDO, A. LOS POEMAS DE
ANTONIO MACHADO.
C. MORÓN ARROYO, 240(HR):OCT70-443
SÁNCHEZ DE BADAJOZ, D. RECOPILACIÓN EN
METRO. (F.W. DE KURLAT, ED)
E.L. RIVERS, 400(MLN):MAR70-290
SÁNCHEZ FERLOSIO, R. INDUSTRIAS Y
ANDANZAS DE ALFANHUÍ. (S. & A.H.
CLARKE, EDS)
E.C. RILEY, 86(BHS):JUL71-280
SÁNCHEZ ROMERALO, A. EL VILLANCICO.
J. CROSBIE, 402(MLR):JAN71-204
J. SAGE, 86(BHS):JUL71-264
SANCHO, I. LETTERS OF THE LATE IGNATIUS
SANCHO AN AFRICAN TO WHICH ARE PRE-
FIXED MEMOIRS OF HIS LIFE BY JOSEPH
JEKYLL.
L.W. BROWN, 173(ECS):SPRING70-415
À SANCTA CLARA, A. - SEE UNDER ABRAHAM À
SANCTA CLARA
SAND, A. DER BEGRIFF "FLEISCH" IN DEN
PAULINISCHEN HAUPTBRIEFEN.
C.K. BARRETT, 182:VOL23#6-263
SAND, G. LETTRES D'UN VOYAGEUR. (H.
BONNET, ED)
R. CHAMBERS, 67:NOV71-247
SANDBERG, K.C. & E.C. TATHAM. FRENCH FOR
READING.
R.E. LEAKE, JR., 399(MLJ):NOV70-538
SANDBERG-BRAUN, B. WEGE ZUR SYMBOLIS-
MUS.*
G.W. REINHARDT, 222(GR):JAN70-68
SANDBERGER, G. DIE NICHTIGKEIT WETTBE-
WERBSBESCHRÄNKENDER VEREINBARUNGEN UND
BESCHLÜSSE IM RECHT DER EUROPÄISCHEN
WIRTSCHAFTSGEMEINSCHAFT.
K.O. NASS, 182:VOL23#11/12-604
SANDBURG, H. TO A NEW HUSBAND.
N. SULLIVAN, 491:NOV71-107
SANDER, V. DIE FASZINATION DES BÖSEN.*
W. HINDERER, 221(GQ):MAR70-298
SANDERS, C.R. - SEE CARLYLE, T. & J.W.
SANDERS, E. THE FAMILY.*
P. DELANY, 99:MAY72-67
R. KEE, 362:11MAY72-627
617(TLS):9JUN72-667
SANDERS, J.B. & D.G. CREIGHTON, EDS. A
TRAVERS LES SIÈCLES.
C. HÉRISSON, 255(HAB):WINTER69-84
A. SZOGYI, 207(FR):OCT69-156
SANDERS, L. LOVE SONGS.
T. MORRISON, 441:1OCT72-41

SANDERS, N. - SEE SHAKESPEARE, W.
SANDERS, W. THE DRAMATIST AND THE
RECEIVED IDEA.*
D. COLE, 405(MP):MAY70-376
M. MINCOFF, 179(ES):APR70-157
SANDFORD, J. IN SEARCH OF THE MAGIC
MUSHROOM.
617(TLS):12MAY72-549
SANDISON, A. THE WHEEL OF EMPIRE.
J. BUTLER, 637(VS):JUN70-418
SANDMAN, J. EATING OUT.
G. ROPER, 627(UTQ):JUL70-339
SANDMEL, S. THE ENJOYMENT OF SCRIPTURE.
C.E. SIMCOX, 441:19NOV72-18
SANDOR, A.I. THE EXILE OF GODS.
J.L.S., 191(ELN):SEP69(SUPP)-104
SÁNDOR, F., ED. MUSICAL EDUCATION IN
HUNGARY.
J.S.W., 410(M&L):JAN71-74
SANDQUIST, T.A. & M.R. POWICKE, EDS.
ESSAYS IN MEDIEVAL HISTORY PRESENTED
TO BERTIE WILKINSON.
J. DAHMUS, 377:MAR71-34
SANDVED, A.O. STUDIES IN THE LANGUAGE OF
CAXTON'S MALORY AND THAT OF THE WIN-
CHESTER MANUSCRIPT.*
M.J. WRIGHT, 597(SN):VOL41#2-475
SANDY, S. ROOFS.
V. YOUNG, 249(HUDR):WINTER71/72-676
SANESI, R. INFORMATION REPORT.
J. BERNARDIN, 493:AUTUMN70-254
SANESI, R. L'IMPROVVISO DI MILANO.
617(TLS):21JUL72-839
SANGSTER, J. YOUR FRIENDLY NEIGHBORHOOD
DEATH PEDLAR.*
N. CALLENDAR, 441:23APR72-43
SANGUINETI, E. WIRRWARR.
617(TLS):29SEP72-1166
SAN JUAN, E. THE ART OF OSCAR WILDE.
E.H. MIKHAIL, 397(MD):FEB68-439
SANJUÁN, J.M. UN PUÑADO DE MANZANAS
VERDES.
F. LACOSTA, 238:MAR70-152
SANKHDHER, B.M. SAMBHAL.
617(TLS):31MAR72-378
SANSOM, W. THE BIRTH OF A STORY.
617(TLS):16JUN72-680
SANSOM, W. HANS FEET IN LOVE.*
G. EWART, 364:OCT/NOV71-159
SANSONE, G.E., ED. IL CARRIAGGIO DI
NIMES.
L.P.G. PECKHAM, 546(RR):OCT70-219
SANTAYANA, G. SELECTED CRITICAL WRITINGS
OF GEORGE SANTAYANA.* (N. HENFREY, ED)
J. MASHECK, 592:MAR69-145
R. NEWSOM, 97(CQ):SUMMER69-292
DE SANTILLANA, G. REFLECTIONS ON MEN AND
IDEAS.
F.K. SANDERS, 569(SR):SPRING71-292
DE SANTILLANA, G. & H. VON DECHEND. HAM-
LET'S MILL.*
A.B. FRIEDMAN, 319:OCT72-479
SANTOLI, V. STORIA DELLA LETTERATURA
TEDESCA.
W. LEPPMANN, 131(CL):SUMMER71-267
SANTORO, M. FORTUNA, RAGIONE E PRUDENZA
NELLA CIVILTÀ LETTERARIA DEL CINQUE-
CENTO.
C. TRINKAUS, 551(RENQ):SUMMER70-165
SANTOS, J.F. - SEE UNDER FERNÁNDEZ SAN-
TOS, J.
SANTUCCI, L. MEETING JESUS.
441:5MAR72-10
SAPORTA, M. HISTOIRE DU ROMAN AMÉRICAIN.
J.L. BROWN, 659:SUMMER72-395
SARACHCHANDRA, E.R. THE FOLK DRAMA OF
CEYLON.
F. BOWERS, 397(MD):SEP67-216

SAREIL, J. ANATOLE FRANCE ET VOLTAIRE.
   D. BRESKY, 131(CL):SUMMER71-273
SAREIL, J. LES TENCIN.
   N.M. LEOV, 67:NOV71-246
SAREIL, J. & J. CONTES CLASSIQUES.
   J. HELLERMANN, 207(FR):FEB70-546
SARGENT, B.N., ED. LE LIVRE DU ROY RAM-
   BAUX DE FRISE.
   R. LATHUILLÈRE, 545(RPH):AUG69-138
   M.L. SWITTEN, 546(RR):APR70-123
SARGENT, B.N. - SEE VILLON, F.
SARGESON, F. MAN OF ENGLAND NOW.
   D.A.N. JONES, 362:11MAY72-628
SARKAR, A.K. CHANGING PHASES OF BUDDHIST
   THOUGHT.
   P.J.H., 543:JUN70-748
SARMIENTO, E. CONCORDANCIAS DE LAS OBRAS
   POÉTICAS EN CASTELLANO DE GARCILASO DE
   LA VEGA.
   617(TLS):25FEB72-226
SARNACKI, J. - SEE MONDRAGÓN, M.
SARNOWSKA-TEMERIUSZ, E. ŚWIAT MITÓW I
   ŚWIAT ZNACZEŃ.
   D. WELSH, 104:SPRING71-126
SAROCCHI, J. JULIEN BENDA, PORTRAIT
   D'UN INTELLECTUEL.
   O. DE MOURGUES, 208(FS):OCT71-488
SAROYAN, W. PLACES WHERE I'VE DONE TIME.
   P. SOURIAN, 441:2APR72-3
   442(NY):29APR72-142
SARRAUTE, N. BETWEEN LIFE AND DEATH.*
   (FRENCH TITLE: ENTRE LA VIE ET LA
   MORT.)
   S. MAX, 207(FR):MAY70-943
SARRAUTE, N. VOUS LES ENTENDEZ?
   617(TLS):25FEB72-208
SARRAZIN, A. LETTRES À JULIEN 1958-60.
   617(TLS):11AUG72-936
SARRIS, A., ED. HOLLYWOOD VOICES.
   617(TLS):4FEB72-125
SARTON, M. A GRAIN OF MUSTARD SEED.
   H. TAYLOR, 651(WHR):AUTUMN71-372
SARTONO KARTODIRDKO. THE PEASANTS'
   REVOLT OF BANTEN IN 1888.
   T. FRIEND, 318(JAOS):APR-JUN70-406
SARTORI, C. BIBLIOGRAFIA DELLA MUSICA
   STRUMENTALE ITALIANA STAMPATA IN ITALIA
   FINO AL 1700.* (VOL 2)
   A.H. KING, 354:DEC69-348
SARTRE, J-P. ESSAYS IN AESTHETICS.
   H.R. WACKRILL, 39:MAR69-246
SARTRE, J-P. L'IDIOT DE LA FAMILLE.*
   (VOLS 1&2)
   J. WEIGHTMAN, 453:6APR72-10
SARTRE, J-P. L'IDIOT DE LA FAMILLE.
   (VOL 3)
   617(TLS):29SEP72-1155
SARTRE, J-P. SITUATIONS, VIII. SITUA-
   TIONS, IX.
   617(TLS):24MAR72-330
SASAMOTO TAKEJI & KAWANO SHIGETŌ, EDS.
   TAIWAN KEIZAI SŌGŌ KENKYŪ.
   R. MYERS, 293(JAST):MAY70-697
SASEK, L.A. - SEE SMITH, W.
SASS, H-M. HEIDEGGER-BIBLIOGRAPHIE.
   J-D.C., 543:SEP69-139
SASSO, G. MACHIAVELLI E CESARE BORGIA.
   R. PARENTI, 548(RCSF):JAN-MAR68-106
SASTRE, A. ESCUADRA HACIA LA MUERTE.
   (A.M. PASQUARIELLO, ED)
   H.N. SEAY, JR., 399(MLJ):JAN70-58
SATPRAKASHĀNANDA, S. METHODS OF KNOW-
   LEDGE ACCORDING TO ADVAITA VEDĀNTA.
   K. HINCK, 485(PE&W):JUL68-220
SATS, I.A. - SEE LUNACHARSKY, A.V.
SATTAR, A. IN THE SYLVAN SHADOWS.
   617(TLS):22SEP72-1124

"SATZ UND WORT IM HEUTIGEN DEUTSCH; PROB-
   LEME UND ERGEBNISSE NEUERER FORSCHUNG."
   H. SITTA, 361:VOL23#1-96
SAUER, C.O. NORTHERN MISTS.*
   S. EISNER, 50(ARQ):WINTER69-367
SAUER, C.O. SIXTEENTH CENTURY NORTH
   AMERICA.
   617(TLS):12MAY72-557
SAUERMANN, D. HISTORISCHE VOLKSLIEDER
   DES 18. UND 19. JAHRHUNDERTS.
   J. ERHARDT, 292(JAF):JAN-MAR70-91
SAUL, N.E. RUSSIA AND THE MEDITERRANEAN,
   1797-1807.
   M.S. ANDERSON, 575(SEER):APR71-302
   B-C. PINCHUK, 32:MAR71-142
ŠAUMJAN, S.K. PRINCIPLES OF STRUCTURAL
   LINGUISTICS.
   617(TLS):22SEP72-1115
SAUNDERS, A.N.W. IMAGINATION ALL COM-
   PACT.
   D. LOCKE, 447(N&Q):FEB70-69
SAUNDERS, J.J. THE HISTORY OF THE MONGOL
   CONQUESTS.
   617(TLS):28JUL72-887
SAUNDERS, J.T. & D.F. HENZE. THE PRI-
   VATE-LANGUAGE PROBLEM.
   E. DOWLING, 63:MAY71-110
   L.C. HOLBOROW, 479(PHQ):APR70-185
   P. HUGLY, 482(PHR):APR70-288
SAUNDERS, N. ALTERNATIVE LONDON.
   S. CLAPP, 362:10AUG72-183
   617(TLS):30JUN72-752
SAUNDERS, N. SURVIVAL GUIDE FOR STRAN-
   GERS.
   S. CLAPP, 362:10AUG72-183
DE SAUSSURE, F. COURS DE LINGUISTIQUE
   GÉNÉRALE. (FASC 1-3) (R. ENGLER, ED)
   K. CONNORS, 545(RPH):NOV69-201
DE SAUSSURE, F. COURS DE LINGUISTIQUE
   GÉNÉRALE. (VOL 1) (R. ENGLER, ED)
   G.C. LEPSCHY, 353:DEC69-82
SAUVAGE, O. - SEE SIGÉE, L.
DE SAUVIGNY, G. - SEE UNDER DE BERTIER
   DE SAUVIGNY, G.
SAUVY, A. GENERAL THEORY OF POPULATION.
   617(TLS):29DEC72-1585
SAVAGE, C. ROGER MARTIN DU GARD.*
   M. O'NAN, 207(FR):OCT69-171
   M. TISON-BRAUN, 546(RR):OCT70-234
SAVAGE, C.W. THE MEASUREMENT OF SENSA-
   TION.*
   M. ATHERTON, 311(JP):3AUG72-422
   A.R. LOUCH, 319:OCT72-495
SAVAGE, E. THE HAPPY ENDING.
   M. LEVIN, 441:5MAR72-35
SAVAGE, E.H. POLICE RECORDS AND RECOL-
   LECTIONS.
   617(TLS):18FEB72-191
SAVATIER, R. LE DROIT COMPTABLE AU SER-
   VICE DE L'HOMME.
   J. PUCELLE, 542:JUL-DEC69-471
SAXENA, K.C. PAKISTAN: HER RELATIONS
   WITH INDIA, 1947-1966.
   R.S. WHEELER, 293(JAST):AUG70-975
SAXL, F. & R. WITTKOWER. BRITISH ART
   AND THE MEDITERRANEAN. (NEW ED)
   90:JUN70-423
SĀYAṆA. SĀYAṆA'S SUBHĀṢITA-SUDHĀNIDHI
   (AN ANTHOLOGY). (K. KRISHNAMOORTHY,
   ED)
   L. ROCHER, 318(JAOS):APR-JUN70-410
SAYCE, R.A. THE ESSAYS OF MONTAIGNE.
   617(TLS):22SEP72-1100
SAYERS, D. LORD PETER.
   N. CALLENDAR, 441:16JAN72-42
SAYERS, J.E. PAPAL JUDGES DELEGATE IN
   THE PROVINCE OF CANTERBURY 1198-1254.
   617(TLS):9JUN72-665

SAYERS, R.S., ED. PORTUGAL AND BRAZIL
IN TRANSITION.*
O. FERNÁNDEZ, 399(MLJ):APR70-293
SAYRE, K.M. PLATO'S ANALYTIC METHOD.*
N. GULLEY, 518:OCT70-30
A.R. LACEY, 483:JUL70-250
SAYWELL, J. QUEBEC 70.
C.I. MILLER, 99:JAN-FEB72-74
617(TLS):28JUL72-861
AL-SAYYID, A.L. EGYPT AND CROMER.
R.L. TIGNOR, 637(VS):JUN70-421
SCADUTO, A. BOB DYLAN.
P. MARIN, 441:20FEB72-4
C. RICKS, 362:1JUN72-724
617(TLS):27OCT72-1296
SCAMMELL, M., ED. RUSSIA'S OTHER WRIT-
ERS.*
D. BROWN, 574(SEEJ):WINTER71-508
SCANNELL, V. SELECTED POEMS.*
J. SYMONS, 364:DEC71/JAN72-128
SCANNELL, V. THE TIGER AND THE ROSE.*
G. EWART, 364:DEC71/JAN72-146
SCARBOROUGH, J. ROMAN MEDICINE.
R.W. DAVIES, 313:VOL60-224
J.G. LANDELS, 123:JUN71-276
L.R. LIND, 124:NOV70-96
G.S. SACHSE, 24:OCT71-757
SCARBOROUGH, W.K. - SEE RUFFIN, E.
SCARFE, N. A SHELL GUIDE TO ESSEX.
J.M.R., 46:JUN69-472
SCARFE, N. THE SUFFOLK LANDSCAPE.
617(TLS):22DEC72-1566
SCARISBRICK, J.J. HENRY VIII.*
A.J. LOOMIE, 613:SPRING69-148
SCARLET, I. THE PROFESSIONALS.
617(TLS):12MAY72-549
SCARLETT, B. SHIPMINDER.
617(TLS):9JUN72-667
VAN DER SCHAAR, J. WOORDENBOEK VAN VOOR-
NAMEN.
G.B. DROEGE, 424:MAR68-58
SCHACHERL, L. MÄHREN.
N.P., 46:JUN69-472
SCHACHERMEYR, F. PERIKLES.
R. SEALEY, 24:OCT71-746
SCHACHERMEYR, F. RELIGIONSPOLITIK UND
RELIGIOSITAT BEI PERIKLES.
S.L. GLASS, 124:FEB71-200
SCHACHT, S. THE DICTIONARY OF EXCEPTIONS
TO RULES OF RUSSIAN GRAMMAR.*
J.F. HENDRY, 104:SUMMER71-269
SCHAEFER, H. THE ROOTS OF MODERN DESIGN.
H. OSBORNE, 89(BJA):SUMMER71-301
SCHAEFER, H. WALTHER VON DER VOGELWEIDE
UND FRAUENLOB.
E.S. FIRCHOW, 406:SUMMER71-188
SCHAEFFER, E. HIDDEN ART.
617(TLS):1SEP72-1034
SCHAEFFER, P. TRAITÉ DES OBJETS MUSI-
CAUX. LA MUSIQUE CONCRÈTE.
N. KAY, 607:SPRING68-29
SCHAEFFNER, A. ORIGINE DES INSTRUMENTS
DE MUSIQUE.
W.P. MALM, 187:MAY72-292
SCHAFER, E.H. SHORE OF PEARLS.
639(VQR):AUTUMN70-CLVI
SCHAFER, W. ECOLOGY AND PALAEOECOLOGY OF
MARINE ENVIRONMENTS. (G.Y. CRAIG, ED)
617(TLS):28JUL72-871
SCHALIT, A. NAMENWÖRTERBUCH ZU FLAVIUS
JOSEPHUS.
D. RUNNALLS, 487:AUTUMN70-272
SCHALK, A. THE GERMANS.
L.L. SNYDER, 561(SATR):29JAN72-65
SCHALLER, G.B. SERENGETI.
G. STADE, 441:3DEC72-6

SCHALLER, G.B. THE SERENGETI LION.
G. STADE, 441:3DEC72-6
561(SATR):28OCT72-78
SCHANE, S.A. FRENCH PHONOLOGY AND MOR-
PHOLOGY.
R. POSNER, 545(RPH):MAY71-625
SCHANZE, H., ED. DIE ANDERE ROMANTIK.
I.C., 191(ELN):SEP69(SUPP)-97
SCHANZE, H., ED. INDEX ZU NOVALIS HEIN-
RICH VON OFTERDINGEN. INDEX ZU HEIN-
RICH VON KLEIST SÄMTLICHE ERZÄHLUNGEN,
ERZÄHLVARIANTEN, ANEKDOTEN.
M. DURZAK, 221(GQ):MAR70-241
SCHANZE, H. ROMANTIK UND AUFKLÄRUNG.*
G. SCHULZ, 564:SPRING68-73
SCHAPIRO, L. THE COMMUNIST PARTY OF THE
SOVIET UNION. (2ND ED)
F.L. CARSTEN, 575(SEER):APR71-307
SCHAPIRO, L. TOTALITARIANISM.
617(TLS):13OCT72-1221
SCHAPIRO, L. - SEE TURGENEV, I.S.
SCHAPIRO, L. & E. DE KADT, EDS. POLITI-
CAL OPPOSITION IN ONE-PARTY STATES.
617(TLS):29DEC72-1575
SCHARANG, M. ZUR EMANZIPATION DER KUNST.
617(TLS):16JUN72-691
SCHARBERTH, I. & H. PARIS, EDS. ROLF
LIEBERMANN ZUM 60. GEBURTSTAG.
E.H., 412:MAY71-183
SCHARPE, K.R. GATTUNGSPOETIK IM 18.
JAHRHUNDERT.
I.C., 191(ELN):SEP70(SUPP)-96
SCHATTER, H.R., ED. SCHARFGESCHOSSEN.
R. HANSER, 19(AGR):VOL36#1-25
SCHEDEL DE CASTELLO BRANCO, T.M. VIDA DO
MARQUÊS DE SANDE.
617(TLS):18AUG72-972
SCHEER, G.F. & H.F. RANKIN. REBELS AND
REDCOATS.
T. LASK, 441:26MAY72-35
SCHEFER, J-L. SCÉNOGRAPHIE D'UN TABLEAU.
LECTURE ET SYSTÈME DU TABLEAU.
L. MARIN, 98:NOV69-953
SCHEFFLER, I. SCIENCE AND SUBJECTIVITY.*
H. LEHMAN, 486:SEP68-291
SCHEFFLER, W. BERLINER GOLDSCHMIEDE,
DATEN, WERKE, ZEICHEN.
C. OMAN, 90:JAN70-68
SCHELER, L. & M-C. BANCQUART - SEE
VALLÈS, J.
VON SCHELIHA, R. FREIHEIT UND FREUND-
SCHAFT IN HELLAS.*
D.W. BRADEEN, 24:APR71-379
SCHELLHORN, L. GOLDENES VLIES.
M-L. VON FRANZ, 182:VOL23#23/24-1021
SCHELLING-SCHÄR, E. DIE GESTALT DER
OTTILIE.
D. ROBERTS, 67:NOV71-254
SCHELP, H. EXEMPLARISCHE ROMANZEN IM
MITTELENGLISCHEN.*
D. MEHL, 38:BAND87HEFT2-253
M. MILLS, 382(MAE):1971/3-291
SCHENKER, A.M., ED. FIFTEEN MODERN
POLISH SHORT STORIES.
G. KOLODZIEJ, 574(SEEJ):FALL71-372
SCHENKER, H. FIVE GRAPHIC MUSIC ANALY-
SES.*
E. SAMS, 415:FEB71-140
SCHER, S.P. VERBAL MUSIC IN GERMAN LIT-
ERATURE.*
H.S. DAEMMRICH, 290(JAAC):SUMMER70-
554
H. LEHNERT, 401(MLQ):DEC70-513
E. SPEIDEL, 447(N&Q):OCT70-392
SCHERER, J. CONTEMPORARY COMMUNITY.
617(TLS):13OCT72-1220
SCHERF, M. TO CACHE A MILLIONAIRE.
N. CALLENDAR, 441:18JUN72-32

SCHMID, M.E. SYMBOL UND FUNKTION DER
MUSIK IM WERK HUGO VON HOFMANNSTHALS.
R. EXNER, 149:JUN71-170
R.T. LLEWELLYN, 220(GL&L):OCT70-98
SCHMIDHÄUSER, E. STRAFRECHT.
P. PADIS, 182:VOL23#6-268
SCHMIDT, A. DIE SCHULE DER ATHEISTEN.
617(TLS):21JUL72-843
SCHMIDT, G. KYPRISCHE BILDWERKE AUS DEM
HERAION VON SAMOS.
R.V. NICHOLLS, 123:MAR71-145
SCHMIDT, H. HUS UND HUSSITISMUS IN DER
TSCHECHISCHEN LITERATUR DES XIX. UND
XX. JAHRHUNDERTS.
W. PROCHAZKA, 574(SEEJ):SPRING71-139
SCHMIDT, J. - SEE GENGENBACH, P.
SCHMIDT, M. JOHN WESLEY. (VOL 2, PT 1)
617(TLS):13OCT72-1234
SCHMIDT, M. & G. LINDOP, EDS. BRITISH
POETRY SINCE 1960.
617(TLS):20OCT72-1249
SCHMIDT, P.L. IULIUS OBSEQUENS UND DAS
PROBLEM DER LIVIUS-EPITOME.
M.H. CRAWFORD, 313:VOL60-269
SCHMIDT, S.J. SPRACHE UND DENKEN ALS
SPRACHPHILOSOPHISCHES PROBLEM VON LOCKE
BIS WITTGENSTEIN.
R.W.K. PATERSON, 479(PHQ):OCT70-398
SCHMIDT, U. DIE REZEPTION DES A-NASALIS
ROMANISCHER LEHNWÖRTER IM MITTELENG-
LISCHEN UND SEINE WEITERENTWICKLUNG IN
STANDARD UND DIALEKTEN.
A.A. PRINS, 179(ES):OCT70-451
SCHMIDT, V. SPRACHLICHE UNTERSUCHUNGEN
ZU HERONDAS.*
I.C. CUNNINGHAM, 123:MAR71-22
SCHMIDT, W. GRUNDFRAGEN DER DEUTSCHEN
GRAMMATIK. (2ND ED)
L. HERMODSSON, 597(SN):VOL40#2-469
SCHMIDT-GÖRG, J. & H. SCHMIDT, EDS. LUD-
WIG VAN BEETHOVEN.*
A. TYSON, 415:OCT70-999
SCHMIDT-MACKEY, I. PHONÉTIQUE PRATIQUE
DE L'ALLEMAND À L'USAGE DES FRANCO-
PHONES.
J.J. BINAMÉ, 564:SPRING68-71
SCHMIED, W. ALFRED KUBIN.
A. WERNER, 58:MAY70-10
SCHMIELE, W. HENRY MILLER.
M. FARZAN, 27(AL):NOV71-479
SCHMITT, C.B. GIANFRANCESCO PICO DELLA
MIRANDOLA (1469-1533) AND HIS CRITIQUE
OF ARISTOTLE.*
W.F. EDWARDS, 258:DEC69-625
C.H. LOHR, 613:SPRING69-140
C.G. NAUERT, JR., 551(RENQ):SPRING70-
55
SCHMITT, F.O. & OTHERS, EDS. NEUROSCI-
ENCES RESEARCH SYMPOSIUM SUMMARIES.
(VOL 3)
M.B.M., 543:JUN70-753
SCHMITT, G. THE GODFORGOTTEN.
P. ADAMS, 61:JUN72-113
G. HICKS, 441:20AUG72-22
SCHMITT, H.A. CHARLES PÉGUY.
G.M., 477:SUMMER69-423
SCHMITT, H.H. DIE STAATSVERTRÄGE DES
ALTERTUMS.* (VOL 3)
D.M. LEWIS, 123:JUN71-296
SCHMITT, L.E., ED. KURZER GRUNDRISS DER
GERMANISCHEN PHILOLOGIE BIS 1500.*
(VOL 1)
P. SALMON, 402(MLR):JUL71-698
SCHMITT, L.E., ED. KURZER GRUNDRISS DER
GERMANISCHEN PHILOLOGIE BIS 1500.
(VOL 2)
P. SALMON, 402(MLR):OCT71-917

SCHMITT, R. DICHTUNG UND DICHTERSPRACHE
IN INDOGERMANISCHER ZEIT.
J. GONDA, 361:VOL23#3-301
SCHMITT, R. MARTIN HEIDEGGER ON BEING
HUMAN.*
J.D.C., 543:SEP69-139
S.A. ERICKSON, 319:OCT72-491
SCHMITZ, W. ÜBUNGEN ZU SYNONYMEN VERBEN.
H. BROCKHAUS, 221(GQ):JAN70-133
SCHNABEL, A. MUSIC AND THE LINE OF MOST
RESISTANCE.
R.T. BECK, 447(N&Q):JUL70-274
SCHNABEL, A. MY LIFE AND MUSIC.
F. DAWES, 415:MAY71-448
SCHNACK, I. RILKES LEBEN UND WERK IM
BILD.
L.B. FOLTIN, 399(MLJ):MAR70-215
SCHNAPP, A. & P. VIDAL-NAQUET. THE
FRENCH STUDENT UPRISING, NOVEMBER 1967-
JUNE 1968.*
R.O. PAXTON, 441:24SEP72-46
SCHNAPP, F. - SEE HOFFMANN, E.T.A.
SCHNAPPER, A. TABLEAUX POUR LE TRIANON
DE MARBRE.
J. MONTAGU, 90:JAN70-59
SCHNECK, S. NOCTURNAL VAUDEVILLE.
P. ADAMS, 61:FEB72-109
J. HENDIN, 441:2APR72-6
SCHNEEWEISS, G. DER PROTREPTIKOS DES
ARISTOTELES.
P.S. COSTAS, 124:OCT70-58
P.M. HUBY, 123:MAR71-128
E. MUEHLENBERG, 319:JAN72-86
SCHNEIDAU, H.N. EZRA POUND.
W.M. CHACE, 598(SOR):WINTER72-225
L.L. MARTZ, 27(AL):MAY71-299
F.K. SANDERS, 569(SR):SUMMER71-433
A.K. WEATHERHEAD, 141:FALL70-358
SCHNEIDER, E.W. THE DRAGON IN THE GATE.*
R. BOYLE, 301(JEGP):APR71-327
F.N. LEES, 637(VS):JUN70-451
N.H. MAC KENZIE, 401(MLQ):JUN70-236
W.D. TEMPLEMAN, 191(ELN):JUN70-315
SCHNEIDER, H. DER FRÜHE BAL'MONT!
T.A. SCHMIDT, 575(SEER):JUL71-464
SCHNEIDER, I. ISADORA DUNCAN, THE RUS-
SIAN YEARS.
D.S. HULL, 550(RUSR):OCT70-482
SCHNEIDER, K. DER "TROJANISCHE KRIEG"
IM SPÄTEN MITTELALTER.*
W.H. JACKSON, 402(MLR):JAN71-211
SCHNEIDER, K.D. DIE MUNDART VON RAMOSCH
(KANTON GRAUBÜNDEN, SCHWEIZ).
J. KRAMER, 72:BAND208HEFT4/6-431
SCHNEIDER, L.A. KU CHIEH-KANG AND
CHINA'S NEW HISTORY.
M. BERNAL, 453:23MAR72-31
SCHNEIDER, N. DIE RHETORISCHE EIGENART
DER PAULINISCHEN ANTITHESE.
F.F. BRUCE, 182:VOL23#15/16-719
SCHNELL, R. RUDOLF VON EMS.
H. ADOLF, 182:VOL23#9-483
D.H. GREEN, 402(MLR):JUL71-703
SCHNETZ, D. DER MODERNE EINAKTER.*
S. MELCHINGER, 52:BAND4HEFT2-217
SCHNITZLER, A. FRÜHE GEDICHTE.* (H.
LEDERER, ED)
R.K. ANGRESS, 406:FALL71-293
SCHNITZLER, A. JUGEND IN WIEN. (T.
NICKL & H. SCHNITZLER, EDS)
H. LEDERER, 221(GQ):JAN70-117
R.O. WEISS, 19(AGR):VOL35#2-22
SCHOCK, R. LOGICS WITHOUT EXISTENCE
ASSUMPTIONS.
R.H.K., 543:MAR70-565
SCHOECK, H. ENVY.
W.C. HAVARD, 639(VQR):AUTUMN70-674

SCHOECK, H. DER NEID.
K. GRUE-SØRENSEN, 462(OL):VOL23#3-251
SCHOELL, K. DAS THEATER SAMUEL BECK-
ETTS.*
R. KUHN, 207(FR):DEC69-324
SCHOENBAUM, S., ED. RENAISSANCE DRAMA.
(NEW SER, VOL 1)
I. DONALDSON, 541(RES):AUG70-352
SCHOENBAUM, S., ED. RENAISSANCE DRAMA.
(NEW SER, VOL 2)
C. LEECH, 541(RES):NOV70-492
SCHOENBAUM, S. SHAKESPEARE'S LIVES.*
M. CHARNEY, 301(JEGP):OCT71-661
L.F. DEAN, 568(SCN):SPRING71-15
D.R.C. MARSH, 67:NOV71-230
M. RUDICK, 651(WHR):SPRING71-184
SCHOENDOERFFER, P. L'ADIEU AU ROI.
M. NAUDIN, 207(FR):APR70-868
SCHOFIELD, H. THE PHILOSOPHY OF EDUCA-
TION.
617(TLS):3NOV72-1349
SCHOGT, H.G. LE SYSTÈME VERBAL DU FRAN-
ÇAIS CONTEMPORAIN.
J. DUBOIS, 361(VOL23#1-103
SCHOKKER, G.H., ED. THE PĀDATĀḌITAKA OF
ŚYĀMILAKA. (PT 1)
S. LEVITT, 318(JAOS):OCT-DEC70-594
SCHOLEFIELD, A. THE YOUNG MASTERS.*
M. LEVIN, 441:30JAN72-26
P. THEROUX, 440:23JAN72-2
SCHOLEM, G. URSPRUNG UND ANFÄNGE DER
KABBALA.
J. SCHLANGER, 542:JAN-MAR69-123
SCHOLES, P.A. THE OXFORD COMPANION TO
MUSIC. (10TH ED) (J.O. WARD, ED)
R. ANDERSON, 415:APR71-346
SCHOLES, R. THE FABULATORS.*
L. CASPER, 613:AUTUMN68-444
SCHOLES, R.J. PHONOTACTIC GRAMMATICALITY.
E. PULGRAM, 353:DEC69-144
SCHOLL, H. DER DIENST DES GEBETES NACH
JOHANNES CALVIN.
A. GANOCZY, 182:VOL23#7-349
SCHOLZ, B.W., WITH B. ROGERS - SEE UNDER
"CAROLINGIAN CHRONICLES"
SCHOLZ, M.G., ED. BIBLIOGRAPHIE ZU
WALTHER VON DER VOGELWEIDE.
C. GRAY, JR., 301(JEGP):JAN71-109
K.J. NORTHCOTT, 406:SUMMER71-162
SCHÖNAU, W. SIGMUND FREUDS PROSA.
D.G. DAVIAU, 222(GR):NOV70-311
H. LEDERER, 400(MLN):OCT70-758
H. RIDLEY, 220(GL&L):OCT70-114
SCHÖNBERG, A. FUNDAMENTALS OF MUSICAL
COMPOSITION.* (G. STRANG & L. STEIN,
EDS)
G.W. HOPKINS, 607:SPRING68-35
SCHÖNHAAR, R. NOVELLE UND KRIMINAL-
SCHEMA.
W.W. HOLDHEIM, 401(MLQ):SEP70-388
SCHÖNZELER, H-H. BRUCKNER.*
R. ANDERSON, 415:SEP71-858
M.C., 410(M&L):JUL71-331
"THE SCHOOL AND THE DEMOCRATIC ENVIRON-
MENT."
J.P. LOVEKIN, 529(QQ):AUTUMN70-458
SCHOPENHAUER, A. IL MONDO COME VOLONTÀ
E RAPPRESENTAZIONE.
G. FAGGIN, 548(RCSF):JUL/SEP69-344
SCHÖPFLIN, G., ED. THE SOVIET UNION AND
EASTERN EUROPE.
617(TLS):30JUN72-757
SCHOTT, H. PLAYING THE HARPSICHORD.
617(TLS):21JAN72-78
SCHOTTELIUS, J.G. AUSFÜHRLICHE ARBEIT
VON DER TEUTSCHEN HAUBTSPRACHE. (W.
HECHT, ED)
J.E. OYLER, 564:FALL69-144

SCHOTTLAENDER, R. RÖMISCHES GESELL-
SCHAFTSDENKEN.*
G.K. GALINSKY, 124:APR71-278
SCHÖWERLING, R. DIE ANEKDOTE IM ENGLAND
DES 18. JAHRHUNDERTS.
J. BOURKE, 72:BAND208HEFT4/6-382
SCHRADER, R.J. - SEE DYCE, A.
SCHRAG, P. THE DECLINE OF THE WASP.
R. ALTER, 441:5MAR72-40
F. DARWIN, 561(SATR):29JAN72-66
E.Z. FRIEDENBERG, 453:24FEB72-30
B.A. WEISBERGER, 440:6FEB72-6
442(NY):4MAR72-116
SCHRAG, P. THE VANISHING AMERICAN.
617(TLS):1SEP72-1012
SCHRAG, P.G. COUNSEL FOR THE DECEIVED.
P. ADAMS, 61:SEP72-110
SCHRAM, I. ASHES, ASHES, WE ALL FALL
DOWN.
D.K. MANO, 441:27AUG72-2
SCHRAMM, G. DER POLNISCHE ADEL UND DIE
REFORMATION, 1548-1607.*
D.W. JELLEMA, 182:VOL23#13/14-692
SCHRAMM, P.E. HITLER.
G. BARRACLOUGH, 453:19OCT72-37
SCHRAMM, P.E. KAISER, KÖNIGE UND PÄPSTE.
(VOLS 1-3)
H.S. OFFLER, 182:VOL23#19/20-889
SCHRECKENBACH, H-J., ED. BIBLIOGRAPHIE
ZUR GESCHICHTE DER MARK BRANDENBURG.
(PT 1)
T. KLEIN, 182:VOL23#9-451
SCHRECKENBERG, H. BIBLIOGRAPHIE ZU
FLAVIUS JOSEPHUS.
D. RUNNALLS, 487:AUTUMN70-272
SCHREINER, J.H. ARISTOTLE AND PERIKLES.
V. EHRENBERG, 303:VOL90-447
P. HUART, 555:VOL44FASC2-324
SCHREMP, W.E. DESIGNER FURNITURE ANYONE
CAN MAKE.
B. GLADSTONE, 441:3DEC72-99
SCHROEDER, A. THE OZONE MINOTAUR.
D. BARBOUR, 150(DR):SPRING70-112
D. FETHERLING, 606(TAMR):#57-80
A. SHUCARD, 102(CANL):SPRING71-80
SCHROEDER, H. & I. KIRCHHOFF. WIR LESEN
DEUTSCH. (PT 1)
H. BROCKHAUS, 221(GQ):JAN70-133
SCHROEDER, H-D., ED. DER STRALSUNDER
LIBER MEMORIALIS. (PTS 2 & 4)
G. THEUERKAUF, 182:VOL23#19/20-892
SCHROETER, J., ED. WILLA CATHER AND HER
CRITICS.
M.R. BENNETT, 502(PRS):SUMMER68-178
SCHRÖTER, K. ANFÄNGE HEINRICH MANNS.
B.A. SØRENSEN, 462(OL):VOL24#4-305
SCHRÖTER, K. HEINRICH MANN: DREI AUF-
SÄTZE.
B.A. SØRENSEN, 462(OL):VOL24#4-305
U. WEISSTEIN, 406:WINTER71-405
SCHRÖTER, K., ED. THOMAS MANN IM URTEIL
SEINER ZEIT.*
A. VON GRONICKA, 222(GR):MAY70-231
SCHUBART, C.F.D. GEDICHTE. (P. HART-
LING, ED)
T.T. KARST, 221(GQ):NOV70-828
SCHUBERT, O. OPTIK IN ARCHITEKTUR UND
STÄDTEBAU.
R. ARNHEIM & E.F. SEKLER, 576:MAR69-
77
SCHUCHHARDT, W-H. GRIECHISCHE KUNST.
J.A. GAERTNER, 124:JAN71-164
SCHUCHART, M. THE NETHERLANDS.
617(TLS):11AUG72-941
SCHUELER, H.J. THE GERMAN VERSE EPIC IN
THE NINETEENTH AND TWENTIETH CENTUR-
IES.*
L. FORSTER, 627(UTQ):JUL69-390

SCHUELLER, H.M. & R.L. PETERS - SEE
SYMONDS, J.A.
SCHUETTINGER, R., ED. THE CONSERVATIVE
TRADITION IN EUROPEAN THOUGHT.
J. REAL, 396(MODA):SPRING71-207
SCHULBERG, B. LOSER AND STILL CHAMPION.
M. WATKINS, 441:1SEP72-30
SCHÜLE, E. & OTHERS, EDS. GLOSSAIRE DES
PATOIS DE LA SUISSE ROMANDE. (FASC
39-48)
G. AUB-BUSCHER, 545(RPH):FEB71-518
SCHULER, F. FLAMEWORKING.
D. SMITH, 139:JAN-FEB69-8
SCHÜLKE, U., ED. KONRADS BÜCHLEIN VON
DER GEISTLICHEN GEMAHELSCHAFT.
P.F. GANZ, 382(MAE):1971/3-312
G.F. JONES, 406:WINTER71-393
R. RUDOLF, 182:VOL23#11/12-611
H.B. WILLSON, 402(MLR):OCT71-931
SCHULKIND, E., ED. THE PARIS COMMUNE
OF 1871.
617(TLS):26MAY72-610
SCHULL, J. THE JINKER.
G. ROPER, 627(UTQ):JUL69-362
SCHULL, J. REBELLION.
J-P. BERNARD, 99:JUN72-34
SCHULMAN, A. BABA.*
617(TLS):25AUG72-986
SCHULMAN, I.A. & M.P. GONZÁLEZ. MARTÍ,
DARÍO Y EL MODERNISMO.
H. CASTILLO, 238:MAY70-343
M.E. VENIER, 400(MLN):MAR70-318
SCHULTZ, G.F. VIETNAMESE LEGENDS.*
R.G. ALVEY, 582(SFQ):DEC68-328
SCHULTZ, H.S. STUDIEN ZUR DICHTUNG
STEFAN GEORGES.
V.J. GÜNTHER, 52:BAND4HEFT3-316
SCHULTZ, J. MOTION WILL BE DENIED.
J.R. WALTZ, 440:20FEB72-4
SCHULTZE, A. THE SULTANATE OF BORNU.
A.H.M. KIRK-GREENE, 69:JAN69-81
SCHULTZE, C.L. & OTHERS. SETTING
NATIONAL PRIORITIES: THE 1973 BUDGET.
E. DREW, 441:4JUN72-3
SCHULZ, G. REZENSIERTE GEDICHTE.
617(TLS):7JAN72-6
SCHULZ, G. - SEE NOVALIS
SCHULZ, J. VENETIAN PAINTED CEILINGS OF
THE RENAISSANCE.
D. ROSAND, 551(RENQ):SPRING70-80
SCHULZ, M.F., W.D. TEMPLEMAN & C. METZ-
GER, EDS. ESSAYS IN AMERICAN AND ENG-
LISH LITERATURE.
F.S., 477:SUMMER69-426
SCHULZ, R.K. THE PORTRAYAL OF THE GERMAN
IN RUSSIAN NOVELS.
A.B. MC MILLIN, 575(SEER):JUL71-469
SCHULZ-BEHREND, G. - SEE OPITZ, M.
SCHULZ-BUSCHHAUS, U. DAS MADRIGAL.
R. HESS, 72:BAND208HEFT4/6-446
SCHULZE, A. TJUTČEVS KURZLYRIK.*
G. DE MALLAC, 32:MAR71-204
SCHULZE, E.J. SHELLEY'S THEORY OF
POETRY.
K.N.C., 191(ELN):SEP69(SUPP)-43
SCHULZE, H., ED. KAS KABINETT SCHEIDE-
MANN.
617(TLS):19MAY72-581
SCHULZE, J. ENTTÄUSCHUNG UND WAHNWELT.*
A.R. OLIVER, 546(RR):DEC70-308
SCHUON, F. IN THE TRACKS OF BUDDHISM.
P.J.H., 543:MAR70-565
SCHUR, M. FREUD: LIVING AND DYING.
R. LOCKE, 441:24JUL72-25
P. RIEFF, 441:18JUN72-23
C. RYCROFT, 453:10AUG72-12
R.S. STEWART, 561(SATR):29JUL72-52

SCHURIG-GEICK, D. STUDIEN ZUM MODERNEN
"CONTE FANTASTIQUE" MAUPASSANTS UND
AUSGEWÄHLTER AUTOREN DES 20. JAHRHUN-
DERTS.
W. PABST, 72:BAND208HEFT3-237
SCHÜTRUMPF, E. DIE BEDEUTUNG DES WORTES
ETHOS IN DER "POETIK" DES ARISTOTELES.
L. GOLDEN, 122:OCT71-286
F. LASSERRE, 182:VOL23#17/18-818
SCHUTTE, W.M., ED. "A PORTRAIT OF THE
ARTIST AS A YOUNG MAN:" TWENTIETH CEN-
TURY INTERPRETATIONS.
502(PRS):WINTER69/70-426
SCHUTZ, A. THE PHENOMENOLOGY OF THE
SOCIAL WORLD.
617(TLS):9JUN72-663
SCHUTZ, A. REFLECTIONS ON THE PROBLEM OF
RELEVANCE.* (R.M. ZANER, ED)
Q. LAUER, 182:VOL23#5-205
SCHÜTZEICHEL, R. ALTHOCHDEUTSCHES WÖR-
TERBUCH.*
D.H. GREEN, 402(MLR):APR71-429
E. HUNERT-HOFMANN, 221(GQ):NOV70-818
SCHUYLER, J. THE CRYSTAL LITHIUM.
D. KALSTONE, 441:5NOV72-6
SCHWAB, R.N., W.E. REX & J. LOUGH. IN-
VENTORY OF DIDEROT'S ENCYCLOPÉDIE.
(VOLS 2&3)
617(TLS):30JUN72-751
SCHWAB, U., ED. WALDERE.
H. DÖLVERS, 72:BAND208HEFT2-141
SCHWAMBORN, F. DAS SPANIENBILD DOMINGO
FAUSTINO SARMIENTOS.
R. GUTIÉRREZ GIRARDOT, 72:BAND208
HEFT2-156
SCHWARTZ, B. IN SEARCH OF WEALTH AND
POWER.
M. BERNAL, 453:23MAR72-31
SCHWARTZ, D. SELECTED ESSAYS OF DELMORE
SCHWARTZ.* (D.A. DIKE & D.H. ZUCKER,
EDS)
I. MALIN, 651(WHR):SUMMER71-270
SCHWARTZ, E. WILL THE REVOLUTION SUC-
CEED?
E. CAPOUYA, 561(SATR):11MAR72-64
SCHWARTZ, H. THE CASE FOR AMERICAN
MEDICINE.
L. LASAGNA, 441:10DEC72-53
SCHWARTZ, J. HART CRANE, AN ANNOTATED
CRITICAL BIBLIOGRAPHY.
A. GALPIN, 659:WINTER72-106
SCHWARTZ, J. & R.C. SCHWEIK. HART CRANE.
617(TLS):14JUL72-825
SCHWARTZ, P. HEARING MUSIC WITH UNDER-
STANDING.
S. ANDERSON, 308:SPRING69-152
SCHWARZ, A. THE COMPLETE WORKS OF
MARCEL DUCHAMP.
R. SHATTUCK, 453:1JUN72-19
SCHWARZ, B. MUSIC AND MUSICAL LIFE IN
SOVIET RUSSIA 1917-1970.
L. KIRSTEIN, 441:16APR72-7
442(NY):6MAY72-148
617(TLS):24MAR72-333
SCHWARZ, S.M. THE RUSSIAN REVOLUTION OF
1905.
S. GALAI, 587:APR69-557
SCHWARZ, S.M. - SEE UNDER SHVARTS, S.M.
SCHWARZ, W.J. DER ERZÄHLER HEINRICH
BÖLL.*
T. ZIOLKOWSKI, 564:SPRING68-75
SCHWARZ, W.J. DER ERZÄHLER GÜNTER GRASS.
J. REDDICK, 402(MLR):JAN71-232
A.L. WILLSON, 301(JEGP):JAN71-127
SCHWARZ, W.J. DER ERZÄHLER UWE JOHNSON.*
R. GRIMM, 406:SUMMER71-172
SCHWARZ-BART, A. LA MULÂTRESSE SOLITUDE.
617(TLS):2JUN72-623

SCHWARZBAUM, H. STUDIES IN JEWISH AND
WORLD FOLKLORE.
W.E. ROBERTS, 292(JAF):JAN-MAR70-83
SCHWARZE, C. DER ALTPROVENZALISCHE
"BOECI."
A-J. HENRICHSEN, 545(RPH):MAY70-592
SCHWARZENBACH, R. DIE STELLUNG DER MUN-
DART IN DER DEUTSCHSPRACHIGEN SCHWEIZ.
R.E. KELLER, 402(MLR):OCT71-915
C.E. REED, 301(JEGP):JUL71-494
E.H. YARRILL, 182:VOL23#3-85
SCHWARZKOPF, U. DIE RECHNUNGSLEGUNG DES
HUMBERT DE PLAINE ÜBER DIE JAHRE 1448-
52.
R. FOLZ, 182:VOL23#10-567
SCHWEICKERT, A. HEINRICH HEINES EIN-
FLÜSSE AUF DIE DEUTSCHE LYRIK 1830-
1900.
J.L.S., 191(ELN):SEP70(SUPP)-105
SCHWEIKERT, U. - SEE "LUDWIG TIECK: DICH-
TER ÜBER IHRE DICHTUNGEN".
SCHWEITZER, B. DIE GEOMETRISCHE KUNST
GRIECHENLANDS.
J.M. COOK, 303:VOL90-259
SCHWEITZER, C.E. - SEE GOES, A.
SCHWEITZER, F.M. A HISTORY OF THE JEWS
SINCE THE FIRST CENTURY A.D.
R. GORDIS, 441:9JAN72-5
SCHWEITZER, G. THE LEDGE.
N. CALLENDAR, 441:20FEB72-27
H. FRANKEL, 561(SATR):25MAR72-104
SCHWEIZER, K. DIE SONATENSATZFORM IM
SCHAFFEN ALBAN BERGS.
M-C., 410(M&L):JAN71-82
SCHWEIZER, W.R. MÜNCHHAUSEN UND MÜNCH-
HAUSIADEN.*
H. MOENKEMEYER, 406:SPRING71-61
W.L. WARDALE, 220(GL&L):JUL71-378
SCHWERIN, K. CLASSIFICATION FOR INTER-
NATIONAL LAW AND RELATIONS. (3RD ED)
I.J. WILDMAN, 356:JUL71-268
SCHWIEBERT, E. REMEMBRANCES OF RIVERS
PAST.
C. LEHMANN-HAUPT, 441:14MAR72-45
SCHWIETERING, J. PHILOLOGISCHE SCHRIF-
TEN.*
D.H. GREEN, 402(MLR):OCT71-916
SCHWINGE, E-R. DIE VERWENDUNG DER STICH-
OMYTHIE IN DEN DRAMEN DES EURIPIDES.*
A.F. GARVIE, 123:MAR71-17
F. LASSERRE, 182:VOL23#9-500
J.R. WILSON, 121(CJ):OCT-NOV70-88
SCHWOB, U.M. KULTURELLE BEZIEHUNGEN
ZWISCHEN NÜRNBERG UND DEN DEUTSCHEN IM
SÜDOSTEN IM 14. - 16. JAHRHUNDERT.
H.L. MIKOLETZKY, 182:VOL23#10-569
SCHWOEBEL, R. THE SHADOW OF THE CRES-
CENT.
P.F. SUGAR, 32:MAR71-193
SCIAMA, D.W. MODERN COSMOLOGY.
617(TLS):18FEB72-198
SCIASCIA, L. IL CONTESTO.
617(TLS):17MAR72-295
SCKOMMODAU, H. DIE SILBE UND DIE STRUK-
TUR DES FRANZÖSISCHEN.
U. BONNEKAMP, 490:JAN68-131
SCOBIE, A. ASPECTS OF THE ANCIENT RO-
MANCE AND ITS HERITAGE.
G. SCHMELING, 124:NOV70-92
SCOTT, A.F., COMP. EVERY ONE A WITNESS.
566:SPRING71-49
SCOTT, A.L. MARK TWAIN AT LARGE.
C.A. BROWN, 613:WINTER69-605
A.E. STONE, 27(AL):NOV71-459
SCOTT, B., ED. FOLK SONGS OF FRANCE.
J.L. JOHNSON, 650(WF):JAN68-58
SCOTT, C. BARTLEBY.
K. GIBSON, 99:APR72-51

SCOTT, C. BONE OF CONTENTION.
A. PAYNE, 607:WINTER69/70-42
SCOTT, D. A.D. LINDSAY.*
617(TLS):10MAR72-272
SCOTT, J., ED & TRANS. LOVE & PROTEST.
617(TLS):3MAR72-258
SCOTT, J.C. POLITICAL IDEOLOGY IN MALAY-
SIA.
D.S. GIBBONS, 293(JAST):NOV69-203
SCOTT, J.H.M., ED. UNIVERSITY INDEPEN-
DENCE.
617(TLS):14JAN72-47
SCOTT, J.M. EXTEL 100.
617(TLS):26MAY72-613
SCOTT, M. - SEE "THE HELIAND"
SCOTT, N.A., JR., ED. ADVERSITY AND
GRACE.
S.O.H., 543:DEC69-361
SCOTT, N.A., JR. ERNEST HEMINGWAY.
E. KRICKEL, 219(GAR):SUMMER69-246
SCOTT, N.A., JR. NEGATIVE CAPABILITY.*
J.M. DUFFY, 340(KR):1969/5-694
SCOTT, N.A., JR. THE WILD PRAYER OF
LONGING.*
R.W. NOLAND, 31(ASCH):WINTER71/72-164
SCOTT, P. THE JEWEL IN THE CROWN. THE
DAY OF THE SCORPION.
N.W. ROSS, 561(SATR):24JUN72-58
SCOTT, P. THE TOWERS OF SILENCE.*
P. BAILEY, 364:DEC71/JAN72-157
A-C. FOOTE, 440:20FEB72-6
M. LEVIN, 441:20FEB72-26
N.W. ROSS, 561(SATR):24JUN72-58
SCOTT, P. & OTHERS. THE SWANS.
617(TLS):26MAY72-611
SCOTT, W. SIR WALTER SCOTT ON NOVELISTS
AND FICTION. (I. WILLIAMS, ED)
K.C., 191(ELN):SEP70(SUPP)-43
T. CRAWFORD, 541(RES):AUG70-385
J.C. MAXWELL, 447(N&Q):OCT70-393
W.D. SCHAEFER, 445(NCF):SEP69-250
SCOTT, W.H. A CRITICAL STUDY OF THE PRE-
HISPANIC SOURCE MATERIALS FOR THE
STUDY OF PHILIPPINE HISTORY.
D.V. HART, 293(JAST):AUG70-994
SCOTT, W.T. ERWIN SCHRÖDINGER.
R.H.K., 543:MAR70-566
"SIR WALTER SCOTT, 1771-1971."
W. BEATTIE, 595(SCS):VOL15PT2-165
SCOTT-HERON, G. THE NIGGER FACTORY.
L.J. DAVIS, 440:12MAR72-11
442(NY):20MAY72-139
SCOTTI, T.G. - SEE UNDER GALLARATI SCOT-
TI, T.
SCOULAR, K.W. NATURAL MAGIC.*
M-S. RØSTVIG, 179(ES):JUN69-308
SCREEN, J.E.O. MANNERHEIM.
D. KIRBY, 575(SEER):JAN71-159
M. RINTALA, 32:MAR71-194
SCULLARD, H.H. SCIPIO AFRICANUS.*
R.M. ERRINGTON, 123:DEC71-425
R.M. HAYWOOD, 124:DEC70-138
J.A.O. LARSEN, 122:JAN71-67
SCULLY, J. AVENUE OF THE AMERICAS.
J.R. REED, 398:VOL3#2-93
SDUN, W. PROBLEME UND THEORIEN DES ÜBER-
SETZENS IN DEUTSCHLAND VOM 18. BIS 20.
JAHRHUNDERT.
I.C., 191(ELN):SEP69(SUPP)-97
SEABY, H.A. ROMAN SILVER COINS. (VOL 3)
C.H.V. SUTHERLAND, 313:VOL60-265
SEAGER, A. THE GLASS HOUSE.*
C. FREER, 50(ARQ):SPRING69-83
SEAGER, R., ED. THE CRISIS OF THE ROMAN
REPUBLIC.
E.W. GRAY, 123:JUN71-298
SEAGER, R. TIBERIUS.
617(TLS):12MAY72-550

SEALE, W. SAM HOUSTON'S WIFE.
   W. GARD, 584(SWR):SPRING71-198
SEALSFIELD, C. AMERICA. (E.L. JORDAN,
ED & TRANS)
   K.J.R. ARNDT, 400(MLN):OCT70-756
   M.L. BROWN, JR., 656(WMQ):JAN70-178
SEALOCK, R.B. & P.A. SEELY. BIBLIOGRAPHY
OF PLACE-NAME LITERATURE. (2ND ED)
   F.L. UTLEY, 424:JUN69-164
SEAMAN, B. FREE AND FEMALE.
   C. BIRD, 561(SATR):26AUG72-55
   R. JAFFE, 441:13AUG72-5
SEAMAN, G.R. HISTORY OF RUSSIAN MUSIC.*
(VOL 1)
   M. VELIMIROVIĆ, 414(MQ):JUL69-408
SEAMAN, J.E. THE MORAL PARADOX OF "PARA-
DISE LOST."
   617(TLS):18FEB72-184
SEARLE, C. THE FORSAKEN LOVER.
   617(TLS):16JUN72-678
SEARLE, J.R. THE CAMPUS WAR.
   617(TLS):11AUG72-932
SEARLE, J.R. SPEECH ACTS.*
   W.P. ALSTON, 479(PHQ):APR70-172
   L.J. COHEN, 482(PHR):OCT70-545
SEARLE, R. & K. DOBBS. THE GREAT FUR
OPERA.
   102(CANL):WINTER71-108
SEARS, S. THE NEGATIVE IMAGINATION.*
   W.F. WRIGHT, 405(MP):MAY70-389
SEAY, J. LET NOT YOUR HART.*
   639(VQR):SUMMER70-LXXXIX
SÉCHAN, L. SEPT LÉGENDES GRECQUES,
SUIVIES DE L'ÉTUDE DES SOURCES.
   F. JOUAN, 555:VOL44FASC2-307
SECO SERRANO, C. - SEE MESONERO ROMANOS,
R.
"SECOND ASSEMBLING."
   617(TLS):21JAN72-66
"SECOND INTERNATIONAL CONFERENCE OF
ECONOMIC HISTORY, AIX-EN-PROVENCE,
1962." (VOL 1)
   R.J. HOPPER, 123:MAR71-108
SECRET, F. BIBLIOGRAPHIE DES MANUSCRITS
DE GUILLAUME POSTEL.
   F. WAGNER, 182:VOL23#21/22-902
SECRET, F. L'ÉSOTÉRISME DE GUY LE FÈVRE
DE LA BODERIE.
   D.B. WILSON, 208(FS):JUL71-331
SEDGWICK, P. - SEE SERGE, V.
SEEBOLD, E. VERGLEICHENDES UND ETYMOLO-
GISCHES WÖRTERBUCH DER GERMANISCHEN
STARKEN VERBEN.
   B.J. KOEKKOEK, 301(JEGP):OCT71-715
SEEGER, L.G. DIE DEMASKIERUNG DER
LEBENSLÜGE.
   W. BRAUN, 406:SPRING71-81
   J.J. WHITE, 220(GL&L):OCT70-119
SEELYE, H.N., ED. A HANDBOOK ON LATIN
AMERICA FOR TEACHERS.
   R.G. MEAD, JR., 399(MLJ):MAY70-384
SEELYE, J. THE KID.
   J. DECK, 441:23JAN72-6
   C. LEHMANN-HAUPT, 441:2FEB72-41
   442(NY):19FEB72-115
   617(TLS):25AUG72-985
SEELYE, J. MELVILLE.*
   H. COHEN, 191(ELN):MAR71-234
   617(TLS):10MAR72-280
SEELYE, J. THE TRUE ADVENTURES OF HUCK-
LEBERRY FINN.
   617(TLS):10MAR72-280
SEGAL, C.P. LANDSCAPE IN OVID'S "META-
MORPHOSES."*
   W.S. ANDERSON, 24:OCT71-685
   D.A. KIDD, 67:MAY71-76
   E.R. MIX, 124:NOV70-92

SEGAL, E. ROMAN LAUGHTER.*
   N.E. COLLINGE, 487:SUMMER70-182
   A.S. GRATWICK, 123:DEC70-333
   E.N. O'NEIL, 122:JAN71-62
SEGAL, J.B. EDESSA, THE "BLESSED CITY."
   J.E. SEAVER, 402(MLR):JUL71-242
SEGAL, O. THE LUCID REFLECTOR.*
   J.M. CAMERON, 89(BJA):WINTER71-100
   K. MC SWEENEY, 529(QQ):SUMMER70-286
   B. RICHARDS, 402(MLR):OCT71-883
SEGALL, B. TRADITION UND NEUSCHÖPFUNG IN
DER FRÜHALEXANDRINISCHEN KLEINKUNST.
   G. ROUX, 555:VOL44FASC1-115
SEGEBRECHT, W. AUTOBIOGRAPHIE UND DICH-
TUNG.*
   V. SANDER, 222(GR):JAN70-59
SEGEL, H.B., ED & TRANS. THE LITERATURE
OF EIGHTEENTH-CENTURY RUSSIA.
   K. CRAVEN, 149:MAR71-89
SEGEL, H.B. - SEE FREDRO, A.
SEGHERS, P. & A BOSQUET, EDS. LES
POÈMES DE L'ANNÉE: 1968.
   L.E. AULD, 399(MLJ):OCT70-470
SEGRE, C. I SEGNI E LA CRITICA.
   F. FERRUCCI, 276:SUMMER70-230
SEGRE, C., ED. LINGUISTICA E FILOLOGIA.
   A. SCAGLIONE, 545(RPH):MAY71-634
SÉGUIN, R-L. LES JOUETS ANCIENS DU
QUÉBEC.
   J-C. BONENFANT, 627(UTQ):JUL70-409
SEIBERT, J. UNTERSUCHUNGEN ZUR GESCHICH-
TE PTOLEMAIOS' I.
   S.I. OOST, 122:OCT71-288
SEIDEL, E. & OTHERS. ZUM 150. GEBURTSTAG
VON FRANZ BOPP, BEGRÜNDER DER SPRACH-
WISSENSCHAFT.
   G.S. LANE, 350:SEP71-700
SEIDEL, G.J. A CONTEMPORARY APPROACH TO
CLASSICAL METAPHYSICS.
   H.B., 543:JUN70-749
SEIDENSTICKER, B. DIE GESPRÄCHSVERDICH-
TUNG IN DEN TRAGÖDIEN SENECAS.
   W.M. CALDER 3D, 124:MAR71-239
SEIDMAN, J., ED. COMMUNISM IN THE UNITED
STATES - A BIBLIOGRAPHY.
   T.T. HAMMOND, 32:MAR71-221
SEIDMANN, G. SPIEGEL DER ZEIT.
   E.M. FLEISSNER, 221(GQ):NOV70-822
SEIFERT, S. HEINE-BIBLIOGRAPHIE 1954-
1964.
   J.L.S., 191(ELN):SEP70(SUPP)-106
SEIFERTH, W. SYNAGOGE UND KIRCHE IM
MITTELALTER.
   J. SHAPLEY, 54:JUN69-184
SEIGEL, J.E. RHETORIC AND PHILOSOPHY IN
RENAISSANCE HUMANISM.*
   W.J. ONG, 377:MAR71-41
   W.A. SESSIONS, 399(MLJ):JAN70-49
SEIGEL, K., ED. TALKING BACK TO THE NEW
YORK TIMES.
   R.R. LINGEMAN, 441:10SEP72-16
SEITLIN, P. IS ANYTHING ALL RIGHT?
   42(AR):SPRING69-110
SEITZ, W.C. GEORGE SEGAL.
   617(TLS):29DEC72-1590
"SĔJARAH MĔLAYU OR MALAY ANNALS." (C.C.
BROWN, TRANS)
   617(TLS):21JAN72-69
SEKHAR, M.C. SOCIAL CHANGE IN INDIA
(FIRST DECADE OF PLANNING).
   R.P. TAUB, 293(JAST):FEB70-481
SELA, O. THE BEARER PLOT.
   617(TLS):8DEC72-1507
SELBY, H., JR. THE ROOM.*
   V. CUNNINGHAM, 362:2MAR72-283
   T.R. EDWARDS, 453:9MAR72-19
   617(TLS):25FEB72-209

SELBY, J. SHAKA'S HEIRS.
617(TLS):12MAY72-557
SELDEN, M. THE YENAN WAY IN REVOLUTION-
ARY CHINA.
J.P. HARRISON, 441:20FEB72-3
617(TLS):11AUG72-951
"SELECTIONS FROM THE GREEK ANTHOLOGY."*
(A. SINCLAIR, TRANS)
J. HUTTON, 121(CJ):DEC70-JAN71-172
SELESKOVITCH, D. L'INTERPRÈTE DANS LES
CONFÉRENCES INTERNATIONALES.
H.W. BRANN, 207(FR):FEB70-550
SELIGER, M. THE LIBERAL POLITICS OF
JOHN LOCKE.
N.S. FIERING, 656(WMQ):APR70-312
A. GEWIRTH, 482(PHR):OCT70-571
J.J. JENKINS, 483:JUL70-244
SELIGMAN, K. MAGIC, SUPERNATURALISM AND
RELIGION.
617(TLS):4FEB72-133
DE SELINCOURT, E. - SEE WORDSWORTH, W. &
D.
SELLARS, R.W. LENDING A HAND TO HYLAS.
M.B.M., 543:SEP69-140
W.P. WARREN, 484(PPR):JUN70-620
SELLARS, W. PHILOSOPHICAL PERSPECTIVES.
W.L. HARPER, 484(PPR):SEP69-146
SELLARS, W. SCIENCE AND METAPHYSICS.
S.A. ERICKSON, 319:JAN72-111
G. HARMAN, 482(PHR):JUL70-404
V.F. LENZEN, 484(PPR):MAR70-464
R. RORTY, 483:JAN70-66
L. STEVENSON, 479(PHQ):JAN70-86
SELLECK, R.J.W. ENGLISH PRIMARY EDUCA-
TION AND THE PROGRESSIVES, 1914-1939.
617(TLS):9JUN72-657
SELLERS, C.C. CHARLES WILLSON PEALE.*
S. SPECTOR, 58:MAR70-12
639(VQR):SPRING70-LXIV
SELLIN, E. THE DRAMATIC CONCEPTS OF
ANTONIN ARTAUD.
A. DEMAITRE, 207(FR):DEC69-325
SELLIN, P.R. DANIEL HEINSIUS AND STUART
ENGLAND.
W. GILBERT, 551(RENQ):SPRING70-87
SELLY, C. ILL FARES THE LAND.
617(TLS):3MAR72-257
SELVON, S. A BRIGHTER SUN.
617(TLS):11FEB72-145
SELVON, S. THOSE WHO EAT THE CASCADURA.
E. MORGAN, 362:27JAN72-120
617(TLS):11FEB72-145
SELZ, P. GERMAN EXPRESSIONIST PAINTINGS.
L.D.E., 90:DEC69-783
SELZER, M., ED. KIKE!
I. MALIN, 561(SATR):26AUG72-64
SELZNICK, D.O. MEMO FROM DAVID O. SELZ-
NICK. (R. BEHLMER, ED)
C. HIGHAM, 441:24SEP72-6
J. KANON, 561(SATR):16DEC72-58
442(NY):18NOV72-246
SEMBACH, K-J. INTO THE THIRTIES.
617(TLS):28APR72-501
SEMBDNER, H. - SEE "HEINRICH VON KLEIST"
SEMCZUK, S. POEZIYA I PROSA.
C.H. ANDRUSYSHEN, 627(UTQ):JUL69-491
SEMCZUK, S. SOTVORENNIA.
C.H. ANDRUSYSHEN, 627(UTQ):JUL69-492
SEMENZATO, C. CORPUS PALLADIANUM. (VOL
1: THE ROTONDA.)
617(TLS):29DEC72-1577
SEMENZATO, C. LA SCULTURA DEL SEICENTO
E DEL SETTECENTO.
P. CANNON-BROOKES, 39:JUL69-84
SEMIONOVA, L.E. RUSSKO-VALAŠKIE OTNO-
ŠENIJA V KONCE XVII-NAČALE XVIII V.
D. DVOICHENKO-MARKOV, 104:FALL71-432

SEMONCHE, J.E. RAY STANNARD BAKER.
N. BETTEN, 330(MASJ):FALL69-83
SEMPER, G. WISSENSCHAFT, INDUSTRIE UND
KUNST. (H.M. WINGLER, ED)
N.P., 46:MAR69-228
SEMPERE, R.S. - SEE UNDER SENABRE SEM-
PERE, R.
SEMPRUN, J. LA DEUXIÈME MORT DE RAMÓN
MERCADER.
M. NAUDIN, 207(FR):MAY70-946
SEN, N.B. - SEE GANDHI, I.
SEN, R.K. AESTHETIC ENJOYMENT.
V.M. AMES, 290(JAAC):SUMMER70-559
SEN, S.D.K. A COMPARATIVE STUDY OF THE
INDIAN CONSTITUTION.
G.H. GADBOIS, JR., 293(JAST):MAY70-
719
SEN, S.P., ED. STUDIES IN MODERN INDIAN
HISTORY. THE INDIAN PRESS.
R.I. CRANE, 293(JAST):FEB70-479
DE SENA, J. OS SONETOS DE CAMÕES E O
SONETO QUINHENTISTA PENINSULAR.
R.S. SAYERS, 238:MAY70-342
SENA, J.F. A BIBLIOGRAPHY OF MELANCHOLY,
1660-1800.
T.L. CANAVAN, 566:SPRING71-74
SENABRE SEMPERE, R. LENGUA Y ESTILO DE
ORTEGA Y GASSET.
C.P. OTERO, 545(RPH):NOV70-301
SENCOURT, R. T.S. ELIOT: A MEMOIR.*
(D. ADAMSON, ED)
F. KERMODE, 61:JAN72-89
W. PLOMER, 364:FEB/MAR72-174
G. STEINER, 442(NY):22APR72-141
SENDREY, A. MUSIC IN ANCIENT ISRAEL.*
P. GRADENWITZ, 415:AUG70-805
L.D. LOEB, 187:SEP72-502
SENECA. NATURALES QUAESTIONES II. (VOL
10) (T.H. CORCORAN, TRANS)
617(TLS):18AUG72-977
SENECA. L. ANNAEUS SENECA, PHILOSOPHIS-
CHE SCHRIFTEN. (VOL 1) (M. ROSENBACH,
ED)
A.L. MOTTO, 24:OCT71-753
SENEFELDER, A. A COMPLETE COURSE OF
LITHOGRAPHY.
J. LAVER, 39:JUN69-488
"HANNAH SENESH: HER LIFE AND DIARY."*
(M. COHN, TRANS)
R. ELMAN, 441:21MAY72-47
SEN GUPTA, A. A CRITICAL STUDY OF THE
PHILOSOPHY OF RĀMĀNUJA.
J. JOHNSON, 485(PE&W):JAN69-91
SEN GUPTA, A. KAṬHA UPANIṢAD.
S.K. SAKSENA, 485(PE&W):JAN-APR68-109
SENN, A.E. THE RUSSIAN REVOLUTION IN
SWITZERLAND 1914-1917.
617(TLS):14JAN72-30
SENNETT, R. & J. COBB. THE HIDDEN
INJURIES OF CLASS.
P. ADAMS, 61:DEC72-144
N. BIRNBAUM, 441:26NOV72-2
442(NY):23DEC72-80
SEOANE, M.C. EL PRIMER LENGUAJE CONSTI-
TUCIONAL ESPAÑOL (LAS CORTES DE CÁDIZ).
191(ELN):SEP70(SUPP)-151
DE SEPÚLVEDA, L. CANCIONERO DE ROMANCES
(SEVILLA, 1584). (A. RODRÍGUEZ-MOÑINO,
ED)
E.M. WILSON, 240(HR):JUL70-324
SERDJUČENKO, G.P., ED. SOVREMENNYE LIT-
ERATURNYE JAZYKI STRAN AZII.
L. ZGUSTA, 353:APR69-127
SERENY, G. THE CASE OF MARY BELL.
617(TLS):17NOV72-1402
SERGE, V. YEAR ONE OF THE RUSSIAN REVO-
LUTION. (P. SEDGWICK, ED & TRANS)
617(TLS):6OCT72-1187

"SERIELLE MANIFESTE 66."
  W.A. KOCH, 490:JUL68-416
SERIS, H. NUEVO ENSAYO DE UNA BIBLIO-
TECA ESPAÑOLA DE LIBROS RAROS Y CURI-
OSOS. (PT 2)
  O.H. GREEN, 240(HR):JAN70-80
SERLE, G. THE RUSH TO BE RICH.
  617(TLS):4AUG72-923
SEROFF, V. SERGEI PROKOFIEV.*
  D. LLOYD-JONES, 415:FEB70-159
SEROFF, V. THE REAL ISADORA.*
  441:30JAN72-33
  617(TLS):2JUN72-635
SERRANO, C.S. - SEE UNDER SECO SERRANO,
C.
SERRANO DE HARO, A. PERSONALIDAD Y DES-
TINO DE JORGE MANRIQUE.
  A. VÁRVARO, 545(RPH):FEB71-538
SERRANO-PLAJA, A. "MAGIC" REALISM IN
CERVANTES.
  K.J. ATCHITY, 651(WHR):SPRING71-182
SERRES, M. LE SYSTÈME DE LEIBNIZ ET SES
MODÈLES MATHÉMATIQUES.
  N. VIALLANEIX, 98:OCT69-895
SÉRULLAZ, M., WITH L. DUCLAUX & G. MON-
NIER. GREAT DRAWINGS OF THE LOUVRE
MUSEUM: THE FRENCH DRAWINGS.
  W. AMES, 54:DEC69-406
SERVADIO, G. A SIBERIAN ENCOUNTER.*
  P. THEROUX, 440:9APR72-7
  442(NY):1APR72-106
  617(TLS):25FEB72-212
SERVOTTE, H. LITERATUUR ALS LEVENSKUNST.
  J. SOUVAGE, 179(ES):FEB69-127
SESSIONS, R. QUESTIONS ABOUT MUSIC.
  J. HARTMAN, 89(BJA):AUTUMN71-412
  R.S.J., 410(M&L):JAN71-71
  E. SAMS, 415:NOV70-1113
  412:FEB71-73
  639(VQR):AUTUMN70-CLIV
SETON-WATSON, H. THE RUSSIAN EMPIRE,
1801-1917.
  S. MONAS, 587:JAN69-395
SETTLE, W.A., JR. JESSE JAMES WAS HIS
NAME.
  M.W. FISHWICK, 650(WF):JAN69-55
SEUPHOR, M. PIET MONDRIAN.
  J-P. ATTAL, 98:APR69-324
SEUPHOR, M. & A. BERNE-JOFFROY. MONDRI-
AN.
  J-P. ATTAL, 98:APR69-324
SEUREN, G. DAS GATTER, LEBECK.
  T. WEYR, 19(AGR):VOL35#4-31
SEUSE, H. DEUTSCHE MYSTISCHE SCHRIFTEN.
  M.J.V., 543:DEC69-355
"SEVEN MONTREAL ARTISTS."
  A. EMERY, 627(UTQ):JUL69-409
SEVERIN, M. & A. REID. ENGRAVED BOOK-
PLATES.
  617(TLS):24NOV72-1440
SEVERS, J.B., GENERAL ED. A MANUAL OF
THE WRITINGS IN MIDDLE ENGLISH, 1050-
1500. (FASC 1)
  N. DAVIS, 541(RES):FEB70-72
  S-W. HOLTON, 597(SN):VOL40#1-240
SEVERY, M. & OTHERS, EDS. GREECE AND
ROME.
  R-V. SCHODER, 121(CJ):DEC70-JAN71-163
SEWARD, D. THE MONKS OF WAR.
  617(TLS):4AUG72-912
SEWELL, J. & OTHERS. INSIDE CITY HALL.
  N. & D. NOWLAN, 99:MAY72-45
"SEX EDUCATION IN PERSPECTIVE."
  617(TLS):6OCT72-1205
SEXTON, A. THE BOOK OF FOLLY.
  M. SWENSON, 441:19NOV72-7
SEXTON, A. LOVE POEMS.*
  R. DURGNAT, 493:SPRING70-81

SEXTON, A. TRANSFORMATIONS.*
  V. YOUNG, 249(HUDR):WINTER71/72-683
  617(TLS):28JUL72-873
SEYERSTED, P. KATE CHOPIN.*
  G. ARMS, 27(AL):MAR71-136
SEYERSTED, P. - SEE CHOPIN, K.
SEYFARTH, W. - SEE AMMIANUS
SEYMOUR, C., JR. MICHELANGELO'S DAVID.
  J.T. PAOLETTI, 54:SEP69-294
SEYMOUR, H. BASEBALL: THE GOLDEN AGE.*
  617(TLS):2JUN72-639
SEYMOUR, R.K. A BIBLIOGRAPHY OF WORD
FORMATION IN THE GERMANIC LANGUAGES.
  J.E. CREAN, JR., 406:FALL71-289
SEYMOUR, W.K. THE CATS OF ROME.
  L. CLARK, 493:SUMMER70-166
SEYMOUR-SMITH, M., ED. LONGER ELIZA-
BETHAN POEMS.
  617(TLS):14APR72-429
SEYMOUR-SMITH, M. REMINISCENCES OF
NORMA.*
  G. EWART, 364:JUN/JUL71-132
SEZNEC, J. - SEE DIDEROT, D.
SGALL, P. & OTHERS. A FUNCTIONAL AP-
PROACH TO SYNTAX IN GENERATIVE DES-
CRIPTION OF LANGUAGE.
  D-G. LOCKWOOD, 350:SEP71-691
SGARD, J. PRÉVOST ROMANCIER.
  J.S. SPINK, 208(FS):APR71-203
SHAABAN ROBERT. DIWANI YA SHAABAN. (NO.
6)
  L. HARRIES, 315(JAL):VOL8PT1-54
SHAABAN ROBERT. DIWANI Y SHAABAN. (NO.
8, 9, 11 & 13)
  G. BENSON & L. HARRIES, 315(JAL):
  VOL8PT1-54
SHABAD, T. BASIC INDUSTRIAL RESOURCES
OF THE USSR.
  D.B. SHIMKIN, 32:DEC71-904
SHABAN, M.A. ISLAMIC HISTORY A.D. 600-
750 (A.H. 132).
  617(TLS):4FEB72-130
SHABERMAN, R.B. & D. CRUTCH, EDS. UNDER
THE QUIZZING GLASS.
  617(TLS):7APR72-402
SHACKLE, C. PUNJABI.
  617(TLS):19MAY72-584
SHACKLETON, R. THE "ENCYCLOPÉDIE" AND
THE CLERKS.
  J. LOUGH, 208(FS):APR71-205
SHACKLETON BAILEY, D.R. CICERO.*
  617(TLS):11FEB72-158
SHADBOLT, J. IN SEARCH OF FORM.*
  A. EMERY, 627(UTQ):JUL69-406
  R. SIMMINS, 96:FEB69-35
  W. TOWNSEND, 592:MAR69-155
SHADBOLT, M. STRANGERS AND JOURNEYS.
  617(TLS):15DEC72-1521
SHADBOLT, M. THIS SUMMER'S DOLPHIN.
  R.A. COPLAND, 368:DEC69-401
SHADEGG, S.C. THE NEW HOW TO WIN AN
ELECTION.
  J. GREENFIELD, 441:4JUN72-40
SHAFFER, H.G. & J.S. PRYBYLA, EDS. FROM
UNDERDEVELOPMENT TO AFFLUENCE.
  J.T. LEBER, 550(RUSR):JAN70-112
SHAFFER, J., ED. VIOLENCE.
  S. GENDIN, 311(JP):6APR72-186
SHAFTESBURY, A. L'ETICA DEL SENTIMENTO.
(A. PLEBE, ED)
  L. TURCO, 548(RCSF):JAN/MAR69-112
SHAGAN, S. SAVE THE TIGER.
  M. LEVIN, 441:10DEC72-58
SHAH, A. FOLK TALES OF CENTRAL ASIA.
  617(TLS):16JUN72-697
SHAKESPEARE, W. MACBETH. (R.A. FOAKES,
ED) JULIUS CAESAR. (M. CHARNEY, ED)
  S. WELLS, 447(N&Q):APR70-155

SHAKESPEARE, W. THE MOST EXCELLENT AND
LAMENTABLE TRAGEDIE OF ROMEO AND JUL-
IET. (G.W. WILLIAMS, ED)
  A. BROWN, 570(SQ):SPRING68-178
SHAKESPEARE, W. ROMEO AND JULIET.
(T.J.B. SPENCER, ED) A MIDSUMMER
NIGHT'S DREAM. (S. WELLS, ED) CORIO-
LANUS. (G.R. HIBBARD, ED) JULIUS
CAESAR. (N. SANDERS, ED) MACBETH.
(G.K. HUNTER, ED) THE MERCHANT OF
VENICE. (W.M. MERCHANT, ED)
  C. SPENCER, 570(SQ):SPRING69-231
SHAKESPEARE, W. THE TEMPEST. (B. CEL-
LINI, ED)
  L.G. CLUBB, 570(SQ):SPRING68-180
SHAKESPEARE, W. THE TRAGEDY OF KING
RICHARD THE THIRD. (K. SMIDT, ED)
  J. GERRITSEN, 179(ES):JUN69-307
  E.A.J. HONIGMANN, 447(N&Q):APR70-150
SHAKESPEARE, W. THE TWO GENTLEMEN OF
VERONA. (C. LEECH, ED)
  J. WILDERS, 541(RES):FEB70-80
SHAKESPEARE, W. THE WARS OF THE ROSES.
(J. BARTON, ED)
  G. NEVIN, 493:WINTER70/71-372
SHAKESPEARE, W. THE WINTER'S TALE.
(J.H.P. PAFFORD, ED)
  B. MAXWELL, 570(SQ):SPRING68-179
SHALES, T. & OTHERS. THE AMERICAN FILM
HERITAGE.
  J. KANON, 561(SATR):16DEC72-58
SHAMBERG, M. & OTHERS. GUERRILLA TELE-
VISION.
  L. ROSS, 453:9MAR72-25
SHAND, R.T., ED. AGRICULTURAL DEVELOP-
MENT IN ASIA.
  P.A. YOTOPOULOS, 293(JAST):AUG70-909
  617(TLS):15SEP72-1066
SHANE, A.M. THE LIFE AND WORKS OF
EVGENIJ ZAMJATIN.*
  P.A. FISCHER, 574(SEEJ):FALL71-388
"SHANG-HAI PO-WU-KUAN TSANG CH'ING-T'UNG
CH'I."
  A.C. SOPER, 57:VOL31#1-81
SHANIN, T. THE AWKWARD CLASS.
  617(TLS):7JUL72-775
SHANNON, D. MURDER WITH LOVE.
  N. CALLENDAR, 441:9JAN72-33
  H. FRANKEL, 561(SATR):26FEB72-71
  617(TLS):1DEC72-1467
SHANNON, D. WITH INTENT TO KILL.
  N. CALLENDAR, 441:10SEP72-41
SHANSKII, N.M. RUSSIAN LEXICOLOGY.
(J.E.S. COOPER, ED)
  J.E. AUGEROT, 399(MLJ):OCT70-468
  G.F. HOLLIDAY, 104:SUMMER71-239
SHANSKII, N.M. RUSSIAN WORD FORMATION.
(J.E.S. COOPER, ED)
  A.F. GOVE, 399(MLJ):NOV70-535
  G.F. HOLLIDAY, 104:SUMMER71-239
SHAO-CH'I, L. - SEE UNDER LIU SHAO-CH'I
SHAPCOTT, T.W. INWARDS TO THE SUN.
  J. TULIP, 581:1971/1-72
SHAPIRO, B.J. JOHN WILKINS 1614-1672.*
  O.S. REDD, 568(SCN):WINTER71-77
SHAPIRO, H. THIS WORLD.*
  P. PETTINGELL, 491:JAN72-234
SHAPIRO, H.I. - SEE RUSKIN, J.
SHAPIRO, M. ASPECTS OF RUSSIAN MORPHOL-
OGY.
  H.S. COATS, 32:JUN71-444
  R.C. DE ARMOND, 574(SEEJ):WINTER71-
  520
SHAPIRO, M. RUSSIAN PHONETIC VARIANTS
AND PHONOSTYLISTICS.
  H.S. COATS, 32:JUN71-444
SHAPIRO, N.R., ED & TRANS. NEGRITUDE.*
  R. LATTIMORE, 249(HUDR):AUTUMN71-508

SHAPLEY, F.R. PAINTINGS IN THE KRESS
COLLECTION - ITALIAN SCHOOLS XV-XVI
CENTURY.
  F. ZERI, 90:JUL69-455
SHARMA, R.S. ASPECTS OF POLITICAL IDEAS
AND INSTITUTIONS IN ANCIENT INDIA.
  D.N. LORENZEN, 293(JAST):NOV69-197
SHARP, D. THE PICTURE PALACE AND OTHER
BUILDINGS FOR THE MOVIES.
  R. DURGNAT, 46:JUN69-472
SHARP, E. THE IQ CULT.
  561(SATR):9DEC72-79
SHARP, J.M. - SEE PEÑUELAS, M.C.
SHARP, M. THE INNOCENTS.*
  442(NY):1JUL72-74
SHARMA, B.L. KASHMIR AWAKES.
  617(TLS):25FEB72-230
SHARMA, I.C. ETHICAL PHILOSOPHIES OF
INDIA. (REV BY S.M. DAUGERT)
  H.T. HAMADA, 485(PE&W):JUL68-225
SHARMAN, G. FILIGREE IN SOUND.*
  R. MASSEY, 415:OCT70-1003
SHATTUCK, C.H. THE HAMLET OF EDWIN
BOOTH.*
  A. GERSTNER-HIRZEL, 182:VOL23#5-227
  J.A. MILLS, 301(JEGP):APR71-297
SHAVER, C.L. - SEE WORDSWORTH, W. & D.
SHAW, A.M., ED & TRANS. PIMA INDIAN
LEGENDS.
  A.L. CAMPA, 582(SFQ):JUN69-131
  292(JAF):JUL-SEP70-363
SHAW, B. OTHER DAYS, OTHER EYES.
  617(TLS):13OCT72-1235
SHAW, G. MEAT ON THE HOOF.
  J. DURSO, 441:3DEC72-40
SHAW, G.B. THE BODLEY HEAD BERNARD
SHAW. (VOL 1) (D.H. LAURENCE, ED)
  M.M. MORGAN, 67:MAY71-111
SHAW, G.B. THE BODLEY HEAD BERNARD SHAW.
(VOL 4)
  617(TLS):4AUG72-917
SHAW, G.B. COLLECTED LETTERS 1898-1910.
(D.H. LAURENCE, ED)
  W.H. AUDEN, 442(NY):25NOV72-190
  N. BALAKIAN, 441:13OCT72-40
  C. JAMES, 362:27JUL72-114
  G. WEALES, 441:24SEP72-42
  617(TLS):4AUG72-917
SHAW, G.B. SAINT JOAN, A SCREENPLAY.
(B.F. DUKORE, ED)
  G. WEALES, 572:MAY69-80
SHAW, G.B. YOU NEVER CAN TELL.
  A.H. NETHERCOT, 397(MD):FEB69-455
SHAW, I. WHISPERS IN BEDLAM.
  J. HUNTER, 362:21DEC72-869
  617(TLS):8DEC72-1477
SHAW, I.S. & D.S. NEWELL. VIOLENCE ON
TELEVISION.
  C. JAMES, 362:17FEB72-203
SHAW, J. ON OUR CONSCIENCE.
  617(TLS):3MAR72-250
SHAW, J.T. THE TRANSLITERATION OF MODERN
RUSSIAN FOR ENGLISH-LANGUAGE PUBLICA-
TIONS.
  C.L. DRAGE, 575(SEER):OCT71-630
SHAW, J.T. - SEE PUSHKIN, A.S.
SHAW, L.R. THE PLAYWRIGHT AND HISTORICAL
CHANGE.
  R. GRIMM, 406:SUMMER71-173
  H. KNUST, 301(JEGP):JUL71-513
  J. OSBORNE, 402(MLR):OCT71-958
SHAW, T. IGBO-UKWU.
  617(TLS):5MAY72-523
SHAW, W.D. THE DIALECTICAL TEMPER.*
  C. TRACY, 627(UTQ):JUL69-373
SHAWN, T. EVERY LITTLE MOVEMENT.
  J. DE LABAN, 290(JAAC):FALL69-112
SHAWN, W. - SEE PANTER-DOWNES, M.

SHAYER, M. POEMS FROM AN ISLAND.
R.B. SHAW, 491:MAR72-342
SHCHERBATOV, M.M. ON THE CORRUPTION OF
MORALS IN RUSSIA.* (A. LENTIN, ED &
TRANS)
J. AFFERICA, 32:MAR71-140
S.A. ZENKOVSKY, 550(RUSR):JUL70-358
SHE, L. - SEE UNDER LAO SHE
SHEA, D.B., JR. SPIRITUAL AUTOBIOGRAPHY
IN EARLY AMERICA.
H. PARKER, 173(ECS):SUMMER70-573
W.C. SPENGEMANN, 141:SPRING70-153
SHEAFFER, L. O'NEILL, SON AND PLAYWRIGHT.
J.Y. MILLER, 397(MD):FEB70-437
S.K. WINTHER, 50(ARQ):AUTUMN69-271
SHEARMAN, J. MANNERISM.*
K.W. FORSTER, 551(RENQ):AUTUMN70-287
H. ZERNER, 453:31AUG72-25
SHEARS, S. GATHER NO MOSS.
617(TLS):20OCT72-1259
SHEARS, S. A VILLAGE GIRL.
441:19MAR72-16
SHECKLEY, R. CAN YOU FEEL ANYTHING WHEN
I DO THIS?
T. STURGEON, 441:14MAY72-34
617(TLS):9JUN72-650
SHEED, F.J. WHAT DIFFERENCE DOES JESUS
MAKE?
617(TLS):5MAY72-527
SHEED, W. THE BLACKING FACTORY (AND)
PENNSYLVANIA GOTHIC.
J.P. DEGNAN, 340(KR):1969/2-272
SHEEHAN, N. THE ARNHEITER AFFAIR.
P. ADAMS, 61:FEB72-110
H. DAREFF, 561(SATR):5FEB72-66
C. LEHMANN-HAUPT, 441:4FEB72-32
S.K. OBERBECK, 440:27FEB72-3
G. SMITH, 441:6FEB72-3
442(NY):12FEB72-103
SHEEHAN, N. & OTHERS - SEE "THE PENTAGON
PAPERS"
SHELBY, L.R. JOHN ROGERS.*
P.F. HOWLETT, 325:APR69-506
SHELDON, R. - SEE SHKLOVSKY, V.
SHELDON, S. THE NAKED FACE.
617(TLS):7JAN72-17
SHELLEY, M.W. FRANKENSTEIN.*
H. KOSOK, 447(N&Q):OCT70-391
SHELLEY, P.B. POSTHUMOUS POEMS OF
SHELLEY. (I. MASSEY, ED)
P.H. BUTTER, 402(MLR):APR71-401
K.N.C., 191(ELN):SEP70(SUPP)-44
N. ROGERS, 541(RES):NOV70-514
SHELLEY, P.B. SELECTED POETRY. (N.
ROGERS, ED)
D.H.R., 191(ELN):SEP69(SUPP)-42
SHELLEY, P.B. SHELLEY'S "PROMETHEUS UN-
BOUND." (L.J. ZILLMAN, ED)
K.N.C., 191(ELN):SEP69(SUPP)-45
N. ROGERS, 541(RES):FEB70-90
R.B. WOODINGS, 597(SN):VOL41#2-439
SHELLEY, S. BOWMANVILLE BREAK.
G. ROPER, 627(UTQ):JUL69-361
SHELTON, R. THE TATTOOED DESERT.*
D. ALLEN, 491:JUL72-235
SHELTON, W. SOVIET SPACE EXPLORATION:
THE FIRST DECADE.
F.J. KRIEGER, 550(RUSR):JAN70-113
SHEPARD, L. CANTATA OF DEATH, WEAKMIND,
& GENERATION.
W. WITHERUP, 502(PRS):WINTER69/70-422
SHEPARD, M. THE LOVE TREATMENT.*
E. WILLIS, 453:31AUG72-7
SHEPARD, M. A PSYCHIATRIST'S HEAD.
J. KOVEL, 441:8OCT72-10
SHEPHERD, W., COMP. SHEPHERD'S GLOSSARY
OF GRAPHIC SIGNS AND SYMBOLS.
617(TLS):4AUG72-926

SHEPPARD, D.K. THE GROWTH AND ROLE OF UK
FINANCIAL INSTITUTIONS 1880-1962.
617(TLS):11FEB72-165
SHEPPARD, F. LONDON 1808-1870.
P. WHITEHEAD, 362:6APR72-455
617(TLS):28JAN72-86
SHEPPARD, F.H.W., ED. SURVEY OF LONDON.
(VOLS 33-35)
A. PORTER, 415:JUN70-604
SHEPPARD, H.L. & N.Q. HERRICK. WHERE
HAVE ALL THE ROBOTS GONE?
N. BIRNBAUM, 441:26NOV72-2
SHEPPARD, L., ED. THE NEW LITURGY.
617(TLS):14APR72-426
SHEPPERD, G.A. ARMS AND ARMOUR 1660-
1918.
617(TLS):25AUG72-1005
SHERBO, A. STUDIES IN THE EIGHTEENTH
CENTURY NOVEL.
A.J. HASSALL, 67:MAY71-99
SHERBO, A. - SEE JOHNSON, S.
SHERESKY, N. & M. MANNES. UNCOUPLING.
S. EDMISTON, 441:22OCT72-42
L. WOLFE, 561(SATR):9SEP72-72
SHERFEY, M.J. THE NATURE AND EVOLUTION
OF FEMALE SEXUALITY.
C. BIRD, 561(SATR):26AUG72-55
C. LEHMANN-HAUPT, 441:31MAY72-43
I. SINGER, 453:30NOV72-29
SHERIDAN, A. VACATION.
617(TLS):8DEC72-1477
SHERRINGTON, R.J. THREE NOVELS BY FLAU-
BERT.*
A. FAIRLIE, 208(FS):APR71-221
SHERRY, N. CONRAD'S EASTERN WORLD.
CONRAD'S WESTERN WORLD.*
M. MUDRICK, 249(HUDR):WINTER71/72-711
SHERRY, P. A THEATRE IN THE FAMILY.
617(TLS):13OCT72-1237
SHERWANI, H.K. CULTURAL TRENDS IN
MEDIEVAL INDIA.
G.R.G. HAMBLY, 293(JAST):AUG70-998
SHERWIG, J.M. GUINEAS AND GUNPOWDER.*
W.M. STERN, 325:OCT70-156
SHERWIN, J.J. THE LIFE OF RIOT.
639(VQR):AUTUMN70-CXXIX
SHERWIN, J.J. URANIUM POEMS.
639(VQR):WINTER70-XII
SHERWIN-WHITE, A.N. - SEE PLINY
SHERWOOD, M. THE LOGIC OF EXPLANATION IN
PSYCHOANALYSIS.
H.P.K., 543:MAR70-566
SHERWOOD, W.R. CIRCUMFERENCE AND CIRCUM-
STANCE.
P. URE, 447(N&Q):SEP70-359
SHESTACK, A. FIFTEENTH CENTURY ENGRAV-
INGS OF NORTHERN EUROPE FROM THE
NATIONAL GALLERY OF ART.
J. SNYDER, 90:MAR69-160
SHESTOV, L. DOSTOEVSKY, TOLSTOY AND
NIETZSCHE. A SHESTOV ANTHOLOGY. (B.
MARTIN, ED)
S. MONAS, 32:DEC71-909
SHETZLINE, D. DE FORD.
C. DEEMER, 448:SUMMER70-118
SHETZLINE, D. HECKLETOOTH 3.
C. DEEMER, 448:SUMMER70-118
639(VQR):WINTER70-VIII
SHEWELL-COOPER, W.E. COMPOST GARDENING.
617(TLS):10NOV72-1377
SHIDELER, M.M. CHARLES WILLIAMS.
E. KRICKEL, 219(GAR):SUMMER69-246
SHIEH, M.J.T., ED. THE KUOMINTANG.
T-L. LEE, 396(MODA):WINTER71-101
SHIELDS, J. & I.I. GOTTESMAN - SEE
SLATER, E.

SHIKES, R.E. THE INDIGNANT EYE.*
  M. LAVANOUX, 363:FEB70-68
  J.R. REED, 141:SUMMER70-256
  R.A. SEGAL, 58:APR70-12
"THE IZUMI SHIKIBU DIARY" - SEE FILED
  UNDER IZUMI
SHIMER, R.H. SQUAW POINT.
  N. CALLENDAR, 441:16APR72-29
  H. FRANKEL, 561(SATR):13MAY72-86
  442(NY):22APR72-144
SHIMONIAK, W. COMMUNIST EDUCATION.
  W.W. BRICKMAN, 32:SEP71-676
SHIN TONG-YOP. KUM RIVER.
  270:VOL20#4-95
SHINAGEL, M. DANIEL DEFOE AND MIDDLE-
  CLASS GENTILITY.*
  J.P. HUNTER, 301(JEGP):APR71-315
  J. SUTHERLAND, 597(SN):VOL41#1-192
SHINE, D.J., ED. AN INTERIOR METAPHYS-
  ICS.
  D.J.M.B., 543:MAR70-572
SHINE, M.G. THE FICTIONAL CHILDREN OF
  HENRY JAMES.*
  Q. ANDERSON, 27(AL):MAY71-294
SHINN, C. & D. THE ILLUSTRATED GUIDE TO
  VICTORIAN PARIAN CHINA.
  617(TLS):7JAN72-8
SHIPLEY, S. CLUB LIFE AND SOCIALISM IN
  MID-VICTORIAN LONDON.
  617(TLS):28JAN72-86
SHIPPEY, T.A. OLD ENGLISH VERSE.
  617(TLS):1SEP72-1020
SHIPTON, C.K. BIOGRAPHICAL SKETCHES OF
  THOSE WHO ATTENDED HARVARD COLLEGE IN
  THE CLASSES 1761-1763, WITH BIBLIO-
  GRAPHICAL AND OTHER NOTES.
  F.A. CASSELL, 432(NEQ):DEC70-649
SHIPTON, C.K. & J.E. MOONEY. NATIONAL
  INDEX OF AMERICAN IMPRINTS THROUGH
  1800, THE SHORT-TITLE EVANS.
  J. CUSHING, 432(NEQ):JUN70-329
  H. EDELMAN, 517(PBSA):APR-JUN71-184
SHIPTON, E. - SEE WHYMPER, E.
SHIPWAY, G. THE IMPERIAL GOVERNOR.
  G. CORE, 219(GAR):FALL69-423
SHIRE, H.M. SONG, DANCE, AND POETRY OF
  THE COURT OF SCOTLAND UNDER KING JAMES
  VI.*
  D.F.C. COLDWELL, 191(ELN):JUN71-317
  J. CURRIE, 415:MAY70-506
  W. KOLNEDER, 182:VOL23#1/2-38
  J. DE LABAN, 399(MLJ):MAY70-359
SHIRER, W.L. THE COLLAPSE OF THE THIRD
  REPUBLIC.*
  B.E. BROWN, 639(VQR):SPRING70-346
SHIRLEY, F.A. - SEE WEBSTER, J.
SHIRLEY, J. - SEE "A PARISIAN JOURNAL
  1405-1449"
SHKLAR, J.N. MEN AND CITIZENS.
  E. GARVER, 185:JUL70-323
SHKLOVSKY, V. A SENTIMENTAL JOURNEY.
  (R. SHELDON, ED & TRANS)
  P. AUSTIN, 104:WINTER71-570
  V. ERLICH, 32:MAR71-209
  G. GIBIAN, 550(RUSR):OCT70-473
  639(VQR):SPRING70-LXX
SHKLOVSKY, V. ZOO, OR LETTERS NOT ABOUT
  LOVE. (R. SHELDON, ED & TRANS)
  J. BAYLEY, 362:24FEB72-249
  C. SIMMONS, 441:24JAN72-31
SHNITMAN, A.M. IZ ISTORIIATA NA INTER-
  NATSIONALNITE VRŬZKI NA V. I. LENIN S
  REVOLIUTSIONNOTO RABOTNICHESKO DVIZ-
  HENIE V BŬLGARIIA (1896-1923 G.).
  M. PUNDEFF, 32:DEC71-922

SHOGAN, R. A QUESTION OF JUDGMENT.
  G. COWAN, 441:28MAY72-1
  N. VON HOFFMAN, 453:29JUN72-14
  T. LASK, 441:3JUN72-31
  E.M. YODER, JR., 440:7MAY72-1
  442(NY):17JUN72-104
SHŌNAGON, S. THE PILLOW BOOK OF SEI
  SHŌNAGON.* (I. MORRIS, ED & TRANS)
  E.A. CRANSTON, 244(HJAS):VOL29-248
SHORES, C.F. PICTORIAL HISTORY OF THE
  MEDITERRANEAN AIR WAR. (VOL 1)
  617(TLS):22DEC72-1566
"SHORT TITLE CATALOGUE OF BOOKS PRINTED
  BEFORE 1801." [LIVERPOOL CATHEDRAL,
  RADCLIFFE LIBRARY]
  P. MORGAN, 354:JUN69-163
SHOTEN, K., ED. A PICTORIAL ENCYCLOPEDIA
  OF THE ORIENTAL ARTS.
  J. BRZOSTOSKI, 58:FEB70-17
SHRADER, S. LEAVING BY THE CLOSET DOOR.
  J. NAIDEN, 491:MAY72-115
SHRAKE, E. STRANGE PEACHES.
  J. DECK, 441:18JUN72-7
SHRESHTHA, B.P. THE ECONOMY OF NEPAL OR
  A STUDY IN PROBLEMS AND PROCESSES OF
  INDUSTRIALIZATION.
  L.E. ROSE, 293(JAST):FEB70-487
SHREWSBURY, J.F.D. A HISTORY OF BUBONIC
  PLAGUE IN THE BRITISH ISLES.
  C.R. YOUNG, 579(SAQ):SUMMER71-435
SHRIMALI, K.L. A SEARCH FOR VALUES IN
  INDIAN EDUCATION.
  617(TLS):31MAR72-378
SHRIVASTAVA, S.N.L. ŠAMKARA AND BRADLEY.
  A. BHARATI, 293(JAST):FEB70-466
  E.J. COLEMAN, 485(PE&W):OCT69-471
SHTEMENKO, S.M. GENERAL'NYI SHTAB V
  GODY VOINY.
  M. PARRISH, 587:OCT69-251
SHU-HUAI, W. - SEE UNDER WANG SHU-HUAI
SHUB, A. THE NEW RUSSIAN TRAGEDY.
  B.R. BOCIURKIW, 550(RUSR):JUL70-328
  J.C. MC CLELLAND, 32:MAR71-159
  L.M. TIKOS, 418(MR):SPRING71-352
SHUB, D. POLITICHESKIYE DEYATELI ROSSII
  (1850-YKH-1920-YKH GG.).
  A. PARRY, 550(RUSR):OCT70-457
SHUKMAN, H. LENIN AND THE RUSSIAN REVO-
  LUTION.
  P. AVRICH, 587:JAN68-449
SHULMAN, A.K. MEMOIRS OF AN EX-PROM
  QUEEN.
  M. BENDER, 441:23APR72-34
  S. BLACKBURN, 440:14MAY72-13
  L. ROSENTHAL, 561(SATR):20MAY72-76
  442(NY):10JUN72-130
SHUMAKER, W. UNPREMEDITATED VERSE.*
  G. BULLOUGH, 175:SPRING69-28
  R.B. HINMAN, 290(JAAC):WINTER69-255
  F.S.K., 477:SUMMER69-402
SHUNKOV, V.I. & S.M. KASHTANOV - SEE
  VESELOVSKY, S.B.
SHUTER, R. THE PSYCHOLOGY OF MUSICAL
  ABILITY.*
  P.R. FARNSWORTH, 290(JAAC):SUMMER70-
  561
SHVARTS [SCHWARZ], S.M. SOTSIAL'NOYE
  STRAKHOVANIYE V ROSSII V 1917-1919
  GODAKH.*
  J. KEEP, 575(SEER):APR71-309
SIBLEY, F.N., ED. PERCEPTION.
  617(TLS):17MAR72-303
SICARD, C. - SEE COPEAU, J. & R. MARTIN
  DU GARD
SICES, D. MUSIC AND THE MUSICIAN IN
  "JEAN-CHRISTOPHE."*
  K. BIEBER, 401(MLQ):MAR70-130

294

SICHIROLLO, L. STORICITÀ DELLA DIALET-
TICA ANTICA.
  P. SOMVILLE, 542:APR-JUN69-271
SICILIANO, I. LES CHANSONS DE GESTE ET
L'ÉPOPÉE.*
  S.G. NICHOLS, JR., 131(CL):SUMMER71-
262
ŠIDAK, J. & OTHERS. POVIJEST HRVATSKOG
NARODA G. 1860-1914.
  C. JELAVICH, 32:JUN71-412
SIDDIQUI, K. CONFLICT, CRISIS AND WAR IN
PAKISTAN.
  617(TLS):1SEP72-1029
SIDER, R.D. ANCIENT RHETORIC AND THE ART
OF TERTULLIAN.
  617(TLS):14APR72-422
SIDERI, S. TRADE AND POWER.
  617(TLS):4FEB72-137
SIDNEY, P. SIR PHILIP SIDNEY, "ASTROPHEL
AND STELLA." (V. GENTILI, ED)
  M. PRAZ, 179(ES):DEC70-551
SIDNEY, P. SIR PHILIP SIDNEY: SELECTED
POETRY AND PROSE. (R. KIMBROUGH, ED)
  K. KOLLER, 568(SCN):SPRING71-14
THE DUCHESS OF MEDINA SIDONIA - SEE UNDER
MEDINA
SIEBERT, H. ZUR THEORIE DES REGIONALEN
WIRTSCHAFTSWACHSTUMS. REGIONALES WIRT-
SCHAFTSWACHSTUM UND INTERREGIONALE
MOBILITÄT.
  G. GAUDARD, 182:VOL23#21/22-931
SIEGEL, J.T. THE ROPE OF GOD.
  E.M. BRUNER, 293(JAST):MAY70-740
SIEGEL, M.B. AT THE VANISHING POINT.
  T. LASK, 441:9DEC72-37
SIEGEL, P.N. SHAKESPEARE IN HIS TIME AND
OURS.
  A.M. EASTMAN, 191(ELN):DEC69-139
SIEGEL, R. GALEN'S SYSTEM OF PHYSIOLOGY
AND MEDICINE.
  E.D. PHILLIPS, 123:DEC71-370
SIEGEL, S. BIG MEN WALKED HERE!
  W. GARD, 584(SWR):AUTUMN71-VI
SIEGMEISTER, E. HARMONY AND MELODY.
  G. WITTLICH, 308:SPRING67-133
SIEGRIST, C. & OTHERS - SEE HEINE, H.
DA SIENA, C. - SEE UNDER ST. CATERINA DA
SIENA
SIERKSMA, F. TIBET'S TERRIFYING DEITIES.
  P.J.H., 543:MAR70-567
SIERRA, S. - SEE BOETHIUS, A.M.S.
SIGÉE, L. [L. SIGEA]. DIALOGUE DE DEUX
JEUNES FILLES SUR LA VIE DE COUR ET LA
VIE DE RETRAITE. (O. SAUVAGE, ED &
TRANS)
  F. WAGNER, 182:VOL23#11/12-619
  R.C. WILLIS, 86(BHS):JUL71-281
SIH, P.K.T., ED. THE STRENUOUS DECADE.
  H. KU, 396(MODA):SPRING71-206
SIHANOUK, N. L'INDOCHINE VUE DE PÉKIN.
  617(TLS):11FEB72-143
ŠIK, O. PLAN AND MARKET UNDER SOCIALISM.
  S. LAMED, 104:SPRING71-110
SILBAJORIS, R. RUSSIAN VERSIFICATION.*
  C.L. DRAGE, 575(SEER):OCT71-612
SILBER, I., ED. REPRINTS FROM "SING
OUT!" (VOL 9)
  E.A. WIENANDT, 650(WF):JAN69-66
SILBER, I., ED. SONGS AMERICA VOTED BY.
  617(TLS):11FEB72-154
SILBERSTEIN, G.E. THE TROUBLED ALLIANCE.
  V.S. MAMATEY, 32:JUL71-421
SILES GUEVARA, J. BIBLIOGRAFÍA DE BIB-
LIOGRAFÍAS BOLIVIANAS. (2ND ED)
  J.R. ARZE, 263:APR-JUN71-208
SILES SALINAS, J. LA LITERATURA BOLIVI-
ANA DE LA GUERRA DEL CHACO.
  A. GUZMÁN, 263:JAN-MAR71-78

SILHOL, R. LES TYRANS TRAGIQUES.
  S.N. GREBSTEIN, 27(AL):MAR71-143
SILK, L. NIXONOMICS.
  H.G. JOHNSON, 441:27AUG72-4
  V.D. OOMS, 440:21MAY72-13
SILKIN, J. AMANA GRASS.*
  M. SCHMIDT, 491:JUN72-170
  I. WEDDE, 364:DEC71/JAN72-118
  V. YOUNG, 249(HUDR):WINTER71/72-679
SILKIN, J. OUT OF BATTLE.
  617(TLS):29SEP72-1131
SILLITOE, A. RAW MATERIAL.
  D.A.N. JONES, 362:26OCT72-557
  617(TLS):3NOV72-1305
SILLITOE, A. A START IN LIFE.*
  F.P.W. MC DOWELL, 659:SUMMER72-361
SILLITOE, A. TRAVELS IN NIHILON.*
  S. BLACKBURN, 441:15OCT72-2
  E. WEEKS, 61:OCT72-134
SILONE, I. EMERGENCY EXIT.
  M. EGAN, 111:30JAN70-94
SILVAIN, P. MÉLODRAME. LES EOLIENNES.
  617(TLS):14JAN72-31
SILVER, H. - SEE "ROBERT OWEN ON EDUCA-
TION"
SILVER, I. THE INTELLECTUAL EVOLUTION OF
RONSARD.* (VOL 1)
  E. ARMSTRONG, 551(RENQ):WINTER70-444
  D. STONE, JR., 400(MLN):MAY70-608
SILVER, I. - SEE DE RONSARD, P.
SILVER, J. & L. GOTTLIEB. LIMBO.
  C. LEHMANN-HAUPT, 441:2MAR72-41
  M. LEVIN, 441:12MAR72-42
SILVER, R.G. THE AMERICAN PRINTER,
1787-1825.*
  N. BARKER, 78(BC):SPRING70-112
  R. STOKES, 354:DEC69-353
SILVERBERG, R., ED. ALPHA 2.
  T. STURGEON, 441:14MAY72-34
SILVERBERG, R. THE BOOK OF SKULLS.
  P. ADAMS, 61:APR72-128
SILVERBERG, R. MOONFERNS AND STARSONGS.
THE WORLD INSIDE. A TIME OF CHANGES.
SON OF MAN.
  T. STURGEON, 441:5MAR72-37
SILVERBERG, R., ED. NEW DIMENSIONS 1.
  T. STURGEON, 441:5MAR72-37
SILVERMAN, B., ED. MAN AND SOCIALISM IN
CUBA.
  D. SEERS, 441:20FEB72-6
SILVERMAN, D.P. RELUCTANT UNION.
  617(TLS):29SEP72-1171
SILVERMAN, J. THE CHORD-PLAYER'S ENCY-
CLOPEDIA.
  J. KAMIN, 650(WF):JAN69-70
SILVERMAN, J. THE FLAT-PICKER'S GUITAR
GUIDE.
  A.J. FIELD, 650(WF):OCT68-278
SILVERMAN, J., ED. THE PANIC IS ON AND
62 OTHER SONGS.
  H.H. MALONE, 650(WF):APR68-140
SILVERMAN, K. - SEE MATHER, C.
SILVERMAN, M.G. DISCONCERTING ISSUE.
  617(TLS):23JUN72-715
SIMENON, G. THE CAT.
  617(TLS):1DEC72-1467
SIMENON, G. MAIGRET AND THE FLEA.
  617(TLS):29SEP72-1174
SIMENON, G. MAIGRET AND THE MADWOMAN.
  O.L. BAILEY, 561(SATR):28OCT72-84
  442(NY):23SEP72-135
  617(TLS):26MAY72-612
SIMENON, G. TEDDY BEAR.
  J. CATINELLA, 561(SATR):26FEB72-78
  442(NY):19FEB72-114
SIMENON, G. WHEN I WAS OLD.*
  617(TLS):24MAR72-335

SIMEON, R. FEDERAL-PROVINCIAL DIPLOMACY.
P. FOX, 99:DEC72-37
SIMIC, C. DISMANTLING THE SILENCE.*
H. CARRUTH, 249(HUDR):SUMMER71-323
F. MORAMARCO, 651(WHR):SUMMER71-280
R.B. SHAW, 491:MAR72-342
SIMIRENKO, A., ED. SOCIAL THOUGHT IN THE
SOVIET UNION.*
D. DIRSCHERL, 550(RUSR):JAN70-102
O.Z., 543:MAR70-568
SIMKIN, C.G.F. THE TRADITIONAL TRADE OF
ASIA.
P. WHEATLEY, 293(JAST):FEB70-421
SIMMEL, J.M. CAIN '67.
H. KEYISHIAN, 440:30JAN72-10
SIMMEN, E., ED. PAIN AND PROMISE. THE
CHICANO.
J. WOMACK, JR., 453:31AUG72-12
SIMMONDS, G.W., ED. SOVIET LEADERS.
R. CONQUEST, 587:OCT68-256
SIMMONDS, J.D., ED. MILTON STUDIES.*
(VOL 1)
D.A. ROBERTS, 551(RENQ):SPRING70-94
A.J. SMITH, 541(RES):NOV70-494
SIMMONDS, J.D., ED. MILTON STUDIES.
(VOL 2)
J.M. ALLEN, 67:NOV71-235
SIMMONS, E. DRIVING TO BILOXI.
B.D.S., 502(PRS):FALL69-326
SIMMONS, E.J. INTRODUCTION TO TOLSTOY'S
WRITINGS.*
I.P. FOOTE, 447(N&Q):JUN70-240
J.L.R., 502(PRS):WINTER68/69-362
SIMMONS, J. IN THE WILDERNESS.
W.P. TURNER, 619(TC):1969/2-45
SIMMONS, J. ST. PANCRAS STATION.
P. HOWELL, 46:OCT69-323
K. ROBERTS, 90:OCT70-704
SIMON, A.L. THE INTERNATIONAL WINE AND
FOOD SOCIETY'S GAZETTEER OF WINE.
(REV)
617(TLS):1DEC72-1469
SIMON, C. THE BATTLE OF PHARSALUS.*
D.A.N. JONES, 362:20JAN72-90
SIMON, C. HISTOIRE.
M.P. LEVITT, 340(KR):1969/1-128
SIMON, D. UNTERSUCHUNGEN ZUM JUSTINIAN-
ISCHEN ZIVILPROZESS.
F.C. BOURNE, 124:SEP70-28
SIMON, E. ARA PACIS AUGUSTAE.*
P. MAC KENDRICK, 121(CJ):FEB-MAR71-
275
SIMON, E. NEIDHART VON REUENTAL.*
R.J. TAYLOR, 220(GL&L):APR71-274
SIMON, I. THREE RESTORATION DIVINES.
T.A. BIRRELL, 179(ES):FEB69-120
SIMON, J. INGMAR BERGMAN DIRECTS.
R. FJELDE, 441:26NOV72-6
SIMON, J. DAS PROBLEM DER SPRACHE BEI
HEGEL.
M.J.V., 543:SEP69-140
SIMON, J.Y. - SEE GRANT, U.S.
SIMON, K. NEW YORK. (4TH ED)
C. SIMMONS, 441:4JUN72-7
SIMON, P. LES CONSONNES FRANÇAISES.
P. DELATTRE, 545(RPH):NOV70-332
SIMON, W.M. EUROPEAN POSITIVISM IN THE
NINETEENTH CENTURY.
A. PACCHI, 548(RCSF):JAN-MAR68-99
SIMON, Y. FREEDOM AND COMMUNITY. (C.P.
O'DONNELL, ED)
A. DONOSO, 258:DEC69-636
SIMONE, F. THE FRENCH RENAISSANCE.
D. COLEMAN, 402(MLR):APR71-404
I.D. MC FARLANE, 208(FS):JUL71-323
SIMONE, F., ED. MISCELLANEA DI STUDI E
RICERCHE SUL QUATTROCENTO FRANCESE.
J.C. LAIDLAW, 208(FS):JAN71-61

SIMONE, F. STORIA DELLA STORIOGRAFIA
LETTERARIA FRANCESE.
I.D. MC FARLANE, 208(FS):JUL71-323
SIMONE, F. UMANESIMO, RINASCIMENTO,
BAROCCO IN FRANCIA.
T.C. CAVE, 402(MLR):JAN71-183
R. LEBÈGUE, 546(RR):DEC70-302
I.D. MC FARLANE, 208(FS):JUL71-323
SIMONIDES & BACCHYLIDES. SIMONIDES,
BAKCHYLIDES: "GEDICHTE." (O. WERNER,
ED)
J. STERN, 122:JUL71-200
SIMONOV, R. STANISLAVSKY'S PROTÉGÉ.
R.L. BELKNAP, 32:JUN71-443
SIMONS, F. INFALLIBILITY AND THE EVI-
DENCE.
B.L. MARTHALER, 142:FALL71-481
SIMONS, G.L. PORNOGRAPHY WITHOUT PREJU-
DICE.
617(TLS):3NOV72-1346
SIMOONS, F.J. THE CEREMONIAL OX OF
INDIA.
F.K. LEHMAN, 293(JAST):NOV69-198
SIMPSON, C. A COMPENDIUM OF PRACTICAL
MUSIC. (P.J. LORD, ED)
M. TILMOUTH, 415:JUN71-557
J.A.W., 410(M&L):APR71-207
SIMPSON, C. KATMANDU.
T. RICCARDI, JR., 318(JAOS):APR-JUN
70-412
SIMPSON, C. LUSITANIA.
617(TLS):3NOV72-1308
SIMPSON, G.W.G. PERISCOPE VIEW.
617(TLS):8DEC72-1482
SIMPSON, J.M., COMP. WITHOUT ADAM.
H. SERGEANT, 175:SPRING69-33
W.P.T., 619(TC):1968/3-58
SIMPSON, L. ADVENTURES OF THE LETTER I.*
J. SYMONS, 364:DEC71/JAN72-128
SIMPSON, L. AIR WITH ARMED MEN.
D. BROMWICH, 362:27JUL72-117
617(TLS):11AUG72-934
SIMPSON, L. ARKWRIGHT.
A. MONTAGNES, 99:JAN-FEB72-75
L. RICOU, 296:SPRING72-90
SIMPSON, L.B. - SEE IGLESIA, R.
SIMPSON, M. SIMPSON THE OBSTETRICIAN.
617(TLS):19MAY72-566
SIMPSON, R. BEETHOVEN'S SYMPHONIES.
R. ANDERSON, 415:OCT70-1001
SIMPSON, R. THE ESSENCE OF BRUCKNER.
R. FREEDMAN, 340(KR):1969/2-264
SIMPSON, R.H. A GAZETTEER AND ATLAS OF
MYCENAEAN SITES.
J. RAISON, 555:VOL44FASC2-301
SIMPSON, R.H. & J.F. LAZENBY. THE CATA-
LOGUE OF THE SHIPS IN HOMER'S "ILIAD."
J.M. COOK, 123:JUN71-173
W. MC LEOD, 487:AUTUMN70-256
C.G. THOMAS, 124:MAR71-236
SIMS, E.H. FIGHTER TACTICS AND STRATEGY,
1914-1970.
617(TLS):4FEB72-138
SIMS, G. DEADHAND.
617(TLS):7JAN72-17
SIMS, O.L. COWPOKES, NESTERS, AND SO
FORTH.
W. GARD, 584(SWR):WINTER71-91
SINCLAIR, A. MAGOG.
P. ADAMS, 61:AUG72-92
J. HUNTER, 362:4MAY72-596
A. THWAITE, 441:2JUL72-7
617(TLS):5MAY72-509
SINCLAIR, A. - SEE "SELECTIONS FROM THE
GREEK ANTHOLOGY"
SINCLAIR, D., ED. NINETEENTH-CENTURY
NARRATIVE POEMS.
J.R. SORFLEET, 296:SPRING72-92

SINCLAIR, K.V. DESCRIPTIVE CATALOGUE OF
MEDIEVAL AND RENAISSANCE MANUSCRIPTS
IN AUSTRALIA.
P. MC GURK, 123:JUN71-286
SINCLAIR, M. FOLIO FORTY-ONE.
N. CALLENDAR, 441:19MAR72-42
SINCLAIR, M. NORSLAG.
D.A.N. JONES, 362:20JAN72-90
SINGER, I.B. ENEMIES, A LOVE STORY.
P. ADAMS, 61:JUL72-96
L. DICKSTEIN, 441:25JUN72-4
T.R. EDWARDS, 453:20JUL72-20
J. HUNTER, 362:16NOV72-682
C. LEHMANN-HAUPT, 441:26JUN72-35
L.E. SISSMAN, 442(NY):30DEC72-70
G. WOLFF, 561(SATR):22JUL72-54
617(TLS):17NOV72-1387
SINGER, I.B. A FRIEND OF KAFKA.
J. HUNTER, 362:9MAR72-317
SINGER, I.B. THE SÉANCE AND OTHER STOR-
IES.*
S. PINSKER, 328:WINTER69-126
SINGER, I.J. STEEL AND IRON.
J. GREENFIELD, 287:DEC69-26
SINGER, M. & B.S. COHN, EDS. STRUCTURE
AND CHANGE IN INDIAN SOCIETY.
E.J. JAY, 318(JAOS):OCT-DEC70-598
SINGH, A. TAKE-OVERS.
617(TLS):24MAR72-345
SINGH, G. LEOPARDI E L'INGHILTERRA.
A. PAOLUCCI, 276:AUTUMN70-321
N.J. PERELLA, 401(MLQ):MAR70-123
W.T.S., 191(ELN):SEP70(SUPP)-138
SINGH, M. HIMALAYAN ART.*
S. KRAMRISCH, 57:VOL31#4-330
SINGH, R.C.P. KINGSHIP IN NORTHERN INDIA
(CIR. 600 A.D. - 1200 A.D.).
J.W. SPELLMAN, 293(JAST):NOV69-199
SINGH, R.J., ED. WORLD PERSPECTIVES IN
PHILOSOPHY, RELIGION, AND CULTURE.
W.A.J., 543:DEC69-367
SINGH, S. THE DUST-STORM AND THE HANGING
MIST.
D.M. SPENCER, 318(JAOS):APR-JUN70-362
SINGH, S.D. ANCIENT INDIAN WARFARE WITH
SPECIAL REFERENCE TO THE VEDIC PERIOD.*
S. KRAMRISCH, 57:VOL31#1-94
SINGHA, R. & R. MASSEY. INDIAN DANCES.*
F. RICHMOND, 397(MD):FEB69-454
SINGLETON, C.S. - SEE TOYNBEE, P.
SINHA, K.K., ED. PROBLEMS OF DEFENSE OF
SOUTH AND EAST ASIA.
L.P. SINGH, 293(JAST):MAY70-684
SINHA, V.B. THE RED REBEL IN INDIA.
J.P. HAITHCOX, 293(JAST):MAY70-729
SINNIGE, T.G. MATTER AND INFINITY IN THE
PRESOCRATIC SCHOOLS AND PLATO.
P.J. BICKNELL, 303:VOL90-240
SINYAVSKY, A. UNGUARDED THOUGHTS.
S. HOOD, 362:24FEB72-248
SINZELLE, C.M. THE GEOGRAPHICAL BACK-
GROUND OF THE EARLY WORKS OF D.H.
LAWRENCE.
R.L. DRAIN, 179(ES):DEC70-570
SIOHAN, R. STRAVINSKY.
E.V. WILLIAMS, 32:SEP71-700
SIPE, D.L. SHAKESPEARE'S METRICS.*
G.R. HIBBARD, 447(N&Q):APR70-147
T.H. HOWARD-HILL, 541(RES):FEB70-110
B. LINDBERG-SEYERSTED, 179(ES):OCT70-
453
K. MAGAREY, 67:MAY71-88
N. MURRAY, 597(SN):VOL41#2-428
SIPOS, P. IMRÉDY BÉLA ÉS A MAGYAR
MEGÚJULÁS PÁRTJA.
N.M. NAGY-TALAVERA, 32:SEP71-686

"SIR GAWAIN AND THE GREEN KNIGHT."
(J.A. BURROW, ED)
617(TLS):8DEC72-1513
"SIR GAWAIN AND THE GREEN KNIGHT."*
(J.R.R. TOLKIEN & E.V. GORDON, EDS;
2ND ED REV BY N. DAVIS)
S.W. HOLTON, 597(SN):VOL41#1-179
"SIR GAWAIN AND THE GREEN KNIGHT." (R.A.
WALDRON, ED)
T.A. SHIPPEY, 402(MLR):OCT71-850
SIRC, L. ECONOMIC DEVOLUTION IN EASTERN
EUROPE.*
S. LAMED, 104:SPRING71-110
SIRCAR, D.C. STUDIES IN INDIAN COINS.
T.R. TRAUTMANN, 293(JAST):NOV69-200
SIRCAR, D.C. STUDIES IN THE SOCIETY AND
ADMINISTRATION OF ANCIENT AND MEDIEVAL
INDIA. (VOL 1)
L. STERNBACH, 318(JAOS):APR-JUN70-410
T.R. TRAUTMANN, 293(JAST):NOV69-200
SIROIS, A. MONTRÉAL DANS LE ROMAN CAN-
ADIEN.
R. GIGUERE, 102(CANL):SUMMER71-86
SISAM, C. & K., EDS. THE OXFORD BOOK OF
MEDIEVAL ENGLISH VERSE.*
J.A. GRAY, 67:NOV71-225
ŠIŠMAREV, V.F. IZBRANNYE STAT'I: FRAN-
CUZSKAJA LITERATURA.
E. BRISTOL, 545(RPH):FEB71-524
SISSMAN, L.E. PURSUIT OF HONOR.*
R. LATTIMORE, 249(HUDR):AUTUMN71-505
SISSMAN, L.E. SCATTERED RETURNS.*
639(VQR):SPRING70-XLVI
SISSON, C.H. THE CASE OF WALTER BAGEHOT.
617(TLS):18AUG72-959
SISSON, C.H. ENGLISH POETRY 1900-1950.
617(TLS):11FEB72-146
SISSON, C.J. THE BOAR'S HEAD THEATRE.
(S. WELLS, ED)
617(TLS):25AUG72-1003
SISSON, C.J. THE LOST PLAYS OF SHAKE-
SPEARE'S AGE.
568(SCN):SUMMER/AUTUMN71-47
SISSON, C.J. SHAKESPEARE'S TRAGIC
JUSTICE.
K. SMIDT, 179(ES):APR70-160
SITHOLE, N. OBED MUTEZO.
617(TLS):20OCT72-1264
SITHOLE, N. THE POLYGAMIST.
J. CAREW, 441:10SEP72-47
442(NY):5AUG72-82
SITTE, C. CITY PLANNING ACCORDING TO
ARTISTIC PRINCIPLES.
C. TUNNARD, 576:MAR68-87
SITWELL, E. SELECTED LETTERS.* (J.
LEHMANN & D. PARKER, EDS)
J.D. BROPHY, 295:VOL2#3-427
G. NEVIN, 493:WINTER70/71-372
SITWELL, E. & W. WALTON. FAÇADE.
617(TLS):7APR72-386
SITWELL, S. GOTHIC EUROPE.
639(VQR):SPRING70-LXXV
SIVAN, E. L'ISLAM ET LA CROISADE.
S.D. GOITEIN, 589:JAN71-184
DE SIVERS, F. ANALYSE GRAMMATICALE DE
L'ESTONIEN PARLÉ.
R.T. HARMS, 574(SEEJ):SUMMER71-249
SIVERTSEN, E. FONOLOGI.
E.S. TALO, 596(SL):VOL22#2-134
SIVIN, N. CHINESE ALCHEMY.
I. VEITH, 318(JAOS):APR-JUN70-414
SIWEK, R.P.P. LE DIEU D'ARISTOTE DANS
LES DIALOGUES.
P. LOUIS, 555:VOL44FASC2-323
"6 DAYS: AN ANTHOLOGY OF CANADIAN CHRIS-
TIAN POETRY."
R. GIBBS, 198:SUMMER72-129

"SIX YÜAN PLAYS." (LIU JUNG-EN, TRANS)
617(TLS):25AUG72-1003
SIZER, T., WITH C. ROLLINS. THE WORKS OF
COLONEL JOHN TRUMBULL.
M.S. YOUNG, 39:APR69-328
SJÖLIN, B. EINFÜHRUNG IN DAS FRIESIS-
CHE.*
J. EICHHOFF, 406:SPRING71-74
SJÖWALL, M. & P. WAHLÖÖ. THE ABOMINABLE
MAN.
O.L. BAILEY, 561(SATR):28OCT72-84
N. CALLENDAR, 441:19NOV72-61
SJÖWALL, M. & P. WAHLÖÖ. THE FIRE
ENGINE THAT DISAPPEARED.*
617(TLS):4FEB72-135
SJÖWALL, M. & P. WAHLÖÖ. MURDER AT THE
SAVOY.*
N. CALLENDAR, 441:9JAN72-33
617(TLS):13OCT72-1235
ŠKARKA, A. FRIDRICH BRIDEL NOVÝ A NEZ-
NÁMÝ.
R.B. PYNSENT, 575(SEER):JAN71-138
SKARMETA, A. DESNUDO EN EL TEJADO.
G.W. PETERSEN, 238:MAY70-345
SKAZKIN, S.D., ED. ROSSIJA I ITALIJA.
W. KIRCHNER, 104:SUMMER71-283
SKAZKIN, S.D. & OTHERS, EDS. ISTORIIA
VIZANTII V TREKH TOMAKH. AN SSSR.
P.J. ALEXANDER, 32:SEP71-635
J. MEYENDORFF, 32:SEP71-619
I. ŠEVČENKO, 32:SEP71-624
SKEAT, T.C. THE REIGNS OF THE PTOLEMIES.
J.G. GRIFFITHS, 123:DEC70-412
SKEAT, W.W. MALAY MAGIC.
R.N. JACKSON, 302:JAN69-118
SKELTON, G. WIELAND WAGNER.*
L. BECKETT, 415:SEP71-859
SKELTON, J. POEMS.* (R.S. KINSMAN, ED)
W. NELSON, 382(MAE):1971/2-208
Z., 179(ES):AUG70-388
SKELTON, R., ED. THE CAVALIER POETS.
D.C. JUDKINS, 568(SCN):SUMMER/AUTUMN
71-38
P. PALMER, 677:VOL2-269
SKELTON, R. A DIFFERENT MOUNTAIN.
S. MOORE, 385(MQR):SUMMER72-217
SKELTON, R. THE HUNTING DARK.
G. NOONAN, 99:JAN-FEB72-81
N. RENNIE, 364:AUG/SEP71-120
SKELTON, R. AN IRISH ALBUM.
M. DOYLE, 491:MAR72-356
SKELTON, R., ED. POETRY OF THE FORTIES.
L. MATEO, 202(FMOD):APR/AUG69-297
SKELTON, R. PRIVATE SPEECH.*
G. NOONAN, 99:JAN-FEB72-81
SKELTON, R. SELECTED POEMS, 1947-1967.*
H. MAC CALLUM, 627(UTQ):JUL69-340
SKELTON, R.A. - SEE PIGAFETTA, A.
SKILLEND, W.E. KODAE SOSOL.
293(JAST):MAY70-745
SKINNER, A.N., M.N. SAKKWATO & M.A.
INGAWA. KAMUS NA TURANCI DA HAUSA.
F.W. PARSONS, 315(JAL):VOL8PT1-62
SKINNER, B.F. BEYOND FREEDOM AND DIG-
NITY.*
A. LEWIS, 362:23MAR72-388
M. WOLFE, 99:MAR72-12
W.I. THOMPSON, 99:MAR72-14
617(TLS):12MAY72-533
SKINNER, J. JOURNAL OF A SOMERSET RECTOR
1803-1834. (H. & P. COOMBS, EDS)
617(TLS):12MAY72-557
SKINNER, M. - SEE EDGAR, F.
SKINNER, T. HOW BLACK IS THE GOSPEL?
J. MC DONNELL, 142:FALL71-469
SKLAR, R. F. SCOTT FITZGERALD.
J.J. MC ALEER, 613:SPRING68-134

SKLARE, M. AMERICA'S JEWS.
441:20FEB72-25
SKLIARSKY, I.I. - SEE VATMAN, D.P. &
V.A. ELIZAROV
SKORNIA, H.J. TELEVISION AND THE NEWS.
W. CANZIANI, 182:VOL23#1/2-4
SKORUPKA, S. SŁOWNIK FRAZEOLOGICZNY
JĘZYKA POLSKIEGO.
J.T. BAER, 574(SEEJ):SPRING71-135
SKOWRONEK, S. ON THE PROBLEMS OF THE
ALEXANDRIAN MINT.
M.H. CRAWFORD, 313:VOL60-232
ŠKREB, Z., ED. THE ART OF THE WORD,
1957-1967.
A.M. MLIKOTIN, 574(SEEJ):FALL71-391
SKRYNNIKOV, R.G. NACHALO OPRICHNINY.
OPRICHNYI TERROR.
J.T. ALEXANDER, 32:MAR71-137
SKRZYNECKI, P. THERE, BEHIND THE LIDS.
J. TULIP, 581:1971/1-72
SKUTSCH, O. STUDIA ENNIANA.*
E.L. BASSETT, 122:JUL71-210
SLADE, T. D.H. LAWRENCE.
M. ALLOTT, 677:VOL2-327
SLADKEVIČ, N.G. & S.S. VOLK. OČERKI PO
ISTORII LENINGRADSKOGO UNIVERSITETA.
(VOL 2)
W.L. MATHES, 104:SUMMER71-287
SLATER, E. MAN, MIND AND HEREDITY. (J.
SHIELDS & I.I. GOTTESMAN, EDS)
617(TLS):14APR72-425
SLATER, M., ED. DICKENS 1970.
A. WELSH, 155:SEP70-248
SLATER, W.J. LEXICON TO PINDAR.
D.E. GERBER, 487:AUTUMN70-275
SLATOFF, W.J. WITH RESPECT TO READERS.
J. KILLHAM, 89(BJA):SPRING71-200
SLATTERY, W.C., ED. THE RICHARDSON-
STINSTRA CORRESPONDENCE AND STINSTRA'S
PREFACES TO "CLARISSA."*
R.E. KELLEY, 481(PQ):JUL70-375
SLAUGHTER, H.K. GEORGE FITZMAURICE AND
HIS ENCHANTED LAND.
617(TLS):29SEP72-1176
SLAVITT, D.R. DAY SAILING.*
639(VQR):SPRING70-XLVI
SLAVUTYCH, Y. PIVNICHNE SIAYVO.
C.H. ANDRUSYSHEN, 627(UTQ):JUL70-451
SLEEPER, C.F. BLACK POWER AND CHRISTIAN
RESPONSIBILITY.
S.O.H., 543:DEC69-356
SLESSAREV, H. EDUARD MÖRIKE.
W. PELTERS, 406:SUMMER71-183
SLESSER, M. THE POLITICS OF ENVIRONMENT.
617(TLS):16JUN72-697
SLETSJØE, L. LE DÉVELOPPEMENT DE "L" ET
"N" EN ANCIEN PORTUGAIS.
C. BLAYLOCK, 545(RPH):AUG70-200
SLETSJÖE, L., ED. LE MYSTÈRE D'ADAM.*
B-M. CRAIG, 399(MLJ):APR70-302
C. RÉGNIER, 545(RPH):FEB70-366
ŚLIWOWSKI, R. OD TURGIENIEWA DO CZECH-
OWA.
J.T. BAER, 574(SEEJ):SUMMER71-221
SLOAN, J.P. THE CASE HISTORY OF COMRADE
V.
P. ADAMS, 61:MAY72-112
J. DECK, 441:18JUN72-6
D. JOHNSON, 440:23APR72-3
C. LEHMANN-HAUPT, 441:13APR72-45
G. MALKO, 561(SATR):15JUL72-57
SLOANE, E. AN AGE OF BARNS.
R.L. WELSCH, 650(WF):JAN68-62
SLOANE, E.A. THE COMPLETE BOOK OF
BICYCLING.
H.C. GARDNER, 441:4JUN72-8
SLOANE, P. COLOR.
G. BATTCOCK, 58:MAR70-12

SLONIM, M. SOVIET RUSSIAN LITERATURE.* (1ST ED)
  M. DEWHIRST, 587:APR68-597
SLOTE, B. - SEE CATHER, W.
SLOTE, M.A. REASON AND SCEPTICISM.
  F.I. DRETSKE, 311(JP):27JAN72-47
  T.E. WILKERSON, 518:MAY71-26
"SLOVAR SLOVENSKEGE KNJIŽNEGA JEZIKA." (VOL 1)
  J. PATERNOST, 104:FALL71-424
"SŁOWNIK JĘZYKA ADAMA MICKIEWICZA." (VOL 7)
  D. WELSH, 104:SPRING71-127
SLUCKIN, W. IMPRINTING AND EARLY LEARNING. (NEW ED)
  617(TLS):18AUG72-978
SMALLEY, P. A WARM GUN.
  617(TLS):3NOV72-1305
SMALLMAN, B. THE BACKGROUND OF PASSION MUSIC.
  R. BULLIVANT, 415:DEC71-1174
SMART, N. THE CONCEPT OF WORSHIP.
  617(TLS):13OCT72-1234
SMEDLEY, R. & J. TETHER. LET'S DANCE - COUNTRY STYLE.
  617(TLS):18AUG72-964
SMEETS, J.R., ED. LA BIBLE DE MACÉ DE LA CHARITÉ. (VOL 1)
  P. MÉNARD, 545(RPH):NOV69-254
SMELSER, M. THE WINNING OF INDEPENDENCE.
  441:26MAR72-37
SMIBERT, J. THE NOTEBOOK OF JOHN SMIBERT.
  639(VQR):WINTER70-XXVI
SMIDT, K. - SEE SHAKESPEARE, W.
SMIRNITSKY, A.L. ESSENTIALS OF RUSSIAN GRAMMAR. (O.S. AKHMANOVA, ED)
  H. LEEMING, 575(SEER):JUL71-460
SMIRNOFF, V. THE SCOPE OF CHILD ANALYSIS.
  617(TLS):14APR72-425
SMITH, A. BESIDE THE SEASIDE.
  617(TLS):8DEC72-1513
SMITH, A.B. IDEAL AND REALITY IN THE FICTIONAL NARRATIVES OF THÉOPHILE GAUTIER.
  H. COCKERHAM, 208(FS):OCT71-473
  R. MERKER, 207(FR):FEB70-516
SMITH, A.H., ED. THREE NORTHUMBRIAN POEMS.
  H. GNEUSS, 72:BAND208HEFT3-214
SMITH, A.J., ED. JOHN DONNE.
  617(TLS):29DEC72-1581
SMITH, A.J.M. - SEE WILKINSON, A.
SMITH, A.W. A GARDENER'S DICTIONARY OF PLANT NAMES. (REV BY W.T. STEARN)
  617(TLS):11FEB72-165
"ADAM SMITH." SUPERMONEY.
  E. FREMONT-SMITH, 561(SATR):21OCT72-69
  C. LEHMANN-HAUPT, 441:12OCT72-49
  P. PASSELL & L. ROSS, 441:15OCT72-6
SMITH, B. THE STATE POLICE.
  617(TLS):18FEB72-191
SMITH, C. RAMÓN MENÉNDEZ PIDAL, 1869-1968.
  R.B. TATE, 86(BHS):JUL71-257
SMITH, C. THE OLD MANOR HOUSE. (A.H. EHRENPREIS, ED)
  P. FAULKNER, 677:VOL2-292
SMITH, C. - SEE "POEMA DE MIO CID"
SMITH, C.B. - SEE UNDER BABINGTON SMITH, C.
SMITH, C.G. SHAKESPEARE'S PROVERB LORE.
  G.H.V. BUNT, 179(ES):DEC69-611

SMITH, C.G. SPENSER'S PROVERB LORE.
  R.F. HILL, 677:VOL2-251
  A. LOW, 568(SCN):SUMMER/AUTUMN71-36
SMITH, C.M. INSTANT STATUS.
  P. SHOWERS, 441:12MAR72-14
SMITH, C.R. AN EXAMINATION OF THE PROCEDURE FOR DEALING WITH COMPLAINTS AGAINST THE POLICE.
  617(TLS):3NOV72-1349
SMITH, D. REPORT FROM ENGINE CO. 82.
  A. BROYARD, 441:1FEB72-39
  J. FLAHERTY, 440:12MAR72-8
  D.W. MC CULLOUGH, 561(SATR):8APR72-68
  441:16APR72-20
  442(NY):19FEB72-116
SMITH, D.E. & G.R. GAY, EDS. "IT'S SO GOOD, DON'T EVEN TRY IT ONCE."
  441:8OCT72-38
SMITH, D.E. & J. LUCE. LOVE NEEDS CARE.*
  M. HALBERSTAM, 31(ASCH):SPRING72-308
SMITH, D.I.B., ED. EDITING EIGHTEENTH-CENTURY TEXTS.
  G. FALLE, 627(UTQ):JUL69-369
  R. LONSDALE, 447(N&Q):NOV70-439
SMITH, D.M. - SEE UNDER MACK SMITH, D.
SMITH, D.R. THE MONITOR AND THE MERRIMAC.
  J.M. PREST, 447(N&Q):DEC70-480
"DAVID SMITH BY DAVID SMITH."* (C. GRAY, ED)
  G. BARO, 592:NOV68-224
SMITH, E. VICTORIAN FARNHAM.
  617(TLS):14JAN72-43
SMITH, E.C. TREASURY OF NAME LORE.
  L.M. HARDER, 424:MAR68-61
SMITH, E.E. & R. LEDNICKY. "THE OKHRANA."
  R.V. ALLEN, 32:SEP71-663
SMITH, F.S. BIBLIOGRAPHY IN THE BOOKSHOP. (REV)
  617(TLS):9JUN72-667
SMITH, G. DEAN ACHESON.
  D.S. CLEMENS, 441:10SEP72-7
  R.R. LINGEMAN, 441:20JUL72-35
SMITH, G. DICKENS, MONEY, AND SOCIETY.
  A. KETTLE, 541(RES):MAY70-233
  R.D. MC MASTER, 637(VS):JUN70-447
  R.E. SHERWIN, 445(NCF):JUN69-117
  R. WILLIAMS, 155:SEP69-178
SMITH, G., ED. 1000 MAKERS OF THE TWENTIETH CENTURY.
  617(TLS):11FEB72-153
SMITH, H.G. CATTLE TRAILS TO TRENCHES.
  W. GARD, 584(SWR):AUTUMN71-VI
SMITH, I.C. - SEE UNDER CRICHTON SMITH, I.
SMITH, I.R. THE EMIN PASHA RELIEF EXPEDITION 1886-1890.
  617(TLS):8DEC72-1478
SMITH, J. NORTHAMPTONSHIRE AND THE SOKE OF PETERBOROUGH.
  S.T.S., 46:FEB69-150
SMITH, J.B. MODERN FINNISH PAINTING AND GRAPHIC ART.
  K. LUNDE, 32:DEC71-913
SMITH, J.E., ED. CONTEMPORARY AMERICAN PHILOSOPHY. (2ND SER)
  A.R. WHITE, 518:JAN71-23
SMITH, J.E. EXPERIENCE AND GOD.
  J. HICK, 483:JAN70-74
  J. NEEDLEMAN, 543:SEP69-102
SMITH, J.E. & OTHERS. THE INVERTEBRATE PANORAMA.
  617(TLS):14JAN72-45
SMITH, J.G., ED. POLITICAL BROKERS.
  441:16APR72-22
SMITH, J.M. ON EVOLUTION.
  617(TLS):23JUN72-727

SMITH, M. EVERYBODY KNOWS AND NOBODY
CARES.*
617(TLS):11FEB72-145
SMITH, M. PALESTINIAN PARTIES AND POLI-
TICS THAT SHAPED THE OLD TESTAMENT.
R. GORDIS, 441:9JAN72-5
SMITH, M. - SEE DE RONSARD, P.
SMITH, M.A. FRANÇOIS MAURIAC.
C.J. GALLANT, 399(MLJ):DEC70-614
SMITH, M.C. DECLARATION OF CONSCIENCE.
(W.C. LEWIS, JR., ED)
L. CARPENTER, 561(SATR):15APR72-66
SMITH, M.G. - SEE MC CULLERS, C.
SMITH, M.N. & V.M. AFANASIEF. INTRODUC-
TION TO RUSSIAN.
M.I. LEVIN, 574(SEEJ):SPRING71-131
"MERRIMAN SMITH'S BOOK OF PRESIDENTS."
(T.G. SMITH, ED)
G.W. JOHNSON, 441:10CT72-36
SMITH, N.J. A BRIEF GUIDE TO SOCIAL
LEGISLATION.
617(TLS):2JUN72-641
SMITH, N.K. FRANK LLOYD WRIGHT.
A. GOWANS, 576:MAY69-140
SMITH, P. - SEE "LORD SALISBURY ON POLI-
TICS"
SMITH, P. & G. SUMMERFIELD, EDS. MATTHEW
ARNOLD AND THE EDUCATION OF THE NEW
ORDER.
B. SIMON, 637(VS):JUN70-403
SMITH, P.J. THE TENTH MUSE.*
W. DEAN, 415:SEP71-859
G. MARTIN, 676(YR):WINTER71-267
J.A.W., 410(M&L):OCT71-433
SMITH, P.J. - SEE "AMERICAN BOOK-PRICES
CURRENT, 1969"
SMITH, R. CAPE BRETON IN THE THOUGHT
CONTROL CENTRE OF CANADA.*
G. ROPER, 627(UTQ):JUL70-340
SMITH, R.A.L. CANTERBURY CATHEDRAL
PRIORY.
U. DIRLMEIER, 182:VOL23#3-113
SMITH, R.H. OSS.
R. JELLINEK, 441:26JUL72-37
C. RYAN, 441:17SEP72-31
617(TLS):130CT72-1228
SMITH, S. SCORPION.
R. BLYTHE, 362:6APR72-457
617(TLS):14JUL72-820
SMITH, T.D. - SEE UNDER D'ARCH SMITH, T.
SMITH, T.G. - SEE "MERRIMAN SMITH'S BOOK
OF PRESIDENTS"
SMITH, V. VANCE PALMER.
L. KRAMER, 71(ALS):OCT72-433
SMITH, V.E., ED. PHILOSOPHICAL PROBLEMS
IN BIOLOGY.
J. WUBNIG, 486:SEP68-300
SMITH, W. THE DIAMOND HUNTERS.
M. LEVIN, 441:23APR72-41
SMITH, W. THE POEMS OF WILLIAM SMITH.
(L.A. SASEK, ED)
J. GRUNDY, 677:VOL2-253
SMITH, W.C. HANDEL. (2ND ED)
S. SADIE, 415:OCT70-1004
SMITH, W.C. & C. HUMPHRIES. A BIBLIO-
GRAPHY OF THE MUSICAL WORKS PUBLISHED
BY THE FIRM OF JOHN WALSH DURING THE
YEARS 1721-1766.*
M. DAWNEY, 78(BC):SPRING70-115
G. HEARD, 503:AUTUMN69-118
SMITH, W.E. WE MUST RUN WHILE THEY WALK.
P. ADAMS, 61:MAR72-108
441:20FEB72-25
SMITH, W.G. GARDENING FOR FOOD.
J. SAVERCOOL, 441:3DEC72-92
SMITH, W.H., ED. HORACE WALPOLE.
R. LONSDALE, 447(N&Q):MAR70-106

SMITH, W.H.C. NAPOLEON III.
617(TLS):19MAY72-578
SMITH, W.J. NEW & SELECTED POEMS.*
W.H. PRITCHARD, 491:DEC71-159
SMITH, W.S. INTERCONNECTIONS IN THE
ANCIENT NEAR EAST.*
J.D. MUHLY, 318(JAOS):APR-JUN70-305
SMITH, W.S. THE LONDON HERETICS, 1870-
1914.*
H.J. FYRTH, 571:SPRING-SUMMER68-17
F.P.W. MC DOWELL, 572:JAN69-32
SMITH BRINDLE, R. CONTEMPORARY PERCUS-
SION.*
G. MELVILLE-MASON, 415:AUG70-806
H. REES, 607:SUMMER70-34
412:FEB71-76
SMITH BRINDLE, R. SERIAL COMPOSITION.
E. BARKIN, 414(MQ):JAN69-125
B. FENNELLY, 308:WINTER67-288
SMITHYMAN, K. FLYING TO PALMERSTON.
R. OPPENHEIM, 368:JUN69-198
SMITS, R., COMP. HALF A CENTURY OF
SOVIET SERIALS, 1917-1968.
W.S. SWORAKOWSKI, 550(RUSR):JAN70-114
SMOCK, A.C. IBO POLITICS.
617(TLS):10MAR72-268
SMOLAR, B. SOVIET JEWRY TODAY AND TOMOR-
ROW.
R.N. LEVY, 441:9JAN72-4
SMOLLETT, T. THE LETTERS OF TOBIAS SMOL-
LETT, M.D.* (L.M. KNAPP, ED)
G.S. ROUSSEAU, 72:BAND208HEFT4/6-392
SMOUT, T.C. A HISTORY OF THE SCOTTISH
PEOPLE 1560-1830.
E. CREGEEN, 595(SCS):VOL15PT2-150
SMYTH, A., ED. THE LONDON SYMPHONY
ORCHESTRA.
K. SPENCE, 415:FEB71-141
SMYTH, C.H. BRONZINO AS DRAUGHTSMAN.
617(TLS):14APR72-414
SMYTHE, C. - SEE LADY GREGORY
SNAGGE, J. & M. BARSLEY. THOSE VINTAGE
YEARS OF RADIO.
F. DILLON, 362:2NOV72-608
617(TLS):17NOV72-1397
SNELGROVE, D., WITH J. MAYNE & B. TAYLOR
- SEE HARDIE, M.
SNELL, B. TYRTAIOS UND DIE SPRACHE DES
EPOS.*
F.M. COMBELLACK, 122:JAN71-45
J.B. HAINSWORTH, 123:JUN71-174
SNELL, W.R. - SEE WATSON, F.S.
SNELLGROVE, D.L., ED & TRANS. FOUR LAMAS
OF DOLPO.* (VOL 1)
P.J.H., 543:JUN70-752
SNODGRASS, A.M. THE DARK AGE OF GREECE.
617(TLS):14APR72-422
SNODGRASS, W.D. AFTER EXPERIENCE.*
P. COOPER, 577(SHR):SPRING70-179
K. SKINNER, 448:SUMMER70-128
W.P.T., 619(TC):1968/4&1969/1-90
SNOOK, I.A., ED. CONCEPTS OF INDOCTRINA-
TION.
617(TLS):11AUG72-939
SNOOK, I.A. INDOCTRINATION AND EDUCA-
TION.
617(TLS):21JUL72-853
SNOW, C.P. LAST THINGS.*
P. CRUTTWELL, 249(HUDR):SPRING71-177
F.P.W. MC DOWELL, 659:SUMMER72-361
SNOW, C.P. THE MALCONTENTS.
A. BROYARD, 441:26APR72-47
D.A.N. JONES, 362:29JUN72-873
A. THWAITE, 441:7MAY72-5
B. WEBER, 561(SATR):17JUN72-76
E. WEEKS, 61:JUN72-110
442(NY):13MAY72-145
617(TLS):30JUN72-737

SNOW, C.P. PUBLIC AFFAIRS.*
   S. HAMPSHIRE, 453:21SEP72-12
SNOW, E. THE LONG REVOLUTION.
   J.K. FAIRBANK, 453:19OCT72-9
   442(NY):28OCT72-159
SNOW, P. HUSSEIN.
   617(TLS):17NOV72-1390
SNOW, S. HALF A DOZEN OF THE OTHER.
   617(TLS):11AUG72-936
SNOWDEN, F.M., JR. BLACKS IN ANTIQUITY.*
   W.O. MOELLER, 124:NOV70-90
   639(VQR):SUMMER70-CXV
SNYDER, F.B. THE LIFE OF ROBERT BURNS.
   J.M. LOTHIAN, 541(RES):MAY70-224
SNYDER, G. EARTH HOUSE HOLD.*
   J. MC GAHEY, 661:FALL/WINTER69-102
   T. PARKINSON, 295:VOL2#3-448
   96:AUG69-47
SNYDER, G. REGARDING WAVE.*
   G. BURNS, 584(SWR):SPRING71-207
   J.R. CARPENTER, 491:JUN72-164
   W. DICKEY, 249(HUDR):SPRING71-159
   G.S. FRASER, 473(PR):WINTER71/72-469
   J. FULLER, 362:24FEB72-251
   T. PARKINSON, 295:VOL2#3-448
SNYDER, W.U. THOMAS WOLFE.
   L. FIELD, 578:FALL72-163
SNYTKO, T.G. RUSSKOE NARODNICHESTVO I
   POL'SKOE OBSHCHESTVENNOE DVIZHENIE,
   1865-1881 GG.
   R.H.W. THEEN, 32:SEP71-665
SOARES, M.N.L. MACHADO DE ASSIS E A
   ANÁLISE DA EXPRESSÃO.
   H.M., 191(ELN):SEP70(SUPP)-147
SOBOLEV, R. ZAPAD.
   617(TLS):12MAY72-549
SOBOUL, A. THE SANS-CULOTTES.
   J.H. PLUMB, 441:21MAY72-6
SOCHEN, J. THE NEW WOMAN.
   442(NY):28OCT72-159
"SOCIÉTÉ RENCESVALS, IVE CONGRÈS INTER-
   NATIONAL (HEIDELBERG, 28 AOÛT - 2
   SEPTEMBRE 1967): ACTES ET MÉMOIRES."
   P. WUNDERLI, 72:BAND208HEFT1-64
"A SOCIETY'S CHIEF JOYS."
   J.D. CUSHING, 432(NEQ):MAR70-141
SÖDERSTRÖM, O. MOLNVANDRINGEN - EN ROMAN
   OM VERNER VON HEIDENSTAM.
   K-I. HILDEMAN, 563(SS):AUTUMN71-455
SOFUE, T., ED. NIPPONJIN.
   H. WAGATSUMA, 293(JAST):MAY70-704
SOI SALON-SOININEN, I. DIE INFINITIVE IN
   DER SEPTUAGINTA.
   R.A. BARCLAY, 182:VOL23#4-146
SOKOLOFF, A.H. COSIMA WAGNER.
   B. MAGEE, 415:MAR70-282
SOKOLOWSKI, F. LOIS SACRÉES DES CITÉS
   GRECQUES.
   K. CLINTON, 24:JUL71-496
DE SOLA PINTO, V. & W. ROBERTS - SEE
   LAWRENCE, D.H.
SOLALINDE, A.G., L.A. KASTEN & V.R.B.
   OELSCHLÄGER - SEE ALFONSO EL SABIO
SOLBERG, W.U. THE UNIVERSITY OF ILLI-
   NOIS, 1867-1894.
   W.B. FAHERTY, 377:JUL71-115
SOLER, A.M.S. DIE SPANISCH-RUSSISCHEN
   BEZIEHUNGEN IM 18. JAHRHUNDERT.
   F.A. WALKER, 32:JUN71-391
SOLIN, H. EINE NEUE FLUCHTAFEL AUS
   OSTIA.
   J. ANDRÉ, 555:VOL44FASC2-351
SOLÍS, S.S. - SEE UNDER SUÁREZ SOLÍS, S.
SOLIVA, C. DAS EIDGENÖSSISCHE STADT-
   UND LANDRECHT DES ZÜRCHER BÜRGER-
   MEISTERS JOHANN JAKOB LEU.
   B. MEYER, 182:VOL23#9-474

SOLLERS, P. LOIS.
   617(TLS):22SEP72-1088
SOLLERS, P. NOMBRES.
   J. DERRIDA, 98:FEB69-99 [AND CONT IN]
   98:MAR69-215
SOLMI, S. DAL BALCONE. QUADERNO DI
   TRADUZIONI.
   G. SINGH, 276:SPRING70-78
SOLMI, S., ED. PENSIERI DI LEOPARDI.
   617(TLS):21JAN72-60
SOLMI, S. SCRITTI LEOPARDIANI.
   617(TLS):21JAN72-60
SOLOMON, B.M. - SEE DWIGHT, T.
SOLOMON, B.P. ARRIVING WHERE WE STARTED.
   R. JELLINEK, 441:21APR72-40
   R. KIELY, 441:23APR72-5
   442(NY):13MAY72-148
SOLOMON, M., ED. THE JOAN BAEZ SONGBOOK.
   C.M. SIMPSON, JR., 650(WF):APR68-136
SOLOMON, M., ED. NOËL: THE JOAN BAEZ
   CHRISTMAS SONGBOOK.
   H. STURM, 582(SFQ):DEC68-337
SOLOMON, M.C. ETERNAL GEOMATER.
   639(VQR):SUMMER70-C
SOLOMON, P.H., JR. SOVIET CRIMINOLOGY.
   I. LAPENNA, 575(SEER):JAN71-166
SOLOMON, R.H. MAO'S REVOLUTION AND THE
   CHINESE POLITICAL CULTURE.*
   J. MATHEWS, 31(ASCH):SPRING72-304
   J. MIRSKY, 561(SATR):4MAR72-86
   R. STEEL, 440:9APR72-1
   617(TLS):24MAR72-324
SOLOTAROFF, T. - SEE "NEW AMERICAN REVIEW
   NUMBER 13."
SOLOUKHIN, V. SEARCHING FOR ICONS IN
   RUSSIA.
   C. ELLIOT, 441:16APR72-26
   617(TLS):31MAR72-368
SOLOUKHIN, V. WHITE GRASS.
   617(TLS):5MAY72-526
SOLOV'EV, V.S. STIXOTVORENIJA I ŠUTOČNYE
   P'ESY.
   J. BAILEY, 574(SEEJ):WINTER71-505
SOLOW, R.L. THE LAND QUESTION AND THE
   IRISH ECONOMY 1870-1903.
   617(TLS):16JUN72-692
SOLT, M.E., ED. CONCRETE POETRY.
   639(VQR):SUMMER70-XCV
SOLTÉSZ, E. - SEE "BIBLIA PAUPERUM"
SOLZHENITSYN, A. AUGUST 1914.* (RUSSIAN
   TITLE: AVGUST CHETYRNADTSATOGO.)
   J. BAYLEY, 362:21SEP72-373
   N. BLIVEN, 442(NY):14OCT72-178
   K. FITZLYON, 364:DEC71/JAN72-139
   S. KARLINSKY, 441:10SEP72-1
   C. LEHMANN-HAUPT, 441:6SEP72-47
   M. MC CARTHY, 561(SATR):16SEP72-79
   P. RAHV, 453:5OCT72-13
   617(TLS):22SEP72-1086
SOLZHENITSYN, A. CANCER WARD. (PT 2)
   (N. BETHELL & D. BURG, TRANS)
   R.D., 619(TC):1968/4&1969/1-92
SOLZHENITSYN, A. THE FIRST CIRCLE.*
   (RUSSIAN TITLE: V KRUGE PERVOM. FRENCH
   TITLE: LE PREMIER CERCLE.)
   F. GALICHET, 98:JUL69-624
SOLZHENITSYN, A. FOR THE GOOD OF THE
   CAUSE.*
   W.H. PRITCHARD, 249(HUDR):SUMMER71-
   362
SOLZHENITSYN, A. THE LOVE GIRL AND THE
   INNOCENT.
   L.M. TIKOS, 418(MR):SPRING71-353
SOLZHENITSYN, A. "ONE WORD OF TRUTH..."
   617(TLS):10NOV72-1369
SOMERS, H.H. ANALYSE STATISTIQUE DU
   STYLE. (VOL 2)
   P. FLOBERT, 555:VOL44FASC1-145

SOMERVILLE, J.M. TOTAL COMMITMENT.
J. MACQUARRIE, 613:SPRING69-144
B.A. NACHBAHR, 258:SEP69-464
SOMFAI, L. JOSEPH HAYDN: HIS LIFE IN
CONTEMPORARY PICTURES.*
S. SADIE, 415:MAR70-278
412:FEB71-73
SOMLYÓ, G., ED. ARION.
P. DEBRECZENY, 32:MAR71-216
SOMMER, R. HOMAGE TO MR. MACMULLIN.
M. HORNYANSKY, 627(UTQ):JUL70-332
SOMMERS, J. AFTER THE STORM.*
L. LEAL, 240(HR):JUL70-338
L. LEAL, 50(ARQ):SUMMER69-169
SONDEREGGER, S. - SEE HEUSLER, A.
SONDHI, M.L. NON APPEASEMENT.
617(TLS):3MAR72-258
SONG UK. A CRITICAL ANALYSIS OF POETRY.
270:VOL20#4-94
"THE SONG OF ROLAND." (D.D.R. OWEN,
TRANS)
617(TLS):11AUG72-954
SONNECK, O.G.T. "THE STAR SPANGLED
BANNER."
H. KOSOK, 447(N&Q):MAY70-198
SONNINO, L.A. A HANDBOOK TO SIXTEENTH
CENTURY RHETORIC.
K. COCHRANE, 541(RES):MAY70-247
B. VICKERS, 148:WINTER70-382
SONTAG, F. THE EXISTENTIALIST PROLEGO-
MENA.
J.M. HEMS, 484(PPR):DEC69-308
SONTHEIMER, K. DEUTSCHLAND ZWISCHEN DEM-
OKRATIE UND ANTIDEMOKRATIE.
617(TLS):18AUG72-960
SONTHEIMER, K. DAS POLITISCHE SYSTEM
GROSSBRITANNIENS.
617(TLS):12MAY72-535
SOONS, A. FICCIÓN Y COMEDIA EN EL SIGLO
DE ORO.*
A.K.G. PATERSON, 402(MLR):JUL71-697
SOPHOCLES. PHILOCTETES. (T.B.L. WEB-
STER, ED)
A.S. HENRY, 67:MAY71-63
A.C. SCHLESINGER, 124:DEC70-121
SOPHOCLES. SOPHOKLES: "ANTIGONE."* (G.
MÜLLER, ED)
H. FLASHAR, 490:OCT68-558
SORDI, M. ROMA E I SANNITI NEL IV
SECOLO A.C.
E.T. SALMON, 487:AUTUMN70-278
SORELIUS, G. THE GIANT RACE BEFORE THE
FLOOD.
W. KLUGE, 38:BAND87HEFT2-265
SORELL, W. FACETS OF COMEDY.
442(NY):16SEP72-126
SORELL, W. HANYA HOLM.
S.J. COHEN, 151:JUL69-65
J. DE LABAN, 290(JAAC):SUMMER70-557
SORELL, W. THE SWISS.
F. BONDY, 441:19NOV72-67
SORIANO, M. LES CONTES DE PERRAULT,
CULTURE SAVANTE ET TRADITIONS POPU-
LAIRES.
J. BARCHILON, 207(FR):OCT69-188
J. BELLEMIN-NOËL, 98:MAR69-250
SOROKIN, J.S. RAZVITIE SLOVARNOGO
SOSTAVA RUSSKOGO LITERATURNOGO JAZYKA
30-90YX GODOV XIX VEKA.
B. BILOKUR, 574(SEEJ):SUMMER71-243
SORRELL, A. ROMAN LONDON.*
A.R. BURN, 123:DEC70-383
SORRENTINO, G. IMAGINATIVE QUALITIES OF
ACTUAL THINGS.*
L. GRAVER, 441:2JUL72-6
SŌSEKI, N. GRASS ON THE WAYSIDE.
639(VQR):SPRING70-LXVI

SŌSEKI, N. I AM A CAT.* [SHOWN IN PREV
UNDER NATSUME SŌSEKI]
442(NY):19AUG72-80
SŌSEKI, N. MON.
617(TLS):7APR72-385
SŌSEKI, N. THE WAYFARER.* [SHOWN IN
PREV UNDER NATSUME SŌSEKI]
E. MC CLELLAN, 318(JAOS):APR-JUN70-
383
C.F.S., 502(PRS):WINTER68/69-363
SOTO, O.N. REPASO DE GRAMÁTICA.
G. FRANKS, 238:SEP70-589
SOTO, O.N. & C.D. MC VICKER - SEE ARCIN-
IEGAS, G.
SOTTOMAYOR, A.P.Q.F. - SEE AESCHYLUS
SOUBIRAN, J. - SEE VITRUVIUS
SOUCHAL, F. LES SLODTZ.*
T. HODGKINSON, 90:MAR69-159
SOUČKOVÁ, M. A LITERARY SATELLITE.
M. BERMAN, 574(SEEJ):FALL71-390
S.E. MANN, 575(SEER):JUL71-467
"SOURCES OF LOCAL HISTORY." (4TH ED)
617(TLS):19MAY72-584
DE SOUSA, F. - SEE DOMINGOS BONTEMPO, J.
DE SOUSA CARVALHO, J. L'AMORE INDUSTRI-
OSO; ABERTURA. (F. DE SOUSA, ED)
R. STEVENSON, 414(MQ):JAN68-111
SOUSTER, R. LOST AND FOUND.*
H. MAC CALLUM, 627(UTQ):JUL69-342
SOUSTER, R. SO FAR, SO GOOD.
M. DOYLE, 491:MAR72-356
M. HORNYANSKY, 627(UTQ):JUL70-331
150(DR):AUTUMN70-427
SOUSTER, R. THE YEARS.
R. GIBBS, 198:SUMMER72-129
SOUSTER, R. & J.R. COLOMBO - SEE ROSS,
W.W.E.
SOUTHAM, B.C., ED. JANE AUSTEN: THE
CRITICAL HERITAGE.*
J.E.J., 191(ELN):SEP70(SUPP)-20
SOUTHAM, B.C., ED. CRITICAL ESSAYS ON
JANE AUSTEN.
J.E.J., 191(ELN):SEP70(SUPP)-19
B.G. MAC CARTHY, 541(RES):NOV70-512
SOUTHERN, R.W. & F.S. SCHMITT, EDS. MEM-
ORIALS OF SAINT ANSELM.*
M.L. COLKER, 589:APR71-396
"SOVIET UKRAINE."
J. BORYS, 104:SUMMER71-295
SOYER, R. SELF-REVEALMENT.
W.D. ALLEN, 58:DEC69/JAN70-10
SOYINKA, W. IDANRE AND OTHER POEMS.*
J. SMITH, 493:SPRING70-89
SOYINKA, W. THE INTERPRETERS.
T. LASK, 441:11AUG72-32
SOYINKA, W. MADMEN AND SPECIALISTS.*
C.R. LARSON, 441:24DEC72-6
SOYINKA, W. THE MAN DIED.
F. WYNDHAM, 362:23NOV72-716
SPAAK, P-H. THE CONTINUING BATTLE.
442(NY):19FEB72-116
SPACKS, B. ORPHANS.
M. LEVIN, 441:14MAY72-36
SPAE, J.J. CHRISTIANITY ENCOUNTERS
JAPAN.
J.F. HOWES, 293(JAST):NOV69-174
SPAETHLING, R. & E. WEBER, EDS. A
READER IN GERMAN LITERATURE.
W. HOFFMEISTER, 221(GQ):JAN70-137
SPAGIS, A.A. PARNYE I NEPARNYE GLAGOLY
V RUSSKOM JAZYKE.
J. FERRELL, 574(SEEJ):SPRING71-95
SPALDING, K. - SEE VON GOETHE, J.W.
SPALEK, J.M. ERNST TOLLER AND HIS
CRITICS.
C. HILL, 221(GQ):JAN70-124
C. ZIEGLER, 397(MD):FEB70-430

SPALTER, M. BRECHT'S TRADITION.*
  G.E. WELLWARTH, 397(MD):FEB68-437
SPANIER, D. EUROPE, OUR EUROPE.
  617(TLS):28JUL72-861
SPANIER, J. GAMES NATIONS PLAY.
  617(TLS):12MAY72-535
SPANOS, W.V. THE CHRISTIAN TRADITION IN
MODERN BRITISH VERSE DRAMA.
  SISTER M. CLEOPHAS, 613:AUTUMN68-446
SPARK, M. COLLECTED STORIES I.
  G. GREENE, 340(KR):1969/2-267
SPARK, M. THE DRIVER'S SEAT.*
  P. CRUTTWELL, 249(HUDR):SPRING71-177
  F.P.W. MC DOWELL, 659:SUMMER72-361
SPARK, M. NOT TO DISTURB.*
  P. ADAMS, 61:APR72-128
  A. BROYARD, 441:29MAR72-45
  E. FEINSTEIN, 364:FEB/MAR72-177
  J.R. FRAKES, 440:16APR72-4
  H. FRANKEL, 561(SATR):8APR72-74
  L. GRAVER, 441:26MAR72-6
  F. KERMODE, 61:JUL72-86
  K. MILLER, 453:20APR72-19
SPARROW, J. VISIBLE WORDS.*
  C. RICKS, 184(EIC):APR70-259
SPARSHOTT, F. A CARDBOARD GARAGE.*
  M. HORNYANSKY, 627(UTQ):JUL70-337
  150(DR):AUTUMN70-424
SPARSHOTT, F.E. THE CONCEPT OF CRITI-
CISM.
  W.H. CLARK, JR., 290(JAAC):SPRING70-
   393
  M. WEITZ, 627(UTQ):JUL69-414
SPASOV, B. & A. ANGELOV. DŬRZHAVNO
PRAVO NA NARODNA REPUBLIKA BŬLGARIIA.
(2ND ED)
  I. SIPKOV, 32:MAR71-192
SPATH, T. DAS MOTIV DER DOPPELTEN
BELEUCHTUNG BEI HERODOT.
  H.C. AVERY, 24:APR71-357
  N.G.L. HAMMOND, 123:MAR71-126
  E. WILL, 555:VOL44FASC1-126
SPÄTH, U. GEBROCHENE IDENTITÄT.
  J.M. MC GLATHERY, 406:SPRING71-85
SPATZ, J. HOLLYWOOD IN FICTION.*
  D. GALLOWAY, 27(AL):NOV71-498
SPEAIGHT, R. THE LIFE OF TEILHARD DE
CHARDIN.
  R.J. O'CONNELL, 613:AUTUMN68-455
SPEAIGHT, R. VANIER.
  A.R.M. LOWER, 529(QQ):WINTER70-637
SPEAIGHT, R. - SEE BRIDGES-ADAMS, W.
SPEAK, H. & J. FORRESTER. OLD WAKEFIELD
IN PHOTOGRAPHS.
  617(TLS):24NOV72-1441
SPEAR, A.T. RODIN SCULPTURE IN THE
CLEVELAND MUSEUM OF ART.
  A. ELSEN, 90:MAR69-161
SPEARS, M.K. DIONYSUS AND THE CITY.
  L.S. DEMBO, 27(AL):MAY71-308
  E. ENGELBERG, 579(SAQ):AUTUMN71-609
  L. FEDER, 385(MQR):SPRING72-138
SPECHT, E.K. THE FOUNDATIONS OF WITT-
GENSTEIN'S LATER PHILOSOPHY.
  J. BURNHEIM, 63:MAY71-119
SPECHT, R. COMMERCIUM MENTIS ET COR-
PORIS.
  G. TONELLI, 319:JAN72-89
SPECK, W.A. TORY AND WHIG.
  C. ROBBINS, 566:AUTUMN70-23
SPEER, D.G. & M.B. A LA BELLE ÉTOILE.
  W. STAAKS, 207(FR):MAY70-949
SPELLMAN, D. & S. VICTORIAN MUSIC
COVERS.
  M. VICINUS, 637(VS):JUN70-433
  592:NOV69-199

SPENCE, J.D. TS'AO YIN AND THE K'ANG-HSI
EMPEROR, BONDSERVANT AND MASTER.
  E-T.Z. SUN, 318(JAOS):APR-JUN70-381
SPENCER, C., ED. FIVE RESTORATION ADAP-
TATIONS OF SHAKESPEARE.*
  J.H. WILSON, 570(SQ):SPRING68-181
SPENCER, E. THE SNARE.
  M. JONES, 441:17DEC72-6
SPENCER, H., ED. THE PENROSE GRAPHIC
ARTS INTERNATIONAL ANNUAL 65, 1972.
  617(TLS):12MAY72-556
SPENCER, J.R. LEON BATTISTA ALBERTI: ON
PAINTING.
  S.Y. EDGERTON, JR., 54:DEC69-397
SPENCER, M.C. THE ART CRITICISM OF
THÉOPHILE GAUTIER.*
  P. COURTHION, 546(RR):DEC70-311
SPENCER, R. THE AESTHETIC MOVEMENT.
  617(TLS):13OCT72-1218
SPENCER, T.J.B. - SEE SHAKESPEARE, W.
SPENCER, T.J.B. & S.M. WELLS - SEE "A
BOOK OF MASQUES"
SPENDER, S. THE GENEROUS DAYS.*
  J. FULLER, 362:24FEB72-251
  R. FULLER, 364:FEB/MAR72-145
SPENSER, E. A VIEW OF THE PRESENT STATE
OF IRELAND. (W.L. RENWICK, ED)
  J.C. BECKETT, 402(MLR):JUL71-658
SPERATTI-PIÑERO, E.S. DE "SONATA DE
OTOÑO" AL ESPERPENTO (ASPECTOS DEL
ARTE DE VALLE-INCLÁN).
  H.L. BOUDREAU, 238:MAY70-338
  R. WHITTREDGE, 241:MAY71-76
SPERLING, J.B. THE HUMAN DIMENSION OF
TECHNICAL ASSISTANCE.
  S.K. KHINDUKA, 293(JAST):AUG70-960
SPERONI, C. THE APHORISMS OF ORAZIO
RINALDI, ROBERT GREENE, AND LUCAS
GRACIAN DANTISCO.
  S. GAROFALO, 276:AUTUMN70-323
SPERONI, C. & C.L. GOLINO. PANORAMA
ITALIANO. (REV)
  W.E. LEPARULO, 276:AUTUMN70-331
SPETTIGUE, D.O. FREDERICK PHILIP GROVE.*
  D. CAMERON, 529(QQ):SUMMER70-282
  S.E. MC MULLIN, 150(DR):SUMMER70-291
SPEVACK, M. A COMPLETE AND SYSTEMATIC
CONCORDANCE TO THE WORKS OF SHAKE-
SPEARE. (VOL 1)
  N.E. ENKVIST, 597(SN):VOL41#1-184
  J.G. MC MANAWAY, 570(SQ):AUTUMN68-393
SPIES, W. SCULPTURE BY PICASSO.
  D.L. SHIREY, 441:10DEC72-47
SPIES, W. VICTOR VASARELY.*
  P. ADAMS, 61:MAY72-112
SPILLANE, M. THE ERECTION SET.
  N. CALLENDAR, 441:27FEB72-50
  H. FRANKEL, 561(SATR):25MAR72-104
SPILLANE, M. ME, HOOD!
  42(AR):SPRING69-110
SPILLEBOUT, G. LE VOCABULAIRE BIBLIQUE
DANS LES TRAGÉDIES SACRÉES DE RACINE.
  H.T. BARNWELL, 208(FS):APR71-198
SPILLER, R.E. - SEE BROOKS, V.W. & L.
MUMFORD
SPINELLA, M. SORELLA H, LIBERA NOS.
  G.P. BIASIN, 275(IQ):FALL69-87
SPINK, I. AN HISTORICAL APPROACH TO
MUSICAL FORM.
  R. JACKSON, 308:WINTER68-309
SPINK, R. HANS CHRISTIAN ANDERSEN AND
HIS WORLD.
  617(TLS):11AUG72-946
SPINK, W. AJANTA TO ELLORA.
  S. KRAMRISCH, 57:VOL31#4-327
SPINOZA, B. PHILOSOPHIE ET POLITIQUE.
(L. GUILLERMIT, ED)
  S. ZAC, 542:JUL-DEC69-458

SPIRO, G. - SEE DAVIS, D., C. WILMER &
R. WELLS
SPIRO, H.J. THE DIALECTIC OF REPRESEN-
TATION, 1619 TO 1969.
J.C. RAINBOLT, 656(WMQ):APR70-334
SPIRO, M.E. BUDDHISM AND SOCIETY.*
617(TLS):10MAR72-283
SPITERIS, T. GREEK AND ETRUSCAN PAINT-
ING.
G. SCAGLIA, 124:OCT70-61
SPIVAK, T. THE BRIDE WORE THE TRADITION-
AL GOLD.
S. BLACKBURN, 440:9APR72-8
A. BROYARD, 441:24APR72-37
J. HARRISON, 441:14MAY72-4
P. WOOD, 561(SATR):10JUN72-68
442(NY):20MAY72-138
SPOCZYNSKA, J.O.I. FOSSILS.
617(TLS):7JAN72-17
SPOERRI, D. THE MYTHOLOGICAL TRAVELS...
S. FRANK, 58:SUMMER70-14
"LOUIS SPOHR'S AUTOBIOGRAPHY."
412:FEB71-81
SPONGANO, R., ED. STUDI E PROBLEMI DI
CRITICA TESTUALE.
L.J. FRIEDMAN, 545(RPH):AUG69-114
SPOO, E., ED. DIE TABUS DER BUNDES-
DEUTSCHEN PRESSE.
617(TLS):26MAY72-596
SPRAGUE, A.C. THE DOUBLING OF PARTS IN
SHAKESPEARE'S PLAYS.
L.F. BALL, 570(SQ):AUTUMN69-478
SPRAGUE, R.K. PLATO'S USE OF FALLACY.
C. VINCENT, 542:APR-JUN68-291
"SPRÅK I NORDEN 1970." (A. HAMBURGER, A.
SUDMANN & B. MOLDE, EDS)
E. HAUGEN, 563(SS):SUMMER71-290
SPREIREGEN, P.D. - SEE PEETS, E.
SPRIGGE, T.L.S. - SEE BENTHAM, J.
SPRING, G.M. MAN'S INVINCIBLE SURMISE.
P. DUBOIS, 542:JUL-DEC69-493
SPRING, J.H. EDUCATION AND THE RISE OF
THE CORPORATE STATE.
441:1OCT72-38
SPRINGER, A. VON BERLIN AUS GESCHEN.
(H. WALLENBERG, ED)
617(TLS):26MAY72-596
SPRISSLER, M. DAS RHYTHMISCHE GEDICHT
"PATER DEUS INGENITE" (11. JH.) UND DAS
ALTFRANZÖSISCHE ALEXIUSLIED.
K.D. UITTI, 545(RPH):AUG70-128
SPROCKEL, C. THE LANGUAGE OF THE PARKER
CHRONICLE. (VOL 1)
P. MERTENS-FONCK, 179(ES):OCT70-442
SPRUTE, J. DER BEGRIFF DER DOXA IN DER
PLATONISCHEN PHILOSOPHIE.
P.M. HUBY, 123:MAR71-127
SPULER, B. HISTORY OF THE MONGOLS.
617(TLS):28JUL72-887
SPURLIN, P.M. ROUSSEAU IN AMERICA.
W.H. BLANCHARD, 385(MQR):SUMMER72-221
V. BURANELLI, 656(WMQ):APR70-330
C.R. METZGER, 173(ECS):SPRING70-412
SPYER, G. ARCHITECT AND COMMUNITY.
617(TLS):14APR72-415
SQUIRE, P.S. THE THIRD DEPARTMENT.
T. EMMONS, 550(RUSR):APR70-217
SQUIRES, R. THE LIGHT UNDER ISLANDS.*
R. MORAN, 598(SOR):WINTER72-243
S.G. RADHUBER, 448:SUMMER68-110
SQUIRES, R. ALLEN TATE.*
M.E. BRADFORD, 27(AL):NOV71-480
"SRI PADUKA: THE EXILE OF THE PRINCE OF
AYODHYA." (S.M. PONNIAH, TRANS)
S. VAIDYANATHAN, 293(JAST):FEB70-506
SRZEDNICKI, J.T.J. FRANZ BRENTANO'S
ANALYSIS OF TRUTH.
J. FOSTER, 393(MIND):OCT70-627

STAAL, J.F. WORD ORDER IN SANSKRIT AND
UNIVERSAL GRAMMAR.*
W.H. MAURER, 485(PE&W):APR69-202
STAAR, R.F., ED. YEARBOOK ON INTERNA-
TIONAL COMMUNIST AFFAIRS, 1969.
B.S. MORRIS, 32:SEP71-678
STABB, M.S. AMÉRICA LATINA EN BUSCA DE
UNA IDENTIDAD.
M.W. NICHOLS, 263:APR-JUN71-200
STABB, M.S. JORGE LUIS BORGES.
C.L. CHUA, 651(WHR):SPRING71-179
STACEY, C.P., ED. HISTORICAL DOCUMENTS
OF CANADA. (VOL 5)
J.L. GRANATSTEIN, 99:SEP72-16
STACHIW, M. & J. SZENDERA. WESTERN
UKRAINE AT THE TURNING POINT OF EUR-
OPE'S HISTORY, 1918-1923. (VOL 1)
O. GERUS, 104:WINTER71-571
STACK, E.M. WORKBOOK FOR "LE PONT NEUF."
E.S. SILBER, 207(FR):APR70-863
STACK, G.J. BERKELEY'S ANALYSIS OF PER-
CEPTION.
H.M. BRACKEN, 319:OCT72-480
STADTFELD, C.K. FROM THE LAND AND BACK.
561(SATR):25NOV72-74
STAEBLER, E. CAPE BRETON HARBOUR.
G. NOONAN, 99:JUL-AUG72-43
"MADAME DE STAËL ET L'EUROPE."
A. FAIRLIE, 208(FS):JAN71-93
MADAME DE STAËL & P-S. DU PONT DE NE-
MOURS. CORRESPONDENCE OF MADAME DE
STAËL AND PIERRE-SAMUEL DU PONT DE
NEMOURS AND OF OTHER MEMBERS OF THE
NECKER AND DU PONT FAMILIES. (J.F.
MARSHALL, ED & TRANS)
N. KING, 208(FS):JAN71-95
STAFFORD, D. FROM ANARCHISM TO REFORM-
ISM.*
102(CANL):AUTUMN71-101
STAFFORD, J. THE COLLECTED STORIES OF
JEAN STAFFORD.
42(AR):SPRING69-109
STAFFORD, P. PSYCHEDELIC BABY REACHES
PUBERTY.
617(TLS):1SEP72-1012
STAFFORD, W. ALLEGIANCES.*
L.L. MARTZ, 676(YR):SPRING71-403
STAFFORD, W.T., ED. PERSPECTIVES ON
JAMES'S "THE PORTRAIT OF A LADY."
R. LEHAN, 445(NCF):JUN68-117
STAFLEU, F.A. LINNAEUS AND THE LINNAE-
ANS.
617(TLS):31MAR72-371
STAGG, J.M. FORECAST FOR OVERLORD.
E. WEEKS, 61:OCT72-133
441:1OCT72-38
617(TLS):25FEB72-229
STAHL, H-P. THUKYDIDES: DIE STELLUNG DES
MENSCHEN IM GESCHICHTLICHEN PROZESS.
M.F. MC GREGOR, 24:OCT71-757
STAHLBERGER, P. DER ZÜRCHER VERLEGER
EMIL OPRECHT UND DIE DEUTSCHE POLI-
TISCHE EMIGRATION 1933-1945.
617(TLS):10MAR72-267
STAINTON, J.D.A. FORESTS OF NEPAL.
617(TLS):22DEC72-1566
STALEY, T.F. & B. BENSTOCK, EDS. AP-
PROACHES TO ULYSSES.
N. HALPER, 329(JJQ):FALL71-161
R.S. ZELENKA, 584(SWR):SUMMER71-286
STALIN, I.V. WORKS (SOCHINENIYA). (R.H.
MC NEAL, ED)
T.H. RIGBY, 587:JUL69-100
STALLARD, J. FOUR IN A WILD PLACE.
A. BROYARD, 441:7JUL72-33
STALLKNECHT, P. & H. FRENZ, EDS. COMPAR-
ATIVE LITERATURE.
C. DE DEUGD, 179(ES):APR70-171

STALLMAN, R.W. STEPHEN CRANE.*
   R.E. PECK, 219(GAR):SPRING69-105
   B.D.S., 502(PRS):SPRING69-140
   E. SOLOMON, 445(NCF):MAR69-485
STALLMAN, R.W. - SEE CRANE, S.
STALLWORTH, A.N. THIS TIME NEXT YEAR.
   A.C. FOOTE, 440:28MAY72-8
STALLWORTHY, J. VISION AND REVISION IN
YEATS'S "LAST POEMS."
   C. BRADFORD, 401(MLQ):MAR70-133
   A.N. JEFFARES, 541(RES):NOV70-532
STAMATIS, E.S. PROSŌKRATIKOI PHILOSO-
PHOI.
   J.S. MORRISON, 123:JUN71-292
STAMM, J.R. A SHORT HISTORY OF SPANISH
LITERATURE.
   D.M., 477:SPRING69-302
STAMM, R. THE SHAPING POWERS AT WORK.
   C.G. MASINTON, 397(MD):SEP69-212
   N.C. DE NAGY, 72:BAND208HEFT1-62
STAMMLER, H.A. - SEE ODOJEWSKIJ, W.F.
STAMPFER, J. JOHN DONNE AND THE META-
PHYSICAL GESTURE.*
   J. BENNETT, 402(MLR):APR71-390
   J.T. SHAWCROSS, 301(JEGP):APR71-301
STAMPP, K.M. & L.F. LITWACK, EDS. RECON-
STRUCTION.
   639(VQR):SUMMER70-CVIII
"THE STANBROOK ABBEY PRESS."
   617(TLS):28JAN72-108
STANDEN, M. THE DREAMLAND TREE.
   D.A.N. JONES, 362:10AUG72-184
   617(TLS):21JUL72-851
STANFORD, A. THE WEATHERCOCK.
   W. ANDERSON, 502(PRS):WINTER68/69-358
STANFORD, A. - SEE "THE BHAGAVAD GITA"
STANFORD, W.B. THE SOUND OF GREEK.*
   V. LEINIEKS, 121(CJ):FEB-MAR71-267
STANFORD, W.B. THE ULYSSES THEME.*
   L.H. PEER, 219(GAR):FALL69-422
STANFORTH, D. & M. STAMM. BUYING AND
RENOVATING A HOUSE IN THE CITY.
   B. GLADSTONE, 441:3DEC72-97
STANG, F. DIE INDISCHEN STAHLWERKE UND
IHRE STÄDTE.
   J. COMTE, 182:VOL23#10-573
STANGOS, N. - SEE BERGER, J.
STANISHEVA, L. & S. SHOPOVA, COMPS. BIB-
LIOGRAFIIA NA DISERTATSIITE, ZASHTITENI
V BŬLGARIIA, 1929-1964.
   M. PUNDEFF, 32:SEP71-710
STANISLAWSKI, D. LANDSCAPES OF BACCHUS.
   639(VQR):SUMMER70-CXVI
STANKIEWICZ, E. - SEE BAUDOUIN DE COURTE-
NAY
STANKIEWICZ, E. & D.S. WORTH. A SELECTED
BIBLIOGRAPHY OF SLAVIC LINGUISTICS.
(VOL 1)
   H. KUČERA, 361:VOL23#4-402
STANLEY, G.F.G. NEW FRANCE: THE LAST
PHASE, 1744-1760.*
   R. ROBIDOUX, 208(FS):OCT71-497
STANLEY, G.F.G. A SHORT HISTORY OF THE
CANADIAN CONSTITUTION.
   J.A. CORRY, 529(QQ):SUMMER70-279
STANSKY, P. - SEE MORLEY, J.
STANSKY, P. & W. ABRAHAMS. THE UNKNOWN
ORWELL.
   A. BROYARD, 441:10NOV72-39
   J. CAREY, 362:26OCT72-552
   R. JELLINEK, 441:12NOV72-7
   M. MADDOCKS, 61:NOV72-122
   V.S. PRITCHETT, 561(SATR):4NOV72-71
   S. SPENDER, 453:16NOV72-3
   617(TLS):20OCT72-1253
STANTON, P. PUGIN.
   J. EMERSON, 362:24AUG72-249
   617(TLS):14JAN72-42

STANTON, P.B. THE GOTHIC REVIVAL AND
AMERICAN CHURCH ARCHITECTURE.
   J.M. CROOK, 46:NOV69-404
   E.M. UPJOHN, 576:DEC69-307
   G.L. WRENN 3D, 505:JUL69-150
STANWOOD, P.G., WITH D. O'CONNOR - SEE
COSIN, J.
VAN DER STAP, P.A.M. OUTLINE OF DANI
MORPHOLOGY.
   V. KRUPA, 353:SEP69-127
STARES, J. MOLECULES OF LIFE. CELL FORM
AND FUNCTION.
   617(TLS):9JUN72-667
STARIKOV, V.S. MATERIALNAYA KULTURA
KITAITSEV SEVERO-VOSTOCHNYKH PROVINTSII
KNR.
   G. GINSBURGS, 293(JAST):NOV69-166
STARK, R. PLUNDER SQUAD.
   O.L. BAILEY, 561(SATR):25NOV72-70
STARK, T. THE DISTRIBUTION OF PERSONAL
INCOME IN THE UNITED KINGDOM 1949-1963.
   617(TLS):4AUG72-920
STARK, W. THE SOCIOLOGY OF RELIGION.
(VOL 5)
   617(TLS):1SEP72-1026
STARKIE, E. FLAUBERT: THE MASTER.*
   P. ADAMS, 61:JAN72-97
   D. SCHIER, 109:SPRING/SUMMER72-144
   442(NY):1JAN72-64
STARKLOFF, C.F. THE OFFICE OF PROCLAMA-
TION IN THE THEOLOGY OF KARL BARTH.
   K. HAMILTON, 150(DR):AUTUMN70-421
STARKWEATHER, F. TRADITIONAL IGBO ART.
   R. BRAIN, 69:JUL69-314
STAROBIN, H. - SEE LOEBL, E.
STAROBIN, J.R. AMERICAN COMMUNISM IN
CRISIS 1943-1957.
   W.C. MC WILLIAMS, 441:16APR72-2
STAROBIN, R.S. INDUSTRIAL SLAVERY IN THE
OLD SOUTH.
   V.J. VOEGELI, 676(YR):SPRING71-449
STAROBINSKI, J. LES MOTS SOUS LES MOTS.
   617(TLS):21JAN72-67
STAROBINSKI, J. J-J. ROUSSEAU.
   617(TLS):10NOV72-1367
STARR, G.A. - SEE DEFOE, D.
STARRING, C.R. & J.O. KNAUSS. THE MICHI-
GAN SEARCH FOR EDUCATION STANDARDS.
   Q.M. WILSON, 377:MAR71-52
STASHEVSKY, D.N. PROGRESSIVNYE SILY
SSHA V BOR'BE ZA PRIZNANIE SOVETSKOGO
GOSUDARSTVA, 1917-1933.
   R.P. BROWDER, 32:JUN71-400
STASIO, M. BROADWAY'S BEAUTIFUL LOSERS.
   441:24SEP72-52
STASOV, V. SELECTED ESSAYS ON MUSIC.*
   B. SCHWARZ, 414(MQ):OCT69-580
STATHAS, T. - SEE CENTLIVRE, S.
STATIUS, P.P. THEBAIS I-III. (J.B.
POYNTON, TRANS)
   617(TLS):3MAR72-257
STAUB, H. LE CURIEUX DÉSIR.
   M. DASSONVILLE, 546(RR):FEB70-52
STÄUBLE, A. LA COMMEDIA UMANISTICA DEL
QUATTROCENTO.*
   M. DE PANIZZA LORCH, 276:WINTER70-438
   L.V.R., 568(SCN):SPRING71-28
STAVAN, H.A. GABRIEL SÉNAC DE MEILHAN
(1736-1803).
   T.E.D. BRAUN, 207(FR):FEB70-522
STAVELEY, E.S. GREEK AND ROMAN VOTING
AND ELECTIONS.
   617(TLS):14JUL72-797
STAVIG, M. JOHN FORD AND THE TRADITIONAL
MORAL ORDER.
   D.K. ANDERSON, JR., 141:WINTER69-102
   R. GILL, 541(RES):MAY70-204

STAVINS, R., R.J. BARNET & M.G. RASKIN.
WASHINGTON PLANS AN AGRESSIVE WAR.*
617(TLS):21APR72-436
STAVROU, T.G., ED. RUSSIA UNDER THE
LAST TSAR.*
J.F. HUTCHINSON, 104:SPRING71-132
W.B. WALSH, 550(RUSR):JAN70-98
STEAD, C. HOUSE OF ALL NATIONS.
M. WOOD, 453:19OCT72-33
STEADMAN, J.M. MILTON AND THE RENAIS-
SANCE HERO.*
E. MINER, 173(ECS):WINTER69-296
STEADMAN, J.M. MILTON'S EPIC CHARAC-
TERS.*
M. FIXLER, 541(RES):AUG70-358
I.G. MAC CAFFREY, 191(ELN):MAR70-219
J.H. SIMS, 577(SHR):SUMMER70-286
STEARN, G.E. BROKEN IMAGE.
C. EBY, 440:19MAR72-4
STEARN, W.T. - SEE SMITH, A.W.
STEARNS, R.P. SCIENCE IN THE BRITISH
COLONIES OF AMERICA.
617(TLS):7JAN72-3
STECHOW, W. NORTHERN RENAISSANCE ART
1400-1600.
G. MARTIN, 39:MAY69-407
STECHOW, W. RUBENS AND THE CLASSICAL
TRADITION.*
J. AGNEW, 90:APR70-248
STEDMAN, J.W. - SEE GILBERT, W.S.
STEEGMULLER, F. - SEE FLAUBERT, G.
STEEGMULLER, F. STORIES AND TRUE STOR-
IES.
E. JANEWAY, 441:27FEB72-4
617(TLS):6OCT72-1193
STEELE, A.J. - SEE UNDER RAYMOND, M.
STEELE, H.C. - SEE MARTEL, F.
STEENBOCK, F. DIE KIRCHLICHE PRACHTEIN-
BAND IM FRÜHEN MITTELALTER.
P. VERDIER, 589:JAN71-186
STEENSMA, R.C. SIR WILLIAM TEMPLE.
K.G. RASMUSSEN, 651(WHR):AUTUMN71-360
566:SPRING71-72
STEER, F.W., ED. SCRIVENERS' COMPANY
COMMON PAPER 1357-1628.
E. WELCH, 325:6OCT70-151
STEEVENS, G. - SEE UNDER HARDINGE, G.
STEFFAN, T.G. LORD BYRON'S CAIN.
E.E.B., 191(ELN):SEP70(SUPP)-29
STEFFEN, H., ED. DAS DEUTSCHE LUSTSPIEL.
(PT 1)
C.P. MAGILL, 220(GL&L):OCT70-109
STEFFEN, H., ED. DIE DEUTSCHE ROMANTIK.
B.M., 191(ELN):SEP69(SUPP)-97
STEGLICH, W., ED. DER FRIEDENSAPPELL
PAPST BENEDIKTS XV. VOM 1. AUG. 1917
UND DIE MITTELMÄCHTE.
A. WAHL, 182:VOL23#11/12-634
STEGMANN, A. L'HÉROÏSME CORNÉLIEN.
W.L. WILEY, 207(FR):MAY70-938
STEGNER, P. HAWKS AND HARRIERS.
W.C. HAMLIN, 561(SATR):15JAN72-41
T. LASK, 441:22JAN72-31
J. SEELYE, 441:23JAN72-7
442(NY):4MAR72-114
STEIBLE, D.J. CONCISE HANDBOOK OF LIN-
GUISTICS.
R.S. MEYERSTEIN, 545(RPH):AUG69-100
STEIG, W. DOMINIC.
S.G. LANES, 231:OCT72-122
STEIN, A. JOHN DONNE'S LYRICS.
M. EVANS, 179(ES):JUN70-256
STEIN, A. GEORGE HERBERT'S LYRICS.
C.C. BROWN, 541(RES):MAY70-206
L.L. MARTZ, 401(MLQ):JUN70-252
STEIN, D.L. MY SEXUAL AND OTHER REVO-
LUTIONS.
D. GUTTERIDGE, 99:JAN-FEB72-78

STEIN, G. SELECTED OPERAS AND PLAYS OF
GERTRUDE STEIN. (J.M. BRINNIN, ED)
G. BURNS, 584(SWR):WINTER71-100
STEIN, J. - SEE "THE RANDOM HOUSE DIC-
TIONARY OF THE ENGLISH LANGUAGE"
STEIN, J.M. POEM AND MUSIC IN THE
GERMAN LIED FROM GLUCK TO HUGO WOLF.
617(TLS):8DEC72-1513
STEIN, R. MEDIA POWER.
441:15OCT72-40
STEIN, R. MEGALOPREPEIA BEI PLATON.
A.W.H. ADKINS, 123:JUN71-290
STEIN, R.B. JOHN RUSKIN AND AESTHETIC
THOUGHT IN AMERICA, 1840-1900.*
C. KEELER, 290(JAAC):WINTER69-252
B.R.M., 477:SUMMER69-425
K. ROBERTS, 90:OCT70-706
STEIN, S.J. & B.H. THE COLONIAL HERI-
TAGE OF LATIN AMERICA.
639(VQR):SUMMER70-CV
STEIN, W.B. THE POETRY OF MELVILLE'S
LATE YEARS.
N. BAYM, 301(JEGP):JUL71-571
617(TLS):21JAN72-53
STEINBECK, J. JOURNAL OF A NOVEL.
639(VQR):SPRING70-LXVI
STEINBERG, A. DOSTOEVSKY.
R. BEERMANN, 587:JAN69-402
STEINBERG, D.D. & L.A. JAKOBOVITS, EDS.
SEMANTICS.
617(TLS):7JAN72-21
STEINBERG, J., ED. INTRODUCTION TO
RUMANIAN LITERATURE.
D. GRIGORESCU, 32:MAR71-218
STEINBERG, J. - SEE RÜHLE, J.
VON DEN STEINEN, W. HOMO CAELESTIS.
G. LADNER, 589:APR71-402
STEINER, G. EXTRATERRITORIAL.*
J. CULLER, 362:27APR72-557
R. FREEDMAN, 440:2JAN72-9
W.H. PRITCHARD, 249(HUDR):WINTER
71/72-702
617(TLS):19MAY72-567
STEINER, G. IN BLUEBEARD'S CASTLE.*
G. GERSH, 99:SEP72-33
STEINER, Z.S. THE FOREIGN OFFICE AND
FOREIGN POLICY, 1898-1914.
C.R. MIDDLETON, 579(SAQ):WINTER71-113
G. NIEDHART, 182:VOL23#13/14-694
STEINGASS, D. BODY COMPASS.*
R. MORAN, 598(SOR):WINTER72-243
639(VQR):WINTER70-XII
STEINHAGEN, H. DIE STATISCHEN GEDICHTE
VON GOTTFRIED BENN.
R. GRIMM, 301(JEGP):JUL71-516
STEINHOFF, J. THE STRAITS OF MESSINA.
617(TLS):11FEB72-166
STEINICKE, D., ED. QUELLENINDEX ZUR
CUBAKRISE.
D. ALBRECHT, 182:VOL23#6-318
STEINITZ, R., WITH E. LANG. ADVERBIAL-
SYNTAX.
B.J. KOEKKOEK, 399(MLJ):MAR70-199
STEINKRAUS, W.E., ED. NEW STUDIES IN
BERKELEY'S PHILOSOPHY.
D.J.M.B., 543:DEC69-365
E. RONCHETTI, 548(RCSF):JAN/MAR69-112
STEINMETZ, H. DIE TRILOGIE.
A. CLOSS, 402(MLR):JAN71-230
STEINMETZ, P., ED. POLITEIA UND RES
PUBLICA.
F. LASSERRE, 182:VOL23#6-305
STEINMEYER, K-J. UNTERSUCHUNGEN ZUR
ALLEGORISCHEN BEDEUTUNG DER TRÄUME IM
ALTFRANZÖSISCHEN ROLANDSLIED.
J. HORRENT, 545(RPH):MAY70-595

STEINMÜLLER, W. EVANGELISCHE RECHTS-
THEOLOGIE.
G. MAY, 182:VOL23#11/12-595
STEMPEL, I. DEUTSCHLAND IN DER "REVUE
GERMANIQUE" VON DOLLFUS UND NEFFTZER
(1858-65).*
J. HÖSLE, 52:BAND4HEFT1-102
STENDHAL. LIFE OF ROSSINI.* (2ND ED)
(R.N. COE, ED & TRANS)
J.W.K., 410(M&L):APR71-189
STENDHAL. LIVES OF HAYDN, MOZART AND
METASTASIO. (R.N. COE, ED & TRANS)
617(TLS):16JUN72-684
STENDHAL. TRAVELS IN THE SOUTH OF
FRANCE.* (E. ABBOTT, TRANS)
617(TLS):25FEB72-226
STENERSON, D.C. H.L. MENCKEN.*
J. DROST, 70(ANQ):DEC71-62
617(TLS):14JUL72-792
STENSTRÖM, T. EXISTENTIALISMEN.
N. EGEBAK, 462(OL):VOL24#1-77
STENTON, F.M. ANGLO-SAXON ENGLAND.
617(TLS):20OCT72-1255
STENTON, F.M. THE FREE PEASANTRY OF THE
NORTHERN DANELAW.
A.G. DYSON, 325:OCT70-151
STÉNUIT, R. TREASURES OF THE ARMADA.
P. ADAMS, 61:DEC72-146
STENZEL, J. - SEE GLEIM, J.W.L.
STEPANOV, V.I. ALPHABET OF MOVEMENTS OF
THE HUMAN BODY.
J. DE LABAN, 290(JAAC):SUMMER70-556
STEPHAN, B. STUDIEN ZUR RUSSISCHEN
ČASTUŠKA UND IHRER ENTWICKLUNG.
J. BAILEY, 574(SEEJ):SPRING71-82
STEPHAN, J.J. SAKHALIN.
617(TLS):30JUN72-744
STEPHANUS, H. - SEE UNDER ESTIENNE, H.
STEPHEN, G. REMODELING OLD HOUSES
WITHOUT DESTROYING THEIR CHARACTER.
B. GLADSTONE, 441:3DEC72-97
STEPHENS, A. TREE MEDITATION AND OTHERS.
R. LATTIMORE, 249(HUDR):AUTUMN71-502
STEPHENS, E.B. JOHN GOULD FLETCHER.
C. BUSH, 447(N&Q):FEB70-72
STEPHENS, J.E. - SEE AUBREY, J.
STEPHENS, M.G. SEASON AT COOLE.
M. LEVIN, 441:16JUL72-30
STEPHENS, R. NASSER.*
M. COPELAND, 441:21MAY72-2
617(TLS):21JAN72-56
STEPHENS, R.O. HEMINGWAY'S NONFICTION.
D.E.S. MAXWELL, 402(MLR):JUL71-682
STEPHENS, R.W. WALTER DURBIN.
W. GARD, 584(SWR):SPRING71-199
STEPHENSON, B. - SEE ANDERSON, W.J.V. &
D. CROSS
STEPHENSON, G. RUSSIA FROM 1812 TO
1945.*
J.D. CLARKSON, 32:MAR71-143
STEPUN, F. MYSTISCHE WELTSCHAU.
B. NØRRETRANDERS, 462(OL):VOL23#3-250
STERLING, C. & M. SALINGER. FRENCH
PAINTINGS. (VOLS 2&3)
J. ISAACSON, 56:SUMMER69-199
STERLING, D. THE MAKING OF AN AFRO-
AMERICAN.
E. & N. FONER, 453:20APR72-39
STERN, F. THE FAILURE OF ILLIBERALISM.
G. BARRACLOUGH, 453:16NOV72-25
D. SCHOENBAUM, 440:30JAN72-11
L.L. SNYDER, 561(SATR):29JAN72-65
441:6FEB72-40
617(TLS):15SEP72-1055
STERN, G., ED. LESSING YEARBOOK I.
S-A. JØRGENSEN, 301(JEGP):OCT71-722
M.K. TORBRUEGGE, 406:WINTER71-418

STERN, H. L'ART BYZANTIN.
H.L. KESSLER, 56:SPRING69-91
STERN, M. - SEE VON GOETHE, J.W.
STERN, M. - SEE SAILER, S.
STERN, M.R. THE GOLDEN MOMENT.*
R.M. ADAMS, 453:27JAN72-26
H.D. PIPER, 27(AL):NOV71-469
STERN, P.M., WITH H.P. GREEN. THE OPPEN-
HEIMER CASE.*
639(VQR):AUTUMN70-CLII
STERN, R. 1968.*
M. CAVELL, 473(PR):1971/1-117
STERN, R.M. YOU DON'T NEED AN ENEMY.
N. CALLENDAR, 441:30JAN72-24
H. FRANKEL, 561(SATR):26FEB72-71
STERN, S.M. - SEE GOLDZIHER, I.
STERNE, L. A SENTIMENTAL JOURNEY THROUGH
FRANCE AND ITALY BY MR. YORICK. (G.D.
STOUT, JR., ED)
R.F. BRISSENDEN, 405(MP):NOV69-196
STERNE, L. VIAȚA ȘI OPINIUNILE LUI TRIS-
TRAM SHANDY GENTLEMAN. (M. MIROIU &
M. SPĂRIOSU, EDS & TRANS)
A.D., 566:AUTUMN70-7
STETLER, R., ED. PALESTINE.
T. LASK, 441:25AUG72-33
STETTLER, M. BEGEGNUNGEN MIT DEM
MEISTER.
F.G. CRONHEIM, 402(MLR):JUL71-713
STETTLER, P. DAS AUSSENPOLITISCHE
BEWUSSTSEIN IN DER SCHWEIZ (1920-30).
H. KRAMER, 182:VOL23#7-381
VON STEUBEN, H. FRÜHE SAGENDARSTELLUNGEN
IN KORINTH UND ATHEN.
M.L. THOMPSON, 124:JAN71-162
VAN DER STEUR, I. DE LYRISCHE METRA VAN
DE GRIEKSE TRAGEDIE.
L.P.E. PARKER, 123:DEC71-455
STEVENS, J. - SEE CHAMIER, G.
STEVENS, J.R. - SEE KENNEDY, D.
STEVENS, P. A FEW MYTHS.
R. GIBBS, 198:SUMMER72-129
STEVENS, P., ED. THE MC GILL MOVEMENT.
D.O. SPETTIGUE, 529(QQ):WINTER70-638
STEVENS, P. NOTHING BUT SPOONS.*
M. HORNYANSKY, 627(UTQ):JUL70-332
STEVENS, P.A. THE LEICESTER LINE.
617(TLS):1SEP72-1034
STEVENS, R. AMERICAN MEDICINE AND THE
PUBLIC INTEREST.*
E. CRAY, 441:23JAN72-4
STEVENS, W. THE CANNIBAL ISLE.
639(VQR):AUTUMN70-CXXIX
STEVENS, W. THE PALM AT THE END OF THE
MIND.* (H. STEVENS, ED)
G. BURNS, 584(SWR):SUMMER71-295
D. HINE, 491:DEC71-171
STEVENS COX, J. & G., EDS. THE THOMAS
HARDY YEAR BOOK 1971.
617(TLS):7JAN72-16
STEVENS COX, J. & G., EDS. THE THOMAS
HARDY YEAR BOOK 1972-1973.
617(TLS):1DEC72-1469
STEVENSON, A. A GAME OF STATUES.
N. CALLENDAR, 441:25JUN72-30
STEVENSON, A. THE PROBLEM OF THE "MIS-
SALE SPECIALE."
A. SCAGLIONE, 545(RPH):FEB71-551
STEVENSON, A.E. THE PAPERS OF ADLAI E.
STEVENSON. (VOL 1) (W. JOHNSON, WITH
C. EVANS, EDS)
E.E. MORISON, 441:1OCT72-4
STEVENSON, B. MIDDLESEX.
617(TLS):9JUN72-667
STEVENSON, C.A. THE END OF NOWHERE.
453:6APR72-35

STEVENSON, D. THE MEDITATIONS OF SHAKE-
SPEARE.
  E.S. & W.F. FRIEDMAN, 570(SQ):
    SPRING68-185
STEVENSON, F. LLOYD GEORGE: A DIARY.*
(A.J.P. TAYLOR, ED)
  N. ANNAN, 453:10FEB72-22
  R.G. MARTIN, 561(SATR):29JAN72-61
  P. STANSKY, 441:30JAN72-4
  E.M. YODER, JR., 440:30JAN72-8
  442(NY):8JAN72-85
STEVENSON, G.T. THE SOUTHWESTERN LIBRARY
ASSOCIATION PROJECT REPORT.
  A. EASTERLY, 356:OCT71-344
STEVENSON, M. A HISTORY OF COUNTY CRICK-
ET: YORKSHIRE.
  617(TLS):13OCT72-1237
STEVENSON, R. MUSIC IN AZTEC & INCA
TERRITORY.
  G. BÉHAGUE, 414(MQ):JAN69-115
STEVENSON, R. WESTERN MUSIC.
  H. KELLER, 362:16MAR72-348
  617(TLS):4FEB72-131
STEVENSON, V. GARDENING WITH GREEN
FINGERS.
  617(TLS):12MAY72-557
STEVICK, P. THE CHAPTER IN FICTION.
  E.A. BLOOM, 301(JEGP):JUL71-524
STEVICK, R.D., ED. FIVE MIDDLE ENGLISH
NARRATIVES.
  R.M. WILSON, 402(MLR):OCT71-846
STEVICK, R.D. SUPRASEGMENTALS, METER,
AND THE MANUSCRIPT OF "BEOWULF."*
  C.J.E. BALL, 541(RES):NOV70-476
STEWART, A.T.Q. THE PAGODA WAR.
  617(TLS):27OCT72-1281
STEWART, D. THE MIDDLE EAST.
  617(TLS):1DEC72-1447
STEWART, D.H. THE OPPOSITION PRESS OF
THE FEDERALIST PERIOD.
  W.E.A. BERNHARD, 656(WMQ):JUL70-489
  M. KAMMEN, 432(NEQ):JUN70-311
STEWART, F.M. LADY DARLINGTON.
  M. LEVIN, 441:9JAN72-32
STEWART, H. A CHIME OF WINDBELLS.
  M. BROCK, 285(JAPQ):JUL-SEP70-339
STEWART, J. - SEE DELACROIX, E.
STEWART, J.D. GODFREY KNELLER.
  617(TLS):25FEB72-229
STEWART, J.I.M. JOSEPH CONRAD.
  C.T. WATTS, 541(RES):FEB70-101
STEWART, J.I.M. A PALACE OF ART.
  V. CUNNINGHAM, 362:20JUL72-89
  M. LEVIN, 441:10DEC72-58
  617(TLS):4AUG72-909
STEWART, J.M. ACROSS THE RUSSIAS.
  T. SHABAD, 32:DEC71-899
STEWART, K. THE TIMES COOKERY BOOK.
  617(TLS):3NOV72-1349
STEWART, M. (LADY WILSON) ENGLISH
SINGER.*
  A. BLYTH, 415:JUN70-608
STEWART, M. KEYNES AND AFTER. (2ND ED)
  617(TLS):14APR72-413
STEWART, P. IMITATION AND ILLUSION IN
THE FRENCH MEMOIR-NOVEL, 1700-1750.*
  J. HECKMAN, 400(MLN):DEC70-929
STEWART, R. THE POLITICS OF PROTECTION.
  617(TLS):7JAN72-10
STEWART, R. REGIONALISM AND BEYOND.
(G. CORE, ED)
  R.S. MOORE, 219(GAR):SPRING69-85
  L.D. RUBIN, JR., 340(KR):1969/1-135
STEWART, R.G. A NINETEENTH CENTURY
GALLERY OF DISTINGUISHED AMERICANS.
  A.A. DAVIDSON, 127:FALL70-122

STEWART, R.W. JAZZ MASTERS OF THE THIR-
TIES.
  453:9MAR72-34
STEWART, S. BOOK COLLECTING.
  617(TLS):18AUG72-976
STEWART, S. COUNTRY KATE.
  617(TLS):10MAR72-285
STEWART, S. THE EXPANDED VOICE.
  A.L. CLEMENTS, 301(JEGP):JUL71-550
  B. DRAKE, 401(MLQ):DEC70-492
  M.E. ITZKOWITZ, 568(SCN):SPRING71-11
STEWART, W. TRUDEAU IN POWER.
  C. COCKING, 561(SATR):8JAN72-30
  B. MOORE, 440:30JAN72-13
STEWART, Z. - SEE NOCK, A.D.
STEWART-BAXTER, D. MA RAINEY AND THE
CLASSIC BLUES SINGERS.
  W.R. FERRIS, JR., 187:JAN72-132
  M. HARRISON, 415:SEP70-898
STICKNEY, T. THE POEMS OF TRUMBULL
STICKNEY. (A.R. WHITTLE, ED)
  J. HOLLANDER, 441:16JUL72-5
STIEBER, Z., ED. ATLAS JĘZYKOWY KASZUB-
SZCZYZNY I DIALEKTÓW SĄSIEDNICH.
  G. STONE, 575(SEER):JAN71-131
STIEBER, Z. THE PHONOLOGICAL DEVELOPMENT
OF POLISH.*
  Z. GOŁĄB, 104:SPRING71-100
STIEBER, Z. ZARYS GRAMATYKI PORÓWNAW-
CZEJ JĘZYKÓW SŁOWIAŃSKICH: FONOLOGIA.
  H. BIRNBAUM, 574(SEEJ):FALL71-347
STIEHM, L., ED. ADALBERT STIFTER.*
  H.R. KLIENEBERGER, 402(MLR):JAN71-226
STIEHM, L. MAX TAU.
  J. STRELKA, 221(GQ):JAN70-126
STIERLIN, H. LIVING ARCHITECTURE:
ANCIENT MEXICAN.
  J.M.R., 46:OCT69-323
"STIL UND BEDEUTUNG DER LITERATUR DES 18.
JH. IN DER GESCHICHTE DER RUSSISCHEN
KULTUR."
  D. TSCHIŽEWSKIJ, 72:BAND208HEFT4/6-
  466
STILL, C. THIRTY-THREE PAINTINGS IN THE
ALBRIGHT-KNOX ART GALLERY.
  D. HALL, 39:JAN69-81
STILLINGER, J. THE HOODWINKING OF MADE-
LINE.
  617(TLS):30JUN72-741
STILLMAN, D. DECORATIVE WORK OF ROBERT
ADAM.
  S. BLUTMAN, 576:MAR68-92
STILLMAN, E. SKI COUNTRY COOK BOOK.
  N. MAGID, 440:20FEB72-8
STILLWELL, M.B. THE AWAKENING INTEREST
IN SCIENCE DURING THE FIRST CENTURY OF
PRINTING 1450-1550.
  D.D. VOGT, 517(PBSA):APR-JUN71-181
STILLWELL, M.B. THE BEGINNING OF THE
WORLD OF BOOKS 1450-1470.
  617(TLS):29SEP72-1175
STINCHCOMBE, W.C. THE AMERICAN REVOLU-
TION AND THE FRENCH ALLIANCE.
  A.H. BOWMAN, 656(WMQ):APR70-328
  P. GOODMAN, 432(NEQ):JUN70-322
STIRLING, B. THE SHAKESPEARE SONNET
ORDER.
  H. LANDRY, 191(ELN):JUN70-300
  A.P. RIEMER, 67:MAY71-91
STIRNER, M. THE EGO AND HIS OWN.* (J.
CARROLL, ED)
  L.S. STEPELEVICH, 319:APR72-230
STIX, G. TRAKL UND WASSERMANN.
  R. GRIMM, 406:WINTER71-413
  S.S. PRAWER, 220(GL&L):OCT70-101
STOCHHOLM, J.M. GARRICK'S FOLLY.
  L. FOX, 570(SQ):WINTER68-99
STOCK, B. - SEE "MEDIEVAL LATIN LYRICS"

STOCK, N. THE LIFE OF EZRA POUND.*
  W. BENNETT, 493:AUTUMN70-258
  W.M. CHACE, 598(SOR):WINTER72-225
  L.S. DEMBO, 27(AL):MAR71-145
  J. ESPEY, 579(SAQ):SUMMER71-424
STOCK, N. READING THE "CANTOS."
  W.M. CHACE, 598(SOR):WINTER72-225
STÖCKER, C. HUMOR BEI PETRON.
  E. DE SAINT-DENIS, 555:VOL44FASC2-341
STOCKING, M.K., WITH D.M. STOCKING - SEE
CLAIRMONT, C.
STOCKTON, B. PHOENIX WITH A BAYONET.
  G. ANASTAPLO, 561(SATR):12FEB72-79
STOCKTON, D. - SEE CICERO
STOIKO, M. SOVIET ROCKETRY.*
  A. PARRY, 32:JUN71-435
STOKES, A. THE IMAGE IN FORM. (R. WOLL-
HEIM, ED)
  A. FORGE, 362:5OCT72-445
  617(TLS):29SEP72-1150
STOKES, A. REFLECTIONS ON THE NUDE.*
THE INVITATION IN ART.
  P.G. KUNTZ, 290(JAAC):FALL69-103
STOKES, R., ED. ESDAILE'S MANUAL OF
BIBLIOGRAPHY.* (4TH ED)
  G.T. TANSELLE, 354:JUN69-160
STÖKL, G. DAS BILD DES ABENDLANDES IN
DEN ALTRUSSISCHEN CHRONIKEN.
  B. UROFF, 32:MAR71-135
STOLTZFUS, B. GIDE'S EAGLES.
  W.M.L. BELL, 208(FS):APR71-232
STOLZ, F., A. DEBRUNNER & W.P. SCHMID.
STORIA DELLA LINGUA LATINA.
  D.O. ROBSON, 487:AUTUMN70-280
STONE, D., JR. FRANCE IN THE SIXTEENTH
CENTURY.
  H. HORNIK, 399(MLJ):FEB70-134
STONE, D., JR. HANDBOOK FOR FRENCH
COMPOSITION.
  E.H. KADLER, 399(MLJ):MAR70-213
STONE, D.D. NOVELISTS IN A CHANGING
WORLD.
  617(TLS):6OCT72-1198
STONE, E. A CERTAIN MORBIDNESS.
  J.B. COLVERT, 579(SAQ):WINTER71-130
  R.B. NYE, 27(AL):NOV71-499
  639(VQR):WINTER70-XV
"EDWARD DURRELL STONE."
  J.T. BURNS, 505:APR68-222
  A.H. LAPIDUS, 505:APR68-222
STONE, G. THE SMALLEST SLAVONIC NATION.
  617(TLS):5MAY72-512
STONE, H. - SEE DICKENS, C.
STONE, L. THE CAUSES OF THE ENGLISH
REVOLUTION 1529-1642.
  J. DUNN, 362:3AUG72-151
  617(TLS):29SEP72-1137
STONE, P.W.K. THE ART OF POETRY 1750-
1820.
  T.P. LOGAN, 399(MLJ):JAN70-45
STONE, R. HALL OF MIRRORS.
  502(PRS):FALL68-280
STONE, R. TOPOGRAPHY AND OTHER POEMS.*
  P. PETTINGELL, 491:JAN72-234
STONE, R.H. REINHOLD NIEBUHR.
  R. COLES, 442(NY):7OCT72-153
  M. NOVAK, 441:5MAR72-30
STONEHOUSE, B. ANIMALS OF THE ARCTIC.
  617(TLS):14JAN72-45
STONERIDGE, M.A. GREAT HORSES OF OUR
TIME.
  G.F.T. RYALL, 441:3DEC72-30
STOPPARD, T. JUMPERS.
  617(TLS):29DEC72-1569
STOREY, A. PLATINUM JAG.
  V. CUNNINGHAM, 362:9NOV72-643

STOREY, D. PASMORE.
  D. MAY, 362:2NOV72-610
  617(TLS):6OCT72-1184
STOREY, E. A MAN IN WINTER.
  617(TLS):4AUG72-910
STOREY, M. SOFT IN THE MIDDLE.
  N. CALLENDAR, 441:25JUN72-30
STORING, H.F., ED. WHAT COUNTRY HAVE I?
  D.R. NOLAN, 396(MODA):SPRING71-214
STORM, H. SEVEN ARROWS.
  W. BRANDON, 561(SATR):1JUL72-50
  W. KITTREDGE, 231:NOV72-120
STORM, T. & P. HEYSE. BRIEFWECHSEL.*
(C.A. BERND, ED)
  W.A. COUPE, 402(MLR):OCT71-953
STORMBOM, N-B., ED. SUOMENRUOTSALAISEN
LYRIIKAN ANTOLOGIA EDITH SÖDERGRANISTA
BO CARPELANIIN.
  G.C. SCHOOLFIELD, 563(SS):SUMMER71-
311
STORR, A. THE DYNAMICS OF CREATION.
  D.W. HARDING, 453:14DEC72-21
  R. WOLLHEIM, 362:16NOV72-674
  617(TLS):22SEP72-1091
STORR, C. BLACK GOD, WHITE GOD.
  E. MORGAN, 362:20APR72-524
  617(TLS):14APR72-409
STORY, G.M. - SEE ANDREWES, L.
STORY, L. A TERMINUS PLACE.
  617(TLS):29SEP72-1138
STORY, N. THE OXFORD COMPANION TO CAN-
ADIAN HISTORY AND LITERATURE.
  D. GRANT, 179(ES):1969SUPP-XC
STORZ, G. EDUARD MÖRIKE.*
  F.H. MAUTNER, 222(GR):NOV70-300
STOUDT, J.J. JACOB BOEHME.
  J.D.C., 543:DEC69-356
STOUGH, C.L. GREEK SKEPTICISM.
  E.L. MINAR, JR., 124:JAN71-159
  R.K. SPRAGUE, 122:JAN71-75
  Z. STEWART, 24:APR71-376
STOUT, G.D., JR. - SEE STERNE, L.
STOUTENBURG, A. & L.N. BAKER. LISTEN
AMERICA.
  W. WHITE, 646(WWR):DEC68-174
STOVALL, F. EDGAR POE THE POET.*
  639(VQR):WINTER70-XIV
STOVER, R. THE NATURE OF HISTORICAL
THINKING.
  P. GARDINER, 479(PHQ):JUL70-297
STOWELL, R.F. A THOREAU GAZETTEER.
(W.L. HOWARTH, ED)
  639(VQR):AUTUMN70-CLV
STRABO. STRABON, "GÉOGRAPHIE."* (VOL 1)
(G. AUJAC & F. LASSERRE, EDS & TRANS)
  D.R. DICKS, 123:JUN71-188
  É. DES PLACES, 555:VOL44FASC2-330
STRABO. STRABON, "GÉOGRAPHIE." (VOL 3)
(F. LASSERRE, ED & TRANS)
  D.R. DICKS, 123:DEC70-326
STRACHAN, M. & B. PENROSE - SEE KEELING,
W. & T. BONNER
STRACHAN, W.J. THE ARTIST AND THE BOOK
IN FRANCE.*
  J.P. HARTHAN, 90:DEC70-837
  P. JAMES, 39:DEC69-541
  L. LAMB, 592:JUL/AUG69-48
STRACHEY, L. LANDMARKS IN FRENCH LITERA-
TURE.
  W.G. MOORE, 208(FS):JUL71-358
STRACHEY, L. THE REALLY INTERESTING
QUESTION AND OTHER PAPERS. (P. LEVY,
ED)
  Q. BELL, 362:7DEC72-802
  617(TLS):8DEC72-1480
STRAKA, G., ED. TRAVAUX DE LINGUISTIQUE
ET DE LITTÉRATURE.
  P. DELATTRE, 545(RPH):AUG69-92

STRAND, M., ED. THE CONTEMPORARY AMERI-
CAN POETS.
D. ALLEN, 491:NOV71-109
STRAND, M. DARKER.*
L.L. MARTZ, 676(YR):SPRING71-403
J. VERNON, 651(WHR):SPRING71-189
STRAND, M. REASONS FOR MOVING.
J. MC MICHAEL, 598(SOR):WINTER72-213
J. WESTON, 50(ARQ):AUTUMN69-276
STRAND, P. A RETROSPECTIVE MONOGRAPH.
617(TLS):18AUG72-978
STRANG, B.M.H. MODERN ENGLISH STRUCTURE.
(2ND ED)
E. TRAUGOTT, 399(MLJ):OCT70-465
STRANG, G. & L. STEIN - SEE SCHÖNBERG, A.
STRANGER, J. LAKELAND VET.
M. LEVIN, 441:25JUN72-26
VON STRASSBURG, G. - SEE UNDER GOTTFRIED
VON STRASSBURG
STRATFORD, P. MARIE-CLAIRE BLAIS.
I. POLL-WATTS, 296:SUMMER72-80
STRATHERN, A. & M. SELF-DECORATION IN
MOUNT HAGEN.
E.H. GOMBRICH, 453:4MAY72-35
617(TLS):2JUN72-620
STRATHERN, G.M., COMP. NAVIGATIONS,
TRAFFIQUES AND DISCOVERIES, 1774-1848.
102(CANL):WINTER71-106
STRATOS, A.N. BYZANTIUM IN THE SEVENTH
CENTURY.
P. CHARANIS, 589:JUL71-544
STRATTON, A. SINAN.
D. PARK, 440:30JAN72-4
441:20FEB72-25
617(TLS):17NOV72-1389
STRAUS, D. THRESHOLDS.*
617(TLS):10MAR72-272
STRAUS, E.W., M. NATHANSON & H. EY. PSY-
CHIATRY AND PHILOSOPHY. (M. NATHANSON,
ED)
M.B.M., 543:JUN70-755
STRAUSS, E. SOVIET AGRICULTURE IN PER-
SPECTIVE.*
J.P. HARDT, 550(RUSR):APR70-236
STRAUSS, K. DIE KACHELKUNST DES 15. UND
16. JAHRHUNDERTS, IN DEUTSCHLAND,
ÖSTERREICH UND DER SCHWEIZ.
R.J.C., 90:FEB70-118
"RICHARD STRAUSS UND LUDWIG THUILLE:
BRIEFE DER FREUNDSCHAFT, 1877-1907."
(A. OTT, ED)
J.A.W., 410(M&L):APR71-208
STRAVINSKY, I. POETICS OF MUSIC IN THE
FORM OF SIX LESSONS.
G.W. HOPKINS, 415:MAY71-442
412:FEB71-73
STRAVINSKY, I. THEMES AND CONCLUSIONS.
H. KELLER, 362:26OCT72-547
617(TLS):22DEC72-1557
STRAVINSKY, I. & R. CRAFT. DIALOGUES AND
A DIARY.
R. SMALLEY, 607:SUMMER68-39
STRAYER, J.R. THE ALBIGENSIAN CRUSADES.
D. KNOWLES, 441:13FEB72-40
STRAYER, J.R. MEDIEVAL STATECRAFT AND
THE PERSPECTIVES OF HISTORY.
617(TLS):2JUN72-636
STRECH, H. THEODOR FONTANE: DIE SYNTHESE
VON ALT UND NEU.
F.M. SUBIOTTO, 402(MLR):OCT71-955
STREET, J. PRUDENCE DICTATES.
V. CUNNINGHAM, 362:27APR72-564
STREETEN, P. & M. LIPTON, EDS. THE
CRISIS OF INDIAN PLANNING.
E. MUELLER, 293(JAST):MAY70-665
STREHLOW, T.G.H. SONGS OF CENTRAL AUS-
TRALIA.
617(TLS):19MAY72-582

STREIKER, L.D. THE JESUS TRIP.*
D. POLING, 561(SATR):22JUL72-57
STREIKER, L.D. & G.S. STROBER. RELIGION
AND THE NEW MAJORITY.
M.E. MARTY, 441:6AUG72-7
STREKALOVA, Z.N. IZ ISTORII POL'SKOGO
GLAGOL'NOGO VIDA.
H. LEEMING, 575(SEER):JAN71-133
STRELKA, J. BRÜCKE ZU VIELEN UFERN.
K. TOBER, 564:FALL68-162
STRELKA, J., ED. PERSPECTIVES IN LITER-
ARY SYMBOLISM.
S. JOHANSEN, 462(OL):VOL23#3-281
STRELKA, J., ED. PROBLEMS OF LITERARY
EVALUATION.
P. HERNADI, 221(GQ):MAY70-503
J. KILLHAM, 89(BJA):SPRING71-200
STRELKA, J. VERGLEICHENDE LITERATUR-
KRITIK.
R.K. ANGRESS, 406:FALL71-311
STRELLER, S. DAS DRAMATISCHE WERK HEIN-
RICH VON KLEISTS.
J.T., 191(ELN):SEP69(SUPP)-113
STREVENS, P., ED. MODERN LANGUAGES IN
EUROPE. (VOL 4)
I.D. MC FARLANE, 208(FS):JUL71-375
STRIEDTER, J., ED. TEXTE DER RUSSISCHEN
FORMALISTEN.* (VOL 1)
W. ARNDT, 550(RUSR):OCT70-475
STRINDBERG, A. GETTING MARRIED. (M.
SANDBACH, TRANS)
J.G. FARRELL, 362:5OCT72-447
STRINDBERG, A. OPEN LETTERS TO THE INTI-
MATE THEATER. (W. JOHNSON, TRANS)
R.B. VOWLES, 397(MD):SEP67-219
STRINDBERG, A. STRINDBERGS BREV. (VOL
12) (T. EKLUND, ED)
W. JOHNSON, 563(SS):AUTUMN71-453
STROBEL, G.W. QUELLEN ZUR GESCHICHTE
DES KOMMUNISMUS IN POLEN 1878-1918.
L. BLIT, 587:APR69-560
R.F. STARR, 497(POLR):SPRING69-111
STRODACH, G.K. - SEE LUCRETIUS
STROLL, A., ED. EPISTEMOLOGY.
B. AUNE, 482(PHR):JUL70-433
VON STROMER, W. OBERDEUTSCHE HOCHFINANZ
1350-1450.
H.S. OFFLER, 182:VOL23#21/22-953
STROMMENBERG, A.G. A PROPHECY CONCERNING
THE SWEDISH MONARCHY AS IT WAS RELATED
IN 1809 BY ANDERS GABRIEL STROMMENBERG.
D.M. MENNIE, 447(N&Q):FEB70-80
STRONG, J. TIKE.
R.H. BAYES, 50(ARQ):WINTER69-373
STRONG, K. MEN OF INTELLIGENCE.*
441:30JUL72-20
STRONG, R. TUDOR & JACOBEAN PORTRAITS.
THE ENGLISH ICON.
O. MILLAR, 90:MAR70-170
STRONG, R. VAN DYCK: CHARLES I ON
HORSEBACK.
617(TLS):11AUG72-940
STRONG, R. & J.T. OMAN. ELIZABETH R.*
617(TLS):3MAR72-257
STRONG, R. & J.T. OMAN. MARY QUEEN OF
SCOTS.
617(TLS):24NOV72-1441
STROUD, D. GEORGE DANCE.
617(TLS):21APR72-457
STROUD, R.S. DRAKON'S LAW ON HOMICIDE.
D.M. LEWIS, 123:DEC71-390
M.F. MC GREGOR, 124:DEC70-129
STROUP, T.B. MICROCOSMOS.*
M. MINCOFF, 179(ES):FEB70-61
STROUP, T.B. RELIGIOUS RITE & CEREMONY
IN MILTON'S POETRY.*
D.P. HARDING, 551(RENQ):SUMMER70-206

STRUEVER, N.S. THE LANGUAGE OF HISTORY
IN THE RENAISSANCE.
L.V.R., 568(SCN):SPRING71-31
"STRUGGLE FOR JUSTICE."
P.P. HALLIE, 31(ASCH):AUTUMN72-674
J. MITFORD, 453:9MAR72-29
STRUGHOLD, H. YOUR BODY CLOCK.
617(TLS):10NOV72-1377
STRUIK, D.J., ED. A SOURCE BOOK IN
MATHEMATICS, 1200-1800.
J.F. DALY, 377:JUL71-111
STRUNK, G. KUNST UND GLAUBE IN DER
LATEINISCHEN HEILIGENLEGENDE.
D.H. GREEN, 402(MLR):JUL71-705
B. NAUMANN, 382(MAE):1971/3-269
F. WAGNER, 182:VOL23#3-95
STRUNK, W., JR. & E.B. WHITE. THE ELE-
MENTS OF STYLE. (NEW ED)
442(NY):24JUN72-95
STRUVE, G. - SEE VALENTINOV, N.
STRUVE, G.P. & B.A. FILIPPOVA - SEE MAN-
DELSTAM, O.
STRYJKOWSKI, J. THE INN.
M. LEVIN, 441:2APR72-23
617(TLS):10MAR72-265
STRYK, L. THE PIT AND OTHER POEMS.*
T. BLACKBURN, 493:SPRING70-85
STRYK, L. & T. IKEMOTO - SEE TAKAHASHI,
S.
STUART, D. A PARTICULAR PLACE.
R. MORAN, 598(SOR):WINTER72-243
STUART, E. ROCK RUDE.
617(TLS):3MAR72-239
STUART, F. BLACK LIST, SECTION H.
L. DURRELL, 441:9APR72-36
D. FORTUNA, 561(SATR):1JAN72-31
F. KERMODE, 362:23MAR72-382
STUART, J. DAWN OF REMEMBERED SPRING.
M. LEVIN, 441:26MAR72-44
STUART, J., COMP. IZIBONGO.
E.J. KRIGE, 69:APR69-193
STUBBINGS, F.H. PREHISTORIC GREECE.
617(TLS):29DEC72-1590
STUBBINGS, H.U. RENAISSANCE SPAIN IN ITS
LITERARY RELATIONS WITH ENGLAND AND
FRANCE.*
A.O.A., 149:JUN71-192
J.G. FUCILLA, 551(RENQ):WINTER70-450
STUBBS, J. THE HOME BOOK OF ENGLISH
COOKERY.
617(TLS):23JUN72-730
STUCKENSCHMIDT, H.H. FERRUCCIO BUSONI.
H.F., 410(M&L):APR71-202
J.C.G. WATERHOUSE, 415:NOV70-1110
STUCKENSCHMIDT, H.H. MAURICE RAVEL.*
A.E.F. DICKINSON, 607:SUMMER70-37
G.W. HOPKINS, 415:MAR70-277
STUCKENSCHMIDT, H.H. TWENTIETH CENTURY
COMPOSERS.* (VOL 2: GERMANY AND CEN-
TRAL EUROPE.)
P. EVANS, 415:APR71-345
STUCKENSCHMIDT, H.H. TWENTIETH-CENTURY
MUSIC.*
S. WALSH, 607:AUTUMN69-43
C. WHITTENBERG, 308:WINTER69-295
STUCKI, P-A. HERMÉNEUTIQUE ET DIALEC-
TIQUE.
F.F. BRUCE, 182:VOL23#21/22-926
"STUDIA BIBLIOGRAPHICA IN HONOREM HERMAN
DE LA FONTAINE VERWEY, AMSTELODAMI,
KALENDIS NOVEMBRIS MDCCCCLXVI."
A.E.C. SIMONI, 354:SEP69-252
"STUDIA GRAMMATICA." (VOLS 1-7)
B.J. KOEKKOEK, 221(GQ):JAN70-84
"STUDIES IN RENAISSANCE AND BAROQUE ART,
PRESENTED TO ANTHONY BLUNT ON THE
OCCASION OF 60TH BIRTHDAY."
P.P. FEHL, 290(JAAC):FALL69-100

"STUDII DE LITERATURĂ COMPARATĂ." [IN-
STITUTUL DE ISTORIE ŞI TEORIE LITERARĂ
"GEORGE GĂLINESCU"]
R. AUSTERLITZ, 104:SUMMER71-272
STUHLMANN, G. - SEE NIN, A.
STUMPF, S.E. MORALITY AND THE LAW.
D.N. MAC CORMICK, 479(PHQ):JUL70-300
STURM, S. THE LAY OF GUINGAMOR.
L.S. CRIST, 207(FR):OCT69-196
STURROCK, J. THE FRENCH NEW NOVEL.*
S.M. BELL, 208(FS):OCT71-491
J.H. MATTHEWS, 401(MLQ):JUN70-266
L.S. ROUDIEZ, 546(RR):OCT70-238
STUTCHBURY, H.E. THE ARCHITECTURE OF
COLEN CAMPBELL.*
J. COOLIDGE, 576:OCT69-229
"DER STUTTGARTER BILDERPSALTER."
E. KITZINGER, 54:DEC69-393
STUVERAS, R. LE PUTTO DANS L'ART ROMAIN.
K. SCHAUENBURG, 182:VOL23#3-98
R.T. SCOTT, 124:JAN71-171
J.M.C. TOYNBEE, 123:DEC71-465
STYAN, J.L. CHEKHOV IN PERFORMANCE.*
T. EEKMAN, 574(SEEJ):WINTER71-504
STYAN, J.L. THE DARK COMEDY.
F. BUSI, 207(FR):DEC69-360
STYAN, J.L. THE DRAMATIC EXPERIENCE.
A.S. DOWNER, 570(SQ):WINTER68-98
STYAN, J.L. SHAKESPEARE'S STAGECRAFT.
M. TAYLOR, 255(HAB):WINTER69-79
SU-GIL, A. - SEE UNDER AN SU-GIL
SU-YONG, K. - SEE UNDER KIM SU-YONG
SUÁREZ, F. INTRODUCCIÓN A DONOSO CORTÉS.
191(ELN):SEP69(SUPP)-152
SUÁREZ SOLÍS, S. EL LÉXICO DE CAMILO
JOSÉ CELA.
J. ALBERICH, 86(BHS):APR71-174
SUBRAHMANIAN, N. SANGAM POLITY.
R.L. HARDGRAVE, JR., 318(JAOS):APR-
JUN70-411
SUBRAMANIAM, V. SOCIAL BACKGROUND OF
INDIA'S ADMINISTRATORS.
617(TLS):27OCT72-1297
SUCH, P. FALLOUT.*
G. ROPER, 627(UTQ):JUL70-340
SUCHOFF, B. GUIDE TO BARTÓK'S MIKRO-
KOSMOS.
F. DAWES, 415:DEC71-1173
SUCHOFF, B. - SEE BARTÓK, B.
SUCIU, C. DICŢIONAR ISTORIC AL LOCALI-
TĂŢILOR DIN TRANSILVANIA. (VOL 1)
E.P. HAMP, 424:SEP69-237
SUCKLING, J. THE WORKS OF SIR JOHN
SUCKLING: THE NON-DRAMATIC WORKS. (T.
CLAYTON, ED) THE WORKS OF SIR JOHN
SUCKLING: THE PLAYS. (L.A. BEAURLINE,
ED)
617(TLS):2JUN72-634
SUCKSMITH, H.P. THE NARRATIVE ART OF
CHARLES DICKENS.
D. MEHL, 72:BAND208HEFT4/6-401
G.W. SPENCE, 67:MAY71-106
SUDA, Z. THE CZECHOSLOVAK SOCIALIST
REPUBLIC.*
Y. JELINEK, 104:FALL71-446
SUERBAUM, W. UNTERSUCHUNGEN ZUR SELBST-
DARSTELLUNG ÄLTERER RÖMISCHER DICHTER.
P.G.M. BROWN, 123:DEC71-373
K. GRIES, 124:DEC70-134
W.C. SCOTT, 122:JAN71-61
SUFFEL, J. - SEE FLAUBERT, G.
SUGAR, P.F. & I.J. LEDERER, EDS. NATION-
ALISM IN EASTERN EUROPE.*
B.M. KIRÁLY, 104:SPRING71-141
SUH CHONG-JU. WINTER SKY.
270:VOL20#4-101
SUHL, B. JEAN-PAUL SARTRE.
R. CHAMPIGNY, 659:SPRING72-261

SUHR, E.G. THE SPINNING APHRODITE.
G. STEINER, 124:APR71-279
SUKENICK, R. WALLACE STEVENS.
H.H. WAGGONER, 405(MP):MAY70-392
SUKHOVO-KOBYLIN, A. THE TRILOGY OF
ALEXANDER SUKHOVO-KOBYLIN. (H.B.
SEGEL, TRANS)
E. WILSON, 442(NY):18MAR72-144
SUKHWAL, B.L. INDIA.
617(TLS):7APR72-402
SULIMIRSKI, T. PREHISTORIC RUSSIA.*
C.S. CHARD, 32:JUN71-379
SULLIVAN, E. WHERE DID THE $13 BILLION
GO?
441:9APR72-34
SULLIVAN, F. WELL, THERE'S NO HARM IN
LAUGHING. (G. OPPENHEIMER, ED)
J. BRYAN 3D, 441:22OCT72-31
SULLIVAN, J. CHESTERTON CONTINUED.
B.C. BLOOMFIELD, 354:DEC69-355
SULLIVAN, J.P. THE "SATYRICON" OF PET-
RONIUS.*
H.T. ROWELL, 24:JAN71-92
SULLIVAN, M. THE BIRTH OF LANDSCAPE
PAINTING IN CHINA.
B. ROWLAND, 54:DEC69-393
SULLIVAN, M. THE CAVE TEMPLES OF
MAICHISHAN.
J. RAWSON, 90:DEC70-834
293(JAST):MAY70-743
SULLIVAN, M. MANDATE '68.
H. MACQUARRIE, 150(DR):AUTUMN70-415
SULLIVAN, M.R. BROWNING'S VOICES IN
"THE RING AND THE BOOK."*
R.D. ALTICK, 401(MLQ):JUN70-260
W.D. SHAW, 627(UTQ):APR70-289
SULLIVAN, M.W. APULEIAN LOGIC.*
I. THOMAS, 486:JUN68-197
SULLIVAN, W., C.H. HOLMAN & L.D. RUBIN,
JR. SOUTHERN FICTION TODAY. (G. CORE,
ED)
F. DURHAM, 577(SHR):SUMMER70-279
SULTANA, D.E. SAMUEL TAYLOR COLERIDGE
IN MALTA AND ITALY.
D.V.E., 191(ELN):SEP70(SUPP)-33
SULZBERGER, C.L. THE LAST OF THE GI-
ANTS.*
617(TLS):14APR72-407
SUMAROKOV, A.P. SELECTED TRAGEDIES OF
A.P. SUMAROKOV. (R. & R. FORTUNE,
TRANS)
A. CROSS, 32:DEC71-906
SUMMERS, G. THE LURE OF THE FALCON.
617(TLS):28JUL72-900
SUMMERS, H. THE GARDEN.
M. LEVIN, 441:17SEP72-42
SUMMERS, J. THE RAGING SUMMER.
617(TLS):25AUG72-985
SUMMERS, J.H. THE HEIRS OF DONNE AND
JONSON.
W.L. GODSHALK, 301(JEGP):JUL71-544
676(YR):WINTER71-VI
SUMMERS, R.S., ED. MORE ESSAYS IN LEGAL
PHILOSOPHY.
J. RAZ, 311(JP):7SEP72-498
SUMMERSON, J., ED. CONCERNING ARCHITEC-
TURE.
R.F. JORDAN, 46:FEB69-148
SUMMERSON, J. INIGO JONES.
P.F. NORTON, 576:OCT69-228
SUMNER, H. THE NEW FOREST. (NEW ED)
617(TLS):1DEC72-1469
SUMNER, L.W. & J. WOODS, EDS. NECESSARY
TRUTH.
I.T. OAKLEY, 63:DEC71-320
SUMOWSKI, W. CASPAR DAVID FRIEDRICH-
STUDIEN.
W. SCHEIDIG, 182:VOL23#8-416

SUN, K.C., WITH R.W. HUENEMANN. THE ECO-
NOMIC DEVELOPMENT OF MANCHURIA IN THE
FIRST HALF OF THE TWENTIETH CENTURY.*
J.C. CHANG, 293(JAST):NOV69-169
SUN-WON, H. - SEE UNDER HWANG SUN-WON
SUNG, K.I. - SEE UNDER KIM IL SUNG
SUNGOLOWSKY, J. ALFRED DE VIGNY ET LE
DIX-HUITIÈME SIÈCLE.
C.C., 191(ELN):SEP69(SUPP)-91
C.G. HILL, 207(FR):OCT69-183
SUPER, R.H. THE TIME-SPIRIT OF MATTHEW
ARNOLD.
M. COOKE, 676(YR):WINTER71-294
P. HONAN, 402(MLR):OCT71-880
SUPER, R.H. - SEE ARNOLD, M.
SUPPES, P. STUDIES IN THE METHODOLOGY
AND FOUNDATIONS OF SCIENCE.
R.H.K., 543:JUN70-749
"A SUPPLEMENT TO THE OXFORD ENGLISH
DICTIONARY." (VOL 1) (R.W. BURCH-
FIELD, ED)
D.A.N. JONES, 362:23NOV72-719
C. LEHMANN-HAUPT, 441:1NOV72-43
G. STEINER, 441:26NOV72-1
617(TLS):13OCT72-1209
SURMELIAN, L. APPLES OF IMMORTALITY.
W.H. JANSEN, 292(JAF):JAN-MAR70-85
SURTEES, V. - SEE RUSKIN, J.
"'SUSANNAH:' AN ALLITERATIVE POEM OF THE
FOURTEENTH CENTURY."* (A. MISKIMIN,
ED)
M. RIGBY, 541(RES):AUG70-342
SUSSMAN, G. SUSSMAN'S COLLEGE MANUAL.
441:16APR72-22
SUSSMAN, H.L. VICTORIANS AND THE MACH-
INE.
V. COLBY, 405(MP):AUG69-100
L. DUDEK, 191(ELN):MAR70-227
E.D.H. JOHNSON, 445(NCF):DEC68-349
SUTCLIFFE, S. MARTELLO TOWERS.
617(TLS):6OCT72-1205
SUTHERLAND, D. TRIED AND VALIANT.
617(TLS):22DEC72-1555
SUTHERLAND, G., ED. STUDIES IN THE
GROWTH OF NINETEENTH-CENTURY GOVERN-
MENT.
617(TLS):16JUN72-679
SUTHERLAND, J. DANIEL DEFOE.
617(TLS):28APR72-461
SUTHERLAND, J. OXFORD HISTORY OF ENGLISH
LITERATURE.* (VOL 6: ENGLISH LITERA-
TURE OF THE LATE SEVENTEENTH CENTURY.)
J. KINSLEY, 541(RES):NOV70-501
D.T. MACE, 191(ELN):MAR70-222
J.M. OSBORN, 481(PQ):JUL70-319
V.D. PINTO, 175:AUTUMN69-108
P.W. ROGERS, 529(QQ):WINTER70-647
D.I.B. SMITH, 627(UTQ):JAN70-188
SUTHERLAND, R. LARK DES NEIGES.
H. ROITER, 296:SPRING72-91
SUTTON, A.C. WESTERN TECHNOLOGY AND
SOVIET ECONOMIC DEVELOPMENT, 1917-1930.*
M.G. CLARK, 550(RUSR):JAN70-94
R. HUTCHINGS, 575(SEER):JAN71-128
SUTTON, A.C. WESTERN TECHNOLOGY AND
SOVIET ECONOMIC DEVELOPMENT 1930-1945.
617(TLS):21APR72-453
SUTTON, D. - SEE FRY, R.
SUTTON, D. & A. CLEMENTS, EDS. AN ITAL-
IAN SKETCHBOOK BY RICHARD TAYLOR, R.A.
R. EDWARDS, 39:JAN69-79
R. PAULSON, 173(ECS):WINTER69-278
J. SUNDERLAND, 90:DEC69-783
SUTTON, G.M. HIGH ARCTIC.
E. WEEKS, 61:FEB72-108

SUTTON, J. & A. BARTRAM. AN ATLAS OF
TYPEFORMS.
K. BAYNES, 46:NOV69-402
N. GRAY, 592:NOV68-220
SUTTON, M.L. JOSEPH CONRAD'S "THE NIG-
GER OF THE NARCISSUS."
J. WALT, 136:SPRING70-139
VON SUTTON, T. QUODLIBETA. (M. SCHMAUS
& M. GONZALEZ-HABA, EDS)
G.J. ETZKORN, 589:APR71-400
SUYIN, H. - SEE UNDER HAN SUYIN
SUŽIEDĚLIS, S., ED. ENCYCLOPEDIA LITU-
ANICA. (VOL 1)
G.B. FORD, 575(SEER):JAN71-147
SUZUKI, D.T. OUTLINES OF MAHAYANA BUD-
DHISM.
P.J.H., 543:JUN70-749
SUZUKI, D.T. SENGAI.
617(TLS):7JUL72-761
ŠVÁB, M. PROLOGY A EPILOGY V ČESKÉ
PŘEDHUSITSKÉ LITERATUŘE.
S.E. MANN, 575(SEER):JUL71-482
SVAGLIC, M.J. - SEE NEWMAN, J.H.
SVANBERG, V. DIKTAREN I SAMHÅLLET.
270:VOL20#2-44
SVARTVIK, J. ON VOICE IN THE ENGLISH
VERB.*
G. NICKEL, 72:BAND208HEFT3-212
A. ZETTERSTEN, 596(SL):VOL22#2-129
SVENAEUS, G. EDVARD MUNCH.
E. HOFFMANN, 39:FEB69-157
A. NEUMEYER, 290(JAAC):WINTER69-261
SVENNUNG, J. JORDANES UND SCANDIA.
A-R. TELLIER, 555:VOL44FASC2-367
"SVENSKA DUDEN BILDLEXIKON."
B. NYSTRÖM, 75:2/1969-115
SVOBODA, L. CESTAMI ŽIVOTA I.
617(TLS):29SEP72-1158
SWADOS, H. STANDING FAST.*
M. MIRSKY, 473(PR):WINTER71/72-480
SWAN, A. THE BRITISH ARCHITECT.
D. STILLMAN, 576:DEC69-300
SWAN, L.A. & C.S. PAPP. THE COMMON IN-
SECTS OF NORTH AMERICA.
442(NY):9DEC72-179
SWANBERG, W.A. LUCE AND HIS EMPIRE.
J. EPSTEIN, 453:2NOV72-11
C. LEHMANN-HAUPT, 441:28SEP72-49
D. MACDONALD, 441:10CT72-1
561(SATR):21OCT72-78
SWANSON, D.C. THE NAMES IN ROMAN VERSE.
D.J. GEORGACAS, 424:SEP68-299
H. PETERSEN, 24:OCT71-750
SWANTON, E.W. SORT OF A CRICKET PERSON.
617(TLS):22DEC72-1566
SWARTHOUT, G. THE TIN LIZZIE TROOP.
M. LEVIN, 441:25JUN72-28
SWEDENBERG, H.T., JR., ED. ENGLISH
POETRY OF THE RESTORATION AND EARLY
EIGHTEENTH CENTURY.
D.G., 173(ECS):SPRING70-422
"THE SWEDISH BALLET 1920-25."
J. ANDERSON, 151:NOV69-85
SWENSON, M. HALF SUN HALF SLEEP. POEMS
TO SOLVE.
H. ZINNES, 502(PRS):SPRING68-86
SWENSON, M. ICONOGRAPHS.*
G-S. FRASER, 473(PR):WINTER71/72-469
N. SULLIVAN, 491:NOV71-107
SWETTENHAM, J. ALLIED INTERVENTION IN
RUSSIA 1918-1919.
R.S. FELDMAN, 587:OCT68-265
SWETTENHAM, J. MC NAUGHTON. (VOL 1)
A.R.M. LOWER, 529(QQ):WINTER70-618
SWETTENHAM, J. MC NAUGHTON. (VOLS 2&3)
A.R.M. LOWER, 529(QQ):WINTER70-618
R.A. MAC KAY, 150(DR):SUMMER70-276

SWIFT, J. GULLIVER'S TRAVELS. (R.A.
GREENBERG, ED)
566:AUTUMN70-29
SWIFT, J. GULLIVER'S TRAVELS. (C. JEN-
KINS, ED)
566:SPRING71-69
SWIFT, J. GULLIVER'S TRAVELS. (L.A.
LANDA, ED)
P. DANCHIN, 179(ES):OCT70-458
SWIFT, J. GULLIVER'S TRAVELS. (P. TUR-
NER, ED)
C.T. PROBYN, 566:SPRING71-69
SWIFT, J. A TALE OF A TUB; THE BATTLE
OF THE BOOKS; THE MECHANICAL OPERATION
OF THE SPIRIT.
C.T.P., 566:SPRING71-50
SWIFT, M.G. THE ART OF THE DANCE IN THE
U.S.S.R.*
S.J. COHEN, 550(RUSR):APR70-228
SWIGG, R. LAWRENCE, HARDY, AND AMERICAN
LITERATURE.
617(TLS):28JAN72-95
SWINBURNE, A.C. SWINBURNE AS CRITIC.
(C.K. HYDER, ED)
617(TLS):15DEC72-1537
SWINBURNE, R. THE CONCEPT OF MIRACLE.*
A. FLEW, 518:MAY71-28
SWINBURNE, R. SPACE AND TIME.
R.H.K., 543:MAR70-568
SWINDLER, W.F. GOVERNMENT BY THE PEOPLE.
J.C. RAINBOLT, 656(WMQ):APR70-334
SWING, T.K. KANT'S TRANSCENDENTAL LOGIC.
H.E. MATTHEWS, 518:MAY70-28
SWINNERTON, F. NOR ALL THY TEARS.
D-A.N. JONES, 362:11MAY72-628
M. LEVIN, 441:5NOV72-40
617(TLS):23JUN72-705
SWINNERTON, F. REFLECTIONS FROM A VIL-
LAGE.
J. GILSDORF, 502(PRS):WINTER69/70-419
SWINSON, A. - SEE TULLOCH, D.
SWORTZELL, L., ED. ALL THE WORLD'S A
STAGE.
G. WEALES, 441:11JUN72-8
SYKES, C. NANCY.
P. GROSSKURTH, 362:5OCT72-445
P. STANSKY, 441:26NOV72-4
617(TLS):20OCT72-1246
SYKES, S.W. & J.P. CLAYTON, EDS. CHRIST,
FAITH AND HISTORY.
617(TLS):20OCT72-1261
SYLVESTER, D. HENRY MOORE.*
M. LAST, 55:OCT69-20
S.R. LEVITT, 592:NOV68-226
SYME, R. AMMIANUS AND THE "HISTORIA
AUGUSTA."*
T.R.S. BROUGHTON, 121(CJ):DEC70-JAN
71-187
M. WOLOCH, 487:SUMMER70-185
SYME, R. THE TRAVELS OF CAPTAIN COOK.
617(TLS):22SEP72-1124
SYMES, R. & D. COLE. RAILWAY ARCHITEC-
TURE OF THE SOUTH-EAST.
617(TLS):16JUN72-697
SYMONDS, J. THE GREAT BEAST.
617(TLS):30JUN72-757
SYMONDS, J. & K. GRANT, EDS. THE MAGICAL
RECORD OF THE BEAST 666.
617(TLS):10NOV72-1370
SYMONDS, J.A. THE LETTERS OF JOHN ADD-
INGTON SYMONDS. (VOL 1) (H.M.
SCHUELLER & R.L. PETERS, EDS)
J. BERTRAM, 447(N&Q):JAN70-25
J.C. MAXWELL, 447(N&Q):JAN70-30
L. POSTON 3D, 502(PRS):FALL68-273
C. RYAN, 447(N&Q):JAN70-26
D. TYLER, 385(MQR):SPRING72-136

SYMONDS, J.A. THE LETTERS OF JOHN
ADDINGTON SYMONDS. (VOL 2) (H.M.
SCHUELLER & R.L. PETERS, EDS)
   C. MARKGRAF, 637(VS):JUN70-464
   D. TYLER, 385(MQR):SPRING72-136
SYMONDS, J.A. THE LETTERS OF JOHN
ADDINGTON SYMONDS. (VOL 3) (H.M.
SCHUELLER & R.L. PETERS, EDS)
   D. TYLER, 385(MQR):SPRING72-136
SYMONS, J., COMP. BETWEEN THE WARS.
   617(TLS):20OCT72-1264
SYMONS, J. BLOODY MURDER.
   P. DICKINSON, 362:27APR72-563
   617(TLS):14APR72-427
SYMONS, J. MORTAL CONSEQUENCES.
   P. ADAMS, 61:APR72-129
   N. CALLENDAR, 441:19MAR72-42
   H. FRANKEL, 561(SATR):13MAY72-86
   442(NY):1APR72-107
SYMONS, J. NOTES FROM ANOTHER COUNTRY.
   M. SULLIVAN, 362:28DEC72-902
   617(TLS):21JUL72-836
SYMONS, J. THE PLAYERS AND THE GAME.
   P. ADAMS, 61:1OCT72-135
   O.L. BAILEY, 561(SATR):30SEP72-80
   N. CALLENDAR, 441:22OCT72-47
   D-A.N. JONES, 362:31AUG72-280
   617(TLS):29SEP72-1174
SYMONS, S. PLACE D'ARMES.
   R.H. BAYES, 448:SUMMER68-130
"SYMPOTICA FRANZ WIEACKER SEXAGENARIO
SASBACHWALDENI A SUIS LIBATA."
   J. CROOK, 123:DEC71-396
SYNGE, J.M. COLLECTED WORKS.* (VOLS
3&4) (A. SADDLEMYER, ED)
   R. DAVIES, 627(UTQ):JUL69-376
   W. HABICHT, 72:BAND208HEFT1-60
SYNGE, J.M. LETTERS TO MOLLY. (A. SAD-
DLEMYER, ED)
   617(TLS):17MAR72-306
SYRETT, D., ED. THE SIEGE AND CAPTURE OF
HAVANA 1762.
   617(TLS):24MAR72-329
SYRIOPOULOS, K.T. HĒ PROISTORIA TĒS
STEREAS HELLADOS. HĒ PROISTORIKĒ KATO-
IKĒSIS TĒS STEREAS HELLADOS.
   H. WATERHOUSE, 303:VOL90-256
SZABÓ, Á. ANFÄNGE DER GRIECHISCHEN
MATHEMATIK.
   C-B. BOYER, 124:SEP70-23
   W. BURKERT, 182:VOL23#3-102
SZANTYR, A. - SEE HOFMANN, J.B.
SZARKOWSKI, J. - SEE EVANS, W.
SZAROTA, E.M. LOHENSTEINS ARMINIUS ALS
ZEITROMAN.
   G. GILLESPIE, 301(JEGP):JUL71-502
SZÁSZ, B. VOLUNTEERS FOR THE GALLOWS.
   S. FREIDIN, 440:5MAR72-8
SZCZESNIAK, B.B. THE KNIGHTS HOSPITAL-
LERS IN POLAND AND LITHUANIA.
   K. VON LOEWE, 32:MAR71-133
SZCZUCKI, L. & J. TAZBIR, EDS. EPITOME
COLLOQUII RACOVIAE HABITI ANNO 1601.
   F. DE MICHELIS, 548(RCSF):JAN-MAR68-
107
SZEMKUS, K. GESELLSCHAFTLICHER WANDEL
UND SPRACHLICHE FORM.
   L.W. KAHN, 222(GR):MAY70-240
SZERTICS, J. TIEMPO Y VERBO EN EL ROMAN-
CERO VIEJO.
   T. MONTGOMERY, 545(RPH):NOV69-228
SZIDAT, J. CAESARS DIPLOMATISCHE TÄTIG-
KEIT IM GALLISCHEN KRIEG.
   F. LASSERRE, 182:VOL23#10-561
"SZIGETI ON THE VIOLIN."
   R. ANDERSON, 415:APR70-394
SZILASI, W. PHANTASIE UND ERKENNTNIS.
   W. SCHWARZ, 484(PPR):JUN70-629

SZPORLUK, R. - SEE POKROVSKY, M.N.
SZULC, T. CZECHOSLOVAKIA SINCE WORLD
WAR II.*
   E. TABORSKY, 32:DEC71-916
SZULC, T. PORTRAIT OF SPAIN.
   S.G. PAYNE, 441:1OCT72-34
SZYDŁOWSKI, J. CMENTARZYSKO Z OKRESU
WPŁYWÓW RZYMSKICH W CHORULI, POW.
KRAPKOWICE.
   K. TACKENBERG, 182:VOL23#21/22-941

"TSG: TRANSFORMATIONELLE SCHULGRAMMATIK."
   D-A. BECKER, 406:SUMMER71-181
TABOADA, J.M.D. & J-M. ROZAS - SEE UNDER
DÍEZ TABOADA, J.M. & J.M. ROZAS
TABOR, P. PAULINE'S.
   A. WHITMAN, 231:MAY72-102
TABORI, P. THE ANATOMY OF EXILE.
   617(TLS):11AUG72-933
TABORI, P. PIONEERS OF THE UNSEEN.
   617(TLS):16JUN72-690
TABORSKI, B. POLISH PLAYS IN ENGLISH
TRANSLATIONS.
   A. LANDSBERGIS, 497(POLR):SUMMER69-95
TACITUS. AGRICOLA, GERMANY, DIALOGUE ON
ORATORS.* (H.W. BENARIO, TRANS)
   J-M. SNYDER, 121(CJ):OCT-NOV70-89
TACITUS. THE ANNALS OF TACITUS. (BOOKS
1-6, VOL 1) (F.R.D. GOODYEAR, ED)
   617(TLS):22DEC72-1566
TACITUS. CORNELIUS TACITUS: "ANNALEN."
(VOL 4) (E. KOESTERMANN, ED)
   N-P. MILLER, 123:DEC70-345
TACITUS, A. AENEAS TACITUS: "POLIOR-
CÉTIQUE." (A. DAIN, ED; A-M. BON,
TRANS)
   S. USHER, 303:VOL90-210
TADIÉ, J-Y. PROUST ET LE ROMAN. LEC-
TURES DE PROUST.
   617(TLS):21JAN72-60
TAGLIACOZZO, G., WITH H.V. WHITE, EDS.
GIAMBATTISTA VICO.*
   G-N.G. ORSINI, 131(CL):FALL71-365
   R-N. STROMBERG, 149(MAR71-79
   639(VQR):SPRING70-LXXVI
TAGMANN, P-M. ARCHIVALISCHE STUDIEN ZUR
MUSIKPFLEGE AM DOM VON MANTUA (1500-
1627).
   G. NUGENT, 317:FALL71-474
TÄHTINEN, U. INDIAN PHILOSOPHY OF VALUE.
   E.J. QUIGLEY, 485(PE&W):OCT69-466
TAIT, C. FLIGHT OF THE KIWI.
   617(TLS):10MAR72-285
TAIT, V. A FAMILY OF BROTHERS.
   W. STONE, 71(ALS):OCT72-437
   617(TLS):30JUN72-757
"TAIWAN NŌGYŌ KANKEI BUNKEN MOKUROKU."
   R. MYERS, 293(JAST):MAY70-698
TAKAHASHI, S. AFTERIMAGES.* (L. STRYK
& T. IKEMOTO, EDS & TRANS)
   D-J. ENRIGHT, 364:AUG/SEP71-123
TAKEDA TSUNEO. THE KYOTO NATIONAL
MUSEUM, RAKUCHŪ RAKUGAI ZU.
   A-C. SOPER, 57:VOL31#4-321
TAKEJI, S. & KAWANO SHIGETŌ - SEE UNDER
SASAMOTO TAKEJI & KAWANO SHIGETŌ
TAKEUCHI RIZŌ, ED. RITSURYŌ KOKKA TO
KIZOKU SHAKAI. SHŌENSEI TO BUKE SHAKAI.
   G-C. HURST, 293(JAST):MAY70-698
TAKTSIS, C. THE THIRD WEDDING.
   R. MAURER, 561(SATR):1JAN72-75
TALESE, G. HONOR THY FATHER.*
   W. SHEED, 453:20JUL72-23
   617(TLS):14APR72-410
TALLIS, D. MUSICAL BOXES.
   H-M. BROWN, 415:NOV71-1073

TALLIS, J. LONDON STREET VIEWS 1838-
1840.
P. WHITTING, 78(BC):SUMMER70-260
TALMADGE, J.E. CORRA HARRIS.
W. TATE, 219(GAR):SPRING69-96
TALON, H. D.H. LAWRENCE, "SONS AND
LOVERS."
M. ALLOTT, 677:VOL2-327
TAMARIN, A.H., ED & TRANS. REVOLT IN
JUDEA.
L.H. FELDMAN, 124:SEP70-29
TAMMELO, I. OUTLINES OF MODERN LEGAL
LOGIC.
F. GILLIARD, 182:VOL23#15/16-721
TAMPION, J. THE GARDENER'S PRACTICAL
BOTANY.
617(TLS):6OCT72-1203
TAMUNO, T.N. THE POLICE IN MODERN NI-
GERIA 1861-1965.
617(TLS):7JAN72-22
TANDON, P. PUNJABI CENTURY: 1857-1947.*
B. RAMUSACK, 293(JAST):FEB70-474
TANG, P.S.H. & J.M. MALONEY. COMMUNIST
CHINA: THE DOMESTIC SCENE 1949-1967.
S.B. THOMAS, 293(JAST):NOV69-167
TANNER, J. WHILE LINCOLN LAY DYING.
D.E. FLOYD, 14:JUL69-274
TANNER, T. CITY OF WORDS.*
H. HARPER, 659:AUTUMN72-523
R. HAYMAN, 364:JUN/JUL71-135
TANNER, T. THE REIGN OF WONDER.
J.T. FLANAGAN, 179(ES):DEC70-569
TANSELLE, G.T. GUIDE TO THE STUDY OF
UNITED STATES IMPRINTS.
617(TLS):24NOV72-1440
TAPER, B. THE ARTS IN BOSTON.
639(VQR):AUTUMN70-CLIV
TAPPER, T. YOUNG PEOPLE AND SOCIETY.
617(TLS):14JAN72-47
TARÁN, L. - SEE ASCLEPIUS OF TRALLES
TARÁN, L. - SEE "PARMENIDES"
TARANOW, G. SARAH BERNHARDT.
617(TLS):30JUN72-735
TARANTINO, R.S. SMALL GARDENS ARE MORE
FUN.
J. SAVERCOOL, 441:3DEC72-92
TARDITI, G. - SEE ARCHILOCHUS
TARLING, A. WILL CARTER, PRINTER.
D.J.C., 503:WINTER68-193
TARN, J.N. WORKING-CLASS HOUSING IN
19TH-CENTURY BRITAIN.
617(TLS):28JAN72-86
TARN, N. A NOWHERE FOR VALLEJO.
617(TLS):4AUG72-910
TARN, N. - SEE NERUDA, P.
TARNÓCZY, L. FORDÍ TÓKALAUZ.
A. SAVAGEOT, 75:1/1969-58
TAROT, R. HUGO VON HOFMANNSTHAL.
J.D. WORKMAN, 406:SUMMER71-195
TAROT, R., WITH W. BENDER & F.G. SIEVEKE
- SEE VON GRIMMELSHAUSEN, H.J.C.
TARSHIS, B. - SEE "JULIE HARRIS TALKS TO
YOUNG ACTORS"
TART, C.T., ED. ALTERED STATES OF CON-
SCIOUSNESS.
J.O. MEANY, 142:FALL71-468
TASIS, R. LA RENAIXENÇA CATALANA.
191(ELN):SEP70(SUPP)-152
TATAKIS, B.N. MELETEMATA CHRISTIANIKĒS
PHILOSOPHIAS.
G.L. KUSTAS, 303:VOL90-243
TATE, A. ESSAYS OF FOUR DECADES.*
L.T. LEMON, 502(PRS):WINTER69/70-416
I. WEDDE, 364:APR/MAY71-171
42(AR):SPRING69-111

TATE, A. THE SWIMMERS AND OTHER SELECTED
POEMS.*
H. CARRUTH, 249(HUDR):SUMMER71-332
R.B. SHAW, 491:JAN72-222
I. WEDDE, 364:APR/MAY71-171
TATE, C., ED. CABLE TELEVISION IN THE
CITIES.
L. ROSS, 453:9MAR72-25
TATE, D.J.M. THE MAKING OF MODERN SOUTH-
EAST ASIA. (VOL 1)
617(TLS):10NOV72-1361
TATE, J. ABSENCES.
J. MOYNAHAN, 441:12NOV72-63
N. ROSTEN, 561(SATR):12AUG72-58
TATE, J. NOTES OF WOE.
R. MORAN, 598(SOR):WINTER72-243
TATE, J. THE OBLIVION HA-HA.*
J. ATLAS, 491:OCT71-45
639(VQR):AUTUMN70-CXXXII
TATE, J. RELIGIOUS WOMEN IN THE MODERN
WORLD.
R. BRADLEY, 142:WINTER71-113
TATE, J. ROW WITH YOUR HAIR.
R. MORAN, 598(SOR):WINTER72-243
639(VQR):WINTER70-XIII
TATE, J. THE TORCHES.*
R. BROTHERSON, 661:FALL/WINTER69-109
V. YOUNG, 249(HUDR):WINTER71/72-669
TATE, R.S., JR. PETIT DE BACHAUMONT.
M.H. WADDICOR, 208(FS):JAN71-91
TATU, M. POWER IN THE KREMLIN.
J. PENNAR, 550(RUSR):JAN70-100
TAUB, R.P. BUREAUCRATS UNDER STRESS.
A. BÉTEILLE, 293(JAST):NOV69-201
TAUBER, G. & S. KAPLAN. THE NEW YORK
CITY HANDBOOK.
C. SIMMONS, 441:4JUN72-7
TAUBERT, S., ED. THE BOOK TRADE OF THE
WORLD. (VOL 1)
617(TLS):22SEP72-1123
TAULI, V. INTRODUCTION TO A THEORY OF
LANGUAGE PLANNING.
V. RŪĶE-DRAVIŅA, 353:DEC69-102
TAVANI, G. POESIA DEL DUECENTO NELLA
PENISOLA IBERICA.*
R.M. WALKER, 382(MAE):1971/2-193
TAVERNIER, B. GREAT MARITIME ROUTES.
617(TLS):13OCT72-1237
TAVERNIER, M. & P. O'REILLY. L'ECRITURE
DE GAUGUIN, ÉTUDE GRAPHOLOGIQUE.
J. HOUSE, 90:OCT70-711
"R.H. TAWNEY'S COMMONPLACE BOOK." (J.M.
WINTER & D.M. JOSLIN, EDS)
617(TLS):28APR72-463
TAYLOR, A. DRUSTAN THE WANDERER.*
M. LEVIN, 441:11JUN72-34
TAYLOR, A. MY SISTER, MY SELF.
V. CUNNINGHAM, 362:3FEB72-156
617(TLS):21JAN72-57
TAYLOR, A.J.P. BEAVERBROOK.
R. FULLER, 362:29JUN72-870
P. SILCOX, 99:DEC72-38
P. STANSKY, 441:8OCT72-3
442(NY):21OCT72-168
617(TLS):30JUN72-747
TAYLOR, A.J.P. - SEE STEVENSON, F.
TAYLOR, A.W. WILD FLOWERS OF SPAIN AND
PORTUGAL.
617(TLS):15DEC72-1541
TAYLOR, A.W. WILD FLOWERS OF THE PYRE-
NEES.
617(TLS):28JAN72-109
TAYLOR, B. STUBBS.*
P. ADAMS, 61:MAR72-108

TAYLOR, E. THE DEVASTATING BOYS AND
OTHER STORIES.
W. BEAUCHAMP, 561(SATR):10JUN72-69
A. BROYARD, 441:24MAY72-49
V. CUNNINGHAM, 362:25MAY72-693
M. LEVIN, 441:23APR72-41
J.C. OATES, 440:30APR72-6
617(TLS):9JUN72-649
TAYLOR, E. MRS. PALFREY AT THE CLARE-
MONT.*
E. FEINSTEIN, 364:DEC71/JAN72-154
TAYLOR, E.R. WELCOME EUMENIDES.
A. RICH, 441:2JUL72-3
TAYLOR, G. RETURN TICKET.
617(TLS):19MAY72-584
TAYLOR, G.O. THE PASSAGES OF THOUGHT.*
B.C. BACH, 613:WINTER69-604
M.F. DEAKIN, 141:WINTER70-87
W.B. DILLINGHAM, 481(PQ):OCT70-570
R. LEHAN, 445(NCF):DEC69-375
TAYLOR, G.R. RETHINK.
617(TLS):17NOV72-1401
TAYLOR, H. BREAKINGS.
J. VERNON, 651(WHR):SPRING71-192
TAYLOR, H.J.F. SCHOOL AND COUNSELLING.
617(TLS):7JUL72-785
TAYLOR, J. FROM SELF-HELP TO GLAMOUR.
617(TLS):19MAY72-578
TAYLOR, J.R. ANGER AND AFTER.
A.P. HINCHLIFFE, 148:SPRING70-95
TAYLOR, J.R., ED. JOHN OSBORNE: "LOOK
BACK IN ANGER," A CASEBOOK.
M. PAGE, 397(MD):SEP69-214
TAYLOR, J.R. THE RISE AND FALL OF THE
WELL-MADE PLAY.
T.F. EVANS, 571:SPRING-SUMMER68-20
TAYLOR, J.R. & A. JACKSON. THE HOLLYWOOD
MUSICAL.
617(TLS):4FEB72-125
TAYLOR, L. DEVIANCE AND SOCIETY.
617(TLS):25FEB72-224
TAYLOR, L.E. PASTORAL AND ANTI-PASTORAL
PATTERNS IN JOHN UPDIKE'S FICTION.
N.Y. YATES, 27(AL):NOV71-484
TAYLOR, M.D. SWORDS AND PLOWSHARES.
S.E. AMBROSE, 440:9APR72-4
A. BROYARD, 441:27MAR72-37
N. SHEEHAN, 441:9APR72-3
TAYLOR, M.J., ED. SEX.
G. DEVINE, 441:26MAR72-14
TAYLOR, S. SOPHY UNDER SAIL. (I. TAY-
LOR, ED)
617(TLS):24MAR72-339
TAYLOR, S.D. THE CHORALE PRELUDES OF
J.S. BACH.
W. EMERY, 415:NOV71-1073
TAYLOR, S.W. & E. LUCIE-SMITH, EDS.
FRENCH POETRY TODAY.
G. MARTIN, 364:FEB/MAR72-164
617(TLS):31MAR72-360
TAYLOR, T. THOMAS TAYLOR THE PLATONIST.*
(K. RAINE & G.M. HARPER, EDS)
D.V.E., 191(ELN):SEP70(SUPP)-13
D. HIRST, 340(KR):1969/5-684
W.J.B. OWEN, 541(RES):NOV70-507
J.B. SKEMP, 123:DEC71-469
TAYLOR, W.D., ED. EIGHTEENTH CENTURY
COMEDY. (NEWLY ED BY S. TRUSSLER)
566:AUTUMN70-31
TÊ-K'UN, C. - SEE UNDER CHÊNG TÊ-K'UN
TEDLOCK, D. - SEE "FINDING THE CENTER"
TEICHMANN, H. GEORGE S. KAUFMAN.
C. BARNES, 441:25JUN72-7
E. FREMONT-SMITH, 561(SATR):22JUL72-
52
T. LASK, 441:14JUN72-49
442(NY):22JUL72-79

TEIJEIRO, A. DIARIOS (1828-1831).
(A.M. BERAZALUCE, ED)
191(ELN):SEP70(SUPP)-152
TEIK, G.C. - SEE UNDER GOH CHENG TEIK
TEIKA, F. FUJIWARA TEIKA: SUPERIOR
POEMS OF OUR TIME. (R.H. BROWER & E.
MINER, TRANS)
M. BROCK, 285(JAPQ):JAN-MAR70-100
TEILHARD DE CHARDIN, P. CHRISTIANITY AND
EVOLUTION.
617(TLS):5MAY72-527
TEILHARD DE CHARDIN, P. HUMAN ENERGY.*
ACTIVATION OF ENERGY.*
D.P. GRAY, 142:SPRING71-238
TEILHARD DE CHARDIN, P. LETTERS TO TWO
FRIENDS, 1926-1952. (R.N. ANSHEN, ED)
D.P. GRAY, 613:WINTER68-620
TEJERA, V. MODES OF GREEK THOUGHT.
J.P. ANTON, 319:OCT72-472
TEL QUEL. THÉORIE D'ENSEMBLE.
J-M. REY, 98:DEC69-1059
TELLE, É.V. - SEE ERASMUS
"TEMENOS." (VOL 5)
J.G. MAC QUEEN, 595(SCS):VOL15PT2-161
TEMPEL, E. NEW FINNISH ARCHITECTURE.
J.M.R., 46:JUL69-84
TEMPEL, G. THE CHAIRMAN AS GOD.*
H. LOMAS, 364:JUN/JUL71-139
TEMPLE, R.Z. NATHALIE SARRAUTE.
H.T. MASON, 447(N&Q):OCT70-394
TEMPLE, R.Z., WITH M. TUCKER, EDS. TWEN-
TIETH CENTURY BRITISH LITERATURE.
W. WARNCKE, 517(PBSA):JAN-MAR71-87
TEMPLIER, P-D. ERIK SATIE.*
P. DICKINSON, 415:SEP70-896
TENIN, V. MOSCOW NIGHTS.
L.J. DAVIS, 440:30JAN72-9
M. LEVIN, 441:9JAN72-32
TENNANT, F.R. PHILOSOPHICAL THEOLOGY.
S.O.H., 543:DEC69-356
TENNYSON, A. THE POEMS OF TENNYSON.*
(C. RICKS, ED)
R.W. FLINT, 453:2NOV72-28
G. JOSEPH, 637(VS):JUN70-425
TERENCE. ANDRIA. (ILLUSTRATIONS BY A.
DÜRER)
617(TLS):4FEB72-124
TERGIT, G. FLOWERS THROUGH THE AGES.
617(TLS):26MAY72-613
TERKEL, S. HARD TIMES.
C. PHILLIPS, 639(VQR):SUMMER70-502
TERLECKI, T., ED. LITERATURA POLSKA NA
OBCZYŹNIE.
D. BIEŃKOWSKA, 497(POLR):SUMMER69-91
TERRACE, E.L.B. & H.G. FISCHER. TREAS-
URES OF THE CAIRO MUSEUM.
R.A. FAZZINI, 676(YR):SUMMER71-600
TERRAS, V. THE YOUNG DOSTOEVSKY (1846 TO
1849).*
R.L. BELKNAP, 574(SEEJ):SUMMER71-217
P. MEYER, 32:DEC71-908
K. SANINE, 182:VOL23#15/16-751
TERRAY, E. MARXISM AND "PRIMITIVE"
SOCIETIES.
617(TLS):22SEP72-1094
TERRELL, J.U. BUNKHOUSE PAPERS.
441:6FEB72-40
TERRELL, J.U. ESTEVANICO THE BLACK.
R.C. EWING, 50(ARQ):SUMMER69-179
TERRILL, R. 800,000,000: THE REAL CHINA.
S.R. SCHRAM, 441:7MAY72-2
R. STEEL, 440:9APR72-1
617(TLS):11AUG72-951
TERRISSE, J-R. LES CÉRAMIQUES SIGILLÉES
GALLO-ROMAINES DE MARTRES-DE-VEYRE
(PUY-DE-DÔME).
G. SIMPSON, 313:VOL60-250

TERRY, A., ED. AN ANTHOLOGY OF SPANISH
POETRY, 1500-1700. (PT 2)
   E.L. RIVERS, 400(MLN):MAR70-301
TERRY, W. MISS RUTH.
   J. ANDERSON, 151:DEC69-22
TERTULLIAN. Q. SEPTIMII FLORENTIS TER-
TULLIANI, "DE BAPTISMO." (B. LUISELLI,
ED)
   J. ANDRÉ, 555:VOL44FASC2-354
TERVOOREN, H. BIBLIOGRAPHIE ZUM MINNE-
SANG UND ZU DEN DICHTERN AUS "DES
MINNESANGS FRÜHLING."
   C. GRAY, JR., 301(JEGP):JAN71-108
   O. SAYCE, 402(MLR):APR71-439
TESAURO, E. IL CANOCCHIALE ARISTOTELICO.
   R. HESS, 72:BAND208HEFT4/6-446
TESTARD, M. SAINT JÉRÔME.
   D. WIESEN, 124:DEC70-133
TETZELI VON ROSADOR, K. MAGIE IM ELISA-
BETHANISCHEN DRAMA.
   J. WESTLAKE, 677:VOL2-255
TEZLA, A. HUNGARIAN AUTHORS.
   I. CSICSERY-RÓNAY, 356:APR71-184
THACKER, C. - SEE DE VOLTAIRE, F.M.A.
THACKERAY, H.S. JOSEPHUS THE MAN AND THE
HISTORIAN.
   L.H. FELDMAN, 318(JAOS):OCT-DEC70-545
THACKRAY, A. ATOMS AND POWERS.*
   M.J. OSLER, 319:JAN72-95
THAKUR, S.C. CHRISTIAN AND HINDU ETHICS.
   D. BASTOW, 479(PHQ):JUL70-310
VAN THAL, H. & J.S. NICKERSON - SEE
BELLOC, H.
THALE, M. - SEE PLACE, F.
THALHEIM, K.C. & H-H. HÖHMANN, EDS.
WIRTSCHAFTSREFORMEN IN OSTEUROPA.
   V. HOLEŠOVSKÝ, 32:MAR71-195
THALHEIMER, S. DER GENTER ALTAR.
   H. PAUWELS, 90:JUN69-390
THALMANN, M. ROMANTIKER ALS POETOLOGEN.
   M. MC INNES, 67:NOV71-259
   T.P. SAINE, 406:SUMMER71-178
   J. TRAINER, 402(MLR):OCT71-950
THALMANN, M. - SEE TIECK, L.
THANI NAYAGAM, X.S. - SEE "ANATAÕ DE PRO-
ENÇA'S TAMIL-PORTUGUESE DICTIONARY,
A.D. 1679"
THARP, L.H. SAINT-GAUDENS AND THE GILDED
ERA.
   S.W. JACKMAN, 432(NEQ):JUN70-346
THARPE, J. NATHANIEL HAWTHORNE.
   R. LEHAN, 445(NCF):JUN68-117
THATCHER, D.S. NIETZSCHE IN ENGLAND,
1890-1914.
   H.W. REICHERT, 301(JEGP):JUL71-522
   G. WOODCOCK, 102(CANL):SUMMER71-67
   617(TLS):24NOV72-1432
   676(YR):SPRING71-XIV
THAYER, H.S. MEANING AND ACTION.*
   D. GREENLEE, 322(JHI):OCT-DEC69-603
   M.B.M., 543:JUN69-750
   R.J. ROTH, 258:JUN69-297
THAYER, N.B. HOW THE CONSERVATIVES RULE
JAPAN.
   J.M. MAKI, 293(JAST):MAY70-706
"LE THÉÂTRE MODERNE DEPUIS LA DEUXIÈME
GUERRE MONDIALE." (VOL 2)
   G. BRÉE, 397(MD):FEB69-447
THEEN, R.H.W. - SEE VALENTINOV, N.
THEILER, W. UNTERSUCHUNGEN ZUR ANTIKEN
LITERATUR.
   H. LLOYD-JONES, 123:DEC71-405
THEINER, J. DIE ENTWICKLUNG DER MORAL-
THEOLOGIE ZUR EIGENSTÄNDIGEN DISZIPLIN.
   G. MAY, 182:VOL23#10-529
THEISS, W. EXEMPLARISCHE ALLEGORIK.*
   E. SOBEL, 222(GR):MAY70-246

THEOBALD, D.W. AN INTRODUCTION TO THE
PHILOSOPHY OF SCIENCE.
   R.A. SHARPE, 479(PHQ):JAN70-90
THEOBALD, L. SHAKESPEARE RESTORED [OR,]
A SPECIMEN OF THE MANY ERRORS, AS WELL
COMMITTED, AS UNAMENDED, BY MR. POPE IN
HIS LATE EDITION OF THIS POET.
   617(TLS):18FEB72-178
THEOCRITUS. THÉOCRITE, "IDYLLES (II, V,
VII, XI, XV)." (P. MONTEIL, ED)
   C. DOBIAS-LALOU, 555:VOL44FASC1-130
THÉOPHILE DE VIAU. LES AMOURS TRAGIQUES
DE PYRAME ET THISBÉ. (G. SABA, ED)
   C. CHERPACK, 546(RR):APR70-133
THEROUX, A. THREE WOGS.
   D. JOHNSON, 440:13FEB72-8
   D.K. MANO, 441:16APR72-4
THEROUX, P. GIRLS AT PLAY.*
   639(VQR):WINTER70-VIII
THEROUX, P. JUNGLE LOVERS.*
   J.M. MORSE, 249(HUDR):AUTUMN71-535
   J. RABAN, 364:AUG/SEP71-152
THEROUX, P. V.S. NAIPAUL.
   R. BRYDEN, 362:9NOV72-641
   617(TLS):17NOV72-1391
THEROUX, P. SINNING WITH ANNIE.
   J. HENDIN, 441:5NOV72-4
THESSALUS OF TRALLES. THESSALOS VON
TRALLES GRIECHISCH UND LATEINISCH.
(H-V. FRIEDRICH, ED)
   E.D. PHILLIPS, 303:VOL90-221
"THINKING ABOUT THE EUCHARIST."
   617(TLS):20OCT72-1261
THIONG'O, N.W. - SEE UNDER NGUGI WA
THIONG'O
THIRSK, J. & J.P. COOPER, EDS. SEVEN-
TEENTH-CENTURY ECONOMIC DOCUMENTS.
   617(TLS):14JUL72-822
THODY, P.M.W. FOUR CASES OF LITERARY
CENSORSHIP.
   G. REES, 208(FS):OCT71-492
THOMAS OF ERFURT. GRAMMATICA SPECULA-
TIVA. (G.L. BURSILL-HALL, ED & TRANS)
   617(TLS):29SEP72-1164
THOMAS, A. HOPKINS THE JESUIT.
   J.M. HAZARD, 541(RES):NOV70-517
THOMAS, A. MRS. BLOOD.*
   A. BOXILL, 198:FALL72-113
   J. COLDWELL, 102(CANL):AUTUMN71-98
THOMAS, A. MUNCHMEYER [AND] PROSPERO ON
THE ISLAND.
   A. BOXILL, 198:FALL72-113
THOMAS, A. THE VEGETARIAN EPICURE.
   N. HAZELTON, 441:3DEC72-97
THOMAS, B. MIGRATION AND URBAN DEVELOP-
MENT.
   617(TLS):6OCT72-1201
THOMAS, B. THALBERG.*
   A.H. WHITHAM, 200:MAR69-175
THOMAS, B. WEEKEND IN '33.
   M. LEVIN, 441:6FEB72-37
THOMAS, C. MARGARET LAURENCE.*
   C. KING, 627(UTQ):JUL70-376
THOMAS, C. LOVE AND WORK ENOUGH.
   E. MOERS, 637(VS):MAR70-370
THOMAS, C.M. RYERSON OF UPPER CANADA.*
   M. ANGUS, 529(QQ):SPRING70-124
   R.S. HARRIS, 627(UTQ):JUL70-401
   D.V. WADE, 627(UTQ):JUL70-392
THOMAS, D. EARLY PROSE WRITINGS. (W.
DAVIES, ED)
   617(TLS):3MAR72-254
"DYLAN THOMAS." [THE TIMES AUTHORS]
   G. NEVIN, 493:WINTER70/71-372
THOMAS, E.W. THE SYNTAX OF SPOKEN BRA-
ZILIAN PORTUGUESE.
   O. FERNÁNDEZ, 399(MLJ):MAR70-203

THOMAS, F. LAST WILL AND TESTAMENT.
617(TLS):22SEP72-1124
THOMAS, G. THE SKY OF OUR LIVES.
617(TLS):22SEP72-1087
THOMAS, H. CUBA.*
N. BLIVEN, 442(NY):2SEP72-68
THOMAS, H. TRISTAN LE DÉPOSSÉDE.
617(TLS):4AUG72-925
THOMAS, J. SCOTLAND: THE LOWLANDS AND
THE BORDERS.
617(TLS):14JAN72-49
THOMAS, J. THE TAY BRIDGE DISASTER.
617(TLS):21APR72-458
THOMAS, J. & D.J. NORDLOH - SEE HOWELLS,
W.D.
THOMAS, J.E. THE ENGLISH PRISON OFFICER
SINCE 1850.
617(TLS):6OCT72-1202
THOMAS, J.I. EDUCATION FOR COMMUNISM.
J.J. TOMIAK, 575(SEER):JUL71-479
THOMAS, J.J. THEORY AND PRACTICE OF
CREOLE GRAMMAR.
R.B. LE PAGE, 315(JAL):VOL8PT1-67
THOMAS, J.W. MEDIEVAL GERMAN LYRIC
VERSE.*
M.E. GIBBS, 220(GL&L):APR71-277
THOMAS, L. ONWARD VIRGIN SOLDIERS.*
M. LEVIN, 441:21MAY72-31
THOMAS, L.B. THE MGM YEARS.
J. KANON, 561(SATR):16DEC72-58
THOMAS, L.L. - SEE VINOGRADOV, V.V.
THOMAS, M. - SEE "THE GRANDES HEURES OF
JEAN, DUKE OF BERRY"
THOMAS, O. METAPHOR AND RELATED SUB-
JECTS.
L. JONES, 399(MLJ):APR70-285
THOMAS, O. TRANSFORMATIONAL GRAMMAR AND
THE TEACHER OF ENGLISH.
G. NICKEL, 72:BAND208HEFT3-208
THOMAS, P. SAVIOR, SAVIOR, HOLD MY HAND.
B. BECKHAM, 441:17SEP72-5
J.D. O'HARA, 561(SATR):30SEP72-80
THOMAS, P.W. SIR JOHN BERKENHEAD, 1617-
1679.*
C. HILL, 184(EIC):APR70-243
THOMAS, R. THE BACKUP MEN.*
617(TLS):4FEB72-135
THOMAS, R. THE PORKCHOPPERS.
O.L. BAILEY, 561(SATR):5AUG72-56
N. CALLENDAR, 441:2JUL72-15
442(NY):24JUN72-94
THOMAS, R. THE SELECTED POEMS OF ROSE-
MARY THOMAS.
V.B. YOUNG, 577(SHR):WINTER70-94
THOMAS, R.G. EDWARD THOMAS.
617(TLS):15SEP72-1048
THOMAS, R.H. & W. VAN DER WILL. THE GER-
MAN NOVEL AND THE AFFLUENT SOCIETY.
R. GRIMM, 406:SUMMER71-191
P. PROCHNIK, 220(GL&L):JUL71-386
E. SPEIDEL, 447(N&Q):FEB70-70
THOMAS, W. & B.G. SEAGRAVE. THE SONGS OF
THE MINNESINGER, PRINCE WIZLAW OF
RÜGEN.* [SHOWN IN PREV UNDER PRINCE
WIZLAW VON RÜGEN]
T. ESHELMAN, 399(MLJ):MAY70-374
THOMIS, M.I., ED. LUDDISM IN NOTTING-
HAMSHIRE.
617(TLS):8DEC72-1513
THOMPSON, A.W. & R.A. HART. THE UNCER-
TAIN CRUSADE.
J.M. THOMPSON, 32:DEC71-887
THOMPSON, E.A. THE GOTHS IN SPAIN.
P.G. WALSH, 123:JUN71-300

THOMPSON, H.S. FEAR AND LOATHING IN LAS
VEGAS.
C. LEHMANN-HAUPT, 441:22JUN72-41
C. WOODS, 441:23JUL72-17
617(TLS):3NOV72-1307
THOMPSON, H.Y. AN ENGLISHMAN IN THE
AMERICAN CIVIL WAR. (C. CHANCELLOR,
ED)
617(TLS):18FEB72-181
THOMPSON, J. ENGLISH STUDIES.
617(TLS):28APR72-501
THOMPSON, J. THE LONELY LABYRINTH.
L. MACKEY, 543:DEC69-316
L.H. MACKEY, 141:SUMMER69-308
THOMPSON, J.A. & A. BERUMAN. SPEAKING
AND UNDERSTANDING SPANISH. (3RD ED)
S. BALDWIN, 399(MLJ):JAN70-55
THOMPSON, J.A. & P.J. LUNARDINI. PRAC-
TICING SPANISH. (3RD ED)
S. BALDWIN, 399(MLJ):JAN70-55
THOMPSON, J.M. RUSSIA, BOLSHEVISM, AND
THE VERSAILLES PEACE.*
R.A. WADE, 587:JUL68-148
THOMPSON, L. ROBERT FROST: THE YEARS OF
TRIUMPH, 1915-1938.*
B.T. SPENCER, 27(AL):MAR71-139
D. TYLER, 385(MQR):SPRING72-135
676(YR):AUTUMN70-VI
THOMPSON, L. & A. GRADE - SEE FROST, L.
THOMPSON, L.A. & J. FERGUSON, EDS.
AFRICA IN CLASSICAL ANTIQUITY.
B.H. WARMINGTON, 123:JUN71-246
THOMPSON, P. WILLIAM BUTTERFIELD.
617(TLS):6OCT72-1181
THOMPSON, P. THE WORK OF WILLIAM MORRIS.
D.J. GORDON, 592:MAR68-156
THOMPSON, S., ED. ONE HUNDRED FAVORITE
FOLKTALES.
E.W. BAUGHMAN, 292(JAF):OCT-DEC70-482
J.E. KELLER, 582(SFQ):JUN69-129
THOMPSON, T. HEARTS.*
G. CANT, 561(SATR):29JAN72-63
THOMPSON, W.B. & J.W. RIDGE, EDS. CATA-
LOGUE OF THE NATIONAL COLLECTION OF
GREEK AND LATIN SCHOOL TEXT-BOOKS
(1800 ONWARDS). (PT 1)
123:MAR71-149
THOMPSON, W.I. THE IMAGINATION OF AN
INSURRECTION.
J.D. BOULGER, 613:SPRING68-145
J.F. LEHMAN, 461:SUMMER69-632
THOMSON, A.W., ED. WORDSWORTH'S MIND
AND ART.
S. GILL, 447(N&Q):MAY70-188
THOMSON, D. HUNGRY AS HUNTERS.
617(TLS):21APR72-438
THOMSON, D. WILD EXCURSIONS.
R. BLYTHE, 362:31AUG72-279
617(TLS):27OCT72-1288
THOMSON, D. & R. SWANSON. CANADIAN
FOREIGN POLICY.
J.L. GRANATSTEIN, 99:SEP72-16
THOMSON, G. FROM MARX TO MAO TSE-TUNG.
617(TLS):28JAN72-84
THOMSON, G.H. THE FICTION OF E.M. FOR-
STER.
T. ROGERS, 175:SUMMER69-73
S.P. ROSENBAUM, 627(UTQ):JUL69-374
THOMSON, G.M. SIR FRANCIS DRAKE.
D.A.N. JONES, 362:27APR72-559
T. LASK, 441:17NOV72-47
617(TLS):12MAY72-536
THOMSON, J. NOT ONE OF US.*
617(TLS):8DEC72-1507
THOMSON, J.C., JR. WHILE CHINA FACED
WEST.
D. BORG, 293(JAST):AUG70-922

THOMSON, S.H. LATIN BOOKHANDS OF THE
LATER MIDDLE AGES, 1100-1500.
J.W. HALPORN, 124:JAN71-173
P. MC GURK, 123:JUN71-284
B. ROSS, 122:OCT71-278
THOMSON, V. AMERICAN MUSIC SINCE 1910.*
H.W. HITCHCOCK, 415:SEP71-861
W. SARGEANT, 442(NY):1JAN72-59
THORARDSON, B. TRUDEAU AND FOREIGN
POLICY.
J.L. GRANATSTEIN, 99:SEP72-16
D. SMILEY, 99:SEP72-18
THORAVAL, J. & M. LÉO. LE COMMENTAIRE
DE TEXTES LITTÉRAIRES.
E.L. DUTHIE, 208(FS):JUL71-372
THOREAU, H.D. THE BEST OF THOREAU'S
JOURNALS.* (C. BODE, ED)
617(TLS):7JAN72-16
THORLBY, A., ED. THE PENGUIN COMPANION
TO EUROPEAN LITERATURE. (BRITISH
TITLE: THE PENGUIN COMPANION TO LITERA-
TURE: EUROPE.)
N. BALAKIAN, 441:28JAN72-42
R. PLANT, 441:5NOV72-31
617(TLS):7JUL72-780
THORNE, A. ROME AND SOUTHERN ITALY.
617(TLS):29DEC72-1586
THORNHILL, W., ED. THE CASE FOR REGION-
AL REFORM.
617(TLS):2JUN72-641
THORNHILL, W., ED. THE GROWTH AND RE-
FORM OF ENGLISH LOCAL GOVERNMENT.
617(TLS):21JUL72-853
THORNHILL, W. THE NATIONALISED INDUS-
TRIES.
617(TLS):2JUN72-637
THORNTON, G. - SEE ANDERSEN, H.C.
THORNTON, R.C. THE COMINTERN AND THE
CHINESE COMMUNISTS, 1928-1931.
639(VQR):SUMMER70-CX
THORNTON, W. ALLUSIONS IN "ULYSSES."*
E. KREUTZER, 52:BAND4HEFT3-324
THOROLD, H. DERBYSHIRE.
617(TLS):24NOV72-1441
THORP, W. SONGS FROM THE RESTORATION
THEATER.
M. LAURIE, 415:MAR71-241
THORPE, E. THE NIGHT I CAUGHT THE SANTA
FE CHIEF.
V. CUNNINGHAM, 362:24AUG72-248
THORPE, J. - SEE ETHEREGE, G.
THORPE, M. MATTHEW ARNOLD.
P. TURNER, 179(ES):FEB70-73
THORPE, M. THE POETRY OF EDMUND BLUNDEN.
617(TLS):26MAY72-607
THORPE, M. SIEGFRIED SASSOON.*
F.J. MC DERMOTT, 613:AUTUMN68-453
F.W. SCHULZE, 38:BAND87HEFT1-103
THORSBERG, B. ÉTUDES SUR L'HYMNOLOGIE
MOZARABE.
S. CORBIN, 545(RPH):AUG70-210
THORSON, G. LIFE IN THE SEA.
617(TLS):30JUN72-754
THOULESS, R.H. FROM ANECDOTE TO EXPERI-
MENT IN PSYCHICAL RESEARCH.
617(TLS):15SEP72-1063
THOYTS, E.E. HOW TO READ OLD DOCUMENTS.
617(TLS):10NOV72-1377
THRAEDE, K. GRUNDZÜGE GRIECHISCH-RÖM-
ISCHER BRIEFTOPIK.
F. LASSERRE, 182:VOL23#9-502
THRASHER, P.A. PASCAL PAOLI, AN ENLIGHT-
ENED HERO, 1725-1807.
P.K., 566:SPRING71-48
THROWER, J. A SHORT HISTORY OF WESTERN
ATHEISM.
617(TLS):9JUN72-665

THULSTRUP, N. KIERKEGAARDS FORHOLD TIL
HEGEL.
G.L. STENGREN, 319:JUL72-366
THULSTRUP, N. - SEE "KIERKEGAARDIANA VI"
THUMMER, E. - SEE PINDAR
THURN, H., ED. DIE HANDSCHRIFTEN DER
ZISTERZIENSERABTEI EBRACH.
W. IRTENKAUF, 182:VOL23#15/16-706
THURSTON, P.T. ARTISTIC AMBIVALENCE IN
CHAUCER'S "KNIGHT'S TALE."*
R.T. DAVIES, 447(N&Q):FEB70-65
D.R. HOWARD, 401(MLQ):MAR70-112
TIBBLE, J.W., ED. THE FUTURE OF TEACHER
EDUCATION.
617(TLS):10MAR72-285
TIBBLE, J.W. & A. JOHN CLARE.
617(TLS):13OCT72-1216
TIBERIUS. TIBERII "DE FIGURIS DEMOS-
THENICIS LIBELLUS CUM DEPERDITORUM
OPERUM FRAGMENTIS." (G. BALLAIRA, ED)
D.C. INNES, 123:DEC71-368
G. KENNEDY, 124:NOV70-87
"TIBET 1950-1967."
293(JAST):MAY70-745
TIBULLUS. THE POEMS OF TIBULLUS. (P.
DUNLOP, TRANS)
617(TLS):29SEP72-1176
TICE, G.A. PATERSON.
S. SCHWARTZ, 441:3DEC72-16
TIDYMAN, E. SHAFT AMONG THE JEWS.
P. ADAMS, 61:JUL72-97
O.L. BAILEY, 561(SATR):26AUG72-61
N. CALLENDAR, 441:6AUG72-24
TIECK, L. WERKE IN VIER BÄNDEN. (M.
THALMANN, ED)
W.J. LILLYMAN, 406:SPRING71-91
"LUDWIG TIECK: DICHTER ÜBER IHRE DICHTUN-
GEN." (U. SCHWEIKERT, ED)
617(TLS):2JUN72-634
TIELSCH, E. DIE PLATONISCHEN VERSIONEN
DER GRIECHISCHEN DOXALEHRE.
F. LASSERRE, 182:VOL23#8-434
TIERNEY, B. ORIGINS OF PAPAL INFALLIBIL-
ITY, 1150-1350.
617(TLS):6OCT72-1201
TIERNEY, P.E. LADIES OF THE AVENUE.
L.C. POGREBIN, 441:27FEB72-34
TIGER, L. MEN IN GROUPS.
M. INGRAM, 362:20JAN72-73
TIGER, L. & R. FOX. THE IMPERIAL ANIMAL.*
M. GLUCKMAN, 453:16NOV72-39
G. GRIGSON, 362:17AUG72-216
M. LEVIN, 99:MAR72-16
617(TLS):14JUL72-791
TIGRID, P. LA CHUTE IRRÉSISTIBLE D'ALEX-
ANDER DUBCEK.
R. LUZA, 32:MAR71-177
TIKHOMIROV, M.N. ISTORICHESKIE SVIAZI
ROSSII SO SLAVIANSKIMI STRANAMI I VIZ-
ANTIEI.
G.P. MAJESKA, 32:JUN71-382
TIKHOMIROV, M.N. & OTHERS - SEE POKROV-
SKY, M.N.
TILANDER, G. LITTRÉ ET REMIGEREAU COMME
LEXICOGRAPHES ET MISCELLANEA CYNEGET-
ICA.*
M.D. LEGGE, 208(FS):APR71-189
TILANDER, G., ED. TRADUCCIÓN ESPAÑOLA
DE "DANCUS REX" Y "GUILLELMUS FALCON-
ARIUS," PUBLICADA SEGÚN EL MANUSCRITO
ESCURIALENSE V-II-19 DE LA SEGUNDA
MITAD DEL SIGLO XIII.
Á. GALMÉS DE FUENTES, 545(RPH):MAY70-
612
TILANDER, G. - SEE DU FOUILLOUX, J.
TILL, B. THE CHURCHES SEARCH FOR UNITY.
617(TLS):15SEP72-1064

TILLETT, L. THE GREAT FRIENDSHIP.*
W.S. VUCINICH, 32:JUN71-402
639(VQR):WINTER70-XXIV
TILLICH, P. AMOUR, POUVOIR ET JUSTICE.
F. HEIDSIECK, 542:JUL-DEC69-494
TILLICH, P. BEGEGNUNGEN.
617(TLS):28JAN72-103
TILLICH, P. THE FUTURE OF RELIGIONS.
(J.C. BRAUER, ED)
R.G.K., 543:DEC69-357
TILLICH, P. PERSPECTIVES ON 19TH AND
20TH CENTURY PROTESTANT THEOLOGY.
(C.E. BRAATEN, ED)
E.A.R., 543:SEP69-141
"PAUL TILLICH: RETROSPECT AND FUTURE."
S.O.H., 543:SEP69-146
TILLINGHAST, R. SLEEP WATCH.*
H. MORRIS, 569(SR):SPRING71-301
639(VQR):SUMMER70-XCV
TILLOTSON, G., P. FUSSELL, JR. & M. WAIN-
GROW, EDS. EIGHTEENTH-CENTURY ENGLISH
LITERATURE.
D.G., 173(ECS):SPRING70-422
481(PQ):JUL70-322
TILLOTSON, K. - SEE DICKENS, C.
"TIME OUT'S BOOK OF LONDON."
S. CLAPP, 362:10AUG72-183
"THE 'TIMES' ANTHOLOGY OF DETECTIVE STOR-
IES."
J. HUNTER, 362:21DEC72-869
"THE TIMES ATLAS OF THE WORLD."
617(TLS):21JUL72-846
"THE TIMES CONCISE ATLAS OF THE WORLD."
(J.C. BARTHOLOMEW & OTHERS, EDS)
617(TLS):22DEC72-1562
TIMM, W. THE GRAPHIC ART OF EDVARD
MUNCH.
D.L. SHIREY, 441:10DEC72-44
A. WERNER, 58:SUMMER70-10
TIMOFIEWITSCH, W. THE CHIESA DEL REDEN-
TORE.
617(TLS):23JUN72-729
TIMPE, D. DER TRIUMPH DES GERMANICUS.*
E.W. GRAY, 123:DEC70-347
TINCTORIS, J. CONCERNING THE NATURE AND
PROPRIETY OF TONES (DE NATURA ET PRO-
PRIETATE TONORUM). (A. SEAY, TRANS)
A. CLARKSON, 308:WINTER68-281
TINDALL, G.B. THE EMERGENCE OF THE NEW
SOUTH 1913-1945.
R.S. KIRKENDALL, 330(MASJ):FALL69-84
TINDALL, W.Y. A READER'S GUIDE TO "FINN-
EGANS WAKE."
A. MAC GILLIVRAY, 613:WINTER69-607
TING, W. HOT AND SOUR SOUP.
S. FRANK, 58:MAY70-12
TINGSTEN, H. VICTORIA AND THE VICTORI-
ANS.
N. ANNAN, 453:30NOV72-12
617(TLS):21JUL72-841
TINKER, H. INDIA AND PAKISTAN.
H. HEIDENREICH, 293(JAST):NOV69-178
TINKLE, L. MR. DE.
S. ACHESON, 584(SWR):WINTER71-V
TIPTAFT, N., ED. RELIGION IN BIRMINGHAM.
617(TLS):10MAR72-285
TIRSO DE MOLINA. EL BURLADOR DE SEVILLA.
(G.E. WADE, ED)
D. ROGERS, 86(BHS):JAN71-69
A.E. SINGER, 238:MAR70-169
TIRSO DE MOLINA. LA VENGANZA DE TAMAR.*
(A.K.G. PATERSON, ED)
J.G. FUCILLA, 551(RENQ):WINTER70-450
TISCHLER, H. A STRUCTURAL ANALYSIS OF
MOZART'S PIANO CONCERTOS.
D. CURRIER, 308:WINTER67-295
TITONE, E. CIVILTÀ DI MOTYÀ.
A. HUS, 555:VOL44FASC1-169

TITOW, J.Z. WINCHESTER YIELDS.
617(TLS):14JUL72-822
TIUSANEN, T. O'NEILL'S SCENIC IMAGES.
F.I. CARPENTER, 397(MD):FEB70-431
S.K. WINTHER, 50(ARQ):AUTUMN69-271
"TO HONOR ROMAN JAKOBSON."
R.E. MATLAW, 149:JUN71-187
TOBIN, J. HANDEL'S MESSIAH.*
W. DEAN, 415:FEB70-161
TOBINO, M. PER LE ANTICHE SCALE.
617(TLS):2JUN72-622
TODD, C. VOLTAIRE'S DISCIPLE: JEAN
FRANÇOIS DE LA HARPE.
617(TLS):20OCT72-1262
TODD, J.M. REFORMATION.
617(TLS):30JUN72-753
TODD, M.E. THE THINKING BODY.
J. DE LABAN, 290(JAAC):FALL69-112
TODD, O. L'ANNÉE DU CRABE.
617(TLS):1DEC72-1449
TODD, W.B. - SEE "GUY OF WARWICK"
TODOROV, T. LITTÉRATURE ET SIGNIFICA-
TION.
K. TOGEBY, 545(RPH):NOV69-248
TOEPFER, A.B. & A.C. DREILING. CONQUER-
ING THE WIND.
S.J. SACKETT, 650(WF):JAN69-56
TOESCA, M. LAMARTINE OU L'AMOUR DE LA
VIE.
J.S.P., 191(ELN):SEP70(SUPP)-73
TOFT, J. THE WEDGE.
V. CUNNINGHAM, 362:6APR72-458
TOGEBY, K., ED. OGIER LE DANOIS.
F. WHITEHEAD, 208(FS):JAN71-56
TOGEBY, K. OGIER LE DANOIS DANS LES
LITTÉRATURES EUROPÉENNES.
F. WHITEHEAD, 208(FS):JAN71-56
M.G. WORTHINGTON, 545(RPH):FEB71-488
TOGEBY, K. STRUCTURE IMMANENTE DE LA
LANGUE FRANÇAISE.* (2ND ED) IMMANENCE
ET STRUCTURE.*
M.G. WORTHINGTON, 545(RPH):FEB71-488
TOKARSKAJA, V.P. JAZYK MALINKE (MAN-
DINGO).
J. KNAPPERT, 353:SEP69-103
TŐKÉS, R.L. BÉLA KUN AND THE HUNGARIAN
SOVIET REPUBLIC.*
A. POLONSKY, 587:JUL68-147
TOLAND, J. THE RISING SUN.*
R.A. MILLER, 676(YR):SUMMER71-576
617(TLS):1SEP72-1029
DE TOLEDANO, R. ONE MAN ALONE.
F.G. WILSON, 396(MODA):SPRING71-195
TOLKIEN, J.R.R. THE HOBBIT. THE LORD
OF THE RINGS.
J.A. SMITH, 453:14DEC72-19
TOLKIEN, J.R.R. & E.V. GORDON - SEE "SIR
GAWAIN AND THE GREEN KNIGHT"
DE TOLLENAERE, F. DE HARIGASTI-INSKRIP-
TIE OP HELM B VAN NEGAU.
W.G. MOULTON, 361:VOL24#4-409
TOLSTOY, I. TOLSTOY, MY FATHER.*
442(NY):6MAY72-146
617(TLS):23JUN72-704
TOLSTOJ, L. XOZJAIN I RABOTNIK. (E.
AITKEN, ED)
E.H. LEHRMAN, 574(SEEJ):SUMMER71-234
TOLSTOY, L. ANNA KARENINA. (G. GIBIAN,
ED)
A. LEONG, 574(SEEJ):SPRING71-71
TOMA, P.A., ED. THE CHANGING FACE OF
COMMUNISM IN EASTERN EUROPE.
J.C. CAMPBELL, 32:SEP71-679
TOMANI, S., ED. I MANOSCRITTI FILOSOFICI
DI PAOLO FRISI.
G. GORI, 548(RCSF):JAN/MAR69-113
TOMAS, A. ATLANTIS.
617(TLS):24NOV72-1441

TOMAŠEVSKIJ, B.V. PUŠKIN UND FRANKREICH.
D. TSCHIŽEWSKIJ, 72:BAND208HEFT4/6-
478
TOMASSONI, I. MONDRIAN.
617(TLS):7JAN72-18
TOMASZEWSKI, W., ED. THE UNIVERSITY OF
EDINBURGH AND POLAND.
L.R. LEWITTER, 575(SEER):APR71-278
TOMBERG, K-H. DIE KAINE HISTORIA DES
PTOLEMAIOS CHENNOS.
N.G. WILSON, 123:MAR71-134
TOMIAK, J.J. THE SOVIET UNION.
617(TLS):7JUL72-785
TOMKINS, C. LIVING WELL IS THE BEST
REVENGE.*
R.M. ADAMS, 453:27JAN72-26
617(TLS):6OCT72-1193
TOMKINS, C. MERCHANTS AND MASTERPIECES.*
J.D. WELDON, 58:MAY70-12
TOMLIN, E.W.F., ED. CHARLES DICKENS, A
CENTENARY VOLUME.
L.C.S., 155:JAN70-54
TOMLINSON, C. WRITTEN ON WATER.
617(TLS):20OCT72-1249
TOMLINSON, R.A. ARGOS AND THE ARGOLID.
617(TLS):25AUG72-992
TOMORY, P. THE LIFE AND ART OF HENRY
FUSELI.
J. CANADAY, 441:3DEC72-90
D.J. ENRIGHT, 362:21DEC72-867
TOMORY, P.A. NEW ZEALAND ART: PAINTING
1890-1950.
W. CURNOW, 368:JUN69-186
TOMPKINS, D.C. SOURCES FOR THE STUDY OF
THE ADMINISTRATION OF CRIMINAL JUSTICE
1938-1948. SOURCES FOR THE STUDY OF
THE ADMINISTRATION OF CRIMINAL JUSTICE
1949-1956.
617(TLS):18FEB72-191
TONCHIA, D. L'ESSERE DEL CIVILE DIVE-
NIRE.
E. NAMER, 542:JUL-DEC69-494
TONG-YOP, S. - SEE UNDER SHIN TONG-YOP
TONKIN, H. SPENSER'S COURTEOUS PASTORAL.
617(TLS):22DEC72-1559
TONKS, R. THE HALT DURING THE CHASE.
E. MORGAN, 362:20APR72-524
617(TLS):28APR72-500
"TÖNNIES FENNE'S LOW GERMAN MANUAL OF
SPOKEN RUSSIAN, PSKOV 1607." (VOLS
1 & 2) (L.L. HAMMERICH & OTHERS, EDS)
B.J. KOEKKOEK, 301(JEGP):OCT71-716
TÖNZ, L. DIE KÜNSTLERISCHE EIGENSTÄNDIG-
KEIT UND EIGENART NESTROYS.
J.D. BARLOW, 406:SPRING71-88
TOPEROFF, S. PILGRIM OF THE SUN AND
STARS.
A. BROYARD, 441:8NOV72-49
TOPLISS, P. THE RHETORIC OF PASCAL.
S.V.O. PRICHARD, JR., 583:SUMMER69-
324
TOPOLSKI, F. SHEM, HAM AND JAPHETH INC.
617(TLS):28JAN72-109
TOPONCE, A. REMINISCENCES OF ALEXANDER
TOPONCE WRITTEN BY HIMSELF. (R.A.
GRIFFEN, ED)
W. GARD, 584(SWR):AUTUMN71-VI
TOPOR, T. TIGHTROPE MINOR.
M. LEVIN, 441:6FEB72-36
TOPPING, S. JOURNEY BETWEEN TWO CHINAS.
T. LASK, 441:28JUL72-34
A. PRAGER, 561(SATR):18NOV72-91
J.C. THOMSON, JR., 441:29OCT72-3
442(NY):14OCT72-181
TORCHIANA, D. W.B. YEATS AND GEORGIAN
IRELAND.
D.H. GREENE, 397(MD):DEC68-336

TORDAI, Z. EXISTENCE ET RÉALITÉ.
S.D. BRAUN, 399(MLJ):JAN70-44
TORMEY, A. THE CONCEPT OF EXPRESSION.
M. WEITZ, 311(JP):23NOV72-791
TÖRNQVIST, E., ED. DRAMA OCH TEATER.
W. JOHNSON, 397(MD):FEB70-430
TORRANCE, T.F. THEOLOGICAL SCIENCE.
H. MEYNELL, 479(PHQ):JUL70-315
TORRAS ELÍAS, J. LA GUERRA DE LOS AGRA-
VIADOS.
191(ELN):SEP70(SUPP)-152
DE TORRE, G. DEL 98 AL BARROCO.*
J.W. SCHWEITZER, 238:SEP70-574
DE TORRE, G. VIGENCIA DE RUBÉN DARÍO Y
OTRAS PÁGINAS.
R.A. CARDWELL, 86(BHS):OCT71-361
V.M. VALENZUELA, 238:SEP70-584
TORREGIAN, S. THE WOUNDED MATTRESS.
J.R. CARPENTER, 491:JUN72-164
TORRES, T. THE OPEN DOORS.
J. GREENFIELD, 287:JUL/AUG69-24
DE TORRES VILLARROEL, D. LA BARCA DE
AQUERONTE (1731). (G. MERCADIER, ED)
R. JOHNSON, 86(BHS):APR71-166
TORTEL, J. LIMITES DU REGARD.
617(TLS):11FEB72-146
TORTEL, J. RELATIONS.
J. GUGLIELMI, 98:OCT69-879
TŌRU, Y. - SEE UNDER YANO TŌRU
TOTMAN, C.D. POLITICS IN THE TOKUGAWA
BAKUFU, 1600-1843.*
R. STORRY, 302:JAN69-127
TOUCHARD, J. LA GLOIRE DE BÉRANGER.
J.S.P., 191(ELN):SEP69(SUPP)-60
TOUCHEFEU-MEYNIER, O. THÈMES ODYSSÉENS
DANS L'ART ANTIQUE.
J. BOARDMAN, 123:MAR71-143
K. MATTHEWS, 124:JAN71-163
TOULMIN, S. HUMAN UNDERSTANDING. (VOL
1)
617(TLS):11AUG72-939
DE TOULOUSE-LAUTREC, H. UNPUBLISHED COR-
RESPONDENCE OF HENRI DE TOULOUSE-
LAUTREC. (L. GOLDSCHMIDT & H. SCHIM-
MEL, EDS)
J. HOUSE, 90:OCT70-711
TOURAINE, A. THE POST-INDUSTRIAL SOCI-
ETY.*
T. BOTTOMORE, 453:6APR72-31
TOURGUENEV, I. - SEE UNDER TURGENEV, I.
TOURNEUR, C. THE REVENGER'S TRAGEDY.
(L.J. ROSS, ED)
M.R.M., 477:SPRING69-293
TOURNIER, M. THE ERL KING.
K. GRAHAM, 362:12OCT72-481
617(TLS):6OCT72-1185
TOURNIER, M. FRIDAY.
R.M. BAINE, 219(GAR):FALL69-420
TOURNIER, M. THE OGRE.
M. ENGEL, 441:3SEP72-7
K. MILLER, 453:30NOV72-40
L.E. SISSMAN, 442(NY):30DEC72-68
TOURNOUX, J-R. JAMAIS DIT.
617(TLS):29SEP72-1134
TOUSSAINT, A. HISTOIRE DES ÎLES MASCAR-
EIGNES.
617(TLS):24NOV72-1424
TOVEY, D. ESSAYS IN MUSICAL ANALYSIS.
617(TLS):27OCT72-1276
TOWLE, T. NORTH.
D. LEHMAN, 491:JAN72-224
F. MORAMARCO, 651(WHR):SUMMER71-281
TOWNEND, P. OUT OF FOCUS.
N. CALLENDAR, 441:9JUL72-30
TOWNEND, P. ZOOM.
N. CALLENDAR, 441:22OCT72-47
TOWNSEND, J.B., ED. THIS NEW MAN.
A.A. DAVIDSON, 127:FALL70-122

TOWNSEND, W., ED. CANADIAN ART TODAY.
B. HALE, 96:JUN70-62
TOYNBEE, A. SOME PROBLEMS OF GREEK HIS-
TORY.
M. CHAMBERS, 124:OCT70-62
N.G.L. HAMMOND, 123:DEC71-415
TOYNBEE, A. A STUDY OF HISTORY. (NEW
ED) (ABRIDGED)
617(TLS):20OCT72-1258
TOYNBEE, A. SURVIVING THE FUTURE.*
441:15OCT72-40
TOYNBEE, P. A DICTIONARY OF PROPER NAMES
AND NOTABLE MATTERS IN THE WORKS OF
DANTE.* (REV BY C.S. SINGLETON)
E. VON RICHTHOFEN, 276:SPRING70-93
C.E. TURNER, 546(RR):FEB70-43
TRABA, M. LOS LABERINTOS INSOLADOS.
270:VOL20#3-61
TRACY, C., ED. BROWNING'S MIND AND ART.*
K. ALLOTT, 541(RES):FEB70-92
TRACY, C. - SEE JOHNSON, S.
TRACY, G.L. & A.R. ANDERSON, EDS. DAUER
IM WECHSEL.
W. HOFFMEISTER, 221(GQ):JAN70-137
TRACY, H. THE BUTTERFLIES OF THE PRO-
VINCE.
F.P.W. MC DOWELL, 659:SUMMER72-361
TRACY, H. THE QUIET END OF EVENING.
P. ADAMS, 61:JUN72-112
L. GRAVER, 441:2JUL72-6
J. HUNTER, 362:13APR72-493
J.D. O'HARA, 561(SATR):24JUN72-60
442(NY):8JUL72-74
617(TLS):21APR72-438
TRACY, T.J. PHYSIOLOGICAL THEORY AND THE
DOCTRINE OF THE MEAN IN PLATO AND ARIS-
TOTLE.
R.K. SPRAGUE, 122:OCT71-292
TRAERUP, B. EAST MACEDONIAN FOLK SONGS.
N. SACHS, 187:JAN72-129
TRAGER, J. THE BIG, FERTILE, RUMBLING,
CAST-IRON, GROWLING, ACHING, UNBUTTONED
BELLYBOOK.
R.A. SOKOLOV, 441:12NOV72-62
TRAGLIA, A., ED. POETAE NOVI.
A. WLOSOK, 182:VOL23#17/18-820
TRAHERNE, T. CHRISTIAN ETHICKS.* (C.L.
MARKS & G.R. GUFFEY, EDS)
M. FIXLER, 405(MP):NOV69-185
TRAILL, W. IN RUPERT'S LAND. (M. AT-
WOOD, ED)
102(CANL):SPRING71-119
TRAKL, G. DICHTUNGEN UND BRIEFE.* (W.
KILLY & H. SZKLENAR, EDS)
W.G. CUNLIFFE, 406:WINTER71-394
TRANI, E.P. THE TREATY OF PORTSMOUTH.
N.G. LEVIN, JR., 432(NEQ):JUN70-335
TRANTER, J.E. PARALLAX.
J. TULIP, 581:1971/1-72
TRANTER, N. PORTRAIT OF THE BORDER
COUNTRY.
617(TLS):25AUG72-1006
TRAPP, F.A. THE ATTAINMENT OF DELA-
CROIX.*
P. GAY, 31(ASCH):AUTUMN72-660
617(TLS):28APR72-497
TRASK, W.R., ED. THE UNWRITTEN SONG.
(VOL 2)
V.L. EDWARDS, 37:APR69-40
TRAUM, H. FINGER-PICKING STYLES FOR
GUITAR.
A.J. FIELD, 650(WF):OCT68-278
TRAUTMAN, K. SPIES BEHIND THE PILLARS,
BANDITS AT THE PASS.
441:23JUL72-16
442(NY):8APR72-132
TRAVEN, B. THE REBELLION OF THE HANGED.
D.K. MANO, 441:27AUG72-2

TRAVERS, P.L. MARIA POPPINA AB A AD Z.
(G.M. LYNE, TRANS)
J.K. COLBY, 124:DEC70-136
TRAVERS, R. THE APARTMENT ON K STREET.
N. CALLENDAR, 441:19NOV72-61
TRAVERSA, V. IDIOMA IN PROSPETTIVA.
M. KUITUNEN, 399(MLJ):FEB70-135
J.A. TURSI, 276:AUTUMN70-329
TRAVERSA, V.P. LUIGI CAPUANA CRITIC AND
NOVELIST.
S.E. SCALIA, 276:SUMMER70-222
TRAVERSARI, G. ASPETTI FORMALI DELLA
SCULTURA NEOCLASSICA A ROMA DAL I AL
III SECOLO D.C.*
M.A.R. COLLEDGE, 313:VOL60-241
TRAWICK, L.M., ED. BACKGROUNDS OF
ROMANTICISM.
D.G., 173(ECS):SPRING70-422
R.S. WOOF, 447(N&Q):JAN70-40
"TRE STUDI SULLA CULTURA SPAGNOLA."
J. HERRERO, 240(HR):APR70-206
TREASE, G. SAMUEL PEPYS AND HIS WORLD.
617(TLS):23JUN72-729
TREFUSIS, V. FROM DUSK TO DAWN.
617(TLS):25AUG72-985
TREGGIARI, S. ROMAN FREEDMEN DURING THE
LATE REPUBLIC.*
M.H. CRAWFORD, 123:JUN71-255
A. LINTOTT, 313:VOL60-221
TREGONNING, K.G. HOME PORT SINGAPORE.
J.D. CLARKSON, 293(JAST):AUG70-990
TREHARNE, R.F. ESSAYS ON THIRTEENTH
CENTURY ENGLAND.
617(TLS):12MAY72-557
TREHER, C.M. SNOW HILL CLOISTER [TO-
GETHER WITH] BARBA, P.A., ED. DIALECT
POEMS.
19(AGR):VOL35#5-25
TREIP, M. MILTON'S PUNCTUATION AND
CHANGING ENGLISH USAGE, 1582-1676.
J.S. DIEKHOFF, 301(JEGP):JUL71-553
M. LIEB, 568(SCN):SUMMER/AUTUMN71-35
J.T. SHAWCROSS, 191(ELN):JUN71-326
S.I. TUCKER, 402(MLR):OCT71-863
TREISTMAN, J.M. THE PREHISTORY OF CHINA.
617(TLS):18AUG72-977
TRELEASE, A.W. RECONSTRUCTION.
E. & N. FONER, 453:20APR72-39
TRELOAR, B. MOLIÈRE: LES PRÉCIEUSES
RIDICULES.
C.B. THORNTON-SMITH, 67:MAY71-128
TREMAYNE, S. THE TURNING SKY.
W.P. TURNER, 619(TC):VOL177#1042-58
TREMBLAY, G. LES SEINS GORGÉS.
J-L. MAJOR, 627(UTQ):JUL70-429
TREMLETT, T.D. & H.S. LONDON, EDS. ROLLS
OF ARMS HENRY III.
J. BROMLEY, 325:APR69-503
TREML, V.G., ED. THE DEVELOPMENT OF THE
SOVIET ECONOMY.
R.W. CAMPBELL, 550(RUSR):JUL70-359
TRENARD, L., ED. HISTOIRE DE LILLE.
(VOL 1)
D.J.A. MATTHEW, 182:VOL23#19/20-893
J. ROGOZINSKI, 589:APR71-377
TRENDALL, A.D. & T.B.L. WEBSTER. ILLUS-
TRATIONS OF GREEK DRAMA.
617(TLS):14JUL72-797
TRENT, P. THE IMAGE MAKERS.
J. KANON, 561(SATR):16DEC72-58
A. TAYLOR, 441:24SEP72-6
"THE TRES RICHES HEURES OF JEAN, DUKE OF
BERRY."
A. KUHN, 58:NOV69-18
M.M. SHEEHAN, 363:MAY70-107
"TRÉSOR DE LA LANGUE FRANÇAISE." (VOL 1)
(P. IMBS, GENERAL ED)
617(TLS):13OCT72-1229

TRETHOWAN, I. THE ABSOLUTE AND THE
ATONEMENT.
617(TLS):11FEB72-163
TRETHOWAN, I. ABSOLUTE VALUE.
C. LYAS, 518:MAY71-30
TREVANIAN. THE EIGER SANCTION.
O.L. BAILEY, 561(SATR):28OCT72-89
A. BROYARD, 441:5OCT72-49
N. CALLENDAR, 441:17SEP72-45
TREVELYAN, G.M. TRINITY COLLEGE.
617(TLS):1SEP72-1033
TREVELYAN, H. THE INDIA WE LEFT.
617(TLS):13OCT72-1214
TREVELYAN, R. PRINCES UNDER THE VOLCANO.
J. VINCENT, 362:7DEC72-793
617(TLS):10NOV72-1360
TREVES, R. DO-IT-YOURSELF HOME PROTEC-
TION.
L.J. DAVIS, 440:28MAY72-9
TREVISAN, D. THE VAMPIRE OF CURITIBA
AND OTHER STORIES.
T. LASK, 441:1DEC72-42
E. RODRÍGUEZ MONEGAL, 441:24DEC72-6
TREVOR, W. THE BALLROOM OF ROMANCE AND
OTHER STORIES.
A. BROYARD, 441:31OCT72-47
J. HUNTER, 362:4MAY72-596
617(TLS):26MAY72-595
TREVOR, W. MISS GOMEZ AND THE BRETHREN.*
E. FEINSTEIN, 364:FEB/MAR72-177
TREVOR-ROPER, H.R. RELIGION, THE REFOR-
MATION AND SOCIAL CHANGE. (2ND ED)
617(TLS):17MAR72-296
TREWIN, J.C. THE POMPING FOLK IN THE
NINETEENTH CENTURY THEATRE.
K.J. WORTH, 155:JAN69-46
TREWIN, J.C. - SEE O'CASEY, E.
TRICKETT, R. THE HONEST MUSE.
H.D. WEINBROT, 173(ECS):FALL69-141
TRIESCH, M., ED. DEUTSCHE GEDICHTE VOM
16. JAHRHUNDERT BIS ZUR GEGENWART.
W. WONDERLEY, 399(MLJ):OCT70-472
TRIESCH, M., COMP. THE LILLIAN HELLMAN
COLLECTION AT THE UNIVERSITY OF TEXAS.
J.S., 78(BC):AUTUMN70-399
TRIFONOV, N.A. - SEE LUNACHARSKY, A.V.
TRIGG, R. PAIN AND EMOTION.
R. PETERS, 518:JAN71-25
TRILLING, L. BEYOND CULTURE.*
R. LEHAN, 445(NCF):DEC68-368
TRILLING, L. MIND IN THE MODERN WORLD.
J.M. CAMERON, 453:30NOV72-18
TRILLING, L. SINCERITY AND AUTHENTICITY.
J. BAYLEY, 362:26OCT72-543
A. BROYARD, 441:25OCT72-49
617(TLS):27OCT72-1269
TRIMPI, W. BEN JONSON'S POEMS.
R. GILL, 179(ES):JUN70-254
TRINGHAM, R. - SEE MASSON, V.M. & V.I.
SARIANIDI
"THE TRINITY COLLEGE APOCALYPSE."* (M.
DULONG, TRANS)
J. BACKHOUSE, 90:JAN69-35
TRIOLET, E. LE CHEVAL ROUX.
617(TLS):22SEP72-1086
TRIOMPHE, R. JOSEPH DE MAISTRE.
191(ELN):SEP69(SUPP)-76
TRIPET, A. PÉTRARQUE OU LA CONNAISSANCE
DE SOI.
N.J. PERELLA, 551(RENQ):SUMMER70-163
TRIPLETT, F. THE LIFE, TIMES AND
TREACHEROUS DEATH OF JESSE JAMES.
R.N. ELLIS, 651(WHR):SUMMER71-271
TRIPP, M. THE CLAWS OF GOD.
617(TLS):29DEC72-1588
TRISELIOTIS, J.P., ED. SOCIAL WORK WITH
COLOURED IMMIGRANTS AND THEIR FAMILIES.
617(TLS):15DEC72-1526

TRISKA, J.F., ED. COMMUNIST PARTY-
STATES.
V.V. ASPATURIAN, 32:SEP71-674
R.E. KANET, 104:SPRING71-139
TRISTAN, F. NAISSANCE D'UN SPECTRE.
S. MAX, 207(FR):FEB70-530
TRIVICK, H.H. THE CRAFT AND DESIGN OF
MONUMENTAL BRASSES.
M.D. ANDERSON, 46:DEC69-482
R.E. TULLY, 363:FEB70-77
TROGER, R. A COMPARATIVE STUDY OF A
BENGAL FOLKTALE.*
E.C. KIRKLAND, 582(SFQ):SEP68-271
TROISFONTAINES, R. WHAT IS EXISTENTIAL-
ISM?
W.A.J., 543:MAR70-569
TROLLOPE, A. THE NEW ZEALANDER. (N.J.
HALL, ED)
617(TLS):28JUL72-862
TROTSKY, L. 1905. (A. BOSTOCK, TRANS)
R. PIPES, 441:19MAR72-37
617(TLS):15SEP72-1061
TROTSKY, L. THE YOUNG LENIN. (M.
FRIEDBERG, ED) (GERMAN TITLE: DER JUNGE
LENIN.)
A. PARRY, 550(RUSR):OCT70-457
442(NY):16SEP72-127
TROTTER, G.D. & K. WHINNOM, EDS. LA
COMEDIA THEBAIDA.
A.D. DEYERMOND, 86(BHS):JAN71-62
J.G. FUCILLA, 551(RENQ):WINTER70-450
TROUNCER, M. CHARLES DE FOUCAULD.
617(TLS):4AUG72-924
TROUP, F. SOUTH AFRICA.
617(TLS):27OCT72-1272
TROWER, P. MOVING THROUGH THE MYSTERY.
D. BARBOUR, 150(DR):SPRING70-112
TROXELL, H.M. THE NORMAN DAVIS COLLEC-
TION.
R.T. WILLIAMS, 123:JUN71-302
TROYANOVICH, J.M. & K.W. SCHILD, EDS.
GERMAN CONVERSATIONAL READER.
H.L. STOUT, 221(GQ):NOV70-825
DE TROYES, C. - SEE UNDER CHRÉTIEN DE
TROYES
TRUBETZKOY, N.S. PRINCIPLES OF PHONOL-
OGY.
C.E. CAIRNS, 350:DEC71-918
J. KRÁMSKÝ, 575(SEER):JUL71-458
TRUC, G. LAMARTINE.
J.S.P., 191(ELN):SEP69(SUPP)-75
TRUCHET, J. - SEE HUGO, V.
TRUCHET, J. - SEE DE LA ROCHEFOUCAULD, F.
TRUDEL, M. INITIATION À LA NOUVELLE-
FRANCE.
J-C. BONENFANT, 627(UTQ):JUL69-452
TRUEBLOOD, P.G. LORD BYRON.
J.D. BONE, 447(N&Q):MAY70-198
TRUEMAN, S. YOU'RE ONLY AS OLD AS YOU
ACT.
J.M. ROBSON, 627(UTQ):JUL69-422
TRUESDALE, C.W. MOON SHOTS.
J. HOPPER, 661:SPRING69-102
TRULLEMANS, U.M. HUELLAS DE LA PICARESCA
EN PORTUGAL.
A.R. CLEMENTE, 400(MLN):MAR70-288
TRUMAN. HARRY S. TRUMAN.
A. BROYARD, 441:26DEC72-35
W.C. MC WILLIAMS, 441:24DEC72-1
442(NY):30DEC72-71
TRUMBULL, H. & M. A SEASON IN NEW YORK,
1801. (H.M. MORGAN, ED)
E.B. SCHLESINGER, 432(NEQ):DEC70-652
B. STILL, 656(WMQ):APR70-336
TRUMP, D.H. MALTA.
617(TLS):6OCT72-1189
TRUNK, I. JUDENRAT.
441:10DEC72-48

TRUSSLER, S., ED. BURLESQUE PLAYS OF THE
EIGHTEENTH CENTURY.
A. SHERBO, 402(MLR):OCT71-867
566:AUTUMN70-31
TRUSSLER, S., ED. EIGHTEENTH-CENTURY
COMEDY.
A. SHERBO, 402(MLR):OCT71-867
TRUSSLER, S. THE PLAYS OF JOHN OSBORNE.
A.P. HINCHLIFFE, 148:SPRING70-95
TRUSSLER, S. - SEE TAYLOR, W.D.
TRYPANIS, C.A., ED. FOURTEEN EARLY
BYZANTINE CANTICA.
J. GROSDIDIER DE MATONS, 303:VOL90-
222
TRYTHALL, J.W.D. FRANCO.*
J. MADDEN, 67:NOV71-266
TSANOFF, R.A. AUTOBIOGRAPHIES OF TEN
RELIGIOUS LEADERS.
W.A.J., 543:DEC69-357
TS'AO CHIH. WORLDS OF DUST AND JADE.
(G.W. KENT, TRANS)
H.H. FRANKEL, 318(JAOS)OCT-DEC70-610
TSCHACBASOV, N. AN ILLUSTRATED SURVEY OF
WESTERN ART.
J.E. ARONIN, 505:JAN69-186
TSCHÖPL, C. VJAČESLAV IVANOV.*
P.R. HART, 104:SUMMER71-280
TSE-TUNG, C. - SEE UNDER CHOW TSE-TUNG
TSE-TUNG, M. - SEE UNDER MAO TSE-TUNG
TSOU, T., ED. CHINA IN CRISIS. (VOL 2)
F.W. NEAL, 293(JAST):NOV69-168
TSUENEO, T. - SEE UNDER TAKEDA TSUNEO
TSUJI, K. KAISEKI.
617(TLS):22DEC72-1561
TSURUMI, K. SOCIAL CHANGE AND THE IN-
DIVIDUAL.
J.M. MAKI, 418(MR):WINTER71-171
R.A. MILLER, 676(YR):AUTUMN70-117
TSVETAYEVA, M. SELECTED POEMS.
J. FULLER, 362:24FEB72-251
TSYBENKO, V.A. MIROVOZZRENIE D.I. PISA-
REVA.
J.A. ROGERS, 32:JUN71-395
TU-JIN, P. - SEE UNDER PAK TU-JIN
TUCHMAN, B. SAND AGAINST THE WIND.*
W. ALLEN, 362:6JAN72-23
TUCHOLSKY, K. WHAT IF--?*
R. HANSER, 19(AGR):VOL35#2-34
M. SONNENFELD, 221(GQ):MAY70-522
TUCKER, H. AND WHERE DOES THE CIRCLE END
BEGINNING.
V.B. YOUNG, 577(SHR):WINTER70-94
TUCKER, R.C. THE MARXIAN REVOLUTIONARY
IDEA.*
H.B., 543:DEC69-358
T.J. BLAKELEY, 550(RUSR):JUL70-359
TUCKER, R.C. THE SOVIET POLITICAL MIND.
(2ND ED)
617(TLS):27OCT72-1297
TUCKER, S.I. ENTHUSIASM.
617(TLS):5MAY72-513
TUCKER, S.I. PROTEAN SHAPE.
P.K. ELKIN, 67:MAY71-100
TUCKER, W. THIS WITCH.*
617(TLS):13OCT72-1235
TUCKEY, J.S. - SEE TWAIN, M.
TUDOR, D. OLTENIA ROMANĂ.
R.A. TODD, 104:WINTER71-524
TUGENDHAT, C. THE MULTINATIONALS.*
H.L. SILBERMAN, 561(SATR):11MAR72-66
TUGWELL, M. AIRBORNE TO BATTLE.
617(TLS):14JAN72-49
TUGWELL, R.G. IN SEARCH OF ROOSEVELT.
K.S. DAVIS, 441:17DEC72-4
TUGWELL, R.G. OFF COURSE.*
J.M. BLUM, 676(YR):SUMMER71-598

TUILIER, A. RECHERCHES CRITIQUES SUR LA
TRADITION DU TEXTE D'EURIPIDE.*
J. DIGGLE, 123:MAR71-19
TULLOCH, D. WINGATE. (A. SWINSON, ED)
617(TLS):30JUN72-734
TUMA, E.H. ECONOMIC HISTORY AND THE
SOCIAL SCIENCES.
617(TLS):7JUL72-772
TUNNEY, C. BIOGRAPHICAL DICTIONARY OF
WORLD WAR II.
617(TLS):14JUL72-825
TUNNEY, K. TALLULAH - DARLING OF THE
GODS.
617(TLS):8DEC72-1482
TUPLIN, W.A. GREAT WESTERN SAINTS AND
SINNERS.
617(TLS):17MAR72-317
TURCAN, R. SÉNÈQUE ET LES RELIGIONS
ORIENTALES.*
J.R.G. WRIGHT, 123:MAR71-133
TURCO, L. AWAKEN, BELLS FALLING.
H. CARLILE, 448:SUMMER70-124
TURGENEV [TOURGUENEV], I. LETTRES INÉD-
ITES À PAULINE VIARDOT ET À SA FAMILLE.
(H. GRANJARD & A. ZVIGUILSKY, WITH D.
PEROVIĆ, EDS)
617(TLS):15SEP72-1062
TURGENEV [TOURGUENEV], I. NOUVELLE COR-
RESPONDANCE INÉDITE. (VOL 1) (A.
ZVIGUILSKY, ED)
617(TLS):14APR72-423
TURGENEV [TOURGUENEV], I. NOUVELLE COR-
RESPONDANCE INÉDITE. (VOL 2) (A. ZVI-
GUILSKY, ED)
617(TLS):22DEC72-1553
TURGENEV, I.S. DVORJANSKOE GNEZDO. (P.
WADDINGTON, ED)
W. JASZCZUN, 574(SEEJ):SPRING71-129
TURGENEV, I.S. SPRING TORRENTS. (L.
SCHAPIRO, ED & TRANS)
617(TLS):28JAN72-100
TURIN, S.P. FROM PETER THE GREAT TO
LENIN.
L. KOCHAN, 587:APR69-565
TURKAY, O. UYURGEZER.
M. ÇATAN, 270:VOL20#2-48
TURLINGTON, B. SOCRATES, THE FATHER OF
WESTERN PHILOSOPHY.
W. CHARLTON, 123:DEC71-458
"THE TURN OF A CENTURY 1885-1910."
H. LEHMANN-HAUPT, 517(PBSA):JUL-SEP
71-334
TURNBULL, A. THOMAS WOLFE.
J.P. LOVERING, 613:SPRING69-129
P. OAKES, 619(TC):1968/2-57
TURNBULL, C.M. THE MOUNTAIN PEOPLE.
P. ADAMS, 61:NOV72-130
R. ARDREY, 561(SATR):14OCT72-73
H. KENNER, 441:12NOV72-3
C. LEHMANN-HAUPT, 441:30OCT72-33
442(NY):18NOV72-246
TURNBULL, C.M. THE STRAITS SETTLEMENTS.
617(TLS):22DEC72-1565
TURNBULL, L. & J.C. TYSON, COMPS. COALS
FROM NEWCASTLE.
W.B. STEPHENS, 325:APR70-83
TURNBULL, P. PROVENCE.
617(TLS):28JUL72-900
TURNELL, M. JEAN RACINE: DRAMATIST.
D.A.N. JONES, 362:24AUG72-247
617(TLS):28APR72-468
TURNER, A.R. THE VISION OF LANDSCAPE
IN RENAISSANCE ITALY.
A.B. HARRIS, 56:SUMMER69-200
TURNER, B. SOLDEN'S WOMEN.
617(TLS):4FEB72-135

TURNER, B.A. EXPLORING THE INDUSTRIAL
SUBCULTURE. (J. WAKEFORD, ED)
617(TLS):13OCT72-1237
TURNER, C.B. AN ANALYSIS OF SOVIET
VIEWS ON JOHN MAYNARD KEYNES.*
J.S. PRYBYLA, 550(RUSR):JUL70-360
A. WALKER, 575(SEER):APR71-312
TURNER, E.G., ED. MÉNANDRE.
E. KEULS, 124:14MAY71-313
TURNER, J.G. & L.L. - SEE "MARY TODD
LINCOLN"
TURNER, P. - SEE SWIFT, J.
"TURNER'S EARLY SKETCHBOOKS." (G. WIL-
KINSON, ED)
617(TLS):21JUL72-840
TURNEY, A.W. DISASTER AT MOSCOW.*
A. DALLIN, 32:MAR71-155
TURP, R. GUNRUNNER.
617(TLS):23JUN72-729
TURVEY, R. ECONOMIC ANALYSIS AND PUBLIC
ENTERPRISES.
617(TLS):2JUN72-637
TUSHNET, L. THE MEDICINE MEN.
E. CRAY, 441:23JAN72-4
TUTEN, F. THE ADVENTURES OF MAO ON THE
LONG MARCH.*
J. UPDIKE, 442(NY):13MAY72-138
M. WOOD, 453:10AUG72-14
TUTTLE, A. SONGS FROM THE NIGHT BEFORE.
M. LEVIN, 441:5MAR72-35
442(NY):4MAR72-115
TUTTLE, A. THIS TIME IN TWILIGHT.
617(TLS):4FEB72-117
TUTTLE, H.N. WILHELM DILTHEY'S PHILOSO-
PHY OF HISTORICAL UNDERSTANDING.
R.A. MAKKREEL, 319:APR72-232
TUTTLE, I. CONCORDANCE TO VAUGHAN'S
"SILEX SCINTILLANS."*
R. DEROLEZ, 179(ES):OCT70-476
TUVE, R. ESSAYS BY ROSEMOND TUVE. (T.P.
ROCHE, JR., ED)
A. LOW, 568(SCN):SUMMER/AUTUMN71-35
TUVESON, E.L. REDEEMER NATION.*
R.E. KNOLL, 502(PRS):SUMMER69-230
TUWIM, J. THE DANCING SOCRATES AND OTHER
POEMS. (A. GILLON, ED & TRANS)
J.J. MACIUSZKO, 574(SEEJ):SPRING71-
125
TWAIN, M. CLEMENS OF THE CALL. (E.M.
BRANCH, ED)
639(VQR):SPRING70-LII
TWAIN, M. MARK TWAIN'S HANNIBAL, HUCK &
TOM.* (W. BLAIR, ED) MARK TWAIN'S
MYSTERIOUS STRANGER MANUSCRIPTS.*
(W.M. GIBSON, ED)
J.M. COX, 639(VQR):WINTER70-144
TWAIN, M. MARK TWAIN'S LETTERS TO HIS
PUBLISHERS: 1867-1894. (H. HILL, ED)
MARK TWAIN'S SATIRES & BURLESQUES.
(F.R. ROGERS, ED) MARK TWAIN'S WHICH
WAS THE DREAM? AND OTHER SYMBOLIC
WRITINGS OF THE LATER YEARS. (J.S.
TUCKEY, ED)
R.A. REES, 445(NCF):JUN68-113
TWAIN, M. & H.H. ROGERS. MARK TWAIN'S
CORRESPONDENCE WITH HENRY HUTTLESTON
ROGERS.* (L. LEARY, ED)
J.M. COX, 639(VQR):WINTER70-144
TWISTLETON-WYKEHAM-FIENNES, R. ICE FALL
IN NORWAY.
E.S. TURNER, 362:3FEB72-154
"293 RENAISSANCE WOODCUTS FOR ARTISTS
AND ILLUSTRATORS/JOST AMMAN'S KUNST-
BÜCHLIN."
B. REISE, 592:NOV69-186
"2,000 YEARS OF CALLIGRAPHY."
617(TLS):22SEP72-1123

TYAGI, R.B. RECENT TRENDS IN THE COOP-
ERATIVE MOVEMENT IN INDIA.
I.J. CATANACH, 293(JAST):AUG70-964
DE TYARD, P. PONTUS DE TYARD: OEUVRES
POÉTIQUES COMPLÈTES. (J.C. LAPP, ED)
R.A. KATZ, 551(RENQ):AUTUMN70-298
TYLER, A. THE CLOCK WINDER.
S. BLACKBURN, 440:14MAY72-13
E. EASTON, 561(SATR):17JUN72-77
M. LEVIN, 441:21MAY72-31
442(NY):29APR72-140
TYLER, P. MAGIC AND MYTH OF THE MOVIES.
617(TLS):4FEB72-125
TYLER, P. THE SHADOW OF AN AIRPLANE
CLIMBS THE EMPIRE STATE BUILDING.
D. BROMWICH, 441:17DEC72-2
TYLER, R. THE VERSE OF ROYALL TYLER.
(M.B. PELADEAU, ED)
M.I. LOWANCE, JR., 432(NEQ):JUN70-317
TYLER, S.A. KOYA.*
H.U. BAYLIS, 293(JAST):FEB70-468
TYNAN, K. TYNAN RIGHT AND LEFT.
571:SPRING-SUMMER68-26
TYNDALE-BISCOE, J. GUNNER SUBALTERN.
617(TLS):4FEB72-132
TYRE, N. TWICE SO FAIR.
M. LEVIN, 441:6FEB72-37
TYRMAND, L., ED. KULTURA ESSAYS.
676(YR):SUMMER71-VI
TYRTAEUS. TIRTEO.* (C. PRATO, ED)
C. MEILLIER, 555:VOL44FASC1-123
TYRWHITT, J. - SEE BARTLETT, W.H.
TYSDAHL, B.J. JOYCE AND IBSEN.
B. HENRICI, 462(OL):VOL23#2-178
TYSON, A. THEMATIC CATALOGUE OF THE
WORKS OF MUZIO CLEMENTI.
L.B. PLANTINGA, 414(MQ):APR68-257
TZABAR, S. THE WHITE FLAG PRINCIPLE.
617(TLS):1SEP72-1021

"USLTA OFFICIAL ENCYCLOPEDIA OF TENNIS."
F. TUPPER, 441:22OCT72-26
UGUZZONI, A. & F. GHINATTI. LE TAVOLE
GRECHE DI ERACLEA.
A.M. DAVIES & D.M. LEWIS, 123:MAR71-
119
UIBLEIN, P., ED. ACTA FACULTATIS ARTIUM
UNIVERSITATIS VINDOBONENSIS, 1385-1416.
P. KIBRE, 589:APR71-398
UITTI, K.D. LINGUISTICS AND LITERARY
THEORY.*
A.P. BERTOCCI, 207(FR):MAR70-702
J. CULLER, 402(MLR):JAN71-161
Y. MALKIEL, 545(RPH):FEB70-323
UK, S. - SEE UNDER SONG UK
UKRAINKA, L. SELECTED WORKS.*
V. REVUTSKY, 575(SEER):JAN71-144
ULČ, O. THE JUDGE IN A COMMUNIST STATE.
617(TLS):25AUG72-1006
ULICH, R. PROGRESS OR DISASTER?
617(TLS):24NOV72-1437
ULLMANN, S. LANGUAGE AND STYLE.
A. VALDMAN, 545(RPH):AUG70-162
ULLMANN, S. - SEE VON WARTBURG, W.
ULLMANN, W. A SHORT HISTORY OF THE
PAPACY IN THE MIDDLE AGES.
617(TLS):7APR72-396
ULRICH VON LIECHTENSTEIN. ULRICH VON
LIECHTENSTEIN'S "SERVICE OF LADIES."
(J.W. THOMAS, TRANS)
S.M. JOHNSON, 406:SPRING71-76
H. SACKER, 220(GL&L):JUL71-376
ULRICH, W. SEMANTISCHE UNTERSUCHUNGEN
ZUM WORTSCHATZ DES KIRCHENLIEDES IM
16. JAHRHUNDERT.
W. FLEISCHHAUER, 301(JEGP):OCT71-712

"ULSTER."
617(TLS):17MAR72-298
"CHARLES UMLAUF, SCULPTOR."
M.S. YOUNG, 39:APR69-329
UNALI, L.G. MENTE E MISURA.
J. WOODRESS, 27(AL):JAN72-670
DE UNAMUNO, M. NIEBLA. (M.J. VALDÉS,
ED)
J. DÍAZ, 241:SEP71-77
M.E.W. JONES, 238:MAY70-357
DE UNAMUNO, M. OUR LORD DON QUIXOTE.*
M. IVENS, 619(TC):1968/2-57
G. RIBBANS, 86(BHS):JAN71-76
UNBEGAUN, B.O. SELECTED PAPERS ON RUS-
SIAN AND SLAVONIC PHILOLOGY.* (R.
AUTY & A.E. PENNINGTON, EDS)
G.H. WORTH, 574(SEEJ):FALL71-355
UNDERHILL, M. GIVE ME THE HILLS.
441:30JAN72-33
UNDERHILL, R.M. SINGING FOR POWER.
B.L. FONTANA, 50(ARQ):AUTUMN69-271
UNDERWOOD, M. A TROUT IN THE MILK.
O.L. BAILEY, 561(SATR):25NOV72-70
N. CALLENDAR, 441:22OCT72-47
UNDERWOOD, P. HORROR MAN.
617(TLS):2JUN72-635
UNDERWOOD, P. INTO THE OCCULT.
617(TLS):5MAY72-529
UNDERWOOD, P.A. THE KARIYE DJAMI.*
W.M.A. GRIMALDI, 613:SPRING68-142
UNGAR, S.J. THE PAPERS & THE PAPERS.
R. HARRIS, 442(NY):26AUG72-73
C. REMBAR, 441:11JUN72-2
P. SCHRAG, 561(SATR):27MAY72-70
UNGARETTI, G. SELECTED POEMS.
J. SYMONS, 364:FEB/MAR72-160
UNGER, H. GEISTLICHER HERZEN BAUNGART.*
H.B. WILLSON, 402(MLR):APR71-443
UNGER, L. T.S. ELIOT.*
H. SERGEANT, 175:SPRING69-33
UNGERN-STERNBERG VON PÜRKEL, J. UNTER-
SUCHUNGEN ZUM SPÄTREPUBLIKANISCHEN
NOTSTANDSRECHT.
S.I. OOST, 122:OCT71-290
C.G. STARR, 24:JAN71-128
"UNICORN FOLIO." (SER 2, NO. 4)
R. BROTHERSON, 661:FALL/WINTER69-109
"UNION LIST OF MANUSCRIPTS IN CANADIAN
REPOSITORIES."
H.P. BEERS, 14:APR69-162
"UNITED STATES-VIETNAM RELATIONS, 1945-
1967."*
J. MIRSKY, 561(SATR):1JAN72-23
"LES UNIVERSITÉS EUROPÉENNES DU XIVe
AU XVIIe SIÈCLE."
L.J. FRIEDMAN, 545(RPH):MAY70-587
"UNIVERSITY OF WITWATERSRAND LIBRARY:
GUIDE TO THE ARCHIVES AND PAPERS."
K.W. DUCKETT, 14:APR69-165
UNRUH, G.G. & W.M. ALEXANDER. INNOVA-
TIONS IN SECONDARY EDUCATION.
J.P. LOVEKIN, 529(QQ):AUTUMN70-458
UNTERECKER, J. VOYAGER.*
A. GALPIN, 659:WINTER72-106
R. HUTSON, 598(SOR):WINTER72-234
P.R. YANNELLA, 399(MLJ):OCT70-455
42(AR):FALL69-447
UNTERMEYER, L., ED. GREAT HUMOR.
P. ADAMS, 61:SEP72-110
UNTERSTEINER, M. POSIDONIO NEI PLACITA
DI PLATONE SECONDO DIOGENE LAERZIO III.
F.M. CLEVE, 319:OCT72-475
UNWIN, P. THE PUBLISHING UNWINS.
E.S. TURNER, 362:3FEB72-154
617(TLS):4FEB72-118

UPDIKE, J. BECH: A BOOK.*
A.B. HAMILTON, 150(DR):AUTUMN70-402
A. & K. HAMILTON, 529(QQ):WINTER70-
624
639(VQR):AUTUMN70-CXXVIII
UPDIKE, J. COEUR DE LIÈVRE. LES PLUMES
DU PIGEON. LE CENTAURE. LA FERME.
COUPLES.
P-Y. PÉTILLON, 98:NOV69-972
UPDIKE, J. MIDPOINT AND OTHER POEMS.
A.B. HAMILTON, 150(DR):AUTUMN70-402
UPDIKE, J. MUSEUMS AND WOMEN.
A. BROYARD, 441:19OCT72-49
J. KANON, 561(SATR):30SEP72-73
T. TANNER, 441:22OCT72-5
R. TODD, 61:DEC72-126
M. WOOD, 453:14DEC72-12
UPDIKE, J. RABBIT REDUX.*
B. GILL, 442(NY):8JAN72-83
E.F. SUDERMAN, 109:SPRING/SUMMER72-
156
F. WYNDHAM, 362:6APR72-454
617(TLS):7APR72-385
UPHILL, A. - SEE POWYS, J.C.
UPTON, L.F.S. THE LOYAL WHIG.
M.B. NORTON, 656(WMQ):JAN70-155
G.A. RAWLYK, 529(QQ):WINTER70-638
URBAN, G.R., WITH M. GLENNY, EDS. CAN WE
SURVIVE OUR FUTURE?
J. CAREY, 362:3FEB72-154
617(TLS):31MAR72-372
URBAN, M. EMIL NOLDE LANDSCAPES.
A. WERNER, 58:MAY70-10
URBANO, V. UNA ESCRITORA COSTARRICENSE,
YOLANDA OREAMUNO.
T-B. IRVING, 238:MAR70-159
URCIOLO, R.G. THE INTERVOCALIC PLOSIVES
IN TUSCAN (-P-, -T-, -C-).*
E-H. YARRILL, 182:VOL23#17/18-792
URDANG, L., ED. A DICTIONARY OF MIS-
UNDERSTOOD, MISUSED, MISPRONOUNCED
WORDS.
617(TLS):20OCT72-1264
URDANG, L. - SEE "THE RANDOM HOUSE DIC-
TIONARY OF THE ENGLISH LANGUAGE: COL-
LEGE EDITION"
URE, P. YEATS THE PLAYWRIGHT.
R. STAMM, 179(ES):APR69-218
URE, P. - SEE FORD, J.
URGOITI, M.S.C. - SEE UNDER CARRASCO
URGOITI, M.S.
URMSON, J.O. THE EMOTIVE THEORY OF
ETHICS.
G. PITCHER, 482(PHR):OCT70-586
URMUZ. PAGINI BIZARE. (S. PANĂ, ED)
V. NEMOIANU, 574(SEEJ):FALL71-398
URWIN, K. - SEE "LANGENSCHEIDT'S STANDARD
DICTIONARY OF THE FRENCH AND ENGLISH
LANGUAGES"
URZIDIL, J. THERE GOES KAFKA.
H. GROSS, 340(KR):1969/3-419
USHER, S. THE HISTORIANS OF GREECE AND
ROME.
P.A. BRUNT, 123:DEC70-404
F.J. FROST, 124:JAN71-163
USINGER, F. DIE VERWANDLUNGEN.
617(TLS):14JAN72-44
USPENSKY, B. PRINCIPLES OF STRUCTURAL
TYPOLOGY.
B. POTTIER, 361:VOL24#4-393
USTINOV, P. KRUMNAGEL.*
S. BLACKBURN, 440:2JAN72-2
USUDA JINGORŌ & OTHERS, EDS. TSUGARU
HYAKUWA BANASHI.
F.H. MAYER, 293(JAST):MAY70-702
UTTLEY, A. SECRET PLACES.
617(TLS):29DEC72-1589

VACALOPOULOS, A.E. ORIGINS OF THE GREEK
NATION. (VOL 1)
  A.E. LAIOU, 32:DEC71-877
VACATELLO, M. LUKÁCS.
  G. OLDRINI, 548(RCSF):JAN/MAR69-116
VACCA, G. POLITICA E FILOSOFIA IN BER-
TRANDO SPAVENTA.
  G. OLDRINI, 548(RCSF):APR-JUN68-238
VACHEK, J. THE LINGUISTIC SCHOOL OF
PRAGUE.
  L. LIPKA, 38:BAND87HEFT3/4-412
VACHON, B., WITH J. & B. CHEETHAM. A
TIME TO BE BORN.
  D. POLING, 561(SATR):22JUL72-57
VACULÍK, L. DIE MEERSCHWEINCHEN. DAS
BEIL.
  N. ASCHERSON, 453:10AUG72-16
VAILLANT, A. L'ÉVANGILE DE NICODÈME.*
  W.F. RYAN, 575(SEER):JUL71-462
VAIZEY, J. SOCIAL DEMOCRACY.
  617(TLS):25FEB72-221
VAIZEY, J., WITH OTHERS. THE POLITICAL
ECONOMY OF EDUCATION.
  617(TLS):25AUG72-997
VAJDA, G. RECHERCHES SUR LA PHILOSOPHIE
ET LA KABBALE DANS LA PENSÉE JUIVE DU
MOYEN AGE.
  J. SCHLANGER, 542:JAN-MAR69-120
VAKALOPOULOS, A. PEGES TES ISTORIAS TOY
NEOY HELLENISMOY, I (1204-1669).
  C.N. TSIRPANLIS, 121(CJ):APR-MAY71-
  364
VALCÁRCEL, E.D. - SEE UNDER DÍAZ VALCÁR-
CEL, E.
DE VALDÉS, J. DIÁLOGO DE LA LENGUA.
(J.M. LOPE BLANCH, ED)
  R. HAMILTON, 86(BHS):APR71-160
VALDÉS, M.J. DEATH IN THE LITERATURE OF
UNAMUNO.
  C. MORÓN ARROYO, 240(HR):JAN70-104
VALDÉS, M.J. - SEE DE UNAMUNO, M.
VALDEZ, L. & S. STEINER, EDS. AZTLÁN.
  J. WOMACK, JR., 453:31AUG72-12
VALDMAN, A., R.J. SALAZAR & M.A. CHAR-
BONNEAUX. A DRILLBOOK OF FRENCH PRO-
NUNCIATION.
  R.W. NEWMAN, 207(FR):DEC69-387
VALE, M.G.A. ENGLISH GASCONY, 1399-
1453.*
  G.P. CUTTINO, 589:JUL71-545
VALENTIN, E. MOZART AND HIS WORLD.
  S. SADIE, 415:OCT71-1003
VALENTINE, C.W. THE EXPERIMENTAL PSY-
CHOLOGY OF BEAUTY.
  P.R. FARNSWORTH, 290(JAAC):FALL69-114
VALENTINE, J. PILGRIMS.*
  639(VQR):SUMMER70-XCV
VALENTINI, F. LA CONTRORIFORMA DELLA
DIALETTICA.
  A.A.D., 477:SUMMER69-421
VALENTINOV, N. [N.V. VOLSKI] DVA GODA S
SIMVOLISTAMI. (G. STRUVE, ED)
  J.D. ELSWORTH, 575(SEER):APR71-294
  D. VON MOHRENSCHILDT, 550(RUSR):
  JUL70-348
  V. TERRAS, 574(SEEJ):SPRING71-123
VALENTINOV, N. [N.V. VOLSKI]. THE EARLY
YEARS OF LENIN.* (R.H.W. THEEN, ED &
TRANS)
  J. KEEP, 104:SPRING71-130
  A. PARRY, 550(RUSR):OCT70-457
  W. ZIMMERMAN, 385(MQR):WINTER72-60
VALENTINOV, N. [N.V. VOLSKI]. ENCOUNTERS
WITH LENIN.
  J. MILLER, 587:JAN69-400
  A. PARRY, 550(RUSR):OCT70-457
  T.D.Z., 543:SEP69-141
  42(AR):SUMMER69-263

VALÉRY, P. COLLECTED WORKS. (J. MAT-
THEWS, GENERAL ED) (VOL 1 TRANS BY
D. PAUL & J.R. LAWLER)
  617(TLS):10MAR72-273
VALÉRY, P. COLLECTED WORKS. (J. MAT-
THEWS, ED) (VOL 2 TRANS BY H. CORKE;
VOL 11 TRANS BY R. SHATTUCK & F.
BROWN; VOL 14 TRANS BY S. GILBERT)
  617(TLS):26MAY72-606
VALÉRY, P. LEONARDO, POE, MALLARMÉ.
  617(TLS):27OCT72-1296
VALÉRY, P. MASTERS AND FRIENDS. (M.
TURNELL, TRANS)
  V.J. DANIEL, 208(FS):JUL71-350
VALÉRY, P. POEMS IN THE ROUGH. (H.
CORKE, TRANS)
  C.M. CROW, 208(FS):OCT71-485
VALÉRY, P. PROSE ET VERS. (H. PEYRE,
ED)
  V.J. DANIEL, 208(FS):JUL71-349
  A. SZOGYI, 207(FR):MAR70-716
VALESIO, P. STRUTTURE DELL'ALLITTERA-
ZIONE.
  K.D. UITTI, 350:SEP71-749
VALETTE, R.M. ARTHUR DE GOBINEAU AND
THE SHORT STORY.
  M.D. BIDDISS, 208(FS):OCT71-480
  A.E. CARTER, 207(FR):MAY70-936
  H.L. ROBINSON, 399(MLJ):NOV70-541
VALETTE, R.M. LECTURES LIBRES.
  R.C. KELLY, 207(FR):DEC69-380
  H.L. ROBINSON, 399(MLJ):OCT70-460
VÁLI, F.A. BRIDGE ACROSS THE BOSPORUS.
  617(TLS):21JUL72-834
VALKHOFF, M.F. STUDIES IN PORTUGUESE AND
CREOLE.*
  J.M. MC CARTNEY, 545(RPH):AUG69-85
DEL VALLE-INCLÁN, R.M. DIVINE WORDS.
(E. WILLIAMS, TRANS)
  R. WHITTREDGE, 241:SEP71-80
VALLÈS, J. L'ENFANT. (E. CARASSUS, ED)
  F.W. SAUNDERS, 208(FS):OCT71-479
VALLÈS, J. SOUVENIRS D'UN ETUDIANT
PAUVRE, LE CANDIDAT DES PAUVRES, LETTRE
À JULES MIRÈS. (L. SCHELER & M-C.
BANCQUART, EDS)
  617(TLS):22DEC72-1560
VALLÈS, J. JULES VALLÈS: CORRESPONDANCE
AVEC HECTOR MALOT. (M-C. BLANCQUART,
ED)
  R. MERKER, 207(FR):MAR70-687
VALLIÈRES, P. L'URGENCE DE CHOISIR.
  617(TLS):28JUL72-861
VALLIÈRES, P. WHITE NIGGERS OF AMERICA.*
(FRENCH TITLE: NÈGRES BLANCS D'AMÉR-
IQUE.)
  J-C. BONENFANT, 627(UTQ):JUL69-457
VALVERDE, J.M. BREVE HISTORIA DE LA LIT-
ERATURA ESPAÑOLA.
  C.A. JONES, 86(BHS):APR71-153
VAN BRUNT, H. ARCHITECTURE AND SOCIETY.
(W.A. COLES, ED)
  D. HOFFMAN, 44:NOV69-62
  W.S. RUSK, 127:WINTER70/71-214
  639(VQR):WINTER70-XXVI
VAN BUITENEN, J.A.B. RĀMĀNUJA ON THE
BHAGAVADGĪTĀ.
  L. ROCHER, 293(JAST):NOV69-202
VANCE, B. COMPANION TO "THE EYE OF THE
BEHOLDER." COMPANION TO "MICROCOSM."
  D. CONWAY, 296:FALL72-101
VANCE, B., ED. THE EYE OF THE BEHOLDER.
MICROCOSM.
  D. CONWAY, 296:FALL72-101
VANDELOO, J. DE COLADRINKERS.
  270:VOL20#3-66

VAN DEN HEUVEL, J. VOLTAIRE DANS SES
CONTES.
J. SAREIL, 546(RR):APR70-140
VANDERBILT, A. AMY VANDERBILT'S ETI-
QUETTE.
C.D.B. BRYAN, 441:19MAR72-27
VANDERBILT, K. THE ACHIEVEMENT OF WIL-
LIAM DEAN HOWELLS.
J. WOODRESS, 445(NCF):SEP69-244
VAN DER STARRE, E. RACINE ET LE THÉÂTRE
DE L'AMBIGUÏTÉ.
J. BRODY, 593:SPRING71-79
VANDERVEEN, B.H. THE OBSERVER'S MILITARY
VEHICLES DIRECTORY FROM 1945.
617(TLS):15DEC72-1528
VAN DEUSEN, G.G. WILLIAM HENRY SEWARD.
V.P. LANNIE, 613:AUTUMN68-473
D.G. MATHEWS, 377:MAR71-50
VAN DEUSEN, M. J.E. SPINGARN.
L. MUMFORD, 453:23MAR72-13
VAN DIJK, H.J. EZEKIEL'S PROPHECY ON
TYRE (EZ. 26,1-28,19).
M. GREENBERG, 318(JAOS):OCT-DEC70-536
VAN DORSTEN, J.A. THE RADICAL ARTS.*
J. REES, 402(MLR):OCT71-856
VAN EERDE, K.S. WENCESLAUS HOLLAR.
F.A. AMES-LEWIS, 89(BJA):AUTUMN71-415
VAN EFFENTERRE, H. L'HISTOIRE EN GRÈCE.
P. GAUTHIER, 555:VOL44FASC1-107
VANEZIS, P.N. MAKARIOS.
617(TLS):7JAN72-4
VAN GELDER, H.A.E. GETEMPERDE VRIJHEID.
617(TLS):24NOV72-1424
VAN HORNE, H. NEVER GO ANYWHERE WITHOUT
A PENCIL.
441:10DEC72-48
VANIER, J. LE BONHEUR PRINCIPE ET FIN
DE LA MORALE ARISTOTÉLICIENNE.
J. BRUNSCHWIG, 542:APR-JUN69-271
VAN LEEUWEN, J. - SEE ARISTOPHANES
VANNIER, F. LE IVE SIÈCLE GREC.
P. GAUTHIER, 555:VOL44FASC1-107
VAN ORSDELL, J. RAGLAND.
M. LEVIN, 441:18JUN72-30
VAN PARYS, J.M. LA VOCATION DE LA
LIBERTÉ.
A. PONCELET, 258:SEP69-467
VAN ROEKEL, G.B. THE JICARILLA APACHES.
W. GARD, 584(SWR):AUTUMN71-VI
VAN SCHREEVEN, W.J. & G.H. REESE - SEE
PORY, J.
VAN SETERS, J. THE HYKSOS.
J. VON BECKERATH, 318(JAOS):APR-JUN
70-309
VAN TRUMP, J.D. & A. ZIEGLER, JR. LAND-
MARK ARCHITECTURE OF ALLEGHENY COUNTY,
PENNSYLVANIA.
F. KOEPER, 576:DEC68-305
VAN TUYL, M. ANTHOLOGY OF IMPULSE.
J. DE LABAN, 290(JAAC):SUMMER70-556
VAN VEEN, C.F. DUTCH CATCHPENNY PRINTS.
617(TLS):11AUG72-953
VAN ZANDT, R., ED. CHRONICLES OF THE
HUDSON.
J. SEELYE, 441:30JUL72-6
VARADARĀJA. SĀRASIDDHĀNTAKAUMUDĪ OF
VARADARĀJA. (G.V. DEVASTHALI, ED &
TRANS)
R. ROCHER, 318(JAOS):APR-JUN70-408
VARANINI, G., ED. CANTARI RELIGIOSI
SENESI DEL TRECENTO.
F.B. AGENO, 545(RPH):FEB71-478
VÁRDY, S.B. HISTORY OF THE HUNGARIAN
NATION.
B.K. KIRÁLY, 104:FALL71-443

VARÈSE, L. VARÈSE. (VOL 1: 1883-1928)
T. LASK, 441:21JUL72-32
J. PEYSER, 441:23APR72-3
V. THOMSON, 453:31AUG72-19
VAREY, J.E., ED. GALDÓS STUDIES.
J. LOWE, 402(MLR):OCT71-911
VAREY, J.E., N.D. SHERGOLD & J. SAGE -
SEE VÉLEZ DE GUEVARA, J.
VARGAS LLOSA, M. GARCÍA MÁRQUEZ. HIS-
TORIA SECRETA DE UNA NOVELA.
617(TLS):29SEP72-1140
VARGISH, T. NEWMAN.*
E.D. MACKERNESS, 402(MLR):OCT71-879
VARGYAS, L. RESEARCHES INTO THE MEDIEVAL
HISTORY OF FOLK BALLAD.*
L. DÉGH, 292(JAF):OCT-DEC70-472
VARGYAS, L. - SEE KODÁLY, Z.
VARLEY, H.P. IMPERIAL RESTORATION IN
MEDIEVAL JAPAN.
617(TLS):5MAY72-524
VARNHAGEN VON ENSE, R. RAHEL VARNHAGEN
IM UNGANG MIT IHREN FREUNDEN. (F.
KEMP, ED)
D.L., 191(ELN):SEP69(SUPP)-118
VARNHAGEN VON ENSE, R. & A. RAHEL VARN-
HAGEN UND AUGUST VARNHAGEN VON ENSE:
BRIEFWECHSEL. (F. KEMP, ED)
D.L., 191(ELN):SEP69(SUPP)-118
VARTAN, V.G. THE DINOSAUR FUND.
M. LEVIN, 441:9APR72-42
VARTY, K. - SEE DE PISAN, C.
VARVARO, A. BEROUL'S "ROMANCE OF TRIS-
TRAN."
617(TLS):8DEC72-1509
VARVARO, A. IL "ROMAN DE TRISTAN" DI
BÉROUL.
J.M. FERRANTE, 545(RPH):MAY71-651
VARVARO, A. STORIA, PROBLEMI E METODI
DELLA LINGUISTICA ROMANZA.
Y. MALKIEL, 545(RPH):FEB70-323
VARVARO, A. - SEE JAUSS, H.R.
VASILEVA, I., COMP. BIBLIOGRAFIIA NA
IZDANIIATA NA SOFIISKIIA UNIVERSITET
"KLIMENT OKHRIDSKI," 1956-1965.
M. PUNDEFF, 32:SEP71-710
VASIL'EVA-ŠVEDE, O.K. & A.M. GAX. AN-
TOLOGIJA PORTUGAL'SKOJ I BRAZIL'SKOJ
LITERATUR (XIX-XX VV.).
B.M. WOODBRIDGE, JR., 545(RPH):NOV69-
260
VASSI, M. THE STONED APOCALYPSE.
441:26MAR72-37
VATIKIOTIS, P.J., ED. REVOLUTION IN THE
MIDDLE EAST.
617(TLS):1DEC72-1447
VATMAN, D.P. & V.A. ELIZAROV. ADVOKAT V
GRAZHDANSKOM PROTSESSE. (I.I. SKLIAR-
SKY, ED)
S. KUCHEROV, 32:MAR71-168
VATUK, V.P. ADVANCE HINDI READER IN THE
SOCIAL SCIENCES.
C. COPPOLA, 293(JAST):FEB70-465
VATUK, V.P. THIEVES IN MY HOUSE.
F.L. NITZBERG, 293(JAST):MAY70-726
VAUGHAN, J.D. THE MANNERS AND CUSTOMS
OF THE CHINESE OF THE STRAITS SETTLE-
MENTS.
617(TLS):22DEC72-1565
VAUGHAN, M. & M.S. ARCHER. SOCIAL CON-
FLICT AND EDUCATIONAL CHANGE IN ENGLAND
AND FRANCE 1789-1848.
617(TLS):25FEB72-229
VAUGHAN, R. GULLS IN BRITAIN.
617(TLS):16JUN72-697
VAUGHAN, R. & M. LYNCH. BRANDYWINE'S
WAR.
M. LEVIN, 441:6FEB72-36

VAUGHAN, T. & G.A. MC MATH. A CENTURY
OF PORTLAND ARCHITECTURE.
M.D. ROSS, 576:MAY68-152
VAUGHAN, W., H. BÖRSCH-SUPAN & H.J. NEID-
HARDT. CASPAR DAVID FRIEDRICH 1774-
1840 - ROMANTIC LANDSCAPE PAINTING IN
DRESDEN.
617(TLS):1DEC72-1448
VAUGHN, R. ONLY VICTIMS.
J.R. WALTZ, 440:26MAR72-8
VAUGHN-JAMES, M. THE PROJECTOR.
G. CURNOE, 99:JUN72-40
VAUX, J.H. THE MEMOIRS OF JAMES HARDY
VAUX.* (N. MC LACHLAN, ED)
D.R. BARNES, 650(WF):JAN69-59
VAWTER, B. BIBLICAL INSPIRATION.
617(TLS):22SEP72-1121
VÁSQUEZ, P.R. - SEE UNDER RAMÍREZ VÁS-
QUEZ, P.
VEALE, E.M. - SEE JAMES, M.K.
VEATCH, H.B. TWO LOGICS.
J.J.R., 543:DEC69-358
R.H. STOOTHOFF, 479(PHQ):JUL70-283
VEEVERS-CARTER, W. ISLAND HOME.
617(TLS):7JAN72-21
DE LA VEGA, G. - SEE UNDER GARCILASO DE
LA VEGA
DE LA VEGA, J.S.L. - SEE UNDER LASSO DE
LA VEGA, J.S.
DE VEGA, L. - SEE UNDER LOPE DE VEGA
VÉLEZ DE GUEVARA, J. LOS CELOS HACEN
ESTRELLAS. (J.E. VAREY, N.D. SHERGOLD
& J. SAGE, EDS)
617(TLS):4AUG72-914
VELLACOTT, P. - SEE EURIPIDES
VELOUDIS, G. ALEXANDER DER GROSSE.
S.I. OOST, 124:DEC70-129
VELZ, J.W. SHAKESPEARE AND THE CLASSICAL
TRADITION.
M.W. LLOYD, 541(RES):MAY70-202
M. TAYLOR, 255(HAB):WINTER69-79
VENABLES, F., ED. THE EARLY AUGUSTANS.
617(TLS):14APR72-429
VAN DEN VEN, P., ED. LA VIE ANCIENNE
DE S. SYMÉON STYLITE LE JEUNE (521-
592). (VOL 2)
G. DOWNEY, 589:JUL71-546
VENDLER, H.H. ON EXTENDED WINGS.*
R. BUTTEL, 295:VOL2#3-431
P.L. MARIANI, 418(MR):WINTER71-162
J. PINKERTON, 141:SPRING70-161
VENDLER, Z. ADJECTIVES AND NOMINALIZA-
TIONS.
D. BICKERTON, 361:VOL24#1-56
VENDLER, Z. LINGUISTICS IN PHILOSOPHY.
B. HARRISON, 483:JAN70-71
VENEZKY, R.L. THE STRUCTURE OF ENGLISH
ORTHOGRAPHY.
J. VACHEK, 350:MAR71-212
VENIARD, J. A FURTHER GUIDE TO FLY
DRESSING. FLYTYING DEVELOPMENT AND
PROGRESS.
617(TLS):3MAR72-258
VENIZELOS, E. I KRITIKI EPANASTASIS TOU
1889. (I.G. MANOLIKAKI, ED)
617(TLS):4FEB72-137
VENKATARAMAN, B. LADDIGAM.
617(TLS):12MAY72-552
VENKATASUBBIAH, A. VEDIC STUDIES. (VOL
2)
E. BENDER, 318(JAOS):APR-JUN70-413
DE VENTADOUR, B. - SEE UNDER BERNARD DE
VENTADOUR
VENTURI, R., D.S. BROWN & S. IZENOUR.
LEARNING FROM LAS VEGAS.
R. JELLINEK, 441:29DEC72-23

VENZMER, G. FIVE THOUSAND YEARS OF MEDI-
CINE.
617(TLS):8DEC72-1512
VERA, L.C. - SEE UNDER CERVERA VERA, L.
VERBEKE, G. - SEE PHILOPON, J.
VERBIT, G.P. TRADE AGREEMENTS FOR DEVEL-
OPING COUNTRIES.
617(TLS):15SEP72-1066
VERCORS. LE SILENCE DE LA MER. (T.
MARK, ED)
J. KOLBERT, 399(MLJ):NOV70-529
VERCRUYSSE, J. & S. MENANT - SEE BOILEAU-
DESPRÉAUX, N.
VERDET, A. LÉGER.
617(TLS):7JAN72-18
VERDI, G. LETTERS OF GIUSEPPE VERDI.*
(C. OSBORNE, ED & TRANS)
W.H. AUDEN, 453:9MAR72-17
G. MARTIN, 440:13FEB72-15
H.C. SCHONBERG, 441:12MAR72-6
VERDIER, P. THE WALTERS ART GALLERY:
CATALOGUE OF THE PAINTED ENAMELS OF THE
RENAISSANCE.*
J.F.H., 90:FEB69-95
VERGER, P. FLUX ET REFLUX DE LA TRAITE
DES NÈGRES ENTRE LE GOLFE DU BÉNIN AT
BAHIA DE TODOS OS SANTOS, DU DIX-SEP-
TIÈME AU DIX-NEUVIÈME SIÈCLE.
H. DESCHAMPS, 69:APR69-194
VERGIL. THE "AENEID" OF VIRGIL. (A.
MANDELBAUM, TRANS)
E. SEGAL, 441:25JUN72-23
617(TLS):12MAY72-550
VERGIL. THE ECLOGUES OF VIRGIL. (D.R.
SLAVITT, TRANS)
P. MURRAY, 491:AUG72-304
VERGIL. P. VERGILI MARONIS OPERA.
(R.A.B. MYNORS, ED)
A. ERNOUT, 555:VOL44FASC2-274
E.J. KENNEY, 313:VOL60-259
W.S. MAGUINNESS, 123:JUN70-197
VERLAINE, P. OEUVRES POÉTIQUES. (J.
ROBICHEZ, ED)
D.J. MOSSOP, 208(FS):JAN71-101
VERLÉE, L. ENSEIGNEMENT DES LANGUES ET
INFORMATION CULTURELLE.
N. GABRIEL, 67:NOV71-271
H.L. NOSTRAND, 399(MLJ):NOV70-545
VERLET, P., ED. OBJETS D'ART FRANÇAIS DE
LA COLLECTION CALOUSTE GULBENKIAN.
90:NOV70-774
VERLINDEN, C. LES ORIGINES DE LA CIVILI-
SATION ATLANTIQUE.
R.H. BOULIND, 182:VOL23#15/16-765
VERMANDEL, J.G. OF MIDNIGHT HONOR.
N. CALLENDAR, 441:30APR72-36
VERMEULE, C.C. ROMAN IMPERIAL ART IN
GREECE AND ASIA MINOR.*
R. HIGGINS, 90:NOV69-691
D. STRONG, 39:APR69-322
VERNADSKY, G. THE TSARDOM OF MOSCOW,
1547-1682.*
J. KEEP, 575(SEER):OCT71-607
N.V. RIASANOVSKY, 550(RUSR):JAN70-90
VERNADSKY, G. & R.T. FISHER, JR. - SEE
PUSHKAREV, S.G.
VERNANT, J-P. MYTHE ET PENSÉE CHEZ LES
GRECS.
A.W.H. ADKINS, 123:MAR71-80
VERNANT, J-P. PROBLÈMES DE LA GUERRE EN
GRÈCE ANCIENNE.*
A.L. BOEGEHOLD, 24:APR71-374
W. MC LEOD, 487:SPRING70-93
VERNANT, J-P. & P. VIDAL-NAQUET. MYTHE
ET TRAGÉDIE EN GRÈCE ANCIENNE.
617(TLS):11AUG72-952
VERNE, J. LES INDES NOIRES.
M. SERRES, 98:APR69-291

VERNON, M.D. HUMAN MOTIVATION.
  V. RÜFNER, 182:VOL23#1/2-6
VERNON, P.E., ED. CREATIVITY.
  J. BELOFF, 89(BJA):SPRING71-196
VERNON, R. SOVEREIGNTY AT BAY.
  P. PASSELL, 441:23JAN72-23
VERRA, V. MITO, RIVELAZIONE E FILOSOFIA
  IN J.G. HERDER E NEL SUO TEMPO.
  C. CESA, 548(RCSF):APR/JUN69-218
VERRALL, J.W. FUGUE AND INVENTION IN
  THEORY AND PRACTICE.
  C. SCHACHTER, 308:SPRING67-157
VERSINI, L. LACLOS ET LA TRADITION.
  A. VARTANIAN, 207(FR):DEC69-351
VERVLIET, H.D.L., ED. THE BOOK THROUGH
  FIVE THOUSAND YEARS.
  617(TLS):15DEC72-1540
VERVLIET, H.D.L. THE TYPE SPECIMEN OF
  THE VATICAN PRESS 1628.
  P. GASKELL, 354:MAR69-65
VERZONE, P. THE ART OF EUROPE.
  A. KUHN, 58:SEP/OCT69-14
VERZOSA, N.P. - SEE BERNARDO, G.A.
VESAAS, T. THE BOAT IN THE EVENING.*
  M. LEVIN, 441:26MAR72-43
VESAAS, T. SPRING NIGHT.
  D.A.N. JONES, 362:20JAN72-90
  617(TLS):4FEB72-117
VESELOVSKY, S.B. ISSLEDOVANIIA PO ISTOR-
  II KLASSA SLUZHILYKH ZEMLEVLADEL'TSEV.
  (V.I. SHUNKOV & S.M. KASHTANOV, EDS)
  R.O. CRUMMEY, 32:JUN71-388
VESEY, G.N.A., ED. THE PROPER STUDY.
  A. FLEW, 518:OCT71-28
VESEY, G.N.A., ED. TALK OF GOD.
  A. FLEW, 479(PHQ):JAN70-91
"THE VESPASIAN PSALTER." (S.M. KUHN, ED)
  H. GNEUSS, 38:BAND87HEFT1-84
  P. MERTENS-FONCK, 179(ES):FEB69-112
"THE VESPASIAN PSALTER."* (D.H. WRIGHT,
  ED)
  C.J.E. BALL, 541(RES):AUG70-339
  P. MERTENS-FONCK, 179(ES):FEB69-117
VETTER, H. WAHRSCHEINLICHKEIT UND LOGI-
  SCHER SPIELRAUM.
  A. MERCIER, 182:VOL23#4-138
VETTER, H.J. LANGUAGE BEHAVIOR AND
  PSYCHOPATHOLOGY.
  J. LINDENFELD, 350:MAR71-244
VEVER, R. LUSTY JUVENTUS. (J.M. NOS-
  WORTHY, ED)
  617(TLS):26MAY72-613
VEVERS, G. THE UNDERWATER WORLD.
  617(TLS):14JAN72-45
VEYRENC, J. LA FORME POÉTIQUE DE SERGE
  ESENIN.*
  A.F. GOVE, 32:JUN71-441
  L. KOEHLER, 550(RUSR):JAN70-115
DE VIANA, J. SUS MEJORES CUENTOS.
  G. FIGUEIRA, 263:JAN-MAR71-79
VIANELLO, N. LA TIPOGRAFIA DI ALVISOPOLI
  E GLI ANNALI DELLE SUE PUBBLICAZIONI.
  J.M. POTTER, 354:MAR69-71
VIANSSON-PONTE, P. HISTOIRE DE LA RÉPUB-
  LIQUE GAULLIENNE. (VOL 2)
  617(TLS):29SEP72-1134
VIARD, J. PHILOSOPHIE DE L'ART LITTÉR-
  AIRE ET SOCIALISME SELON PÉGUY (ET
  SELON BALZAC, BERDIAEV, BERNANOS,
  BERNARD-LAZARE, HUGO, LEROUX, MICHELET,
  PROUDHON, PROUST, SIMONE WEIL ETC.).
  E. CAHM, 208(FS):APR71-235
VIARRE, S. LA SURVIE D'OVIDE DANS LA
  LITTÉRATURE SCIENTIFIQUE DES XIIE ET
  XIIIE SIÈCLES.*
  W. SAYERS, 545(RPH):NOV70-346
DE VIAU, T. - SEE UNDER THÉOPHILE DE VIAU

VICENTE, A.Z. - SEE UNDER ZAMORA VICENTE,
  A.
VICKERS, B. FRANCIS BACON AND RENAIS-
  SANCE PROSE.
  P.H. KOCHER, 551(RENQ):AUTUMN70-335
  J. ROBERTS, 541(RES):FEB70-77
VICKERS, B. CLASSICAL RHETORIC IN
  ENGLISH POETRY.*
  L. CATALDI, 402(MLR):APR71-380
  J.L. LIEVSAY, 579(SAQ):SUMMER71-428
  T.G.A. NELSON, 67:NOV71-233
VICKERS, B., ED. THE WORLD OF JONATHAN
  SWIFT.*
  C.J. RAWSON, 541(RES):FEB70-84
VICKERY, B.C. TECHNIQUES OF INFORMATION
  RETRIEVAL.
  S.P. HARTER, 356:JAN71-68
VICKERY, W.N. ALEXANDER PUSHKIN.
  R. GREGG, 32:MAR71-202
"VICTORIA AND ALBERT MUSEUM YEARBOOK."
  (NO. 3)
  617(TLS):20OCT72-1248
"VICTORIA R.I."
  S. NOWELL-SMITH, 78(BC):SUMMER70-245
VIDAL, G. HOMAGE TO DANIEL SHAYS.
  R. SALE, 441:31DEC72-7
  442(NY):30DEC72-72
  561(SATR):16DEC72-71
VIDAL, G. TWO SISTERS.*
  P. CRUTTWELL, 249(HUDR):SPRING71-177
VIDAL-NAQUET, P. LE BORDEREAU D'ENSE-
  MENCEMENT DANS L'ÉGYPTE PTOLÉMAÏQUE.
  P. GAUTHIER, 555:VOL44FASC1-131
VIDAL-NAQUET, P. LA TORTURE DANS LA
  RÉPUBLIQUE.
  617(TLS):28APR72-464
VIDAL I BARRAQUER, A. ARXIU VIDAL I
  BARRAQUER: ESGLÉSIA I ESTAT DURANT LA
  SEGONA REPÚBLICA ESPANYOLA 1931-1936.
  (VOL 1) (M. BATLLORI & V.M. ARBELOA,
  EDS)
  617(TLS):29SEP72-1171
VIDMAN, L. ISIS UND SARAPIS BEI DEN
  GRIECHEN UND RÖMERN.
  E.A. FREDRICKSMEYER, 124:MAR71-243
VIDMAN, L. SYLLOGE INSCRIPTIONUM
  RELIGIONIS ISIACAE ET SARAPIACAE.
  J.R. HARRIS, 123:JUN71-305
  R.E. WITT, 313:VOL60-233
VIDOVIĆ, R. KAKO NE VALJA - KAKO VALJA
  PISATI.
  R. DUNATOV, 574(SEEJ):SUMMER71-246
VIERECK, W. PHONEMATISCHE ANALYSE DES
  DIALEKTS VON GATESHEAD-UPON-TYNE/CO.
  DURHAM.*
  W. KÜHLWEIN, 38:BAND87HEFT1-80
VIETH, D.M. ATTRIBUTION IN RESTORATION
  POETRY.
  D.R.M. WILKINSON, 179(ES):DEC69-612
VIETH, D.M. - SEE WILMOT, J.
VIGA, D. LOS SUEÑOS DE CÁNDIDO.
  E.S. URBANSKI, 263:JAN-MAR71-80
VIGNAU-SCHUURMAN, T.A.G.W. - SEE UNDER
  WILBERG VIGNAU-SCHUURMAN, T.A.G.
VIGNEAULT, G. TALES SUR LA POINTE DES
  PIEDS.
  B. GODARD, 99:OCT/NOV72-87
  K. O'DONNELL, 296:FALL72-89
VIGNERON, P. LE CHEVAL DANS L'ANTIQUITÉ
  GRÉCO-ROMAINE (DES GUERRES MÉDIQUES
  AUX GRANDES INVASIONS).
  S. BENTON, 303:VOL90-265
VILAR, E. THE MANIPULATED MAN.
  617(TLS):1SEP72-1019
VILAS, S. EL HUMOR Y LA NOVELA ESPAÑOLA
  CONTEMPORÁNEA.
  E.L. PLACER, 238:SEP70-579

VILJAMAA, T. STUDIES IN GREEK ENCOMIAS-
TIC POETRY OF THE EARLY BYZANTINE
PERIOD.*
R. BROWNING, 123:MAR71-140
VILJOEN, H.G. - SEE RUSKIN, J.
VILLA, E. SCAPIGLIATURA E VERISMO A
GENOVA.
W.T.S., 191(ELN):SEP70(SUPP)-132
VILLA, P. CORPUS OF CYPRIOTE ANTIQUI-
TIES. (VOL 1)
J. BOARDMAN, 123:DEC70-408
V. KARAGEORGHIS, 303:VOL90-260
VILLAFUERTE, C. VOCES Y COSTUMBRES DE
CATAMARCA.
D.L. CANFIELD, 545(RPH):AUG69-132
VILLARROEL, D.D. - SEE UNDER DE TORRES
VILLARROEL, D.
VILLAS, J. GÉRARD DE NERVAL, A CRITICAL
BIBLIOGRAPHY, 1900 TO 1967.*
R.B. JOHNSON, 207(FR):OCT69-182
VILLASANTE, C.B. - SEE UNDER BRAVO VILLA-
SANTE, C.
DE VILLEFOSSE, L. & J. BOUISSOUNOUSE.
L'OPPOSITION À NAPOLÉON.
O. POZZO DI BORGO, 546(RR):DEC70-304
DE VILLEFOSSE, L. & J. BOUISSOUNOUSE.
THE SCOURGE OF THE EAGLE. (M. ROSS,
ED & TRANS)
617(TLS):4AUG72-912
VILLENEUVE, P. J'AI MON VOYAGE!
R. ROBIDOUX, 627(UTQ):JUL70-435
VILLIERS, A. THE WAR WITH CAPE HORN.
441:20FEB72-24
617(TLS):4FEB72-132
VILLIERS, A. & H. PICARD. THE BOUNTY
SHIPS OF FRANCE.
617(TLS):8DEC72-1513
VILLON, F. THE LEGACY AND OTHER POEMS.
617(TLS):13OCT72-1217
VILLON, F. LE "TESTAMENT" ET POÉSIES
DIVERSES. (B.N. SARGENT, ED)
E. BAUMGARTNER, 545(RPH):FEB70-357
W.L. HENDRICKSON, 207(FR):DEC69-386
VINAVER, E. - SEE MALORY, T.
VINCE, J. FARMS AND FARMING.
617(TLS):4FEB72-137
VINCENT, H.P. THE TAILORING OF MEL-
VILLE'S "WHITE-JACKET."
W. BRASWELL, 27(AL):NOV71-451
617(TLS):21JAN72-53
VINCENT, J.R. & M. STENTON, EDS. MC CAL-
MONT'S PARLIAMENTARY POLL BOOK OF ALL
ELECTIONS, 1832-1918.
617(TLS):18FEB72-172
DE VINCENZ, A. TRAITÉ D'ANTHROPONYMIE
HOUTZOULE.
J.B. RUDNYĆKYJ, 574(SEEJ):WINTER71-
522
VINGE, L. THE NARCISSUS THEME IN WESTERN
EUROPEAN LITERATURE UP TO THE EARLY
19TH CENTURY.*
M. BELLER, 462(OL):VOL24#4-315
A. FOULET, 546(RR):FEB70-45
F. GOLDIN, 545(RPH):NOV69-220
J.C. VAN MEURS, 179(ES):DEC69-614
VINOGRADOV, V.V. THE HISTORY OF THE RUS-
SIAN LITERARY LANGUAGE FROM THE SEVEN-
TEENTH CENTURY TO THE NINETEENTH.
(L.L. THOMAS, ED & TRANS)
G.M. ERAMIAN, 104:FALL71-423
F.J. OINAS, 550(RUSR):JAN70-115
W. VICKERY, 32:DEC71-906
VINSON, J.C. THOMAS NAST.
O.M. COLEMAN, JR., 219(GAR):SPRING69-
98
VIOLA, R. EMILIO CECCHI, SCRITTORE DEL
NOSTRO TEMPO.
L.C. BORELLI, 399(MLJ):APR70-285

VIORST, J. YES, MARRIED.
A. YOUNGMAN, 441:22OCT72-43
VIORST, M. HUSTLERS AND HEROES.
441:13FEB72-14
VIRGIL - SEE UNDER VERGIL
VIRIEUX, D. - SEE MADAME DE DURAS
VIRTANEN, R. ANATOLE FRANCE.
H.H. WEINBERG, 399(MLJ):JAN70-35
"THE VISCONTI HOURS."
P. ADAMS, 61:NOV72-131
D. KNOWLES, 441:1OCT72-27
T. LASK, 441:23SEP72-33
VISCOTT, D.S. THE MAKING OF A PSYCHIA-
TRIST.
P. ADAMS, 61:DEC72-144
T. LASK, 441:27DEC72-41
561(SATR):23DEC72-68
VISHNIAK, M. GODY EMIGRATSII, 1919-1969.
L.K-D. KRISTOF, 32:DEC71-888
"VISIONS 2020."
A. APPENZELL, 102(CANL):AUTUMN71-96
VISSER, F.T. AN HISTORICAL SYNTAX OF THE
ENGLISH LANGUAGE.* (PT 3)
S.R. LEVIN, 301(JEGP):OCT71-649
K.C. PHILLIPPS, 179(ES):AUG70-344
VITAL, D. THE SURVIVAL OF SMALL STATES.
617(TLS):17MAR72-312
VITALIS, O. - SEE UNDER ORDERIC VITALIS
VITRUVIUS. VITRUVE, "DE L'ARCHITEC-
TURE."* (BK 9) (J. SOUBIRAN, ED &
TRANS)
H. PLOMMER, 123:DEC70-349
VITTORINI, E. LE DUE TENSIONI. (D.
ISELLA, ED)
G.P. BIASIN, 275(IQ):SUMMER69-81
VIVA. SUPERSTAR.
M. MUDRICK, 249(HUDR):SPRING71-185
VIVAS, E. CONTRA MARCUSE.
D.A. ZOLL, 396(MODA):FALL71-425
VIVIAN, F. IL CONSOLE SMITH.
617(TLS):4AUG72-905
VIVIANI, A. DAS DRAMA DES EXPRESSIONIS-
MUS.
H.G. HERMANN, 406:FALL71-297
VIZINCZEY, S. THE RULES OF CHAOS.*
R.C. ELLSWORTH, 529(QQ):SPRING70-128
VLAD, R. STRAVINSKY. (2ND ED)
S. WALSH, 607:SPRING69-63
VLASTO, A.P. THE ENTRY OF THE SLAVS
INTO CHRISTENDOM.*
C.A. MACARTNEY, 382(MAE):1971/1-90
G.P. MAJESKA, 32:DEC71-876
VOEGELIN, C.F. & F.M. LANGUAGES OF THE
WORLD: INDO-EUROPEAN. (FASC 1)
L. ZGUSTA, 353:MAY69-97
DE VOGEL, C.J. PYTHAGORAS AND EARLY
PYTHAGOREANISM.*
P. SOMVILLE, 542:APR-JUN69-270
VOGEL, E. CANTON UNDER COMMUNISM.
R. BAUM, 293(JAST):AUG70-931
VOGEL, V.J. THIS COUNTRY WAS OURS.
M. ROGIN, 441:24DEC72-4
VOGT, A.M. BOULLÉES NEWTON-DENKMAL.
N. PEVSNER, 182:VOL23#5-234
VOGT, M. DIE ENTSTEHUNG DES YOUNG-PLANS.
617(TLS):19MAY72-581
VOGT, M., ED. DAS KABINETT MÜLLER I.
DAS KABINETT MÜLLER II.
617(TLS):19MAY72-581
"LES VOIES DE LA CRÉATION THÉÂTRALE."
(VOLS 1&2)
D. GRONAU, 182:VOL23#7-369
VOIGT, M. SWIFT AND THE TWENTIETH CEN-
TURY.
P. DANCHIN, 179(ES):JUN70-261
VOLIN, L. A CENTURY OF RUSSIAN AGRICUL-
TURE.
M. MC CAULEY, 575(SEER):OCT71-620

VÖLKER, K. IRISCHES THEATER I. IRISCHES
  THEATER II.
    K. TETZELI VON ROSADOR, 72:BAND208
    HEFT1-49
VOLKMANN, H-E. DIE RUSSISCHE EMIGRATION
  IN DEUTSCHLAND, 1919-1920.
    G. STRUVE, 32:MAR71-152
VOLLENWEIDER, M-L. DER JUPITER-KAMEO.
    D.E. STRONG, 123:JUN71-305
VOLLMER, A. THE POLICE AND MODERN
  SOCIETY.
    617(TLS):18FEB72-191
VOLLRATH-REICHELT, H. KÖNIGSDANKE UND
  KÖNIGTUM BEI DEN ANGELSACHSEN BIS ZUR
  MITTE DES 9. JAHRHUNDERTS.
    617(TLS):20OCT72-1255
VOLSKI, N.V. - SEE UNDER VALENTINOV, N.
DE VOLTAIRE, F.M.A. CANDIDE, OU L'OPTI-
  MISME. (A. MAGNAN, ED)
    C. THACKER, 208(FS):JUL71-338
DE VOLTAIRE, F.M.A. CANDIDE OU L'OPTIM-
  ISME. (A. MORIZE, ED) CANDIDE. (REV)
  (G.R. HAVENS, ED) CANDIDE.* (J.H.
  BRUMFITT, ED)
    C. FLEISCHAUER, 399(MLJ):MAR70-200
DE VOLTAIRE, F.M.A. CANDIDE OU L'OPTIM-
  ISME. (C. THACKER, ED)
    R.L. FRAUTSCHI, 207(FR):MAR70-693
DE VOLTAIRE, F.M.A. THE COMPLETE WORKS
  OF VOLTAIRE. (VOL 59 ED BY J.H. BRUM-
  FITT; VOL 85 ED BY T. BESTERMAN)
    A. AGES, 141:SUMMER70-251
    M. LUNDLIE, 529(QQ):WINTER70-658
DE VOLTAIRE, F.M.A. THE COMPLETE WORKS
  OF VOLTAIRE. (VOLS 81&82) (T. BESTER-
  MAN, ED)
    A. AGES, 141:SUMMER70-251
    J.H. BRUMFITT, 208(FS):JAN71-84
    M. LUNDLIE, 529(QQ):WINTER70-658
DE VOLTAIRE, F.M.A. THE COMPLETE WORKS
  OF VOLTAIRE. (VOL 86) (T. BESTERMAN,
  ED)
    A. AGES, 141:SUMMER70-251
    J.H. BRUMFITT, 208(FS):JAN71-84
    M. LUNDLIE, 529(QQ):WINTER70-658
DE VOLTAIRE, F.M.A. THE COMPLETE WORKS
  OF VOLTAIRE. (VOLS 87 & 88) (T. BES-
  TERMAN, ED)
    J.H. BRUMFITT, 208(FS):OCT71-459
VOMPERSKIJ, V.P. STILISTIČESKOE UČENIE
  M.V. LOMONOSOVA I TEORIJA TRECH STILEJ.
    D. TSCHIŽEWSKIJ, 72:BAND208HEFT4/6-
    476
VON GOEBEN, A. CUATRO AÑOS EN ESPAÑA.
  (L. RUIZ HERNÁNDEZ, ED & TRANS)
    191(ELN):SEP69(SUPP)-147
VOORHEES, R.J. P.G. WODEHOUSE.
    502(PRS):FALL68-280
VOORHIS, J. THE STRANGE CASE OF RICHARD
  MILHOUS NIXON.
    M.F. NOLAN, 441:27AUG72-5
VOORHOEVE, J. & P.P. DE WOLF. BENUE-
  CONGO NOUN CLASS SYSTEMS.
    P.R. BENNETT, 315(JAL):VOL8PT2-120
"VOPROSSI NA SAVREMENNATA BULGARSKA LIT-
  ERATURA."
    270:VOL20#2-35
VORDTRIEDE, W. - SEE HEINE, H.
VORDTRIEDE, W. & U. SCHWEIKERT. HEINE-
  KOMMENTAR.
    S. ATKINS, 406:SUMMER71-171
VORMWEG, H. EINE ANDERE LESART.
    617(TLS):12MAY72-554
VORPAHL, B.M. MY DEAR WISTER-.
    E. WEEKS, 61:AUG72-89
VORTRIEDE, W. - SEE KUHLMANN, Q.

VOSGERAU, H-J. ÜBER OPTIMALES WIRT-
  SCHAFTLICHES WACHSTUM.
    A. HÜFNER, 182:VOL23#10-549
VOSPER, C. THE MIND BENDERS.
    617(TLS):12MAY72-545
VOSS, R. DER PROSA-LANCELOT.
    D.H. GREEN, 402(MLR):OCT71-932
VOURVERIS, C.J. KLASSIKĒ PAIDEIA KAI
  ZŌĒ.
    A.R. BURN, 123:DEC70-409
    J.E. REXINE, 24:OCT71-758
VOVELLE, M. LA CHUTE DE LA MONARCHIE,
  1787-1792.
    617(TLS):22SEP72-1113
"VOX SHORTER SPANISH AND ENGLISH DICTION-
  ARY." "VOX CONCISE SPANISH AND ENGLISH
  DICTIONARY." "VOX NEW COMPACT SPANISH
  AND ENGLISH DICTIONARY."
    617(TLS):13OCT72-1231
VOYCE, A. MOSCOW AND THE ROOTS OF
  RUSSIAN CULTURE.
    617(TLS):24MAR72-345
DE VRIES, L., WITH I. VAN AMSTEL. VIC-
  TORIAN INVENTIONS.*
    E. FREMONT-SMITH, 561(SATR):30SEP72-
    72
    H. KRAMER, 441:3DEC72-34
VRIESEN, G. & M. IMDAHL. ROBERT DELAU-
  NAY.
    M. BRUMER, 58:SEP/OCT69-16
VROONEN, E. LES NOMS DES PERSONNES DANS
  LE MONDE.
    G.B. DROEGE, 424:JUN69-169
VUCINICH, A. SCIENCE IN RUSSIAN CULTURE,
  1861-1917.*
    M. MC CAULEY, 575(SEER):OCT71-629
VUCINICH, W.S., ED. CONTEMPORARY YUGO-
  SLAVIA.*
    F.W.D. DEAKIN, 575(SEER):OCT71-627
    J.B. HOPTNER, 32:JUN71-415
    639(VQR):AUTUMN70-CLI
VUĆO, N. AGRARNA KRIZA U JUGOSLAVIJI,
  1930-1934.
    L. SIRC, 32:MAR71-191
VUILLEMIN, J. DE LA LOGIQUE À LA THÉOLO-
  GIE.*
    R. LAURENTI, 548(RCSF):APR/JUN69-228
VYNAR, L. [L. WYNAR] MYKHAILO HRUSHEV-
  S'KYI I NAUKOVE TOVARYSTVO IM. TARASA
  SHEVCHENKA, 1892-1930.
    G.S.N. LUCKYJ, 32:SEP71-671
VYVYAN, C.C. LETTERS FROM A CORNISH
  GARDEN.
    617(TLS):25AUG72-1006

WAARDENBURG, J-J. L'ISLAM DANS LE MIROIR
  DE L'OCCIDENT.
    G. MAKDISI, 318(JAOS):APR-JUN70-280
WACKER, M. - SEE HOFFMANN, E.T.A.
WACKERNAGEL, H.G., ED. DIE MATRIKEL DER
  UNIVERSITÄT BASEL.
    I. IBEN, 182:VOL23#5-193
WACKETT, L.J. AIRCRAFT PIONEER.
    617(TLS):18AUG72-977
WADDELL, J.R.E. AN INTRODUCTION TO
  SOUTH-EAST ASIAN POLITICS.
    617(TLS):10NOV72-1361
WADDINGTON, C.H. BEHIND APPEARANCE.
    676(YR):AUTUMN70-XX
WADDINGTON, M. A.M. KLEIN.
    D. BARBOUR, 99:MAY72-68
WADDINGTON, M. SAY YES.*
    M. HORNYANSKY, 627(UTQ):JUL70-329
WADDINGTON, P. - SEE TURGENEV, I.S.
WADE, G.E. - SEE TIRSO DE MOLINA

WADE, I.O. THE INTELLECTUAL DEVELOPMENT
OF VOLTAIRE.*
  A.O. ALDRIDGE, 131(CL):SPRING71-186
  J. SAREIL, 401(MLQ):DEC70-511
WADE, I.O. THE INTELLECTUAL ORIGINS OF
THE FRENCH ENLIGHTENMENT.
  617(TLS):22SEP72-1118
WADE, R.A. THE RUSSIAN SEARCH FOR
PEACE, FEBRUARY-OCTOBER 1917.
  R.P. BROWDER, 32:MAR71-150
  O.H. RADKEY, 550(RUSR):OCT70-464
WADE, R.G. & K.J. O'CONNELL, EDS. THE
GAMES OF ROBERT J. FISCHER.
  617(TLS):25AUG72-1006
WADELL, M-B. FONS PIETATIS.
  N. GRASS, 182:VOL23#8-421
WADIA, A.R. THE PHILOSOPHY OF MAHATMA
GANDHI AND OTHER ESSAYS PHILOSOPHICAL
AND SOCIOLOGICAL.
  W.A.J., 543:DEC69-359
WADLEY, N. MANET.
  P. POOL, 39:DEC69-542
WADSWORTH, M.E.J., W.J.H. BUTTERFIELD &
R. BLANEY. HEALTH AND SICKNESS.
  617(TLS):14JAN72-49
DE WAELHENS, A. LA PHILOSOPHIE ET LES
EXPÉRIENCES NATURELLES.
  A. FOREST, 542:OCT-DEC68-497
WAGENKNECHT, E. WILLIAM DEAN HOWELLS.*
  R. TUERK, 432(NEQ):SEP70-517
WAGENKNECHT, E. JAMES RUSSELL LOWELL.*
  H.A. POCHMANN, 27(AL):JAN72-659
WAGENKNECHT, E. MARK TWAIN.
  R. LEHAN, 445(NCF):JUN68-117
WAGENKNECHT, E. JOHN GREENLEAF WHIT-
TIER.*
  S.J. HASELTON, 613:WINTER68-615
  G. VAN CROMPHOUT, 179(ES):APR70-170
WAGER, W., ED. THE PLAYWRIGHTS SPEAK.
  T. ROGERS, 175:AUTUMN69-110
WAGER, W. SWAP.
  N. CALLENDAR, 441:8OCT72-46
WAGGONER, H.H. AMERICAN POETS.*
  D. HOFFMAN, 141:SUMMER69-297
  G.M. WHITE, 502(PRS):SUMMER69-224
  G.M. WHITE, 646(WWR):DEC68-177
WAGLE, N. SOCIETY AT THE TIME OF THE
BUDDHA.*
  R.G. FOX, 293(JAST):FEB70-461
WAGNER, A.R. ENGLISH GENEALOGY. (2ND
ED)
  617(TLS):2JUN72-641
WAGNER, G. FIVE FOR FREEDOM.
  617(TLS):22DEC72-1560
WAGNER, G. "FRECH" IM HEUTIGEN ENGLISCH.
  K. SCHIBSBYE, 179(ES):AUG69-411
WAGNER, H. GAEILGE THEILINN.
  R.A. BREATNACH, 182:VOL23#3-88
WAGNER, H.L. DIE KINDERMÖRDERIN. (J-U.
FECHNER, ED)
  R.K., 221(GQ):JAN70-145
WAGNER, L.W. THE PROSE OF WILLIAM CARLOS
WILLIAMS.*
  A. PARSONS, 301(JEGP):JUL71-576
  W. SUTTON, 27(AL):NOV71-472
WAGNER, M.L. DIZIONARIO ETIMOLOGICO
SARDO.
  J.L. BUTLER, 545(RPH):AUG70-108
WAGNER, R. WAGNER ON MUSIC AND DRAMA.
(A. GOLDMAN & E. SPRINCHORN, EDS)
  B. MAGEE, 415:JUL70-711
WAGNER, S. CIGARETTE COUNTRY.*
  E. EDELSON, 440:9JAN72-6
WAGNER, V. THE SUSPENSION OF HENRY
ADAMS.*
  J.W. CROWLEY, 432(NEQ):MAR70-154

WAGNER, W.J., ED. POLISH LAW THROUGHOUT
THE AGES.
  K. GRZYBOWSKI, 32:JUN71-429
WAGONER, D. NEW AND SELECTED POEMS.*
  R. BOYERS, 340(KR):1970/1-176
  N. JACOBS, 447(N&Q):DEC70-476
WAGONER, D. RIVERBED.
  J.W. HUGHES, 561(SATR):26FEB72-62
WAGONER, D. WORKING AGAINST TIME.
  R. DURGNAT, 493:WINTER70/71-366
WAGONER, D. - SEE ROETHKE, T.
WAHL, J. IL PENSIERO MODERNO IN FRANCIA.
  G. OLDRINI, 548(RCSF):JAN/MAR69-115
WAHLUND, P.E. RIDÅFALL.
  B. HELLSTRÖM, 270:VOL20#2-46
WAHRIG, G., ED. DEUTSCHES WÖRTERBUCH.
  A.L. LLOYD, 221(GQ):JAN70-91
WAIN, J., ED. INTERPRETATIONS. (2ND ED)
  617(TLS):22SEP72-1112
WAIN, J. LETTERS TO FIVE ARTISTS.*
  T. BLACKBURN, 493:SUMMER70-171
  R. DURGNAT, 493:SPRING70-81
WAIN, J. THE LIFE GUARD.*
  M. LEVIN, 441:19MAR72-41
  442(NY):13MAY72-146
WAIN, J. A WINTER IN THE HILLS.*
  F.P.W. MC DOWELL, 659:SUMMER72-361
WAINGROW, M. - SEE BOSWELL, J.
WAINWRIGHT, A. MOVING OUTWARD.
  D. FETHERLING, 606(TAMR):#57-80
WAINWRIGHT, A. & J. LUDWIG, EDS. SOUND-
INGS.
  G. WOODCOCK, 102(CANL):AUTUMN71-6
WAINWRIGHT, G. EUCHARIST AND ESCHATOL-
OGY.
  617(TLS):21APR72-454
WAINWRIGHT, G.J. & I.H. LONGWORTH. DUR-
RINGTON WALLS: EXCAVATIONS 1966-1968.
  617(TLS):3MAR72-241
WAINWRIGHT, J. NIGHT IS A TIME TO DIE.
  617(TLS):26MAY72-612
WAINWRIGHT, J. REQUIEM FOR A LOSER.
  617(TLS):29SEP72-1174
WAIS, K. STUDIEN ZU RILKES VALÉRY-
ÜBERTRAGUNGEN.
  E.C. MASON, 52:BAND4HEFT1-102
WAITES, N., ED. TROUBLED NEIGHBOURS.
  617(TLS):21JAN72-71
WAKAYAMA, T. SIGNS OF LIFE.
  T. EMERY, 627(UTQ):JUL70-383
WAKEFIELD, G.S. ROBERT NEWTON FLEW 1886-
1962.
  617(TLS):10MAR72-283
WAKEFIELD, W.L. & A.P. EVANS, EDS &
TRANS. HERESIES OF THE HIGH MIDDLE
AGES.*
  639(VQR):SPRING70-LXXI
WAKEFORD, J. - SEE TURNER, B.A.
WAKELIN, M.F., ED. PATTERNS IN THE FOLK
SPEECH OF THE BRITISH ISLES.
  617(TLS):4FEB72-136
WAKOSKI, D. INSIDE THE BLOOD FACTORY.*
  B.D.S., 502(PRS):FALL69-274
WAKOSKI, D. THE MAGELLANIC CLOUDS.
  J.R. CARPENTER, 491:JUN72-164
WAKOSKI, D. THE MOTORCYCLE BETRAYAL
POEMS.*
  M. WATERS, 398:VOL3#1-42
WAKOSKI, D. SMUDGING.
  T. LASK, 441:18AUG72-31
WAKOSKI, D. THE GEORGE WASHINGTON POEMS.
  N. MARTIEN, 473(PR):1971/1-122
WALBANK, F.W. THE AWFUL REVOLUTION.
  R. BROWNING, 123:MAR71-101
  D. KAGAN, 124:SEP70-30
  O. MURRAY, 313:VOL60-264
WALCH-SCHUMANN, K. - SEE WIECK, F.

WALCKER-MAYER, W. DIE RÖMISCHE ORGEL VON
AQUINCUM.
S.J., 410(M&L):JUL71-323
WALCOT, P. GREEK PEASANTS.
E. FRIEDL & H.L. LEVY, 124:JAN71-165
WALCOTT, D. THE GULF AND OTHER POEMS.*
B. QUINN, 491:FEB72-301
WALCUTT, C.C. MAN'S CHANGING MASK.
R. CHRIST, 613:SUMMER68-301
WALDAPFEL, J. A TRAVERS SIÈCLES ET
FRONTIÈRES.
G.F. CUSHING, 575(SEER):JAN71-139
A. DEMAITRE, 149:JUN71-175
L. PÁLINKÁS, 52:BAND4HEFT3-305
WALDECK, P.B. DIE KINDHEITSPROBLEMATIK
BEI HERMANN BROCH.
H. STEINECKE, 405(MP):MAY70-396
WALDER, D. THE CHENAK AFFAIR.
H.G.I., 619(TC):1968/4&1969/1-97
WALDMAN, A. BABY BREAKDOWN.*
A. OSTRIKER, 473(PR):1971/2-218
WALDMAN, A. GIANT NIGHT.
D. LEHMAN, 491:JAN72-224
WALDMAN, A., ED. THE WORLD ANTHOLOGY.
F.D. REEVE, 491:OCT71-39
WALDRON, R.A. - SEE "SIR GAWAIN AND THE
GREEN KNIGHT"
WALES, H.G.Q. DVĀRAVATĪ.
S.J. O'CONNOR, 293(JAST):FEB70-493
WALGRAVE, J.H. UNFOLDING REVELATION.
617(TLS):4AUG72-924
WALICKI, A. THE CONTROVERSY OVER CAPI-
TALISM.*
A. WALKER, 575(SEER):JAN71-155
A.L. WEEKS, 550(RUSR):JUL70-360
WALICKI, A. W KRĘGU KONSERWATYWNEJ
UTOPII.*
E.C. THADEN, 497(POLR):SPRING69-116
WALKER, A. STANLEY KUBRICK DIRECTS.
G. MILLAR, 362:1JUN72-726
WALKER, A. LISZT.
H. SEARLE, 415:AUG71-761
WALKER, A., ED. FRANZ LISZT, THE MAN AND
HIS MUSIC.
E.N. WATERS, 415:OCT70-1002
WALKER, A. THE THIRD LIFE OF GRANGE
COPELAND.*
J. MC DONNELL, 142:FALL71-469
WALKER, A. & G. WILLCOCK - SEE PUTTENHAM,
G.
WALKER, D. DEVIL'S PLUNGE.
G. ROPER, 627(UTQ):JUL69-361
WALKER, D. THE LORD'S PINK OCEAN.
M. LEVIN, 441:20AUG72-26
WALKER, M. GERMAN HOME TOWNS.
617(TLS):7JUL72-771
WALKER, M., ED. METTERNICH'S EUROPE.
617(TLS):4AUG72-912
WALKER, M.H. COME WIND, COME WEATHER.
617(TLS):11FEB72-153
WALKER, N.M. WHEN I PUT OUT TO SEA.
617(TLS):2JUN72-639
WALKER, P.D. ÉMILE ZOLA.
F.W.J. HEMMINGS, 208(FS):JAN71-99
WALKER, P.G. - SEE UNDER GORDON WALKER,
P.
WALKER, P.N. PUNISHMENT.
617(TLS):6OCT72-1205
WALKER, S.A. SPORTING ART: ENGLAND 1700-
1900.
617(TLS):17NOV72-1389
WALL, B. HEADLONG INTO CHANGE.
J. ELLIOTT, 619(TC):1969/2-57
WALLACE, D.H. JOHN ROGERS - THE PEOPLE'S
SCULPTOR.
W.H. GERDTS, 56:WINTER69-429

WALLACE, I. THE WORD.
W. ABRAHAMS, 61:SEP72-96
S. KROLL, 441:19MAR72-39
R.R. LINGEMAN, 441:15MAR72-49
WALLACE, J.M. DESTINY HIS CHOICE.
R.J. BAUER, 568(SCN):SUMMER/AUTUMN71-
44
F. FOGLE, 551(RENQ):SUMMER70-207
J.M. NEWTON, 97(CQ):AUTUMN68-393
M-S. RØSTVIG, 179(ES):FEB70-67
WALLACE, M. THE IRISH.
617(TLS):12MAY72-557
WALLACE, R. UNGAINLY THINGS.
R. MORAN, 598(SOR):WINTER72-243
WALLACE, W. FOREIGN POLICY AND THE POL-
ITICAL PROCESS.
617(TLS):9JUN72-666
WALKER, W.S. & A.E. UYSAL. TALES ALIVE
IN TURKEY.
W.H. JANSEN, 292(JAF):JAN-MAR70-95
WALLACE-HADRILL, J.M. EARLY GERMANIC
KINGSHIP IN ENGLAND AND ON THE CONTI-
NENT.
617(TLS):20OCT72-1255
WALLASCHEK, R. PRIMITIVE MUSIC.
S. SADIE, 415:FEB71-140
WALLENBERG, H. - SEE SPRINGER, A.
WALLER, R., ED. JUST CONSEQUENCES.
617(TLS):28JAN72-109
WALLIS, H.F. THE NEW BATTLE OF BRITAIN.
617(TLS):23JUN72-727
WALLIS, J. GRAMMAR OF THE ENGLISH LAN-
GUAGE. (J.A. KEMP, ED & TRANS)
617(TLS):21JUL72-849
WALLIS, M. PRZEŻYCIE I WARTOŚĆ.
M. RIESER, 290(JAAC):SUMMER70-548
WALLIS, R.T. NEOPLATONISM.
617(TLS):28JUL72-896
WALLMANN, J. PHILIPP JAKOB SPENER UND
DIE ANFÄNGE DES PIETISMUS.
F.W. KANTZENBACH, 182:VOL23#10-533
WALLNER, B. - SEE GUY DE CHAULIAC
WALLWORK, J.F. LANGUAGE AND LINGUISTICS.
A. TRAILL, 180(ESA):SEP70-421
WALPOLE, H. HORACE WALPOLE'S CORRESPON-
DENCE WITH SIR HORACE MANN AND SIR
HORACE MANN THE YOUNGER. (W.S. LEWIS
& OTHERS, EDS)
R. HALSBAND, 561(SATR):26FEB72-64
617(TLS):25AUG72-986
WALSER, G. - SEE HERZFELD, E.
WALSER, M. DIE GALLISTL'SCHE KRANKHEIT.
617(TLS):28APR72-465
WALSER, M. THE UNICORN.*
617(TLS):14JAN72-31
WALSER, R. DAS GESAMTWERK. (VOL 2 ED BY
J. GREVEN; VOL 11 ED BY R. MÄCHLER)
617(TLS):16JUN72-680
WALSER, R. JAKOB VON GUNTEN.*
G.C. AVERY, 406:SPRING71-64
WALSH, D. LITERATURE AND KNOWLEDGE.*
G.P. HENDERSON, 479(PHQ):JUL70-316
S.E. MARSHALL, 518:OCT70-31
M. RADER, 290(JAAC):SUMMER70-552
WALSH, D., ED. A HANDBOOK FOR THE
TEACHING OF SPANISH AND PORTUGUESE.
(REV)
J.P. LAWLOR, 238:MAR70-165
J.E. MC KINNEY, 238:MAR70-166
J. MIRSKY, 238:MAR70-163
WALSH, J. POE, THE DETECTIVE.*
R. LEHAN, 445(NCF):DEC68-372
WALSH, J. STRANGE HARP, STRANGE SYM-
PHONY.*
P. DANCHIN, 179(ES):FEB70-74
WALSH, J.E. THE HIDDEN LIFE OF EMILY
DICKINSON.*
L. PERRINE, 27(AL):NOV71-457

WALSH, J.P. FAREWELL GREAT KING.
  617(TLS):7APR72-385
WALSH, P.G. THE ROMAN NOVEL.
  H.T. ROWELL, 24:OCT71-701
  A. SCOBIE, 67:MAY71-77
WALSH, W. A MANIFOLD VOICE.*
  W.H. NEW, 102(CANL):SUMMER71-98
WALSH, W. R.K. NARAYAN.
  617(TLS):3MAR72-252
WALSHE, M.O. MEDIEVAL GERMAN LITERATURE.
  R. HARVEY, 220(GL&L):JUL71-382
WALTER, A., ED. ASPECTS OF MUSIC IN
  CANADA.
  W. MELLERS, 415:JUL70-710
WALTERS, J. THE ROYAL GRIFFIN.
  617(TLS):4AUG72-926
WALTHER, H., ED. INITIA CARMINUM AC
  VERSUUM MEDII AEVI POSTERIORIS LATIN-
  ORUM... (2ND ED)
  R.W. HUNT, 382(MAE):1971/1-64
WALTON, H., JR. BLACK POLITICAL PARTIES.
  N.I. HUGGINS, 441:12NOV72-42
WALTON, L. THE GALÁPAGOS KID.
  M. LEVIN, 441:23JAN72-36
WALTON, P.H. THE DRAWINGS OF JOHN RUS-
  KIN.
  617(TLS):10NOV72-1353
WALTON, R.C. ZWINGLI'S THEOCRACY.
  W.A.J., 543:DEC69-359
WALTON, R.J. COLD WAR AND COUNTERREVO-
  LUTION.
  G.W. JOHNSON, 440:23JAN72-6
  D. SCHOENBRUN, 441:19MAR72-6
  R. STEEL, 453:19OCT72-43
  E.B. TOMPKINS, 561(SATR):20MAY72-68
  442(NY):26FEB72-103
WAMBAUGH, J. THE BLUE KNIGHT.
  A. FOOTE, 440:5MAR72-6
  E. PACE, 441:13FEB72-4
  442(NY):1APR72-105
"THE WANDERER." (T.P. DUNNING & A.J.
  BLISS, EDS)
  H. BOYD, 180(ESA):SEP70-414
  S.B. GREENFIELD, 447(N&Q):MAR70-113
  R.F.S. HAMER, 382(MAE):1971/3-262
WANDYCZ, P.S. SOVIET-POLISH RELATIONS,
  1917-1921.*
  W. SUKIENNICKI, 550(RUSR):APR70-237
WANG CHIA-CHIEN. WEI YÜAN NIEN PU.
  J.J. WRENN, 293(JAST):MAY70-688
WANG ERH-MIN. HUAI-CHUN CHIH.
  R.W.H. CHU, 293(JAST):FEB70-427
WANG P'ING. HSI-FANG LI-SUAN-HSUEH CHIH
  SHU-JU.
  N. SIVIN, 293(JAST):AUG70-914
WANG SHU-HUAI. WAI-JEN YÜ WU-HSÜ PIEN-
  FA.
  J-P. LO, 293(JAST):FEB70-429
WANG YÜ-CHÜN. CHUNG-SU WAI-CHIAO TI
  HSÜ-MO.
  H. MAST 3D, 293(JAST):FEB70-433
WÄNGLER, H.H., E. BIRKMAIER & K. ANDER-
  SON. DEUTSCHE UNSERER ZEIT.
  M.A.S. FIELDS, 399(MLJ):APR70-284
WÄNGLER, H-H. AN OUTLINE OF GERMAN
  PHONETICS. (PT 2)
  B.J. KOEKKOEK, 221(GQ):MAR70-306
WANKE, C. SENECA LUCAN CORNEILLE.
  R. HESS, 72:BAND208HEFT4/6-446
WANLEY, H. THE DIARY OF HUMFREY WANLEY,
  1715-1726. (C.E. & R.C. WRIGHT, EDS)
  H.H. CAMPBELL, 517(PBSA):JAN-MAR71-84
WAPNEWSKI, P. DIE LYRIK WOLFRAMS VON
  ESCHENBACH.
  617(TLS):27OCT72-1296
WARBECK, V. DIE SCHÖNE MAGELONA. (H-G.
  ROLOFF, ED)
  M.L. BAEUMER, 406:SPRING71-69

WARBEY, W. HO CHI MINH AND THE STRUGGLE
  FOR AN INDEPENDENT VIETNAM.
  617(TLS):21APR72-436
WARD, B. & R. DUBOS. ONLY ONE EARTH.
  A. MANNING, 362:1JUN72-731
  E. WEEKS, 61:AUG72-89
WARD, D. THE DIVINE TWINS.
  D.R. SKEELS, 292(JAF):JUL-SEP70-358
  W.L. WARDALE, 220(GL&L):JUL71-379
WARD, D. 1848.
  617(TLS):4AUG72-912
WARD, J.A. THE SEARCH FOR FORM.
  D. HEWITT, 541(RES):MAY70-252
  B.R. MC ELDERRY, JR., 445(NCF):JUN68-
  111
WARD, J.O. - SEE SCHOLES, P.A.
WARD, J.T. & R.G. WILSON, EDS. LAND AND
  INDUSTRY.
  617(TLS):24MAR72-321
WARD, K. THE DEVELOPMENT OF KANT'S VIEW
  OF ETHICS.
  617(TLS):29SEP72-1153
WARD, M. THE BLESSED TRADE.
  617(TLS):21JAN72-70
WARD, M. ROBERT BROWNING AND HIS WORLD.*
  (VOL 1)
  J.F. SCOTT, 613:AUTUMN68-448
WARD, M. ROBERT BROWNING AND HIS WORLD.*
  (VOL 2)
  639(VQR):WINTER70-XXII
WARD, M. IN THIS SHORT SPAN.
  617(TLS):29DEC72-1589
WARD, P. SPANISH LITERARY APPRECIATION.
  R.A. CARDWELL, 86(BHS):APR71-152
WARD, P. TOURING CYPRUS.
  617(TLS):14JAN72-49
WARD, R. SHEDDING SKIN.
  T. LASK, 441:29JAN72-27
  D.K. MANO, 441:16APR72-4
WARD, R.R. THE LIVING CLOCKS.
  617(TLS):17MAR72-299
WARD, W.R. RELIGION AND SOCIETY IN ENG-
  LAND 1790-1850.
  617(TLS):1DEC72-1468
WARDEN, G.B. BOSTON 1689-1776.
  R.J. CHAFFIN, 432(NEQ):DEC70-682
WARDHAUGH, R. READING.
  R-M. WEBER, 351(LL):JUN70-135
WARDLE, R.M. HAZLITT.
  617(TLS):24NOV72-1427
WARDROPER, J. - SEE "THE DEMAUNDES JOY-
  OUS"
WARDROPPER, B.W., ED. TEATRO ESPAÑOL DEL
  SIGLO DE ORO.
  J.A. CASTAÑEDA, 238:DEC70-1028
WARK, R.R. EARLY BRITISH DRAWINGS IN
  THE HUNTINGTON COLLECTION, 1600-1750.
  J. SUNDERLAND, 90:MAR70-179
WARK, R.R. - SEE "ROWLANDSON'S DRAWINGS
  FOR THE ENGLISH DANCE OF DEATH"
WARMINGTON, B.H. NERO, REALITY AND
  LEGEND.
  P.A. BRUNT, 123:JUN71-258
  S.I. OOST, 122:APR71-144
  H.B. WOLMAN, 124:JAN71-169
WARNANT, L. DICTIONNAIRE DE LA PRONON-
  CIATION FRANÇAISE. (3RD ED)
  F.J. BARNETT, 208(FS):JUL71-370
WARNER, C.K., ED. FROM THE ANCIEN RÉGIME
  TO THE POPULAR FRONT.
  N. HAMPSON, 208(FS):OCT71-495
WARNER, L. LANGDON WARNER THROUGH HIS
  LETTERS. (T. BOWIE, ED)
  B.M. LEEPER, 57:VOL31#2/3-226
WARNER, P. BRITISH BATTLEFIELDS. (VOL
  1)
  617(TLS):28JUL72-875

WARNER, P. THE CRIMEAN WAR.
617(TLS):13OCT72-1232
WARNER, P. LOOSE ENDS.
N. CALLENDAR, 441:14MAY72-35
WARNER, P. THE MEDIEVAL CASTLE.
442(NY):1APR72-108
WARNER, P. THE SPECIAL AIR SERVICE.
617(TLS):28JAN72-109
WARNER, R. ATHENS AT WAR.
G. MASLAKOV, 67:MAY71-66
WARNER, R. MEN OF ATHENS.
617(TLS):1DEC72-1466
WARNER, S.B., JR. THE PRIVATE CITY.*
W. KIDNEY, 505:JAN69-204
E.E. MELVIN, 219(GAR):SPRING69-92
WARNOCK, G.J. THE OBJECT OF MORALITY.
R.D.L. MONTAGUE, 518:OCT71-30
WARNOCK, R.G., ED. DIE PREDIGTEN
JOHANNES PAULIS.
R. RUDOLF, 182:VOL23#11/12-614
H.B. WILLSON, 402(MLR):OCT71-928
WARR, B. ACKNOWLEDGMENT TO LIFE. (L.
GASPARINI, ED)
L.T. CORNELIUS, 102(CANL):SUMMER71-95
D. FETHERLING, 606(TAMR):#57-80
WARRACK, J. TCHAIKOVSKY SYMPHONIES AND
CONCERTOS.
D. BROWN, 415:JUL70-712
412:NOV71-362
WARREN, A. CONNECTIONS.
M. LEBOWITZ, 598(SOR):SUMMER72-696
E.R. MARKS, 676(YR):AUTUMN70-135
WARREN, E. A REPUBLIC, IF YOU CAN KEEP
IT.
R. CLARK, 441:27AUG72-19
WARREN, P. IRISH GLASS.
617(TLS):3MAR72-240
WARREN, P. MINOAN STONE VASES.
R.J. BUCK, 124:JAN71-163
WARREN, P. MYRTOS.
617(TLS):22DEC72-1564
WARREN, R.P. AUDUBON: A VISION.
N. MARTIEN, 473(PR):1971/1-122
H. MORRIS, 569(SR):SPRING71-301
639(VQR):AUTUMN70-CXXXII
WARREN, R.P. MEET ME IN THE GREEN GLEN.*
D.A.N. JONES, 362:11MAY72-628
G. WEALES, 249(HUDR):WINTER71/72-716
617(TLS):21APR72-439
WARSH, L. MOVING THROUGH AIR.*
J. HOPPER, 661:SPRING69-107
VON WARTBURG, W. PROBLEMS AND METHODS
IN LINGUISTICS. (REV WITH S. ULLMANN)
S. POTTER, 402(MLR):JAN71-160
N.C.W. SPENCE, 208(FS):OCT71-501
VON WARTBURG, W., H-E. KELLER & R. GEUL-
JANS. BIBLIOGRAPHIE DES DICTIONNAIRES
PATOIS GALLOROMANS (1550-1967). (NEW
ED)
H.J. WOLF, 72:BAND208HEFT4/6-429
WARTOFSKY, M. CONCEPTUAL FOUNDATIONS OF
SCIENTIFIC THOUGHT.
J.W. SWANSON, 486:JUN69-221
WARTOFSKY, V. YEAR OF THE YAHOO.
N. CALLENDAR, 441:24DEC72-14
WARWICK, J. THE LONG JOURNEY.
D.M. HAYNE, 399(MLJ):FEB70-127
R. ROBIDOUX, 208(FS):JUL71-360
B-Z. SHEK, 207(FR):OCT69-201
G. TOUGAS, 627(UTQ):JUL69-381
WASHBURN, W.E., ED. PROCEEDINGS OF THE
VINLAND MAP CONFERENCE.
P. ADAMS, 61:JAN72-97
617(TLS):28APR72-498
WASIOLEK, E. - SEE DOSTOEVSKY, F.M.
WASKOW, H.J. WHITMAN.*
F. GADO, 597(SN):VOL40#1-252

WASMUTH, E. DER UNBEKANNTE PASCAL.
P. LÖNNING, 462(OL):VOL23#4-328
WASON, P.C. & P.N. JOHNSON-LAIRD. PSY-
CHOLOGY OF REASONING.
617(TLS):15SEP72-1063
WASOWICZ, A. OBRÓBKA DREWNA W STAROŻYT-
NEJ GRECJI.
R. HEIDENREICH, 182:VOL23#4-179
WASSERMAN, J. OTTAVIANO MASCARINO AND
HIS DRAWINGS IN THE ACCADEMIA NAZIONALE
DI SAN LUCA.
J-J. GLOTON, 576:MAR68-74
WASSERSTROM, W. THE LEGACY OF VAN WYCK
BROOKS.
S. PAUL, 301(JEGP):OCT71-699
WASSON, R.G. SOMA.*
J. KAYALOFF, 550(RUSR):APR70-238
WÄSTBERG, P. THE AIR CAGE.
T. LASK, 441:24JUN72-29
442(NY):8JUL72-74
WASTI, S.R. - SEE AMEER ALI, S.
WATANABE, M. KINSEI-CHOSEN KYOYUKU-SHI
KENKYU.
H.C. KIM, 293(JAST):FEB70-455
WATERER, J.W. SPANISH LEATHER.
617(TLS):28JUL72-899
WATERHOUSE, E.K. THE JAMES A. DE ROTHS-
CHILD COLLECTION AT WADDESDON MANOR:
PAINTINGS.*
J. HAYES, 90:APR69-227
WATERMAN, J.T. A HISTORY OF THE GERMAN
LANGUAGE.
M. RICHTER, 564:FALL68-165
WATERMEIER, D.J. - SEE BOOTH, E. & W.
WINTER
WATERS, D.W. THE RUTTERS OF THE SEA.
R.O. LINDSAY, 656(WMQ):JUL70-495
WATERS, F. BOOK OF THE HOPI.
D. PRINGLE, 96:DEC69-48
WATERS, F. CONVERSATIONS WITH FRANK
WATERS. (J.R. MILTON, ED)
W. BRANDON, 561(SATR):1JUL72-50
WATERSTON, E. - SEE PARKER, G.
WATKIN, D. THOMAS HOPE, 1769-1831, AND
THE NEO-CLASSICAL IDEA.
J. HARRIS, 46:MAY69-386
D. IRWIN, 39:MAY69-402
WATKINS, M., ED. THE EAST ANGLIAN BOOK.
617(TLS):21JAN72-77
WATKINS, O.C. THE PURITAN EXPERIENCE.
617(TLS):9JUN72-665
WATKINSON, R. WILLIAM MORRIS AS DESIGN-
ER.*
D-J. GORDON, 592:MAR68-156
WATSON, A. THE LAW OF PROPERTY IN THE
LATER ROMAN REPUBLIC.*
J. CROOK, 123:DEC70-359
WATSON, A.G. THE MANUSCRIPTS OF HENRY
SAVILE OF BANKE.
T-A. VAN, 517(PBSA):APR-JUN71-182
WATSON, B., ED & TRANS. CHINESE RHYME-
PROSE.
617(TLS):19MAY72-573
WATSON, C. BROOMSTICKS OVER FLAXBOROUGH.
617(TLS):7JUL72-783
WATSON, C. KISSING COVENS.
N. CALLENDAR, 441:25JUN72-30
WATSON, C. SNOBBERY WITH VIOLENCE.*
R. GADNEY, 364:DEC71/JAN72-151
WATSON, C.P. & A.C. REYNELL - SEE OVID
WATSON, D. BIRDS OF MOOR AND MOUNTAIN.
617(TLS):6OCT72-1203
WATSON, D.R. THE LIFE AND TIMES OF
CHARLES I.
617(TLS):15SEP72-1053
WATSON, E.P. - SEE GASKELL, E.

WATSON, F.S. FORGOTTEN TRAILS. (W.R.
SNELL, ED)
C. DELANEY, 9(ALAR):JAN69-77
WATSON, G. THE ENGLISH PETRARCHANS.
C. FAHY, 354:MAR69-59
WATSON, G., ED. THE NEW CAMBRIDGE
BIBLIOGRAPHY OF ENGLISH LITERATURE.
(VOL 3)
R.D. ALTICK, 301(JEGP):JAN71-139
G. THURLEY, 67:MAY71-125
WATSON, G. NUTRITION AND YOUR MIND.
441:13FEB72-16
WATSON, G. THE STUDY OF LITERATURE.*
C. RICKS, 97(CQ):AUTUMN/WINTER69/70-
395
WATSON, G.R. THE ROMAN SOLDIER.*
R.W. DAVIES, 313:VOL60-220
R.O. FINK, 24:JUL71-506
P. SALWAY, 123:JUN71-263
WATSON, J.D. THE DOUBLE HELIX.
I. FLEMING, 97(CQ):AUTUMN68-389
WATSON, J.G. THE SNOPES DILEMMA.*
J.V. HAGOPIAN, 27(AL):MAY71-304
E. HOWELL, 579(SAQ):SUMMER71-430
WATSON, W. CULTURAL FRONTIERS IN ANCIENT
EAST ASIA.
617(TLS):29SEP72-1168
WATT, D. - SEE HUXLEY, A.
WATT, I., ED. THE AUGUSTAN AGE.
D.G., 173(ECS):SPRING70-422
WATT, R.M. THE KINGS DEPART.
K.H. JARAUSCH, 19(AGR):VOL35#6-28
WATTERS, P. DOWN TO NOW.
P. ADAMS, 61:FEB72-109
WATTS, A. IN MY OWN WAY.
J. KANON, 561(SATR):11NOV72-67
T. LASK, 441:16DEC72-33
N.W. ROSS, 441:12NOV72-50
WATTS, A.C. THE LYRE AND THE HARP.
D.C. BAKER, 191(ELN):MAR70-215
S.B. GREENFIELD, 301(JEGP):APR71-279
A.I. GYGER, 382(MAE):1971/2-172
WATTS, C.T. - SEE CONRAD, J.
WAUGH, A. A BED OF FLOWERS.
E. MORGAN, 362:24FEB72-252
617(TLS):3MAR72-239
WAY, P. A PERFECT STATE OF HEALTH.
M. LEVIN, 441:28MAY72-16
WEALES, G. TENNESSEE WILLIAMS.
S. FALK, 397(MD):DEC67-318
WEALES, G. - SEE WYCHERLEY, W.
WEATHERHEAD, A.K. THE EDGE OF THE IMAGE.
E.L. MAYO, 448:SUMMER68-116
M.B. QUINN, 131(CL):WINTER71-72
H. SERGEANT, 175:SPRING69-33
WEATHERS, W. THE ARCHETYPE AND THE PSY-
CHE.
J.R. RAPER, 577(SHR):SPRING70-188
WEAVER, M. WILLIAM CARLOS WILLIAMS.*
C. TOMLINSON, 364:FEB/MAR72-166
617(TLS):14JAN72-32
WEAVER, P.R.C. FAMILIA CAESARIS.
617(TLS):22SEP72-1110
WEAVER, R.M. LANGUAGE IS SERMONIC.
(R.L. JOHANNSEN, R. TRICKLAND & R.T.
EUBANKS, EDS)
H. REGNERY, 396(MODA):FALL71-437
WEBB, A. A CURATOR'S NOTEBOOK.
D. MC VEAGH, 415:MAR70-283
WEBB, E. SAMUEL BECKETT.
E. KERN, 659:AUTUMN72-530
R. PEARCE, 295:VOL2#3-442
WEBB, J., ED. POOR RELIEF IN ELIZABETHAN
IPSWICH.
B.R. MASTERS, 325:APR69-505
WEBB, P. SELECTED POEMS 1954-1965.
G. FOX, 99:MAY72-70
M.T. LANE, 198:WINTER72-110

WEBBER, J. THE ELOQUENT "I."*
L.A. BEAURLINE, 219(GAR):SPRING69-103
J.I. COPE, 401(MLQ):MAR70-92
L. NATHANSON, 141:SPRING69-209
V.D. PINTO, 175:AUTUMN69-108
B. VICKERS, 541(RES):AUG70-361
C.F. WILLIAMSON, 447(N&Q):NOV70-426
WEBBER, R. THE VILLAGE BLACKSMITH.
617(TLS):25AUG72-1006
WEBER, B. SHERWOOD ANDERSON.
S. FALK, 397(MD):DEC67-318
WEBER, B.J. THE CONSTRUCTION OF "PARA-
DISE LOST."
617(TLS):3MAR72-252
WEBER, D.J. THE TAOS TRAPPERS.
W. GARD, 584(SWR):SUMMER71-V
WEBER, E. JOHN GOWER: DICHTER EINER
ETHISCH-POLITISCHEN REFORMATION. JOHN
GOWER: ZUR LITERARISCHEN FORM SEINER
DICHTUNG.
W.F. SCHIRMER, 38:BAND87HEFT3/4-452
WEBER, E. DIE RÖMERZEITLICHEN INSCHRIF-
TEN DER STEIERMARK.
R.P. WRIGHT, 313:VOL60-235
WEBER, L. THE ENGLISH INFANT SCHOOL AND
INFORMAL EDUCATION.*
J. BREMER, 441:13FEB72-38
WEBER, R.W. DER AUSSAGE DER FORM.
H. FRIEDL, 72:BAND208HEFT4/6-421
WEBER, S.A. THEOLOGY AND POETRY IN THE
MIDDLE ENGLISH LYRIC.
R.E. KASKE, 589:JAN71-188
S. MANNING, 401(MLQ):DEC70-504
WEBSTER, B. ONE BY ONE.
M. LEVIN, 441:29OCT72-59
WEBSTER, G. THE ROMAN IMPERIAL ARMY OF
THE FIRST AND SECOND CENTURIES A.D.
R.W. DAVIES, 313:VOL60-226
WEBSTER, J. THE DEVIL'S LAW-CASE. (F.A.
SHIRLEY, ED)
617(TLS):26MAY72-613
WEBSTER, J.C.B., ED. HISTORY AND CONTEM-
PORARY INDIA.
617(TLS):26MAY72-613
WEBSTER, M. DON'T PUT YOUR DAUGHTER ON
THE STAGE.
P. ADAMS, 61:OCT72-135
WEBSTER, N. A KILLING IN MALTA.
N. CALLENDAR, 441:13AUG72-20
WEBSTER, N.W. BRITAIN'S FIRST TRUNK
LINE.
617(TLS):25AUG72-1006
WEBSTER, T.B.L. EVERYDAY LIFE IN CLASSI-
CAL ATHENS.
B.A. SPARKES, 303:VOL90-255
WEBSTER, T.B.L. THE GREEK CHORUS.
D.D. FEAVER, 124:APR71-268
WEBSTER, T.B.L. AN INTRODUCTION TO
SOPHOCLES. (2ND ED)
H. LLOYD-JONES, 123:DEC70-299
WEBSTER, T.B.L. TRADITION IN GREEK DRA-
MATIC LYRIC.
L.P.E. PARKER, 123:DEC71-455
WEBSTER, T.B.L. THE TRAGEDIES OF EURI-
PIDES.*
D.J. CONACHER, 487:SPRING70-74
A.F. GARVIE, 123:JUN71-180
WEBSTER, T.B.L. - SEE SOPHOCLES
"WEBSTER'S GUIDE TO AMERICAN HISTORY."
617(TLS):11FEB72-152
"WEBSTER'S THIRD NEW INTERNATIONAL DIC-
TIONARY OF THE ENGLISH LANGUAGE."
(P.B. GOVE, ED)
617(TLS):13OCT72-1209
WECHSBERG, J. THE OPERA.
617(TLS):1DEC72-1469
WECHSBERG, J. SOUNDS OF VIENNA.
N. HENDERSON, 39:MAY69-407

WECHSLER, J.A., WITH N.F. WECHSLER & H.W.
KARPF. IN A DARKNESS.
  J. BRENNER, 561(SATR):1JUL72-54
  R. COLES, 453:18MAY72-18
WEDDERBURN, D. & R. CROMPTON. WORKERS'
ATTITUDES AND TECHNOLOGY.
  617(TLS):1SEP72-1034
WEDECK, H.E., WITH W. BASKIN. DICTIONARY
OF SPIRITUALISM.
  617(TLS):17MAR72-317
WEDGWOOD, C.V. SEVENTEENTH-CENTURY
ENGLISH LITERATURE. (2ND ED)
  J.H. SIMS, 568(SCN):WINTER71-70
WEEKS, A.L. THE OTHER SIDE OF COEXIS-
TENCE.
  H.S. DINERSTEIN, 32:JUN71-401
WEEKS, D. CORVO.*
  H. ACTON, 453:16NOV72-24
WEEKS, D. - SEE ROLFE, F.
WEESNER, T. THE CAR THIEF.
  C. LEHMANN-HAUPT, 441:28JUN72-47
  J. MC ELROY, 441:18JUN72-7
  R. SALE, 453:5OCT72-34
  442(NY):15JUL72-81
WEGNER, M. MUSIK UND TANZ.*
  L.B. LAWLER, 121(CJ):OCT-NOV70-85
WEGNER, M. UNTERSUCHUNGEN ZU DEN LATEIN-
ISCHEN BEGRIFFEN "SOCIUS" UND "SOCIE-
TAS."*
  F. LASSERRE, 182:VOL23#5-241
WEHRLE, E.S. BRITAIN, CHINA, AND THE
ANTIMISSIONARY RIOTS, 1891-1900.*
  P.A. KUHN, 637(VS):MAR70-367
WEHRLI, C. ANTIGONE ET DÉMÉTRIOS.
  J. BRISCOE, 123:DEC71-420
  R.M. ERRINGTON, 303:VOL90-250
  S.I. OOST, 122:APR71-139
WEHRLI, F. DIE SCHULE DES ARISTOTELES.
(PTS 2 & 8)
  G.B. KERFERD, 123:DEC70-400
WEHRLI, F. DIE SCHULE DES ARISTOTELES.
(PTS 3 & 6) (2ND ED)
  P. CHANTRAINE, 555:VOL44FASC2-328
  G.B. KERFERD, 123:DEC70-400
WEHRLI, F. DIE SCHULE DES ARISTOTELES.
(PT 4) (2ND ED)
  P. CHANTRAINE, 555:VOL44FASC1-130
  G.B. KERFERD, 123:DEC70-400
WEHRLI, M. FORMEN MITTELALTERLICHER
ERZÄHLUNG.
  D.H. GREEN, 402(MLR):OCT71-924
WEIBULL, C. DROTTNING CHRISTINA OCH
SVERIGE 1646-1651.
  H.A. BARTON, 563(SS):AUTUMN71-440
WEIDHORN, M. DREAMS IN SEVENTEENTH-
CENTURY ENGLISH LITERATURE.
  R. SHARROCK, 677:VOL2-265
WEIDHORN, M. RICHARD LOVELACE.
  P. PALMER, 402(MLR):OCT71-864
  E-A. TAYLOR, 568(SCN):SUMMER/AUTUMN
  71-42
WEIDMAN, J. LAST RESPECTS.
  M. LEVIN, 441:23JAN72-36
  R.C. STERNE, 561(SATR):22JAN72-69
  442(NY):19FEB72-116
WEIGAND, H.J. WOLFRAM'S PARZIVAL.* (U.
HOFFMANN, ED)
  M. CURSCHMANN, 589:JAN71-190
  H.B. WILLSON, 402(MLR):APR71-436
WEIGEL, H. KARL KRAUS ODER DIE MACHT
DER OHNMACHT.
  H-F. GARTEN, 270:VOL20#1-12
WEIHRAUCH, H.R. EUROPÄISCHE BRONZESTATU-
ETTEN, 15.-18. JAHRHUNDERT.*
  J. MONTAGU, 90:JUN69-393

WEIL, A. THE NATURAL MIND.
  R. COLES, 61:AUG72-80
  L. GRINSPOON, 441:15OCT72-27
  M. WATKINS, 441:30SEP72-33
WEIL, G. & J. CHASSARD. LES GRANDES
DATES DES LITTÉRATURES ÉTRANGÈRES.
  L.R. FURST, 208(FS):JUL71-366
WEIL, I. GORKY.
  J.B. WOODWARD, 397(MD):DEC67-323
WEIL, S. FIRST AND LAST NOTEBOOKS.*
(R. REES, ED & TRANS)
  G.A. PANICHAS, 396(MODA):SPRING71-211
WEIL, S. POÈMES, SUIVIS DE "VENISE
SAUVÉE."
  J.P. LITTLE, 208(FS):JAN71-113
WEILER, C. JAWLENSKY.
  617(TLS):5MAY72-508
WEILER, I. AGONALES IN WETTKÄMPFEN DER
GRIECHISCHEN MYTHOLOGIE.
  H-A. HARRIS, 123:DEC71-467
WEIMANN, R. SHAKESPEARE UND DIE TRADI-
TION DES VOLKSTHEATERS.
  G.K. HUNTER, 447(N&Q):JUN70-233
  D. MEHL, 52:BAND4HEFT3-311
  M. RIESER, 290(JAAC):WINTER69-260
WEIMAR, K. VERSUCH ÜBER VORAUSSETZUNG
UND ENTSTEHUNG DER ROMANTIK.
  I.C., 191(ELN):SEP69(SUPP)-98
  L.R. FURST, 220(GL&L):APR71-282
WEINBERG, G. SOCIETY AND THE HEALTHY
HOMOSEXUAL.
  J. JOHNSTON, 441:20FEB72-5
WEINBERG, G.L. THE FOREIGN POLICY OF
HITLER'S GERMANY.
  J.L. SNELL, 32:DEC71-891
WEINBERG, H.A. THE NEW NOVEL IN AMER-
ICA.*
  B.H. GELFANT, 27(AL):MAR71-147
  D.M. KARTIGANER, 418(MR):WINTER71-174
WEINBERG, H.G., COMP. THE COMPLETE
GREED.
  J. KANON, 561(SATR):16DEC72-58
WEINBERG, K. ON GIDE'S PROMÉTHÉE.
  617(TLS):20OCT72-1262
WEINBERG, W. DIE RESTE DES JÜDISCH-
DEUTSCHEN.*
  B. MURDOCH, 402(MLR):JUL71-717
WEINBERGER, M. MICHELANGELO, THE SCULP-
TOR.*
  M. HIRST, 90:DEC69-762
WEINBROT, H.D. THE FORMAL STRAIN.*
  H. FOLTINEK, 182:VOL23#15/16-753
  C.E. FRANK, 577(SHR):FALL70-379
  M. KALLICH, 481(PQ):JUL70-323
  F.M.L., 502(PRS):SUMMER69-233
  42(AR):SPRING69-112
WEINER, M. THE SOVEREIGN REMEDY.
  617(TLS):11FEB72-152
WEINER, P. OLD PEWTER IN HUNGARIAN COL-
LECTIONS.
  617(TLS):14JUL72-825
WEINGARTEN, V. A WOMAN OF FEELING.
  P. ADAMS, 61:MAY72-112
  E. EASTON, 561(SATR):25MAR72-101
  A. FOOTE, 440:5MAR72-7
  M. LEVIN, 441:12MAR72-41
WEINGARTNER, P., ED. DESKRIPTION, ANAL-
YTIZITÄT, UND EXISTENZ.*
  I. DAPUNT, 484(PPR):DEC69-310
WEINGARTNER, T. STALIN UND DER AUFSTIEG
HITLERS.
  H.S. ROBINSON, 32:DEC71-890
WEINREICH, U. MODERN ENGLISH-YIDDISH,
YIDDISH-ENGLISH DICTIONARY.
  E. STANKIEWICZ, 328:SUMMER69-368
WEINSTEIN, M.A. WILLIAM EDMONDSTOUNE
AYTOUN AND THE SPASMODIC CONTROVERSY.*
  J. LUCAS, 637(VS):SEP69-111

WEINSTEIN, P.M. HENRY JAMES AND THE
REQUIREMENTS OF THE IMAGINATION.
617(TLS):18AUG72-957
WEINSTOCK, H. VINCENZO BELLINI.*
D. ARNOLD, 362:15JUN72-796
R. JACOBSON, 561(SATR):26FEB72-66
W. SARGEANT, 442(NY):8JAN72-81
617(TLS):16JUN72-684
WEINSTOCK, H. ROSSINI.*
G. AUDETTE, 418(MR):SPRING71-261
WEINSTOCK, S. DIVUS JULIUS.
617(TLS):12MAY72-550
WEINTRAUB, S. BEARDSLEY.*
E. HOFFMANN, 90:FEB70-118
WEIR, M. BEST FOOT FORWARD.
617(TLS):31MAR72-378
WEISBERGER, B.A. THE AMERICAN HERITAGE
HISTORY OF THE AMERICAN PEOPLE.
W. LORD, 441:19MAR72-24
WEISBORD, R.G. & A. STEIN. BITTERSWEET
ENCOUNTER.
M. KEMPTON, 453:29JUN72-3
WEISE, C. EIN WUNDERLICHES SCHAU-SPIEL
VOM NIEDERLÄNDISCHEN BAUER. (H. BUR-
GER, ED)
R.K., 221(GQ):JAN70-144
WEISGAL, M. ...SO FAR.
E. WIESEL, 441:27FEB72-6
617(TLS):12MAY72-553
WEISGAL, M.W. - SEE WEIZMANN, C.
WEISGERBER, J. FAULKNER ET DOSTOÏEVSKI.*
C.S. BROWN, 131(CL):WINTER71-84
M.J. HANAK, 149:MAR71-102
WEISGERBER, J.L. DIE NAMEN DER UBIER.*
L. SEIFFERT, 447(N&Q):JUN70-224
WEISKOPF, W. ALIENATION AND ECONOMICS.
R.L. HEILBRONER, 453:9MAR72-9
WEISS, A. HÉROINES DU THÉÂTRE DE HENRY
DE MONTHERLANT.
D.E. NEVILLE, 399(MLJ):NOV70-536
WEISS, A. LE MONDE THEATRAL DE MICHEL DE
GHELDERODE.
R. TROUSSON, 397(MD):DEC67-327
WEISS, G. JOANNES KANTAKUZENOS - ARISTO-
KRAT, STAATSMANN, KAISER UND MÖNCH.
J.W. BARKER, 589:OCT71-751
WEISS, P. THE CONVERSATION OF THE THREE
WALKERS [AND] THE SHADOW OF THE COACH-
MAN'S BODY.
J.G. FARRELL, 362:7SEP72-312
617(TLS):29DEC72-1588
WEISS, P. DRAMEN.*
I. HILTON, 220(GL&L):JUL71-385
WEISS, P. DAS DUELL.
617(TLS):29DEC72-1588
WEISS, P. NOTES ON THE CULTURAL LIFE OF
THE DEMOCRATIC REPUBLIC OF NORTH VIET-
NAM.*
H. LOMAS, 364:JUN/JUL71-139
WEISS, P. PHILOSOPHY IN PROCESS. (VOLS
1&2)
J. COLLINS, 613:AUTUMN68-463
WEISS, P. PHILOSOPHY IN PROCESS. (VOL
3)
S.O.H., 543:SEP69-142
WEISS, P. TROTSKY IN EXILE. HÖLDERLIN.
617(TLS):14APR72-408
WEISS, R. THE RENAISSANCE DISCOVERY OF
CLASSICAL ANTIQUITY.
R.J. BARNETT, JR., 124:SEP70-30
J.M. COOK, 123:JUN71-279
A. MOLHO, 589:JAN71-193
WEISS, T. THE WORLD BEFORE US.
J. KOETHE, 491:APR72-49
WEISS, W.T. & C.S. PROCTOR. UMPHREY LEE.
H. GAMBRELL, 584(SWR):SPRING71-V
WEISSBORT, D. IN AN EMERGENCY.
617(TLS):29SEP72-1146

WEISSBORT, D. - SEE GORBANEVSKAYA, N.
WEISSENBERGER, K. DIE ELEGIE BEI PAUL
CELAN.*
R.E. LORBE, 301(JEGP):JUL71-518
WEISSENBERGER, K. FORMEN DER ELEGIE VON
GOETHE BIS CELAN.*
A. CLOSS, 402(MLR):APR71-456
WEISSMAN, P. LORDS OF POWER.
M. LEVIN, 441:17SEP72-42
WEISSTEIN, U. HEINRICH MANN.
B.A. SØRENSEN, 462(OL):VOL24#4-305
WEISSTUB, D. HEAVEN TAKE MY HAND.*
H. MAC CALLUM, 627(UTQ):JUL69-351
WEITZMAN, A.J. - SEE MARANA, G.P.
WEITZMANN, C.F. A HISTORY OF PIANOFORTE-
PLAYING AND PIANOFORTE LITERATURE.
R. ANDERSON, 415:AUG70-808
WEITZMANN, K. STUDIES IN CLASSICAL AND
BYZANTINE MANUSCRIPT ILLUMINATION.
(H.L. KESSLER, ED)
617(TLS):7JAN72-18
WEITZMANN, K. & OTHERS. A TREASURY OF
ICONS.*
B. BETTINSON, 363:FEB70-75
WEIZMANN, C. THE LETTERS AND PAPERS OF
CHAIM WEIZMANN. (VOL 3) (M.W. WEISGAL,
ED)
617(TLS):29DEC72-1574
WELBON, G.R. THE BUDDHIST NIRVĀṆA AND
ITS WESTERN INTERPRETERS.
L. ROCHER, 318(JAOS):OCT-DEC70-589
WELCH, E., ED. THE ADMIRALTY COURT BOOK
OF SOUTHAMPTON: 1566-1585.
R.C. JARVIS, 325:APR70-76
WELCH, E., ED. PLYMOUTH BUILDING AC-
COUNTS OF THE SIXTEENTH AND SEVENTEENTH
CENTURIES.
J.G. WOODWARD, 325:APR69-504
WELCH, P. AMERICAN FOLK ART.
J.D. LABAN, 650(WF):JAN69-70
WELCH, W. AMERICAN IMAGES OF SOVIET
FOREIGN POLICY.
P.S. GILLETTE, 32:DEC71-892
S. HOROWITZ, 104:WINTER71-582
WELKER, K-E. DIE GRUNDSÄTZLICHE BEUR-
TEILUNG DER RELIGIONSGESCHICHTE DURCH
SCHLEIERMACHER.
M.J.V., 543:DEC69-360
WELLEK, A. WITZ, LYRIK, SPRACHE.
L. BORNSCHEUER, 406:SUMMER71-197
WELLEK, R. DISCRIMINATIONS.*
R.G. COX, 89(BJA):SPRING71-204
E.R. MARKS, 676(YR):AUTUMN70-135
WELLEK, R. A HISTORY OF MODERN CRITICISM
1750-1950.* (VOLS 1-4)
B. WEINBERG, 322(JHI):JAN-MAR69-127
WELLER, A.S. THE JOYS AND SORROWS OF
RECENT AMERICAN ART.
S.G.L., 330(MASJ):FALL69-79
WELLERSHOFF, D. A BEAUTIFUL DAY.
J. HENDIN, 441:2APR72-6
WELLERSHOFF, D. GOTTFRIED BENN, PHÄNOTYP
DIESER STUNDE.
J. BOUVERESSE, 98:AUG-SEP69-713
WELLERSHOFF, D. EINLADUNG AN ALLE.
617(TLS):24NOV72-1415
WELLERSHOFF, D. - SEE BENN, G.
WELLES, C.B. ALEXANDER AND THE HELLEN-
ISTIC WORLD.
T.W. AFRICA, 124:APR71-269
WELLESZ, E. ARNOLD SCHOENBERG. (NEW ED)
617(TLS):3MAR72-253
WELLINGS, E.M. A HISTORY OF COUNTY
CRICKET: MIDDLESEX.
617(TLS):29SEP72-1176
WELLMER, A. CRITICAL THEORY OF SOCIETY.
T. BOTTOMORE, 453:6APR72-31

WELLS, C.M. THE GERMAN POLICY OF AUGUS-
TUS.
617(TLS):1DEC72-1466
WELLS, D.A. THE VORAU "MOSES" AND
"BALAAM."
K. NORTHCOTT, 406:WINTER71-406
F. RÄDLE, 182:VOL23#19/20-858
P. SALMON, 402(MLR):APR71-434
WELLS, G.A. THE PLAYS OF GRILLPARZER.
P.K. WHITAKER, 399(MLJ):OCT70-467
W.E. YATES, 402(MLR):JAN71-223
WELLS, H.G. THE OUTLINE OF HISTORY.
(REV BY R. POSTGATE & G.P. WELLS)
617(TLS):30JUN72-750
WELLS, H.W., ED & TRANS. SANSKRIT PLAYS
FROM EPIC SOURCES.*
P.S. JAINI, 293(JAST):FEB70-469
WELLS, S. - SEE SHAKESPEARE, W.
WELLS, S. - SEE SISSON, C.J.
WELLS, T. A DIE IN THE COUNTRY.
N. CALLENDAR, 441:17DEC72-23
WELLS, T. HOW TO KILL A MAN.
N. CALLENDAR, 441:30APR72-36
WELMERS, B.F. & W.E. IGBO: A LEARNER'S
DICTIONARY.
M.M. GREEN, 315(JAL):VOL8PT1-48
WELSCH, R.L., COMP. A TREASURY OF NEB-
RASKA PIONEER FOLKLORE.*
E.T. HERBERT, 650(WF):JAN68-62
WELSFORD, E. THE FOOL. (NEW ED)
J. STAROBINSKI, 98:DEC69-1033
WELSFORD, E. FOWRE HYMNES AND EPITHALA-
MION.
S. JAYNE, 551(RENQ):AUTUMN70-321
WELSH, A. THE CITY OF DICKENS.*
H.P. SUCKSMITH, 677:VOL2-310
K. TETZELI VON ROSADOR, 72:BAND208
HEFT4/6-405
WELSH, D.J. IGNACY KRASICKI.*
Z. FOLEJEWSKI, 32:JUN71-445
WELSH, R.P. PIET MONDRIAN.
J-P. ATTAL, 98:APR69-324
WELTI, M.E. DER BASLER BUCHDRUCK UND
BRITANNIEN.
J. HASLER, 179(ES):APR70-163
WELTY, E. LOSING BATTLES.*
P.E. GRAY, 676(YR):AUTUMN70-101
T.H. LANDESS, 569(SR):AUTUMN71-626
639(VQR):SUMMER70-LXXXVIII
WELTY, E. THE OPTIMIST'S DAUGHTER.
A. BROYARD, 441:18MAY72-49
E. JANEWAY, 561(SATR):1JUL72-60
H. MOSS, 441:21MAY72-1
P. THEROUX, 440:14MAY72-5
E. WEEKS, 61:JUN72-111
M. WOOD, 453:29JUN72-8
WELWEI, K.W. RÖMISCHES GESCHICHTSDENKEN
IN SPÄTREPUBLIKANISCHER UND AUGUSTEI-
SCHER ZEIT.
J. ANDRÉ, 555:VOL44FASC2-366
WENDLER, W. CARL STERNHEIM.
J.M. RITCHIE, 220(GL&L):OCT70-118
WENIGER, D. CACTI OF THE SOUTHWEST.
W. GARD, 584(SWR):WINTER71-91
WENK, K. THE RESTORATION OF THAILAND
UNDER RAMA I, 1782-1809.
W.F. VELLA, 318(JAOS):OCT-DEC70-628
WENKAM, R. MAUI.
617(TLS):4AUG72-923
WENNER, J. LENNON REMEMBERS.
P. MARIN, 441:20FEB72-4
WENSINGER, A.S. & W.B. COLEY - SEE LICHT-
ENBERG, G.C.
WENZEL, M. HOUSE DECORATION IN NUBIA.
E.H. GOMBRICH, 453:4MAY72-35
617(TLS):2JUN72-620

WENZEL, S. THE SIN OF SLOTH.
P. DAMON, 545(RPH):FEB70-370
P. ENGELHARDT, 52:BAND4HEFT1-91
S. NEUIJEN, 179(ES):DEC69-605
WEÖRES, S. & F. JUHÁSZ. SELECTED POEMS.*
M.D. BIRNBAUM, 574(SEEJ):WINTER71-515
R.B. SHAW, 491:MAR72-342
WERBA, H. BASIC CONVERSATIONAL GERMAN.
N.A. BUSCH, 399(MLJ):JAN70-39
G.B. MATHIEU, 221(GQ):MAR70-307
WERCKMEISTER, O-K. IRISCHE-NORTHUMBRIS-
CHE BUCHMALEREI DES 8. JAHRHUNDERTS UND
MONASTISCHE SPIRITUALITÄT.
P. MEYVAERT, 589:APR71-408
WERFEL, F. DAS LYRISCHE WERK. (A.D.
KLARMANN, ED)
L.B. FOLTIN, 221(GQ):NOV70-789
WERIN, A. GOETHE-LYRIKERN.
G. ORTON, 220(GL&L):APR71-276
WERKMEISTER, L. A NEWSPAPER HISTORY OF
ENGLAND, 1792-1793.*
D.V.E., 191(ELN):SEP69(SUPP)-14
WERKMEISTER, W.H. HISTORICAL SPECTRUM OF
VALUE THEORIES.
S.C. PEPPER, 319:APR72-237
WERNER, O. - SEE SIMONIDES & BACCHYLIDES
WERNHAM, J.C.S. TWO RUSSIAN THINKERS.*
R. BEERMANN, 587:JAN69-402
W. KERR, 484(PPR):DEC69-309
WERTH, A. RUSSIA.
M. MC CAULEY, 575(SEER):JAN71-168
J.C. MC CLELLAND, 32:MAR71-159
WERTHEIMER, R. THE SIGNIFICANCE OF
SENSE.
617(TLS):24MAR72-345
WESLAGER, C.A. THE LOG CABIN IN AMERICA
FROM PIONEER DAYS TO THE PRESENT.
M.C. DONNELLY, 656(WMQ):APR70-340
WESSEL, K. BYZANTINE ENAMELS FROM THE
5TH TO THE 13TH CENTURY.
J.D. BRECKENRIDGE, 589:JAN71-195
P. HETHERINGTON, 90:MAY70-316
WESSÉN, E. SCHWEDISCHE SPRACHGESCHICHTE,
I, II, III.
N. HASSELMO, 301(JEGP):OCT71-700
WESSON, R.G. SOVIET FOREIGN POLICY IN
PERSPECTIVE.
T. GILBERG, 32:MAR71-157
R. LANE, 550(RUSR):OCT70-469
WEST, A. - SEE BERKOVITS, I.
WEST, A.C. AS TOWNS WITH FIRE.
F.P.W. MC DOWELL, 659:SUMMER72-361
WEST, D. THE IMAGERY AND POETRY OF
LUCRETIUS.*
W.S. ANDERSON, 121(CJ):FEB-MAR71-275
M.L. CLARKE, 123:MAR71-41
W.H. OWEN, 24:APR71-380
WEST, E. THESE LONELY VICTORIES.
N. CALLENDAR, 441:16JUL72-32
WEST, F. - SEE MURRAY, H.
WEST, F.J., JR. THE VILLAGE.
B. FARWELL, 440:5MAR72-9
441:17SEP72-44
WEST, G.D. FRENCH ARTHURIAN VERSE
ROMANCES 1150-1300.
D.J.A. ROSS, 447(N&Q):AUG70-317
WEST, G.P. RABIES IN ANIMALS AND MAN.
617(TLS):15DEC72-1527
WEST, J. RUSSIAN SYMBOLISM.*
V.D. BAROOSHIAN, 574(SEEJ):SUMMER71-
226
S.D. CIORAN, 104:FALL71-426
S. KARLINSKY, 659:WINTER72-129
WEST, M.L., ED. IAMBI ET ELEGI GRAECI.
(VOL 1)
617(TLS):31MAR72-374

WEST, M.L., ED. IAMBI ET ELEGI GRAECI
ANTE ALEXANDRUM CANTATI. (VOL 2)
  617(TLS):25AUG72-992
WEST, P. ALLEY JAGGERS.
  J.W. ALDRIDGE, 340(KR):SEP66-559
WEST, P. BELA LUGOSI'S WHITE CHRISTMAS.
  P. ADAMS, 61:SEP72-110
  V. CUNNINGHAM, 362:3FEB72-156
  G. WOLFF, 441:10SEP72-4
  617(TLS):28JAN72-85
WEST, P. COLONEL MINT.
  D. JOHNSON, 440:28MAY72-3
WEST, P. I'M EXPECTING TO LIVE QUITE
  SOON.*
  639(VQR):SUMMER70-LXXXIX
WEST, R. RIVER OF TEARS.
  J. VAIZEY, 362:190CT72-509
WEST, R.H. SHAKESPEARE AND THE OUTER
  MYSTERY.*
  M.B. ACKERMAN, 50(ARQ):AUTUMN69-280
  J.B. ARNOLD, 141:WINTER70-73
  W.F. MC NEIR, 149:JUN71-166
  R. SANER, 191(ELN):JUN70-298
WESTERBERGH, U., ED. GLOSSARIUM TILL
  MEDELTIDSLATINET I SVERIGE (GLOSSARIUM
  MEDIAE LATINITATIS SUECIAE).* (VOL 1,
  FASC 1)
  J. ANDRÉ, 555:VOL44FASC1-174
WESTERINK, L.G. - SEE ARETHAS
WESTHEIMER, D. OVER THE EDGE.
  N. CALLENDAR, 441:5NOV72-44
WESTIN, A.F., ED. INFORMATION TECHNOLOGY
  IN A DEMOCRACY.
  617(TLS):31MAR72-372
WESTLAKE, D. COPS AND ROBBERS.
  O.L. BAILEY, 561(SATR):280CT72-89
  N. CALLENDAR, 441:19NOV72-61
WESTLAKE, D.E. BANK SHOT.
  N. CALLENDAR, 441:16APR72-29
  442(NY):29APR72-144
  617(TLS):29SEP72-1174
WESTLAKE, D.E. I GAVE AT THE OFFICE.*
  617(TLS):29DEC72-1588
WESTLAKE, D.E. UNDER AN ENGLISH HEAVEN.
  561(SATR):25NOV72-74
WESTLAKE, H.D. ESSAYS ON THE GREEK
  HISTORIANS AND GREEK HISTORY.
  M.E. WHITE, 487:AUTUMN70-277
WESTLAKE, H.D. INDIVIDUALS IN THUCYDI-
  DES.*
  G.L. CAWKWELL, 123:DEC71-357
  R.J. LENARDON, 121(CJ):DEC70-JAN71-
  176
  L. PEARSON, 24:JAN71-108
"WESTMINSTER ABBEY."
  617(TLS):22DEC72-1562
WESTON, C. POOR, POOR, OPHELIA.
  N. CALLENDAR, 441:19MAR72-42
WESTON, J.C. - SEE MAC DIARMID, H.
WESTPHALEN, T. BEOWULF 3150-55.
  G. NICKEL, 72:BAND208HEFT2-129
  E.G. STANLEY, 597(SN):VOL41#1-209
  L. WHITBREAD, 179(ES):1969SUPP-LXXV
WESTRUP, J. MUSICAL INTERPRETATION.
  S. SADIE, 415:JUL71-670
WESTRUP, J. - SEE BLOM, E.
WESTRUP, J.A. SCHUBERT CHAMBER MUSIC.
  A.F.L.T., 412:AUG71-275
WESTRUP, J.A. - SEE FELLOWES, E.H.
WESTWOOD, J.N. WITNESSES OF TSUSHIMA.
  J.W. LONG, 31:MAR71-148
WETHEY, H.E. EL GRECO Y SU ESCUELA.
  E. WATERHOUSE, 90:MAY69-328
WETHEY, H.E. THE PAINTINGS OF TITIAN.
  (VOL 1)
  J. MAXON, 90:DEC70-830

WETHEY, H.E. THE PAINTINGS OF TITIAN.
  (VOL 2)
  617(TLS):25FEB72-222
WETZEL, H. KLANG UND BILD IN DEN DICH-
  TUNGEN GEORG TRAKLS.
  T. FIEDLER, 221(GQ):JAN70-121
  R. GRIMM, 406:WINTER71-413
  S.S. PRAWER, 220(GL&L):OCT70-101
WETZEL, H. KONKORDANZ ZU DEN DICHTUNGEN
  GEORG TRAKLS.
  R. GRIMM, 406:WINTER71-413
WEVERS, R.F. ISAEUS.*
  D.M. MACDOWELL, 123:MAR71-24
WEYDT, G. NACHAHMUNG UND SCHÖPFUNG IM
  BAROCK.*
  G. HILLEN, 221(GQ):MAR70-273
  B.L. SPAHR, 222(GR):NOV70-303
WHALEN, R.J. CATCH THE FALLING FLAG.
  C. LEHMANN-HAUPT, 441:23MAY72-43
  J.P. ROCHE, 441:4JUN72-38
  I.F. STONE, 453:1JUN72-11
WHALLON, W. FORMULA, CHARACTER, AND
  CONTEXT.*
  F.M. COMBELLACK, 122:JAN71-41
  S.B. GREENFIELD, 301(JEGP):APR71-279
  J.B. HAINSWORTH, 123:MAR71-69
  W. MC LEOD, 487:AUTUMN70-262
  R.M. WILSON, 402(MLR):OCT71-846
WHARTON, E. A BACKWARD GLANCE.
  617(TLS):8DEC72-1482
WHATELY, T. REMARKS ON SOME OF THE CHAR-
  ACTERS OF SHAKESPERE. (R. WHATELY, ED)
  617(TLS):18FEB72-178
WHATMOUGH, J. THE DIALECTS OF ANCIENT
  GAUL.
  G.M. MESSING, 122:JAN71-38
WHEATLEY, J.H. PATTERNS IN THACKERAY'S
  FICTION.*
  J. MC MASTER, 637(VS):DEC69-224
WHEATLEY, R. & B. THE LAST DAYS OF
  STEAM ON AUSTRALIA'S RAILWAYS.
  617(TLS):270CT72-1297
WHEELER, A. - SEE MUUS, B.J.
WHEELER, M. THE INDUS CIVILIZATION.
  (3RD ED)
  L. ROCHER, 318(JAOS):APR-JUN70-409
WHEELER, M. THE OXFORD RUSSIAN-ENGLISH
  DICTIONARY.
  617(TLS):21JUL72-838
WHEELER, T. FROM HOME IN HEAVEN.*
  P. BAILEY, 364:DEC71/JAN72-157
WHEELER-BENNETT, J. & A. NICHOLLS. THE
  SEMBLANCE OF PEACE.
  617(TLS):22SEP72-1081
WHEELER-BENNETT, J.W. A WREATH TO CLIO.
  W.A. SPRAY, 255(HAB):WINTER69-78
WHEELOCK, C. THE MYTHMAKER.*
  J. AYORA, 263:OCT-DEC71-448
  R.S. MILLS, 86(BHS):JUL71-286
WHEELOCK, J.H. BY DAYLIGHT AND IN
  DREAM.*
  H. TAYLOR, 569(SR):SUMMER71-460
WHELAN, J.P. THE SPIRITUALITY OF FRIED-
  RICH VON HÜGEL.
  617(TLS):25FEB72-225
WHETHAM, E.H. & J.I. CURRIE. THE ECONOM-
  ICS OF AFRICAN COUNTRIES.
  617(TLS):15SEP72-1066
WHETTEN, L.L. GERMANY'S OSTPOLITIK.
  N. ASCHERSON, 453:20APR72-26
  617(TLS):17MAR72-312
WHINNEY, M. EARLY FLEMISH PAINTING.*
  D.F. ROWE, 363:NOV69-33
WHINNEY, M. ENGLISH SCULPTURE 1720-1830.
  617(TLS):16JUN72-694
WHINNEY, M. HOME HOUSE, NO. 20 PORTMAN
  SQUARE.
  L. LEWIS, 90:SEP70-632

WHINNEY, M. WREN.
617(TLS):28JAN72-98
WHITAKER, C.S., JR. THE POLITICS OF
TRADITION.
J. SMITH, 579(SAQ):SUMMER71-429
"WHITAKER'S ALMANACK 1972."
617(TLS):7JAN72-7
WHITBREAD, N. THE EVOLUTION OF THE
NURSERY-INFANT SCHOOL.
617(TLS):18AUG72-977
WHITE, B.T. TANKS AND OTHER AFVS OF THE
BLITZKRIEG ERA 1939-41.
617(TLS):15DEC72-1528
WHITE, D.H. POPE AND THE CONTEXT OF
CONTROVERSY.
J.M. ADEN, 579(SAQ):AUTUMN71-608
D.R. HOILMAN, 566:SPRING71-66
R. PARKIN, 301(JEGP):OCT71-674
WHITE, E.W. ANNE BRADSTREET.
W.J. SCHEICK, 165:FALL72-204
617(TLS):18AUG72-967
WHITE, E.W. BENJAMIN BRITTEN.
W. DEAN, 415:JAN71-32
P.H., 410(M&L):JAN71-72
WHITE, H.C. TUDOR BOOKS OF SAINTS AND
MARTYRS.
T.A. BIRRELL, 179(ES):OCT70-452
WHITE, J. NATIONAL GALLERY OF IRELAND.
A. NEUMEYER, 290(JAAC):SUMMER70-561
WHITE, J.F. PROTESTANT WORSHIP AND
CHURCH ARCHITECTURE.
G.L. HERSEY, 576:MAY68-153
WHITE, J.J. MYTHOLOGY IN THE MODERN
NOVEL.
617(TLS):16JUN72-680
WHITE, J.M. THE MOUNTAIN LION.
617(TLS):28JAN72-94
WHITE, J.M. DIEGO VELAZQUEZ.
T. CROMBIE, 39:NOV69-447
WHITE, L. MACHINA EX DEO.
W.A.J., 543:MAR70-569
WHITE, L.A. THE SCIENCE OF CULTURE.
J. GREENWAY, 292(JAF):JUL-SEP70-357
WHITE, L.J. THE AUTOMOBILE INDUSTRY
SINCE 1945.
E. ROTHSCHILD, 453:24FEB72-40
WHITE, M. FOUNDATIONS OF HISTORICAL
KNOWLEDGE.
J.J. LEACH, 486:MAR68-76
WHITE, M. SCIENCE AND SENTIMENT IN
AMERICA.
P. CAWS, 441:12MAR72-7
WHITE, M.E. CON.
T. MORRISON, 441:3SEP72-6
WHITE, N. & E. WILLENSKY, EDS. AIA GUIDE
TO NEW YORK CITY.
C. SIMMONS, 441:4JUN72-7
WHITE, P. THE VIVISECTOR.*
R.N. COE, 381:VOL29#4-526
P. CRUTTWELL, 249(HUDR):SPRING71-177
T. HERRING, 581:1971/1-3
F.P.W. MC DOWELL, 659:SUMMER72-361
WHITE, P.W. & R. GLOUCESTER. ON PUBLIC
VIEW.
617(TLS):14JAN72-49
WHITE, R. BE NOT AFRAID.
C.C. PARK, 440:21MAY72-1
P. WEST, 441:14MAY72-27
617(TLS):15DEC72-1527
WHITE, R.J. THE AGE OF GEORGE III.
D.V.E., 191(ELN):SEP70(SUPP)-15
WHITE, R.J. A CONCISE HISTORY OF ENG-
LAND.
617(TLS):18AUG72-972
WHITE, R.J. FROM PETERLOO TO THE CRYSTAL
PALACE.
617(TLS):21JUL72-841
WHITE, R.L. - SEE ANDERSON, S.

WHITE, T.D. THE ANGLO-IRISH.
617(TLS):15SEP72-1052
WHITE, W.L. THE IMAGE OF MAN IN C.S.
LEWIS.
R.M. KAWANO, 651(WHR):WINTER71-93
WHITE, W.S. THE RESPONSIBLES.
441:9JAN72-28
WHITEHEAD, S.B. THE OBSERVER'S BOOK OF
HOUSE PLANTS.
617(TLS):17NOV72-1405
WHITEHILL, W.M. ANALECTA BIOGRAPHICA.
A.W. WILLIAMS, 432(NEQ):JUN70-319
WHITEHILL, W.M. DUMBARTON OAKS.
J.D. FORBES, 576:MAY69-150
WHITEHILL, W.M. MUSEUM OF FINE ARTS,
BOSTON.*
D.V. THOMPSON, 432(NEQ):SEP70-520
90:OCT70-716
WHITEHORN, K. HOW TO SURVIVE IN HOS-
PITAL.
617(TLS):24NOV72-1441
WHITEHOUSE, A. HERO WITHOUT HONOR.
M. LEVIN, 441:10DEC72-58
WHITELEY, W.H. SOME PROBLEMS OF TRANSI-
TIVITY IN SWAHILI.
L. HARRIES, 69:JUL69-315
WHITELEY, W.H. A STUDY OF YAO SENTENCES.*
J. KNAPPERT, 353:SEP69-107
WHITEMAN, J.H.M. THE MYSTICAL LIFE.
LORD HALSBURY, 483:JAN70-61
WHITEMAN, M. PHILOSOPHY OF SPACE AND
TIME.
LORD HALSBURY, 483:JAN70-61
WHITEN, C. PUTTING THE BIRTHDATE INTO
PERSPECTIVE.*
M. HORNYANSKY, 627(UTQ):JUL70-337
150(DR):AUTUMN70-424
WHITESIDE, D.T. - SEE NEWTON, I.
WHITESIDE, T. THE INVESTIGATION OF
RALPH NADER.
442(NY):1JUL72-74
WHITFIELD, I.T. LOUISIANA FRENCH FOLK
SONGS.
F. HOWES, 415:JUN70-610
WHITFIELD, J.H. - SEE LEOPARDI, G.
WHITING, B.J., WITH H.W. WHITING, COMPS.
PROVERBS, SENTENCES, AND PROVERBIAL
PHRASES FROM ENGLISH WRITINGS MAINLY
BEFORE 1500.
E.G. STANLEY, 447(N&Q):MAY70-187
WHITING, C. GEHLEN.
R.G. DEINDORFER, 561(SATR):24JUN72-61
WHITING, C. WEREWOLF.
617(TLS):1SEP72-1034
WHITLEY, J.S. & A. GOLDMAN - SEE DICKENS,
C.
WHITMAN, A. THE OBITUARY BOOK.*
617(TLS):4FEB72-118
WHITMAN, G. INTRODUCTION TO MICRO-TONAL
MUSIC.
J. BULLER, 607:AUTUMN70-34
WHITMAN, W. THE CORRESPONDENCE OF WALT
WHITMAN. (VOLS 4&5) (E.H. MILLER, ED)
S.E. MC MULLIN, 150(DR):SPRING70-135
K. MC SWEENEY, 529(QQ):SPRING70-126
WHITMAN, W. SPECIMEN DAYS.*
442(NY):23SEP72-132
WHITMAN, W. THE TENDEREST LOVER. (W.
LOWENFELS, ED)
W.M. WHITE, 569(SR):AUTUMN71-650
WHITMAN, W. WALT WHITMAN'S BLUE BOOK.*
(A. GOLDEN, ED) LEAVES OF GRASS.
(H.W. BLODGETT & S. BRADLEY, EDS)
LEAVES OF GRASS: A SELECTION OF THE
POEMS. A CHOICE OF WHITMAN'S VERSE.
(D. HALL, ED)
W. WHITE, 646(WWR):DEC68-174

WHITMAN, W. WALT WHITMAN'S COMPLETE
LEAVES OF GRASS. (W.L. MOORE, ED)
W. WHITE, 646(WWR):JUN68-61
WHITMORE, T., WITH R. WEBER. MEMPHIS
NAM SWEDEN.
441:9JAN72-28
WHITNEY, C.A. THE DISCOVERY OF OUR GAL-
AXY.
617(TLS):6OCT72-1203
WHITNEY, J.D. TRACKS.
J. HOPPER, 661:SUMMER70-123
WHITNEY, P.A. LISTEN FOR THE WHISPERER.
N. CALLENDAR, 441:20FEB72-27
WHITROW, G.J. WHAT IS TIME?
617(TLS):10NOV72-1376
WHITROW, M. - SEE "ISIS CUMULATIVE BIBLI-
OGRAPHY"
WHITSON, W.W., P. YANG & P. LAI - SEE
"MILITARY CAMPAIGNS IN CHINA"
WHITTAKER, H. CANADA'S NATIONAL BALLET.
A. EMERY, 627(UTQ):JUL69-408
WHITTAKER, N. & U. CLARK. HISTORIC
ARCHITECTURE OF COUNTY DURHAM.
617(TLS):25FEB72-229
WHITTAKER, P. THE FLYING MEN.*
G. EWART, 364:JUN/JUL71-132
WHITTEMORE, L.H. FEELING IT.*
W.H. PRITCHARD, 249(HUDR):SUMMER71-
355
WHITTEMORE, R. FIFTY POEMS FIFTY.*
G.S. FRASER, 473(PR):WINTER71/72-469
E. NELSON, 590:WINTER71-41
M.L. ROSENTHAL, 491:NOV71-99
WHITTING, C.E.J. HAUSA AND FULANI PRO-
VERBS.
A.H.M. KIRK-GREENE, 69:JUL69-319
WHITTINGTON, G. THE PREDICTION OF PROF-
ITABILITY.
617(TLS):31MAR72-378
WHITTINGTON-EGAN, R. THE ORDEAL OF
PHILIP YALE DREW.
617(TLS):16JUN72-697
WHITTLE, A.R. - SEE STICKNEY, T.
WHITTOCK, T. A READING OF THE "CANTER-
BURY TALES."*
H. BOYD, 180(ESA):SEP70-415
E. REISS, 589:JAN71-197
R.M. WILSON, 175:SPRING69-27
"WHO WAS WHO." (VOL 6)
617(TLS):7APR72-395
WHONE, H. THE SIMPLICITY OF PLAYING THE
VIOLIN.
617(TLS):26MAY72-613
"WHO'S WHO IN ALABAMA."
W.S. HOOLE, 9(ALAR):JUL69-238
"WHO'S WHO IN COMMUNIST CHINA."
M. BERNAL, 453:23MAR72-31
WHYMPER, E. TRAVELS AMONGST THE GREAT
ANDES OF THE EQUATOR. (E. SHIPTON, ED)
617(TLS):29DEC72-1589
WHYTHORNE, T. THE AUTOBIOGRAPHY OF
THOMAS WHYTHORNE. (J.M. OSBORN, ED)
B. PATTISON, 179(ES):1969SUPP-LXXXIV
WIARDA, H.J. THE DOMINICAN REPUBLIC.
W. BARBER, 150(DR):SPRING70-131
WIBBERLY, L. MEETING WITH A GREAT
BEAST.*
S. BLACKBURN, 440:12MAR72-7
617(TLS):10NOV72-1375
WICK, D. TROMBONE TECHNIQUE.
A. LUMSDEN, 415:OCT71-972
WICK, G.L. ELEMENTARY PARTICLES.
617(TLS):9JUN72-667
WICKES, G. AMERICANS IN PARIS.
H.W. BRANN, 207(FR):MAR70-722
W.L. MINER, 27(AL):JAN72-677
639(VQR):WINTER70-XX

WICKHAM, A. SELECTED POEMS.
617(TLS):28JAN72-94
WICKHAM, G. EARLY ENGLISH STAGES 1300
TO 1660. (VOL 2, PT 2)
617(TLS):9JUN72-662
WICKHAM, G. SHAKESPEARE'S DRAMATIC HERI-
TAGE.
T.W. CRAIK, 541(RES):AUG70-350
WICKMANN, D. EINE MATHEMATISCH-STATIS-
TISCHE METHODE ZUR UNTERSUCHUNG DER
VERFASSERFRAGE LITERARISCHER TEXTE.
J.L.S., 191(ELN):SEP70(SUPP)-99
J.L. SAMMONS, 222(GR):NOV70-309
WICKRAM, G. SÄMTLICHE WERKE.* (VOLS
3&4) (H-G. ROLOFF, ED)
P.V. BRADY, 402(MLR):APR71-445
L.E. KURTH, 400(MLN):APR70-402
WICKRAM, G. SÄMTLICHE WERKE. (VOL 5)
(H-G. ROLOFF, ED)
L.E. KURTH, 400(MLN):APR70-402
WICKWIRE, F. & M. CORNWALLIS: THE AMERI-
CAN ADVENTURE.*
J.A. SCHUTZ, 432(NEQ):DEC70-674
639(VQR):SUMMER70-CV
WIEBE, R., ED. STORIES FROM WESTERN
CANADA.
D. ARNASON, 296:SPRING72-89
T. COLSON, 198:SUMMER72-124
WIEBE, R., ED. THE STORY-MAKERS.
J.G. MOSS, 296:WINTER72-79
WIEBE, R.H. PEACE SHALL DESTROY MANY.
J.R. SORFLEET, 296:SPRING72-92
WIEBENSON, D. TONY GARNIER: THE CITÉ
INDUSTRIELLE.
R.G. HOWES, 363:MAY70-105
WIECK, F. FRIEDRICH WIECK BRIEFE AUS
DEN JAHREN 1830-1838. (K. WALCH-
SCHUMANN, ED)
L.E. PEAKE, 317:SPRING71-136
WIECZERZAK, J.W. A POLISH CHAPTER IN
CIVIL WAR AMERICA.
J.F. KUTOLOWSKI, 497(POLR):WINTER68-
104
WIEDEMANN, C., ED. DER GALANTE STIL:
1680-1730.
R.K., 221(GQ):MAY70-533
WIEDEMANN, C. JOHANN KLAJ UND SEINE
REDEORATORIEN.
G. PAULINE, 182:VOL23#5-229
WIELAND, G.F. & H. LEIGH, EDS. CHANGING
HOSPITALS.
617(TLS):10MAR72-278
WIENER, J.H. GREAT BRITAIN: FOREIGN
POLICY AND THE SPAN OF EMPIRE, 1689-
1971.
617(TLS):15DEC72-1519
WIENERS, J. SELECTED POEMS.
617(TLS):28JUL72-873
WIENPAHL, P. ZEN DIARY.
A.W. SADLER, 142:WINTER71-117
WIERLACHER, A. DAS BÜRGERLICHE DRAMA.*
J. BIRKE, 222(GR):MAY70-226
WIERSCHIN, M., ED. HANDSCHRIFTEN DER
RATSBÜCHEREI LÜNEBURG.
H. KNAUS, 182:VOL23#23/24-962
WIERZBICKA, A. DOCIEKANIA SEMANTYCZNE.
H. RÖSEL, 182:VOL23#3-90
VON WIESE, B., ED. DEUTSCHE DICHTER DER
MODERNE.
R. PASCAL, 402(MLR):APR71-464
VON WIESE, B., ED. DEUTSCHE DICHTER DES
19. JAHRHUNDERTS.
W.J. LILLYMAN, 301(JEGP):JAN71-123
R. PASCAL, 402(MLR):APR71-464
VON WIESE, B., ED. DEUTSCHE DRAMATURGIE
DES 19. JAHRHUNDERTS.*
R.K., 221(GQ):MAY70-534

VON WIESE, B. KARL IMMERMANN.
  J.L. SAMMONS, 221(GQ):NOV70-803
WIESE, W-D. DIE "NEUEN ENGLISCHEN DRA-
MATIKER" IN IHREM VERHÄLTNIS ZU BRECHT
(UNTER BESONDERER BERÜCKSICHTIGUNG VON
WESKER, OSBORNE UND ARDEN).
  K. TETZELI VON ROSADOR, 72:BAND208
  HEFT1-45
WIESEL, E. LEGENDS OF OUR TIME.
  J. GREENFIELD, 287:SEP69-32
WIESEL, E. SOULS ON FIRE.
  A.H. FRIEDLANDER, 561(SATR):26FEB72-
  76
  T. LASK, 441:10MAR72-38
  C.E. SILBERMAN, 441:5MAR72-1
  442(NY):15APR72-148
WIESELGREN, T. LUNI SUL MIGNONE: THE
IRON AGE SETTLEMENT ON THE ACROPOLIS.
  E.L. OCHSENSCHLAGER, 124:SEP70-23
  R.M. OGILVIE, 123:DEC71-463
WIESENFARTH, J. THE ERRAND OF FORM.
  L.W. BROWN, 173(ECS):FALL69-145
  J.E.J., 191(ELN):SEP69(SUPP)-19
  J.W. LOOFBOUROW, 613:SUMMER69-296
  W.D. SCHAEFER, 445(NCF):MAR69-489
WIESNER, H., I. ZIVSA & C. STOLL, EDS.
BIBLIOGRAPHIE DER PERSONALBIBLIOGRAPH-
IEN ZUR DEUTSCHEN GEGENWARTSLITERATUR.
  K.L. BERGHAHN, 406:SUMMER71-157
WIESNER, J. FAHREN UND REITEN.
  J. BOARDMAN, 123:MAR71-143
  F.M. COMBELLACK, 122:JAN71-50
WIESSNER, E. DER WORTSCHATZ VON HEINRICH
WITTENWILERS "RING."
  J. FLECK, 301(JEGP):OCT71-711
LORD WIGG. GEORGE WIGG.
  T. DRIBERG, 362:18MAY72-657
  617(TLS):19MAY72-566
WIGGIN, M. FACES AT THE WINDOW.
  617(TLS):22DEC72-1554
WIGGINS, D. IDENTITY AND SPATIO-TEMPORAL
CONTINUITY.
  S. SHOEMAKER, 482(PHR):OCT70-529
WIGGINTON, E., ED. THE FOXFIRE BOOK.
  N. BRYANT, 441:19MAR72-20
  T. LASK, 441:25MAR72-33
WIGHAM, P. ASTAPOVO.
  J. SMITH, 493:AUTUMN70-243
WIGHTMAN, W.P.D. SCIENCE IN A RENAIS-
SANCE SOCIETY.
  617(TLS):15SEP72-1057
WIJEYEWARDENE, G., ED. LEADERSHIP AND
AUTHORITY.
  J. GROSSHOLTZ, 293(JAST):MAY70-680
WIJSENBEEK, L.J.F. MONDRIAN.
  N. LYNTON, 592:NOV69-188
WILBER, C.K. THE SOVIET MODEL AND UNDER-
DEVELOPED COUNTRIES.
  J.O. BRAY, 550(RUSR):JUL70-361
WILBERG VIGNAU-SCHUURMAN, T.A.G. DIE
EMBLEMATISCHEN ELEMENTE IM WERKE JORIS
HOEFNAGELS.
  M. PRAZ, 182:VOL23#5-236
WILBERT-COLLINS, E. A BIBLIOGRAPHY OF
FOUR CONTEMPORARY GERMAN-SWISS AUTHORS.
  L. NEWMAN, 220(GL&L):JAN71-212
WILBUR, R. DIGGING FOR CHINA.
  T. LUCAS, 590:FALL70-39
WILBUR, R. WALKING TO SLEEP.*
  T. LUCAS, 590:FALL70-39
  N. RENNIE, 364:JUN/JUL71-129
WILBYE, J. THE SECOND SET OF MADRIGALS
1609.
  617(TLS):16JUN72-684
WILCOX, D.J. THE DEVELOPMENT OF FLOREN-
TINE HUMANIST HISTORIOGRAPHY IN THE
FIFTEENTH CENTURY.*
  F.S. FUSSNER, 551(RENQ):WINTER70-439
  C. GRAYSON, 589:JUL71-546

WILCZYNSKI, J. THE ECONOMICS AND POLI-
TICS OF EAST-WEST TRADE.
  A. ABOUCHAR, 32:SEP71-693
  S. LAMED, 104:FALL71-447
WILD, J. THE RADICAL EMPIRICISM OF WIL-
LIAM JAMES.
  W.J. EARLE, 479(PHQ):JUL70-274
  J.M. EDIE, 543:MAR70-481
  H.A. LARRABEE, 432(NEQ):JUN70-298
  R.J. ROTH, 613:WINTER69-621
WILD, P. MICA MOUNTAIN POEMS.
  W. WITHERUP, 502(PRS):WINTER69/70-422
WILDBOLZ, H. MENSCH UND STAND IM WERKE
GOTTFRIED KELLERS.
  L.W. KAHN, 222(GR):MAY70-240
WILDE, F-E. KIERKEGAARDS VERSTÄNDNIS DER
EXISTENZ.
  P. ROUBICZEK, 182:VOL23#19/20-842
WILDE, O. THE ARTIST AS CRITIC. (R.
ELLMANN, ED)
  J.B. GORDON, 340(KR):1970/1-152
WILDEN, A. SYSTEM AND STRUCTURE.
  617(TLS):8DEC72-1510
WILDENSTEIN, G. CHARDIN.
  J.T. ROSASCO, 58:MAR70-14
WILDER, A. AMERICAN POPULAR SONG. (J.T.
MAHER, ED)
  W. CLEMONS, 441:23APR72-6
  442(NY):29APR72-143
  617(TLS):27OCT72-1283
"WILDERNESS CANADA."
  A. APPENZELL, 102(CANL):AUTUMN71-96
WILDERS, J. - SEE BUTLER, S.
WILDGANS, F. ANTON WEBERN - EINE STUDIE.
  W.M. STROH, 513:FALL-WINTER68-144
WILDING, M., ED. MARVELL.
  G.K. HOLZKNECHT, 67:MAY71-95
WILDING, M. MILTON'S "PARADISE LOST."
  W.M. BECKETT, 180(ESA):SEP70-419
  M.M. BYARD, 551(RENQ):WINTER70-487
  617(TLS):3MAR72-252
WILDMAN, A.K. THE MAKING OF A WORKERS'
REVOLUTION.* (VOL 1)
  H. SHUKMAN, 587:APR69-559
WILES, J. THE GRAND TRUNK ROAD.
  617(TLS):24NOV72-1441
WILES, P.J.D., ED. THE PREDICTION OF
COMMUNIST ECONOMIC PERFORMANCE.
  617(TLS):21JAN72-77
WILEY, W.L. THE FORMAL FRENCH.
  A. LÉVÊQUE, 546(RR):FEB70-57
WILGUS, D.K., ED. FOLKLORE INTERNATIONAL.
  D. EMRICH, 650(WF):JAN69-52
WILHELM, J.J., ED & TRANS. MEDIEVAL
SONG.
  617(TLS):28JUL72-884
WILHELM, K. DER NOUVEAU ROMAN.
  Z. TAKACS, 182:VOL23#19/20-869
WILKES, B.S. NAUTICAL ARCHAEOLOGY.
  617(TLS):3MAR72-241
WILKES, G.A. - SEE GREVILLE, F.
WILKES, J.J. DALMATIA.
  S.L. DYSON, 124:NOV70-96
  S.I. OOST, 122:APR71-131
  P. SALWAY, 123:JUN71-267
  I. WEILER, 24:OCT71-707
WILKIE, B. ROMANTIC POETS AND EPIC
TRADITION.
  M. PRAZ, 402(MLR):JUL71-670
WILKINS, C. FINGER.
  V. CUNNINGHAM, 362:3FEB72-156
  617(TLS):18FEB72-173
WILKINS, K.S. A STUDY OF THE WORKS OF
CLAUDE BUFFIER.
  N. SUCKLING, 208(FS):JAN71-90

WILKINS, N. ONE HUNDRED BALLADES, RON-
DEAUX AND VIRELAIS FROM THE LATE MIDDLE
AGES.*
    N.J. LACY, 399(MLJ):OCT70-460
    J.R. ROTHSCHILD, 207(FR):MAY70-942
WILKINSON, A. ANCIENT EGYPTIAN JEWEL-
LERY.
    617(TLS):21JAN72-72
WILKINSON, A. THE COLLECTED POEMS OF
ANNE WILKINSON.* (A.J.M. SMITH, ED)
    H. MAC CALLUM, 627(UTQ):JUL69-345
WILKINSON, G. - SEE "TURNER'S EARLY
SKETCHBOOKS"
WILKINSON, H.E. THE LATINITY OF IBERO-
ROMANCE.
    P.M. LLOYD, 545(RPH):NOV70-363
WILKINSON, L.P. THE "GEORGICS" OF VIR-
GIL.*
    R.G. AUSTIN, 313:VOL60-262
    G. WILLIAMS, 123:MAR71-50
WILKINSON, P. SOCIAL MOVEMENT.
    617(TLS):4FEB72-119
WILKINSON, R., ED. GOVERNING ÉLITES.*
    O. MURRAY, 123:DEC71-459
WILKINSON, R.J., ED. PAPERS ON MALAY
SUBJECTS. (P.L. BURNS, COMP)
    617(TLS):24NOV72-1441
WILKINSON, W. AN AMERICAN - BUT DIFFER-
ENT.
    617(TLS):14JAN72-31
WILKS, Y.A. GRAMMAR, MEANING AND THE
MACHINE ANALYSIS OF LANGUAGE.
    617(TLS):19MAY72-569
WILL, É. HISTOIRE POLITIQUE DU MONDE
HELLÉNISTIQUE (323-30 AV. J-C.).*
(VOL 2)
    J. BRISCOE, 123:DEC70-371
    R.A. DE LAIX, 24:APR71-354
VAN DER WILL, W. PIKARO HEUTE.
    M. NERLICH, 490:APR68-279
WILLCOX, W.B. & OTHERS - SEE FRANKLIN, B.
WILLEFORD, C. COCKFIGHTER.
    M. LEVIN, 441:16JUL72-30
    442(NY):15JUL72-81
WILLEFORD, W. THE FOOL AND HIS SCEPTER.*
    J.L. STYAN, 401(MLQ):JUN70-245
WILLETTS, P. HANDLIST OF MUSIC MANU-
SCRIPTS ACQUIRED 1908-67.
    J.A.W., 410(M&L):APR71-184
WILLETTS, P.J. BEETHOVEN AND ENGLAND.
    D. JOHNSON, 415:FEB71-134
    J.A.W., 410(M&L):APR71-194
WILLETTS, R.F. EVERYDAY LIFE IN ANCIENT
CRETE.
    J. BOARDMAN, 303:VOL90-245
WILLETTS, R.F., ED & TRANS. THE LAW CODE
OF GORTYN.*
    C. BRIXHE, 555:VOL44FASC2-313
WILLETTS, W. FOUNDATIONS OF CHINESE ART
FROM NEOLITHIC POTTERY TO MODERN ARCHI-
TECTURE.
    W. WATSON, 90:FEB69-93
WILLEY, B. SAMUEL TAYLOR COLERIDGE.
    617(TLS):31MAR72-354
WILLIAM OF OCKHAM - SEE UNDER OCKHAM
WILLIAM OF SHERWOOD. WILLIAM OF SHER-
WOOD'S TREATISE ON SYNCATEGOREMATIC
WORDS. (N. KRETZMANN, ED & TRANS)
    D.P. HENRY, 482(PHR):OCT70-568
    M. KNEALE, 479(PHQ):APR70-180
WILLIAMS, A.D. - SEE GALBRAITH, J.K.
WILLIAMS, A.R. JOURNEY INTO REVOLUTION.*
(L.S. WILLIAMS, ED)
    W.B. WALSH, 550(RUSR):APR70-219
WILLIAMS, B. FOOD FOR THE EAGLE. MASTER
OF RAVENSPUR.
    J. ARNASON, 296:SUMMER72-89

WILLIAMS, C.K. LIES.*
    R. HOWARD, 340(KR):1970/1-130
    M.L. ROSENTHAL, 491:NOV71-99
WILLIAMS, E. INWARD HUNGER.
    442(NY):4MAR72-116
WILLIAMS, F.B., JR. - SEE ROGERS, T.
WILLIAMS, G. THE BEST OF GLUYAS WIL-
LIAMS.
    E. WEEKS, 61:APR72-127
WILLIAMS, G. EASTERN TURKEY.
    617(TLS):21JUL72-846
WILLIAMS, G. TRADITION AND ORIGINALITY
IN ROMAN POETRY.*
    D. HENRY, 122:JUL71-196
    B. OTIS, 24:APR71-316
    C. SEGAL, 121(CJ):DEC70-JAN71-164
    L.P. WILKINSON, 313:VOL60-255
WILLIAMS, G. WALK DON'T WALK.
    617(TLS):29SEP72-1138
WILLIAMS, G. - SEE BEWICK, T.
WILLIAMS, G. - SEE GRAHAM, A.
WILLIAMS, G. - SEE HORACE
WILLIAMS, G. - SEE OGDEN, P.S.
WILLIAMS, G.M. THE UPPER PLEASURE GAR-
DEN.
    F.P.W. MC DOWELL, 659:SUMMER72-361
WILLIAMS, G.R. THE HIDDEN WORLD OF SCOT-
LAND YARD.
    617(TLS):28APR72-501
WILLIAMS, G.W. - SEE CRASHAW, R.
WILLIAMS, G.W. - SEE SHAKESPEARE, W.
WILLIAMS, H. AC/DC.
    617(TLS):29DEC72-1569
WILLIAMS, H. SUGAR DADDY.*
    R. DURGNAT, 493:WINTER70/71-366
WILLIAMS, H.A. TRUE RESURRECTION.
    617(TLS):28JAN72-93
WILLIAMS, I. - SEE SCOTT, W.
WILLIAMS, J. AUGUSTUS.
    T. LASK, 441:28OCT72-33
    442(NY):25NOV72-199
WILLIAMS, J. GIVE ME YESTERDAY.
    617(TLS):25FEB72-229
WILLIAMS, J. THE HOME FRONTS.
    617(TLS):15SEP72-1065
WILLIAMS, J. THE OTHER BATTLEGROUND.
    A. CALDER, 441:20AUG72-4
WILLIAMS, J.A. CAPTAIN BLACKMAN.
    G. DAVIS, 441:21MAY72-4
    L. FLEISCHER, 561(SATR):13MAY72-85
    R. SALE, 453:5OCT72-34
WILLIAMS, J.A. THE KING GOD DIDN'T
SAVE.*
    J. MC DONNELL, 142:FALL71-469
WILLIAMS, J.A. THE NATURAL WORK OF ART.
    L.F. BALL, 570(SQ):AUTUMN69-479
WILLIAMS, K. JONATHAN SWIFT.
    566:AUTUMN70-5
WILLIAMS, K., ED. SWIFT: THE CRITICAL
HERITAGE.*
    O.W. FERGUSON, 579(SAQ):WINTER71-121
    566:AUTUMN70-4
WILLIAMS, L. CHALLENGE TO SURVIVAL.
    617(TLS):11FEB72-160
WILLIAMS, L. I, JAMES MC NEILL WHISTLER.
    R. LYNN, 561(SATR):15JUL72-52
WILLIAMS, L.F.R. THE EAST PAKISTAN
TRAGEDY.
    617(TLS):28JAN72-90
WILLIAMS, L.P. - SEE FARADAY, M.
WILLIAMS, M. THOMAS HARDY AND RURAL
ENGLAND.
    617(TLS):16JUN72-687
WILLIAMS, M. INSIDE NUMBER 10.
    D. CANDLER, 362:19OCT72-510
    617(TLS):27OCT72-1286

WILLIAMS, M. JAZZ MASTERS IN TRANSITION
1957-69.
M. HARRISON, 415:NOV71-1075
WILLIAMS, M. THE ONLY WORLD THERE IS.
H. CARRUTH, 249(HUDR):SUMMER71-327
P. PETTINGELL, 491:JAN72-234
WILLIAMS, N. THE LIFE AND TIMES OF
ELIZABETH I.
617(TLS):14JUL72-799
WILLIAMS, O., ED. A LITTLE TREASURY OF
MODERN POETRY. (3RD ED)
G. BURNS, 584(SWR):WINTER71-100
WILLIAMS, P. BACH ORGAN MUSIC.
617(TLS):21JUL72-853
WILLIAMS, P. THE EUROPEAN ORGAN, 1450-
1850.
H. GLEASON, 414(MQ):APR68-252
WILLIAMS, P. FIGURED BASS ACCOMPANI-
MENT.*
D. ARNOLD, 415:MAR71-239
J.A.W., 410(M&L):JUL71-321
WILLIAMS, R. THE ENGLISH NOVEL FROM
DICKENS TO LAWRENCE.
J. BAYLEY, 111:29MAY70-198
L. STEVENSON, 676(YR):AUTUMN70-126
WILLIAMS, R. MODERN TRAGEDY.*
W.A. ARMSTRONG, 397(MD):DEC67-326
WILLIAMS, R. GEORGE ORWELL.*
S. SPENDER, 453:16NOV72-3
WILLIAMS, R. POLITICS AND TECHNOLOGY.
617(TLS):9JUN72-666
WILLIAMS, R. THE WORKS OF SIR ROGER
WILLIAMS. (J.X. EVANS, ED)
617(TLS):14JUL72-799
WILLIAMS, R.C. CULTURE IN EXILE.
617(TLS):19MAY72-584
WILLIAMS, R.M. THE BONDS.*
441:13FEB72-16
WILLIAMS, S.A. GIVE BIRTH TO BRIGHT-
NESS.
M. WATKINS, 441:8JUL72-23
WILLIAMS, T.C. THE CONCEPT OF THE CATE-
GORICAL IMPERATIVE.
W. SCHWARZ, 185:OCT69-82
R.W. SIMPSON, 479(PHQ):JAN70-90
WILLIAMS, T.H. HUEY LONG.*
D.W. GRANTHAM, 639(VQR):WINTER70-168
WILLIAMS, W. THE FAR SIDE.
M. LEVIN, 441:27AUG72-26
WILLIAMS-ELLIS, C. ARCHITECT ERRANT.*
617(TLS):4FEB72-116
WILLIAMSON, G. THE INGENIOUS MR. GAINS-
BOROUGH.
617(TLS):14APR72-429
WILLIAMSON, G. THE PROPER WIT OF POETRY.
R.P. DRAPER, 179(ES):APR70-161
WILLIAMSON, H. THE SCANDAROON.
J. CAREY, 362:7DEC72-797
617(TLS):29DEC72-1589
WILLIAMSON, H.R. KIND KIT.
617(TLS):17NOV72-1405
WILLIAMSON, J. CHARLES KEMBLE, MAN OF
THE THEATRE.
P. THOMSON, 402(MLR):JUL71-673
WILLIAMSON, K. A GRAMMAR OF THE KOLOKUMA
DIALECT OF IJQ.*
J. KNAPPERT, 353:SEP69-105
WILLIAMSON, K. & K. SHIMIZU. BENUE-CONGO
COMPARATIVE WORDLIST. (VOL 1)
P.R. BENNETT, 315(JAL):VOL8PT2-120
WILLIAMSON, S.R., JR. THE POLITICS OF
GRAND STRATEGY.
617(TLS):21APR72-444
WILLINGHAM, C. RAMBLING ROSE.
J.R. FRAKES, 441:29OCT72-56
WILLIS, I. - SEE MACROBIUS
WILLIS, R. PORTRAIT OF YORK.
617(TLS):6OCT72-1205

WILLISON, I.R., ED. THE NEW CAMBRIDGE
BIBLIOGRAPHY OF ENGLISH LITERATURE.
(VOL 4)
617(TLS):29DEC72-1582
WILLOWEIT, G. DIE WIRTSCHAFTSGESCHICHTE
DES MEMELGEBIETS.
W. KIRCHNER, 32:DEC71-878
WILLS, G. BARE RUINED CHOIRS.
J. GARDNER, 441:29OCT72-1
C. LEHMANN-HAUPT, 441:20OCT72-45
WILLS, G. ENGLISH FURNITURE.
617(TLS):7JAN72-8
WILLS, G. NIXON AGONISTES.*
F.G. WILSON, 396(MODA):SPRING71-195
WILLS, G., WITH OTHERS. TECHNOLOGICAL
FORECASTING.
617(TLS):26MAY72-609
WILMERDING, J. WINSLOW HOMER.
D.L. SHIREY, 441:10DEC72-47
442(NY):18NOV72-248
WILMOT, J. THE COMPLETE POEMS OF JOHN
WILMOT, EARL OF ROCHESTER.* (D.M.
VIETH, ED)
H. ERSKINE-HILL, 541(RES):NOV70-496
VON WILPERT, G. & A. GÜHRING. ERSTAUSGA-
BEN DEUTSCHER DICHTUNG.
E. ALKER, 182:VOL23#23/24-991
WILSHERE, J. WILLIAM GARDINER OF LEI-
CESTER (1770-1853).
C. CUDWORTH, 415:JAN71-35
WILSHIRE, B. WILLIAM JAMES AND PHENOMEN-
OLOGY.*
J.M. EDIE, 543:MAR70-481
D.C. MATHUR, 484(PPR):SEP69-142
WILSHIRE, B. METAPHYSICS.
H.B., 543:JUN70-750
LADY WILSON - SEE UNDER STEWART, M.
WILSON, A. THE WORLD OF CHARLES DICKENS.
K.J. FIELDING, 155:SEP70-248
J.M. LALLEY, 396(MODA):SPRING71-185
WILSON, A.B. - SEE GALSWORTHY, J.
WILSON, A.M. DIDEROT.
E. CHILL, 441:17SEP72-6
T. LASK, 441:15JUL72-21
442(NY):29JUL72-80
WILSON, C. THE OCCULT.*
P. ADAMS, 61:JAN72-96
R. LIMA, 561(SATR):15JAN72-48
WILSON, C. ORDER OF ASSASSINS.
617(TLS):8DEC72-1507
WILSON, C. VOYAGE TO A BEGINNING.
42(AR):SUMMER69-264
WILSON, D. ASIA AWAKES.
S.A.M. ADSHEAD, 67:MAY71-142
WILSON, D. THE GALLEY GOURMET.
N. MAGID, 440:20FEB72-8
WILSON, D. THE LIFE AND TIMES OF VUK
STEFANOVIĆ KARADZIĆ, 1787-1864.
D.E. BYNUM, 32:JUN71-447
M. COOTE, 574(SEEJ):FALL71-395
E.D. GOY, 575(SEER):APR71-287
639(VQR):AUTUMN70-CXLIII
WILSON, D. THE LONG MARCH.* (BRITISH
TITLE: THE LONG MARCH 1935.)
J.P. HARRISON, 441:20FEB72-3
R. STEEL, 440:9APR72-1
442(NY):18MAR72-154
WILSON, D. THE SCIENCE OF SELF.
H. MILLER, 362:24AUG72-241
617(TLS):28JUL72-879
WILSON, D. A TUDOR TAPESTRY.
617(TLS):11AUG72-949
WILSON, D.B. DESCRIPTIVE POETRY IN
FRANCE FROM BLASON TO BAROQUE.
A. SPINA, 545(RPH):FEB71-534
WILSON, D.F. DOCKERS.
K. HINDELL, 362:21SEP72-375
617(TLS):15SEP72-1051

346

WILSON, E. DIARY OF THE "TERRA NOVA"
EXPEDITION TO THE ANTARCTIC 1910-1912.
617(TLS):10NOV72-1358
WILSON, E. THE SHOW BUSINESS NOBODY
KNOWS.
N. EPHRON, 441:23APR72-7
WILSON, E. TO THE FINLAND STATION. (NEW
ED)
M. BERMAN, 441:20AUG72-1
C. LEHMANN-HAUPT, 441:24AUG72-43
V.S. PRITCHETT, 442(NY):23DEC72-75
WILSON, E. UPSTATE.*
L.M. DABNEY, 31(ASCH):WINTER71/72-169
R. DWORKIN, 362:23MAR72-387
617(TLS):19MAY72-561
WILSON, E. A WINDOW ON RUSSIA.
P. ADAMS, 61:SEP72-110
V. ERLICH, 441:10CT72-28
WILSON, E.M. & D. MOIR. THE GOLDEN AGE
DRAMA 1492-1700.
617(TLS):14APR72-419
WILSON, E.O. THE INSECT SOCIETIES.
C.P. HASKINS, 441:19MAR72-3
WILSON, F.P. THE ENGLISH DRAMA 1485-
1585.* (G.K. HUNTER, ED)
D. MEHL, 541(RES):MAY70-197
S.G. PUTT, 175(AUTUMN69-107
P.W. ROGERS, 529(QQ):WINTER70-647
WILSON, F.P. SHAKESPEARE AND THE NEW
BIBLIOGRAPHY.* (REV & ED BY H. GARD-
NER)
P. DAVISON, 402(MLR):OCT71-859
D. MEHL, 72:BAND208HEFT1-54
WILSON, G. MURRAY OF YARRALUMLA.
639(VQR):WINTER70-XXI
WILSON, G.B. A HISTORY OF AMERICAN ACT-
ING.
G. WEALES, 397(MD):DEC67-319
WILSON, G.M. RADICAL NATIONALIST IN
JAPAN: KITA IKKI, 1883-1937.*
R.J. WALD, 293(JAST):FEB70-444
WILSON, H.S. MC CLURE'S MAGAZINE AND THE
MUCKRAKERS.
D. AARON, 27(AL):NOV71-496
WILSON, J. PRACTICAL METHODS OF MORAL
EDUCATION.
617(TLS):22DEC72-1552
WILSON, J. THE WORKS OF JAMES WILSON.
(R.G. MC CLOSKEY, ED)
J.F. COSTANZO, 613:SPRING69-155
WILSON, J.D. AN INTRODUCTION TO THE
SONNETS OF SHAKESPEARE FOR THE USE OF
HISTORIANS AND OTHERS.
S. BALDI, 570(SQ):SPRING68-175
WILSON, J.F. PULPIT IN PARLIAMENT.*
D.B. RUTMAN, 432(NEQ):JUN70-342
WILSON, J.H. THE ORDEAL OF MR. PEPYS'S
CLERK.
617(TLS):18AUG72-967
WILSON, J.H. A PREFACE TO RESTORATION
DRAMA.*
H.N. DAVIES, 677:VOL2-270
S.G. PUTT, 175:AUTUMN69-107
I.Z. SHERWOOD, 131(CL):SPRING71-181
WILSON, J.R. BARRINGTON.
M. LEVIN, 441:9JAN72-32
WILSON, J.R., ED. TWENTIETH CENTURY IN-
TERPRETATIONS OF EURIPIDES' "ALCES-
TIS."*
A.D. FITTON BROWN, 123:DEC70-300
WILSON, J.R.S. EMOTION AND OBJECT.
617(TLS):7JUL72-779
WILSON, K. GRAVES REGISTRY AND OTHER
POEMS.*
R. SQUIRRU, 37:OCT69-41
WILSON, M. PASSION TO KNOW.
C.P. SNOW, 441:18JUN72-4

WILSON, M. E.J. PRATT.*
C. KING, 627(UTQ):JUL70-376
WILSON, M. SPANISH DRAMA OF THE GOLDEN
AGE.*
E.L. RIVERS, 400(MLN):MAR70-302
A. VALBUENA-BRIONES, 238:SEP70-571
WILSON, R.A. PLAYBOY'S BOOK OF FORBIDDEN
WORDS.
R.W. BURCHFIELD, 441:26NOV72-22
WILSON, R.M. EARLY MIDDLE ENGLISH LIT-
ERATURE.
H. GNEUSS, 72:BAND208HEFT3-214
WILSON, R.M. THE LOST LITERATURE OF
MEDIEVAL ENGLAND.
R.T. DAVIES, 402(MLR):OCT71-849
WILSON, W. THE PAPERS OF WOODROW WIL-
SON.* (VOL 7) (A.S. LINK, ED)
L. VEYSEY, 639(VQR):AUTUMN70-666
R.L. WATSON, 579(SAQ):WINTER71-112
WILSON, W. THE PAPERS OF WOODROW WIL-
SON.* (VOL 8) (A.S. LINK, ED)
L. VEYSEY, 639(VQR):AUTUMN70-666
WILSON, W. THE PAPERS OF WOODROW WILSON.
(VOL 10) (A.S. LINK, ED)
617(TLS):19MAY72-578
WIMMEL, W. DER FRÜHE TIBULL.
J.H. GAISSER, 121(CJ):FEB-MAR71-260
J. HELLEGOUARC'H, 555:VOL44FASC2-336
E.J. KENNEY, 123:DEC70-337
WIMSATT, J. CHAUCER AND THE FRENCH LOVE
POETS.*
A.E. HARTUNG, 546(RR):OCT70-219
R.M. JORDAN, 149(JUN71-160
H. NEWSTEAD, 545(RPH):NOV70-349
WIMSATT, W.K. THE PORTRAITS OF ALEXANDER
POPE.
M. ALLENTUCK, 54:DEC69-400
WINCH, P., ED. STUDIES IN THE PHILOSOPHY
OF WITTGENSTEIN.
R.J.B., 543:JUN70-756
J. BURNHEIM, 63:MAY71-119
C.A. LYAS, 483:OCT70-330
H.O. MOUNCE, 518:JAN70-27
J. TEICHMANN, 479(PHQ):JUL70-276
WINCHESTER, B. BEYOND THE TUMULT.
442(NY):20MAY72-140
617(TLS):4AUG72-921
WINCHESTER, R.G. JAMES PINCKNEY HENDER-
SON, TEXAS' FIRST GOVERNOR.
W. GARD, 584(SWR):SUMMER71-V
WINCKELMANN, J.J. WINCKELMANN: WRITINGS
ON ART. (D. IRWIN, ED)
617(TLS):2JUN72-620
WIND, E. PAGAN MYSTERIES IN THE RENAIS-
SANCE. (NEW ED)
W.M. JOHNSON, 56:WINTER69-428
WIND, E., WITH G.L. HARRISS - SEE MC FAR-
LANE, K.B.
WIND, H.W. THE WORLD OF P.G. WODEHOUSE.
J.K. HUTCHENS, 561(SATR):12FEB72-69
P. THEROUX, 440:30JAN72-6
WINDCHY, E.G. TONKIN GULF.*
D.I. DAVIDSON, 61:FEB72-96
WINDFUHR, M. HEINRICH HEINE.*
J.L.S., 191(ELN):SEP70(SUPP)-107
WING, D. A GALLERY OF GHOSTS.
J. HORDEN, 354:MAR69-67
WING, G. DICKENS.
A.B., 155:SEP70-244
WING, J.K. & G.W. BROWN. INSTITUTIONAL-
ISM AND SCHIZOPHRENIA.
617(TLS):21JAN72-75
WINGLER, H.M. THE BAUHAUS.
W.J. MALARCHER, 363:AUG70-132
WINGLER, H.M. GRAPHIC WORK FROM THE BAU-
HAUS.
S. ABERCROMBIE, 505:OCT69-218
WINGLER, H.M. - SEE SEMPER, G.

WINKLER, G. DIE REICHSBEAMTEN VON NORI-
CUM UND IHR PERSONAL BIS ZUM ENDE DER
RÖMISCHEN HERRSCHAFT.
A.R. BIRLEY, 313:VOL60-214
S.L. DYSON, 124:JAN71-169
WINN, D. I SERVED CAESAR.
D.A.N. JONES, 362:11MAY72-628
WINNER, V.H. HENRY JAMES AND THE VISUAL
ARTS.*
D.K. KIRBY, 579(SAQ):SUMMER71-420
WINNICOTT, D.W. THERAPEUTIC CONSULTA-
TIONS IN CHILD PSYCHIATRY. PLAYING AND
REALITY.
V. HAMILTON, 362:13APR72-490
C. RYCROFT, 453:1JUN72-17
M. SCARF, 441:16APR72-34
VON WINNING, H. PRE-COLUMBIAN ART OF
MEXICO AND CENTRAL AMERICA.
J.B. LYNCH, 127:SUMMER71-426
J. SPENCER, 363:AUG70-129
WINNY, J. THE MASTER-MISTRESS.
D.J. PALMER, 148:WINTER70-383
C. SCHAAR, 551(RENQ):SUMMER70-198
WINSTOCK, L. SONGS AND MUSIC OF THE
REDCOATS.
F. HOWES, 415:JUL70-709
WINSTON, R. & C. - SEE MANN, T.
WINT, G. - SEE WOLFF, J.
WINTER, F.E. GREEK FORTIFICATIONS.
617(TLS):1DEC72-1466
WINTER, G. PAST POSITIVE.
G. ANNAN, 362:6JAN72-24
WINTER, J.M. & D.M. JOSLIN - SEE "R.H.
TAWNEY'S COMMONPLACE BOOK"
WINTER, W., ED. EVIDENCE FOR LARYNGEALS.*
B. PANZER, 353:JUL69-86
WINTER-BERGER, R. THE WASHINGTON PAY-
OFF.
G. VIDAL, 453:10AUG72-8
453:18MAY72-37
WINTERICH, J.T. & D.A. RANDALL. A PRIMER
OF BOOK COLLECTING.* (3RD ED)
R.C., 503:SPRING68-41
WINTERNITZ, E. MUSICAL INSTRUMENTS OF
THE WESTERN WORLD.
E. KENTON, 414(MQ):APR68-255
WINTERS, Y. FORMS OF DISCOVERY.*
L.T. LEMON, 502(PRS):FALL68-277
A. LØSNES, 179(ES):JUN69-314
WINTERS, Y. EDWIN ARLINGTON ROBINSON.
P. MURRAY, 491:JUL72-230
WINTON, C. SIR RICHARD STEELE, M.P.
A.R. HUMPHREYS, 677:VOL2-277
S.S. KENNY, 566:SPRING71-68
WINTOUR, C. PRESSURES ON THE PRESS.
W. HARDCASTLE, 362:23NOV72-723
617(TLS):24NOV72-1425
WIORA, W. DAS DEUTSCHE LIED.
E. SAMS, 415:OCT71-971
WIRTH, J.D. THE POLITICS OF BRAZILIAN
DEVELOPMENT, 1930-1954.
D. CARNEIRO, 263:JUL-SEP71-337
WISBEY, R. DAS ALEXANDERBILD RUDOLFS VON
EMS.*
E. SCHRADER, 406:WINTER71-390
WISBEY, R.A. A COMPLETE CONCORDANCE TO
THE "ROLANDSLIED" (HEIDELBERG MANU-
SCRIPT).*
D.J.A. ROSS, 402(MLR):JAN71-209
WISBEY, R.A. A COMPLETE CONCORDANCE TO
THE VORAU AND STRASSBURG "ALEXANDER."*
A COMPLETE WORD-INDEX TO THE "SPECULUM
ECCLESIAE" (EARLY MHG AND LATIN).*
D.J.A. ROSS, 402(MLR):JAN71-209
P. SALMON, 220(GL&L):JUL71-374
WISBEY, R.A., ED. THE COMPUTER IN LIT-
ERARY AND LINGUISTIC RESEARCH.
617(TLS):4FEB72-136

WISE, A. THE HISTORY AND ART OF PERSONAL
COMBAT.
617(TLS):25AUG72-1005
WISE, S.F. - SEE HEAD, F.B.
WISEMAN, C. WAITING FOR THE BARBARIANS.
D.S. MC NEAL, 99:SEP72-39
WISEMAN, D.J. THE CAMBRIDGE ANCIENT
HISTORY. (REV) (VOL 2, CHAPTER 31)
D.B. WEISBERG, 318(JAOS):APR-JUN70-
330
WISEMAN, T.P. CATULLAN QUESTIONS.*
J.P. ELDER, 124:SEP70-26
E.J. KENNEY, 123:MAR71-43
G.N. SANDY, 24:JAN71-126
J. WOHLBERG, 124:APR71-270
WIŚNIEWSKI, B. KARNEADES' FRAGMENTE.
F. LASSERRE, 182:VOL23#13/14-680
WIŚNIEWSKI, B. L'IMPORTANCE DES SOPHIS-
TES SUR ARISTOTE, ÉPICURE, STOÏCIENS
ET SCEPTIQUES.
M. BUCCELLATO, 548(RCSF):JAN-MAR68-
103
WISSMANN, W. & E. HOFMANN - SEE KUR-
SCHAT, A.
WISSMANN, W. & H-F. ROSENFELD - SEE
ILKOW, P.
WITCOVER, J. WHITE KNIGHT.
W. JACOBSON, 440:14MAY72-1
C. LEHMANN-HAUPT, 441:17APR72-35
442(NY):22APR72-142
WITEMEYER, H. THE POETRY OF EZRA POUND.*
W.M. CHACE, 598(SOR):WINTER72-225
F.K. SANDERS, 569(SR):SUMMER71-433
639(VQR):SPRING70-LVI
WITHERS, C. A WORLD OF NONSENSE.
T.B. UNTHANK, 582(SFQ):DEC69-372
WITHERSPOON, M.E. THE MORNING COOL.
T. LASK, 441:8APR72-31
WITKE, C. ENARRATIO CATULLIANA.*
E.J. KENNEY, 123:MAR71-43
WITT, H. POP.
C. MOLESWORTH, 491:MAY72-107
WITT, H. UM DIESER WELTEN LUST.
G.F. JONES, 222(GR):MAR70-151
WITT, P-C. DIE FINANZPOLITIK DES
DEUTSCHEN REICHES VON 1903-13.
H.F. YOUNG, 182:VOL23#11/12-636
WITTE, B. DIE WISSENSCHAFT VOM GUTEN UND
BÖSEN.
F.E. SPARSHOTT, 124:JAN71-159
WITTGENSTEIN, L. LECTURES AND CONVERSA-
TIONS ON AESTHETICS, PSYCHOLOGY AND
RELIGIOUS BELIEF.* (C. BARRETT, ED)
L. GRIFFITHS, 393(MIND):JUL70-464
WITTGENSTEIN, L. LEZIONI E CONVERSAZIONI
SULL'ETICA, L'ESTETICA, LA PSICOLOGIA
E LA CREDENZA RELIGIOSA. (M. RAN-
CHETTI, ED)
A.G. GARGANI, 548(RCSF):OCT-DEC68-475
WITTGENSTEIN, L. ON CERTAINTY.* (G.E.M.
ANSCOMBE & G.H. VON WRIGHT, EDS)
A.R. WHITE, 518:MAY70-30
WITTGENSTEIN, L. PHILOSOPHISCHE GRAM-
MATIK.* (R. RHEES, ED)
R.L. GOODSTEIN, 518:JAN71-28
WITTGENSTEIN, L. PROTOTRACTATUS.*
(B.F. MC GUINNESS, T. NYBERT & G.H.
VON WRIGHT, EDS)
A.R. LOUCH, 319:OCT72-490
WITTGENSTEIN, L. TRACTATUS LOGICO-PHILO-
SOPHICUS. (P. KLOSSOWSKI, TRANS; A.
PATRI, ED)
M. CHASTAING, 542:JAN-MAR68-133
WITTGENSTEIN, L. ZETTEL. (G.E.M. ANS-
COMBE & G.H. VON WRIGHT, EDS)
H. MORICK, 258:MAR69-151

"WITTGENSTEIN ET LE PROBLÈME D'UNE PHIL-
OSOPHIE DE LA SCIENCE."
    A. MERCIER, 182:VOL23#11/12-589
VON WITTKOP-MÉNARDEAU, G., ED. E.T.A.
HOFFMANNS LEBEN UND WERK IN DATEN UND
BILDERN.
    R.M., 191(ELN):SEP70(SUPP)-116
WITTNER, L.S. REBELS AGAINST WAR.*
    C.A. BARKER, 639(VQR):WINTER70-158
WITTSCHIER, H.W. GIANNOZZO MANETTI.
    R. KLESCZEWSKI, 72:BAND208HEFT4/6-440
PRINCE WIZLAW VON RÜGEN - SEE UNDER
THOMAS, W. & B.G. SEAGRAVE
WLOSOK, A. ROM UND DIE CHRISTEN.
    J.E. SEAVER, 124:JAN71-172
WODDIS, J. NEW THEORIES OF REVOLUTION.
    617(TLS):1DEC72-1450
WODEHOUSE, P.G. JEEVES AND THE TIE THAT
BINDS.*
    J.K. HUTCHENS, 561(SATR):12FEB72-69
WODEHOUSE, P.G. PEARLS, GIRLS AND MONTY
BODKIN.
    D.A.N. JONES, 362:26OCT72-557
WODTKE, F.W. - SEE BENN, G.
WOEHRLIN, W.F. CHERNYSHEVSKII.
    617(TLS):16JUN72-683
WOHMANN, G. SELBSTVERTEIDIGUNG. GEGEN-
ANGRIFF.
    617(TLS):21JUL72-851
WÖHRMANN, K-R. HÖLDERLINS WILLE ZUR
TRAGÖDIE.*
    L. WELCH, 290(JAAC):FALL69-110
WOIWODE, L. WHAT I'M GOING TO DO, I
THINK.*
    42(AR):SUMMER69-261
WOJACZEK, G. DAPHNIS: UNTERSUCHUNGEN
ZUR GRIECHISCHEN BUKOLIK.
    W. BERG, 24:OCT71-735
    G. LAWALL, 124:DEC70-123
WOLANSKY, W.D. WOODWORKING MADE EASY.
    B. GLADSTONE, 441:3DEC72-99
WOLD, R. "EL DIARIO DE MÉXICO."
    G. FIGUEIRA, 263:OCT-DEC71-458
WOLF, C. NACHDENKEN ÜBER CHRISTA T.
    T. WEYR, 19(AGR):VOL35#6-27
WOLF, C. THE QUEST FOR CHRISTA T.*
    I. WEDDE, 364:OCT/NOV71-149
WOLF, D. FOUL!
    J.B. SEGAL, 441:26MAR72-38
WOLF, E. PLATON, DIALOGE DER MITTLEREN
UND SPÄTEREN ZEIT, BRIEFE.
    F. LASSERRE, 182:VOL23#5-246
WOLF, G. BESCHREIBUNG EINES ZIMMERS.
    617(TLS):5MAY72-509
WOLF, H. DIE SPRACHE DES JOHANNES
MATHESIUS.
    R. RUDOLF, 182:VOL23#1/2-22
WOLF, L., ED. TEXTE UND DOKUMENTE ZUR
FRANZÖSISCHEN SPRACHGESCHICHTE: 16.
JAHRHUNDERT.
    P. RICKARD, 208(FS):JAN71-64
WOLF, M. RECHTSGESCHÄFTLICHE ENTSCHEI-
DUNGSFREIHEIT UND VERTRAGLICHER INTER-
ESSENAUSGLEICH.
    P. PADIS, 182:VOL23#15/16-722
WOLF, W. FASCHISMUS IN DER SCHWEIZ.
    P. HOFFMANN, 182:VOL23#3-117
WOLF, W. FRÜHE HOCHKULTUREN: ÄGYPTEN,
MESOPOTAMIEN, ÄGÄIS.
    J.A. GAERTNER, 124:JAN71-164
"THE WOLF-MAN: HIS MEMOIRS."* (BRITISH
TITLE: THE WOLF-MAN AND SIGMUND FREUD.)
(M. GARDINER, ED)
    R. WOLLHEIM, 362:2MAR72-280
    617(TLS):28APR72-499
WOLF-PHILLIPS, L. COMPARATIVE CONSTITU-
TIONS.
    617(TLS):9JUN72-666

WOLFE, B. MEMOIRS OF A NOT ALTOGETHER
SHY PORNOGRAPHER.
    H. GOLD, 441:22OCT72-40
WOLFE, B.D. THE BRIDGE AND THE ABYSS.*
    D. FOOTMAN, 587:OCT68-258
WOLFE, B.D. AN IDEOLOGY IN POWER.*
    J.D. WALZ, 550(RUSR):APR70-220
WOLFE, L., ED. MC CALL'S INTRODUCTION TO
SCANDINAVIAN COOKING.
    N. MAGID, 440:20FEB72-6
WOLFE, T. THE LETTERS OF THOMAS WOLFE TO
HIS MOTHER.* (C.H. HOLMAN & S.F. ROSS,
EDS)
    R.S. KENNEDY, 219(GAR):SUMMER69-247
    M.J. LYDE, 577(SHR):SPRING70-181
WOLFE, T. THE NOTEBOOKS OF THOMAS
WOLFE.* (R.S. KENNEDY & P. REEVES,
EDS)
    R. WALSER, 639(VQR):WINTER70-141
WOLFE, T. RADICAL CHIC & MAU-MAUING THE
FLAK CATCHERS.*
    A. OSTRIKER, 473(PR):1971/3-355
WOLFE, T.W. SOVIET POWER AND EUROPE,
1945-1970.
    P.S. GILLETTE, 32:DEC71-892
WÖLFEL, E. SEINSTRUKTUR UND TRINITÄTS-
PROBLEM.
    M.J.V., 543:SEP69-142
WOLFENSBERGER, H. MUNDARTWANDEL IM 20.
JAHRHUNDERT.
    S.E. BELLAMY, 400(MLN):APR70-399
    W.G. MOULTON, 350:DEC71-938
WOLFF, H.C. OPER: SZENE UND DARSTELLUNG
VON 1600 BIS 1900.
    E. SURIAN, 317:SUMMER71-306
WOLFF, J. A MISSION TO BOKHARA. (G.
WINT, ED)
    R.A. PIERCE, 550(RUSR):OCT70-483
WOLFF, K. THE TEACHING OF ARTUR SCHNA-
BEL.
    617(TLS):24MAR72-333
WOLFF, R.P. IN DEFENSE OF ANARCHISM.*
    S. BATES, 311(JP):6APR72-175
WOLFF, R.P. THE POVERTY OF LIBERALISM.
    R.H.K., 543:MAR70-570
WOLFF-WINDEGG, P. SWIFT.
    H. CASTROP, 72:BAND208HEFT4/6-386
WOLFFE, B.P. THE CROWN LANDS 1461 TO
1536.
    C.R. YOUNG, 579(SAQ):SUMMER71-427
WOLFSKEHL, K. & A. VERWEY. DIE DOKUMENTE
IHRER FREUNDSCHAFT 1897-1946. (M.
NIJLAND-VERWEY, ED)
    T. WEEVERS, 220(GL&L):OCT70-102
WOLITZ, S.L. THE PROUSTIAN COMMUNITY.
    441:16APR72-20
WOLKENFELD, J. JOYCE CARY.
    C.G. HOFFMANN, 141:SPRING69-215
WOLLASTON, N. THE TALE BEARER.
    617(TLS):7JUL72-765
WOLLHEIM, D.A. THE UNIVERSE MAKERS.
    T. STURGEON, 441:5MAR72-36
WOLLHEIM, R. ART AND ITS OBJECTS.
    T.J. DIFFEY, 536:DEC70-182
    A. FORGE, 592:NOV68-229
    M. WEITZ, 482(PHR):OCT70-580
WOLLHEIM, R. - SEE STOKES, A.
WOLOHOJIAN, A.M., ED & TRANS. THE RO-
MANCE OF ALEXANDER THE GREAT BY PSEUDO-
CALLISTHENES.
    E.A. FREDRICKSMEYER, 124:SEP70-22
WOLTERS, M. AUSSENPOLITISCHE FRAGEN VOR
DER VIERTEN DUMA.
    W.B. WALSH, 32:MAR71-149
WOLTERS, O.W. EARLY INDONESIAN COMMERCE.
    R.N. JACKSON, 302:JAN69-112
    E.H. SCHAEFER, 57:VOL31#2/3-224

WOLTERS, O.W. THE FALL OF SRIVIJAYA IN
   MALAY HISTORY.
      617(TLS):21JAN72-69
"WOMAN SUFFRAGE: ARGUMENTS AND RESULTS,
   1910-1911."
      617(TLS):18FEB72-180
WOOD, C. CHAUCER AND THE COUNTRY OF THE
   STARS.
      R.M. DAWSON, 150(DR):SUMMER70-271
      639(VQR):SUMMER70-XCVIII
WOOD, C.T. THE AGE OF CHIVALRY, MANNERS
   AND MORALS, 1000-1450.
      N. DOWNS, 589:APR71-412
WOOD, G.S. THE CREATION OF THE AMERICAN
   REPUBLIC, 1776-1787.
      C.F. MULLETT, 377:JUL71-112
WOOD, G.S. REPRESENTATION IN THE AMERI-
   CAN REVOLUTION.
      J.C. RAINBOLT, 656(WMQ):APR70-334
WOOD, H.H. TWO SCOTS CHAUCERIANS.
      H. BOYD, 180(ESA):SEP70-413
WOOD, J., ED. POWELL AND THE 1970 ELEC-
   TIONS.
      A.A. SHENFIELD, 396(MODA):SPRING71-
      190
WOOD, J.S. - SEE ZOLA, É.
WOOD, R. VICTORIAN DELIGHTS.
      M. VICINUS, 637(VS):JUN70-433
WOODCOCK, G. CANADA AND THE CANADIANS.*
      C.J. FOX, 102(CANL):SUMMER71-92
WOODCOCK, G. DAWN AND THE DARKEST HOUR.
      F. KERMODE, 362:27APR72-555
      453:15JUN72-36
      617(TLS):12MAY72-544
WOODCOCK, G. GANDHI.
      617(TLS):31MAR72-351
WOODCOCK, G., ED. MALCOLM LOWRY.*
      D. JEWISON, 296:WINTER72-83
WOODCOCK, G. HUGH MAC LENNAN.
      D. CAMERON, 529(QQ):SUMMER70-282
      P. STEVENS, 102(CANL):WINTER71-84
WOODCOCK, G. ODYSSEUS EVER RETURNING.
   MORDECAI RICHLER.
      P. STEVENS, 102(CANL):WINTER71-84
WOODCOCK, G. HERBERT READ.
      617(TLS):1DEC72-1457
WOODCOCK, G. & I. AVAKUMOVIC. THE DOUK-
   HOBORS.*
      P. AVRICH, 550(RUSR):JUL70-362
WOODHAM-SMITH, C. QUEEN VICTORIA. (VOL
   1)
      N. ANNAN, 453:30NOV72-12
      N. BLIVEN, 442(NY):9DEC72-173
      M. DRABBLE, 362:26OCT72-546
      C. LEHMANN-HAUPT, 441:17NOV72-49
      P. QUENNELL, 441:26NOV72-5
      P. STANSKY, 561(SATR):18NOV72-84
      E. WEEKS, 61:DEC72-141
      617(TLS):20OCT72-1247
WOODHEAD, A.G. THUCYDIDES ON THE NATURE
   OF POWER.
      A. BURNETT, 122:JUL71-209
      C.W. FORNARA, 24:APR71-358
      A.R. RAUBITSCHEK, 124:SEP70-21
      639(VQR):SUMMER70-CXIV
WOODHOUSE, A.S.P. & D. BUSH. A VARIORUM
   COMMENTARY ON THE POEMS OF JOHN MILTON.
   (VOL 2)
      617(TLS):29SEP72-1162
WOODHOUSE, J.R. ITALO CALVINO.
      C. FANTAZZI, 276:SUMMER70-228
WOODHOUSE, M. MAMA DOLL.
      N. CALLENDAR, 441:23JUL72-22
      617(TLS):7JUL72-783
WOODHULL, V.C. A LECTURE ON CONSTITU-
   TIONAL EQUALITY.
      617(TLS):18FEB72-180

WOODMAN, R.G. JAMES REANEY.
      D. LIVINGSTONE, 99:JUN72-42
WOODRESS, J. WILLA CATHER.
      H.H. CLARK, 659:SPRING72-258
      T. MARTIN, 27(AL):NOV71-465
      A.F. SCOTT, 579(SAQ):AUTUMN71-610
WOODRESS, J. & S.P. ANDERSON. A BIBLIO-
   GRAPHY OF WRITING ABOUT WILLIAM DEAN
   HOWELLS.
      U. HALFMANN, 72:BAND208HEFT4/6-406
WOODRING, C. POLITICS IN ENGLISH ROMAN-
   TIC POETRY.
      B. WILKIE, 301(JEGP):JUL71-559
      676(YR):SUMMER71-X
WOODRING, C. WORDSWORTH.*
      J. COLMER, 402(MLR):APR71-399
WOODS, F. - SEE CHURCHILL, W.S.
WOODS, G., P. THOMPSON & J. WILLIAMS,
   EDS. ART WITHOUT BOUNDARIES, 1950-
   1970.
      617(TLS):3NOV72-1311
WOODS, G.A. CATCH A KILLER.
      R. BRADFORD, 441:19NOV72-58
WOODS, J. KEEPING OUT OF TROUBLE.
      B.D.S., 502(PRS):FALL69-326
WOODS, S. THEY LOVE NOT POISON.
      N. CALLENDAR, 441:17DEC72-23
WOODSIDE, A.B. VIETNAM AND THE CHINESE
   MODEL.
      617(TLS):21APR72-436
WOODWARD, C.V. AMERICAN COUNTERPOINT.*
      R. COLES, 442(NY):15APR72-141
WOODWARD, D.H. - SEE FLETCHER, R.
WOODWARD, G.S. POCAHONTAS.
      P.L. BARBOUR, 656(WMQ):JAN70-176
WOODWARD, J.B. LEONID ANDREYEV.
      J.M. NEWCOMBE, 575(SEER):APR71-292
      T. PACHMUSS, 574(SEEJ):SPRING71-116
      639(VQR):AUTUMN70-CXLIII
WOODWARD, J.B. - SEE BLOK, A.
WOODWARD, L. BRITISH FOREIGN POLICY IN
   THE SECOND WORLD WAR. (VOL 3)
      617(TLS):5MAY72-514
WOODWARD, L. PRELUDE TO MODERN EUROPE
   1815-1914.
      617(TLS):19MAY72-581
WOODWARD, M. - SEE GERARD, J.
WOODWORTH, R.S. & H. SCHLOSBERG. EXPERI-
   MENTAL PSYCHOLOGY. (REV BY J.W. KLING
   & L.A. RIGGS)
      617(TLS):12MAY72-534
WOOLDRIDGE, D. CONDUCTOR'S WORLD.*
      H.R., 412:FEB71-79
WOOLF, J. A CHALKED HEART.
      J.G. FARRELL, 362:15JUN72-797
      617(TLS):30JUN72-737
WOOLF, R. THE ENGLISH RELIGIOUS LYRIC
   IN THE MIDDLE AGES.*
      S.W. HOLTON, 597(SN):VOL41#2-425
      S. MANNING, 301(JEGP):JAN71-145
      J. STEVENS, 382(MAE):1971/1-72
WOOLFOLK, W. THE OVERLORDS.
      N. CALLENDAR, 441:24DEC72-14
WOOLLER, W. GLAMORGAN.
      617(TLS):28JAN72-109
WORCESTER, D.E. & W.G. SCHAEFFER. THE
   GROWTH AND CULTURE OF LATIN AMERICA.
   (VOL 1) (2ND ED)
      P.T. BRADLEY, 86(BHS):OCT71-365
WORCESTER, G.R.G. THE JUNKS AND SAMPANS
   OF THE YANGTZE.
      V.D. TATE, 441:12MAR72-18
WORCESTRE, W. WILLIAM WORCESTRE "ITINER-
   ARIES." (J.H. HARVEY, ED)
      A.G. DYSON, 325:OCT70-150
      R.H. ROUSE, 589:APR71-375

WORDSWORTH, J. THE LETTERS OF JOHN
   WORDSWORTH. (C.H. KETCHAM, ED)
   M. MONTGOMERY, 219(GAR):FALL69-412
   M.T. SOLVE, 50(ARQ):WINTER69-375
WORDSWORTH, J. THE MUSIC OF HUMANITY.*
   K.K., 191(ELN):SEP70(SUPP)-51
WORDSWORTH, W & D. THE LETTERS OF WIL-
   LIAM AND DOROTHY WORDSWORTH. (VOL 1)
   (2ND ED) (E. DE SELINCOURT, ED; REV BY
   C.L. SHAVER)
   H. SCHNYDER, 179(ES):JUN70-263
WORDSWORTH, W. & D. THE LETTERS OF WIL-
   LIAM AND DOROTHY WORDSWORTH.* (VOL 2,
   PT 1) (2ND ED) (E. DE SELINCOURT, ED;
   2ND ED REV BY M. MOORMAN)
   J.C. MAXWELL, 447(N&Q):MAY70-189
WORDSWORTH, W. & D. THE LETTERS OF WIL-
   LIAM AND DOROTHY WORDSWORTH. (VOL 3,
   PT 2) (E. DE SELINCOURT, ED) (2ND ED
   REV BY M. MOORMAN & A.G. HILL)
   D.V.E., 191(ELN):SEP70(SUPP)-49
   W.J.B. OWEN, 402(MLR):APR71-397
"THE WORLD OF LEARNING 1971-72."
   617(TLS):7JAN72-7
"THE WORLD OF LIFE: THE BIOSPHERE."
   617(TLS):30JUN72-754
"THE WORLD OF VOLTAIRE."
   J.H. BRUMFITT, 208(FS):OCT71-463
WORMHOUDT, A. - SEE AL-MUTANABBĪ,
   A.T.A.H.
WORONOFF, D. LA RÉPUBLIQUE BOURGEOISE DE
   THERMIDOR À BRUMAIRE.
   617(TLS):22SEP72-1113
WOROSZYLSKI, W. THE LIFE OF MAYAKOVSKY.*
   J. BAYLEY, 362:24FEB72-249
   617(TLS):18FEB72-177
WORRINGER, W. L'ART GOTHIQUE.
   P. GUERRE, 98:MAR69-265
WORSLEY, P., ED. PROBLEMS OF MODERN
   SOCIETY.
   617(TLS):15SEP72-1071
WORSLEY, P., ED. TWO BLADES OF GRASS.
   617(TLS):4FEB72-137
WORSLEY, T.C. FELLOW TRAVELLERS.*
   F. MC GUINESS, 364:JUN/JUL71-148
WORTH, C.B. OF MOSQUITOES, MOTHS, AND
   MICE.
   P. ADAMS, 61:JUL72-96
WORTH, D.S., A.S. KOZAK & D.B. JOHNSON.
   RUSSIAN DERIVATIONAL DICTIONARY.
   Z.F. OLIVERIUS, 67:NOV71-267
WORTH, G.H. FOREIGN WORDS IN RUSSIAN.
   V.B. EMMONS, 545(RPH):NOV69-250
WORTHAM, J.D. BRITISH EGYPTOLOGY, 1549-
   1906.
   617(TLS):26MAY72-613
WORTLEY, B.A., ED. AN INTRODUCTION TO
   THE LAW OF THE EUROPEAN ECONOMIC COM-
   MUNITY.
   617(TLS):28JUL72-861
WOSIEN, M-G. THE RUSSIAN FOLK-TALE.
   P. ARANT, 574(SEEJ):SPRING71-124
   F.J. OINAS, 32:MAR71-212
   L. WARNER, 575(SEER):APR71-319
VAN DER WOUDE, S., ED. STUDIA BIBLIO-
   GRAPHICA IN HONOREM HERMAN DE LA FON-
   TAINE VERWEY.
   R. STOKES, 503:WINTER68-191
WOYCENKO, O. THE UKRAINIANS IN CANADA.
   C.H. ANDRUSYSHEN, 627(UTQ):JUL69-490
WREDE, J. ARVID MÖRNES LYRIK FRÅN OCH
   MED DEN POETISKA FÖRNYELSEN OMKRING
   1920.
   G.C. SCHOOLFIELD, 563(SS):SUMMER71-
   307
WREN, J. THE GREAT BATTLES OF WORLD WAR
   I.
   617(TLS):1DEC72-1469

WREN-LEWIS, J. WHAT SHALL WE TELL THE
   CHILDREN?
   617(TLS):28JAN72-101
WRIGHT, A. BLAKE'S JOB.
   617(TLS):29SEP72-1145
WRIGHT, B.A. MILTON'S "PARADISE LOST."
   W.M. BECKETT, 180(ESA):SEP70-419
WRIGHT, C. THE DREAM ANIMAL.*
   H. CARLILE, 448:SUMMER70-124
WRIGHT, C. FANNY KEMBLE AND THE LOVELY
   LAND.
   442(NY):30DEC72-72
WRIGHT, C. THE WORKING CLASS.
   617(TLS):17NOV72-1405
WRIGHT, C.E. & R.C. - SEE WANLEY, H.
WRIGHT, C.J. A GUIDE TO THE PILGRIMS'
   WAY.
   617(TLS):20OCT72-1264
WRIGHT, D.H. - SEE "THE VESPASIAN PSAL-
   TER"
WRIGHT, D.M. A FISH WILL RISE.
   617(TLS):21JUL72-853
WRIGHT, F.L. GENIUS AND THE MOBOCRACY.
   (NEW ED)
   617(TLS):19MAY72-568
"FRANK LLOYD WRIGHT: THE EARLY WORK."
   E. TAFEL, 45:MAR69-148
VON WRIGHT, G.H. AN ESSAY IN DEONTIC
   LOGIC AND THE GENERAL THEORY OF ACTION.
   A.N. PRIOR, 536:DEC70-175
VON WRIGHT, G.H. EXPLANATION AND UNDER-
   STANDING.
   617(TLS):21JAN72-61
VON WRIGHT, G.H. TIME, CHANGE AND CON-
   TRADICTION.
   R.H.K., 543:MAR70-569
WRIGHT, G.T. W.H. AUDEN.*
   E. MENDELSON, 677:VOL2-337
WRIGHT, H.B. & M.K. SPEARS - SEE PRIOR,
   M.
WRIGHT, J. COLLECTED POEMS.*
   H. CARRUTH, 249(HUDR):SUMMER71-331
   P. DAVISON, 61:FEB72-106
   L. GOLDSTEIN, 385(MQR):SUMMER72-214
   H. TAYLOR, 651(WHR):AUTUMN71-368
   A. WILLIAMSON, 491:FEB72-296
WRIGHT, J. THE HOMECOMING SINGER.
   D. KALSTONE, 441:30JUL72-4
WRIGHT, J., ED & TRANS. THE PLAY OF
   ANTICHRIST.*
   A.S. DOWNER, 597(SN):VOL41#1-174
WRIGHT, J. SHALL WE GATHER AT THE
   RIVER.*
   T. BLACKBURN, 493:SPRING70-85
WRIGHT, J.W. SHELLEY'S MYTH OF METAPHOR.
   P.H. BUTTER, 677:VOL2-299
WRIGHT, L.B., ED. THE ELIZABETHANS'
   AMERICA.
   F. PATTERSON, 570(SQ):SPRING68-183
WRIGHT, L.B. GOLD, GLORY AND THE GOSPEL.
   J. FENNELL, 263:JUL-SEP71-339
WRIGHT, L.B., ED. SHAKESPEARE CELEBRAT-
   ED.
   S.G. PUTT, 175:SPRING69-30
WRIGHT, L.R. THE ORIGINS OF BRITISH
   BORNEO.
   617(TLS):11AUG72-941
WRIGHT, M. ZAMBIA - I CHANGED MY MIND.
   617(TLS):11AUG72-951
WRIGHT, M.C., ED. CHINA IN REVOLUTION,
   THE FIRST PHASE, 1900-1913.
   J. CHESNEAUX, 293(JAST):FEB70-432
WRIGHT, N. - SEE IRVING, W.
WRIGHT, N., JR., ED. BIRACIAL POLITICS.
   N.I. HUGGINS, 441:12NOV72-42
WRIGHT, P. CONFLICT ON THE NILE.
   617(TLS):21APR72-455

WRIGHT, R.B. THE WEEKEND MAN.*
  J.M. MORSE, 249(HUDR):AUTUMN71-535
  K. THOMPSON, 198:FALL72-110
WRIGHT, R.L. SWEDISH EMIGRANT BALLADS.
  W.H. JANSEN, 650(WF):JAN68-57
WRIGHT, T. THE DISENCHANTED ISLES.
  441:24SEP72-53
WRIGHT, W. A GRAMMAR OF THE ARABIC LAN-
  GUAGE. (3RD ED)
  S.A. HANNA, 399(MLJ):APR70-287
WRIGHT, W.D.C. & D.H. STEWART, EDS. THE
  EXPLODING CITY.
  617(TLS):18AUG72-963
WRIGHT, W.F. THE SHAPING OF THE DYNASTS.
  B.R.M., JR., 477:SPRING69-294
WRIGLEY, E.S., COMP. SUPPLEMENT TO THE
  FRANCIS BACON LIBRARY HOLDINGS IN THE
  SHORT TITLE CATALOGUE OF ENGLISH
  BOOKS.
  568(SCN):SPRING71-19
WUNDERLI, P., ED. LE LIVRE DE L'ESCHIELE
  MAHOMET.
  P.B. FAY, 545(RPH):MAY70-601
  G. HOLMER, 597(SN):VOL40#2-450
WURLITZER, R. QUAKE.
  M. DICKSTEIN, 441:22OCT72-4
WÜRZBACH, N., ED. BRITISH THEATRE:
  EIGHTEENTH-CENTURY ENGLISH DRAMA.
  D. MEHL, 72:BAND208HEFT1-58
"WÜRZBURGER PROSASTUDIEN I."
  V. GÜNTHER, 182:VOL23#13/14-669
WUST, K. THE VIRGINIA GERMANS.
  J.W. HEISEY, 656(WMQ):JAN70-181
WYATT, R. THE STRING BOX.
  L. WOODS, 606(TAMR):#56-85
WYATT, T. COLLECTED POEMS OF SIR THOMAS
  WYATT.* (K. MUIR & P. THOMSON, EDS)
  J. DAALDER, 67:MAY71-83
  R. HARRIER, 551(RENQ):WINTER70-471
WYATT, W.F., JR. INDO-EUROPEAN /A/.
  A.M. DAVIES, 402(MLR):OCT71-842
WYATT, W.F., JR. METRICAL LENGTHENING IN
  HOMER.
  C. CALAME, 182:VOL23#21/22-947
  G.M. MESSING, 24:JUL71-494
  S.L. SCHEIN, 124:NOV70-86
WYCHERLEY, W. THE COMPLETE PLAYS OF
  WILLIAM WYCHERLEY. (G. WEALES, ED)
  G. KRIEGER, 38:BAND87HEFT1-93
WYCZYNSKI, P. NELLIGAN ET LA MUSIQUE.
  617(TLS):7APR72-399
WYCZYNSKI, P., ED. RECHERCHE ET LIT-
  TÉRATURE CANADIENNE-FRANÇAISE.
  617(TLS):7APR72-399
WYKES, A. 1942.
  617(TLS):27OCT72-1294
WYLIE, L. & A. BÉGUÉ. LES FRANÇAIS.
  E.C. KNOX, 399(MLJ):NOV70-545
WYLIE, P. THE END OF THE DREAM.
  M. LEVIN, 441:23JUL72-19
WYLLER, E.A. PLATONS PARMENIDES IN
  SEINEM ZUSAMMENHANG MIT SYMPOSIUM UND
  POLITEIA.
  C. VINCENT, 542:APR-JUN68-289
WYLLER, E.A. DER SPÄTE PLATON.
  R.S. BRUMBAUGH, 124:JAN71-160
WYMAN, D.S. PAPER WALLS.
  H.L. FEINGOLD, 390:MAY69-75
WYNAR, B.S. - SEE "AMERICAN REFERENCE
  BOOKS ANNUAL, 1970"
WYNAR, L. - SEE UNDER VYNAR, L.
WYNDHAM, F. & D. KING. TROTSKY.
  617(TLS):15DEC72-1541
WYNNE-TYSON, J. THE CIVILISED ALTERNA-
  TIVE.
  617(TLS):23JUN72-724
WYSLING, H. - SEE MANN, T. & H.

WYSS, H., ED. DAS LUZERNER OSTERSPIEL.
  W.F. MICHAEL, 221(GQ):JAN70-114
WYTRZENS, G. - SEE PASEK, J.C.

CAPTAIN X. SAFETY LAST.
  441:24SEP72-52
  561(SATR):7OCT72-109
XENAKIS, F. THE FIG TREE.
  S. BLACKBURN, 440:6FEB72-5
  M. LEVIN, 441:30JAN72-26
XENAKIS, I. FORMALIZED MUSIC.
  V. THOMSON, 453:31AUG72-19
XENAKIS, I. PITHOPRAKTA.
  M. SERRES, 98:FEB69-140
XENOPHON. MEMOIRS OF SOCRATES AND THE
  SYMPOSIUM. (H. TREDENNICK, TRANS)
  D. MACNEAL, 124:APR71-268
XENOPHON. XÉNOPHON, "L'ART DE LA
  CHASSE." (E. DELEBECQUE, ED & TRANS)
  J.K. ANDERSON, 124:JAN71-159
XIRAU, R. OCTAVIO PAZ.
  617(TLS):29SEP72-1144

YADIN, Y. BAR-KOKHBA.*
  617(TLS):24MAR72-342
YAKER, H., H. OSMOND & F. CHEEK, EDS.
  THE FUTURE OF TIME.
  617(TLS):10NOV72-1376
YAKIR, P. A CHILDHOOD IN PRISON. (R.
  CONQUEST, ED)
  617(TLS):29DEC72-1575
YALLOP, D.A. TO ENCOURAGE THE OTHERS.
  617(TLS):7JAN72-5
YAMADA, C.F. DECORATIVE ARTS OF JAPAN.
  J. BRZOSTOSKI, 139:JUL/AUG69-6
YAMAK, L.Z. THE SYRIAN SOCIAL NATIONAL-
  IST PARTY.
  L. MEO, 318(JAOS):APR-JUN70-283
YAMAMOTO, K. A CLASSIFIED DICTIONARY OF
  SPOKEN MANCHU.
  J.E. BRUMBAUGH, 350:DEC71-970
YANAGITA, K. JAPANESE FOLK TALES.
  G.K. BRADY, 650(WF):OCT68-284
YANES, S. & C. HOLDORF, EDS. BIG ROCK
  CANDY MOUNTAIN.
  R. GROSS, 441:21MAY72-44
YÁÑEZ, A. THE LEAN LANDS.*
  J. RUTHERFORD, 86(BHS):APR71-181
YANO TORU. TAI-BIRUMA GENDAI SEIJI-SHI
  KENKYŪ.
  E.T. FLOOD, 293(JAST):FEB70-495
YANOVSKY, V.S. OF LIGHT AND SOUNDING
  BRASS.
  R. HOWARD, 441:17DEC72-7
YARDEN, L. THE TREE OF LIGHT.
  617(TLS):26MAY72-608
YARLOTT, G. EDUCATION AND CHILDREN'S
  EMOTIONS.
  617(TLS):3MAR72-250
YARMOLINSKY, A. DOSTOEVSKY: WORKS AND
  DAYS.
  442(NY):15JAN72-92
YARMOLINSKY, A. THE RUSSIAN LITERARY
  IMAGINATION.*
  639(VQR):SPRING70-LXIV
YASHIRO YUKIO & OTHERS, EDS. ARTS OF
  CHINA. (VOL 1) (JAPANESE TITLE: CHŪ-
  GOKU BIJUTSU.)
  A.C. SOPER, 57:VOL31#1-82
YASUSHI, N. - SEE UNDER NISHIKAWA YASUSHI
YATES, B. SUNDAY DRIVER.
  J. DURSO, 441:3DEC72-6

YATES, D.A., J. PALLEY & J. SOMMERS, EDS.
TRES CUENTISTAS HISPANOAMERICANOS.
J. STAIS, 238:MAY70-351
YATES, F.A. THE ART OF MEMORY.*
C.H. CLOUGH, 39:MAR69-246
YATES, F.A. THEATRE OF THE WORLD.*
D.S. BLAND, 551(RENQ):WINTER70-482
M. DEL VILLAR, 191(ELN):MAR71-217
YATES, J.M., ED. CONTEMPORARY POETRY OF
BRITISH COLUMBIA.* (VOL 1)
M. DOYLE, 491:MAR72-356
R. GUSTAFSON, 102(CANL):WINTER71-77
150(DR):AUTUMN70-431
YATES, J.M. THE GREAT BEAR LAKE MEDITA-
TIONS.*
M. DOYLE, 491:MAR72-356
D. FETHERLING, 606(TAMR):#57-80
YATES, J.M., ED. VOLVOX.
D. ARNASON, 198:SUMMER72-127
YATES, R. A SPECIAL PROVIDENCE.
42(AR):FALL69-443
YATES, W.E. GRILLPARZER.
617(TLS):3MAR72-254
YATES, W.E. - SEE GRILLPARZER, F.
YAVETZ, Z. PLEBS AND PRINCEPS.*
E. BADIAN, 487:SPRING70-93
M.A.R. COLLEDGE, 123:DEC71-427
S.I. OOST, 122:APR71-137
J. SCARBOROUGH, 121(CJ):FEB-MAR71-264
"YEARBOOK OF SCIENCE AND TECHNOLOGY."
[1972]
M.F. GIBBONS, JR., 70(ANQ):JUN72-157
YEARSLEY, M. THE FOLKLORE OF THE FAIRY
TALE.
L. ROBERTS, 582(SFQ):DEC69-374
YEATS, W.B. JOHN SHERMAN & DHOYA. (R.J.
FINNERAN, ED)
J.L. ALLEN, JR., 295:VOL2#1-148
YEATS, W.B. A TOWER OF POLISHED BLACK
STONES. (D.R. CLARK & G. MAYHEW, EDS)
617(TLS):17MAR72-311
YEATS, W.B. UNCOLLECTED PROSE BY W.B.
YEATS.* (VOL 1) (J.P. FRAYNE, ED)
J.L. ALLEN, JR., 295:VOL2#1-148
R. LANGBAUM, 31(ASCH):SUMMER72-460
A. SADDLEMYER, 301(JEGP):JUL71-567
YELTON, D.C. MIMESIS AND METAPHOR.
T.C. MOSER, 445(NCF):MAR69-476
YEO, M. GAME FOR SHUT-INS.
T.L. WEPPLER, 99:JUL-AUG72-46
YERBY, F. THE GIRL FROM STORYVILLE.
G. DAVIS, 441:17SEP72-49
YEVTUSHENKO, Y. STOLEN APPLES.*
Y. BLUMENFELD, 441:6FEB72-30
YEVTUSHENKO, Y., L. MARTYNOV & E. VINO-
KUROV. THREE NEW SOVIET POETS.
S. MC PHERSON, 448:SUMMER68-104
YGLESIAS, H. HOW SHE DIED.
M. HAYNES, 561(SATR):18MAR72-74
C. LEHMANN-HAUPT, 441:8FEB72-35
S. SCHOONOVER, 441:13FEB72-36
P. THEROUX, 440:16APR72-9
M. WOOD, 453:6APR72-25
442(NY):26FEB72-101
YGLESIAS, J. THE TRUTH ABOUT THEM.
T.R. EDWARDS, 453:9MAR72-19
A.C. FOOTE, 440:16JAN72-10
M. LEVIN, 441:9JAN72-32
YGLESIAS, R. HIDE FOX, AND ALL AFTER.
H. KEYISHIAN, 440:30JAN72-10
D.K. MANO, 441:16APR72-4
R. SALE, 453:4MAY72-3
YIP, W-L. EZRA POUND'S "CATHAY."*
W.M. CHACE, 598(SOR):WINTER72-225
F.K. SANDERS, 569(SR):SUMMER71-433
639(VQR):SPRING70-LVI

"YIVO ANNUAL OF JEWISH SOCIAL SCIENCE."
(VOL 14)
B. MURDOCH, 402(MLR):JUL71-719
YNDURÁIN, F. CLÁSICOS MODERNOS.
K. SCHWARTZ, 238:SEP70-573
D.L. SHAW, 86(BHS):JAN71-75
YOHANNAN, J.D., ED. JOSEPH AND POTI-
PHAR'S WIFE IN WORLD LITERATURE.
G. COSTA, 545(RPH):FEB71-550
A.E. SINGER, 149:JUN71-155
YOLTON, J.W. LOCKE AND THE COMPASS OF
HUMAN UNDERSTANDING.
W.L. FOGG, 566:SPRING71-75
R.S. WOOLHOUSE, 319:APR72-224
YOLTON, J.W., ED. JOHN LOCKE: PROBLEMS
AND PERSPECTIVES.
N.S. FIERING, 656(WMQ):APR70-312
P.M.S. HACKER, 393(MIND):JAN70-150
W.J. HUGGETT, 627(UTQ):JUL70-345
J.J. JENKINS, 483:JUL70-244
D.O. THOMAS, 518:JAN70-30
YOLTON, J.W. METAPHYSICAL ANALYSIS.
M. KITELEY, 482(PHR):JAN70-139
J. NARVESON, 627(UTQ):JUL69-416
A.R. WHITE, 479(PHQ):JUL70-282
YOORS, J. CROSSING.*
617(TLS):1SEP72-1017
YORK, A. THE EXPURGATOR.
617(TLS):26MAY72-612
YOSHIDA, J., WITH B. HOSOKAWA. TWO
WORLDS OF JIM YOSHIDA.
441:17SEP72-44
"YOSHIKAWA HAKUSHI TAIKYŪ KINEN CHŪGOKU
BUNGAKU RONSHŪ."
J.R.H., 244(HJAS):VOL29-335
YOSHINO, M.Y. JAPAN'S MANAGERIAL SYSTEM.
B.K. MARSHALL, 293(JAST):NOV69-175
YOUINGS, J. THE DISSOLUTION OF THE
MONASTERIES.
617(TLS):17MAR72-317
YOUNG, A. THE POETIC JESUS.
617(TLS):10MAR72-285
YOUNG, D.P. SWEATING OUT THE WINTER.*
R. HOWARD, 340(KR):1970/1-130
YOUNG, E. THE CORRESPONDENCE OF EDWARD
YOUNG 1683-1765. (H. PETTIT, ED)
H. TREVOR-ROPER, 362:13APR72-489
617(TLS):14APR72-405
YOUNG, E. A FAREWELL TO ARMS CONTROL?
617(TLS):24NOV72-1413
YOUNG, I. YEAR OF THE QUIET SUN.
D. BARBOUR, 150(DR):SPRING70-112
M. DOYLE, 491:MAR72-356
A. SHUCARD, 102(CANL):SPRING71-80
YOUNG, I. - SEE GAFURIUS, F.
YOUNG, J.M. THE BRAZILIAN REVOLUTION OF
1930 AND THE AFTERMATH.
J.F. THORNING, 613:SUMMER68-313
YOUNG, J.Z. AN INTRODUCTION TO THE STUDY
OF MAN.
617(TLS):23JUN72-714
YOUNG, M. NEW ZEALAND ART: PAINTING 1950-
1967.
W. CURNOW, 368:JUN69-186
YOUNG, P. THREE BAGS FULL.
T. LASK, 441:5FEB72-27
L. MARX, 441:14MAY72-4
YOUNG, P., ED. THE WAR GAME.
617(TLS):24NOV72-1413
YOUNG, P. & C.W. MANN. THE HEMINGWAY
MANUSCRIPTS.
R.M. DAVIS, 577(SHR):SUMMER70-284
D.E.S. MAXWELL, 402(MLR):JUL71-682
YOUNG, P.M. THE BACHS, 1500-1850.*
W. EMERY, 415:JUN70-605
W.S. NEWMAN, 579(SAQ):SUMMER71-434
YOUNG, P.M. SIR ARTHUR SULLIVAN.*
442(NY):1APR72-108

YOUNG, P.M. - SEE ELGAR, E.
YOUNG, T.D., ED. JOHN CROWE RANSOM.*
R. BUFFINGTON, 219(GAR):SPRING69-82
YOUNG, W. FOUNDATIONS OF THEORY.
J.B.L., 543:SEP69-142
YOUNG, W.D. THE ANATOMY OF A PARTY.*
I.M. ABELLA, 529(QQ):AUTUMN70-462
YOUNGER, C. A STATE OF DISUNION.
617(TLS):15SEP72-1046
YOUNGSON, A.J. THE MAKING OF CLASSICAL
EDINBURGH, '1750-1840.*
A. FORWARD, 576:MAY68-151
YOURCENAR, M. L'OEUVRE AU NOIR.
A-C. DOBBS, 207(FR):DEC69-375
YÜ-CHÜN, W. - SEE UNDER WANG YÜ-CHÜN
YU-SHU, L. - SEE UNDER LI YU-SHU
YUDHISHTAR. CONFLICT IN THE NOVELS OF
D.H. LAWRENCE.*
K. MC LEOD, 541(RES):NOV70-521
YUDKIN, J. SWEET AND DANGEROUS.
E. EDELSON, 440:7MAY72-6
YUKICHI, F. - SEE UNDER FUKUZAWA YUKICHI
YUKIO, Y. & OTHERS - SEE UNDER YASHIRO
YUKIO & OTHERS
YULE, H., COMP. A NARRATIVE OF THE MIS-
SION TO THE COURT OF AVA IN 1865.
M.E. SPIRO, 293(JAST):AUG70-985
YURICK, S. SOMEONE JUST LIKE YOU.
C. LEHMANN-HAUPT, 441:1SEP72-29
J.C. OATES, 441:3SEP72-6
"YWAIN AND GAWAIN." (A.B. FRIEDMAN &
N.T. HARRINGTON, EDS)
U. JACOBSSON, 179(ES):OCT69-525

ZABEEH, F. WHAT IS IN A NAME?
K.B. HARDER, 424:DEC69-303
ZABOLOTSKY, N. SCROLLS. (D. WEISSBORT,
TRANS)
617(TLS):14JAN72-49
ZAEHNER, R.C. DRUGS, MYSTICISM AND MAKE-
BELIEVE.
617(TLS):6OCT72-1200
ZAFRULLA KHAN, M. - SEE "THE QURAN"
ZAHAREAS, A.N., R. CARDONA & S. GREEN-
FIELD, EDS. RAMÓN DEL VALLE-INCLÁN.*
I-M. GIL, 240(HR):OCT70-439
G.E. WELLWARTH, 397(MD):FEB70-434
R. WHITTREDGE, 241:MAY71-69
ZAHRNT, H. WHAT KIND OF GOD?
617(TLS):28JAN72-93
ZAIONCHKOVSKY, P.A. OTMENA KREPOSTNOGO
PRAVA V ROSSII.
S.F. STARR, 32:JUN71-394
ZAJACZKOWSKI, A. TURECKA WERSJA SAH-NAME
Z EGIPTU MAMELUCKIEGO.
J. STEWART-ROBINSON, 318(JAOS):APR-
JUN70-277
ZALESKI, E. PLANNING FOR ECONOMIC
GROWTH IN THE SOVIET UNION, 1918-1932.
(M-C. MAC ANDREW & G.W. NUTTER, EDS &
TRANS)
617(TLS):25FEB72-229
ZAŁUCKI, H. DICTIONARY OF RUSSIAN TECH-
NICAL AND SCIENTIFIC ABBREVIATIONS.
J.F. HENDRY, 104:SUMMER71-270
ZAMJATIN, Y. - SEE UNDER ZAMYATIN, Y.
ZAMORA VICENTE, A. LA REALIDAD ESPER-
PÉNTICA (APROXIMACIÓN A "LUCES DE
BOHEMIA").*
E. WILLIAMS, 238:MAY70-338
ZAMPETTI, P. - SEE "LORENZO LOTTO"
ZAMYATIN, Y. THE DRAGON.
V. CUNNINGHAM, 362:20JUL72-89
ZAMYATIN [ZAMJATIN], Y. POVESTI I RASS-
KAZY.
J.P. MANSON, 574(SEEJ):FALL71-373

ZAMYATIN, Y. A SOVIET HERETIC. (M.
GINSBURG, ED & TRANS)
J. BAYLEY, 453:19OCT72-18
D.J. RICHARDS, 575(SEER):APR71-296
ZAMYATIN, Y. WE. (M. GINSBURG, TRANS)
P. ADAMS, 61:JUN72-112
J. BAYLEY, 453:19OCT72-18
S. KOCH, 441:9JUL72-7
T. LASK, 441:29JUL72-23
V.D. MIHAILOVICH, 561(SATR):6MAY72-88
ZANARDO, A. - SEE ENGELS-MARX
ZANDER, W. ISRAEL AND THE HOLY PLACES OF
CHRISTENDOM.
617(TLS):31MAR72-377
ZANER, R.M. - SEE SCHUTZ, A.
ZANES, J. ATHENA AND HIGH VOLTAGE.
M. HORNYANSKY, 627(UTQ):JUL70-332
ZAPATA, C. CANTOS DE EVOCACIÓN Y EN-
SUEÑO.
J.V., 37:JUL69-42
ZARDOYA, C. POESÍA ESPAÑOLA DEL 98 Y
DEL 27.
J. PALLEY, 238:MAR70-150
M.A. SALGADO, 241:JAN71-79
ZASLOW, M. THE OPENING OF THE CANADIAN
NORTH, 1870-1914.
J. WARKENTIN, 99:MAY72-62
ZATKO, J.J. DESCENT INTO DARKNESS.
M. KLIMENKO, 32:JUN71-403
ZAVALA, I.M. UNAMUNO Y SU TEATRO DE
CONCIENCIA. LA ANGUSTIA Y LA BÚSQUEDA
DEL HOMBRE EN LA LITERATURA.
C. MORÓN ARROYO, 240(HR):JUL70-331
ZAZOFF, P. ETRUSKISCHE SKARABÄEN.*
D.E. STRONG, 123:JUN71-303
VAN DER ZEE, J. CANYON.
A. GOTTLIEB, 441:27FEB72-32
ZEITLER, R. & OTHERS. DIE KUNST DES 19.
JAHRHUNDERTS.
A. NEUMEYER, 54:JUN69-194
ZEITLIN, A. LIDER FUN KHURBN UN LIDER
FUN GLOYBN.
E.S. GOLDSMITH, 328:SPRING69-245
ZELL, H. & H. SILVER, EDS. A READER'S
GUIDE TO AFRICAN LITERATURE.
D.A.N. JONES, 362:30MAR72-426
ZELNIK, R.E. LABOR AND SOCIETY IN TSAR-
IST RUSSIA.
617(TLS):5MAY72-512
ZEMAN, J.K. THE ANABAPTISTS AND THE
CZECH BRETHREN IN MORAVIA, 1526-1628.*
F.G. HEYMANN, 32:MAR71-131
ZEMAN, Z.A.B. TWILIGHT OF THE HABSBURGS.
617(TLS):11FEB72-144
ZENKOVSKY, S.A. RUSSIA'S OLD BELIEVERS.
C.B.H. CANT, 575(SEER):APR71-286
ZENKOVSKY, S.A. & D.L. ARMBRUSTER. A
GUIDE TO THE BIBLIOGRAPHIES OF RUSSIAN
LITERATURE.
C.J.G. TURNER, 104:WINTER71-568
ZENOFF, D.B. PRIVATE ENTERPRISE IN THE
DEVELOPING COUNTRIES.
J.N. ANDERSON, 293(JAST):MAY70-682
ZERNER, H. THE SCHOOL OF FONTAINEBLEAU:
ETCHINGS AND ENGRAVINGS.
H. MILES, 90:OCT70-709
VON ZESEN, P. SÄMTLICHE WERKE. (VOL 8:
SIMSON.) (F. VAN INGEN, ED)
E.A. PHILIPPSON, 301(JEGP):OCT71-720
ZETTERSTEN, A. A STATISTICAL STUDY OF
THE GRAPHIC SYSTEM OF PRESENT-DAY
AMERICAN ENGLISH.
J.M. SINCLAIR, 447(N&Q):MAR70-102
ZETTERSTEN, A. STUDIES IN THE DIALECT
AND VOCABULARY OF THE "ANCRENE RIWLE."
K. FAISS, 353:JUL69-107
ZHUKHOVITSKY, L. ASTRIDE A DOLPHIN.
617(TLS):5MAY72-526